Jürg Niehans

INTERNATIONAL MONETARY ECONOMICS

E R R A T U M

The figures, but not the legends,
on pages 40 and 49 have been interchanged.

INTERNATIONAL MONETARY ECONOMICS

JÜRG NIEHANS

International Monetary Economics

The Johns Hopkins
University Press

Baltimore and London

The Johns Hopkins University Press, Baltimore, Maryland 21218
The Johns Hopkins Press Ltd., London

Library of Congress Cataloging in Publication Data

Niehans, Jürg.
    International monetary economics.

    Bibliography: p. 319
    Includes index.
    1. Foreign exchange.   2. International finance.
3. Monetary policy.   I. Title.
HG3821.N595   1984   332′.042   83–14960
ISBN 0–8018–3021–4

Contents

Preface

Since the final collapse of the Bretton Woods system, experience and research about floating exchange rates have rapidly accumulated. Though much is still unclear, and in some cases more unclear than ever, it is evident that the working of floating rates is different from what both their protagonists and their opponents imagined it to be in the 1960s. This book tries to provide a comprehensive, balanced, and integrated survey of international monetary economics as it emerges from this decade of rapid learning. Its main topic is floating rates, but pegged exchange rates are considered wherever they shed light on fundamental problems.

In a sense, this volume may be regarded as an open-economy sequel to my *Theory of Money*. Like the latter, it provides a closely reasoned synthesis of received doctrine, recent contributions, and original developments. The international perspective adds a new analytical dimension to the theory of money inasmuch as relative prices appear in a decisive role. This combination of money and relative prices gives international monetary economics its specific fascination. At the same time, the microeconomics of the demand for money and of financial intermediation drop into the background.

The emphasis is on economic theory. Except for illustrative references to recent events, the reader will find no historical, empirical, or institutional material. In particular, there are no chapters on the working of the gold standard, the institutions of Bretton Woods, or the European Monetary System. (For the theory of the gold-exchange standard the reader is referred to my earlier volume.) There is also no discussion of exchange controls. The theory, however, is strongly policy-oriented. More specifically, it is focused on monetary policy in open economies under floating rates. The international aspects of fiscal policy, which attracted so much attention in the 1960s, are hardly touched upon.

ix

This book does not subscribe to one or the other of the "approaches" between which economists supposedly have to choose. It is based on the conviction that different approaches help to illuminate different aspects of our complex world, each finding its appropriate place in an integrated analysis. Whether a particular adjustment process is described in terms of cash accumulation or of elasticities is not a matter of principle but of analytical convenience. The same is true with respect to the choice between a monetary approach and an asset approach to exchange dynamics. It is consistent with this philosophy that the exposition is not based on a single core model, gradually taken through its paces, as, for example, in Allen and Kenen (1980). The book is problem-oriented rather than model-oriented, each problem being discussed in terms of a model that expresses the essential points in a particularly simple way. A strong effort is made, however, to relate and integrate the various analytical tools. I hope the reader will not leave this volume with the frustrating impression of a bewildering variety of competing models.

The exposition is aimed at advanced undergraduates with a theoretical bent and first-year graduate students. It makes extensive use of mathematics, but the techniques do not go beyond elementary calculus and simple differential equations. Wherever possible, the argument is supported by graphs. Technical details are sacrificed where the marginal return in economic insight does not seem to warrant the marginal cost.

The first part of the book discusses the interaction of money, prices, and exchange rates in the absence of capital flows. In chapter 1, a summary review of the pure theory of international trade provides the "real" framework for monetary analysis. The second chapter introduces money, prices, and exchange rates, mostly in comparative-static terms, but including an analysis of price dynamics. The case of flexible exchange rates leads to purchasing-power parity; the case of fixed rates leads to the specie-flow mechanism. In full equilibrium, devaluation (under fixed rates) and money-supply changes (under floating rates) are neutral. During the adjustment process, both have powerful real effects. These are analyzed in chapters 3, 4, and 5. Each of these chapters focuses on one particular aspect. It is shown that the monetary approach, the elasticity approach, and the expenditure approach, often regarded as rivals, differ more in the choice of concepts than in economic substance. It turns out, in particular, that, under suitable assumptions, there is a precise correspondence between the Bickerdike/Robinson/Metzler condition familiar from the elasticity approach and an analogous condition in terms of hoarding coefficients under the monetary approach.

The subject of part II is international assets and capital flows, considered from a macroeconomic point of view. Chapter 6 discusses the determinants of net international indebtedness, the welfare implications of international lending, and the capital flows resulting from capital market integration. This results in a "q- theory" of capital flows as determined mainly by investment opportunities, whereas the role of interest rates is shown to be secondary and ambiguous. This "new view" of capital flows, while rooted in the classical tradition, represents perhaps the book's most pronounced departure from prevalent notions. Chapter 7 introduces heterogeneous assets and asset diversification. It develops a theory of asset arbitrage based on the comparative advantages and preferences of each country for different types of assets in close analogy to international trade theory.

The following two chapters are about particular markets in financial assets. Chapter 8 argues that forward exchange markets owe their economic significance to transaction costs; with costless transactions they would be redundant. Though forward markets are important for microeconomic efficiency, their macroeconomic significance, therefore, is easily overestimated. Chapter 9 discusses the structure, economic function, and policy implications of Eurocurrency markets. It is based on an interpretation that explains the location of financial intermediaries in terms of transaction costs and regulatory constraints. Chapter 10 returns to the topic of chapter 6 by providing a detailed analysis of the influence of income, capital goods prices, interest rates, and exchange rates on capital movements. One of the recurring themes is the fundamental difference between asset arbitrage and net capital flows and the illegitimacy of equating the rapidity of arbitrage with the mobility of capital flows.

Part III considers monetary policy in open economies under floating rates with interacting trade and capital flows. Chapter 11 analyzes the dynamic adjustment of the economy to a change in monetary policy, focusing particularly on the "overshooting" of exchange rates. From a general model, three submodels are derived by alternative simplifications, shedding light on different aspects of the dynamic process. The remaining chapters gradually lead from pure theory to policy implications. Chapter 12 examines the differential effects of open-market operations and foreign-exchange operations on exchange rates, output, and interest rates over different time spans. This is followed in chapter 13 by a discussion of alternative strategies for central-bank intervention into the foreign-exchange market. It is argued that "leaning against the wind" and purchasing-power parity rules are not promising, whereas temporary exchange-rate ceilings may be useful as emergency measures against "imported" overshooting. Chapter 14 surveys the debate about pegged and floating rates, the literature about optimum currency areas, and the various proposals for introducing some flexibility into pegged exchange rates. For a noninflationary world, fixed rates emerge as the best solution, but floating rates appear second-best under inflationary conditions.

The book concludes with a largely nontechnical discussion of possible guidelines for monetary policy in open economies under floating rates. These guidelines, though largely derived from the preceding analysis, clearly involve elements of personal judgment. Pure theorists may perhaps deplore this. I believe, however, that judgment still is, and will probably remain, an essential part of economics. I also believe that, once doctrinal and political antagonisms are put on one side, there is more consensus about such guidelines than is commonly supposed.

In writing this book, I received help, support, and stimulation from many people and institutions. My greatest debt is to my wife, who not only accompanied me to faraway places wherever I was doing my work but also was a most dedicated editorial assistant, sometimes under difficult conditions. Mrs. Margrit Shannon, Mrs. Jeannette Regan, and Mrs. Carola Duff typed various parts of the manuscript and helped me to improve its style. Critical comments and questions from students and colleagues at Bern, Johns Hopkins, Kobe, and other universities left their traces in many chapters. Substantive contributions were made, in particular, by Ailsa Roëll. The graphs were expertly drawn by Jürg Grünig. As part of a larger project, the Swiss National Science Foundation enabled me to obtain the successive help of Carlo Graziani, Beat Moser, and Tobias Rötheli as research assistants. For five months, the Federal Reserve Bank of San Francisco provided me with an office, a library, and a stimulating environment. The Japan Society for the Promotion of Science, on the initiative of Kazuhiro Igawa, gave me the opportunity to work for another two months at Kobe University. For all these contributions I express my sincere thanks.

I

MONEY, TRADE, AND EXCHANGE RATES

CHAPTER 1

The International
Division of Labor

Introduction

The subject of this book is the influence of money on the international flows of goods, services, and assets. The primary determinants of these flows are nonmonetary, arising from "real" factors like resource endowments, tastes, and knowledge analyzed in the "pure theory" of international trade. The monetary aspects are best understood as a layer of secondary modifications superimposed on the real factors. While these modifications are sometimes so powerful, dramatic, and even catastrophic that the real factors are in danger of being lost from sight, they cannot be understood in isolation.

Consistent with this perspective, this introductory chapter offers a thumbnail summary of the real aspects of international economics. It is intended to provide the nonmonetary background for the monetary aspects of international economics discussed in the following chapters. Inevitably, the exposition must be reduced to a bare minimum of analytical building blocks. It is designed for a reader who has some familiarity with international trade theory without, however, being an accomplished expert in it. The competent international trade theorist will find that many important qualifications and extensions are disregarded; he will learn nothing from this chapter. The complete novice, on the other hand, may find the exposition excessively terse and undesirably abstract; he should consult the literature on international trade theory.[1]

The discussion is limited to two countries and two commodities. The first section concentrates on the demand side, exhibiting the prominent role of

1. In particular, the following expositions may be useful: Caves and Jones 1977, pts I and II; Heller 1973, ch. 6; Krauss 1979, chs. II and VI.

price elasticities. The second section concentrates on the supply side, emphasizing differences in factor endowments and technology. In the third section, demand and supply elements are combined into a concise restatement of the international division of labor with imperfect specialization. It is followed by a brief discussion of the terms of trade. The final section introduces rigid wages and thus unemployment.

1.1 Diversified Consumption with Specialization in Production

Suppose there are two countries, Portugal and England, and two goods, wine and cloth. Transportation costs are disregarded. Each country is endowed with certain factors of production. In reality these are of various kinds, including capital goods of different types, labor of different skills, and land of different quality and location. For the present purpose it will be assumed, however, that there are only two kinds of factors, called land and resources. Land may be visualized as actually found on the map. Resources, on the other hand, should be visualized rather abstractly as consisting of standardized "bundles" of labor inputs and capital goods. As a consequence, the quantity of resources can be measured in a single number. The question is what quantities of wine and/or cloth each country will consume, produce, export, and import. The complete answer is complex. It will be developed in stages by concentrating in each stage on one particular aspect. The present section focuses on the significance of demand, an aspect emphasized by John Stuart Mill and analytically elaborated by Alfred Marshall (1923, 1930). At the same time, the influence of cost factors is pushed into the background by the assumption that each country specializes in one product. With its land and resources, Portugal produces wine but is assumed to be unable to produce cloth. England, on the other hand, produces cloth but is unable to grow wine. It is clear that, with fully employed resources, Portugal produces a fixed quantity of wine, $\bar{W}_P$, while England produces a fixed quantity of cloth, $\bar{C}_E$. Production is thus predetermined.

Under these assumptions, Portugal's demand can be described as follows. Her income, measured in barrels of wine, is $\bar{W}_P$. Her consumption of cloth depends on this income and on the relative price of cloth in terms of wine, π, called the terms of trade:

$$C_P = C_P(\pi, \bar{W}_P). \tag{1.1.1}$$

The same can be said about the demand for wine,

$$W_P = W_P(\pi, \bar{W}_P),$$

but this function does not contain new information, because the consumption of wine is just what is left of income after the payment for cloth. This is expressed by the budget constraint

$$W_P = \bar{W}_P - \pi C_P. \tag{1.1.2}$$

What can be said about the demand functions? If Portuguese income increases, the demand for both commodities will normally rise. In this case the goods are called "normal" (or sometimes "superior"). It may happen, however, that demand declines as income rises; such goods are called "inferior." Clearly, not all goods can simultaneously be inferior, since additional income must be spent on something.

If the price of cloth rises, Portugal will probably demand less of it; the exceptional "Giffen case," while logically conceivable for strongly inferior goods with a high budget share, is extremely unlikely and, in the present context, can practically be disregarded. It may seem that the same argument can be applied to wine. A rising relative price of cloth is equivalent to a falling relative price of wine, which should induce an increase in the demand for wine. However, this argument is deficient. In fact, it is quite possible that the decline in the demand for cloth is accompanied by a decline in the demand for wine. At the higher price of cloth, even a reduced quantity may have to be bought with a higher quantity of wine, leaving less of the latter for Portuguese home consumption.

To illustrate with an extreme example, imagine a happy state in which Portugal can obtain cloth free, so that she can satiate herself with cloth without sacrificing any of her wine. If England now started to charge a price for her cloth, Portugal's consumption of wine, though it had become relatively cheaper, would certainly decline. Suppose, on the other hand, the price of cloth is initially so high that none is consumed in Portugal. If the price of cloth now declines to a level at which some is consumed, the consumption of wine will have to be reduced to pay for the cloth. In this case, the price of cloth and the consumption of wine necessarily move in the same direction. Between these extremes, we cannot be quite sure whether a rise in the relative price of cloth (and thus a fall in the relative price of wine) will raise or lower the Portuguese demand for wine. The microeconomic theorist would trace this ambiguity to the opposing signs of a substitution effect and an income effect in the case of a supplier of a normal good. While the lower relative price of wine, taken at the same real income level, would tend to raise Portugal's wine consumption, the lower purchasing power of her wine in terms of English cloth reduces her real income and would thus, taken by itself, tend to reduce her consumption of wine.

What do these demand reactions imply for Portugal's imports and exports? Since home production is fixed, a decline in cloth consumption is associated with an equal decline in import demand. For wine, exports increase as consumption decreases, and vice versa. The effect of a price change on cloth imports, C_P, and wine exports, $\bar{W}_P - W_P$, can be summarized in a familiar graph (fig. 1.1.1). With a falling relative price of cloth, cloth imports rise as expressed by the falling demand curve. Wine exports, $\bar{W}_P - W_P$, are measured by the area of the shaded rectangle (see 1.1.2). It is clear that with falling π this area can increase, stay constant, or decrease depending on the price elasticity of the demand for cloth.

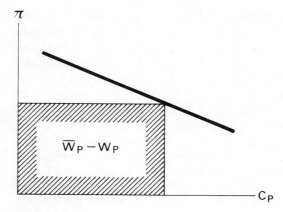

FIGURE 1.1.1
Portugal's Imports and Exports

The precise relationship between import demand and export supply of the same country can be expressed in terms of two elasticities. By taking the total differential of the budget constraint (1.1.2) one obtains

$$d(\bar{W}_P - W_P) = \pi dC_P + C_P d\pi.$$

Using the budget constraint (1.1.2), this can be written

$$\frac{d(\bar{W}_P - W_P)}{d\pi} \cdot \frac{\pi}{(\bar{W}_P - W_P)} = \frac{dC_P}{d\pi} \cdot \frac{\pi}{C_P} + 1.$$

Defining the elasticity of the Portuguese import demand for cloth with respect to its relative price as

$$\epsilon_{PC} = \frac{dC_P}{d\pi} \cdot \frac{\pi}{C_P}$$

and the elasticity of the Portuguese export supply of wine with respect to its relative price, $\pi^* = 1/\pi$, as

$$\eta_{PW} = \frac{d(\bar{W}_P - W_P)}{d\pi^*} \cdot \frac{\pi^*}{(\bar{W}_P - W_P)} = -\frac{d(\bar{W}_P - W_P)}{d\pi} \cdot \frac{\pi}{(\bar{W}_P - W_P)},$$

this can be written

$$\epsilon_{PC} + \eta_{PW} = -1. \tag{1.1.3}$$

In words, the elasticities of import demand and export supply, each in terms of its own relative price, sum to -1.

In the preceding argument, Portugal's demand function for cloth was regarded as one of the ultimate data. On the assumption that the behavior of the Portuguese economy can be analyzed in the same way as the behavior of a single individual, the demand functions can, in turn, be derived from Portugal's preferences or "tastes" as described by indifference curves. Consider figure 1.1.2. Consumption of cloth and wine are marked off, respectively, on the vertical axis and the horizontal axis. For cloth, import demand is equal to consumption. For wine, export supply is equal to the difference between domestic production, $\overline{W}_P$, and consumption, W_P. The Portuguese tastes for wine and cloth are expressed by the indifference curves. At a given relative price, π, Portugal maximizes her utility

$$U_P = U_P(C_P, W_P) \tag{1.1.4}$$

subject to the budget constraint (1.1.2). The optimum, Q_1, is realized where the budget line is tangent to an indifference curve. This implies that the marginal rate of substitution in consumption is equal to the terms of trade,

$$\frac{\partial U_P/\partial C_P}{\partial U_P/\partial W_P} = \pi. \tag{1.1.5}$$

As the relative price of cloth rises, demand and supply move along the P line to Q_2 and further on to Q_3. Disregarding the Giffen paradox, it is clear that C_P declines; W_P, however, may either decline or increase. The same is true, with opposite sign, for export supply.

The economic content of figure 1.1.2 can be expressed in still another way by measuring exports, instead of consumption, along the horizontal axis. The resulting graph (fig. 1.1.3) is just like figure 1.1.2, read from right to left.

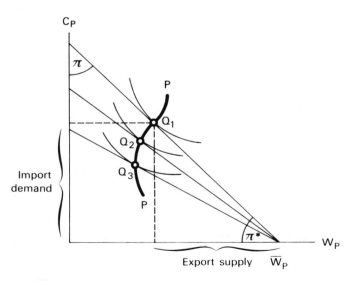

FIGURE 1.1.2
Portugal's Consumption

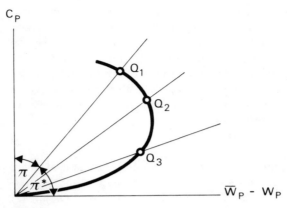

FIGURE 1.1.3
Portugal's Offer Curve

The curve connecting Q_1, Q_2, etc., is called Portugal's "reciprocal demand curve" or "offer curve," a concept introduced by Alfred Marshall. It shows how much wine Portugal is willing to give up for given quantities of cloth. As the curve is drawn, higher quantities of cloth are initially bought with larger quantities of wine, but after a point larger quantities of cloth are being regarded as worth less wine. Other shapes of the curve are easily possible.

So far, the discussion has been about Portugal. The same kind of analysis can obviously be applied to England. England's demand for imports can be written

$$W_E = W_E(\pi^*, \bar{C}_E), \tag{1.1.6}$$

with the budget constraint

$$C_E = \bar{C}_E - \pi^* W_E. \tag{1.1.7}$$

Again the demand function can be thought to be derived by postulating that, for each relative price, England maximizes a social utility function

$$U_E = U_E(C_E, W_E), \tag{1.1.8}$$

subject to the budget constraint. This results in the marginal condition

$$\frac{\partial U_E / \partial C_E}{\partial U_E / \partial W_E} = \pi. \tag{1.1.9}$$

The relationship between England's import demand and export supply resulting from variations in the terms of trade can be expressed in another reciprocal demand curve as illustrated by figure 1.1.4.

Since each country was considered in isolation, it has so far been assumed that the terms of trade are parametrically given. By considering both

$\bar{C}_E - C_E$

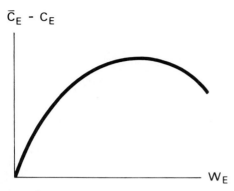

W_E

FIGURE 1.1.4
England's Offer Curve

countries together, it can be shown how the terms of trade are, in turn, determined by the interplay of demand and supply. If some arbitrary price is taken as a starting point, it will probably turn out that the Portuguese demand for cloth is either larger or smaller than the English supply; the opposite must then hold for wine. If there is excess demand for cloth and excess supply of wine, π has to be corrected upward. If there is excess demand for wine and excess supply of cloth, π has to be reduced. The adjustment in π will continue until demand and supply for cloth are equal, which implies the same for wine. This means that, in addition to the two budget constraints (1.1.2) and (1.1.7) and the two demand functions (1.1.1) and (1.1.6), there is now an equilibrium condition for the trade balance,

$$\bar{W}_P - W_P = \pi(\bar{C}_E - C_E). \tag{1.1.10}$$

It states that Portuguese wine exports must be equal in value (measured in wine) to English exports of cloth. If these conditions are simultaneously satisfied, Portugal's import demand for cloth is automatically equal to the English export supply and English import demand for wine is automatically equal to Portuguese export supply. At the same time, since the marginal rates of commodity substitution are both equal to the terms of trade, they are equal to each other. Efficient international exchange sees to it that Portuguese and English consumers are willing to sacrifice the same amount of wine for a unit of cloth.

Market equilibrium can be graphically determined by combining the two offer curves (see fig. 1.1.5). Equilibrium will be reached where the two offer curves intersect. The equilibrium terms of trade are represented by the slope of the ray through that point. It may well be that there are several equilibrium prices as illustrated by figure 1.1.6. At the equilibrium terms of trade, Portugal's import demand for cloth matches England's export supply, and England's import demand of wine matches Portugal's export supply. With given

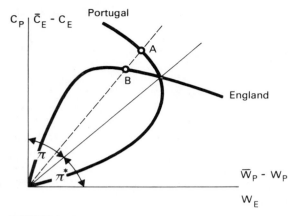

FIGURE 1.1.5
Diversified Consumption Equilibrium

production, the terms of trade and international trade depend on the countries' preferences in consumption.

What exactly happens if the terms of trade are "wrong" in the sense that they do not produce equilibrium? It has sometimes been said that trade would be unbalanced in this case, with the excess of imports over exports being paid in money. This is incorrect. If the terms of trade correspond, say, to the broken ray in figure 1.1.5, each country is ready to pay for all of its imports by its exports, Portugal at point *A* and England at point *B*. The trouble is that Portugal wants to maintain a higher level of balanced trade than England. There are two alternative interpretations of this situation. According to the "tâtonnement" interpretation, no actual exchange takes place before equilibrium is reached. The two countries just submit bids at the price announced by some imaginary broker, who then raises or lowers the price until the bids match. According to the "buffer stock" interpretation, countries do not trade directly, but through an international commodity board which announces the terms at which it is willing to trade. If the price of cloth is "too low," the agency finds itself with declining stocks of cloth, while the stock of wine grows. In the next period it will thus raise the relative price of cloth, proceeding in this fashion until its stocks remain stable. While the buffer stock interpretation looks more realistic than the tâtonnement interpretation, it is also theoretically less satisfactory, since the transactions that take place at "wrong" prices leave a permanent effect on the level of stocks and may affect the demand functions in subsequent periods.

Can we be sure that a small price reduction in the case of excess supply (or a small price increase in the case of excess demand) will actually bring the system closer to equilibrium? This is the question of stability. The system is (locally) stable if a small increase in price reduces excess demand. Consider wine. Excess demand is

$$E_W = W_E - (\bar{W}_P - W_P). \tag{1.1.11}$$

Stability requires

$$\frac{dE_W}{d\pi^*} = \frac{dW_E}{d\pi^*} - \frac{d(\bar{W}_P - W_P)}{d\pi^*} < 0, \tag{1.1.12}$$

where $\pi^* = 1/\pi$. At an equilibrium point, where $W_E = \bar{W}_P - W_P$, this can be written in terms of elasticities in the form

$$\frac{dW_E}{d\pi^*} \cdot \frac{\pi^*}{W_E} - \frac{d(\bar{W}_P - W_P)}{d\pi^*} \cdot \frac{\pi^*}{\bar{W}_P - W_P} = \epsilon_{EW} - \eta_{PW} < 0. \tag{1.1.13}$$

The first term is the price elasticity of England's demand for wine; the second term is the price elasticity of Portugal's supply of the same commodity. Using the fact that the negative value of this supply elasticity is equal to the price elasticity of Portugal's demand for cloth plus one (see 1.1.3), we obtain the stability condition

$$\epsilon_{EW} + \epsilon_{PC} + 1 < 0. \tag{1.1.14}$$

Stability thus requires that the sum of the absolute values of the two demand elasticities exceed unity.

Inequality (1.1.14) is often called the Marshall/Lerner condition. This is a somewhat unfortunate terminology. The formula was indeed derived by Marshall (1923, p. 354) in the sense of a stability condition for barter. It was also used by Lerner (1946, pp. 378 f.), but in the very different sense of a condition for a positive effect of a devaluation on the trade balance in a monetary economy with infinite supply elasticities. This is a case where the same symbols have very different meanings. In particular, the price elasticities in (1.1.14) do not relate to absolute money prices, but to the terms of trade. The equivalent expression (1.1.13), together with (1.1.3), also makes clear that the relevant elasticities incorporate both demand and supply elements. There is no direct correspondence between the elasticities of the offer curves and the usual demand elasticities. The significance of price elasticities for the effect of a devaluation is discussed in chapter 4.

While a given equilibrium may well be unstable, unstable equilibria are always "framed" by stable ones. This is illustrated in figure 1.1.6. It means that the tâtonnement process, if continued long enough, will eventually lead to a stable equilibrium. At the wine price corresponding to the broken line, English demand for wine exceeds Portuguese supply. The broker will thus raise the wine price. By so doing, he will lead the market further away from the unstable equilibrium E_1; for a time excess demand becomes even larger. In due course, however, excess demand will begin to shrink. The market will

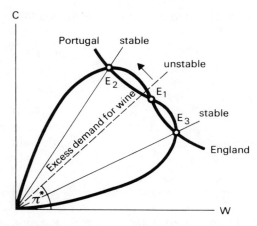

FIGURE 1.1.6
Multiple Equilibria

eventually settle at stable equilibrium E_2, with the terms of trade indicated by the slope of the solid ray.

1.2 Diversified Production with Specialization in Consumption

The preceding analysis was designed to exhibit the significance of demand for international trade. It assumed that each country's production is exogenously fixed. In particular, there was complete specialization in production. This assumption will now be dropped. It will be replaced by the assumption that, with the given resources, each country can produce both commodities in variable proportions. On the other hand, any substitution in consumption will now be eliminated by the assumption that each country wishes to consume only one of the two commodities. In particular, Portugal is imagined to be interested only in wine, while England demands only cloth. The assumption of complete specialization in consumption, while highly artificial, serves to focus attention on the production side of international exchange. Comparative cost, emphasized by Ricardo and expressed in terms of opportunity cost by Haberler (1933), thus moves to the center of the stage. The more general case of diversification in both production and consumption will be taken up in section 1.3.

Supply conditions in Portugal can be thought to be described by supply functions for wine and cloth, each in terms of the relative price:

$$\overline{C}_P = \overline{C}_P(\pi), \tag{1.2.1}$$

$$\overline{W}_P = \overline{W}_P(\pi^*), \tag{1.2.2}$$

where again $\pi^* = 1/\pi$. It is clear that the supply of each commodity increases with its price. The quantity of wine available for consumption in Portugal is the sum of domestic production (since Englishmen do not drink wine) and what can be obtained for exported cloth,

$$W_P = \bar{W}_P + \pi\bar{C}_P = \bar{W}_P\left(\frac{1}{\pi}\right) + \pi\bar{C}_P(\pi). \tag{1.2.3}$$

With an increasing price of cloth, domestic wine production clearly declines while the export supply of cloth rises. Wine imports, benefiting from the increases in both the quantity and the price of cloth exports, rise even more. What happens to the domestic consumption of wine seems less clear, since an increase in imports is associated with a decline in domestic production. Clarity can be gained by considering the more fundamental data from which the supply functions are derived.

These data can be summarized in Portugal's production frontier for wine and cloth (fig. 1.2.1). For a given factor endowment and given technology, this curve indicates the maximum amount of cloth Portugal can produce for each amount of wine. It is clear that more cloth can be produced if less land and resources are allocated to wine growing; the curve thus has a negative slope. It is also clear that there is a finite amount of wine (cloth) that can be obtained if no cloth (wine) is produced. In addition, the laws of production

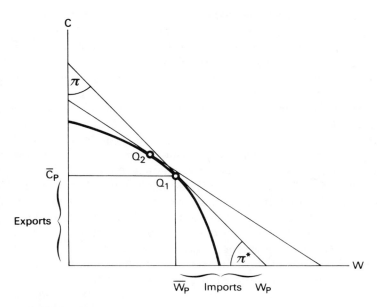

FIGURE 1.2.1
Portugal's Production Possibilities

and the difference in input requirements between the two industries will normally see to it, as the theory of production shows, that the curve is concave downward. As more wine is produced, more and more cloth must be sacrificed for an additional barrel.

Competition, if it works to perfection, will see to it that Portugal finds herself somewhere on the production frontier; inside the frontier, some factors would be unemployed or inefficiently used. Competition will also see to it that the total amount of wine available for consumption is maximized. Output combinations with the same wine consumption are found along a straight line whose slope corresponds to the terms of trade, π (or π^*). The highest income is reached at Q_1, where the production frontier is tangent to such an "iso-income line." Mathematically, the Portuguese commodity supply can be determined by maximizing wine consumption (1.2.3) subject to the implicit transformation function

$$R_P(\bar{W}_P, \bar{C}_P) = \bar{R}_P, \tag{1.2.4}$$

where $\bar{R}_P$ denotes the given quantity of Portuguese resources. The solution of this problem leads to the familiar optimality condition that the marginal rate of transformation in production must be equal to the terms of trade,

$$\frac{\partial R_P/\partial \bar{C}_P}{\partial R_P/\partial \bar{W}_P} = \pi. \tag{1.2.5}$$

If the relative price of cloth rises, the production point moves upward from Q_1 to, say, Q_2. As stated above, $\bar{C}_P$ rises and $\bar{W}_P$ declines. Both exports and imports rise. In addition, the graph makes clear that Portuguese income, and thus her wine consumption, W_P, also rise. This is intuitively plausible: a country cannot fail to gain if the terms of trade, *ceteris paribus*, move in favor of its exports.

The relationship between export supply and import demand with changing terms of trade can again be graphed in an offer curve. In figure 1.2.2 the offer curve for Portugal shows that with rising π both the supply of cloth and the import demand for wine are increasing. A similar curve can be drawn for England, with $\pi^* = 1/\pi$ taking the place of π. Equilibrium is reached where the two curves intersect. If π is "too high," Portugal's demand for wine exceeds England's supply and Portugal's supply for cloth exceeds England's demand. If π is too low, it is the other way around. In equilibrium the marginal rates of transformation of the two countries are equal, since each is equal to the terms of trade. Under the pressure of perfect competition, international trade thus sees to it that the opportunity costs are equalized internationally.

It is instructive to describe the equilibrium situation in still another graph (see fig. 1.2.3). The lower left-hand part reproduces the production diagram for Portugal in figure 1.2.1. To this is added the corresponding diagram for England, put on its head, with the origin in the upper right-hand

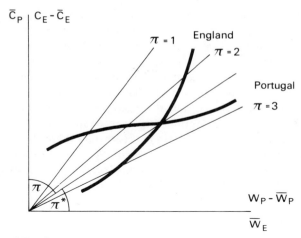

FIGURE 1.2.2
Diversified Production Equilibrium

corner. The dimensions of the box express total world production of wine
(along the horizontal axis) and cloth (along the vertical axis). Since the two
production frontiers just touch, the international division of labor is efficient
in the sense of promising the maximum amount of cloth that can be obtained
for the given amount of wine. Since the two curves could be made tangent to

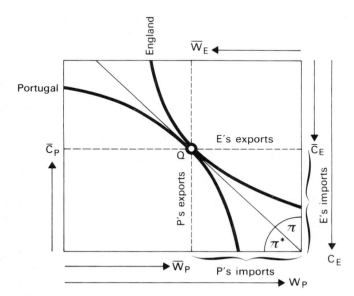

FIGURE 1.2.3
"Production Box"

each other at many other points, there are many international divisions of labor, each yielding a different combination of outputs, that satisfy this efficiency criterion. Of these, we have to select that combination for which supply matches demand. This means that the tangent to the two production frontiers at Q must go through the lower right-hand corner. If it passes left of the corner, the quantities Portugal wishes to trade are smaller than those England wants to exchange; if it passes above the corner, it is the other way around.

This analysis was based on the assumption that each country is interested in only one of the products. It shows that even in this case, if there is any trade at all, both countries will usually end up with diversified production. In this case, the international division of labor depends only on factor endowments and technology.

1.3 Diversified Consumption and Production

The preceding sections served mainly to introduce basic concepts and relationships. In reality, of course, international trade flows depend on both demand and supply factors. The two sets of elements will thus have to be combined.

Mathematically this results in the following system. Each country maximizes its utility

$$U_P = U_P(C_P, W_P), \tag{1.3.1}$$

$$U_E = U_E(C_E, W_E), \tag{1.3.2}$$

subject to the resource constraints (with land omitted)

$$R_P(\bar{C}_P, \bar{W}_P) = 0, \tag{1.3.3}$$

$$R_E(\bar{C}_E, \bar{W}_E) = 0, \tag{1.3.4}$$

and the budget constraints

$$\bar{W}_P + \pi\bar{C}_P = W_P + \pi C_P, \tag{1.3.5}$$

$$\bar{W}_E + \pi\bar{C}_E = W_E + \pi C_E. \tag{1.3.6}$$

In addition, total demand for wine must equal total supply,

$$W_P + W_E = \bar{W}_P + \bar{W}_E. \tag{1.3.7}$$

There is, of course, a similar condition for cloth, but it is implied by the preceding conditions. Equations (1.3.5) through (1.3.7) also guarantee that international trade is balanced. The system consisting of (1.3.1) through (1.3.7) determines production and consumption for each commodity in each country as well as the terms of trade. Trade flows are implicitly determined as the difference between consumption and production.

Graphically, this system can be represented by the "Mill/Marshall/

Meade international trade butterfly" depicted in figure 1.3.1, one of the most compact, and also prettiest, graphs in economics (Meade 1952). Wine is again measured horizontally, both to the right and to the left of the origin. Cloth is measured vertically, both upward and downward. The indifference curves for Portugal are drawn in the NW quadrant, while those for England are found in the SE quadrant. The NE quadrant contains information on foreign trade, horizontal distances measuring Portugal's exports (and England's imports) of wine, while vertical distances measure Portugal's imports (and England's exports) of cloth. Trade flows in the opposite direction would be recorded in the SW quadrant. The wing-shaped contours, finally, represent the production possibilities of the two countries. They are sometimes called the "production blocks."

Suppose some foreign trade broker announced an arbitrary relative price, π. This fixes a ray through the origin, indicating the exchange opportunities open to each country. At these terms of trade Portugal will choose that trade volume which, together with domestic production, promises the highest utility. It can be determined by sliding the production block up or down the exchange ray until it reaches the highest possible indifference curve. The origin of the production block then fixes a point on Portugal's offer curve. By

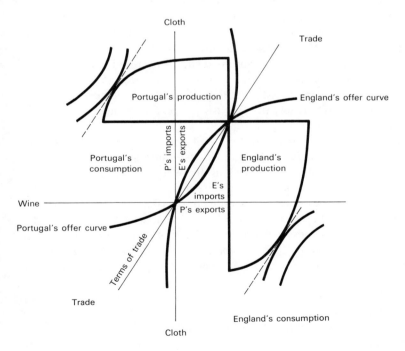

FIGURE 1.3.1
Consumption and Production Equilibrium

repeating this operation for other values of π, the whole offer curve for Portugal can be traced. England's offer curve is determined in a similar way.

The system is in equilibrium where the two offer curves intersect. If the two production blocks have their origin at this point and if each country chooses consumption in such a way that the indifference curve just touches the production frontier, then the terms of trade will be equal to the marginal rate of substitution in consumption and to the marginal rate of transformation in production in both countries. In this way, production, consumption, trade flows, and relative prices must be thought to be jointly determined by factor endowments, technology, and tastes without any reference to monetary factors. This is the "real" part of the international economic system, albeit in a highly abstract form and reduced to just two countries, two factors, and two commodities.

1.4 Shifts in the Terms of Trade

One of the more controversial problems in the field of international monetary economics is the effect of real factors on exchange rates. For example, was the discovery of North Sea oil one of the major causes of the appreciation of sterling in the late 1970s? Many aspects of this problem, since they are of a monetary nature, have to be postponed to subsequent chapters. However, the debate often involves the question of the effect of real factors on the terms of trade. This question is the subject of the present section.

To make the discussion look more realistic, it may be imagined that W stands for oil instead of wine. England thus exports cloth to obtain Portuguese oil. It may also be imagined that large oil deposits have been discovered in England. As a consequence, the English production frontier shifts to the right as indicated in figure 1.4.1.

What is the effect of such a shift on the terms of trade? The answer depends (1) on the resulting *shift* in England's offer curve and (2) on the *slope* of Portugal's offer curve. Most likely, the oil discovery reduces England's willingness to export cloth for oil at any given terms of trade. England's offer curve therefore swivels around the no-trade point as described in figure 1.4.2. At the same time it probably changes its shape. As a matter of fact, for certain terms of trade the willingness to export cloth for oil may even be replaced by a desire to export oil for cloth. The larger the "inward" shift in the English offer curve at given terms of trade, the larger—with other things equal—is the effect on the terms of trade.

The extent of the inward shift in the offer curve depends, in turn, (1) on the type of the underlying shift in resources and (2) on the income effects on English consumption. Suppose the initial situation for England is described by the production point P_1 and the consumption point Q_1 in figure 1.4.3. The cloth exports offered for oil imports at the terms of trade π are then repre-

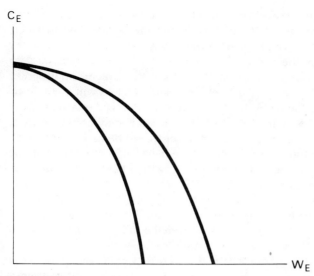

FIGURE 1.4.1
Technological Progress

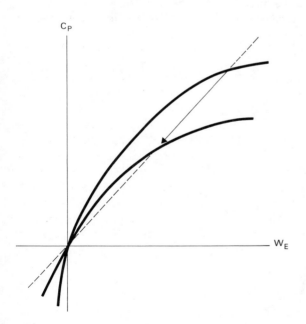

FIGURE 1.4.2
Shift in England's Offer Curve

sented by the difference between P_1 and Q_1. Now the production frontier shifts to the right. At unchanged terms of trade, the new situation is described by the production point P_2 and the consumption point Q_2. The change in trade clearly depends on the two arrows.

Consider first the shift in production from P_1 to P_2. If technical progress consists of a large oil discovery, it is likely that some factors will move from clothing into oil, thus reducing cloth production at unchanged relative prices. This case is illustrated in figure 1.4.3. In other cases it may be that factors formerly employed in the oil industry are now set free to be used in clothing, thus raising clothing production. The larger the increase in oil production at unchanged terms of trade, the more pronounced, with other things equal, the inward shift in the offer curve.

Now consider the shift in consumption from Q_1 to Q_2. It depends on the marginal propensity to consume cloth and oil. Except for inferior goods, consumption of oil is certain to increase. The lower the marginal propensity to consume oil, the lower the increase in consumption.

If both goods are noninferior and if the oil discovery attracts resources from the textile industry, we can be sure that oil production will rise more than oil consumption, thereby reducing both the import demand for oil and the export supply of cloth. In extreme cases, Q_2 may actually be to the left of P_2, indicating a reversal in the direction of trade. It is logically conceivable, however, that the increase in oil consumption exceeds the increase in produc-

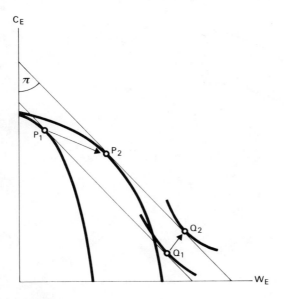

FIGURE 1.4.3
Effects of Technological Progress

tion; P_2 and Q_2 will then be farther apart than P_1 and Q_1. In such a case, the offer curve moves outward. It is important to note that the shift in the English offer curve does not depend on price elasticities. What matters is the reaction of output and consumption to increases in income at constant terms of trade.

Once the shift in the English offer curve is known, its effect on the terms of trade depends on the slope of the Portuguese offer curve. The latter, in turn, depends on the elasticity of the Portuguese import demand with respect to the terms of trade, ϵ_{PC}. If this elasticity is infinite, the Portuguese offer curve is a ray through the origin. In this case, the oil discovery, no matter how much it may have shifted the English offer curve, has no effect on the terms of trade. England will continue to trade at given world market prices. A small open economy trading in a large world market may come close to this limiting case. Even large shifts in natural resources may have little influence on the terms of trade.

In reality, the relevant demand elasticities for the rest of the world will often be clearly finite. In this case, the Portuguese offer curve in figure 1.3.1 is concave to the left. As a consequence, an inward shift in the English offer curve moves the terms of trade in favor of England; oil becomes cheaper relative to cloth. How much cheaper depends both on the size of the inward shift and the elasticity of Portuguese demand. In the exceptional case of an outward shift in the English offer curve, the terms of trade would move against England.

This discussion of real factors affecting the terms of trade has been limited to aspects which are potentially important as a background for exchange rate analysis. The main points can be summarized as follows:

1. The analytical framework for the determination of terms-of-trade effects is provided by the pure theory of international trade.

2. The shifts in the terms of trade resulting from real factors depend not only on price elasticities but also on the nature of the real factors and on income effects.

3. In the case of a small open economy in a large world market even a large shift in real factors may be accommodated without a large change in the terms of trade.

It should finally be noted that all of these considerations apply to the long run once all adjustments have run their course. During the adjustment process the terms of trade may be subject to more pronounced fluctuations. In the explanation of these temporary fluctuations, monetary factors will turn out to play a decisive role.

1.5 Factor Prices and Unemployment

The model of section 1.3 has implications for factor prices. These will now be made explicit. For this purpose, resources are labeled "labor" and their price is called "wage." Competition among employers will see to it that the real wage is equal to the marginal product of labor. In terms of the model of section 1.3, Portugal's marginal product of labor in terms of wine is the reciprocal of $\partial R_P / \partial \bar{W}_P$. The other marginal products are defined analogously.

Marginal products may be regarded as determined by the following mental experiment. Consider the Portuguese economy at an original point of international equilibrium as determined by the model of section 1.3. Assume now, however, that the quantity of resources is variable instead of being fixed. In this situation, imagine an increase in the production of wine obtained by a small increase in the amount of labor. The marginal product of labor is the increment in wine per unit of additional labor. A similar experiment yields the marginal product of labor in the Portuguese cloth industry. If Portuguese wages are paid in wine, workers in the wine industry simply keep their marginal product, while textile workers receive the quantity of wine that their marginal product can buy in the market at the given terms of trade. Denoting wages by w, this can be written as

$$w_P = \frac{1}{\partial R_P / \partial \bar{W}_P} = \frac{\pi}{\partial R_P / \partial \bar{C}_P}. \tag{1.5.1}$$

English wages are determined in the same way.

If there is competition in the labor market, all resources will be fully employed while wages are flexible. This is the assumption underlying the preceding sections. From a long-run point of view this is the relevant case. In the short run, however, it may well be that wages are "sticky" in the sense that they fail to decline promptly under the pressure of an emerging excess supply of labor. In this case there may be unemployment. Although in principle this will be temporary, it may nevertheless be serious. This Keynesian idea may be made more precise by assuming that the real wage is fixed above the full-employment level while resource utilization is variable. In terms of the previous model, this means that there is now a family of production frontiers, each for a different level of employment. In figure 1.5.1, these frontiers are represented by the iso-resources curves $R_1 \cdots R_6$.

If increasing quantities of labor are applied to given land, the iso-resources curves are more and more closely spaced, reflecting the law of diminishing returns. At each point of the diagram, there will be a certain marginal product of labor in terms of wine, measured by the horizontal distance between the iso-resources curves. Fixing the real wage (in terms of wine) means that the economy is restricted to a certain iso-wage path. Suppose that the Portuguese economy has originally been at point O with all resources fully employed. Now there is a change in the demand and supply conditions in England in such a way that the new equilibrium would be at F with a lower level of Portuguese real wages. In the short run, however, Portuguese wages

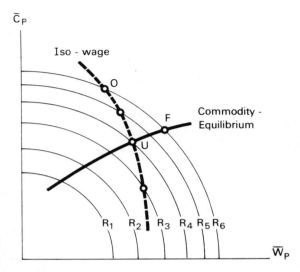

FIGURE 1.5.1
Factor Prices and Unemployment

are rigid. As a consequence, the economy can only move along the broken iso-wage curve.

On the other hand, for any given resource input, the economy must satisfy all the conditions for commodity-market equilibrium described in the model of section 1.3. With full employment (but after the change in the international situation), this equilibrium would be at F, as stated above. A corresponding commodity-equilibrium point can be constructed for each of the different employment levels. This determines another path, represented by the solid curve in figure 1.5.1. Overall short-run equilibrium at the predetermined wage rate is reached where the two curves intersect; in the graph this is at the underemployment point U. Employment will be at the level $R = 4$, which falls short of full employment.

This is only a short-run equilibrium, to be sure. In the course of time, the underemployment of resources will exert pressure on real wage rates. These will gradually decline, moving the economy outward along the commodity-equilibrium curve to higher employment levels. Finally, full employment will be restored at point F, but with wages below the initial level. While in the short run a shift in real demand and supply conditions leads to a change in employment at unchanged wages, in the long run it leads to a change in wage rates at unchanged employment.

Alternatively, we can start out with the commodity-equilibrium path corresponding to the new international situation. At each point along this path we determine the marginal product of labor in terms of wine by measuring the

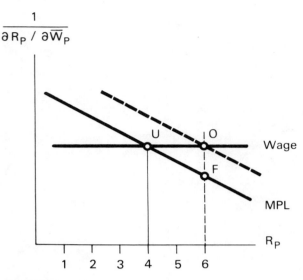

FIGURE 1.5.2
Marginal Product of Labor and Real Wage

horizontal distance between two successive iso-resources curves. In figure 1.5.2 these marginal products are plotted as a function of resources. In the same diagram we draw the fixed real wage rate. Employment will then be at the resource level $R = 4$, where the wage rate is equal to the marginal product of labor. The situation before the change in the international situation is added for comparison. For each employment level the marginal product of labor was higher, as expressed by the broken line. The same wage rate thus produced full employment at $R = 6$.

This chapter has shown how the "real" factors of the economy determine production, consumption, trade, and relative prices in economic equilibrium. The determinants are tastes, resources, and technology. Monetary factors have so far played no role. The way in which they extend and modify the picture resulting from the real factors is the central topic of the remainder of this book.

CHAPTER 2

Money, Prices, and Exchange Rates

Introduction

The introductory discussion of the international division of labor in chapter 1 was based on a model of barter: wine was directly exchanged for cloth, both nationally and internationally. The present chapter makes the step to a monetary economy. Money supplies, price levels, and exchange rates thus move to the center of the stage, which they will occupy through the remainder of this book. Prices are assumed to be perfectly flexible and the factors of production are thus fully employed.

The topic of the first section is the (relatively trivial) transition from barter terms of trade to relative money prices in different currencies. The second section considers the determination of commodity prices and exchange rates for given national money supplies. It is followed by a discussion of the special topic of purchasing-power parities. The converse case of the determination of commodity prices and money supplies for given exchange rates is the subject of the fourth section, again followed by a special-topic section on the transfer problem. While this discussion is in terms of a gold standard, the concluding section extends the analysis to fiat money. The exposition is restricted to commodity trade throughout. The chapter thus provides the foundations of international monetary economics in the absence of interest-bearing debt and international capital flows.

2.1 Relative Money Prices: Commodity Arbitrage

The subject matter of this section hardly deserves a separate title. However, this organization helps to make clear that the simple propositions discussed on the following pages are independent of any particular monetary arrangements and, in particular, have nothing to do with the purchasing-power parity doctrine and the specie-flow mechanism discussed in the remainder of this chapter.

In the barter world of the preceding chapter, if transportation costs and other trade impediments are abstracted from, the price of cloth in terms of wine, π, must clearly be the same everywhere in the trading area, both nationally and internationally. More generally, there can be only one equilibrium set of barter terms of trade. This is the "Law of One Price" for a barter economy. If it were violated, traders could make unlimited, riskless, and instant profits by selling cloth against wine where it is relatively dear and simultaneously buying it where it is relatively cheap. The Law of One Price is enforced through commodity arbitrage.

Basically, the Law of One Price has nothing to do with money. Nevertheless, it has implications for the relative money prices in monetary economics. Imagine that both the Portuguese and the English economies, while using different currencies, are fully monetized. The implications of the Law of One Price can then be expressed in three propositions:

1. In each country, the relative money prices must be equal to the barter terms of trade. Thus

$$\frac{p_{CE}}{p_{WE}} = \pi, \qquad \frac{p_{CP}}{p_{WP}} = \pi, \tag{2.1.1}$$

where p_{CE} is the money price of cloth in England, expressed in sterling, while p_{CP} is the money price of cloth in Portugal, expressed in escudos, and similarly for wine.

2. It follows from the preceding statement that the relative money prices for any two commodities must be the same in both countries:

$$\frac{p_{CE}}{p_{WE}} = \frac{p_{CP}}{p_{WP}}. \tag{2.1.2}$$

3. The sterling price of cloth must equal the escudo price of cloth converted into sterling. The same must be true for wine and any other traded commodity. If the exchange rate e is defined as the price of escudos in terms of sterling, this can be written

$$\frac{p_{CE}}{p_{CP}} = \frac{p_{WE}}{p_{WP}} = e. \tag{2.1.3}$$

While these propositions relate to relative money prices, they do not depend on any sort of monetary equilibrium or on a particular monetary arrangement. All they require is costless commodity trading. Whenever they are violated, this creates opportunities for profitable commodity arbitrage, which will quickly eliminate the discrepancy. Specifically, these arbitrage conditions do not constitute the purchasing-power parity doctrine. As will be shown in section 2.3, the latter may be valid even though there is not a single good that can be costlessly traded. Conversely, the arbitrage condition may be satisfied even though exchange rates deviate from purchasing-power parity.

The commodity arbitrage conditions are clearly restricted to costlessly tradeable goods. Such goods are usually called "international goods" or "traded goods." At the other end of the spectrum are goods that cannot be traded at all. They are often called "nontraded" or "home" goods. Land is an obvious example. Since international exchange is technically possible for most goods and services, though perhaps at a prohibitive cost, nontraded goods are also to some extent an idealization. From the present point of view, their essential feature is that the equalizing force of commodity arbitrage is inoperative. As Heckscher (1949) and Ohlin (1933) have shown, there are indeed economic forces linking the price of land in different countries,[1] but arbitrage does not do the job.

Most goods are found somewhere between these extremes, being tradeable at a cost. These costs may include transportation, transaction costs, tariffs, and other trade impediments. For such "imperfectly-traded goods," trading costs drive a wedge between the two sides of the above equalities. Suppose, to give an example, cloth is exported by England to Portugal, while wine is exported by Portugal to England, with transportation provided by English shipping at rates of, respectively, t_{CE} and t_{WE}. In this case the Law of One Price requires

$$e = \frac{p_{CE} + t_{CE}}{p_{CP}} = \frac{p_{WE} - t_{WE}}{p_{WP}}. \tag{2.1.4}$$

The price of cloth in Portugal, expressed in sterling, is equalized to the English price of cloth after shipping costs have been added to the latter. In the case of wine, shipping costs must be subtracted from the sterling price before it can be compared to the sterling equivalent of the Portuguese wine price. A similar condition could be written for any good entering into international trade. Which commodities are exported and imported, and at what costs, is determined in the real part of the system. While these problems are analytically difficult, they do not have to concern us in this monetary context. For the present purpose it is enough to note two points. First, any one of these arbitrage conditions is enough to provide a link between the two price systems. The others convey no additional information, since they can be derived from the first together with the relative prices determined in the real part. Second, while costlessly traded goods are easy to work with, their existence is

---

1. Samuelson's factor-price equalization theorem demonstrates that, under certain conditions, factor prices are completely equalized internationally even in the absence of international factor movements. In such cases, arbitrage is not necessary for factor-price equalization. In reality, however, the required conditions are unlikely to be satisfied, and international factor-price equalization thus seems to depend largely on factor mobility.

not essential; the required link between the price systems can just as well be provided by a commodity traded at a cost.

If price index numbers included only traded goods with identical weights, price levels would, of course, be equalized internationally through mere commodity arbitrage. Since, in reality, comprehensive price indices cover a wide spectrum of traded, imperfectly traded, and nontraded goods, commodity arbitrage, even with identical weights, provides no reason why the price levels of different countries or the purchasing power of their currencies should be equalized. In addition, countries generally use different weights corresponding to their consumption patterns. As a consequence, price levels would not be equalized even if all goods could be costlessly traded. Historical experience shows, in fact, that considerable differences in purchasing power may persist over indefinite periods. Arbitrage certainly links the price levels of different countries, but with costly trading it does not make them equal.

2.2 Prices and Exchange Rates with Given Money Supplies

This section makes the step from relative prices to absolute prices. Suppose the analysis of the real factors has determined the international division of labor and thus the quantities of all goods produced, traded, and consumed. At what money prices will these goods change hands? The answer to this question depends on the monetary arrangements. There are two basic variants of such arrangements. In one case, the money supply in each country is given while exchange rates are variable. In the other case, the exchange rate is fixed while the money supply adjusts. The present section is about the first of these cases.

For the purpose of this discussion it will be assumed that each country is on a "paper standard," using a fiat currency. Its money supply is exogenously given, being a legacy of past periods of money-financed budget deficits. Interest-bearing government debt (like, in fact, any sort of debt) is disregarded. The various currencies can be exchanged at freely fluctuating exchange rates. Gold plays no monetary role and is traded like any other commodity. Otherwise the underlying assumptions are the same as in chapter 1.

These assumptions are designed to focus attention on some basic features of the present system of floating exchange rates that emerged from the collapse of the gold-exchange standard in 1973. While the analysis is highly simplified, the main conclusions are nevertheless directly relevant for the interpretation of recent developments. In the present section, the discussion of dynamic aspects is narrowly limited; an extensive analysis of exchange dynamics is provided in chapter 11.

Again using the example of England and Portugal, the two money supplies can be denoted, respectively, by M_E (measured in sterling) and M_P (measured in escudos). In each country the nominal demand for cash balances, under full employment and disregarding other assets, depends on the absolute money prices:

$$L_E = L_E(p_{CE}, p_{WE}), \qquad L_P = L_P(p_{CP}, p_{WP}). \tag{2.2.1}$$

In the absence of money illusion, these money demand functions are linear-homogeneous in all prices. With wine as numéraire, they can thus be written

$$L_E = p_{WE}L_E\left(\frac{p_{CE}}{p_{WE}}, 1\right) = p_{WE}l_E(\pi),$$

$$L_P = p_{WP}L_P\left(\frac{p_{CP}}{p_{WP}}, 1\right) = p_{WP}l_P(\pi). \tag{2.2.2}$$

This means that the demands for real cash balances, l_E and l_P, measured in terms of the quantity of wine they can buy, depend on relative prices only. The terms of trade or relative price, π, are determined in the real part of the system as shown in chapter 1. The only variables left to be determined in the monetary part are the two absolute price levels, measured by the wine prices p_{WE} and p_{WP}, and the exchange rate.

The absolute price levels are determined by the condition that in each country the demand for money must be equal to the given money supply:

$$M_E = p_{WE}l_E(\pi), \qquad M_P = p_{WP}l_P(\pi). \tag{2.2.3}$$

If the demand for money exceeds the money supply, individuals, in the aggregate, try to accumulate more cash by selling goods, thus driving commodity prices down. The reverse happens if there is an excess supply of money. The quantity theory of money is valid in each country: in the absence of government debt, an exogenous, one-time increase in the supply of fiat money, once all adjustments have run their course, produces a proportional increase in all commodity prices. It would not be true to say, however, that all movements in the price level reflect movements in the money supply, since any change in real factors can produce changes in absolute prices at the given money supply. Fortunately, the acceptance of the quantity theory of money does not depend on a monetary interpretation of history.[2]

Once the absolute commodity prices are known for each country, the exchange rate can be determined from the commodity arbitrage condition for traded goods,

$$e = \frac{p_{WE}}{p_{WP}}. \tag{2.2.4}$$

---

2. A continuing expansion of the money supply, since it produces inflation, may result in a marked reduction in the demand for real balances. It may also have repercussions on real incomes. Inflation indeed has real effects. In this case, the relevant quantity-theory proposition says that a one-time change in the rate of monetary expansion does not produce a *progressive* change in the demand for real balances and in real income. If inflation rises from 5 to 10 percent, there is no reason why cash balances should continue to decline forever and why long-term economic growth should change.

As long as the right-hand side exceeds the left-hand side, it will be profitable to buy wine in Portugal for escudos, sell it in England for sterling, and convert the sterling into escudos at the going rate of exchange. This operation would tend to raise the escudo price of wine, lower the sterling price of wine, and raise the sterling rate of the escudo until equality is established. If the inequality is reversed, the arbitrage mechanism operates in the opposite direction.

This argument implies that the exchange rate for any two countries reflects their relative money supplies. In the present model

$$e = \frac{M_E}{M_P} \cdot \frac{l_P(\pi)}{l_E(\pi)}. \tag{2.2.5}$$

Once the real factors have determined π, the exchange rate depends on nothing but the two money supplies. Since the exchange rate is also affected by real factors, it would clearly be false to say that it is a "purely monetary phenomenon." It is true, however, that with the real factors unchanged the exchange rate moves in step with the relative money supplies. While this proposition has so far been derived for the special case of costlessly traded goods, it remains valid for a more general class of cases. In the long run, any change in relative money supplies tends to produce a similar change in exchange rates (compared to what exchange rates would have been at unchanged money supplies). The relationship between money supplies, prices and the exchange rate in the presence of nontraded goods will be the subject of the following section.

The relationships in the preceding analysis can be represented in a simple graph. In figure 2.2.1, the upward sloping ray in the NE quadrant represents the English demand for money, plotted along the horizontal axis, as a function of the absolute price level, measured vertically. The downward sloping ray in the SW quadrant contains the same information for Portugal. These are the graphs of (2.2.2). Once the money supplies, M_E and M_P, are marked off on the respective money axes, the two rays determine the corresponding national price levels. According to (2.2.4), the exchange rate is then obtained by taking the ratio of the two price levels; this is indicated in the NW quadrant.

The comparative statics of this model with respect to monetary factors are straightforward. If the English money supply rises (or the English demand for money declines), the English price level and the sterling rate of the escudo will rise in the same proportion, while Portuguese prices are not affected. If the Portuguese money supply increases (or the Portuguese demand for money declines), the result will be the same with the countries reversed. Each country, in the long run, has full control over its prices through the money supply. This is the fundamental feature of systems with fully flexible exchange rates and prices. A valid justification of floating exchange rates must ultimately be based on this feature (for an elaboration see ch. 14).

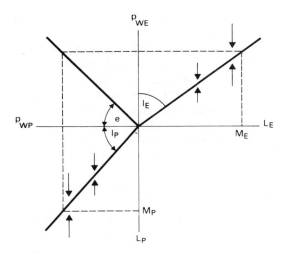

FIGURE 2.2.1
Prices and Exchange Rates with Given Money Supplies

The comparative statics with respect to real factors are less clear. Suppose some technological progress in agriculture permits England to grow wine at lower costs, thus shifting England's production frontier to the right as in figure 1.4.1. What is the effect on the exchange rate? The answer has a real and a monetary part.

The real part concerns the effect on the terms of trade, π. It was explained in section 1.4 that π is likely to rise, though in a small open economy facing given world market prices, it would remain constant, and in exceptional cases it might even decline.

The monetary part of the answer concerns the effect of π on e. Equation (2.2.5) shows that this depends on the effect of relative prices on the demand for real cash balances. The important point is that no general statement can be made about this effect. In particular, $\partial l_P / \partial \pi$ and $\partial l_E / \partial \pi$ can just as well be positive as negative. As a consequence, the effect of a real disturbance of this kind on the equilibrium exchange rate is entirely unclear.

The discovery of North Sea oil provides a modern illustration of this argument. The marked reduction in the English net demand for oil was often regarded as a compelling reason for a lasting appreciation of sterling. Concentrating on the English side, (2.2.5) shows that this argument is correct if at least one of the following statements applies:

1. The discovery of North Sea oil is associated with a contraction of the English money supply, M_E.

2. The discovery of North Sea oil produces an expansion in the English demand for real balances at given relative prices, that is, in an upward shift in $l_E(\pi)$.

3. The discovery of North Sea oil shifts the terms of trade in such a way that the English demand for money rises.

Relationship 1, if observed, seems fortuitous; economic science supplies no general justification for it. The same must be said about 3. It is true that π is likely to rise, but there is no particular reason why this should result in an increase in l_E. This leaves relationship 2. Inasmuch as the advent of North Sea oil increases the real resources of the British economy, it may indeed be expected to result in some increase in the demand for real balances. This seems to be the only reasonably solid basis for expecting a lasting appreciation of sterling. It should be noted that (1) this basis is of an entirely monetary nature, (2) it would, at best, explain a minor appreciation, and (3) the latter could easily be counteracted by an appropriate expansion in the English money supply.

So far, the analysis has been restricted to full equilibrium. What happens during the transition from one equilibrium to another? This is the basic question of exchange rate dynamics. The present discussion will have to be limited to the most elementary part of the answer; other aspects are taken up in subsequent chapters. The fundamental adjustment mechanism can be exhibited most clearly by assuming that prices in all commodity and factor markets are fully flexible, keeping these markets in equilibrium at all times. This leaves the sluggish adjustment of real cash balances to their desired level as the only reason for delays in the adjustment process. To formalize this idea, (2.2.2) can be reinterpreted as giving *desired real balances*, denoted by an asterisk, as a function of the terms of trade,

$$\left[\frac{L_E}{p_{WE}} \right]^* = l_E{}^*(\pi), \qquad \left[\frac{L_P}{p_{WP}} \right]^* = l_P{}^*(\pi). \qquad (2.2.6)$$

The accumulation of real cash balances in any given period may then be assumed to close a certain fraction of the gap between desired and actual balances:

$$\frac{dl_E}{dt} = \lambda_E \left[l_E{}^*(\pi) - \frac{M_E}{p_{WE}} \right],$$

$$\frac{dl_P}{dt} = \lambda_P \left[l_P{}^*(\pi) - \frac{M_P}{p_{WP}} \right]. \qquad (2.2.7)$$

The fractions λ_E and λ_P measure the speed of the adjustment process in each country. With infinite speed, the adjustment is instantaneous; full equilibrium is continuously maintained. Sluggish adjustment expresses the notion that economic agents, for reasons not explained in the model, find it costly or inconvenient to make up the whole shortfall of their cash balances by an immediate reduction in commodity purchases relative to sales. This model will be further analyzed in chapter 3.

With an exogenously given money supply and flexible prices, gradual adjustment of real cash balances translates into gradual adjustment of the price level. More precisely, a given percentage increase in real cash balances is achieved by bidding down the price level by the same percentage. In figure 2.2.1 this adjustment mechanism is expressed by vertical arrows. Whenever, at the given prices, the nominal cash balances are "too high," prices adjust upward; whenever cash balances are "too low," prices adjust downward. The strength of these adjustments, expressed by the length of the arrows, is in proportion to the excess or shortfall of cash balances.

It should be noted that this fundamental adjustment mechanism does not involve any imbalances in international trade, however short-lived. Trade is constantly balanced, and the terms of trade are in equilibrium at all times. "Hoarding" and "dishoarding" are not reflected in temporary gaps between sales and purchases of commodities, but in the increase and decline of the purchasing power of existing cash balances through falling and rising prices. This is a pure stock adjustment without any disturbances in flows. Of course, once prices cease to be fully flexible, temporary deviations of commodity flows and relative prices from their equilibrium values may appear. In the real world, they are the source of most problems. It is essential to realize, however, that these aspects, while often important, are analytically not crucial for the adjustment mechanism under flexible exchange rates.

2.3 Purchasing-Power Parity

The analysis of the preceding section was limited to traded goods. We shall now consider two economies which, besides the two costlessly traded goods, also produce and consume nontraded goods. There may also be any number of goods that can be internationally traded at a cost. The remaining assumptions are the same as before. This is the case to which the purchasing-power parity (PPP) doctrine is meant to apply. While its ancestry has been traced back to preclassical times, it was named and fully developed by Gustav Cassel (1916, 1918, 1921, 1922). Though occasional ambiguities in Cassel's arguments have given rise to misunderstandings up to the present day, the main lines of his analysis still retain their validity.[3]

Again, as in the previous case, the real factors determine which goods and services each country produces, consumes, and trades. In the presence of costly trading, the analytical solution of these problems is more difficult than before, to be sure, but international monetary theory may be excused for leaving these difficulties to the pure theory of international trade (see Samuelson

---

3. For surveys of the history and literature see Officer (1976) and Frenkel (1978). The interpretation of purchasing-power parity in this section is essentially identical to the one given by Haberler in 1933 (pp. 34 f.).

1964). The following discussion thus concentrates on the monetary aspects, taking the relative prices in each country as predetermined.

The demand for money must now be written as a function of many prices,

$$L_E = L_E(p_{CE}, p_{WE}, p_{1E}, \ldots, p_{nE}),$$

$$L_P = L_P(p_{CP}, p_{WP}, p_{1P}, \ldots, p_{nP}),$$

(2.3.1)

where $p_1 \cdots p_n$ denote the prices of nontraded goods or goods traded at a cost. For each country we can specify a commodity bundle that is, in some sense, regarded as representative for the economy in question. The two bundles may well be different. Their prices, p_E and p_P, are functions of the constituent commodity prices:

$$p_E = p_E(p_{CE}, p_{WE}, p_{1E}, \ldots, p_{nE}),$$

$$p_P = p_P(p_{CP}, p_{WP}, p_{1P}, \ldots, p_{nP}).$$

(2.3.2)

More specifically, the index numbers p_E and p_P are weighted averages of individual prices with nonnegative weights. They measure the absolute price levels.

In view of the linear homogeneity of the money demand functions, the latter can be expressed as functions of the respective price level and relative prices:

$$L_E = p_E l_E\left(\frac{p_{CE}}{p_E}, \frac{p_{WE}}{p_E}, \frac{p_{1E}}{p_E}, \ldots, \frac{p_{nE}}{p_E}\right),$$

$$= p_E l_E(\pi_{CE}, \pi_{WE}, \pi_{1E}, \ldots, \pi_{nE}),$$

(2.3.3)

$$L_P = p_P l_P(\pi_{CP}, \pi_{WP}, \pi_{1P}, \ldots, \pi_{nP}).$$

The relative prices expressed by the π's are predetermined by the real part of the system. What remains to be explained are the two absolute price levels p_E and p_P. As before, they are determined by the condition that the demand for money must equal the given supply:

$$M_E = p_E l_E(\ )$$

(2.3.4)

$$M_P = p_P l_P(\ )$$

(2.3.5)

The quantity theory is still valid in each country; it is not impaired by the presence of nontraded goods.

It also remains true that the exchange rate must be such that the English price of each costlessly traded good is equal to the Portuguese price converted into sterling at the current exchange rate as expressed in (2.1.3). In the absence of costlessly traded goods, this arbitrage condition is replaced by one like those in (2.1.4). As Haberler (1975, p. 24) has noted, the arbitrage condition, since it provides a link between price levels, may, in some sense, be regarded as the foundation of the PPP doctrine. However, Keynes (1930, 1:72) was also right in remarking that it is trivial. Though providing a necessary underpinning for the PPP doctrine, it is not its essence. It relates the exchange rate to the prices of traded (or imperfectly traded) goods, but it does not relate it to the purchasing power of the national currencies. For the essential elements we again have to turn to the monetary factors.

The relationship between the exchange rate and the two money supplies now becomes slightly more complicated. Assuming wine can be costlessly traded, the exchange rate is related to the two price levels through

$$e = \frac{p_{WE}/p_E}{p_{WP}/p_P} \cdot \frac{p_E}{p_P} = \frac{\pi_{WE}}{\pi_{WP}} \cdot \frac{p_E}{p_P} = k\frac{p_E}{p_P}, \tag{2.3.6}$$

where k is the ratio of the *relative* prices of wine in England and Portugal. If these relative prices are constant, the exchange rate is proportionate (but generally not equal) to the relative purchasing power of the two currencies. This is the proposition that gave the doctrine its name.

Behind the two price levels there are, of course, the respective money supplies:

$$e = k\frac{p_E}{p_P} = k\frac{M_E}{M_P} \cdot \frac{l_P(\ )}{l_E(\ )}. \tag{2.3.7}$$

This expression is the core of the purchasing-power parity postulate. It says essentially that the quantity theory of money applies not only to commodity prices, but also to the price of foreign exchange. If England doubles her money supply while Portugal leaves hers constant, the sterling price of escudos will double just like the sterling price of wine, cloth, haircuts, land, and everything else. There is no reason why one-time changes in money supplies should have lasting effects on k, π, or the demand for real balances. That the sterling rate of the escudo is proportional to the relative purchasing power of the two currencies is just a corollary to this basic postulate. For percentage changes we can write

$$\frac{de}{e} = \frac{dp_E}{p_E} - \frac{dp_P}{p_P} = \frac{dM_E}{M_E} - \frac{dM_P}{M_P}. \tag{2.3.8}$$

This expression holds whether or not $k = 1$.

It has been customary to distinguish an absolute version of the purchasing-power parity postulate in which $k = 1$ and a relative version in which $k \neq 1$. In criticism of absolute purchasing-power parity, Samuelson (1964) seems to have said all there is to say. Absolute PPP is valid provided (1) both price indices cover only costlessly traded goods and (2) the same weights are used in both indices. In this case, however, it is also trivial and uninteresting, reflecting nothing but commodity arbitrage. In less special (and more interesting) cases it is invalid. In general, there are just no economic forces making the purchasing power of one pound sterling equal to the purchasing power of its counterpart in escudos at the current exchange rate. The absolute PPP postulate is also unnecessary, since the relevant propositions can be obtained from the relative version. In fact, no serious economist seems to have defended it as an empirical proposition. It is true, however, that even Cassel was not always clear about the difference between the arbitrage conditions, which belong to the underpinnings of PPP, and PPP itself.

The relative version of the PPP postulate recognizes that k will generally be different from unity because (1) the two index numbers include nontraded or imperfectly traded goods and/or (2) the two index numbers are constructed with different weights. Being the ratio of two relative prices, k depends on all the real factors behind the international division of labor. It was Cassel's view that economic theory would find it difficult to make general statements about the determination of k, and he has yet to be proved wrong. The point is that international monetary theory does not need to know the level of k. Equation (2.3.8), based on the knowledge that k is not permanently affected by one-time changes in money supplies, is all that is required.

The preceding argument makes clear that the PPP postulate does not maintain that fluctuations in commodity prices cause exchange rate movements or vice versa. The association between exchange rates and price levels expressed by (2.3.6) comes about, rather, because these endogenous variables are jointly dependent on the money supply, as expressed in (2.3.4) and (2.3.7). The discussion about causation is thus beside the point. In particular, it makes no sense to "test" the direction of causation by observing leads and lags. It may well be that exchange rates run ahead of prices, the latter being often quite sluggish while the former, as will be shown in subsequent chapters, react quickly and even tend to overshoot.

Nor does the PPP doctrine maintain that exchange rates are expected to move parallel to the ratio of price levels in the course of economic history. Comparisons of price changes and exchange rate changes in the course of time, therefore, do not provide meaningful tests of the doctrine (see, for example, Officer 1980). As a matter of fact, the real factors behind the international division of labor are continuously changing, producing changes in k, l_E^*, and l_P^*, and thus deviations of exchange rates from relative purchasing power. The most familiar example of systematic deviations of this sort is the observation that domestic prices tend to increase relative to traded-goods prices in the course of economic development (Balassa 1964; Samuelson 1964). It is clear that such observations, while interesting for other reasons, do not impair the validity of the PPP principle. From the point of view of PPP, the changes in real factors may even dominate the monetary changes as determinants of exchange rate fluctuations. The PPP principle maintains that changes in the money supply affect price levels and exchange rates in a parallel fashion; it does not maintain that price levels and exchange rates are affected by nothing but money supplies. Rather than relating to the total movements in exchange rates and price levels, it relates to the partial effects of monetary changes. To put it negatively, the principle says that k, by whatever forces it may otherwise be determined, is *not* influenced by changes in money supplies. As a consequence, meaningful testing of PPP must be based on a comparison, not of the total variations in exchange rates and prices, but of the partial effects attributable to monetary factors.

This quantity-theoretic interpretation of PPP provides the proper perspective on the choice of price indices. The main point is that, in principle, this choice does not matter. Since the money supply, under the assumptions of this chapter, has no influence on relative prices, the PPP postulate is valid for any composition of commodity bundles. Specifically, price indices might include land rents, the wages of labor, and the prices of nontraded goods, along with the prices of traded goods. In fact, they might even be restricted to nontraded goods. The perennial question about the choice of the appropriate index number is thus largely irrelevant (a potential exception to this statement is noted in footnote 4 below). It should be kept in mind, however, that for costlessly traded goods, PPP is trivially satisfied through arbitrage. Whatever interest PPP may have derives, as Keynes (1930, 1:73) emphasized, from its application to nontraded and imperfectly traded goods. It would be unfortunate, therefore, to use price indices of traded goods only. A considerable component of nontraded and imperfectly traded goods is necessary for a meaningful application of PPP.

Not surprisingly, the PPP postulate is subject to the same qualifications as the quantity theory from which it is derived. Some of these were already mentioned in the preceding discussion. Three more will now be added. First, the PPP postulate relates only to full long-run equilibrium of stocks and flows after all temporary adjustments have run their course. It is well understood that in the short run money can have powerful real effects on the economy, reflected in temporary deviations of relative prices and real cash balances from their equilibrium values. The international counterpart of these effects is the short-run deviation of exchange rates from purchasing-power parity, possibly of a violent sort. These deviations are, in fact, the main subject of international monetary theory under flexible rates, to which the PPP doctrine only provides the long-run background.[4]

4. The fact that individual prices, if disturbed by a monetary change, approach their new long-run level with unequal speed and smoothness, may provide a criterion for the construction of appropriate price indices. One would probably want to include prices that are likely to approach their new equilibrium levels rapidly and monotonically, while one would want to exclude prices that are particularly sluggish or subject to overshooting. Similar considerations may be relevant in determining the appropriate devaluation rate in disequilibrium situations under fixed exchange rates. While the PPP postulate is not strictly valid under such conditions and relative prices are distorted, one would probably want to construct the price index in such a way that the distortions are as small as possible.

Second, the PPP principle, like the quantity theory, strictly applies only to fiat money exogenously supplied by the government. It would not be strictly (though perhaps roughly) valid, for example, under a gold standard, where the purchasing power of money, in the last analysis, depends on the production costs in gold mining relative to other industries, while the quantity of money is endogenous.[5]

Third, the strict validity of the PPP postulate requires either that there be no interest-bearing government debt or that this debt expand and contract in proportion to the money supply. This corresponds to the fact, familiar from monetary theory, that the quantity theory does not relate to money as such but to the whole array of financial assets exogenously supplied by the government. Violations of this requirement may lead to lasting deviations of the exchange rate from PPP. Deviations of this sort will be taken up in the final section of chapter 12.

2.4 Prices and Money Supplies with Given Gold Prices

Sections 2.2 and 2.3 discussed the determination of absolute commodity prices for given money supplies under flexible exchange rates. In this and the following sections the perspective is reversed by regarding the money supply of each country as variable while exchange rates are fixed. Attention is thus focused on the working of a system with fixed exchange rates as it existed before 1973. In this system, gold played an important role. The present discussion concentrates on the idealized case of a pure gold standard. Reality was more complex even before World War I. Since then, the monetary role of gold declined further. Nevertheless, the gold standard case exhibits important aspects of international monetary arrangements before the collapse of the Bretton Woods system in a particularly clear form.

The central problem of the gold standard is the centuries-old question of how gold is distributed between countries if each maintains a fixed gold price in terms of its own currency. The classical answer to this question is the so-called specie-flow mechanism. It is the main topic of the present section.

The real aspects of the system may again be thought to be determined by the model of chapter 1. This will now be combined with the following set of monetary assumptions:

1. Each country is on a gold specie standard where gold coins actually circulate as money. Alternatively, it could be assumed that bank notes are fully covered by the gold reserves of the central bank.

2. The world gold supply, $\bar{G}$, is given, and there is neither current production nor nonmonetary use of gold.

3. Each country defines the gold content of its coins, and each mint is

---

5. For an elaboration see Niehans (1978, pp. 142 f.).

ready to recoin foreign currency into domestic currency free of charge in unlimited amounts.

These assumptions are designed to eliminate any influence of monetary factors on the real side of the economy. They are highly artificial inasmuch as the distinctive feature of the gold standard is exactly the relationship between the monetary system on one hand and the production and nonmonetary consumption of gold.[6] They are nevertheless appropriate for the purpose of the present section, since they help to put the discussion in a classical context.

The question is how the world money supply is distributed among countries. The mercantilists concentrated their efforts on attracting as much gold as possible to their own economies. In opposition to them, David Hume (1752/1898) was able to show that national gold stocks have a natural level, from which, he argued, they cannot be permanently diverted by mercantilist measures. It will now have to be explained how this level is determined. Hume's argument, while valid in substance, is analytically defective. It is remarkable that economists did not succeed in correcting its defects, and indeed hardly felt the need for doing so, for more than two centuries. (Their subterfuges are entertainingly exposed in Samuelson 1980.) The following exposition, in its static part, substantially follows Collery (1971). A different graphical depiction, instructive despite a drawing error, is given in Samuelson (1971a).

According to assumptions 1 and 2 the gold stocks of England and Portugal add up to the world gold stock:

$$G_E + G_P = \bar{G}. \tag{2.4.1}$$

By assumption 3, the two gold prices, $\bar{p}_{GE}$ and $\bar{p}_{GP}$, are given. Gold arbitrage will see to it that the exchange rate corresponds to the ratio of these prices:

$$e = \frac{\bar{p}_{GE}}{\bar{p}_{GP}}. \tag{2.4.2}$$

Surely, fixed gold parities for national currencies (in the absence of transaction costs) imply fixed exchange rates. In addition, in each country the gold stock and the commodity price level have to be such that the demand for money at the predetermined relative prices is satisfied:

$$\bar{p}_{GE}G_E = M_E = p_{WE}l_E(\pi),$$
$$\bar{p}_{GP}G_P = M_P = p_{WP}l_P(\pi). \tag{2.4.3}$$

Since commodity and gold arbitrage will result in $\bar{p}_{GE}/\bar{p}_{GP} = p_{WE}/p_{WP}$, it follows that

$$\frac{G_E}{G_P} = \frac{l_E(\pi)}{l_P(\pi)}. \tag{2.4.4}$$

6. For a detailed discussion of commodity money see Niehans (1978, ch. 8).

This means that the division of gold between the two economies is entirely demand-determined. The gold stocks stand in the same proportion as the demands for real cash balances. This proportion, together with the total gold stock, then determines the absolute amount of gold and the absolute commodity price level in each country.

This is expressed graphically in figure 2.4.1. Its skeleton is similar to figure 2.2.1, but the east and south axes are now used for the national stocks of monetary gold. The exchange rate, depicted in the NW quadrant, is fixed by the given gold prices. It determines the ratio, but not the level, of national prices. The rays in the NE and the SW quadrants relate to each national price level the corresponding demand for gold, derived from the demand for real cash balances. The line going SE indicates the ratio between the two gold demands at a given exchange rate. Since the ratio is the same for all price levels, this line is a ray through the origin. The 45° line in the SE quadrant, finally, connects those national gold stocks that add up to the given world gold supply. The equilibrium division of available gold supplies is reached at A, where the curves in the SE quadrant intersect. This, in turn, fixes the price level in both countries.

The *comparative statics* of this gold standard system can be summarized in the following propositions:

1. If new gold is found, both countries share in the increase in the world

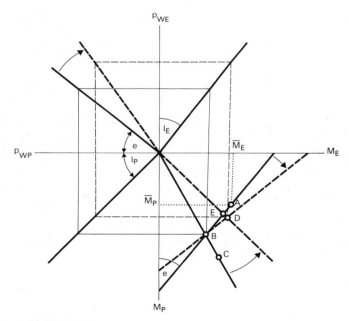

FIGURE 2.4.1
Prices and Money Supplies with Given Gold Prices

gold stock in proportion to their previous gold stocks. It does not matter in which country the gold is initially discovered.[7] Both price levels rise in proportion to the additional gold supply, leaving relative prices unchanged. After the discovery of America, Spain could not prevent its gold and silver from being dissipated all over Europe, producing a general "price revolution." In the nineteenth century, the Californian and South African gold discoveries had similar effects. It is the fundamental property of fixed exchange rates that they "internationalize" the money supply.

2. If Englishmen try to "hoard" gold in the sense of an increased demand for cash balances, they will attract a higher share of the world gold supply. At the same time, the price level will fall by the same percentage in both countries, reconciling Portugal with a lower gold stock and reducing the required accumulation in England. The same would be true if England's demand for money increased because of economic growth. Under fixed exchange rates, the demand for money creates its own supply, partly through money flows and partly through adjustments in the world price level.

3. If England raises the price of gold, the only effect is a proportional increase in English prices. The distribution of gold is unaffected and so is the Portuguese price level. Devaluation is neutral.

Comparative statics does not tell us how an economy moves from one equilibrium to another. This is a question of *dynamics*. What happens, for example, if the initial distribution of gold is "wrong," say at *B*, England having paid a one-time subsidy (for reparations, development aid, etc.) to Portugal? In this case, the English money supply at the previous prices will fall short of the demand for money. Englishmen will try to replenish their cash balances, probably by cutting down on their purchases of both wine and cloth. As a consequence, they import less wine and leave more cloth for export. Conversely, excess cash balances will induce the Portuguese to purchase more wine and cloth, thus increasing cloth imports and leaving less wine for export. The result will be a trade deficit for Portugal, which has to be paid for in gold. Gold will continue to flow back to England until the initial position is restored. The initial subsidy in the form of gold will thus be gradually converted into a flow of commodities. Once equilibrium is restored, the only lasting effect of the subsidy is the pleasant memory among the Portuguese of a period of good living, while the English will bear the permanent burden in the form of the memory of hard times. (Any accumulation or loss of durable capital goods would, of course, leave a permanent effect on relative prices.) The international distribution of gold is thus shown to be regulated by automatic feedback-control. This dynamic argument was the centerpiece of Hume's specie-flow mechanism.

This dynamic mechanism can be made analytically more precise by using

---

7. Of course, if the new gold, contrary to the present assumptions, has to be mined at a cost, it affects the real part of the system and thus relative prices.

the partial-adjustment model of (2.2.7), where, in each period, the accumulation of real cash balances closes a certain fraction of the gap between desired and actual balances. But since exchange rates are now fixed while money supplies are variable, the model has to be reinterpreted in certain respects. To simplify the analysis without loss of generality, it will be assumed that both gold prices are fixed at $\bar{p}_{GE} = \bar{p}_{GP} = 1$, implying $e = 1$, $p_{WE} = p_{WP} = p_W$, and $p_{CE} = p_{CP} = p_C$. Money stocks thus become equivalent to gold stocks, $L_E = \bar{p}_{GE}G_E = G_E$ and $L_P = \bar{p}_{GP}G_P = G_P$. A further, and quite considerable, simplification can be obtained by assuming that the desired demand for real balances is independent of *relative* prices and can thus be written $l_E{}^*(\pi) = \bar{l}_E$ and $l_P{}^*(\pi) = \bar{l}_P$.[8] The crucial modification concerns the way real cash balances are accumulated. Under fixed exchange rates with variable money supplies this takes place through the accumulation or decumulation of nominal cash balances at the prices determined by the market. With these modifications, the accumulation functions can be written

$$\frac{dG_E}{dt} = \lambda_E(p_W\bar{l}_E - G_E),$$

$$\frac{dG_P}{dt} = \lambda_P(p_W\bar{l}_P - G_P).$$

$$(2.4.5)$$

Graphically, the accumulation function for England can best be visualized by taking the negative

$$-\frac{dG_E}{dt} = \lambda_E(G_E - p_W\bar{l}_E).$$

For a given "world price level," the reduction in cash balances, originating from a cash surplus and associated with a trade deficit, is a rising linear function of G_E as depicted in figure 2.4.2. The slope of such a line reflects the adjustment speed, while the G_E intercept corresponds to the desired amount of money. For a given money supply, a rising price level gradually transforms excess supply of money into excess demand. A similar graph can be drawn for Portugal.

During the adjustment process, England's gains of gold must always be equal to Portugal's losses, which means $dG_E/dt = -dG_P/dt$. Starting with any initial distribution of gold, however "wrong," the adjustment process is then determined as follows. For a given subperiod or "week," the gold stocks inherited from the previous week determine the price level at which the desired cash accumulation in England equals the desired cash decumulation in

8. If in a two-goods model the price level is measured by one of the prices, this assumption cannot be strictly valid. Suppose the wine price used as numéraire remains constant while the cloth price rises. The demand for cash balances must certainly rise. A change in relative prices at a constant "price level" thus influences the demand for money. With less simplistic index numbers the assumption may well be satisfied.

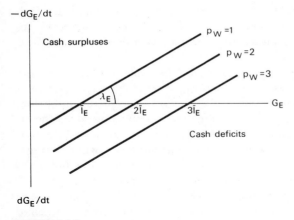

FIGURE 2.4.2
Cash Accumulation

Portugal. This produces a short-run flow equilibrium characterized by a certain trade balance. The resulting changes in cash balances are then added to (or subtracted from) the existing stocks, thus determining the money supplies at the beginning of next week, and so on. This is illustrated in figure 2.4.3, which is a combination of figure 2.4.2 for England with the corresponding graph for Portugal, the latter with both axes reversed. The horizontal dimension corresponds to the given world gold stock, $\bar{G} = G_E + G_P$. Along the

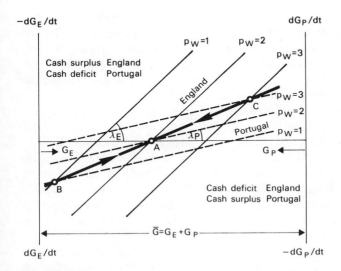

FIGURE 2.4.3
Specie-flow Mechanism

vertical axis, English trade deficits (originating from cash surpluses) and Portuguese trade surpluses (originating from cash deficits) are measured upward, while English trade surpluses and Portuguese trade deficits are measured downward.

It is clear that commodity prices must be the same in both countries. This requirement is satisfied where the English curve for a given p_W intersects the Portuguese curve for the same price. The locus of these price-equilibrium points is the heavy line. It describes the adjustment path along which the international system moves toward equilibrium. Consider an initial point B (corresponding to B in fig. 2.4.1). England is short of money, while Portugal has an excessive money supply. At a price level of $p_W = 1$ there is equilibrium between the cash England wishes to acquire in the next period and the cash Portugal is willing to give up. At the beginning of the following period, the system will have moved to the right. Again England will have a balance of payments surplus, though of a somewhat smaller amount. Gradually, the system moves in the direction of the arrow. The same would happen, though with opposite direction, if the initial cash deficit had occurred on the side of Portugal as exemplified by C. Stationary equilibrium with full adjustment of both stocks and flows is reached at A (corresponding to A in fig. 2.4.1), where the demand for money is equal to the supply for both countries. This seems to be the dynamic adjustment mechanism Hume had in mind, reduced to its bare essentials.

2.5 The Transfer Problem

Hume's mechanism is traditionally called the "price/specie-flow mechanism." The name seems to suggest that prices play a crucial role in it, but what exactly this role may be has been a subject of controversy since Hume's time. (On the history of this debate, see Viner 1937, ch. 6; Samuelson 1971b; Frenkel and Johnson 1976; Frenkel 1976.) The present section outlines the answer that is implied by the model of section 2.4.

As the mechanism was described by Hume, its decisive element appears to be the ratio between the prices in different countries, with the abundance of money driving up Portuguese prices while scarcity of money drives English prices down. For nontraded and imperfectly traded goods such international price differentials may indeed appear. For costlessly traded goods, however, they are excluded, arbitrage keeping foreign and domestic prices, expressed in the same currency, continuously in line. The present model is restricted to such traded goods, and yet the mechanism works. It follows that international price differentials cannot play an essential role in it.

Other economists, including J. S. Mill, suggested that the crucial ratio was the one between the prices of the traded goods—in other words, the terms of trade. However, in the above account of the mechanism, π does not appear either. It was, in fact, explicitly eliminated by the assumption that the demand for money is independent of relative prices. Nevertheless a coherent description of the mechanism could be given. Thus Mill must have been wrong, too.

If any price can be said to play a crucial role, it is the common international price level, here measured by p_W, because, in general, this must continuously adjust to provide equilibrium between cash accumulation and cash decumulation in different countries. However, no general statements can be made about the direction in which p_W is moving during the adjustment process. This depends entirely on the relative adjustment speeds. If the gold-gaining country (that is, the subsidy-paying country with the initial cash deficit) has the higher adjustment speed, p_W will instantly decline when the subsidy is paid and rise again during the adjustment process. This case is illustrated in figure 2.4.3. If the gold-losing country has the higher adjustment speed, p_W will instantly rise and then gradually decline. If, finally, the adjustment speeds are equal, the price level will remain constant.[9] Surely, these common price movements, of which economists were hardly aware, were not what gave the mechanism its name.

There is still the possibility that the crucial role may be played by a price that was omitted from this model. In particular, one might wonder if Hume's argument was supposed to apply to the prices of nontraded or domestic goods. If Portugal, because of the subsidy, has excess money while England is short of cash, does this produce an increase in the Portuguese prices of domestic goods relative to those in England? Theoretical research on this problem has shown that in a wide class of cases this is indeed so, but the opposite outcome cannot be excluded. In any case, this cannot be called a crucial aspect of the mechanism either.[10] In the light of these considerations we have to conclude that the mechanism has been misnamed: it is indeed a specie-flow mechanism, but prices do not play a crucial role in it. The decisive element is the reaction of commodity demand to excess cash balances.[11]

There remains the question whether the terms of trade, while not being a

---

9. The fact that $dG_E/dt = -dG_P/dt$ implies $\lambda_E(p_W \bar{L}_E - G_E) = -\lambda_P(p_W \bar{L}_P - G_P)$. Taking the total differential, $\lambda_E \bar{L}_E dp_W - \lambda_E dG_E = -\lambda_P \bar{L}_P dp_W + \lambda_P dG_P$, letting $dG_P = -dG_E$, and rearranging, one obtains

$$\frac{dp_W}{dG_E} = \frac{\lambda_E - \lambda_P}{\lambda_E \bar{L}_E + \lambda_P \bar{L}_P}.$$

While the English money supply gradually rises to its former level, the international price level will thus rise, remain constant, or fall according to whether $\lambda_E \gtreqless \lambda_P$. The instant reaction at the time the subsidy is paid goes, of course, in the opposite direction.

10. See Chipman (1974, pp. 70 f.).

11. It should be noted that the demand functions for desired real balances (2.2.6) do not include actual cash balances. As a consequence, the model does not exhibit "real balance effects" in full equilibrium. Actual balances, working through (2.2.7), play their dynamic role only during the adjustment process.

crucial element of the mechanism, nevertheless react in a typical way. Keynes (1929) thought they did. In the discussion about German reparations under the Treaty of Versailles he argued that Germany, in addition to the primary burden of reparations, had to bear a secondary burden consisting of an adverse shift in the terms of trade. Ohlin (1929) replied that this was not necessarily true, the terms of trade moving possibly in favor of Germany. The subsequent debate about what came to be called the "transfer problem" showed that Ohlin was right.[12]

The basic argument is straightforward. Suppose England has paid Portugal a subsidy consisting of gold, which was collected in England by taxes and distributed in Portugal among the population. How will this affect the price ratio between cloth and wine? The answer depends on whether at *unchanged* relative prices the subsidy creates overall excess demand for cloth (necessarily accompanied by excess supply of wine) or excess supply of cloth (necessarily accompanied by excess demand for wine). At unchanged terms of trade, production remains unchanged. Overall excess demand for cloth thus depends entirely on the shifts in consumption. These, in turn, depend on the fraction of every ounce of excess gold that is used in Portugal to buy additional cloth after deducting the fraction of every ounce of gold shortfall that is saved up in England by buying less cloth. What matters is the difference between the two marginal propensities to spend excess money on cloth.

If for every ounce of gold transferred to Portugal, Portuguese demand for cloth rises more than the English demand declines, there will be an overall excess demand for cloth, accompanied by an excess supply of wine. As a consequence, π will rise. On the other hand, if for every ounce of gold transferred to Portugal, Portuguese demand for cloth rises less than the English demand declines, there will be an overall excess supply of cloth, accompanied by an excess demand for wine. As a consequence, π will fall. It follows that the *direction* of the shift in the terms of trade during the adjustment process depends *only* on the division of excess cash balances between cloth and wine. In particular, it does not depend on the price elasticities of demand and on the shape of the production function.[13] The extent of the shift, however, also depends on the other aspects of the model.

This argument may be made clearer with the aid of figure 2.5.1. The solid lines describe, respectively, the Portuguese excess demand for cloth and the English excess supply of cloth, both depending on the terms of trade, before the disturbance in the money supply. By the transfer of money from England to Portugal both curves are shifted to the right. Whether π rises or falls depends entirely on the relative magnitude of these horizontal shifts.

12. The most important single contribution to this debate is by Samuelson (1952). An up-to-date summary and restatement, though in highly mathematical terms, is given in Chipman (1974).

13. This is no longer true in the presence of nontraded goods.

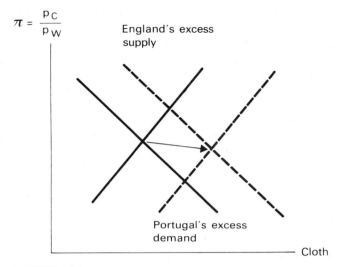

$$\pi = \frac{p_C}{p_W}$$

FIGURE 2.5.1
Transfer Effect on Terms of Trade

However, once the magnitude of the shifts is known, the extent of the rise or fall also depends on the slopes of the two curves.

During the last fifty years, the debate about the transfer problem has absorbed a large amount of analytical energy. This is not only because it is a neat intellectual puzzle, but also because it is an ingredient in many important problems in international monetary economics. The main general result of this debate, despite the brilliance of some contributions, was a warning to mistrust seemingly clear-cut statements in this area, no matter how plausible they may appear. Prices may move in almost any direction and still the specie-flow mechanism works.

2.6 Fiat Money with Fixed Exchange Rates

Section 2.2 above discussed fiat money with flexible exchange rates; section 2.4 was about a gold standard with fixed rates. Neither of these models seems to be immediately applicable to arrangements like the European Monetary System, which are based on fiat money but nevertheless maintain fixed exchange rates subject to occasional devaluation or revaluation. The same is true for the later stages of the Bretton Woods system, when monetary policy was increasingly conducted as if the fixed gold price did not matter. The present section is intended to close this gap by concentrating on the case of fiat money with fixed exchange rates. It will turn out that this case is closely related to the gold standard, but with an important difference in the dynamics of devaluation.

The gold standard described in section 2.4 is now replaced by the following assumptions:

1. Both England and Portugal use fiat money; gold is treated like any other commodity.

2. Each country has originally issued a fixed amount of its own currency, denoted, respectively, by $\bar{M}_E$ and $\bar{M}_P$; this fixes the world money supply.

3. Each central bank is willing to issue additional amounts of its own currency against payment in foreign currency at a fixed exchange rate;[14] the money supply in each country thus remains variable.

These assumptions can be summarized in the statement that the sum of the national money supplies, expressed in sterling, is equal to the world money supply,

$$M_E + eM_P = \bar{M}_E + e\bar{M}_P. \tag{2.6.1}$$

The remaining assumptions are the same as before. In particular, in full equilibrium the demand for money equals the supply,

$$M_E = p_{WE}l_E(\pi), \qquad M_P = p_{WP}l_P(\pi), \tag{2.6.2}$$

and arbitrage sees to it that the international price ratio for each traded good is equal to the exchange rate,

$$e = \frac{p_{WE}}{p_{WP}}. \tag{2.6.3}$$

Prices are again fully flexible, and nontraded goods are disregarded.

The graphical representation of this model is similar to the gold-standard case. In figure 2.6.1 everything except the SE quadrant corresponds exactly to figure 2.4.1. In the SE quadrant the two axes now measure, respectively, the national money supplies. The initial quantities are marked off as $\bar{M}_E$ and $\bar{M}_P$. Starting from A, the public is then free to obtain escudos for sterling from the Portuguese central bank or sterling for escudos from the English central bank according to (2.6.1). In graphical terms the public can move along the solid line, whose slope reflects the exchange rate. The intercepts of this line measure the world money supply, to the south in escudos and to the east in sterling. As the graph is drawn, the system will be in equilibrium at point B, with the Portuguese central bank holding some sterling.

The comparative statics of this model are easily derived. Suppose one of the countries, say Portugal, exogenously increases its money supply, moving $\bar{M}_P$, and thus A, vertically downward. The effects can be summarized as follows:

14. This assumption is chosen to eliminate the reserve constraint from the present model. In reality, convertibility is at least as much a question of the willingness and ability of central banks to sell foreign exchange against payment in domestic currency at fixed rates.

1. Both countries will share in the increase in the world money supply in proportion to their previous money supplies.[15] Some of the additional money issued in Portugal will thus spill over to England. In figure 2.6.1, the money supply curve in the SE quadrant will shift downward in a parallel fashion. The equilibrium will thus move along the SE ray to a position like *C*. This means that under fixed rates individual countries have no control over their money supplies; the money supply is "internationalized." When the Federal Reserve switched to a policy of rapid credit expansion around 1961, the additional money spilled over to the rest of the world, producing increases in national money supplies abroad.

2. Both price levels will rise in proportion to the world money supply. Under fixed rates it is impossible for a country to insulate its price level against inflationary or deflationary pressures originating abroad. In the 1960s, monetary expansion in the United States inexorably led to inflation in the rest of the world; efforts to combat imported inflation were futile.

3. The English central bank will experience an inflow of Portuguese money in exchange for English money. Once the bank is no longer willing to accumulate escudos, the system collapses. This moment may be postponed if the Portuguese central bank is willing and able to convert these escudos into sterling, but then the Portuguese foreign exchange reserves decline. Relatively expansionary policies lead to a shortage of reserves, while high reserves

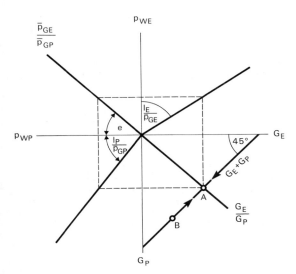

FIGURE 2.6.1
Fiat Money with Fixed Rates

15. Note that the SE ray, whose slope expresses the ratio of the national money supplies, does not change.

are the counterpart of relatively restrictive policies. U.S. monetary expansion in the 1960s was associated with a loss of reserves, while the rest of the world accumulated dollar balances. No such problems appear if both sides expand their money supplies in the same proportion. Long-run viability of a fiat-money system with fixed rates requires that pronounced international discrepancies in monetary policies are avoided. Indeed, the need for "harmonization" of monetary policies is one of the basic characteristics of fixed exchange rates in a fiat-money system. It should be noted, though, that even the most perfect harmonization could not have saved the Bretton Woods system because it was ultimately based on gold.

The other comparative-static question concerns the effects of a devaluation.[16] If sterling is devalued (and thus the escudo revalued), the exchange ray in the NW quadrant and the money-supply ray in the SE quadrant swivel around in the proportion of the devaluation as indicated by the broken lines. At the same time, the money-supply line in the SE quadrant swivels around B in the same proportion.[17] The joint effect of these changes is a movement of the equilibrium from B to D. Its implications can be summarized in the following propositions:[18]

1. The money supply of the devaluing country expands. The expansion is in direct proportion to the share of the other (revaluing) country in the world money supply. In small countries, the money supply is more strongly affected by devaluation than in large countries.

2. The money supply of the revaluing country contracts. The contraction is again in direct proportion to the share of the other (devaluing) country in the world money supply.

3. In each country, the national price level changes in the same direction and proportion as the national money supply. Devaluation is thus followed by rising prices, while revaluation results in falling prices.

4. The devaluing country gains reserves and/or the revaluing country loses reserves.

16. It is left to the reader to trace out the effects of a decline in the demand for money, since this is closely analogous to an increase in the money supply.

17. It follows that the new money-supply line no longer runs through A. If people, moving upward and to the right from B, exchange escudos for sterling at the *new* exchange rate, they will now get a higher amount of escudos at any given amount of sterling than under the old rate.

18. These propositions, if not self-evident, can easily be proved. From (2.6.2) and (2.6.3) it follows that $\dot{M}_E = \dot{p}_{WE}$, $\dot{M}_P = \dot{p}_{WP}$, and $\dot{p}_{WE} - \dot{p}_{WP} = \dot{e}$, where the dotted variables denote percentage changes. Equation (2.6.1) means that conversions at the central bank are subject to the constraint $M_E \dot{M}_E + e M_P \dot{M}_P = 0$. From this it is easily derived that

$$\dot{M}_E = \frac{e M_P}{M_E + e M_P} \dot{e}$$

and

$$\dot{M}_P = -\frac{M_E}{M_E + e M_P} \dot{e}.$$

All real variables are the same after the devaluation as before; devaluation has, in the long run, no real effects. Its only effects are on the money supplies and thus on the national price levels. From this perspective, devaluation turns out to be a "purely monetary phenomenon."

These comparative-static propositions relate to full equilibrium. There remains the question of the dynamic adjustment path of such a system. To analyze it, we can use accumulation functions similar to those used for the gold standard. Again assuming that the demand for money is independent of relative prices, they can be written

$$\frac{dM_E}{dt} = \lambda_E[p_{WE}l_E(\pi) - M_E] = \lambda_E(p_{WE}\bar{l}_E - M_E),$$

$$\frac{dM_P}{dt} = \lambda_P[p_{WP}l_P(\pi) - M_P] = \lambda_P(p_{WP}\bar{l}_P - M_P).$$

(2.6.4)

These expressions represent not only the rates of increase (or decrease) in national money supplies, but also the trade surplus (or deficit) of the country in question. There is, under the assumed circumstances, no way for an economy to increase its money supply except by exporting more than it imports, and vice versa. In addition, it is clear that the English surplus must continually be equal to the Portuguese deficit, expressed in the same currency:

$$\frac{dM_E}{dt} = -e\frac{dM_P}{dt}.$$

(2.6.5)

This corresponds to the fact that more sterling currency can only be obtained at the central bank in exchange for escudos. Substituting from (2.6.4) into (2.6.5) and considering that $ep_{WP} = p_{WE}$, one obtains

$$\lambda_E(p_{WE}\bar{l}_E - M_E) = -\lambda_P(p_{WE}\bar{l}_P - eM_P).$$

(2.6.6)

This is the same system as that under the gold standard, but with gold stocks replaced by nominal money supplies. As a consequence, the analysis of section 2.5 remains valid. Again, relative prices do not play an essential role in the adjustment process. In particular, the terms of trade, though generally changing, do not change in a characteristic way, and the price elasticities of demand and supply, though not irrelevant, are not decisive for the direction of the change in the terms of trade. The international price ratio, on the other hand, is continuously held at the level set by the exchange rate through arbitrage; the real exchange rate remains constant. The essential function of prices in the adjustment process concerns the absolute level of p_{WE}, which continually adjusts in such a way that, for the given adjustment speeds, the trade surplus of one country is matched by the trade deficit of the other.

The dynamic adjustment in a fiat-money system depends on the initial disturbance. If the disturbance concerns the international distribution of money at given exchange rates, the analogy of the adjustment process under a fixed-rate fiat-money system with the specie-flow mechanism is perfect. Suppose in figure 2.6.1 the system had initially been at A. The adjustment process that takes it to the equilibrium point B is exactly like the process described by Hume. With fixed exchange rates, it makes no difference whether the initial subsidy is paid in gold or in convertible fiat money.

If the initial disturbance is produced by a devaluation, the adjustment is different under the two systems. In the case of the gold standard it was found that a devaluation of sterling, carried out through an increase in the sterling price of gold, affects nothing but English prices. In particular, it leaves Portugal completely unaffected and does not initiate a period of English trade surpluses. No money flows are required to restore equilibrium.

In a fiat-money system, on the other hand, a devaluation of sterling (equivalent to a revaluation of the escudo) initiates a period of English surpluses (and Portuguese deficits) to adjust the money supplies to the new exchange rate. In fact, a devaluation is now just about equivalent to the payment of a subsidy, while the revaluing country is in the position of the receiver of the subsidy.

The one difference can be explained in terms of figure 2.6.1. Suppose a disturbance in money supplies (for instance, by a transfer) had initially moved the system from the equilibrium point B to a disequilibrium point like E. The adjustment process would then lead the system back to B along the unchanged money-supply curve (represented by the solid line). In the case of a devaluation, however, the system adjusts along a new money-supply curve (represented by the broken line) to a point like D. From a practical point of view, the difference between E and D is surely minor. The adjustment from E to B is almost the same, though of opposite sign, as the adjustment from B to D.

This shows that, under a fiat-money system with fixed exchange rates, devaluation is an almost perfect antidote for disturbances in relative money supplies. If, once the monetary disturbance has occurred, the correction through the money-flow mechanism appears onerous, devaluation may promise a reduction of the burden. Under pegged exchange rates, devaluation is typically used as a substitute for the money-flow mechanism. The following chapters will extend this brief analysis of devaluation in various directions.

The models considered in this chapter are extremely simplified. In particular, unemployment, interest, capital flows, and many important aspects of exchange dynamics are left out. These omissions are necessary to make the fundamental aspects of the international monetary system stand out as clearly as possible. Despite their stark simplicity, these aspects explain much of the history of the international monetary system.

CHAPTER 3

The Adjustment Process:
The Monetary Approach

Introduction

The main subject of chapter 2 was the relationship between money, prices, and exchange rates in full economic equilibrium with only an occasional sidelight on transitional processes. These processes are the subject of this and the following two chapters. This does not mean that the discussion is entirely in terms of dynamic models. Economic analysis has often succeeded in capturing important elements of transitional phases in static models. This is also true in the field of trade and exchange rates. As a consequence, a considerable part of the discussion is cast in terms of static analysis.

The dichotomy between floating-rate models with exogenous money supplies and mobile-money models with exogenous exchange rates will continue to be useful. Most of the important contributions in this area were originally developed in the analysis of devaluation. The effect of devaluation on trade under a system of exogenous exchange rates and mobile money may thus be regarded, metaphorically, as the "primal" problem. It has a "dual," however, in the effect of monetary shifts on the exchange rate under a system of exogenous money supplies and floating exchange rates. Thus the question whether the appreciation of sterling in 1979–80 was caused by the emergence of North Sea oil or by monetary policy is analytically similar to the question how large a devaluation of sterling would be required to eliminate a given trade deficit. In the following chapters, each problem is first taken up in its primal form and then translated into the dual form.

In full equilibrium, as pointed out in the preceding chapter, devaluation (in the primal case) and money supply changes (in the dual case) are neutral, leaving relative prices and commodity flows unaffected. In transition, however, both may have powerful real effects. These effects make devaluation and money supply changes important policy instruments.

Suppose an economy with fixed exchange rates finds itself out of equilibrium with a payments deficit. Most certainly, a new equilibrium would eventually be reached through monetary contraction, but this may take a long time and subject the economy to severe unemployment. As suggested at the end of chapter 2, these disturbances might be reduced by devaluation. The question is how large the devaluation should be.

Suppose, on the other hand, the disequilibrium occurs under floating rates. Eventually, a new equilibrium will be reached through adjustments in prices and exchange rates, but again this may be a costly process that can be made more tolerable by appropriate changes in monetary policies. Despite their long-run neutrality, devaluation and money supply changes thus play potentially important roles in correcting economic disequilibrium.

It has become customary to distinguish a monetary approach, an elasticity approach, and an expenditure (or absorption) approach to devaluation. The present discussion follows this tradition. It will be shown, however, that these approaches, far from being mutually exclusive, are largely equivalent, describing the same economic process, though in different terms and emphasizing different aspects.

The analysis continues to abstract from interest, credit, and foreign assets. Capital flows appear only in the form of shifts of reserves between central banks. Important aspects of exchange dynamics, like the much-discussed "overshooting," are still excluded. They will be taken up in parts II and III.

In its modern form, the monetary approach to devaluation is the most recent of the three approaches. It was first labeled as a separate "approach" by H. G. Johnson (1972c), who built on important contributions by Hahn (1959) and particularly by Mundell (1968, 1971). Suggestive hints can be found in an influential paper by Alexander (1952). However, with respect to its basic idea, the monetary approach is the oldest, being derived from the classical tradition of the specie-flow mechanism. References to its early literature are given in Frenkel and Johnson (1976) and Frenkel (1976). It can also be said to be the most fundamental of the three. That is why it is here considered first.

The basic idea can be summarized in three points:

1. Devaluation involves a change in absolute commodity prices, which rise in the devaluing country and decline in the revaluing country.

2. These commodity price changes involve a change in real cash balances, which decline in the devaluing country and rise in the revaluing country.

3. These changes in real balances are gradually eliminated through trade balances, namely, a trade surplus in the devaluing country to replenish cash balances and a deficit in the revaluing country to reduce cash balances.

This idea will now be made more precise.

3.1 A One-Good Model of Devaluation

An outline of devaluation analysis was given at the end of section 2.6. This and the following section fill in the details. Basically, devaluation works its effects, not through relative prices, but through absolute prices or, equivalently, the purchasing power of money. As a consequence, the crucial points stand out most clearly in a one-good model. With two and more goods, the monetary approach, while certainly no less valid, loses much of its lucidity.[1] The present chapter will thus be restricted to the one-good case, while the two-goods case is more naturally handled in terms of the elasticity approach.

It is first assumed that both economies are fully employed. England and Portugal produce and consume the same commodity (or commodity bundle). As a consequence, there is no trade in full equilibrium and no terms-of-trade problem. The commodity can be costlessly traded. Its sterling price p_E, therefore, is always equal to its escudo price p_P, converted at the current exchange rate. All relative-price problems are thus excluded by assumption. The point is that relative prices, while important in reality, are not crucial for the devaluation mechanics. In this model, devaluation is reduced to a "purely monetary phenomenon."

The static part of the model consists of three elements, familiar from section 2.6. Each country is equipped with an initial supply of fiat money denoted, respectively, by $\bar{M}_E$ and $\bar{M}_P$. Central banks are willing to convert sterling into escudos and vice versa at the exogenous exchange rate e. The two economies are thus free to determine their own money supplies subject to the constraint

$$M_E + eM_P = \bar{M}_E + e\bar{M}_P. \tag{3.1.1}$$

Costless arbitrage implies absolute purchasing-power parity,

$$e = p_E/p_P. \tag{3.1.2}$$

In each country, the supply of cash balances must equal the demand, where the latter is proportionate to the price level:

$$M_E = p_E l_E^*, \qquad M_P = p_P l_P^*. \tag{3.1.3}$$

Again l_E^* and l_P^* denote desired real balances; these depend on real factors outside the scope of this analysis. This is the model of section 2.6 reduced to one good.

The model can be solved to give the national price levels in terms of the initial money supplies and the exchange rate:

$$p_E = \frac{\bar{M}_E + e\bar{M}_P}{l_E^* + l_P^*}, \qquad p_P = \frac{(1/e)\bar{M}_E + \bar{M}_P}{l_E^* + l_P^*}. \tag{3.1.4}$$

---

1. For two-goods models of devaluation, see Dornbusch (1973), where the monetary approach first found a clear analytical expression, and Dornbusch (1980).

The English price level turns out to be equal to the world money supply, measured in sterling, divided by the world demand for real balances. An analogous statement holds for Portugal. National price levels are determined by world conditions.

The national money supplies can be written

$$M_E = \frac{l_E{}^*}{l_E{}^* + l_P{}^*} (\bar{M}_E + e\bar{M}_P),$$

$$M_P = \frac{l_P{}^*}{l_E{}^* + l_P{}^*} ((1/e)\bar{M}_E + \bar{M}_P).$$

(3.1.5)

Each country's share in the world money supply thus corresponds to its share in the world demand for real balances. The relative money supplies are demand-determined. The initial quantity of sterling $\bar{M}_E$ affects the English money supply M_E only as a component of the world money supply. The same is true for Portugal.

Differentiation of this model reveals the comparative-static effects of devaluation. For prices, these can be written

$$\frac{dp_E}{p_E} = \frac{l_P{}^*}{l_E{}^* + l_P{}^*} \cdot \frac{de}{e},$$

$$\frac{dp_P}{p_P} = -\frac{l_E{}^*}{l_E{}^* + l_P{}^*} \cdot \frac{de}{e}.$$

(3.1.6)

A devaluation of sterling, reflected in $de/e > 0$, thus raises sterling prices, while escudo prices decline. For each country, the elasticity of the price level with respect to the exchange rate is equal (in absolute value) to the share of the *other* country in the world demand for real balances. In a small country, the price level thus changes proportionately more than in a large country. Of course, the sum of the two (absolute) price changes, measured in percentages, is equal to the devaluation rate. Equation (3.1.3) makes clear that the two money supplies exhibit the same proportionate variation as the corresponding price levels. This is consistent with the argument about the comparative statics of devaluation in section 2.6.

3.2 Devaluation Dynamics

The main question concerns, of course, the dynamics of devaluation. If cash balances could instantaneously adjust to their desired levels, the economy would "jump" immediately to the new equilibrium. In fact, the adjustment is likely to be gradual. The nature of this process can best be visualized by again assuming that a certain fraction of the gap between desired and actual balances is closed per unit of time:

$$\frac{dM_E}{dt} = \lambda_E(p_E l_E{}^* - M_E),$$

$$\frac{dM_P}{dt} = \lambda_P(p_P l_P{}^* - M_P).$$

(3.2.1)

This assumption is illustrated in figure 3.2.1. For a given price level p_E, the accumulation of sterling balances is a declining linear function of the money supply M_E. At $M_E = p_E l_E{}^*$ accumulation is zero; for $M_E < p_E l_E{}^*$ it is positive; and for $M_E > p_E l_E{}^*$ it is negative. The higher the price level, the more money will be accumulated at a given level of cash balances. The accumulation function for England can thus be represented by a family of straight lines as depicted on the left-hand side of figure 3.2.1. A similar graph is drawn for Portugal on the right-hand side. The slopes of the two curves measure the respective adjustment speeds.

The accumulation and decumulation of cash balances is constrained by the requirement that England can accumulate only what Portugal is willing to give up. This requirement can be formalized by taking the time derivative of (3.1.1):

$$\frac{dM_E}{dt} + e\frac{dM_P}{dt} = 0.$$

(3.2.2)

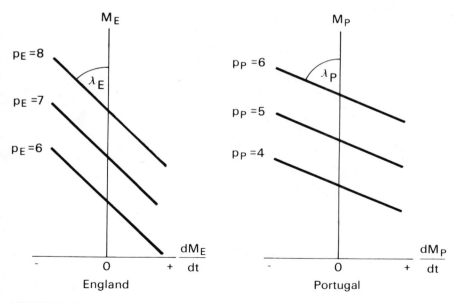

FIGURE 3.2.1
Accumulation of Cash Balances

The accumulation of cash balances takes place through a trade surplus, while decumulation requires a trade deficit. Trade flows thus appear in this model as concomitants of the dynamic adjustment of cash balances. Of course, the English trade surplus must be equal to the Portuguese deficit or vice versa.

The implications of this requirement can be visualized by combining the two sides of figure 3.2.1. The result is figure 3.2.2, a graph very similar to figure 2.4.3. This similarity reflects the fact that, from the point of view of the monetary approach, a devaluation in a fiat-money system acts essentially like a transfer of gold under a gold standard. In the devaluing country, the initial increase in the price level reduces real balances in much the same way as gold losses do under a gold standard. In the revaluing country, real balances are increased by price declines much as if gold had been received under the gold standard. In the course of the adjustment process, the initial real balances are gradually restored, in close analogy to the return flow of gold, by the payments for trade deficits.

Suppose at the initial exchange rate $e = 1$, England held money supply $\bar{M}_E$ while Portugal held $\bar{M}_P$. At the new exchange rate $e = 2$, the money supply constraint is thus $M_E + 2M_P = \bar{M}_E + 2\bar{M}_P$. This constraint is expressed by the horizontal dimension of the graph. The initial distribution of

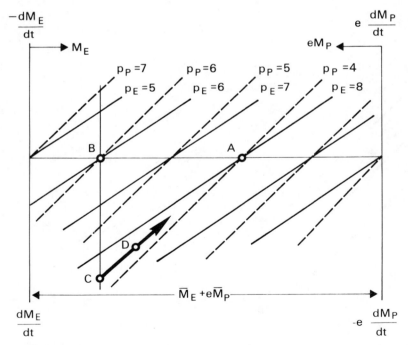

FIGURE 3.2.2
Monetary Dynamics

money, but at the new exchange rate, is indicated by point B. (It should be noted that before the devaluation the graph looked different; the situation before cannot be directly compared with the situation after.) B is not an equilibrium point. True, both England and Portugal would be happy with their former money supplies if prices remained at their previous levels. However, because of the devaluation these prices are no longer consistent with arbitrage equilibrium in the commodity market. Whereas the price levels were equal before devaluation, English prices must now be twice as high as Portuguese prices. Since, in the absence of transaction costs, arbitrage works very rapidly, the price adjustment takes place virtually instantaneously. On the vertical line through B we have to find the point at which $p_E = 2p_P$. Since we must move downward to produce an increase in p_E and a decline in p_P, this point must be below B. In the graph it is at C, with $p_E = 8.5$ and $p_P = 4.25$. At this point, England, in view of her increased prices, wishes to accumulate additional cash balances in the same amount in which Portugal, in view of her reduced prices, is willing to give them up. The English trade surplus exactly matches the Portuguese deficit.[2] Point C thus represents a temporary equilibrium.

Clearly, the system cannot remain at C. In the next period, the shift in money balances will have moved it to the right, say to D. If both countries have the same adjustment speeds, prices will not change from C to D; they will have jumped directly to their final equilibrium. However, if Portugal adjusts cash balances faster than England (as drawn in the graph), both price levels will gradually decline in the course of the adjustment process. If, on the other hand, adjustment is faster in England, both price levels will gradually rise.[3]

Final equilibrium is reached at A, where both countries are content with their cash balances while prices correspond to purchasing-power parity. Compared to the initial distribution of money at B, devaluation has thus resulted in a permanent increase in the English money supply at the expense of Portugal. England has paid for this money by a temporary reduction in consumption, while Portugal's consumption has been correspondingly increased. Initially, English prices are certain to rise while Portugal's prices decline, but subsequent price movements are uncertain.

This graphical analysis can be restated in mathematical terms. The dynamic model consists of (3.2.1), (3.2.2), and the arbitrage condition (3.1.2). It can be solved for prices at given money supplies and a given exchange rate:

$$p_E = \frac{\lambda_E M_E + \lambda_{pe} M_P}{\lambda_E l_E{}^* + \lambda_P l_P{}^*}, \qquad p_P = \frac{\lambda_E(1/e) M_E + \lambda_P M_P}{\lambda_E l_E{}^* + \lambda_P l_P{}^*}. \qquad (3.2.3)$$

2. Note that, in a vertical direction, English accumulation is paired with Portuguese decumulation.
3. For the corresponding argument in the case of a gold transfer, see section 2.5.

The products $\lambda_E l_E{}^*$ and $\lambda_P l_P{}^*$ indicate the desired accumulation of cash balances for a given change in commodity prices. To simplify the exposition they will be called "hoarding coefficients," denoted by $h_E = \lambda_E l_E{}^*$ and $h_P = \lambda_P l_P{}^*$. It is characteristic of the monetary approach that the adjustment process is explained in terms of hoarding behavior.

The impact effects of devaluation on national price levels are determined by taking the derivatives of (3.2.3) with respect to e. Using (3.1.3), these can be written in the form of elasticities as follows:

$$\frac{dp_E}{p_E} = \frac{h_P}{h_E + h_P} \cdot \frac{de}{e}, \qquad \frac{dp_P}{p_P} = -\frac{h_E}{h_E + h_P} \cdot \frac{de}{e}. \qquad (3.2.4)$$

It is interesting to compare these impact effects with the comparative-static effects given in (3.1.6). Like the latter, the impact effects depend on the desired real balances, but each of these is now weighted with the corresponding adjustment speed. With equal adjustment speeds—that is, $\lambda_E = \lambda_P$—each impact effect is equal to the corresponding comparative-static effect; prices will jump immediately to their new equilibrium. If England adjusts faster, the impact effects will leave both prices below their final equilibrium; if Portugal adjusts faster, they will first push them beyond their equilibrium values. This confirms the conclusions from the graphical analysis.

The dynamic system can also be solved for the changes in the money supplies:

$$\frac{dM_E}{dt} = \lambda_E \lambda_P \frac{l_E{}^*eM_P - l_P{}^*M_E}{\lambda_E l_E{}^* + \lambda_P l_P{}^*},$$

$$\frac{dM_P}{dt} = -\lambda_E \lambda_P \frac{l_E{}^*M_P - l_P{}^*(1/e)M_E}{\lambda_E l_E{}^* + \lambda_P l_P{}^*}. \qquad (3.2.5)$$

Starting from initial values $M_E{}^\circ$ and $M_P{}^\circ$, these differential equations describe the adjustment paths of M_E and M_P for a given exchange rate. The process is clearly stable, since dM_E/dt declines, and dM_P/dt rises, as M_E rises and M_P declines. In terms of figure 2.6.1 this means that whenever the system finds itself on the money supply constraint in the SE quadrant, it will gradually move toward the equilibrium ray. If, after a devaluation, it still finds itself at the old equilibrium point B, it will thus move toward the new equilibrium D.

It can be ascertained that in the initial equilibrium, where $M_P = p_P l_P{}^*$ and $M_E = p_E l_E{}^*$, both expressions in (3.2.5) are zero. If an increase in e now occurs, dM_E/dt becomes positive and dM_P/dt negative. This impact effect can again be formalized by taking the derivatives of (3.2.5) with respect to e. Making use of the fact that initially $M_E = p_E l_E{}^*$ and $M_P = p_P l_P{}^*$, the result can be written in elasticity form as

$$\frac{d(dM_E/dt)}{M_E} = \lambda_E \frac{h_P}{h_E + h_P} \cdot \frac{de}{e} = \lambda_E \frac{dp_E}{p_E},$$

$$\frac{d(dM_P/dt)}{M_P} = -\lambda_P \frac{h_E}{h_E + h_P} \cdot \frac{de}{e} = \lambda_P \frac{dp_P}{p_P}. \tag{3.2.6}$$

This means that, for each country, the impact effect of devaluation on the trade balance, expressed as a percentage of the initial money supply, is proportionate to the impact effect on its price level. The adjustment speeds appear as factors of proportionality. It would not be correct to say, though, that the increase in the English money supply pushes up English prices. It is more correct to say that the increase in English prices, because it creates a shortage of cash balances, attracts an inflow of money. The reverse applies for Portugal.

It is instructive to rewrite (3.2.6) in terms of commodity units as

$$\frac{d(dM_E/dt)}{p_E} = -\frac{d(dM_P/dt)}{p_P} = \frac{h_E h_P}{h_E + h_P} \cdot \frac{de}{e}. \tag{3.2.7}$$

This says that the impact of devaluation on the trade balance is proportionate to the devaluation rate, the factor of proportionality depending on the hoarding coefficients. While the elasticity approach explains the impact effect of devaluation on the trade balance in terms of the demand and supply of commodities, the monetary approach explains it in terms of hoarding. It will be shown in the following chapter that the economic content of the two expressions is actually very similar.

Devaluation has so far been considered on the assumption of continuous full employment. One of the main reasons for resorting to devaluation was thereby excluded. Even in this limiting case, however, devaluation has at least two significant economic effects.

First, the adjustment to devaluation involves money flows. With fractional reserves these may create reserve problems, since the deficit country may run out of reserves before the new equilibrium is reached. Usually this problem presents itself from a different angle. Suppose at the original exchange rate there is a trade imbalance associated with reserve flows. In principle, this is self-correcting through adjustments in money stocks and price levels, but reserves may be insufficient. Devaluation may then offer a shortcut, restoring equilibrium instantly without further reserve movements. Devaluation is important practically, not because it disturbs an initial equilibrium, but because it may restore equilibrium after a disturbance.

Second, the adjustment to equilibrium involves temporary welfare gains and losses even under full employment. The counterpart of reserve gains is a reduction in consumption, while reserve losses are associated with additional consumption. It was pointed out above that devaluation initially acts like a transfer, reducing the real balances of the devaluing country and increasing those of the revaluing country. In the course of time, these real balance effects are gradually transformed into consumption effects, and the old real balances are restored. Again it is more relevant practically to consider this process from the other side. A disequilibrium situation is characterized by a real transfer, that is, a transfer of commodities from the surplus country to the deficit country. In such a situation, devaluation may be able to stop the transfer long before the monetary mechanism would have brought it to a halt. For these reasons, devaluation would be of potential significance for economic policy even in the absence of unemployment.

3.3 Devaluation with Unemployment

From a policy point of view, one of the most important aspects of devaluation is its relationship to unemployment. In particular, wages are often slow in adjusting to price movements, giving the short-run impression of rigid wages. Seen from one side, the price fluctuations induced by devaluation become associated with fluctuations in output and employment. Seen from the other side, the price adjustments required in the absence of devaluation would involve a contraction in output and employment, which devaluation may forestall. This aspect will now have to be incorporated into the model of the preceding section. The analytical framework was provided in section 1.5. It will now be applied to the case of two economies with one good.

The full-employment model consists of equations (3.1.1), (3.1.2), and (3.2.1). These can still be used as the monetary part of the unemployment model. This implies that the desired amounts of real balances, as represented by l_E^* and l_P^*, depend on available resources (or full-employment output) and not on resources employed (or actual output). This assumption may be defended by the argument that the "lapses from full employment" appearing in this model are recognized as temporary. In addition, it will turn out that the fluctuations in consumption are smaller than those in output. To the extent that the demand for money depends on consumption expenditure, its sensitivity to output fluctuations is correspondingly reduced. The main justification for the assumption, however, is the simplification it permits. The consequences of allowing for an effect of output on the demand for real balances are briefly discussed at the end of this section.

To the monetary part we will now add a real part to determine output. It consists of three simple components. The production functions relate English output and Portuguese output, respectively, to the amount of resources employed:

$$Q_E = Q_E(R_E) \qquad Q_P = Q_P(R_P) \tag{3.3.1}$$

$$Q'_E > 0, Q_E'' < 0 \qquad Q'_P > 0, Q_P'' < 0.$$

Employment is such that the marginal products of resources are equal to their real wages:

$$\frac{w_E}{p_E} = Q_E', \qquad \frac{w_P}{p_P} = Q_P'. \tag{3.3.2}$$

Money wages, finally, vary under the pressure of gaps between actual employment and normal (or "full") employment:

$$\frac{dw_E}{dt} = \omega_E(R_E - R_E^*), \qquad \frac{dw_P}{dt} = \omega_P(R_P - R_P^*). \tag{3.3.3}$$

This is a rudimentary form of the Phillips curve. Expected inflation can be disregarded because price movements are generally recognized as temporary.

Thanks to the simplifying assumption about desired real balances, there is no feedback from the real part to the monetary part. The monetary part can be used separately to determine prices. Once these are known, the real part can be used to determine wages, output, and employment.

Since there is also no interaction between the two countries in the real part, it is enough to consider one of them. In any given period, English prices and wages are predetermined by past history. Equations (3.3.1) and (3.3.2) then determine employment as a declining function of real wages. Once employment is known, (3.3.3) determines the wage adjustment. At the same time, the monetary part has determined the price adjustment. Together these determine the level of real wages, and thereby employment, in the next period. The paths of output and employment thus depend on the path of prices, determined in the monetary part, and the path of wages, determined in the real part.

In the light of this model, the impact effects of devaluation on output and employment are easily identified. Suppose sterling is devalued. The impact effect, as shown above, is an increase in p_E and a decline in p_P. At the given money wages, English output rises while Portuguese output declines. Devaluation thus stimulates output, while revaluation tends to produce a contraction. At the same time, English wages begin to rise while Portuguese wages fall.

The further path of output and employment depends on prices. Suppose prices, in view of equal adjustment speeds, immediately leap to their new equilibrium level, remaining constant thereafter. In this case, the gradual rise in English wages pushes output back down towards its full-employment level, while Portuguese output gradually recovers. The employment effects of devaluation thus turn out to be temporary.

If English prices first overshoot their final equilibrium, the initial output expansion is more pronounced, but the subsequent price decline supports the normalization. In Portugal, on the other hand, the contraction is milder initially, but recovery is impeded by further price declines. The reverse is true if English prices initially fall short of their final equilibrium.

The temporary gains and losses identified in the real part have to be set against those originating in the monetary part. It was shown in the preceding section that Portugal, by running a deficit, gains consumer goods at the expense of England. It has now been shown that, at the same time, Portugal's output contracts while England's output expands. The overall effect on consumption is not clear. In England, the aggregate gain in output may be either larger or smaller than the cumulative export surplus. In Portugal, on the other hand, the aggregate output loss may be either larger or smaller than the cumulative import surplus. Devaluation does not promise a clear welfare gain nor does it impose a clear welfare loss.

I shall now return to the assumption that desired real balances are not affected by output fluctuations. First, it should be noted that the uncertainty about the overall consumption effect helps to justify the assumption. To the extent that desired real balances depend on consumption rather than output, their behavior during the adjustment process is indeed unclear and their fluctuations may well be small.

Second, one might conjecture that a marked positive effect of output on desired real balances would tend to strengthen the monetary effects of devaluation. In England, the expansion would further increase the demand for real balances, while Portugal's desired balances would be further reduced by output contraction. As a consequence, the temporary trade balance would be larger.

As an instrument of economic policy, devaluation is hardly ever used in economic equilibrium for the sake of hoped-for temporary benefits. It is, rather, used in a state of disequilibrium in order to prevent threatened output losses. Commodity prices, perhaps due to past policy errors, are out of line with the exchange rate. The economy is in the same state as if, starting from equilibrium, the exchange rate had just been arbitrarily revalued, initiating a deflationary adjustment process associated with uncertain net benefits and in any case with unemployment. In such a case, devaluation may spare the economy such an adjustment process.

3.4 Floating Exchange Rates

The preceding discussion concentrated on the effects of devaluation. As explained in the introduction to this chapter, this "primal" problem has a "dual" in the effects of monetary shifts under floating rates. These effects are the subject of the present section, which continues the discussion of price and exchange-rate dynamics with given money supplies in section 2.2.

In contrast to the devaluation discussion, it is now assumed that England and Portugal both determine their own money supply, offering no convertibility of sterling against escudos. At the same time, the exchange rate fluctuates freely. Since private capital flows are still abstracted from, exchange rates must be such that trade is balanced at all times. There can be no money flows. In the one-good model, which still provides the framework for the analysis, there never occurs any trade at all. Although this is not a realistic picture, it does help to isolate essential features of exchange dynamics.

The model of section 2.2, reduced to a single commodity, may be briefly restated. It is also the model of 3.1 as modified for floating rates. The desired amounts of real balances, l_E* and l_P*, are again determined by factors outside the scope of this analysis. In each country, real cash balances adjust to discrepancies between desired and actual balances with a distributed lag according to

$$\frac{d}{dt}\left(\frac{M_E}{p_E}\right) = \lambda_E\left(l_E* - \frac{M_E}{p_E}\right) \tag{3.4.1}$$

and

$$\frac{d}{dt}\left(\frac{M_P}{p_P}\right) = \lambda_P\left(l_P* - \frac{M_P}{p_P}\right). \tag{3.4.2}$$

In view of costless commodity arbitrage, absolute purchasing-power parity holds, whence

$$e = \frac{p_E}{p_P}. \tag{3.4.3}$$

The first thing to note is the independence of the two countries. The dynamic equations can be used for each separately without feedback from the other. The exchange rate links the two economies without influencing them. Suppose England experiences an exogenous increase in its money supply. At the given price level, M_E/p_E now exceeds l_E*. As a consequence, real cash balances begin to decline.

This decline can take place only through an increase in the price level. The speed of the price increase can be determined as follows. At any given level of M_E, equation (3.4.1) reduces to

$$-\frac{M_E}{p_E{}^2}\frac{dp_E}{dt} = \lambda_E\left(l_E* - \frac{M_E}{p_E}\right).$$

This can be rewritten

$$\dot{p}_E = \frac{dp_E}{dt}\cdot\frac{1}{p_E} = \lambda_E\left(1 - \frac{p_E l_E*}{M_E}\right). \tag{3.4.4}$$

If M_E is now exogenously increased, the rate of price increase reacts according to

$$\frac{d\dot{p}_E}{dM_E/M_E} = \lambda_E\frac{p_E l_E*}{M_E} = \lambda_E. \tag{3.4.5}$$

This makes use of the observation that initially $p_E l_E{}^* = M_E$. The interpretation is simple. Due to the adjustment lag in cash balances, the immediate effect of money on prices is only partial, its strength depending on the adjustment speed. In subsequent periods, the money supply remains constant at its new level. As $p_E l_E{}^*$ rises toward M_E, the percentage increase in the price level, according to (3.4.4), gradually declines toward zero.

The implications for the exchange rate are simple: it just follows the path of prices. There are no effects on Portugal at all. It should be noted that there is no overshooting of the exchange rate in this case. Overshooting, which has received so much attention in recent years, will be discussed in chapter 11.

In principle, a monetary approach can also be used to analyze the effect of changes in real factors on the exchange rate. However, the present one-good model leaves room for real changes only insofar as they express themselves in an increase in desired real balances. Increases in real resources, technological progress, and changes in tastes (here restricted to the demand for real balances) can indeed affect the exchange rate, but they can do so only through $l_E{}^*$ and $l_P{}^*$. It is evident from the model that an increase in $l_E{}^*$ produces exactly the same adjustment paths of prices as a reduction in the money supply by the same percentage.

With flexible wages, the economy adjusts to the exogenous increase in the money supply without unemployment. If wages are sticky, a depreciation of the exchange rate, due to an increase in the money supply or a decline in the demand for real balances, is accompanied by temporary overemployment. Conversely, an appreciation of the exchange rate, due to a contraction of the money supply or an increase in the demand for money, is associated with unemployment. For example, if North Sea oil, as was sometimes argued, really produced an increase in the demand for sterling, sterling would appreciate, rapidly at first and then progressively more slowly. At the same time, there would be deflationary pressure on the British economy, resulting in unemployment. The effect would be indistinguishable, at this aggregative level, from that of a contraction in the money supply.

The monetary approach describes fluctuations in price levels, exchange rates, and trade as monetary phenomena, determined by hoarding behavior. This has sometimes been regarded as a hypothesis about the real world. Such a hypothesis would have little chance of being empirically confirmed, because in general, price levels, exchange rates, and trade depend on many factors besides hoarding behavior. It makes little sense to argue whether the exchange rate is really a "purely monetary phenomenon." Rather than being regarded as a hypothesis about the real world, the monetary approach, like other theoretical models, should be regarded as a partial picture that sheds light on limited, but important, aspects of reality. Other aspects will be taken up in subsequent chapters.

CHAPTER 4

The Adjustment Process:
The Elasticity Approach

Introduction

If sterling is devalued, the escudo price of English exports declines. As a consequence, Portugal imports more cloth. In view of this increase in sales, the sterling price of English cloth is certain not to decline and it may possibly rise. Since the quantity of English exports rises and their sterling price does not decline, the English receipts for exports, measured in sterling, are certain to increase.

On the other hand, the sterling price of Portuguese wine increases. As a consequence, England imports less. Since the quantity of imports declines while their price rises, the English payments for imports, measured in sterling, may either rise or fall. If the English balance of payments is measured in terms of escudos, it can be shown by analogous reasoning that import payments are certain to decline, while export receipts may either increase or decline.

Taking export receipts and import payments together, it seems likely that a devaluation produces an improvement in the balance of payments, measured in either currency, but a deterioration cannot be excluded.

The exact result clearly depends on the reaction of exports and imports to price changes. It should thus be possible to explain the reaction of the balance of payments to devaluation on the basis of the price elasticities of exports and imports. This is the basic idea behind the elasticity approach. While the monetary approach concentrates on the demand and supply of money, the elasticity approach focuses on commodity markets.

4.1 A Two-Goods Model of Devaluation

To bring out the characteristic features of the elasticity approach, the underlying model has to include at least two goods. Such a model is presented in this section, followed by a graphical representation. The mathematical analysis is given in section 4.2.

In the discussion of the monetary approach it was emphasized that devaluation can be regarded as a transfer of real cash balances resulting in money flows. With two goods, there is the additional question how the money flows are allocated to those goods. Following the monetary approach, this question can be answered by specifying the demand for cash balances as depending on both prices. Traditionally, however, it has been answered in terms of demand and supply elasticities. It will be shown in section 4.4 that the two approaches are entirely compatible, giving the same answers if correctly applied to the same problems.

In the interest of lucidity, the notation in this chapter will be different from that in the preceding chapters. Small letters are used for England, while capital letters refer to Portugal. For wine, English import demand is denoted by x with sterling price p, while Portuguese export supply is X with escudo price P. For cloth, Portuguese import demand is Y with escudo price Q, while English export supply is y with sterling price q.

The Law of One Price is still regarded as valid for each good,

$$p = eP, \qquad q = eQ, \tag{4.1.1}$$

and both markets must be cleared,

$$x = X, \qquad y = Y. \tag{4.1.2}$$

The English trade balance, measured in sterling, is defined as

$$b = qy - px = -eB, \tag{4.1.3}$$

where B is the Portuguese balance.

The elasticity approach is characterized by the assumption that demand and supply for each good depend only on its own price. Cross elasticities are assumed to be zero. In pure logic, it is certainly possible to introduce cross elasticities, but the results become cumbersome and difficult to interpret.[1] The demand and supply functions can be specified as follows:

England

			(4.1.4)
Demand for wine: $x = x(p)$	$x_p < 0$	$\epsilon_x = x_p(p/x) < 0$	
Supply of cloth: $y = y(q)$	$y_q > 0$	$\eta_y = y_q(q/y) > 0$	

Portugal

Supply of wine: $X = X(P)$	$X_P > 0$	$\eta_x = X_P(P/X) > 0$
Demand for cloth: $Y = Y(Q)$	$Y_Q < 0$	$\epsilon_y = Y_Q(Q/Y) < 0.$

---

1. About this generalization, see Negishi (1968).

The question concerns db/de, the change in the English trade balance due to a given (small) change in the exchange rate. The present discussion is restricted to the case of initially balanced trade.[2]

The dependence of devaluation effects on elasticities is first demonstrated in terms of a graph (fig. 4.1.1).[3] The axes of this graph are in terms of logarithms. The right-hand side refers to wine, and the left-hand side to cloth. Escudo prices are measured vertically, starting from the solid horizontal axis. Sterling prices are equal to escudo prices times the exchange rate. They are obtained (remembering the log scale) by shifting the origin of the price scale downward by e_1. Sterling prices are thus measured from the broken horizontal axis.

The solid upward-sloping $X(P)$ curve in the wine quadrant is the Portuguese supply curve for wine, drawn with reference to the (solid) Portuguese price scale. The broken downward-sloping $x(p)$ curves are English demand curves for wine, drawn with reference to the (broken) English price scale. The corresponding curves for the English supply of cloth, $y(q)$, and the Portuguese demand for cloth, $Y(Q)$, are found on the left-hand side.

If sterling is devalued, the English price scale shifts downward by de to e_2. The English curves $x(p)$ and $y(q)$ move in step, while the Portuguese curves stay in place. If the English axes and curves were drawn on transparent paper, the latter could simply be shifted downward on the Portuguese graph.

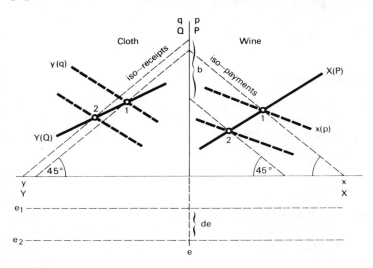

FIGURE 4.1.1
Elasticity Approach

2. The modifications due to initial surpluses or deficits are analyzed in Hirschman (1949).
3. See Niehans (1974). This graphical approach is more compact than the one used by Haberler (1949) and reproduced in many textbooks. Some readers may thus prefer the latter.

The market equilibrium thus moves from position 1 to position 2. It is clear that the effects on the quantities traded and on prices (both in sterling and escudos) depend on the slopes of the four curves. In view of the logarithmic scales, these slopes represent elasticities.

The important question is what happens to receipts and payments. In figure 4.1.1 these are measured in escudos. The logarithm of payments is the sum of the logarithms of the import quantity and the import price. The iso-payments curves, therefore, are 45° lines with negative slopes and drawn with reference to the escudo axes. Similarly, the iso-receipts curves are 45° lines with positive slopes. Total payments and receipts can be measured by the vertical intercepts of these lines. For the initial position 1 the iso-payments line and the iso-receipts line have the same intercept; trade is initially balanced.

A devaluation is certain to reduce payments (in foreign currency); the new iso-payments intercept is necessarily below the old one. However, depending on the slopes of $Y(Q)$ and $y(q)$, the iso-receipts curve for position 2 may be below or above that for position 1. As the graph is drawn, receipts rise as payments decline, thus indicating a surplus for the devaluing country. A surplus may still result if receipts decline, provided they decline less than payments. It is easy (yet instructive) to redraw the curves in such a way that receipts decline even more than payments, indicating that devaluation has resulted in a deficit. It is also easy to derive the trade effect of devaluation for special cases involving horizontal or vertical demand and/or supply curves. The reader may find it helpful to refer back to this graph when such special cases are discussed in the following section.

4.2 The Bickerdike Condition

The argument of the preceding section can be made more precise by mathematical analysis. The result is the Bickerdike condition.[4] By taking differentials of (4.1.1) one obtains a relationship between price changes and devaluation, both in percentage terms:

$$\frac{de}{e} = \frac{dp}{p} - \frac{dP}{P} = \frac{dq}{q} - \frac{dQ}{Q}. \tag{4.2.1}$$

For each commodity, the sterling price change and the escudo price change, taken in absolute value, add up to the devaluation rate. The question is how the devalution of sterling is divided between English price increases and Portuguese price decreases.

The answer depends on price elasticities. Taking the differential of (4.1.2) and using the demand and supply functions (4.1.4), one obtains the

---

4. Bickerdike (1920). The same condition was derived by Joan Robinson (1937). See Metzler (1948) about early interpretations. The condition is often called the Bickerdike/Robinson/Metzler condition.

relationships between the sterling price changes and the escudo price changes necessary to maintain market equilibrium,

$$x_p dp = X_P dP, \qquad y_q dq = Y_Q dQ. \tag{4.2.2}$$

In terms of elasticities, these can be written

$$\epsilon_x \frac{dp}{p} = \eta_x \frac{dP}{P}, \qquad \eta_y \frac{dq}{q} = \epsilon_y \frac{dQ}{Q}. \tag{4.2.3}$$

By substituting from (4.2.3) into (4.2.1), the percentage changes in sterling prices can be expressed as a function of the devaluation rate:

$$\frac{dp}{p} = \frac{\eta_x}{\eta_x - \epsilon_x} \frac{de}{e},$$

$$\tag{4.2.4}$$

$$\frac{dq}{q} = \frac{\epsilon_y}{\epsilon_y - \eta_y} \frac{de}{e}.$$

Assuming nonzero elasticities, it is evident that both sterling prices rise. In the same way it can be shown that both escudo prices decline.

The difference between the two price effects is the effect of devaluation on the terms of trade,

$$\frac{d\pi}{de} \frac{e}{\pi} = \frac{dq}{de} \frac{e}{q} - \frac{dp}{de} \frac{e}{p} = \frac{\epsilon_y}{\epsilon_y - \eta_y} - \frac{\eta_x}{\eta_x - \epsilon_x}$$

$$= \frac{\epsilon_x \epsilon_y - \eta_x \eta_y}{(\eta_x - \epsilon_x)(\eta_y - \epsilon_y)} \gtreqless 0. \tag{4.2.5}$$

Devaluation may thus result in either an improvement or a deterioration in the terms of trade. There is an improvement (for the devaluing country) if the demand elasticities dominate the supply elasticities. In the reverse case there is a deterioration. It is entirely possible that a devaluation leaves the terms of trade virtually unchanged even though there may be a marked effect on the trade balance. According to the elasticity approach, just as according to the monetary approach, changes in the terms of trade are not an essential aspect of devaluation.[5]

The change in the trade balance due to given price changes is obtained by differentiating (4.1.3) and writing the result in terms of elasticities:

$$db = qdy + ydq - pdx - xdp$$

$$= (qy_q + y)\, dq - (px_p + x)\, dp \tag{4.2.6}$$

$$= qy\,(\eta_y + 1)\, \frac{dq}{q} - px\,(\epsilon_x + 1)\, \frac{dp}{p}.$$

5. On the surface, (4.2.5) may seem to be inconsistent with the outcome of the transfer debate, the latter having shown that changes in the terms of trade depend, not on price elasticities, but on the propensities to spend. As a matter of fact, there is no inconsistency. The transfer debate related to relative prices, while the price elasticities of the elasticity approach relate to absolute money prices and are thus alternative measures of the propensity to spend.

By substituting from (4.2.4) and considering that $qy = px$, the change in the trade balance as a percentage of exports (or imports) can be expressed as a function of the devaluation rate:

$$\frac{db}{px} = \left\{(\eta_y + 1)\frac{\epsilon_y}{\epsilon_y - \eta_y} - (\epsilon_x + 1)\frac{\eta_x}{\eta_x - \epsilon_x}\right\}\frac{de}{e}$$

$$= \frac{\epsilon_x\epsilon_y(\eta_x + \eta_y + 1) - \eta_x\eta_y(\epsilon_x + \epsilon_y + 1)}{(\eta_x - \epsilon_x)(\eta_y - \epsilon_y)}\frac{de}{e}. \qquad (4.2.7)$$

This formidable-looking expression precisely relates the improvement in the trade balance resulting from devaluation to the underlying elasticities of demand and supply. It may be called the "Bickerdike formula." It is the mathematical counterpart to the graphical analysis in the preceding section.

What can be said about the sign of this expression? The denominator is unambiguously positive. A devaluation thus improves the trade balance if the numerator is positive. This is the Bickerdike condition

$$\epsilon_x\epsilon_y(\eta_x + \eta_y + 1) - \eta_x\eta_y(\epsilon_x + \epsilon_y + 1) > 0. \qquad (4.2.8)$$

It is convenient to rewrite it in such a way that all parentheses are positive (or, more precisely, nonnegative):

$$(-\epsilon_x)(-\epsilon_y)(\eta_x + \eta_y + 1) + \eta_x\eta_y[(-\epsilon_x) + (-\epsilon_y) - 1] > 0.$$

The first term is clearly positive, but the second term becomes negative if the absolute values of ϵ_x and ϵ_y are low enough. In general, therefore, we cannot say whether the Bickerdike condition is satisfied.

The outcome is an empirical question on which, over the decades, a large number of empirical studies have been made.[6] While opinions have ranged from "elasticity pessimism" to "elasticity optimism," the prevalent view now seems to be that, if the proper adjustment period is chosen, devaluation can be expected to improve the trade balance. An important qualification will be added in the following section, however, where it is shown that elasticities are bound to change in the course of the adjustment process. Starting from full equilibrium, devaluation can have no permanent effect on trade.

By and large, one can say that the Bickerdike condition is satisfied if the foreign trade elasticities are "high enough," but that it may be violated if the elasticities are "too low." Yet, this is strictly true only for the demand side. The opposite may be true for supply elasticities if the bracketed expression is negative. It should be noted that there is no direct relationship between the Bickerdike condition and the terms of trade.

An understanding of the condition is helped by considering special

---

6. For representative examples, see Houthakker and Magee (1969) and, more recently, Goldstein and Khan (1978). Magee (1975) provides a comprehensive survey, and there is an exhaustive annotated bibliography by Stern, Francis, and Schumacher (1976).

cases.[7] First, it is easily seen that the Marshall/Lerner condition $(-\epsilon_x) + (-\epsilon_y) \geq 1$ is sufficient (but not necessary) for the Bickerdike condition. Whatever the supply elasticities may be (provided they are nonnegative), if the (absolute) demand elasticities sum to at least 1, a devaluation is sure to improve the trade balance.

Second, with infinite supply elasticities, and thus fixed domestic prices, the Bickerdike condition reduces to the Marshall/Lerner condition. The latter then becomes both necessary and sufficient for a positive effect of devaluation on the trade balance. This case is often regarded as typical for underemployment, but this argument is based on doubtful, if perhaps plausible, reasoning.

Third, consider the case of a "small" economy facing given world market prices. In this case, $-\epsilon_x = \infty$ and $\eta_x = \infty$. As a consequence, the Bickerdike condition reduces to $\eta_y - \epsilon_x > 0$, which is always satisfied. For a "small" economy there can be no elasticity paradoxes.

4.3 Latent Dynamics

On the surface, the elasticity approach is strictly static. Taken at face value, this may give the impression that, starting from full equilibrium, a devaluation can produce a trade surplus that lasts indefinitely. It has long been recognized that such an impression would be seriously in error. In the long run, as the comparative-static analysis of chapter 2 showed, devaluation is neutral. Its only lasting effects are on money supplies and prices, while trade is again balanced in the new equilibrium. The devaluation effects derived in this chapter must thus be interpreted as essentially transitory, presenting a static picture of a dynamic adjustment process. Behind the static surface there must be latent dynamics.

The most basic dynamic factor is the *money supply*. In the course of the postwar period, it became increasingly recognized that the demand and supply functions for imports and exports do not depend just on prices but also on cash balances.[8] This is easily understood once it is realized that the relevant prices are not relative prices but absolute money prices. Imagine an experiment with just one import good, considered in isolation. A price increase results in a reduction in demand and, assuming an elastic demand, also in expenditure. The latter, in turn, produces an increase in cash balances, which will eventually cause demand to rise again to its former level. The virtual price elasticity of demand, taking account of the varying cash balance, thus declines in the course of the adjustment process, ultimately approaching zero.

7. The reader may find it instructive to express these in terms of the graphical approaches of the preceding section.
8. The contributions by Hahn (1959) and Negishi (1968) were important in this context.

This reasoning also applies to the elasticity model as a whole. Since every trade surplus has as its counterpart a change in cash balances, the demand and supply functions in (4.1.4) are subject to continuous shifts. In particular, the import demand curve of the surplus country shifts to the right, while its export supply curve shifts to the left. The reverse is true for the deficit country. This tends to reduce the trade balance, and ultimately any effect on commodity flows is bound to disappear. Of course, this is precisely the effect which is prominently featured in the monetary approach.[9]

Under the pressure of these monetary factors, in view of the gradual decline of elasticities toward zero, the effect of devaluation on the trade balance, starting from full equilibrium, would follow a path like *b* in figure 4.3.1.[10] This is not the complete picture, though.

The second dynamic factor may be called the *allocation lag*. With two or more goods, a change in trade requires a reallocation of resources, involving changes in production, transportation, inventories, marketing, distribution, plants, foreign subsidiaries, and the like. Such shifts take time, some perhaps a few days, others (like new subsidiaries and the building of new plants) perhaps years. The adjustment of trade to price changes thus takes place with a rather long distributed lag.

If everything else remains equal, the reaction of the Portuguese demand for cloth to a one-time reduction in its escudo price can be described by a curve like log *Y* in figure 4.3.2. English receipts, measured in escudos, are expressed by log *R*. Since at first a virtually unchanged quantity is sold at a

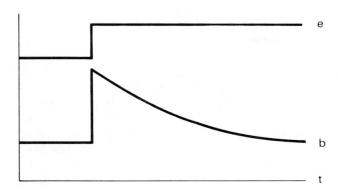

FIGURE 4.3.1
Money Supply Dynamics

9. The effects of devaluation on the terms of trade, by the same reasoning, are also bound to disappear.

10. Multiply all elasticities in the Bickerdike equation (4.2.7) by λ and let λ go to zero. It can be verified that the effect of devaluation on the trade balance declines with λ and that it reaches zero for $\lambda = 0$, provided the effect of devaluation on the terms of trade is zero.

lower price, receipts are lower. If the (absolute) price elasticity of demand ultimately exceeds unity, this initial revenue loss gradually disappears and is replaced by a revenue gain.

This reasoning has often been applied to the trade balance as a whole, leading to the expectation that a devaluation would immediately be followed by a worsening of the trade balance and that the full effect would only emerge after several years.[11] The result looks like the broken curve for b in figure 4.3.3, commonly called the J-curve. It helps to explain why in the short run the results of devaluation so often seem to be disappointing.

If the devaluation was expected in advance, this would tend to produce a deterioration even before devaluation, as imports are accelerated and exports are held back to beat the devaluation. Once devaluation has occurred, there would be a corresponding lull in imports and a rush of exports. This speculative component is indicated by the dotted variant to the J-curve. It would take two to four years to bring the adjustment close to completion.[12]

However, other things do not (and cannot) remain equal as prices change in response to devaluation. Specifically, trade flows are necessarily associated with changes in money supplies. As a consequence, the J-curve does not, in itself, describe the reaction of trade to devaluation. Starting from equilibrium, a one-time devaluation cannot possibly result in a permanent trade surplus. In each period, the addition to the money supply, resulting from the

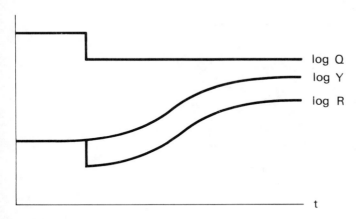

FIGURE 4.3.2
Allocation Lag

11. Note that with $\epsilon_x = \epsilon_y = 0$, the Bickerdike equation gives $(db/px) = -(de/e)$. Devaluation in a given proportion produces a *deficit* in the same proportion of trade.

12. For representative empirical studies, see Junz and Rhomberg (1973) and Wilson and Takacs (1979). The argument in the text assumes that contracts are denominated in the exporter's currency. This aspect is analyzed in Magee (1973).

current surplus, increases the demand for both imports and exportables in the next period, thus reducing the trade balance. Once cash balances have reached the desired level, the trade surplus will have disappeared. In the early phases, on the other hand, the initial trade deficit reduces cash balances, speeding up the emergence of a surplus. The trade balance must thus follow an S-shaped path like the solid *b* curve in figure 4.3.3.[13]

So far, the initial position has been assumed to be full equilibrium with balanced trade. Most devaluations actually take place in disequilibrium with a trade deficit and persistent reserve losses. In such a situation, devaluation serves, not to initiate money flows, but to bring them to an end. Once the deficit has disappeared, there is no further change in money balances and thus no reason for further trade adjustments. The improvement of the trade balance will be permanent. In this case, the J-curve presents a valid picture. For devaluations under pegged rates, it is the normal case.

There may still be a third dynamic factor, namely, the *prices of non-traded goods*. In the elasticity approach, such goods are not explicitly accounted for. In reality, however, they usually play an important role. In their absence, elasticities reflect only the substitution between goods and money. In their presence, elasticities also reflect the substitution between home goods

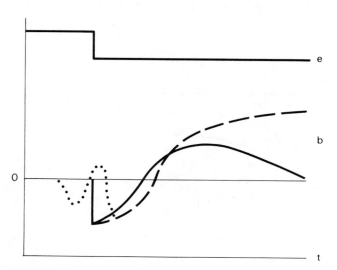

FIGURE 4.3.3
The J-curve

13. At the point where the broken curve crosses the zero line, trade is momentarily balanced, but there is still a cumulative shortfall of cash balances. As a consequence, the solid curve is still above the broken curve. The curves intersect at the point at which cash balances again reach their initial level.

and traded goods. In the course of the adjustment process, prices of non-traded goods sooner or later begin to rise in the devaluing country while they decline in the revaluing country. This, in turn, raises import demand and reduces export supply in the devaluing country; the reverse takes place in the revaluing country. Again this tends to counteract the improvement in the trade balance derived from the pure elasticity approach.

Overall, the elasticity approach presents a static shorthand expression for a complicated dynamic process. The elasticities appearing in the Bickerdike equation clearly cannot be interpreted as constants. In the very short run, demand elasticities may be close to zero while supply elasticities are very high, reflecting the free availability of goods at given domestic prices. In the intermediate run, both demand and supply elasticities may have absolute values between, say, one and four. In the long run, the neutrality of devaluation requires that all elasticities approach zero. Depending on the time span considered, the effect of devaluation on the trade balance thus appears to be very variable. This is the usual price one has to pay for the convenience of analyzing a dynamic process in terms of a static model.

4.4 The Correspondence between the Monetary Approach and the Elasticity Approach

Those who, in the early seventies, revived and developed the monetary approach to devaluation often envisaged themselves as being in sharp opposition to the dominant elasticity approach. The two approaches seemed irreconcilable, giving conflicting answers to the same question. The preceding restatement of the two approaches suggests that, in fact, the two approaches are largely equivalent, expressing the same economic content in different terms.

The correspondence can best be seen by focusing on the nature of the price elasticities that appear in the elasticity approach. The essential points are that the relevant prices are absolute money prices and that cross elasticities are assumed to be zero. This implies that the price elasticities express the substitution of commodities against cash balances. Whenever, at a given elasticity, less money is spent on goods, it is implicitly added to the cash balance. The elasticities thus express the same relationship as the hoarding coefficients of the monetary approach; the two are like the two sides of the same coin.

It is consistent with this interpretation that the elasticity model includes no budget constraint. The English supply function for cloth cannot be derived from the demand function for wine, and an analogous statement holds for Portugal. As a consequence, there will generally be differences between receipts and expenditures, reflected in changes in cash balances. This was sometimes expressed by stating that Say's Law is not assumed to hold.

Is it not possible to establish an exact correspondence between the two approaches? A look at the price effects of devaluation suggests that this should be possible. In the monetary approach, the effect of sterling devaluation on English prices is given in (3.2.4) as

$$\frac{dp_E}{p_E} = \frac{h_P}{h_P + h_E} \cdot \frac{de}{e}.$$

For the elasticity approach, the effect of sterling devaluation on the English wine price is stated in (4.2.4) to be

$$\frac{dp}{p} = \frac{\eta_x}{\eta_x - \epsilon_x} \cdot \frac{de}{e}.$$

The formal similarity of these expressions is striking. The elasticities indeed seem to play the same role in the elasticity approach as the hoarding coefficients in the monetary approach.

A similar correspondence can be established for the terms of trade and the trade balance. This requires an extension of the monetary model to two commodities. There is, however, a difficulty because the assumption about the invariant characteristics of economic behavior is different in the two cases. According to the elasticity approach, traders react to a given percentage change in a commodity price with an invariant percentage change in the quantity traded; this generally implies that hoarding is variable. The monetary approach, on the other hand, assumes that an increase in price by a given amount of money per unit requires a certain addition to cash balances; this generally implies variable price elasticities. For the present purpose, the difficulty can be overcome by choosing artificial assumptions under which the difference disappears.

First consider the terms of trade. As a counterpart to the assumption of zero cross elasticities, it is assumed that separate cash balances are held for each commodity. This results in four accumulation functions:

$$\frac{dM_x}{dt} = \lambda_x(pl_x^* - M_x) \qquad \frac{dM_X}{dt} = \lambda_X(Pl_X^* - M_X)$$

$$\frac{dM_y}{dt} = \lambda_y(ql_y^* - M_y) \qquad \frac{dM_Y}{dt} = \lambda_Y(Ql_Y^* - M_Y).$$

$$\text{(4.4.1)}$$

In the notation of this chapter, the lowercase subscripts (on the left-hand side) refer to England, while the capital subscripts (on the right-hand side) refer to Portugal. The two commodities are again denoted x (or X) and y (or Y). The symbol M_x, for example, thus represents the cash balance England holds against wine.

It must also be assumed that there are no spillovers of cash balances from one commodity to the other. This means that there are, so to say, separate payments balances for each commodity:

$$\frac{dM_x}{dt} = -e\frac{dM_X}{dt}, \qquad \frac{dM_y}{dt} = -e\frac{dM_Y}{dt}. \qquad \text{(4.4.2)}$$

Production is assumed to be fixed at, respectively, $\bar{x}$, $\bar{X}$, $\bar{y}$, and $\bar{Y}$. As a consequence, any changes in export demand and import supply are entirely due to shifts in consumption. If, for each commodity, the demand for cash balances depends on output, then l_x^*, l_X^*, l_y^*, and l_Y^*, and thus the corresponding hoarding coefficients, can be treated as constants.

Substituting from (4.4.1) into (4.4.2) yields

$$\lambda_x(pl_x^* - M_x) = -e\lambda_X(Pl_X^* - M_X),$$

$$\lambda_y(ql_y^* - M_y) = -e\lambda_Y(Ql_Y^* - M_Y).$$

(4.4.3)

At the same time, the arbitrage conditions $p = eP$ and $q = eQ$ must, of course, be satisfied. After taking differentials, these equations can be solved for the effect of devaluation on English prices. The result is

$$\frac{dp}{p} = \frac{h_X}{h_x + h_X}\frac{de}{e}, \qquad \frac{dq}{q} = \frac{h_Y}{h_y + h_Y}\frac{de}{e}.$$

(4.4.4)

The effect on the terms of trade, therefore, turns out to be

$$\frac{d\pi}{de}\frac{e}{\pi} = \frac{dq}{de}\frac{e}{q} - \frac{dp}{de}\frac{e}{p} = \frac{h_Y}{h_y + h_Y} - \frac{h_X}{h_x + h_X},$$

(4.4.5)

which can be written

$$\frac{d\pi}{de}\frac{e}{\pi} = \frac{h_x h_Y - h_y h_X}{(h_y + h_Y)(h_x + h_X)}.$$

(4.4.6)

There is a one-to-one correspondence between the hoarding coefficients in this expression and the elasticities in (4.2.5).

The effect of devaluation on the trade balance depends on the changes in the two English (or Portuguese) cash balances:

$$d\left(\frac{dM_x}{dt}\right) = \lambda_x l_x^* dp = h_x dp = h_x\frac{h_X}{h_x + h_X}p\frac{de}{e},$$

(4.4.7)

$$d\left(\frac{dM_y}{dt}\right) = \lambda_y l_y^* dq = h_y dq = h_y\frac{h_Y}{h_y + h_Y}q\frac{de}{e}.$$

The effect on the trade balance is the sum of these:

$$d\left(\frac{dM}{dt}\right) = \left\{q\frac{h_y h_Y}{h_y + h_Y} + p\frac{h_x h_X}{h_x + h_X}\right\}\frac{de}{e}.$$

(4.4.8)

This is the counterpart of (3.2.7) for a two-goods model.

Equation (4.4.8) cannot be directly compared to the Bickerdike equation, because the latter is not written for zero initial trade. The required modification is easily determined. The change in the trade balance reduces to

$$db = qdy - pdx.$$

Redefining elasticities in terms of quantities produced, this can be written

$$db = [y_q(q/\bar{y})]\bar{y}dq - [x_p(p/\bar{x})]\bar{x}dp = \eta_y\bar{y}dq - \epsilon_x\bar{x}dp.$$

Substituting for the price effects from (4.2.4), this is seen to be[14]

$$db = \left\{ q\bar{y}\,\frac{\epsilon_y\eta_y}{\epsilon_y - \eta_y} + p\bar{x}\,\frac{\epsilon_x\eta_x}{\epsilon_x - \eta_x} \right\}\frac{de}{e}. \tag{4.4.9}$$

After suitable modifications for zero initial trade, the Bickerdike equation thus corresponds closely to equation (4.4.8), derived from the monetary approach.[15]

These comparisons were based on highly artificial assumptions, to be sure. In general, the relationship between the monetary approach and the elasticity approach, for the reasons indicated, cannot be expressed by a pairwise correspondence between hoarding coefficients and elasticities. The comparisons demonstrate, however, that the two approaches have the same economic content. The artificial assumptions were necessary only to overcome the dimensional differences in the parameters.

The comparative advantages of the two approaches depend on the nature of the question. The monetary approach provides a complete dynamic model, while the elasticity approach provides only a static, one-shot picture. On the other hand, the elasticity approach makes it relatively easy to incorporate the allocation lag as expressed in the J-curve and information about specific markets and commodities. By and large, the monetary approach is most lucid for a one-commodity model, while the elasticity approach was constructed for two or more commodities. There is also the important empirical question whether hoarding coefficients or price elasticities tend to be more invariant in the course of the adjustment process, particularly if this process leads from disequilibrium to equilibrium.

4.5 Floating Exchange Rates

In the preceding sections, the elasticity approach was used to determine the trade balance resulting from devaluation. The same approach can be used to solve the "dual" problem of the exchange fluctuations resulting from exogenous shifts in trade under floating exchange rates. Obvious examples of such shifts are price increases for imported oil, which can be represented as an

---

14. Equation (4.2.4) made use of the fact that $x = X$. For the present purpose, elasticities are based on outputs, $\bar{x}$ and $\bar{X}$. To make (4.2.4) valid, one is forced to make the further artificial assumption $\bar{x} = \bar{X}$.

15. The appearance of $\bar{y}$ and $\bar{x}$ in (4.4.9) reflects the fact that the elasticities are pure numbers, whereas the hoarding coefficients have the dimension of commodity units.

upward shift in the supply curve for imports, or the emergence of North Sea oil, which, in the case of the United Kingdom, can be represented by a downward shift of the p demand curve for imports.

On the face of it, the inversion of the problem seems to be straightforward. If under fixed rates a 10 percent devaluation, on the basis of the relevant elasticities, results in a 20 percent trade surplus (measured in terms of total exports or imports), then, under floating rates, the maintenance of trade balance after a 20 percent reduction in import demand seems to require a 10 percent appreciation of the exchange rate. The solution of the floating-rate problem seems to consist in a simple inversion of the Bickerdike formula. In fact, the appreciation of sterling attributable to North Sea oil has sometimes been estimated in this way.

In principle, the application of the elasticity approach to floating rates is as valid as its application to devaluation. It implies that the initial disturbance is primarily a shift between some commodities and money. Thus the emergence of North Sea oil would be implicitly interpreted as a reduction of English import demand associated with a desired accumulation of cash balances. Again, the elasticity approach to devaluation has the same basic content as the monetary approach. Without a desired accumulation of cash balances, the English demand for exportables would at once increase by the full amount of the decline in import demand, leaving no incipient trade surplus to be eliminated by appreciation.

Nonetheless, the simple inversion of the Bickerdike formula is correct only in special cases. In general, it is incorrect because it leaves the exact nature of the exogenous shift in the trade balance out of account. For example, it does make a difference for the exchange rate whether the demand for imports shrinks or the supply of exports increases, though the incipient trade surplus may be the same.

This will now be made more precise. The model is the same as in section 4.1 except for two modifications. On one hand, the English demand function for wine now includes a shift parameter, thus reading $x = x(p) + \alpha$. On the other hand, the exchange rate adjusts in such a way that trade is continuously balanced, and thus $b = qy - px = 0$. The question is how a change in α affects e and possibly individual commodity prices and the terms of trade as well.

With these modifications, the relationship between price changes and exchange rate changes is transformed from (4.2.4) into

$$(\epsilon_x - \eta_x)\frac{dp}{p} + \eta_x\frac{de}{e} = -\frac{d\alpha}{x}. \qquad (4.5.1)$$

$$(\eta_y - \epsilon_y)\frac{dq}{q} + \epsilon_y\frac{de}{e} = 0. \qquad (4.5.2)$$

At the same time, the balance-of-payments constraint (4.2.6) becomes

$$(\epsilon_x + 1)\frac{dp}{p} - (\eta_y + 1)\frac{dq}{q} = -\frac{d\alpha}{x}. \tag{4.5.3}$$

In these equations, $d\alpha/x$ measures the exogenous increase in import demand as a fraction of total imports.

These equations can be solved for de/e in terms of $d\alpha/x$. The result is

$$\frac{de}{e} = \frac{(\eta_y - \epsilon_y)(\eta_x + 1)}{\epsilon_x\epsilon_y(\eta_x + \eta_y + 1) - \eta_x\eta_y(\epsilon_x + \epsilon_y + 1)}\frac{d\alpha}{x}. \tag{4.5.4}$$

The numerator of this expression is unambiguously positive. It can be ascertained that the denominator is identical with the numerator of the Bickerdike formula (4.2.7). In the absence of stabilizing capital flows, a positive sign of the denominator is necessary for stability.[16] An exogenous increase in the demand for imports thus produces a depreciation of the currency.

The main point is that the numerator of (4.5.4) is not, in general, identical with the denominator of the Bickerdike formula. An exception is the special case in which $\epsilon_x = -1$. If $|\epsilon_x| > 1$, the simple inversion of the Bickerdike expression would have been in error, resulting in an overestimation of the exchange reaction. In the reverse case, there would be an underestimation.

For shifts in other demand or supply functions, the effect on the exchange rate is different. Clearly, an increase in the English demand (or in the Portuguese supply) of wine produces a sterling depreciation. An increase in the English supply (or in the Portuguese demand) for cloth, on the other hand, produces an appreciation. Numerically, an increase in the demand for a given commodity does not have the same effect on the exchange rate as an equal increase in supply. In particular, the effect of a shift in a given demand or supply function on the exchange rate can be obtained from the inverted Bickerdike expression by replacing in the numerator, which is now $(\eta_y - \epsilon_y)(\eta_x - \epsilon_x)$, the corresponding elasticity by -1 and taking the result with a negative sign in the case of supply shifts. This can easily be checked by rewriting (4.5.1) through (4.5.3) for shifts in the other functions. In the case of supply shifts, with positive supply elasticities, the Bickerdike inversion is certain to overestimate the exchange fluctuations.

The Bickerdike inversion turns out to be valid in the special case of infinite supply elasticities. It can be verified that, with $\eta_y = \eta_x = \infty$,

$$\frac{de}{e} = -\frac{1}{\epsilon_x + \epsilon_y + 1}\frac{d\alpha}{x}, \tag{4.5.5}$$

16. Actually, the Bickerdike condition was originally derived as a stability condition for floating rates. From the stability of floating rates it does not necessarily follow that devaluation improves the trade balance under fixed rates, because the relevant elasticities can be different under the two regimes.

which is the inverse of the Marshall/Lerner condition. In this case it does not matter (except for the sign) where the shift occurs.

An increase in import demand, with other things equal, usually results in a deterioration of the terms of the trade. This is plausible, since the price of imports is driven up relative to exports. It can be verified by solving the equations (4.5.1) through (4.5.3) for $(dq/d\alpha)(x/q)$ and $(dp/d\alpha)(x/p)$ and taking the difference

$$\frac{d\pi}{d\alpha}\frac{x}{\pi} = \frac{dq}{d\alpha}\frac{x}{q} - \frac{dp}{d\alpha}\frac{x}{p} = \frac{1}{D}\,\eta_y(\epsilon_y - \eta_x) < 0, \tag{4.5.6}$$

where $D > 0$ is the denominator of (4.5.4). If all elasticities are finite and have the normal signs, (4.5.6) is negative. This terms-of-trade effect is the one feature the two-goods elasticity model adds to the one-good monetary model of section 3.4.

The effect on the terms of trade was sometimes regarded as the crucial aspect of depreciation. In the case of an increase in import demand, so it was argued, a depreciation is necessary precisely in order to cheapen exports relative to imports. The present model shows that this argument is not correct. With infinite supply elasticities, the terms-of-trade effect is zero, but the exchange rate nevertheless depreciates. The same is true for a completely inelastic supply of cloth, $\eta_y = 0$.

The secondary role of the terms of trade for the exchange rate can be seen even more vividly by visualizing an increase in the English demand for wine, $d\alpha > 0$, accompanied by an increase in the home demand for cloth and thus a reduction in the export supply of cloth, $d\beta < 0$. Suppose the two shifts, expressed as a fraction of the respective quantities, are exactly proportionate to the respective elasticities—that is,

$$\frac{d\beta}{y} = \frac{\eta_y}{\epsilon_x}\frac{d\alpha}{x}.$$

By introducing such an additional supply shift into (4.5.2) and (4.5.3), it can easily be ascertained that the demand shifts, though they certainly affect the exchange rate, leave the terms of trade unchanged. Prices and the exchange rate now move hand in hand; there are no repercussions on the other country. This case thus corresponds exactly to the one-good model analyzed in section 3.4.

Rather than the effect on the terms of trade, if any, the crucial aspect of a demand shift is the implicit desire to accumulate or decumulate cash balances. This can best be seen by visualizing a demand shift without such a desire. Suppose there is a shift in English consumption from imports to exportables in such a way that the effects on imports and exports at given price levels cancel out. This means that there is no implicit change in desired cash balances. The resulting system can be written

$$(\epsilon_x - \eta_x) \frac{dp}{p} + \eta_x \frac{de}{e} = -\frac{d\gamma}{xp}, \qquad (4.5.7)$$

$$(\eta_y - \epsilon_y) \frac{dq}{q} + \epsilon_y \frac{de}{e} = -\frac{d\gamma}{xp}, \qquad (4.5.8)$$

$$(\epsilon_x + 1) \frac{dp}{p} - (\eta_y + 1) \frac{dq}{q} = 0, \qquad (4.5.9)$$

where $d\gamma/xp$ denotes both the increase in the English demand for wine and the reduction in the demand for cloth, measured in value terms and expressed as a fraction of export value. These equations can be solved for the exchange rate effect of the demand shift, namely,

$$\frac{de}{e} = \frac{1}{\Delta} [(\epsilon_x + 1)(\eta_y - \epsilon_y) + (\eta_y + 1)(\eta_x - \epsilon_x)] \frac{d\gamma}{xp} \gtreqless 0, \qquad (4.5.10)$$

where $\Delta > 0$ is the denominator of the Bickerdike formula (4.2.7). There is no reason for the exchange rate to be constant, but since $(\epsilon_x + 1)$ can easily be negative, it is no longer clear that the currency depreciates. The terms-of-trade effect, on the other hand, is now even stronger. This demonstrates that the decisive factor for depreciation is not the shift in demand between different commodities, but the shift between commodities and money.

From this point of view, the depreciation of the exchange rate which results from an increase in import demand (at an unchanged demand for exportables) takes the place of the trade deficit that would have occurred under fixed rates. The desired reduction in real balances, under fixed rates achieved through the trade deficit, is in the present case achieved through the increase in commodity prices. Conversely, a contraction of import demand due to the discovery of domestic oil is implicitly interpreted by the elasticity approach as an increase in desired real balances. Under floating exchange rates, this is realized by an appreciation of the currency accompanied by falling prices.

The preceding argument was based on a formal application of the static elasticity model. Even if correctly executed, this application is subject to stringent qualifications. First, it must be remembered that the elasticity approach is inherently short-run in nature. The shift in demand that gives rise to the exchange adjustment can only be temporary; once the desired accumulation of cash balances is accomplished, the demand shift disappears while the exchange rate effect remains. In a mechanical application of (4.5.4), $(de/e)/(d\alpha/x)$ would thus go to infinity, which is consistent with the gradual decline of elasticities noted at the beginning of section 4.3.

What is more, in many cases the desired increase in cash balances is itself only temporary, cash balances serving as buffer stocks while the reallocation of resources is under way. Once this reallocation is completed, a shift in tastes, resources, or technology in favor of increased imports will usually have a counterpart in an increase in export supply, while desired cash balances remain more or less at their initial level. In this case, the initial depreciation will gradually be reversed, and the long-term effect on the exchange rate is uncertain. By the same token, if the emergence of North Sea oil initially had as its counterpart an increase in desired cash balances, thus resulting in an appreciation of sterling, the latter will largely disappear as the ensuing reallocation of resources is gradually completed.

The steady-state effect of an exogenous shift in trade on the exchange rate was analyzed in section 2.2. It turned out to be ambiguous, depending on the effects, if any, of the trade shift on the demand for and supply of money. These stock effects are not captured in the elasticity model, which relates prices to money flows and not to money stocks. Though it is clear that the elasticities decline in the course of time, the steady-state result cannot be derived from the elasticity approach.

In addition, the relevant elasticities under floating rates are likely to be different from those under fixed exchange rates. The reason is the difference in expectations about the future course of exchange rates. In particular, if economic agents regard a depreciation under floating rates as a brief episode, they will probably make fewer adjustments than if depreciation results from a devaluation under pegged exchange rates.[17]

---

17. The adjustment of trade to floating rates has been empirically studied by Wilson and Takacs (1980).

CHAPTER 5

The Adjustment Process:
The Expenditure Approach

Introduction

The expenditure approach to devaluation analysis grew out of Keynesian multiplier analysis for open economies as developed by, among others, Metzler (1942) and Machlup (1943). Disregarding the government, the social accounts represent national income, y, as the sum of expenditures on consumption and investment, a, and the excess of exports, x, over imports, i:

$$y = a + x - i. \tag{5.0.1}$$

They also show that the trade surplus is equal to the net accumulation of foreign assets. In the absence of capital flows, the latter can consist only of cash balances, M.

The trade surplus can therefore be written in three alternative ways, namely,

$$b = y - a = x - i = \Delta M. \tag{5.0.2}$$

The monetary approach focuses primarily on M. The starting point of the elasticity approach is $x - i$. In the expenditure approach, the center of attention is the excess of income over expenditure, $y - a$. This approach thus emphasizes the fact that the trade balance can be controlled by controlling national output and expenditure.[1]

The basic idea of the expenditure approach is simple: as (5.0.2) demon-

---

1. Setting a bad precedent, Sidney Alexander (1952) called expenditures "absorption." The approach thus became known as the "absorption approach." It is evident, however, that it is nothing but the aggregate demand approach made familiar by Keynesian macroeconomics.

strates, any effect of devaluation on the trade balance can be explained by determining its effect on aggregate supply, y, and aggregate demand, a. Aggregate demand, in turn, depends on aggregate income, $a = a(y) + \alpha$. As a consequence, the trade balance can be written

$$b = y - a(y) - \alpha. \tag{5.0.3}$$

Again denoting the exchange rate by e, the effect of devaluation becomes

$$\frac{db}{de} = (1 - a_y)\frac{dy}{de} - \frac{d\alpha}{de}. \tag{5.0.4}$$

Devaluation analysis thus seems to turn on the effect of the exchange rate on (1) output as reflected in dy/de and (2) the level of the expenditure function as expressed by $d\alpha/de$. Price elasticities seem to play no role.

It was soon recognized, however, that this impression is misleading. Equation (5.0.3) alone is insufficient to determine either y or b. As a consequence, Alexander's (1952) devaluation analysis did not progress beyond suggestive hints on the possible factors behind dy/de and $d\alpha/de$. In order to obtain a determinate solution, another blade has to be added to the analytical scissors. It is provided by the export surplus, $x - i$, the very element the "pure" absorption approach proposed to discard.[2]

This can best be seen in graphical terms. In figure 5.0.1, $y - a(y) - \alpha$ is an upward-sloping curve that intersects the horizontal axis at the point where

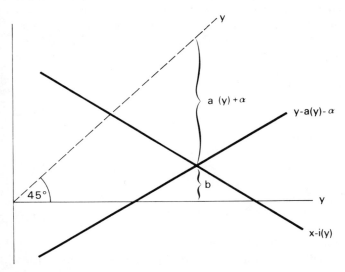

FIGURE 5.0.1
Expenditure Approach, Single Country

2. For early criticism of Alexander, see Machlup (1955).

aggregate output is just enough to satisfy aggregate demand. This curve alone is clearly not enough to determine b, because it is not known at what point the economy finds itself. The missing element is provided by $x - i(y)$. This curve must slope downward because, with a given foreign demand for exports, the demand for imports rises with income. The trade balance b is determined, jointly with y, by the intersection of the two curves. The effect of devaluation on trade is then seen to depend on the shifts it produces in each of these curves.

This argument, though fragmentary, indicates clearly that the expenditure approach, like the monetary approach, is not a rival to the elasticity approach but its companion. In the elasticity approach, changes in aggregate output are either excluded by the assumption of full employment or left implicit. In the expenditure approach, they occupy the center of the stage. The relationships between the three approaches will be made more precise by the following analysis.

5.1 Demand Shifts and Devaluation

The analysis is based on a model for two interdependent economies along the lines of Harberger's (1950) model. Again, variables for England are denoted by lower-case letters, while capital letters refer to Portugal. The government sector, foreign assets, and interest rates are disregarded. Currencies are convertible at a fixed exchange rate, and central banks have enough reserves to maintain convertibility. Countries are assumed to be specialized in production. The analysis is short-run in the sense that domestic prices are fixed, each country supplying any desired amount of output at given prices, normalized at unity.

The submodel for England can be written

$$y = a + x - ei, \tag{5.1.1}$$

with the expenditure function

$$a = a(y, e) + \alpha, \tag{5.1.2}$$

and import demand

$$i = i(y, e), \tag{5.1.3}$$

where α is an autonomous demand component.[3]

If England is a small economy in a large world market, x can be regarded as independent of i and thus of y. In this case, an autonomous increase in

---

3. The model differs from Harberger's inasmuch as a includes both foreign and domestic components.

demand (with e normalized at 1) can be easily calculated to have the following effect on output:

$$\frac{dy}{d\alpha} = \mu_s = \frac{1}{1 - a_y + i_y}. \tag{5.1.4}$$

This is the familiar small-economy multiplier. If investment does not depend on income, $(1 - a_y)$ is the marginal propensity to save. If income also affects investment, $(1 - a_y)$ represents the marginal excess saving relative to investment. In any case, it is the marginal propensity to hoard, while i_y is, of course, the marginal propensity to import. Compared to the closed-economy multiplier, $\mu = 1/(1 - a_y)$, the small-economy multiplier is lower, provided the openness of the economy does not affect a_y. The "import leakage" weakens the effect of demand shifts on output and employment.

However, we want to consider England as a "large" economy in a two-country world in which an increase in imports has repercussions on the foreign demand for exports. We thus have to add the corresponding submodel for Portugal:

$$Y = A + X - EI, \tag{5.1.5}$$

$$A = A(Y, E), \tag{5.1.6}$$

$$I = I(Y, E). \tag{5.1.7}$$

Of course, $E = 1/e$. In addition, equilibrium requires $x = I$ and $i = X$. It is assumed that trade is initially balanced, whence $i = I$. Note that each country's income and expenditure are measured in units of its own output. Arbitrage sees to it that, for each good, the price in the importing country is equal to the price in the country of origin times the exchange rate.

The model can be condensed to two equations

$$y = a(y, e) + I(Y, E) - ei(y, e) + \alpha, \tag{5.1.8}$$

$$Y = A(Y, E) + i(y, e) - EI(Y, E). \tag{5.1.9}$$

It is first used to determine the effect of a shift in England's demand, $d\alpha$, on output in both countries. With $de = 0$ and normalizing $e = 1$, differentiation yields

$$(1 - a_y + i_y)dy \qquad\qquad -I_Y dY = d\alpha \tag{5.1.10}$$

$$-i_y dy + (1 - A_Y + I_Y)dY = 0. \tag{5.1.11}$$

This can be solved for

$$\frac{dy}{d\alpha} = \frac{1 - A_Y + I_Y}{(1 - A_Y + I_Y)(1 - a_y + i_y) - I_Y i_y}$$

$$= \frac{\dfrac{1}{1 - a_y + i_y}}{1 - \dfrac{i_y}{1 - a_y + i_y} \dfrac{I_Y}{1 - A_Y + I_Y}} \tag{5.1.12}$$

$$= \frac{\mu_E}{1 - (i_y \mu_E)(I_Y \mu_P)}.$$

In this expression, μ_E and μ_P are, respectively, the small-economy multipliers for England and Portugal. It turns out that the large-economy multiplier (including foreign repercussions) is definitely larger than the small-economy multiplier (in the absence of repercussions).

The corresponding effect on the other country is

$$\frac{dY}{d\alpha} = \frac{i_y}{(1 - A_Y + I_Y)(1 - a_y + i_y) - I_Y i_y} = \frac{i_y \mu_E \mu_P}{1 - (i_y \mu_E)(I_Y \mu_P)}.$$

$$\tag{5.1.13}$$

A positive sign of the denominator in these expressions is a necessary condition for stability. It follows that an exogenous expansion in England results in an expansion in Portugal, too. There is positive transmission of demand impulses in this model. On the basis of this mechanism, one would expect that prosperity in one country helps to produce prosperity in other countries. The same applies for depression. Both prosperity and unemployment are, in part, automatically "exported." In fact, it may easily happen that, as a percentage of output, the secondary expansion (or contraction) in Portugal is stronger than the primary expansion (or contraction) in England, particularly if Portugal is considerably smaller. In such a case it might be said, "If England catches a cold, Portugal gets pneumonia."

The working of the model and its stability requirement can be illustrated graphically. In figure 5.1.1, the *EE* curve connects all those income combinations that provide equilibrium between output and expenditure in England. Higher English income is associated with higher Portuguese income, because it leaves a larger part of output available for export, for which higher Portuguese income provides a market. Similarly, the *PP* curve connects the income combinations that equilibrate aggregate demand and supply in Portugal. The system is in equilibrium at Q_1, where the curves intersect. To the right of the *EE* curve, say at A, there is an excess supply of English goods; the dynamic reaction thus leads to a contraction of English output as indicated by the horizontal arrow. Point A is also characterized by excess supply of Portuguese goods; the vertical arrow thus points downward. The other arrows are explained in a similar way. If the *EE* curve is steeper than the *PP* curve, the adjustment paths lead toward the equilibrium point; the system is stable. In

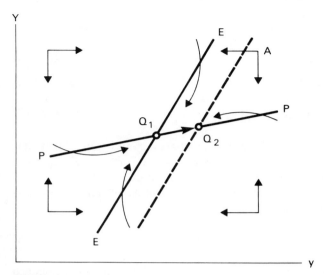

FIGURE 5.1.1
Demand Shift, Fixed Exchange Rates

the opposite case, the system is unstable. A positive denominator in (5.1.13) is the mathematical condition for the relative steepness of *EE*.

Now consider an exogenous increase in English demand. The *EE* curve shifts to the right as indicated by the broken curve. The equilibrium point thus moves upward along the *PP* curve to Q_2 with a higher income for both countries.

The same model can be used to determine the income effects of devaluation. In this case, $d\alpha = 0$ and $de \neq 0$. Normalizing $e = 1$, we have $dE = -de$. Differentiating (5.1.8) and (5.1.9), one obtains

$$(1 - a_y + i_y)dy \qquad\qquad -I_Y dY = \quad (a_e - i - i_e - I_E)de,$$

$$(5.1.14)$$

$$-i_y dy + (1 - AY + I_Y)dY = -(A_E - I - I_E - i_e)de.$$

$$(5.1.15)$$

Stability requires that $\Delta = (1 - a_y + i_y)(1 - A_Y + I_Y) - i_y I_Y > 0$. The most troublesome terms in these equations are a_e and A_E. In the remainder of this section, they are temporarily excluded from consideration by the assumption $a_e = A_E = 0$. Their significance will be taken up in the following section.

Equations (5.1.14) and (5.1.15) can be solved for the effect of sterling devaluation on English output,

$$\frac{dy}{de} = \frac{1}{\Delta} \{I_Y(I + i_e + I_E) - (1 - A_Y + I_Y)(i + i_e + I_E)\}.$$

(5.1.16)

Considering that $i = I$, this can be written

$$\frac{dy}{de} = -\frac{i}{\Delta}(1 - A_Y)(1 + \epsilon_E + \epsilon_P),$$

(5.1.17)

where ϵ_E and ϵ_P are the price elasticities of import demand. This shows that sterling devaluation stimulates English output if (1) the Portuguese propensity to hoard is positive and (2) the Marshall/Lerner condition is satisfied.

In the same way, it can be determined that the effect of sterling devaluation on Portuguese output is

$$\frac{dY}{de} = \frac{I}{\Delta}(1 - a_y)(1 + \epsilon_E + \epsilon_P).$$

(5.1.18)

Portuguese output thus declines provided (1) the English propensity to hoard is positive and (2) the Marshall/Lerner condition is satisfied. Just as under the monetary approach, devaluation tends to produce an expansion in the devaluing country accompanied by a contraction in the revaluing country.

We are finally in a position to determine the effect of sterling devaluation on trade. It is

$$\frac{db}{de} = \frac{dx}{de} - \frac{di}{de} - i = I_Y \frac{dY}{de} - i_y \frac{dy}{de} - (i + i_e + I_e)$$

$$= I_Y \frac{dY}{de} - i_y \frac{dy}{de} - i(1 + \epsilon_E + \epsilon_P).$$

(5.1.19)

Substituting for dy/de and dY/de from (5.1.17) and (5.1.18), this can, after rearrangement, be written

$$\frac{db}{de}\frac{e}{I} = -\frac{1}{\Delta}(1 - a_y)(1 - A_Y)(1 + \epsilon_E + \epsilon_P).$$

(5.1.20)

A sterling devaluation improves the English balance of payments if (1) the marginal propensities to hoard are positive and (2) the Marshall/Lerner condition is satisfied.

5.2 The Expenditure Effect of the Exchange Rate

The model of the preceding section originally included a possible effect of the exchange rate on expenditure. In the comparative-static analysis of devaluation, however, this effect was excluded by the assumption $a_e = A_E = 0$. The significance of this expenditure effect is the subject of the present section.

The question how the exchange rate may affect expenditure at a given income first came up in the early fifties, and it still provokes occasional controversy.[4] In view of the most prominent contribution, the phenomenon is sometimes called the Laursen/Metzler effect (1950). It raises the fundamental problem how aggregate demand may be affected by changes in relative prices and casts some doubt on the effects of devaluation derived in the preceding section.

By the inclusion of a_e and A_E, (5.1.17) is modified to read

$$\frac{dy}{de} = \frac{1}{\Delta} \{a_e(1 - A_Y) + (a_e - A_E)I_Y - i(1 - A_Y)(1 + \epsilon_E + \epsilon_P)\}.$$

$$(5.2.1)$$

As a consequence, it is no longer certain that devaluation raises output, the outcome depending greatly on the signs and size of a_e and A_E. Suppose, for example, that a_e is negative and has a high absolute value, while the absolute value of A_E is small. In this case it can easily be imagined that the effect of devaluation on output becomes negative.

Similarly, the effect of sterling devaluation on Portuguese output, described by (5.1.18), is now modified to read

$$\frac{dY}{de} = \frac{1}{\Delta} \{-A_E(1 - a_Y) - (A_E - a_e)i_y + I(1 - a_y)(1 + \epsilon_E + \epsilon_P)\}.$$

$$(5.2.2)$$

This means that Portuguese output is no longer certain to decline, and depending on A_E and a_e, it may conceivably rise.

The same ambiguity appears in the trade effect. Substituting from (5.2.1) and (5.2.2) into (5.1.19) and rearranging, the effect of sterling devaluation on the English trade balance can now be written

$$\frac{db}{de}\frac{e}{I} = -\frac{1}{\Delta}\left\{A_E\frac{I_Y}{I}(1 - a_y) + a_e\frac{i_y}{i}(1 - A_Y)\right.$$

$$\left. + (1 - a_y)(1 - A_Y)(1 + \epsilon_E + \epsilon_P)\right\}. \quad (5.2.3)$$

If both A_E and a_e are positive and large enough, this expression will be negative, a devaluation producing a trade deficit. The intuitive interpretation is that devaluation stimulates demand in England, and revaluation depresses

4. The papers and notes in *Kyklos*, vol. 27, no. 3 (1974) and vol. 29, no. 1 (1976), give the flavor of such discussions.

demand in Portugal, to such an extent that the substitution effects connected with the Marshall/Lerner term are overcompensated.

These considerations show that the expenditure effects of the exchange rate are potentially important for the economic effects of devaluation. What can be said about them? It should first be noted that in the model of section 5.1, expenditures include domestic goods, a^*, and imports:

$$a = a^* + ei.$$

The partial effect of the exchange rate on expenditures can thus be written

$$a_e = a_e^* + i + ei_e = a_e^* + i(1 + \epsilon_E). \tag{5.2.4}$$

If the exchange rate affects only imports, leaving the domestic demand for domestic goods unchanged, then $a_e^* = 0$. In this case, an elastic demand for imports implies $a_e < 0$. At given domestic income, a devaluation produces a contraction of aggregate demand.[5] However, the assumption $a_e^* = 0$ seems arbitrary. The question is whether it can be replaced by an economic argument.

Such an argument was developed by Laursen and Metzler along Keynesian lines. Note, first, that income is measured in units of domestic goods. A true measure of real income would be in terms of bundles of both domestic and foreign goods, their weights depending on tastes. A devaluation, by raising the domestic price of imports, results in a decline of real income for any given level of measured income. With a Keynesian consumption function, consumers would reduce saving at a given measured income and spend more on consumption. As a consequence, $a_e > 0$ and $A_E > 0$.[6] At the time when Keynesian thinking dominated international monetary economics, this reasoning was widely accepted. It casts doubts on the view that devaluation is sure to produce a trade surplus.

There is, however, also a monetary consideration. Devaluation reduces the real value of cash balances. In order to restore cash balances, it is necessary to reduce aggregate expenditures and increase hoarding. This implies $a_e < 0$ and $A_E < 0$. To achieve the increase in cash balances, it is not necessary that the expenditures on domestic goods be reduced, and thus it does not follow that $a_e^* < 0$ and $A_E^* < 0$. With elastic import demand, some additional cash balances are already provided by reduced expenditures on imports. It is sufficient that domestic expenditures be increased by less than import expenditures are reduced. On the basis of this monetary consideration, the expectation that devaluation will produce a trade surplus is strengthened.

---

5. This was assumed by Stolper (1950).

6. Dornbusch (1980, p. 78) shows neatly that the Laursen/Metzler assumption is equivalent to assuming that the elasticity of real spending with respect to real income is smaller than unity. This is another way of saying that, in the Keynesian diagram, the consumption function is flatter than a ray through the origin.

Both of these arguments are logically correct. Laursen and Metzler emphasized that devaluation amounts to a reduction in real income (at any level of measured income), and lower real income tends to reduce saving. The monetary argument emphasizes that devaluation amounts to a reduction in real wealth, which tends to stimulate saving. It seems to be an empirical question which of the two effects dominates.

5.3 Floating Exchange Rates

The expenditure approach has so far been applied to the problem of demand shifts and devaluation under fixed rates. Like the monetary and elasticity approaches, it can readily be applied to the "dual" problem of fluctuations in output and exchange rates under floating rates. In this case, the question concerns the effects of given shifts in the demand for domestic or foreign goods on domestic output, foreign output, and the exchange rate. This question is the subject of the present section.

The basic model is the same as in section 5.1, and the exposition can start from (5.1.8) and (5.1.9). The principal modification concerns the balance of payments. The exchange rate now fluctuates in such a way that, in the absence of capital flows, trade is always balanced. Any effects of income fluctuations on the trade balance are neutralized by an appreciation or depreciation of the currency. At the same time, a shift parameter is added in the English import demand function. This results in the condition

$$I(Y, E) - ei(y, e) - \beta = 0. \tag{5.3.1}$$

Substituting this condition into (5.1.8) and (5.1.9), one obtains the following system of equations:

$$y - a(y, e) = \alpha \tag{5.3.2}$$

$$Y - A(Y, E) = 0 \tag{5.3.3}$$

$$I(Y, E) - ei(y, e) = \beta. \tag{5.3.4}$$

These equations determine y, Y, and e for any values of α and β.

Some important aspects of floating rates are understood most easily by first considering the small-economy case. In the present model, repercussions on England from Portuguese demand fluctuations are excluded by dropping income as an argument in the Portuguese import demand function. With $I = I(E)$, (5.3.2) and (5.3.4) determine y and e without reference to (5.3.3).

This simplification makes the model amenable to graphical representation. In figure 5.3.1 the D curves are three possible graphs of (5.3.2). Each connects those combinations of y and e that maintain domestic balance between aggregate demand and aggregate supply. Their slopes depend on a_e. In the Laursen/Metzler case, with $a_e > 0$, the D curve is rising, as illustrated by

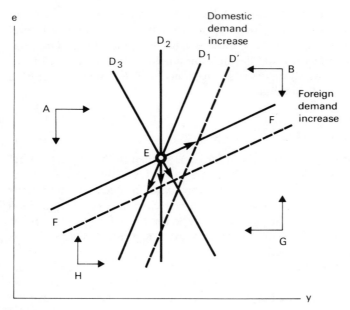

FIGURE 5.3.1
Floating Exchange Rate

D_1. In the monetary case, with $a_e < 0$, it is falling, as expressed by D_3. With $a_e = 0$, finally, the D curve is vertical.

The F curve, on the other hand, is the graph of (5.3.4), connecting all those combinations of y and e that maintain foreign balance between exports and imports. If the Marshall/Lerner condition is satisfied, its slope is positive. The economy is in equilibrium at E, where the curves intersect.

If the economy is at a point like A, there is excess demand domestically, which is combined with an export surplus and thus excess supply of foreign exchange internationally. As a consequence, domestic output rises and the price of foreign exchange declines as indicated by the arrows. Similar arrows can be drawn at points like B, G, and H. These arrows indicate the direction of dynamic adjustments in income and the exchange rate if the system is out of equilibrium. As the graph is drawn, the adjustment will eventually lead to equilibrium at E; the system is stable. Stability requires either that the D curve be falling or, if rising, that it be steeper than the F curve.

An exogenous increase in domestic demand expresses itself as a rightward shift of the D curve, as illustrated for D_1 by the broken curve. This clearly produces an expansion of output associated with a depreciation of the currency. This qualitative result holds for all D curves and is thus independent of a_e.

An increase in the exogenous demand for exports can be interpreted as a decline in β. In the graph this is represented by a rightward shift in the F curve. It clearly produces an appreciation of the currency. Alternatively, the decline in β can be interpreted as an exogenous decrease in import demand. It follows that the latter also leads to a currency appreciation. This seems to be the reasoning on which, implicitly or explicitly, most arguments about the effect of exogenous trade shifts on floating exchange rates are based.

The associated effect on domestic output is, remarkably, much less certain, since it depends crucially on the sign of a_e. If $a_e = 0$, exogenous trade shifts, no matter how large, leave output unaffected. In the monetary case, an increase in export demand or a decline in import demand produces a domestic expansion, as indicated by the arrow along D_3; this is the intuitively plausible result. In the Laursen/Metzler case, however, domestic output declines, the appreciation producing a contraction in expenditure. While it seems paradoxical that an increased demand for exports should produce a contraction, it is tempting (though probably misleading) to regard the combination of sterling appreciation and recession accompanying the decline in the British import demand due to North Sea oil as a case in point.

This graphical analysis was restricted to the small-country case; I now return to the complete two-country model of (5.3.2) through (5.3.4). This means that foreign income is allowed to have repercussions on import demand. For the purpose of comparative statics, the equations are differentiated. This yields

$$(1 - a_y)dy \qquad\qquad -a_e de = d\alpha \qquad (5.3.5)$$

$$(1 - A_Y)dY \qquad +A_E de = 0 \qquad (5.3.6)$$

$$i_y dy - I_Y dY + i(1 + \epsilon_E + \epsilon_P)de = -d\beta. \qquad (5.3.7)$$

The determinant of the left-hand coefficients is

$$\Delta = a_e i_y(1 - A_Y) + A_E I_Y(1 - a_y) + i(1 - A_Y)(1 - a_y)(1 + \epsilon_E + \epsilon_P). \qquad (5.3.8)$$

If the Marshall/Lerner condition, $1 + \epsilon_E + \epsilon_P < 0$, is satisfied and if $a_e < 0$, $A_E < 0$, then $\Delta < 0$ unambiguously. In fact, $\Delta < 0$ is necessary for stability. We can interpret β as excess demand for English exports and thus as excess demand for sterling. Under plausible dynamic assumptions, an excess demand for sterling produces appreciation and thus a decline in e. Stability requires that this decline in e reduce excess demand β. This is equivalent to requiring that $de/d\beta > 0$. An increase in the English demand for imports must depreciate sterling. Assuming $d\alpha = 0$ and solving (5.3.5) through (5.3.7) one obtains

$$\frac{de}{d\beta} = -\frac{(1 - a_y)(1 - A_Y)}{\Delta} > 0. \qquad (5.3.9)$$

Given positive marginal propensities to hoard, the numerator of this expression is positive. It follows that $\Delta < 0$ is necessary for stability.

The first question concerns the effects of an increase in English demand. In the model, such a shift is expressed by assuming $d\beta = 0$, $d\alpha > 0$. The consequent reaction of the exchange rate is

$$\frac{de}{d\alpha} = -\frac{i_y(1 - A_Y)}{\Delta} > 0. \tag{5.3.10}$$

With positive hoarding, this is positive. An expansion of domestic demand certainly results in a depreciation of the currency.

The effect on English output is somewhat less simple, but no less certain:

$$\frac{dy}{d\alpha} = \frac{1}{\Delta}\{(1 - A_Y)i(1 + \epsilon_E + \epsilon_P) + A_E I_Y\}. \tag{5.3.11}$$

If the Marshall/Lerner condition is satisfied and $A_E < 0$, this is clearly positive. In fact, the positive output effect is more reliable than this conditional statement suggests, because it can be derived as an additional stability condition. For this purpose, α is interpreted as excess supply of English goods. The dynamic effect of excess supply is surely a contraction of output. Stability requires that this output contraction, in turn, reduce excess supply, implying $dy/d\alpha > 0$.

By assuming $I_Y = 0$, the model is reduced to the small-economy case without foreign demand repercussions. In this case, the output effect reduces to

$$\frac{dy}{d\alpha} = \frac{(1 - A_Y)i(1 + \epsilon_E + \epsilon_P)}{i(1 - A_Y)(1 - a_y)(1 + \epsilon_E + \epsilon_P) + a_e i_y(1 - A_Y)}$$

$$= \frac{1}{(1 - a_y) + i_y\dfrac{a_e}{i(1 + \epsilon_E + \epsilon_P)}}. \tag{5.3.12}$$

This can be compared to the small-economy multiplier under fixed rates (5.1.4), $\mu_s = 1/(1 - a_y + i_y)$. Whether the multiplier effect of autonomous demand is stronger under fixed rates or under floating rates is seen to depend on whether $a_e/i(1 + \epsilon_E + \epsilon_P) \gtrless 1$. If the Marshall/Lerner condition is satisfied and if $a_e < 0$ and (absolutely) large relative to $(1 + \epsilon_E + \epsilon_P)$, then floating rates reduce the multiplier effect of domestic disturbances compared to fixed rates, thus acting as an additional stabilizer. If $a_e < 0$, but relatively small, this effect is stronger than under fixed rates. For $a_e = 0$, the multiplier effect is, with equal a_y, as strong as in a closed economy. Floating rates then "bottle up" domestic disturbances, preventing the dampening through international trade. For $a_e > 0$, finally, floating rates make the multiplier even larger than in a closed economy, increasing domestic disturbances.

The effect of domestic demand on foreign output is given by

$$\frac{dY}{d\alpha} = \frac{A_E i_y}{\Delta}. \tag{5.3.13}$$

This depends crucially on A_E. With $A_E = 0$, domestic demand impulses are not transmitted abroad. Each country is insulated against foreign disturbances. In the Laursen/Metzler case $A_E > 0$, there is inverse transmission of disturbances. Demand expansion at home produces contraction abroad. This is the "Laursen/Metzler paradox." In the monetary case $A_E < 0$, on the other hand, the transmission is parallel as under fixed rates (see eq. 5.1.13).

In the preceding argument, the increase in expenditures was supposed to leave import demand unaffected, thus being concentrated on domestic goods. The counterpart is an increase in import demand at unchanged demand for domestic goods. In this case, total demand increases by the same amount as import demand. This can be expressed in the model by assuming $d\alpha = d\beta$.

In this case, the depreciation is even stronger than before:

$$\frac{de}{d\beta} = -\frac{1}{\Delta}(1 - a_y + i_y)(1 - A_Y) > 0. \tag{5.3.14}$$

Correspondingly, an exogenous reduction in import demand, say because of North Sea oil, would result in an appreciation of the currency.

The effect of an import increase on English output turns out to be

$$\frac{dy}{d\beta} = \frac{1}{\Delta}\{[(1 - A_Y)i(1 + \epsilon_E + \epsilon_P) + A_E I_Y] - a_e(1 - A_Y)\}. \tag{5.3.15}$$

For $a_e = 0$, this is identical to the domestic expenditure multiplier (see eq. 5.3.11), which must be positive for stability. In the absence of a direct expenditure effect, an increase in import demand thus stimulates domestic output in the same way as an equal increase in domestic demand. In the Laursen/Metzler case of $a_e > 0$, the impulse from import demand is even stronger than that from domestic demand, because the more pronounced depreciation reenforces the expansion. In the opposite case of $a_e < 0$, however, the multiplier effect is weakened. In extreme cases it is conceivable that the increase in import demand actually produces a recession. Conversely, a spontaneous decline in import demand would normally result in a domestic contraction, but the opposite case is logically conceivable.

The international transmission of the import impulse, as can easily be verified, again depends crucially on the sign of A_E. Nothing more needs to be added to the discussion of an expenditure impulse in this respect. It should be noted that under floating rates even a spontaneous increase in the demand for imports cannot be relied upon to stimulate aggregate demand abroad. It is

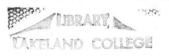

common that policymakers in one country, faced with a recession, blame it on the recession in some other country, often the United States. Under floating rates, such alibis are weak.

5.4 Comparison with the Monetary Approach and the Elasticity Approach

It was pointed out in section 4.4 that, from the point of view of economic content, the monetary approach and the elasticity approach are largely equivalent, though with significant differences in emphasis and in the choice of simplifications. The same can be said of the expenditure approach.

I shall first compare the latter with the elasticity approach. Both use static analysis to describe phenomena which are essentially transitory. The common element of this analysis is the dependence of trade flows on demand elasticities. The differences are at two levels. On one hand, the elasticity approach is more general, inasmuch as it makes allowance for finite supply elasticities, while the expenditure approach assumes an infinitely elastic supply. This is not a matter of doctrinal principles, to be sure, but of analytical convenience. Once supply prices are allowed to vary, the expenditure approach tends to become quite complex. The difference means that the expenditure approach, as usually developed, is more suitable for the Keynesian short run, before domestic prices have had time to adjust.

On the other hand, the expenditure approach introduces the effect of the exchange rate on expenditure and the effect of variable income on aggregate demand and imports. It would not be correct to say that the elasticity approach abstracts from these effects. The elasticity model does not require the assumption of continuous full employment, and a change in the exchange rate may well exert its effect on demand and supply in part through variations in output. The point is that this relationship is left implicit, while in the expenditure model it is made explicit. This means that the price elasticities in the elasticity approach differ from those of elementary microeconomics inasmuch as they are defined not for constant income but for variable income. As it was sometimes explained, they are meant to apply not *ceteris paribus* but *mutatis mutandis*. In the expenditure approach, however, they are for given income, the income effect being explicitly accounted for.[7]

Similarly, it would not be true to say that the elasticity approach does not allow for effects of exchange rates on expenditure. In fact, the expenditure effect of the exchange rate is, like its demand or supply effect, an alternative way to specify its effect on hoarding. Measuring the effect of a price change in terms of the quantity demanded, in terms of expenditures, and in terms of the change in cash balances all amount to the same thing. Again, however, the two approaches express the same economic relationship in different ways.

---

7. It should be noted that, for this reason, econometric estimates of "pure" price elasticities are not directly relevant for the elasticity approach.

In comparing the expenditure approach with the monetary approach, one clearly has to consider the unemployment version of the latter. One should not be diverted by the fact that, in the present exposition, a one-good model was used for the monetary approach, while a two-goods model was used for the expenditure approach. These are differences in exposition, not in essence. More important is the fact that the relationships between prices and spending are again captured by different parameters in the two approaches. The most important difference is that the expenditure approach, like the elasticity approach, is restricted to a still picture of an adjustment process while the monetary approach provides a complete dynamic model. As a consequence, the results derived from the expenditure approach can be only temporary and not permanent. If a devaluation takes place in economic equilibrium, all real effects are eventually bound to disappear while domestic prices are fully adjusted. The effect on real expenditures will decline to zero, real income will be back at the original level, and there will be no effect of the exchange rate on the demand for imports. Behind the static surface of the expenditure approach, just as behind the elasticity approach, there is an implicit dynamics.

II

INTERNATIONAL ASSETS AND CAPITAL FLOWS

CHAPTER 6

The Balance of International Indebtedness

Introduction

The analysis of part I abstracted from foreign assets and capital flows except in the form of gold and foreign-exchange holdings of central banks. In part II they are the main topic. The present chapter considers the determinants of international indebtedness and capital flows in the absence of money. It may thus be regarded as a counterpart to the review of "real" determinants of international trade in chapter 1. Commodity markets are in full equilibrium throughout.

Financial assets are assumed to be homogeneous in every respect. There are not even exchange rate risks to produce potential preferences between foreign and domestic securities. As a consequence, there is no reason for a given country to be both a creditor and a debtor at the same time; the net international creditor or debtor position is all that matters. Chapter 7 will then take account of the fact that there is usually a broad spectrum of assets, both financial and nonfinancial, with different risks and yields. The composition of gross foreign assets and liabilities thus moves into the foreground.

The first section of this chapter is about the basic determinants of international debts and claims in full steady-state equilibrium. Section 6.2 discusses the welfare implications of capital mobility compared with isolated capital markets. Section 6.3 makes the step from capital stocks to capital flows by considering the changes in international debts and claims during the transition from one steady state to another.

Capital flows cannot be understood in isolation. They must be seen in the context of the national accounts. The balance of payments tells us that the net capital outflow, C, has its counterpart in the sum of the excess of exports over imports and net interest receipts on foreign assets,

$$C = X - I + iA. \tag{6.0.1}$$

From the national income accounts we know that, omitting the government, the right-hand side of this expression is equal to the excess of saving, S, over net domestic investment, NDI. It follows that the capital outflow corresponds to excess saving:

$$C = S - NDI. \tag{6.0.2}$$

From the point of view of the national wealth accounts, the capital outflow must be interpreted as the increase in net foreign assets, ΔA; saving is defined as the increase in wealth, ΔW; and net domestic investment corresponds to the increase in the stock of real capital goods, ΔK. As a consequence,

$$C = \Delta A = \Delta W - \Delta K.$$

Explaining net capital flows is tantamount to explaining changes in national wealth relative to the changes in the stock of real capital goods. From the international accounts it is also clear that any change in wealth relative to real capital in one country must be matched by an opposite change in the rest of the world.

It has become customary in recent years to treat international capital flows primarily as a financial phenomenon, reflecting shifts in supply and demand for assets in different currencies. Their most important determinants are supposed to be interest rates, a higher relative yield on domestic assets calling forth a capital inflow. Covered interest arbitrage in the forward exchange market is often used as the paradigm of this mechanism. The rapid reaction of asset arbitrage to interest differentials under present-day conditions is taken as an indication that the mobility of international capital flows is very high. I believe this purely financial orientation of capital flow analysis is a source of serious error.

In this and the following chapters, financial capital flows are considered in close connection with real phenomena, reflecting differences in aggregate saving and investment between residents of different countries. Purely financial transactions, no matter how large, do not have the power to move a single dollar's worth of net capital across national borders except inasmuch as they influence investment and saving. In particular, forward exchange transactions, since they leave the net asset position of a country unchanged, are the paradigm of financial transactions that do not produce net capital flows. Asset arbitrage, no matter how prompt, gives no clue about the mobility of net capital flows, and it is not evident that the latter is higher today than it was, say, in the nineteenth century. Surely asset arbitrage has virtually nothing to do with changes in relative wealth and real capital stocks between the residents of different countries. As a consequence, it has virtually nothing to do with net capital movements. The principal determinants of net capital flows must be sought among the "real" factors.

6.1 Creditor Countries and Debtor Countries

This section concerns the basic question why some countries are international debtors while others are creditors. In very general terms, the answer is that countries are debtors if their investment opportunities exceed their wealth and are creditors if their wealth exceeds their investment opportunities. It may well be, therefore, that a wealthy country, since its investment opportunities are particularly favorable, turns out to be a net borrower, while a poor country, since its investment opportunities are even poorer, ends up as a net lender. This answer will now have to be made more precise.

Portugal and England will again serve as paradigms, the former in the role of debtor, the latter as creditor. In order to focus attention on the basic elements of the problem, it will also be assumed that both countries produce and consume the same homogeneous good, simply called "output." As a consequence, there is no international division of labor, and in the absence of indebtedness and transfers there would be no trade.

To introduce the elements of the model, it is convenient to consider first a single country, either England or Portugal, in isolation. In this one-sector economy, output is either consumed or used as a capital good, called a "machine." One machine can be obtained by foregoing $\bar{q}$ units of consumption, where $\bar{q}$ is regarded as constant throughout. Once a machine is installed, either in England or in Portugal, it is immobile; there is no international trade in capital goods. While this is unrealistic for airplanes and tankers, it is a reasonable first approximation for a dominant part of the real capital stock, including buildings, roads, railways, harbors, and mines.

Assuming that land and labor are given and immobile, output (net of depreciation), Q, depends only on the stock of capital goods, K, with a positive, but diminishing, marginal product. Using starred symbols for the isolation equilibrium, this relationship can be expressed by the production function

$$Q^* = Q(K^*) \qquad \frac{\partial Q^*}{\partial K^*} > 0 \qquad \frac{\partial^2 Q^*}{\partial K^{*2}} < 0. \qquad (6.1.1)$$

Competition will see to it that the rental on a machine equals its marginal product:

$$r^* = \frac{\partial Q^*}{\partial K^*}. \qquad (6.1.2)$$

Property rights in machines are embodied in securities, each representing one machine. Rentals on machines are paid to the security owners in the form of dividends. If the price of the machine (and thus of the security) is denoted by q, the yield (or interest rate) is

$$i^* = r^*/q^*. \tag{6.1.3}$$

In full equilibrium the market price of a machine must be equal to its replacement cost, $\bar{q}$,

$$q^* = \bar{q}. \tag{6.1.4}$$

National wealth, measured in terms of machines, is assumed to be given,

$$K^* = \bar{V}. \tag{6.1.5}$$

In a more general formulation, V would presumably depend also on both the rate of interest and income, which would add an equation

$$V = V(i^*, Q^*), \tag{6.1.6}$$

but these elements, while certainly modifying the results, do not offer additional insights into the basic determinants of international indebtedness. The five equations (6.1.1) through (6.1.5) determine K^*, Q^*, r^*, i^*, and q^*. In figure 6.1.1, the upward-sloping curve represents output for different amounts of capital. The dividend (rental) per machine corresponds to the slope of the output curve. It declines as more machines are added. By multiplying the rental by the amount of capital, one obtains the aggregate income going to the wealth owners; the remainder goes to the other resources. Suppose capital is at $K^* = \bar{V}$. Capital income is then measured by the distance

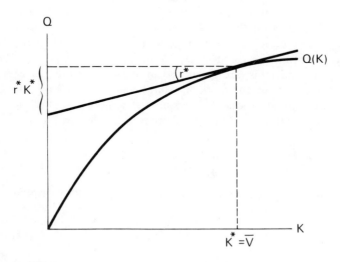

FIGURE 6.1.1
Production Function

$r*K*$. If wealth increases, aggregate capital income may either rise or fall, depending on the relationship between the increase in the amount of capital and the decline in the per-unit rental.

This is all we need for an individual country. We will now consider two such countries, but still in isolation, without international indebtedness and thus without international trade. For each, Portugal and England, we have four equations:

$$K_P^* = \bar{V}_P \qquad\qquad K_E^* = \bar{V}_E \qquad\qquad\qquad (6.1.7)$$

$$Q_P^* = Q_P(K_P^*) \qquad Q_E^* = Q_E(K_E^*) \qquad\qquad (6.1.8)$$

$$r_P^* = \frac{\partial Q_P^*}{\partial K_P^*} \qquad r_E^* = \frac{\partial Q_E^*}{\partial K_E^*} \qquad\qquad (6.1.9)$$

$$i_P^* = \frac{r_P^*}{\bar{q}} \qquad\qquad i_E^* = \frac{r_E^*}{\bar{q}} \qquad\qquad\qquad (6.1.10)$$

The production functions may have different shapes, but in relation to land and labor Portugal is assumed to have lower wealth than England. More exactly, it is assumed that $r_P^* > r_E^*$. However, replacement costs for capital goods in terms of output are the same in both countries, and thus $\bar{q}_P = \bar{q}_E = \bar{q}$. It is clear, therefore, that the higher rental in Portugal implies a higher interest rate.

This model is represented in figure 6.1.2. The left-hand side relates to Portugal, while the right-hand side relates to England. The upper part expresses the content of (6.1.7) through (6.1.10) in terms of marginal products. On each side, the given wealth, measured in machines, is confronted with the demand for machines, represented by the downward-sloping schedule of the marginal product of capital. Without an international capital market, the rental of capital in the capital-poor country, r_P^*, is higher than the rental in the capital-rich country, r_E^*.

The lower part of figure 6.1.2 expresses the same economic content in terms of total output. It thus resembles figure 6.1.1 turned on its head. It is clear that at capital stocks K_P^* and K_E^*, the Portuguese curve must be steeper than the English curve.

Suppose Portugal and England now establish complete mobility of financial assets, wealth owners in each country being free to choose either domestic or foreign securities. At the original prices, it now becomes profitable for English wealth holders to sell English securities and to buy Portuguese securities. This temporarily lowers the price of English machines below replacement cost. The price of Portuguese machines, on the other hand, temporarily rises above replacement cost. A positive gap between the market price of capital goods and their replacement cost calls forth investment, while a

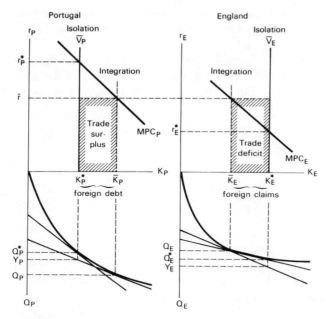

FIGURE 6.1.2
Isolation and Integration of Capital Markets

negative gap results in disinvestment. The basic determinant of investment can be identified as Tobin's q.[1] It will turn out that it is also the basic force behind international capital movements. In England the capital stock is thus reduced by disinvestment, and in Portugal it is increased by investment. This, in turn, results in an increase in English, and a decline in Portuguese, rentals. Equilibrium in the integrated capital market will be established when rentals are internationally equalized and both capital-goods prices are again at the level of replacement cost.

With integrated capital markets, interest rates are equalized internationally. If securities are homogeneous, there is no reason for interest rates to be higher in the debtor country than in the creditor country (and if securities are heterogeneous, prices might just as well be higher for the securities of the debtor country than for those of the creditor country). Capital indeed flows from countries which, in isolation, would have lower interest rates to those which, in isolation, would have higher interest rates, but arbitrage promptly eliminates such differences for homogeneous securities. We cannot expect to find any trace of them in international comparisons of interest rates.

----

1. Tobin (1969), Tobin and Brainard (1977). For recent developments, see Yoshikawa (1980) and Hayashi (1982). In the present exposition, q denotes the price of capital goods, while the ratio of the latter to replacement cost is denoted by $q/\bar{q}$.

The two-country model with an integrated capital market can be written as follows:

$$(K_P + K_E) = \bar{V}_P + \bar{V}_E \tag{6.1.11}$$

$$Q_P = Q_P(K_P) \qquad Q_E = Q_E(K_E) \tag{6.1.12}$$

$$r = \frac{\partial Q_P}{\partial K_P} \qquad r = \frac{\partial Q_E}{\partial K_E} \tag{6.1.13}$$

$$i = \frac{r}{\bar{q}}. \tag{6.1.14}$$

Instead of the two wealth constraints (6.1.7), there is now the integrated constraint (6.1.11). Subject to this constraint, capital is distributed in such a way that its marginal products are equalized, which results in a single world interest rate.

At this point, international trade makes its appearance, even in a one-good world. Portugal, using more capital than she owns, has to pay dividends to England on the borrowed funds. In the steady state these payments take the form of commodity exports. The Portuguese balance of payments thus consists of a debit item on service account and an equal credit item on merchandise account. The English balance of payments is simply the reverse. As a counterpart, Portuguese income is now lower than domestic product, while the reverse is true in England:

$$Y_P = Q_P - \bar{r}(K_P - \bar{V}_P) \qquad Y_E = Q_E + \bar{r}(\bar{V}_E - K_E). \tag{6.1.15}$$

This is illustrated in figure 6.1.2. With integrated capital markets, the equilibrium rental rate $\bar{r}$ must be such that English foreign claims are equal to Portuguese foreign debts. Compared to capital isolation, the English capital stock shrinks while Portuguese capital expands by the same amount. At the equilibrium interest rate, the Portuguese trade surplus, measured by the shaded rectangle, is equal to the English deficit, and both correspond to interest on foreign debts (or claims). The lower part of the graph shows that Portugal, thanks to capital mobility, produces more than under capital isolation while England produces less. Portugal pays some part of the additional output, namely $Q_P - Y_P$, to England as interest on foreign debt. The same payment appears on the English side as additional income, $Y_E - Q_E$.

So far, international equilibrium with integrated capital markets has been compared with national isolation. Another comparative-static question concerns the effect of shifts in wealth on the international equilibrium. This question can be answered by considering first differences of the two-country model. Suppose there is an increase in English wealth while Portuguese wealth is unchanged. The increases in capital stocks must sum to the wealth increase

$$dK_P + dK_E = dV_E. \tag{6.1.16}$$

They are allocated in such a way that the rental changes by the same amount in both countries:

$$Q_P'' \, dK_P = Q_E'' \, dK_E. \tag{6.1.17}$$

Equations (6.1.16) and (6.1.17) can be solved for dK_P and dK_E in terms of dV_E. The result is

$$\frac{dK_P}{dV_E} = \frac{Q_E''}{Q_E'' + Q_P''} > 0$$

$$\frac{dK_E}{dV_E} = \frac{Q_P''}{Q_E'' + Q_P''} > 0. \tag{6.1.18}$$

The wealth increase in one country results in an increase in the use of capital goods in both countries. It can also be ascertained that it makes no difference for the allocation of capital goods in which country the wealth increase occurs. For an increase in Portuguese wealth, the effects would be exactly the same. With integrated capital markets, savings in one country increase capital in all countries. Not unexpectedly, each country's share of new capital is inversely related to the slope of its marginal product curve. If additional machines can be absorbed with but a small decline in their marginal product, a country will get many new machines; if the marginal product declines rapidly, it will get only a few.

The output effects, according to (6.1.12), depend on nothing but the capital inputs:

$$\frac{dQ_P}{dV_E} = Q_P' \frac{dK_P}{dV_E} = Q_P' \frac{Q_E''}{Q_E'' + Q_P''} > 0,$$

$$\frac{dQ_E}{dV_E} = Q_E' \frac{dK_E}{dV_E} = Q_E' \frac{Q_P''}{Q_E'' + Q_P''} > 0. \tag{6.1.19}$$

An increase in English wealth produces an expansion of output in both countries, and again it makes no difference where the wealth increase occurs. Integrated capital markets spread the output effect of higher wealth, regardless of where it occurs, over all countries.

This is achieved by the equalization of rental rates, because a wealth increase in one country produces the same decline in rentals in both:

$$\frac{dr}{dV_E} = Q_P'' \frac{dK_P}{dV_E} = \frac{Q_P'' Q_E''}{Q_E'' + Q_P''} < 0. \tag{6.1.20}$$

At the same time, English lending to Portugal increases, since the whole increase in Portuguese capital goods is financed by international borrowing.

It is tempting to argue that, as a consequence of increased international lending, the Portuguese export surplus increases. This is not certain, however. The Portuguese trade surplus is the excess of production over consumption, which is equal to dividend payments to England:

$$B_P = Q_P - Y_P = r(K_P - V_P). \tag{6.1.21}$$

The effect of the increase in English wealth is, therefore,

$$\frac{dB_P}{dV_E} = r\frac{dK_P}{dV_E} + (K_P - V_P)\frac{dr}{dV_E}$$

$$= r\frac{Q_E''}{Q_E'' + Q_P''} + (K_P - V_P)\frac{Q_P''Q_E''}{Q_E'' + Q_P''} \gtreqless 0. \tag{6.1.22}$$

The first term on the right-hand side, measuring the effect through the increased lending at given interest rates, is positive. In addition, however, the decline in interest rates lowers the exports required to finance a given volume of foreign debt, which is reflected in the negative sign of the second term. It is not clear, therefore, how increased wealth affects trade balances.

One might also be tempted to conjecture that an increase in English wealth certainly raises English income, while the effect on Portuguese income, in view of higher borrowing, is unclear. Again, however, the conjecture would be false. In fact, the opposite is true. The reaction of Portuguese income is, from (6.1.15),

$$\frac{dY_P}{dV_E} = \frac{dQ_P}{dV_E} - r\frac{dK_P}{dV_E} - (K_P - V_P)\frac{dr}{dV_E}$$

$$= -(K_P - V_P)\frac{dr}{dV_E} > 0. \tag{6.1.23}$$

The first two terms on the right-hand side cancel out. This means that the increase in Portuguese production just pays for the dividends on the additional debt. What remains is the income effect of the decline in the dividend rate, and this is certainly positive. An increase in English wealth is certain to raise Portuguese income.

The reaction of English income, on the other hand, is

$$\frac{dY_E}{dV_E} = \frac{dQ_E}{dV_E} - r\frac{dK_E}{dV_E} + r + (V_E - K_E)\frac{dr}{dV_E}$$

$$= r + (V_E - K_E)\frac{dr}{dV_E} \gtreqless 0. \tag{6.1.24}$$

Again the first two terms cancel out. What remains is the dividend income on the additional wealth and the loss in income from the decline in dividends on the foreign assets. Since it is not clear which term dominates, England's income may either rise or decline. The possibility of a decline is an example of "immiserizing growth," the positive effect of capital growth being more than offset by a negative price effect. Total world income, however, certainly increases, the increase being simply the dividends on the additional wealth.

It can be left to the reader to trace the comparative-static effects of an increase in the borrowing country's wealth. In this case, international lending will be reduced. Eventually, if the shift is large enough, the roles may be reversed, the former borrower becoming the lender and vice versa. The effects of technological progress, as expressed by shifts in the marginal product curves of lenders or borrowers, can be determined by the same technique.

In the preceding analysis, as throughout this chapter, wealth was regarded as independent of interest rates. Given this assumption, it was shown how international indebtedness is determined by the interplay of wealth and the demand for capital goods. With homogeneous assets, interest differentials cannot occur; they are not a determinant of the structure of international indebtedness. In a more general analysis, the influence of interest rates on wealth could also be included. In this case, the supply curves for capital goods in figure 6.1.2, instead of being vertical, would presumably slope upward; the interest sensitivity of wealth would appear in the mathematical analysis. Nevertheless, international interest differentials would still play no role. Whenever such interest differentials occur in long-run equilibrium, they simply reflect risk differentials without having any particular connection with the debtor or creditor status of the countries concerned.

6.2 Welfare Effects of Capital Mobility

What can be said about the welfare effects of free capital movements? The answer to this question has many aspects, only the most elementary of which are considered in this section.[2] A first observation concerns the effect of capital market integration on income. The basic proposition is that real national income is higher with capital mobility than with isolation for both the debtor country and the creditor country. This is already apparent from the lower part of figure 6.1.2, since for Portugal the gain in output necessarily exceeds the interest payments to England, whereas for England the income payments received from Portugal exceed the loss in output.

This graphical argument can also be expressed in terms of the upper part of figure 6.1.2. It is reproduced as figure 6.2.1 with the English side reversed and the horizontal dimension equal to the world capital stock.[3] Without capital mobility, the situation is described by the vertical line labeled "isolation." With capital-market integration the system moves to point E, where the mar-

2. For a comprehensive discussion, see MacDougall (1968). Readers familiar with international trade theory will note the close correspondence between the welfare effects of capital mobility and the gains from trade. In fact, capital services may be interpreted as a second good, in which England has a comparative advantage, while Portugal's advantage is in commodity output.
   3. The same graph is used in Stern (1973, p. 272).

ginal product curves intersect. The rectangle *EGFH* represents interest payments from Portugal to England. The area *EGFD* measures Portuguese production gains. The triangle *DEH* thus measures the net gain for Portugal. By analogous reasoning, *EKH* is the net gain for England.[4] At this level of analysis, there is no conflict of interest between the borrowing country and the lending country, though the relative size of their gains, depending on the slopes of the marginal product curves, may be different.[5]

It does not follow that international lending cannot produce a conflict of interest. In fact, there may well be one, but it is a conflict between different groups within the same country. Suppose there are two social classes, "workers," earning only wages, and "capitalists," earning only dividends (or interest). Consider the borrowing country. In isolation, the Portuguese capitalists earn *OBDF*. With capital mobility their income is *OCHF*, which is certainly less. The Portuguese workers, on the other hand, see their income rise from *ABD* to *ACE*. Foreign borrowing thus makes wage income rise while capital income declines. In the lending country it is the other way around. Dividend income of English capitalists increases from *QNKF* to *QMHF*, but the wage income of English workers declines from *PNK* to *PME*.

Two points should be noted, however, before far-reaching social conclusions are drawn from this analysis. First, since total income rises, the winners

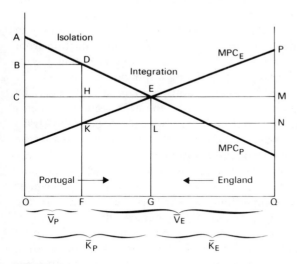

FIGURE 6.2.1
Welfare Gains and Losses

4. For a proof that isolation is not Pareto-optimal and that capital mobility is, see Kareken and Wallace (1977).
5. While this argument relates to stationary economies, Amano (1965) pointed out that in a Harrod/Domar model the income gain from capital mobility stimulates growth.

in each country gain more than the losers lose. By appropriate taxes and/or transfers it is thus possible, in principle, to redistribute income in such a way that capital mobility is to everybody's advantage. In the borrowing country, such a policy would involve heavier taxes on wages to relieve the tax burden on dividends; in the lending country, it would involve a relatively heavier burden on dividends to relieve wage earners. To the extent that such a policy is successful, it would establish harmony of interests in favor of capital mobility.[6]

Second, it should be remembered that in reality functional income shares do not correspond to clearly separated social classes. Some capital income goes to workers through savings, pension funds, social security, and the like. Some wages, on the other hand, go to people we are rather inclined to regard as "capitalists," such as managers. In some incomes—as in those of farmers, professionals, and independent business people—wage elements and capital returns are inseparably intertwined. To the extent that this is so, the shifts in the functional distribution of income due to capital mobility permit no direct inference about shifts in the personal distribution between social groups.

From the observation that each country has a net gain from capital mobility, it does not follow that this gain could not perhaps be increased by unilateral restrictions on international borrowing or lending. In the pure theory of international trade, the discussion of optimal tariffs has shown that a country can often gain by imposing a unilateral tariff. The same reasoning can be applied to international indebtedness. Suppose lenders have a monopoly in the capital market while borrowers are in pure competition.[7] Starting from isolation, such a lender could obtain for the first "dose" of international lending an interest rate of DF (see fig. 6.2.2). Being a monopolist, he will now base his lending policies, not on the average return of loans as represented by the MPC_P curve, but on the marginal return. If the MPC_P curve is linear, this MRL curve will slope downward from D with twice the slope of the MPC_P curve. The marginal cost of lending, on the other hand, is represented by the MPC_E curve, indicating the domestic returns foregone for the sake of foreign lending. The lender's optimum is reached at interest rate RT, where the marginal revenue from lending equals its marginal cost. At this point, the lender is better off than under pure competition, but the borrower is worse off, the borrower's loss exceeding the lender's gain by the deadweight loss from monopoly, RSE. Essentially, this deadweight loss occurs because the capital rental of the borrowing country now remains higher than that of the lending country. This difference RS indicates that some machines now used in England could have been more efficiently used in Portugal. The same advantage

6. Kareken and Wallace also showed that capital mobility is not Pareto-superior to isolation, but can be made so by suitable taxes and/or transfers.
7. This monopoly argument is found in Jasay (1960). For the following discussion, see Stern (1973).

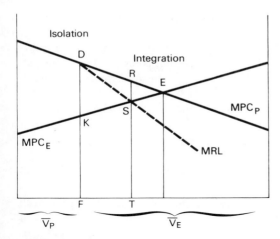

FIGURE 6.2.2
Monopolistic Lending

can be obtained by the lending country even without monopoly by imposing an appropriate tax on interest payments from abroad.[8]

A similar profit can be obtained by the borrower at the expense of the lender either by monopoly (more exactly: monopsony) control of borrowing or by imposing an appropriate tax on dividends paid to foreign lenders, provided the lenders remain in pure competition. It is clear that such monopolistic (or monopsonistic) exploitation depends on the absence of competition from other lenders (or borrowers) and on the absence of retaliation. In practice, its scope will thus be quite limited, and there is a danger that everybody will lose in the end.

The preceding welfare analysis of international indebtedness, since it is based on a one-good model, abstracted completely from terms-of-trade effects. In reality, these may play an important role. To visualize this role, we have to return to the two-product case of chapter 1, with England and Portugal exchanging cloth and wine. At the same time, the capital good, still called a "machine" and given in a fixed aggregate amount, is now differentiated from the two outputs. This extension of the model raises the new question how international lending affects welfare through the terms of trade. Would England, since its output contracts, obtain an additional benefit through an increase in the relative price of cloth, and would Portugal, since its output expands, have to bear an additional burden through a decline in the relative

8. On the simultaneous determination of an optimal tariff on commodities and an optimal tax on foreign investment income, see Kemp (1976, chs. 15–16) and Jones (1967). Suitably chosen taxes and tariffs could also be used to avoid the danger of "immiserizing" capital flows mentioned at the end of the preceding section.

price of wine? Since this question resembles the transfer problem, it might seem plausible to answer it in close analogy to the latter. Such an analogy would be misplaced, however, because the present problem has to do primarily with transfers of factors of production and not of income or wealth. In fact, at unchanged terms of trade, income increases in both countries, while wealth remains constant by assumption.

The analytical discussion of this problem has been extensive. It has often been argued that the export surplus required for the payment of interest would shift the terms of trade permanently against the borrowing country.[9] More recent research has shown that general statements about the terms-of-trade effects of capital mobility are difficult to obtain; almost everything depends on the circumstances of the case.[10]

More clear-cut results can be obtained on the assumption that each country, while still consuming both goods, specializes in the production of one of them. Suppose that England specializes in cloth while Portugal produces only wine. An intuitive argument would now run as follows. By virtue of international lending, Portuguese wine production rises and English cloth production declines. This shift in supply, taken alone, tends to shift the terms of trade in favor of the lender. At the same time, income rises in both countries. Assuming both goods are normal (non-inferior), demand therefore increases for both goods. One is thus driven to the tentative conclusion that excess demand at unchanged terms of trade, since it is the combined result of both demand and supply shifts, is uncertain, leaving the terms-of-trade effect ambiguous. Fortunately, more precise analysis reveals that the terms of trade (assuming non-inferior goods) shift definitely in favor of the lender.

This can be shown as follows. Suppose the terms of trade are held constant and normalized at $\pi = 1$. As a consequence, the outputs, incomes, marginal products, and rentals of the two countries, though measured in terms of physically different goods, can be directly compared. Suppose further that the two countries are at an arbitrary intermediate point between isolation and capital integration, where Portugal's rental rate is still higher than England's. International lending takes place at a rate r, which is no higher than r_P and no lower than r_E.[11] The price of capital goods is normalized at $q = 1$. Now imagine one further machine is added in Portugal, financed with English capital, while the English capital stock is correspondingly reduced. Will this, at unchanged terms of trade, call forth excess demand for cloth (and thus excess supply of wine) or excess supply of cloth (and thus excess demand for wine)?

---

9. See Keynes (1930, pp. 343–46) and Singer (1950). The following discussion is restricted to permanent steady-state effects, thus leaving out the terms-of-trade effects of transitory capital flows.

10. This is the view taken by MacDougall (1968, p. 187) and analytically supported by Pearce and Rowan (1966) and Pearce (1970, pp. 602–12).

11. It is most convenient to assume that all international lending takes place at the ultimate equilibrium rate $r = \bar{r}$. The gradual adjustment of r is analyzed at the end of section 6.3.

Excess demand for cloth is

$$\beta = C_P + C_E - Q_E = C_P + C_E - (Y_E - r(\bar{V}_E - K_E))$$
$$= C_P + C_E - Y_E + r(K_P - \bar{V}_P). \tag{6.2.1}$$

In both countries the demand for cloth depends only on income,

$$C_P = C_P(Y_P), \qquad C_E = C_E(Y_E). \tag{6.2.2}$$

The two incomes can be written

$$Y_P = Q_P(K_P) - r(K_P - \bar{V}_P), \tag{6.2.3}$$

$$Y_E = Q_E(K_E) + r(\bar{V}_E - K_E),$$

with

$$K_P + K_E = \bar{V}_P + \bar{V}_E. \tag{6.2.4}$$

Taking differentials and substituting from (6.2.2) through (6.2.4) into (6.2.1), the change in the excess demand for cloth can be expressed as a function of the capital shift:

$$d\beta = dC_P + dC_E - dY_E + r\,dK_P$$

$$= \frac{\partial C_P}{\partial Y_P}dY_P + \left(\frac{\partial C_E}{\partial Y_E} - 1\right)dY_E + r\,dK_P$$

$$= \left[\frac{\partial C_P}{\partial Y_P}\left(\frac{\partial Q_P}{\partial K_P} - r\right) + \left(\frac{\partial C_E}{\partial Y_E} - 1\right)\left(r - \frac{\partial Q_E}{\partial K_E}\right) + r\right]dK_P$$

$$= \left[\frac{\partial C_P}{\partial Y_P}(r_P - r) + \left(\frac{\partial C_E}{\partial Y_E} - 1\right)(r - r_E) + r\right]dK_P \tag{6.2.5}$$

$$= \left[\frac{\partial C_P}{\partial Y_P}(r_P - r) + \frac{\partial C_E}{\partial Y_E}(r - r_E) + r_E\right]dK_P.$$

If $\partial C_P/\partial Y_P \geqq 0$ and $\partial C_E/\partial Y_E \geqq 0$, the three terms in the square bracket are all positive. For normal (non-inferior) goods, therefore, an increase in Portuguese borrowing unambiguously increases the excess demand for cloth at unchanged terms of trade. This argument related to an arbitrary intermediate point between isolation and integration. Now imagine that Portuguese borrowing begins at the isolation point and continues, at fixed terms of trade, to the point of full integration. As the preceding argument has shown, this process is associated with a continuous increase in the excess demand for cloth. It follows that there is excess demand for cloth in the final situation.

Intuitive understanding of this result may be helped by considering two limiting cases. Suppose the marginal propensity to spend income on cloth is zero. In this case, the capital shift does not affect the demand for cloth. The supply of cloth, however, declines by the marginal product in England, r_E. There is thus excess demand in this amount. Suppose, on the other hand, the marginal propensity to spend income on cloth is unity. In this case the demand for cloth increases by the aggregate increase in income, which is the difference between the two marginal products, $r_P - r_E$. Supply shrinks again by r_E. There is thus excess demand for cloth in the amount r_P. These limiting cases suggest that, as long as none of the goods is inferior, there is always excess demand for cloth.

From the emergence of excess demand for cloth at constant terms of trade it follows that in order to restore equilibrium in the commodity markets the relative price of cloth must rise. With complete specialization in production, the transition to capital mobility thus shifts the terms of trade unambiguously in favor of the lending country at the expense of the borrowing country. For the lending country, the income gain from capital mobility is thereby increased. For the borrowing country, it is reduced, and it is conceivable that the total effect is actually negative. [12]

As pointed out above, the terms-of-trade effect becomes ambiguous once each country produces both goods. However, since pronounced creditor countries and pronounced debtor countries are often characterized by marked differences between their respective imports and exports, the case of complete specialization, though not deciding the issue, is still likely to indicate which side the terms of trade will usually favor. In any case, in an international system consisting of many countries, each with different comparative advantages and with a minor share in the production and consumption of each commodity, the change in the terms of trade, whatever its direction, is likely to be rather small.

6.3 Capital Movements

The analysis of international indebtedness in section 6.1 was concerned with stocks of foreign claims and liabilities in stationary equilibrium. Capital movements do not explicitly appear in such an analysis. To make room for them, the analytical framework has to be extended. Such an extension can be sought in two directions.

On one hand, there may be permanent capital flows as a concomitant of economic growth. If both the debtor economy and the creditor economy grow, the mere maintenance of the initial proportions between wealth and capital stocks requires continuing capital flows. To illustrate by the simplest possible example, suppose the stationary model for capital mobility in section 6.1 is transformed into a model of balanced growth. This can be achieved by rein-

---

12. To give an extreme example, if the debtor's *MPC* curve is horizontal, his income gain at unchanged terms of trade is zero. At the same time, there is still a secondary burden from the adverse shift in the terms of trade. This is another case of "immiserizing growth."

terpreting all stocks and flows in a per capita sense and assuming that labor (and other resources) grow at a constant rate g. In this case, the maintenance of equilibrium requires a continuous capital flow from England to Portugal in the amount of $g\bar{q}(K_P - \bar{V}_P) = g\bar{q}(\bar{V}_E - K_E)$. The Portuguese export surplus will thus be reduced to $(i - g)\bar{q}(K_P - \bar{V}_P)$. If the rate of growth exceeds the rate of interest, it is even changed into an import surplus, but this case can perhaps be ruled out on efficiency grounds. These long-term growth aspects of capital flows, since they are not closely related to international monetary problems, are not further considered in this study. [13]

On the other hand, there may be temporary capital flows associated with the dynamic adjustment process that leads from one stationary equilibrium to another. The comparative-static analysis of section 6.1 showed, for example, that an increase in the wealth of the lending country will ultimately result in a higher stock of foreign assets. During the transition, the lending country must export capital; there must be a temporary capital outflow. This aspect of capital flows, briefly described in section 6.1, will now be analyzed in detail. For the purpose of this discussion, wealth in each country is again regarded as given; saving is zero by assumption. This means that the analysis concentrates on the investment aspects of capital flows.

The model is the same as in section 6.1. In particular, it is a one-good model; England and Portugal produce the same good (and thus, in the absence of international indebtedness, would have no trade), and this good can be either consumed or accumulated as real capital. Capital goods, once installed, are immobile, but financial claims to capital good embodied in securities, can be costlessly traded.

The analysis best begins with an initial situation of isolation. This is the situation described in section 6.1 and formalized in (6.1.7) through (6.1.10). Portugal is again the potential borrower and England the potential lender. This implies $r_P^* > r_E^*$ and $i_P^* > i_E^*$. We imagine that the two capital markets now become unified in the sense that wealth owners in each country are free to buy securities issued in the other country. As a consequence, the Law of One Price becomes operative not only for the commodities but also for securities; yields will be equalized and thus $i_P = i_E$. As long as this equality is not reached, English wealth owners find it profitable to sell English securities in order to buy Portuguese securities. Portuguese wealth holders do the same, provided they can sell English securities short.

Under the pressure of arbitrage, the equalization of interest rates will be virtually instantaneous. It requires no net capital movements, no savings (or dissavings) and no investment (or disinvestment). Its speed has nothing to do with the mobility of net capital flows. A few telephone calls are all that is necessary. It should be noted, in particular, that there is no need for English

13. These aspects were elaborated by Gale (1974).

capitalists to buy securities from Portuguese capitalists (as in the case of a net capital flow). In fact, arbitrage has nothing to do with security shifts between residents of different countries. Both English and Portuguese capitalists are simultaneously trying to do the same thing, namely, to sell English, and to buy Portuguese, securities.

Since there are no immediate changes in capital stocks, the rentals (or dividends) r_P and r_E cannot adjust instantaneously. With unchanged rentals, the equalization of yields can take place only through an instantaneous adjustment in security (or capital-goods) prices in the sense that q_P rises while q_E declines. The instantaneous adjustment to the opening of the capital markets thus takes place through the valuation of existing assets. So far, however, we do not know how the world interest rate is determined; we only know that it must be somewhere between i_P^* and i_E^*.

As the foregoing discussion shows, it would be wrong to argue that the transitional capital flows are determined by temporary differentials between national security yields. [14] It is true, of course, that no capital flows will appear after market unification unless interest rates have been different in isolation. Once markets are unified, however, interest rates are equalized by mere arbitrage before net capital flows can even appear, and they remain equal (though not necessarily constant) throughout the adjustment process. To try to explain net capital flows by interest differentials is an exercise in futility. It would also be wrong to argue that the relevant differential relates to the yield of real capital goods. In the present model, this yield is identical to the security yield; like the latter, it is equalized instantaneously through arbitrage. The crucial differential is in the margin between market prices, q_E and q_P, and the replacement cost, $\bar{q}$, for capital goods. There is no way to eliminate this margin instantaneously. This can only be accomplished gradually through the time-consuming process of capital accumulation.

This process can be made analytically precise in terms of the model of section 6.1. The production functions for England and Portugal are still

$$Q_E = Q_E(K_E), \qquad Q_P = Q_P(K_P), \tag{6.3.1}$$

and rentals correspond to the marginal products,

$$r_E = Q_E', \qquad r_P = Q_P'. \tag{6.3.2}$$

The slopes of the marginal product curves, measured by $Q_E'' < 0$ and $Q_P'' < 0$, are assumed to be constant. Marginal products are diminishing, to be sure, but at a constant rate. In the initial situation, all variables are at their (starred) isolation levels.

Once the capital market is integrated, the English price of existing ma-

---

14. This point was forcefully made by Floyd (1969). While the present model is quite different from his, the general perspective is the same.

chines, q_E, falls below replacement cost $\bar{q}$. As a consequence, worn-out machines will not be replaced. Resources that would otherwise have been allocated to the production of replacement machines are now allocated to the production of consumer goods. These consumer goods may be imagined to be distributed to security owners in redemption of the shares of worn-out machines.

In Portugal, on the other hand, the market price of machines, as reflected in the security price, is now above replacement cost. This creates an incentive to build new capital goods with resources that would otherwise have been used to produce consumer goods.

To keep the model as simple as possible, it may be postulated that the speed of this disinvestment/investment process depends, in each country, on the margin between the market price of capital goods and their replacement cost according to

$$\frac{dK_E}{dt} = \dot{K}_E = \beta_E(q_E - \bar{q}) < 0,$$

$$\frac{dK_P}{dt} = \dot{K}_P = \beta_P(q_P - \bar{q}) > 0. \tag{6.3.3}$$

The adjustment speeds β_E and β_P, regarded as constant, are intended to reflect all other determinants of investment, including planning periods and the rate of obsolescence. Their detailed analysis would clearly lead into difficult problems of microeconomic dynamics.

With isolation of capital markets, since output is assumed to be homogeneous, there is no international trade. The investment/disinvestment process now calls forth a flow of English exports to Portugal. If machines could simply be dismantled in England to be reinstalled in Portugal, this commodity flow would consist of machines. This is not, however, an essential aspect of the process. International movements of capital do not require international movements of capital goods. For this reason, the above description of the process was based on the notion that machines, once installed, are immobile. In this case, the English wealth owners export the consumption goods they receive in redemption of English securities, using the proceeds to buy Portuguese securities. Even with immobile capital goods, disinvestment and investment can thus take place without any changes in consumption (and thus without any saving or dissaving) on either side, the Portuguese using the consumption goods imported from England to replace those they had to forego in order to build additional capital goods.

In the absence of saving or dissaving, English disinvestment must be exactly matched by Portuguese investment:

$$-\dot{K}_E = \dot{K}_P. \tag{6.3.4}$$

On the left appear the English capital exports; on the right, the Portuguese capital imports. With given wealth, any international capital movements are reflected in domestic investment and disinvestment. Purely financial transactions, however large, cannot move capital across international borders. The counterpart is, of course, an English export surplus on merchandise account.

Equations (6.3.3) and (6.3.4) can be solved for q_P. The result is

$$q_P = \frac{\beta_E + \beta_P}{\beta_P}\bar{q} - \frac{\beta_E}{\beta_P}q_E = a - \frac{\beta_E}{\beta_P}q_E, \tag{6.3.5}$$

where $a = \bar{q}(\beta_E + \beta_P)/\beta_P > 0$.

The interplay between capital flows and capital-goods prices is illustrated in figure 6.3.1. The curve in the NW quadrant graphs Portugal's investment, $\dot{K}_P$, as a function of its capital-goods price, q_p (see 6.3.3); the slope of this curve reflects the adjustment speed. The corresponding curve for England is drawn in the SE quadrant with *dis*investment measured vertically downward. Equilibrium requires that Portugal's investment be equal to England's disinvestment (6.3.4). This condition is expressed by the 45° line in the SW quadrant. By following this line and marking off at each point the corresponding capital-goods prices, one obtains the downward-sloping line in

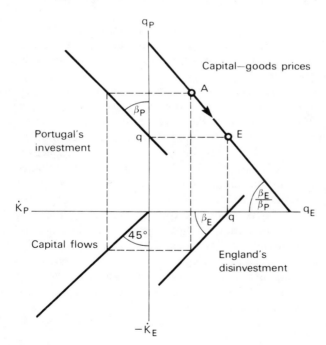

FIGURE 6.3.1
Capital-goods Prices

the NE quadrant; this is the graph of (6.3.5). It connects those combinations of capital-goods prices that provide equilibrium of international capital flows. With isolated capital markets, the system is at E, both capital-goods prices being at their equilibrium levels. Integration will displace the system. Eventually, however, in the new integration equilibrium, capital-goods prices will again have returned to their initial levels at E. According to (6.3.5), they reach this point along a path with constant slope $-\beta_E/\beta_P$. It follows that at the instant markets are integrated the two capital-goods prices must "jump" to a point like A.

The behavior of rentals during the adjustment process depends on the shape of the marginal product curves. If they are linear, the deviation of rentals from their isolation levels is proportional to the deviation of the capital stocks from their isolation levels, with Q_E'' and Q_P'' as factors of proportionality:

$$r_E - r_E^* = Q_E'' (K_E - K_E^*),\tag{6.3.6}$$

$$r_P - r_P^* = Q_P'' (K_P - K_P^*).\tag{6.3.7}$$

But Portugal always gains the capital England loses:

$$K_P - K_P^* = -(K_E - K_E^*).\tag{6.3.8}$$

As a consequence, r_P can be written as a linear function of r_E:

$$r_P = r_P^* - \frac{Q_P''}{Q_E''}(r_E - r_E^*) = b - \frac{Q_P''}{Q_E''}r_E,\tag{6.3.9}$$

where

$$b = r_P^* + \frac{Q_P''}{Q_E''}r_E^* > 0.$$

The adjustment of rentals is depicted in figure 6.3.2. The downward-sloping line is the graph of (6.3.9). The initial position, inherited from the state of isolation, is at B. Rentals adjust along a path with constant slope $-Q_P''/Q_E''$ until they reach the 45° line at E, where rentals are equalized.

So far only the direction of the respective adjustment paths has been determined. To determine the speed with which the international system travels along these paths, it is also necessary to consider interest rates or yields. The relevant yields consist of the sum of the rental and the capital gain per unit of time, both expressed as a fraction of the current capital-goods price:

$$i_E = \frac{r_E + \dot{q}_E}{q_E}, \qquad i_P = \frac{r_P + \dot{q}_P}{q_P}.\tag{6.3.10}$$

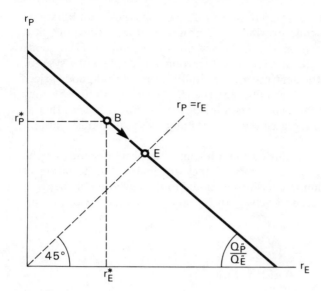

FIGURE 6.3.2
Rentals

This assumes that the capital gains (or losses) on capital goods are correctly anticipated.[15] Arbitrage implies that the two yields are equal at all times, so that

$$\frac{r_E + \dot{q}_E}{q_E} = \frac{r_P + \dot{q}_P}{q_P}. \tag{6.3.11}$$

An additional relationship between $\dot{q}_E$ and $\dot{q}_P$ is implied in (6.3.5), namely,

$$\dot{q}_P = -\frac{\beta_E}{\beta_P}\dot{q}_E. \tag{6.3.12}$$

In conjunction with (6.3.5) and (6.3.9), equations (6.3.11) and (6.3.12) can be solved for $\dot{q}_E$ as a function of q_E and r_E:

$$\dot{q}_E = \frac{b}{a}q_E - r_E + \frac{1}{a}\left(\frac{\beta_E}{\beta_P} - \frac{Q_P''}{Q_E''}\right)r_E q_E. \tag{6.3.13}$$

The change in English rentals can be derived by differentiating (6.3.2) and substituting from (6.3.3):

$$\dot{r}_E = Q_E''\frac{dK_E}{dt} = Q_E''\beta_E(q_E - \bar{q}). \tag{6.3.14}$$

15. The suggestion to include capital gains as a component of the asset yield on the basis of perfect foresight is due to Ailsa Röell.

The differential equations (6.3.13) and (6.3.14) determine the path of English capital-goods prices and rentals. A corresponding path for Portugal is implied in the model.

The exposition can be further simplified by the special assumption that the adjustment speeds are inversely proportional to the marginal product slopes, that is,

$$\frac{\beta_E}{\beta_P} = \frac{Q_P''}{Q_E''}. \tag{6.3.15}$$

It will turn out that this is the condition for the constancy of the international interest rate during the adjustment process. In this special case, (6.3.13) reduces to

$$\dot{q}_E = \frac{b}{a} q_E - r_E. \tag{6.3.16}$$

The resulting adjustment path is best described in graphical terms.[16] According to (6.3.14), the English rental remains constant if $q_E = \bar{q}$. This rental-equilibrium curve is the vertical line in figure 6.3.3. To the right of this line, r_E declines (remember that $Q_E'' < 0$), while on the left, r_E rises, as indicated by the vertical arrows. There is also a price-equilibrium line along which the English capital-goods price is constant. In the special case of (6.3.16) it is a ray through the origin with slope b/a as depicted in figure 6.3.3. In the general case, represented by (6.3.13), this line would be curved. To the right of the price-equilibrium curve the capital-goods price rises, while to the left it declines, as expressed by the horizontal arrows.

Full international equilibrium is reached at the intersection point E. In isolation, the English economy was at a point like A, with $q_E^* = \bar{q}$ but $r_E^* < r_E$. Once capital markets are integrated, q_E will instantaneously decline. The rental r_E, however, can adjust only gradually through disinvestment. Immediately upon capital integration, the English economy is thus displaced along a horizontal line to the left. The question is how far. From a point like B it would never reach equilibrium, moving along the curved arrow to the left. Nor would it reach E from a point like C, since it would then follow a downward-curving path.

In fact, there is one and only one point, denoted by D, from which the adjustment path leads to equilibrium. This is the path the economy has to follow if wealth owners, once financial markets are (unexpectedly) integrated, have perfect foresight about the ensuing adjustments. Competitive pressure thus lowers the price of English capital goods from A to D. From there, the gradual disinvestment/investment process leads the economy to the new inte-

---

16. For the mathematical analysis of dynamic systems of this sort, though based on a different economic model, see Gray and Turnovsky (1979).

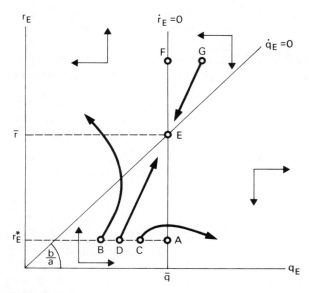

FIGURE 6.3.3
Capital-goods Prices and Rentals

grated equilibrium E. If England had been the capital-poor economy, her isolation equilibrium would be at a point like F. The instantaneous rise in capital-goods prices resulting from integration would then bring her to a point like G, from where she would also approach the final equilibrium at E.

Trade flows during the adjustment process depend on the rental paid on foreign capital. Clearly, all owners of Portuguese capital goods receive the same rental regardless of their nationality. In the stationary state, English rentals are also the same as Portuguese rentals. During the adjustment process, however, Portuguese rentals are higher than English rentals. This does not mean that capitalists have a reason to prefer Portuguese investments to English investments, because the difference in rentals is always matched by the difference between the capital gains on English machines and the capital losses on Portuguese machines.

The balance of payments for Portugal can thus be written

$$I_P + r_P(K_P - V_P) = q_P \dot{K}_P. \tag{6.3.17}$$

On the left appear commodity imports, I_P, and rental payments on the foreign debt, summing to the deficit on current account. This is equal to the capital inflow, evaluated at the current capital-goods price, appearing on the right. In the early stages after the integration of the capital market, $K_P - V_P$ is small while $\dot{K}_P$ is large. As a consequence, there must be an import surplus. In later stages, close to the new steady state, it is the other way around. The imports will have changed into exports. Once the steady state is reached, capital flows will have vanished again, and there will be permanent exports.[17]

There remains the question of interest rate adjustments. In general, yields will continually change. The important point is that it is impossible to generalize about the direction of these changes. Surely once capital markets are opened, the rate of interest will instantaneously fall in the borrowing country and rise in the lending country, but subsequent changes may go in either direction.

By substituting for $\dot{q}_E$ from (6.3.13) into (6.3.10) and canceling terms, the world interest rate can be written

$$i = \frac{r_E + \dot{q}_E}{q_E} = \frac{b}{a} + \left(\frac{\beta_E}{\beta_P} - \frac{Q_P''}{Q_E''} \right) \frac{r_E}{a}. \qquad (6.3.18)$$

By substituting for Q_P''/Q_E'' from (6.3.9), this becomes

$$i = \frac{b}{a} + \frac{\beta_E}{\beta_P} \frac{r_E}{a} + \frac{r_P - b}{a}$$

$$= \frac{1}{a\beta_P}(\beta_E r_E + \beta_P r_P), \qquad (6.3.19)$$

$$= \frac{1}{\bar{q}} \frac{\beta_E r_E + \beta_P r_P}{\beta_E + \beta_P}.$$

This is a neat result: at every moment, the world interest rate is an adjustment-speed–weighted average of national rentals expressed as a fraction of the equilibrium capital-goods price.

The change in the rate of interest during the adjustment process, as derived from (6.3.18), is

$$\frac{di}{dt} = \frac{1}{a} \left(\frac{\beta_E}{\beta_P} - \frac{Q_P''}{Q_E''} \right) \dot{r}_E. \qquad (6.3.20)$$

It is clear that $\dot{r}_E > 0$, since England's capital stock is reduced. Also remember that $Q_E'' < 0$, $Q_P'' < 0$. It follows that the world interest rate rises or declines according to whether the product of the adjustment speed and the absolute slope of the marginal product curve is higher in England or in Portugal:

$$\frac{di}{dt} \gtreqless 0 \quad \text{depending on} \quad \beta_E(-Q_E'') \gtreqless \beta_P(-Q_P''). \qquad (6.3.21)$$

---

17. With more than one commodity, the temporary capital flow also affects the terms of trade. In contrast to the permanent effect of capital mobility on the terms of trade, this is a pure transfer problem, and the usual agnostic conclusions apply.

If the adjustment speeds are equal, the interest rate rises provided the English marginal product curve is steeper than its Portuguese counterpart. If the marginal product curves have the same slope, the interest rate rises if England's capital stock adjusts faster than Portugal's. If both adjustment speeds and the slopes of the marginal product curves are equal internationally, the interest rate jumps immediately to its equilibrium level and stays there. The same is true, more generally, if the adjustment speeds of the two capital stocks are inversely proportional to the slopes of the marginal product curves; this is the special case of (6.3.15).

The preceding analysis assumed that international security arbitrage is perfect in the sense that yields are instantaneously equalized. In the recent literature, this assumption is often identified with "perfect mobility" of capital. This terminology is unfortunate, because it suggests that net international capital movements are able to close any gap between desired and actual indebtedness with high speed. In fact, the promptness of arbitrage has little to do with the mobility of net international capital flows. In the present model, despite the assumption of perfect arbitrage, the adjustment process may take any length of time because the international equalization of rentals and capital-goods prices requires an accumulation or decumulation of real capital goods like factories, houses, and roads. This takes years rather than days or weeks. For net international capital flows as recorded in balance-of-payments statistics, "perfect mobility" would require that existing capital goods (like houses) be internationally traded and transported without costs or delays. For the world we live in, this is not a fruitful assumption to make.

The main topic of this section has been the interaction between interest rates, capital-goods prices, and capital flows. In order to focus attention on the basic elements of this interaction, the analysis has been based on a very simple model with highly restrictive assumptions. Many aspects that may be important in the real world have been omitted. Some of them will be taken up in subsequent chapters. In a less restrictive model, the results would most certainly have been more complicated. I would conjecture, however, that the main conclusion from the present analysis would still be valid. This conclusion is that net capital flows cannot be assumed to be controlled by interest rates. Economic theory simply does not suggest any particular association between market rates of interest and net capital flows. Empirical efforts to establish such an association thus seem to lack a firm analytical basis. The true determinants of international capital flows must, rather, be sought among the relative rentals and prices of capital goods. [18]

It is interesting to note the analogy between this result and the outcome

---

18. It should be remembered, however, that each country's wealth was regarded as given. In a more general analysis, wealth would also be variable through saving. Inasmuch as saving is influenced by the rate of interest, this would establish an additional link between interest rates and capital flows. This aspect is further discussed in chapter 10.

of the transfer debate (see section 2.5). This debate showed that international specie flows are not controlled by price differentials and that the movement of the world price level during the adjustment process depends on the adjustment speed of money balances. The present discussion has shown that international capital flows are not controlled by interest differentials and that the movement of the world interest level depends on the adjustment speed of real capital stocks. Just as the initial error in the transfer debate consisted in confusing commodity arbitrage with trade flows, so the error in the capital flow debate arises from confusing asset arbitrage with capital flows.

CHAPTER 7

Asset Diversification

Introduction

The analysis of international indebtedness and capital flows in chapter 6 was based on the assumption that assets are homogeneous. As a consequence, a country would not simultaneously be a debtor and a creditor; the problem of asset diversification could not arise. What remained was the problem of the net international asset position. In reality, most countries are both gross creditors and gross debtors, with domestic residents holding assets abroad while domestic assets are owned by foreign residents. The United States, for example, is a net creditor, chiefly because of extensive foreign loans and direct investments abroad. Nevertheless, foreigners hold large amounts of dollars and own firms and real estate in the United States, making the latter a large gross debtor as well.

The reason is that assets are heterogeneous, some consisting of currency, others of interest-bearing debt, still others of real capital goods. For assets of the same type, it also makes a difference in what currency they are denominated, in which country the debtor (or the capital good) is located, and who the debtor is. Debt may be further differentiated by maturity. This raises the question of gross international claims and debt, the question of international asset diversification. This question is the subject of the present chapter.

While the analysis of net indebtedness and capital flows in chapter 6 abstracted from asset diversification, the analysis of asset diversification in the present chapter abstracts from net capital flows. Attention is thus focused on the composition of given net claims or liabilities. While net foreign assets are adjusted by capital flows, the composition of foreign assets is adjusted by arbitrage. It was shown in the preceding chapter that capital flows have little to do with security arbitrage. The present chapter will confirm this conclusion.

132

The distinctive feature of the approach developed in this section is its close correspondence to the pure theory of international trade. Just as countries exchange goods with different technical characteristics, so they exchange assets with different risk characteristics. Just as countries have comparative advantages in the production of different goods, so they have comparative advantages in the production of different assets. Just as countries have different tastes with respect to goods, so they have different tastes with respect to assets. What emerges is the equivalent of a Mill/Marshall/Meade model for international asset diversification. Sections 7.1 and 7.2 develop the basic approach. In section 7.3 this approach is applied to country risk and exchange risk.

7.1 Asset Risk in a Closed Economy

This section provides tools and concepts for the analysis of international asset diversification. These tools are chosen in such a way that the analogy between the theory of asset diversification and the pure theory of international trade is as close as possible. Since the tools are to be used for the analysis of national economies as a whole, the microeconomics of the underlying portfolio decisions—again in analogy with the pure theory of international trade—will be indicated only in rough outline.

For the purpose of this preparatory discussion the economy is assumed to be closed. It is equipped with a given stock of real capital goods, K. The marginal product of capital has an expected value r, determined by K; it is subject to random fluctuations with given variance.

Capital goods are owned by firms and financed by securities called "stocks." In reality, firms typically issue various types of assets. Some of them may be rather risky and relatively illiquid, while others are relatively riskless and liquid. One of the interesting problems of financial analysis concerns the choice of these assets. In the present model it is simply assumed that firms issue only stocks. Stocks are measured in units whose annual return has an expected value of \$1 (or, more exactly, one unit of consumer goods) in perpetuity. While in chapter 6 assets were denominated in machines, they are now denominated in units of real income. In contrast to conventional perpetuities, the return on stocks is assumed to be subject to random fluctuations with the same variance as the marginal product of capital. The mean stock price in terms of consumer goods is p_S and the mean stock yield, therefore, is $i_S = 1/p_S$. The mean stock price is determined by the requirement that firms should have no incentive either to expand their capital stock by investment or to reduce it by disinvestment.

While stocks are supposed to stand for a class of relatively risky and illiquid assets, there is also a class of riskless assets called "deposits." For the sake of simplicity, these deposits are assumed to be rather different from most real-life deposits inasmuch as they, too, are defined as perpetuities with a coupon of one unit of consumer goods. Since the coupon on deposits, in contrast to that on stocks, is riskless, the deposits are nevertheless highly liquid. The price of deposits is p_D and their yield is $i_D = 1/p_D$. While the mean stock price is determined by the stationarity of the capital stock, the price of deposits (and thus the ratio of asset prices) are determined endogenously by the model.

Deposits are created by financial intermediaries called "banks." In general, financial intermediaries perform two basic functions. First, they act as brokers or middlemen, exchanging financial assets between firms and households at lower transaction costs than if the ultimate buyers and sellers had traded directly. In the present model this function is left in the background; it is further examined in chapter 9. Second, financial intermediaries modify the composition of portfolios by buying assets that are qualitatively different from those they are selling. For example, a bank may use the money deposited in checking accounts to make commercial loans, or it may use saving deposits to buy mortgages. This is the function relevant in the present context. Specifically, it is assumed that banks issue deposits to households, using the proceeds, except for a fraction held in reserves, to buy stocks. To perform this function, the banking industry is assumed to be equipped with given factors of production. It should be noted that non–interest-bearing cash balances do not appear in the model. This reflects the view that so-called international currency substitution relates more to interest-bearing time deposits than to actual cash balances.

Asset transformation by banks is depicted in figure 7.1.1. The (mean) incomes on stocks and deposits are measured, respectively, along the vertical and horizontal axes. The stocks issued by firms are marked off at C. The distance OC represents rK, the (mean) rental on capital goods. Some of the stocks are bought up by banks to be transformed into deposits, as indicated by the downward-sloping asset frontier. In the present context, this curve is not derived from an explicit banking model but must be based on more intuitive reasoning; some elements of an explicit model can be found in, among many other sources, Niehans (1978).

The (absolute) slope of the asset frontier can be interpreted as the marginal rate of asset transformation. For each relative interest rate i_S/i_D (or for each relative asset price p_D/p_S), banks find it profitable to perform asset transformation up to the point where the marginal rate of asset transformation is equal to the interest (or price) ratio. As a consequence, the level of asset transformation depends on relative interest rates. It is plausible to assume that it increases with i_S/i_D. If stock yields are low relative to deposit interest, the level of intermediation is low; bank balance sheets are small. With increasing i_S/i_D, banks will gradually buy more stocks, financed by more and more deposits. At extremely high relative stock yields, banks would probably

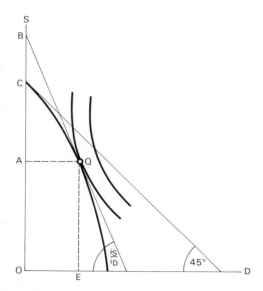

FIGURE 7.1.1
Asset Transformation in a Closed Economy

be willing to absorb all of the stocks issued by firms; no stocks would be left for households. This reasoning implies that the asset transformation curve is concave to the origin.

The curve is steeper than 45° throughout, because for a dollar of dividends a bank will not be willing to issue claims to a full dollar of deposit interest. The difference between stock earnings and deposit interest of banks pays for the cost of intermediation and also for the banker's risk. It is expressed by the horizontal distance between the asset frontier and the 45° line. The concavity of the asset frontier implies that banking is an increasing-cost industry. The higher the efficiency of intermediation, the closer is the asset frontier to the 45° line. For a very inefficient banking industry, it would be close to the vertical axis.

If the system is, for example, at Q, the distance AQ, abstracting from equity capital, measures the banks' liabilities in terms of deposits. Since the slope of the tangent at Q is the asset-price ratio, the distance AB measures the same magnitude in terms of stocks. It is necessarily equal to total assets. The difference BC shows that the value of the banks' assets is higher than the value of their stocks. BC can be interpreted as the banks' reserves and the ratio BC/BA as the reserve ratio. As the level of asset transformation is increased, the banking system moving gradually downward from C, the reserve ratio rises or declines depending on the decrease or increase in the elasticity of the asset transformation curve.

Firms and banks, taken together, determine the supply of financial assets as embodied in the asset frontier. Asset demand is determined by households as wealth owners. These are assumed to have a utility function for assets reflecting their risk preference. For risk-averse investors, asset indifference curves are convex, as indicated in figure 7.1.1. To be induced to replace riskless deposits by risky stocks, the investor must be offered the stocks at increasingly favorable prices. With riskless deposits, indifference curves, too, will be steeper than 45° throughout; starting with an all-deposit portfolio, a risk-averse investor would never be willing to replace $1 of deposit interest by $1 of (mean) stock returns unless the price of the stocks is lower (which means that their yield is higher). There are probably relative stock yields high enough to result in an all-stock portfolio, and there are probably relative stock yields low enough to result in an all-deposit portfolio. In an intermediate range, portfolios are diversified.

In the closed economy, relative asset prices (or yields) and asset shares are determined by the condition that demand and supply must be equal for each asset. This point is reached at Q, where the production-possibility curve for assets is tangent to an asset indifference curve. The intercepts of the budget line can be interpreted as a measure of household wealth in terms of, respectively, deposits and stocks. Asset transformation certainly makes the economy better off; Q is on a higher indifference curve than C. The gain is clearly greater the more efficient the banking system. By being at Q instead of at C, households sacrifice some expected returns, but this loss is more than offset by the reduction in risk.

This is all that is needed for the purpose of this chapter. Leaving the underlying risk calculus in the background, the graphic analysis of this section was intended to bring out the main point as simply as possible. This point is that supply and demand of financial assets can be described in terms of concepts closely analogous to those commonly used for the supply and demand of commodities.

7.2 Asset Risk in an Open Economy

The preparatory discussion of section 7.1 considered asset diversification for a closed economy. In the present section, the tools and concepts developed in the course of that discussion are applied to the international diversification of assets in open economies. The risks that underlie this diversification have different origins. Some are due to differences in the type of assets and in the debtors; thus bonds may be regarded as less risky than stocks, government bonds as less risky than corporate bonds, and debts of corporation X as less exposed to default risk than those of corporation Y. These risks will be classified here as asset risks. Other risks are due to the country in which the assets are located; these will be called country risks. Still other risks, called currency risks, depend on the currency in which the assets are denominated. The present section concentrates on asset risks; country risks and currency risks are the subject of the following section.

Progressing from the simple to the more complicated, the exposition begins with the case of a *small open economy* that has no appreciable influence on the world market prices of assets. The assumptions are the same as those for the closed economy in the preceding section. In particular, there are still two homogeneous assets, stocks and deposits, with a downward-sloping and concave asset frontier and downward-sloping and convex asset indifference curves as in figure 7.1.1. There is still no international exchange of commodities, and *net* international indebtedness is not allowed. The country in question thus has a given stock of real capital and there is no international equalization of real capital rentals of the sort described in chapter 6. In fact, until further notice, wealth owners are not even allowed to exchange assets for consumer goods; the only exchange is pure asset arbitrage between stocks and deposits. Exchange rates are fixed.

Suppose we start with a closed economy as described in figure 7.1.1. In figure 7.2.1 the economy would thus find itself at Q. This economy is now given the opportunity to exchange assets with the rest of the world. In world capital markets, the relative price of deposits and stocks is $p^* = p_D^*/p_S^*$. If the national asset price ratio, $p = p_D/p_S$, is different from p^*, there will be opportunities for profitable arbitrage. Suppose, for example, that $p > p^*$,

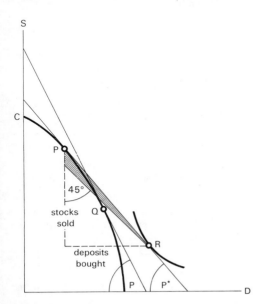

FIGURE 7.2.1
Asset Transformation in a Small Open Economy

which means that at home deposits are relatively expensive while stocks are relatively cheap. In this case, people will sell deposits domestically against stocks, send the stocks abroad to sell them in the international market for deposits, bring the deposits home to sell them in the domestic market against stocks, etc. As a result of such arbitrage operations, p_D is lowered while p_S is raised until p is in line with p^*.

In figure 7.2.1, the international asset price ratio is described by the slope of the line going through P and R. At this relative price, banks will absorb stocks as indicated by the vertical distance between C and P. Compared with the closed economy with its higher relative price of deposits, the banks will buy fewer stocks and issue less deposits. The banking system has to contract in order to bring its marginal rate of asset substitution into line with the international price ratio. Wealth owners, on the other hand, will demand assets as indicated by R. Compared to the closed economy, assuming both assets are non-inferior, they will want to hold more deposits and often (but not necessarily) fewer stocks.

The resulting international asset position can be judged by comparing the supply point P with the demand point R. The country will have sold stocks in the international market in the amount of the vertical distance between P and R; to this extent it is a gross debtor. On the other hand, the country will have bought deposits in the international market in the amount of the horizontal distance between P and R; to this extent it is a gross creditor. At the international asset price ratio p^*, the value of liabilities is equal to the value of assets. On a net basis, therefore, the country is neither a creditor nor a debtor.

While there is no net indebtedness, there may still be net interest payments. According to the assumptions specified at the beginning of section 7.1, (mean) interest payments are one unit of consumer goods per unit of stocks or deposits. If the prices of the two assets were identical, equal asset values would thus imply equal interest payments. In general, however, the prices of stocks and deposits will differ. In particular, if deposits are risk-free, p_D will exceed p_S. This means that the annual dividend payments on the stocks sold abroad will exceed the annual interest receipts on the deposits made abroad. If the international price ratio p^* is lower than the closed-economy price ratio p, the country will thus end up with net payments on interest and dividend account. In figure 7.2.1, these are represented by the distance between the price line and the 45° line (shaded). Net interest has to be paid for in terms of consumer goods. Exports of goods and services thus pay for a net outflow on account of capital returns, while the current account as a whole is balanced.

This does not mean that a country with a net outflow of interest and/or dividend payments is worse off than it would be in the absence of international asset diversification. In fact, it is better off. Its wealth owners can lower their risk and this is worth more to them, in general, than the exports they have to give up in compensation.[1] Welfare gains and losses from international asset diversification cannot be judged by looking at net returns on foreign assets.

This discussion started from the assumption that in the closed economy the deposit price is higher in relation to the stock price than in the international market. The same argument applies, *mutatis mutandis*, if $p < p^*$. In this case, international diversification results in an expansion of the banking industry. The additional deposits created by banks are held abroad, while domestic households actually hold less deposits. At the same time, households and banks now hold more stocks than domestic firms have issued, the difference consisting of stocks bought abroad. The country will thus hold foreign stocks, while foreigners hold domestic deposits. As a consequence, there will be net receipts on foreign assets, for which the country will receive imports. Again there will generally be a net benefit, since the welfare gain from these imports exceeds the welfare loss through higher risk.

Instead of assuming a fixed ratio of international asset prices, we can imagine a continuous variation in this ratio. Each ratio would be associated with amounts of deposits bought (sold) and stocks sold (bought) in the international market. These would trace out an "asset offer curve," or "reciprocal asset demand curve," analogous to the Marshallian curves for commodities presented in chapter 1. Such a curve is illustrated in figure 7.2.2. With a

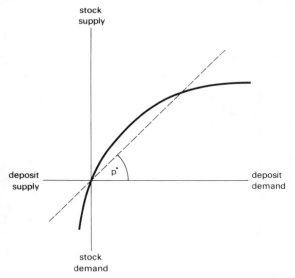

FIGURE 7.2.2
Asset Offer Curve

1. This was pointed out by Grubel (1968) in a paper that provided a significant impulse to the analysis of international portfolio diversification.

falling relative price of deposits, the amount of deposits demanded is certain to rise, but the amount of stocks supplied may either increase or decrease. As usual, this ambiguity is due to the interplay of a substitution effect, which works in favor of the now-cheaper deposits at the expense of stocks, and an income or wealth effect, which for net importers of deposits works in favor of both assets. For a net exporter of deposits it would, of course, be the other way around.

The analysis of asset diversification is now extended to two *interdependent economies* with the international asset price ratio, the asset terms of trade, determined by the interaction of demand and supply in the international asset market. The result may be called a Mill/Marshall/Meade model of international indebtedness. It can be illustrated by an "international asset butterfly" as drawn in figure 7.2.3. Its economic content may be described as follows.

The two countries are again called England and Portugal. England has a comparative advantage in supplying stocks, reflected in a relatively steep asset frontier. Portugal, on the other hand, is assumed to have a comparative advantage in supply deposits; as a consequence, its asset frontier is relatively flat. England's asset preferences are given in the NE quadrant while Portugal's preferences are described by the indifference curves in the SW quadrant.

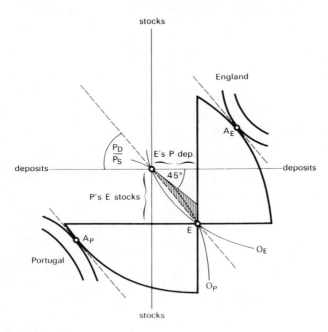

FIGURE 7.2.3
Interdependent Economies

A point on England's asset offer curve can be obtained in the following way. Select an international asset price ratio as represented by one of the rays through the origin running from NW to SE. Slide the English asset block along this price line until its common tangent with an indifference curve has the same slope as the price line. The origin of the asset block on the price line is then a point on the English asset offer curve. If the experiment is repeated (with the same price line) for Portugal, the corresponding point on the price line will generally be different. This means that the initial price line did not represent the equilibrium terms of trade. England wants to supply and demand a larger amount of assets than Portugal wants to demand and supply, or vice versa. Equilibrium is reached where the two offer curves intersect. At this point, both the marginal rates of asset substitution and the marginal rates of asset transformation are equalized internationally and among each other.

As figure 7.2.3 is drawn, English wealth owners hold Portuguese deposits while Portuguese wealth owners hold English stocks. England thus uses the international asset market to reduce the risk on her assets while Portugal uses it to increase her returns. As a consequence, there is a net annual income payment from England to Portugal, which may be regarded as a risk premium. In figure 7.2.3 it is represented by the difference between the equilibrium asset price ratio and the 45° line. The annual return, as specified above, is one unit of consumer goods per unit of assets. The annual net return on a country's foreign assets and liabilities is thus measured simply by the difference between the foreign deposits held domestically and the domestic stocks held abroad (or vice versa).

What is the meaning of "disequilibrium" in such a model? It has often been argued that disequilibrium requires temporary capital flows involving balance-of-payments surpluses or deficits.[2] This, just like the corresponding argument in the pure theory of international trade, is incorrect. Suppose the given relative price of deposits is too low compared with the equilibrium price. Both England and Portugal are still constrained to maintain equality between the values of their international assets and liabilities, but England wants to do this at a higher level of assets and liabilities than Portugal. This means that England's demand for deposits is higher than Portuguese supply and England's supply of stocks exceeds Portugal's demand. As a consequence, the deposit price rises relative to the stock price. There is no "incipient" capital flow in either direction. If governments insisted on maintaining "wrong" asset price ratios, they would have to set up a buffer-stock agency for assets in the form of a bank selling deposits against stocks at a fixed relative price. No matter in what country such an agency is located, its operations would never show up as a capital flow from one country to the other. Arbitrage between

2. This argument, too, can be found in Grubel (1968).

assets simply has no direct relationship with net capital flows between countries as reflected in their balance of payments.

How does an improvement in asset transformation affect international portfolio diversification? Suppose in the two-country model of the present section English banks experience technological progress. This makes England's asset frontier flatter than before. The result is a relative decline in the price of deposits, implying a relative increase in deposit interest, in both countries. England's comparative advantage in stocks is weakened and eventually may even be reversed. In the latter case, England, thanks to its more efficient banking industry, becomes a net supplier of risk-free deposits and a net buyer of risky stocks. The net flow of interest and dividends is reversed, England now receiving a net inflow. It should be noted that there is no corresponding increase in risk for British wealth owners; risk actually tends to decline in both countries. The net inflow of interest payments in this case is, rather, an income from efficient intermediation, England now playing the role of international banker. At the present time, the United States and Switzerland illustrate this point. The preceding analysis thus leads naturally to the view of international liquidity presented by Despres, Kindleberger, and Salant (1966) in their well-known article.

In conclusion, it should be noted that the analysis of this section has been limited to pure asset arbitrage. The only exchange was between stocks and deposits. This, in itself, is not enough to produce full asset equilibrium. The missing elements can be visualized in two steps. The first step consists in admitting the exchange of securities against consumer goods. As a result, the prices of stocks (and thus the stock yields) are equalized internationally, and the same is true for deposits. While the previous analysis led to the international equalization of the relative prices (or interest rates) of different assets, the present step leads to the international equalization of the prices of each security, expressed in units of consumer goods.

This arbitrage process, too, takes place virtually instantaneously. Rapid communication is all it requires. In particular, it does not require capital flows. Suppose the English deposit price exceeds the Portuguese price while the exchange rate is unity. Suppose further that buffer-stock agencies stand ready to exchange unlimited amounts of deposits against consumer goods at the given prices. It is clear that under these circumstances wealth owners could make riskless profits by selling English deposits and buying Portuguese bonds. The buffer-stock agencies would incur a corresponding loss.

The international distribution of gains and losses depends entirely on the location of traders and buffer-stock agencies. If wealth owners in each country trade with an agency in the same country, there is no international wealth shift. If the agency is located in Portugal while wealth owners are scattered throughout both countries, England gains at the expense of Portugal. Other examples can easily be constructed. In reality, of course, no agency would persist in maintaining "wrong" prices for any length of time; the disparity of prices would promptly disappear. The important point is that such an arbitrage process, while it lasts, does not involve a net capital flow from the low-interest country to the high-interest country.

The second step to full equilibrium consists in the equalization of capital-goods prices at their equilibrium levels. This is the process described in section 6.3. It requires an expansion or contraction of real capital goods by, respectively, investment or disinvestment associated with net capital flows. In terms of the concepts used in the two-asset model of the present section, the asset frontier of the capital-exporting country shrinks toward the origin, while the asset frontier of the capital-importing country expands. While the arbitrage analyzed in this section is virtually timeless, this adjustment of real capital goods through capital flows may take a long time.

7.3 Country Risk and Currency Risk

The model of section 7.2 was constructed to analyze differences in asset risks. Each class of assets was assumed to be completely homogeneous internationally. English bonds were interchangeable with Portuguese bonds, and the same was true for stocks. In reality this is often not so. In particular, English securities may be different from Portuguese securities because the debtor is subject to different laws and policies or because the securities are denominated in a different currency. In the first case the associated risks may be classified as country risks, in the second, as currency risks. These risks are the subject of the present section.

Country risks may originate from nationalization risks, tax policies, government regulation, foreign trade policies, and the like. In practice they may be difficult to assess, but their basic nature can readily be interpreted in terms of the model of section 7.2 by suitable adaptation. In fact, all we have to do is assume that each country specializes in the production of only one type of security with its own risk characteristics. At the same time, the asset demand of wealth holders continues to be diversified. In the context of such a model it is then possible to study the effect, say, of an increase in nationalization risk on Portuguese securities.

This modification clearly amounts to a simplification of the model. In fact, the simplified model is an exact asset counterpart of the trade model of section 1.1 with diversified consumption and specialization in production. It is convenient to discuss it graphically in terms of an Edgeworth Box for assets (see figure 7.3.1). The given supply of English securities determines the horizontal dimension of the box, while the quantity of Portuguese assets is measured by its height. Point Q may be called the endowment point for assets. English asset indifference curves, with their origin in the lower left-hand corner, are described by the solid lines, while the Portuguese asset indifference

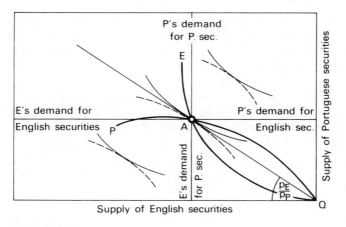

FIGURE 7.3.1
Supply of English Securities

curves, with their origin in the upper right-hand corner, are represented by the broken lines. International asset equilibrium is attained at A, where the ray from the endowment point is tangent to both indifference curves. England's and Portugal's asset offer curves are, respectively, QE and QP. The slope of the price line QA reflects the relative price of English securities, p_E/p_P. The international asset position of the two countries is expressed by the dimensions of the rectangle in the lower right. Its horizontal dimension measures Portuguese holdings of English securities, while the vertical dimension measures English holdings of Portuguese securities.

The question is how this international asset position is affected by an increase in the risk on, say, Portuguese securities. It cannot be answered in a general, yet precise way, because an increase in risk changes the whole shape of the asset indifference curves. It can nevertheless be assumed that at every point of the diagram the English asset indifference curve is now steeper than it was before, which expresses the fact that for the marginal unit of English securities wealth owners are now demanding a larger amount of Portuguese securities. As a consequence, the English offer curve shifts to the right as indicated in figure 7.3.2 by the difference between E and E'. For any given quantity of Portuguese securities, English wealth owners now give up a lower amount of English securities. Portuguese indifference curves are twisted in the same direction and for the same reason. As a consequence the Portuguese asset offer curve shifts from the P curve to the P' curve; the Portuguese are now willing to give up a higher amount of their own assets for any given amount of English securities. Because of these shifts, the relative price of Portuguese securities declines and their relative yield rises. Wealth holders are worse off in both countries because of the higher risk of Portuguese assets, but they suffer more in Portugal than in England because of the adverse change in asset terms of trade. These losses will have to be compared with the gain, if any, from the circumstances or policies that caused the increase in risk.

It has often been argued that an increased country risk would result in a capital outflow, perhaps associated with a depreciation of the exchange rate. A reduction in country risk, on the other hand, would attract capital inflows, perhaps associated with an exchange appreciation. Up to this point, the discussion of country risk provides no basis for this argument. The portfolio adjustments just described are entirely due to instant asset arbitrage; they do not require international capital flows. The picture is not complete, however. The rise in Portuguese interest rates is accompanied, at a given real capital stock, by a decline in capital-goods prices below replacement cost, while the decline in English interest rates has the opposite effect. This, in turn, will set in motion the disinvestment/investment process, described in section 6.3, associated with a capital flow from Portugal to England. Whereas the arbitrage adjustment is instantaneous, this capital stock adjustment will take time. It is worth noting that during the adjustment process higher interest rates will be associated with a capital *out*flow.

The other risk to be discussed in this section is *currency risk*. It differs from country risk inasmuch as Portuguese bonds, subject to Portuguese legislation and policies, may be denominated either in escudos or in sterling. With the emergence of the Eurocurrency markets the distinction has become quite important, since investors can now combine country risk and currency risk in a large number of ways. The following discussion concentrates on currency risk, regarding assets as homogeneous in all respects except the currency in which they are denominated. The only risk thus relates to exchange rates.

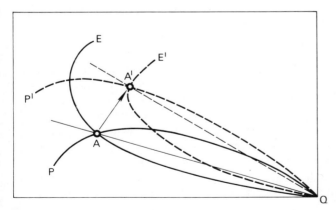

FIGURE 7.3.2
Shift in Country Risk

It must first be noted that the level of the exchange rate, if held constant, is irrelevant for the yield or profitability of foreign assets. As long as payments on principal and interest are converted at the same exchange rate, the level of the exchange rate is of no concern to the investor. What matters is the expected change in the exchange rate.

For a Portuguese investor holding English bonds, an appreciation of sterling constitutes income, just as much as the payment of interest does. In choosing his portfolio, he takes this income, positive or negative, into account. If English securities and Portuguese securities are identical except for the currency, under fixed exchange rates they are perfect substitutes and interest rates are equalized. If exchange rates are expected to change, this is no longer true. To make the investor indifferent, the two interest rates must then differ by the expected exchange-rate change. More exactly, if $\dot{e}$ is the expected annual appreciation of escudos in terms of sterling while i_E and i_P denote the two interest rates, the condition is

$$(1 + i_P)(1 + \dot{e}) = (1 + i_E). \tag{7.3.1}$$

This is the so-called interest parity.[3] Compared with the other terms, $i_P\dot{e}$ is usually small. Neglecting it, the condition can be approximated by

$$\dot{e} = i_E - i_P. \tag{7.3.2}$$

Interest parity states that, for assets with equal risk, arbitrage sees to it that the interest differential corresponds to the expected rate of change of the exchange rate. The more a currency is expected to depreciate, the higher its relative interest rate. This may also be turned around by saying that a higher interest rate must be associated with a more rapid rate of expected depreciation. As long as the interest parity condition is continuously satisfied, even large fluctuations in exchange rates provide no reason to reshuffle portfolios. The problem is, of course, that expectations about exchange rates are subjective and may differ widely among individuals. At a time when some investors see good reasons to shift from sterling into escudos others may decide to do the reverse.

It should be noted that interest parity relates to nominal interest rates. If at the end of the year an Englishman has £1,000, he is always better off, regardless of inflation or deflation, than if he has only £900. It would be wrong, therefore, to relate the expected change in nominal exchange rates to the differential in real interest rates. If the latter are used, they must be compared with the expected change in the real exchange rate; inflation must be taken into account either on both sides of the equation or not at all.

The effect of the expected exchange-rate changes on international asset markets, if not accompanied by corresponding interest changes, may be very

---

3. The same designation is often used for a similar-looking expression in which $\dot{e}$ is replaced by the premium of the forward rate relative to the spot rate. This will be discussed in chapter 8.

strong. In one sense this is perhaps disturbing, because relatively small changes in expected exchange rates trigger a large reshuffling of portfolios. In another sense, however, it is reassuring, because it means that even large shifts in international asset markets can be neutralized by moderate exchange rate fluctuations. The first oil crisis provided a telling example. While international organizations, conferences, and committees gravely debated the seemingly crucial and intractable problem of the "recycling" of petrodollars, the fluctuations in exchange rates, together with the Eurocurrency market, had quietly disposed of it. One of the main contributions to the solution was the depreciation of weak currencies to the point where they were regarded as *under*valued and thus expected to appreciate; as a consequence, these currencies were more in demand than the experts had expected.

In the absence of uncertainty, any deviation of the expected future exchange rate from interest parity, however small, would result in a switch of all assets from one currency into the other. There would never be diversified portfolios with marginal adjustments to expected exchange-rate changes. To explain asset diversification and marginal adjustments, we have to appeal to uncertainty about the future course of exchange rates. In the field of international corporate finance, an extensive literature about the portfolio effects of currency risk has grown up. This literature cannot be surveyed here.[4] The present discussion is limited to a brief explanation of three basic reasons for currency diversification.

The first reason is that currency risk acts as an impediment to foreign-asset holding. Suppose $\dot{e} > i_E - i_P$ because, for example, sterling is expected to depreciate while interest rates are equal. In the absence of currency risk, both English and Portuguese wealth holders would hold only escudo assets in this case. Usually, however, expected exchange rates are more or less uncertain. For Portuguese wealth owners this makes no difference. If sterling assets, because of the expected depreciation, are unattractive for them in the absence of uncertainty, they will be even more unattractive in its presence. English wealth holders, on the other hand, now find the attraction of escudo assets reduced by the uncertainty of appreciation. As a consequence, they may be induced to diversify their portfolios, keeping some of their wealth in sterling.

This reasoning can be illustrated in terms of the familiar return/risk diagram (Tobin 1958). In figure 7.3.3, the share of escudo assets in English portfolios, denoted by a, is measured downward. The risk of English wealth owners, measured to the right, is proportionate to the escudo share as expressed by the solid ray sloping downward from 0. The mean return from escudo appreciation, measured upward, is also proportionate to the share of escudos. For each risk, it is found along the solid ray sloping upward from 0. The

---

4. Representative contributions, including empirical estimates, are by Levy and Sarnat (1975, 1978).

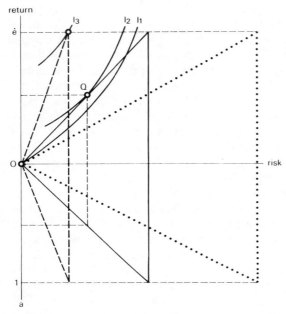

FIGURE 7.3.3
Currency Diversification

optimum is located at Q, where this ray reaches the highest possible indifference curve, I_1, I_2, I_3, etc. If currency risk is sufficiently small, English wealth is held exclusively in the form of escudo assets; this case is illustrated by the broken lines. If currency risk rises, the ray in the lower part of the diagram becomes gradually flatter. As a consequence, English portfolios begin to be diversified, as expressed by the solid lines. Finally, currency risk may become so large that no escudo assets are held, the mean return from expected appreciation being outweighed by its uncertainty. This case is illustrated by the dotted lines. If a corresponding graph were drawn for Portuguese asset holders, the ray in the upper part would be replaced by a straight line declining to the right. As a consequence, the share of sterling assets in Portuguese portfolios would be zero regardless of currency risk. The overall conclusion is that currency risk reduces the share of foreign assets in wealth holders' portfolios. At moderate risk levels, this may increase the international diversification of portfolios, but at high risk levels this diversification tends to disappear.

The second reason for diversification arises from the fact that, given purchasing-power parity, the foreign currency may be an effective inflation hedge for consumers of domestic goods.[5] Suppose wealth holders have the

5. This motive is analyzed in Wihlborg (1978) and, together with other motives, in Kouri and de Macedo (1978).

choice between sterling balances and escudo balances, both bearing no interest. Consider an English wealth owner who is interested in consuming only English goods. Both English prices, p_E, and Portuguese prices, p_p, are subject to change, and the same is true for the exchange rate. Denoting initial prices and terminal prices by, respectively, superscripts 0 and t, the proportionate gain in purchasing power from holding £1 from 0 to t is

$$r_E = \frac{1/p_E^t - 1/p_E^0}{1/p_E^0} = \frac{p_E^0}{p_E^t} - 1. \tag{7.3.3}$$

The "yield" from holding sterling is, naturally, equal to the English deflation rate; with inflation, it is negative.

The alternative is to convert sterling into escudos at the present exchange rate e^0, hold escudos during the period, and convert them back into sterling at e^t. In this case the proportionate gain in purchasing power is

$$r_P = \frac{(e^t/e^0)(1/p_E^t) - (1/p_E^0)}{1/p_E^0} = \frac{e^t}{e^0} \frac{p_E^0}{p_E^t} - 1. \tag{7.3.4}$$

This may be regarded as the "yield" from holding escudos.

So far, Portuguese prices do not appear. They become relevant, however, to the extent they are related to the exchange rate. Suppose (relative) purchasing-power parity is valid. In this case

$$\frac{e^t}{e^0} = \frac{p_E^t}{p_E^0} \cdot \frac{p_P^0}{p_P^t}, \tag{7.3.5}$$

whence

$$r_P = \frac{p_P^0}{p_P^t} - 1. \tag{7.3.6}$$

The yield on escudos thus reduces to the Portuguese deflation rate, and through this yield the latter becomes relevant even for Englishmen who do not consume Portuguese goods. If purchasing-power parity applies and if Portuguese prices are perfectly stable, then escudos are a perfect inflation hedge for English wealth holders.

We now have to introduce uncertainty about prices and thus about the exchange rate and currency yields. Let the English deflation rate be characterized by an expected value $E(r_E)$ and variance $V(r_E) = \sigma_E^2$, while the Portuguese inflation rate is characterized by $E(r_P)$ and $V(r_P) = \sigma_P^2$ with $\text{Cov}(r_E, r_P) = \rho_{EP}\sigma_E\sigma_P$. Suppose an individual allocates a proportion, a, of his funds to sterling, leaving a share of $1 - a$ for escudos. The expected yield on his total currency holdings then is

$$E(r) = aE(r_E) + (1 - a)E(r_P). \tag{7.3.7}$$

We now make the additional assumption that expected inflation is the same in both countries, so that $E(r_E) = E(r_P)$. This means that, from the point of view of expected yield, diversification makes no difference. While this is certainly a special case, it helps to bring out the significance of exchange risk in the simplest possible way.

The risk about portfolio yield, measured by its variance, depends on diversification according to

$$V(r) = a^2\sigma_E^2 + 2a(1 - a)\rho_{EP}\sigma_E\sigma_P + (1 - a)^2\sigma_P^2. \tag{7.3.8}$$

With expected yield given, a utility-maximizing wealth holder will choose a in such a way that portfolio risk is minimized. By taking the derivative of $V(r)$ with respect to a and putting it equal to zero, we obtain the condition

$$\frac{\partial V}{\partial a} = 2a\sigma_E^2 + 2(1 - 2a)\rho_{EP}\sigma_E\sigma_P - 2(1 - a)\sigma_P^2 = 0. \tag{7.3.9}$$

With floating rates it is plausible to assume that, over periods for which purchasing-power parity applies, the correlation between price levels is zero. In this case, the condition reduces to

$$\frac{a}{1 - a} = \frac{\sigma_P^2}{\sigma_E^2}. \tag{7.3.10}$$

This means that, normally, currency diversification pays for wealth holders in both countries. It is not true that all balances should be held in the more stable currency; risk can be reduced by holding some in the less stable currency. The higher the purchasing-power risk for a given currency, however, the lower its share in the optimal portfolio. Pure portfolios will be chosen only if some currency is completely free of purchasing-power risk. If both currencies are equally risky, each will be allocated half of the portfolio in this simple case. While reality is, of course, more complicated, the basic considerations brought out in this simple example are still valid in more general cases. In particular, for currency diversification to be efficient, it is not necessary for (relative) purchasing-power parity to be strictly valid; a significant correlation between exchange rates and prices is enough.

The third reason for currency diversification has to do with the diversification of consumption. Even without purchasing-power parity, currency diversification may be efficient if an Englishman consumes both English and Portuguese goods. Suppose sterling prices of English goods and escudo prices of Portuguese goods are fixed; there is no inflation risk. The exchange rate, on the other hand, is variable and uncertain, implying deviations from purchasing-power parity. The English consumer receives his income in sterling in the base period, and he spends it on consumer goods at a later time t. Depending on his utility function, he consumes both English and Portuguese goods, and he can hold his wealth in any combination of sterling and escudos.

Suppose he holds all in sterling. He then suffers no uncertainty about his eventual purchasing power in terms of English goods, but there is uncertainty about his purchasing power in terms of Portuguese goods. If he holds all in escudos, it is the other way around. The optimum will, in general, be somewhere in between, depending on his relative preference for imported and domestic goods. For detailed analysis, the reader is referred to the literature.[6]

In all cases of currency diversification, the demand for each currency becomes dependent on exchange risk. Fluctuations in this risk produce shifts in the demand for money. It should be noted, however, that these demand shifts do not require capital flows. If the demand for sterling increases relative to the demand for escudos, the market will react by lowering sterling prices relative to escudo prices accompanied by an appreciation of sterling.

From the point of view of subsequent chapters, three important conclusions can be drawn from the brief analysis of currency risk in this section:

1. It is not generally true that exchange risk, because it makes foreign assets more risky, is a barrier against asset diversification. Quite to the contrary, exchange risk may be a potent motive for the international diversification of portfolios.

2. With floating exchange rates, interest differentials have to balance not only the expected changes in exchange rates, but also exchange risk. If this risk is not explicitly allowed for, there may be deviations of the expected exchange rate from interest parity even in equilibrium.

3. There may be a foreign demand for domestic cash balances even though foreign residents have no direct transactions demand for domestic currency. The same applies to the domestic demand for foreign cash balances. These demands are subject to fluctuations depending on exchange risk and inflation risk.

6. See, in particular, Heckerman (1973); Grauer, Litzenberger, and Stehle (1976); Roll and Solnik (1977); and Kouri and de Macedo (1978).

CHAPTER **8**

Forward Exchange

Introduction

Foreign financial assets and liabilities were discussed in chapter 7 in general terms. The present chapter concentrates on one particular segment of the foreign asset market, namely, the forward exchange market.

Forward transactions are basically simple and commonplace. They occur, in general, whenever a contract provides for both delivery and payment at a future time. For example, a contractor may promise to deliver a building for $1 million in two years, a mail-order house promises to deliver merchandise within a month c.o.d., or an employee is hired at $2,000 a month. In certain fields there is an organized market for such transactions. One of them is the foreign-exchange market. In the spot market two currencies are exchanged on the spot. In the forward market contracts are made now, but the exchange of currencies takes place at a stipulated later date. For example, an American importer may obtain from a bank a promise to deliver £1 million three months hence against the promise to pay the bank $2 million. Economically (though not legally) a forward transaction is equivalent to an exchange of IOUs; no cash changes hands. Forward contracts can be made, in principle, for any maturity, from a day to several years. In practice, few maturities exceed one year, and the financial press usually quotes rates for one, two, and three months.

The forward exchange rate is the price at which one currency is traded against another in the forward market. For the same pair of currencies it is usually different for different maturities. For the same maturity, the rate at which the dealer is willing to buy a currency is lower than the selling rate. For

example, on August 25, 1981, the Zurich rates for dollars in terms of Swiss
francs were quoted as follows:

	Buy	*Sell*
Spot	2.1600	2.1900
1 month	2.1400	2.1700
2 months	2.1225	2.1525
3 months	2.1075	2.1375

The dollar thus stood at a discount, which amounted to roughly 2.5 percent
for three months or 10 percent per annum. The spread between the buying
and the selling price was about 1.5 percent. Note that the headings "Buy"
and "Sell" refer to the dealer. For the customer, the relevant rate is the less
favorable one.

The forward exchange market has two main functions. First, it enables
traders to eliminate exchange risk on future transactions. For example, a
Swiss importer who has to pay $100,000 in three months can eliminate his
exchange risk by buying the dollars at the current forward rate for delivery in
three months. Such an operation is called hedging. Second, the forward market can be used for speculative operations. Suppose, for example, a speculator expects to sell spot dollars in three months for Sfr. 2.25. He can then make
a profit by buying dollars three months forward at Sfr. 2.1375. These types of
transactions are analyzed in more detail on the following pages.

It should always be kept in mind, though, that hedging and speculation
can also take place through the spot market. The importer can avoid exchange risk by just buying the needed dollars spot. Similarly, the speculator
can profit from an expected appreciation of the dollar by buying dollars spot
and holding them for three months. In the absence of transaction costs, hedgers and speculators should actually be indifferent between the forward and
the spot market. In a basic sense, forward exchange markets are redundant.
Their significance depends crucially on transaction costs. Risk, while often
present in the background, is not explicitly considered in the following analysis. This is based on the impression that from a macroeconomic point of view,
risk is a secondary factor in the forward exchange market. For an explicit
analysis of uncertainty in the forward exchange market, see Feldstein (1968).

The fundamental redundancy of the forward market appears readily
from the description given above. If a forward transaction consists in an exchange of two IOUs, it should be possible to calculate the forward rate from
the spot exchange rate of two currencies and the interest rates on the IOUs. In
the absence of transaction costs this would indeed be the case, and under
present conditions transaction costs are so low that it comes close to being
true in reality.

The literature on forward exchange is vast and complicated.[1] The com-

---

1. For a standard treatment, see Grubel (1966).

plications mostly arise either from an effort to analyze the implications of transaction costs without introducing them explicitly or from the inherent intricacies of transaction costs. The vastness of the literature seems to be due partly to an exaggerated view of the significance of the forward market for economic policy and partly to a continuing feeling of dissatisfaction with the state of the art in this field.

By and large, forward exchange markets are important for the banker and businessman, whose job it is to shave a few pennies from the costs of every transaction, thereby increasing the efficiency of the economy. The policy maker, however, might almost as well forget about their existence. This view seems to be in contrast with much of the recent literature; the following pages will try to substantiate it in detail. In the first section, forward exchange will be discussed on the assumption of costless transactions. The second section introduces transaction costs, resulting in an interpretation of forward market functions closely analogous to domestic banking functions. The brief final section draws conclusions about central-bank intervention as an instrument of economic policy.

8.1 Forward Exchange without Transaction Costs

This section presents a detailed analysis of the basic forward operations in the absence of transaction costs.[2] Transaction costs are meant to include all those costs that drive a wedge between the buying price and the selling price of foreign exchange and between the borrowing rate and the lending rate on funds like Eurocurrencies. For the purpose of this section, there is assumed to be a uniform exchange rate at which currencies can be bought or sold and also a uniform interest rate at which funds can be borrowed or lent. This assumption does not mean, of course, that there is no risk or that individual traders are not subject to a wealth constraint.

The exposition is limited to two countries, called the United States and England, and to two currencies, called dollars and sterling. The relevant interest rates are, respectively, i_{US} and i_E. They may be visualized as the rates on highly liquid money-market instruments. Under present circumstances, Eurocurrency rates are probably the best choice. The rates are meant to be for the maturity in question and not necessarily per annum. The exchange rate, e, is defined as the price of sterling in terms of dollars. For the present purpose it is enough to consider one particular maturity, t, which may be imagined to be three months. While e_0 denotes the spot rate, e_t is the rate on forward contracts maturing at time t. It should be noted that both of these rates are current market rates; they do not involve risk.

Users of the forward market are traditionally divided into hedgers, arbitrageurs, and speculators. This approach is open to the familiar criticism that

2. For a survey of important contributions, see Hodjera (1973).

the same agent may appear in the market in several of these roles and that a satisfactory microtheory of the forward market thus requires a portfolio analysis of such agents. The present exposition nevertheless follows the traditional approach because, despite its microeconomic shortcomings, it makes it easy to grasp the general economic significance of the forward market. In particular, this procedure helps to bring out the fact that the three functions are basically more similar than most of the literature seems to indicate.

The analysis conveniently begins with *hedging*. Merchants, banks, industrial firms, and private individuals often find themselves exposed, by the nature of their business, to foreign exchange risk. Hedging is the activity by which they cover themselves against this risk.[3] Hedgers typically have a choice between different techniques. Suppose an American importer wishes to hedge the exchange risk on a sterling payment due in three months. He can accomplish this either by buying sterling spot or by buying it forward, his choice probably depending on relative costs. If he buys forward, his cost per pound at time t is simply e_t. If he buys spot, he first has to borrow dollars at the U.S. interest rate (or to impute the corresponding opportunity cost to his own funds), then he pays e_0 for spot sterling, and finally he can invest the sterling for three months at the U.K. interest rate. Hedging in the forward market is cheaper if

$$e_t < e_0 \frac{1 + i_{US}}{1 + i_E}. \tag{8.1.1}$$

If the inequality is reversed, the importer will prefer to buy sterling in the spot market.

Consider, on the other hand, an American exporter who expects to receive a sterling payment in three months. He, too, can hedge his exchange risk either in the forward market or in the spot market. In the forward market his proceeds at time t will be e_t. If he sells sterling spot at e_0, he first has to borrow it at the U.K. interest rate, but he can then invest the proceeds at the U.S. rate. He will prefer the forward sale to the spot sale if

$$e_t > e_0 \frac{1 + i_{US}}{1 + i_E}. \tag{8.1.2}$$

If the inequality is reversed, he will prefer the spot transaction. Analogous computations can be made for English merchants, and with the same result.

It turns out that in all cases the merchant's choice depends decisively on whether the forward rate is above or below the critical level

$$\bar{e}_t = e_0 \frac{1 + i_{US}}{1 + i_E}, \tag{8.1.3}$$

---

3. A more comprehensive analysis would have to explain the hedging activities simultaneously with the underlying business transactions. For example, exchange risk can be avoided by abstaining from international transactions in the first place.

where $\bar{e}_t$ may be called the interest parity rate. The essential point is that the hedgers never simultaneously buy and sell sterling in the forward market at a rate different from $\bar{e}_t$. If they find it profitable to buy sterling forward, their sales move through the spot market. If they find it profitable to sell sterling forward, their purchases will be made spot. There is only one point at which demand and supply in the forward market match, and this is where the forward rate is exactly at interest parity. At this point, however, the forward market has no advantage over the spot market; merchants are indifferent between the two.

This is described in figure 8.1.1. The forward rate is measured along the vertical axis, while the volume of forward sales and forward purchases is measured, respectively, to the left and to the right. Sterling is sold forward if $e_t \geqq \bar{e}_t$; at the same time, other merchants buy sterling spot. It is plausible to assume that the forward volume expands with an increasing differential, at first rapidly and then gradually more slowly. This is mostly due to risk, but the reasons are not explicitly analyzed here. If $e_t \leqq \bar{e}_t$, hedgers will buy sterling forward, again probably in increasing amounts, while others sell it spot. At the parity forward rate, $e_t = \bar{e}_t$, the curve has a flat segment, indicating indifference between forward-market hedging and spot-market hedging.

Hedgers help to keep the forward rate at interest parity by switching their operation from the forward market to the spot market and vice versa at any deviation of the forward rate from interest parity. In addition, such deviations create opportunities for *covered interest arbitrage*. This is an operation in which the arbitrageur, usually a professional foreign-exchange dealer, exploits an international interest differential while simultaneously hedging his exchange risk. The operation is profitable if the interest differential exceeds the cost of hedging. Suppose the forward rate is below interest parity, $e_t < \bar{e}_t$. In this case it is profitable to

—borrow sterling at i_E,
—sell the sterling for dollars spot at e_0,
—lend the dollars at i_{US},
—buy sterling forward at e_t.

The right-hand side of the inequality represents the dollar proceeds after three months from £1 borrowed now, sold spot, and invested in the United States; the left-hand side is the cost of £1 bought forward. If the inequality holds, the transaction is profitable without exposing the arbitrageur to exchange risk. In the reverse case with $e_t > \bar{e}_t$, arbitrageurs would, of course, operate in the opposite direction by

—borrowing dollars at i_{US},
—buying sterling against dollars spot at e_0,
—lending sterling at i_E,
—selling sterling forward at e_t.

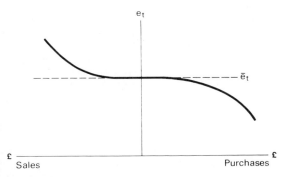

FIGURE 8.1.1
Forward Hedging

It should be noted that all of these transactions are in terms of current market rates; subsequent developments, expected or unexpected, are immaterial as long as all parties fulfill their contractual obligations. As a consequence, even small profit margins may call forth large transactions; credit risks and liquidity considerations are the most relevant limiting factor.[4] As a practical matter, in the absence of transaction costs, covered interest arbitrage would be enough to prevent any significant deviations of forward rates from interest parity. The supply curve for arbitrage funds would be virtually horizontal. The supply curve for covered interest arbitrage in figure 8.1.2 is thus drawn with a large flat segment at $e_t = \bar{e}_t$. It is likely, though, that for very large volumes an increasing gap between e_t and $\bar{e}_t$ would be necessary to compensate the arbitrageurs for increasing default risks. It is important to note that in the absence of transaction costs there is no significant difference between covered interest arbitrage and hedging. Both hedgers and arbitrageurs perform the same calculations and have supply functions with similar characteristics.

It has traditionally been argued that covered interest arbitrage involves international capital flows.[5] In the case of forward purchases, sterling is borrowed while dollars are lent, which seems to involve a flow of short-term funds from England to the United States. Forward sales of sterling, on the other hand, seem to be associated with a flow of short-term funds in the opposite direction. Keynes seems to have initiated the tradition of regarding short-term capital flows as controlled by deviations of exchange rates from interest parity (1923, pp. 125f., esp. pp. 149f.). Further developed by Spraos (1953, pp. 87–92), Tsiang (1959), and Branson (1968), this tradition dominates the literature on capital flows to the present day.

4. The best concise and nontechnical explanation of these limiting factors is still to be found in Keynes (1923, pp. 137 f.).
5. Branson has, in fact, used forward operations as a paradigm for short-term capital flows (1968).

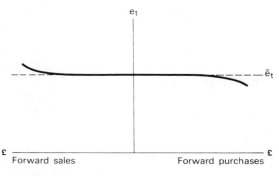

FIGURE 8.1.2
Covered Interest Arbitrage

In view of the weight of this tradition, it is important to realize that the underlying argument is valid only in a quite restricted sense. It is true, of course, that in the case of $e_t < \bar{e}_t$ there is an increased supply of sterling assets and an increased demand for dollar assets. However, the apparent capital flow to the United States is exactly matched by the forward commitments to sell dollars for sterling. If the ledgers are correctly kept, these have to be counted as foreign assets and liabilities, too. As a matter of fact, the arbitrageurs' net foreign asset position is not changed at all, nor is the net foreign asset position of England relative to the United States. If capital flows are considered in the usual sense as the counterpart of current-account surpluses or deficits, no capital flow takes place. Clearly, a trade deficit cannot be "financed" by covered interest arbitrage operations.

This can also be seen from another point of view. Capital flows in the sense of the balance of payments have to do with payments and receipts of residents of one country in their transactions with residents of other countries. Covered interest arbitrage, however, has nothing to do with residency. It can take place among U.S. residents or among U.K. residents without any transactions between the two groups. The implication is that covered interest arbitrage has nothing to contribute to the analysis of capital flows between countries in the balance-of-payments sense. All it helps to explain are the shifts between assets of different maturities within the same net foreign asset position.

The forward market can also be used by *speculators*. Speculators are characterized by the fact that they try to profit from differences between current market rates, spot or forward, and market rates expected to rule in the future. The spot rate expected to rule at time t will be denoted by ϵ_t. Expectations are assumed to be held with certainty and to be identical for all speculators.

It is profitable for speculators to buy sterling forward if $\epsilon_t > e_t$. In this case, the speculator contracts today to buy sterling three months hence at a price of e_t, and he expects to sell the sterling at the higher rate ϵ_t. If the inequality is reversed, speculation runs in the opposite direction.

It has often been argued that the relationship between the forward rate and the expected future spot rate is all that matters for the speculator under the given assumptions. It was then pointed out that speculation differs from hedging and covered interest arbitrage inasmuch as it depends on the comparison of the forward rate, not with the interest parity rate, but with the expected future spot rate. As a consequence, there might be a range of exchange rates in which hedgers and/or arbitrageurs buy forward, while speculators simultaneously wish to sell forward, or vice versa. Excess demand in one segment of the market would be balanced by excess supply in the other.

Unfortunately, this argument is incomplete and, as a consequence, misleading. In reality, things are more complicated. The complication arises because speculators, like hedgers, have the option of channeling their operations through the spot market.[6] Expecting an appreciation of sterling, the speculator can borrow dollars at i_{US}, buy sterling spot, and invest the proceeds at i_E, expecting to sell the sterling later at the future spot rate. This is profitable if

$$\epsilon_t > \bar{e}_t. \tag{8.1.4}$$

With the inequality sign reversed, spot speculation is profitable in the opposite direction.[7]

The available options can be graphed in a diagram with ϵ_t and e_t, respectively, on the horizontal axis and the vertical axis (see fig. 8.1.3). Above the broken 45° line it is profitable to sell sterling forward; below this line it is profitable to buy forward. The broken vertical line indicates the level of ϵ_t at which the expected future spot rate is equal to interest parity. To the right of this line it is profitable to speculate by buying sterling spot; to the left sterling is sold spot. Whatever e_t and ϵ_t, it always pays to speculate one way or another. The trouble is that there are always two profitable alternatives, one in the forward market, the other in the spot market. Of course, the speculator will presumably choose the one with the higher profit per dollar of operations. Thus, forward speculation can be profitable and still not take place because spot speculation is even more profitable.

It is necessary, therefore, to determine the dividing lines between spot speculation and forward speculation. To begin in the lower left of figure 8.1.3, selling spot is preferred to buying forward if

$$\frac{e_0}{\epsilon_t} \frac{1 + i_{US}}{1 + i_E} > \frac{\epsilon_t}{e_t},$$

---

6. This was clearly pointed out by Tsiang (1959).

7. It has often been pointed out that spot speculation is equivalent to a combination of forward speculation and covered interest arbitrage. The profit rate on speculative forward purchases of sterling can be expanded to $\epsilon_t/e_t = (\epsilon_t/\bar{e}_t)(\bar{e}_t/e_t)$, which is the product of the profit rates on speculative spot purchases and on covered spot sales. It has to be kept in mind, however, that the equivalence only applies in the absence of transaction costs, in which case the forward market is redundant anyhow.

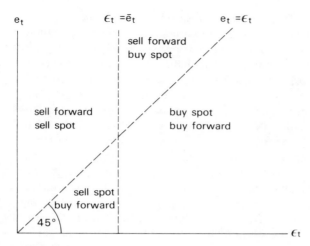

FIGURE 8.1.3
Profitable Speculation

where the profit rate for speculative spot purchases appears on the left, while the profit rate for speculative forward purchases is shown on the right. Using (8.1.3), this condition can be rewritten as

$$e_t > \frac{\epsilon_t^2}{\bar{e}_t} . \qquad (8.1.5)$$

Exactly the same condition emerges for forward sales to be more profitable than spot purchases. In both cases the watershed between the spot market and the forward market is thus characterized by the equation

$$e_t = \frac{\epsilon_t^2}{\bar{e}_t} .$$

For a given parity rate $\bar{e}_t$, the graph of this equation is a parabola that intersects the 45° line at the point $\bar{e}_t = e_t$ (see fig. 8.1.4).

There is also another watershed. Selling forward is more profitable than selling spot if

$$\frac{e_t}{\epsilon_t} > \frac{e_0}{\epsilon_t} \frac{1 + i_{US}}{1 + i_E} ,$$

or

$$e_t > \bar{e}_t. \qquad (8.1.6)$$

The same condition determines the superior profitability of spot purchases relative to forward purchases. The dividing line, characterized by the equa-

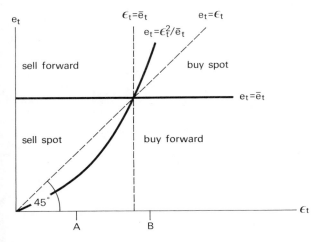

FIGURE 8.1.4
Optimal Speculative Transactions

tion $e_t = \bar{e}_t$, is a horizontal line that intersects the 45° line at the same point as the parabola.[8]

This analysis shows that sterling will not necessarily be sold forward whenever $e_t > \epsilon_t$ and that it will not necessarily be bought forward if this inequality is reversed. In fact, the 45° line is not of critical importance at all. On the other hand, the interest parity rate, previously shown to be relevant for hedging and interest arbitrage, turns out to be of critical importance for speculators as well.[9]

The main points of this argument can be visualized in a graph of the type of figures 8.1.1 and 8.1.2. Suppose in panel (*a*) of figure 8.1.5, the expected rate ϵ_t is at a level like A. Sterling will be sold forward if $e_t \geqq \bar{e}_t$, the amount presumably increasing with increasing profitability. Sterling will be bought forward if $e_t \leqq \epsilon_t^2/\bar{e}_t$, again presumably in increasing amounts. In the intermediate range the forward market will be deserted, speculators preferring to sell sterling spot.

A different picture emerges if, other things equal, ϵ_t is at a point like B in panel (*b*) of figure 8.1.5. In this case, ϵ_t is above the parity rate $\bar{e}_t$, but below $\epsilon_t^2/\bar{e}_t$. Again there is an upper range for e_t, in which sterling is sold forward, and a lower range, in which it is bought forward, but the two are now sepa-

---

8. The choice between spot and forward transactions in a given direction, since it is independent of ϵ_t, is also independent of the risk about ϵ_t. Even if risk were explicitly considered in this analysis, it would not affect this choice. This is not so for the choices between selling spot and buying forward and between buying spot and selling forward, because the parabolic curve depends on ϵ_t.

9. This, too, was noted by Tsiang (1959).

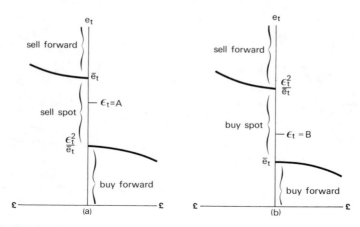

FIGURE 8.1.5
Forward Speculation

rated by a range of speculative spot purchases. The important point is that at the level $e_t = \bar{e}_t$, which is critical for hedging and covered interest arbitrage, speculative demand for (or speculative supply of) forward exchange also disappears.

Finally we consider the *forward market as a whole*. Aggregate demand and supply of forward exchange are obtained by adding the respective curves for hedgers, arbitrageurs, and speculators. If panel (*a*) of figure 8.1.5 is relevant for speculators, the result is a graph like figure 8.1.6. If panel (*b*) is relevant, the curve would look more or less as if figure 8.1.6 were wheeled around its intersection with the e_t line by 180°, but its main characteristics would remain the same.

The essential observation is that, in the absence of transaction costs,

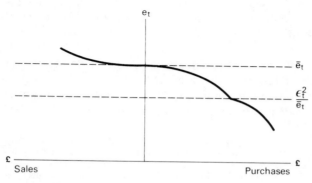

FIGURE 8.1.6
Forward Market as a Whole

there is no forward rate different from interest parity at which there can be both positive demand and positive supply of forward exchange. It never happens that one group of traders wants to buy sterling forward while another group wants to sell it forward. The only forward rate at which aggregate excess demand is zero is the interest parity rate. At this rate, however, the forward market becomes redundant. All transactions could as well be channeled through the spot market.

This indicates that the forward market depends on transaction costs in an essential way: without transaction costs it simply would not exist. Impressions to the contrary are usually the result of faulty analysis of speculative forward operations, disregarding the option of spot speculation. On the positive side, the analysis showed that in the absence of transaction costs, forward rates can be expected to be at interest parity. Hedgers, arbitrageurs, and speculators all contribute to keeping it continuously at this level.

While this exposition was limited to a single maturity of forward contracts, it actually applies to any and all maturities. For any maturity, t, the parity condition can be written

$$f = \frac{e_t - e_0}{e_0} = \frac{i_{US} - i_E}{1 + i_E} , \qquad (8.1.7)$$

where f is the forward premium as a fraction of the spot rate. If the product fi_E is small enough to be disregarded, this can be simplified to

$$f = i_{US} - i_E. \qquad (8.1.8)$$

For any maturity, the forward premium on the price of the foreign currency (or the forward discount on the dollar) is (approximately) equal to the interest differential in favor of the United States.[10] The forward market sees to it that, in the absence of transaction costs, the term structure of the forward exchange rates is an exact reflection of the term structure of interest rates. Since the term structure of forward rates provides no information that is not contained in the term structure of interest rates it is, in a fundamental sense, redundant. Only transaction costs can invest it with economic meaning.

8.2 Forward Exchange with Transaction Costs

In this section, the model of the forward-exchange market is extended to include transaction costs. Frenkel and Levich (1975) first drew attention to the significance of transaction costs for a proper understanding of the forward market. The critical inequalities that guide the choice between spot and

---

10. Consider the exchange rates quoted in the Introduction. On August 25, 1981, the interest rate on three-month Eurodollars was 18 7/8 percent. The corresponding rate on Swiss francs was 8 7/8 percent. For all practical purposes, the interest differential was indeed equal to the forward discount on the dollar.

forward operations in the presence of transaction costs are developed in Deardorff (1979). The picture of the forward market emerging from the following analysis is in many respects similar to that presented by McKinnon (1979). This is especially true with respect to the similarity of private hedgers and speculators as opposed to banks as arbitrageurs.

Transaction costs can be introduced in different ways. They can be visualized, for example, as resource inputs required by traders to carry out a given transaction. Alternatively, they can be visualized as a fee that traders pay to a middleman or broker. The following analysis, in an effort to stay close to actual arrangements in the forward market, uses the second approach. Forward exchange and credit transactions are thus assumed to be channeled through banks. Banks cover their operating costs partly by selling foreign exchange (both spot and forward) above the central rate and buying it below. The selling rate for spot exchange is supposed to be $\eta_s e_0$ while the buying rate is e_0/η_s, where η_s is a number like 1.01. The corresponding margin for the forward rate is η_f.

Banks cover another part of operating costs by lending funds at higher rates than those at which they are borrowed. It is assumed that for a dollar borrowed from a bank today the nonbank borrower has to repay $\gamma_{US}(1 + i_{US})$ dollars at time t, while for a dollar lent to a bank today the nonbank lender receives $(1/\gamma_{US})(1 + i_{US})$ at the end of the period, where γ_{US}, like η_s, is a number slightly above unity. For sterling, the corresponding margin would be expressed by $\gamma_E > 1$. These assumptions agree reasonably well with the picture that emerges every day from the financial pages while still keeping computations simple.

It may first be imagined that banks operate at constant marginal costs equal to the quoted margins. This is not quite realistic, to be sure, but it helps to simplify the main argument. The assumption means that at a (central) forward rate equal to the interest-parity rate—that is, at $e_t = \bar{e}_t$—banks are willing to buy and sell any amount of forward sterling. They behave like private arbitrageurs in the absence of transaction costs, either selling sterling spot to buy it forward or vice versa along a horizontal arbitrage supply schedule.

Under these circumstances *covered interest arbitrage* will not be undertaken by nonbank traders. In order to make forward sales of sterling profitable, the forward rate would have to rise above $\bar{e}_t$, and in order to make forward purchases profitable, the forward rate would have to fall below $\bar{e}_t$, to compensate the arbitrageurs for the transactions margins. However, with the banks maintaining a horizontal supply curve at the parity level, this is not possible. Covered interest arbitrage thus becomes concentrated in the hands of banks. This conclusion from the model is close to reality inasmuch as exchange rates and interest rates quoted in the financial press hardly ever offer any significant arbitrage opportunities to nonbank traders.[11] This leaves open

11. This was brought out by Frenkel and Levich (1975).

the question why all traders do not establish themselves as banks. The answer is that, if they did, their transaction costs, not specified in the present model, would be higher than the existing transactions margins. Interest arbitrage simply becomes concentrated in the hands of traders with particularly low transaction costs, who then act as brokers for others.

A different picture emerges for the *hedgers*. Assuming that they use none of their own funds,[12] a purchase of sterling will be made forward if

$$\eta_f e_t < \eta_s e_0 \frac{\gamma_{US}(1 + i_{US})}{(1/\gamma_E)(1 + i_E)}$$

or

$$e_t < \frac{\eta_s \gamma_{US} \gamma_E}{\eta_f} \bar{e}_t = \bar{e}_t^B, \qquad (8.2.1)$$

where $\bar{e}_t^B$ may be called the critical forward buying rate. With η_f sufficiently close to η_s, we can be sure that $\bar{e}_t^B > \bar{e}_t$. Sales of sterling will be made forward if

$$\frac{e_t}{\eta_f} > \frac{e_0}{\eta_s} \frac{(1/\gamma_{US})(1 + i_{US})}{\gamma_E(1 + i_E)}$$

or

$$e_t > \frac{\eta_f}{\eta_s \gamma_{US} \gamma_E} \bar{e}_t = \bar{e}_t^S, \qquad (8.2.2)$$

where $\bar{e}_t^S$ is the critical forward selling rate. With η_f sufficiently close to η_s, we can be sure that $\bar{e}_t^S < \bar{e}_t$. This means that the demand curve on the right-hand side of figure 8.1.1 is shifted upward, while the supply curve on the left-hand side is shifted downward. This results in a diagram like figure 8.2.1. As a consequence of transaction costs, there is now a range of e_t in which some hedgers wish to sell sterling forward while others simultaneously wish to buy it forward. At the interest parity rate, in particular, there is now both demand and supply.

What is depicted in figure 8.2.1 may be regarded as the normal case. If, for some reason, the spread in the forward market is very much larger than in the spot market while the interest margins are small, it is conceivable that $\bar{e}_t^B < \bar{e}_t < \bar{e}_t^S$. This is clearly an exception, however.

Transaction costs also affect the calculations of *speculators*. In the first place, the scope for profitable speculation is reduced. Selling sterling forward is now profitable if

$$\eta_s \epsilon_t < \frac{e_t}{\eta_s}$$

---

12. In the presence of transaction costs, the initial position of the trader makes a difference. In particular, the opportunity cost of funds lent is usually lower than that of funds borrowed. It must be left to the interested reader to work out various cases. For a good discussion, see McKinnon (1979).

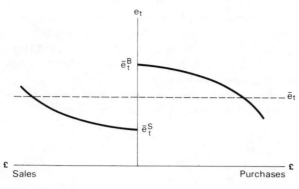

FIGURE 8.2.1
Hedging with Transaction Costs

or

$$e_t > \eta_s^2 \epsilon_t, \tag{8.2.3}$$

while forward purchases are profitable if

$$e_t < (1/\eta_s^2)\epsilon_t. \tag{8.2.4}$$

In figure 8.2.2 these two areas are separated by a cone in which any forward speculation is unprofitable. The profitability of spot sales requires

$$\eta_s \epsilon_t < \frac{1}{\eta_s}\, e_0\, \frac{(1/\gamma_{US})(1 + i_{US})}{\gamma_E(1 + i_E)}\,,$$

or

$$\epsilon_t < \frac{1}{\eta_s^2 \gamma_{US} \gamma_E}\, \bar{e}_t, \tag{8.2.5}$$

while the corresponding condition for spot purchases is

$$\frac{\epsilon_t}{\eta_s} > \eta_s e_0\, \frac{\gamma_{US}(1 + i_{US})}{(1/\gamma_E)(1 + i_E)}$$

or

$$\epsilon_t > \eta_s^2 \gamma_{US} \gamma_E \bar{e}_t. \tag{8.2.6}$$

In figure 8.2.2 these two areas are separated by the vertical corridor in which no spot speculation is profitable. Whereas in the absence of transaction costs some speculation was always profitable, there is now a "white" area around $e_t = \epsilon_t = \bar{e}_t$ in which no speculation takes place.

What is more important, transaction costs also affect the relative profitabilities of the two types of profitable transactions in each segment of figure

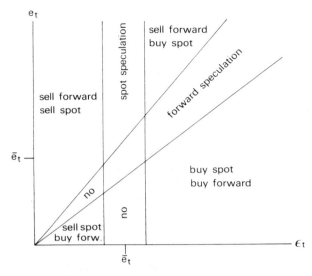

FIGURE 8.2.2
Profitable Speculation with Transaction Costs

8.2.2. It can be left to the reader to work out the details by rewriting (8.1.4), (8.1.5), and (8.1.6) with due allowance for transactions margins. The main result can be summarized in the statement that the range of e_t in which forward transactions are preferred is enlarged while the range of spot transactions shrinks.[13] This is plausible because the margins on exchange operations are likely to be of the same order of magnitude in both types of transactions, while the spot operations have to bear the additional burden of transaction costs on borrowing and lending.

In figure 8.1.5 these modifications are reflected in a downward shift of the supply curves and an upward shift of the demand curves. The result is illustrated in figure 8.2.3. The important point is that in panel (*a*) there is now a positive supply of forward sterling even below $\bar{e}_t$ and that in panel (*b*) there is now a demand for forward sterling even above $\bar{e}_t$. Even though banks, by providing unlimited arbitrage, keep the forward rate at the parity level, transaction costs see to it that there is still some positive demand or supply for speculative forward exchange. It should be noted that with uniform expectations as expressed by ϵ_t, speculative demand and speculative supply of forward exchange cannot coexist. Simultaneous supply and demand may appear, however, if speculators have different expectations about the future exchange rate, some expecting appreciation while others expect depreciation.

13. Exceptions would require that the transactions margin in the forward market be considerably larger than in the spot market while interest margins are small.

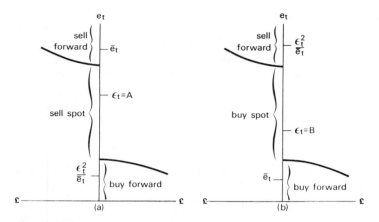

FIGURE 8.2.3
Forward Speculation with Transaction Costs

If banks provide any amount of arbitrage at the given transactions margins, the preceding analysis can be summarized as follows. The forward rate is continuously at interest parity. At this forward rate, nonbank arbitrage is not profitable and does not occur. There may, however, be both demand and supply for hedging purposes; the more hedging is burdened by interest margins in the spot market, the more it will be shifted to the forward market. With the forward rate at interest parity, there may also be either speculative demand or speculative supply of forward exchange and, with differing expectations, possibly both.

Whatever forward exchange is demanded (or supplied) by hedgers and speculators is supplied (or bought) by the banks, who, unless they also wish to speculate, promptly cover themselves by spot purchases (or sales), calculating the forward rate by adjusting the spot price for interest differentials. The forward market thus gives the impression of being just a reflection of the spot market in combination with the current interest rates. This description is close to the picture the forward market actually presents today.

However, a potentially important feature is still missing in this picture. This is the *determination of transactions margins*. It has so far been assumed that marginal transaction costs are constant for all levels of bank operations and identical for all banks. Under these conditions, transactions margins can be treated as being exogenously determined by bank technology. As a matter of fact, different banks may have different marginal transaction costs for the same level of output, and transaction costs may vary depending on the capacity utilization of their foreign exchange departments. As a consequence, transactions margins become endogenous variables, determined jointly with exchange rates and the volume of operations. A complete treatment of this problem for all transactions margins would be cumbersome and also uninteresting from the viewpoint of the economy as a whole. The discussion will thus be limited to the transactions margin on forward exchange, η_f, while the other margins are still regarded as exogenous.

Suppose the representative bank has marginal operating costs on forward transactions of η_f^*, while the market margin is η_f. For spot transactions and credit transactions, the market margins just cover transaction costs, so they can be disregarded. In this case, the bank finds it profitable to buy sterling forward if

$$\frac{\eta_f^*}{\eta_f} e_t < e_0 \frac{1 + i_{US}}{1 + i_E}$$

or

$$e_t < \frac{\eta_f}{\eta_f^*} \bar{e}_t. \tag{8.2.7}$$

Forward sales, on the other hand, are profitable if

$$\frac{\eta_f}{\eta_f^*} e_t > e_0 \frac{1 + i_{US}}{1 + i_E}$$

or

$$e_t > \frac{\eta_f^*}{\eta_f} \bar{e}_t. \tag{8.2.8}$$

The ratio of operating costs to the market margin, η_f^*/η_f, will be denoted by α.

It is plausible to assume that α rises with the level of operations. For efficient banks, it will be below unity for some range of α, but sooner or later increasing capacity utilization and/or jointness of exchange operations with services of other bank departments will cause it to rise above unity, making further expansion unprofitable. The critical level at which forward purchases of sterling by banks cease to be profitable can be written

$$\bar{e}_t^{B_b} = \frac{1}{\alpha(B_b)} \bar{e}_t, \tag{8.2.9}$$

where B_b is the amount bought forward by banks. The critical level of e_t for forward sales by banks, on the other hand, is

$$\bar{e}_t^{S_b} = \alpha(S_b)\bar{e}_t, \tag{8.2.10}$$

where S_b denotes the volume of forward sales by banks.[14]

The amounts bought and sold forward as a function of the forward rate

14. Perhaps it would be more realistic to let α depend on the sum of B_b and S_b, but this would make a graphical representation of the argument almost impossible.

can be described by curves like those in figure 8.2.4. At a low level of purchases, $\bar{e}_t^{Bb}$ is above interest parity. It then declines as the volume increases and eventually falls below interest parity. For forward sales, the critical level of the forward rate begins below interest parity and rises gradually above it.

The demand and supply curves for bank arbitrage have to be confronted with the demand and supply curves of nonbank agents. These can be derived by adding the respective curves for hedgers and speculators. They show a branch rising to the left from below $\bar{e}_t$ and a branch declining to the right from above $\bar{e}_t$, as illustrated by the solid curves in figure 8.2.5. The buy and sell curves for banks from figure 8.2.4 are reproduced in figure 8.2.5, but with the sides reversed so that nonbank sales are matched with bank purchases and vice versa.[15]

Selecting an arbitrary market margin η_f, the demand and supply for forward sales (as seen from the nonbank point of view) on the left-hand side of figure 8.2.5 will probably not be equalized at the same forward rate as the demand and supply for forward purchases on the right-hand side. This means that the initial margin η_f was not at its equilibrium value and has to be adjusted. An increase in η_f lowers $\bar{e}_t^B$ but raises $\bar{e}_t^S$. This is plausible because a higher spread in the forward market makes forward hedging relatively less attractive compared with spot market hedging, thus reducing the volume of both forward purchases and forward sales at a given forward rate. The nonbank curves thus shift inward. The bank curves, on the other hand, shift out-

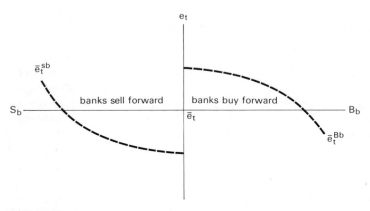

FIGURE 8.2.4
Forward Transactions by Banks

15. To the extent that private forward purchases and private forward sales collect simultaneously in the same bank, the bank will probably find it advantageous to "marry" them directly. In this case, the bank would not provide cover for each side separately, but only for net purchases or net sales. The exposition assumes that this does not take place. For the *representative* bank, this assumption, while not entirely realistic, seems appropriate because at any given time the banking system is typically engaged on both sides of the market.

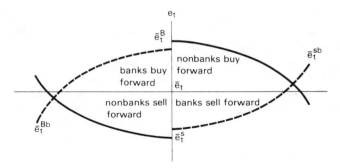

FIGURE 8.2.5
Determination of Transactions Margins

ward because at higher market margins higher amounts will be offered and demanded at any given forward rate. These shifts reduce the equilibrium rate for nonbank forward purchases and increase the equilibrium rate for nonbank forward sales. The equilibrium forward spread will be reached where demand and supply are equilibrated on both sides of the market at the same central forward rate. If initially the two left-hand curves had intersected at a higher forward rate than the two right-hand curves, the required adjustment of η_f would have been in the opposite direction. In this fashion, endogenous adjustments in the forward margin bring about equilibrium between non-bank traders and covered interest arbitrage by banks.

This analysis considered banks only as arbitrageurs. In reality, banks can also hedge their own foreign-exchange commitments and speculate in foreign exchange. In both cases, the basic considerations are the same as for nonbank firms, but again banks appear on the opposite side of the market margins. In the presence of transaction costs the interaction of all these elements is bound to be quite intricate, and from a macroeconomic point of view it is probably not very illuminating. For this reason, these aspects are not worked out here.

While transaction costs make the details of the forward exchange market look complicated, they lead to an overall picture that is simple, straightforward, and closely analogous to financial intermediation in the domestic economy.[16] There are individuals and firms, exemplified by the hedgers, who find themselves with foreign-exchange claims and debts of different maturities yet would like to avoid the associated exchange risk. At the same time, there are other individuals and firms, exemplified by the speculators, who would like to acquire foreign-exchange claims and debts of various maturities in order to profit from expected future exchange-rate changes. Foreign exchange dealers

16. For a corresponding interpretation of domestic intermediation, see Niehans (1978, chs. 9 and 12).

or banks, acting as brokers or middlemen, make it their business to "marry" desired forward purchases and desired forward sales of the same maturity at lower transaction costs than hedgers and speculators would have incurred in the absence of banks.[17] What is more important, banks also make it their business to transform the maturity of debts and claims through covered interest arbitrage, thus transforming, say, spot sterling into thirty-day sterling, thirty-day sterling into sixty-day sterling, and vice versa. They will, again, stay in business if they can provide this service at a lower cost than nonbank agents. Seen from this perspective, the forward market is not a mysterious tangle of intricate technical detail, but rather a straightforward extension of basic intermediation functions to the foreign exchange market.

8.3 Forward Intervention

Shortly after the beginning of this century, the Austrian central bank, as Paul Einzig reports, made an interesting discovery: by selling foreign currencies in the forward market, it could stop, and possibly even reverse, an outflow of reserves without any tightening of credit policy.[18] After World War I this mechanism was rediscovered and popularized by Keynes.[19] Since then, central-bank intervention into the forward market has come to be regarded as an important instrument of central-bank policy. The question is to what extent this claim is justified.

In recent years, swap operations between central banks and commercial banks have been the main tool of forward intervention. A swap is a covered interest arbitrage operation in which the exchange of spot currencies and the exchange of forward currencies are combined in a single transaction. If the Swiss National Bank offers a commercial bank a dollar swap, the commercial bank obtains Swiss francs for dollars spot against the promise to return the same amount of Swiss francs for the same amount of dollars after, say, thirty days. The interest rate on such an operation, the swap rate, would thus correspond to the difference between the appropriate U.S. money-market rate and the appropriate Swiss money-market rate.

Forward intervention by the central bank means that covered interest arbitrage in a given direction is made available at a marginally lower cost than if the central bank had abstained. The result is a shift in the relative levels of the spot rate, the forward rate, and money-market rates. In the above example, the Swiss National Bank makes the swap attractive to the commercial bank by offering a rate that is slightly higher than the differential between the U.S. interest rate and the Swiss interest rate that the commercial bank could

17. This figure of speech was used by Keynes (1923, p. 138).
18. Einzig (1937, p. 329).
19. Keynes (1923, ch. 3, sec. 4). This is an ironic example of an "academic scribbler" putting into words what men of affairs had long done without bothering to write about it.

have otherwise obtained. As a consequence, the bank's market demand for spot francs declines, thus lowering the price of francs in terms of dollars. At the same time, the supply of Swiss money-market funds increases, lowering the Swiss interest rate relative to the U.S. rate. Finally, the forward supply of Swiss francs is reduced, thus raising the forward premium.

Overall, the effect of central-bank intervention is a "twist" in the term structure of interest rates, Swiss short-term rates being lowered relative to longer-term rates. This is associated with a corresponding twist in the term structure of the forward premium. The effect is closely analogous to the twists in the term structure of interest rates, so widely discussed in the early 1960s, that can be produced by shifts in central-bank portfolios in the domestic economy.

The question is what significance such twists, obtained through forward intervention, have as a policy instrument. In trying to answer it, it is convenient to distinguish between fixed exchange rates and floating rates. Under fixed rates, a depreciation of the currency, once the intervention point is reached, is translated into a loss of reserves. By selling foreign exchange forward and thus lowering the forward price of foreign exchange in terms of domestic currency, the central bank can make it profitable for hedgers, speculators, and arbitrageurs to buy the foreign currency forward rather than spot and to sell it spot rather than forward. This helps to stop the outflow of spot funds and may even enable the central bank to make covering spot purchases at or near the intervention rate, thus acquiring reserves. The main point is that this can be achieved without any tightening of domestic credit conditions. Forward intervention may thus be an effective technique for reducing reserve fluctuations in the face of short-run disturbances. It is also clear, however, that a continuing loss of reserves would require forward intervention on an ever-larger scale and that an eventual devaluation would involve the central bank in foreign-exchange losses to the extent that its forward sales were uncovered.

Under floating rates, the purpose of forward intervention is less clear. Special cases of temporary disturbances can readily be imagined. End-of-quarter window dressing by Swiss banks offers a good example. In their quarterly balance sheets these banks wish (or are required) to exhibit a higher liquidity in terms of Swiss francs than they find it profitable and necessary to maintain in the course of the quarter. As a consequence, daily money-market rates at the end of the quarter may rise to a per annum level between 50 and 100 percent. A few days later, the transactions are reversed, interest rates returning to their normal level. By offering to commercial banks end-of-quarter swaps, the Swiss National Bank can reduce these short-run fluctuations in interest rates. While this is profitable to both the central bank and the commercial banks, the general economic purpose of this sort of intervention is questionable. The sharp fluctuations in bank liquidity cannot, in themselves, be efficient and desirable. Either the end-of-quarter liquidity is unnecessarily high or the in-between liquidity is precariously low. It may be argued that in both cases the central bank, rather than supporting the liquidity fluctuations by its interventions, should help to remove their underlying cause. If the cause is excessive legal requirements, these might be relaxed. If the cause is the laxity of reserve requirements for the in-between period, these might be tightened. If window dressing is intended to project a more solid public image, the banks should perhaps be required to publish more frequent balance sheets. However, while these arguments may be plausible, it is clear that the question requires much further study.

Aside from such special cases, debatable as they are, marginal twists in the maturity structure of foreign-exchange commitments seem to have little economic significance. Whatever can be achieved by swaps can generally be achieved just as effectively by operations in domestic and foreign securities together with spot exchange operations. If swap operations have an advantage, that advantage must again be looked for in a reduction of transaction costs for the central bank. This is a relevant consideration, of course. It should be kept in mind, however, that from the point of view of general monetary policy the central bank might just as well refrain from forward intervention under floating rates.

CHAPTER 9

The Eurodollar
Market

Introduction

The Eurodollar market is a network of financial intermediation. Since it is, by definition, located outside the United States, it is necessarily international in character. The subject of this chapter, therefore, is the international aspects of financial intermediation.

The emergence of the Eurodollar system in the postwar period is one of the more impressive examples of financial innovation in recent monetary history. The most relentless force behind financial innovation is transactions technology. This chapter takes the view that the Eurodollar market owes its existence largely to the lowering of transaction costs in the external money market relative to the domestic market. I first expressed this view in 1971. It was further developed by Hewson (1975) and particularly Niehans and Hewson (1976). The present chapter is, in the main, based on this work. For a comprehensive recent analysis the reader is referred to the excellent monograph by Dufey and Giddy (1978).

The first section is intended as a summary description of the Euromarket. The second section describes the Euromarket as a network for the efficient distribution of short-term funds based on transaction-cost differentials. The third section takes up the question of liquidity creation; this involves, naturally, a discussion of alternative models of financial intermediation. In the fourth section, the Eurocurrency market is considered from the viewpoint of economic policy. The main conclusion is similar to the conclusion of chapter 8 about the forward market: while the Euromarket raises welfare by improving the allocational efficiency of financial markets, its macroeconomic significance is usually overestimated.

9.1 The Structure of the Eurodollar Market

This section provides a concise description of financial assets and institutions in the Eurodollar market. For details the reader is referred to the voluminous literature.[1]

The Eurodollar market, in a literal sense, is a money market for U.S. dollars located in Europe. Its center is London, but other cities like Paris, Frankfurt, and Zurich are also important. It has become customary, however, to stretch the meaning of the term in two directions. First, dollar markets outside of Europe like those in Canada, Japan, Hongkong, Singapore, and in the Caribbean islands are regarded as part of the Eurodollar market, provided they are external to the United States. Second, the term is often stretched to include markets in nondollar currencies like sterling, German marks, or Swiss francs, as long as they are located outside the issuing country. It would clearly be more exact to speak more generally of "external money markets," but common usage often takes the part for the whole.

In the early period of Eurodollars, the existence of external money markets tended to be regarded as extraordinary. In fact, it is nothing of the sort. One of the basic functions of a bank is to act as broker or middleman for liquid funds. In this respect banks are similar to commodity brokers. There is no reason why a commodity broker should generally be located in the country where the commodity originates. American wheat can be bought and sold just as well in London or Zurich as in Chicago. The same is true for banks. There is no general reason why a broker in U.S. dollars should be located in the United States; he can operate just as well in London or Zurich. Like the location of a commodity broker, his location will usually depend on the proximity to his customers, on relative transaction and information costs, and on local laws, taxes and regulations. The size of the external market in a given currency relative to the internal market is basically a question of the comparative advantages of foreign and domestic financial centers for brokerage services.

Euromarkets are essentially banking markets. At least one of the parties in a Eurodollar transaction is always a bank. The external market in the currency of a given country, therefore, is best regarded as a part of its own financial intermediation system. Economically, London Eurodollar banks are an important part of the U.S. banking system, and a significant part of the Swiss money market happens to be located in Frankfurt.

In fact, in a majority of Eurodollar transactions both parties are banks. The Eurodollar market is largely an interbank money market. Its ultimate function is, of course, the channeling of funds from a nonbank lender to a nonbank borrower. However, between the ultimate lender and the ultimate

1. For an introduction, see Einzig and Quinn (1977). An up-to-date source of information is Dufey and Giddy (1978). Current developments are reported in the *Quarterly Bulletin* of the Bank of England, particularly March 1982, and in the quarterly releases "International Banking Developments" of the Bank for International Settlements.

borrower there is, on average, a chain of several banks. As a consequence, the volume of interbank "wholesale" transactions is considerably larger than the volume of "retail" transactions with nonbank customers, and the gross amount of Eurodollars is several times the amount held by nonbank agents.

Although some Eurobanks are specialized institutions,[2] most of them are departments of banks that also engage in other banking activities. Many important Eurodollar banks are foreign subsidiaries of American banks. For the purpose of the present chapter, however, it is convenient to use the fiction that all Eurobanks are specialized institutions.[3]

Eurodollar transactions do not involve the exchange of one currency against another. What is exchanged is U.S. money against a nonmonetary dollar asset or liability of a bank outside the United States. The same is true, *mutatis mutandis*, for other currencies. Conceptually, the Eurocurrency market is completely separate from the foreign-exchange market. In practice, Eurodollar operations are often handled by the same bank department as foreign-exchange operations.

The risks associated with the country in which the borrowing or lending bank is located are often called country risks. In domestic money markets, currency risk and country risk go together. An essential feature of the Eurocurrency system is that it permits the dissociation of currency risk and country risk. By holding dollars in England, a firm combines the currency risk on the dollars with the political risk with respect to England.

The paradigmatic Eurodollar asset is a large time deposit or a certificate of deposit with a specified maturity. The latter may be as short as overnight or as long as several years. While these funds may be highly liquid, they are not actual means of payments. There is no significant amount of checking deposits. Eurodollar loans, too, range over a broad spectrum of maturities, sometimes reaching ten years.

The fulcrum of the Eurodollar interest structure is the London Interbank Offered Rate (LIBOR), the rate at which major banks are prepared to offer funds for deposit in the London interbank market. This rate is determined in a highly competitive way. Nonbank borrowers pay more than LIBOR, the spread depending on their creditworthiness and the transaction costs they impose on the bank. These spreads are sometimes as low as 0.5 percent, but they may be as high as 3 percent. By the same token, nonbank depositors will often obtain less than LIBOR. Such spreads are familiar from domestic banking systems. The essential point is that in the Eurodollar market they are often smaller. This is the main (but not sole) explanation for the rapid growth of the Euromarket.

2. They are discussed in Davis (1980).
3. Aliber (1980) has emphasized the implications of the fact that most banks active in the Euromarket are subsidiaries of U.S. banks, considering their portfolio and reserves on an integrated basis.

In the early period of the Euromarket, interest rates were usually fixed for the full term of the loan or deposit. Since then, it has become increasingly common to use floating interest rates based on LIBOR. Under such a "roll-over" arrangement the interest rate on a long-term loan is adjusted every three or six months to stay by a fixed spread above the LIBOR. In many cases, the loan becomes due if at a rollover date the lender is unable to borrow the required amount. With such provisions, the concept of maturity becomes blurred: the legal commitment period dissociates itself from the economic maturity, and a long-term loan becomes virtually equivalent to a succession of short-term loans.

There is, of course, continuous arbitrage between Eurodollars and domestic dollar assets like time deposits, commercial paper, or certificates of deposit. As a consequence, interest rates in external money markets tend to correspond closely to the interest rates on similar funds in the domestic market for the same currency. In view of transaction costs and risk differentials, the correspondence is not perfect, though. Naturally, the less similar the assets, the larger the interest differential can be. Considerable differences may be introduced particularly by taxation and bank regulation.[4]

In view of their standardized form and low transaction costs, Eurodeposits are the preferred medium for covered interest arbitrage operations between different currencies. (This largely explains why they are handled by the banks' foreign-exchange departments.) Under the pressure of such operations, the deviations of the forward premia from interest parity in the Euromarket tend to be extremely small.

Eurobanks usually hold some U.S. dollars in the form of demand deposits with American banks. Their amount, however, is usually very small and seems to be determined by transaction motives rather than by reserve considerations. If a deposit is withdrawn, the bank relies on its ability to raise the amount by new borrowing. The relevant risks do not relate so much to illiquidity as to the interest rates that may have to be paid on such borrowing. The Euromarket is the paradigm of a nearly perfect money market.

9.2 Financial Intermediation in the Euromarket

The Eurodollar market has often been described as very complicated, defying the understanding of the uninitiated. As a matter of fact, it is probably the simplest large network of financial intermediation in existence. In particular, it is considerably simpler than most national credit systems. It is also highly efficient. What puzzled or even mystified some observers was exactly the absence of those complications and inefficiencies they were accustomed to find in national credit systems.

---

4. The relationship between interest rates on Eurodollars and domestic assets is analyzed in Johnston (1979) and in Giddy, Dufey, and Min (1979).

The relative simplicity and efficiency of the Euromarket is largely due to three characteristics:

1. The credit instruments are highly standardized, mostly consisting of large time deposits. In addition, the significance of maturity differences is reduced by the rollover arrangements, and the differences between creditors are reduced by the fact that most of them are large corporations or government agencies.

2. The market is relatively free from interest ceilings, reserve requirements, special taxes, and other forms of government regulation.

3. The market is highly competitive and relatively perfect in the sense that even large additional demands can be met at interest rates close to the current market rate.

For the purpose of this section these characteristics are idealized by the triple assumption that (1) there is only one standard deposit of given maturity, (2) there is no government intervention, and (3) everybody can borrow or lend any amount at the going market rate, plus or minus the relevant transaction costs. These assumptions exclude important aspects of the Eurodollar market. In particular, they exclude the problem of liquidity creation, which is the subject of section 9.3. They help, however, to obtain a clear picture of the economic function of the Euromarket and of the factors behind its phenomenal growth.

I first consider the world market for dollar funds in the absence of financial intermediation.[5] This market consists of a large number of firms, scattered all over the globe. Each firm is assumed to act as a price taker; it may be imagined that each is representative of a group of identical firms in pure competition. The behavior of each firm can be characterized by a schedule indicating desired borrowing or desired lending as a function of the relevant interest rate. It is natural to postulate that with a rising interest rate desired borrowing declines and desired lending increases. The absence of financial intermediation means, furthermore, that there is no interest rate at which a firm both borrows and lends. However, there will often be a range of interest rates at which it neither borrows nor lends.

In evaluating the relevant interest rate, a firm has to consider its own internal transaction costs on borrowing and lending. For the purpose of the present discussion, transaction costs should be interpreted in a wide sense, including costs of information, communication, and risk. The net borrowing rates are the market rates plus internal transaction costs; the net lending rates are the market rates minus internal transaction costs. The transaction costs of a given firm are generally different for different market partners. As a consequence, there is potentially a separate loan market for every pair of repre-

5. The following discussion is largely based on Niehans and Hewson (1976, sec. III.2), but the underlying model is more general.

sentative firms, each with its own interest rate. Many of these potential markets will usually be inactive, however.

If an auctioneer announces a market rate of interest for every potential market, a firm can calculate its net borrowing rates by adding to the market rates the respective transaction costs. Since the firm will borrow only from the cheapest source, the relevant net borrowing rate is the lowest of the net borrowing rates. If the relevant net borrowing rate applies to several lenders, the firm is indifferent to how its total borrowing is divided up among them.

Similarly, the firm can calculate its net lending rates by subtracting from the announced market rates the respective transaction costs. Since the firm will lend only in the most lucrative market, the relevant net lending rate is the highest of the net lending rates. Again the firm may be indifferent among several borrowers. It is evident that the relevant net lending rate cannot be higher than the relevant net borrowing rate; if it were, there would be room for profitable intermediation.

The relevant net borrowing and lending rates, juxtaposed to the firm's borrowing/lending schedule, reveal the desired borrowing or lending and the desired partner (or, in the case of indifference, partners). The auctioneer then compares desired borrowing with desired lending between any two firms. Whenever borrowing exceeds lending, the announced market rate is raised, and vice versa. Equilibrium is reached when borrowing matches lending (possibly at zero) in every market. It is worth repeating that in a world with transaction costs there is generally no "world interest rate."

It may help to illustrate this argument graphically. In figure 9.2.1 the dashed curve represents A's borrowing or lending as a function of the relevant net interest rate. The B curve represents lending to, and borrowing from, firm B. The lending branch is shifted upward from the dashed curve by the amount of A's transaction costs on loans from A to B. The borrowing branch is shifted downward by the amount of A's transaction costs on loans from B to A. The C curve contains the same information for dealings with C.

Market equilibrium is illustrated in figure 9.2.2. As the graph is drawn, A is lending to C at interest rate i_{AC} and B is lending to C at interest rate i_{BC}. Interest rate i_{BC} must exceed i_{AC} by the same amount as C's transaction costs on borrowings from A exceed those on borrowings from B. If C's transaction costs are added to the respective market rate, we obtain C's net rate. Equilibrium requires that the sum of A's lending at i_{AC} and of B's lending at i_{BC} be equal to C's borrowing at the corresponding net rate.

So far, firms have been lending directly to firms. I now introduce financial intermediaries, called banks. It is assumed that they are pure intermediaries in the sense that their lending equals their borrowing. The absolute level of interest rates is immaterial to banks. What matters to them is the margins between borrowing and lending rates. We may assume that each bank has a basic margin reflecting general costs. In addition it has transaction costs de-

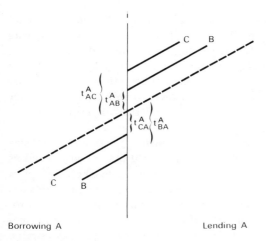

FIGURE 9.2.1
Eurodollar Borrowing and Lending

pending on the borrower or lender in question. If firm A lends directly to firm C, the relevant transaction costs are those discussed in the preceding paragraphs. If A lends to C through a bank, these costs are replaced by the transaction costs of A's lending to the bank, the transaction costs of C's borrowing from the bank, and the bank's own internal costs. The important point is that in lending to a bank, A usually incurs lower transaction costs than in lending directly to C. The same is true for C's borrowing. The combined savings are

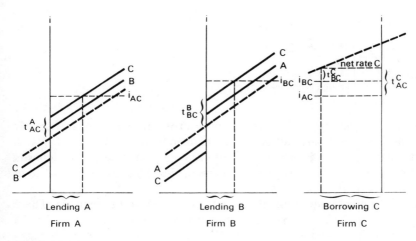

FIGURE 9.2.2
Market Equilibrium

often higher than the bank's own costs. If this is so, it is efficient to channel lending through the bank. As for different pairs of firms, transaction costs will generally be different for different pairings of a firm and a bank. As a result, there is usually room for several banks, and possibly a large number of them, each having a comparative advantage in dealing with particular firms. At the same time, it is evident that a bank attracts more business the lower its transaction costs, both those it incurs itself and those it imposes on its customers.

In the light of this general discussion I now consider the function and size of the Eurodollar market. For this purpose, the world may be visualized as consisting of the U.S. money market and the Eurodollar market. For given borrowing/lending schedules of firms, the division between these markets depends on the relative transaction costs of banks. If transaction costs of Eurobanks are very high while transaction costs of U.S. banks are low, all intermediation is provided by U.S. banks; the Euromarket is deserted. This extreme case is depicted in figure 9.2.3. This was broadly the picture before the end of the 1950s.

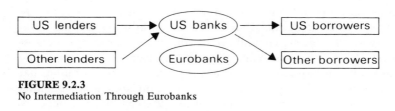

FIGURE 9.2.3
No Intermediation Through Eurobanks

FIGURE 9.2.4
All Intermediation Through Eurobanks

If, on the other hand, the transaction costs of Eurobanks are sufficiently below those of U.S. banks, all borrowing and lending, even by U.S. firms, is done through Eurobanks. The U.S. banks are reduced to accepting deposits from Eurobanks and holding government securities. This case is illustrated in figure 9.2.4.

Under present conditions, these extremes are clearly unrealistic. There will always be some U.S. borrowers and lenders for which some U.S. banks have a comparative advantage. Usually there will even be some other borrowers or lenders for which this is true. There will also be firms, both U.S. and foreign, for which Eurobanks have a comparative advantage. One of the main reasons is that close contact between a firm and its bank often lowers transaction costs. Under these circumstances, the banking business of both U.S. and other firms, taken as a whole, will generally be divided between U.S. banks and Eurobanks. This is illustrated in figure 9.2.5.

The size of the Euromarket relative to the U.S. banking market may be expected to be higher, *ceteris paribus*,

1. the lower the transaction costs of Eurobanks relative to those of U.S. banks;

2. the lower the transaction costs of firms in dealing with Eurobanks relative to those incurred in dealing with U.S. banks;

3. the larger the proportion of ultimate borrowing and lending that originates with non-U.S. firms.

Perhaps the last point requires a word of explanation. It may be assumed that U.S. banks often have a comparative advantage for U.S. firms, whereas non-U.S. banks have an advantage for non-U.S. firms. As a consequence, the Eurodollar market tends to expand if the dollar lending and borrowing of non-U.S. firms expand. An increasing role of the dollar in international transactions thus tends to enhance the position of the Euromarket relative to the U.S. money market.

It should be clear from this discussion that one should not expect any specific relationship between the size of the Eurodollar market and either the balance of payments or the foreign asset position of the United States. First, U.S. foreign liabilities are not necessarily denominated in dollars. More importantly, balance-of-payments deficits are not necessarily paid for in liquid funds but may have their counterpart in, say, foreign direct investments in the United States or foreign purchases of U.S. stocks. Most importantly, there is no particular relationship between the size of the Euromarket and *net* foreign dollar holdings. The Euromarket consists of both dollar lending and dollar borrowing. In the case of U.S. deficits, foreign dollar lending may increase relative to borrowing. The reverse may be true in the case of U.S. surpluses. It is not clear what this should have to do with the gross flow of dollars through European banks.

The preceding discussion ignored the fact that the Eurodollar market is

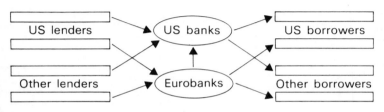

FIGURE 9.2.5
Some Intermediation Through Eurobanks

primarily an interbank market in which "wholesale" banks intermediate between "retail" banks. The latter, sometimes called "peripheral" banks, collect deposits from, and make loans to, nonbank firms. The wholesale banks, sometimes called "center" banks, besides doing their own retail business, channel the funds from peripheral banks with net nonbank deposits to those with net nonbank loans. In the context of the Euromarket, U.S. banks belong to the periphery; they are sometimes net lenders to the center while at other times they are net borrowers. This pattern, illustrated in figure 9.2.6, is basically due to the fact that the transaction costs between peripheral banks, say in Latin America or Southeast Asia, are often higher when they deal with each other directly than when they conduct their business indirectly through the center. This is particularly true in view of the fluctuations in ultimate lending and borrowing. While some areas are typically net lenders and others are usually net borrowers, it is characteristic of the Euromarket that the direction of the flows is subject to marked and rapid changes. The high ability of the market to accommodate such changes without large variations in interest rates was vividly illustrated during the various "oil shocks" and sometimes surprised even the experts.[6]

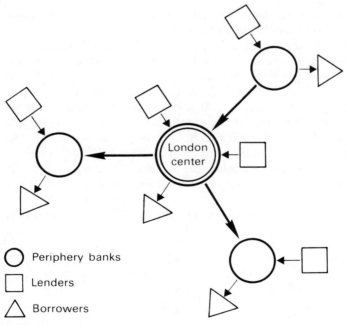

FIGURE 9.2.6
Center and Periphery

6. This is the grain of truth in Heller's phrase (1979) that the size of the Euromarket is "demand-determined."

In the preceding discussion, the factors explaining the existence and the size of the Euromarket were all subsumed under the very general and abstract heading of transaction costs. I shall now be more concrete by listing several important sources of transaction-cost differentials.

1. *Reserve requirements* act like a tax on bank borrowing, thus widening the required margin between borrowing and lending rates. The dollar money market reacted to this tax by partial emigration to Europe.

2. *Interest ceilings* may prevent banks from paying competitive deposit rates, again widening the interest margin. In the United States, regulation Q became one of the main forces behind the development of the Euromarket, particularly in its early phases.

3. *Monopolistic practices* in national banking systems may have a similar effect. In Switzerland, for example, interest rates on many classes of deposits are kept low by agreements among banks. This caused some funds to flow into the Eurofranc market, where rates might be much higher.

4. Money markets will tend to move to locations with *low taxes*. This is often quite easy because a "bank" is essentially a bookkeeping operation not strongly tied to particular locations. As a consequence, Caribbean islands, even though not financial centers in any real sense of the term, became important Eurodollar centers.

5. In comparing the interest rates on U.S. deposits and Eurodeposits, a firm may also consider *political risks*. Such risks include the danger of the blocking, attachment, or expropriation of assets in the case of war or economic warfare. Historically, the Eurodollar market owed some of its early attraction to the efforts of Soviet banks to protect their dollar holdings against cold war risks. This is a particularly clear illustration of the separation of political risk from currency risk.

6. *Restrictions on international capital movements* may create incentives for the money market to move abroad. Thus the Swiss restrictions on capital inflows around the middle of the 1970s tended to divert foreign deposits to the Eurofranc market. Similarly, the earlier U.S. attempt to restrict loans to foreigners under the Voluntary Foreign Credit Restraint Program helped to divert dollar lending to London.

7. Important cost differentials may simply be due to *location*. If a California firm borrows from a California bank, the transaction costs on both sides will often be smaller than if it borrows from a Swiss bank, not only because of lower communications costs but also because of easier risk evaluation, long-established relationships, and lower legal costs. Similarly, the transaction costs for a Swiss dollar deposit will often be lower in Zurich than in San Francisco. In view of this proximity factor, some part of the Eurodollar market would probably survive even if the aforementioned factors ceased to be relevant.

8. Finally, potential sources of transaction-cost differentials are, of

course, *differences in bank efficiency*. The higher the efficiency of London banks relative to U.S. banks, the larger, *ceteris paribus*, the Eurodollar market. It is not clear, however, that this factor has actually been of major importance in the development of the Euromarket.

This enumeration of factors is meant to be illustrative rather than exhaustive. It suggests that the Euromarket is to a large extent the result of government regulation. If national money markets are discriminated against by government regulation, external money markets tend to take their place. To some extent, the development of the Eurocurrency market is also the result of progress in banking technology, which has made it increasingly advantageous to take the dollar bank to the international customer instead of bringing the international customer to the U.S. bank. The next stage in this process now seems to be the emergence of multinational banking, where the same bank offers its intermediary services in many countries and in many currencies.

9.3 Liquidity Creation in the Euromarket

In the early 1970s, the breathtaking growth and the already amazing size of the Eurodollar market were puzzling to many observers. Enormous amounts of dollars seemed to be "sloshing around" in the market. Where did they come from? What were their effects? Would they create the danger of a collapse? Would they fuel inflation?

In answering these questions, economists tended to do what they usually do in such situations: they interpreted the Eurodollar market in terms of the models or paradigms they were familiar with. For almost half a century they had done their best to convince undergraduate students that most of the money is created by fractional-reserve banking as formalized in the Phillips multiplier. Naturally, they tried the same argument with Eurodollars. It was at once observed that the "reserves" of Eurobanks are very low. The inference was that the "Euromultiplier" must be extremely high (Friedman 1969). It was also noticed, however, that only a small fraction of new Euroloans is likely to remain in the Euromarket; the "redeposit ratio" seemed to be low. This was enough to reduce the apparent multiplier to quite moderate levels (Klopstock 1968). It was further recognized that the Eurodollar market should not be considered in isolation but as a segment of the whole dollar banking system. From this perspective, Eurodollar banks, since they hold their "reserves" not in the form of Federal Reserve deposits but of correspondent bank deposits, seemed analogous to nonbank financial intermediaries in the United States.[7]

7. For a detailed analysis of the Eurodollar multiplier in a three-stage banking system, see Willms (1976).

This leads to a model of the following sort. The money supply consists of currency, U.S. deposits, and Eurodeposits:

$$M = C + D + E. \tag{9.3.1}$$

The demand for U.S. deposits is a linear function of the total money supply:

$$D = mM + \mu. \tag{9.3.2}$$

The same is true for Eurodollars:

$$E = eM + \epsilon. \tag{9.3.3}$$

Eurobanks hold a fraction r_E of their deposits as reserves with U.S. banks:

$$R_E = r_E E. \tag{9.3.4}$$

U.S. banks, in turn, hold a fraction r_D of their total deposits as reserves with the Federal Reserve:

$$R_D = r_D(D + R_E). \tag{9.3.5}$$

The Federal Reserve determines the monetary base, consisting of currency and bank reserves:

$$C + R_D = B. \tag{9.3.6}$$

By routine steps this model can be used to determine various multipliers. A shift in deposit demand from U.S. dollars to Eurodollars can be expressed by assuming $d\epsilon = -d\mu > 0$, while $dB = 0$. The effect on the size of the Eurodollar market is

$$\frac{dE}{d\epsilon} = \frac{1}{1 + \dfrac{er_D(1 - r_E)}{(e + m)(1 - r_D) - 1}}. \tag{9.3.7}$$

Since $(e + m)(1 - r_D) < 1$, this multiplier exceeds one. The Euromarket seems to expand by more than one dollar for every dollar shifted into it. If currency is disregarded, $e + m = 1$. In this case the demand-shift multiplier simplifies to the familiar form

$$\frac{dE}{d\epsilon} = \frac{1}{1 - e(1 - r_E)}. \tag{9.3.8}$$

It is higher for a high share of Eurodeposits and a low reserve ratio of Eurobanks, but with realistic parameters it will be only slightly higher than one.

The effect of a shift into Eurodollars on the total money supply is

$$\frac{dM}{d\epsilon} = \frac{r_D(1 - r_E)}{1 - (1 - r_D)m - (1 - r_D r_E)e}. \tag{9.3.9}$$

There is clearly an expansion. It would be wrong to say that this is due to the relatively low reserve ratio of Eurobanks; there would be an expansion even with $r_E = r_D$. The crucial aspect is that Eurobanks hold their reserves not with the Federal Reserve but with a U.S. bank and thus do not absorb base money.

From the same model we can calculate the effect of a given change in the monetary base on the total money supply. This base multiplier, again disregarding currency, is

$$\frac{dM}{dB} = \frac{1}{r_D[1 - e(1 - r_E)]}. \tag{9.3.10}$$

In the absence of Eurodollars, the corresponding multiplier is $1/r_D$. It follows that the presence of the Eurodollar market raises the value of the base multiplier.[8]

Multiplier models of this sort can be extended and refined in various directions, particularly by considering a larger variety of deposits with different reserve requirements. Their characteristic feature is that behavior is described by fixed coefficients, independent of market conditions. The next phase in paradigm assimilation was the interpretation of the Euromarket in terms of the general-equilibrium, or "Yale," approach, which assigns a crucial role to the interest mechanism. It was shown early (Niehans 1971) that this may transform the demand-shift multiplier into a divisor. The basic reason is easily understood. Eurodollars and U.S. dollars are close substitutes, like butter and margarine. Suppose demand shifts from butter to margarine. This raises the price of margarine relative to the price of butter, which causes some consumers, who at the old prices would have eaten margarine, to switch to butter. The net shift to margarine consumption, therefore, is smaller than the spontaneous demand shift. Similarly, a demand shift into the Euromarket, by lowering Eurodollar rates relative to U.S. interest rates, produces some reverse shift into U.S. dollars. As a consequence, the multiplier is likely to be smaller than one.[9]

Eurodollars have so far been treated as if they were money. In fact, except for insignificant amounts, they are not. Even in the case of short-term deposits they cannot be used as means of payment, but have to be converted into a checking deposit with a U.S. bank before a payment can be made. Therefore, if the question concerns the creation of money in the sense of M_1, the answer for the Eurodollar market is clearly negative. To the extent that Eurodollar banks hold demand deposits with their U.S. correspondent banks, the Eurodollar market actually reduces the money supply to the non-bank sector. There is no compelling reason why this should remain so forever. It is quite conceivable that the development of international banking will lead to the widespread use of external checking accounts. At the present time, this stage has not been reached. It follows that the preceding discussion of liquid-

---

8. For a recent survey of Eurodollar multipliers, see Swoboda (1980).
9. A detailed analysis is given in Niehans and Hewson (1976, sec. I.2).

ity creation in the Eurodollar market is meaningful only for a concept of liquid assets that includes a considerable amount of interest-bearing money substitutes. The conclusion from this discussion can so far be summarized by the statement that the Eurodollar market may be able to create some additional liquidity, but, at most, in quite moderate amounts.

The most basic problem, however, still remains to be considered. So far, the supply of liquidity to nonbank firms has been measured by aggregating the liquid funds on the asset side of their balance sheets (or on the liability side of the bank balance sheets). This may be called a concept of gross liquidity. In general, liquid funds also appear on the liability side of the firms' (or on the asset side of the banks') balance sheets. Thus a multinational firm may obtain a two-day dollar loan from a Eurobank. It is evident that the behavior of this firm depends not only on its liquid assets but also on its liquid liabilities.

Without doing violence to reality it may be postulated that the relevant magnitude for the firms' behavior is net liquidity, obtained by subtracting the liquid liabilities from liquid assets. Suppose firms, without using intermediaries, exchange commercial paper of the same maturity and quality among each other. Their gross liquidity clearly increases, but their net liquidity remains unchanged. The above postulate implies that such an experiment, no matter what its scale, does not lead to inflation. I believe no economist would argue that it does. Passing a dollar bill around in a circle in exchange for IOUs does not produce inflation; though it increases gross liquidity, it does not create net liquidity.

In the multiplier models it is implicitly assumed that the monetary liabilities of the banks have their counterpart in nonmonetary assets. To the extent that this is true, the gross liquidity of firms may be reasonably close to their net liquidity. In this case, the multiplier approach is a valid idealization of reality. For the U.S. banking system, this has in the past been the relevant case, at least as a first approximation. However, to the extent that the monetary liabilities of banks are matched by monetary assets, the multiplier is entirely misleading; it may easily give the impression of monetary expansion or contraction where none has taken place. This case seems to be the relevant first approximation for the Eurodollar market.[10]

The Euromoney market is essentially a market for time deposits. Uncertainty about withdrawals, which since Edgeworth (1888) plays a crucial role in domestic banking theory, is relatively unimportant. Whatever funds may be required can be borrowed at close to the going market rate in a near-perfect market. Surplus funds can be invested in a similar way. Under these conditions, the primary concern of the bank, besides default risk, is not liquidity,

---

10. The same problem arises if the money supply is measured by a wide aggregate including large components of interest-bearing assets. To the extent that these assets have a counterpart in liquid liabilities, the aggregate may give a misleading picture of liquidity in the relevant net sense. By including Eurodeposits in a monetary aggregate, the problem is further aggravated.

but rather the interest rates at which it will be able to borrow and lend in the future. If long-term rates are high relative to short-term rates and uncertainty about interest rates is small, the bank will tend to finance longer-term loans with shorter-term deposits. If, with low uncertainty, long-term rates are low relative to short-term rates, the bank will tend to finance shorter-term loans with longer-term deposits. If the uncertainty about future interest rates is high compared with any difference between short and long rates, the bank will strive for a portfolio with closely matched maturities.[11] It should be noted that for the purpose of this calculus the rollover period is more relevant than the commitment period. A five-year loan with a three-month rollover is more like a succession of three-month loans than a five-year loan.

By and large, this calculus tends to result in a relatively close matching of the liquidity of assets and liabilities in the Eurodollar market. The "moneyness" of bank assets is not much higher, and sometimes even lower, than the "moneyness" of bank liabilities. It is true that in the course of the last two decades the maturities of Euroloans have tended to lengthen,[12] but the effect of this development on the liquidity of bank assets has been offset, to a large extent, by the rollover practice. It can hardly be doubted that for a given amount of gross liquidity Eurobanks supply relatively little net liquidity, certainly much less than most domestic banking systems. As a first approximation, it seems legitimate to assume that they supply no net liquidity at all, the "moneyness" of their assets being the same as that of their liabilities.[13] In this case, Eurobanks are pure distributors of liquid assets. The more efficient they are in this function, the larger will be the gross amount of their liquid liabilities. No matter how large their liabilities, however, the amount of net liquidity creation is zero. While this simplified picture certainly does not convey the whole truth, it is not too far away from it. It makes clear that multiplier models and even general-equilibrium models are likely to give misleading answers about liquidity creation in the Eurocurrency market.

9.4 Euromarkets and Economic Policy

Before the development of large external money markets, banking in a given currency was regarded as an immobile activity, a natural monopoly of the country issuing that currency. There was little international competition for banking business in a given currency. Government regulation of banking was hardly restrained by the fear that business might be driven elsewhere. The rapid expansion of external money markets made this attitude unten-

---

11. This calculus is worked out in the appendix to Niehans and Hewson (1976).
12. This has been noted by Heinevetter (1979).
13. This is consistent with the observation that Eurobanks hold no reserves in the sense in which this term is used in the United States; their deposits with correspondent banks, as noted in section 9.1, have largely the character of transactions balances.

able. The international competition for banking business in the domestic currency was seen to require a reexamination of inherited concepts of monetary and banking policy. Euromarkets thus became a policy problem. This problem has many aspects, several of them controversial. Some of the more important aspects will be briefly examined in this section.

The most basic consideration relates to the *allocation of resources*. External money markets owe their expansion to the fact that they operate with smaller transaction costs than the respective domestic markets, performing their intermediary function at a smaller margin between borrowing and lending rates. The result is an improvement in the allocation of resources. A given amount of intermediation can be performed at lower cost. Banking may, of course, absorb more resources overall, but in this case the amount of intermediation increases in an even higher proportion. This basic effect is clearly beneficial. On the whole, Euromarkets are a particularly efficient sector of the banking industry, and their expansion has contributed to the efficiency of the economy.

Another basic aspect concerns *risk*. Euroloans are, of course, subject to default risk, against which the bank holds equity capital. If this risk is misjudged, the bank's stockholders will suffer losses. Default risk may well be higher for loans to foreign governments than for private domestic loans, because there is usually no collateral security and no bankruptcy court to hand over the assets of the defaulting debtor to the creditors. In fact, the only effective incentive for the debtor to fulfill his obligations may be the hope of obtaining still higher loans in the future. Once this hope, in view of excessive debt growth in the past, has disappeared, the temptation to default may be almost irresistible. This means that the growth of debt should be geared to the economic growth of the debtor; if this requirement is violated there might well be a "debt crisis." There may also be an externality problem inasmuch as individual banks, when extending a loan, probably give little consideration to the additional risk this loan imposes on other creditors. The result would be "congestion" in the international loan market. Furthermore, since a lending bank may be separated from the ultimate borrower by several layers of intermediaries, it may often find it difficult to assess its own risk. For such reasons, competition in the international loan market may have to be supplemented by certain elements of coordination, which have yet to be developed. However, these problems, serious as they may be, are not specific to the Euromarket, and there is no reason to believe that they would be significantly lessened if each bank made international loans in its domestic currency only.

Eurodeposits, on the other hand, raise the question of liquidity risk and thus of liquidity requirements for the protection of depositors. Eurobanks tend to lend virtually every dollar the moment it is deposited, thereby minimizing their cash balances. Because of this observation, the liquidity risk has sometimes been regarded as alarmingly high. In fact, it is probably lower than in domestic banking. Since the typical Eurodeposit is for a definite maturity, there is little withdrawal risk. The Eurobank is thus in a position to match the maturities of deposits with the maturities of loans and typically takes great care in doing so. In addition, the large size and near-perfection of the market enable a bank to borrow any required funds at close to market rates. This is consistent with the historical experience that the Eurodollar market easily survived situations which seemingly competent observers had forecast to become serious crises.

It is nevertheless conceivable that a liquidity crisis may originate in the external market. If such a crisis develops in the domestic market, it is regarded as a basic function of the central bank to counteract it by stepping in as a lender of last resort. The consequences of such a crisis for the U.S. economy are likely to be the same if it originates in London as if it originates in New York. It follows that the responsibility of the central bank for countermeasures should be similar in the two cases. This argument is entirely in terms of the general economic effects of a liquidity contraction in the banking system. Since participants in the Euromarket are large firms, who presumably understand the risks involved, there is little basis for the protection of individual depositors.

It has often been alleged that the Eurodollar market, by increasing the international mobility of capital, may give rise to undesirable *capital movements*. There seems to be little basis for this allegation. First, capital flows originate from differences in saving and investment between residents of different countries. It is not clear why the existence of external money markets should have a significant effect on such differences. Second, Euromarket operations as such do not consist in exchanges of one currency against another, but in exchanges of different assets denominated in the same currency. As a consequence, the Euromarket is not very important even for the currency composition of asset portfolios. While Eurofunds are often used in foreign-exchange operations, the same operations could have been undertaken, albeit somewhat less efficiently, in their absence. Third, as pointed out in section 9.2, there is no particular relationship between the growth of Eurodollar deposits and the U.S. balance of payments. The size of the Eurodollar market depends on the extent to which both dollar borrowing and dollar lending take place abroad rather than in the United States. It is not clear how this, in turn, depends on the net foreign assets position of the United States. On the other hand, a shift from the U.S. money market to the Eurodollar market, no matter how large, does not constitute a capital outflow; the net foreign asset position of the United States remains unchanged.

One of the most widely debated questions concerns *international liquidity*. The rising tide of Eurodollars was interpreted as an "uncontrolled" and potentially malignant growth in international liquidity. There may be some grains of truth in this fear. To the extent that Eurobanks hold no reserves with the Federal Reserve, a shift of funds into the Euromarket may free some reserves for additional lending. This amount is minor, though. It is probably more important that the Eurodollar market has made time deposits a better substitute for demand deposits, thus reducing the demand for (or increasing the velocity of) the latter. This is yet another phase in the continuing progress of financial technology.

These grains of truth, however, are few and small. For the most part, the fear about international liquidity is unfounded. To begin with, the transition to floating rates made the concept of "international liquidity" as obsolete as the concept of "world inflation." There are now only national money supplies and national inflation rates. More importantly, the expansion of the Eurodollar market, as explained in the preceding section, does not imply an increase in dollar liquidity. This is true for two reasons. First, to the extent that Eurodollars expanded at the expense of U.S. dollars, there was no overall increase in dollar borrowing and lending. Second, since Eurodeposits are closely matched by Euroloans with largely similar economic characteristics, the gross expansion of Eurodeposits is not associated with a comparable expansion in net liquidity. Of course, any shift in asset demand from demand deposits to time deposits has, in principle, an expansionary effect. Thus if a central bank shifts its dollar reserves from demand deposits to Eurodollars, the effect is similar to that of an open-market purchase by the Federal Reserve. However, this is not peculiar to the Euromarket, and central banks are not likely to hold large demand deposits.

The real policy problems are at a different level. They generally concern the *efficacy of national banking regulation and monetary policy*. It is convenient to distinguish two types of policy measures. In one case, the central bank acts like any other agent, buying or selling assets in the market. Open market operations are the prime example, but the announcement of an interest rate at which the central bank is willing to discount in unlimited amounts also belongs to this category. In the other case, the authorities impose regulating constraints on banks and possibly other agents. Reserve requirements, interest ceilings, taxes, credit allocation schemes, and restrictions on foreign borrowing or lending serve as examples.

The efficacy of market actions is not impaired by Eurocurrency markets. If the Federal Reserve System sells treasury bills in the open market, dollar liquidity contracts regardless of the existence of a Eurodollar market. There is no escape from market actions by moving funds from New York to London. The tightening of dollar liquidity will immediately be reflected in higher dollar interest rates in external markets as well as at home.

For regulatory constraints this is different. Governments have tended to leave the foreign-currency operations of banks operating within their borders quite free from regulatory constraints. By shifting funds into external markets, the constraints can thus be largely avoided; the efficacy of the constraints is correspondingly reduced. As was pointed out in section 9.2, this was, in fact, the principal force behind the expansion of external markets. By the same token, the international mobility of financial activities acts as a powerful brake against the imposition of new regulations and as a stimulus to the relaxation of old ones.

The policy conclusions from these considerations depend on one's views about financial regulation. Those who regard reserve requirements, interest ceilings, credit allocation schemes, or restrictions on bank activities as necessary for the health of the financial system will press for an extension of these constraints to the external markets. They will be joined by the domestic banks, who, though they may not be convinced of the wisdom of regulation, at least wish to be protected against the loss of business. The chances for international agreement on the regulation of external markets are slim, though. The host country will usually be only too happy to benefit from another country's regulative efforts and refuse to kill the goose that lays the golden eggs. In addition, the nonbank firms have every reason to oppose measures that would prevent their escape to more efficient markets.

Those, on the other hand, who regard such regulative measures as largely obsolete and counterproductive will welcome the competition from external markets as an important contribution to greater efficiency. By and large, I am inclined to share this view. In particular, neither reserve requirements nor interest ceilings are necessary or even useful for an effective monetary policy. If competition from external markets hastens their demise, so much the better for the domestic economy. Exchanges of different financial assets at market rates are enough, under present circumstances, for an effective monetary policy, and they fully retain their effectiveness in the presence of Euromarkets.

CHAPTER 10

Determinants of
Capital Flows

Introduction

Capital flows, as the mirror image of current-account surpluses or deficits, play an essential role in the explanation of international monetary phenomena. It is important, therefore, to establish as definitely as possible by what factors they are determined. The literature on this question is extensive; there seems to be little that has not been explored. Nevertheless, it is fair to say that even some of the most elementary aspects are far from clear. Such aspects are the subject of this chapter, which continues the analysis of net capital flows in chapter 6, but now with diversified financial assets as discussed in chapters 7 through 9.

Capital flows are regarded as temporary stock adjustment phenomena. Factors like economic growth, which might give rise to permanent capital flows, are not taken into account. In principle, explanatory variables like interest rates, other asset yields, and incomes are used to explain the level of international asset stocks. Capital flows, reflecting changes in stocks, are thus explained by changes in the explanatory variables. This is consistent with the approach Branson (1968, 1970), building on Meade (1951, pp. 103 f.), helped to initiate and later called the "new view" of capital movements. It is in contrast to the flow approach, where capital flows are explained by the levels of the explanatory variables.

The adjustment of asset stocks usually takes time. During this time, given levels of yields and incomes will indeed be associated with capital flows. This results in capital-flow functions that look formally similar to those used in the flow approach. The capital-flow functions of the present chapter must be assumed to be derived in this fashion. While valid in the short run, they cannot stay invariant in the course of time. In the long run, capital flows, like savings, vanish for any (constant) levels of the explanatory variables.

For the purpose of this chapter, the capital-flow function may be written

$$c = c(y_1, y_2, q_1, q_2, i, j, e). \qquad (10.0.1)$$

where the symbols have the following meanings:

c capital outflow
y_1 domestic income
y_2 foreign income
q_1 price of domestic capital goods
q_2 price of foreign capital goods
i yield on domestic securities
j yield on foreign securities
e exchange rate.

What can be said about the signs of the partial derivatives of the capital-flow function? Interest rates turn out to present the most difficult problems. In most macroeconomic models for open economies it is regarded as self-evident that lower interest rates produce a capital outflow. The typical reasoning behind this assumption was clearly stated by Meade (1951, p. 103): if interest rates in country A are lower than in country B, B's borrowers will have an incentive to borrow in A rather than in B and asset holders in A will shift their funds from A to B.

The following discussion will show that the traditional assumption is partly correct, but hard to substantiate, and partly false. The essential point is that a shift by asset holders in both countries from A securities to B securities does not, in itself, constitute an increase in A's wealth at the expense of B's wealth as required, at unchanged real capital, for a net capital flow from A to B. Suppose some agency, holding a large portfolio of both assets, is ready to exchange securities in a given ratio. Suppose further the agency now announces an increase in the number of B securities offered for each A security. According to Meade's argument, asset holders in both countries would turn in A securities and acquire B securities. However, net foreign assets of each country would remain unchanged. Regardless of the country in which the agency is located, the net change in private foreign assets would be exactly matched by the change in the agency's net foreign assets. Meade's argument, therefore, is inconclusive. Interest rates are a dubious determinant of international capital flows.

It has been customary to treat different types of capital flows in isolation. This has resulted in a separate literature on short-term capital, long-term capital, direct investments, and the like, in each case reaching far into the microeconomics of asset decisions.[1] In contrast, the present chapter, consis-

---

1. For surveys, including references to empirical work, see Spitäller (1971), Hodjera (1973), Bryant (1975), Lee (1977) and Agarwal (1980).

tent with the macroeconomic orientation of this book, considers capital movements as a whole. The emphasis is on the interaction of the separate components in determining the aggregate net capital flow.

The international asset position of two countries is first considered in the
context of the national wealth accounts. In the second section, the accumulation of each asset is related to yields, incomes, and the exchange rate. Sections 10.3 and 10.4 then develop the implications for aggregate capital flows.
The final section draws the corresponding implications for the special case of
perfect substitutability of capital goods.

10.1 Foreign Assets in the National Wealth Accounts

In chapter 7, the diversification of assets was discussed on the assumption that net foreign assets are zero. What mattered was the composition of
gross foreign assets. It was pointed out at the end of section 7.2 that pure
arbitrage is generally not enough to produce full equilibrium. As a consequence, arbitrage initiates an adjustment in net foreign assets of the kind
described in section 6.3. The discussion will now return to net foreign assets.
In contrast to chapter 6, however, assets are assumed to be heterogeneous and
thus diversified. In particular, the analysis will distinguish between real capital goods, bonds, and cash balances. For each of these assets it also makes a
difference whether they are domestic or foreign. As a consequence, arbitrage
will not, in general, lead to a complete equalization of yields.

The analysis of such problems has often been simplified by the assumption that some balance-sheet items are zero. An extreme example is the assumption that all international assets take the form of bonds and that foreigners hold no domestic bonds. It will turn out that such simplifications may
have far-reaching consequences for economic results. In particular, they may
convey the impression that the effect of interest rates on capital flows is more
clear-cut than it actually is. This effect will be discussed in section 10.3. The
present section provides the analytical background by considering foreign assets in the context of national wealth accounts.

The exposition is again restricted to two countries, with England and
Portugal identified, respectively, by subscripts 1 and 2. There are three assets, namely, cash balances M, bonds B, and real capital goods R. Bonds may
be regarded as representing all interest-bearing assets, whereas R, if held
abroad, stands for direct investments. The first subscript refers to the issuing
country while the second refers to the owner country. To give two examples,
M_{21} denotes escudos held in England and R_{21} denotes English direct investments in Portugal. Bonds are visualized as consols, paying one unit of the
debtor country's money per period. The English bond yield is i; the Portuguese yield is j. The exchange rate is assumed to be normalized at $e = 1$, and
the prices of capital goods are $q_1 = q_2 = 1$. Commodity prices are constant at
$p_1 = p_2 = 1$; the significance of price changes is not discussed in this chapter.

National wealth can be taken as the starting point. For England it is defined as

$$W_1 = R_{11} + R_{21} + B_{21}/j - B_{12}/i + M_{21} - M_{12}. \qquad (10.1.1)$$

National wealth is the sum of real capital goods owned by domestic residents, both at home and abroad, and the net amount of foreign financial assets, the latter being the difference between British-held Portuguese bonds and cash balances and Portuguese-held British bonds and cash balances. The corresponding expression for Portugal is

$$W_2 = R_{22} + R_{12} + B_{12}/i - B_{21}/j + M_{12} - M_{21}. \qquad (10.1.2)$$

Foreign wealth, taken in a gross sense, consists of the foreign components of total wealth. For England it is

$$F_1 = R_{21} + B_{21}/j + M_{21} = W_1 - R_{11} + B_{12}/i + M_{12}, \qquad (10.1.3)$$

and for Portugal it can be written

$$F_2 = R_{12} + B_{12}/i + M_{12} = W_2 - R_{22} + B_{21}/j + M_{21}. \qquad (10.1.4)$$

The net international asset position for England is the difference between F_1 and F_2,

$$A = R_{21} + B_{21}/j + M_{21} - R_{12} - B_{12}/i - M_{12}. \qquad (10.1.5)$$

Substituting for the first three terms from F_1, this is seen to be equivalent to

$$A_1 = W_1 - R_{11} + B_{12}/i + M_{12} - R_{12} - B_{12}/i - M_{12}$$
$$= W_1 - R_{11} - R_{12}. \qquad (10.1.6)$$

The net international asset position of England thus turns out to be equal to the difference between English national wealth and total real capital employed in the English economy. An analogous expression is obtained for Portugal by substituting in (10.1.5) for the second three terms from F_2:

$$A_2 = R_{21} + B_{21}/j + M_{21} - (W_2 - R_{22} + B_{21}/j + M_{21})$$
$$= -(W_2 - R_{22} - R_{21}). \qquad (10.1.7)$$

These expressions demonstrate that the net foreign asset position of a country depends on nothing but total national wealth and the total stock of real capital employed in the economy. Financial transactions have an effect on the net foreign asset position if, and only if, they influence these magnitudes. Equations (10.1.6) and (10.1.7) also make clear that the net asset position can be looked at from the side of either country with identical results.

So far, the discussion has been entirely in terms of stocks. It can easily be translated into flow terms. The increase in wealth at constant prices is defined as saving, the increase in real capital is investment, and the increase in net foreign assets is the capital outflow. We thus obtain the statement that the capital flow from England to Portugal is necessarily equal to (1) the excess of English saving over England's domestic investment and (2) the excess of Portugal's domestic investment over Portuguese saving. Even in the presence of a large number of financial assets, net international capital flows, just as described in chapter 6, reduce to a question of saving and investment.

The preceding analysis used the concept of total national wealth, which includes government wealth. This means that government debt, whether interest-bearing or not, is implicitly counted as a negative item. For the discussion of capital flows it is often more enlightening to base the analysis on private wealth. This is because it may be difficult to say anything definite about the effect of interest rates, exchange rates, or incomes on desired total wealth (or about the effect of a rising interest rate on saving) if one component of total wealth is government wealth.

English private wealth can be written as

$$V_1 = R_{11} + R_{21} + B_{11}/i + B_{21}/j + M_{11} + M_{21}. \tag{10.1.8}$$

It differs from W_1 by the amount of English government debt, $B_{11}/i + B_{12}/i + M_{11} + M_{12}$. The corresponding expression for Portugal is

$$V_2 = R_{22} + R_{12} + B_{22}/j + B_{12}/i + M_{22} + M_{12}. \tag{10.1.9}$$

In terms of private wealth, the gross foreign asset positions are

$$F_1 = R_{21} + B_{21}/j + M_{21} = V_1 - R_{11} - B_{11}/i - M_{11} \tag{10.1.10}$$

and

$$F_2 = R_{12} + B_{12}/i + M_{12} = V_2 - R_{22} - B_{22}/j - M_{22}. \tag{10.1.11}$$

The net foreign asset position thus turns out to be either

$$\begin{aligned} A_1 &= V_1 - R_{11} - B_{11}/i - M_{11} - R_{12} - B_{12}/i - M_{12} \\ &= V_1 - R_{11} - R_{12} - (B_{11}/i + B_{12}/i + M_{11} + M_{12}) \end{aligned} \tag{10.1.12}$$

or

$$\begin{aligned} A_2 &= R_{21} + B_{21}/j + M_{21} - (V_2 - R_{22} - B_{22}/j - M_{22}) \\ &= -[V_2 - R_{22} - R_{21} - (B_{22}/j + B_{21}/j + M_{22} + M_{21})]. \end{aligned} \tag{10.1.13}$$

If the net asset position is considered from the point of view of private wealth, financial assets are seen to contribute to the overall result along with total wealth and real capital. In particular, government debt appears on both the English and the Portuguese side of the balance sheet.

This discussion has been entirely in terms of accounting identities. While containing no causal propositions, these identities are nevertheless relevant for causal analysis inasmuch as they state certain logical requirements any causal proposition must satisfy. For example, the proposition that higher interest rates attract capital inflows cannot be true unless higher interest can be shown to increase domestic investment relative to saving. More generally, international financial transactions, no matter how large, do not involve net capital flows as long as national wealth and the stock of real capital goods remain unchanged. Basically, international capital movements, though influenced by financial factors, are not a financial phenomenon.

10.2 The Determinants of Asset Accumulation

In the preceding section, the net foreign asset position of a country was decomposed into different types of assets. Since capital flows are defined as the change in net foreign assets, they can be similarly decomposed into the accumulation or decumulation of individual assets under the influence of income, yields, and the exchange rate. These individual components are the subject of the present section.

For each asset, we can postulate a stock demand function

$$X^* = X(y_1, y_2, q_1, q_2, i, j, e), \tag{10.2.1}$$

where X stands for any of the assets considered in the preceding section. Determinants that do not appear in the demand function are assumed to be constant. The asterisk is meant to indicate that these demand functions relate to the steady state. Whenever the representative individual holds assets corresponding to these functions, he sees no reason either to accumulate or decumulate assets at the current income, yields, and exchange rate. The functions are, in general, not subject to a wealth constraint, since steady-state wealth is endogenously determined as the sum of desired assets.

The effects of income, yields, and the exchange rate on desired asset stocks are expressed by the partial derivatives of the above functions. Their postulated signs are given in table 10.2.1. The income effects in the first two rows reflect the assumption that an increase in English income has a positive effect on the desired quantity of each English-owned asset, but no effect on Portuguese asset demand, and vice versa. The remainder of the table expresses the assumption that all assets are gross substitutes. The higher the market value of real capital goods relative to their (given) production costs, the higher the demand for them, while the demand for financial assets is reduced.[2] A higher bond yield has a positive effect on the demand for bonds but a negative effect on real capital and cash balances.[3] A depreciation of ster-

2. If new capital goods could not be produced at unchanged cost, a higher market price of existing capital goods would, of course, reduce demand. This assumption will be used in chapter 11.

3. Branson noted an ambiguity in the effect of the U.S. interest rate on the volume of U.S. short-term liabilities to foreigners (1968, pp. 71, 16 f.). One might suspect that in the present context this should be reflected in an uncertain sign of $\partial B_{12}/\partial i$. This is not so, however. Branson's ambiguity relates to the change in U.S. short-term liabilities to foreigners that can be observed once the excess demand created by the increase in U.S. interest rates is eliminated by an appropriate adjustment in the spot exchange rate. The present analysis relates to the excess demand at unchanged exchange rates. It is clear from elementary price theory that the first is generally ambiguous even if the second has a definite sign.

ling, expressed by an increase in e, is assumed to have a positive effect on sterling assets and a negative effect on escudo assets. This assumption is largely based on speculative considerations; more will be said about it in section 10.4.

Capital flows occur because actual asset stocks differ from desired stocks. Without going into the optimizing calculus that may govern the stock adjustment, the investment in asset X may be thought to be determined by the accumulation function

$$x = \frac{dX}{dt} = \gamma(X^* - X),\tag{10.2.2}$$

where $\gamma > 0$ measures the adjustment speed. In a more general formulation, the accumulation of each asset would be influenced by the deviation of desired stocks from actual stocks for *every* asset, each with its own (positive or negative) adjustment speed. [4]

In these accumulation functions, X reflects the influence of current asset levels, the "wealth effects." While important during the adjustment process, their influence disappears in the steady state. This is as it should be, because current asset levels are indeed a constraint on the individual's behavior during transition, but in full equilibrium they can be made whatever the individual wants them to be under given market conditions.

The effect of, say, the interest rate i on the accumulation of X depends on the partial derivative of X^* with respect to i and on the adjustment speed:

$$x_i = \frac{d}{di}\left(\frac{dX}{dt}\right) = \gamma\,\frac{\partial X^*}{\partial i}.\tag{10.2.3}$$

Since $\gamma > 0$ for all assets, the signs in table 10.2.1 are also the signs of the partial derivatives of asset accumulation or asset flows.

The adjustment speeds reflect the various impediments that stand in the way of a prompt adjustment of asset stocks. These impediments include information lags, information costs, transaction costs, planning periods, con-

TABLE 10.2.1

Partial Derivatives of Asset Demand Functions

	R_{11}	R_{12}	R_{22}	R_{21}	B_{11}/i	B_{12}/i	B_{22}/j	B_{21}/j	M_{11}	M_{12}	M_{22}	M_{21}
y_1	+	0	0	+	+	0	0	+	+	0	0	+
y_2	0	+	+	0	0	+	+	0	0	+	+	0
q_1	+	+	−	−	−	−	−	−	−	−	−	−
q_2	−	−	+	+	−	−	−	−	−	−	−	−
i	−	−	−	−	+	+	−	−	−	−	−	−
j	−	−	−	−	−	−	+	+	−	−	−	−
e	+	+	−	−	+	+	−	−	+	+	−	−

4. For an example, see Niehans (1978).

struction periods, and the like. In general, different assets will adjust with different speeds. With present-day financial technology, adjustment speeds for foreign cash balances (M_{12}, M_{21}) and foreign and domestic interest-bearing assets $(B_{11}, B_{12}, B_{22}, B_{21})$ are likely to be high, perhaps virtually infinite. On the other hand, adjustment speeds for capital goods $(R_{11}, R_{12}, R_{22}, R_{21})$ are often very low. Modern technology does not seem to have increased them significantly. A casual comparison of the development of cities and transportation systems in the nineteenth century with that toward the end of the twentieth century suggests that they may actually have declined. Domestic cash balances, largely playing the role of a buffer stock, seem to have an intermediate position.

The overall mobility of international capital movements, as (10.1.6) and (10.1.7) show, depends on the adjustment speeds of total wealth and real capital goods. There is little reason to believe that these are higher today than in earlier centuries, and perhaps they are lower than in, say, the nineteenth century. As a consequence, the familiar notion of a high mobility of present-day capital flows, derived from the promptness of arbitrage, seems to have little foundation. Even instantaneous adjustment of certain financial assets would be perfectly consistent with slow adjustment in overall wealth and real capital stocks.

10.3 Income, Capital-Goods Prices, and Interest Rates

The concepts and assumptions introduced in the preceding sections will now be used to evaluate the effect of income, capital-goods prices, and interest rates on aggregate net capital flows.

Questions of this sort can be raised at two entirely different levels. Consider the domestic interest rate. At one level, the question then relates to the comparative statics of a macroeconomic model for an open economy in which the level of interest is an exogenous policy variable while the other variables, including capital flows, adjust endogenously. In this case, the interest sensitivity of capital flows is, in principle, the joint result of all behavior relationships in the model. This question will not be taken up in the present section. At a more modest level, the question relates to the capital flows wealth holders wish to carry out if interest rates change while all other determinants of capital flows remain constant. At this level, the question is concerned with the partial derivatives of a capital flow equation like (10.0.1), taken in isolation. This is the sense in which the question will be discussed here. This means that postulates derived from macroeconomic equilibrium cannot be used. Budget constraints, however, must be satisfied.

To simplify the exposition, it will be assumed that all adjustment speeds are equal. In this special case, the effects of, say, the domestic rate of interest on the accumulation of various assets are proportionate to its effects on the desired stocks. It is left to the reader to generalize to the case of different adjustment speeds.

Income effects can be determined from (10.1.5) and table 10.2.1. An increase in English income, y_1, raises the English demand for assets abroad, composed of R_{21}, B_{21}, and M_{21}, while the Portuguese demand for assets in England is not affected. It is clear, therefore, that the result is a capital export and thus $\partial c/\partial y_1 > 0$. By the same token, an increase in Portuguese income raises desired Portuguese assets abroad while foreign assets in Portugal are unchanged. The result is a capital inflow into England and thus $\partial c/\partial y_2 < 0$. These postulated signs conflict with H. G. Johnson's (1972b) argument, according to which an income expansion tends to produce a capital inflow. The conflict is more apparent than real, however, because Johnson had in mind the associated stimulation of investment, working through the q's, rather than income itself.

The effect of capital-goods prices is equally straightforward. According to (10.1.6), desired net foreign assets are the difference between desired wealth and real capital goods desired by both domestic and foreign holders. An increase in the market price of English capital goods, q_1, certainly raises the demand for English capital goods by more than it raises the desired wealth of English wealth owners. As a consequence, A_1 declines, indicating a capital inflow and thus $\partial c/\partial q_1 < 0$. Conversely, an increase in Portuguese capital-goods prices results in a capital outflow from England, as expressed by $\partial c/\partial q_2 > 0$. In fact, capital-goods prices, together with saving, must be regarded as the most basic determinant of international capital flows.

The effect of security yields is much less clear. It has often been regarded as a truism that an increase in the rate of interest tends to produce, *ceteris paribus*, a capital inflow. It has already been shown in chapter 6 that, in reality, capital flows cannot be said to be controlled by the market yields on financial assets. However, the model of chapter 6 was restricted to homogeneous assets. The question remains whether in the presence of diversified financial assets the familiar proposition is perhaps valid after all. As a matter of fact, it will turn out that, while not generally correct, it may be correct under certain conditions.

Equations (10.1.6) and (10.1.7) show that an increase in i can produce capital flows only inasmuch as it influences desired wealth and/or the demand for real capital. In particular, an increase in i results in a capital inflow if, and only if, it (1) produces an excess of investment over saving in England and (2) simultaneously produces an excess of saving over investment in Portugal. While the latter seems likely, the former looks quite implausible. Surely higher English interest rates tend to discourage investment in the English economy, and it is not evident that saving, if reduced at all, is reduced even more. The effect of interest rates on capital flows seems unclear indeed, and the obvious effect on bond demand does not seem to matter for the overall result.

In part, this lack of clarity arises from the use of total concepts. In total wealth, increases in government debt enter with a negative sign. As a consequence, it is difficult to relate total wealth to the behavior functions of asset holders. A clearer picture can be made to emerge by using private wealth. In this perspective, the question relates to the effect of interest rates on private asset demand. This approach will be followed here.

For the purpose of this discussion, the partial derivative of R_{11}/i with respect to i is denoted by $\partial(R_{11}/i)/\partial i = r_{11}$. The analogous notation is used for the other assets. From (10.1.5) we obtain

$$\partial A/\partial i = a = r_{21} + b_{21} + m_{21} - r_{12} - b_{12} - m_{12} \gtreqless 0. \qquad (10.3.1)$$

The signs of these coefficients appear in row 5 of table 10.2.1. Since the expression includes both negative and positive terms, it is not possible, at this point, to establish a definite sign. It is true that the domestic demand for foreign assets, represented by the first three terms, declines, while the foreign demand for domestic bonds increases. At the same time, however, foreign demand for domestic capital goods and cash balances declines, and it is conceivable that these terms dominate the others. As a consequence, there is no general reason to exclude the possibility that an increase in interest rates produces a capital outflow.

It may be argued, however, that this is a somewhat unlikely possibility. It requires that the negative cross effects of the domestic interest rate on the foreign demand for domestic cash balances and domestic capital goods, taken together, exceed their positive direct effect on domestic bonds. In symbols, it requires $|m_{12}| + |r_{12}| > b_{12}$. The contrary assumption is sufficient to assure that an increase in interest rates produces a capital inflow. The conventional result can also be assured by the assumption that all foreign assets have the form of bonds. In this case (10.3.1) reduces to $a = b_{21} - b_{12} < 0$. This special case has, explicitly or implicitly, often been the basis for the view that an increase in interest rates is certain to produce a capital inflow.

Fortunately, it is possible to eliminate the ambiguity even in the general case by considering the effect of the bond yield on desired private wealth. From (10.1.12) and (10.1.13) we obtain, respectively,

$$a_1 = s_1 - r_{11} - r_{12} - (b_{11} + b_{12} + m_{11} + m_{12}) \gtreqless 0, \qquad (10.3.2)$$

and

$$a_2 = -[s_2 - r_{22} - r_{21} - (b_{22} + b_{21} + m_{22} + m_{21})] < 0, \qquad (10.3.3)$$

where s_1 and s_2 represent, respectively, the effects of i on English and Portuguese wealth, namely,

$$s_1 = r_{11} + r_{21} + b_{11} + b_{21} + m_{11} + m_{21}, \qquad (10.3.4)$$

$$s_2 = r_{22} + r_{12} + b_{22} + b_{12} + m_{22} + m_{12}. \qquad (10.3.5)$$

It is plausible to assume that higher asset yields cause people, in the steady state, to hold higher wealth, whence $s_1 > 0$ and $s_2 > 0$. Given this assumption, a_2 is unambiguously negative. An increase in the yield on English bonds thus results, *ceteris paribus*, in a capital inflow. The traditional proposition is vindicated.

It should be noted that in the case of a change in the British bond yield, the direction of the resulting capital flow is derived from Portuguese saving together with the demand for Portuguese assets by both Portuguese and English owners. No definite sign can be established for a_1, which is the capital flow in terms of English saving and the demand for English assets. The only negative terms in this expression are those for the demand for British bonds; the other items are positive. In particular, the increase in British saving and the discouragement of investment in the British economy together with the decline in the demand for sterling balances all pull in the direction of a capital outflow. Of course, the sign of a_1 cannot, in fact, be different from that of a_2, both being alternative and equivalent expressions for a. The negative sign for a_2 just tells us that under the stated assumptions the increase in demand for British bonds necessarily dominates the remaining terms in the expression for a_1. The important point is that in the presence of foreign cash balances and direct investment, the usual assumption about the effect of interest rates on desired capital flows depends on the reaction of saving. No clear-cut proposition can be established if higher interest rates reduce the desired amount of wealth.

The interest effects on capital flows have often been considered on the assumption that there is no effect on saving and investment. To disregard saving effects is equivalent to imposing a wealth constraint. What is left is just a reshuffling of bonds and cash balances. In this case, the expressions for capital flows reduce to

$$a = b_{21} + m_{21} - b_{12} - m_{12} \gtreqless 0 \tag{10.3.6}$$

$$a_1 = -(b_{11} + b_{12} + m_{11} + m_{12}) \gtreqless 0 \tag{10.3.7}$$

$$a_2 = b_{22} + b_{21} + m_{22} + m_{21} < 0. \tag{10.3.8}$$

Even under these restrictive assumptions it is not possible to derive the direction of the interest-induced capital flows directly from (10.3.6), because it seems the Portuguese demand for British cash balances might well decline more than the Portuguese demand for British bonds increases and the British demand for Portuguese assets declines. In fact, this is impossible. This is again revealed by a_2, whose sign is still unambiguously negative. Only in the extreme case in which foreign assets are restricted to bonds can the direction of the capital flow be directly established from (10.3.6).

It has so far been assumed that all bonds are denominated in the currency of the debtor country. In reality, this is not necessarily so, since many international loans are denominated in the currency of the creditor country. This injects an element of uncertainty into the interest effects on capital flows. This is most clearly seen in the limiting case in which there are no international assets except creditor-denominated loans. In this case, an increase in the English interest rate clearly raises the English demand for Portuguese sterling bonds. At the same time, it lowers the Portuguese demand for English escudo bonds. The result is a capital outflow.

In general, there will be both debtor-denominated and creditor-denominated bonds. In this case it is not possible to establish general propositions about the effect of interest rates on capital flows. Consider the expression for a_2, which in the case of debtor-denominated bonds yielded an unambiguous sign. It now reads

$$
\begin{aligned}
a_2 = -[s_2 - r_{22} - r_{21} - (b_{22}^1 + b_{22}^2 + b_{21}^1 + b_{21}^2 \\
+ m_{22} + m_{21})] \gtreqless 0,
\end{aligned}
\tag{10.3.9}
$$

where the superscripts indicate the currency of denomination. For the debtor-denominated bonds the partial derivatives are those given in table 10.2.1, and thus $b_{22}^2 < 0$ and $b_{21}^2 < 0$. For the creditor-denominated bonds, however, we have $b_{22}^1 > 0$ and $b_{21}^1 > 0$. As a consequence, the sign of a_2 remains ambiguous, depending on the relative strength of the various effects.

This ambiguity of interest effects is more than a technical paradox. Interest rates relate to different assets, but capital flows relate to residents of different countries. We may be able to establish a more or less definite association between interest rates and capital flows, provided there is a definite relationship between assets and countries. While such an association often exists, there is no intrinsic reason why it should always exist. In principle, a country can issue any sort of assets. As a consequence, the effect of interest rates on aggregate capital flows, unlike the effect of income and capital-goods prices, must be regarded as fundamentally ambiguous.

10.4 Exchange Rates

The last question concerns the effect of a change in the exchange rate, *ceteris paribus*, on capital flows. It has different aspects. A depreciation of sterling results in a relative shrinking of the share of sterling funds in both Portuguese and English portfolios, while the share of escudo funds correspondingly expands. As a consequence, the given asset composition may no longer be optimal. Its modification will generally require capital flows. These are the wealth effects of exchange-rate changes. Other effects are due to exchange-rate changes expected in the future; they may be called speculative effects. The remaining effects, if any, are those that would arise even in the absence of wealth and speculative effects; they are here called relative price effects. These effects will now be taken up in reverse order.

To isolate the relative price effects, if any, it may be assumed that in the initial situation, by coincidence, there are no international assets. As a consequence, an exchange-rate change has no wealth effect. It is also assumed that the new exchange rate is expected to persist forever. As a consequence, there are no speculative effects either. The question is whether the shift in the relative price of foreign and domestic assets nevertheless causes the previous position to be non-optimal, thus requiring temporary capital flows. The answer is no. It is true that after a depreciation of sterling one pound buys a smaller amount of escudo bonds, but it is also true that an escudo's worth of interest payments converts into more sterling. The relative yields of foreign and domestic assets, as pointed out in section 7.3, remain the same. The change in relative asset prices as such does not produce capital flows.

To isolate speculative effects we continue to assume that initially there are no international assets and thus no wealth effects. We now assume, however, that any change in the current exchange rate is regarded as temporary, the level of expected future exchange rates remaining constant. In this case, any present depreciation automatically creates the expectation of a future appreciation. This raises the relative yield on sterling assets while the relative yield on escudo assets declines, thus causing both Portuguese and English wealth holders to increase sterling assets at the expense of escudo assets. This reasoning is reflected in the bottom row of table 10.2.1. These signs can be used to determine the change in net foreign assets from (10.1.5). The exchange-rate effect on the first three items, appearing with a positive sign, is negative, whereas the exchange-rate effect on the second three items, appearing with a negative sign, is positive. It follows that depreciation, *ceteris paribus*, produces a capital inflow, implying $\partial c/\partial e < 0$.

The preceding argument assumed that all bonds are debtor-denominated. Creditor-denominated bonds again inject an element of uncertainty. Net foreign assets can now be written

$$A = R_{21} + B^1_{21}/i + B^2_{21}/j + M_{21} - R_{12}$$
$$- B^1_{12}/i - B^2_{12}/j - M_{12}, \tag{10.4.1}$$

where the superscripts again refer to the currency of denomination. B^1_{21}, for example, denotes Portuguese sterling bonds held by England. The problem is that the exchange-rate effects on creditor-denominated bonds and debtor-denominated bonds go in opposite directions. In symbols, $\partial(B^1_{21}/i)/\partial e > 0$ and $\partial(B^1_{12}/i)/\partial e > 0$, while $\partial(B^2_{21}/j)/\partial e < 0$ and $\partial(B^2_{12}/j)/\partial e < 0$. If sterling depreciates, the English demand for Portuguese sterling bonds rises while the English demand for Portuguese escudo bonds declines, and similarly for the Portuguese bond demand. As a consequence, it is no longer certain that a depreciation of sterling produces a capital inflow into England.

Similar conclusions can be derived for the wealth effects of depreciation. To isolate the wealth effects, we assume that expected exchange rates vary hand in hand with the current rate, thus excluding speculative motives. If all bonds are debtor-denominated, a depreciation raises the domestic-currency value of foreign assets of the depreciating country. At the same time, it lowers the domestic-currency value of foreign assets of the appreciating country. In each country, total wealth in terms of domestic currency is affected in the same direction and by the same amount as the value of foreign assets. As a consequence, the proportion of foreign assets in total wealth rises in the depreciating country and declines in the appreciating country. *Desired* assets, on the other hand, do not change. To bring actual assets again in line with desired assets, there has to be a capital inflow into the depreciating country. Again, $\partial c/\partial e < 0$.[5]

Once creditor-denominated bonds are admitted, the wealth effects of depreciation, like the speculative effects, become ambiguous. Various cases are summarized in table 10.4.1. The first column specifies the denomination assumption. The following two columns list the direction of the wealth effects of an exchange-rate change. The last column lists the implications for the wealth effect of a depreciation on capital flows.

In the first case, described above, bonds are debtor-denominated. If the exchange rate changes, the depreciating country gains while the appreciating country loses. If bonds are creditor-denominated, it is the other way around, as indicated on line 2. In this case, depreciation results in a capital outflow expressed by $\partial c/\partial e > 0$. This illustrates the proposition that the wealth effects of depreciation depend crucially on the type of assets.

In the following two cases, all assets are denominated in the same currency, possibly because it is the "leading" currency. Suppose this is sterling. In this case, a depreciation of sterling leaves English wealth unaffected. In

TABLE 10.4.1

Wealth Effects of Exchange-Rate Changes

Asset Denomination	Depreciating Country	Appreciating Country	$\partial c/\partial e$
1. Debtor currency	gains	loses	<0
2. Creditor currency	loses	gains	>0
3. Depreciating currency	unchanged	gains if debtor	>0
	unchanged	loses if creditor	<0
4. Appreciating currency	loses if debtor	unchanged	>0
	gains if creditor	unchanged	<0
5. Mixed; creditor depreciates	gains	gains	$\lessgtr 0$
6. Mixed; debtor depreciates	loses	loses	$\lessgtr 0$

5. This portfolio-balance effect was stressed by Boyer (1977) and Kouri (1976, 1980). For recent developments, see Henderson and Rogoff (1981). The argument in the text is purely in terms of nominal wealth. A more complete analysis would also have to take into account that real wealth is affected by commodity prices.

Portugal, the wealth effect depends on the net asset position. If Portugal is a net debtor, sterling depreciation reduces her debt in terms of escudos. The restoration of portfolio balance then requires an increase in Portuguese debt and thus a capital outflow from England. If Portugal is a net creditor, the capital flow goes in the opposite direction. Case 4 provides the corresponding results for an appreciation of the leading currency.

In the last two cases, the denominations are mixed, but if a country is a creditor for one type of bonds it is also a creditor for the other. Suppose England has given Portugal both sterling loans and escudo loans. If sterling now depreciates, both England and Portugal register a gain in wealth, England on its escudo claims, Portugal on its sterling debts. While the first component tends to produce a capital inflow into England, the second tends to result in an outflow. The net result is uncertain. The same is true, *mutatis mutandis*, if the escudo depreciates.

The detailed casuistry of such cases is not particularly illuminating. The main point is that the wealth effects of exchange-rate fluctuations depend crucially on the precise composition of international assets. In reality, the assets and liabilities of a given country are usually denominated in various currencies. As a consequence, it is difficult to generalize about wealth effects.

This argument about the exchange-rate effects on capital flows can be summarized as follows. If all bonds are debtor-denominated, a change in the exchange rate causes capital to flow from the appreciating country to the depreciating country. In symbols, $\partial c/\partial e < 0$. Both speculative and wealth effects contribute to this result. With a more complex asset structure in which some or all bonds are creditor-denominated, this may no longer be true. One may nevertheless be inclined to regard a capital inflow as the normal effect of depreciation. It should be remembered, however, that this analysis is confined to the partial effects of exchange-rate changes on desired capital flows while all other determinants are held constant. It therefore provides no answer to the question about the association between depreciation and capital flows in the macroeconomic system as a whole.

10.5 Perfect Substitutability of Bonds

In the preceding sections it was assumed that domestic and foreign bonds are imperfect substitutes. As a consequence, the exchange rate and the two interest rates could each be separately varied while the other determinants remained constant. The expected change in the exchange rate was not necessarily equal to the interest differential, the difference presumably being accounted for by a (variable) risk premium. It would be important to know to what extent the influence of interest rates and exchange rates on capital flows depends on the degree of substitutability of bonds. Under present-day conditions, there are usually classes of interest-bearing assets which are virtually perfect substitutes internationally. Eurodeposits are a prime example. Do the results derived in the preceding sections still hold in the presence of such assets?

It is first assumed that the exchange rate, still normalized at $e = 1$, is not expected to change. Perfect substitutability of domestic and foreign bonds then implies that interest rates are equalized and thus $i = j$. The English supply of bonds, measured by their coupon, is exogenously given as $\bar{B}_1$ while the Portuguese bond supply is $\bar{B}_2$. The two bond demands are denoted, respectively, by B_1 and B_2. There is no need to distinguish between English and Portuguese bonds. To eliminate wealth effects, the initial value of foreign assets is assumed to be zero.

Under these assumptions, table 10.2.1 takes the form of table 10.5.1. The zeros in the bottom row reflect the fact that in the absence of speculative and wealth effects, a change in the exchange rate, as explained in section 10.4, has no influence on the desired asset level. If no foreign assets were held at the old exchange rate, none will be desired at the new one. The interest effects are, of course, positive for bonds and negative for other assets.

From the effect of interest rates on desired assets one can derive their effect on capital flows. Suppose, for simplicity, that all foreign assets consist of bonds, while real capital and cash balances are held only domestically. In this case, the effect of a change in the interest rate on the desired amount of England's net foreign assets is simply the difference between its effect on English bond demand and on Portuguese bond demand. If the partial derivatives of asset demand functions are again denoted by lower-case letters, this can be written

$$\partial A/\partial i = a = b_1 - b_2 \gtreqless 0. \tag{10.5.1}$$

An increase in the rate of interest thus results in a capital outflow from the country with the stronger interest effect on bond demand. For the other country there is a capital inflow. With a uniform world interest rate, it is intuitively evident that a change in this rate cannot have a clear-cut effect on capital flows.[6] It is also evident that the inclusion of foreign currencies and direct investments does not remove the ambiguity.

It has so far been assumed that the exchange rate is not expected to change. The analysis is now extended to include the speculative effects of expected exchange-rate changes. Perfect substitutability then means that interest parity is continuously maintained. In symbols, $\dot{e} = i - j$. Wealth effects are still excluded by the assumption that initial foreign assets are zero. It is also assumed that asset owners are interested in asset returns in terms of domestic goods only.

---

6. It should be noted that b_1 and b_2 represent the effects of interest changes in absolute money terms and not in terms of elasticities. Thus they depend on the size of the country. As a consequence, the larger country is more likely to experience a capital outflow.

TABLE 10.5.1

Partial Derivatives of Asset Demand Functions with Homogeneous Bonds

	R_{11}	R_{12}	R_{22}	R_{21}	B_1/i	B_2/j	M_{11}	M_{12}	M_{22}	M_{21}
y_1	+	0	0	+	+	0	+	0	0	+
y_2	0	+	+	0	0	+	0	+	+	0
q_1	+	+	−	−	−	−	−	−	−	−
q_2	−	−	+	+	−	−	−	−	−	−
i	−	−	−	−	+	+	−	−	−	−
e	0	0	0	0	0	0	0	0	0	0

Under these assumptions, the asset yields relevant for English and Portuguese owners are those given in table 10.5.2. For English owners, sterling balances have zero yield, but the yield on escudo balances may be positive or negative depending on exchange-rate changes. For Portuguese owners it is the other way around. English bonds have, of course, the same yield as Portuguese bonds, but for English owners this yield is generally different from the yield for Portuguese owners. In the case of capital goods, yields may differ both between English and Portuguese capital goods and between English and Portuguese owners.

Now consider an increase in i at given q_1, q_2, r_1, r_2, and j, but with $\dot{e}$ adjusting as required by interest parity. For English owners, the yield on escudo balances rises while the yield on sterling balances remains zero. The demand for escudos is thus likely to increase relative to the demand for sterling. For Portuguese owners, the sterling yield declines while the escudo yield remains zero, initiating the same sort of currency substitution as for English owners.

The yields on English and Portuguese bonds are, of course, equal for each group of owners, but for English owners both yields rise while for Portuguese owners they remain unchanged. It is reasonable to assume that the English bond demand increases, but the Portuguese reaction, if any, is uncer-

TABLE 10.5.2

Asset Yields with Interest Parity

Asset	English owners	Portuguese owners
English cash	0	$-\dot{e} = j - i$
Portuguese cash	$\dot{e} = i - j$	0
English bonds	i	$i - \dot{e} = j$
Portuguese bonds	$j + \dot{e} = i$	j
English capital goods	$\dfrac{r_1}{q_1}$	$\dfrac{r_1}{q_1} - \dot{e} = \dfrac{r_1}{q_1} + j - i$
Portuguese capital goods	$\dfrac{r_2}{q_2} + \dot{e} = \dfrac{r_2}{q_2} + i - j$	$\dfrac{r_2}{q_2}$

tain. It may perhaps be argued that an increase in Portuguese bond demand is likely, because for Portuguese owners the yields on both English cash balances and English capital goods decline, thus making bonds relatively more attractive.

For capital goods, an increase in i produces an increase in the yield of Portuguese capital relative to English capital for both groups of owners. Most likely, this will tend to raise the demand for Portuguese capital goods at the expense of English capital goods, but in view of the changes in other yields this is not absolutely certain. The results of these considerations are summarized in the following row of probable signs, relating to the partial derivatives of asset demand with respect to the English interest rate:

	R_{11}	R_{12}	R_{22}	R_{21}	B_1/i	B_2/j	M_{11}	M_{12}	M_{22}	M_{21}
i	$-$	$-$	$+$	$+$	$+$	$+$	$-$	$-$	$+$	$+$

There is a similar row of signs for the exchange-rate effects. It is implied in the interest parity condition. The latter says that $di = d(\dot{e})$ where $\dot{e} = f(e)$. Assuming that an increase in the level of the exchange rate tends to reduce the expected rate of its future increase (or to increase the expected rate of its future decline), we have $f'(e) < 0$. This implies that an increase in the rate of interest is associated with a decline in e. If interest rates rise, the currency appreciates. It follows that the exchange rate effects have the opposite signs from the interest effects:

	R_{11}	R_{12}	R_{22}	R_{21}	B_1/i	B_2/j	M_{11}	M_{12}	M_{22}	M_{21}
e	$+$	$+$	$-$	$-$	$-$	$-$	$+$	$+$	$-$	$-$

On the basis of these partial derivatives we now consider capital flows. With perfect substitutability of bonds, England's net asset position, corresponding to (10.1.5), is

$$A = R_{21} - R_{12} + (B_1 - \bar{B}_1)/i - (B_2 - \bar{B}_2)/j + M_{21} - M_{12}.$$

Portuguese private wealth, corresponding to (10.1.9), is

$$V_2 = R_{22} + R_{12} + B_2/j + M_{22} + M_{12}.$$

England's net asset position can thus be expressed in terms of Portugal's private wealth as

$$A_2 = -(V_2 - R_{22} - R_{21} - B_1/i - M_{22} - M_{21} - \bar{B}_2/j + \bar{B}_1/i).$$

In the light of table 10.5.2, the effect of an increase in i on Portuguese desired wealth may be assumed to be negative, since some yields decline, and none rise. As a consequence, $\partial V_2/\partial i < 0$. The partial derivatives of the desired asset stocks were shown to be positive, while $\bar{B}_1$ and $\bar{B}_2$ are constants. It follows that an increase in the interest rate results in a capital *out*flow.

Whoever finds this result paradoxical may find it helpful to note that the capital outflow can just as well be attributed to the appreciation of sterling. Surely an appreciation of the currency, producing an expected depreciation, most likely produces a capital outflow. It should also be noted that the continuous maintenance of interest parity does not eliminate interest rates (or the exchange rate) as an initiator of capital flows. It is not true that capital moves only if exchange rates deviate from interest parity. Even with perfect arbitrage, changes in interest rates, as table 10.5.2 shows, can give rise to capital flows.

The overall picture about the effect of interest rates on capital outflows thus appears to be quite complex. Depending on the circumstances of the case, both negative and positive reactions seem to be perfectly possible. The picture can be somewhat simplified by disregarding creditor-denominated bonds. For heterogeneous assets it was found that the "traditional" negative effect prevails in this case. For homogeneous assets under given exchange rates no presumption could be established either way. With homogeneous assets and interest parity, an increase in the domestic interest rate is likely to result in a capital outflow. No such complications appeared in determining the effects of incomes and capital-goods prices on capital flows, but creditor-denominated debt also makes exchange-rate effects somewhat ambiguous.

In summary, the capital flow equation (10.0.1) is likely to have the following partial derivatives:

$$\frac{\partial c}{\partial y_1} > 0 \qquad \frac{\partial c}{\partial q_1} < 0 \qquad \frac{\partial c}{\partial i} \gtreqless 0 \qquad \frac{\partial c}{\partial e} < 0 \ (?)$$

$$\frac{\partial c}{\partial y_2} < 0 \qquad \frac{\partial c}{\partial q_2} > 0 \qquad \frac{\partial c}{\partial j} \gtreqless 0$$

The influence of incomes and prices of capital goods is clear and straightforward, the influence of the exchange rate is somewhat less certain, and the influence of interest rates is ambiguous. There is a strong presumption that an increase in the market price of capital goods will attract a capital inflow. There is no clear presumption that a capital inflow will also be attracted by higher interest rates.

As a final remark, it should be reemphasized that the effects derived in this chapter are partial effects as they would appear in a structural equation or behavior function for capital flows. If the macroeconomic system is considered as a whole, the exogenous changes that produce a change in the bond yield would, as a rule, also produce changes in other determinants of capital flows. As a consequence, the actual capital flows associated with interest changes may be different, both in size and direction, from the partial derivatives derived above.

This becomes particularly relevant if the capital-flow function is misspecified by omitting capital-goods prices. In open-economy macroeconomics such misspecification seems to be the rule rather than the exception. The consequences can best be explained in terms of (10.0.1) by disregarding y_1, y_2, q_2, j, and e, thus concentrating on q_1 and i. Suppose the change in capital flows is written as

$$dc = \frac{\partial c^*}{\partial i} di$$

whereas, in fact, it should have been written as

$$dc = \frac{\partial c}{\partial q_1} dq_1 + \frac{\partial c}{\partial i} di.$$

What sign should be attributed to $\partial c^*/\partial i$? The answer depends on the relationship between i and q_1. If the exogenous change occurred in monetary policy, the association between i and q_1 will typically be negative, so that $dq_1 = adi$ with $a < 0$. For the apparent effect of the interest rate on capital flows one thus obtains

$$dc = \left(\frac{\partial c}{\partial q_1} a + \frac{\partial c}{\partial i} \right) di.$$

Now suppose both partial effects conform to traditional assumptions, which means $\partial c/\partial q_1 < 0$ and $\partial c/\partial i < 0$. In view of the negative sign of a, the apparent effect of the interest rate on capital flows may nevertheless be positive. I am inclined to conjecture that this is the normal case. It follows that in the misspecified function, $\partial c^*/\partial i$ should have been attributed a positive sign, higher interest rates seemingly producing a capital outflow. This means that under a restrictive monetary policy, because it starts out by depressing domestic capital-goods prices, higher interest rates seem to result in a capital outflow, even if their partial effect is the opposite. Under an expansionary monetary policy, on the other hand, lower interest rates will often give the impression of producing a capital inflow, because such a policy stimulates investment. Whenever in a macroeconomic model the capital-flow function is misspecified by omitting the market prices of capital goods, the apparent interest effect on capital flows is likely to be the opposite of what is commonly supposed. It will turn out that this may have far-reaching consequences for the theory of monetary policy under floating exchange rates.

III

MONETARY POLICY UNDER FLOATING EXCHANGE RATES

CHAPTER **11**

Dynamics of
Monetary Policy

Introduction

The subject of the final part of this book is monetary policy in an open economy under floating exchange rates. This does not mean that monetary policy played no role in the preceding chapters. In fact, the analysis of parts I and II is largely intended to provide tools for a better understanding of monetary policies. In this and the following chapters these tools are used for an explicit analysis of policy questions.

The first question concerns the sequence of the effects of monetary policy on exchange rates, prices, interest rates, output, trade, capital flows, and foreign assets. This is the subject of the present chapter. It was shown in chapter 2 that in the long run an exogenous change in the money supply affects only commodity prices and exchange rates, while real variables like interest rates, output, trade, capital flows, and the terms of trade remain unchanged. The quantity theory of money and purchasing-power parity rule the field.

In the short run, however, monetary policy may have powerful real effects. The classical tradition of monetary macroeconomics views these effects as beginning with a rapid, almost instantaneous reaction of the prices of existing assets like stocks, bonds, land, houses, and other capital goods. This initiates, as a second stage, repercussions on output flows and employment while output prices and wages are relatively inert. After a time, however, the monetary impulse is increasingly transmitted to the prices of current output and productive factors while output reactions gradually subside.[1] Recent work on the "microfoundations" of macroeconomics has supplied a somewhat bewil-

---

1. A more detailed account of this sequence of events in a closed economy is given in chapters 10 and 11 of Niehans (1978).

dering array of hypotheses about the fundamental reasons for this sequence, in which transaction, information and planning costs, and the formation of expectations often play a prominent role. For the present purpose it is enough to recognize the typical sequence of events as a fact of economic life. The present chapter is concerned with the international aspects of this sequence.

The key concept of the analysis is the "overshooting" of the exchange rate. The phenomenon was known to Cassel more than sixty years ago (Cassel 1921), but during the period of fixed exchange rates it was largely forgotten and had to be rediscovered around the middle of the 1970s. The term "over-shooting" can be given different meanings. First, the exchange rate may be said to overshoot if in the course of the adjustment process it temporarily exceeds its ultimate equilibrium value. This is illustrated by the top curve of figure 11.0.1. Second, overshooting can be interpreted in the sense of a temporary reversal of direction as illustrated by curve 2. Third, overshooting may be interpreted as relating to the path of commodity prices. In this case, illustrated by curve 3, the exchange rate is said to overshoot if it exceeds purchasing-power parity.[2]

It is the deviation of the exchange rate from purchasing-power parity that creates potential economic problems. It may well be associated with over-shooting in the first and/or second sense, but this is by no means necessary. Consider an economy with continuing inflation in a world with stable prices. In this case, there is no equilibrium level of the exchange rate, the latter

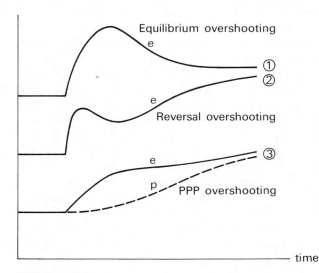

FIGURE 11.0.1
Meanings of Overshooting

2. The meaning of overshooting is explained in more detail in Levich (1981).

sooner or later exceeding any specified level. As a consequence, there can be no overshooting in the first sense. In addition, the inflationary trend may be strong enough to transform any reversal into an increase at a slower rate, so that overshooting in the second sense does not appear either. Overshooting in the third sense, however, remains important regardless of the underlying inflationary trend. Whenever overshooting is mentioned in the following discussion, it is always meant in the PPP sense.

11.1 A General Model of Exchange Dynamics

The first section provides the building blocks for the subsequent sections. Together, these blocks form a model of exchange dynamics. However, the complete model is difficult to interpret. In each of the following sections it is therefore reduced to a simpler model by omitting one particular aspect. From a general model this procedure thus generates three submodels, each shedding light on particular aspects of the dynamic process. The model of this section is general in a relative sense only. It is indeed more general than the submodels derived from it, but it still disregards many aspects of exchange dynamics that may be important in the real world. Wealth effects and the J-curve are two of them.

The exposition of the model conveniently begins with the static part. There are three assets: domestic real balances l, domestic capital goods k, and an international asset a. Money and capital goods are held only by domestic residents, who, on the other hand, hold no foreign money or capital goods. The amount of capital goods is exogenously fixed at $\bar{k}$; capacity effects of domestic investment are disregarded. The inclusion of capital goods and their price takes account of the argument in chapters 6 and 10.

The international asset is assumed to consist of perfectly homogeneous money-market instruments, called "bonds," traded at par. Arbitrage sees to it that interest parity is continuously maintained. The symbol a represents the stock of net foreign assets measured in domestic currency. In principle, it can be positive or negative. It is assumed, however, that $a = 0$ in the initial situation. This serves to exclude wealth effects from currency depreciation or appreciation. It is true that, in reality, such wealth effects may play a significant role.[3] It is also true, however, that they depend entirely on the denomination of assets (see section 10.4), so that general statements can hardly be made. In addition, the assumption that initially $a = 0$ helps to justify the exclusion of interest payments as a component of the current account.

The demand for each asset depends on income y, the relative market price of existing capital goods q, and the domestic interest rate i. The foreign interest rate j is assumed to be given. As a consequence, with homogeneous

3. This role has been emphasized by Kouri (1976, 1980).

bonds, the exchange rate does not appear as a separate determinant of asset demand. All variables except interest rates are expressed in logarithmic form; their coefficients thus represent elasticities. Constant terms are suppressed.

Denoting the desired levels of variables by an asterisk, the demand functions for real balances and foreign assets are written

$$l^* = l_y y + l_i i, \qquad\qquad l_y > 0 \qquad l_i < 0 \qquad\qquad (11.1.1)$$

$$a^* = a_y y + a_i i + a_q q. \qquad a_y > 0 \qquad a_i \gtreqless 0 \qquad a_q < 0 \qquad (11.1.2)$$

The positive income effects and the negative effect of the rate of interest on cash balances require no explanation. The negative reaction of desired foreign assets to the relative price of capital goods is based on the analysis of sections 6.3 and 10.3. It should be born in mind that q is the market price of capital goods at a given production cost. A high level of q makes it profitable to increase planned investment in domestic capital goods at the expense of foreign assets.

That the effect of the interest rate on net foreign assets is ambiguous in the case of homogeneous assets was explained in detail in section 10.5. For the purpose of this chapter this will be made more specific either by the assumption $a_i = 0$ or by the less stringent assumption

$$(-a_i) < \frac{(-a_q)}{(-k_q)} (-k_i).$$

Since the coefficients on the right-hand side, as explained in the following paragraph, are negative, the parentheses are positive. The assumption thus means that the direct effect of the interest rate on foreign assets, if negative, is absolutely smaller than its indirect effect through the associated decline in the price of capital goods. In any case, the channel through capital goods dominates.

The capital-goods sector is reduced to a bare minimum by the assumption that no investment goods are actually completed. As a consequence, movements in income, interest rates, and capital-goods prices have to see to it that the stock demand for capital goods is equal to the given supply:

$$\bar{k} = k_y y + k_i i + k_q q \qquad k_y > 0 \qquad k_i < 0 \qquad k_q < 0. \qquad (11.1.3)$$

The negative sign of k_q requires an explanation. It was pointed out in sections 6.3 and 10.2 that an increase in q, since it promises investors a capital gain, stimulates the accumulation of capital goods. The effect of q_i on R_{ij} in table 10.2.1 was thus assumed to be positive. In the present context, no investment is allowed to take place; what matters is the stock demand for existing capital goods, which declines with a rising market price.

Output is assumed to gravitate to "normal" (or "full employment") output $\bar{y}$. It may deviate from the latter due to an excess of actual cash balances over desired cash balances or "excess liquidity":

$$y - \bar{y} = \phi(l - l^*). \qquad \phi > 0 \tag{11.1.4}$$

This makes it possible to investigate output fluctuations during the adjustment process. A more general model would also include a direct output effect of the terms of trade. Real balances are linked to the (exogenous) nominal balances, $\bar{m}$, through the price level:

$$l = \bar{m} - p. \tag{11.1.5}$$

At given l^*, rising prices would thus be associated with declining output.

In addition to these static relationships we have to specify the laws of motion for p, e, and a. Price adjustments are assumed to be primarily determined by the speed with which people adjust cash balances to their desired levels. A second component expresses the influence of the exchange rate through import prices. The rate of change of domestic prices is thus written

$$\dot{p} = \lambda(l - l^*) + \gamma(e - p). \qquad \lambda > 0 \qquad \gamma > 0 \tag{11.1.6}$$

The rate of change of the exchange rate is equal to the interest differential:

$$\dot{e} = i - \bar{j}. \tag{11.1.7}$$

With homogeneous assets, interest parity is continuously maintained. This implies that actual changes in the exchange rate are equal to expected changes. With perfect foresight, this condition is satisfied over periods of any length. As a consequence, the time profile of the interest differential is identical to the time profile of exchange-rate changes. In reality, of course, human foresight is far from perfect. However, perfect foresight is the only assumption about expectations that is not arbitrary, and there is no particular reason why forecasting errors should not be random.[4]

The stock of net foreign assets is assumed to adjust to its desired level with a given adjustment speed according to

$$\dot{a} = \alpha(a^* - a), \tag{11.1.8}$$

where α reflects all the factors that impede the process of saving and investment (see chapter 6). At the same time, the accumulation of foreign assets must be equal to the current-account surplus, which is assumed to depend

---

4. Dornbusch (1976), for example, used the assumption that a certain fraction of the gap between the actual exchange rate and the equilibrium rate is closed in each period. He correctly pointed out that in his model, given the appropriate adjustment speed, this is equivalent to perfect foresight. However, this is not true in general, and with continuing inflation an equilibrium exchange rate does not even exist.

negatively on the terms of trade and on the deviation of output from its normal level,

$$\dot{a} = \beta(p - e) + \eta(y - \bar{y}). \qquad \beta < 0 \qquad \eta < 0 \tag{11.1.9}$$

The coefficient β summarizes the elasticity aspects, while η expresses the expenditure aspects of balance-of-payments determination.[5] By combining (11.1.8) with (11.1.9) and substituting for a^* from (11.1.2), we obtain another static relationship

$$\alpha(a_y y + a_q q + a_i i - a) = \beta(p - e) + \eta(y - \bar{y}). \tag{11.1.10}$$

It should be noted that even with perfect arbitrage, as reflected in interest parity, foreign assets may adjust with any speed, rapid or slow. There is no direct relationship between capital mobility and arbitrage.

This completes the exposition of the model. For any values of the exogenous variables $\bar{y}$, $\bar{k}$, and $\bar{m}$, the static equations (11.1.1), (11.1.3) through (11.1.5), and (11.1.10) can be used to express l, l^*, y, q, and i in terms of p, e, and a. By substituting these expressions into the dynamic equations (11.1.6), (11.1.7), and (11.1.8), one obtains a system of three linear differential equations in p, e, and a. Starting from initial values p_0, e_0, and a_0, this system determines the dynamic sequence of events. In particular, it can be used to determine the adjustment path of income, exchange rate, interest rate, prices, and capital flows following an exogenous change in the money supply.

The system is in equilibrium if (1) actual balances are equal to desired balances, $l = l^*$, (2) purchasing-power parity obtains, $e = p$, and (3) the domestic interest rate is equal to the foreign rate, $i = \bar{j}$. It was explained in chapter 2 that an exogenous increase in the money supply ultimately leads to an equiproportionate increase in p and e while all real variables remain unchanged. It can easily be confirmed that the equilibrium solution of the present model has the same property; if $\bar{m}$ is raised, an equal increase in p and e is enough to maintain equilibrium. The present model goes beyond the comparative statics of chapter 2 by determining the adjustment path leading from the old equilibrium to the new.

In principle, the problem posed in the introduction to this chapter is thus solved. Unfortunately, a model with three simultaneous differential equations is too complex for intuitive interpretation, and it is hard to extract general economic propositions from it. Intuitive insight, though of a less general nature, can be gained by analyzing different simplified versions, each characterized by the elimination of one differential equation. By assuming perfectly flexible prices, we obtain a full-employment model with capital flows and interest-parity dynamics. By disregarding capital flows, we can analyze the in-

---

5. This specification disregards the *J*-effect. If the effect of the real exchange rate on trade is at first perverse and reaches its final value with a lag, this fact is likely to be another source of exchange-rate overshooting not analyzed in this chapter.

teraction of interest-parity dynamics and output fluctuations. By assuming non-substitutability of bonds and thus discarding interest parity, we can investigate the interaction between trade, capital flows, and output. These submodels are discussed, one after another, in the following sections.

It should be noted that these submodels do not represent rival "approaches" to exchange-rate dynamics. It is true that each submodel sheds light on certain aspects of what recent literature has called, respectively, the "monetary approach," the "portfolio approach," and the "current-account approach." However, the parent model from which these submodels are derived makes clear that these "approaches" are not rivals but complements, each motivated by the need for simplification.

11.2 Capital Flows and Interest-Parity Dynamics with Flexible Prices

The first submodel serves to highlight the crucial role of lags in real-balance adjustment (or, equivalently, of the imperfect flexibility of prices) for the reaction of the economy to monetary changes. It also sheds light on the exchange-rate dynamics initiated by real factors like shifts in import demand and the demand for foreign assets.

The submodel is derived from the general model by postulating that perfect flexibility of prices keeps actual cash balances continuously at their desired level. As a consequence, (11.1.6) disappears. This is the crucial modification. With $l = l^*$ it also follows from (11.1.4) that $y = \bar{y}$, which means that output is continuously at its full-employment level. This is as it should be, because deviations from full-employment are basically due to the imperfect flexibility of prices.[6] As a consequence, y can be disregarded. For further simplification it is assumed that foreign assets are continuously at their desired levels; this is formally expressed by $\alpha = \infty$.

With these modifications, the model of section 11.1 reduces to the following full-employment submodel:

Static part:

$$\bar{m} - p = l_i i \tag{11.2.1}$$

$$a = a_i i + a_q q \tag{11.2.2}$$

$$\bar{k} = k_i i + k_q q. \tag{11.2.3}$$

Dynamic part:

$$\dot{e} = i - \bar{j} \tag{11.2.4}$$

$$\dot{a} = \beta(p - e). \tag{11.2.5}$$

6. For a full-employment model of exchange dynamics, but with sluggish price adjustment, see Dornbusch (1976).

The last two equations formalize the essential dynamic elements of this model, namely, the interest-parity mechanism and the current-account (or capital-flow) mechanism.

The static equations determine i, q, and p in terms of a, $\bar{m}$, and $\bar{k}$:

$$i = \frac{1}{\Delta_1} (k_q a - a_q \bar{k}), \tag{11.2.6}$$

$$q = -\frac{1}{\Delta_1} (k_i a - a_i \bar{k}), \tag{11.2.7}$$

$$p = \bar{m} - \frac{l_i}{\Delta_1} (k_q a - a_q \bar{k}), \tag{11.2.8}$$

where $\Delta_1 = a_i k_q - k_i a_q < 0$ as explained in section 11.1.

By substituting for i from (11.2.6) and for p from (11.2.8), equations (11.2.4) and (11.2.5) can be written as differential equations in e and a:

$$\dot{e} = \frac{1}{\Delta_1} (k_q a - a_q \bar{k}) - \bar{j} \tag{11.2.9}$$

$$\dot{a} = -\beta e - \frac{\beta l_i}{\Delta_1} (k_q a - a_q \bar{k}) + \beta \bar{m}. \tag{11.2.10}$$

In the light of this dynamic model we can now determine the consequences of a one-time increase in the money supply. At the initial level of a, the instantaneous reaction of i, q, and p is given by (11.2.6), (11.2.7), and (11.2.8). It turns out that the rate of interest and the price of capital goods do not change at all, while prices increase at once in the same proportion as the money supply.

With unchanged i, (11.2.4) tells us that there is no reason for gradual appreciation or depreciation of the currency. The exchange rate jumps immediately to the new purchasing-power parity without any subsequent change. With this instantaneous adjustment in the exchange rate, (11.2.10) shows that there is no incentive for capital flows. In this flexible-price model, monetary policy is neutral even in the short run. Prices and the exchange rate move at once to their long-run equilibrium values, and all real variables remain unchanged. It has long been recognized in closed-economy macroeconomics that with perfectly flexible prices money has no real effects even in the short run. The present analysis confirms this for an open economy.

The flexible-price model can also be used to determine the effects of changes in real factors. The consequences of an exogenous shift in imports or exports turn out to be remarkably similar to those of a shift in the money supply. Suppose the demand for imports declines. This can be formalized by adding a shift parameter to (11.2.5):

$$\dot{a} = \beta(p - e) + \beta_0. \tag{11.2.11}$$

At the inherited level of a, in view of (11.2.2) and (11.2.3), i and q remain unchanged. Since, at given $\bar{m}$, prices are determined by the rate of interest, they do not change either. The constancy of i also precludes the activation of the interest-parity mechanism (11.2.4). All that takes place is an instantaneous and permanent appreciation of the currency, expressed in a step-wise decrease in e. This serves to reduce exports and/or stimulate other imports in such a way that trade is continuously balanced (which means that capital flows remain zero). With perfect flexibility of domestic prices the only consequences of the exogenous decline in import demand is a compensating appreciation of the currency and a shift in the internal composition of trade flows.[7]

The preceding results were largely negative, inasmuch as they revealed the absence of a dynamic adjustment process. Richer results are obtained for exogenous shifts in the stock demand for foreign assets. The analysis is best conducted in terms of a phase diagram (see fig. 11.2.1). By letting $\dot{e} = 0$ in (11.2.9), one obtains those combinations of a and e for which the exchange rate is constant. Since e does not appear in (11.2.9), the resulting exchange-equilibrium line is vertical. To the left of this line the exchange rate declines while to the right it rises, as indicated by the vertical arrows.

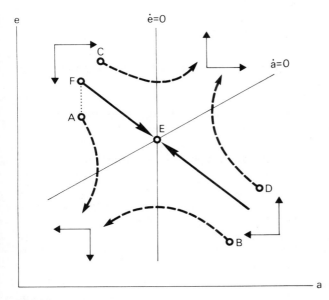

FIGURE 11.2.1
Dynamics of Exchange Rate and Capital Flows

7. The contrast between these results and those of section 2.2 is due to the fact that the present model, assuming perfect specialization in production, takes no account of the international equilization of commodity prices.

The asset-equilibrium line can be derived from (11.2.10) by letting $\dot{a} = 0$. Since the coefficients of e and a have opposite signs, this line has a positive slope. This is intuitively plausible. At a given level of the exchange rate, a higher level of foreign assets would call forth a capital inflow. At a given level of assets, an increase in e, since it stimulates exports relative to imports, would result in a capital outflow. To maintain asset equilibrium, a higher level of foreign assets must thus be associated with a higher exchange rate. To the right of this line capital flows in, while to the left there is a capital outflow as indicated by the horizontal arrows.

Inspection of the phase diagram reveals that the system is unstable.[8] From points like A and B, the adjustment path curves around, leading eventually to progressive appreciation of the currency associated with capital inflows. From points like C and D, the economy would end up with progressive depreciation and capital accumulation. However, there are points from which the economy will indeed reach the equilibrium E. These points are connected by the solid arrows pointing towards E.

If the economy, after an exogenous change in some real factor, had to start from the inherited values of e and a, the chance that it would find itself on one of the stable arrows would be slight indeed. In fact, the exchange rate, immediately upon the exogenous change, can jump to a new level. It can choose, so to say, its own initial value. Suppose the economy was initially in equilibrium at A. The exogenous change now shifts both curves so that the new equilibrium is at E. If the economy follows the broken arrow, it will never reach E. If, however, the exchange rate first jumps to F, the economy can follow the solid arrow to E.

Why should the exchange rate jump instantaneously to F? Correct foresight about the future path provides an answer. If individuals, once they have been surprised by the exogenous change, have correct expectations about its consequences, they will instantaneously bid the exchange rate up to F. They do this because this is the only rate from which they can expect interest parity, as required by (11.2.4), to be satisfied forever. To express it differently, suppose individuals correctly perceive the new equilibrium to be at E. They also know that interest parity must be continuously satisfied. Reckoning backward from E, they will arrive at F. Trying to put their knowledge to profitable use, they will immediately bid the price of foreign exchange up to the level of F.[9] This is the basic mechanism by which changes in exogenous factors can produce instantaneous jumps in exchange rates. It is important to note that these jumps, erratic as they might seem to observers, are not due to irrational behavior or speculative excesses. Quite to the contrary, they are basically due to correct anticipation of the consequences of current events by rational traders.

8. This can be checked mathematically.
9. For a detailed technical analysis of this point, see Gray and Turnovsky (1979) and Gray (1982).

We are now in a position to determine the consequences of an exogenous shift in the demand for foreign assets. Suppose asset demand increases by a_0, as indicated by the modified asset demand curve

$$a = a_i i + a_q q + a_0. \tag{11.2.12}$$

In figure 11.2.1, this is expressed by a rightward shift in both curves by the same amount.[10] This means that in the new equilibrium the exchange rate is the same but net foreign assets are higher. The rate of interest cannot permanently change because it is tied to the foreign rate. Prices cannot permanently change because (1) there is no change in the money supply and (2) real balances are tied to the rate of interest. The exchange rate cannot permanently change because otherwise, at unchanged prices, trade cannot be in balance.

The interesting question is how the new equilibrium is reached. Figure 11.2.2 summarizes the contours of the adjustment process. The path of the exchange rate is explained in figure 11.2.3. The initial and the final equilibrium are, respectively, at E_0 and E. Immediately upon the shift in asset demand, the price of the foreign currency rises to F. From there it begins to decline again until it finally reaches the initial level at E. The increase in

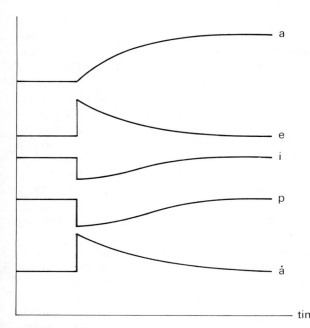

FIGURE 11.2.2
Adjustments to Asset-Demand Shift

10. This can be verified by replacing a by $a - a_0$ in (11.2.9) and (11.2.10), letting $\dot{e} = \dot{a} = 0$, and solving for a.

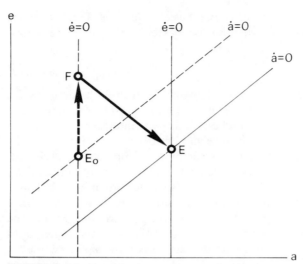

FIGURE 11.2.3
Exchange-Rate Adjustment

foreign-asset demand thus leaves no permanent trace in the exchange rates, but it produces a period of a depreciated, yet gradually appreciating, domestic currency. The exchange rate clearly "overshoots" its ultimate equilibrium.

The rate of interest, as shown in figure 11.2.2, reacts to the shift in foreign-asset demand with an instantaneous decline.[11] As (11.2.4) indicates, it remains below the foreign interest rate as long as the domestic currency appreciates. At the same time, it gradually rises toward its initial level.[12] The temporary decline in the rate of interest is consistent with the fact that the increase in foreign-asset demand is equivalent to an increase in desired wealth and thus accompanied by saving.

The path of prices can be derived from that of interest rates by (11.2.1). The initial decline in interest rates raises the demand for real balances. With a given money supply and flexible prices, this is satisfied by a decline in prices. The initial price fall is followed by a gradual return to the previous level as the interest differential disappears.

Once the paths of e and p are known, capital flows (or the trade balance) can be determined from (11.2.5). The increase in asset demand is associated with an immediate improvement in the competitiveness of the domestic economy. The domestic currency is seen to be "undervalued" relative to purchasing-power parity. With normal elasticities, summarized by a negative value of β, this calls forth an export surplus accompanied by a capital outflow. In the

11. This can be seen from (11.2.6) by replacing a by $a - a_0$ and considering the effect of a_0 at given a.

12. In (11.2.6), i is positively related to a; interest rises as the asset stock grows.

course of the adjustment process the initial deviation from PPP is gradually reduced; it will have disappeared once capital outflows have raised foreign assets by the desired amount.

The price of capital goods, finally, as (11.2.3) shows, is first shifted upwards. When interest rates are low, capital-goods prices are high. This helps to choke off the demand for foreign assets during the interval in which the stock of foreign assets has not had enough time to adjust.

11.3 Interest-Parity Dynamics and Output Fluctuations with Balanced Trade

With perfectly flexible prices, monetary policy has no influence on interest rates. As a consequence, interest parity, as the preceding section showed, is inoperative as a dynamic mechanism. Once sluggish price adjustments give money the power to affect interest rates, interest parity becomes a powerful lever in exchange-rate dynamics. This mechanism is the subject of the present section. Its main consequence is the overshooting of exchange rates after an unexpected change in monetary policy. Overshooting of this type, though recognized by Cassel and others, was first described in a theoretical model by Dornbusch (1976). In the light of recent experience it appears to be the crucial problem of floating exchange rates.

It is important to note, however, that the interest-parity mechanism, and thus overshooting, is not confined to foreign-exchange markets. In fact, it is a very general phenomenon. Asset holders continually shift their investments in such a way that the expected yields, after allowing for differences in risk, are equal. The yields consist of the expected current return (like interest payments, dividends, or rent) and expected capital gains (positive or negative). Suppose some bad news about a company reduces the expected dividends for a limited period. To keep the yield at the (unchanged) level of other assets, this temporary decline in expected returns must be compensated by an expected capital gain. We thus arrive at the apparent paradox that bad news must be associated with expected capital gains. The paradox is resolved by recognizing that the expected capital gains are achieved by a present decline in the stock price to such an extent that it seems to be "undervalued," thus creating the expectation of future appreciation. What is to go up, must first come down; what is to go down, must first go up. This is the common sense of overshooting in asset markets.

To capture this phenomenon, it is now assumed that real cash balances respond to changes in market conditions with a lag. With a given money supply, this means that the flexibility of prices is imperfect. As a counterpart, output can now deviate from its normal level in both directions. This introduces one of the important aspects of exchange dynamics, which is a potential problem for policy makers precisely because it may involve fluctuations in output and employment.

To keep the model tractable, the addition of price dynamics must be combined with the omission of another dynamic aspect. In the present sub-model this is the accumulation of foreign assets through current-account surpluses. It is accordingly assumed that no capital flows can take place and that trade is balanced at all times. The interest-parity dynamics, on the other hand, are retained. The emerging submodel belongs to the same family as the underemployment version in Dornbusch (1976).

The required modifications of the model of section 11.1 can be more formally restated as follows. In the money demand function, income now appears as an argument:

$$l* = l_y y + l_i i. \tag{11.3.1}$$

Income is also assumed to influence the demand for foreign assets, but at the same time the rate of interest is dropped. The function thus reads

$$\bar{a} = a_y y + a_q q. \tag{11.3.2}$$

Interest is a prime candidate for omission because it was shown in section 10.4 that the direction of its influence is unclear and that the primary determinants of asset demand are the price of capital goods and income. In the demand for capital goods, income is omitted to keep the model as simple as possible. As a consequence it is unchanged from (11.2.3):

$$\bar{k} = k_i i + k_q q. \tag{11.3.3}$$

Output is determined as in the general model by

$$y - \bar{y} = \phi(l - l*). \tag{11.3.4}$$

In the dynamic part, the interest-parity condition

$$\dot{e} = i - \bar{j} \tag{11.3.5}$$

is retained. It is now accompanied by the dynamic price equation of (11.1.6),

$$\dot{p} = \lambda(l - l*) + \gamma(e - p). \qquad \lambda > 0 \qquad \gamma > 0 \tag{11.3.6}$$

Since the model is used to analyze a one-time increase in the money supply, the price equation does not include a term for expected inflation.

Using the definition $l = \bar{m} - p$, the "static" variables i, q, and y can be expressed in terms of p together with the exogenous asset stocks $\bar{m}$, $\bar{a}$, and $\bar{k}$. The results are

$$i = \frac{1}{\Delta_2} \{a_y k_q [\phi(p - \bar{m}) - \bar{y}] + (1 + \phi l_y)(k_q \bar{a} - a_q \bar{k})\},$$

$$\tag{11.3.7}$$

$$q = \frac{1}{\Delta_2} \{-a_y k_i [\phi(p - \bar{m}) - \bar{y}] - (1 + \phi l_y)k_i \bar{a} - \phi a_y l_i \bar{k}\},$$

$$\tag{11.3.8}$$

$$y = \frac{1}{\Delta_2} \{ a_q k_i [\phi(p - \bar{m}) - \bar{y}] - \phi k_q l_i \bar{a} + \phi a_q l_i \bar{k} \},$$

$$(11.3.9)$$

where $\Delta_2 = -(1 + \phi l_y) a_q k_i - \phi l_i a_y k_q < 0$. These can be substituted into the dynamic equations to yield

$$\dot{e} = \frac{1}{\Delta_2} \{ a_y k_q [\phi(p - \bar{m}) - \bar{y}] + (1 + \phi l_y)(k_q \bar{a} - a_q \bar{k}) \} - \bar{j},$$

$$(11.3.10)$$

$$\dot{p} = \left(\frac{\lambda}{\Delta_2} a_q k_i - \gamma \right) p + \gamma e - \frac{\lambda}{\Delta_2} a_q k_i \bar{m}$$

$$+ \frac{\lambda}{\Delta_2} (a_q k_i l_y + a_y k_q l_i) \bar{y} - \frac{\lambda}{\Delta_2} k_q l_i \bar{a} + \frac{\lambda}{\Delta_2} a_q l_i \bar{k}.$$

$$(11.3.11)$$

This is conveniently rewritten, omitting the constant terms,[13]

$$\dot{e} = Ap, \qquad\qquad (11.3.12)$$

$$\dot{p} = Bp + Ce, \qquad\qquad (11.3.13)$$

with

$$A = \frac{\phi a_y k_q}{\Delta_2} > 0,$$

$$B = \left(\frac{\lambda}{\Delta_2} a_q k_i - \gamma \right) < 0,$$

$$C = \gamma > 0.$$

The indicated signs are derived from the stated assumptions about the signs of coefficients.

The phase diagram of this system looks like figure 11.3.1. The exchange-equilibrium line is vertical. There is just one price level at which the domestic interest rate is equal to the foreign rate and thus $\dot{e} = 0$. On the right of this line the exchange rate rises, whereas on the left it declines. The price-equilibrium curve has a positive slope. An increase in the price level at a given exchange rate produces, of course, downward pressure on prices. An increase in

---

13. The constant terms represent the equilibrium values of e and p. By letting $\dot{e} = \dot{p} = 0$, solving for the equilibrium values $\bar{e}$ and $\bar{p}$, and substituting these into (11.3.10) and (11.3.11), these equations can be written

$$\dot{e} = A(p - \bar{p}),$$

$$\dot{p} = B(p - \bar{p}) + C(e - \bar{e}).$$

the exchange rate (that is, a depreciation) at a given price level, on the other hand, pushes prices up. To keep prices constant, a rise in p must thus be associated with a rise in e. By comparing B and C it can also be shown that the price-equilibrium line is steeper than 45°. Above this line prices rise, below they decline.

The phase diagram reveals that this system, like the one of section 11.2, is generally unstable. From arbitrary initial points the trajectories will curve around either to the northeast or to the southwest. Again, however, there is a stable path SS which, once it is reached, leads the system to equilibrium at E. As pointed out in section 11.2, this is the only path consistent with perfect foresight into an indefinite future. It is the essential economic function of exchange overshooting to bring the economy to this path.

The adjustment process following an exogenous increase in the money supply can be described in the context of this phase diagram. Its outlines are summarized in figures 11.3.2 and 11.3.3. Suppose with the initial money supply the economy is in equilibrium at price level p_0 and exchange rate e_0, where p and e are normalized so that $e_0 = p_0$. If there is now an unexpected one-time increase in the money supply, the equilibrium price level and the exchange rate increase in the same proportion to, respectively, $\bar{p}$ and $\bar{e}$. This reflects the comparative statics of chapter 2.

The economy cannot move instantly to E, however. With imperfectly

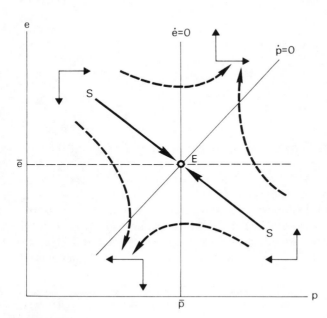

FIGURE 11.3.1
Dynamics of Exchange Rate and Prices

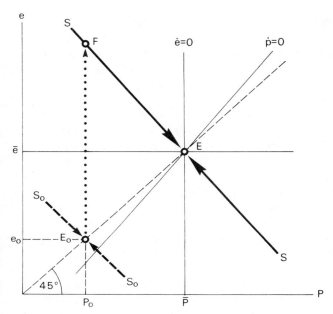

FIGURE 11.3.2
Exchange Rate and Prices: Money-Supply Shift

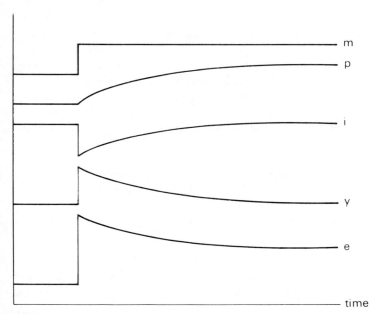

FIGURE 11.3.3
Adjustments (Including Interest Rate) to Money-Supply Shift

flexible prices, the rightward movement can only be gradual. Equation (11.3.11) shows that at the initial price level p_0, the increase in $\bar{m}$ imparts an upward impulse to the rate of price change. Another impulse is added by the currency depreciation. Both impulses are subsequently reduced by the gradual increase in the price level. The resulting adjustment path of prices is illustrated in figure 11.3.3.

Sluggish prices are accompanied by depressed interest rates. The path of interest rates can now be determined from (11.3.7). At the initial price level p_0 the rate of interest declines the instant $\bar{m}$ is increased. From then on, with $\bar{m}$ remaining at its new level, i rises hand in hand with the price level.[14]

An increase in the money supply, since it involves easy money, is accompanied by a temporary increase in output beyond its normal level. Equation (11.3.9) shows that y rises the instant $\bar{m}$ is increased and thereafter declines again as prices and interest rates rise. In reality, the initial impulse is likely to be more gradual, reaching its peak several months after the change in monetary policy. However, the model is a valid idealization of reality in the sense that output recedes as prices rise.[15]

As explained in the introduction to this section and formalized in (11.3.5), depressed interest rates must be associated with a continuous appreciation of the currency and thus declining e. In terms of figure 11.3.2, the new equilibrium must be reached from the NW. With perfect foresight, this is achieved by an instantaneous "jump" in a vertical direction. More precisely, in the initial situation the stable adjustment path was S_0S_0. After the increase in the money supply it is SS. Immediately upon this increase, the exchange rate thus rises to F, from which point it gradually follows the stable path to E. In the present model, the exchange rate clearly overshoots its eventual equilibrium value. With continuing inflation, as pointed out in the introduction to this chapter, this is not necessarily so.[16] The essential point is that the exchange rate, by jumping to F, overshoots the purchasing-power parity. This is most conveniently summarized in the proposition that a low level of the real interest rate is associated with a decline in the real exchange rate.

It should be noted that this overshooting does not create opportunities for profitable speculation. Though at F everybody is assumed to have recognized the domestic currency as "undervalued," there are no profits in this

14. Note that the iso-interest curves in figure 11.3.2, if drawn, would be vertical with i rising to the right. In figure 11.3.3, the path of q would be a mirror image of that of i (see eq. 11.3.8); easy money is associated with high capital-goods prices.

15. In figure 11.3.2, iso-income curves would also appear as vertical lines, but with y declining to the right.

16. The sequence following a change in the rate of monetary expansion is briefly described and graphed in Niehans (1980a). A more detailed analysis can be found in Frankel (1979). Overshooting relative to the final equilibrium may be absent even without continuing inflation if individuals are slow in perceiving the increase in the money supply. See Baltensperger (1981) and Moser (1983).

knowledge, because the expected appreciation, period by period, is offset by the interest differential.

11.4 Output Fluctuations and Capital Flows without Domestic Securities

One of the important aspects of monetary dynamics with floating exchange rates is the development of the current account or, equivalently, of capital movements. In section 11.2 it could not be considered, because with perfectly flexible prices money is neutral even in the short run. In section 11.3 capital movements were excluded by assumption. They are the main topic of the present section. The principal question concerns the trade balances and capital flows associated with fluctuations in output and exchange rates following a change in the money supply.

To keep the complexity of the analysis at a manageable level, the addition of the capital flow mechanism has as its counterpart the exclusion of domestic securities and capital goods. The interest-parity mechanism no longer operates. At the same time, it now makes sense to relate the desired level of foreign assets to the real exchange rate. This is intended to capture the speculative aspects of currency substitution. It is still assumed that foreign assets are continuously at their desired levels. This results in the following submodel.

The static part reduces to the three equations

$$l^* = l_y y, \qquad l_y > 0 \tag{11.4.1}$$

$$a = a_y y + a_e(e - p), \qquad a_y > 0 \qquad a_e < 0 \tag{11.4.2}$$

$$y - \bar{y} = \phi(l - l^*), \qquad \phi > 0 \tag{11.4.3}$$

together with the definition $l = m - p$. The coefficient a_e is intended to express the speculative effects of the real exchange rate on desired asset stocks. If e rises relative to p, investors expect a future decline in the real value of foreign assets. As a consequence, they wish to reduce their foreign assets as discussed in chapter 10. It would be easy to add an equation for domestic bonds to determine the domestic interest rate, which would then appear as an additional argument in (11.4.1) and (11.4.2).[17]

The dynamic part now consists of the differential equations for prices, simplified by the omission of the direct exchange-rate effect, and foreign assets:

$$\dot{p} = \lambda(l - l^*), \qquad \lambda > 0 \tag{11.4.4}$$

$$\dot{a} = \beta(p - e) + \eta(y - \bar{y}). \qquad \beta < 0 \qquad \eta < 0 \tag{11.4.5}$$

---

17. This is the type of model analyzed in Branson (1979).

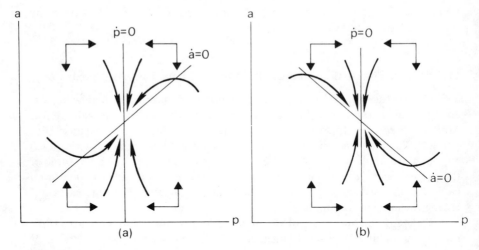

FIGURE 11.4.1
Dynamics of Capital Flows and Prices

This model is similar in spirit to Calvo and Rodriguez (1977), Niehans (1977), Branson (1979), Driskill (1980), and Dornbusch and Fischer (1980). However, while these contributions explain foreign-asset demand largely on the basis of wealth effects, the present model emphasizes income effects.

The static part can be used to express y and e each as a function of p, a, m, and $\bar{y}$:

$$y = -\frac{1}{1 + l_y\phi}\left[\phi(p - \bar{m}) - \bar{y}\right], \qquad (11.4.6)$$

$$e = \left(1 + \frac{a_y}{a_e}\frac{\phi}{1 + l_y\phi}\right)p + \frac{1}{a_e}a - \frac{a_y}{a_e}\frac{1}{1 + l_y\phi}(\phi\bar{m} + \bar{y}). \qquad (11.4.7)$$

Substituting these expressions into the dynamic equations results in two differential equations in p and a:

$$\dot{p} = -\frac{\lambda}{1 + l_y\phi}(p - \bar{m} + l_y\bar{y}), \qquad (11.4.8)$$

$$\dot{a} = -\left(\beta\frac{a_y}{a_e} + \eta\right)\frac{\phi}{1 + l_y\phi}(p - \bar{m})$$

$$- \frac{\beta}{a_e}a + \left[\left(\beta\frac{a_y}{a_e} + \eta\right)\frac{1}{1 + l_y\phi} - \eta\right]\bar{y}. \qquad (11.4.9)$$

In the phase diagrams of figure 11.4.1, the price-equilibrium curve, defined by $\dot{p} = 0$, is vertical. To the left prices rise and to the right they decline, as indicated by the horizontal arrows. The asset-equilibrium curve, defined by $\dot{a} = 0$, can be positively or negatively inclined depending on

$$-\left(a_y + \frac{\eta}{\beta} a_e\right) \frac{\phi}{1 + l_y \phi} \gtreqless 0. \qquad (11.4.10)$$

The first case is illustrated in panel (*a*), the second, in panel (*b*). Above the asset-equilibrium curve foreign assets are reduced; below it they are increased, as expressed by the vertical arrows. In both cases the system is stable.

An exogenous increase in the money supply expresses itself as a rightward shift in both equilibrium curves by the same amount (see fig. 11.4.2). This means that in the new equilibrium prices are higher in proportion to the money supply while the amount of foreign assets is unchanged. The question is how this new equilibrium is reached (for the following discussion, see fig. 11.4.3).

Prices rise monotonically toward their new level. Their rate of increase, as (11.4.8) shows, is highest immediately after the monetary expansion. It declines gradually towards zero as p rises to its new level. We can also be sure

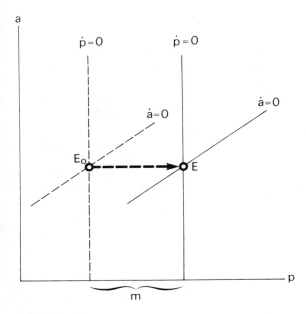

FIGURE 11.4.2
Capital Flows and Prices: Money-Supply Shift

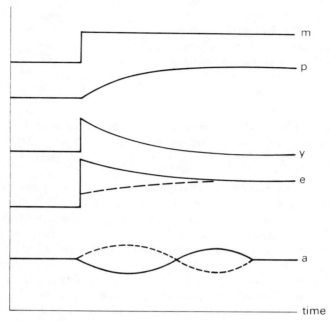

FIGURE 11.4.3
Adjustments (Including Trade Balance) to Money-Supply Shift

that the increase in the money supply, just as in the model of section 11.3, is accompanied by an instantaneous expansion of output. As prices rise, this expansion subsides (see eq. 11.4.6).

As (11.4.7) shows, the increase in m results in an instantaneous depreciation of the domestic currency. Since prices are inert, this implies overshooting relative to PPP. In contrast to the preceding section, the lever of the overshooting mechanism is not interest parity but the speculative effect of the exchange rate on asset demand.

While the initial overshooting is clear, the further course of the exchange rate is not. In particular, it is not clear whether e overshoots its new equilibrium value, the initial depreciation being followed by appreciation, or whether the initial depreciation, falling short of the new equilibrium, is followed by further depreciation. This depends on whether

$$-\frac{a_y}{a_e}\; \frac{\phi}{1 + l_y\phi} \gtreqless 1. \tag{11.4.11}$$

The development of the trade balance, and thus of capital flows, is even less clear. It is evidently impossible for monetary expansion to result either in surpluses without eventual deficits or vice versa, because this would leave the economy with a permanently higher (or lower) stock of foreign assets. Unless trade is continuously balanced, there must be both surplus periods and deficit periods.

The sequence depends on the slope of the asset-equilibrium curve. If this is positive, as illustrated in panel (*a*) of figure 11.4.1, monetary expansion is immediately followed by a period of trade deficits and thus of capital inflows. The stock of foreign assets declines. After a while, deficits turn into surpluses associated with capital outflows until the former asset level is restored. With a negative slope, as illustrated in panel (*b*), the sequence is reversed, initial surpluses being followed by deficits.

According to (11.4.10), the first case requires

$$\frac{(-\eta)}{(-\beta)} > \frac{a_y}{(-a_e)},$$

where all parentheses are positive. This means that the current account is relatively more sensitive to income, whereas the demand for foreign assets reacts more sensitively to the exchange rate. As a consequence, the initial expansion in income combined with the overshooting of the exchange rate produces an import surplus and a shift away from foreign assets. The sequence is reversed if the inequality goes in the opposite direction. This implies that income has a relatively strong effect on the demand for foreign assets, whereas the real exchange rate has a more powerful effect on the trade balance. Equation (11.4.10) may be said to play a similar role in the dynamic model as the extended Marshall/Lerner condition in the static expenditure approach.

With constant coefficients it is difficult to say which case is more likely. If long-run values of the coefficients are used, the second case may well dominate because β then tends to be quite high while the speculative effect of a_e vanishes. With short-run coefficients, however, the first case is more likely to be relevant because β is initially held low by the *J*-effect while a_e is high. For the initial phases of a dynamic process we should clearly look at these short-run values. I conclude that a one-time monetary expansion is likely to initiate a period of trade deficits and capital inflows, followed later by surpluses and capital outflows.

It is important to note that in either case there is no simple relationship between the exchange rate and the trade balance. With given parameters, a depreciating currency may be associated with a trade deficit in one phase, but with a surplus in another; the same is true for appreciation. Every change in one of the parameters of the model can change the pattern of this association. As a consequence, efforts to predict the trade balance on the basis of the exchange rate or vice versa do not look promising. While any such effort may seem to be successful in some cases, it is likely to fail in others.

This skeptical conclusion applies only to a change in the money supply; it does not necessarily apply to changes in other exogenous variables. Consider an exogenous increase in export demand (or a decline in import demand). It can be expressed by adding a shift variable to (11.4.5):

$$\dot{a} = \beta(p - e) + \eta(y - \bar{y}) + \beta_0. \tag{11.4.12}$$

In the phase diagram, an increase in β_0 is reflected in an upward shift in the asset-equilibrium curve, while the price-equilibrium curve is not affected. The new equilibrium is thus characterized by a higher stock of foreign assets at unchanged prices. There is no instantaneous "jump" in the exchange rate. At the old exchange rate, the shift in β_0 creates a trade surplus which initiates the accumulation of foreign assets. This is accompanied by a gradual appreciation of the currency. The appreciation, in turn, reduces the trade surplus. In the new equilibrium the appreciation will have reached the point at which it just offsets the initial shift in β_0. Prices and income remain constant throughout.

The sequence of events is quite similar if the exogenous shift is in the demand for foreign assets as expressed by

$$a = a_y y + a_e(e - p) + a_0. \tag{11.4.13}$$

This means that a in (11.4.7) and (11.4.9) is replaced by $a - a_0$. Again the asset-equilibrium curve shifts upward as a_0 is increased. In contrast to the previous case, the trade surplus that "finances" the asset accumulation is now called forth by an instantaneous depreciation. As the stock of foreign assets rises, the gradual appreciation reduces the trade surplus. In the final equilibrium the exchange level is back at the initial level, but the asset stock is permanently higher. In both cases, appreciation of the domestic currency is associated with trade surpluses.[18]

This and the two preceding sections have presented three pictures of exchange dynamics following a change in the money supply. These pictures were partial and complementary, each stressing different aspects of the general model of section 11.1. An additional mechanism, not analyzed in this chapter, has its origin in the *J*-curve. Overall, economic theory has provided compelling reasons to expect overshooting of real, and perhaps also of nominal, exchange rates in the wake of monetary disturbances. The same is true for many real disturbances. In addition, historical experience, particularly in the recent past, strongly suggests that overshooting may be large enough to be a serious problem.

Under these circumstances it would clearly be desirable to have quantitative estimates of the likely range of overshooting. The adjustment pattern of exchange rates was recently estimated by Driskill (1981) for the case of the dollar price of Swiss francs. The estimates imply that a one-time increase in

---

18. This agrees with the conclusions in Dornbusch and Fischer (1980, p. 964).

the U.S. money supply tended to be followed by an overshooting of the (nominal) Swiss franc rate in the proportion of 2.3 in the first quarter. It is quite likely, however, that other cases, circumstances, and specifications would lead to rather different results. This suspicion follows from the observation that overshooting is a characteristic of a highly volatile endogenous variable in a complex dynamic model with a number of interacting overshooting mechanisms. In fact, a more recent study (Moser 1983) suggests that after the elimination of endogenous foreign-exchange interventions, overshooting turns out to be much lower. It is unlikely, therefore, that the degree of overshooting will ever become one of the "great constants" of economics. Unpredictability may well remain one of its main characteristics.[19]

11.5 The Consequences of Overshooting

In the final section I shall try to draw general conclusions from the preceding analysis. The significance of exchange overshooting must be sought mainly at two levels:

1. Overshooting is likely to increase the fluctuations in output and employment following a change in monetary policy.

2. Through overshooting exchange rates, monetary policy in one country affects prices and output in other countries.

These propositions will now be elaborated by pulling together, albeit in a nonrigorous fashion, the various strands of the arguments in the preceding sections.

In all three submodels an increase in the money supply results in a virtually instantaneous depreciation of the currency. With perfectly flexible prices, as the submodel of section 11.2 shows, there is also an immediate increase in commodity prices. Real exchange rates remain unchanged; money has no real effects even in the short run. With imperfectly flexible prices, prices can react only gradually. As a consequence, the real exchange rate shoots up; the competitiveness of the country in international markets improves. Those who take the sequence of events as an indicator of causality will (wrongly) conclude that the change in the exchange rate causes the price changes. Those who (again wrongly) regard the purchasing-power parity doctrine as postulating a chain of causality from prices to the exchange rate will also be misled into concluding that the doctrine is falsified by facts.

The depreciation of the currency, since it raises foreign prices in terms of the domestic currency, accelerates the inflationary effects of monetary expansion on commodity prices. Conversely, the appreciation of the exchange rate following a monetary contraction accelerates the deflationary price effects. If there was inflation, it seems to subside more rapidly than expected. These

19. This assessment is consistent with the critical evaluation of some econometric estimates in Meese and Rogoff (1981).

price effects of overshooting exchange rates are only temporary, however. As the overshooting disappears, they are necessarily followed by a reaction. If there was a monetary expansion, inflation declines again. In the case of an anti-inflationary contraction, inflation seems to reappear. In view of their temporary character, these price effects of overshooting must be regarded as undesirable disturbances, as an enemy rather than an ally of an effective monetary policy.

The exchange depreciation may also overshoot its eventual equilibrium, though this is by no means certain. As the submodel of section 11.3 shows, it is particularly likely under the influence of the interest-parity mechanism. To the extent that monetary expansion is accompanied by a temporary reduction in interest rates, it must, under perfect foresight, also be accompanied by an appreciation of the currency. The appreciation, in turn, is called forth by an instantaneous depreciation. In an inflationary environment, the association of low interest and currency appreciation may only appear in the real interest rates and real exchange rates, while nominal interest rates continue to be high (though less so) and the nominal exchange rate continues to depreciate (though more slowly).

In a closed economy, monetary expansion typically initiates an expansion of output, followed by a later decline as prices rise. In an open economy with floating rates, the improvement in competitiveness due to overshooting adds a further impulse. Conversely, the recessionary effects resulting from monetary contraction are further aggravated by the loss of competitiveness in foreign markets resulting from currency appreciation. While conclusive empirical estimates are still lacking, recent examples (like that of the United Kingdom) seem to indicate that the additional impulse from overshooting, positive or negative, can be quite large compared to the effect of monetary policy in a closed economy.[20]

If the impulse from overshooting takes effect simultaneously with the domestic impulse, the variability of output and employment is increased. I regard this as the likely case.[21] It is logically conceivable, however, that the overshooting effect takes hold when the domestic effect is already receding. In this case the output effect of monetary expansion would be spread over a longer period than in a closed economy.

The effect of overshooting on foreign trade and capital flows is less clear. Suppose the income effect on foreign-asset demand and the price elasticity of foreign trade, at least initially, are relatively weak. Suppose further that trade reacts strongly to income expansion and that the demand for foreign assets is quite sensitive to capital-goods prices. In this case, monetary expansion first

20. For a simulation study based on the U.K. case, see Buiter and Miller (1982).
21. As noted above, the submodels of sections 11.3 and 11.4 are not realistic inasmuch as output reaches its peak immediately upon the increase in the money supply. In reality, the peak is likely to be reached after several months.

produces a period of deficits and capital inflows, later followed by surpluses and capital outflows. This seems to be the likely case, particularly with a strong *J*-effect in foreign trade elasticities. In the opposite case the sequence of events is reversed. There is, in general, no clear-cut relationship between the exchange rate and the current account. Eventually, possibly after several oscillations, aggregate surpluses will match aggregate deficits, and foreign assets will return to their initial level.

Through real exchange rates, monetary policy in one country affects prices, interest rates, output, real income, and trade in other countries. It is true that in the long run each country's monetary policy affects only its own price level. In the short run, however, floating exchange rates do not generally insulate an economy against imported deflation or inflation and the associated underemployment or overemployment.[22]

In the case of a monetary expansion abroad, the primary effect on the domestic economy is an immediate appreciation of the real exchange rate. It may be called "imported overshooting." Interest rates now show a differential in favor of domestic assets. At an unchanged exchange rate, there would thus be an excess demand for the domestic currency. As a consequence, the domestic currency appreciates to the point where the interest differential is just offset by the expected depreciation. The most conspicuous recent example is the appreciation of currencies like the yen, the pound sterling, the mark, and the Swiss franc in terms of the dollar as a consequence of the weakening monetary policy of the United States in 1977-78. The later tightening of U.S. monetary policy provided an example in the opposite direction.

If domestic interest rates are held constant, the burden of adjustment will be borne first by the exchange rate alone. In the case of foreign expansion, the domestic central bank will probably find that interest rates can be held constant only by some contraction of the domestic money supply. If, on the other hand, the money supply is held constant while domestic interest rates are free to adjust, some part of the adjustment will probably be provided by a decline in domestic interest rates.[23] The initial currency appreciation is correspondingly reduced.

At first, the trade balance is likely to show an export surplus. One reason is the expansion in foreign income. Another reason is the J-effect, which reduces the negative influence of appreciation on the current account and may even make it positive initially. The export surplus has its counterpart in an outflow of capital, attracted by the favorable investment opportunities created by the monetary expansion abroad. At the same time, however, new or-

22. The "bottling up" of domestic disturbances by floating exchange rates is discussed in section 5.3.

23. A rigorous analysis of the instantaneous effect of monetary policy on foreign interest rates is provided in section 12.2. It shows that, in strict logic, the possibility of an increase in interest rates in the case of foreign monetary expansion cannot be excluded.

ders from abroad begin to decline under the impact of the reduced competitiveness, and domestic industry suffers from increasing import competition. In due course, this will lead to a reversal in the current account associated with a capital inflow. As pointed out above, the sequence of these phases may well be different. The main point is that foreign monetary expansion is likely to produce a wave of disturbances in foreign trade and capital flows.

These disturbances are normally associated with fluctuations in domestic output and employment. In fact, in view of the lag between the placement of orders and the shipment of goods, the effects of overshooting on output may precede those on recorded exports. The reaction of export quantities may be further reduced by the acceptance of orders at depressed prices. At the same time, the decline in domestic income helps to counteract the effect of overshooting on imports. For these reasons, the consequences of imported overshooting may actually be more pronounced in income and employment than they are in foreign trade. In the midst of recession there may be talk of a "foreign trade miracle." In the later phases, the income effects of exchange overshooting will, of course, vanish and eventually be reversed.[24]

Again, there is no certainty that the sequence of events may not be different. However, it seems virtually inevitable that shifts in foreign monetary policy, through the overshooting of exchange rates, produce disturbances for the domestic economy. This is probably the most serious consequence of floating exchange rates.

24. These repercussions of the exchange rate on output and trade are well illustrated in an investigation of the Swiss case by Zenger (1982).

CHAPTER 12

Comparative Advantages of Alternative Policy Instruments

Introduction

The dynamic processes analyzed in chapter 11 are initiated by the simplest type of policy, namely, a one-time increase in the money supply. For the purpose of economic theory this increase may be thought to be achieved, for example, by handing out currency in the form of randomly distributed transfer payments. In the real world, monetary policy is not conducted in this way. In fact, central banks, as the principal suppliers of money, do not have the ability to increase the money supply without at the same time reducing the supply of some other financial asset. Monetary policy of the central bank typically consists of an exchange of money against some nonmonetary financial instrument. In general, its economic effects are different depending on the instrument used. It may be said that different instruments have different comparative advantages.[1] These comparative advantages are the subject of this chapter. The alternative policy instruments are specified in section 12.1. Their effects are analyzed in the following three sections, beginning with instantaneous stock adjustments, progressing to the Keynesian flow aspects, and concluding with the steady state.

The analysis is conducted in comparative-static terms. For each policy measure there is, in fact, a dynamic adjustment process similar to those dis-

1. That a given change in the money supply may have different effects depending on how it is brought about was recognized by Keynes (1936, pp. 200 f.). The classic paper on the subject is Metzler (1951). Research on the comparative advantages of fiscal and monetary policies was brought to maturity by Mundell (1960, 1962, 1968) and Fleming (1962), building on Meade (1951) and Tinbergen (1952). The literature in this field is vast. Allen and Kenen (1980) provide a detailed taxonomy of results for a two-country model with three goods and three assets.

cussed in the preceding chapter. In the present chapter, however, the description of this process is reduced to three still pictures of successive phases.

12.1 The Policy Instruments

If a government runs a deficit, the deficit is financed by selling financial assets like bonds or treasury bills to the private sector of the economy. At any given moment, the net aggregate stock supply of financial assets reflects the history of past deficits and surpluses. The central bank supplies the private sector with money by buying financial assets (both government and private) and paying in currency or central-bank deposits. To what extent and in what forms this has been done in the past can be seen from the central bank's balance sheet.

In the simplified balance sheet of table 12.1.1, the liability side shows the amount of currency and central-bank deposits supplied or "created."[2] This is called the monetary base. Whereas the currency is held mostly by the private sector, the deposits largely serve as reserves of commercial banks. The monetary base differs from what is usually called the money supply inasmuch as it includes, besides currency, the deposits of commercial banks, while the money supply includes the deposits of the nonbank sector with commercial banks. In the following discussion, banks are lumped together with the private sector, and the term "money supply" is used in the sense of the monetary base.

Money is created by making domestic loans and buying domestic securities (usually government securities), or by buying foreign assets (here called foreign exchange), or by buying gold. For the theoretical purpose of the present discussion, domestic loans and securities are assumed to consist of homogeneous perpetuities with a fixed coupon of $1.00. This is unrealistic, to be sure, because most central-bank assets are short-term. However, the gain in simplicity is worth the loss in realism. The number of such bonds held by

TABLE 12.1.1

Central-Bank Balance Sheet

Assets	*Liabilities*
Loans and securities (b)	Currency
Foreign exchange (f)	Deposits
Gold (g)	
Monetary base	Monetary base (M)

2. Net worth is omitted throughout. It should be noted that capital gains due to changes in asset prices are reflected in net worth.

the central bank is denoted by b. Their market value is, of course, $1/i$, where i is the domestic interest rate.

Foreign assets of the central bank typically consist of foreign short-term securities (like treasury bills), time deposits (like Eurodeposits), and claims against foreign central banks. The discussion is again simplified by assuming that they consist of perpetuities, denoted by f, with a coupon of 1 unit of foreign currency. Their foreign-currency value is $1/j$ and their domestic-currency value is e/j, where j is the foreign interest rate. It is assumed that domestic and foreign assets are more or less imperfect substitutes.

Gold consists either of gold ingots or, in the case of the Federal Reserve, of certificates on gold held by the Treasury. The gold, g, is measured in physical units and assumed to be valued at the going market price, p_g. In recent years, most central banks have been inactive in the gold market except for the gold sales of the U.S. Treasury and the International Monetary Fund. In central-bank balance sheets, gold reserves are often carried at historical or conventional prices. It is worth noting, however, that in principle, gold operations are still an instrument of monetary policy, having their specific comparative advantages. [3]

In symbols, the content of table 12.1.1 can be expressed by the equation

$$\frac{1}{i}b + \frac{e}{j}f + p_g g = M. \tag{12.1.1}$$

In terms of this rudimentary balance sheet the following "pure" policies can be defined:

1. Open-market operations (OMO) consist of central-bank purchases or sales of domestic securities. In this case, $(1/i)db = dM$ and $df = dg = 0$.

2. Foreign-exchange operations (FEO) are defined as purchases or sales of foreign securities, which means $(e/j)df = dM$ and $db = dg = 0$.

3. Gold operations (GO) consist of gold purchases at the going gold price as expressed by $p_g dg = dM$ and $db = df = 0$.

In addition, the central bank can use any two of these policies, but in the opposite direction, in such a way that the money supply remains constant. For three pure instruments there are, in principle, three "mixed" policies of this sort. However, since the subsequent analysis does not give any further attention to gold, it is enough to specify just one mixed policy as follows:

4. A portfolio shift (PS) is assumed to consist of an increase in foreign assets at the expense of domestic securities with an unchanged monetary base. It can be written $(e/j)df = -(1/i)db$, $dM = dg = 0$. This may be called a policy of complete sterilization.

The question is how these policies affect interest rates, exchange rates, prices, output, and capital flows. Answers are provided in the following sections. [4]

---

3. These are analyzed in Niehans (1982b).
4. The following discussion is based on Niehans (1981a).

12.2 Instantaneous Effects: Asset Prices

The instantaneous effects of monetary policy are confined to the prices of existing assets as reflected in interest rates and exchange rates. Production, consumption, saving, investment, output prices, and trade can change only gradually. At the first instant they may be regarded as given. A pure stock or asset approach is appropriate in this case. The stock of private foreign assets is also among the constants; it can only gradually be changed by capital flows. As a consequence, it is unnecessary to distinguish between domestic and foreign-asset holders. What matters is only the equilibrium between stock demand and stock supply in the market as a whole.[5]

The private sector holds four assets, namely, domestic money M, domestic bonds B, foreign bonds F, and foreign money M^*. The stock demand for each asset depends on the exchange rate, the domestic interest rate, and the foreign interest rate:

$$M = L(e, i, j) \qquad L_e > 0 \quad L_i < 0 \quad L_j < 0 \tag{12.2.1}$$

$$B/i = B(e, i, j) \qquad B_e > 0 \quad B_i > 0 \quad B_j < 0 \tag{12.2.2}$$

$$F/j = F(e, i, j) \qquad F_e < 0 \quad F_i < 0 \quad F_j > 0 \tag{12.2.3}$$

$$M^* = L^*(e, i, j). \qquad L_e^* < 0 \quad L_i^* < 0 \quad L_j^* < 0 \tag{12.2.4}$$

Without loss of generality, the initial exchange rate may be normalized at $e = 1$.

On the assumption that assets are gross substitutes, the partial derivatives with respect to interest rates are straightforward. The exchange-rate effects reflect mainly speculative motives. An increase in the price of foreign currency reduces the likelihood of a future increase and raises the risk of a future decline. As a consequence, the demand for foreign assets is reduced and the demand for domestic assets rises. (This is discussed in more detail in chapter 10.) With given asset stocks, one of these functions depends on the other three. This is assumed to be L^*. The dependence implies that

$$L_e + B_e + F_e = -L_e^* > 0,$$

$$L_i + B_i + \frac{B}{i^2} + F_i = -L_i^* > 0, \tag{12.2.5}$$

$$L_j + B_j + F_j + \frac{F}{j^2} = -L_j^* > 0.$$

The total supply of foreign and domestic bonds by the respective governments is given. As a consequence, the supply to the private sector changes by the same amount as the central-bank portfolio:

---

5. This approach was first used by Black (1973) and developed by Girton and Henderson (1976, 1977). Similar models are found in Branson (1979) and Kouri (1980).

$$dB = -db,$$
$$dF = -df.$$
(12.2.6)

The effect of given policies on the exchange rate and interest rates can be determined by taking differentials of (12.2.1) through (12.2.3), keeping in mind (12.2.6):

$$L_e de + \qquad L_i di + \qquad L_j dj = \frac{1}{i} db + \frac{1}{j} df \quad (12.2.7)$$

$$B_e de + \left(B_i + \frac{B}{i^2}\right) di + \qquad B_j dj = -\frac{1}{i} db \qquad (12.2.8)$$

$$F_e de + \qquad F_i di + \left(F_j + \frac{F}{j^2}\right) dj = \qquad -\frac{1}{j} df. \quad (12.2.9)$$

Before the results are given in mathematical terms, a simplified version of the model is represented graphically. The simplification consists in assuming that the foreign central bank, by suitable open-market operations, is keeping the foreign interest rate at a fixed level so that $dj = 0$. This makes foreign money and foreign securities perfect substitutes, thereby eliminating the equilibrium condition for foreign assets (12.2.9). As a consequence, the model can be represented in two dimensions.

In figure 12.2.1 the money-equilibrium curve *MM* connects all those combinations of i and e which, for a given central-bank balance sheet, satisfy (12.2.7). An increase in e raises the demand for domestic money while an increase in i lowers it. To maintain equilibrium, an increase in e must thus be associated with an increase in i; the curve slopes upward. Combinations of e and i that satisfy (12.2.8) are found along the bond-equilibrium curve *BB*. Since B_e and B_i have the same sign, it must be sloping downward. The initial equilibrium is at the intersection point E.

If the central bank engages in open-market purchases, the increase in the money supply shifts the *MM* curve to the right. At the same time, the reduction in the bond supply shifts the *BB* curve to the left. The new equilibrium is at a point like G. It is evident that the interest rate declines. It is less evident, but nevertheless true, that the currency depreciates, as drawn. This is most easily seen by considering that there must also be an equilibrium curve *FF* for foreign assets (not drawn). Since $F_e < 0$ and $F_i < 0$, it has negative slope and, by virtue of the wealth constraint, goes through E. It is also steeper than B. Since open-market operations leave this curve unaffected, the economy must move along it. This implies that e rises.

In the case of foreign-exchange purchases, the *MM* curve again shifts to the right, but now the *BB* curve stays in place (which implies that the imaginary *FF* curve shifts to the right). The economy thus moves to a point like H. Again the interest rate declines (but less than for OMO) and the currency depreciates (but more than for OMO).

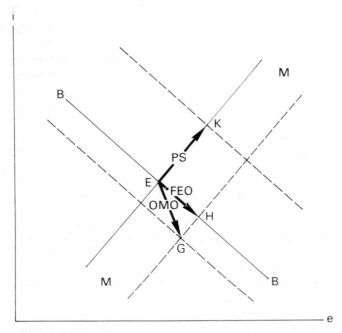

FIGURE 12.2.1
Instantaneous Effects of Monetary Policies

This means that the effects of open-market operations and foreign-exchange operations are qualitatively the same. In particular, it would be seriously wrong to believe that domestic open-market operations have no effect on the exchange rate and that foreign-exchange operations have no effect on the domestic credit market. As long as the central bank does anything, it is virtually certain also to influence the exchange rate. Under these circumstances it is difficult to see what "pure floating," under which the central bank abstains from "intervening" in the foreign-exchange market, is supposed to mean.

At the same time, the graphical analysis indicates that open-market operations have a comparative advantage in influencing the domestic interest rate, while foreign-exchange operations have an advantage in influencing the exchange rate. Consider a portfolio shift in which foreign-exchange purchases are associated with domestic bond sales, while the money supply remains unchanged. This moves the economy along the *MM* curve to a point like *K*. The price of foreign currency rises, confirming the dominating influence of the foreign-exchange purchases, and the interest rate also rises, confirming the dominating influence of the bond sales.

I now return to the more general model with variable foreign interest rates. The results of different policies depend crucially on the sign of the determinant Δ, formed by the coefficients on the left-hand side of (12.2.7) through (12.2.9). It can be shown by standard techniques that $\Delta > 0$ is necessary for the stability of the system. The following discussion assumes that this condition is satisfied.

The effects of open-market operations can be determined by letting $db > 0$ and $df = 0$ and then solving (12.2.7) through (12.2.9) for de, di, and dj in terms of db. The results can be further simplified by using the implied coefficients of the demand function for foreign cash balances as given in (12.2.5). Open-market purchases clearly result in a depreciation of the home currency:

$$\frac{de}{db/i} = \frac{1}{\Delta}\left[F_i L_j^* - \left(F_j + \frac{F}{j^2}\right)L_i^*\right] > 0. \tag{12.2.10}$$

At the same time, the domestic interest rate declines:

$$\frac{di}{db/i} = -\frac{1}{\Delta}[(L_j + B_j)L_e^* - (L_e + B_e)L_j^*] < 0. \tag{12.2.11}$$

This confirms the conclusions from the graphical analysis. The effect on foreign interest rates, however, is ambiguous:

$$\frac{dj}{db/i} = \frac{1}{\Delta}(F_e L_i^* - F_i L_e^*) \gtreqless 0. \tag{12.2.12}$$

In the case of open-market operations it is not certain, therefore, that cheaper money in one country also tends to produce cheaper money in the rest of the world. Interest rates move in a parallel fashion if the demand for foreign currency is relatively more sensitive to the exchange rate while the demand for foreign bonds is relatively more sensitive to the domestic interest rate. This is indeed the more likely case. Interest rate movements in opposite directions cannot generally be excluded, however.

The effects of foreign-exchange purchases, defined by $df > 0$ and $db = 0$, are qualitatively similar. Again the domestic currency depreciates as indicated by

$$\frac{de}{df/j} = \frac{1}{\Delta}\left[B_j L_i^* - \left(B_i + \frac{B}{i^2}\right)L_j^*\right] > 0, \tag{12.2.13}$$

the domestic interest rate declines according to

$$\frac{di}{df/j} = -\frac{1}{\Delta}(B_j L_e^* - B_e L_j^*) < 0, \tag{12.2.14}$$

and the reaction of foreign interest rates,

$$\frac{dj}{df/j} = \frac{1}{\Delta}\left[\left(B_i + \frac{B}{i^2}\right)L_e^{**} - B_e L_i^*\right] \gtreqless 0, \tag{12.2.15}$$

is ambiguous but more likely to be negative.

Quantitatively, however, the effects of open-market operations and foreign-exchange operations are different. In particular, open-market operations have a relatively stronger effect on domestic interest rates and a relatively weaker effect on the exchange rate. This can easily be checked by calculating the effects of a portfolio shift, defined by $df = -(j/i)db$. The results are

$$\frac{de}{df/j} = \frac{1}{\Delta}(L_i L_j^* - L_j L_i^*) > 0, \tag{12.2.16}$$

$$\frac{di}{df/j} = \frac{1}{\Delta}(L_j L_e^* - L_e L_j^*) > 0, \tag{12.2.17}$$

$$\frac{dj}{df/j} = -\frac{1}{\Delta}(L_i L_e^* - L_e L_i^*) < 0. \tag{12.2.18}$$

It is evident that purchases of foreign assets at the expense of domestic assets must lower the interest rate on the former and raise it on the latter. The depreciation of the domestic currency requires that in each country the demand for money be relatively more sensitive to the domestic interest rate than to the foreign interest rate; it is difficult to see how it could be otherwise. If the demand for domestic and foreign cash balances is almost insensitive to the domestic interest rate, but highly sensitive to exchange speculation, the central bank loses its power over the exchange rate. The *MM* curve, and thus the PS arrow, comes close to being vertical. If, on the other hand, the demand for money is little affected by the exchange rate, a portfolio shift has its main effect on the exchange rate, leaving interest rates virtually unchanged. In this case the MM curve would be close to the horizontal.

The comparative advantages of alternative policy instruments can be exploited by the central bank to achieve, by suitable combination of the instruments, the desired configuration of exchange rates and interest rates.[6] It is possible, for example, to produce a depreciation of the currency at unchanged domestic interest rates by combining foreign-exchange purchases with open-market sales, though in a smaller amount. It is also possible to lower domestic interest rates at unchanged exchange rates by combining open-market purchases with a smaller amount of foreign-exchange sales. The availability of such options is the main reason why central banks may find it advantageous to have a choice among different instruments of monetary policy. This requires, of course, that their balance sheets include both foreign and domestic assets.[7]

6. The required levels of the policy instruments can be determined from (12.2.7) through (12.2.9) by assigning the desired values to *de* and *di* and then solving for *db* and *df*.
7. Gold operations would add another dimension to policy making. By combining them with the appropriate open-market operations and foreign-exchange operations it would be possible, for example, to expand the money supply without any change in either the rate of interest or the exchange rate (see Niehans 1982b).

The comparative advantages of policy instruments have, as Mundell has shown, an interesting implication for the day-to-day conduct of monetary policy. In most cases, the parameters of the relevant economic model are very imperfectly known. As a consequence, it cannot be determined numerically how large the operations must be in order to reach given interest and exchange-rate targets. In such a case, knowledge of the comparative advantages of policy instruments makes it possible to reach the targets by trial and error. The required procedure consists in assigning each instrument to the target on which it has the relatively stronger effect. This amounts to a division of labor between policy instruments on the basis of comparative advantage. Each instrument should then be used gradually, paying attention only to the assigned target, until the latter is attained. Mundell showed that if this is done with both instruments simultaneously, but in a decentralized fashion, both targets will eventually be reached.

This proposition can be illustrated by inverting figure 12.2.1. Along the axes are now measured, respectively, the volumes of foreign-exchange operations and open-market operations (see fig. 12.2.2). The interest-target line $\bar{i}$ connects those levels of f and b which keep the domestic interest rate on target. The exchange-target line $\bar{e}$ does the same for the exchange rate. Since the effects of both instruments are qualitatively the same, both curves have a negative slope; constant target levels thus require the combination of open-market purchases with foreign-exchange sales. However, in view of the compara-

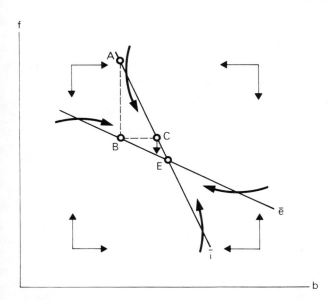

FIGURE 12.2.2
Stable Assignment of Policy Instruments

tive advantages of the policy instruments, the interest line is steeper than the exchange line.

Now suppose Mundell's principle is followed by assigning to f the task of looking after $\bar{e}$, while b is used to reach $\bar{i}$. This means increasing f whenever it is below, and reducing it whenever it is above, the $\bar{e}$ line as indicated by the vertical arrows. At the same time, b is increased whenever it is to the left, and reduced whenever it is to the right, of the $\bar{i}$ line, as indicated by the horizontal arrows. If this is continuously done in small steps, the economy will eventually end up at E. [8]

If each instrument is assigned to the wrong target, this is not so. In this case, the direction of the horizontal and vertical arrows in the NW and SE sectors would be reversed. As a consequence, decentralized policy control would lead progressively farther away from E.

The existence of comparative advantages of policy instruments depends crucially on the heterogeneity of domestic and foreign assets. If assets are completely homogeneous, interest parity being continuously maintained, it makes no difference whether the central bank creates money by buying foreign or domestic assets. [9] If the central bank wants to exploit the comparative advantage of assets, it should see to it, therefore, that the assets it uses are not very close substitutes. Treasury bills, for example, would be a better choice than, say, Eurodeposits. However, given the short-term character of most central-bank assets, the scope for the exploitation of comparative advantages will usually be quite limited.

12.3 Short-Term Effects: Output

Sooner or later, the effects of monetary policy on asset prices cannot fail to affect the flows of goods and services and thus output, employment, and trade. This reaction largely takes place before domestic prices have had time to react. In fact, it takes place exactly because domestic prices are slow in adjusting. As a first approximation it may be assumed that domestic prices are fixed. These are essentially the characteristics of the Keynesian short run.

The introduction of flows requires an extension of the model. [10] In the demand functions for assets, income fluctuations now begin to play an impor-

---

8. Alternatively it may be supposed that those in charge of a given instrument move this instrument to its target level in one step, leaving the next move to those in charge of the other instrument. Starting from a point like A, foreign-exchange operations would first lead to B, open-market operations would then take the economy to C, and so on, along a step-like path toward E.

9. Mathematically this is expressed by the fact that B_i, F_i, B_j and F_j go to (plus or minus) infinity. Infinity of one of these coefficients is enough for $\Delta = \infty$. The (inconclusive) evidence about the effectiveness of "sterilized" portfolio shifts is reviewed in Genberg (1981).

10. The following model is in the spirit of Mundell (1960, 1962) and Fleming (1962). It differs from them by focusing on the bond market instead of the domestic-goods market and by including exchange-rate effects on asset demand and capital flows.

tant role. On the other hand, the model is simplified by the assumption, already used in figure 12.2.1, that foreign interest rates are held constant by foreign central banks. This leaves two independent asset demand functions,

$$M = L(y, e, i), \qquad L_y > 0 \qquad L_e > 0 \qquad L_i < 0 \qquad (12.3.1)$$

$$\frac{B}{i} = B(y, e, i). \qquad B_y > 0 \qquad B_e > 0 \qquad B_i > 0 \qquad (12.3.2)$$

It may be assumed that the interest rate has a stronger effect on bonds than on cash balances, which implies $L_i + B_i + B/i^2 > 0$. These demand functions still include both domestic and foreign holders.

The main extension is the introduction of the balance of payments. Income, the exchange rate, and the rate of interest must be such that the current account surplus is continually equal to the capital outflow. The picture is simplified by assuming that we are looking at an economy without an accumulated stock of foreign assets and/or liabilities. This excludes wealth effects on foreign assets and interest payments in the current account. The balance-of-payments condition can then be written

$$X(e) - eI(y, e) - C(y, e, i) = 0. \qquad (12.3.3)$$

Exports and imports depend on the exchange rate in the normal way, and imports also depend positively on domestic income. The capital-export function is similar to that discussed in chapter 10. It relates not to particular assets but to relative shifts in saving and investment between domestic and foreign residents. Since this is a model for heterogeneous assets, it is appropriate to assume $C_y > 0$, $C_e < 0$, $C_i < 0$. It should be noted that the capital flow function cannot be expected to remain constant in the course of the adjustment process. As foreign assets (or liabilities) are accumulated, the function is bound to shift, and in the eventual equilibrium C is again zero. Equation (12.3.3) can be condensed to

$$T(y, e, i) = 0 \qquad (12.3.4)$$

with partial derivatives

$$T_y = -eI_y - C_y < 0,$$
$$T_e = X_e - eI_e - I - C_e > 0,$$
$$T_i = -C_i > 0.$$

The Marshall/Lerner condition is sufficient, but not necessary, for $T_e > 0$.

A further simplification is achieved by assuming that foreign-exchange operations are conducted in terms of non–interest-bearing foreign cash balances. Monetary policy is then characterized by the fact that the increase in the money supply is equal to the increase in the central-bank portfolio of domestic bonds, b, and foreign currency, $m*$, while the increase in the private bond supply is equal to central-bank bond sales:

$$dM = \frac{1}{i}db + dm*,$$ (12.3.5)

$$dB = -db.$$ (12.3.6)

For comparative-static analysis, the model is written in differential form with the exchange rate normalized at $e = 1$:

$$T_y dy + T_e de + \qquad\qquad T_i di = \quad 0$$

$$L_y dy + L_e de + \qquad\qquad L_i di = \quad \frac{1}{i}db + dm* \qquad (12.3.7)$$

$$B_y dy + B_e de + \left(B_i + \frac{B}{i^2}\right)di = -\frac{1}{i}db.$$

It can be ascertained that the determinant D, formed by the left-hand coefficients, must be negative for stability. It is thus assumed that $D < 0$. Stability also requires $T_e(B_i + B/i^2) - T_i B_e > 0$; the exchange rate must have a relatively stronger effect on payments while the rate of interest has a relatively stronger effect on the demand for bonds.

Open-market operations are defined by $db > 0$, $dm* = 0$. Their effects can be determined to be

$$\frac{dy}{db/i} = \frac{1}{D}\left[T_i(L_e + B_e) - T_e\left(L_i + B_i + \frac{B}{i^2}\right)\right] \gtreqless 0, \qquad (12.3.8)$$

$$\frac{de}{db/i} = \frac{1}{D}\left[T_y\left(L_i + B_i + \frac{B}{i^2}\right) - T_i(L_y + B_y)\right] > 0, \qquad (12.3.9)$$

$$\frac{di}{db/i} = -\frac{1}{D}[T_y(L_e + B_e) - T_e(L_y + B_y)] < 0. \qquad (12.3.10)$$

That open-market purchases still produce a depreciation of the home currency and a decline in interest rates is no surprise. The surprise is that their output effect is ambiguous. If the exchange-rate effect on the balance of payments and the interest effect on bonds are strong enough, the normal expansionary effect prevails. If, however, the interest effect on the balance of payments and the speculative exchange-rate effect on the demand for money and bonds dominate, open-market operations may result in a contraction. The apparent paradox is due to the fact that both the increased demand for foreign assets, induced by lower interest rates, and the speculative demand for domestic assets are associated with a decline in the domestic demand for goods and services. It can easily be imagined that the output effects of open-market operations change sign in the course of the adjustment process, most likely from perverse to normal, as T_e gradually rises to its full value.

No such ambiguity appears in the case of foreign-exchange operations, defined by $dm^* > 0$, $db = 0$. As expected, there is an expansion of output,

$$\frac{dy}{dm^*} = \frac{1}{D}\left[T_iB_e - T_e\left(B_i + \frac{B}{i^2}\right)\right] > 0, \tag{12.3.11}$$

a depreciation of the currency,

$$\frac{de}{dm^*} = \frac{1}{D}\left[T_y\left(B_i + \frac{B}{i^2}\right) - T_iB_y\right] > 0, \tag{12.3.12}$$

and a decline in interest rates,

$$\frac{di}{dm^*} = \frac{1}{D}(T_eB_y - T_yB_e) < 0. \tag{12.3.13}$$

The sign of the output effect is based on the stability condition given above. It is interesting to note that it is more clear-cut than in the case of open-market operations.

To complete the picture, we consider a portfolio shift, consisting of foreign-exchange purchases associated with open-market sales, at a given money supply. It is characterized by $-db/i = dm^*$. The results are

$$\frac{dy}{dm^*} = \frac{1}{D}(T_eL_i - T_iL_e) > 0, \tag{12.3.14}$$

$$\frac{de}{dm^*} = \frac{1}{D}(T_iL_y - T_yL_i) \gtreqless 0, \tag{12.3.15}$$

$$\frac{di}{dm^*} = \frac{1}{D}(T_yL_e - T_eL_y) > 0. \tag{12.3.16}$$

Output clearly expands, suggesting that its reaction is dominated by the acquisition of foreign assets. Interest rates rise, indicating that they are dominated by the sale of domestic securities. Remarkably, the reaction of exchange rates is ambiguous; it is not generally clear whether the depreciation due to the foreign-exchange purchases or the appreciation due to the bond sales dominates.

These effects are summarized in table 12.3.1. Its most interesting aspects are the two indeterminate signs. They raise the question of the comparative advantages of the policy instruments. The answer is obtained in the way indicated in section 12.2. The main argument can be represented graphically as follows.

In figure 12.3.1, the levels of domestic securities and foreign exchange held by the central bank are marked off along, respectively, the horizontal axis and the vertical axis. The solid iso-income lines connect portfolios resulting in the same output. If both instruments have a positive effect on output, these curves have a negative slope, as drawn. With a perverse effect of open-

TABLE 12.3.1

Direction of Short-Term Effects

	Output	Exchange Rate	Interest Rate
Open-market purchases	?	+	−
Foreign-exchange purchases	+	+	−
Portfolio shift	+	?	+

market operations they would slope upward. In any case, a higher level of foreign exchange is associated with higher output. We also know that a portfolio shift in favor of foreign exchange raises output. Such a shift is graphically expressed as a move along a 45° line. This means that the iso-income curves, if negatively sloped, are flatter than 45°.

The broken iso-exchange lines are the loci of policy combinations resulting in the same exchange rate. Since both de/dm^* and $de/(db/i)$ are positive, their slope is unambiguously negative, with higher m^* (or b/i) associated with a higher exchange rate. Since a portfolio shift along the 45° line can either raise or lower the exchange rate, the iso-exchange curves can be steeper or flatter than the 45° line.

The dotted iso-interest curves, finally, indicate the policies required to maintain a given interest rate. Again their slope is negative, with higher port-

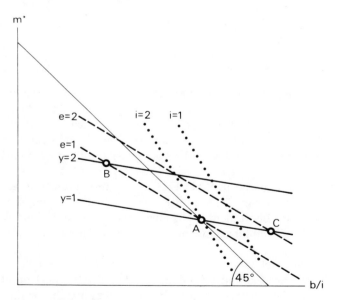

FIGURE 12.3.1
Short-Term Effects of Monetary Policies

folio levels associated with lower interest rates. These curves, however, are steeper than 45°, since a portfolio shift results in a higher interest rate.

The remarkable point is that even if both the iso-income lines and the iso-exchange lines are sloping downward at less than 45°, the former are flatter than the latter. This means that foreign-exchange operations have a comparative advantage in influencing domestic output, while domestic open-market operations have an advantage in influencing the exchange rate. The proof for this proposition, valid for the model of this section, is given in the appendix to this section. If foreign-exchange operations are conducted in terms of interest-bearing assets, the comparative advantages may be reversed.

The preceding argument illustrates the fact that the effects of economic policies on interest rates often give misleading clues about their effects on output. Open-market operations certainly have a stronger effect on interest rates, both instantaneously and in the short run, while foreign-exchange operations are relatively more effective in influencing the exchange rate. This is indicated by the slopes of the iso-exchange and the iso-interest curves in figure 12.3.1. Nevertheless, in comparing the output effect with the exchange-rate effect, open-market operations have a comparative disadvantage with respect to the exchange rate.

By exploiting the comparative advantages of policy instruments, the central bank can achieve different combinations of output, exchange rates, and interest rates. Suppose the bank is initially at a point like *A* in figure 12.3.1. It wishes to stimulate output without depreciating the currency, moving to a point like *B*. This can be achieved by selling domestic securities and using a part, but only a part, of the proceeds to buy foreign exchange. In another situation the central bank may wish to move to a point like *C* with a depreciated currency but no stimulation of output. This requires foreign-exchange sales accompanied by domestic-security purchases in an even larger amount.

The short-run model used in this section is in many respects highly simplified. It represents one particular, though interesting and important, case. In other cases the conclusions may be different. It may also happen that the comparative advantages are too small to be exploited. The preceding argument nevertheless yields three general propositions:

1. From the short-term point of view, as from the instantaneous point of view, it may be important for the central bank to have a choice among different policy instruments. The greater the difference between them, the more relevant this choice.

2. The comparative advantages of different policy instruments are not obvious but, rather, require detailed analysis.

3. In particular, foreign-exchange operations may be more potent in influencing domestic output, while open-market operations may have a relatively stronger effect on the exchange rate.

Appendix to Section 12.3: Comparative Advantages of Policy Instruments

Consider the model of (12.3.7). To determine the rate at which foreign assets can be substituted for bonds without changing output, let $dy = 0$ and transpose dm^* to the left-hand side. The system of equations can then be solved for $dm^*/(db/i)$ and the result can be written

$$-\frac{dm^*}{db/i}(\bar{y}) = 1 + \frac{L_i - T_i(L_e/T_e)}{(B_i + B/i^2) - T_i(B_e/T_e)} = 1 + A_y, \qquad \text{(A.1)}$$

with $A_y < 0$ in view of stability requirements. This means that the iso-income curves have a slope of no less than -1.

To determine the slope of the iso-exchange curves, let $de = 0$ and solve again for $dm^*/(db/i)$. The result is

$$-\frac{dm^*}{db/i}(\bar{e}) = 1 + \frac{L_i - T_i(L_y/T_y)}{(B_i + B/i^2) - T_i(B_y/T_y)} = 1 + A_e, \qquad \text{(A.2)}$$

where $A_e \gtreqless 0$. This indicates that the iso-exchange curves can be either steeper or flatter than 45°.

If $A_e > 0$, since $A_y < 0$, the iso-exchange curves are evidently steeper than the iso-income curves. The same is true, though less evident, if $A_e < 0$. The difference between (A.2) and (A.1) is

$$A_e - A_y = \frac{(-L_i) + T_i(L_e/T_e)}{(B_i + B/i^2) - T_i(B_e/T_e)}$$

$$- \frac{(-L_i) + T_i(L_y/T_y)}{(B_i + B/i^2) - T_i(B_y/T_y)},$$

but

$$T_i\frac{L_e}{T_e} > 0, \qquad T_i\frac{L_y}{T_y} < 0$$

and

$$T_i\frac{B_e}{T_e} > 0, \qquad T_i\frac{B_y}{T_y} < 0.$$

It follows that $A_e - A_y > 0$, which establishes the proposition.

12.4 Long-Term Effects: Resource Allocation

In the long run, the output effects of monetary policy are bound to vanish. Whatever policy instrument is used, employment eventually goes back to its normal level. If the money is supplied by transfers, as assumed in chapter 11, while government debt is zero, there are no long-run real effects at all.

Money is neutral, its sole effect being a proportionate increase in prices and exchange rates. The quantity theory and purchasing-power parity rule the field. This is different in the presence of government debt. In this case, even "dropping money from helicopters" would have permanent effects on resource allocation. Moreover, these effects differ depending on how the money is created. These long-run real effects of monetary policy are the subject of the present section.[11]

To reduce the argument to the simplest possible terms, consider an economy with given resources producing a traded good, x, at price p and a nontraded good, y, at price q. Resources grow at rate g both at home and abroad. The world economy is in balanced growth, and all stocks and flows are written in per capita terms. The world price of the traded good, p^*, is given, and its domestic price is $p = ep^*$. The economy holds net foreign assets. These are assumed to have the form of perpetuities with a coupon of one unit of foreign currency per year. Their amount, A, is measured by these coupon payments, and their value is A/j. The continuous adjustment of foreign assets to economic growth requires annual capital exports of $(g/j)A$. At the same time, interest is earned at the foreign rate j. If the rate of interest exceeds the rate of growth, there is a trade deficit in the amount of $(1 - g/j)A$. The economy can afford to consume more traded goods than it produces and simultaneously export capital, paying the balance with the income on foreign investments. This is the case considered in this section.

The allocation of resources between the two sectors depends on the amount of foreign assets in the portfolios of both the private sector and the central bank. The private demand for foreign assets, in turn, depends on the rate of interest. Both by its direct asset holding and by its influence on the domestic interest rate the central bank thus influences the allocation of resources as measured by the relative size of the traded-goods sector and the home sector.[12] This influence is now analyzed in more detail.

The demand for domestic money and domestic bonds is written

$$M = pL(i) = ep^*L(i), \qquad L_i < 0 \tag{12.4.1}$$

$$\frac{B}{i} = pB(i) = ep^*B(i). \qquad B_i > 0 \tag{12.4.2}$$

Exchange rates influence asset demand through their effect on traded-goods prices. The assumption that the relevant deflator includes only traded-goods prices permits a considerable simplification of the exposition.

These demand functions determine the exchange rate and the domestic interest rate for given supplies of money and bonds. Consider figure 12.4.1.

---

11. The following analysis is based on Niehans (1981b).

12. At the same time, the central bank influences the capital intensity of the domestic economy and thereby the level of consumption, but this aspect, since it is not specific to an open economy, is not further pursued here.

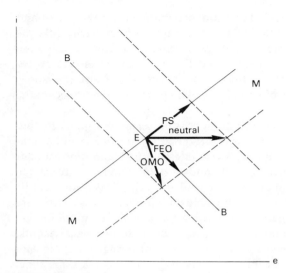

FIGURE 12.4.1
Long-Term Effects of Monetary Policies

The money-equilibrium curve *MM* connects those exchange rates and interest rates that satisfy (12.4.1); its slope is clearly positive. The bond-equilibrium curve *BB*, resulting from (12.4.2) has negative slope. Equilibrium is attained where the curves intersect. [13]

The supply of domestic assets to the private sector depends on the central bank portfolio (see eq. 12.1.1),

$$M = \frac{1}{i}b + \frac{e}{j}f,$$ (12.4.3)

and the given supply of government debt,

$$\bar{B} = B + b.$$ (12.4.4)

Money creation through foreign-asset purchases expresses itself in a rightward shift of the *MM* curve while the *BB* curve stays in place. It produces an increase in the exchange rate and a decline in the rate of interest (see FEO arrow). If the central bank creates domestic money by buying domestic bonds, the rightward shift in *MM* is accompanied by a leftward shift in the *BB* curve. Again the exchange rate rises, but less than in the preceding case, while interest rates decline even more. [14] Suppose the central bank decides on

13. Note that these curves, while they look similar to those in figure 12.2.1, have different economic content inasmuch as there are no speculative effects.
14. That *e* unambiguously rises is not evident from the graph but can be verified mathematically, provided the direct effect of the rate of interest on the demand for bonds is no weaker absolutely than its indirect effect on the demand for money.

a permanent portfolio shift characterized by a higher proportion of foreign-exchange purchases at the expense of open-market purchases. In this case, the economy moves along the PS arrow to higher interest rates and a higher exchange rate.

Aren't there ways to change the money supply in a neutral manner so that the exchange rate rises in accordance with purchasing-power parity while the interest rate remains unchanged? Indeed there are. They require a combination of foreign-exchange purchases and portfolio shifts (or open-market sales) in such proportions that the economy moves along the horizontal arrow. Neutrality can also be achieved, in coordination with government fiscal policy, by buying no foreign exchange at all and expanding government debt at the same rate as the money supply. [15]

An increase in the foreign assets of the central bank, assuming these are interest-earning, amounts to a direct increase in the foreign assets of the economy. An indirect, but potentially more important, effect is exerted through interest rates on private foreign assets. The demand for the latter can be written

$$\frac{F}{j} = \frac{p}{e}F(i) = p^*F(i). \qquad F_i < 0 \qquad (12.4.5)$$

Total returns on foreign assets are, therefore,

$$A = jp^*F(i) + f. \qquad (12.4.6)$$

An increase in f thus raises A both directly and indirectly through the lowering of i. In the case of domestic open-market operations the direct effect is missing, but the indirect effect is even stronger. [16] Through foreign assets, monetary policy influences the structure of the economy. Suppose A is initially zero. We can then draw a production frontier for domestic goods and traded goods (see fig. 12.4.2). In the absence of trade, it also represents the consumption possibilities. If preferences are as indicated by the indifference curves, perfect competition would guide the economy to point Q. Now suppose central-bank policy results in an increase in foreign assets to $A = 1$, $A = 2$, etc. As a consequence, the production block moves to the right. The difference between consumption and production, $x - \bar{x}$, is paid for by the excess of interest receipts over growth-induced capital exports,

$$x - \bar{x} = \left(1 - \frac{g}{j}\right)(A/p^*). \qquad (12.4.7)$$

With increasing A, consumption moves along the expansion path EE. If both goods are superior, it is clear that resource allocation is shifting increasingly

---

15. Note that debt expansion is essentially similar to a portfolio shift by the central bank.
16. It is shown in Niehans (1981b) that, on balance, foreign-exchange purchases are likely to have the stronger effect on A.

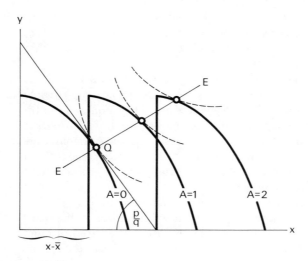

FIGURE 12.4.2
Allocation Effects of Foreign Assets

in favor of nontraded goods, while the traded-goods sector shrinks. This shift is associated with an increase in domestic prices relative to international prices.

By creating money through foreign-asset purchases instead of using a neutral policy, the central bank thus causes consumption to be permanently more import-oriented while domestic production is more home-oriented. The same is true, though probably to a lesser extent, if open-market purchases are used. If there is a lasting shift from a neutral policy to foreign-exchange operations, the traded-goods sector will shrink and the foreign currency will appear to be "undervalued" relative to purchasing-power parity. It is interesting to note that precisely the continuous buying of foreign assets by the central banks leads to the impression that the foreign currency is "undervalued."

I conclude this chapter with a general comment about the significance of nonmonetary assets. It has been customary in recent years to contrast a monetary approach and an asset approach to exchange-rate determination. The monetary approach is supposed to be characterized by the proposition that exchange rates are determined by relative money supplies, whereas the asset approach attributes a significant role to nonmonetary assets. This chapter has clearly shown that, in general, nonmonetary assets indeed matter. The exchange rate is not a purely monetary phenomenon.

It has sometimes been argued that the validity of the monetary approach depends crucially on the international substitutability of nonmonetary assets. This is incorrect. Even with perfect substitutability, an increase in the bond supply, either at home or abroad, through temporary budget deficits generally has an effect on exchange rates, both in the short and the long run. Other assumptions must be added to the perfect substitutability of assets to make the monetary approach strictly valid. [17]

It may nevertheless be true that in many cases nonmonetary assets do not matter very much, so that the exchange rate is largely, though not purely, a monetary phenomenon. In such cases the monetary approach would be valid as a first approximation. The experience and evidence accumulated since the collapse of the Bretton Woods system seems to indicate that this is indeed so. Clearly this is not a question of doctrinal controversy, but of the pragmatic selection of a suitable model for particular cases.

17. In the models of this chapter, suitable assumptions can be found by determining the exchange rate effect of an exogenous increase in government debt at an unchanged central bank portfolio and selecting parameter values in such a way that this effect is zero.

CHAPTER 13

Strategies for Floating Rates

Introduction

The analysis of chapter 11 showed that in the short run exchange rates are likely to deviate considerably from purchasing-power parity. In chapter 12 it was further shown that the effects of foreign-exchange operations are generally different from those of domestic credit operations. This raises the question which strategies the central bank should follow in its foreign-exchange operations.

It must at once be added that the discussion in this chapter is incomplete inasmuch as it is restricted to a limited number of aspects. Other aspects are discussed in chapter 14, and an effort to integrate these elements is made in chapter 15. For the purpose of the present chapter it is assumed that exchange rates are floating, but it is "managed floating," in the sense that central banks have the option of buying and selling foreign-currency assets. The question is what use they should make of this option.

Three particular strategies are considered. According to the first, discussed in section 13.2, the central bank tries to reduce exchange-rate fluctuations by counterspeculative interventions. The second strategy, taken up in section 13.3, uses monetary policy to keep exchange rates continuously at the purchasing-power parity. The third strategy, considered in section 13.4, uses temporary exchange-rate ceilings to prevent massive deviations of exchange rates from purchasing-power parity. The discussion of these strategies is preceded in section 13.1 by a discussion of the choice between a strategy based on the control of monetary aggregates and an exchange-rate strategy.

13.1 The Choice between Money Control and Exchange-Rate Control

In a closed economy, the central bank has the familiar choice between controlling the quantity of base money and controlling the rate of interest. In an open economy, there is a similar choice between setting the quantity of domestic base money to be created by foreign-exchange purchases and setting the exchange rate at which such purchases are made. This choice is the subject of the present section.

The discussion will be limited to the case of a country that creates all of its money by foreign-exchange purchases. No domestic securities are held by the central bank. From the point of view of the United States this is unrealistic, but for some other countries it is reasonably close to reality; Switzerland, at least up into the late 1970s, is a good example. The assumption serves to exclude all questions of alternative policy instruments. The problems discussed in chapter 12 are left in the background.[1]

The decision to control the money supply is not meant to imply a constant quantity or a constant rate of expansion; it can relate to any path of the money supply. Similarly, the decision to control the exchange rate does not imply fixed exchange rates or any other specific pattern; as a consequence, the chosen path of the exchange rate may exhibit any sort of fluctuation. The choice between fixed and floating rates is discussed in the following chapter.

It should first be observed that the central bank, with qualifications to be noted presently, can indeed control the exchange rate. All it has to do is to announce the rate at which, on a given day, it is willing to buy or sell foreign exchange. If all domestic money, as assumed, was originally created by foreign-exchange purchases, the central bank will generally be able to live up to such an announcement regardless of the choice of the exchange rate. If at the announced rates the market wishes to buy domestic currency, it will always be able to do so because there is no limit to the quantity the bank can create. If the announced rates are such that the market wishes to buy foreign exchange, the central bank has to sell the latter from its own reserves, which are limited. Nevertheless, since reserves are assumed to "cover" the whole money supply, it is unlikely to run out of reserves. Long before reserves are exhausted, the increasing tightness of the money supply will have stopped the reserve loss. Reserves may impose a constraint, however, if the central bank offers to sell foreign exchange much cheaper than it was originally bought. In this case the loss of foreign exchange may force the central bank to raise its price. The main point is that the central bank, if it decides to do so, can indeed control the exchange rate within a considerable margin. If, contrary to the present

---

1. Note that it is impossible for all countries to create all of their money by the acquisition of foreign central bank deposits, because in this case all base money would end up in the portfolio of a central bank; nothing would be left for the private sector.

assumptions, a sizable part of the portfolio consists of domestic securities, this margin is, of course, much smaller.

At the same time, it is clear that the central bank cannot control more than one exchange rate. It can control either the dollar price of its currency or the sterling price, but not both. The other rates are then determined by the market.[2]

The corollary of exchange-rate control is, inevitably, the lack of money control. The central bank has to accept passively the amount of money the private sector wishes to hold. With a high price of foreign exchange this amount will be high and with a low price it will be low. Conversely, if the bank decides to control the domestic money supply, it has to accept passively the exchange rates at which the private sector, day by day, is willing to hold that money.

If the central bank knew exactly at what exchange rates different quantities of money would be held, the choice between money control and exchange-rate control would be meaningless. The bank could simply select a point on the demand curve for money (or, equivalently, for foreign exchange). It would make no difference whether this point was reached by announcing the price or by controlling the quantity. This is an unlikely case, though. In most situations, the central bank is quite uncertain about the result of its policy. In this case, the choice between money control and exchange-rate control makes a difference. The following argument is intended to explain the essential point as simply as possible.[3]

Consider an open economy with only one good. The private sector holds domestic money and foreign money, and the two currencies are imperfect substitutes. The analysis relates to the short run, in which prices are given and output is variable. The surplus in the balance of payments, including both trade and capital flows, depends negatively on income and positively on the exchange rate; in equilibrium it must be zero. The central bank's notions about the balance of payments are expressed by

$$P(y, e) = 0. \qquad P_y < 0 \qquad P_e > 0 \qquad (13.1.1)$$

The demand for domestic money must equal the supply

$$L(y, e) = M, \qquad L_y > 0 \qquad L_e > 0 \qquad (13.1.2)$$

where $L(y, e)$ summarizes the central bank's notions about the demand for money.

In figure 13.1.1, equation (13.1.1) is represented by the payments-

2. If a central bank holds a diversified foreign-exchange portfolio, it may be able to exert a slight influence on cross rates too.

3. The argument was originally developed by Poole (1970a) with respect to the choice between money-supply control and interest-rate control in a closed economy. For the application to exchange rates, see Boyer (1978) and Parkin (1978). Related contributions are Turnovsky (1976), Fischer (1977), and Henderson (1979).

equilibrium curve *PP*. It slopes upward because an increase in *y* must be off-set by an increase in *e*. The money-equilibrium curves *LL*, one for each value of *M*, have negative slopes, because an increase in *y* requires a reduction in *e*. By the appropriate monetary policy, the central bank can, in principle, reach any point along the *PP* curve. In figure 13.1.1, the desired point is denoted by *Q* with exchange rate *e** and income *y**. If the bank's notions are correct, *Q* can be reached *either* by setting the money supply at *M* = 2 *or* by setting the exchange rate at *e* = *e**. In the latter case, the *LL* curve is replaced by the horizontal supply curve of the central bank. In reality, the central bank's no-tions about both the balance of payments and the demand for money are sub-ject to error. It will turn out that the choice between a money policy and an exchange-rate policy depends on the relative size of the two errors.

Suppose, first, that the demand for money is correctly estimated, but along the *PP* curve there turns out to be a deficit. This means that the actual payments-equilibrium curve is further to the left, as illustrated in figure 13.1.2 by the solid *PP* curve. As a consequence, *Q* is not attained. The devia-tion of actual income from *y** depends on the policy chosen. Under a money-supply policy, the central bank would have set the money supply at *M* = 2, resulting in the solid *LL* curve. The economy would thus end up at *R* with income y_M. Under an exchange-rate policy, the central bank would have set the exchange rate at *e**. This would have resulted in the economy ending up at *T* with income y_e. It follows that the shortfall in income resulting from the

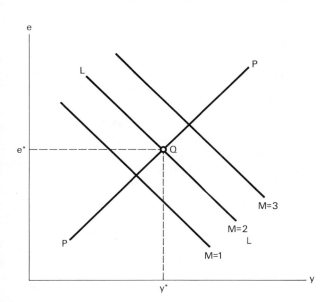

FIGURE 13.1.1
Correct Information

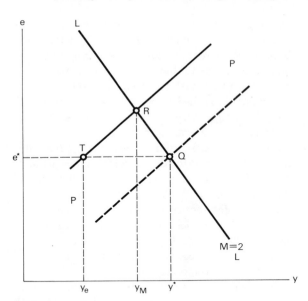

FIGURE 13.1.2
Error About Balance of Payments

forecasting error would have been larger for the exchange-rate policy than for the money-supply policy. If the errors are likely to concern mostly "real" aspects of the economy like trade and capital flows, their adverse consequences can be reduced by using a money-supply policy.

Suppose, on the other hand, that the balance of payments is correctly estimated, but the demand for money is underestimated. As a consequence, the actual LL curve for $M = 2$, drawn in figure 13.1.3 as a solid line, lies to the left of the broken curve. If the central bank controls the money supply, the economy ends up at S with income y_M, but if it chooses to control the exchange rate, it actually attains Q with income $y_e = y^*$. In this case, the substitution of a horizontal money-supply curve for the imperfectly known demand curve of the private sector reduces the policy error to zero. This suggests that an exchange-rate policy should be used if the errors tend to concern mostly the monetary aspects of the economy.

The preceding argument was restricted to the simplest possible case. It cries out for elaboration and extension in several directions.[4] This may affect the results, to be sure, but the main conclusions are likely to survive, though perhaps in a modified form. If the central bank is sure about the monetary aspects, it should control the money supply; if it is sure about the real aspects,

---

4. Henderson (1982) extends the analysis to two instruments, namely, *either* the money supply and the foreign-exchange portfolio *or* the interest rate and the exchange rate.

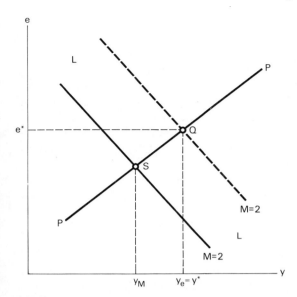

FIGURE 13.1.3
Error About Demand for Money

it should set the exchange rate. What if it is not sure about anything? Then the choice of policy should presumably depend on where the ignorance is smaller. In particular, the more volatile the demand for money, the stronger the case for an exchange-rate policy; the more predictable the demand for money, the stronger the case for a money-supply policy.

While this approach to the problem of policy choice is valid in principle, its relevance depends on the planning horizon of policy makers. If decisions are made for a considerable period, perhaps many months at a time, the risk of forecasting errors may be considerable. If, on the other hand, decisions are subject to frequent, perhaps almost continuous revision, this risk may be minor. In the preceding model, forecasting errors would soon be revealed by unexpected developments in the money supply or in exchange rates. The central bank could then adjust either the quantity of foreign-exchange transactions or the exchange rate. As a consequence, errors could most likely be corrected before they become large.

13.2 Stabilizing Intervention

The reduction of exchange-rate fluctuations is often regarded as one of the important tasks of the central bank. The question is whether such efforts are likely to succeed.

It must first be noted that the central banks are themselves the principal creators of exchange-rate fluctuations. By maintaining different inflation rates, they produce long-run trends of exchange depreciation or appreciation. By shifting their monetary policies, they give rise to the overshooting of exchange rates, often of a violent nature. Such fluctuations may occur even in the absence of any central-bank intervention in the foreign-exchange market, simply as a consequence of domestic monetary policy. The primary contribution of central banks toward more stable exchange rates thus consists in a steady course of domestic monetary policy. Compared with the latter, stabilizing interventions into the foreign-exchange market are, at best, of secondary importance.

The present section is about these secondary aspects. It is based on the assumption that the course of the domestic money supply is predetermined. The remaining decisions concern the timing, direction, and amount of sterilized foreign-exchange transactions. Any purchase of foreign exchange is assumed to be matched by a sale of domestic assets and vice versa, leaving the money supply unchanged. It was pointed out in chapter 12 that the effectiveness of such portfolio shifts, in view of the substitutability between foreign and domestic assets, is likely to be limited. This means that the discussion in the present section is not necessarily applicable to large exchange-rate fluctuations. Counteracting the latter most certainly involves the course of the money supply itself.

The call for stabilizing intervention usually originates from the notion that exchange fluctuations are often due to destabilizing speculation. The view that the activities of "speculators" cause exchange rates to fluctuate is popular among financial writers, politicians, and government officials and also with the public at large. It found an influential expression in Nurkse (1944). "Anticipatory purchases of foreign exchange," Nurkse wrote, "tend to produce or at any rate to hasten the anticipated fall in the exchange value of the national currency, and the actual fall may set up or strengthen expectations of a further fall.... Exchange rates in such circumstances are bound to become highly unstable, and the influence of psychological factors may at times be overwhelming" (p. 118). "If currencies are left free to fluctuate, 'speculation' in the widest sense is likely to play havoc with exchange rates" (p. 138). The basic idea is that, given the largely irrational psychology of speculators, small disturbances tend to be magnified and prolonged by "bandwagon" effects.

This view, though popular, is not universally accepted, particularly among economists. According to another view the speculator tends to act more like Joseph in Egypt, who, expecting seven fat years to be followed by seven lean years, was able by his speculative operations to benefit not only the pharaoh and himself, but also, by stabilizing grain supplies, his fellow men. This view was expressed forcefully, though with careful qualifications, by Friedman (1953). He made the point that profit-seeking speculators would, by and large (though not without exceptions), try to buy a currency when its price is low and sell it when its price is high, thereby reducing the exchange fluctuations. Destabilizing speculation, though conceivably profitable (particularly at the expense of other speculators), would usually cause the speculator to lose money and thus carry its own penalty. The ensuing discussion tended to support Friedman's view that a large part of speculation tends to be stabilizing, but that cases of destabilizing, and yet profitable, speculation can readily be imagined.

From the point of view of the present topic the relationship between the stabilizing effect of speculation and its profitability is a side issue. The main question is whether the central bank can devise intervention rules that make its own transactions much more likely to have a stabilizing than a destabilizing effect. It is true, however, that this depends at least in part on the behavior of private speculators.

For the purpose of the following discussion the meaning of "speculation" must be made more precise. While some traders in the foreign-exchange market may be nothing but speculators, it is advisable not to visualize the latter as a separate group of people. Whoever in his market transactions pays attention to the likely future course of exchange rates acts, in fact, as a speculator. As a consequence, there is hardly a traveler, migrant worker, businessman, bank, or investor who can afford not to act as a speculator. In order to isolate the effect of speculation it is not possible, therefore, to compare an economy in the presence of speculators with the same economy in their absence. Rather, one has to compare the actual economy with a fictitious economy in which, *ceteris paribus*, the prospective capital gains or losses from exchange-rate changes do not affect people's behavior. Such an economy may be constructed by assuming that all those capital gains are completely taxed away while capital losses are made up by transfer payments. The question is whether such a "speculation tax" could be expected to make foreign-exchange markets less volatile.

The answer depends, of course, on the way expectations are formed. Two cases may be distinguished. In the case of unstable expectations, a given increase in the current exchange rate results in a larger increase in expected future exchange rates. With stable expectations, on the other hand, the increase in expected future rates is smaller than the underlying increase in the current rate, and there may actually be no increase in expected rates at all. With unstable expectations, speculation tends to be destabilizing, whereas with stable expectations it is stabilizing.

The prevalent opinion today is that stable expectations predominate. Modern portfolio analysis describes investors as deciding on the prices at which they are willing to hold given assets on a certain day in the light of the information available at that time.[5] Prices change because new information becomes available, and in the absence of new information prices would re-

5. For a general introduction, see Fama (1970, 1976).

main (approximately) the same. The essence of new information is unpredictability. It follows that price changes should not be predictable from past prices. There should be no "bandwagons."

This is not quite exact, however, at least for the foreign-exchange market. The basic message of foreign-exchange theory is that there are systematic, predictable components in exchange-rate fluctuations. Precisely with perfect foresight about the consequences, an unexpected shift in exogenous factors should give rise to a definite path of exchange-rate adjustments. The point is that even perfect knowledge of this path does not offer opportunities for speculative profits because, over every future time span, expected exchange-rate changes are matched by interest differentials. The path itself involves no speculative bandwagons; the latter would have to be sought, rather, in the deviations of the exchange rate from this path.[6]

Empirical research on bandwagons and profitable speculation opportunities in foreign-exchange markets has been extensive.[7] The task is not easy. Inspecting graphs of exchange rates, the eye often detects seemingly obvious sequences of rising or falling rates. The trouble is that the eye is likely to detect such sequences even in numbers changing at random. Problems of a different nature are posed by the systematic components mentioned in the preceding paragraph. Testing for bandwagons thus requires sophisticated techniques and is fraught with frustration. The general outcome of the discussion seems to be that it is very difficult, and perhaps impossible, to find evidence of bandwagon effects, at least beyond the shortest periods of a few hours or days. There is no evidence that expectations are predominantly unstable, but there is substantial evidence that they are predominantly, though not invariably, stable.

In the argument of chapters 11 and 12, this view was reflected in the assumptions $L_e > 0$, $B_e > 0$, $F_e < 0$, $L_e^* < 0$, and $C_e < 0$. To determine the significance of these assumptions for exchange-rate fluctuations, it may be assumed that a fraction τ of speculative gains, positive or negative, is taxed away, leaving the individual with a fraction of $\delta = 1 - \tau$. Each of the speculative effects is thus multiplied by δ. The influence of speculative effects on exchange fluctuations is then determined by finding the effect of δ on the exchange-rate change resulting from given monetary policies.

In the instantaneous asset model of section 12.2, the common denominator Δ is now replaced by $\delta\Delta$. In the case of the exchange-rate effect of open-market operations, represented by (12.2.10), this is the only place where δ appears. This means that a reduction in δ raises the exchange-rate effect of monetary policy. As a larger and larger proportion of speculative gains is taxed away, the exchange rate becomes more volatile. There is no such influence of δ on the interest effects, described by (12.2.11) and (12.2.12), because δ

---

6. This point is forcefully made in Kohlhagen (1979).

7. Excellent surveys are provided by Kohlhagen (1978), Sweeney (1978), and Levich (1979a, b).

also appears as a common factor in the numerator. For foreign-exchange operations and portfolio shifts the result is the same as for open-market operations.

In the short-term stock/flow model of section 12.3, the influence of δ is less evident. Since δ does not appear in the numerators of (12.3.9), (12.3.12), and (12.3.15), its influence on the exchange rate depends solely on the common denominator. The latter is not proportionately affected, because the speculation tax influences only asset demands and capital flows, while the exchange-rate effects on commodity trade remain the same. Denoting the latter by $G_e = X_e - I_e - I$, so that $T_e = G_e - C_e$, the denominator can be written

$$D^* = \begin{vmatrix} T_y & G_e - \delta C_e & T_i \\ L_y & \delta L_e & L_i \\ B_y & \delta B_e & B_i + \dfrac{B}{i^2} \end{vmatrix} \tag{13.2.1}$$

It can be shown to be necessary for stability that $D^* < 0$.

The reaction of D^* to a change in δ is

$$\frac{\partial D^*}{\partial \delta} = C_e\left[L_y\left(B_i + \frac{B}{i^2}\right) - B_y L_i\right] + L_e\left[T_y\left(B_i + \frac{B}{i^2}\right) - B_y T_i\right]$$

$$- B_e[T_y L_i - L_y T_i]. \tag{13.2.2}$$

This happens to be the value D^* would take in the special case $\delta = 1$ and $G_e = 0$. It is reasonable to postulate that the system should still be stable in this case, which requires that (13.2.2) be negative. It follows that an increase in δ lowers D^* algebraically, which means that the absolute value of D^* rises. The conclusion is that under the stated assumptions more intense speculation reduces the exchange-rate fluctuations resulting from monetary policy.

For the dynamic models of chapter 11, the results are likely to be similar. In the model of section 11.4 with imperfect asset substitution, speculation expresses itself through the effect of the exchange rate on foreign asset demand, a_e. Equation (11.4.7) shows that a larger absolute value of a_e reduces the impact effect of a monetary disturbance on the exchange rate. In the perfect-substitutability model of section 11.3, the interest-parity condition (11.3.5) can be rewritten

$$\dot{e} = \frac{1}{\delta}(i - \bar{j}).$$

A reduction of δ through a speculation tax thus magnifies the exchange-rate change necessary to offset a given interest differential.[8] The general conclu-

---

8. This argument is incomplete because δ may also affect i. For the Dornbusch (1976) model, the instantaneous overshooting is fully analyzed in Gray and Turnovsky (1979, p. 654, eq. 26). An inflation tax would be equivalent to a reduction in the adjustment speed of expectations, θ, thus increasing the overshooting of the exchange rate.

sion is that speculative effects, wherever they appear in these models, tend to dampen exchange fluctuations. Speculation acts as a stabilizer.[9] To the extent that exchange-rate fluctuations are due to speculation, they would have to be attributed to its insufficiency rather than to its excess.[10]

In the short run, in fact, speculation is likely to be the main stabilizer. Disturbances occur all the time, often of a sudden and violent nature. In the absence of speculation they would often result in extreme, and indeed almost unlimited, exchange-rate fluctuations. Suppose an oil-importing country experiences a marked increase in the price of oil. In the absence of speculation, there might be a drastic depreciation, and in view of the J-effect, it may only make things worse. This is where speculation steps in. Sooner or later, the depreciation cannot fail to reach a point at which it seems to have gone "too far" and the currency appears to be "undervalued." At this point, the speculators begin to buy. Their activity will see to it that the undervaluation of the currency relative to some expected future exchange rate does not exceed the relevant interest differential except by a risk premium. This provides a floor to depreciation that otherwise would not exist.[11]

The preceding argument does not mean that speculative "bubbles" might not occasionally occur in the foreign-exchange market. Most likely they do. The argument means, however, two things. First, most fluctuations in the foreign-exchange market are not due to "irrational" speculation. Large fluctuations may occur even with perfect foresight about the consequences of each unexpected disturbance, and speculation seems to be largely, though not exclusively, a stabilizing force. Second, the central bank would find it exceedingly difficult to devise any rules or procedures which would ensure that exchange rates are made less, rather than more, volatile. To act as reliable stabilizer, the central bank would have to be a superior speculator, having better foresight than private traders.[12] There is no evidence that central banks possess this superiority, and if they did, sharing their knowledge with the public would be even better than profiting from it at the expense of the public.[13] In the light of these considerations, counterspeculative interventions of the central bank into the foreign-exchange market cannot be regarded as a promising undertaking.

9. The Swiss National Bank learned this lesson in 1977–78, when strong stabilizing speculation made it very difficult to influence the rate of the Swiss franc by interventions in the exchange market.

10. This is the view taken by Whitman (1975) and McKinnon (1976).

11. The significance of speculation as a stabilizer in the presence of the *J*-effect was brought out by Britton (1970). For an extended analysis, see Levin (1980).

12. Grubel (1977) contended that by merely "leaning against the wind," selling foreign exchange at rising rates and buying at falling rates, central banks could reduce exchange-rate fluctuations even without superior (in fact, without any) foresight. His argument, however, is insufficient to prove his proposition.

13. Actually, the most effective approach may be either to subsidize speculation (which means $\tau < 0$ and $\delta > 1$) or to behave like a subsidized speculator. However, while this might reduce exchange fluctuations, it would probably not be efficient.

13.3 The Purchasing-Power Parity Rule

Both experience and analysis (see chapter 11) lead to the conclusion that the temporary lapses from purchasing-power parity caused by exchange-rate overshooting are the most serious aspect of floating exchange rates. From this insight it is but a short step to the proposal to keep exchange rates continuously on the purchasing-power parity track by suitable monetary policies. A proposition about the long-run consequences of monetary policy would thereby be transformed into a short-run monetary rule.

PPP-based monetary guidelines have been widely debated in recent years. A formal proposal has been made by the OPTICA group of experts set up by the Commission of the European Communities (1977). Its main point is that exchange rates should be managed to stay close to their purchasing-power parity, calculated on the basis of wholesale prices, from month to month. Rules of this type are the subject of the present section.[14]

For the purpose of this discussion it is assumed that all purchases and sales of foreign exchange by the central bank are fully reflected in the domestic money supply. This is not strictly realistic inasmuch as sterilized intervention along the lines of chapter 12 may offer additional policy alternatives. It is nevertheless a valid simplification because for the massive deviations from purchasing-power parity that gave rise to those proposals, sterilized intervention would most certainly not be potent enough. The main conclusion from this section will be that purchasing-power parity should not be used as a short-run rule for monetary policy. The reasons can be summarized under four headings.[15]

The first point concerns the partial nature of the purchasing-power parity principle. It was observed in section 2.3 that changes in the real determinants of the international division of labor are continually producing deviations of equilibrium exchange rates from PPP. An effort to offset them by means of monetary policy would be self-defeating. Suppose in a given country technological progress is producing an increase in domestic prices relative to the prices of traded goods, thus resulting in an apparent overvaluation of the currency relative to PPP. According to the PPP rule, this would have to be offset by an expansion of the money supply through foreign-exchange purchases. In view of overshooting, such an effort may well seem to succeed in the short run. In due course, however, domestic price increases are bound to catch up with the exchange rate; the apparent "overvaluation" reemerges. The PPP rule would then require a further "dose" of monetary expansion, and so on. The long-run result of these efforts would be nothing but inflation.

Proponents of the PPP rule would probably argue that the rule was never

---

14. The OPTICA proposal was also discussed by Basevi and De Grauwe (1977, 1978); De Grauwe, Steinherr, and Basevi (1980); and Genberg (1981).

15. For a more detailed analysis, see Niehans (1980b). Similar conclusions, though based on a different analysis, are obtained in Dornbusch (1982).

meant to apply to changes in real factors. The problem is that it is not possible at the present time to separate monetary disturbances from real disturbances from week to week and from month to month. All that can be observed are the actual exchange rates and commodity prices; the debate about the relative contribution of real and monetary factors is usually inconclusive. This would be enough to rob the PPP rule of most of its usefulness. The following argument will show that the PPP rule would not be useful even in the absence of real disturbances.

The second point relates to monetary autonomy. The main purpose of the PPP rule is to insulate the domestic economy against the overshooting resulting from shifts in foreign monetary policies. In principle, such "imported" overshooting can indeed be avoided. This requires, however, that the domestic monetary policy parallel faithfully the path of foreign monetary policy. Inasmuch as overshooting is caused by a divergence between foreign and domestic monetary policies, overshooting is eliminated by the avoidance of such divergences. The domestic economy thereby becomes the monetary satellite of the foreign economy. Both economies are forced to accept the same inflation rates. Yet, the ability of different countries to maintain different inflation rates is usually regarded as the main advantage of floating exchange rates. Under the PPP rule this advantage would be lost.

The third observation concerns the persistence of output fluctuations. The PPP rule proposes to eliminate deviations from PPP in the hope of reducing fluctuations in output and employment. As a matter of fact, this hope may not be realized. By faithfully imitating the shifts in foreign monetary policy, the output disturbances resulting from overshooting can indeed be eliminated, at least in principle. At the same time, the "imported" shifts in monetary policy produce domestic output effects of their own. If foreign monetary policy becomes more expansionary, there will be a positive (but temporary) impulse on the domestic economy too. If foreign monetary policy becomes more restrictive, the temporary recession will be transmitted to the domestic economy. These disturbances will often go in the opposite direction from those that would have resulted from overshooting, but there is no guarantee that they will be milder.

It is indeed possible to imagine a monetary policy that insulates domestic output from imported fluctuations. Such a policy, however, requires departures from the PPP rule. In particular, only a fraction of the initial deviations from PPP should be eliminated, the fraction to be determined in such a way that the negative impulse from the remaining overshooting is just offset by the positive impulse from the monetary expansion.[16] This observation should not be regarded as a recommendation for a modified rule. The required fine-

---

16. In order to insulate both output and real exchange rates from foreign disturbances, the central bank would need (at least) two policy instruments.

tuning of the exchange rate would be virtually impossible to carry out in practice, and other deficiencies of the PPP rule would not be eliminated.

The fourth point is probably the most important. It has to do with stability. Suppose there are no disturbances abroad. How does the economy react to domestic disturbances, particularly those of a monetary character? The basic elements of the answer can be given in terms of a highly simplified model.

Domestic prices are assumed to depend on past and present money supplies according to

$$p_t = a_o m_t + a_1 m_{t-1} + (1 - a_o - a_1)m_{t-2}, \qquad (13.3.1)$$

where p_t is an inflation rate and m_t, m_{t-1}, and m_{t-2} are percentage changes in the money supply. The coefficients are nonnegative, but in view of the familiar inertia of prices, a_o and a_1 may be small. The sum of the three coefficients, however, is unity; the quantity theory asserts itself with a lag of two periods.

Since the foreign money supply is constant by assumption, the exchange rate depends on domestic monetary policy only. Denoting the percentage change in the exchange rate by e_t, this can be formalized by

$$e_t = b_o m_t + b_1 m_{t-1} + (1 - b_o - b_1)m_{t-2}. \qquad (13.3.2)$$

Over two periods, purchasing-power parity rules the field. In view of overshooting, however, the early effects show up much more strongly in exchange rates than in prices. As a consequence, $b_o > a_o$ (and perhaps $b_o > 1$) and $b_1 < 0$ while $(1 - b_o - b_1)$ is probably small.

According to the PPP rule, m_t should be chosen in such a way that, for any m_{t-1} and m_{t-2}, we have $e_t = p_t$. By equating (13.3.1) and (13.3.2), this can be shown to require

$$m_t = -\frac{a_1 - b_1}{a_o - b_o} m_{t-1} + \left(1 + \frac{a_1 - b_1}{a_o - b_o}\right) m_{t-2}, \qquad (13.3.3)$$

or

$$m_t - m_{t-1} = -(1 + c)(m_{t-1} - m_{t-2}), \qquad (13.3.4)$$

where $c = (a_1 - b_1)/(a_o - b_o)$. This says that the required increase in the rate of monetary expansion depends on the corresponding increase between the two preceding periods. Through the PPP rule, current monetary policy is linked to past policy.

The resulting adjustment process is stable if $|(1 + c)| < 1$, which implies

$$-2 < \frac{a_1 - b_1}{a_o - b_o} < 0.$$

Initial overshooting relative to PPP means $a_o - b_o < 0$. Initial overshooting in the sense of being followed by a reaction in the nominal exchange rate means $b_1 < 0$ and thus $a_1 - b_1 > 0$. It follows that overshooting in both senses is sufficient for the right-hand inequality. The left-hand inequality is equivalent to

$$a_o - b_o < (1 - a_o - a_1) - (1 - b_o - b_1),$$

which means that the immediate reaction is stronger for the exchange rate, whereas the later reaction is stronger for prices. Again this is a typical aspect of overshooting. It is interesting to note that the very overshooting that the PPP adjustment is supposed to correct helps to make this adjustment stable. In the absence of overshooting the process may well be unstable.

The adjustment path is monotonic if $c < -1$ or $a_o + a_1 > b_o + b_1$. Since the exchange rate tends to approach equilibrium faster than prices, this condition will usually not be satisfied. It is likely, therefore, that the PPP rule requires alternate expansions and contractions of the money supply. The effort to insulate the domestic economy from disturbances produces economic fluctuations.

Even if the adjustment process, in view of $-2 < c < -1$, is both stable and monotonic, the PPP rule still produces permanent inflation (or deflation). What approaches zero in this case is the year-to-year increase in the inflation rate. Inflation itself persists, gradually approaching the rate of $1/(2 + c)$, whose value can range between one and infinity. If in period 1 some domestic disturbance or error produces an increase in the monetary expansion rate by 1 percent, the PPP rule would transform this temporary disturbance into permanent inflation at a rate of more (and possibly much more) than 1 percent. The initial disturbance is never corrected but, in fact, is magnified.

In the light of these dynamic considerations, the PPP rule does not appear promising, and most likely its consequences would be harmful. Present monetary policy should not be made the slave of past and foreign monetary policies. It still remains true that shifts in foreign monetary policy may impose serious disturbances on the domestic economy. It is also true that these disturbances tend to be concentrated mostly in the early periods. This suggests that perhaps some less automatic measures of limited duration might accomplish a large part of the objective of the PPP rule without suffering from its weaknesses. This question will be taken up in the concluding section of this chapter.

13.4 Temporary Exchange-Rate Ceilings

The PPP rule is intended to eliminate the destabilizing effects of overshooting by continuous fine-tuning of exchange rates. It was argued in the preceding section that this is not a promising approach. It does not follow that monetary policy is powerless against overshooting, but there is a need for a better approach. The analysis of the preceding section indicates, in fact, that partial correction of overshooting may be better than total correction. It also suggests that the danger to dynamic stability inherent in the PPP rule can be avoided by limiting any countermeasures to the early stages. An approach that is based on the partial correction of overshooting for a limited period is discussed in this section.

The approach is first described, without any claim to historical realism, in a schematic fashion (see fig. 13.4.1). Consider two countries, called the United States and Switzerland. Up to time t_o both followed a non-inflationary course. At t_o the United States switches to a higher rate of monetary expansion with clearly inflationary consequences. In the absence of any other measures, both the ratio between U.S. and Swiss commodity prices and the dollar price of the Swiss franc would eventually rise at the same rate. Since inflation lowers the demand for real balances, the trend line of prices and exchange rates would also be shifted upward in a parallel fashion. The resulting long-run trend of prices and exchange rates is illustrated by the dotted line.

The approach to the new trend line is likely to be slow, however. In the early stages, U.S. prices will rise but little, as expressed by the broken curve. The exchange rate, on the other hand, may well overshoot, as expressed by

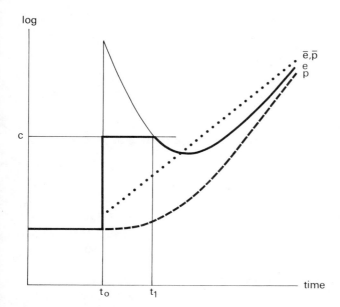

FIGURE 13.4.1
Temporary Exchange-Rate Ceilings

the thin solid curve. The result is a marked appreciation of the Swiss franc in real terms. Its consequences were described in section 11.5.

In this situation, the Swiss National Bank could announce that it would not tolerate a dollar price of the Swiss franc of more than c dollars. This price thus becomes an exchange-rate ceiling. This would, of course, be equivalent to announcing a floor rate of $1/c$ for the franc price of the dollar. The Swiss central bank would implement this announcement by buying any dollars offered at less than $1/c$ francs. As a consequence, the exchange rate would be prevented from moving along the thin line and instead be forced to move along the thick horizontal line.

It is an essential aspect of this strategy that there is no effort to completely suppress overshooting. The central bank does not try to move the exchange rate along the broken price curve. There is also no effort to move it along the dotted equilibrium line. All the central bank seeks to achieve is a significant reduction of overshooting. As a rule of thumb it may try to cut the initial overshooting in half.

Another essential aspect of this strategy is its temporary character. *If the overshooting diagnosis was correct*, there is bound to come a time at which the Swiss franc declines below the ceiling. In figure 13.4.1 this is t_1. At this point, the exchange ceiling becomes inoperative. It is clear that the real exchange rate may still be significantly off its eventual equilibrium level, but the deviation will be much reduced.

This strategy does not require any sophisticated intervention tactics. The central bank just has to convince the market that it means what it says. As long as the market is not convinced, the Swiss central bank will probably be forced to buy large amounts of dollars. It may well turn out that sterilized dollar purchases are insufficient and that an increase in the Swiss money supply cannot be avoided. Once the market is convinced, however, the process will be reversed. With depreciation risk effectively eliminated, the dollar is again an attractive asset. As a consequence, the Swiss central bank will be able to sell dollars against francs. Ideally, its balance sheet at t_1 would be the same as at t_o.

Exchange-rate ceilings of this sort are clearly unsuitable for small disturbances. Their function is as an emergency measure in the case of major disturbances. Once this is understood, they do not require elaborate computations of purchasing-power parities. As long as the deviations from purchasing-power parity are not of major proportions by any reasonable statistic, they are probably not large enough to require countermeasures. As a rule of thumb, the appearance of a deviation from long-run PPP by 10 percent over a period of less than two years might be regarded as a prima facie case for intervention. In no case, however, would the announcement of temporary exchange ceilings be automatic. The central bank would always have to make its decision in the light of the given situation.

It is also evident that exchange rate ceilings are primarily applicable to absolute overshooting, as described by curves 1 and 2 in figure 11.0.1. If overshooting is limited to the real exchange rate as described by curve 3, the concept of a temporary ceiling is much more difficult to define and to implement.

So far the argument has been purely schematic. It will now be brought closer to reality by the example of the Swiss National Bank during 1977–79. In 1977, Switzerland was just emerging from a severe recession. Before the recovery was completed, the economy was hit by a rapid appreciation of the currency. Between the fall of 1977 and the fall of 1978, the Swiss franc appreciated by about one-third in terms of the currencies of its principal trading partners. A part of this was offset by the differential in inflation rates, but in real terms the Swiss franc still appreciated by about 20 percent. In the fall of 1978 it stood roughly 10 percent above its long-run trend. Though the Swiss franc also appreciated against other European currencies, a change in expectations about the course of U.S. monetary policies was generally regarded as the basic reason behind this development. The consequence was a marked decline in Swiss export orders and declining profit rates.

In the fall of 1977 the Swiss National Bank began to intervene heavily in the foreign-exchange market. At the same time it imposed assorted restrictions against foreign holdings of Swiss francs. These measures turned out to be ineffective. Since the market regarded the central bank as committed to its money-supply targets, even large interventions had no significant effect on the exchange rate. A spirit of gloom descended upon the Swiss economy. The central bank seemed to have shot its guns without effect. In fact, it had hardly started to fire them. At the beginning of October 1978 it switched to a different strategy. It announced that for the foreseeable future it would keep the German mark "clearly above" Sfr. 0.80 and that it would not tolerate the dollar to decline "much below" Sfr. 1.70. At the same time, the money-supply targets were suspended.

The immediate consequence was a rapid increase in the money supply. In imposing the ceilings upon a doubting market, the central bank increased its foreign-exchange holdings by roughly 50 percent in three months. At the same time, central-bank deposits of banks and business firms approximately doubled; the monetary base increased by about one-fourth. At this rate, the money supply would have doubled in about nine months.

The bold policy of the central bank succeeded in producing a prompt normalization of business conditions. The stage was set for several years of full employment, though at modest profit margins. At the same time, the monetary expansion brought fears of renewed inflation, nourished by the inevitable spurt in import prices. The Swiss National Bank warned that severe monetary restraint might be necessary to bring the money supply back on track. The warning turned out to be unnecessary. With the downside exchange risk on dollars eliminated, the interest differential in favor of the dollar did its work; asset demand switched rapidly out of the Swiss franc. Less than a year after the ceiling was imposed, the Swiss money supply was back on the former trend line without any explicit contractive measures. In fact, by July 1979 the monetary base was below the level of September 1978. Money-supply targets could be reinstituted, though in a modified form and with the proviso that similar emergency measures might again be taken if required by circumstances. It gradually became clear that monetary targets had persistently been higher than stable prices would have warranted. As a consequence, the trend of prices continued to be somewhat inflationary, requiring a gradual lowering of the expansion rates. However, only a small, if any, part of this can be attributed to the episode of 1978–79.

In the Swiss episode, the imposition of temporary exchange-rate targets succeeded because the overshooting diagnosis was correct, because the overshooting was massive, and because the attempted correction was only partial and of short duration. It is evidently not a remedy that can be applied mechanically. In particular, it is much better suited for imported overshooting than for self-inflicted overshooting. In the latter case, the primary remedy is clearly the avoidance of abrupt shifts in monetary policy.

It is tempting to apply this argument to the United Kingdom at the end of the seventies. From the fall of 1976 to the middle of 1980 sterling appreciated by almost one-half in real terms. Up to the end of 1978 it shared the fate of currencies like the yen, the mark, and the Swiss franc, with overshooting caused largely by expectations about U.S. policies. Under the circumstances, corrective measures of the sort discussed in this section might have been in order. The continued appreciation of sterling in 1979 and 1980 must be attributed largely to the abrupt monetary contraction initiated in the summer of 1979. In such a case of self-inflicted overshooting the primary corrective is clearly a more gradual tightening of the money supply. Though temporary exchange-rate ceilings might still be useful as an emergency measure, they cannot be more than a secondary corrective.

For adherents of a strict money-supply rule, temporary exchange-rate ceilings are, of course, anathema. It must be realized, however, that they are not incompatible with the spirit of a pragmatic monetarism. Money-supply targets are based on the notion that the demand for money does not vary much over short periods. If large variations occur, the spirit, if not the letter, of the money-supply targets requires that they be offset by appropriate central-bank action.[17] Overshooting signals such a variation in the relative demand for national currencies. If not offset, it may impose on the economies concerned the same inflationary or deflationary pressures as other demand shifts. Temporary exchange-rate ceilings represent an effort to compensate for such demand variations without compromising the long-run course of monetary policy.

---

17. It is precisely in this spirit that Friedman prefers an M_1 target to a base target, because an M_1 target forces the central bank to offset fluctuations in the bank demand for base money.

CHAPTER 14

Pegged Exchange Rates

Introduction

Since the final collapse of the Bretton Woods System in the spring of 1973, each country has been free to let its currency float. It also has the option to peg it to another currency. The question is under what circumstances it should make use of this option. This question is the subject of the present chapter.

The discussion is limited to fiat money, excluding any sort of gold standard. With respect to the gold standard, I have nothing to add to the chapter on commodity money in Niehans (1978) at the present time. The discussion is also limited to fully convertible currencies, excluding any form of exchange control or multiple exchange rates.

Section 14.1 offers a concise comparison of pegged and floating rates. Section 14.2 surveys the problem of optimal currency areas. Section 14.3 considers various sources of limited flexibility under pegged rates.

14.1 A Comparison of Pegged and Floating Rates

To identify the comparative advantages of pegged and floating rates, I begin with the question whether country A should peg its currency permanently to that of country B. The alternative is "pure" floating; various strategies for exchange-market intervention were discussed in chapter 13.

The question is first considered from the point of view of the *efficiency of resource allocation*. For this purpose it is assumed that prices are flexible enough to maintain continuous full employment and that both countries succeed in steering a non-inflationary course.

It has sometimes been argued that floating rates are necessary for efficiency because (1) efficiency requires market-clearing prices[1] and (2) only floating rates provide for continuous clearing of the foreign-exchange market (H. G. Johnson 1972a). This may be called the "naive" welfare argument. It is fallacious because market-clearing exchange rates can also be achieved under fixed rates by supplying the appropriate amount of money. Whenever at the given money supply there would be excess demand for foreign exchange, the domestic money supply is contracted to reduce demand for foreign exchange relative to supply, and vice versa. The choice, therefore, is not between market-clearing and non–market-clearing exchange rates, but between market clearing with an exogenous money supply by a fluctuating exchange rate and market clearing with an exogenous exchange rate by a fluctuating money supply.

The relevant welfare considerations have to do with risk and transaction costs. With fixed rates, both are very small.[2] As a consequence, each national currency comes close to being a common currency. The national moneys are thereby made more useful. The international division of labor, as reflected in trade flows, is not significantly distorted by currency risk. The same is true for the international allocation of capital as reflected in the balance of international indebtedness.

With floating rates, on the other hand, exchange risks become important, and transaction costs in the foreign-exchange market as measured by the spread between buying and selling rates become larger. In the sixties, many economists expected that under non-inflationary conditions exchange-rate fluctuations would remain small. Recent experience has disappointed these expectations, and the improved understanding of exchange-rate overshooting does not leave much hope for rapid improvement.

At the same time, recent experience has allayed the fear that floating rates would result in a shrinking of world trade and capital movements. Except for cyclical fluctuations, both seem to be larger than ever. This observation does not dispose of the welfare argument, however, for the latter relates not to the size of trade and capital flows, but to their composition and direction. In fact, the distortion may well appear in the form of an inefficiently large size of these flows. In the case of capital, exchange risk has most likely produced a larger international diversification of portfolios and, in particular, larger direct investments by multinational corporations than would have been efficient in its absence.

It has often been pointed out that foreign-exchange risk can be eliminated by hedging in the forward market. In fact, spot transactions together

---

1. Consider excess demand in a commodity market. For the quantity consumed, the marginal cost is higher than the marginal benefit; consumption is "too high." For the quantity produced, the marginal benefit exceeds the marginal cost; production is "too low."
2. There will still be some exchange risk because of fluctuations between the intervention points.

with money-market operations are enough to achieve this purpose (see sec. 8.1). However, this does not invalidate the welfare argument. First, efficient forward markets and/or money markets may not exist for all relevant maturities. Second, hedging operations are usually not costless (though, as Sohmen used to emphasize, they do not necessarily involve a risk premium). Third, hedging, even if it permits the costless elimination of exchange risk for a given transaction, does not eliminate the potential misallocation of resources, because it may still turn out that the transaction took place at an exchange rate which, in the light of later developments, was "wrong."

This argument leads to the conclusion that, under full employment and with a non-inflationary price trend, efficiency considerations speak clearly in favor of fixed rates. Fixed rates indeed impose a basic welfare cost, but it appears at a different level. Consider first a closed economy. A non-inflationary price trend can be defined in terms of the long-run constancy of a certain index number. Ideally, this index is the price of a commodity bundle that reflects the tastes of the respective community. Now consider two economies with different tastes. In their preferred index numbers, given commodities will have different weights. If each country keeps its own ideal index constant, fluctuations in relative prices will generally result in a fluctuating exchange rate. Conversely, if the exchange rate is fixed, at least one of the countries has to accept fluctuations in its ideal price index; its money does not have constant purchasing power. I believe this is analytically the most fundamental cost of fixed exchange rates. It is clearly larger the more the tastes of two communities differ. In most practical cases, however, it will hardly be large enough to outweigh the welfare benefits of fixed rates, and often it will be quantitatively insignificant.

The comparative advantage of pegged and floating exchange rates has so far been considered from the point of view of allocative efficiency. Another aspect concerns *fluctuations in output and employment*. To isolate this question from the problem of inflation, it will still be assumed that monetary policy succeeds in keeping the long-run trend of prices stable.

Fluctuations in output and employment are, in one way or another, due to the imperfect flexibility of output prices and wages. It was sometimes argued that rigid wages require flexible exchange rates, whereas fixed exchange rates require flexible wages. As a general proposition this is clearly false. In fact, if wages and prices were really rigid, the maintenance of fixed rates would be much facilitated. It is precisely the drifting-away of wages and prices from the levels required by fixed exchange rates that makes fixed rates often difficult to maintain. The real question is whether the output fluctuations due to imperfectly flexible prices are likely to be smaller under fixed or flexible rates. The answer depends (1) on the relative frequency and severity of disturbances and (2) on the relative effectiveness of stabilizing monetary policies.

To begin with subquestion (2), according to the traditional argument, floating exchange rates increase the efficacy of monetary policy. One reason is that under fixed rates national monetary policy is constrained by international reserves, whereas under flexible rates it is not. Indeed, in the 1960s national autonomy of stabilization policies was the central argument in the Keynesian case for floating rates (see H. G. Johnson 1972a). From today's perspective it is easy to see that the reserve constraint was usually not binding for genuine short-run policies. Experience under the Bretton Woods system showed that international reserves together with international lending were more than sufficient for cyclical disturbances. It was long-run inflation that pushed countries against the reserve constraint. If prices are kept on a horizontal trend, there is no reason why reserves and lending should not provide a pegged exchange-rate system with ample room for stabilizing monetary policies.[3]

A more important question concerns the effectiveness of given policy instruments. Mundell's analysis led to the proposition that monetary policy is more potent under flexible rates than under fixed rates. The ensuing discussion is reviewed in more detail in section 15.3. It showed that Mundell's proposition cannot be relied upon and that its reverse may easily be true. The theory of exchange dynamics and the experience with overshooting exchange rates strengthened the doubts about the increased efficacy of monetary policy under floating rates. In the light of these developments, the effects of monetary policy, if not clearly stronger, must certainly be regarded as more reliable and predictable under fixed rates.

This leaves subquestion (1) regarding the frequency and severity of disturbances. The traditional view is best explained by a metaphor. Suppose there are two ponds, one of which is subdivided by dams. Suppose further that numerous rocks are thrown at random into both ponds. In the open pond the resulting waves will probably be smaller because each concentric wave is partially offset by waves produced by other rocks. Similarly, fixed exchange rates help to dilute domestic disturbances by spreading them over the international system, where they are partially offset by other disturbances. Under floating rates, on the other hand, disturbances are "bottled up" at home.[4]

The analysis of section 5.3 confirmed that the effect of domestic demand shifts on domestic output is smaller under fixed rates than under floating rates except in the case of a large negative expenditure effect of the exchange rate (see eq. 5.3.12). The analysis also showed, however, that the "bottling up" argument is strictly valid only in the absence of an expenditure effect. If this effect is positive, we obtain the "Laursen-Metzler paradox" of inverse

---

3. It is consistent with this argument that the transition to floating rates did not contribute to higher freedom of international trade, as many advocates had hoped.

4. This point was early made by Triffin (1968) and Bernstein (1966). More elaborate versions were presented by Mundell (1973) and Laffer (1973).

transmission of disturbances; if it is negative, there is parallel transmission, as under fixed rates.[5]

The traditional argument is based on purely static considerations, usually in a Keynesian framework. It leads to the conclusion that the consequences of demand disturbances are likely to be less severe under fixed rates. Again exchange overshooting adds a new dimension. By revealing an additional source of potentially serious disturbances under floating rates, it further strengthens the case for fixed rates. In fact, there can hardly be a doubt today that output is more volatile under floating rates than under fixed rates. To sum up, from the point of view of output fluctuations, pegged rates probably have an advantage over floating rates because, in the absence of corrective policies, given disturbances are likely to result in smaller output fluctuations and because corrective monetary policies, while not clearly less effective, are certainly more reliable.

Finally, the comparative advantages of pegged and floating rates have to be considered from the point of view of the long-run trend of *prices*. The basic proposition is that under floating rates, inflation in each country essentially depends on its own national policy, while under fixed rates it depends jointly on monetary policies in all countries. By pegging its exchange rate, a country sacrifices its monetary autonomy and makes itself the inflation satellite of the country it is pegging to.

This proposition has two important corollaries. First, floating rates rob the concept of international liquidity of its meaning. International reserves cease to be significant for monetary policy.[6] What matters for the long-run price trend is national monetary policy.

Second, whereas under floating rates each country gains the benefits, and bears the costs, of the inflation it produces, fixed rates spread these benefits and costs over all countries. Floating rates internalize benefits and costs of inflation; under fixed rates they are largely external. This leads to the conjecture that under floating rates the benefits and costs of inflation have a stronger influence on monetary policy than under fixed rates. In particular, if inflation is regarded as a social evil, floating rates tend to make it more likely that effective measures will be taken. Characteristically, the Western world slid into secular inflation under the Bretton Woods system and is now using floating rates to escape from inflation.

During the sixties, monetary autonomy was often related to the Phillips curve. By choosing its own rate of monetary expansion, it was argued, a country could select the preferred combination of inflation and employment. Depending on its social-welfare function, one country might choose higher em-

---

5. It should be noted that the disturbances are here assumed to occur in the demand for goods and services. If they occur in the demand for money, their output effects correspond exactly to the output effects of monetary policy discussed in the preceding paragraphs.

6. This point has been forcefully made by Haberler (1977).

ployment at the price of higher inflation while another might be willing to accept more unemployment for the sake of price stability (H. G. Johnson 1972a). Today it is widely recognized that, in the long run, output and growth have no clear-cut relationship to inflation. While the elimination of inflation usually exacts a price in the form of temporary recession, the long-run output cost of price stability is low and there might well be a long-run output gain.[7]

Why do governments still succumb to the "Phillips illusion" that growth can be permanently stimulated at the price of moderate inflation? I believe this must be attributed primarily to political myopia, which assigns to nearby benefits an irrationally large weight compared with distant costs. Long-run inflation, therefore, is essentially a measure of the political weakness of governments. In the present context, the important point is that governments too weak to keep inflation near zero are likely to be too weak to keep it at any predetermined level. Rather, they will be forced by changing political pressures to make frequent policy changes, resulting in seemingly erratic shifts in inflation rates.

This argument leads to the conclusion that in an inflationary world the permanent pegging of exchange rates is neither desirable nor possible. It is not desirable because it deprives each country of the opportunity to eliminate inflation by its own action. It is, in all probability, not possible because a government too weak to follow a non-inflationary course will not be strong enough to follow any particular monetary rule. In an inflationary environment there is no serious alternative to floating rates.[8] The loss in allocative efficiency and the probable increase in output disturbances are part of the price that has to be paid for inflation. Under non-inflationary conditions, however, there are no compelling reasons in favor of floating rates. By keeping exchange rates constant, the allocation of resources can be improved and macroeconomic disturbances can be reduced.

Under the conditions of 1983, efforts to return to fixed exchange rates would be clearly premature. The problem of inflation still dominates the scene. However, if the United States should ever succeed in keeping its prices reasonably stable for several years at satisfactory employment levels, the argument for pegging to the dollar may well become irresistible.

14.2 Optimal Currency Areas

Suppose pegged rates and floating rates each have both benefits and costs. Suppose further that these benefits and costs depend on economic con-

---

7. H. G. Johnson also argued that floating rates can assist in the recovery of "structurally distressed" areas, but it is difficult to see how the development of, say, Appalachia could be helped by a floating Appalachian dollar.

8. This was essentially also Milton Friedman's argument (1953). It is important to recognize its second-best character. Friedman, therefore, made a much stronger case for flexible rates than H. G. Johnson (1972a), who tried to develop a first-best argument.

ditions. The question then arises how the world should be divided into currency areas, each with a common currency or fixed exchange rates internally and floating rates relative to the other areas, in such a way that the net benefit is maximized. This is the optimum currency-area problem, formulated by Mundell (1961).[9]

The problem is logically similar to the problem how a country should be divided into voting districts in such a way that the parliamentary seats for a given party are maximized. In its full generality, it is obviously a prohibitively difficult problem, and it is therefore not surprising that twenty years of academic efforts have brought little progress toward its solution. What we have is a variety of suggestions about certain elements that may play a role in the solution.

Mundell's formulation of the problem must be understood in the context of the academic debate at the beginning of the sixties. This was the high tide of Keynesianism. Most leading economists advocated floating rates, primarily because of their alleged advantages from the point of view of medium-term stabilization policies. If pursued to its logical conclusion, this argument seemed to imply that each village, if not each house, should have its own currency, linked to other currencies by floating exchange rates. Since this was obvious nonsense, floating exchange rates must have some hidden costs that made them inappropriate under certain circumstances. The question was what these costs and circumstances might be. The concept of the optimum currency area must thus be seen as a defense of pegged exchange rates against the academic arguments for floating rates.

According to Mundell, the crucial factor is labor mobility.[10] Suppose the world produces two goods, wheat and wine. In any particular location, only one good is produced, but both are consumed.[11] Wages are sticky downward, so that wage reductions are accompanied by unemployment. Now consider a shift in demand from wheat to wine. With immobile factors, this requires a decline in the relative price of wheat. If the world has a common currency, the consequence is unemployment in the wheat-producing regions and/or inflation in the wine-growing regions. Both evils can be avoided by giving the wheat regions and the wine regions separate currencies and devaluing the wheat currency relative to the wine currency. Devaluation is regarded as a means to change relative consumer prices without changing absolute producer prices.

Labor mobility would obviate the need for devaluation. Instead of counteracting the demand shift by a shift in relative prices, it could be accommo-

9. A useful survey is provided by Ishiyama (1975). For a recent discussion of monetary integration with extensive bibliographical references see Allen and Kenen (1980).

10. The possible significance of factor mobility for a currency area was already mentioned by Meade (1957).

11. This corresponds to the case of specialization in production with diversified consumption, treated in section 1.1.

dated by a shift in production achieved by a movement of workers from the wheat regions to the wine regions. If it were possible to delineate areas with high factor mobility that include wine regions and wheat regions in the appropriate proportions, such areas could maintain a common currency without suffering from the above-mentioned evils. It would be advantageous for them to do so because of the basic welfare advantages of fixed exchange rates discussed in the preceding section.

The cutting edge of Mundell's argument is the implication that nations are not, in general, optimal currency areas. Although migration is often impeded by national borders, it might also be impeded between wheat regions and wine regions within the same country. In such a case, an optimum currency area might theoretically include the wine-growing regions of several countries or the wheat-growing regions of several countries. Of course, it was clear to Mundell that such an arrangement of the currency map is not practicable. His point was that floating along national lines would not generally be optimal.

Today it is easy to see that Mundell's analysis is sketchy, that most macroeconomic disturbances are not caused by relative demand shifts, and that in the case of relative demand shifts, inventories of wheat and wine could be used as stabilizers even with immobile factors. It is also clear that the general problem how a two-commodity world is best divided into currency areas is analytically quite intractable. However, Mundell's argument, despite its limitations, helped to revive the interest of economists in the virtues of fixed exchange rates.

The discussion of an intractable problem often casts more shadow than light. This was also true of the optimum currency-area problem. Subsequent contributions tended to make explicit certain aspects that Mundell had left in the background. At the same time, the fundamental problem how to define optimal currency areas in the absence of nations disappeared from sight. Its place was taken by the more mundane problem under what conditions existing nations should form a currency area.

McKinnon (1963) emphasized the significance of the openness of the economy as measured by the share of the traded-goods sector in national income. Suppose an economy with rigid home-goods prices and given world-market prices finds it necessary to correct a trade deficit. If this is achieved by devaluation, the consequence is a rise in traded-goods prices and thus in average consumer prices. Trade adjustment through exchange-rate changes is therefore associated with undesirable fluctuations in real income and in the value of money, and these fluctuations are larger for high-trade economies than for low-trade economies. The effect of devaluation on output, on the other hand, does not depend on the openness of the economy in a clear-cut way. This argument is summarized in the upper part of table 14.2.1. The conclusion is that the price criterion makes devaluation more attractive to low-trade economies.

Alternatively, the required trade adjustment could be achieved by a contraction in autonomous demand at unchanged exchange rates. For a given improvement in the trade balance, the consequent contraction in domestic output is larger in a low-trade economy than in a high-trade economy, while consumer prices are constant in either case.[12] This argument is summarized in the lower part of table 14.2.1. It means that the output criterion gives demand contraction an edge for high-trade economies.

McKinnon's conclusion was that wide-open economies should preferably use demand policies at constant exchange rates, while relatively self-sufficient economies should rely on exchange-rate adjustments. Again, the analysis was not fully worked out and left many questions open. In particular, the argument about the relative burden of demand policies is inconclusive. Consider a large country and a small country engaged in mutual exchange. The share of trade is obviously low in the large country and high in the small country. The same will probably be true for the marginal propensity to import. As a consequence, a given correction in the trade balance, at least in a simple model, will indeed produce a larger absolute contraction of output in the large country than in the small country. However, relative to national income, the contraction in the large country may well be lower than in the small country. It follows that the openness of an economy in the sense of the traded-goods share may not determine the relative burden of demand policies.

The problem as defined by McKinnon also suffers from the fact that the relative advantages of pegged and floating rates are considered for a single country only. In reality, pegging requires that both partners prefer it to floating. If the choice depends mainly on relative size, this requirement is unlikely to be satisfied. The real question was how the openness criterion could be used to subdivide a given set of countries into optimal currency areas, but this question was never investigated. While the treatment of demand policies in

TABLE 14.2.1

Significance of Openness

Openness	*Price Fluctuations*	*Output Fluctuations*
	Devaluation	
High trade	large	indifferent
Low trade	small	indifferent
	Demand Contraction	
High trade	none	small
Low trade	none	large

12. The crucial factor is the marginal propensity to import, which is likely to be directly related to the average propensity. For a detailed analysis of demand and devaluation effects in a Keynesian framework, see chapter 5.

McKinnon's analysis is therefore deficient, the argument about price fluctuations is, in principle, valid. Floating exchange rates indeed produce fluctuations in consumer prices, which are particularly important in wide-open economies. McKinnon thus drew attention to the fact that wide-open economies may have a higher stake in fixed exchange rates than nearly closed ones. He did not succeed in showing that any economy has a reason to prefer floating rates.

Nor have subsequent contributions succeeded in closing this analytical gap. Kenen (1969) proposed yet another structural criterion for currency areas, namely, the degree of product diversification. Diversified economies, he suggested, are less likely to suffer from demand shifts and may thus be able to afford fixed rates, while monocultural economies may require floating rates. Again, an explicit optimizing calculus linking the exchange-rate regime to structural characteristics was lacking.[13] It is clear, furthermore, that Kenen's criterion leads back to labor mobility because, in the absence of interindustry mobility, diversification does not help. Kenen's argument, therefore, was not so much an alternative principle as a variation on a theme by Mundell. A detailed survey of further developments sprouting from these suggestions is provided by Tower and Willett (1976). The picture it conveys is not encouraging. Optimum currency areas are still a concept in search of a theory.

In the early stages of the discussion, the relevant costs of fixed exchange rates were sought in the greater difficulties of output stabilization. These difficulties, in turn, were supposed to depend on certain characteristics of the economic structure. This effort to link the exchange-rate regime to structural characteristics had disappointing results. Gradually, the long-run trend of monetary policy moved to the foreground. It had always been recognized that countries with significant differences in inflation rates cannot maintain fixed exchange rates. After the advent of the Phillips curve, this naturally led to the argument that fixed rates would force some countries to move away from their preferred point on the Phillips curve. A country that attaches great weight to employment might be forced to accept more unemployment for the sake of lower inflation. A country that attaches a higher weight to price stability might have to do the opposite.[14] For alternative delineations of currency areas the losses resulting from these considerations could then be compared with the allocational welfare gains to determine the optimum size of currency areas. The realization that the downward-sloping Phillips curve is a short-term phenomenon and that there is no stable inflation/unemployment trade-off deprived this approach of its analytical foundation.

---

13. Stein's early paper (1963) stands out as an exception.

14. Fleming (1971) tried to show that in view of the curvature of the Phillips curve, the formation of a currency area is likely to worsen the inflation/unemployment trade-off. His analysis is inconclusive, however, and he did not establish his point.

The fact that a common currency requires similar inflation raises the further question whether it also requires a common government. Meade (1957) argued early that it does. If this is true, the optimal currency area is the nation. The economic problem merges into the much wider political problem. In a Phillips-curve world there is much to be said for this view. If effective stabilization policies involve inflation and deflation at varying rates, the harmonization of inflation rates can hardly be achieved over long periods of time without a central government. This is why in an inflationary world fixed-rate systems tend to be short-lived.

In fact, the acceptance of inflation does not make output stabilization more effective nor does it permit a higher long-term growth rate. From the point of view of stabilization and growth, there is no reason to prefer an inflationary price trend to one without inflation. If, based on this insight, a number of nations succeed in keeping their long-run price trend horizontal, there is no reason why they should not maintain fixed exchange rates. By letting their reserves rise and fall they could obtain any desirable autonomy for their short-term monetary policies. The history of the gold standard shows that, in fact, a common currency does not require a common government.

The conclusions from the discussion of optimal currency areas thus coincide with those about pegged and floating rates. Considerations of allocational efficiency always speak in favor of fixed rates; in a wide-open economy this advantage is clearly larger than in an economy close to self-sufficiency. Short-run stabilization of output cannot be demonstrated to give an edge to floating rates, no matter what the structure of the economy. Differences in inflation rates, however, clearly prohibit a common currency, making the nation the optimal currency area.

14.3 Flexibility in Pegged Rates

From many points of view, pegged exchange rates are similar to a common currency. There is an important difference, though, inasmuch as a common currency fixes the exchange rate immutably at unity whereas pegged rates still exhibit a certain amount of flexibility. During the final decade of the Bretton Woods system this flexibility and the means to increase it was the main subject of expert discussion.[15] Three sources of flexibility are discussed in this section.

The basic source is, of course, the possibility of parity changes. The literature sometimes conveys the impression that there is a choice between an "adjustable peg" and immutably fixed rates.[16] In reality, a currency is never im-

---

15. A representative, if perhaps depressing, picture of the state of this discussion shortly before the collapse can be obtained from the "Bürgenstock Papers," edited by Halm (1970).

16. Friedman (1953) argued that the adjustable peg combines the vices of fixed and floating rates without their virtues.

mutably pegged to another; short of a common currency there are simply no means to exclude the possibility of devaluation. Under the Bretton Woods system, this fact was reflected in the provision that parities could be changed in cases of "fundamental disequilibrium." It is inherent in the nature of such formulas that they defy the experts' diligent efforts to spell out their exact meaning.

The curse of the adjustable peg is currency speculation. Whenever it looks as if a currency might be officially devalued, people tend to be virtually certain that it will not be officially revalued. It hardly ever happens that some expect revaluation when others expect devaluation. Speculation against a currency may thus promise a capital gain without a corresponding risk of capital loss if devaluation fails to take place. In the latter case, the speculator simply liquidates his position at the parity rate, losing nothing but the transaction costs. Under fixed exchange rates, speculation is a one-way street. As a consequence, any rumors about possible exchange-rate adjustments tend to call forth large speculative asset shifts. Under floating rates this is different, because a speculator's hope to profit from future depreciation is always associated with the risk that the currency might, in fact, appreciate. This risk will tend to dampen speculative fervor.

Under the curse of currency speculation, a system of fixed exchange rates is unlikely to survive for long unless parity adjustments are truly exceptional.[17] Whenever a devaluation occurs, there must be confidence that the new parity will be maintained indefinitely. If this condition is satisfied, speculative positions will be promptly liquidated after a parity change. In the opposite case, a devaluation tends to create the expectation of further devaluations, thus giving rise to increased speculation. In determining the devaluation rate, governments will have good reason to err on the high side in order to create confidence that no further devaluations are in store.

This leads to the conclusion that discretionary adjustments in pegged rates are an appropriate technique for providing flexibility if they are used as highly exceptional emergency measures, say, after wars or revolutions. When discretionary adjustments are made frequently, the system of fixed exchange rates is likely to become unworkable for freely convertible currencies. The efforts to save the Bretton Woods system by facilitating par value adjustments were, therefore, basically misguided.

Flexibility of a very different kind is provided by the margin between the central bank's buying and selling prices for foreign exchange. This margin is the fiat-money counterpart to the gold points under the gold standard. In view of the cost of gold shipments, an exchange rate could rise slightly above parity before gold exports became profitable and it could fall slightly below parity before gold would be imported. Between these gold points, the exchange rate was free to fluctuate. Classical economists were aware that mone-

---

17. Adjustments must also be made as unexpectedly as possible, which leads to the familiar prevarications by otherwise honest officials.

tary policy thereby obtains a higher degree of autonomy than it would otherwise have (see Viner 1937, pp. 206 f.).

With fiat money, the margin partly reflects the transaction costs of the central bank. For the most part, however, it is used as an instrument of monetary policy. Under the Bretton Woods system, the margin was ±1 percent. Whenever the price of the dollar in terms of a given currency had risen 1 percent above par value, the respective central bank had to sell any desired amount of dollars, thus preventing a further depreciation of its currency. Whenever the price of the dollar had declined 1 percent below par value, the central bank had to buy any offered amount of dollars, thus preventing a further appreciation. Between these limits, exchange rates could fluctuate, with all the consequences for competitiveness, speculation, and interest rates that exchange-rate fluctuations have.

One of the more convincing proposals for improvements in the Bretton Woods system, called the "band" proposal (Halm 1965, 1969), envisaged the widening of this margin to, say, ±2.5 percent or even ±5 percent. The main advantage of a wider band is the dampening of speculation by making it a two-way street. If speculators, expecting a devaluation, have bought foreign currency at the ceiling rate, they run the risk that they will have to liquidate their positions at the floor rate if their expectations are disappointed. In addition, a wide band brings into play the adjustment mechanisms of exchange-rate changes without having the serious disadvantages of floating rates. It is clear, however, that some of the allocational advantages of fixed rates are sacrificed and that a band, no matter how wide, is powerless against long-run inflation and deflation. Overall, it seems, a relatively wide margin between intervention points can contribute significantly to the stability of a fixed-rate system.

The third source of flexibility in a pegged exchange rate is the "crawling peg." Originally suggested by Harrod in 1933, first applied by Chile in 1965, and named by Williamson (1965), this contrivance began to stimulate the ingenuity of economists in the waning years of Bretton Woods.[18] The basic idea is to adjust exchange rates frequently and in small steps, but without any long-run limits. At any moment the rate would be pegged, the central bank freely buying or selling at the respective intervention points.[19] The intervention points, however, would be adjusted monthly, weekly, or even daily. Proposals differed about the formula that should control these adjustments, some using past exchange-rate changes, others recommending reserve changes or the deviations of reserves from a target level, still others advocating differences in inflation rates.

Originally, the crawling peg was primarily regarded as an alternative to the Bretton Woods system of adjustable par values. From this point of view,

18. These references are based on the excellent survey by Williamson (1981).
19. It is worth noting, however, that practical applications were apparently confined to countries with exchange controls.

its principal advantage consists in drawing out any significant parity changes, necessitated by differences in inflation rates, over long periods. As a consequence, a speculator has to hold his assets for a long time and his profit rate is correspondingly reduced. Suppose he is right in expecting a devaluation by 20 percent. If he has to wait one week, his profit rate is about 1,000 percent per annum; if he has to wait three years, the profit rate is only about 7 percent. Speculative asset shifts, it was hoped, would thereby be discouraged; exchange rates could be adjusted without the curse of speculation.

This objective cannot be realized if, in addition to the crawl, there is still the possibility of large discretionary parity changes. The difficulty is that there does not seem to exist any effective guarantee against this possibility. Whatever governments may declare and agree to, the risk of large-step devaluations will reappear whenever the prescribed crawl looks insufficient. As a consequence, the crawling peg may fail to reach its objective. It is still true that in an inflationary world almost any crawling peg, if technically workable, is preferable to the fiction of fixed parities with occasional adjustments. It is also true, however, that in a non-inflationary world there is no need for a crawl.

With the collapse of the par-value system the perspective has changed. What has moved to the foreground is the advantage of the crawling peg compared with floating rates. Couldn't a formula crawl be an effective device to reduce the short-run overshooting of exchange rates without impeding the long-run adjustment to inflation and real factors? The answer depends on the dynamics of exchange rates under the two systems.[20]

The essential part of the dynamic mechanism is the relationship between the exchange rate and monetary policy. Under a crawling peg this relationship is, in principle, the same as under fixed exchange rates. In particular, the autonomy of monetary policy is similarly constrained. On any given day, the central bank is committed to defend that day's parity by buying or selling foreign exchange. Within the limits imposed by its reserves, it can do this by "sterilized" portfolio shifts without repercussions on its money supply. However, once the expected rate of the crawl begins to exceed the interest differential, reserve losses (or gains) may become intolerably large. At this point, the central bank is forced to adjust its domestic monetary policy. In recent years, fluctuations in exchange rates have often been violent. It is fairly evident that they could not have been slowed down to a crawl without large adjustments in monetary policies. The assumption of full sterilization thus excludes the most important part of the problem.[21]

The monetary dynamics of a crawling peg depends, of course, on the

20. Arndt (1971) drew attention to the necessity of a dynamic analysis.
21. Kenen's simulations (1975) were limited to a flow model of the foreign-exchange market, disregarding monetary policy. Levin (1975) investigated the stability of alternative assignments of money supply and exchange rate as policy instruments to output and trade balance as targets on the assumption of unlimited sterilization. A more recent paper by Levin (1977) is limited to speculative capital flows at given output, prices and interest rates, again with full sterilization.

adjustment formula. With the collapse of the par-value system, formulas based on reserves and on past exchange rates became obsolete. Formulas based on prices or past monetary policies remain the only serious candidates. As a consequence, the crawling peg becomes very similar to the purchasing-power parity rule discussed in section 13.3. In fact, a crawling peg based on deviations of exchange rates from PPP, as suggested in Williamson (1981, p. 27), would be like a PPP rule with partial adjustment. At any moment the current peg, since it is based on the past history of prices and exchange rates, is the result of (among other things) past monetary policies, both domestic and foreign. The current peg determines, in turn, current monetary policy.

This raises the question of stability.[22] The relevant analysis for the crawling peg is still lacking. However, the close analogy with the PPP rule permits the conjecture that the dynamic mechanism is likely to be stable in some cases but unstable in others. In the unstable cases it would lead the economy either into progressive inflation or deflation or else into oscillations of increasing amplitude. Monetary policies and inflation rates in the pegging country would again become dependent on the monetary policy of the country to which it is pegging its currency. Though intended to combine important advantages of pegged and floating rates, the crawling peg is likely to combine their disadvantages.

This chapter may be concluded with a general remark. In the great debate of the Keynesian generation about fixed and floating rates, the issue seemed to be the weighing of the static welfare advantages of fixed rates against the dynamic advantages of floating rates for economic stabilization and growth. It is easy to see today that this was the wrong issue, because in the long run, monetary policies that require floating rates produce neither more stability nor more growth. There is no need to compare cost and benefits. The ideal regime is one of fixed exchange rates; the optimal currency area is indeed the world. However, this ideal requires non-inflationary national policies. If national governments are politically too weak to keep price fluctuations on a horizontal trend, exchange rates between sovereign nations cannot be held constant beyond limited periods no matter what their advantages may be. Floating becomes inevitable.

The doom of the par-value system of Bretton Woods was sealed when the United States, under the spell of the Phillips curve, switched to an inflationary course in the early sixties.[23] As long as countries stay on such a course, there is no serious alternative to floating rates, though pairs or groups of countries may be able to operate an adjustable peg for limited periods. The return to fixed exchange rates, therefore, is not a question of ingenious schemes the experts may invent; it is primarily a question of an elimination of the "Phillips illusion" from national monetary policy.

22. Concern about this question is expressed in McKinnon (1981).
23. That the switch in the credit policy of the Federal Reserve took place in the early sixties is statistically documented in Niehans (1976).

CHAPTER 15

The Art of Central Banking under Floating Rates

Introduction

The preceding chapters shed light on different aspects of monetary policy. The concluding chapter pulls the various strands of the argument together to provide an integrated summary of the principles of central banking under floating exchange rates in economies with highly developed financial systems.*

The orientation is frankly normative. The subject is the guidelines a central bank should follow in conducting monetary policy. I wish to add at once that I do not visualize such guidelines as negating the use of discretion. They are not meant to replace the responsible decision-maker by a computer program. I have always regarded the antithesis "rules versus discretion" as false. In our ever-changing world, the decision-maker is constantly faced with what seem to be new situations in which the old rules appear to be in need of modification. It is precisely in the choice of rules that he is forced to use discretion. If the Federal Open Market Committee should ever be replaced by a computer program, it would inevitably be succeeded by a Federal Open Market Program Committee to decide (presumably again monthly) on the required changes in the program. There is no escape from decision-making.

In such a discussion, personal judgment inevitably plays a larger role than in the preceding chapters. There are many points on which the evidence is inconclusive and on which competent opinions differ. In such matters of macroeconomic policy it will always be so. Without dogmatic claims, the chapter presents one fallible observer's conclusions from the historical experience and academic work of recent years.

*A paper based on this chapter was given at the conference of the International Economic Association on monetary theory and economic institutions in Florence in September 1982.

The "Art of Central Banking" was also the subject of the last chapter of my *Theory of Money*.[1] There the discussion was limited to a closed economy. It is now extended to an open economy under floating rates. The unifying framework is again provided by the "three-frequency approach" developed in the earlier book. The exposition cannot be made intelligible without some repetition. The latter will, however, be held to a minimum and the reader is referred to the original presentation for supplementary explanations.

15.1 Objectives and Instruments

The most general objective of the central bank is the efficiency of the economy. At the microeconomic level, this means that it should contribute to the efficiency of the payments system, of financial intermediation, and of asset markets. These aspects will not be further considered here. At the macroeconomic level, the primary objective is price stability. A secondary objective is the reduction of fluctuations in output and employment.[2] To these must be added, third, the prevention of liquidity crises in the banking system. This list is the same for both open and closed economies. There is no need to recognize separate exchange rate or balance-of-payments objectives. Whatever the central bank may do to influence exchange rates or the balance of payments is clearly done in the service of the three stated objectives.

In pursuing these objectives, the central bank's principal instrument is the supply of base money. As an auxiliary instrument it can also use portfolio shifts between different types of assets with an unchanged monetary base (see ch. 12). These shifts are classified as auxiliary because, dollar for dollar, a change in base money is likely to be much more potent than a mere portfolio shift. In addition, the central bank may use regulatory constraints like reserve requirements, credit rationing, and interest ceilings. Some of their implications were discussed in chapter 9 in connection with the Eurodollar market. Since these constraints are not basic to the argument, they will not be considered further. There is, however, an alternative set of instruments. Instead of supplying a certain amount of base money, the central bank can set the interest rate at which it supplies base money, thus treating the rate of interest as the principal policy instrument. Correspondingly, instead of converting a certain amount of foreign assets into domestic assets, the central bank can set the exchange rate at which it is willing to perform such portfolio shifts. For every policy instrument expressed as a quantity there is a "dual" instrument expressed as a price or interest rate. This is the price/quantity problem, fa-

---

1. The phrase is, of course, from the title of Hawtrey's well-known book (1932).
2. This statement is not meant to imply that price stability is socially more important than employment; rather it reflects the fact that monetary policy is more effective in controlling prices than in controlling employment. Some qualifications are noted below.

miliar from the closed economy. Floating exchange rates in an open economy add another dimension to it.

In addition, there is the problem of the targeting procedure. Consider a military analogy. A handgun is aimed directly at the target. With a mortar, the gunner learns to train his sight on an auxiliary target, with a spotter measuring the deviation of this auxiliary from the actual target. Monetary policy can be treated like a handgun, the base money supply (or the interest rate) being aimed directly at the ultimate targets—prices, output, and bank liquidity. Under the alternative two-stage procedure, the policymaker selects an intermediate target like, for instance, the supply of money held by the nonbank sector. In the first stage he determines the desired level for this intermediate target in view of the ultimate objectives. In the second stage, he aims the policy instruments at the intermediate target.

In a military context, auxiliary targets are used as second-best procedures because the gunner cannot see the target. In monetary policy, the field of application is less evident because all members of a central bank can be given access to the same information. The traditional protagonist of two-stage procedures has been, characteristically, the Federal Reserve System, whose decision-making happens to be divided between the Federal Open Market Committee in Washington, acting as "spotter," and the manager of the Open Market Account in New York, acting as "gunner." To this institutional tradition was later added the influence of Milton Friedman, who hoped a two-stage procedure would permit a reduction of complicated decision problems to a simple rule. Over the years, two-stage procedures were tried by a number of countries but, sooner or later, were often found wanting. It should be clear that the decision for or against using an intermediate target has nothing to do with a decision for or against "monetarism." A central bank can follow strict monetarist policies without using intermediate targets, and intermediate targets can be used to implement nonmonetarist policies.

At present, the procedure debate, though far from settled, seems to be going against intermediate targets. Deficiencies of the two-stage approach appear at two levels. Analytically, it seems evident that decisions made in the light of all information can hardly be systematically inferior to decisions based on extremely limited information and indeed will often be better. To exclude potentially valuable information is generally inefficient, a point made forcefully by Benjamin Friedman (1975, 1977). At the more practical level, no particular economic variable seems to survive as an intermediate target for more than a few years. Changes in interest rates, financial institutions, and financial technology necessitate almost-continuous revisions. The wide aggregate called Sterling M_3 was a dismal failure in the United Kingdom. Since it includes a large amount of interest-bearing assets, it tended to respond to monetary contraction by expanding. M_1 was abandoned in Switzerland because its credibility was undermined by the frequent adjustments, often appearing ad hoc, required by international asset substitution. In the United

States, confidence in intermediate targets similarly suffered from frequent revisions of the statistical series. In addition, the large random element in the target series has caused frantic speculation about the short-run reaction of monetary policy. The conclusion is that central banks have nothing to gain, and possibly much to lose, by elevating a particular statistical series to the exalted rank of an intermediate target. They can generally do better by aiming their policy instruments directly at the ultimate objectives in the light of all relevant information, including various monetary series.

No matter what procedures are used, the fundamental problem is how much base money should be supplied at each moment in order to reach these ultimate objectives. We note at once that there is only one primary policy instrument for three objectives. We also note, however, that these objectives have very different time dimensions. The desired stability for prices relates to the long-run trend. What matters are price changes from, say, one decade to the next; short-run price fluctuations do not require particular attention. The relevant fluctuations in output show up in annual figures, while long-run growth is beyond the scope of monetary policy. Liquidity crises, finally, are short-run phenomena, reversing their course in a matter of weeks or months.

This opens up the possibility of using money-supply variations of different duration for different objectives. The long-run trend of the money supply determines the trend of prices. Medium-term deviations from this trend can be used, if that seems advisable, to influence output. In prices, in view of their inertia, such deviations will leave hardly a trace. In the short run, from week to week, the central bank can intervene in the money market to relieve threatening liquidity crises; output will be little affected by such interventions, since it reacts to credit conditions with a distributed lag of many months. Using a physical analogy, the total fluctuations in the base money supply may be imagined as decomposed into three waves of different frequencies, with each frequency assigned to one policy objective. In the remainder of this paper, this "three-frequency approach" to monetary policy (Niehans 1978) will be applied to an open economy with floating rates.

15.2 Stabilizing the Price Trend

The basic long-run objective of monetary policy is a non-inflationary price trend. In pursuing this objective, the central bank can take guidance from the quantity theory of money (see sec. 2.2). This says that in a fiat-money economy without nonmonetary public debt a given change in the rate of monetary expansion will, in the long run, result in an equal change in the rate of inflation.[3] By determining the rate of growth of the monetary base, the

---

3. The quantity theory recognizes that a permanent change in the rate of monetary expansion may have permanent effects on the levels of the cash ratio and real income. Inflation may be far from neutral. The quantity theory maintains, however, that a permanent change in the rate of monetary expansion does not have significant permanent effects on the *rates of change* of the cash ratio and real income.

central bank can thus control the long-run trend of prices. Some qualifications to this fundamental proposition will be noted below.

There is little hope that the central bank will be able to prevent medium- and short-term deviations of prices from their long-run trend. In particular, it is often difficult to establish a causal relationship between short-run fluctuations in prices and those in monetary policy. This problem is not serious, however, because the economy is well able to cope with price fluctuations. What matters is secular inflation or deflation, which can be controlled.[4]

In an open economy, the fundamental quantity-theory proposition has an important corollary: the central bank has no long-run influence on real exchange rates. The long-run trends of *nominal* exchange rates and of prices are affected by monetary policy in the same way. The purchasing-power parity (PPP) proposition, correctly interpreted, is valid (see sec. 2.3). It follows that the long-run trend of exchange rates does not require the attention of central bankers. Once they have determined the price trend, there is little they can do about the trend of exchange rates.

There is a minor exception to this statement inasmuch as the central bank, by increasing the share of foreign assets in its portfolio at the expense of domestic securities, can produce a real appreciation of the domestic currency. This possibility was analyzed in section 12.4. This exception does not invalidate the statement, however, because it is not likely that a central bank will continue to shift its portfolio in the same direction for very long.

The central bank can control the price trend because the economy has a demand for non–interest-bearing currency and demand deposits supplied by the central bank. More precisely, it is, as Tobin (1969) has shown, not the absence of interest on base money but its exogenous nature that gives base money its special significance. Yet this distinction is hardly important in practice. If non–interest-bearing base money should disappear, with all means of payment consequently bearing interest at market rates, the control of the central bank over the price level would disappear with it. The central bank would be reduced to exchanging different interest-bearing assets at fluctuating market prices, and it is not clear how such exchanges affect the price level. Control of the price level would probably shift from the central bank to the treasury, the supplier of government debt (Niehans 1982a). While it is not certain, therefore, that the central bank will be able to control the price level forever, it can quite certainly control it under present circumstances. This conclusion has received renewed support from the marked reaction of inflation rates to monetary restraint in recent years.

The PPP proposition implies that a non-inflationary price trend is gener-

---

4. Under a gold standard, there is no such control since the central bank is forced to accept the price trend resulting from production costs in gold mining. With fiat money, good monetary policy can therefore make prices more stable than under a gold standard. Bad monetary policy, on the other hand, will make price instability much worse.

ally incompatible with the stabilization of a particular exchange rate or an average of exchange rates. Stable domestic prices generally require variable exchange rates, and vice versa. To allow a country to pursue a non-inflationary course is indeed the basic virtue of floating exchange rates. Whenever a country pegs an exchange rate, this virtue is lost; the country becomes the price satellite of the partner to whose currency it is pegging.

Again there is an exception, in this case an important one. If there is a trading partner with superior monetary policies, a country may find it advantageous to behave as a price satellite. Suppose the United States succeeded in following an inflation-free course at, on average, satisfactory employment levels. More and more countries would probably find it to their advantage to stabilize their own prices by pegging their currencies to the dollar. It is true that the price index which each country would prefer to stabilize may differ from the U.S. price index, but this would probably be regarded as a negligible drawback in this case. Countries with good monetary policies may thus become gravitation centers for currency areas.

The next question is how the rate of monetary expansion should be determined in order to produce a non-inflationary price trend. I shall develop the answer in stages. First, the required rate of monetary expansion is probably neither constant nor equal to the rate of real economic growth. There are several reasons for this. One is the presence of government debt. It is well known that, in the presence of government debt, the quantity theory of money is not generally valid. It would be valid if the amount of bonds held by the private sector expanded in proportion to the money supply. Except in this special case, the course of prices also depends on government debt. If debt expands faster than money, the inflation rate will rise more than the money supply, and vice versa. To keep prices stable, monetary policy will thus have to take account of fiscal policy. As long as a large proportion of the net financial assets of the private sector consists of base money, the required correction will be small, but if the share of the base money supply is shrinking, it may assume increasing importance.[5]

Another reason for shifts in the required rate of monetary expansion is technical progress in financial services, often called "financial innovation." In a fundamental sense, the demand for money is due to transaction costs, defined in a wide sense to include information and accounting costs.[6] In the absence of transaction costs, no money would ever be held. Technical progress is typically associated with a decline in transaction costs. Thanks to computers and telecommunications, a given volume of stock, bond, credit, or for-

---

5. Once progressive inflation has reduced the level of non–interest-bearing real balances to a very low level, the central bank may be almost powerless; inflation will then depend almost entirely on fiscal policies.

6. For a detailed analysis of transaction costs as a determinant of the demand for money, see Niehans (1978, chs. 3–6).

eign exchange transactions is being handled at progressively lower cost. It is becoming increasingly profitable to invest idle cash balances, even for a few hours. As a consequence, the demand for cash balances declines.[7] It is quite likely, therefore, that in periods of rapid technical progress in the financial sector, the rate of inflation associated with a given rate of monetary expansion will increase.

A third reason arises from the shifts in real factors as reflected in relative prices. The quantity theory is sometimes represented as maintaining that all price changes are due to monetary factors. Nothing could be farther from the truth. Besides money, all kinds of real factors act on prices and the price level. If these factors change, a constant rate of monetary expansion may result in accelerating or decelerating inflation. The price of oil is a prime example. If the relative price of oil rises continually, constancy of the price trend in an oil-importing country would require a lowering of the rate of monetary expansion.

Foreign monetary policy may be a fourth reason for variations in that rate. In fact, the domestic central bank is not necessarily the sole supplier of domestic base money. Domestic money may also be held, bought, and sold by foreign central banks in the pursuit of their own monetary policy. Federal Reserve sales of Swiss francs against dollars are just as much an increase in the Swiss money supply as Swiss National Bank purchases of dollars for Swiss francs. What determines the course of Swiss prices is, in principle, the combined activities of all central banks.

In the light of these considerations, efforts to predetermine a fixed rate of monetary expansion do not look promising. Nor are they necessary. All the central bank has to do is to make marginal corrections in its monetary course based on price behavior observed in the recent past. This is how people steer an automobile. They usually have no idea by how many degrees the front wheels turn for a 90° turn of the steering wheel—and they could not care less. All they do is adjust the steering wheel until the car is headed in the right direction. The same feedback-control approach can be used for the money supply. It is complicated, however, by the fact that the quantity theory acts with a considerable lag. In this respect the money supply is more like the rudder of a sailboat than the steering wheel of a car. Adjustments should, therefore, be made in small steps in order to avoid oversteering.

Such an approach can be made to work if the policy instrument is the base money supply. If policy-makers use interest rates as their main policy instrument, they are likely to fail. Suppose the aim is to reduce inflation. To accomplish this through interest rates, the latter would first have to be raised and then lowered gradually. The required trajectory would be complicated

---

7. Not all phenomena that are commonly labeled "financial innovation" are of this nature. Some are merely the consequence of distortions in interest rates due to inflation and interest ceilings. In this case, they are, in principle, reversible.

and virtually impossible to determine. Feedback control would be of little help. Any errors would threaten to induce cumulative inflation or deflation. With money supply control, a gradual lowering of the expansion rate is enough.[8]

The central problem of long-run price stabilization is the reduction of inflation. It is a problem because disinflation is inevitably accompanied by recession, and a given disinflation should presumably be achieved with the smallest possible recession. There is a near-consensus today that, under conditions of moderate inflation, the key to the success of long-run price stabilization is "gradualism."[9] At the beginning of the 1980s, few, if any, economists urged an abrupt reduction in monetary expansion rates to a non-inflationary level. Virtually all advocated a gradual procedure. If, as in the case of the United Kingdom in 1979, an abrupt contraction actually occurred, it was unintended, resulting from a faulty implementation of gradualism.

Although the near-consensus is impressive, the precise reasoning behind it is not clear. It must have something to do with imperfect foresight. Suppose the choice is between the announcement of an abrupt reduction in the rate of monetary expansion by 8 percent and the announcement of four annual reductions, each by 2 percent. If in each case everyone correctly anticipates all consequences of the announcement, the economic effects should be virtually the same. Perfect foresight telescopes a gradual adjustment into an abrupt adjustment. Suppose, on the other hand, that each of the 2 percent reductions comes as a surprise. In this case, the effects are clearly different from those of an unexpected 8 percent reduction. In its pure form, the second case is hardly more realistic than the first, but gradualism seems to be based on the notion that it is not too far from reality. If this is so, a gradual adjustment of monetary policy can reduce the amplitude of the resulting disturbances by spreading them over a longer period. In an open economy, in particular, the overshooting of the exchange rate can be reduced, but it lasts longer.

The question is why a spreading of adjustment should be desirable. A possible answer is that adjustment costs rise more than in proportion to the amplitude of the adjustment. Two price reductions of 2 percent may be less costly than one of 4 percent. Exchange overshooting by 20 percent for one year may create a smaller disturbance than overshooting by 40 percent for six months. An output decline of 6 percent for one year may have secondary effects which a 2 percent output loss does not have, even if it lasts for three years. Though such non-linearities are intuitively plausible, most economic

8. As Wicksell (1898/1936) showed, for a given capital stock only one interest rate results in a stable price level. For the money supply, however, any level, if held constant, leads to price stability.

9. The term was introduced by Poole (1970b). The statement leaves open the possibility that very high inflation rates are best lowered in large steps.

models imply that the adjustment costs are proportionate to the size of the adjustment. The cumulative output loss during a monetary contraction is thus proportional to the cumulative reduction in the inflation rate. In this case, gradualism cannot lower the total burden of disinflation. (For a recent example, see Buiter and Miller 1982).

This is where a second possible answer comes in. Even if gradualism cannot lower the total burden of disinflation, the burden may be more easily borne by society if it is spread over time. In economic theory, this idea is often formalized by the use of a quadratic social welfare function. In practical politics, it is reflected in the notion that a government may survive three years, each with a 2 percent employment loss, more easily than one year with a 6 percent loss. It is also likely that gradualism will permit a more equal distribution of the adjustment costs among different economic sectors and social groups. In this context, it is important to bear in mind that one of the basic requirements of a successful monetary policy in a democracy is popular support. In the long run, this is difficult to obtain if the burden of adjustment is very unequally distributed.

In an open economy, the case for gradualism is reenforced by the overshooting of exchange rates. Though the evidence is not conclusive, there is little doubt that abrupt shifts in monetary policy produce much more overshooting than do gradual adjustments. The undershooting of the dollar in 1977–78 and the overshooting of sterling in 1979–80 are warning examples. From this point of view, gradualism may be regarded as the basic international rule of conduct for national monetary policy.

It was noted above that the price level in any country is the joint outcome of the monetary policies of all countries. Floating exchange rates do not guarantee complete autonomy of prices. The more the portfolios of individuals, firms, and banks are diversified among highly substitutable assets in different currencies, the more autonomy is reduced. While this is true in principle, for the long-run stabilization of prices it does not matter much. Central bank control over the price level is based on the demand for non–interest-bearing base money. For base money, international substitutability is small. As a consequence, a country's inflation rate over, say, twenty years is little influenced by the action of other countries; it depends almost exclusively on its own policies. Any foreign influences can be compensated for, as pointed out above, by the domestic central bank. In practice, floating exchange rates make each country responsible for its own inflation.

15.3 Reducing Output Fluctuations

The medium-term objective of monetary policy is to reduce output fluctuations. The central bank will try to achieve it by expanding the money supply to counteract an impending recession. These efforts are subject to the constraint that long-term price stability must not be compromised. A monetary expansion for the purpose of output stabilization must thus be followed by a compensatory contraction within one or two years.

I shall first provide a nontechnical summary of "mainstream" views about the output effects of monetary policy in a closed economy. Despite the perennial controversies, there is a fair amount of consensus. The basic contribution of the central bank to output stabilization is the avoidance of abrupt shifts in the long-run course of the money supply. If this course is steady and if necessary corrections are made gradually, as described in the preceding section, the number of serious output fluctuations will be greatly reduced. There is also broad agreement that an expansion of the money supply beyond what was previously expected will indeed stimulate output; monetary contraction, on the other hand, will produce recession. Though theorists might construct models in which money is neutral even in the short run, in the world we live in it is not so. The proximate reason is the limited flexibility of prices. This, in turn, may be due to several factors, including imperfect foresight, the existence of old contracts, the cost of price changes, and the need to distribute new money throughout the economy.[10] While the precise interaction of these factors has not yet been disentangled, their combined result has long been fairly clear. The recessions accompanying the recent monetary contractions in the United Kingdom, the United States, and other countries have provided new evidence for the "mainstream" view.

The output effects of monetary policy are likely to occur with a lag of several quarters. The lag is difficult to forecast and appears to be variable. The output effect will be temporary, being followed by a period of contraction associated with further price increases. The dominant, though far from unanimous, view seems to be that monetary expansion is, in principle, effective in shifting some output from one year to another, but quite ineffective in raising long-run average output or the rate of output growth. In addition, the output shifts are hard to control, and reliable feedback rules are difficult to devise. As a consequence, the use of monetary policy to stimulate output should be regarded more as an exceptional—and thus largely unpredictable—measure than as a normal routine. The "fine-tuning" of output does not seem feasible at the present time.

The preceding summary ignored the openness of the economy. The question is how the medium-term effectiveness of monetary policy may be affected by foreign trade, capital flows, and exchange rates. It is first considered from a static point of view.

In the 1960s, the discussion, largely stimulated by Canadian experiences, focused on the relative effectiveness of monetary and fiscal policies in

---

10. The literature on rational expectations reaffirmed the crucial role of imperfect foresight. An excellent survey is provided by McCallum (1980). For a recent analysis of staggered wage contracts, including references to earlier work, see Taylor (1979).

achieving "internal balance" (characterized by a certain target output) and "external balance" (characterized either by constant reserves or by a certain exchange rate). Mundell (1960, 1962) and Fleming (1962), building on Meade and Tinbergen, brought this approach to maturity. Monetary expansion was interpreted as a rightward shift in the *LM* curve, raising output and lowering the rate of interest. Fiscal expansion was expressed as a rightward shift in the *IS* curve, raising both output and the rate of interest. In a closed economy, both instruments could be used, in many combinations, to reach the desired output. In an open economy, however, the requirement of external balance was seen to add another target. Only with one particular combination of instruments could the economy reach both targets.[11] In addition, the targets could not be reached through decentralized policy-making unless instruments were assigned to targets on the basis of their comparative advantages. This was Mundell's "assignment" problem (see ch. 12 and references given there).

The main conclusion from this analysis was that the comparative advantages depend largely on the exchange rate regime. Under floating rates, both monetary and fiscal policies tend to be more effective in an absolute sense than under fixed rates.[12] At the same time, floating rates tend to increase the effectiveness of monetary policy relative to that of fiscal policy in influencing output. The main reason is that the low level of interest rates associated with monetary expansion is assumed to produce a capital outflow and thus an expansionary export surplus; the high level of interest rates associated with fiscal expansion has the reverse effect.

In addition, the comparative advantages of policy instruments are seen to depend on capital mobility, interpreted in the sense of the interest elasticity of capital flows. With sufficiently high capital mobility, monetary policy would be certain to have a comparative advantage in influencing domestic output, while fiscal policy would be relatively more effective in controlling the exchange rate.[13] In a small economy with infinite mobility of capital, fiscal policy would be entirely powerless. Since interest rates would be set in the international market, the expansionary effect of government expenditures would be neutralized by the contractionary effect of the import surplus that was associated with the capital inflow.

This approach gave rise to a mushrooming taxonomy. It also became

---

11. In principle, there is no reason to regard targets as given. If a given output and a given level of reserves are good, higher output and higher reserves are usually better. A more general analysis would thus consider target trade-offs from the point of view of social welfare (see Niehans, 1968).

12. While the following discussion concentrates on floating rates, an excellent survey of the fixed-rate case is provided by Swoboda (1973).

13. This is analogous, though not equivalent, to the proposition, derived in section 11.3, that foreign-exchange operations have a comparative advantage for domestic output, while open-market operations have a comparative advantage for the exchange rate.

clear, however, that fiscal policy was too unwieldy an instrument to control volatile exchange rates and that the exchange rate cannot be regarded as a policy target in its own right. After the collapse of the Bretton Woods system, fiscal policy thus dropped into the background. The remainder of this section is limited to monetary policy.

Imagine a Keynesian model for an open economy with floating exchange rates. Output supplied equals domestic expenditure plus the trade balance:

$$y = A(i, y) + T(y, e). \qquad A_i < 0 \quad A_y > 0$$
$$T_y < 0 \quad T_e > 0 \qquad (15.3.1)$$

The trade balance is equal to capital exports:

$$T(y, e) = C(i, y, e). \qquad C_i < 0 \quad C_y \gtrless 0 \quad C_e \gtrless 0 \qquad (15.3.2)$$

The demand for (base) money equals the supply:

$$L(i, y) = M. \qquad L_i < 0 \quad L_y > 0 \qquad (15.3.3)$$

In a closed economy, characterized by $T = C = 0$, equation (15.3.1) can be represented by a downward-sloping *IS* curve and (15.3.3) by an upward-sloping *LM* curve (see fig. 15.3.1). Monetary expansion would be reflected in a rightward shift of the *LM* curve; the economy would thus move along the *IS* curve from *O* to *P*.

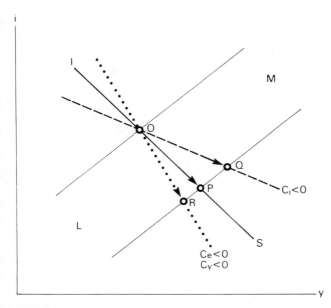

FIGURE 15.3.1
Effects of Monetary Policy

The modifications required for an open economy with floating exchange rates depend crucially on the behavior of capital flows. In the absence of capital flows, the openness of the economy makes no difference. Since trade must be balanced, there can be no additional effect from trade surpluses or deficits. The increase in imports due to higher income is matched by the trade effects of depreciation. This implies that there is no international transmission of domestic expansion. The output effects of monetary policy are "bottled up" at home.[14] The result is the same, even in the presence of capital flows, so long as these are insensitive to interest rates, income, and exchange rates.

Mundell (1964) drew attention to the significance of the interest effects on capital outflows (C_i). If higher interest rates result in a capital inflow ($C_i <$ 0), the *IS* curve is flatter than in the closed economy. This is illustrated by the broken *IS* curve in figure 15.3.1. As a consequence, an expansion of the money supply moves the economy from O to Q, where output is higher than in P. The openness of the economy increases the potency of monetary policy under floating rates.[15] This is intuitively plausible. The capital outflow resulting from the decline in interest rates must be matched by a trade surplus, and this gives an added impulse to the domestic economy. The counterpart is a contractionary effect in the rest of the world. The higher potency of monetary policy at home is thus associated with a contraction abroad; there is inverse transmission of output fluctuations.[16]

H. G. Johnson (1972b) extended the analysis to the income effects on capital flows (C_y). He argued that an increase in income, by improving investment opportunities, is likely to attract a capital inflow, so that $C_y < 0$. This in itself makes the *IS* curve steeper, as illustrated by the dotted *IS* curve in figure 15.3.1. By comparing R with P, one finds that the output effect of monetary policy is weaker than in a closed economy, because domestic expansion is associated with a capital inflow and thus with a trade deficit. By the same token, domestic expansion would be accompanied by expansion abroad. The speculative effect of exchange rates on capital flows (C_e), mentioned but not discussed by Johnson, works in the same direction. With $C_e < 0$ (see sec. 10.4), this effect again makes the *IS* curve steeper and thus reduces the output effects of monetary policy.[17]

A further aspect has been added in the preceding chapters. It has been

14. Regarding the "bottling up" of domestic disturbances by floating rates, see also section 5.3.

15. For Sohmen (1973) this was, in fact, the main motive for advocating floating rates.

16. If low interest rates are caused by an exogenous decline in investment demand, transmission occurs in the same way as under fixed rates, the contraction in the rest of the world being associated with contraction at home. This was pointed out by Modigliani and Askari (1973).

17. This case is analyzed in Niehans (1975), where it is shown that the effect of monetary policy on output may well be smaller under floating rates than under fixed rates. If at the same time $C_i < 0$, it is even conceivable that monetary expansion may reduce output, though this seems an unlikely paradox.

shown that, in fact, the dominant determinant of capital flows is likely to be the market price of capital goods relative to their replacement cost, as reflected in Tobin's "q". With monetary expansion, q is likely to rise, initiating a capital inflow. I believe that this is actually what Johnson had in mind, since, in his argument, income is clearly a proxy for investment opportunities. Once these are explicitly introduced, the remaining "pure" income effect should be positive. The main point is that monetary expansion, by improving investment opportunities, is likely to result in a capital inflow and, therefore, a trade deficit; the output effects are correspondingly reduced. The overall conclusion is that floating rates are far from certain to increase the potency of monetary policy and are, in fact, quite likely to reduce it.

Recent work has yielded another insight. The comparative statics of *IS/LM* analysis provide only a still picture of the dynamic process following a change in monetary policy. In the long run, any effects on output are bound to disappear. In the short run, as shown in chapter 11, a wide variety of effects are possible depending on the period considered. If floating rates make monetary policy less potent in the expansionary phase, they also dampen the subsequent contraction. If monetary expansion, in view of the J-effect, initially produces a trade deficit, this must later be followed by a surplus. The same is true with respect to repercussions on the rest of the world. As a consequence, the output effects of monetary policy now appear to be even less foreseeable and more erratic than before.

This does not mean that monetary policy should never be used to stabilize output; it means that, in the case of domestic disturbances, monetary policy should be used with great restraint. At the same time, monetary policy may be even more indispensable as a defensive weapon against "imported" disturbances. Floating exchange rates do not insulate an economy against output fluctuations imposed by foreign monetary policy, but there is no reason to accept such fluctuations passively. Policy-makers have no excuse for tolerating a serious recession resulting from overshooting exchange rates, while imploring other countries to mend their ways.

It seems, however, that such defensive measures should not take the form of continuous fine-tuning of exchange rates. Such fine-tuning is unnecessary, because the economy is able to cope with considerable fluctuations in real exchange rates. It is also undesirable because mechanical rules based on purchasing-power parity threaten to be destabilizing rather than stabilizing (see sec. 13.3). For counterspeculative interventions into the exchange markets no satisfactory rules have yet been discovered (see sec. 13.2). It was argued in section 13.4 that temporary exchange rate ceilings, though certainly controversial, may offer a more promising defensive strategy. If used infrequently, but in every case decisively, they seem to provide an effective means for reducing the overshooting of real exchange rates. Such ceilings (or floors) are also consistent with the basic objective of long-run price stability.

A successful defense against imported overshooting requires close coordination between the foreign-exchange operations and the domestic credit policies of the central bank. In the first instance, an exchange-rate ceiling would have to be enforced by foreign exchange operations. In the absence of domestic credit operations these would exert upward pressure on output and, at a later date, on prices. Domestic credit operations can help to reduce these side effects. Their nature depends on the comparative advantages of alternative policy instruments discussed in section 12.3. It was there conjectured that foreign-exchange operations are likely to have a short-run advantage for output, while open-market operations have a short-run advantage in influencing the exchange rate. If this is indeed true, the side effects of exchange-rate ceilings can be reduced by initiating a domestic credit expansion associated with a reduction in foreign-exchange purchases. One will also have to bear in mind that such ceilings are intended to be temporary. This may be a valid reason for using domestic credit operations to a lesser extent than would otherwise be the case. It is clear, however, that this question requires further study and that the appropriate solution depends on the circumstances of the case.

It has often been argued that foreign-exchange operations also require close cooperation among central banks. The reasons are far from obvious. The basic international rule of conduct is the avoidance of abrupt shifts in monetary policy. Once a central bank has violated this rule, it is not clear how it can help other central banks to defend themselves. Suppose a relaxation of U.S. monetary policy has produced an overshooting of, say, the Swiss franc. Suppose further that the Swiss National Bank decides to dampen that overshooting by buying dollars against Swiss francs. The United States "cooperation" envisaged in such cases typically consists in U.S. borrowings of Swiss francs from the Swiss National Bank and their sale against dollars in the foreign-exchange market. It is not clear why the Swiss National Bank should regard this as helpful; instead of first lending the francs to the Federal Reserve, it can just as well use them for direct dollar purchases. In fact, the Swiss National Bank has good reason to prefer direct intervention because it thereby retains full control over the Swiss money supply. Historically, "concerted action" by central banks in the foreign exchange market has not been a success. Whatever concerted action can do, individual central banks can usually do just as well and often better.

There may, however, be a need for international cooperation of another kind. If the central bank of country A buys B's currency, it influences the supply not only of its own currency but also that of B's currency. In principle, whatever a central bank does affects not only its home economy but also foreign economies. Conversely, monetary conditions in each country are, in principle, the joint result of the monetary policies of all countries; one country's benefit may be another country's loss. The analysis of these interactions would clearly lead us into oligopoly theory and the theory of games. It is likely to show that only extensive international coordination of policies could assure a mutually beneficial result.[18]

While the detailed analysis of such interactions may be intellectually rewarding, from a practical point of view it does not seem to be of primary importance. The reason is that, by following certain rules of conduct, the mutual interference of central banks can probably be held to a tolerable level. The guiding principle is that in the interest of monetary autonomy each central bank should select its foreign assets in such a way that interference with foreign monetary policies is minimized. This may be called the "principle of minimum interference."

The principle implies that central banks should buy and sell foreign interest-bearing assets rather than foreign cash balances. This is not a stringent requirement, since the profit motive pulls in the same direction. What matters here is the relative weakness, dollar for dollar, of the macroeconomic effects of changes in foreign short-term assets, as compared to changes in foreign cash balances.[19]

It also follows from the principle of minimum interference that central banks, in their foreign exchange operations, should use either a "large" currency (like the dollar) or a broadly-based composite currency (like the SDR or the ECU). To give an illustration: by conducting extensive operations in Swiss francs, the Federal Reserve could completely swamp the monetary policy of the Swiss National Bank. The proposed rule would effectively prevent this.

If these rules are followed, each country, large or small, would, I believe, have enough monetary autonomy to defend itself against excessive overshooting of its exchange rate. From the point of view of short-run output stabilization, it is not clear that international cooperation could be expected to achieve more.

15.4 Preventing Liquidity Crises

The short-term objective of monetary policy is the prevention of liquidity crises in the financial system. In the nineteenth century and up to the Great Depression, business fluctuations were punctuated by "bank panics." Central banks developed largely in response to this challenge. It was recognized that commercial banks were subject to drastic fluctuations in their liquidity requirements, depending on business conditions and on expectations. In an

---

18. Elements of such an analysis can be found in Cooper (1968), Niehans (1968), and Hamada (1974).

19. A switch by central bank A from cash balances to money-market assets of country B, since it is equivalent to domestic open-market purchases of central bank B, would create a particularly strong disturbance. Such disturbances were widely discussed when central banks moved into the Eurodollar market. It should be noted that the disturbance would have been similar if they had moved into U.S. treasury bills.

imperfect credit market, a single failure might trigger a chain reaction of failures. Acting as a "lender of last resort," the central bank, so it was hoped, might be able to forestall such developments.[20]

By and large, this hope was fulfilled. During the last fifty years, liquidity crises have not been a primary problem. In part, this was probably due to the development of increasingly perfect credit markets. In part, it was certainly due to the presence of powerful central banks, equipped to step in at short notice as lenders of last resort. They can do this without compromising their output and price objectives, provided that any intervention is neutralized within, say, six months.

It is neither possible nor necessary here to discuss the short-run functions of the central bank in a closed economy. The relevant question is how this function is affected if one considers instead an open economy with floating exchange rates. I see three main considerations. The first relates to the need for domestic measures. Conflicting forces seem to be at work. On one hand, the possibility that there may be large flows of funds into and out of a given currency may subject bank liquidity to additional strains. On the other hand, the existence of large, international interbank credit markets, particularly the Euromarkets, reduces those market imperfections that in the past often created a need for central-bank assistance. In general, it is not clear which of these forces dominates. I am inclined to believe that in recent years the international market has tended to act as a stabilizer rather than as a destabilizer of bank liquidity. Even moderate-sized banks can now rely on a large and highly perfect world market, which reduces their exposure to local and national disturbances. The need for central-bank action is correspondingly reduced.

The second consideration has to do with the size of fluctuations in the foreign-exchange markets. The main point is that the central bank has good reason to welcome and encourage a wide, deep,and resilient foreign-exchange market with active speculation (see sec. 13.2). In such a market, the seemingly erratic fluctuations caused by real disturbances are probably much smaller than in a thin market with little speculation. Indeed, in the absence of a well-developed foreign-exchange market, floating exchange rates may become unworkable.

The third consideration concerns possible guidelines for short-term intervention in the foreign-exchange market. The main rule seems to be negative. It is true that the central bank, if it were omniscient, could dampen exchange-rate fluctuations. In many cases, sterilized intervention with unchanged money supplies would be enough. A shift of demand in the Euromarket from dollars into Swiss francs, accompanied by an appreciation of the

---

20. Milton Friedman advocated the use of the money supply as an intermediary target precisely in order to force the central bank to offset fluctuations in bank liquidity.

franc could, in principle, be neutralized by a portfolio shift by the Swiss National Bank from domestic assets into dollars. However, central banks are not omniscient. Given their imperfect foresight, no system has yet been discovered which would ensure that their interventions are stabilizing rather than destabilizing. If intervention consists of "leaning against the wind," based on past exchange rates, it is unlikely to be an effective stabilizer (see sec. 13.2). If it is based on PPP, it is likely to be actually destabilizing (see sec. 13.3). The main short-run contribution of the central bank, therefore, seems to consist in the promotion of a large and efficient foreign-exchange market..

This applies to both spot and forward markets (see sec. 8.3). With floating rates, the motives for forward intervention expounded by Keynes have ceased to be relevant. All the central bank can achieve through swap operations is a slight twist in the term structure of both interest rates and exchange rates; such twists seem to serve no useful macroeconomic purpose. It is true that special factors like bank window dressing may produce seasonal fluctuations in both interest rates and exchange rates, which central bank operations can mitigate. Nevertheless, the general economic benefits of such efforts are hard to see. The conclusion is that the central bank, in channeling its foreign exchange operations through either the spot or the forward market, can rely on the same cost considerations as a private foreign-exchange trader.

To those absorbed in doctrinal issues, economics always looks in disarray. Doctrinaires forever fight yesterday's battle, and none of them ever admits defeat. However, I believe that a pragmatic, yet critical, central banker can find in recent monetary economics many developments that give him useful guidance. With hindsight, it is not difficult to see that the Bretton Woods system collapsed because, in the 1960s, economists understood neither fixed nor floating exchange rates. Though many important problems of international monetary economics still remain unsolved, I believe that the last ten years have brought considerable progress. Based on these developments, this chapter has proposed some tentative guidelines for central-bank policy under floating rates, as they seem to appear at the beginning of the 1980s. At the purely intellectual level, such guidelines may look rather simple. They are certainly simpler than the foundations of microeconomic policy. The difficult part is to implement them in the political arena.

Bibliography

Agarwal, J. P. 1980. Determinants of foreign direct investment: a survey. *Weltwirtschaftliches Archiv* 116(4):739–73.

Alexander, S. S. 1952. Effects of a devaluation on a trade balance. *International Monetary Fund Staff Papers* 2:263–78.

Aliber, R. Z. 1980. The integration of the offshore and domestic banking system. *Journal of Monetary Economics* 6(4):509–26.

Allen, P. R., and P. B. Kenen. 1980. *Asset Markets, Exchange Rates, and Economic Integration: A Synthesis.* Cambridge: Cambridge University Press.

Amano, A. 1965. International capital movements and economic growth. *Kyklos* 18:693–99.

Arndt, S. W. 1971. The comparative merits of fixed vs. flexible exchange rates: a comment. *Journal of Money, Credit, and Banking* 3(2):356–62.

Balassa, B. 1964. The purchasing-power parity doctrine: a reappraisal. *Journal of Political Economy* 72(6):584–96.

Baltensperger, E. 1981. Geldpolitik und Wechselkursdynamik. *Kredit und Kapital* 14(2):320–40.

Basevi, G., and P. De Grauwe. 1977. Vicious and virtuous circles: a theoretical analysis and a policy proposal for managing exchange rates. *European Economic Review* 10(3):277–301.

Basevi, G., and P. De Grauwe. 1978. Vicious and virtuous circles and the OPTICA proposal: a two-country analysis. In *One Money for Europe*, ed. M. Fratianni and T. Peeters, pp. 144–57. London: Macmillan.

Bernstein, E. M. 1966. Comment. In *International Payments Problems*, pp. 83–87. Washington, D.C.: American Enterprise Institute for Public Policy Research.

Bickerdike, C. F. 1920. The instability of foreign exchange. *Economic Journal* 30(1):118–22.

Black, S. W. 1973. *International Money Markets and Flexible Exchange Rates.* Princeton Studies in International Finance, no. 32.

319

Boyer, R. S. 1977. Devaluation and portfolio balance. *American Economic Review* 67(2):54–63.

Boyer, R. S. 1978. Optimal foreign exchange market intervention. *Journal of Political Economy* 86(6):1045–55.

Branson, W. H. 1968. *Financial Capital Flows in the U.S. Balance of Payments*. Amsterdam: North-Holland.

Branson, W. H. 1970. Monetary policy and the new view of international capital movements. *Brookings Papers on Economic Activity* 2:235–62.

Branson, W. H. 1979. Exchange rate dynamics and monetary policy. In *Inflation and Employment in Open Economies*, ed. A. Lindbeck, pp. 189–224. Amsterdam: North-Holland.

Britton, A.J.C. 1970. The dynamic stability of the foreign exchange market. *Economic Journal* 80(317):91–96.

Bryant, R. C. 1975. Empirical research on financial capital flows. In *International Trade and Finance: Frontiers for Research*, ed. P. B. Kenen, pp. 321–62. Cambridge: Cambridge University Press.

Buiter, W. H., and M. Miller. 1982. Real exchange rate overshooting and the output cost of bringing down inflation. *European Economic Review* 18(1):85–123.

Calvo, G. A., and C. A. Rodriguez. 1977. A model of exchange rate determination under currency substitution and rational expectations. *Journal of Political Economy* 85(3):617–25.

Cassel, G. 1916. The present situation of the foreign exchanges. *Economic Journal* 26(1):62–65.

Cassel, G. 1918. Abnormal deviations in international exchanges. *Economic Journal* 28(4):413–15.

Cassel, G. 1921. *The World's Monetary Problems: Two Memoranda to the League of Nations*. London: Constable.

Cassel, G. 1922. *Money and Foreign Exchange after 1914*. New York: Macmillan.

Caves, R. E., and R. W. Jones. 1977. *World Trade and Payments: An Introduction*. 2nd ed. Boston: Little, Brown.

Chipman, J. S. 1974. The transfer problem once again. In *Trade, Stability, and Macroeconomics*, ed. G. Horwich and P. A. Samuelson, pp. 19–78. New York: Academic Press.

Collery, A. 1971. *International Adjustment, Open Economies, and the Quantity Theory of Money*. Princeton Studies in International Finance, no. 28.

Commission of the European Communities. 1977. *Inflation and Exchange Rates: Evidence and Policy Guidelines for the European Community*. OPTICA Report 1976. Brussels.

Cooper, R. N. 1968. *The Economics of Interdependence: Economic Policy in the Atlantic Community*. New York: McGraw-Hill.

Davis, S. I. 1980. *The Euro-Bank: Its Origins, Management, and Outlook*. 2nd ed. New York: Wiley.

Deardorff, A. V. 1979. One-way arbitrage and its implications for the foreign exchange markets. *Journal of Political Economy* 87(2):351–64.

De Grauwe, P., A. Steinherr, and G. Basevi. 1980. The dynamics of intervention in foreign exchange markets: purchasing power parity as a guideline. In *The Economics of Flexible Exchange Rates*, ed. H. Frisch and G. Schwödiauer, *Kredit und Kapital*, Beiheft 6, pp. 88–112.

Despres, E., C. P. Kindleberger, and W. S. Salant. 1966. *The Dollar and World Liquidity: A Minority View*. Washington, D.C.: Brookings.

Dornbusch, R. 1973. Currency depreciation, hoarding, and relative prices. *Journal of Political Economy* 81(4):893–915.

Dornbusch, R. 1976. Expectations and exchange rate dynamics. *Journal of Political Economy* 84(6):1161–76.

Dornbusch, R. 1980. *Open Economy Macroeconomics*. New York: Basic Books.

Dornbusch, R. 1982. PPP exchange-rate rules and macroeconomic stability. *Journal of Political Economy* 90(1):158–65.

Dornbusch, R., and S. Fischer. 1980. Exchange rates and the current account. *American Economic Review* 70(5):960–71.

Driskill, R. A. 1980. Exchange rate dynamics, portfolio balance, and relative prices. *American Economic Review* 70(4):776–83.

Driskill, R. A. 1981. Exchange-rate dynamics: an empirical investigation. *Journal of Political Economy* 89(2):357–71.

Dufey, G., and I. H. Giddy. 1978. *The International Money Market*. Englewood Cliffs, N.J.: Prentice-Hall.

Edgeworth, F. Y. 1888. The mathematical theory of banking. *Journal of the Royal Statistical Society* 51:113–27.

Einzig, P. 1937. *The Theory of Forward Exchange*. London: Macmillan.

Einzig, P., and B. S. Quinn. 1977. *The Euro-Dollar System: Practice and Theory of International Interest Rates*. 6th ed. London: Macmillan.

Fama, E. F. 1970. Efficient capital markets: a review of theory and empirical work. *Journal of Finance* 25(2):383–417.

Fama, E. F. 1976. *Foundations of Finance*. New York: Basic Books.

Feldstein, M. S. 1968. Uncertainty and forward exchange speculation. *Review of Economics and Statistics* 50(2):182–92.

Fischer, S. 1977. Stability and exchange rate systems in a monetarist model of the balance of payments. In *The Political Economy of Monetary Reform*, ed. R. Z. Aliber, pp. 59–73. London: Macmillan.

Fleming, J. M. 1962. Domestic financial policies under fixed and under floating exchange rates. *International Monetary Fund Staff Papers* 9:369–79.

Fleming, J. M. 1971. On exchange rate unification. *Economic Journal* 81(323):467–88.

Floyd, J. E. 1969. International capital movements and monetary equilibrium. *American Economic Review* 59(4):472–92.

Frankel, J. A. 1979. On the mark: a theory of floating exchange rates based on real interest differentials. *American Economic Review* 69(4):610–22.

Frenkel, J. A. 1976. Adjustment mechanisms and the monetary approach to the balance of payments: a doctrinal perspective. In *Recent Issues in International Monetary Economics*, ed. E. Claassen and P. Salin, pp. 29–48. Amsterdam: North-Holland.

Frenkel, J. A. 1978. Purchasing power parity: doctrinal perspective and evidence from the 1920s. *Journal of International Economics* 8(2):169–91.

Frenkel, J. A., and H. G. Johnson. 1976. The monetary approach to the balance of payments: essential concepts and historical origins. In *The Monetary Approach to the Balance of Payments*, ed. J. A. Frenkel and H. G. Johnson, pp. 21–45. London: Allen & Unwin.

Frenkel, J. A., and R. M. Levich. 1975. Covered interest arbitrage: unexploited profits? *Journal of Political Economy* 83(2):325–38.

Friedman, B. M. 1975. Targets, instruments, and indicators of monetary policy. *Journal of Monetary Economics* 1(4):443–73.

Friedman, B. M. 1977. The inefficiency of short-run monetary targets for monetary policy. *Brookings Papers on Economic Activity* 2:293–335.

Friedman, M. 1953. The case for flexible exchange rates. In *Essays in Positive Economics*, pp. 157–203. Chicago: University of Chicago Press.

Friedman, M. 1969. The Eurodollar market: some first principles. *Morgan Guaranty Survey* Oct., pp.4–14.

Gale, D. 1974. The trade imbalance story. *Journal of International Economics* 4(2):119–37.

Genberg, H. 1981. Purchasing power parity as a rule for a crawling peg. In *Exchange Rate Rules: The Theory, Performance, and Prospects of the Crawling Peg*, ed. J. Williamson, pp. 88–106. New York: St. Martin's Press.

Giddy, I. H., G. Dufey, and S. Min. 1979. Interest rates in the U.S. and Eurodollar markets. *Weltwirtschaftliches Archiv* 115(1):51–67.

Girton, L., and D. W. Henderson. 1976. Financial capital movements and central bank behavior in a two-country, short-run portfolio balance model. *Journal of Monetary Economics* 2(1):33–61.

Girton, L., and D. W. Henderson. 1977. Central bank operations in foreign and domestic assets under fixed and flexible exchange rates. In *The Effects of Exchange Rate Adjustments*, ed. P. B. Clark, D. E. Logue, and R. J. Sweeney, pp. 151–79. Washington: U.S. Government Printing Office.

Goldstein, M., and M. S. Khan. 1978. The supply and demand for exports: a simultaneous approach. *Review of Economics and Statistics* 60(2):275–86.

Grauer, F.L.A., R. H. Litzenberger, and R. E. Stehle. 1976. Sharing rules and equilibrium in an international capital market under uncertainty. *Journal of Financial Economics* 3(3):233–56.

Gray, J. A. 1982. *Dynamic Instability in Rational Expectations Models: An Attempt to Clarify*. International Finance Discussion Papers, no. 197.

Gray, M. R., and S. J. Turnovsky. 1979. The stability of exchange rate dynamics under perfect myopic foresight. *International Economic Review* 20(3):643–60.

Grubel, H. G. 1966. *Forward Exchange, Speculation, and the International Flow of Capital*. Stanford, Calif.: Stanford University Press.

Grubel, H. G. 1968. Internationally diversified portfolios: welfare gains and capital flows. *American Economic Review* 58(5):1299–1314.

Grubel, H. G. 1977. How important is control over international reserves? In *The New International Monetary System*, ed. R. A. Mundell and J. J. Polak, pp. 133–61. New York: Columbia University Press.

Haberler, G. 1933. *Der internationale Handel*. Berlin: Springer.

Haberler, G. 1949. The market for foreign exchange and the stability of the balance of payments: a theoretical analysis. *Kyklos* 3(3):193–218.

Haberler, G. 1975. Inflation as a worldwide phenomenon: an overview. In *The Phenomenon of Worldwide Inflation*, ed. D. I. Meiselman and A. B. Laffer, pp. 13–25. Washington, D.C.: American Enterprise Institute for Public Policy Research.

Haberler, G. 1977. How important is control over international reserves? In *The New*

International Monetary System, ed. R. A. Mundell and J. J. Polak, pp. 111–32. New York: Columbia University Press.

Hahn, F. H. 1959. The balance of payments in a monetary economy. *Review of Economic Studies* 26(2):110–25.

Halm, G. N. 1965. *The "Band" Proposal: The Limits of Permissible Exchange Rate Variations.* Special Papers in International Economics, no. 6, Princeton University.

Halm, G. N. 1969. *Toward Limited Exchange-Rate Flexibility.* Essays in International Finance, no. 73, Princeton University.

Halm, G. N., ed. 1970. *Approaches to Greater Flexibility of Exchange Rates: The Bürgenstock Papers.* Princeton: Princeton University Press.

Hamada, K. 1974. Alternative exchange rate systems and the interdependence of monetary policies. In *National Monetary Policies and the International Financial System*, ed. R. Z. Aliber, pp. 13–33. Chicago: University of Chicago Press.

Harberger, A. C. 1950. Currency depreciation, income, and the balance of trade. *Journal of Political Economy* 58(1):47–60.

Hawtrey, R. G. 1932. *The Art of Central Banking.* London: Longmans, Green.

Hayashi, F. 1982. Tobin's marginal q and average q: a neoclassical interpretation. *Econometrica* 50(1):213–24.

Heckerman, D. 1973. On the effects of exchange risk. *Journal of International Economics* 3(4):379–87.

Heckscher, E. 1949. The effect of foreign trade on the distribution of income. In *Readings in the Theory of International Trade*, ed. H. S. Ellis and L. A. Metzler, pp. 272–300. Philadelphia: Blakiston.

Heinevetter, B. 1979. Liquiditätsschaffung und -vermittlung an den Eurowährungsmärkten und die Struktur des internationalen Bankensystems. *Kredit und Kapital* 12(2):221–44.

Heller, H. R. 1973. *International Trade: Theory and Empirical Evidence.* 2nd ed. Englewood Cliffs, N.J.: Prentice-Hall.

Heller, H. R. 1979. Assessing Euro-market growth: why the market is demand-determined. *Euromoney* Feb., pp. 41–47.

Henderson, D. W. 1979. Financial policies in open economies. *American Economic Review Papers and Proceedings* 69(2):232–39.

Henderson, D. W. 1982. *The Role of Intervention Policy in Open Economy Financial Policy: A Macroeconomic Perspective.* International Finance Discussion Papers, no. 202.

Henderson, D. W., and K. Rogoff. 1981. *Net Foreign Asset Positions and Stability in a World Portfolio Balance Model.* International Finance Discussion Papers, no. 178.

Hewson, J. 1975. *Liquidity Creation and Distribution in the Eurocurrency Markets.* Lexington, Mass.: Heath.

Hirschman, A. O. 1949. Devaluation and the trade balance: a note. *Review of Economics and Statistics* 31(1):50–53.

Hodjera, Z. 1973. International short-term capital movements: a survey of theory and empirical analysis. *International Monetary Fund Staff Papers* 20:683–740.

Houthakker, H. S., and S. P. Magee. 1969. Income and price elasticities in world trade. *Review of Economics and Statistics* 51(2):111–25.

Hume, D. 1898. Of the balance of trade (1752). In *Essays, Moral, Political and Literary*, 1:330–45. London: Longmans, Green.

Ishiyama, Y. 1975. The theory of optimum currency areas: a survey. *International Monetary Fund Staff Papers* 22:344–83.

Jasay, A. E. 1960. The social choice between home and overseas investment. *Economic Journal* 70(1):105–13.

Johnson, H. G. 1972a. The case for flexible exchange rates, 1969. In *Further Essays in Monetary Economics*, pp. 198–228. London: Allen & Unwin.

Johnson, H. G. 1972b. Some aspects of the theory of economic policy in a world of capital mobility (1966). In *Further Essays in Monetary Economics*, pp. 151–66. London: Allen & Unwin.

Johnson, H. G. 1972c. The monetary approach to balance-of-payments theory. *Journal of Financial and Quantitative Analysis* 7(2):1555–72.

Johnston, R. B. 1979. Some aspects of the determination of Euro-currency interest rates. *Bank of England Quarterly Bulletin* 19(1):35–46.

Jones, R. W. 1967. International capital movements and the theory of tariffs and trade. *Quarterly Journal of Economics* 81(1):1–38.

Junz, H. B., and R. R. Rhomberg. 1973. Price competitiveness in export trade among industrial countries. *American Economic Review* 63(2):412–18.

Kareken, J., and N. Wallace. 1977. Portfolio autarky: a welfare analysis. *Journal of International Economics* 7(1):19–43.

Kemp, M. C. 1976. *Three Topics in the Theory of International Trade: Distribution, Welfare, and Uncertainty*. Amsterdam: North-Holland.

Kenen, P. B. 1969. The theory of optimum currency areas: an eclectic view. In *Monetary Problems of the International Economy*, ed. R. A. Mundell and A. K. Swoboda, pp. 41–60. Chicago: University of Chicago Press.

Kenen, P. B. 1975. Floats, glides, and indicators: a comparison of methods for changing exchange rates. *Journal of International Economics* 5(2):107–51.

Keynes, J. M. 1923. *A Tract on Monetary Reform*. London: Macmillan.

Keynes, J. M. 1929. The German transfer problem. *Economic Journal* 39(1):1–7.

Keynes, J. M. 1930. *A Treatise on Money*. 2 vols. London: Macmillan.

Keynes, J. M. 1936. *General Theory of Employment, Interest, and Money*. London: Macmillan.

Klopstock, F. H. 1968. *The Euro-Dollar Market: Some Unresolved Issues*. Essays in International Finance, no. 65, Princeton University.

Kohlhagen, S. W. 1978. *The Behavior of Foreign Exchange Markets: A Critical Survey of the Empirical Literature*. Monograph Series in Finance and Economics. New York: New York University.

Kohlhagen, S. W. 1979. The identification of destabilizing foreign exchange speculation. *Journal of International Economics* 9(3):321–40.

Kouri, P.J.K. 1976. The exchange rate and the balance of payments in the short run and in the long run: a monetary approach. *Scandinavian Journal of Economics* 78(2):280–304.

Kouri, P.J.K. 1980. Monetary policy, the balance of payments, and the exchange rate. In *The Functioning of Floating Exchange Rates: Theory, Evidence, and Policy Implications*, ed. D. Bigman and T. Taya, pp. 79–111. Cambridge, Mass.: Ballinger.

Kouri, P.J.K., and J. B. de Macedo. 1978. Exchange rates and the international adjustment process. *Brookings Papers on Economic Activity* 1:111–50.

Krauss, M. B. 1979. *A Geometric Approach to International Trade.* Oxford: Blackwell.

Laffer, A. B. 1973. Two arguments for fixed rates. In *The Economics of Common Currencies*, ed. H. G. Johnson and A. K. Swoboda, pp. 25–34. London: Allen & Unwin.

Laursen, S., and L. A. Metzler. 1950. Flexible exchange rates and the theory of employment. *Review of Economics and Statistics* 32:281–99.

Lee, C. H. 1977. A survey of the literature on the determinants of foreign portfolio investments in the United States. *Weltwirtschaftliches Archiv* 113(3):552–69.

Lerner, A. P. 1946. *The Economics of Control.* New York: Macmillan.

Levich, R. M. 1979a. Further results on the efficiency of markets for foreign exchange. In *Managed Exchange-Rate Flexibility: The Recent Experience.* Federal Reserve Bank of Boston, Conference Series no. 20.

Levich, R. M. 1979b. On the efficiency of markets for foreign exchange. In *International Economic Policy: Theory and Evidence*, ed. R. Dornbusch and J. A. Frenkel, pp. 246–67. Baltimore: Johns Hopkins University Press.

Levich, R. M. 1981. *Overshooting in the Foreign Exchange Market.* Group of Thirty, Occasional Papers, no. 5, New York.

Levin, J. H. 1975. Monetary policy and the crawling peg. *Economic Journal* 85(337):20–32.

Levin, J. H. 1977. Speculation and the crawling peg. *Economica* 44(173):57–62.

Levin, J. H. 1980. Devaluation, the *J*-curve, and flexible exchange rates. *Manchester School* 48(4):355–77.

Levy, H., and M. Sarnat. 1975. Devaluation risk and the portfolio analysis of international investment. In *International Capital Markets*, ed. E. J. Elton and M. J. Gruber, pp. 177–206. Amsterdam: North-Holland.

Levy, H., and M. Sarnat. 1978. Exchange rate risk and the optimal diversification of foreign currency holdings. *Journal of Money, Credit, and Banking* 10(4):453–63.

MacDougall, G.D.A. 1968. The benefits and costs of private investment from abroad: a theoretical approach. In *Readings in International Economics*, ed. R. E. Caves and H. G. Johnson, pp. 172–94. Homewood, Ill.: Irwin.

Machlup, F. 1943. *International Trade and the National Income Multiplier.* Philadelphia: Blakiston.

Machlup, F. 1955. Relative prices and aggregate spending in the analysis of devaluation. *American Economic Review* 45(3):255–78.

Magee, S. P. 1973. Currency contracts, pass-through, and devaluation. *Brookings Papers on Economic Activity* 1:303–23.

Magee, S. P. 1975. Prices, incomes, and foreign trade. In *International Trade and Finance: Frontiers for Research*, ed. P. B. Kenen, pp. 175–252. Cambridge: Cambridge University Press.

Marshall, A. 1923. *Money, Credit, and Commerce.* London: Macmillan.

Marshall, A. 1930. *The Pure Theory of Foreign Trade* (privately printed 1879). London: London School of Economics.

McCallum, B. T. 1980. Rational expectations and macroeconomic stabilization policy: an overview. *Journal of Money, Credit, and Banking* 12(4):716–46.

McKinnon, R. I. 1963. Optimum currency areas. *American Economic Review* 53(4):717-25.

McKinnon, R. I. 1976. Floating foreign exchange rates, 1973-74: the emperor's new clothes. In *Institutional Arrangements and the Inflation Problem*, Carnegie-Rochester Conference Series on Public Policy, ed. K. Brunner and A. H. Meltzer, pp. 79-114. Amsterdam: North-Holland.

McKinnon, R. I. 1979. *Money in International Exchange*. New York: Oxford.

McKinnon, R. I. 1981. Monetary control and the crawling peg. In *Exchange Rate Rules: The Theory, Performance, and Prospects of the Crawling Peg*, ed. J. Williamson, pp. 38-49. New York: St. Martin's Press.

Meade, J. E. 1951. *The Balance of Payments*. London: Oxford University Press.

Meade, J. E. 1952. *A Geometry of International Trade*. London: Allen & Unwin.

Meade, J. E. 1957. The balance-of-payments problems of a European free-trade area. *Economic Journal* 67(267):379-96.

Meese, R., and K. Rogoff. 1981. *Empirical Exchange Rate Models of the Seventies: Are Any Fit to Survive?* International Finance Discussion Papers, no. 184.

Metzler, L. A. 1942. Underemployment equilibrium in international trade. *Econometrica* 10:97-112.

Metzler, L. A. 1948. The theory of international trade. In *A Survey of Contemporary Economics*, ed. H. S. Ellis, pp. 210-54. Philadelphia: Blakiston.

Metzler, L. A. 1951. Wealth, saving, and the rate of interest. *Journal of Political Economy* 59(2):93-116.

Modigliani, F., and H. Askari. 1973. The international transfer of capital and the propagation of domestic disturbances under alternative payment systems. *Banca Nazionale del Lavoro Quarterly Review* 107:295-310.

Moser, B. 1983. *Der Frankenkurs des Dollars 1973-1980: Ein Test der Kaufkraftparitätentheorie*. Berner Beiträge zur Nationalökonomie Band 43. Bern: Haupt.

Mundell, R. A. 1960. The monetary dynamics of international adjustment under fixed and flexible exchange rates. *Quarterly Journal of Economics* 74(2):227-57.

Mundell, R. A. 1961. A theory of optimum currency areas. *American Economic Review* 51(4):657-65.

Mundell, R. A. 1962. The appropriate use of monetary and fiscal policy for internal and external stability. *International Monetary Fund Staff Papers* 9:70-77.

Mundell, R. A. 1964. A reply: capital mobility and size. *Canadian Journal of Economics and Political Science* 30(3):421-31.

Mundell, R. A. 1968. *International Economics*. New York: Macmillan.

Mundell, R. A. 1971. *Monetary Theory*. Pacific Palisades: Goodyear.

Mundell, R. A. 1973. Uncommon arguments for common currencies. In *The Economics of Common Currencies*, ed. H. G. Johnson and A. K. Swoboda, pp. 114-32. London: Allen & Unwin.

Negishi, T. 1968. Approaches to the analysis of devaluation. *International Economic Review* 9(2):218-27.

Niehans, J. 1968. Monetary and fiscal policies in open economies under fixed exchange rates: an optimizing approach. *Journal of Political Economy* 76(4):893-920.

Niehans, J. 1971. Geldschaffung und Kreditvermittlung im Eurodollarmarkt. In *Verstehen und Gestalten der Wirtschaft: Festgabe für F. A. Lutz zum 70. Geburtstag*, pp. 279-94. Tübingen: Mohr.

Niehans, J. 1974. The effect of devaluation on the balance of payments: a graphical device. *Weltwirtschaftliches Archiv* 110(4):710–12.

Niehans, J. 1975. Some doubts about the efficacy of monetary policy under flexible exchange rates. *Journal of International Economics* 5(3):275–81.

Niehans, J. 1976. How to fill an empty shell. *American Economic Review Papers and Proceedings* 66(2):177–83.

Niehans, J. 1977. Exchange rate dynamics with stock/flow interaction. *Journal of Political Economy* 85(6):1245–57.

Niehans, J. 1978. *The Theory of Money.* Baltimore: Johns Hopkins University Press.

Niehans, J. 1980a. Purchasing-power parity under flexible rates. In *Issues in International Economics*, ed. P. Oppenheimer, pp. 255–72. Stocksfield, England: Oriel.

Niehans, J. 1980b. Dynamic purchasing power as a monetary rule. In *Flexible Exchange Rates and the Balance of Payments: Essays in Memory of E. Sohmen*, ed. J. S. Chipman and C. P. Kindleberger, pp. 213–30. Amsterdam: North-Holland.

Niehans, J. 1981a. Volkswirtschaftliche Wirkungen alternativer geldpolitischer Instrumente in einer kleinen offenen Volkswirtschaft. In *Probleme der Währungspolitik*, Schriften des Vereins für Socialpolitik, ed. W. Ehrlicher and R. Richter, 120:55–111. Berlin: Duncker & Humblot.

Niehans, J. 1981b. Static deviations from purchasing-power parity. *Journal of Monetary Economics* 7(1):57–68.

Niehans, J. 1982a. Innovation in monetary policy: challenge and response. *Journal of Banking and Finance* 6(1):9–28.

Niehans, J. 1982b. Gold operations as an instrument of monetary policy. In *The Gold Problem: Economic Perspectives*, Proceedings of the World Conference on Gold, ed. A. Quadrio-Curzio, pp. 271–79. Oxford: Oxford University Press.

Niehans, J., and J. Hewson. 1976. The Eurodollar market and monetary theory. *Journal of Money, Credit, and Banking* 8(1):1–27.

Nurkse, R. 1944. *International Currency Experience: Lessons of the Inter-War Period.* League of Nations.

Officer, L. H. 1976. The purchasing-power-parity theory of exchange rates: a review article. *International Monetary Fund Staff Papers* 23(1):1–60.

Officer, L. H. 1980. Effective exchange rates and price ratios over the long run: a test of the purchasing-power-parity theory. *Canadian Journal of Economics* 13(2):206–30.

Ohlin, B. 1929. The reparation problem: a discussion. *Economic Journal* 39(2):172–78.

Ohlin, B. 1933. *Interregional and International Trade.* Cambridge: Harvard University Press.

Parkin, M. 1978. A comparison of alternative techniques of monetary control under rational expectations. *Manchester School* 46(3):252–87.

Pearce, I. F. 1970. *International Trade.* New York: Norton.

Pearce, I. F., and D. C. Rowan. 1966. A framework for research into the real effects of international capital movements. In *Essays in Honor of Marco Fanno*, ed. T. Bagiotti, 2:505–35. Padua: Cedam.

Poole, W. 1970a. Optimal choice of monetary policy instruments in a simple stochastic macro model. *Quarterly Journal of Economics* 84(2):197–216.

Poole, W. 1970b. Gradualism: a mid-course view. *Brookings Papers on Economic Activity* 2:271–95.

Robinson, J. 1937. *Essays in the Theory of Employment*. London: Macmillan.

Roll, R., and B. Solnik. 1977. A pure foreign exchange asset pricing model. *Journal of International Economics* 7(2):161–79.

Samuelson, P. A. 1952. The transfer problem and transport costs. *Economic Journal*: Part I, vol. 62(2), 1952, pp. 278–304. Part II, vol. 64(2), 1954, pp. 264–89.

Samuelson, P. A. 1964. Theoretical notes on trade problems. *Review of Economics and Statistics* 46(2):145–54.

Samuelson, P. A. 1971a. An exact Hume-Ricardo-Marshall model of international trade. *Journal of International Economics* 1(1):1–18.

Samuelson, P. A. 1971b. On the trail of conventional beliefs about the transfer problem. In *Trade, Balance of Payments, and Growth: Papers in International Economics in Honor of C. P. Kindleberger*, ed. J. N. Bhagwati et al., pp. 327–51. Amsterdam: North-Holland.

Samuelson, P. A. 1980. A corrected version of Hume's equilibrating mechanisms for international trade. In *Flexible Exchange Rates and the Balance of Payments: Essays in Memory of E. Sohmen*, ed. J. S. Chipman and C. P. Kindleberger, pp. 141–58. Amsterdam: North Holland.

Singer, H. W. 1950. The distribution of gains between investing and borrowing countries. *American Economic Review Papers and Proceedings* 40(2):473–85.

Sohmen, E. 1973. *Wechselkurs und Währungsordnung*. Tübingen: Mohr.

Spitäller, E. 1971. A survey of recent quantitative studies of long-term capital movements. *International Monetary Fund Staff Papers* 18:189–217.

Spraos, J. 1953. The theory of forward exchange and recent practice. *Manchester School* 21:87–117.

Stein, J. L. 1963. The optimum foreign exchange market. *American Economic Review* 53(3):384–402.

Stern, R. M. 1973. *The Balance of Payments: Theory and Economic Policy*. Chicago: Aldine.

Stern, R. M., J. Francis, and B. Schumacher. 1976. *Price Elasticities in International Trade: An Annotated Bibliography*. London: Macmillan.

Stolper, W. F. 1950. The multiplier, flexible exchanges, and international equilibrium. *Quarterly Journal of Economics* 64(4):559–82.

Sweeney, R. J. 1978. Report on technical studies on speculation and market efficiency. In *Exchange Rate Flexibility*, ed. J. S. Dreyer, G. Haberler, and T. D. Willett, pp. 89–96. Washington, D.C.: American Enterprise Institute for Public Policy Research.

Swoboda, A. K. 1973. Monetary policy under fixed exchange rates: effectiveness, the speed of adjustment, and proper use. *Economica* 40(158):136–54.

Swoboda, A. K. 1980. *Credit Creation in the Euromarket: Alternative Theories and Implications for Control*. Group of Thirty, Occasional Papers, no. 2, New York.

Taylor, J. B. 1979. Staggered wage setting in a macro model. *American Economic Review Papers and Proceedings* 69(2):108–13.

Tinbergen, J. 1952. *On the Theory of Economic Policy*. Amsterdam: North-Holland.

Tobin, J. 1958. Liquidity preference as behavior towards risk. *Review of Economic Studies* 25(2):65–86.

Tobin, J. 1969. A general equilibrium approach to monetary theory. *Journal of Money, Credit, and Banking* 1(1):15–29.

Tobin, J., and W. C. Brainard. 1977. Asset markets and the cost of capital. In *Economic Progress, Private Values, and Public Policy: Essays in Honor of W. Fellner*, ed. B. Balassa and R. Nelson, pp. 235–62. Amsterdam: North-Holland.

Tower, E., and T. D. Willett. 1976. *The Theory of Optimum Currency Areas and Exchange-Rate Flexibility*. Special Papers in International Economics, no. 11, Princeton University.

Triffin, R. 1968. *Our International Monetary System*. New York: Random House.

Tsiang, S. C. 1959. The theory of forward exchange and effects of government intervention on the forward exchange market. *International Monetary Fund Staff Papers* 7:75–106.

Turnovsky, S. J. 1976. The relative stability of alternative exchange rate systems in the presence of random disturbances. *Journal of Money, Credit, and Banking* 8(1):29–50.

Viner, J. 1937. *Studies in the Theory of International Trade*. New York: Harper.

Whitman, M.v.N. 1975. The payments adjustment process and the exchange rate regime: what have we learned? *American Economic Review Papers and Proceedings* 65(2):133–46.

Wicksell, K. 1898/1936. *Interest and Prices*. Trans. R. F. Kahn. London: Macmillan.

Wihlborg, C. 1978. *Currency Risks in International Financial Markets*. Princeton Studies in International Finance, no. 44.

Williamson, J. 1965. *The Crawling Peg*. Essays in International Finance, no. 50, Princeton University.

Williamson, J. ed. 1981. *Exchange Rate Rules: The Theory, Performance, and Prospects of the Crawling Peg*. New York: St. Martin's Press.

Willms, M. 1976. Money creation in the Euro-currency market. *Weltwirtschaftliches Archiv* 112(2):201–30.

Wilson, J. F., and W. E. Takacs. 1979. Differential responses to price and exchange rate influences in the foreign trade of selected industrial countries. *Review of Economics and Statistics* 61(2):267–79.

Wilson, J. F., and W. E. Takacs. 1980. Expectations and the adjustment of trade flows under floating exchange-rates: leads, lags, and the *J*-curve. *International Finance Discussion Papers*, no. 160.

Yoshikawa, H. 1980. On the "*q*" theory of investment. *American Economic Review* 70(4):739–43.

Zenger, C. 1982. *Kursschwankungen des Schweizerfrankens in ihren Auswirkungen auf Produktion, Export, Import, und Fremdenverkehr*. Berner Beiträge zur Nationalökonomie Band 41. Bern: Haupt.

Name Index

331

Subject Index

334

JÜRG NIEHANS is professor of economics at the
University of Bern; until 1977, he was Abraham
G. Hutzler Professor of Political Economy at the
Johns Hopkins University. He is the author of
numerous articles, and of *The Theory of Money*,
published by Johns Hopkins.

Introducing Neuropsychology

Second Edition

John Stirling and Rebecca Elliott

Psychology Press
Taylor & Francis Group
HOVE AND NEW YORK

First published 2008
by Psychology Press
27 Church Road, Hove, East Sussex BN3 2FA

Simultaneously published in the USA and Canada
by Psychology Press
270 Madison Avenue, New York, NY 10016

Psychology Press is an imprint of the Taylor & Francis Group, an informa business

Typeset in Times and Frutiger by RefineCatch Limited, Bungay, Suffolk
Printed and bound in Great Britain by Bell & Bain Ltd, Thornliebank, Glasgow
Paperback cover design by Terry Foley

British Library Cataloguing in Publication Data
A catalogue record for this book is available from the British Library

Library of Congress Cataloging-in-Publication Data
A catalog record for this book is available from the Library of Congress
Stirling, John D., 1951–
    Introducing neuropsychology / John Stirling and Rebecca Elliott. – 2nd ed.
        p. ; cm.
    Includes bibliographical references and index.
    ISBN 978-1-84169-653-9 (hardcover) – ISBN 978-1-84169-654-6 (pbk.)
    1. Neuropsychology.   I. Elliott, Rebecca, 1969–   II. Title.
    [DNLM: 1. Neuropsychology.   WL 103.5 S861i 2008]
    QP360.S793 2008
    612.8–dc22   2007048903

ISBN: 978–1–84169–653–9 (hbk)
ISBN: 978–1–84169–654–6 (pbk)

In

N

Introducing Neurops... ...n in separate focus
gates the functions ...sections allow the
relationships betwe... ...regular intervals.
behaviour. The mat... ...cular expertise on
easy to understan... ...chology or brain
students new to the... ...at interest not only
research. ...ogy and cognitive

Following a bri... ...dical and nursing
description of me... ...ho is interested in
remaining chapters review traditional and recent learning about recent progress in understanding
research findings. Both cognitive and clinical aspects brain–behaviour relationships.
of neuropsychology are addressed to illustrate the
advances scientists are making (on many fronts) in **John Stirling** has worked at Manchester Polytechnic/
their quest to understand brain–behaviour relation- MMU for over 30 years, teaching Bio- and Neuro-
ships in both normal and disturbed functioning. The psychology, Psychopathology and Experimental
rapid developments in neuropsychology and cogni- Design and Statistics. He has published over 30
tive neuroscience resulting from traditional research scientific journal articles, and three books.
methods as well as new brain-imaging techniques are
presented in a clear and straightforward way. Each **Rebecca Elliott** has worked at the University of
chapter has been fully revised and updated and new Manchester for 8 years, using brain-imaging tech-
brain-imaging data are incorporated throughout, niques to study emotion and cognition in psychiatric
especially in the later chapters on Emotion and disorders. She has published over 50 scientific
Motivation, and Executive Functions. As in the first research articles.

Psychology Focus

Series editor: Perry Hinton, Oxford Brookes University

The Psychology Focus series provides students with a new focus on key topic areas in psychology. It supports students taking modules in psychology, whether for a psychology degree or a combined programme, and those renewing their qualification in a related discipline. Each short book:

- presents clear, in-depth coverage of a discrete area with many applied examples
- assumes no prior knowledge of psychology
- has been written by an experienced teacher
- has chapter summaries, annotated further reading and a glossary of key terms.

Also available in this series:

Friendship in Childhood and Adolescence
Phil Erwin

Gender and Social Psychology
Vivien Burr

Jobs, Technology and People
Nik Chmiel

Learning and Studying
James Hartley

Personality: A Cognitive Approach
Jo Brunas-Wagstaff

Intelligence and Abilities
Colin Cooper

Stress, Cognition and Health
Tony Cassidy

Types of Thinking
S. Ian Robertson

Psychobiology of Human Motivation
Hugh Wagner

Stereotypes, Cognition and Culture
Perry R. Hinton

Psychology and "Human Nature"
Peter Ashworth

Abnormal Psychology
Alan Carr

Attitudes and Persuasion
Phil Erwin

The Person in Social Psychology
Vivien Burr

The Social Psychology of Behaviour in Small Groups
Donald C. Pennington

Attention: A Neuropsychological Perspective
Antony Ward

Attention, Perception and Memory
Elizabeth A. Styles

Introducing Cognitive Development
Laura M. Taylor

CONTENTS

PREFACE

TO THE SERIES

The Psychology Focus series provides short, up-to-date accounts of key areas in psychology without assuming the reader's prior knowledge in the subject. Psychology is often a favoured subject area for study, because it is relevant to a wide range of disciplines such as sociology, education, nursing, and business studies. These relatively inexpensive but focused short texts combine sufficient detail for psychology specialists with sufficient clarity for non-specialists.

The series authors are academics experienced in undergraduate teaching as well as research. Each takes a topic within their area of psychological expertise and presents a short review, highlighting important themes and including both theory and research findings. Each aspect of the topic is clearly explained with supporting glossaries to elucidate technical terms.

The series has been conceived within the context of the increasing modularisation which has been developed in higher education over the last decade and fulfils the consequent need for clear, focused, topic-based course material. Instead of following one course of study, students on a modularisation programme are often able to choose modules from a wide range of disciplines to complement the modules they are required to study for a specific degree. It can no longer be assumed that students studying a particular module will necessarily have the same background knowledge (or lack of it!) in that subject. But they will need to familiarise themselves with a particular topic rapidly because a single module in a single topic may be only 15 weeks long, with assessments arising during that period. They may have to combine eight or more

modules in a single year to obtain a degree at the end of their programme of study.

One possible problem with studying a range of separate modules is that the relevance of a particular topic or the relationship between topics may not always be apparent. In the Psychology Focus series, authors have drawn where possible on practical and applied examples to support the points being made so that readers can see the wider relevance of the topic under study. Also, the study of psychology is usually broken up into separate areas, such as social psychology, developmental psychology, and cognitive psychology, to take three examples. While the books in the Psychology Focus series will provide excellent coverage of certain key topics within these "traditional" areas, the authors have not been constrained in their examples and explanations and may draw on material across the whole field of psychology to help explain the topic under study more fully.

Each text in the series provides the reader with a range of important material on a specific topic. They are suitably comprehensive and give a clear account of the important issues involved. The authors analyse and interpret the material as well as present an up-to-date and detailed review of key work. Recent references are provided along with suggested further reading to allow readers to investigate the topic in more depth. It is hoped, therefore, that after following the informative review of a key topic in a Psychology Focus text, readers not only will have a clear understanding of the issues in question but will be intrigued, and challenged to investigate the topic further.

PREFACE

TO THE SECOND EDITION

For this revised and fully updated edition of *Introducing Neuropsychology*, John Stirling has been joined by Rebecca Elliott as co-author.

Although the first edition of *Introducing Neuropsychology* was published just 5 years ago, such has been the growth of interest in research into brain–behaviour relationships that we felt an updated edition would be timely. Much of this growth has been driven by the more widespread availability of in-vivo imaging techniques, an area of expertise for the second author. Such techniques, of course, provide opportunities for researchers to identify brain regions that are engaged as participants undertake all manner of activities. Recently, these have ranged widely, from basic cognitive tasks designed to tap working memory processes (Fletcher et al., 2003) to more elaborate "emotional" challenges aimed, for example, at invoking sympathy/empathy in healthy controls and/or psychopaths (Farrow et al., 2001; Vollm et al., 2004).

Data from such studies have been amalgamated with more basic science research in the areas of molecular genetics, neurophysiology, and psychopharmacology, initially in the US but increasingly in the rest of the world, to provide a knowledge-base for the discipline called "cognitive neuroscience" (Gazzaniga, Ivry, & Mangun, 2003). We considered whether we too should acknowledge this emerging enterprise by re-titling our book "Introducing Cognitive Neuroscience". On balance, however, we felt that neuropsychology, as a subject area, was not yet ready to be subsumed under the cognitive neuroscience banner. This may be seen as an exercise in hair-splitting, but

the facts of the matter are that not everything in this second edition could be said to be either strictly "cognitive" or even strictly "neuroscientific"—yet we hope all our material falls within the domain of neuropsychology.

In truth of course, such dividing lines are seen as more important by some people than others. Take, for instance, animal research, which is quite widespread in the field of cognitive neuroscience, but rare in neuropsychology—rare, but not unheard of (see Rizzolatti et al.'s study of mirror neurons in macaque monkeys which we review in Chapter 5). Case study, on the other hand, could reasonably claim to be the modus operandi of traditional "clinical" neuropsychology. But combine it with longitudinal neuroimaging or some other basic science assaying—such as analysis of cerebrospinal fluid (CSF) or blood, for example—and it would unquestionably qualify as cognitive neuroscience research. In short, what we have is a difference of emphasis, but with many areas of overlap. Both authors have published research in cognitive neuroscience journals, and attended/spoken at neuroscience conferences. However, both are psychologists by training, and this edition, like the first, is written primarily with the needs of psychology students in mind. Thus, on balance we felt we should retain the original title yet be entirely open to describing research that some authors might consider more cognitive neuroscience than neuropsychology. Three later chapters in this edition, covering Attention and Consciousness (Chapter 9), Emotion and Motivation (Chapter 10), and Executive Functions (Chapter 11), attest to the common ground between the two approaches and we expect that such instances of overlap will become more commonplace in the years to come. However, it is instructive to note that just as the rise of "cognitive science" in the US in the early 1960s (Miller, 2003) did not bring about the demise of mainstream psychology, so the rise of "cognitive *neuro*science" from the 1990s onwards has not yet brought about the demise of *neuro*psychology.

In planning the format of this second edition we have tried to adapt and revise the first in light of a dramatically expanded research base and important refinements of existing research techniques and methods, plus the arrival on the scene of some completely new procedures that are now beginning to bear fruit. In no particular order, this work has included the following:

- Promising efforts to further characterise the fractionation (functional subdivisions) of the frontal lobes and the anterior cingulate gyrus (Botvinick, Cohen, & Carter, 2004; Wagner et al., 2001).
- New insights into and models of consciousness (Cooney & Gazzaniga, 2003).
- Expansion and refinement of the concept of brain modularity (Catani & ffytche, 2005; Cavanna & Trimble, 2006).
- Refinement of paradigms aimed at informing models of attention, including attentional blink and inattentional blindness (Rensink, 2002; Sergent, Baillet, & Dehaene, 2005).
- Confirmation of the existence of mirror neurons, and their possible role in imitation and perhaps even in empathy (Brass & Heyes, 2005; Rizzolatti & Buccino, 2004).
- Development of the field sometimes called "social neuroscience" encompassing research into autism and Asperger's syndrome, psychopathy, and pathological gambling (Frith & Frith, 2003; Rilling et al., 2007).
- Developments in the field of brain plasticity and recovery of function coupled with confirmation of the growth of new neurons (neurogenesis) in specific regions of the mature adult mammalian brain (Brown et al., 2003; Carlen et al., 2002; Mirescu, Peters, & Gould, 2004).
- Refinements in functional imaging including pathway tracing using diffusion tensor imaging (DTI) (e.g., Minati & Aquino, 2006).
- The use of transcranial magnetic stimulation

(TMS) to reversibly manipulate brain activity, and as a possible therapeutic procedure (Heiser et al., 2003; Hilgetag, Theoret, & Pascual-Leone, 2001).

Of course, these changes need to be accommodated within the framework of the Psychology Focus series, meaning that we have tried to adhere to the criteria set out by Perry Hinton (series editor) outlined above. As with the first edition, our book is written principally with the "interested beginner" in mind but we have not used this as an excuse for failing to be up to date. Nevertheless, two early warnings may be in order: First, some readers might find sections of coverage in this edition rather complicated for an introductory text. Our only excuse is that the brain, the principal subject of our book, has rightly been characterised as *the most complex entity known to man.* We have tried hard to keep things simple wherever possible, but admit to not always succeeding. However, skipping complex sections (often separated from the general text in boxes) should not, we hope, detract from your general understanding of the material. Second, despite the rapid growth in research, many fundamental neuropsychological questions remain to be answered. Our view is that in such instances it is better to admit to uncertainty (while presenting the relevant material) than to offer glib but premature conclusions, even if the reader may find such lack of resolution frustrating.

As in the first edition, we have made liberal use of "interim comment" sections in each chapter in order variously to pull ideas together, identify inconsistencies in the data, describe continued uncertainties about what particular research findings mean, or simply to summarise a body of research before the "gist" is lost. We have tried to avoid unnecessary jargon, and where this has been impossible have sought to explain or define a term or concept there and then, with additional information provided in the expanded glossary. We have included an appendix (also somewhat expanded in this edition) on the structure and basic workings of the brain and its key constituent components as a reference for information rather than as obligatory reading. Our book should be understandable to readers with a fairly modest working knowledge of the structure and functioning of the mammalian nervous system, but if you want to know more, we offer sources in the Further Reading section at the end of the book. We have identified some key journal articles/reading assignments for each chapter to aid further understanding of particular topics and issues, along with some general recommended reading and some interesting, accessible, and relevant web-pages for you to explore.

In the interests of continuity we have retained the broad chapter structure of the first edition, although each has been revised and updated. One entirely new chapter, on Emotion and Motivation (Chapter 10), has been added, and the Summary and Conclusions chapter from the first edition has been removed to make space for it. The methods chapter (Chapter 2) has been expanded to accommodate recent advances in imaging technology now available to the researcher, such as magnetoencephalography (MEG) and diffu-sion tensor imaging, and consideration is also given to recent research in which TMS has been used to induce temporary reversible disruptions to brain functioning. The chapter on somatosensation (Chapter 4) now additionally includes an extended section on neuro-plasticity. The chapter on attention (Chapter 9) has been extensively revised and now includes an extended section reviewing neuropsychological investigations into consciousness, an area that has recently seen dramatic and exciting new developments. Other chapters have changed more modestly, being updated wherever possible to provide a flavour of the direction that research (in that area) is going, and how it is affecting the way we think about the subject material.

Nevertheless, this edition contains over 600 new journal references, many post-dating publication of the first edition, and 60 or more additional/revised figures and diagrams.

We are particularly grateful to Andrew Parker from MMU who has contributed Chapter 7: Memory and Amnesia, and made helpful comments on other sections of the book. We would also like to thank Marilyn Barnett from MMU both for her work on collating references for this edition and for her help with numerous other administrative chores. Elsewhere in writing the book, while one or other of us has initially taken the role of lead author for a section or chapter, the other has edited, revised, and even re-drafted. Thus, in the spirit of collective responsibility, we (JS and RE) consider ourselves equally culpable!

We hope you find the second edition of *Intro-ducing Neuropsychology* a useful entry point into the neuropsychology literature, and that our interest in trying to understand brain–behaviour relationships through neuropsychological (and cognitive neuro-science) research whets your appetite to learn more about the structure and functioning of the astonishing 1200 to 1500 grams of tissue we call the (mature) human brain.

JOHN STIRLING AND REBECCA ELLIOTT
Manchester, August 2007

PREFACE

TO THE FIRST EDITION

Just over 18 months ago I completed the first draft of an introductory book about the brain entitled *Cortical Functions*, subsequently published by Routledge in the *Modular Psychology* series in 1999. While researching the material for that book, I accumulated more information than could be shoe-horned into the *Modular* series format, and in discussing the fate of my surplus chapters/material with the editors at Routledge the idea of writing a concise up-to-date introductory text in the area of neuropsychology slowly took shape. *Introducing Neuropsychology* is, somewhat belatedly, the result.

As with other books in the "Psychology Focus" series, this one is intended as an accompanying text for courses in neuropsychology for students new to the subject area. I have written the book in such a way that a detailed understanding of neurophysiology (neurons, action potentials, synapses and so on) is not a necessary prerequisite to getting something out of it, so the book should also be accessible to non-psychology students too. However, to be on the safe side, I have included an appendix to which the reader may want to refer for a quick reminder of the basic layout of the nervous system, the structure and function of neurons, and the ways we might usefully wish to divide up the central nervous system in order to make more sense of it. Complete novices may prefer to read the entire appendix before tackling the rest of the book. This is allowed!

Mindful of the difficulties students sometimes have with the subject matter of neuropsychology, I have tried to write *Introducing Neuropsychology* in a jargon-free style (insofar as this is possible). However, a glossary is included to cover highlighted first use terms that may be new to the reader. I have also provided a large number of figures and diagrams to illustrate key points, and I have included several boxes dotted throughout the book encompassing key research findings or, in some cases, the results of neuropsychological case studies. Shaded "interim comment" sections can also be found at regular intervals in every chapter. As their name suggests, these summaries are intended to allow the reader to make sense of particular passages of material in manageable chunks, before progressing further.

Although *Introducing Neuropsychology* aims to do what the title says—with coverage of the core ideas, concepts and research findings in each of the substantive chapters—I have also tried to add a flavour of recent/current research in each area, but particularly in the later chapters. The recommended reading for each chapter (set out in the "Further reading" section) also reflects my wish to encourage readers to seek out up-to-date research reports if they want to take their studies of a topic further. There are several excellent texts with a broader and deeper coverage of the material than can be achieved in *Introducing Neuropsychology*, and I would urge enthusiastic readers to research these resources too. I have listed some of my preferred texts in the "Further reading" section. Similarly, there is some valuable material available on the Internet. The sites listed in the "Selected neuropsychology web sites" section provide an entry point to this material, and links will soon take you to 3D images of the brain, lists of gory neurological disorders and the web pages of research institutions and even individual neuroscientists and neuropsychologists. Happy surfing!

For me, neuropsychology represents a confluence of most of the things I am interested in as a psychologist: normal and particularly abnormal behaviour, the workings of the brain, lifespan changes, the common ground between neurology, psychology and psychiatry, and even the concept of "consciousness". The more we learn about neuropsychology the more amazed I am about how a structure weighing as little as an adult human brain (usually less than 1500 grams) can do everything it does, often faultlessly, for 70, 80 or even more years! I hope that as you read this book, you come to share my wonder about this rather insignificant-looking lump of tissue, and that *Introducing Neuropsychology* whets your appetite to learn more about it.

JOHN STIRLING
Manchester, July 2001

"Into the highlands of the mind let us go"

(Adapted from the emblem on the portico of the State Supreme Court, Capital Building, Sacramento, CA. Source: "Shakespeare", from *A hundred poems by Sir William Watson, selected from his various volumes.* New York: Dodd-Mead & Co., 1923.)

CHAPTER 1

The foundations of neuropsychology

INTRODUCTION

We take the view that a proper understanding of the current status of neuro-psychology cannot be formed without at least a rudimentary appreciation of its origins. Thus, in this chapter we offer a brief history of the beginnings of scientific research into the brain, and we introduce some of the theories (and debates) that have surfaced as our understanding of the relationship between structure and functions has developed. We describe some discoveries that led to the development of the so-called "brain hypothesis", a concept that is central to neuropsychology (if not to psychology as a whole). We then introduce the "localisation of function" debate, which has rumbled on from its origins in the work of the 19th-century neuroanatomists, and continues to influence the distinct approaches and method-ologies of clinical and cognitive neuropsychologists that we describe towards the end of the chapter. Fodor's concept of modularity (of mind: he is a philosopher rather than a researcher) is introduced and re-assessed in light of recent findings. Its current status is considered, by way of illustration, in relation to the neuro-anatomy and connectivity of a little-known region of cortex called the precuneus (Cavanna & Trimble, 2006).

NEUROPSYCHOLOGY AS A DISTINCT DISCIPLINE

Neuropsychology is a bridging discipline that draws on material from neurology, cognitive psychology, and even psychiatry. However, its principal aim is to try to understand the operation of *psychological* processes in relation to brain structures and systems. It is the oldest branch of scientific psychology and it retains a degree of distinctiveness that distinguishes it from other related areas. It has, for example, historically relied on small N or even single-case study designs, a tradition that continues to this day. Like cognitive neuroscience (see preface to this edition) it embraces the concept of *converging operations* (in which research findings from different sources and even different levels of inquiry are "used" to inform a par-ticular debate). But unlike cognitive neuroscience, we should expect some fairly direct reference to human behaviour, and also unlike cognitive neuroscience, the brain itself may seem quite marginalised from the debate. Brain structures barely merit mention in Ellis and Young's classic text *Human cognitive neuropsychology* (1996), for example. (See also Coltheart, 2001, whose ideas are summarised later in this chapter.)

The term "neuropsychology" was used as a subtitle in Donald Hebb's influential book *The organisation of behaviour: A neuropsychological theory*, published in 1949, although the term itself was not defined. With the demise of **behaviourism** (terms in bold type in the text indicate that the term is included in the Glossary section at the end of the book) and renewed interest in cognitive processes in the 1950s and 1960s, the term appeared with increasing frequency, although its definition remained vague and it was used in different senses by different people. Although, as you will see, researchers had been interested in the effects of brain damage and disease on behaviour for many years, it was arguably some time after behaviourism's fall from grace that neuropsychology came to develop a distinct identity within psychology, and its parameters were further clarified by the publication of the first edition of Kolb and Whishaw's *Fundamentals of human neuropsychology* and Lezak's *Neuropsychological assessment* in 1980 and 1983 respectively.

It would be misleading for us to suggest that, following its protracted birth, neuropsychology has emerged as an entirely unified discipline. In reality there remain different emphases among practitioners and researchers, which broadly divide into two domains: those of **clinical** and **cognitive neuropsychology**. At the risk of oversimplifying the distinction, the former tends to focus on the effects of brain damage/disease on psychological processes such as memory, language, and attention, and often has a clinical remit for assessment and even treatment. Conversely, the latter tries to understand impairments to psychological processes in terms of disruptions to the information-processing elements involved. In other words, the clinical approach goes from the damaged brain to psychological dysfunction and its remediation, whereas the cognitive approach goes from psychological dysfunction to hypothetical models about the individual stages of information processing that could explain such dysfunctions, which may (or may not) then be "mapped" onto various brain regions. This division has led to quite heated debates among neuropsychologists about, for instance, the merits/shortcomings of single-case versus group research designs, and the extent to which cases of localised brain damage can *ever* definitively be used as evidence in support of functional localisation. (We take up each of these points in the following chapters. However, see the special issue of the journal *Cognitive Neuropsychology*, 2004, vol 21, for a flavour of the arguments.)

Incidentally, a glimpse at the chapter titles in this book might suggest to the reader that we too have chosen to take a cognitive approach to neuropsychology. However, this is not the case, and it is our hope that you will see that both approaches have much to offer in our quest to understand the relationship(s) between psychological processes and brain functioning. Besides, the ever-increasing use of **in-vivo imaging techniques** has inevitably blurred this distinction, chiefly because they provide the researcher with the opportunity to observe brain activity in healthy individuals as they undertake some sort of cognitive or other psychological challenge, arguably permitting a more direct (i.e., less inferential) link between structure and function.

THE ORIGINS OF THE BRAIN HYPOTHESIS

We know from historical records from the Middle East (e.g., the Edwin Smith Surgical Papyrus, found in Luxor, Egypt, in 1862) that the importance of the brain as a "behaviour control centre" (henceforth referred to as the brain hypothesis) was first considered at least 5000 years ago, although the predominant view then, and for many centuries thereafter, was that the heart was the organ of thinking and other mental processes. The ancient Greeks debated the relative merits of heart and brain, and Aristotle, noting that the brain was relatively cool in comparison with the heart, came down in support of the heart as the seat of mental processes, arguing that the brain's principal role was to cool blood. Hippocrates and Plato, on the other hand, both had some understanding of brain structure, and attributed various aspects of behaviour to it: Hippocrates, for example, warned against probing a wound in the brain in case it might lead to **paralysis** in the opposite side of the body.

In first-century (AD) Rome, the physician Galen spent some time working as a surgeon to gladiators and became all too well aware of the effects that brain damage could have on behaviour. The "heart hypothesis" was fundamentally undermined by Galen's descriptions of his clinical observations: he showed that **sensory nerves** project to the brain rather than the heart, and he also knew that physical distortion of the brain could affect movement whereas similar manipulation of the heart could not.

For reasons that are never entirely clear, the knowledge and understanding of these early writers was lost or forgotten for the next 1500 years or so of European history. Those with any interest in the brain concentrated on attempts to find the location of the soul. Their search focused on easily identifiable brain structures including the pineal gland and the corpus callosum, structures that today are known to be involved in the control of bodily rhythms and communication between the two sides of the brain respectively.

LOCALISATION OF FUNCTION

The renewed interest in rationalism and science that accompanied the Renaissance in Europe in the 15th and 16th centuries prompted scientists of the day to revisit the brain and to try to establish the functions of particular brain structures. Because a lot of brain tissue appears relatively undifferentiated to the naked eye, these researchers also concentrated their efforts on the same easily identified structures as the earlier "soul-searchers". They explored, for example, the functions of the fluid cavities of the brain (the ventricles), the pineal and pituitary glands, and corpus callosum. However, their ideas about the functions of these structures were usually well wide of the mark: **Descartes** (1664), for example, mistakenly argued that the pineal gland was the point of convergence of bodily sensory inputs giving rise to a non-physical sense of awareness—thus encapsulating the key idea of the **mind–body problem**, although it should, perhaps, have been more aptly described as the mind–brain (or even the brain–mind) problem! To reiterate, the pineal gland is today regarded as an entirely soul-less endocrine gland involved in the control of bodily rhythms.

Nevertheless, implicit in this early work was the core idea of **localisation of function**—that different regions of the brain are involved in specific and separate aspects of (psychological) functioning. This idea later intrigued both Gall, the

KEY TERMS
Paralysis: Loss of movement in a body region (such as a limb).
Sensory nerves: Nerves carrying action potentials from sensory receptors towards the CNS (e.g., the optic nerve).
Descartes: French philosopher famous for his ideas about the separate identities of mind and body.
Mind–body problem: Explaining what relationship, if any, exists between mental processes and bodily states.
Localisation of function: The concept that different parts of the brain carry out different functions and, conversely, that not all parts of the brain do the same thing.

Austrian physician, and his student Spurzheim, whose work represents the starting point of what we might call the modern era of brain–behaviour research. It should be noted at the outset that Gall and Spurzheim, like modern-day neuropsychologists, were more interested in localisation of function within the **cerebral cortex** (the outer surface of the brain), with its characteristic bumps (**gyri**) and folds (**sulci**), than in the subcortical structures mentioned earlier. Gall (1785–1828) readily accepted that the brain rather than the heart was the control centre for mental function and, with Spurzheim, made several important discoveries about the anatomy of the brain, its connections with the spinal cord, and its ability to control muscles that have stood the test of time. For example, Gall was the first person to distinguish between grey and white matter (**neuron cell bodies** and their bundled **axons** respectively) in the brain, and also described the first case of **aphasia** (impaired language production) associated with frontal damage resulting from a fencing injury.

THE RISE AND FALL OF PHRENOLOGY

Despite their other notable lasting contributions, Gall and Spurzheim are primarily remembered for their ideas about what is sometimes called "strict" localisation of function in the brain. Through a combination of serendipity and chance observations, Gall came to the view that each of the two sides of the cerebral cortex (also sometimes called the left and right *cerebral hemispheres*) consisted of 27 compartments or regional faculties. These ranged from commonsense (or at least recognisable) ones such as language and perception, to ambiguous and obscure ones including hope and self-esteem. Accordingly, the more a person used particular faculties, the bigger the brain in that region grew, causing the shape of the skull to be distorted. Thus was born the "science" of phrenology, which claimed to be able to describe an individual's personality and other "faculties" on the basis of the physical size and shape of the skull (see Figure 1.1a and b). Interest in phrenology gradually spread widely through both Europe and the US (thanks largely to Spurzheim's efforts; he and Gall fell out over the matter of phrenology's popularisation and the attendant commercial benefits). In England, for example, it received royal support when Queen Victoria had her children's heads measured and analysed, and gradually an entire industry of phrenological "science" was spawned, involving journals, books, and pamphlets offering advice on marital compatibility and, of course, the opportunity for a personal assessment.

Over time, thousands of phrenology measurements were collected, including a series taken from the skulls of 25 murderers, and even from an amorous widow who was described as having prominent features (bumps) behind her ears. Each observation was simply taken as confirmation of the general theory, except that the number of faculties crept up to 35. When, for example, cases were found of individuals with unilateral (one-sided) cortical damage but incomplete loss of function, phrenologists were able to say that the other (intact) hemisphere had taken over responsibility for the faculty in question. However, doubts about phrenology first arose when it became apparent that the shape of the skull bore little relationship to the shape of the underlying brain. Obviously, Gall and Spurzheim had no way of measuring internal brain structure in living people, save for those rare instances of individuals surviving (and often not for very long)

KEY TERMS

Cerebral cortex: The outer surface of the brain which has, in higher mammals, a creased and bumpy appearance.

Gyri: Elongated bumps (convexities) in the cortex (singular: gyrus).

Sulci: The smaller folds or indents on the surface of the cortex (singular: sulcus). Larger ones are called fissures.

Neuron cell bodies: The central part of neurons (nerve cells) that contain the nucleus.

Axon: Long, thin projection from a neuron that carries electrical impulses from the cell body.

Aphasia: Deficit in the production and/or comprehension of language.

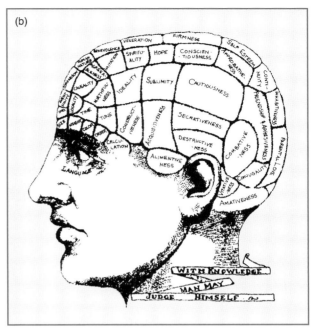

FIG. 1.1   (a) Franz Joseph Gall (1785–1828). (b) A phrenology skull. The concept of phrenology stemmed from Gall's ideas but was developed by Spurzheim. Although most scientists dismissed it as a pseudo-science, it enjoyed popular support in the mid-1800s, gaining royal patronage in the UK and spawning a mini-industry in charts, journals, and consultants.

open head injuries. Actually, records show that Gall had access to a small number of such cases, but unfortunately he seemed to regard them as being of only anecdotal interest, failing to realise that brain-injured people could offer an important test of his theory. Instead, he and Spurzheim continued to accumulate more and more measurements from members of the general population that "confirmed" their ideas.

Just as phrenology was catching on with the general population in Victorian England, Europe, and North America, the French scientist Pierre Flourens (1824) provided the first scientific evidence questioning its validity. Working mainly with birds, he developed the technique of surgically removing small areas of brain tissue and, after a period of recovery, observing the effects of the surgery on behaviour. (We now refer to these procedures as **lesion** and **ablation**, and they are described more extensively in Chapter 2.) Flourens' research led him to the conclusion that the degree of behavioural impairment was more closely linked to the *amount* of damage than to its *location*, a finding that runs counter to the principle of localisation of function that Gall and Spurzheim had so vigorously promoted. Flourens believed that the entire brain operated as a single faculty to serve the functions of perception, memory, volition, and so on, as required—an idea that came to be known as "aggregate field theory". He also believed that undamaged regions could take over the responsibilities of damaged ones—an idea giving rise to the popular (but mistaken) belief that people only use a small proportion of their brains, keeping other areas in reserve for learning new skills or replacing damaged areas.

KEY TERMS

Open head injuries: Head injuries involving damage to the cranium so that the brain is exposed or visible. Often compared with "closed head injury" in which brain damage has occurred although the cranium has not been penetrated: for example, dementia pugilistica (brain damage associated with boxing).

Lesion: A cut in (or severing of) brain tissue. This may occur as the result of an accident or may be part of a surgical procedure.

Ablation: The surgical removal of brain tissue.

Although Flourens' findings dealt something of a blow to Gall and Spurzheim's ideas about localisation (and, by implication, phrenology), hindsight suggests that his conclusions were probably wrong. First, he worked with pigeons and chickens, which are now known to have almost no cortex. Second, his behavioural measures assessed activities (such as eating, movement, and so on) unrelated to Gall and Spurzheim's faculties. Third, his surgical procedure was imprecise, leaving open the possibility that behavioural changes were caused by damage or lesions to brain structures beyond the cortex.

INTEREST IN APHASIA

Despite Flourens' lack of enthusiasm for localisation of function, interest in it was rekindled following a series of case studies of aphasia. French physicians Bouillaud and Dax had independently described a handful of patients they had seen who had lost the power of speech after brain damage. Those with left-sided damage often became paralysed in the right side of their bodies too, despite no apparent loss in intelligence. Bouillaud's work was reported in 1825, and Dax's in 1836 (although neither actually published their findings in a journal), yet little interest was shown until Auburtin (who happened to be Bouillaud's son-in-law) described the same work at a conference in 1861 that was also attended by Paul Broca. A few days later, Broca met Monsieur Leborgne, a patient who became known as Tan because this was almost the only sound he could utter. However, Tan could understand speech well and could, for example, follow quite complicated instructions. Like many of Dax's patients, he too was paralysed on his right side. Broca proposed that Tan had suffered damage to the same area of cortex (the left frontal region) earlier identified as crucial for language production by Dax and Bouillard. When Tan died from an unrelated disease later that year, Broca conducted a superficial post-mortem on his brain and confirmed that he had indeed incurred damage to the left frontal cortical region variously attributed to epilepsy, syphilis, or a **stroke**.

Within two years, Broca had collected post-mortem data on eight similar cases. This research led him to conclude that language production depended on intact left frontal function, and that, in more general terms, the two sides of the brain controlled the opposite sides of the body. (In fact, neither of these ideas was new—the relationship of one side of the brain to the opposite side of the body had been described by Galen at the beginning of the first millennium, and the link between left-sided damage and aphasia could be dated back to Gall.) Nevertheless, Broca seemed to gain the credit, and the region of brain he described (part of the left frontal cortex) is now known as Broca's area.

Soon, other regions of the cortex on the left side were identified as being important for various aspects of language. In 1874 Carl Wernicke described two additional forms of aphasia that were distinct from Broca's type. In **fluent aphasia** the patient could speak at a normal rate but what was said usually made little sense. In **conduction aphasia** the patient seemed able to understand what was said to them but was unable to repeat it. Wernicke surmised (on the basis of just one documented post-mortem investigation) that fluent aphasia was caused by damage to the posterior region of the left **temporal lobe**. He speculated that conduction aphasia was caused by a **disconnection** (literally a break in the pathway) between this region (which we now know as Wernicke's area) and Broca's area.

INTERIM COMMENT

Two important consequences followed from Wernicke's observations. First, language could no longer be considered a unitary "faculty" and would have to be subdivided (at least) in terms of receptive and expressive functions. Second, it was clear that focal disease could cause specific deficits. The first observation meant that the scientists of the day would have to rethink the concept of "faculty". The second lent considerable weight to the idea of localisation of function. When, in 1892, Dejerine identified the cortical area (these days called the **angular gyrus**) related to the loss of the ability to read from text (known as **alexia**), three language areas, all on the left side, had been identified, and the localisation of function concept had received a major boost (see Figure 1.2).

To this work on aphasia, we might add the pioneering work of Fritsch and Hitzig (1870) who showed that discrete electrical stimulation of dogs' brains could induce movement of specific body parts in a consistent and predictable way. We might also note the subsequent cytoarchitectonic maps (maps of cortical regions differentiated by cell type and density) of Vogt (Vogt & Vogt, 1903) and Brodmann (1909). The latter has stood the test of time (with minor modification to some of his regional boundaries), and present-day researchers still frequently identify cortical locations by their Brodmann number (see Figure 1.3). BA 44 (and into BA 45) on the left, for example, correspond with Broca's area, and BA 7 corresponds to the precuneus, which we will discuss towards the end of this chapter. Cytoarchitectonic maps are primarily concerned with structure, but there is general agreement that most of the mappers anticipated there would be correspondences between structurally distinct regions and underlying functions.

KEY TERMS

Angular gyrus: A region of cortex on the temporal/parietal border roughly equivalent to Brodmann's area 39. The left side is probably involved in reading (sentences).

Alexia: Inability to read.

MASS-ACTION AND EQUIPOTENTIALITY

Despite the evidence presented in the previous section, it would be misleading to suggest that after Dejerine's findings all researchers quickly accepted the basic principles of cortical localisation. For instance, the renowned British neurologist John Hughlings-Jackson supported localisation for some cortical functions, but was also aware that focal damage rarely led to complete loss of the function. As if to underline this point, the German physiologist Goltz regularly attended scientific meetings in the 1880s with a dog whose behaviour seemed relatively "normal" despite Goltz himself having removed a large chunk of its cortex!

At the beginning of the 20th century European psychology came under the influence of the "Gestalt" movement, which emphasised the importance of "the whole as being greater than the

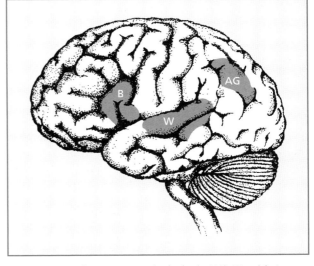

FIG. 1.2   Some language areas in the brain. W is Wernicke's area, conceptualised as the region responsible for linking speech sounds to stored representations of words. B is Broca's area, identified as involved in the generation of speech. AG depicts the angular gyrus, known to be important in understanding visually presented material.

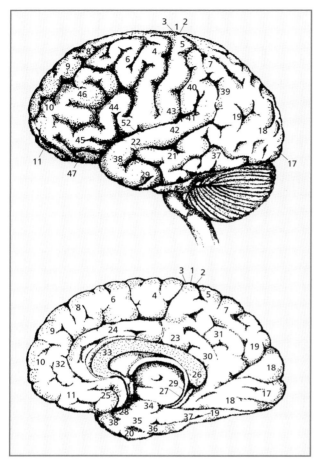

FIG. 1.3 Brodmann areas. Brodmann used a light microscope to analyse the cellular organisation of the cortex, identifying 52 distinct regions. Many (though not all) of these are still recognised and used today to identify particular locations.

sum of its parts". This view was anathema to localisationists but it prompted other scientists, such as the British neurologist Henry Head, to describe the brain as a dynamic, interconnected system that should be considered in its own right rather than as a collection of independently functioning units. Head's ideas were shared by Karl Lashley, an American psychologist, whose theories of **mass-action** (that the entire cortex is involved in all functions), and **equipotentiality** (that each cortical region can assume control for any given behaviour) were based on the same "holistic" principles, and were, for a while, extremely influential, particularly in psychology.

Lashley's ideas can be traced back to the earlier work of Flourens: like him, Lashley used brain lesions and worked exclusively with animals. Many of his studies were designed in an attempt to establish the anatomical location of the "engram"—the representation of memory in the brain. To address this, he measured the effects of lesions and ablations (cutting or removal of brain tissue) on maze learning in rodents (see Figure 1.4a). Initially there would be a period of orientation during which an animal learned its way around a maze to locate a food pellet. Then Lashley would remove a small region of cortex and, following a period of recovery, see how many trials it took the animal to relearn the maze and find the food pellet (see Figure 1.4b). After many such experiments, Lashley came to the view that his quest to locate the engram would never succeed. On the contrary, his research had shown that the amount of lesioned brain tissue rather than its location best predicted how long it would take the rat to relearn the maze. This finding is clearly at odds with the idea of a localised memory system, and lends weight to the ideas of mass-action and equipotentiality.

These findings jibed well with new ideas about behaviourism emanating from American experimental psychology at the beginning of the 20th century. This approach stressed the importance of learning and **reinforcement** at the expense of interest in the brain. However (and notwithstanding the difficulties in generalising from rat to human behaviour), there are a number of flaws in Lashley's argument, and his findings could, in fact, be used to support localisation of function. Think for a moment about the information a rat might use to find food in a maze—this is likely to include sensory information from the visual, tactile, and olfactory modalities, in addition to any more sophisticated conceptual information such as sense of direction, distance travelled, and so on. Indeed, effective maze learning probably depends on the integration of all this information. When Lashley

KEY TERMS

Mass-action: The principle (alongside equipotentiality) that cortical regions of the brain are inherently non-specialised, and have the capacity to engage in any psychological function.

Equipotentiality: The term associated with Lashley, broadly meaning that any region of cortex can assume responsibility for a given function (memory being the function of interest for Lashley).

Reinforcement: Typically some form of reward (positive reinforcement) or punishment (negative reinforcement) that affects the likelihood of a response being repeated.

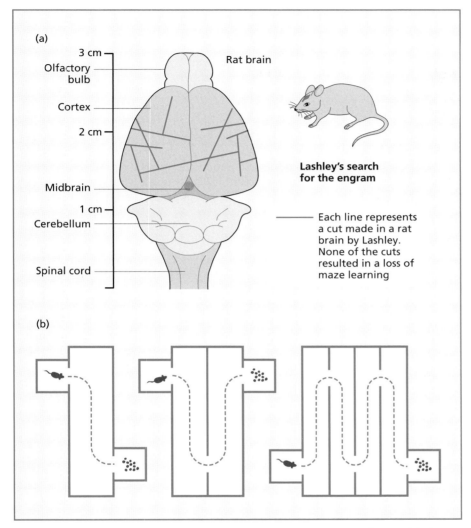

FIG. 1.4 Lashley's lesions and one of his mazes. (a) The anatomical location of some of the lesions performed by Lashley. (b) The types of maze used by Lashley in his search for the engram in rodents' brains.

lesioned different parts of cortex, he might have interfered with the animal's tactile skills or sense of smell, while leaving other functions intact. The animal could still learn the maze using the "localised" functions that remained, but perhaps not as quickly as before.

INTERIM COMMENT

In fact, sound experimental support for Lashley's ideas has been hard to come by, and it is probably helpful to know that most neuropsychologists continue to favour some form of localisation. Indeed, at present the main questions in this area are less to do with *whether or not* the human cortex is organised locally, than the *extent* to which localisation of function applies, and whether it applies equally on both the left and right sides of the brain (an issue we consider in Chapter 3). There is, additionally, a very important lesson for neuropsychologists embedded in the alternative explanation of Lashley's findings. This concerns the interpretation of results about "recovery of function" in brain-damaged individuals, and we will return to it later in the book.

THE (RE)EMERGENCE OF NEUROPSYCHOLOGY

Historians seem unsure why, after such a promising start in the late 19th century, neuropsychology seemed to go into a form of hibernation until after World War II. In reality a combination of factors was responsible, notably the increased interest shown by mainstream psychology in behaviourism and **psychoanalysis**, rivals perhaps, but both understandable without direct reference to the brain. During this period there was also a distinct lack of progress in understanding basic brain physiology. Cajal and Golgi engaged in a protracted argument about whether the brain was, in effect, a single complex nerve field (as Golgi thought), or comprised individual structurally distinct units (neurons) as Cajal believed. More-over, the discovery of chemically mediated **synapses** was made only in the 1930s by Otto Loewi, and even then there was a further delay of several years before the chemical that Loewi had found in his classic experiment was identified as acetyl-choline (see Box 1.1).

Box 1.1 Brain discoveries in the early 20th century

Early in the 20th centruy Camillo Golgi, a neuroanatomist working in a small university in northern Italy, discovered that a silver salt could be used to stain brain tissue. For reasons that are still not fully understood, some tissue absorbed the stain giving it a distinct black appearance, and it could then be examined more closely under the light microscope. Golgi's stain highlighted individual neurons, but he was convinced that he was actually staining small regions of a continuous mass of relatively undifferentiated tissue. Santiago Ramon y Cajal (1913, 1937), a Spanish neuroanatomist, used Golgi's method to show that the regions of stained tissue were, indeed, individual neurons and, moreover, that they carried electrical information (we would now identify this as volleys of action potentials) in one direction only, from the cell body (or more specifically the axon hillock) to the end of the axon (see Appendix). Despite jointly receiving the Nobel prize in 1906, the two men remained fierce rivals, Golgi in particular rebuffing Cajal's ideas—although time has shown that Cajal, rather than Golgi, was right.

By the time Otto Loewi discovered chemically mediated synaptic trans-mission in 1931, most researchers accepted the "neuron" hypothesis (the direct conclusion from Cajal's work) but assumed that "contacts" between neurons were electrically mediated. Loewi is reputed to have come up with the idea for his "frog-heart" perfusion experiment following a dream. He was aware that a frog's heart could be slowed down by electrical stimulation of its vagus nerve, but he did not know what actually caused this effect. He repeated his experiment on a live frog, stimulating its vagus nerve while bathing the exposed heart with water. The "run-off" fluid was collected then trickled over the exposed heart of a second

---

KEY TERMS

Psychoanalysis: The school of psychology initiated by Freud that emphasises the role(s) of unresolved subconscious conflicts in psychological disorder.

Synapses: The tiny fluid-filled gaps between neurons where synaptic transmission (see below) may occur. Typically 20–30 nanometres (millionths of a millimetre) wide.

frog, which slowed down. This showed that some chemical in the perfused water from the first frog mediated the effect seen following vagus nerve stimulation. Some 8 years after this study, the chemical in question was identified as acetylcholine (ACh), now recognised as one of the most widespread neurotransmitter substances. Among its many vital functions in our own nervous system, ACh is a key neurotransmitter at neuromuscular synapses, and also plays many critical roles in the brain.

CONNECTIONISM TO MODULARITY

As we have already suggested, the 1950s and 1960s were marked by a gradual increase (or perhaps re-emergence) of interest in both physiological and cognitive psychology, each making important contributions to the subject matter that we now consider under the heading of neuropsychology. Meanwhile, the concepts of mass-action and equipotentiality gained little support from the new wave of brain research, and interest in them dwindled. New understanding about the connectivity of the brain, on the other hand, prompted a revival of interest in "connectionist models" of brain function. Such models had first appeared almost a century earlier as explanations of how, for instance, the various aphasic conditions might be related to one another, and how they in turn might be linked to pathology in different but interconnected left-sided brain regions (Lichtheim, 1885). Similar types of model were also proposed to explain **agnosia(s)** (loss of ability to recognise visually presented commonplace objects; Lissauer, 1890) and **apraxia(s)** (inability to perform or copy gestures on demand; Liepmann, 1905). However, in each case, a combination of problems with the original conceptualisation of the model (for instance, the identification of cases whose profile did not conform to the stereotypic disorder) coupled with the rise in 20th-century (non-brain) psychology worked to marginalise them, and connectionist models fell out of favour with researchers.

In neuropsychology, their re-emergence in the 1960s as "neural wiring diagrams" was an attempt to clarify the different cortical regions that might be responsible for particular psychological processes. One of the most influential was Geschwind's neo-associationist model of language and aphasia (Geschwind, 1965), considered in Chapter 6. That the model itself contained a number of flaws is not now, some 40 years later, seen as being as important as the impetus it gave to neuropsychological thinking at a critical time in the subject's re-emergence. Most neuropsychologists now think that the human brain coordinates mental processes through the collaboration of (and interconnections between) multiple brain regions. It thus follows that circumscribed deficits in higher brain function should be attributable to (1) loss through damage or disease of some specialised cortical function, or (2) loss through damage or disease to connecting pathways, or (3) both. At present the first alternative is better understood, mainly because of the continuing difficulty in establishing functional connections within the brain, but new "in-vivo" pathway-tracing techniques such as diffusion tensor imaging (DTI) are likely to lead to rapid developments in this area (see Chapter 2)

The circuits comprising areas of specialised cortical function and their interconnections are sometimes called "distributed control networks". Although this sounds rather complicated, think of it as meaning that psychological functions (such as language or movement) depend on the activity of, and connections between, several (many) different but specific locations. Clearly this is a different idea from the "strict" localisation of function concept mentioned earlier, because it implies that no one region has sole responsibility for a particular psychological function (or faculty in Gall's terms). However, it is also quite distinct from Lashley's ideas of mass-action and equipotentiality, because it suggests that some regions of cortex are fundamentally involved in particular psychological processes while others are not.

In a way, the concept of distributed control is a compromise between the two approaches, because it implies cortical specialisation (localisation of function) but also suggests that several (perhaps many) interconnected but anatomically distributed centres may be involved in the overall process. As Kosslyn and Anderson (1992) have commented, the problem for the strict localisationists was of thinking that psychological processes like memory, attention, or language were equivalent to Gall's faculties, and therefore could be localised to one particular brain region. In reality, such processes are complex and multi-tiered, involving the collaborative efforts of many underlying mechanisms. These subsidiary elements could, of course, be "localised" to very specific cortical regions, but the network as a whole may nonetheless actually "engage" broad swathes of cortex when the subsidiary elements interact to serve the particular psychological process.

For some neuropsychologists, Jerry Fodor captured the essence of this emerging view in his influential book *The modularity of mind* (1983). He argued that it was necessary to distinguish between two classes of cognitive processes: central systems and **modules**. The former are non-specific in the sense of operating across cognitive domains: attention, thinking, and memory have been suggested as examples. Modules, on the other hand, are domain specific in that they only process very particular types of input information: colour, shape, movement, faces, and so on. In Fodor's view, modules are likely to be hard-wired (immutable), autonomous, and localised. Critically, they can process information rapidly, and without reference to other modules; something that Fodor called "informational encapsulation".

It must be said at this point that debating the relative merits of different conceptual models of brain functioning takes us into "difficult" territory, certainly beyond the scope of this introductory text. However, we can say that Fodor's model (presented, by the way, without detailed reference to particular brain structures) had at least one advantage over Geschwind's. It allowed for, and indeed presumed that, the brain used **parallel information processing**, at least at the lower "modular" level, so different modules could become simultaneously active, whereas Geschwind's was essentially a serial processing model.

As for the distinction between localised modules and non-localised higher-order cognition, here we must tread very carefully. Certainly there is good evidence for modularity within perceptual systems: Zeki et al. (1991) have described over 30 "modules" in the mammalian visual system for example. But as for non-localised higher-order cognitive processes, current thinking envisages these as mediated by networks of multiple specialised cortical areas, connected through parallel, bi-directional pathways. Thus it could be argued that even processes such as attention and memory, though not localisable to singular specific locations (modules), are nevertheless localisable to networks (or is this a contradiction in terms?). The extent to which components in networks are then dedicated to particular higher-order cognitive functions, or shared between several, is another current matter of debate. (See Box 1.2 for further consideration of this complicated issue, and Chapter 9 for an introduction to the concept of the global workspace model of consciousness.)

Box 1.2 The precuneus: Trying to make sense of its many connections and behavioural correlates

In this focus box we hope to illustrate how our understanding of brain–behaviour relationships has advanced beyond the early connectionist models described in the text, as in-vivo imaging procedures, coupled with ingenious psychological challenges, have been refined. The precuneus (BA [**Brodmann area**] 7) is located medially (in the longitudinal fissure) above the occipital lobe, forming part of the posterior parietal cortex (see Figure 1.5). You actually have both a right and a left precuneus (one in the right hemisphere and another in the left). The precuneus has reciprocal cortical connections (inputs to and outputs from) with other parietal regions: parts of the frontal and temporal lobes and the anterior cingulate gyrus. It has reciprocal subcortical connections with the **thalamus**, and sends outputs to the **striatum** and several **brainstem** areas.

Functional investigations have identified at least four roles for this hitherto poorly understood region. A series of PET and fMRI studies suggest that the precuneus is part of a network (also involving other parietal areas and the supplementary motor region of the frontal lobes) concerned with visuospatial processing and imagery, particularly self-referential imagery such as imagining reaching or pointing, or planning of movements in environments with lots of obstacles that have to be avoided (Malouin et al., 2003). Second, the precuneus has been strongly implicated (along with the prefrontal and anterior cingulate regions) in imagery components of episodic memory retrieval (memory for previously experienced events sequenced in time, in which, presumably, one might use imagery to run through the sequence of events to be recalled) and was labelled by Fletcher et al. (1995) as "the mind's eye". Closer investigation has indicated that the anterior part may be particularly involved in imagery, while the posterior region is associated with successful retrieval in general. A third important observation about the precuneus is that it is more active in tasks related to self—"seeing" things from one's own as opposed to another person's perspective. This network also includes other medial and lateral parietal regions, and a lateral frontal region known as the insula. Fourth, and most intriguing of all, it appears that the precuneus (in combination with posterior cingulate and medial prefrontal regions) is more metabolically active during conscious resting states (such as during meditation) than during goal-directed active tasks. The opposite side of this coin is that it becomes markedly inactive during altered conscious states including slow-wave sleep, hypnosis, and anaesthesia. This preliminary evidence has been marshalled to suggest that the precuneus may be an important node in the neural network mediating consciousness.

Taken together, these findings suggested to Cavanna and Trimble (2006) that: "the precuneus may be involved in the integration of multiple neural systems producing a conscious self-percept" (p. 579). A somewhat more modest interpretation might be that it plays a key role in the modulation of conscious processes, perhaps supporting mental representations of "self".

KEY TERMS
Brodmann area: A region of the cortex defined on the basis of cytoarchitecture.
Thalamus: A multi-functional subcortical brain region.
Striatum: A collective name for the caudate and putamen; key input regions in the basal ganglia.
Brainstem: The lower part of the brain, adjoining and structurally continuous with the spinal cord.

Cognitive neuropsychologists have also made extensive use of diagrams and models to identify both the component processing units (modules) and the way they collaborate to enable psychological processes such as memory, object recognition, or attention to operate. In certain respects, however, the cognitive neuropsychology approach and methodology is quite distinct from that of clinical neuropsychology (as exemplified by Geschwind). Whereas clinical neuropsychologists develop models that are anatomically referenced to specific cortical regions, cognitive neuropsychologists generate hypothetical models that more closely resemble "box and arrow" flow diagrams, and may make little or no reference to possible underlying brain regions (see, for example, Riddoch & Humphreys' 2001 model of visual object recognition, introduced in Chapter 8 and illustrated in Figure 1.6). Such models serve as templates (hypotheses) that attempt to account for *known* cases—of a neuropsychological deficit such as prosopagnosia (difficulty in recognising faces), or amnesia (loss of some aspect of memory) for example—but which must be amended if other cases come to light that do not fit. Cognitive neuropsychologists therefore put great weight on detailed case study of individuals with particular disorders, eschewing research based on groups of individuals, on the grounds that brain damage is infinitely variable and it therefore makes little sense (they would say) to

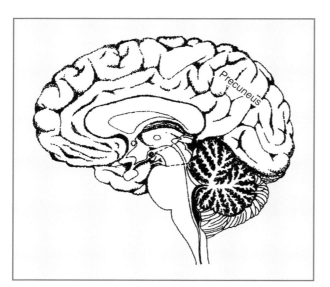

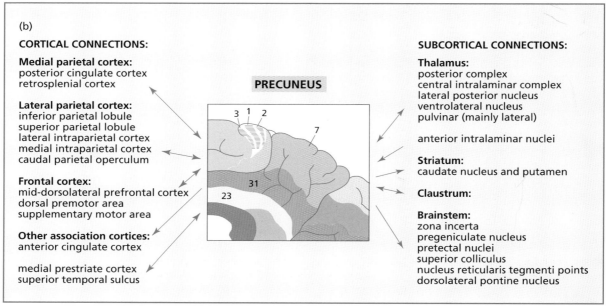

(b)

CORTICAL CONNECTIONS:

Medial parietal cortex:
posterior cingulate cortex
retrosplenial cortex

Lateral parietal cortex:
inferior parietal lobule
superior parietal lobule
lateral intraparietal cortex
medial intraparietal cortex
caudal parietal operculum

Frontal cortex:
mid-dorsolateral prefrontal cortex
dorsal premotor area
supplementary motor area

Other association cortices:
anterior cingulate cortex

medial prestriate cortex
superior temporal sulcus

PRECUNEUS

SUBCORTICAL CONNECTIONS:

Thalamus:
posterior complex
central intralaminar complex
lateral posterior nucleus
ventrolateral nucleus
pulvinar (mainly lateral)

anterior intralaminar nuclei

Striatum:
caudate nucleus and putamen

Claustrum:

Brainstem:
zona incerta
pregeniculate nucleus
pretectal nuclei
superior colliculus
nucleus reticularis tegmenti points
dorsolateral pontine nucleus

FIG. 1.5   The location and connections of the precuneus. (a) The precuneus forms part of the medial parietal lobe. It is hidden in the posterior part of the longitudinal fissure [after Critchley, M. (1953). *The parietal lobes*. London: Edward Arnold]. (b) Cortical and subcortical connections of the precuneus. [Adapted from Cavanna, A. E. & Trimble, M. R. (2006). The precuneus: A review of its functional anatomy and behavioural correlates. *Brain*, *129*, 564–583. Reproduced with permission.]

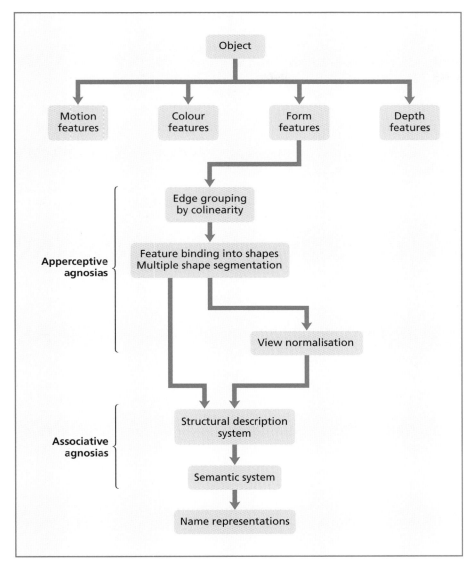

FIG. 1.6   Riddoch and Humphreys' (2001) model of visual object recognition. Typical of the cognitive neuropsychological approach, the model describes the component processes (and their connections) assumed to underpin normal and faulty object recognition. We describe this model in more detail in Chapter 8. [Adapted from Riddoch & Humphreys (2001) in B. Rapp (Ed.), *Handbook of cognitive neuropsychology*. Hove, UK: Psychology Press. Reproduced with permission.]

group individuals together simply because they may have vaguely overlapping areas of damage. Coltheart et al.'s (1998) review of the case of AC (neuro-psychological cases are often identified by initials in this way) provides a typical illustration of this approach which we have summarised in Box 1.3.

According to Coltheart (2001), cognitive neuropsychology attempts to interpret cognitive disorders in terms of selective impairments of functional architectures. (Note his use of the term "*functional* architectures" referring to "box and arrow" diagrams, rather than reference to brain regions or "*structural architectures*", i.e., anatomically referenced neural networks, loops, or circuits.) The approach is premised on four key assumptions:

- *Functional modularity*: simply stated, this means that cognitive systems are actually configurations of modules, each of which has quite specific functions (see our earlier reference to "modularity of mind").
- *Anatomical modularity*: meaning that such modules probably occupy rather specific anatomical locations.
- *Uniform functional architecture*: meaning that the above relationship is consistent from one person to the next.
- *Subtractivity*: meaning that damage may impair or "knock out" a module or connection in a system (or architecture), but not replace it with a new one.

Are these assumptions legitimate? According to Coltheart if they were not, cognitive-neuropsychological research would have run into severe difficulties by now, whereas in fact the approach continues to be very informative. However, this is a rather glib answer, and a more prudent approach may be to consider these not as "key assumptions underlying cognitive neuropsychology" but simply as working hypotheses about brain functionality. So, as with any other hypotheses, the scientist retains them until the evidence dictates that they should be rejected (Popper, 1934).

Box 1.3 The case of AC (Coltheart et al., 1998)

AC, a 67-year-old male, had recently suffered a major stroke, creating an area of damage on the left side of his brain. A CT scan additionally indicated evidence of earlier cerebrovascular incidents (probably minor strokes) in both hemispheres. Not surprisingly in view of the left-hemisphere damage, AC's language ability was severely compromised, both in terms of reading and writing and in relation to verbal expression, where it was apparent that although he knew what he wanted to say, he struggled to find the appropriate words to say it. However, careful examination of his cognitive impairments revealed an additional specific problem with his knowledge of objects, suggesting a profound semantic impairment. When asked how many legs an oyster had, he replied "a few", and for a seagull, "four". Yet he had a 95% success rate in classifying animals as dangerous (or not), and a 96% success rate in determining whether or not an animal would be considered "edible". In other words, he certainly retained considerable semantic information about animals despite not knowing how many legs they had. Further testing indicated that AC's deficit was, in fact, related to loss of knowledge about the *appearance* of objects including animals, as he also struggled to identify those with tails, or indeed their general shape.

From a cognitive neuropsychological perspective, the implication of these findings is that there must be separate independent systems of knowledge about the properties of objects and their visual appearances. Of course there may, in fact, be separate systems of perceptual knowledge (about objects) for each of our senses, in addition to a system for non-perceptual object knowledge.

INTERIM COMMENT

Although the cognitive neuropsychology approach has been useful in certain domains such as language (see Chapter 6) and object recognition (see Chapter 8), its reliance on case study rather than group comparisons and its indifference towards brain structures have not been to everyone's taste. Small *N* research makes for problems of generalisability in any discipline, and neuropsychology cannot be excepted. As for the inclination to marginalise, or even ignore, matters of brain neuroanatomy, it should be noted that the continuing development of in-vivo techniques (see Chapter 2) means that data about functional activation in the brains of people both with and without damage as they undertake various psychological challenges are now readily accessible, and this is likely to mean that cognitive neuropsychologists will, in the future, have to take more notice of the brain. A concise account of the key events in the history and development of neuropsychology is offered by Selnes (2001).

CHAPTER SUMMARY

Scientific interest in the relationship between brain structure and function can be traced back to the work of the 19th-century European neurologists. In the intervening years, researchers have debated the extent to which the brain operates on the basis of localisation of function or according to the principles of equipotentiality and mass-action. Although still a matter of considerable debate, most modern-day researchers favour some form of localisation, albeit one involving specialised distributed networks, as providing the best account for our understanding of how the brain actually operates. Equipotentiality and mass-action currently have few advocates among brain scientists.

In this chapter we have traced the development of scientific brain research, and introduced some of the theories that have surfaced as our understanding of these relationships has developed. A promising start in the 19th century gave way to a period in the first half of the 20th when psychology was dominated by theories and ideas that made only passing reference to the brain. Renewed interest in physiological psychology in the second half of the 20th century, along with greater interest in cognitive processes within psychology, set the scene for the birth (rebirth?) of the discipline we recognise today as neuropsychology. Although it is not an entirely unified enterprise, its cognitive and clinical strands complement one another in many respects. The rapid increase in access to, and consequent use of, in-vivo imaging procedures (which brings into the equation both clinical and non-brain-damaged cases) is likely to lead to greater convergence. These techniques also provide exciting new insights into the functions of particular cortical regions, and the precuneus is an excellent example of this.

CHAPTER 2

CONTENTS

Methods in neuropsychology

INTRODUCTION

In this chapter we introduce some of the methods that are used in neuropsychology to explore the relationship between brain structure and function. In Chapter 1 we described neuropsychology as a "bridging discipline" and consequently there are a wide range of methodologies involved—from neuroanatomical procedures at one end of the spectrum, through to experimental psychology assessments at the other. The advent of in-vivo neuroimaging techniques over the last 20 years has revolutionised neuropsychology, providing research opportunities that were previously unthinkable. In-vivo imaging has, for example, confirmed some of the long-suspected roles of particular brain regions in certain psychological processes (e.g., the role of **anterior cingulate** cortex in attention: see Chapter 9). Imaging techniques have also revealed the complexity inherent in functions that traditional neuropsychology had previously oversimplified. Imaging of language processes is an example of this, as discussed in Chapter 6.

While imaging techniques have undoubtedly provided a wealth of new information, it is important to be aware that they are not without limitations. Older techniques have therefore remained valuable, in spite of predictions of their demise. In fact imaging and traditional neuropsychology techniques provide complementary methodologies, generating more information when used in conjunction than either could do alone. A key element of imaging studies in neuropsychology is the vital importance of good experimental design aimed at testing specific hypotheses. In the excitement of newly available techniques, it is important to remember that they are simply techniques to answer interesting questions—neuroimaging is a means not an end.

An important though sometimes unspoken concept in neuropsychological methodology is that of **converging operations**. Human neuropsychology is inevitably constrained by many practical and ethical concerns: for example, repeating Lashley's research with human subjects would be impossible. Putting this another way, definitive, theory-changing experiments are actually few and far between in neuropsychology. Rather, researchers develop ideas (and ultimately theories) about different aspects of neuropsychology by "being receptive" to

KEY TERMS

Anterior cingulate: A midline frontal lobe structure implicated in attention, response inhibition, and emotional response (especially to pain).

Converging operations: The use of several research methods to solve a single problem so that the strengths of one method balance out the weaknesses of the others.

research findings derived from quite distinct approaches. For example, as discussed in Chapter 3, current ideas about the differing responsibilities of the left and right sides of the brain derive from:

- case studies of individuals with localised brain damage;
- individuals who have been surgically operated on;
- experimental psychological studies of healthy individuals;
- imaging studies of both healthy and brain-damaged individuals.

All these data should additionally be "evaluated" in relation to both basic neuro-anatomical observations of similarities and differences between the two sides of the brain, and (we suggest) broader comparative/evolutionary perspectives. Using all this information to generate neuropsychological theories would, in effect, be to endorse the concept of converging operations—something that the authors of this text are, with certain caveats, happy to do. However, it is important to know that this approach is not to everyone's liking, and most neuropsychological methods have their critics (see, for example, Caramazza's objections to studying groups of individuals with similar brain damage: Caramazza, 1986).

Interestingly, a "new take" on converging operations derives from combining methods in a single study (as we hinted earlier), and we review this potentially fruitful line of inquiry towards the end of this chapter. However, we start with a brief review of classic techniques that are, for the most part, neuroanatomical in origin. We then consider the use of electrical stimulation and electrical recording in the brain. Then we review the in-vivo neuroimaging procedures that have been increasingly used to characterise brain structure and function. Lastly we review the neuropsychological approach. Where possible, we try to refer readers to specific examples of the use of these techniques described elsewhere in this book.

INVASIVE TECHNIQUES FOR MEASURING BRAIN STRUCTURE AND FUNCTION

EXAMINING TISSUE

Until quite recently, the only options for measurement of brain structure were post-mortem investigation or, very occasionally, **biopsy**. The latter technique involves the removal and examination of small (but irreplaceable) samples of brain tissue from the brain region in question. Biopsy is essentially somewhat "hit and miss" and also causes inevitable damage to the brain. It is therefore hardly ever used in humans. Post-mortem analysis by contrast, has a long and sometimes colourful history in medicine. It does, of course, require the subject to be dead, and therefore early signs of disease are typically masked by changes that have occurred as the disease process has progressed.

Sometimes the damage that is revealed in post-mortem is blatantly obvious. In one of neuropsychology's classic cases, Broca observed the brain of his aphasic patient "Tan". His very superficial post-mortem revealed clear damage to the left frontal cortex (in the region still referred to as "Broca's area"). The brain of a patient who has died due to **Alzheimer's disease** or **Huntington's disease** will look abnormal even to the naked eye. It will appear shrunken, with deflated gyri (surface bumps) and widened sulci (surface grooves). These changes are, however,

KEY TERMS

Biopsy: The removal of tissue (in a living individual) for analysis.

Alzheimer's disease: A form of dementia involving progressive loss of psychological functions as a result of widespread loss of cortical and subcortical neurons.

Huntington's disease: A rare, genetically determined, neurological disorder causing dementia and death due to progressive loss of neurons in the striatum.

probably of less interest to researchers than the more subtle brain changes that occurred at the start of the disease, or even before clinical symptoms of the disease were noted. Since the patient would still have been alive at this point, post-mortem investigation would not have been an option.

In other cases, a brain can appear externally normal at post-mortem, and it is only on closer inspection of internal structures and tissues that damage or disease becomes apparent. Brain tissue looks solid to the naked eye, so such closer inspection depended on two crucial developments. The first was the invention and gradual refinement of light microscopy: Van Leeuwenhoek first used a microscope to examine biological tissue in 1674, and since then improvements in lens manufacture have led to the technique becoming ever more effective. Light microscopes can now magnify by a factor of several hundred. The newer technique of electron microscopy provides magnification by a factor of several thousand. It is now possible to view images of individual synapses or even individual **receptor sites** for **neurotransmitters**.

The second crucial development for post-mortem analysis was the discovery of staining techniques that can be used to "highlight" particular component structures of tissue. Staining was pioneered by Golgi in the late 19th century and his silver-staining method ("Golgi staining") is still used today to highlight neurons. Other staining techniques, such as horseradish peroxidase (HRP), have been developed to enable the tracing of connections between neurons. This stain is absorbed by the **distal** (remote) parts of neurons but is carried back to the cell bodies, thus revealing the path that the axons take. A combination of these staining techniques in post-mortem tissue provides evidence of functional connectivity between brain regions, such as the innervation of the striatum by the **substantia nigra**, which deteriorates progressively in **Parkinson's disease** (see Chapter 5).

At the start of the 20th century, Brodmann used a combination of microscopy and staining to map the cytoarchitecture of the human cortex. His research revealed that different cortical locations are characterised by structurally distinct cell types. His comprehensive map, which is still used today (with minor modifications) for reference and anatomical location, identified 52 numbered regions (Brodmann, 1909). For example, the primary visual cortex is known as Brodmann's area 17 (BA 17), while Broca's area spans Brodmann's areas (BA) 44 and 45 in the left hemisphere (see Figure 2.1).

LESION AND ABLATION

Lesion (cutting) and ablation (removal) of nerve tissue are long-standing techniques in neurology. Lashley, whose work we introduced in Chapter 1, put forward the theory of mass-action based on lesion studies in animals. For obvious reasons, these procedures are not used experimentally in humans. However, brain tissue is sometimes ablated for medical reasons (e.g., the removal of a tumour). Surgical lesioning is also occasionally undertaken. For example, lesioning the corpus callosum has been used as a treatment for **epilepsy**, which will be discussed further in Chapter 3. Sometimes lesions or ablations may occur as the result of accidents. A famous case is that of Phineas Gage, who had an accident involving an iron rod and some dynamite that resulted in extensive damage to his prefrontal cortex. Another less famous case is NA, who developed amnesia after an accident with a fencing foil (see Chapters 7, 10, and 11).

KEY TERMS

Receptor sites: Molecular structures on (or in) the membranes of neurons that neurotransmitter substances (and hormones) can "influence" when they occupy them, usually by making the neuron more or less excited.

Neurotransmitters: A heterogeneous group of chemical messengers usually manufactured by, stored in, and released by neurons that can influence the excitability of other neurons (or muscles).

Distal: Far away; as opposed to proximal, meaning near to.

Substantia nigra: Another component of the basal ganglia. Neurons originating in the substantia nigra terminate in the striatum, where they release the neurotransmitter dopamine.

Parkinson's disease: A neurological disorder in which movements become slowed or are lost altogether. Rigidity and tremor are also found. Associated with loss of cells in and around the basal ganglia.

Epilepsy: The term for a group of neurological disorders characterised by synchronised but excessive neuronal activity.

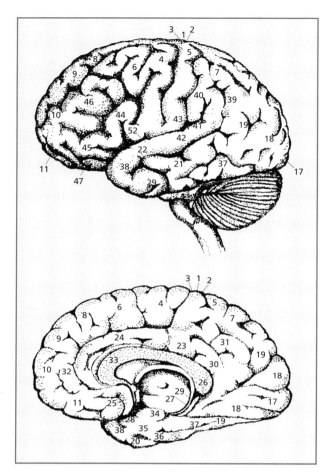

FIG. 2.1 Brodmann's cortical areas revisited. Brodmann identified 52 cortical areas on the basis of the type and density of neurons present.

Lesions can also be induced through the use of chemicals or drugs. The **Wada test** (Wada & Rasmussen, 1960) involves the administration of a fast-acting barbiturate via the carotid artery to one hemisphere at a time. This causes a temporary lesion lasting a matter of minutes, and has historically been used to establish hemispheric dominance for language prior to brain surgery. Other chemicals may induce permanent lesions via toxic influence. The substance MPTP, a toxin that was inadvertently mixed with synthetic heroin by recreational drug users in 1980s California, irreversibly destroys **dopamine** neurons in the substantia nigra, resulting in a very severe form of induced Parkinsonism. (We review the case of the "frozen addicts" in Chapter 5.)

"VIRTUAL LESIONS": TRANSCRANIAL MAGNETIC STIMULATION

Transcranial magnetic stimulation (TMS) was originally investigated as a possible treatment in various therapeutic settings, however it also provides a potential tool for neuropsychologists because it can be used to induce a "virtual lesion". TMS uses strong pulses of magnetisation that can be focally administered via a hand-held coil (see Figure 2.2). Thus, different areas of cortex can be stimulated depending on the positioning of the coil. Single pulses of TMS or brief trains of repetitive TMS at higher frequencies typically increase neuronal excitability. However, continuous stimulation at lower frequencies suppresses neuronal excitability, an effect that can last several minutes after TMS is stopped (Hoffman & Cavus, 2002). Essentially, it is this low-frequency TMS that induces the "virtual lesion". The potential value of this technique is highlighted by a study by Hilgetag et al. (2001) who reproduced the classic neurological symptom of **spatial neglect** (see Chapter 8) by stimulating the parietal cortex in normal subjects.

TMS can also be used in conjunction with structural neuroimaging to investigate the effects of virtual lesions in anatomically localised brain regions. Various studies have shown the utility of the technique in diverse areas of perception and cognition. However, despite its obvious potential, the technique is not without limitations. Concerns have been raised about the safety of the procedure, particularly in subjects who may be vulnerable to developing neurological abnormalities such as epilepsy. Also, TMS is better suited for the investigation of superficial brain regions (the cortex for example) than for probing less accessible regions and deeper structures.

ELECTRICAL PROCEDURES

ELECTRICAL STIMULATION

The neurosurgeon Wilder Penfield was responsible for much of the pioneering work on mapping primary somatosensory and motor cortex. His subjects were patients who required surgery for life-threatening conditions, typically the removal of tumours or blood clots. He asked these patients whether during the course of surgery he could apply mild electrical stimulation to the surface of their brains. Brain surgery is typically carried out with the patient awake, due in part to the lack of pain receptors in the brain, and resultant pain insensitivity. Therefore Penfield was able to talk to his patients about their sensory impressions and motor responses as he stimulated specific regions. Penfield was the first researcher to discover the amazing topographic representation of body parts in the primary motor and somatosensory cortex (which we describe in Chapters 4 and 5). (See Penfield & Rasmussen, 1950.)

ELECTRICAL RECORDING

We can also learn about brain function by recording its electrical activity. In electroencephalography (EEG) and the closely related procedure of event-related potential (ERP) recording, this involves

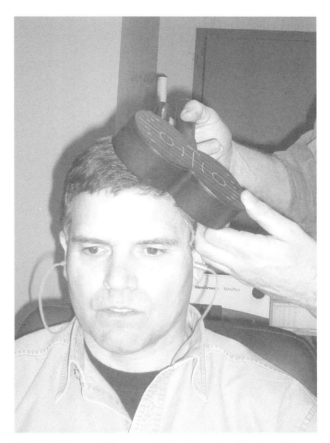

FIG. 2.2 Transcranial magnetic stimulation. A subject receiving stimulation with a typical "figure of eight" TMS stimulator.

attaching electrodes to the scalp. The underlying activity is detected and amplified, and usually displayed on a chart recorder or computer screen. Surface recording is possible because electrical activity in the brain is conducted passively through the **meninges** (protective membranes surrounding the brain) and the skull to the scalp. Of course, voltages recorded represent the sum of activity from millions of neurons in the area of brain closest to the recording electrode. So, in order to get an idea about the spatial distribution of activity, several separate channels of EEG corresponding to electrodes in different positions on the head can be recorded simultaneously. This procedure has been widely used in research and also has clinical relevance, having proved invaluable in the diagnosis of epilepsy and in the identification of sleep-related disorders (see Figure 2.3).

In a research study with ERPs, a series of stimuli such as tones or light flashes are presented to a participant. The raw EEG for a precise 1- or 2-second period following each stimulus is recorded and fed into a computer where it is summed and averaged. There will be a response (or "event-related potential") in the brain to each separate stimulus but this will be small (millionths of a volt) in comparison with the background EEG (thousandths of a volt). By summing all the EEGs and averaging them, the more-or-less random EEG averages to zero, to leave an ERP that has a characteristic waveform when shown on the computer screen. Abnormalities in this waveform have been linked to clinical disorders, for example

KEY TERM
Meninges: The system of membranes that enclose the central nervous system.

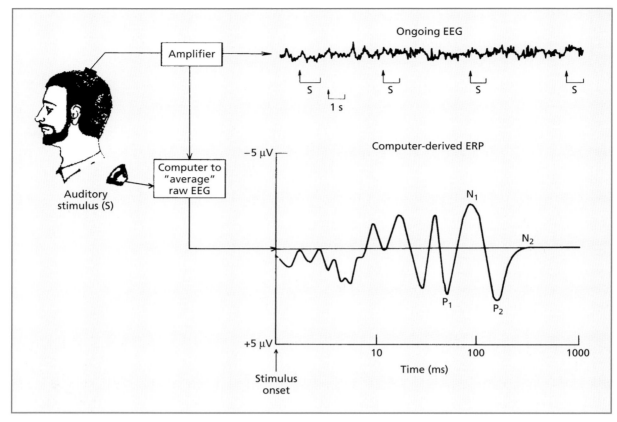

FIG. 2.3   Recording of EEGs and ERPs. Raw EEG can be recorded from surface electrodes on the scalp. If a series of stimuli are presented to the respondent there will be a small but characteristic response to each stimulus but this will be "hidden" in the EEG. ERPs are obtained by feeding brief "epochs" of the EEG (typically 500 to 1000 ms following each stimulus) into a computer that averages them. The random background EEG tends to average to zero, leaving the characteristic ERP waveform.

a predisposition to alcoholism or schizophrenia. The ERP technique has also been useful as a tool to explore the mechanisms of attention, and we describe some of this research in Chapter 9.

Recently, a variant of ERP known as magnetoencephalography (MEG) has been developed. (Mogilner et al.'s 1993 study of remapping in the cortex described in Chapter 4 employs this procedure.) MEG involves upwards of 60 electrodes attached to the participant's scalp, and takes advantage of the fact that when neurons are active they generate tiny magnetic fields. Event-related fields (ERFs) can be detected by an MEG analyser in much the same way as ERPs, but they provide a more accurate means of identifying the origin of particular signals. MEG can therefore locate the source of maximum magnetic field activity in response to stimuli and, if required, map these areas three-dimensionally and in real time. This technique has been of use in identifying the precise focal origins of epileptic seizures and, as hinted above, it has also been used to map areas of the somatosensory cortex. Perhaps surprisingly, MEG had not, until recently, become a widely used research technique. Although it has superior spatial resolution compared to EEG, both techniques are constrained by the fact that they are only suitable for looking at surface structures of the brain. The MEG technology was developed at the same time as the spatially superior in-vivo imaging techniques discussed below, and historically relatively few research groups have chosen to invest in MEG. However, this appears to be changing, as more groups recognise the advantages of combining MRI and MEG technologies. Many leading research centres are opting for MEG technology and the technique is likely to become increasingly influential over the next few years.

IN-VIVO IMAGING

The first of the in-vivo imaging techniques was computerised tomography (CT, or sometimes CAT) scanning, which came on stream in the early 1970s. As technologies developed, and the value of scanning became clearer, it was soon followed by other procedures including PET (positron emission tomography), rCBF imaging (regional cerebral blood flow), and MRI (magnetic resonance imaging). The common feature of these procedures is that researchers can produce images of the structure or functional activity of the brains of *living* people (see Figure 2.4).

STRUCTURAL IMAGING

Computerised tomography (CT, but also known as computerised axial tomography or CAT) provides structural images of the brain. To generate brain scans, low levels of X radiation are passed through an individual's head at a series of different angles (through 180°). A computer analyses each "image" and generates what is, effectively, a compound X-ray. It can produce a "slice-by-slice" picture of the entire brain, or other parts of the nervous system such as the spinal cord. A drawback of CT scanning is that the contrast between more and less dense tissue is not particularly good, although this can be improved by the administration of a dye (injected into the bloodstream just before the scan is taken). CT scans cannot measure functional activity but they have provided valuable information about *structural* changes seen in the brains of some people with dementia, and about the effects and location of brain damage in general.

Magnetic resonance imaging (MRI) is a more recent development and the technique is very

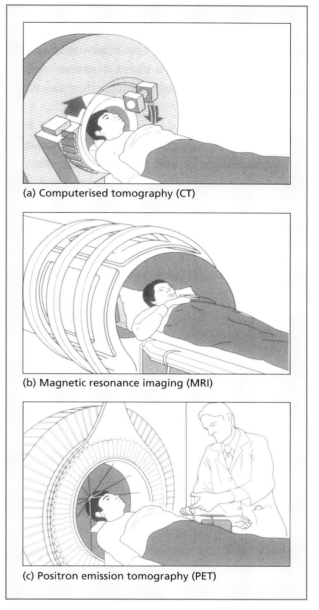

(a) Computerised tomography (CT)

(b) Magnetic resonance imaging (MRI)

(c) Positron emission tomography (PET)

FIG. 2.4   CT, MRI, and PET scanning. CT scans provide reasonably well-defined images of brain structure. PET scans generate images of functional activity, although structure is only poorly defined. MRI can generate "photographic"-quality images of brain structure, and functional MRI (see Figures 2.5 and 2.6) can produce integrated structural and functional images. Source: Rosenzweig et al. (1999). *Biological psychology*. Sunderland, MA: Sinauer Associates Inc. Reproduced by permission of Sinauer Associates Inc.

complex. In summary, it depends on the fact that protons in tissue act as little bar magnets that spin. When a strong magnetic field is applied externally by the MRI scanner, these spinning protons interact with the external field in a way that produces small but detectable changes in magnetic signal that the scanner can measure. Different types of (brain) tissue have different concentrations of protons and different chemical environments which influence the magnetic properties. Thus different tissues produce different signals and the scan data can be computer-processed to generate images that clearly show, in remarkable detail, the structures of the brain. The entire brain can be imaged in successive slices, which can be produced in **sagittal** (side), **coronal** (front), or horizontal transverse planes. Structural MRI has significant advantages over CT; for example, the images are much higher resolution and do not involve exposing people to X radiation.

FUNCTIONAL IMAGING

PET scanning was the first widely used functional imaging technique and provides images of a person's brain that show which regions are activated as they undertake different sorts of task, such as reading words, solving mental arithmetic, and listening to music. There are different types of PET scanning. One of the commonly used techniques involves injecting subjects with water that has been labelled with the short-lived radio-isotope oxygen 15. When a region of the brain is more active, blood flow to that region increases and therefore more radio-labelled water will be carried to active areas. As the oxygen 15 decays, with a half-life of around 2 minutes, gamma rays are emitted that can be detected by the PET scanner. The scanner can determine whereabouts in the brain the gamma rays were produced, and thus provide a picture of regions where blood flow is increased, indirectly determining areas of enhanced neural activity.

Another PET technique uses radio-labelled glucose rather than water. More active regions of the brain need more glucose (as a fuel), so again the radiotracer becomes concentrated in the more active regions and this can be detected as it decays. It is also possible to use PET to look at neurotransmitter function by manufacturing more complex radiotracers. For example, raclopride is a molecule that binds to dopamine receptors in the brain. A radio-labelled form of raclopride can be prepared that uses the isotope carbon 13. If this tracer is used, it will bind directly to dopamine receptors, in competition with endogenous dopamine, and therefore provides information about dopamine function. This technique has been used to study reward systems in the brain (Koepp et al., 1998; and see Chapter 10).

PET is thus a powerful means of assessing *functional* brain activity, although it does not directly measure neuronal events. Rather, it indicates relative levels of (or changes in) activity under different conditions. To do this, "image subtraction" is often employed, meaning that activity during a control condition is (literally) subtracted by computer from activity during the active test condition, and the remaining PET activity taken as an index of the activation specific to the test condition (see Box 2.1 below). Two other variants of the PET technique that you may read about are regional cerebral blood flow (rCBF) and single photon emission computerised tomography (SPECT). In rCBF, the participant inhales a small amount of a radioactive gas such as xenon, which is absorbed into the bloodstream and thus transported around the body. The participant sits in a piece of apparatus that looks a little like a dryer seen in old-fashioned hair-salons. This has a series of sensors that detect the radioactivity from the transported xenon,

Box 2.1 Cognitive subtraction, conjunction, and factorial designs

Many early neuroimaging experiments used a technique called "cognitive subtraction". This is based on the idea that a complex process involves a number of stages, and if you are interested in a particular stage you need an active task that involves that stage and a control task that involves all other stages but for the critical one. By subtracting brain activity in the control task from brain activity in the active task, you isolate brain activity associated with the process of interest. For example, if we are interested in object naming we might have an active task involving naming pictures of objects and a control task involving passively viewing the same pictures. On the face of it, the critical difference is that the object is only named in the active condition. One obvious problem with this is that there may well be incidental naming in the passive condition. It is likely that participants instructed to view pictures of objects passively will nevertheless find themselves mentally naming the objects. Many experiments using the cognitive subtraction approach have used "serial subtraction" where they attempt to isolate a series of stages in processing. So in our object-naming experiment we might also include a condition of viewing meaningless shapes. Subtracting this from the passive viewing condition might identify regions involved in object recognition. The serial subtraction approach makes the assumption of "pure insertion"; that is, it assumes that each process of interest is independent. In fact, many cases are likely to involve a degree of interaction between component processes, such that adding (or subtracting) a cognitive component may affect the other components.

To overcome these limitations, many of the best functional imaging experiments use "cognitive conjunction" or "factorial designs". The logic of cognitive conjunction is to select several tasks that activate the same process of interest, each with an appropriate control. By considering *common* activations across these tasks, we can be confident that we are identifying the core process of interest. Factorial designs explicitly tackle the issue of interactions between processes. This type of design can best be illustrated using an example. Imagine we are still interested in object recognition and naming. We develop a task with four conditions:

1 Naming pictures of objects (naming and object recognition both present).
2 Naming colour of a meaningless design (naming present, object recognition absent).
3 Viewing pictures of objects (object recognition present, naming absent).
4 Viewing a meaningless design (naming and object recognition both absent).

Subtracting 3 and 4 from 1 and 2 will show us the main effect of naming. However we can also look at the interaction between object recognition and naming. By performing the subtraction (1-2) − (3-4), we can see whether the process of retrieving a name has an effect on object recognition, thus identifying whether or not the processes are independent. These types of designs can provide important clarification of models from cognitive neuropsychology.

and because more blood is required by "active" brain regions, a computer can build up an image of areas of greater (and lesser) activity based on the detection rates. SPECT differs from PET in certain technical respects, the upshot of which is that the clarity of the scans is less precise because they take longer to generate.

PET and its associated techniques were a major step forward in understanding brain function. However there are certain limitations with these methods. At a practical level, PET is a very time-consuming and expensive technique. It also involves exposing subjects to ionising radiation, and this precludes repeat scanning of the same person. The approach is also very limited in terms of temporal resolution—each PET image takes a matter of minutes to generate and represents activity across that period. It is therefore not possible to study activity related to brief or transient stimuli. Thus PET is being superseded by functional MRI for many applications. However, it still has a place in brain research, particularly in the area of neurochemistry. As more sophisticated **radio-ligands** are developed, it is becoming possible to use PET to ask questions about neurotransmitter function that other techniques simply cannot address. For example, Thomasius et al. (2006) have studied directly the effect of the drug ecstasy on brain serotonin function (using a PET ligand that binds to serotonin receptors), and related this to mood and cognitive function.

For many purposes, however, functional magnetic resonance imaging (fMRI) has become the imaging technique of choice. fMRI is carried out using the same scanner as structural MRI (see Figure 2.5)—in fact an advantage of the technique is that both structural and functional information can be obtained in a single scanning session. fMRI depends on a lucky chance of biology: that oxygenated and deoxygenated haemoglobin (the molecule in the blood that transports oxygen) have different magnetic properties. Changes in the relative concentrations of oxygenated and deoxygenated blood therefore produce a detectable magnetic signal.

This is referred to as "BOLD (blood oxygenation level dependent) contrast". BOLD contrast provides an indirect measure of neural activity, as neuronal firing has an effect on relative concentrations of oxygenated and deoxygenated blood (see Figure 2.6). These changes are subtle and detection depends on careful "tuning" of the MRI scanner. Using more powerful magnets also improves fMRI sensitivity.

fMRI has been enthusiastically embraced by neuroscience, and there has been a huge proliferation of research papers in which the technique has been used. However, fMRI is not without its limitations. Although the temporal resolution is better than that of PET, allowing neuronal responses to single events to be measured, it is still not in the league of EEG. The BOLD response occurs over a number of seconds and therefore the millisecond accuracy of EEG or MEG is not possible. It is also important to remember that fMRI measures secondary changes in haemodynamic activity and metabolism rather than directly measuring neuronal activity. This causes problems in spatial

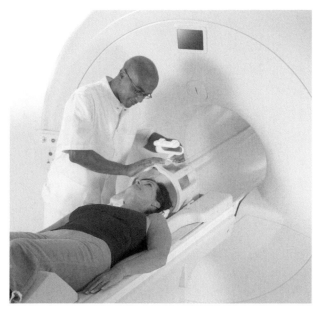

FIG. 2.5   A subject being set up in an MRI scanner. Photo courtesy of Philips Medical Systems.

accuracy and in quantitative measurement (although these are now being addressed to some extent; see Ugurbil, Toth, & Kim, 2003). Good fMRI studies also depend on good experimental design. Using fMRI to make inferences about cognitive processes is only possible if carefully designed, theory-driven experiments are used (see Henson, 2006; Poldrack, 2006).

In-vivo imaging continues to develop. In particular, MRI scanners are being used in new ways to explore different questions about brain structure and function. One example is diffusion tensor imaging or tractography, a technique that allows bundles of **white-matter** fibres, not identifiable using CT or conventional MRI, to be visualised. This allows the investigation of connectivity within neural networks (Minati & Aquino, 2006). Another example is magnetic resonance spectroscopy (MRS), a technique that studies the concentration of particular neurochemicals within specified regions of the brain. Both of these techniques have enormous potential for research as well as clinical applications.

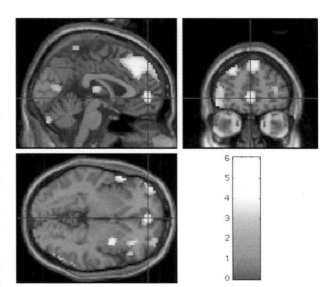

FIG. 2.6   An fMRI scan. These scans identify brain regions involved in winning money during a simple target detection task (scans obtained in the Wellcome Trust Clinical Research Facility, University of Manchester, UK).

Developments in analysis procedures are also opening up new possibilities. In particular, it is now possible to analyse patterns of connectivity between brain regions as well as region-specific activations. Thus we can determine the strength of connections between brain regions under different task conditions, and assess how these are modulated by neurological and psychiatric disease.

INTERIM COMMENT

The development of in-vivo scanning marked the beginning of a new era in brain research. For the first time scientists could examine the structure or functioning of *the living brain*. It became possible to see exactly how extensive a patient's internal brain injury or damage was, and researchers could begin to do valuable brain research in individuals with "intact" brains. By using special "labelling" techniques it even became possible to observe for the first time where in the brain drugs were acting.

Despite the scientific advances that have been made as a result of the wider availability of CT, PET, and MRI, there are drawbacks to each technique, as discussed. One additional practical drawback is worth remembering. All scanning techniques currently require the respondent to lie in a scanner. Not only can this be uncomfortable and, in the case of MRI, very noisy, but it also places significant constraints on the sorts of psychological investigation that can be conducted. Additionally, it raises questions about whether we are imaging the "normal" function of the brain. In drawing inferences from scanning results, we implicitly assume that the brain would act in the same way if a person was going about their day-to-day life as it does when they are lying in a strange scanning environment. That assumption is obviously questionable.

KEY TERM
White matter: Parts of the brain comprising axons of nerve cells, mainly responsible for neuronal transmission rather than information processing.

NEUROPSYCHOLOGICAL ASSESSMENT

The neuropsychological approach relies on using tests designed to reflect, usually in a relatively specific way, different aspects of cognitive function. Poor performance on a test may indicate focal (localised) brain damage. Poor performance on a series of tests may, on the other hand, reflect diffuse (widespread) damage. Neuropsychological assessment serves several purposes. First, it can give a "neurocognitive" profile of an individual, identifying both strengths and weaknesses in cognitive performance. For example, an individual's initial assessment may highlight a specific problem with spatial memory set against a background of above average IQ. Since many tests are "standardised", a person's performance can be readily compared with scores generated by other age- and/or sex-matched respondents (a process known as norm-referencing). Second, repeated testing over time can give an insight into changes in cognitive functioning that may relate either to recovery after accident/injury or to the progression of a neurological illness.

STANDARD AND CUSTOMISED TEST BATTERIES

In a typical neuropsychological assessment, a series of tests (called a test battery) will be given. One widely used battery is the Halstead-Reitan, which includes measures of verbal and non-verbal intelligence, language, tactile and manipulative skills, auditory sensitivity, and so on (Reitan & Wolfson, 1993). Some of the tests are very straightforward: for example, the tapping test, which assesses motor function, requires nothing more than for the respondent to tap as quickly as possible with each of his/her fingers for a fixed time period on a touch-sensitive pad. The Corsi block-tapping test measures spatial memory using a series of strategically placed wooden blocks on a tray (see Figure 2.7a). A third test measures memory span for sets of digits. Another example of a test battery is the Luria-Nebraska (Luria, 1966; see also Christensen, 1979), an even more exhaustive procedure that takes about 3 hours to administer and includes over 250 test items. Today, this battery is regarded as somewhat unwieldy, poorly standardised, and biased towards sensory, verbal, and motor functions—away from core cognitive domains of current interest such as attention, memory, and executive functioning. The battery is probably of more use as a clinical tool.

The administration of a standard lengthy test battery may be unsuitable for some individuals (such as demented or psychiatric patients) who simply do not have the requisite attention span. In such instances a customised battery may be more appropriate. Such assessments typically include some overall index of intelligence: the comprehensively norm-referenced WAIS-R (the revised Wechsler Adult Intelligence Scale; Wechsler, 1981) is still commonly used (though see below). In addition, specific measures may be adopted to test particular hypotheses about an individual. For example, if the person has received brain damage to his/her frontal lobes, tests might be selected that are known to be especially sensitive to frontal damage. The Wisconsin card sort test (see Figure 2.7b), the trails test (in which respondents have to join up numbered dots on a page according to particular rules), and verbal fluency (generating words starting with a particular letter or belonging to a specific category) are typical examples.

(a)

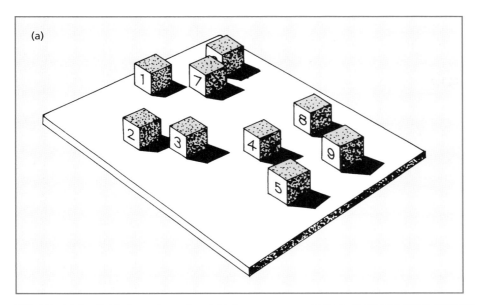

FIG. 2.7 (a) Corsi's block tapping task and (b) the Wisconsin card sort test. Corsi's test assesses spatial memory. The tester taps out progressively longer sequences of blocks to establish spatial memory "span". The respondent cannot see the numbers, so must memorise the correct sequence using spatial memory. In the Wisconsin test, the respondent sorts cards into four piles according to an "unspoken" rule: by colour, shape, or number. The only feedback received from the tester is whether or not a particular card has been correctly sorted. The respondent must use this feedback to guide future card sorts. Every so often the tester changes the sorting rule and the respondent must try to adjust to it. Source of 2.7(b): Gazzaniga et al. (1998). *Cognitive neuroscience: The biology of the mind* (Figure 11.5). © 1998 by W. W. Norton & Company, Inc. Reproduced by permission of W. W. Norton & Company, Inc.

The CANTAB (Cambridge Automated Neuropsychological Assessment battery; Robbins et al., 1994) has been developed as a battery of some 12–14 tests administered via a touch-sensitive screen. Many of the tests resemble computer games in certain respects, and are essentially computerised versions of standard pen and paper neuropsychological tests. For example the "stockings of Cambridge test" is analogous to the Tower of Hanoi test (see Figure 2.8), and the "intra/extra dimensional shift" test is based on the Wisconsin card sort test. Test norms are built into the CANTAB software, so that a particular respondent's performance on any given test can be interpreted in relation to age- and sex-matched peers (norms). The majority of the CANTAB tests are non-verbal—predominantly aimed at assessing

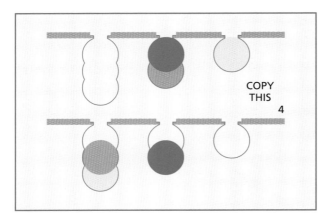

COPY
THIS
4

FIG. 2.8 Stockings of Cambridge test from the CANTAB battery. This is a test of executive function from the widely used CANTAB battery of neuropsychological tests. This particular image shows a four-move problem; respondents must try to copy the template pattern in four moves. Image kindly provided by Cambridge Cognition (© 2007 Cambridge Cognition Limited. All rights reserved. Reproduced in 2-colour from coloured original with permission).

executive and memory functions. This fully computerised battery has quickly become particularly popular with researchers and, at time of writing, has formed at least part of the neuropsychological assessment of participants in over 400 published studies. While the CANTAB battery is widely used, other computerised test batteries have also been developed in recent years and different neuropsychological research centres advocate different batteries.

Poor across-the-board performance on test batteries may indicate generalised damage, while poor performance on a particular test may signal possible localised damage or dysfunction. (In general, non-specific deficits across tests are relatively less interesting than more specific problems.) A patient with advanced dementia may perform poorly on all tests, commensurate with the widespread brain damage seen in severely demented individuals. But the neuropsychologist needs to be aware that apparent generalised deficits might alternatively represent a fundamental problem with concentration or motivation. If a person simply can't or won't make the effort to perform tests, they will typically do badly on all measures; this is sometimes seen in psychiatric patients. There are various strategies neuropsychologists can use to get round this problem, for example offering incentives or performing testing over a number of very short sessions. However, in some cases, it may remain a significant concern.

Where a subject has very selective deficits, neuropsychological test batteries can be extremely informative and allow inferences to be drawn about the location of brain damage. For example, inability to recognise objects by touch (**astereognosis**) may be a sign of damage to a fairly specific region in the **parietal lobe** (see Chapter 4). A poor verbal test score (compared with a normal non-verbal test score) may indicate generalised left hemisphere damage (see Chapter 3). In a patient with very early Alzheimer's disease, selective deficits on certain learning and memory tasks are seen, which has contributed to understanding how the pathology of the disease develops.

ASSESSING GENERAL COGNITIVE FUNCTIONING

The WAIS-R, referred to earlier, has been particularly useful for studying selective deficits because the 11 component subtests address a wide range of psychological functions. Moreover, it is possible to derive separate verbal and non-verbal estimates of IQ by amalgamating scores on the six verbal and five non-verbal subtests. Norms for each of these were derived from a sample of almost 2000 (US) respondents. The WAIS III was launched in 1997 as an updated and extended battery. Now comprising 14 subtests (the original 11 plus 3 new ones), with updated norms and the removal of items deemed to be culturally biased, subtest scores can be used to calculate verbal, performance, and general IQ as before. But additionally, four so-called "index" scores (of verbal comprehension, perceptual organisation, working memory, and processing speed) can be derived, which are said to better reflect the underlying factor structure of cognitive function than the older binary distinction.

On the minus side, it should be remembered that all three of the Wechsler intelligence scales were devised primarily to assess cognitive function in non-pathological groups, although they have in fact been extensively used with both psychiatric and neurological patients. None has proper parallel versions, and this makes retesting of individuals (who may be of interest to neuropsychologists wishing to plot change in function over time) complicated by carry-over—that is, residual learning from the first exposure to the tests. Perhaps with this problem in mind, the WASI (Wechsler Abbreviated Scale of Intelligence (Wechsler, 1999) was developed *with* parallel versions to facilitate retesting, and has quickly become an important tool for neuropsychologists. It comprises alternate versions of the most-informative four tests from the WAIS III: block design, matrix reasoning, vocabulary, and similarities. In fact a reliable assessment of general IQ can, the author claims, be derived in less than 15 minutes from just the vocabulary and matrix reasoning subtests.

An even briefer measure of IQ is the National Adult Reading Test (NART; Nelson, 1982). This allows the researcher to obtain an estimate of an individual's IQ prior to damage or disease onset. This may be useful if a neuropsychologist is making an initial assessment of a person who has been brain damaged/ill for some time. The NART rather cunningly comprises 50 words that sound different from their spelling (such as yacht, ache, and thought). The respondent reads through the list until they begin to make pronunciation errors. Such words were almost certainly learned before the onset of illness or brain damage, and because this test has been referenced against the WAIS, the cut-off point can be used to estimate IQ prior to illness, disease, or accident.

COMBINING IN-VIVO IMAGING TECHNIQUES WITH NEUROPSYCHOLOGICAL CHALLENGES

The use of neuropsychological tests in combination with in-vivo techniques promises to be one of the most informative research approaches. If a test is known to draw on the capacity of a particular brain region, it could be given to a person while he or she is being scanned. This combined technique was used by Smith and Jonides (1994) to examine the role(s) of the frontal lobes in **working memory**. They selected various neuropsychological tests of verbal and non-verbal working memory, and recorded PET scans of normal people as they completed them. The results showed a clear division of labour: non-verbal working memory led to increased right frontal activation, whereas verbal working memory caused greater activation in the left frontal (and parietal) regions (see Chapter 7 for a further discussion of Smith and Jonides' findings). Many other examples of combining neuropsychological challenge with functional imaging are discussed in subsequent chapters. For instance, see Chapter 11 for a discussion of how neuroimaging has informed our understanding of executive function using classic tests such as the Tower of London.

A slightly different way of combining neuropsychology and imaging is to perform detailed neuropsychological testing outside the scanner and then scan the people during performance of specific tasks. One area where this approach is

KEY TERM
Working memory: A form of short-term memory, first characterised by Alan Baddeley, which allows a person to hold "on-line" (and manipulate) a certain amount of information for a few seconds after it has been presented. For example, keeping a phone number in mind until you have dialled it.

proving particularly useful is in studying the early stages of dementia. Mild cognitive impairment (MCI) is relatively common in elderly populations, but in some cases MCI can progress to Alzheimer's disease. Early diagnosis of Alzheimer's disease is very important for optimal treatment and care, however it is not always easy. Recent research that combines focal neuropsychological assessment and functional imaging has suggested that this combined approach facilitates early detection. Cabranes et al. (2004) showed that lower test scores and lower left frontal blood flow predicted progression from MCI to Alzheimer's disease with high sensitivity and specificity. Similarly, Elgh et al. (2003) found that people at high risk for developing Alzheimer's disease showed poorer scores on episodic memory tasks and reduced prefrontal activation during cognitive challenge fMRI. Thus the combined neuropsychology and neuroimaging approach has clinical implications as well as furthering our theoretical understanding of how the brain works.

INTERIM COMMENT

Neuropsychological testing has gained considerable respect in recent years. However, it would be wrong to think that a battery of neuropsychological tests alone could somehow provide the researcher or clinician with a complete map of brain functioning. At best they give an indication of underlying problems. Two further concerns also merit consideration. First, an apparently normal performance on neuropsychological tests can be deceptive. We know that, as individuals recover from brain damage, they often develop alternative strategies or techniques to overcome remaining deficits—see, for example, the case study of the brain-damaged architecture student (Clarke, Assal, & DeTribolet, 1993) which we present in Chapter 4. Second, although neuropsychological and in-vivo assessments usually agree about what regions of brain are dysfunctional or damaged, they do not always do so and the reasons for this are usually unclear.

A further concern about neuropsychological testing that has received attention recently is the ecological validity of tests. A puzzling conundrum for neuropsychologists is that patients' performance on neuropsychological tests can, in fact, be inconsistent with their performance in everyday life (Wilson, 1993). Ideally, test performance should predict this, but ecological validity actually varies from test to test. For example, Chaytor, Schmitter-Edgecombe, and Burr (2006) have studied the ecological validity of executive function measures and found some standard tests "wanting" in this regard. Some researchers are now starting to develop more ecologically valid tests that aim to mimic real-life scenarios (see Burgess et al., 2006). Obviously, the test situation is likely to be different from everyday life, but the continuing challenge for researchers is to develop tests that capture everyday performance as well as possible. We return to this issue in Chapter 11.

DISSOCIATIONS AND DOUBLE DISSOCIATIONS

Neuropsychologists typically try to design studies that provide evidence of the differential performance of brain-damaged and control participants because such studies can inform structure–function relationships. Consider the following example: The right frontal lobe is thought to be important for memorising designs. To test this hypothesis, a researcher assesses memory for designs (MemD) and memory for words (MemW) in a group of people with known right frontal damage and a second group of non-brain-damaged controls.

Hypothetical results from this study are shown in Table 2.1a. At first glance they seem to support the hypothesis, because the right frontal participants appear to be selectively impaired on the MemD condition. Many neuropsychological investigations employ this sort of design, and might use the evidence of a (*single*) *dissociation* between groups in the MemD but not the MemW conditions as support for the hypothesis under investigation. However, there is a design problem with single dissociation studies stemming from the assumption that the two conditions are equally "sensitive" to differences between the two groups of participants (which may or may not be the case). For example, it could be that right frontal participants have poor attention, which happens to affect the MemD task more than the MemW task.

A much "stronger" design is one with the potential to show a *double dissociation*. For example, if we also thought that left frontal damage impaired MemW but not MemD, we could recruit two groups of patients—one with left and the other with right frontal damage—plus a control group—and test all participants on both measures. Hypothetical results from this design are shown in Table 2.1b. They indicate that one group of patients is good at one test but not the other, and the reverse pattern is true for the second group of patients. In other words, we have evidence of a double dissociation (similar to the one found by Smith and Jonides and described earlier), which suggests to neuropsychologists that the two tasks involve non-overlapping component operations that may be anatomically separable too.

TABLE 2.1 A SINGLE AND A DOUBLE DISSOCIATION EXPERIMENT (% CORRECT)

(a) Single dissociation experiment

Group	MemD	MemW
Right frontal	70%	90%
Control	95%	95%

(b) A double dissociation experiment

Group	MemD	MemW
Right frontal	70%	90%
Left frontal	93%	60%
Control	95%	95%

In the single dissociation experiment, frontal patients appear worse on the MemD task than controls, and about the same on the MemW task. However, this result might be due to poor attention (or some other extraneous variable) which happens to affect the patients on this test. In the double dissociation experiment, the "opposite" performance of right and left frontal patients suggests that damage to the different brain regions has a specific and selective effect on the two memory tests.

CHAPTER SUMMARY

Researchers interested in understanding brain function and its relations to psychological function can now draw on a wide range of investigative techniques. In this chapter we have introduced lesion and ablation, electrical/magnetic stimulation and recording, and the structural and functional in-vivo imaging procedures. Consideration is also given to the widespread use of neuropsychological testing. Researchers have moved rapidly from an era in which analysis of brain structure could usually only be assessed post-mortem to an era in which the various in-vivo imaging techniques are quickly becoming almost as commonplace as X-radiography. Their use, in combination with neuropsychological procedures, is a particularly promising research area. Imaging techniques are still evolving and the next few years hold further promise of more exciting developments in this approach to understanding brain function.

CHAPTER 3

CONTENTS

Lateralisation

INTRODUCTION

We should not be surprised that Gall regarded the cortical hemispheres as "mirror image duplicates" of one another, with the same mental faculties located **homotopically** (at the same relative location) in each—after all, the brain, like most other components of the nervous system, is superficially symmetrical along the **midline**. But closer inspection reveals many differences in structure, and behavioural studies suggest intriguing differences in function too.

The reason for these so-called asymmetries is unclear although, as the blue-print for the basic structure (and functioning) of our nervous system is under genetic control, asymmetries too are assumed to depend on the action of genes. Some researchers have suggested that they are particularly linked to the "arrival" of *Homo sapiens* as a species, an event that is thought to have occurred between 100,000 and 150,000 years ago, coincidental with the development of a sophisticated language system (Mitchell & Crow, 2005). Others have argued that the asymmetries pre-dated the appearance of language and are related to tool use, gesture, and hand preference. Corballis (1991, 2003), among others, has suggested that language skills, being analytical and sequential in nature, emerged as left hemisphere functions because this hemisphere had already been operating preferentially in this way for hundreds of thousands of years to mediate gestural (i.e., non-verbal) language and dominant hand use more generally.

Humans are not the only animals to show hemispheric specialisation (see Box 3.1) although it is undoubtedly more marked and consistent in humans than any other species. This observation alone points to an ancient evolutionary origin of laterality as being more likely. But whatever the cause or causes of asymmetry, hemispheric differences in psychological functions encompass many areas in addition to language. In this chapter we consider the various ways that scientists have examined lateralisation/hemispheric specialisation/asymmetry—the terms are sometimes used interchangeably although asymmetry in particular carries connotations about structure (see next section) as well as function—and the conclusions that they have drawn from their research.

KEY TERMS
Homotopical: Occurring at the same relative location.
Midline: Anatomically, in mammals, the imaginary line separating the left from the right side.

Box 3.1 Asymmetries in non-humans

Song birds, chickens, rodents, cats, and primates all show evidence of functional asymmetry. Nottebohm (1980), for example, has illustrated convincingly that song production in canaries depends on left brain structures, and can be disrupted by lesions here, but not by equivalent lesions in the right hemisphere. Rose (1992) showed that imprinting (the formation of early attachments and thus a form of memory) could be impaired in newborn chicks following left brain (but not right brain) lesions. Chickens appear to have right foot preference for scratching the ground when searching for food, and cats too show preferential paw use when reaching for food (Warren, Abplanalp, & Warren, 1967).

Several primate species show structural as well as functional asymmetries similar to those seen in humans: for example, old-world monkeys show both asymmetry of the Sylvian fissure and cortical torque (forward expansion; see above) of the right hemisphere, although how these relate to function remains unclear. At an individual level, non-human primates may show a preference for using one particular hand, but collectively they do not display predominant right-handedness. However, rhesus monkeys, like humans, are better able to make tactile discriminations with their left than their right hand (Hatta & Koike, 1991), whereas fine motor skills are better performed by the right than the left hand (Morris, Hopkins, & Bolser-Gilmore, 1993).

In sum, while both functional and structural asymmetries are apparent in other species, these are somewhat inconsistent, and certainly less pronounced than for humans. Some authors conclude that hemispheric specialisation is an adaptive general design principle which has simply evolved further in humans than other animals.

STRUCTURAL DIFFERENCES

Despite their superficial similarity, the two hemispheres of the human brain consistently differ in a number of characteristic ways that are summarised in Table 3.1.

TABLE 3.1 ANATOMICAL HEMISPHERIC ASYMMETRIES

- Viewed from the top of the head, the right frontal lobe extends several millimetres further forward, and the left occipital lobe further back (known as cortical torque).
- The Sylvian fissure, which is the dividing line between the frontal and temporal lobes, is less sloped on the left side than on the right.
- A region of the temporal lobe known as the planum temporale, which is adjacent to the Sylvian fissure and encompasses Wernicke's area, is significantly larger on the left than on the right.
- Cells in the region of the left frontal lobe that we now call Broca's area have many more synapses (contacts with other neurons) than the equivalent region on the right side.
- The angular gyrus (located in the posterior parietal lobe), which may be important in reading and semantic aspects of language, is larger on the left than on the right side.
- The parietal area on the right side (just behind the location of the angular gyrus on the left) is larger and has more synaptic contacts. This region is linked with visual perception and spatial processing.

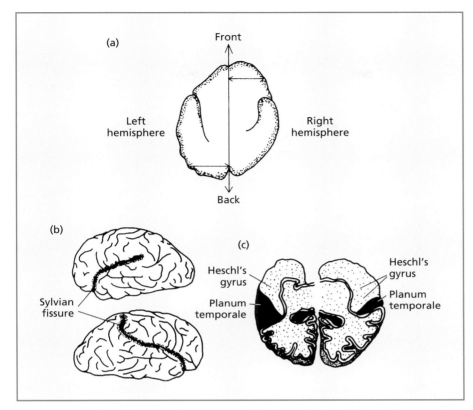

FIG. 3.1 Externally visible structural asymmetries of the human brain. (a) The right frontal region typically projects further forward and is wider than the left frontal region. The reverse pattern is seen in the occipital lobes. (Adapted from Hellige, 1990.) (b) The Sylvian fissure extends further back horizontally on the left side than the right (where it takes a more upward course). (Adapted from Kolb & Whishaw, 1996.) (c) The planum temporale is larger on the left side than on the right.

(Externally visible asymmetries are also shown in Figure 3.1.) Some of these are, so to speak, visible to the naked eye (assuming the brain is exposed), whereas others are only detectable using a microscope. Even at this relatively coarse level of analysis there are tantalising glimpses of the possible links between structure and function, with the left hemisphere's language responsibilities (function) corresponding to more complex cellular connectivity (structure) here. For example, Hutsler, Galuske, and Ralf (2003) have recently confirmed that the columnar structure (and the neuronal connections within columns) in the auditory cortex of the left hemisphere are distinct from the homotopic regions on the right. However, despite the appeal of these observations, Hutsler et al. themselves point out that actually relating structure to function, especially at this level of complexity, is notoriously problematic (see Chapter 2) and must remain, for the moment, speculative.

UNILATERAL NEUROLOGICAL DAMAGE

We cannot manipulate brain damage experimentally in humans but we can assess function in individuals whose brains have been damaged or have become diseased. However, it is important to bear in mind that the degree and extent of damage is variable and idiosyncratic, and it is difficult to generalise on the basis of case studies alone. Nevertheless, damage to the left hemisphere seems to result in a greater impairment to language-related skills than to spatial (or non-linguistic) skills, whereas the reverse is true for right hemisphere damage. A stroke affecting the left hemisphere frequently leads to aphasia (think of Broca's "Tan" for instance), whereas right hemisphere damage can lead to deficits in spatial skills such as mental rotation, map reading, orientation, and, in the most severe cases, spatial neglect, but rarely aphasia (although more subtle language deficits such as impaired prosody may arise; see Chapter 6).

More control is possible when tissue must be surgically removed for medical reasons. An early report by Taylor (1969) described two patients who underwent temporal lobectomies (ablation of temporal lobe) to remove brain tumours. Each patient completed a battery of neuropsychological and IQ tests both before and after surgery. For the patient whose left temporal lobe was removed, a significant decline in performance on tasks with a verbal component was noted, but there was little change in non-verbal function. For the patient who underwent a right temporal **lobectomy**, the exact reverse pattern of outcome was observed. Verbal skills were preserved, but spatial performance dipped markedly.

You may recall from Chapter 2 that this pattern of distinct/opposite impairment is referred to by neuropsychologists as a double dissociation, and it is also observed in patients with left and right frontal and parietal lesions. Once again (in general terms) left-sided damage tends to impact more on verbally based skills, and right-sided damage on non-verbally based skills. For example, surgical removal of tissue from the left frontal lobe may lead to a decline in verbal fluency (*"Think of as many words beginning with the letter S as possible"*), but not to design fluency (*"Draw as many patterns made of four lines as possible"*), and vice versa for right frontal ablation. Removal of tissue on the right side has additionally been associated with impairments in a wide range of psychological skills, including spatial orientation, discrimination of auditory tones, and face recognition (see also Chapter 8).

Very occasionally, and usually only in young children, it is deemed necessary to surgically ablate an entire hemisphere, or most of it (van Empelen et al., 2004). This is usually because the hemisphere has become irreparably damaged, perhaps following vascular pathology (an extensive stroke for example), or following encephalitis, or even in order to remove a widely invasive tumour. Such unfortunate cases nevertheless present fascinating opportunities for researchers to examine what functions are lost post-surgery, and more intriguingly, which ones recover. In very general terms, such individuals often show a marked recovery of function after surgery, but nevertheless remain impaired in comparison with age-matched controls. Following left hemisphere removal, a number of children have gone on to develop near-normal language function, which *must* be mediated by their right hemisphere.

The willingness of the opposite hemisphere to take over the work of the ablated one is often attributed to the remarkable degree of neuronal plasticity that is apparent in the "developing" mammalian nervous system (Isaacs et al., 1996).

KEY TERM
Lobectomy: Surgical removal of all or part of a cortical lobe (as in temporal lobectomy for removal of the temporal lobe).

Curiously however, if the lesion is localised, say to Broca's area in the left hemisphere, the recovery of language function post-surgery appears to be mediated by undamaged tissue adjacent to the lesioned site but still in the left hemisphere, suggesting a "reluctance" to relocate to the opposite hemisphere if it can be avoided—still evidence of remarkable plasticity, but not quite to the extent seen in complete hemispherectomy (Liégeois et al., 2004).

There have been no comparable studies of the effects of complete right hemispherectomy on spatial functioning, although a recent report by Backlund et al. (2005) of four hemispherectomised children (three right hemisphere) indicated "recovered" (normal) touch sensitivity for a static stimulus on the side of the body opposite to the ablation, but a failure to "recover" sensitivity to the direction of a moving tactile stimulus on the contralateral side.

These data can arguably be interpreted in two ways depending on one's viewpoint: either they can be taken as evidence of the fantastic inherent plasticity of the developing brain and the "irrelevance" of pre-determined hemispheric specialisation under these circumstances; or, more prudently perhaps, they can be viewed as evidence of the "desire" of the developing brain to adhere to the preferred blueprint if possible, and an inability to completely overcome wholesale early damage. Whatever your view, it must be said that the degree of neuronal plasticity apparent in young children is rarely seen in individuals who incur similar damage as adults.

INTERIM COMMENT

Notwithstanding the previous discussion, neuropsychologists are rightly cautious about oversimplifying the structure–function relationship (left hemisphere (language); right hemisphere (spatial functions)) to the extent that some writers, working in applied settings such as education and business, have (see Kaminski da Rosa, 1984, for an illustration of this). This is because a slightly more detailed analysis of the lesion/surgical data indicates that although left-sided damage *is* more likely to be associated with some loss of language function, other non-language functions may also be affected. For example, certain forms of apraxia (disorders of purposeful movement, introduced in Chapter 5) are linked to left-sided damage. Moreover, failure to detect emotional intonation in verbal messages, or to impart language with emotional tone (known as aprosody), both clearly para-linguistic skills, are common features of right-sided damage (see above and Chapter 6). The simplistic analysis is also complicated by both sex and handedness, and we return to these issues later in this chapter. A slightly more detailed synopsis of asymmetries is offered in Figure 3.2.

THE SPLIT-BRAIN SYNDROME

Fifty years ago, anti-convulsants (drugs for epilepsy) were not as effective as those available today, and for some people even the highest safe levels of medication could not prevent regular seizures. As these could occur 10 or even 15 times each day, normal life could be profoundly compromised by epilepsy. Scientists were also beginning to realise that the seizures themselves could cause progressive

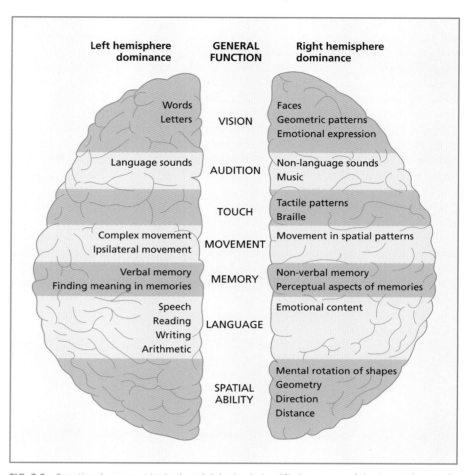

Left hemisphere dominance	GENERAL FUNCTION	Right hemisphere dominance
Words Letters	VISION	Faces Geometric patterns Emotional expression
Language sounds	AUDITION	Non-language sounds Music
	TOUCH	Tactile patterns Braille
Complex movement Ipsilateral movement	MOVEMENT	Movement in spatial patterns
Verbal memory Finding meaning in memories	MEMORY	Non-verbal memory Perceptual aspects of memories
Speech Reading Writing Arithmetic	LANGUAGE	Emotional content
	SPATIAL ABILITY	Mental rotation of shapes Geometry Direction Distance

FIG. 3.2   Functional asymmetries in the adult brain. A simplified summary of the "specialisms" of the two cerebral hemispheres. Source: (Adapted from) Pinel (2006). Published by Allyn & Bacon, Boston, MA. Copyright © 2006 by Pearson Education. Reprinted by permission of the publisher.

cumulative damage to the brain, so there were two imperatives for the development of new epilepsy treatments.

Seizures usually originate in a particular location known as the **ictal focus**, but may then spread (rather like ink on a blotter) to affect adjacent cortical regions. Sometimes, they pass via the corpus callosum (see Box. 3.2) to the opposite hemisphere to bring about a bilateral seizure. Having exhausted other treatments, two Californian surgeons, Bogen and Vogel, decided to try to contain seizure activity to just one hemisphere by lesioning the corpus callosa of their patients. Although this sounds drastic, remember that at the time (in the 1950s) scientists did not fully understand what the corpus callosum did, and they knew that animals given this surgical procedure seemed to suffer no lasting ill effects (see Figure 3.3).

Over a period of several years about 100 people underwent "sectioning" of the corpus callosum. In some cases the lesion was partial; just the anterior (front) or posterior (rear) region would be cut. For some patients, however, complete sectioning was performed, rendering the two hemispheres anatomically almost

KEY TERM
Ictal focus: The point of origin of epileptic activity, often a discrete region of damaged cortical tissue.

completely isolated from one another. Many individuals were assessed on batteries of psychological tests both before and after their operations, and at first glance the procedure appeared remarkably effective. Post-surgery, some patients were initially hemiplegic, mute, and confused, but after a period of recovery these features abated, and both the intensity and frequency of epileptic activity were almost always reduced, with some patients no longer experiencing major seizures at all. Moreover, patients' IQ scores and scores on many other tests often improved and, perhaps because of reduced seizure activity, most people claimed to feel better too. These preliminary data presented a paradox: How could a surgical procedure that involved lesioning the major inter-hemispheric pathway not have a significant effect on psychological functioning? To address this question, a group of researchers led by Sperry, Myers, and Gazzaniga developed a series of tests that were designed to shed more light on the true nature of the split-brain syndrome (see Gazzaniga & Sperry, 1967, for an early account of this work).

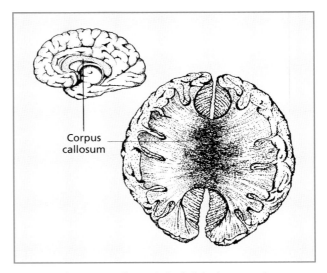

FIG. 3.3 The corpus callosum is (by far) the largest pathway linking the two sides of the brain. In adult humans it comprises several hundred million myelinated axons carrying information from the left to the right hemisphere and vice versa.

Box 3.2 The corpus callosum

This is the largest of the four nerve tracts bridging the hemispheres (the others being the anterior, thalamic, and hippocampal commissures). It develops slowly during childhood, reaching full maturity only in late adolescence, and much of this maturation process actually involves the progressive deposition of myelin, so that by early adulthood the human corpus callosum comprises between 200 and 800 million myelinated axons running transversely from one hemisphere to the other. At this stage, the structure is about 10 cm in length and more than 1 cm deep in places. The anterior section bends under and back on itself—the bend is known as the genu (knee). The mid section comprises the anterior and posterior mid-bodies and isthmus, and the most posterior "bulbous" section is known as the splenium.

The majority of callosal fibres appear to "course" from particular regions in one hemisphere to homologous (homotopic) regions in the other, although connections to non-homologous regions are also seen. Moreover, the left and right frontal lobes communicate via the anterior body, whereas the occipital lobes exchange information via the splenium. Similar precise mapping of temporal and parietal exchanges is apparent in the mid-body regions. This detail is important because it is now clear that when surgeons lesioned this structure to restrict the spread of seizure activity, their procedures were sometimes imprecise, and thus incomplete. (This has been established by MRI scanning of split-brain patients many years post-surgery.) Additionally, in other cases, surgeons deliberately sought to spare anterior or posterior regions, reasoning, in view of a patient's ictal focus, that complete sectioning would serve no additional purpose.

Individual differences in the size of the corpus callosum are of interest: for example, it has been reported that men have a larger anterior corpus callosum, whereas in women, both the isthmus and splenium are larger. However, these findings have not always been replicated and thus remain controversial (see Witelson, 1985; see also Holloway & Lacoste, 1986). Similarly, Witelson reported that individuals with mixed handedness had larger corpus callosa than right-handed individuals, but this too has been questioned by other researchers. A recent study by Chung, Dalton, and Davidson (2004) has reported that the corpus callosa of a group of autistic individuals were smaller than normal. Intriguing though this is, the significance of the finding remains, for the moment, a matter of debate.

EXPERIMENTAL STUDIES

To fully understand the experimental procedures that Sperry, Gazzaniga, and others developed it is important to realise that in higher mammals, including humans, most visual information from the right visual field (that is, everything to your right if you look straight ahead) travels from both eyes, via the visual pathways, to the *left* occipital lobe. Similarly, most information from the left visual field travels to the *right* hemisphere. Auditory and **somatosensory** input is also predominantly, though not completely, "crossed", so the left ear sends most of its sensory input to the right auditory cortex, and the left hand is controlled by, and sends sensory information back to, the right hemisphere, and vice versa for the right hand (see Figure 3.4). Sperry and colleagues were interested to know what would happen if information was presented to the split-brain patient *one hemisphere at a time*. Using a **tachistoscope**, they presented visual stimuli very briefly to either the left or right of a central fixation point on a screen in front of the patient. (A presentation duration of under 200 ms allowed for accurate recognition while ensuring that the participant did not have time to move their eyes towards the stimulus, which would have meant that the image went to both hemispheres.) After each presentation the participant had to say what (if anything) they had seen. Sometimes, they were also given the opportunity to reach behind a screen to feel items (with either their left or right hand) that might be related to the stimuli presented via the tachistoscope. On other occasions, they were invited to draw (again with either their left or right hand) images of the presented material.

With these procedures the true nature of the split-brain syndrome was revealed. Consider, for example, the results of an early study reported by Sperry (1968). If a picture of a car was flashed to the right of the fixation point, the patient reported seeing a car. This would be expected because the image travelled to the left (talking) hemisphere so the patient could say what they saw. If the same picture was flashed to the left of the fixation point, the patient usually reported seeing nothing: now the image went to the "non-speaking" right hemisphere. However, if the patient was allowed to reach behind a screen with their left hand, they could usually select a model car from among other out-of-sight objects. (Remember that the left hand connects to the right hemisphere.) Similarly, if the patient was allowed to "doodle" with their left hand, a drawing of

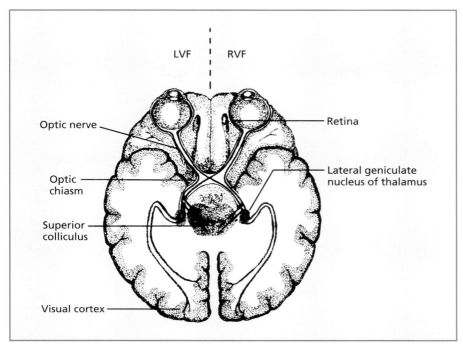

FIG. 3.4   Visual pathways from eye to brain: the route from retina to occipital cortex via the lateral geniculate nuclei of the thalamus. Note that information from the right visual field (everything to the right as you look straight ahead) entering *both* eyes will be channelled to the left occipital lobe. Visual input from the left visual field will be fed to the right occipital lobe.

a car often appeared! Even more amazingly, when asked why they had drawn a car, patients usually expressed surprise and were unable to give the right answer (see Figure 3.5a). We return briefly to consider the significance of this last observation for recent ideas about consciousness in Chapter 9.

THE SPLIT-BRAIN SYNDROME AND LANGUAGE

The results of these early split-brain studies supported the view that for almost all right-handers, and the majority of left-handers, control of speech was localised to the left hemisphere. Did this mean that the right hemisphere was devoid of all language functions? How, for example, would spilt-brain patients deal with letters or words presented to the right hemisphere? The results of such studies are not quite as clear-cut as we might expect. Gazzaniga and Hillyard (1971) reported that when words were briefly presented to the left visual field (right hemisphere) they could not be read aloud, but split-brain patients could often select related items with their left hand from behind a screen. This and other similar observations soon led to the counter-claim that the right hemisphere also possessed language skills but was simply mute (see Figure 3.5b).

This view was partly supported by Zaidel (1978) who developed a lens system (as an alternative to the tachistoscope) as a means of selectively presenting visual input to just one hemisphere. This apparatus comprised a contact lens with one visual field occluded (blacked out). A stalk attached to the lens held a display area at the other end, thus ensuring that any eye movements would cause

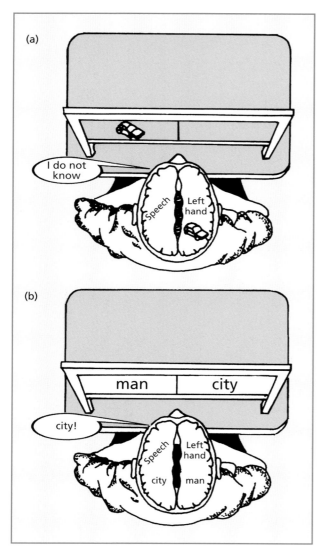

FIG. 3.5 A typical split-brain experiment with objects and words. In (a) the respondent is unable to "say" what image has been briefly projected to the non-speaking right hemisphere. In (b) the respondent reports only the word appearing in the right visual field which projects to the "speaking" left hemisphere. (Adapted from Temple, 1993.)

KEY TERMS
Lexicon: Loosely equates to stored vocabulary: that is, one's long-term memory of native-tongue words (estimated to be about 50,000 for English speakers).
Syntax: The rules governing the structure of sentences.

corresponding display movements. This, along with the occluded visual field, ensured that whatever was shown on the display would only register in one hemisphere. Because Zaidel's system was not restricted to brief presentations he could present longer words. Alternatively, he could present linguistic material aurally (and thus bilaterally), but require participants to make response selections unilaterally from a choice of alternatives presented to just one or other visual field via his lens. Using this method, and working in depth with two spilt-brain patients, Zaidel reported that the right hemisphere had an extensive **lexicon** (vocabulary) equivalent to that of a normal 10-year-old. A schematic diagram of Zaidel's lens system is shown in Figure 3.6.

Clearly then, the right hemisphere was not devoid of all language functions. However, notwithstanding the discovery of a right hemisphere lexicon in a small number of split-brain patients, Zaidel found little evidence of right hemisphere **syntax**. This was apparent, for example, from his participants' difficulties in completing the Token Test (DeRenzi & Vignolo, 1962) in which respondents have to follow a set of simple verbal instructions, such as "*Place the yellow circle above the blue square*". Zaidel's participants performed at about the same level as patients with severe aphasia. In other words, despite an extensive vocabulary, the right hemisphere's ability to extract meaning from sentences was clearly limited.

The debate about the extent of right hemisphere language function has nevertheless rumbled on. Critics have pointed out that only a small proportion of the split-brain cohort (probably no more than six right-handed cases) have shown any notable right hemisphere linguistic skills, and that even for these individuals there was no evidence of right hemisphere "generative syntax" (the ability to produce grammatically structured word strings assessed by left-handed writing: see Gazzaniga, 2000).

Indeed, the integrity of lexical organisation (the way in which words are assumed to be stored in terms of sound, meaning, physical properties, and so on) in the right hemisphere has now also been questioned in view of the absence of a "priming effect" for letters presented to the left visual field of split-brain patients. This effect is apparent in intact individuals by dint of faster reaction times to upper-case single letters that are preceded by lower-case identical letters, compared with non-identical ones. In one intensely researched patient (JW) priming was apparent only for stimuli presented to the right visual field. This patient also

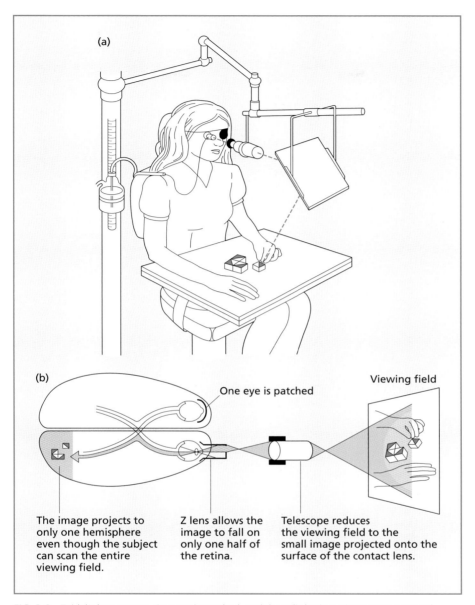

(a)

(b)

One eye is patched

Viewing field

The image projects to only one hemisphere even though the subject can scan the entire viewing field.

Z lens allows the image to fall on only one half of the retina.

Telescope reduces the viewing field to the small image projected onto the surface of the contact lens.

FIG. 3.6   Zaidel's lens system. One eye is patched, and the split-brain patient wears a special contact lens on the other eye to circumvent eye movements (the lens moves with the eye). Visual images are projected to just one half of the lens, enabling Zaidel to present material to just one hemisphere for extended periods of time. Source: Adapted from Zaidel (1978) in Caramazza & Zurif (Eds.) *Language acquisition and language breakdown* (p. 233) © 1978 The Johns Hopkins University Press. Adapted with permission of The Johns Hopkins University Press.

had difficulties in judging which of two words presented to the right hemisphere was sub/superordinate (e.g., animal–rabbit) or in deciding whether two words were antonyms (semantic opposites) of each another. These findings suggest that the right hemisphere is unable to access so-called parallel processing mechanisms, and relies instead on less efficient serial ones.

Nevertheless, on rare occasions, right-handed split-brain patients may develop the ability to speak single words with their right hemisphere! For patient JW, referred to above, speech only developed 13 years after surgery. This is an astonishing finding, although there are parallels in the neurology literature which includes several reports of adults who, having lost their left hemisphere (through accident or surgery), subsequently developed rudimentary right hemisphere language skills. Recovery of function is, of course, much more likely in children, as discussed earlier.

THE SPLIT-BRAIN SYNDROME AND OTHER PSYCHOLOGICAL FUNCTIONS

The split-brain studies support the idea of a key role for the left hemisphere in linguistic skills, but do they tell us anything about the particular roles and responsibilities of the right hemisphere? Franco and Sperry (1977) reported a study in which right-handed split-brain patients were tested using both their right and left hands on a range of visuospatial tasks including route finding and solving jigsaw puzzles. These patients consistently performed better with their non-preferred left hand than with their right hand. This finding is similar to that reported by Sperry, Gazzaniga, and Bogen (1969) in which split-brain patients were tested using a version of the block design test (see Chapter 8 for an example). In this test, geometric visual patterns must be "built" using individual coloured blocks. Right-handed split-brain patients could do this spatial construction test much more effectively with their non-preferred left hand (which is connected to the right hemisphere) than with their dominant hand.

Levy, Trevarthen, and Sperry (1972) presented data consistent with the view that face processing may also be dealt with preferentially in the right hemisphere. Split-brain patients were shown images of pairs of half-faces via a tachistoscope. These "chimeric" images might, for example, comprise half the face of a girl on the left side, and half the face of a man on the right (see Figure 3.7). The fixation point was exactly on the joint at the bridge of the nose. When a participant was asked to say what they had seen, they usually reported seeing an intact (i.e., complete) picture of a man. We might have predicted this, because this half-image went to the left/talking hemisphere. However, when asked to select what they had seen from a set of complete pictures, the same split-brain patient invariably chose the picture of the girl, which had gone to their right hemisphere (see Figure 3.8). It is important to note that we have referred to this as evidence of a *preferential* effect, because further work has confirmed that both hemispheres can "recognise" faces (Gazzaniga, 1989). Indeed, the left hemisphere may be better than the right at processing familiar faces, whereas

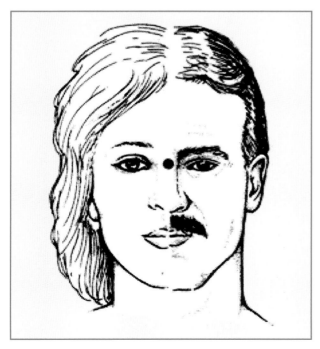

FIG. 3.7   Example of a chimeric image showing fixation point.

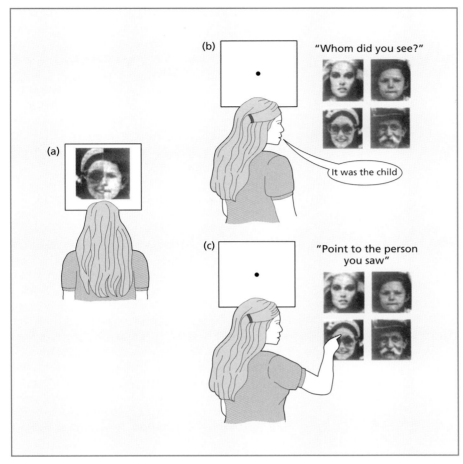

FIG. 3.8 Summary of Levy et al.'s (1972) split-brain study. The split-brain patient views chimeric figures (a). When she is asked to say what she saw (b), she describes the whole image of the half chimeric figure from her right visual field (the child). When asked to "select" what she saw, the right hemisphere tends to dominate (c) and she chooses the whole image of the half chimeric figure from her left visual field that projected to her right hemisphere (the woman wearing glasses). Source: Levy, J., Trevarthen, C. W., & Sperry, R. W. (1972). Perception of bilateral chimeric figures following hemispheric deconnection. *Brain*, *95*, 61–78. Reproduced with permission.

the right hemisphere seems specialised for dealing with unfamiliar or novel faces (Gazzaniga & Smylie, 1983).

In fact, right hemisphere advantages equivalent to the left hemisphere advantage for generative syntax (and other language functions) are hard to come by in split-brain research. However, one illustration is seen in the work of Corballis, Funnell, and Gazzaniga (1999) on perceptual grouping using figures derived from the Kanizsa illusion. Figures similar to those used by Corballis are illustrated in Figure 3.9. In one condition, split-brain and control respondents had to judge whether the illusory rectangle (formed by the four segmented circles) was fat or thin. With the versions on the left in Figure 3.9, although patients were not as good in general at this discrimination as controls, there was no laterality effect: left and right hemispheres were equally proficient. But when outlines were added to the segmented circles (versions on the right in Figure 3.9) in the so-called amodal

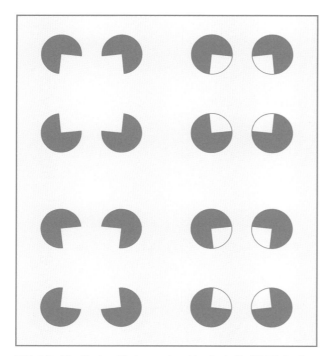

FIG. 3.9 The Kanizsa illusion explored by Corballis (1999). Both hemispheres can decide whether the illusory shapes (left) are "fat" or "thin". When outlines are added so that shapes can only be perceived by amodal completion (right), a more difficult task, only the right hemisphere can still tell the difference. Adapted from Corballis, P. M., Funnell, M. G., and Gazzaniga, M. S. (1999). A dissociation between spatial and identity matching in callosotomy patients. *Neuroreport*, *10*, 2183–2187. Reproduced with permission of Lippincott Williams & Wilkins.

completion condition (which is generally thought to be harder), a clear laterality effect emerged, with the right hemisphere significantly out-performing the left. This finding has been interpreted in a number of different ways, but one explanation is that the right hemisphere has an inherently more "holistic" processing style attuned to the **gestalt** nature of this task, which becomes particularly apparent in the harder amodal condition. We will return to the question of differential processing styles later in this chapter.

The surgery that brings about the split-brain syndrome effectively disconnects the two hemispheres. The amazing thing is that it has so little effect on routine daily activities for the patients themselves. Just occasionally, however, anecdotal accounts from individuals suggest that in particular situations there may be some disagreement between hemispheres (a phenomenon known as hemispheric rivalry). One female split-brain patient complained that as she went to select a dress from her wardrobe with her right hand, she found her left hand reaching for a different one. On another occasion the right hand turned the heating up, only for the left hand to turn it down again! Experimentally, this apparent absence of inter-hemispheric collaboration is best illustrated by the general failure of split-brain patients to combine (in any meaningful sense) potentially linkable information sent simultaneously to separate hemispheres. For example, tachistoscopic presentation of the words "sky" and "scraper" briefly to the two hemispheres failed to generate any drawings of skyscrapers. Instead, patients drew images depicting clouds in the sky and scraper-like tools (Kingstone & Gazzaniga, 1995).

That these examples of rivalry or absence of collaboration are few and far between is probably because in ordinary day-to-day activities visual, auditory, and most other sensory information actually finds its way into both hemispheres. (It takes a group of cunning researchers to think of situations in which input is restricted to just one.) Patients additionally develop strategies to try to ensure that sensory information gets to both hemispheres. The use of exaggerated head movements is one trick. Another is to make more use of "cross-cueing", essentially converting the sensory input into a different modality that will be available to both hemispheres, as illustrated by the following example: a split-brain patient trying to identify a comb by touch alone might tweak the teeth, which will make sounds that travel to both ears, and hence to both hemispheres. It is additionally likely that some "recovery" of inter-hemispheric communication may be achieved through the "recruitment" either of spared corpus callosum tissue (tissue that was not lesioned in the original surgery) or by increased use of one or more of the other non-lesioned commissures.

KEY TERM

Gestalt: A collection of physical, biological, psychological, or symbolic entities that creates a unified concept, configuration, or pattern.

INTERIM COMMENT

Despite the wealth of findings to have emerged from more than 40 years of research into the split-brain syndrome, caution is required in evaluating it. First, the individuals who underwent the surgery could not be regarded as a normal or random sample. They were, in reality, a very atypical group of individuals who had suffered from intractable epilepsy and, in the process, had usually been treated with a range of powerful drugs for many years. Second, it is likely that the cumulative effects of seizure activity will have led to discrete areas of damage and the possibility of shifts in lateralisation prior to any surgery. Third, background information about IQ or other basic cognitive abilities such as memory or attention is missing from some split-brain cases. Fourth, the extent of callosal lesion described in a patient's medical notes has not always been confirmed by later scan (although not all split-brain patients have subsequently been scanned). Finally, most of the published work on the syndrome has actually been based on intensive research with just a small proportion of the entire cohort of cases. Overall, it is probably best to regard the evidence from individuals who have had spilt-brain surgery as just one strand of a comprehensive research quest (applying the principle of converging operations, so to speak) to establish the true nature of the different psychological specialisms of the cerebral hemispheres.

CALLOSAL AGENESIS

The split-brain procedure was, of course, usually carried out on adults who had been born with an intact corpus callosum. However, a small number of people are born with a grossly malformed or entirely missing corpus callosum (see Figures 3.10a and b). Callosal agenesis, as the condition is known, is a very rare disorder

(a)   (b)

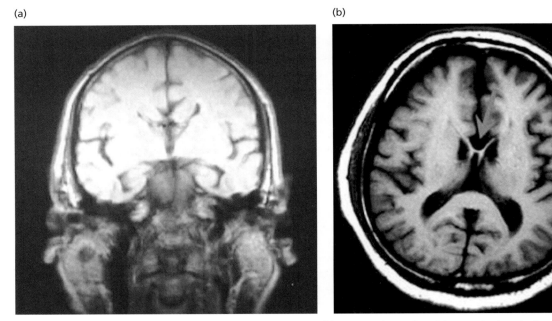

FIG. 3.10   Callosal agenesis. (a) Coronal MRI of complete agenesis. (b) Horizontal MRI of partial agenesis; the splenium is spared. The arrow depicts the intact optic chiasm (the point where about half the axons of the optic nerve from each eye cross to the other side).

of unknown cause, and is often associated with other structural anomalies. In particular, there are more pathways linking the front and back of each hemisphere, and pathways between the hemispheres other than the corpus callosum (notably the anterior commissure and/or the hippocampal commissure) are sometimes more fully developed. Other congenital abnormalities are often apparent, including various brain malformations and ventricular enlargement/displacement. In view of these structural anomalies we might expect acallosal children to have multiple handicaps, and in reality the majority (perhaps four out of five) do. But some do not, and these children are of particular interest because, in principle, they offer an opportunity to examine the role of the corpus callosum during development. If these individuals show the "usual" pattern of asymmetry, this would suggest that lateralisation is determined very early on in life and that the corpus callosum is not necessary for its development. If, on the other hand, lateralisation is partly a developmental process that depends on the corpus callosum, we should find abnormalities of lateralisation in acallosal cases. It is also of interest to compare such individuals with split-brain cases (Geffen & Butterworth, 1992).

In general, research on acallosal children has indicated that they too have language skills lateralised to the left hemisphere, and spatial skills lateralised to the right—findings that tend to support the first hypothesis that lateralisation is not gradually acquired during childhood. However, people with callosal agenesis do have certain difficulties with aspects of *both* language *and* spatial processing. In language tasks, difficulties are frequently reported when the "sound" of a word (testing the integrity of the phonological processing) is important. This becomes apparent in rhyming tasks or when the participant is asked to generate words that sound alike (Jeeves & Temple, 1987). Adding to this picture, acallosal people also have difficulties with spatial tasks such as jigsaws, copying drawings, puzzles, depth perception, and so on (Temple & Ilsley, 1993). The reasons for these deficits are not known but it is likely that, as with other tasks, these are ordinarily best dealt with by a collaborative brain effort involving networks of neurons spanning both hemispheres, which, of course, would be compromised in acallosal people. A recent illustration of the subtle "higher-order" psychological deficits resulting from this "mis-wiring" is provided by Brown et al. (2005). They reported that a group of acallosal adults struggled to understand narrative jokes that depended on verbal nuance, double meanings, and so on, even after controlling for verbal IQ. Anecdotal reports from relatives of acallosal individuals also attest to subtle psychosocial impairments linked to over-literal interpretation, superficiality, and impaired performance on tests that address "**theory of mind**" skills (similar deficits to those observed in autistic individuals; see Chapter 10).

Nevertheless, the most consistent and obvious deficits seen in callosal agenesis relate directly to the general problem of inter-hemispheric transfer. Indeed, a strong hint about the role of the corpus callosum in cortical functioning comes from the observation that acallosal children and adults are very clumsy in tasks that require bimanual cooperation. Examples include playing a musical instrument, doing certain sports, or even tying shoelaces. In certain respects, acallosal adults are rather like normal young children whose corpus callosum is immature. Its presence seems less involved in the process of shaping asymmetry than in promoting interaction between the hemispheres.

INTERIM COMMENT

In many cases of callosal agenesis other brain abnormalities are also apparent, so it is difficult for neuropsychologists to identify with any confidence those behavioural disturbances that have resulted specifically from the absence of a corpus callosum. In cases where meaningful data have been collected, asymmetries occur regardless, indicating that the corpus callosum is not necessary for lateralisation to develop.

Actually, some inter-hemispheric transfer is still apparent in acallosal people, who can, for example, sometimes tell whether two objects held in the left and right hand (but out of sight) are the same or different, although response speeds are invariably slower than for "intact" controls. It is widely presumed that this occurs via one or more of the remaining intact transverse pathways, illustrating once again the brain's ability to adapt in order to overcome adversity. However, the general clumsiness and lack of two-handed coordination seen in acallosal individuals are reminders of the importance of rapid inter-hemispheric exchange of information (via the corpus callosum) for normal behaviour.

ASYMMETRIES IN NORMAL INDIVIDUALS

A variety of experimental procedures permit investigation of lateralisation in normal individuals. Dichotic listening tasks take advantage of the fact that most auditory input to the right ear is relayed to the opposite auditory cortex for detailed processing, and vice versa for the left ear. Different auditory stimuli can thus be presented simultaneously to both ears (via stereo headphones) and participants can be asked to report what is heard. Most research of this kind shows a small but consistent right ear advantage for linguistic material (Kimura, 1973). This is thought to occur because words heard by the right ear are processed directly by the left hemisphere, whereas words heard by the left ear are initially processed by the right hemisphere, before being relayed to the left hemisphere for fuller analysis.

Of course, it could be argued that these findings simply illustrate a superiority of the right ear for auditory materials, but Bartholomeus (1974) established a double dissociation using dichotic presentation of letter strings sung to well-known tunes (for example, the letters p-g-t-v-l-m-d to the tune of "Twinkle, twinkle, little star"). In a subsequent recognition test, respondents showed a right ear advantage for letter recognition and a left ear advantage for tune recognition. Brancucci et al. (2005) have recently additionally confirmed a left ear (right hemisphere) advantage for discrimination of "intensity" for dichotically presented auditory tones and speech sounds.

The same general pattern of left hemisphere advantage for verbal material and right hemisphere advantage for non-verbal material appears to hold in other modalities too. Normal participants can recognise words more quickly when they are presented briefly (using a tachistoscope or computer) to the right visual field, and faces more efficiently when presented to the left visual field (Levine, Banich, & Koch-Weser, 1988). Asymmetry can also be seen in relation to movement. While most humans are right-handed, a motor skill performed with the right hand is more likely to be interfered with by a concurrent language task than the same skill performed by the left hand. You can illustrate this in a very simple experiment. Ask a friend to balance a stick on the end of the first finger of either their left or right hand. When they have mastered this task, ask them to shadow (i.e., repeat as soon as they hear it) a paragraph of text that you read aloud. The concurrent verbal task will usually affect right-hand balance sooner than left-hand balance.

WHAT IS LATERALISED?

Despite our previous reservations about oversimplistic interpretations of data, the accumulating evidence from brain-damaged, split-brain, acallosal, and normal individuals reviewed so far does suggest a general division of labour along the lines of language (left hemisphere) and non-language (right hemisphere), and it is easy to see why this model has been the dominant one until quite recently. However, in recent years a somewhat different explanation of laterality effects has grown in popularity. The "processing styles" approach (Levy & Trevarthen, 1976) suggests that the main functional difference between the hemispheres is not so much "what" they process, but "how" they process it. According to this view, the left hemisphere is specialised to process information in an "analytical-sequential" way, whereas the right hemisphere adopts a more "holistic-parallel" mode of processing. In other words, the left hemisphere's modus operandi is to break tasks down into smaller elements that are dealt with one by one, whereas the right hemisphere tends to ignore the fine detail, paying more attention to the "whole image".

One advantage of this approach is that it allows for the possibility that *both* hemispheres will be involved in linguistic *and* spatial tasks (as strongly suggested by the deficits apparent in acallosal individuals), but that they will differ in the type of processing that is undertaken. For example, the right hemisphere is better at judging whether two photographs are of the same person. Face recognition is a holistic skill in the sense that it involves putting together "the facial image" from its individual elements. However, the left hemisphere is better at identifying individual facial features that may distinguish between two otherwise identical faces. This is an analytic skill, because it requires the "whole" to be broken down into its constituent parts. Language is both sequential and analytical—sequential because word order is critical for meaning; analytical because the meaning of (spoken) language depends on breaking up what is, in effect, a continuous stream of verbal sounds in order to identify words and understand the message. It is thus dealt with mainly by the left hemisphere, whereas facial recognition requires a holistic analysis and is thus dealt with more effectively by the right hemisphere.

The different processing styles of the two hemispheres were very clearly illustrated in a study by Sergent (1982). She used stimuli (similar to those developed by Navon, 1977) that were large capital letters, made up of small letters that were either the same as, or different from, the capital letter. The stimuli were shown briefly via a tachistoscope to either the left or right visual fields of normal participants who had to indicate whether or not particular target letters were present. On some trials participants were directed to attend to the large capital letters and at other times to the small letters (that made up the capitals). Sergent found that the left hemisphere (right visual field presentation) was better at detecting the small letters, and the right hemisphere (left visual field presentation) was better for the large letters. The left hemisphere focused on the fine detail, while

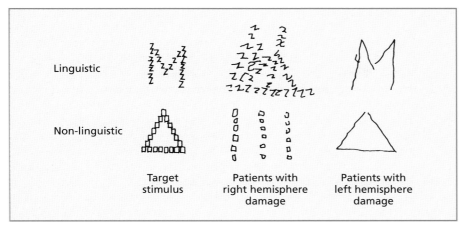

FIG. 3.11   Figures similar to those used by Delis et al. (1986) which comprise large images made up of smaller, different components. Patients with left-sided damage tend to make identification or memory errors relating to the fine detail. Those with right-sided damage are more likely to make "holistic" errors.

the right hemisphere attended to the "big picture". Similar findings have been reported by Delis, Robertson, and Efron (1986) in their study of memory impairment in unilaterally damaged individuals (see Figure 3.11).

INTERIM COMMENT

These studies show us that rather than having absolute and exclusive responsibilities, the cortical hemispheres may have complementary processing roles: The right hemisphere preferentially sees (so to speak) the forest, while the left hemisphere sees the trees. The right hemisphere preferentially processes information at a coarser level than the left, which deals with information at a more detailed and local level. Analytical and sequential aspects of language are thus dealt with predominantly (but not exclusively) by the left hemisphere, whereas more holistic aspects of language such as emotional intonation or interpretation are dealt with by the right. Likewise, spatial tasks, which usually involve integrative rather than analytic skills, are handled more efficiently by the right hemisphere. This model of hemispheric specialisation, with its emphasis on processing style rather than psychological function, arguably makes better sense of the laterality research data than the traditional left brain (language), right brain (spatial skills) model, and is becoming widely accepted by neuropsychologists. However, it is important to remember that with the possible exception of fluent speech production, *both* hemispheres can actually mediate *most* skills; so what we have is a preferential (or more efficient) processing style for one or other hemisphere rather than an absolute division of labour.

INTER-HEMISPHERIC TRANSFER VIA THE CORPUS CALLOSUM

Despite its heuristic appeal, the processing styles approach still doesn't entirely explain the "seamless" nature of psychological functioning. People intuitively "feel" they have a single brain in their heads, not two separate processors set to operate at different levels of analysis. Moreover, we also tend to respond serially; humans actually have difficulty doing two different things at once. You will probably be aware of the playground prank in which a child tries to pat their head and rub their stomach at the same time! This phenomenon can be examined experimentally by asking respondents to draw shapes simultaneously with both hands. Intact individuals can do this with simple shapes that are either identical or mirror images of one another, but not (easily) for shapes where one is rotated 90° in relation to the other. Split-brain patients, however, can do this easily. This suggests that the spatial representations of movements remain independent for split-brain patients, but not for healthy controls ... and this leads to their impaired performance (Franz, Ivry, & Gazzaniga, 1996). On the other hand, in a study by Sergent (1990), split-brain patients had difficulty deciding whether (or not) pairs of photographs presented briefly and simultaneously to right and left visual fields were of the same or different people. As we mentioned earlier, normal people can usually complete this task without error, even when the photographs are taken from a variety of different angles and perspectives. Both these observations illustrate the importance of the corpus callosum for integrating the activity of the two hemispheres. Although other pathways connecting the two sides of the brain exist, the corpus callosum is the largest commissure, and it enables the two hemispheres of the cortex to relay information backwards and forwards almost instantaneously: ERP recording has shown that inter-hemispheric transfer takes no more than 20 ms. When this pathway is absent from the outset (as in callosal agenesis) other pathways may take on some of the work normally done by it, but they generally fail to work as efficiently or as quickly in the cause of inter-hemispheric transfer, hence the slower response speeds seen on tasks requiring inter-hemispheric comparisons. From the first example however, it is clear that inter-hemispheric transfer does not always facilitate "cooperation" between the hemispheres, and several scientists have argued that a significant proportion of callosal transfer actually involves inhibition rather than facilitation of the "rival" hemisphere (Ringo et al., 1994). As we shall see (in Chapter 9), others, most notably Gazzaniga (cf. Gazzaniga, 2002), have argued that at the highest level of conscious cognitive control, it is the left hemisphere that wins this particular rivalry.

INDIVIDUAL DIFFERENCES IN BRAIN ORGANISATION

The evidence we have considered thus far indicates that both structural and functional asymmetries are intrinsic features of nervous system development. However, it is also of interest to know whether (or not) the degree of lateralisation described above varies between people, and if so, why. Two areas where these questions seem particularly relevant (and controversial) are handedness and gender.

HANDEDNESS

Neuropsychologists are now sure that handedness is something you are born with rather than something you acquire with experience, although researchers continue to debate whether it is genetic in origin as Annett (1985) has argued, or related to intrauterine factors such as the position of the foetus in the womb (Previc, 1991). In fact, the two accounts may not be mutually exclusive, and it is interesting to note that researchers using **ultrasound** have reported that hand preference is already apparent in foetuses at 15 weeks of gestation, judging by their preference for sucking either left or right hand digits (Hepper, Shalidullah, & White, 1991). A recent follow-up of this cohort (now aged 10–12 yrs) has, incidentally, confirmed that early thumb preference is an excellent predictor of later handedness, especially for right-handers (Hepper, Wells, & Lynch, 2005). Hepper, McCartney, and Alyson (1998) also reported a strong preference for right (over left) arm movements in 10-week-old foetuses. This is a fascinating finding because this laterality preference pre-dates, by several weeks, any overt indications of asymmetry in the developing brain.

About one in ten humans is left-handed according to Annett (1985), although *degree* of left- or right-handedness certainly varies. Left-handedness has, historically, been frowned on and, at one time, it was common practice for "natural" left-handers to be forced to use their non-dominant right hands both at school and at home. Interestingly, as this practice has faded the proportion of left-handers has increased, but only to the figure cited above.

For many years it was more or less assumed by psychologists that the organisation of the left-hander's brain was the mirror image of that of the right-hander. However, data from the Wada test (see Chapter 2) put paid to this idea (Rasmussen & Milner, 1977). As expected, results indicated a pattern of left-lateralised language for almost all right-handed individuals. But for left-handers a different result emerged. About two-thirds have the same arrangement as right-handers. Of the remainder, about half show the opposite pattern (reversed asymmetry) and half show language and non-language skills both distributed in each hemisphere (bilateral distribution). Nevertheless, combining these figures, about 96.5% of the population has left hemisphere specialisation for language generation. These data have recently been broadly confirmed by Knecht et al. (2000a; 2000b) using "functional transcranial Doppler sonography". This new procedure can measure speed of blood flow independently in each hemisphere, indicating which is more active during verbal tasks and, by implication, dominant for language.

HANDEDNESS AND COGNITIVE FUNCTION

What, if any, then, are the psychological consequences of left- or right-handedness? Researchers have tried to answer this question by examining psychological deficits in right- and left-handed individuals who have incurred brain damage. In one of the most comprehensive reviews of such cases, Hardyck and Petrinovich (1977) found that, on average, left-handers with damage to the right hemisphere were more likely to experience language problems than right-handers with similar damage (14% versus 7%). The incidence of aphasia following left-sided damage was more or less the same for right- and left-handers. Similarly, spatial skills were more likely to be affected after right hemisphere damage in right-handers than in left-handers. Taken together, these findings suggest that left-handers as a group may be less "lateralised" than right-handers. Research on healthy left-handers using tests of both dichotic listening and divided visual attention has also led to the suggestion that left-handers show less functional asymmetry than right-handers (Springer & Deutsch, 1998). However, are these

KEY TERM
Ultrasound: An antenatal procedure for generating images of unborn children.

results so surprising? Remember that some left-handers show left hemisphere dominance for language, some show right hemisphere dominance, and some show mixed patterns. So, as a group, we might expect to find that left-handers were less lateralised, on average, than right-handers. The more interesting question would be to compare test performance between left-handers with left, right, and mixed dominance patterns, but at present large-scale studies of this type have yet to be undertaken.

It has long been known that left-handedness is more common among both developmental- and reading-delayed individuals. Developmental dyslexia is, for example, several times more common in left- than right-handed children (Geschwind & Behan, 1982; and see also Tonnessen et al., 1993). Is there any evidence that this relationship generalises to the "normal" population? Several research projects have set out to compare performances of normal left- and right-handers on measures that tap higher mental functions, but the results have been rather inconsistent. In Hardyck and Petrinovich's (1977) **meta-analysis** of 14 studies, left-handers did marginally worse than right-handers on some tests, and better than right-handers on others. In one study for example, left-handers were reported to have a small but consistent generalised non-verbal IQ deficit as measured by the WAIS (Levy, 1969). However, her data were drawn from a sample of just 10 left-handers and 15 right-handers, all of whom were graduate students. It would, we think, be fair to describe this as a small and unrepresentative sample.

Levy's research findings have not been well supported in follow-up studies, and where differences have been reported, they have usually been so small (Ratcliff & Newcombe, 1973) that critics have raised the possibility that they are statistical artifacts rather than genuine effects (Vogel, Bowers, & Vogel, 2003). A study unlikely to draw criticisms about sample size is that of Halpern, Haviland, and Charles (1998) who looked at the relations between handedness and intelligence in 174,547 adults who had completed the (US) Medical College Admissions Test. There was no evidence of an overall handedness effect; rather a mixed pattern of outcomes, with left-handers scoring lower overall on a writing test, and higher on a test of verbal reasoning. Frankly, we should not be surprised at the absence of effect on generalised measures of cognitive functioning. After all, as far as we know, left-handers have never actually formed either an elite or an under-class of humans (notwithstanding historic stigma for left-handedness based on religious or cultural prejudices), an observation strongly indicative of a de facto parity with right-handers.

But if generalised cognitive differences between left- and right-handers have been somewhat elusive, perhaps there are nevertheless specific cognitive domains that may distinguish the two groups. The answer to our rhetorical question, however, would seem to be that absences of difference outweigh instances of difference, unless, perhaps, one examines the extremes of the handedness distribution. For example, Coren (1992) has argued that left-handedness is over-represented among both the extraordinarily intelligent and the mentally disabled. Kopiez, Galley, and Lee (2006) have recently reported that sight-reading skills are better in left- than right-handed professional musicians, although the effect only reached statistical significance in males. Schachter and Ransil (1996) reported that left-handedness was much more common than would be expected among architects, and Coren (1995) has similarly suggested that left-handedness is more common among chess masters and mathematicians. On the other hand, Gabbard, Hart, and Gentry (1995) reported that in young children, motor performance was

KEY TERM
Meta-analysis: A research technique in which data from similar but separate projects are pooled into a single data set to increase statistical power.

impaired in left- (and mixed-) handers compared to right-handers, whereas Kilshaw and Annett (1983) argued that poor motor coordination was worst in extreme right-handed individuals. Finally, although Leask and Crow (2001) reported that both verbal and non-verbal cognitive abilities were more likely to be impaired in individuals with ambidexterity than in clear left- or right-handers, Francks et al. (2003) failed to replicate this finding.

In sum, the available data provide a somewhat confused picture of the relationship between cognition and handedness. While there is clear evidence that left- and right-handers may "recruit" different brain regions in order to perform cognitive tasks (see, for instance, the differential effect of left and right TMS on perception for left- and right-handers; Mevorach, Humphreys, & Shalev, 2005), the evidence of consistent differential performance is lacking. (However, see Box 3.3 for a different take of handedness effects.)

Box 3.3 Is being left-handed a health risk?

In 1988, Halpern and Coren published their analysis of the relationship between death rates and handedness based on data garnered from the 1979 Baseball Yearbook which included information about pitching/throwing and batting hand preference for over 2000 professional US baseball players. Their analysis indicated that beyond the age of 33, the proportion of surviving right-handers consistently exceeded that of left-handers, and that the former group lived, on average, 8 months longer than the latter. They argued that this effect might be caused by several factors: two suggestions were that left-handers are more susceptible to a range of illnesses relating to reduced or impaired immune function (Geschwind & Behan, 1982), and/or that left-handers are more accident prone, leading to a greater likelihood of life-threatening injuries.

Needless to say, their report caused something of a storm, and other researchers challenged Halpern and Coren's interpretation of their data: Why, for example, were mixed-handers omitted? Could the effect be related to a greater social pressure to switch from left-handedness for men born earlier in the century? Other surveys were undertaken, variously involving an updated analysis of over 5000 baseball players in the 1993 yearbook (Hicks et al., 1994), a study of death rates amongst Swedish conscripts (Persson & Allerbeck, 1994), and a study of English "first-class" cricketers (Aggleton et al., 1994; Aggleton, Kentridge, & Neave, 1993). Interestingly, none of these studies entirely undermined Halpern and Coren's original claims, and the potential role of accidental injury leading to death was actually reinforced. Both the Hicks et al. and Persson and Allerbeck studies reported an elevated accident rate amongst non-right-handers, and the study of cricketers indicated an apparent 25-month difference in longevity (right-handers living longer), although this effect disappeared when deaths due to "unusual causes" and/or warfare were removed from the analysis.

In one of the largest studies ever undertaken (Ellis & Engh, 2000), the deaths of over 5000 North Americans were considered in relation to "degree" of right- or left-handedness. One category—those described as "generally left-handed"—had statistically significantly shorter life-spans, although the reasons for this remain something of a mystery.

SEX DIFFERENCES

One of the most contentious areas of research has been the question of psychological differences between the sexes and, among other things, their relation to brain organisation. It is worth remembering that human embryos have "bipotential", meaning that for the first 6 weeks following conception they are sexually undifferentiated and could develop into either sex. Then, at this point in genetic males, hormonal actions driven by a single gene on the y chromosome throw a developmental switch that differentiates, once and for all, males from females (a so-called organising effect). Of course, if no y chromosome is present, nature's default setting of female will develop.

This may be one of the reasons why scientists have, until recently, seemed somewhat uninterested in exploring brain sex differences, although a second reason is certainly the hostility meted out by some academics towards colleagues bold enough to suggest that such differences might exist: Witness, for example, the recent acrimony between Doreen Kimura (2004) who has published extensively about the possible evolutionary origins of brain sex differences and Tone Bleie (2004) who has questioned such origins and argued that differences between the sexes depend on experiential (learned) factors. Yet there is now convincing evidence of structural differences, and additional evidence of (some) functional differences too.

Structurally, female brains are slightly lighter, but contain proportionately more grey matter (cell bodies and dendrites). Male brains have more white matter and larger ventricles. There are particular local differences in the structure of the hypothalamus, some of which are linked to hormonal differences between the sexes. Perhaps of most interest in the context of this chapter is the observation we noted earlier: that females have a larger anterior commissure and a larger splenium (the most posterior part of the corpus callosum). It has been estimated that at birth the general level of tissue development in boys is between 4 and 6 weeks behind that of girls, and they are known to be about twice as likely to be born with a range of neurodevelopmental disorders as girls. It is also well documented that cognitive developmental disorders including **autism**, **hyperactivity**, stutter, aphasia, and **dyslexia** are all four to six times more common in boys.

Turning to functional differences, Maccoby and Jacklin's (1974) text remains one of the most comprehensive reviews of sex differences and behaviour. Although their research also encompassed the study of social play and aggression, critical attention has focused on their conclusion that girls tend to do better than boys (more or less from the word go) at language-related tasks, and that boys tend to do better at visuospatial tasks. Consider, for example, language: girls begin to talk earlier, they learn to read earlier, and they develop a greater vocabulary. These differences begin to emerge almost as soon as it is possible to measure them, and they increase through childhood and adolescence: teenage girls have consistently higher scores for comprehension, fluency, and translation. Boys, on the other hand, are better at tasks of visual tracking, aiming, maze learning, mental rotation, and map reading. Clearly, we cannot rule out the possibility that some of these differences are acquired through experience: for example, male advantage at mathematics becomes more pronounced in adolescence (Hyde, Fennema, & Lamon, 1990) but boys are more likely to be studying maths courses at this stage of schooling. However, the appearance of at least some differences so early in

KEY TERMS

Autism: A developmental disorder characterised by aloofness, automaticity, and aphasia.

Hyperactivity: In neurological terms, excess functional activity. In behavioural terms, a developmental disorder marked by excess excitability, inattentiveness, restlessness, and reckless/antisocial behaviour.

Dyslexia: A specific reading difficulty found in a person with otherwise normal intelligence.

development suggests that they are, in part, a consequence of differential brain organisation.

As with the earlier debate about the functions of the left and right hemispheres, the rather simplistic conclusions drawn by early researchers (that boys are better at visuospatial skills and girls are better at linguistic skills) have required revision in light of more thorough research. For example, a maths bias favouring males is seen in reasoning tasks (*If it takes 20 workers 3 days to dig a hole 6 metres deep, how many days would it take . . .* etc.) but for females in mental arithmetic tasks. Thus the overall male advantage is smaller than was once thought and may also be reducing further with time (Friedman, 1989). Although a male visuospatial advantage is most apparent on tests of mental rotation and targeting, females outperform males on other non-verbal measures such as manual dexterity and "spot the difference" tests where subtle differences between similar figures must be found (Kimura, 2002). Most measures of language function clearly favour females, but males are better at generating verbal analogies (Halpern, 2005). Bourne (2005) has recently shown that both males and females are "right lateralised" for the interpretation of facial emotions, but males significantly more so than females. Yet Lewin and Herlitz (2002) have confirmed previous findings that females are better than males at facial recognition.

Further study of route learning, traditionally thought to favour males, has also revealed the intriguing subtlety of male–female cognitive differences: In one variant of this visuospatial task, participants were required to learn a route from point A to B depicted on a map. Boys as young as 3 years old found this task easier to do than age-matched girls (Kimura, 1992). However, once learned, girls remembered more landmarks along the route than boys. As with the earlier laterality research, these findings raise again the possibility that boys and girls employ somewhat different strategies to complete the task—boys forming a holistic plan of the relationship between points A and B, and girls negotiating the route via a series of landmarks. In support of this hypothesis Kimura (2002) reported that girls are consistently better at the party game in which they are allowed to look around a room, then blindfolded, and then, when the blindfold is later removed, asked to identify objects in the room that have been moved or taken away. Boys, on the other hand, having seen a particular room layout, are better at avoiding bumping into things when blindfolded.

The neurological literature has been cited as supporting the view that women's brains are functionally less lateralised than men's. McGlone (1980) reported on a series of case studies of people who had suffered damage to just one side of their brain. Left-sided damage was more likely to result in impaired language function in men than women. Right-sided damage was more likely to impair visuospatial function in men than women. Although these data suggest that both language and spatial abilities are more bilaterally distributed (i.e., less lateralised) in women than men, an alternative explanation is that women tend to use verbally mediated strategies to solve *both* linguistic and visuospatial problems. At present it is not possible to say which of these is more likely, but the second explanation tallies well with Kimura's theory of strategy differences between the sexes. However, in two reviews of tachistoscopic and dichotic listening studies of sex/laterality differences, Hiscock et al. (1994, 1995) concluded that the evidence in support of sex differences in degree of lateralisation was inconsistent, and at best indicative of only very small differences. In similar vein, Sommer et al. (2004) have recently raised doubts about the assumption of greater bilateral language representation in females in a meta-analysis of functional imaging studies.

An interesting footnote to this debate comes from research that considers within-subject variability rather than differences between sexes. Although this work takes us some way from the central issue of lateralisation, it has nevertheless become apparent that cortical functioning is influenced by hormonal factors, and these in turn may affect measures of lateralisation. Kimura and Hampson (1994) have studied differences in psychological function in relation to the menstrual cycle. Immediately after ovulation (when levels of oestrogen and progesterone are relatively high) women tend to perform better at tasks involving fine motor control, thought to depend on left hemisphere function, and worse on spatial tasks that tap right hemisphere function. The opposite pattern is seen at menstruation when levels of these hormones are low. Hausmann et al. (2002) have also reported reliable within-subject changes in lexical matching ability, face discrimination, and figural comparison in relation to different stages of the menstrual cycle.

INTERIM COMMENT

The study of sex and handedness differences in relation to lateralisation continues to generate heat and light in roughly equal measure. In each domain, the results of countless investigations have been pored over in order to establish the presence/absence of meaningful group differences, and their consequences for ideas about lateralisation. In the case of handedness, we know that at least a proportion of left-handers (perhaps one in three) have a functional asymmetry that differs from the "right-hander" asymmetry, but we have no reliable data to judge whether (or not) this has consequences in terms of basic psychological functioning. As for the question about general cognitive skills in left- and right-handers, the evidence is equivocal, and a prudent interpretation would have to be that if we steer clear of the extremes of the ability range, left- and right-handers do not differ.

We are obliged to come to a slightly different conclusion in respect of sex differences: Our reading of the available literature suggests that while the early ideas of generalised superior language functions in females and superior non-language functions in males have not been supported by recent research, there are now numerous examples of sex differences relating to specific aspects of both language (e.g., verbal fluency superiority in females) and visuospatial skills (e.g., superior mental rotation skills in males). Indeed, they appear to go beyond these domains. Tranel et al. (2005) have recently reported that unilateral damage to the ventromedial prefrontal cortex influences social functioning, personality, and risk taking in males and females quite differently, right-sided damage affecting males much more than females, and left-sided damage only affecting females. Such instances of specific psychological difference are unlikely to be wholly attributable to developmental influences, and merit serious attention.

However, we do not know how these functional differences relate to more general aspects of brain organisation. A long-standing hypothesis, first mooted by Geschwind and Behan, held that the male brain is more lateralised (i.e., asymmetrical) than the female brain as a result of the inhibitory effects of testosterone on the development of the left hemisphere in males (in utero).

Although support for this model has been difficult to come by in terms of endocrinology (see Mathews et al., 2004), and patchy at best in terms of consequent functional lateralisation (see Sommer et al., 2004), the idea that males have a right hemisphere advantage and a left hemisphere disadvantage compared with females has become ingrained in popular accounts of sex differences.

Yet the issue is complicated by at least two factors not necessarily related to functional laterality differences between males and females. First, females appear to have more efficient inter-hemispheric transfer, which may or may not be related to greater bilateral functionality; at present, we just do not know. Second, males and females may use different strategies to solve identical problems (Kimura's example of landmark memory in females would be one case in point). To demonstrate unequivocally that males and females have different brain organisation, one would need to show that different brain regions are activated when both males and females are unambiguously using the *same* strategy to perform a particular task, something that, so far as we know, has yet to be demonstrated.

Thus, while there appear to be significant "pockets" of functional difference between the sexes, wholesale differences of the sort mooted 20 or 30 years ago have not been confirmed by subsequent research. How such instances of difference, where they are revealed, relate to organisational differences in the brain remains, for the time being, unknown. Further functional imaging studies (similar to Tranel et al.'s recent study) will shed light on this relationship.

LATERALISATION: A FOOTNOTE ON THE EVOLUTIONARY PERSPECTIVE

Whatever one's views about the degree of lateralisation in left- and right-handers or in males and females, the research reviewed in this chapter overwhelmingly supports the idea of hemispheric specialisations. Most researchers think it unlikely that these will all have been acquired exclusively through experience, so genetic factors come into play. Indeed, although we consider it to be beyond the remit of this text, interested readers might wish to explore two recent models on the role of genes in lateralisation by Annett (1987, 2002) and McManus (1992). But if genes are implicated—and caution is required because no one has yet found Annett's right-shift gene (which, according to the model, brings about left hemisphere dominance and right-handedness if present: if absent, chance effects determine either left or right hemispheric dominance)—this usually means that some evolutionary advantage accrues (or accrued) from its possession. According to Gazzaniga (2000), the advantage is computational: it simply makes more sense for overall control (language dominance if you will) to be in one place than to be distributed in both hemispheres. Passingham (1981) made the same point in somewhat different terms by identifying the potential problems (duplication of effort, conflict, etc.) of having bilateral control of the midline structures such as the tongue, larynx, and mouth that enable sound production, be it grunts, wails, or speech. In a sense, other asymmetries follow from this: Unilateral control of articulation frees up space on the contralateral side, to enable this region to undertake other responsibilities such as visuospatial processing, so this hemisphere becomes dominant for non-language functions.

We began this chapter with reference to Corballis (1991), who developed an evolutionary explanation for the asymmetries in cortical function seen in humans. Initially he argued that although the overall blueprint for nervous system structure is symmetry, not asymmetry, the presence of what he called a "generative assembly device" (GAD) in just one hemisphere allows us to think and act in a "generative" manner (combining things/actions/sounds into more sophisticated entities according to set rules). Not only does this mechanism enable us to generate almost endless utterances from a pool (in English at least) of fewer than 50 phonemes (the sounds that make up spoken words), it also provides an explanation of why most humans have a preferred hand, especially when skilled actions (such as those linked to tool use) are required.

Unfortunately, the original version of this account failed to explain fully why the GAD should occupy the same left hemisphere location for almost all humans. This point has more recently been addressed by relating currently observed asymmetry of language dominance to pre-speech communication, involving hand gesture, facial expression, and non-verbal vocalisation. According to Corballis (2003), the GAD evolved for tool use, and later for language as we now know it, from asymmetries already apparent in our forebears, and perhaps even in other primates. Whatever their ultimate origin, they certainly pre-date the arrival of our species. Of course, once the genetic shift occurred, there would be "no going back" because of the advantages outlined above, although the designation of this effect to the left hemisphere was probably a chance occurrence.

CHAPTER SUMMARY

The research that we have reviewed in this chapter supports a model of hemispheric specialisation in humans. While it would be an oversimplification to call the left hemisphere the language hemisphere and the right hemisphere the spatial (or non-language) hemisphere, it is easy to see why earlier researchers jumped to this conclusion. Research conducted on people with brain damage, with surgically lesioned or absent corpus callosa, and on normal people all points to left hemisphere dominance for language. This does not mean that all language skills are, somehow, contained within this hemisphere; rather that, on balance, it "has the final say" when it comes to language, particularly its generation. Whether this is because the left hemisphere is preordained for language, or because it is innately better at analytic and sequential processing, is currently a matter of debate. Certainly, right hemisphere processing seems to be more holistic and integrative, although Corballis has suggested that this happens by default rather than because of any non-verbal equivalent of the GAD mechanism in the right hemisphere. Finally, we have seen that lateralisation can, to some extent, be modified by both handedness and sex differences.

CHAPTER 4

CONTENTS

4

Somatosensation and neuroplasticity

INTRODUCTION

We are used to hearing of *Homo sapiens'* five senses: vision, hearing, touch, smell, and taste. Yet most neuropsychologists would argue that this list underestimates our true sensory capacities. Consider, for example, balance: As bipeds, humans, above most other animals, rely on their sense of balance to teeter around on two legs, sacrificing stability for the opportunity to use their hands and arms for other purposes. How about our sensitivity to temperature? Humans might be able to survive extremes of both high and low temperature, but they are exquisitely sensitive to temperature changes of very small increments. Next, consider pain. Humans (like other mammals) have a highly evolved pain sensitivity system, and are able to differentiate between many types of pain induced by a wide range of focal or diffuse stimuli, including heat, pressure, chemical irritant, and injury. Finally, what about the experience of sensory input when clearly there should be none? We need to have a model of sensory processing that can accommodate "phantom limb" experiences of amputees too.

Our list is clearly in need of revision, but rather than extending it the solution has been to replace "touch" with "somatosensation". In this chapter, rather than offering a brief synopsis of each sense system we have chosen to describe this multi-faceted sensory system in detail. This is not altogether an accident. First, in certain respects somatosensation relies on the same sort of neural wiring as other senses, so it may serve as an approximate model for them too. Second, we know quite a lot about the neural wiring itself, which is arguably less complex than that of the visual or auditory system.

Additionally, we are beginning to realise that although the blueprint for the lay-out of the somatosensory system is, as with the rest of the central nervous system, genetically programmed, the view that it is consequently "hard-wired" and there-fore immutable must now be challenged. On the contrary, the system is demon-strably capable of remarkable "plastic" changes, certainly during development, but also to a significant extent, it seems, in its mature (adult) state. An understanding of how the somatosensory system responds to damage offers an insight into the re-cuperative functions of the brain in other domains. We therefore examine examples of plasticity in this system, before considering neuroplasticity more generally.

To set us on our way, however, we need to review some general features of sensory systems, and familiarise ourselves with some of the confusing terminology.

GENERAL FEATURES OF SENSORY SYSTEMS

Sensory information travels from sensory receptors along afferent pathways towards the central nervous system. Some of this information gets no further than the spinal cord where, at the same segment at which it enters, there is a synapse, and output leaves the cord via motor neurons to innervate the appropriate muscles to complete what is known as the reflex arc. Most information, however, reaches the brain by a series of relays where it is interpreted in the processes of perception.

Sensory receptors may either be modified nerve endings, as is the case with pressure receptors, or separate cellular structures such as rod or cone cells in the retina. In either case, their job is to respond to particular stimulus parameters (distortion of the skin in the case of Pacinian corpuscles; light in the case of rods and cones) by a change in their own electrical "excitability". Most receptors demonstrate three further critical features. First, even within a sensory modality, they are "tuned" to be selectively most sensitive to a particular limited range of sensory input (certain cones in the retina respond maximally only to green–red colours, others to blue–yellow for example). Second, they quickly adapt, meaning their responsivity leads to fewer and fewer nerve impulses the longer the stimulus continues. A consequence of adaptation is that sensory systems are more responsive to changes in stimulation than constant stimulation. Third, there is a physical limit to their excitability, and therefore an upper limit to the number of nerve impulses that can be generated and conveyed from the receptor to other regions of the nervous system in a given period of time (about 200 per second in humans).

In the nervous system information is "conveyed" from point to point in the form of nerve impulses, so all receptors must be able to convert external energy (be it light, pressure, temperature, etc.) into nerve impulses: this process is referred to as **transduction**. (The pick-up on an electric guitar does more or less the same job, converting vibration into electric current.) If the receptor is just a modified nerve ending, as is the case for most touch receptors, we refer to this transducing process as giving rise to a receptor potential. If the receptor is a separate cell such as a rod or cone, a receptor potential (in it) gives rise to a generator potential in the sensory neuron. In either case, these potentials are graded, meaning that they are roughly proportionate to the intensity of the applied stimulus, allowing, of course, for adaptation, and a maximal rate of firing (see Figure 4.1). Thus the intensity, duration, location, variability (or other quality) of a stimulus will be relayed to the spinal cord and brain in the form of volleys of nerve impulses. As these always have the same amplitude in a given neuron (sometimes known as the all or none principle), their frequency rather than any other characteristic enables us to distinguish quiet from loud, dim from bright, or bearable from noxious.

THE SOMATOSENSORY SYSTEM

As we hinted earlier, the somatosensory system is a polymodal system, meaning it accommodates a variety of sensory inputs. First, it provides us with a constantly

KEY TERM
Transduction: Process by which a cell converts one kind of signal or stimulus into another.

Environment	Sense organ	Nerve	CNS
External energy	Accessory structures receptor cell	Sensory neuron	Spinal cord/ brain
Light, temperature, or sound	→ Modification/formation of nerve impulses	→ Frequency coded nerve impulses	

FIG. 4.1   The process of sensory transduction, which involves the conversion of one form of energy into another. In the nervous system this job is performed by sensory receptors, or by separate receptor cells. In either case they must respond to (i.e., be activated by) external stimuli (light, temperature, sounds, etc.) and convert this energy into nerve impulses. Within limits a frequency coding rule usually operates in which more intense stimuli lead to the generation of more nerve impulses.

updated picture of tactile (touch, pressure, vibration) input on the body surface (called "exteroceptive information", because it originates outside the body). Second, it provides the central nervous system (CNS) with information about the relative position of body parts, and the position of the body in space (so-called "interoceptive information", from within the body). Third, it processes information about heat and cold, and pain too.

Transduction is performed by a matrix of receptors in the skin, joints, muscles, or tendons. In humans and other mammals there are at least 20 different types of receptor dealing with information about touch, temperature, stretch, pain, and so on. In common with receptors in other sensory modalities, somatosensory receptors generate action potentials when stimulated. They also tend to be individually "tuned" to be most "responsive" to different intensities of stimulation. For example, some of the touch receptors are particularly sensitive to light touch, others to tickle, and still others to vibration, stretch, or pressure. Finally, many receptors adapt extremely quickly: hair follicle receptors only respond to movement (of the hair), and not at all even if the hair is held "out of position".

SOMATOSENSORY PATHWAYS

In the somatosensory system, receptors are modified nerve endings of sensory neurons, whose axons run from the point of stimulation towards the spinal cord. In some cases (e.g., pain receptors) the receptor is, literally, just a bare nerve ending. In other cases, the nerve ending is modified or even enveloped by an accessory structure such as a hair follicle, or a Pacinian corpuscle (a sort of multi-layered structure that resembles a spring onion when viewed through a microscope, and which responds to pressure and vibration). The accessory structure simply aids in the transduction process.

Once transduction has occurred, the volleys of nerve impulses must be relayed from the receptors towards the CNS. The majority of sensory neurons carrying these impulses are myelinated, which improves the speed of conduction of action potentials dramatically: sensory neurons can convey impulses at up to 100 metres per second. On entering the spinal cord, some sensory neurons continue uninterrupted (without a synapse) up to the brainstem along pathways forming the dorsal column medial lemniscal system (so-called because they are located medially at the back of the cord). Neurons in this pathway are all myelinated. In other cases, sensory neurons synapse as they enter the spinal cord, in a region known as the substantia gelatinosa, on to spinal neurons that then convey the information along their axons to the brain rather like a relay race. This second set of pathways are known as the spinothalamic (or anterolateral) tracts (actually comprising three separate pathways) and many axons in this pathway are unmyelinated (see Figure 4.2). The pathways can also be distinguished in terms of

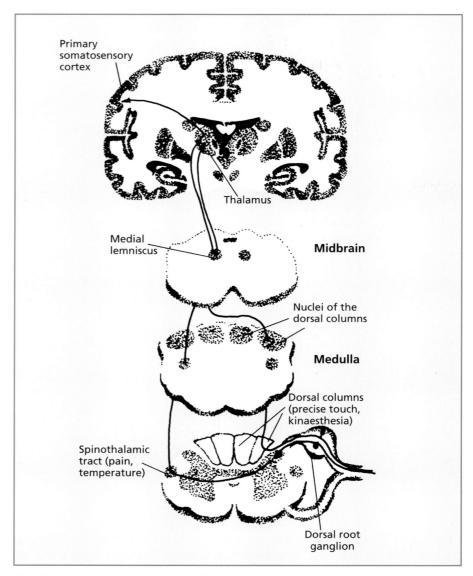

FIG. 4.2 The somatosensory pathways. There are two major sets of spinal pathways carrying somatosensory input. The dorsal columns (found at the back of the spinal cord) convey precise "fine-grain" somatosensory information. The spinothalamic tracts (at the side of the spinal cord) convey less anatomically precise somatosensory information. In each case the final destination for most of this input is the primary somatosensory cortex on the opposite side.

the information they convey. The former carries precise "fine-grained" localised information such as touch, pressure, and **kinaesthetic** information from joints: the latter carries coarser less precisely localised information to do with pain and temperature. A third important distinction between these two pathways is that in the former there is relatively little **convergence**, whereas in the latter there is a considerable amount. One obvious effect of this is that information about "localisation" is more easily retained in the dorsal column pathways than in the spinothalamic tracts.

Most somatosensory input crosses on its way to the brain from one side of the body to the other. In the dorsal columns this occurs in the medulla, whereas in the spinothalamic tracts it occurs at the segment of entry in the spinal cord after the synapse in the substantia gelatinosa. In each case, however, information from the left side of the body mostly finds its way to the right thalamus in the brain, from where it is relayed on to the cortex. In the spinothalamic system, some neurons send out collateral branches that terminate in the ascending reticular activating system (see Chapter 9) and are involved in brain arousal, and others that terminate in the tectum and are concerned with low-level (unconscious) sensory processing (also covered in Chapter 9). The route from receptor to cortex has involved relays of just two or three neurons (and one or two synapses) and the time it takes to convey information along the pathways is, typically, measured in fractions of a second (see Box 4.1 and Figure 4.2).

Box 4.1 Conduction speeds in sensory pathways

Sensory neurons carrying fine-touch information from your toes are the longest neurons in your body at up to 2 metres. Assuming a conduction speed of 100 metres per second, how long would it take for nerve impulses to get to your brain from your toe? (Answer [a] below.)

In some notable cases, speed of conduction is significantly slower. Pain information is predominantly carried along narrow unmyelinated neurons, and travels as slowly as 1 metre per second. This explains why there is sometimes a significant delay between incurring injury (say a burn to the skin) and feeling pain. How long might it take to "register" the fact that someone has trodden (painfully) on one of your toes? (Answer [b] below.)

Answers: [a] 20 ms assuming typical height. [b] 2 seconds assuming typical height.

THE SOMATOSENSORY CORTEX

Like other sensory systems the somatosensory cortex has a primary area for stimulus registration, and other areas (known as secondary and tertiary regions) for further processing, perception, and sensory integration. In humans, the primary area (known as S1) occupies a strip of cortex that runs approximately from ear to ear across the top of the brain. Strictly speaking, it is the most anterior (forward) gyrus (bump) of the parietal lobe and comprises Brodmann's areas 3 (a and b), 1, and 2. (See Figures 4.3 and 4.4.)

KEY TERMS
Kinaesthetic: Anything related to the sensation of body movement/location. Sensory information about the status of joints and muscles.
Convergence: In the nervous system, the process of many (converging) inputs influencing one component (for example, a neuron).

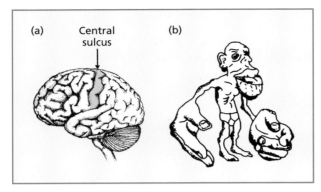

FIG. 4.3 The somatosensory cortex and sensory homunculus.
(a) The primary somatosensory strip (S1) actually comprises several
parallel bands of cortical neurons responsive to sensory inputs from
particular body regions on the opposite side. (b) The topographic
representation is precise but not proportionate, with some body
regions (notably the lower face and hands) having a
disproportionately large S1 representation. This disproportionate
allocation is represented in the relative size of body regions in the
homunculus ("little man").

A truly remarkable feature of this band of cortex is that the entire body is, in effect, mapped or "topographically represented" upside-down and left–right reversed along its length. To illustrate this, imagine you could record the activity of neurons in this band. Starting in the region of cortex located roughly behind the left ear, you would find that these neurons would only become active if there was stimulation to the right side of the tongue or jaw. A little further up, you would find neurons that were activated only to stimulation of the right cheek and forehead. Still further up, you would find neurons that respond to tactile stimulation of different parts of the right hand (with each part of each finger, and the palm, and the back of the hand represented separately), and so on. Towards the top of the left side of the brain you would find neurons that respond to tactile input from the right side of the body and the right leg. This somatotopic representation (meaning specifically that adjacent body locations are represented

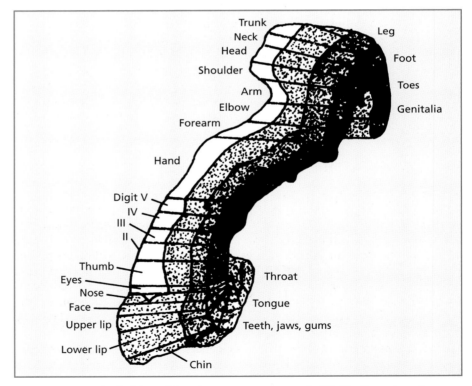

FIG. 4.4 A more detailed view of the primary somatosensory strip (S1). The figure shows how
different body regions (and component parts within those regions) are "mapped" in S1. Note the
disproportionate allocation (in humans) of "cortical space" for dealing with input from the hands
and face. Source: Rosenzweig et al. (1999). *Biological psychology*. Sunderland, MA: Sinauer
Associates Inc. Reproduced by permission of Sinauer Associates Inc.

by adjacent cortical areas) continues into the region of S1 located within the longitudinal fissure, where neurons receptive to input from the right foot and the genitals are found. The identical mirror image pattern would be apparent on the right side of S1 too. Incidentally, much of the initial work on "mapping" S1 (and the primary motor strip) was undertaken by Wilder Penfield, a Canadian neurosurgeon. He managed to persuade patients on whom he was about to operate to let him electrically stimulate areas of exposed cortex, and ask them to report what they felt (or in the case of the motor strip, to observe which body regions began to twitch!). For instance, stimulation of S1 might lead to a patient reporting that they could feel a "tingling" sensation in the palm of their hand. Moving the electrode a few millimetres along S1 might result in the same sensation now appearing to derive from their thumb.

As methods of investigation have improved, Penfield's observations have been broadly confirmed. However, it has become clear that S1 comprises not one but at least three parallel strips of neurons, each receiving distinct combinations of somatosensory input, while retaining the general pattern of topographic representation mentioned above (Kaas, 1983). The pattern of input to these parallel strips is specified in Figure 4.4. However, topographic representation in S1 is distorted. Body areas that are more sensitive, such as the hands and lips, have proportionately very much larger areas of somatosensory cortex to project to than body regions that are less sensitive, such as the upper limbs or the back of the head. The evidence suggests that for primates, including humans, about half the total number of neurons in this region receive input from either the face or hands. Researchers have illustrated this disproportionate relationship by drawing or modelling so-called homunculi (little men) whose bodies are proportionate to the area of cortex sensitive to the various body regions (see Figure 4.3b). The same relationship (of sensitivity and dedicated cortex) is also seen in other species. Mice, for example, have disproportionately large regions of somatosensory cortex dedicated to snout and whiskers, while monkeys have distinct regions dedicated to receiving input from their tails.

SECONDARY AND TERTIARY SOMATOSENSORY CORTEX

S1 is only the initial point of processing of somatosensation. While damage to it leads to reduced sensitivity for the particular body region sending inputs to it, identification of objects by touch depends on other regions of cortex. S1 projects (sends outputs) to a secondary area (S2), the role of which is to integrate input from the three (or possibly more) independent primary cortical strips, but now from both sides (i.e., bilaterally). Both of these areas project to other areas (the tertiary or association areas) of the parietal lobes behind (posterior to) the primary somatosensory strip. In fact, a significant amount of input via the anterolateral tract goes directly to S2 and tertiary regions including BA (Brodmann's areas) 5 and 7.

We can get an idea of the sort of processing that takes place in the secondary and tertiary regions by considering the effects of localised damage here. As a general rule, damage to more posterior regions affects higher-order processing while leaving basic sensitivity unimpaired. In fact, parietal damage often leads to one of the so-called agnosias, a curious and perplexing cluster of disorders that are described in more detail in Chapter 8. To give just one example here, damage to tertiary somatosensory regions can lead to a condition known as astereognosis, in which blindfolded subjects can describe accurately the main physical features of objects that they feel, yet are unable to match them with other similar objects, or identify them by name.

INTERIM COMMENT

Somatosensory input from all over the body is relayed via the spinal cord into the brain and eventually to S1. This strip of cortex comprises neurons waiting (in effect) for input from just one particular body region. The strip maps out the entire body contralaterally and upside-down, and we refer to this relationship between body region and cortical space as topographic representation. From here, secondary and tertiary regions in the parietal lobe process the sensory input further, to enable perception and integration with other sensory modalities.

PLASTICITY IN THE SOMATOSENSORY CORTEX

The topographic representation we described in the previous section is very consistent from one person to another, which reinforces the view that the basic wiring diagram for neurons here is indeed "hard-wired". However, data from a series of studies initiated in the early 1960s (e.g., Bennett et al., 1964) had already cast some doubt on the immutability of the wiring of the brain, at least in rodents. Bennett's group showed that adult brain structure depended in part on the environment in which animals were raised from shortly after birth to maturity, a period of about 60 days. In a typical study there would be a standard (control) condition in an animal laboratory, in which several animals were housed in a cage together. There would be an impoverished condition, which was the same except that animals were caged alone, and an enriched condition in which animals had larger cages, lived in bigger social groups, and had plentiful play opportunities. In a series of experiments the researchers found not only that rats in the enriched environment developed heavier brains, but also that these had more connections between neurons (synapses) (Turner & Greenhough, 1985), and more neuro-transmitter substance (Chang & Greenhough, 1982). The enriched environment rats were also quicker at problem solving and learning (Renner & Rosensweig, 1987). Although these findings were not directly related to the somatosensory cortex, they were important because they provided experimental evidence that challenged the then-current view that cortical connectivity was fixed (hard-wired) early on in development, and could not be affected by experiential factors.

The first indications that plasticity may also be observed in the somatosensory system came with the findings from Woolsey and Wann (1976). In mice there is precise topographic representation of snout whiskers contralaterally in sensory cortex. The cortical region can be mapped, with each whisker sending sensory input primarily to just one cell cluster (known as a barrel). Woolsey knew that if all whiskers (on one side) were removed in infancy, the area of cortex that would normally receive input from them fell silent. However, if a row or column of whiskers was removed, neurons in the whisker barrels that would otherwise have responded to input from these whiskers begin to respond to adjacent intact whiskers. In effect, the barrels for remaining whiskers absorb the cells from the "silent" barrels, and become larger than normal, so that cortical space is not wasted (see Figure 4.5).

Merzenich and Kaas (1980) extended Woolsey's paradigm to primates. In the macaque monkey there is topographic representation of the hand area contralaterally in the monkey equivalent of S1 that is very similar to that in humans. In one study, Merzenich and his colleagues removed a digit from a monkey early in infancy, and later on when the monkey had matured, examined the topographic representation in S1. Like Woolsey, they found that the cortical area that would have received input from the amputated digit had, in effect, been absorbed into adjacent regions responding to other digits. In fact the cortical areas for adjacent digits were now bigger than would normally have been expected.

In subsequent research the group has shown that simply preventing or encouraging use of digits, or otherwise interfering with the sensory input from them, can influence cortical maps even in mature monkeys. In one study by Merzenich and Jenkins (1995), animals were trained to receive food only if they used particular digits to rotate a wheel, which they had to do for several hours each day. This "exercise" brought about enhanced "tactile input" from the trained digit. After just a few weeks of training, these monkeys were found to have significantly larger cortical representation areas in S1 for the trained digits. If training then ceased, the cortical mapping slowly reverted (over a period of several weeks) to its pre-training layout. In another study by Allard et al. (1991), the middle two fingers of a group of adult owl monkeys were surgically "fused" (sewn together) in

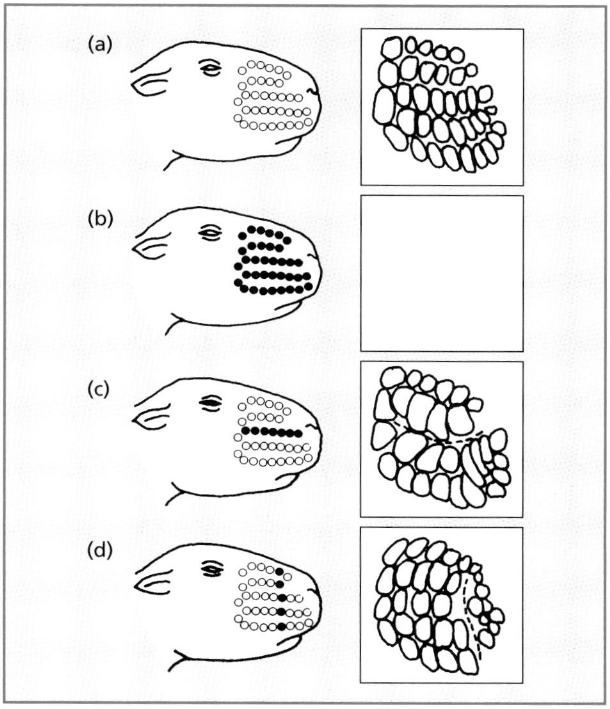

FIG. 4.5 Woolsey's whisker barrel study. (a) The usual topographic representation of snout whiskers and cortical barrels. If all the whiskers are removed (b) from one side of the snout of a new-born mouse the entire cortex that would have received sensory input from these whiskers remains silent (i.e., unused). On the other hand, if only a row (c) or column (d) of whiskers is removed, the whisker barrels (areas of S1) receiving inputs from adjacent whiskers grow, effectively absorbing much of the "silent" cortex, which now responds to the remaining adjacent whiskers. Source: Woolsey & Wann (1976); © 1976 Wiley-Liss, Inc. Reprinted with permission of Wiley-Liss, Inc., a subsidiary of John Wiley & Sons, Inc.

order to change the somatosensory input emanating from them. Some months later, cortical mapping revealed that the usual somatotopic boundaries between digits had effectively disappeared.

Can similar effects be seen in humans? Obviously, scientists cannot go around removing babies' fingers (or sewing them together) and waiting to see how this will influence adult cortical representations. However, Mogilner et al. (1993) have reported on a small number of individuals with syndactyly, a congenital disorder in which the fingers are malformed and fused together. Such individuals can have their fingers surgically separated. The researchers used magnetoencephalography (MEG) (see Chapter 2) to record activity in the "hand" region of the primary somatosensory cortex of these patients before, and again after, surgery to "free" their fused fingers. Prior to surgery, the cortical mapping of the hand region in each case was quite distinct and unusual in comparison with the controls. In particular, presurgical digit representation was displaced within S1. Moreover, the relevant cortical areas were unusually close to one another, and partly

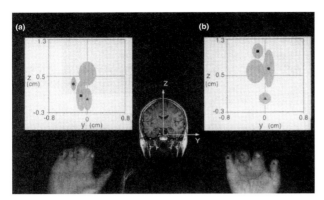

FIG. 4.6 Mogilner et al.'s (1993) syndactyly surgery study. The representation of the hand in the somatosensory cortex changes following surgical correction for syndactyly of digits two to five. (a) A pre-operative map shows that the cortical representation of the thumb, index, middle, and little fingers is abnormal and lacks any somatotopic organisation. For example, the distance between sites of representation of the thumb and little finger is significantly smaller than normal. (b) Twenty-six days after surgical separation of the digits the organisation of the hand area is somatotopic, and the distance between the sites of representation of the thumb and little finger has increased to 1.06 cm. Source: Mogilner et al. (1993). Somatosensory cortical plasticity in adult humans revealed by magnetoencephalography. *Proceedings of the National Academy of Sciences, 90*, 3593–3597. Copyright (1993) National Academy of Sciences, USA. Reproduced with permission.

overlapping. In comparison post-surgery, MEG maps indicated marked reorganisation in the cortical hand area in both cases. The resulting arrangement now more closely resembled the cortical maps of controls, and there was no longer overlap. Astonishingly, these changes were apparent within 1 week, and further MEGs recorded 3 and 6 weeks later indicated relatively little additional change. The remapping appeared to occur over distances of between 5 and 10 mm (see Figure 4.6). Readers will probably recognise the fact that Mogilner et al.'s study is, in effect, the obverse of Allard et al.'s. Together they show that, far from being hard-wired, the mammalian cortex is a dynamic place capable of undergoing remarkable functional plastic change.

As if to underline the effects of experience (as opposed to surgical intervention) on cortical representation in humans, Pascual-Leone and Torres (1993) used MEG to map the changes in cortical representations of (blind) adults who were learning to use Braille. Results indicated an expansion of the cortical representation for the single digit (usually the right or left index finger) that Braille readers used, and a corresponding reduction in the representation of hand regions not used.

INTERIM COMMENT

Mogilner et al.'s (1993) study was the first to illustrate that functional remapping is possible (albeit in rather dramatic circumstances) in the human adult somatosensory cortex, and that this region is not, as was once believed, "hard-wired". The more surprising finding was that areas of cortex responsive to input from individual fingers "appear" to move within a few days of surgery. Clearly, the cortex does not actually move, but new regions several millimetres away from the original site began to respond to sensory input from the newly freed fingers. It is important to remember that Mogilner et al.'s study was based on individuals who had the abnormality (syndactyly) from birth. However, in certain respects this makes the speed of change all the more remarkable, and scientists are now trying to identify the mechanisms that permit such remapping to occur. Further studies have now confirmed that drastic surgical interventions are not necessary for remapping to occur: experiental change (over time) is just as likely to bring it about.

THE PHANTOM LIMB SYNDROME

The observation that experience alone can influence cortical mapping in S1 is important for researchers interested in trying to understand the neurobiological correlates of "practice" (for skill acquisition) and physiotherapy to aid recovery, and we return to consider these issues later in this chapter. Before that however, we want to introduce one further line of research that bears on our understanding of plasticity in the somatosensory system.

A sense of residual (and often painful) feeling emanating from an amputated body region (referred to as phantom limb experience) is felt, at least intermittently, by between 50% and 80% of amputees (Ehde, Czerneicki, & Smith, 2000). The experience is graded, usually being most pronounced soon after surgery, and gradually reducing ("shrinking back") over time (Melzak, 1992). However, some phantom limb feelings can persist for many years. It is important to emphasise that phantom limb experiences are not "made up". Indeed, a remarkable feature of them for the amputee is their realistic nature. Sometimes, the experience will be so real that the individual might forget that their leg has been amputated, and try to stand up, or may start to reach for something with their "amputated" arm.

Until recently, little was known about the physiology of the phantom limb phenomenon, and it was generally assumed that phantom experiences were caused by residual neuronal activity from nerves in the stump. Painful phantom limb experiences can sometimes be so severe that further surgery is conducted (often at the behest of the amputee) to try to eliminate the pain. Unfortunately, this is rarely very effective and scientists now think that the phantom limb experience is, effectively, "recreated" in the brain.

An insight into the possible mechanisms that are involved has been offered by Ramachandran (1994). He reported the case of a young man who had lost his lower left arm in a traffic accident. Four weeks later, the subject reported a series of sensations in his (amputated) arm and hand whenever the left side of his face was "gently stimulated" (Ramachandran used a cotton bud/q-tip to do this). In fact, different regions of the face elicited "sensations" in different parts of the phantom hand. Touching his cheek evoked feelings in his first finger, whereas touching his lower jaw evoked sensations in his little finger, and so on (see Figure 4.7). Ramachandran collected several similar anecdotal reports of phantom experiences being evoked during stimulation of intact body regions. In one case, a woman who had had her foot amputated experienced phantom feelings in it whenever she had sexual intercourse!

Ramachandran explained these observations by proposing that the cortical region that should have received input from the missing limb was now receiving stimulation from the region that evoked the phantom experience—the face in the case of the traffic accident victim and the genitals in the case of the woman. Ramachandran put forward his theory after considering the layout of the somatosensory homunculus. He knew that this was very consistent from one person to another, and he also knew that the evocation of the phantom experience could be achieved by stimulating body regions whose cortical receptive fields were close to the region attendant on input from the amputated limb. For example, you may recall that the hand area is adjacent to the face area, and reference to Figure 4.4 will show that the genital region is immediately adjacent to the foot region.

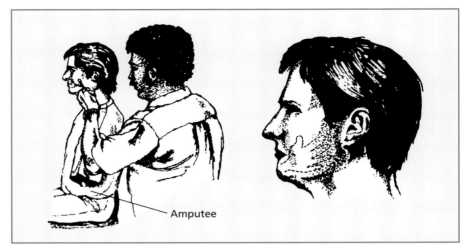

FIG. 4.7   Referred phantom experiences from facial stimulation. The amputee experienced phantom limb sensations when his cheek was gently touched. Ramachandran (1994) observed that different regions of the face evoked sensations in different parts of the amputated limb in a quite precisely mapped way: brushing the lower jaw evoked feelings in his little finger and brushing his cheek evoked feelings in his thumb. Source: Gazzaniga et al. (2002). *Cognitive neuroscience: The biology of the mind* (Figure 12.23). Copyright © 2002 by W. W. Norton & Company, Inc. Reproduced with permission of W. W. Norton & Company, Inc. Reproduced with permission.

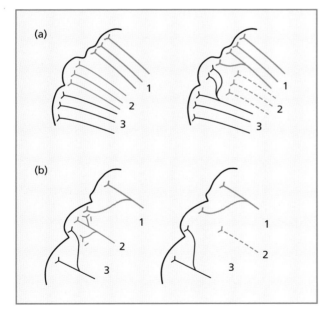

FIG. 4.8   Ramachandran's explanation of phantom limb experiences. Sensory input from the face region now begins to stimulate adjacent hand regions of S1. (a) This could be due to the growth of new axon branches—offshoots from the inputs to the face region (1 and 3) as input 2 is lost—but the speed of the effect is too quick to be accounted for by the relatively slow growth of new axons. (b) A more likely explanation is that previously inhibited (silent) inputs to the hand region become active because they are no longer inhibited by the missing input (2) from the hand itself.

To explain how inputs to one area of cortex can begin to exert an influence at adjacent regions, the growth of new axons (from adjacent inputs) has been suggested. Axons can sprout new branches, but this can be discounted in this case because of the speed with which the effect is observed: axons just do not grow this quickly. Ramachandran's explanation invoked the activation of previously **silent synapses**. He argued that although sensory input travels preferentially to target cortical regions, some also travels to adjacent (non-target) regions, but that this is normally inhibited by the direct inputs to that region. However, loss of this input (after amputation) means loss of **lateral inhibition**, so that neighbouring regions' inputs now get through, and this is what evokes the phantom experience (see Figure 4.8).

Ramachandran also argued that at least some phantom limb discomfort stemmed from a mismatch between the patient's "perceived" and actual sensory experience. To remedy this, he invented the "mirror box", an example of which is shown in Figure 4.9. Essentially the idea is that the amputee places his/her intact arm/hand in the box in such a way that s/he cannot directly see it but the position of the mirror gives the appearance of both limbs being present. Once positioned, s/he is encouraged

FIG. 4.9   Ramachandran's mirror. A mirror is positioned in relation to the seated patient, so that the reflection of the remaining intact arm appears in the position that the now amputated arm would have appeared. When asked to imagine making movements with both arms, some amputees find this arrangement provides relief from phantom pain, and a sense of well-being. Ramachandran has suggested that this is because the patient now experiences movement in the phantom limb from the "illusory" visual feedback. Source: Adapted from Ward, J. (2006). *The student's guide to cognitive neuroscience*. Hove, UK: Psychology Press. Reproduced with permission.

to make synchronous movements with "both" limbs! This means that the individual "intends" actions that are consistent with the visual feedback from both the real and the mirror-image limb. Astonishing though it may seem, this simple procedure seems to be beneficial for some phantom limb sufferers. In Box 4.2 we invite you to play a game closely related to Ramachandran's mirror box which demonstrates the power of illusory feedback suggested by the famous neuroscientist himself.

Box 4.2 Illusory feedback and fake limbs

Purchase a realistic but fake arm/hand.

- Sit at a table with one hand resting on the table, the other beneath the table.
- Position the fake arm/hand on the table in the corresponding position as though both hands/arms are resting on the table.
- Have an associate tap both the real hand that is beneath the table and the fake hand in synchrony, as you watch the fake hand.
- Notice how sensations appear to originate from the fake hand/arm.

Carry out the same procedure on a naïve associate.

- Once the effect has been achieved for a while, pull out previously hidden hammer and hit the fake arm/hand.
- Run!

INTERIM COMMENT

As is so often the case, further research, including in-vivo imaging of phantom limb patients, has painted a somewhat more complex picture than the one proposed by Ramachandran (see Flor, Nikolajsen, & Jensen, 2006, for a concise review of some of these developments). For example, contrary to Ramachandran's observations, phantom experiences can sometimes be evoked by stimulating body regions somatotopically distant from the amputated limb. Additionally, although MEG studies indicate both somatosensory and primary motor strip remapping after amputation, this is apparent in *all* cases, not just in those who experience the phantom phenomenon. Actually, phantom *pain* rather than phantom *experience* best correlates with the extent of remapping, and vivid memories of chronic pain from the now-amputated body part are actually the best predictor of post-amputation phantom pain (Flor et al., 2002).

Additionally, touching the stump itself usually evokes some feelings, suggesting that peripheral input is still involved. Moreover, phantom limb sensations are also often evoked when an amputee tries to move his/her amputated limb, suggesting that re-afference or feed-forward* of motor output directly into somatosensory cortex is also involved. This idea would fit well with the findings from the mirror box, which, in effect, tries to re-establish connections between "the wish/intention to make movements" and the observation of those same movements. Lotze et al. (1999) have reported that amputees fitted with a myoelectric prosthesis (a fake limb that moves in relation to residual nerve impulses in the stump) not only experience less phantom pain but also evince less somatosensory reorganisation.

These are important findings because they may lead to the development of new strategies to help people to overcome a range of phantom experiences—not, incidentally, restricted to limb amputation but also seen following breast removal, ear surgery, and even removal of genitals. This work may additionally aid recovery of lost function after nerve damage.

* In this context feed-forward refers to nerve impulses from the motor strip that travel directly to somatosensory regions (S1 and S2) where they appear to be used to compare intended with actual movements in order, if necessary, to make fine anticipatory adjustments to subsequent movements.

NEUROPLASTICITY BEYOND S1

PLASTICITY IN THE MOTOR CORTEX

It is now time to broaden our brief review of neuroplasticity beyond the focus of our attention thus far, namely S1. For example, in their study of "phantom-limb-experiencing" amputees, Lotze et al. (2001) reported plastic changes in primary motor strip (M1) as well as S1, confirming earlier reports by Karni and colleagues. In this study (Karni et al., 1998), healthy volunteers were asked to practise a simple sequence of digit movements (touching fingers to thumb in a particular order) for a few minutes every day over a period of weeks. Unsurprisingly, both the speed and accuracy of participants at this task improved markedly over time. However, when subsequently required to perform both the practised task and a different unpractised sequence in an fMRI scanner, there was significantly more activation in M1 for the former than the latter, and this difference was still apparent 8 weeks later although no further practice had been undertaken in the interim. These important findings bear on our understanding of both functional brain changes that underpin skill acquisition, and recovery of motor function through physio-therapy: an issue to which we return briefly later.

PLASTICITY IN AUDITORY AND VISUAL CORTEX

Several studies have reported evidence of plastic changes in auditory and visual cortices in relation to both damage and training/change in use (although we should note that for obvious reasons, most of this work has been undertaken with animals). In the auditory modality, Recanzone, Schreiner, and Merzenich (1993) found evidence of remapping in the primary auditory cortex of monkeys trained over a period of weeks on an auditory discrimination task. Behavioural performance was, in fact, directly related to the extent of cortical reorganisation. Robertson and Irvine (1989) reported that discrete monaural lesions in the cochlea (of guinea pigs) brought about a functional reallocation of auditory cortex resource within 1 month.

In the visual modality, Kaas et al. (1990) lesioned discrete regions of a monkey's retina and subsequently showed that the region of V1 (primary visual cortex) previously responsive to the lesioned area had become responsive to adjacent retinal inputs. Hubel and Weisel (1977) showed that both V1 functionality and the integrity of the "ocular dominance column" arrangement usually seen here could be permanently compromised by occluding visual input from one eye during a critical period of post-natal development: roughly the first 6 months in macaques.

CROSS-MODAL PLASTICITY?

In the film "SNEAKERS", a team of investigators finally track down the criminal gang thanks to the extra-sensitive hearing of a blind agent. There are, in fact, many anecdotal reports of individuals with various sensory impairments who seem to overcome adversity by developing increased "acuity" in their intact sensory systems, although scientific investigations of this phenomenon have produced mixed findings. For example, a range of measures of absolute sensory threshold (for an intact sensory modality) usually fail to distinguish healthy from sensory-impaired individuals, suggesting absence of compensation at least at this level (Finney & Dobkins, 2001). However, ERP studies of congenitally blind or deaf people have provided convincing evidence of enhanced functionality in more integrative tasks involving remaining intact sensory systems. For example, congenitally blind people can process sounds faster than sighted people, and localise them more precisely (Roder et al., 1999), and congenitally deaf people show enhanced visual acuity and visual attention (Bavelier et al., 2000). Functional imaging studies of such individuals usually show evidence of enhanced activity in both the primary sensory region and in adjacent multimodal (i.e., non-specific/association) cortical regions such as posterior temporal and inferior parietal lobes (responsive to both visual and auditory input) (Buchel et al., 1998). These effects are either absent or markedly less pronounced in individuals who develop sensory impairments later in life (Bavelier & Neville, 2002).

These are, in themselves, impressive examples of neuroplasticity, but not specifically of cross-modal plasticity, for which we should additionally expect evidence of activations in regions of sensory cortex linked to the congenitally damaged sensory system. Early evidence of this came from a PET study of Braille readers (Sadato et al., 1996). The researchers reported enhanced activation in both primary and secondary *visual cortex* in congenitally blind Braille readers, though not in sighted but blindfolded Braille readers. Moreover, simple non-Braille tactile stimuli failed to recruit these regions in any respondents. The functional significance of these findings was later tested by the same group (Cohen et al., 1997). They showed that the application of TMS (see Chapter 2) to occipital cortex interfered with efficient Braille reading for the blind respondents, strongly hinting that they were recruiting visual cortex to facilitate the tactile skill of reading Braille. Incidentally, equivalent findings of enhanced activation in auditory cortex to visual stimuli in profoundly deaf individuals were reported by Finney, Fine, and Dobkins (2001). These studies *do* provide evidence consistent with cross-modal plasticity.

More recently, both Fine et al. (2005) and Lambertz et al. (2005) have provided further evidence consistent with cross-modal plasticity in deaf people. In the former study, activations in right *auditory* cortex were apparent in congenitally deaf adults viewing a moving peripheral *visual* stimulus, although it should be noted that the areas in question (BA 41, 42, and 22) are known to be involved in the perception of *auditory* motion in intact individuals. In the latter study, deaf participants familiar with German sign language showed increased fMRI activations in their auditory cortex (BA 42 and 22) when viewing videos of people signing. In other words, visual input activated auditory cortex. Bringing the debate up to date, Ptito et al. (2005) used PET to show that a tactile stimulus applied to the tongue (the so-called Snellen task) could, after a short period of training, lead to activations in occipital cortex in a group of blind people, but not in a matched group of sighted controls.

INTERIM COMMENT

To the evidence cited above in support of cross-modal plasticity in humans with particular long-standing sensory deficits, we might add a wealth of experimental data from well-controlled animal studies, which are also consistent with it (e.g., Kahn & Krubitzer, 2002; Lee, Lo, & Erzurumlu, 2005). However, the existence of this type of neuroplasticity remains a matter of debate for the following reasons:

- First, there is a possibility that the recorded activity in the "wrong" cortex is an ephiphenomenon brought about by disinhibition, rather than a genuine functional effect. In other words, it is irrelevant activity that would normally be inhibited in non-sensory-impaired individuals. However, Cohen et al.'s study would tend to count against this.
- Second, the activations may be functionally relevant, but only in so far as they reflect the use of mental imagery: i.e., the blind person uses visual imagery to perceive the configuration of dots and lines that make up the Braille figures. This is hard to discount but runs counter to subjective reports of some blind people who claim never to use/experience visual imagery.
- A third problem is that we presently have no hard evidence of the formation of new connections or pathways into "wrong" cortical regions: Supporters of cross-modal plasticity simply assume either that existing minor pathways are strengthened or silent pathways are activated—the speed of change observed in the Ptito study (over 1 week) favours the latter explanation over the former. However, the reality is that cross-modal

plasticity will stand or fall only when DTI (tractography; see Chapter 2) has been used to look for the presence of new functional connections between sensory inputs and the "wrong" regions of sensory cortex.

NEUROPLASTICITY AND PHYSIOTHERAPY

Physiotherapy aims to restore body function that has been lost through disease, injury, disability, or ageing. The therapist will probably employ a raft of techniques to achieve this: exercise, massage, manipulation, and increasingly, technological procedures such as ultrasound. Often, the problem may be muscular or skeletal (and thus of little interest to the neuropsychologist): for example, the need to build up muscle strength or develop greater joint flexibility following a period of enforced inactivity. Increasingly, however, physiotherapists will be called on to help people rehabilitate after brain damage or disease that might, at one time, have been fatal. (Up-to-date figures in this area are hard to come by, but even 14 years ago in the US alone, Dobkin (1993) estimated there were 300,000 survivors of stroke and 100,000 survivors of traumatic brain injury each year.)

Physiotherapy research has, for the most part, tended to be about optimising practical outcomes rather than developing neuropsychological models to explain its efficacy. However, Randolph Nudo is a pioneer of a more experimental approach to physiotherapy for brain injury, and his work merits attention in the present context. One of his enduring interests has been recovery of function following circumscribed (small, localised) strokes. These typically lead to a permanent loss of tissue in the vicinity of the stroke itself, and a ring (sometimes called a penumbra) of adjacent tissue whose functioning, while initially compromised, may recover over time (the phenomenon of depressed but redeemable functioning is referred to as **diaschisis**). To examine this issue experimentally, Nudo et al. (1996) dealt not with human stroke victims, but with animals in which localised strokes were deliberately induced by manipulating blood supply to the "hand" area of the motor cortex. Five days later the researchers initiated a regime of "physiotherapy" in which the stroke-induced monkeys had to pluck hundreds of tiny food pellets from different-sized containers for several hours each day. Exercise was associated with both a greater recovery of function in the affected hand and with a reduction in the amount of long-term damage (tissue loss) in the penumbra region adjacent to the stroke site. These experimental findings are represented schematically in Figure 4.10.

A second example of research linking physiotherapy and neuroplasticity is the study by Weiller and Rijntjes (1999) (see Taub, Uswatte, & Elbert, 2002) employing "constraint-induced" therapy. The rationale for this study was that during development neurons seem to be in a form of competition, with active ones surviving at the expense of inactive ones. The researchers reasoned that if the same situation prevailed after brain damage, some inactive neurons may die simply through lack of use. They therefore sought to promote recovery of function in a limb in which movement was compromised following unilateral stroke, by "forcing" the recovering patient to use it (the unaffected limb would be tied up or otherwise immobilised in a sling). Even after just 2 weeks of constraint, functioning in the affected limb improved significantly, and there was a noticeable functional increase in the area of motor cortex controlling it. That is, enforced practice led to improved behavioural functioning which corresponded to increased

KEY TERM
Diaschisis: Sudden loss of function in a region of the brain connected to, but at a distance from, a damaged area.

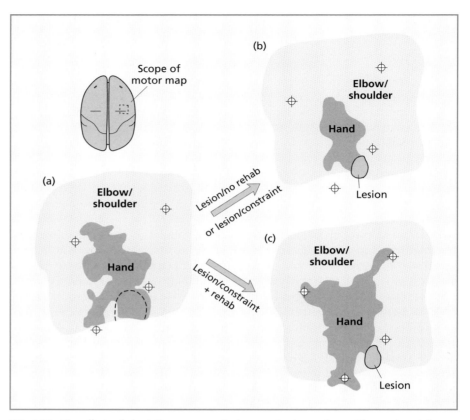

FIG. 4.10   The effects of physiotherapy on cortical remapping in monkeys with experimentally induced strokes (Nudo et al., 1996). Functional mapping of the spared motor cortex adjacent to the location of induced stroke reveals expansions of motor representations of the hand area related to the rehabilitative task + constraint of the unaffected hand (lower right figure), compared to "control" animals (upper right figure). Source: Nudo, R. J., Milliken, G. W., Jenkins, W. M., and Merzenich, M. M. (1996). Use dependent alterations of movement representations in primary motor cortex of adult squirrel monkeys. *Journal of Neuroscience, 16*, 785–807. © 1996 by the Society of Neuroscience, reproduced with permission.

functional activation in motor cortex. Landers (2004) has provided a succinct review of this line of research. A variant of constraint-induced therapy in which patients are strongly discouraged from using partial or para-linguistic utterances rather than "proper" verbal communications has also been shown to be effective in speeding up recovery of function in stroke-induced aphasic individuals (Pulvermuller et al., 2001; Wittenberg et al., 2003).

OTHER EXAMPLES OF NEUROPLASTICITY

Browsing through this book, readers will come across several other examples of observed (or inferred) neuroplasticity. To avoid duplication, we simply list some of these here, identifying the relevant chapter(s) for reference.

● The relocation of language function in individuals with localised or generalised left hemisphere damage in childhood (Chapter 3).

- The development of rudimentary language skills in the right hemisphere of split-brain adults post-surgery (Chapter 3).
- The functional and structural enhancement of remaining commissures in individuals with callosal agenesis (Chapter 3).
- The compensatory actions of surviving nigro-striatal dopamine cells in the pre-symptomatic stages of Parkinson's disease (Chapter 5)
- The control of prosthetic limbs using the BrainGate set-up (Chapter 5).
- Behrmann et al.'s (2005) fMRI study of remedial training of an agnosic individual, indicating that behavioural improvement was accompanied by functional reorganisation in the fusiform gyrus (Chapter 8).

THE PLASTIC BRAIN: A DEVELOPING PICTURE

As we have already mentioned, a long-standing view in neuropsychology held that the brain was, essentially, a "hard-wired" organ: its structure and connectivity genetically pre-determined and, once mature, immutable (except, of course, for age- or disease-related loss of tissue). Rare observations running counter to this viewpoint were, for the most part, accounted for by the idea of **critical periods** early in development where some flexibility may, under extreme circumstances, be possible. How things have changed: The genetic blueprint certainly exists, but what it lays out is not a fixed wiring diagram, but a plan for a highly flexible dynamic system whose components (neurons) are capable of sustaining enduring functional changes and probably enduring structural changes too. Certainly, scope for flexibility may be greatest during development, but more limited neuro-plasticity seems possible at some sites well into adulthood, and even old age (Buonomano & Merzenich, 1998).

Even the long-held view that the brain cannot generate new neurons once it is fully developed now requires revision following recent discoveries of **neurogenesis** in adult hippocampus and olfactory bulb, albeit in rodents. A detailed review of this research is beyond the scope of our text but interested readers might wish to browse papers by Cameron and McKay (2001), Brown et al. (2003), and Ziv et al. (2006) for more information. When Merzenich, Kaas, and colleagues first described S1 neuroplasticity, two mechanisms were mooted to explain it: axon sprouting and disinhibition (freeing of silent synapses). As with neurogenesis, evidence of these processes is now well documented in animals (O'Leary, Ruff, & Dyck, 1994; Sengelaub et al., 1997) although not explicitly yet in humans, where they remain putative rather than established mechanisms. Mogilner et al. proposed the freeing of "silent synapses" as the most likely explanation of the rapid remapping observed in his syndactyly cases, and Ramachandran evoked the same mechanism to explain the rapid development of "phantom" experiences in amputees.

To this list of possible mechanisms of neuroplasticity we can now add a fourth, related to changes in dendritic structure of cortical neurons. Working with rodents, Hickmott and Steen (2005) have shown that peripheral denervation (severing sensory inputs) in rats leads to rapid changes (within 4 weeks) in the **arborial structure** of dendrites of neurons in S1, presumably reflecting loss of some synaptic inputs and the gaining of others during remapping.

Finally, our list would not be complete without mention of **long-term potentiation** (LTP) which refers to enduring changes in the functional connectivity

KEY TERMS
Critical periods: The early stages of an organism's life during which it displays a heightened sensitivity to certain environmental stimuli, and develops in particular ways.
Neurogenesis: The process by which neurons are generated.
Arborial structure: The branching pattern of neuronal dendrites.
Long-term potentiation: The enduring increase in functional activity (at synapses) that may be related to memory storage in the brain.

between neurons (strengthening of synaptic connections) mediated by changes at glutamate synapses (Bliss & Lomo 1973; Sheng & Kim, 2002; and see Appendix). This mechanism is thought to underpin some aspects of both long-term memory (see Chapter 7) and long-term changes in pain sensitivity (allodynia) in which, for example, innocuous stimuli can invoke extreme discomfort following nerve damage (Svendsen, Tjolsen, & Hole, 1998). In sum, we now have several possible neurobiological mechanisms to explain the functional changes seen in studies of neuroplasticity A key task for researchers in coming years will be to establish which of these mechanisms underpins the various examples of functional plasticity that we have reviewed.

However, to complete the picture, alongside these (and other) examples of neuroplasticity, we must consider instances of behavioural plasticity: deliberate adaptive changes to achieve the same (or similar) outcome by alternative means, either in the face of adversity or simply in response to change. Humans are, arguably, the most resourceful of all animals, and countless examples of behavioural adaptation attest to this. The ability of deaf people to communicate effectively with one another using sign language is one obvious example.

CHAPTER SUMMARY

Somatosensation depends on a polymodal sensory system handling exteroceptive information about touch, pressure, and vibration, and interoceptive information from muscles and joints. It also deals with temperature and pain. The sensory input is garnered from at least 20 different types of receptor located predominantly in the skin or muscles, and each relays sensory information in the form of frequency-coded volleys of action potentials via one of two major afferent pathways—the dorsal columns and the spinothalamic tracts—towards the brain. Much of this sensory input is received by S1, which is a topographically organised gyrus at the front of the parietal lobe, along which the entire body is, in effect, mapped contralaterally and upside-down. Further bilateral and higher-order perceptual processing is undertaken in S2 and posterior regions of parietal cortex.

Despite its highly consistent topography S1 can, under certain circumstances, undergo quite marked functional changes. Initially it was thought that this capacity was only present in the immature nervous system, but further investigation has confirmed that plasticity can also be observed in "adult" mammalian nervous systems under certain circumstances, even after relatively short periods of "changed" input. One particular example of functional plasticity is thought to be responsible for some of the features of the phantom limb phenomenon. After injury, it appears that input from body regions mapped cortically adjacent to the missing limb can invade and "innervate" the cortex attendant to the missing limb and evoke phantom limb experiences. However, other mechanisms contribute to the overall experience too.

Neuroplasticity is by no means restricted to primary somatosensory cortex and, under appropriate circumstances, can also be observed in primary motor, auditory, and visual cortices, and subcortical structures too. There is additional evidence to support the idea of cross-modal plasticity although it is difficult to completely rule out alternative explanations at present. Recent research has strongly hinted that the success of physiotherapy following brain injury/damage is underpinned by neuroplastic changes.

Five neurobiological mechanisms have been proposed to explain neuroplasticity: neurogenesis, axonal growth and sprouting, the freeing of silent synapses, changes in dendritic structure (and by implication, changes to the pattern of synaptic inputs), and synaptic plasticity itself, as exemplified by LTP.

CHAPTER 5

CONTENTS

5

Motor control and movement disorders

INTRODUCTION

The psychological study of overt behaviour is, substantially, the study of movement. But even if you were just imagining movements, you would be activating many of the same brain regions that become active during *actual* movement (Roland, 1993). For all of your waking lives, "behaviour" is fundamentally and inextricably linked to action, whether of discrete muscles in our mouth and throat to bring about spoken language, or of massive muscle systems in our trunk and limbs giving rise to the movements required to approach and then hit a tennis ball.

There is no escaping the fact that the nervous system's control of movement is complex: it has to be in order for individuals to engage successfully in behaviours requiring precise muscle coordination. Think, for example, of the skill of a trained acrobat or the dexterity of a concert pianist. Yet skilled movement is something that most of us can develop with a little practice. When considered objectively, riding a bicycle is quite clever, so too is touch-typing, and even tying a shoelace requires bimanual coordination of a series of accurately timed precise movements.

Movement is possible only through the control of "skeletal" muscles (muscles attached to bones). These are under voluntary control and can obviously stretch, but this is a passive process: movement only occurs when muscles are made to contract. In all mammals, the contraction results from the release of the neurotransmitter acetylcholine from the terminals of motor neurons, although there will, of course, be passive expansion of any "oppposor" muscles. The cell bodies of motor neurons are to be found in the spinal cord. They are controlled by a variety of descending neurons from the brain and some ascending neurons in the cord itself, and whether or not they fire will depend on the summed influence of inputs (both excitatory and inhibitory) on them. But to understand the control of movement we need to work backwards: to examine the origin of the inputs that can influence motor neurons.

For many years it was thought that intentional (voluntary) movement was under the direct control of the motor cortex via the so-called pyramidal system, and that all other movement was controlled by a separate so-called extrapyramidal system and/or the spinal cord itself. But, as usual, the true picture turns out to be rather more complicated. First, there are not one but several pathways from different parts of the cortex to the spinal cord, and thus to the cell bodies of motor neurons. Second, in the brain itself there are several regions that are involved in the control of movement: the frontal lobes of the cortex, the sub-cortical structures of the basal ganglia, and the cerebellum, to name but three. Finally, there is good evidence that the parietal lobes, traditionally associated with various sensory and perceptual functions, may also be important in certain kinds of motor function. Our review of the nervous system's control of movement must give due consideration to all these components, and should also take into account certain characteristic movement disorders linked to nervous system damage or disease.

BRAIN–SPINAL CORD PATHWAYS

Although neurons in the cortex do not make direct contact with muscles, it has been known since the pioneering work of Fritsch and Hitzig (1870) that electrical stimulation of the brain can rapidly induce movement. In fact, there are at least four major tracts from the brain that can convey nerve impulses about movement (see Figure 5.1), and we need to consider briefly the specialised roles of each in turn.

THE CORTICOSPINAL TRACT

As the name suggests, this pathway comprises neurons whose cell bodies are found in the cortex (mainly the primary motor strip, also known as M1). This strip is the most posterior gyrus of the frontal lobes, and is located immediately forward of the primary somatosensory cortex (S1) on the other side of the central sulcus. Like S1, the motor strip is highly topographically organised. The axons of pyramidal neurons in this region descend within the brain to the medulla, where most cross (decussate) to the opposite side, before continuing into the spinal cord to synapse with motor neurons. These then relay the impulses to the muscles themselves. Actually, this pathway comprises two functionally distinct tracts: the "lateral" tract helps to control distal muscles (in the forearm, lower limb, hand, and fingers) mainly on the opposite side of the body, while the "ventral" tract controls more medial muscles (in the trunk, upper limbs, and so on) on both sides. Damage to the former will compromise skilled movement involving hands or fingers; damage to the latter will affect posture and ambulation.

THE CORTICOBULBAR PATHWAY

This pathway also has its origins in the primary motor strip, although the axons descend no further than the pons where they innervate some of the cranial nerves to control facial, mouth, and tongue muscles. Projections to the upper part of the face tend to be bilateral, whereas those to the lower face and mouth regions tend to be contralateral: you can, for example, easily raise one side of your mouth, but it is harder to raise one side of your forehead.

THE VENTROMEDIAL PATHWAY

Once again, this pathway actually comprises several interlinked tracts, but unlike the corticospinal tract and corticobulbar pathways, the point of origin of each

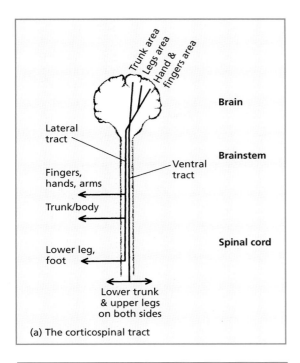

(a) The corticospinal tract

Trunk area
Legs area
Hand & fingers area

Brain

Lateral tract

Brainstem

Ventral tract

Fingers, hands, arms

Trunk/body

Spinal cord

Lower leg, foot

Lower trunk & upper legs on both sides

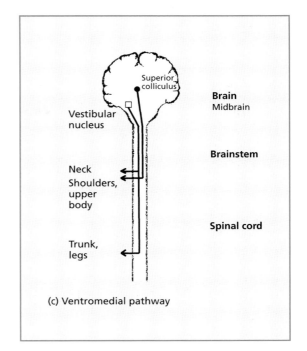

(c) Ventromedial pathway

Superior colliculus

Brain
Midbrain

Vestibular nucleus

Brainstem

Neck
Shoulders, upper body

Spinal cord

Trunk, legs

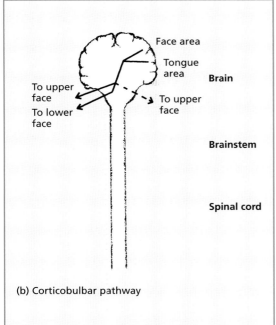

(b) Corticobulbar pathway

Face area

Tongue area

Brain

To upper face

To upper face

To lower face

Brainstem

Spinal cord

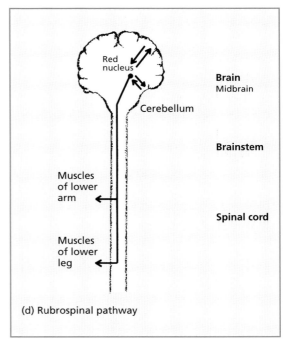

(d) Rubrospinal pathway

Red nucleus

Brain
Midbrain

Cerebellum

Brainstem

Muscles of lower arm

Spinal cord

Muscles of lower leg

FIG. 5.1 Descending "movement" control pathways. (a) The corticospinal tract originates in the primary motor strip and comprises a "lateral" component to control distal muscles on the opposite side of the body, and a "ventral" component that controls medial muscles in the trunk and upper limbs on both sides. (b) The corticobulbar pathway also originates in the primary motor strip, sending axons to innervate some of the cranial nerves in the pons to control facial, mouth, and tongue muscles. (c) The ventromedial pathway comprises several interlinked tracts that originate in the brainstem or midbrain and project to trunk, shoulders, and neck. This pathway is concerned with body posture and balance, and the coordination of various automatic processes such as sneezing, breathing, and so on. (d) The rubrospinal pathway. In non-humans this pathway runs from the red nucleus of the midbrain to distal limb muscles (excluding fingers) to coordinate movement of limbs independent of movements of trunk. The functional significance of this pathway has been questioned in humans.

component is in the brainstem or midbrain rather than the cortex, and projections terminate in proximal (i.e., close to midline) muscles in the trunk, shoulders, and neck. One component whose cells originate in the superior colliculus is important for coordinating eye movements in relation to body posture. A second component whose cell bodies reside in the vestibular nuclei of the brainstem helps to coordinate balance. Other brainstem components coordinate relatively automatic processes such as sneezing, breathing, and so on.

THE RUBROSPINAL PATHWAY

The point of origin of this pathway is the red nucleus of the midbrain, which receives inputs from both the motor cortex and the cerebellum (with which it has reciprocal connections). The main projections, however, are to distal limb parts (excluding fingers), and the primary function of the tract is thought to be the movement of limbs independent of movements of trunk. The importance of this pathway in humans has come into question because, in comparison with other primates, and especially other mammals, the size of the red nucleus is small, and the axons of the pathway are unmyelinated.

INTERIM COMMENT

Earlier we introduced the terms "pyramidal" and "extra-pyramidal" to delineate two separate systems of motor control. Although these terms have, to some extent, fallen into disuse (because they oversimplify the organisation of motor control both in the brain and the spinal cord) it is easy to see how the distinction came about in the first place. Two major descending pathways link the motor cortex to muscles in different body regions in a fairly direct way, and two other pathways (which in the case of the ventromedial system may be further subdivided) act on muscles in an indirect or more automatic way. Incidentally, the pyramidal tract got its name from the wedge-shaped structures that are visible in the brainstem at the point where the axons decussate to the contralateral side. Fibres that did not form part of this pathway were "extra-pyramidal". Today, a more useful distinction (supported by lesion studies) is that between lateral and medial pathways. Animals with lesions to lateral pathways lose the ability to engage in skilled digit coordination (such as reaching for food), whereas animals with ventromedial lesions manifest enduring postural and whole body movement abnormalities (Kuypers, 1981).

THE CEREBELLUM

This structure accounts for at least 10% of the brain's complement of neurons yet, perhaps because it lies outside the cortex, it has received relatively little attention until recently. Two vital observations should be noted at the outset. First, although this structure is now known to be involved in a range of psychological phenomena (such as learning, and self-monitoring) in addition to movement, its pivotal role in movement coordination is unquestioned. In the higher mammals at least, the cerebellum is fundamentally involved both in the modulation of motor coordination and the acquisition of motor skills. This is made possible by the large number of reciprocal connections between the cortex and parts of the cerebellum. Second, we should note that a quirk in the nervous system's wiring diagram (the right side of the cerebellum connects to the left cortical hemisphere, and the left side to the right cortex) means that the cerebellum influences motor control on the **ipsilateral** side, so right-sided damage affects movement on the right side of the body. We consider some of the deficits associated with cerebellar damage in due course. First, we need to summarise the key anatomical regions and functional components of the structure.

CEREBELLAR STRUCTURE

The cerebellum vaguely resembles (and is about the same size as) two walnuts connected to each other and, via two short stalks, to the brainstem in the pons region. The structure is bilaterally symmetrical, and each hemisphere comprises a highly regular neuronal structure. In fact, the cerebellum contains just four different neuron types. The innermost (medial) regions of each hemisphere comprise the vermis. This region receives somatosensory and kinaesthetic information from the spinal cord. The next region (moving outwards) is the intermediate zone. This region receives information from the red nucleus, and returns output to it. Finally, the lateral zones (the left and right outer sections of the cerebellum) receive information from motor and association cortex. Embedded deep within the cerebellum on each side are three nuclei. The vermis projects to the fastigial nuclei, which in turn influence medial descending motor systems. The intermediate zones project to the interpositus nuclei, which influence lateral descending motor systems. The lateral zones project to the dentate nuclei, which in turn project to motor and premotor cortex, and these regions are thought to be involved in motor planning (see Figure 5.2).

CEREBELLAR FUNCTIONS IN HUMANS

In view of its somatosensory inputs and its descending medial outputs, we should not be surprised to learn that damage to the vermis is likely to affect balance and posture, and may lead to a person staggering or even falling over as they try to carry out some simple movement such as bending to pick up an object. Damage to the intermediate zone gives rise to a phenomenon known as "intentional tremor": an action can still occur, but the execution of it is jerky or staggered. This observation reinforces the view that a normal function of the intermediate zone is to "smooth out" otherwise poorly coordinated actions, especially of the distal regions of limbs.

Damage to the lateral zones also affects movement of limbs, especially for tasks that require complex muscle coordination (sometimes called "ballistic" movements) over a short period of time. This type of skilled movement requires the concerted and temporally organised action of many muscles, but in a particular sequence that is too quick for the action to be modified by feedback. An excellent example would be a well-practised tennis serve, or playing a scale on the piano. After lateral damage the movement may still be attempted, and even completed, but instead of being smooth and well rehearsed, it is tentative and often inaccurate. The more joints involved in the action, the worse the deficit seems

KEY TERM
Ipsilateral: Same-sided. An unusual anatomical "wiring" arrangement in which brain function is linked to behaviour function on the same side (the norm being contralateral or opposite side control).

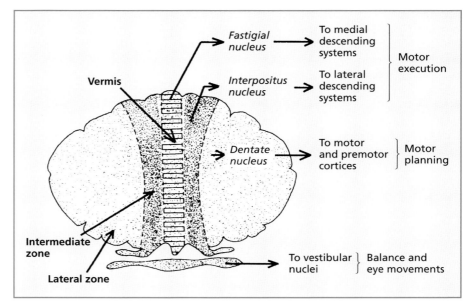

FIG. 5.2   The cerebellum and its connections. Output from the vermis influences medial descending systems to affect motor execution. In similar vein, output from the intermediate zone affects more lateral descending systems. Output from the lateral zone is primarily to the frontal lobes. The lateral zone is thought to be involved in motor planning, particularly in relation to responding to external stimuli. (Adapted from Kandel et al., 1991.)

to be. Moreover, it will probably not improve much with practice because people with this type of brain damage are not only clumsy, they also find it difficult to learn new motor skills.

INTERIM COMMENT

The cerebellum (translation, "little brain") can be subdivided into three anatomically separate regions. These can also be distinguished in terms of inputs and outputs: the medial regions modulate and "smooth out" movements initiated elsewhere, whereas the lateral regions coordinate skilled movements enacted "in time". The cerebellum is involved in a wide range of motor skills including balance, posture, multi-limb movement and, of course, the acquisition and enacting of ballistic movements. It is important to realise that damage to the cerebellum does not eliminate movement per se: rather it seems that tasks that were once effortless become a struggle after cerebellar damage. A modern-day take on the functions and modus operandi of the cerebellum is provided by Ohyama et al. (2003)

THE BASAL GANGLIA

KEY TERM
Subcortical: The portion of the brain immediately below the cerebral cortex.

These are a group of **subcortical** structures that connect with each other and the cortex in a series of at least five parallel "closed loops" first characterised by

Alexander, Delong, and Strick (1986). They also have important reciprocal connections with various brainstem and midbrain structures (McHaffie et al., 2005). Because of the likely involvement of the basal ganglia in a raft of conditions and disorders of interest to the neuropsychologist, in the following sections we pay particular attention to their circuitry and functionality.

BASAL GANGLIA COMPONENTS AND CIRCUITRY

Earlier we described the brain's control of movement as complex; this is the moment where our case is proved! Each of Alexander et al.'s circuits originates from, and ultimately returns output to, a particular region of cortex. The routing of these circuits through the basal ganglia is substantially parallel but segregated, hence the authors' reference to "closed loops". Actually, the segregation is relative rather than absolute as there is evidence of (some) "cross-talk" between them, but it is easier to understand their functions if we think of them as working independently. Readers wanting to know more might refer to a concise review of this circuitry by Tekin and Cummings (2002). A simplified description of the anatomy and possible functions of the cortical → basal ganglia → cortical circuits is provided in Box 5.1.

Box 5.1 Alexander, DeLong, and Strick's taxonomy of closed cortical → basal ganglia → cortical loops

Motor loop

- originates in the supplementary motor area (SMA);
- inputs (mainly) to the putamen;
- then the internal segment of the globus pallidus;
- then the thalamus and back to the SMA.

Main function: The initiation, maintenance, and switching of actions.

Oculomotor loop

- originates in the frontal eye fields (FEFs) region of the frontal lobes;
- inputs mainly to the caudate nucleus;
- then the internal segment of the globus pallidus;
- then the thalamus and back to the FEFs;
- an output also travels from the substantia nigra pars reticulata (SN-pr) directly to the superior colliculus.

Main function: The direction of voluntary (and probably involuntary) eye movements.

Dorsolateral prefrontal loop

- originates in the dorsolateral prefrontal cortex (DLPFC);
- inputs to the caudate nucleus;
- output travels to the internal segment of the globus pallidus;
- then to the thalamus and back to the DLPFC.

Main function: Probably related to the maintenance of spatial working memory and other executive functions, shifting sets, and temporal ordering of recent events.

Orbitolateral loop

- originates in the lateral orbitofrontal cortex;
- and inputs to the caudate nucleus;
- output travels to the internal segment of the globus pallidus;
- then to the thalamus and back to the orbitofrontal region.

Main functions: Switching/inhibiting behaviours, perhaps including the inhibition of inappropriate behaviours in relation to social setting. Possibly also involved in empathy and imitation.

Limbic loop

- originates in the anterior cingulate area (plus additional inputs from the hippocampus, entorhinal cortex, and amygdala);
- inputs to the ventral striatum (especially the nucleus accumbens);
- output travels to the internal segment of the globus pallidus;
- via the thalamus and back to the limbic cortical regions.

Functions remain vague but likely to involve selection of emotional expression(s) or tone, and motivated behaviour.

Before delving any deeper, we suggest that a working understanding of what follows may more easily be achieved if you think of an excitatory effect as one that encourages activation in the "innervated" tissue, whereas an inhibitory effect tends to reduce activation in "innervated" tissue (sometimes likened to an accelerator and brake effect respectively). Incidentally, and critical for the following discussion, inhibition of an inhibitory neuron or pathway will probably give rise to a "net" excitation because, in our simple terms, the "brake" itself would be inhibited (i.e., be less effective).

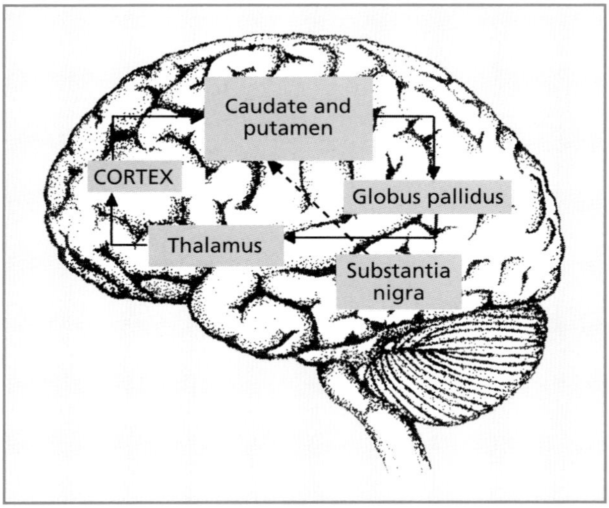

Returning to the main theme of this section, the principal components of the basal ganglia include the caudate, putamen, and ventral striatum (referred to collectively as the striatum), the internal and external segments of the globus pallidus, the subthalamic nucleus, and the substantia nigra, which actually divides into a pars compacta (SN-pc) and a pars reticulata (SN-pr). The former has reciprocal connections with the caudate and putamen whereas the latter projects outside the basal ganglia to contribute to the control of head and eye movements. (see Figure 5.3). The main inputs to the striatum are excitatory, chiefly via the closed loops from the frontal lobes identified in Box 5.1. Generally (and simplistically), it is possible to distinguish between the cognitive-limbic inputs which tend to project preferentially to the caudate and ventral striatum, and motor inputs which project more to the putamen. As

FIG. 5.3 Components and connections of the basal ganglia. The structures form a series of loops with the frontal cortex (particularly the supplementary motor area). A current idea is that plans and intentions for movement are channelled through the basal ganglia prior to being put into effect. The overall excitability of the basal ganglia can be influenced by release of dopamine from neurons originating in the substantia nigra (dotted line in figure). (Adapted from Wichmann & Delong, 1996.)

mentioned above the striatum also receives both excitatory and inhibitory inputs from the SN-pc, and a further excitatory input from the thalamus. For good measure, both excitatory and inhibitory interneurons are found in the striatum itself.

The caudate and putamen send outputs to inhibit the globus pallidus, whose principal output to the thalamus is also inhibitory (remember that inhibition of an inhibitory relay usually leads to net excitation). One path additionally diverts to innervate the subthalamic nucleus (of which more below). The final part of each pathway is an excitatory output from one of the thalamic nuclei back to the frontal lobes, and a smaller output direct to the spinal cord. However, at rest, we might fairly characterise the activity level of the striatum as quiescent (low). This will of course change depending on the balance of inputs mentioned above. In this respect the SN-pc is particularly important because it has the ability to modulate the overall activity of the striatum.

Direct and indirect routes

If this is not already sufficiently complicated, a further twist is that for each of the major parallel loops, two competing paths through the basal ganglia, known as the direct and indirect routes, have also been proposed (Albin, Young, & Penny, 1989, 1995; and see Figure 5.4). The direct route is in fact well established, comprising a path from the striatum to the internal region of the globus pallidus, then on to the thalamus and back to the cortex. There are two serial inhibitory synapses (into the globus pallidus from the striatum, and from the globus pallidus into the thalamus), and then an excitatory output from the thalamus back to the cortex (the double inhibition effectively gives rise to an excitatory influence). Thus, activity in the direct route could be thought of as excitatory, enabling or facilitatory. In essence, in respect of motor function for example, *actions are more likely*.

Now consider the indirect route. There is an inhibitory output from the striatum into the globus pallidus (the external part this time), which in turn sends inhibitory outputs to the subthalamic nucleus (double inhibition again). But this structure exerts an excitatory effect on the internal region of the globus pallidus, which we know (from the direct route circuitry) tends to inhibit the thalamus, so if the indirect route is active, the overall effect will be inhibitory and, in terms of the motor loop, *actions will be less likely*. The precise functional role of this route has recently been questioned (Redgrave, Prescott, & Gurney, 1999) and redefined as a "control" route rather than an

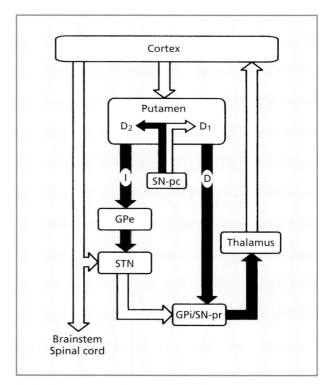

FIG. 5.4 Direct and indirect basal ganglia pathways. Activation of the direct (D) pathway permits selection of a desired action. The exact function(s) of the indirect (I) pathway are currently under review. However, activation of this route, either via the striatum to STN path or directly via cortical control of the STN, appears to put "on hold" possible alternative actions, and put a "brake" on current actions, respectively. (Key: GP = globus pallidus; STN = subthalamic nucleus; SN = substantia nigra; white arrows indicate excitatory influences and black arrows indicate inhibitory influences.)

"inhibitory" alternative to the direct route by Wood, Gurney, and Redgrave (2001). Whatever functions are eventually attributed to it, activation in this indirect route will tend to put a rapid "brake" on ongoing actions.

The final piece of this complicated jigsaw is that dopamine release into the striatum from neurons originating in the SN-pc has opposite effects on the direct and indirect routes: it stimulates the direct route by exciting D_1 dopamine **receptors**, while inhibiting the indirect route by stimulating D_2 **receptors** (Wichmann & DeLong, 1996). In other words, in the motor loop, the net effect of dopamine release into the striatum is to promote actions by simultaneously activating the direct route and inhibiting the indirect route.

BASAL GANGLIA FUNCTIONS

That the basal ganglia are important in movement now seems self-evident although there is still no firm agreement on the extent of basal ganglia influence. An early model held that they were concerned primarily with slow medial postural adjustments, because people with basal ganglia damage sometimes have "writhing"-like movements or other postural disturbances. Another idea was that the basal ganglia were important for initiating movements: damaged individuals sometimes struggle to start movements but are OK once they get going. However, recent research has indicated far more extensive roles for the basal ganglia, for they are ideally placed to selectively enable certain actions/behaviours (via the direct route) while holding others in check. Moreover, a direct excitatory influence from the cortex into the subthalamic nucleus provides a means for rapid termination of an action or actions that were being "enabled" by the direct route. As Grillner et al. (2005) comment, being able to terminate an action with precision is probably as important as being able to initiate one. The basal ganglia are thus able to select and promote particular actions/behaviours, but rapidly terminate these, if necessary, to enable alternative actions to be implemented. We have provided a (simplistic) example of the selective and switching capacity of the basal ganglia in Box 5.2. A modern view of basal ganglia function, based on more extensive neurological investigation in human disease (which we review below) and experimental studies with animals, is that they operate rather like a "gatekeeper" for behavioural action plans locked away in the frontal lobes (Bradshaw & Mattingley, 1995). The upshot of the arrangements described above (and illustrated in Figure 5.5) is that the direct loop effectively works as an "enabling" mechanism that, if active, facilitates ongoing or preferred activity. This regulatory function is supported by the observation that electrical activity in the basal ganglia increases in anticipation of, rather than initiation of, intended movements, and again as movements are about to be terminated (Steg & Johnels, 1993).

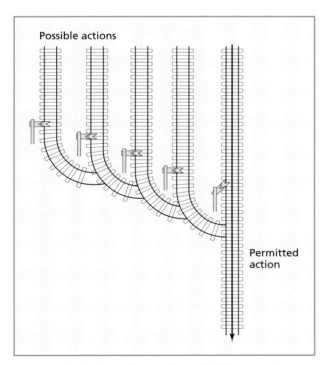

Possible actions

Permitted action

FIG. 5.5 The basal ganglia as facilitators/inhibitors of action plans. Conceptually, we might think of the basal ganglia as facilitating selection of the appropriate movement by holding in check all but the most desired response.

According to Bolam and Magill (2004), an unresolved question concerns the funnelling of competing action plans from the cortex into the striatum, and the selection process that is presumed to occur there. This issue currently represents a major challenge for researchers.

Box 5.2 Approach–avoidance behaviour and the basal ganglia

A hungry animal is contemplating moving towards some food (perhaps another animal). It wants to approach the prey, but is anxious that other predators may be in the area. In the end, hunger dictates that it should approach the food; a movement plan for this is fed though the direct route, and the animal approaches. But, ever wary, it has an alternative escape plan at the ready should a predator show up. As the animal closes in on its prey, it notices a predator in its field of vision. Simultaneous cessation of dopamine release into the striatum and cortical influences on the subthalamic nucleus would enable rapid cessation of the approach behaviour, and the chance to switch to the avoidance plan which would now gain access to the direct route.

THE CORTEX

At one time, motor function (in the brain) was thought to involve all cortical tissue forward of the central sulcus—"the motor unit" in Luria's terms (1973). With more research, this view has required revision. First, it ignores the fact that the frontal lobes have various non-motor functions in addition to responsibilities for the control of movement (see Chapters 10 and 11). Second, it ignores the apparently critical role of parts of the parietal lobe, especially on the left side, in controlling movement in particular circumstances. Today, attention has turned to unravelling the relative responsibilities of different cortical regions in organising and controlling movement, and to trying to understand how these regions interact with each other and with the subcortical structures already mentioned. The emerging model remains essentially hierarchical; region A is controlled by region B which, in turn, is controlled by region C. But the further away from A one looks, the more abstract and widely distributed are the mental operations linked to movements. Researchers have, additionally, found it necessary to make the important distinction between internally generated movement and stimulus-driven or externally prompted movement.

THE MOTOR STRIP

As we have already mentioned, the primary motor cortex or motor strip (BA 4), like the somatosensory cortex, is highly topographically organised (also referred to as somatotopic organisation). In our analogy, this would be region A. All regions of the body that have voluntary muscles are represented, and there is predominantly contralateral control: the right motor cortex coordinates muscles in the left side of the body, and vice versa. As with the somatosensory cortex, the relationship between cortical "space" in the motor strip and body region is not proportionate: there is over-representation of regions capable of fine motor control, such as the hands and fingers, and the mouth area of the face, and under-representation of less "movement-critical" regions such as the back and top of the head, the trunk, and the upper limbs. The axons of pyramidal neurons, whose cell bodies are found here, make up much of the corticospinal and corticobulbar pathways identified earlier.

With more precise instrumentation (basically amounting to finer electrodes), researchers have discovered that the primary motor strip comprises not one but several parallel bands of topographically mapped pyramidal neurons (as many as nine have been proposed). Moreover, Georgopoulos, Taira, and Lukashin (1993) have shown that muscles actually require a pattern of activity in several adjacent cortical cells in order to bring about movement. (Such patterns of activity are referred to as "population vectors", and understanding these has been critical in the development of prosthetic aids that can be controlled by brain activity. We briefly consider this exciting field or research in Box 5.3.) Georgopoulus et al.'s finding also explains why damage to one or a few pyramidal cells weakens, but rarely eliminates entirely, movement in the corresponding body region. However, it is also clear that more extensive damage to this region can bring about a widespread loss of muscle function and paralysis. In cases where accident or stroke has damaged the entire left or right primary motor cortex, the result is contralateral **hemiplegia**, which usually involves lasting impairments. In addition to his aphasia, Broca's "Tan" was hemiplegic on his right side.

Box 5.3 Neural prosthetics and the "bionic man"

In recent years, the goal of achieving recovery of motor function in individuals with extensive damage to their nervous systems resulting from disease or injury has been pursued with renewed vigour. Recall that the outlook for someone with a broken neck is (currently) a life of quadriplegic paralysis (and loss of sensory input) that will probably include inability to breathe independently. The actor Christopher Reeve suffered such an injury when he was thrown from his horse, and lived the remainder of his life as a quadriplegic, although he did appear to regain very modest motor function some years after his accident. He campaigned tirelessly for more research into the nature of spinal injury and for the development of procedures to aid subsequent recovery.

Reeve became interested in neural repair—the promotion of growth of new connections in the nervous system to circumvent the loss of function caused by the traumatic event itself. He believed that this process was somehow activated in him by the intense physiotherapy he underwent, and that this perhaps unpinned his own modest degree of recovery. Although this approach is intriguing, progress has been slow, and Reeve's explanation remains an open question at present. The field of neural prosthetics represents an alternative but equally promising line of inquiry, which takes advantage of the rapid developments in computing, to bypass the area of injury altogether and connect brain to muscle via a microprocessor interface.

KEY TERM
Hemiplegia: Loss of sensory awareness from, and muscle control of, one side of the body.

Recall that earlier we described muscle contraction (and hence movement) as depending on the collaborative actions of many primary motor strip neurons, to generate a so-called "population vector". This composite neural activity, rather than one or a few neurons acting in isolation, is what determines the force and direction of a particular movement. Obviously the motor strip contains millions of neurons and it is not currently possible to record individually all the neuronal activity here. However, researchers have found that a reasonable proxy for this activity can be gleaned from a sensor with about 100 microelectrodes in it.

An American company, "Cyberkinetics", has developed a system called BrainGate for this purpose (see Figure 5.6). It comprises a microelectrode array that has to be implanted so the electrode tips are in direct contact with the brain (usually a particular part of the motor strip), and a computer that "interprets" the recorded activity with a complex software algorithm (which generates quasi-population vectors). These can be used to drive either a cursor on a computer screen or a prosthetic limb.

Initially, researchers tested the system with primates, reporting on a series of monkeys with motor strip implants who could reach with a prosthetic limb to grasp food (their own limbs were restrained) (Schwartz, 2004). Most intriguingly, the monkeys were able to demonstrate "learning" through biofeedback on how to refine the limb's movements by modifying the firing patterns of the recorded neurons.

Then, early in 2006, a group led by Hochberg reported on two humans with the same implants. One was forced to drop out of the study for technical reasons but the other, known as MN, quadriplegic following a knife attack in 2001, has so far been able to use the cursor interface to open emails, do simple drawings, play video games, and adjust the volume and channel of his TV. When the system was linked up to a robotic limb, MN was able to open and close the hand, and grasp an object and move it from one location to another . . . all by imagining (or willing) the desired action that he had been unable to perform since his injury (Hochberg et al., 2006).

Obviously, these are very preliminary research findings and considerable work needs to be done to refine both the hardware and software of the BrainGate system. For example, there is currently intense research underway to identify other brain locations that may be better sources of motor control output than the motor strip; the posterior parietal lobe and the premotor cortex are two such candidate regions (Anderson et al., 2004). Progress will be slow but the concept of a bionic man or woman can no longer be written off as sci-fi nonsense!

The main inputs to the primary motor strip are bilaterally from BA 6 (see below). It also receives rather precise inputs from primary somatosensory cortex, which appear to be intimately involved in providing rapid feedback to motor neurons from, for example, sensory input during manual manipulation of objects (Evarts, 1974).

FIG. 5.6 BrainGate technology. This experimental technology involves implanting microelectrodes in the brain to detect neuronal activity about *intended* movements. This information is fed into a computer that, in turn, generates signals to drive limbs or interact with another computer or TV. The hope is that in due course the technology may permit individuals with profoundly damaged nervous systems to move about and interact with their environment through the power of thought. Source: Adapted from illustration by Leigh Hochberg, Massachusetts General Hospital, with permission from Cyberkinetics Neurotechnology Systems, Inc.

THE SUPPLEMENTARY MOTOR AREA AND PREMOTOR CORTEX

Having established the link between the primary motor cortex and muscles, we now need to consider how a person "initiates" a movement. As we hinted earlier, cortical control of movement is organised "hierarchically" by different regions of the frontal lobes. As we have already seen, pyramidal cells in the primary motor cortex (region A) control muscle contractions via their connections with motor neurons in the spinal cord. These pyramidal cells are, in turn, partly controlled by neurons in the region of frontal lobe just forward of the primary motor cortex; in our analogy, this would be region B. This area actually divides into two functionally distinct regions (both occupying BA 6 as mentioned above): the more medial supplementary motor area or SMA (towards the top of the brain) and the more lateral premotor cortex or PMC (towards the sides). Cells in each region influence neurons in the motor strip when a particular movement is carried out. In other words, SMA and PMC neurons control hierarchically the activity of individual pyramidal cells (see Figure 5.7). People with damage to these regions retain fine motor control of fingers but are impaired on tasks that require the coordination of two hands (such as tying a knot).

The main outputs from the SMA are to the primary motor cortex bilaterally. The main inputs are from the prefrontal cortex and the basal ganglia. This arrangement places the SMA in a strategic position (in the hierarchy) to coordinate motor plans (which, as we saw earlier, have been "approved" by the basal ganglia for execution) via the pyramidal neurons of the primary motor strip. It provides a buffer store for such plans prior to their execution. Several important observations reinforce this view. First, it is possible to record a negative ERP (see Chapter 2) from the SMA that builds over a period of 1 or 2 seconds prior to executing the movement. This is known as the readiness potential (also called the *bereitschaftspotential*), and is observable even when movements are only imagined (Roland, 1993; Tyszka et al., 1994). Second, stimulation of the SMA is reported to produce an urge to perform movements (Bradshaw & Mattingley, 1995). Third, bilateral damage of the SMA can bring about complete loss of voluntary movement including speech (Freund, 1984). Fourth, Gerloff et al. (1997) have reported that the subjective experience of temporary SMA "lesions" induced by TMS is one of apparent loss/forgetting of the goal that the ongoing actions were intended to achieve.

In many respects, the PMC works in analogous fashion to the SMA, except that it is more concerned with coordinating motor plans related to external cues. Like the SMA, the main outputs from the PMC are to the primary motor strip. The main inputs are from the parietal lobe, the cerebellum, and, to a lesser extent, the prefrontal cortex. Activity is greater in the PMC in response to external cues (than internally generated plans). For example, Roland et al. (1980) showed that blood flow increased markedly in this region as the subject was required to keep a spring in a state of compression between the fingers. The PMC, along with the prefrontal cortex, also appears to be more active during the acquisition of skilled movements, whereas the SMA becomes more active when well-practised movements are required (Jenkins et al., 1994).

OTHER FRONTAL REGIONS INVOLVED IN MOVEMENT

As we mentioned earlier, both the SMA and, to a lesser extent, the PMC receive inputs from the area of frontal lobe in front of them (area C, to return to our analogy). This "association" area is known as the prefrontal region, and it becomes active when an individual begins to plan behaviours in a relatively abstract way, or when new motor skills are being acquired. Prefrontal damage actually impairs an individual's ability to plan, whether or not movement is involved. For example, frontal patients often perform badly on strategy tests such as the "Tower of Hanoi", which we discuss in more detail in Chapter 11. And in the Jenkins et al. study mentioned above, increased metabolic activity was observed in the lateral prefrontal cortex *only* during the motor learning stage, not once the skill had been acquired.

These findings support the idea of a three-stage hierarchy in the frontal lobes to control movement, which we illustrate, in very simple terms, in Box 5.4. However, it would be grossly misleading of us to suggest that area C was localised in the way that area A is. In fact, our understanding of where "ideas" (that may become actions) originate from is distinctly hazy and based, as often as not, on case studies of brain-damaged individuals with deficits in this realm. Frontal damage can affect idea generation, but so too can damage to other cortical and subcortical regions. The initial representation, perhaps a goal that the individual wishes to achieve, may be highly abstract, and shaped by any number of influences: prior experience, current predicament, motivational state, desirability of outcome, feasibility of the action plan, and so on. And there will usually be a raft of alternative ways of achieving the goal, necessitating a competitive process to select the most appropriate actions (Rosenbaum et al., 1991). It seems likely that this initial stage of action planning must be underpinned by distributed and parallel processing rather than

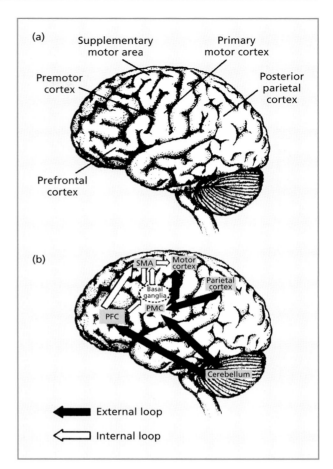

FIG. 5.7   (a) The four hierarchically organised areas of the frontal lobe (the prefrontal cortex, the SMA and PMC, and the motor strip.). (b) "Motor" areas outside the frontal lobes. In general terms, internal (self-generated) actions involve the prefrontal cortex, SMA, and primary motor strip mediated by the subcortical basal ganglia (internal loop). Actions prompted by external events engage the cerebellum and probably the parietal lobe, both of which send outputs to the PMC that, in turn, outputs to the primary motor strip (external loop).

hierarchical serial processing. Teasing apart the constituent mental operations involved will be a major challenge for researchers in coming years.

Scientists have, however, begun to identify some of the other brain regions, in addition to the prefrontal cortex, involved in this early stage of motor control. The anterior cingulate is active when attention must be directed towards novel stimuli that require effortful responses, particularly where there is conflict between response options (Rushworth et al., 2004). A region of medial frontal cortex, tagged the pre-SMA by Matsuzaka and Tanji (1996), appears to be important in organising sequential actions together (Kennerley, Sakai, & Rushworth, 2004). The "frontal eye fields" are of critical importance in controlling **voluntary gaze**. And, as we shall see below, the parietal lobe may be important in storing memories of actions and perhaps their semantic connotations too.

Box 5.4 A motor hierarchy for quenching your thirst

- Dehydration leads to activation of "osmoreceptors" in the anterior hypothalamus. This is translated into consciously feeling thirsty, leading to a motivational state represented in the prefrontal areas (area C) as a *plan* or *intention* to drink.
- The act of raising a glass, tipping, and swallowing (the appropriate *motor pattern*) is coordinated by the SMA and/or the premotor cortex (area B). Remember that these areas exert bilateral control: after all, you could pick up the glass with either hand.
- The SMA and PMC control the pyramidal cells in the primary motor strip (area A) in the coordination of individual muscles as the glass is raised and the drink consumed.
- Moment by moment sensory feedback from touch receptors in the fingers and hand holding the glass ensures that it is gripped tightly enough to prevent it falling, and not too tightly to cause it to break.

INTERIM COMMENT

Motor control is organised hierarchically. Plans or intentions to act are "hatched" in a distributed network including, but extending well beyond, the prefrontal cortex. Motor plans are coordinated in the SMA and PMC, and control of muscles is mediated by the primary motor strip. Although this organisational hierarchy has been speculated about for many years, the use of in-vivo imaging procedures such as SPECT and rCBF (see Chapter 2) has confirmed it. Roland (1993) reported that when an individual was asked to complete a simple repetitive movement such as wiggling a finger, only the contralateral primary motor cortex showed increased activity. However, if a more complex sequence such as touching the ends of each finger with the thumb was required, both the SMA and the prefrontal cortex showed increased activity, as well as the primary motor cortex. Even asking the subject to imagine the complex sequence caused increased activation in the SMA and prefrontal regions.

The distinction between internally and externally cued movement is also important. The basal ganglia interact with the SMA to enable (or inhibit)

KEY TERM
Voluntary gaze: Intentional adjustments of eyes in the deliberate process of attending to a feature in the visual field.

internally generated movement plans. The cerebellum interacts with the PMC to regulate actions related to *external* stimuli or events. Thus the novice tennis player will rely mainly on the second set of connections to return serve, hoping to make contact with the ball (the external stimulus) and hit it anywhere in their opponent's court. The experienced player, on the other hand, will use both systems: the cerebellar–cortical connections will control contact with the ball, and the basal ganglia–cortical connections will allow them (via internally generated intentions) to place their shot deliberately, to maximum advantage. The same distinction probably underpins the different areas of brain activity seen during skill acquisition (learning) and performance of a well-learned skill (Jenkins et al., 1994). This is because there is a high degree of dependence on external cues during skill acquisition, whereas skilled individuals may (not unrealistically) boast of being able to do "such-and-such" with their eyes shut!

PARIETAL INVOLVEMENT IN MOVEMENT

The parietal lobes make at least two independent contributions towards motor control (in addition to their primary role in somatosensation). Proprioceptive information from muscles and joints arrives in the primary somatosensory strip, relaying details about the position of body parts in relation to one another. This information is, in turn, fed to superior-posterior parietal regions BA 5 and BA 7, which also receive "feedback" from more anterior motor regions. This region is therefore in the position to both guide and correct movements, especially when actual movements do not correspond to those intended. A significant minority of pyramidal neuron cell bodies are located in these parietal areas and, as we have seen, the region also has reciprocal links with motor regions in the frontal lobes. More lateral regions of the left parietal lobe (the rostral inferior parietal lobule) seem to have a different motor role involving the storage of complex gesture and action representations. Damage here is associated with a condition known as apraxia in which the patient appears to lose the sense of what a particular movement is for (the concept of it, so to speak), so may be unable to either recognise a gesture made by others or implement a movement to order. We consider this, and other forms of apraxia, below.

THE FRONTAL-PARIETAL "MIRROR NEURON" CIRCUIT

In the early 1990s, a group of Italian researchers discovered a region of premotor cortex in the macaque containing neurons that became "active" *both* when the animal engaged in a particular meaningful action in relation to an object (such as grasping an item of food: a so-called transitive gesture) *and* when it observed another animal engaging in the same (or similar) action. These cells quickly came to be known as "mirror neurons" (Gallese et al., 1996). Further investigation revealed that the rostral (front) part of the inferior parietal lobule also contained mirror neurons that respond to a range of specific biological movements or actions. Subsequently, the superior temporal sulcus, which feeds into the inferior parietal lobule, has also been implicated in this "mirror neuron circuit" although neurons here do not possess motor properties (they only respond to observed actions/gestures).

Interest in this system has intensified following the realisation that the human brain too has a "mirror neuron circuit". Far from being an evolutionary "quirk", researchers have realised that the mirror neuron system might have played a critical evolutionary role in the development of several cognitive faculties that are either unique to or more highly developed in humans than any other species. These include imitation (as a form of learning) and the emergence of a spoken language from hand gestures (as discussed in Chapter 3). Some researchers have argued that humans routinely use this system to understand other people's actions (and emotions) in order to "mind-read" (Baron-Cohen, 2003) and empathise (Dapretto, 2006). Interest in the human mirror neuron circuit is currently intense, and one recent line of inquiry related to movement is the possible overlap between it and apraxia, a condition that we examine below (see, for example, Lewis, 2006). We have provided an outline of ongoing research developments in this exciting area in Box 5.5, and we briefly revisit some of the links between it and other cognitive processes and emotion in Chapter 10.

Box 5.5 The mirror neuron system

Mirror neurons are a particular class of sensory-motor neuron, first discovered in area F5 of the monkey premotor cortex (DiPellegrino et al., 1992). Their unique feature is that they become "active" *both* when the animal engages in a particular meaningful (transitive) action in relation to, for example, an item of food, *and* when it observes another animal engaging in a similar action. It is important to realise that neither the sight of the object alone nor a "meaningless action" unrelated to a specific object (a so-called intransitive gesture) will activate mirror neurons in monkeys. On the other hand, mirror neurons seem to show considerable generalisation in the sense that quite different representations of the same object–action interaction will all activate them to varying degrees. To give just one example, monkey mirror neurons that respond to seeing another monkey grasp a food pellet will also respond if a human hand grasps a food pellet (Rizzolatti et al., 1996). (See Figure 5.8 for an illustration of Rizzolatti et al.'s study.)

In the "early" primate studies, researchers initially sought to establish the proportion of neurons in F5 with "mirror" properties. In the upper sector of this region, at least 20% of neurons showed such properties in relation to hand movements and gestures, and in the lower sector, at least 15% of neurons showed "mirror" properties related to mouth movements, which in turn subdivided into ingestive (eating-related) and communicative functions. (In the macaque, lip smacking was one such example.) Further investigation revealed that the rostral (front) part of the inferior parietal lobule also contained neurons with "mirror" properties, responding to a range of species-specific movements, gestures, or actions. Subsequently, the superior temporal sulcus, which feeds into the inferior parietal lobule, has also been implicated in this "mirror circuit". However, although it contains movement-sensitive neurons, relatively few of these also possess true "mirror" properties, so its role is thought to be somewhat peripheral. Incidentally, these functions are essentially bilaterally distributed in monkeys.

Researchers have been able to measure the functional activity of individual neurons in primates using electrode implantation and unit recording, techniques

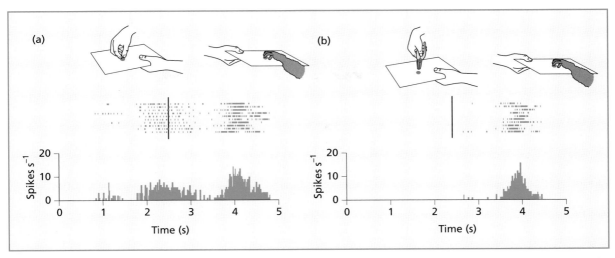

FIG. 5.8   Unit recording of mirror neurons in a macaque's area F5. (a) A piece of food is placed on a tray in front of the macaque. The experimenter grasps it, then replaces it and moves the tray (with the food) towards the macaque. Neuronal firing over a period of 5 seconds is indicated in the lower panels. Note the strong firing both when the experimenter grasps the food and when the macaque grasps it. (b) As (a) except the experimenter initially grasps the food with a pair of pliers, before moving the tray (with food) towards the macaque. Note the absence of neuronal firing when the observed action is performed with a tool rather than a hand. Source: Rizzolatti, G., Fadiga, L., Gallese, V., and Fogassi, L. (1996). Premotor cortex and the recognition of motor actions. *Cognitive Brain Research*, *3*, 131–141. Reproduced with permission, © Elsevier, 1996.

not ordinarily possible with humans. But using a range of procedures such as EEG, fMRI, and TMS it has become clear that humans too possess a mirror neuron system. Anatomically, this includes the human homologue of macaque area F5 which is Broca's area (specifically BA 44). However, the circuit also appears to extend into superior temporal and inferior parietal regions. Although both left and right cortical regions are implicated, bilateral symmetry of the system may not be as complete in humans as in other primates (Aziz-Zadeh et al., 2006). For example, Iacoboni et al. (1999) used fMRI to identify activations when human volunteers made imitative finger movements compared with when they made the same movements in response to a cue. Activation in the imitative condition was greater than in the cue condition in the left inferior frontal lobe, and right inferior parietal and superior temporal regions. In a very similar study to Iacoboni's, Heiser et al. (2003) used TMS to disrupt imitative but not cue-initiated finger movements. This effect could most reliably be induced with TMS to BA 44 on either the left or right side.

   Despite these anatomical similarities, comparison of the mirror neuron systems of macaques and humans has revealed at least two functional differences (Rizzolatti & Buccino, 2004). First, the human system appears responsive to mimed actions without an object (macaques require both a transitive action and an object to activate). Second, even meaningless intransitive gestures can activate the system in humans (Maeda, Kleiner-Fisman, & Pascual-Leone, 2002). These differences are important because they raise the possibility that the systems as a whole may have slightly different functions in humans than in other primates. Animal studies have generated two main hypotheses: imitation (Jeannerod, 1994) and action understanding (Rizzolatti, Fogassi, & Gallese, 2001). The first,

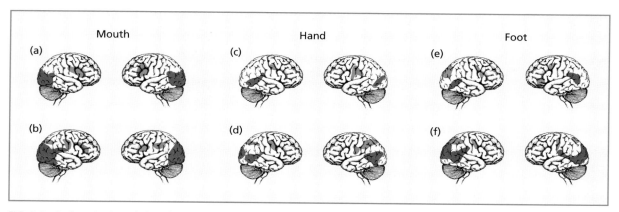

FIG. 5.9 Brain activations during observed mouth, hand, and foot actions (adapted, with permission from Blackwell Publishing, from Buccino et al., 2001). The upper images indicate (bilaterally) areas of activation during observation of movements not involving objects: (a) chewing; (c) mimed hand grasping; and (e) mimed kicking. The lower images indicate (bilaterally) activity to observed actions when objects are involved: (b) biting food; (d) grasping an object; and (f) kicking an object.

imitation, is an obvious candidate because, as we have seen, the system activates when there is correspondence between observed and actioned behaviour. However, there is considerable debate among animal behaviourists as to whether non-human primates actually do much "imitating", although, of course, humans certainly do. Thus the fMRI study of imitation by Buccino et al. (2001) is of interest. Respondents observed a series of transitive or mimed actions involving hand, mouth, or foot, and the main findings are summarised in Figure 5.9. In each case, action observation activated a network of inferior frontal and parietal regions bilaterally (but more pronounced on the right). And parietal activation seemed to be particularly associated with object-directed (as opposed to mimed) actions.

There is, however, more support for involvement of the mirror neuron system in action understanding in both humans and other primates. Consider the findings from Umilta et al.'s (2001) study. Macaques observed either complete transitive actions (a hand moving to grasp some food), or a partially obscured action sequence in which a food pellet was first clearly placed behind a screen and the approaching hand also disappeared behind the screen as it neared the food. (In a control condition the same actions were mimed without a food pellet.) Researchers found that at least 50% of the neurons that activated in the fully visible condition also activated just as vigorously in the obscured condition (though not in the mimed condition). These findings strongly suggest that activations related to the animal's understanding of the "purpose" of the action rather than simply to its mimicry. In essence, each time an animal observes a transitive action, the action activates neurons in its premotor cortex corresponding to when it makes the same action itself, the outcome of which it knows. So, the mirror system rather neatly transforms visual input directly into knowledge for the observer.

As we hinted earlier, the human and non-human mirror systems are similar but not identical. This has led to considerable speculation about other possible roles for it in humans. In particular, its established role in facilitating imitation has led to suggestions about its importance for skill and language acquisition

(Ramachandran, 2006). Its role in action understanding has led to speculation about its importance for human communication in general, and in predicting the actions of others in particular (Ramnani & Miall, 2004). In this context, damage to the system might be relevant in disorders of human communication such as autism and Asperger's syndrome, and some psychotic disorders (Blakemore et al., 2005). We revisit this line of inquiry in Chapter 10 when we review the neuropsychology of emotion and motivation.

PERIPHERAL AND SPINAL MOVEMENT DISORDERS

By now, it should be apparent that movement disorders can result from damage or loss of function to many different regions of the nervous system. Literally dozens of disorders, often thankfully very rare, are described in the neurology literature, but for present purposes we will restrict our list to specific examples that either illustrate the importance of particular components of the motor system or are of special interest to neuropsychologists. We begin the review in distal regions of the nervous system with a brief mention of some disorders related to peripheral or spinal cord abnormalities, before moving into the brain. Here we will consider a small number of disorders related to cortical damage, but spend more time reviewing motor disorders associated with basal ganglia or other subcortical structures.

MYASTHENIA GRAVIS

The main symptoms of myasthenia gravis (which are highly variable and range from mildly disabling to life threatening) are those of muscle weakness or fatigue, especially in the head–neck region. (A tell-tale early symptom is drooping eyelids.) The weakness results not from damage to, or loss of tissue from, the muscles themselves, but from impaired neuromuscular synaptic transmission. In most cases, normal amounts of the neurotransmitter acetylcholine (ACh) are released from motor neurons but this fails to have the expected effect on the target muscles. In the 1970s it became apparent that myasthenic individuals have a reduced number of ACh receptors (Albuquerque et al., 1976), which is thought to occur as a result of an inappropriate immune response in which (for reasons that are not currently known) the body's immune system inadvertently attacks the receptors as if they were "foreign". Myasthenia gravis therefore joins a growing list of auto-immune diseases (Engel, 1984; Shah & Lisak, 1993).

If the symptoms are mild they can be treated quite effectively with drugs that have the effect of boosting activity in the synapses between motor neurons and muscles. It is not presently possible to promote the growth of new ACh receptors, but certain drugs can partially override the problem by ensuring that released neurotransmitter remains in the synapse for longer before it is inactivated. The drugs in question achieve this by inhibiting the enzyme that normally breaks down ACh soon after it is released. The enzyme is acetylcholinesterase (AChE) and the drugs are therefore known as acetylcholinesterase inhibitors (AChEIs). Examples include physostigmine and neostigmine. However, these medications are far from ideal, because they influence all ACh synapses including many in the brain, where they may induce unwanted side effects including sleep disturbances, cognitive impairments, and even **hallucinations**.

KEY TERM
Hallucinations: Perceptual experiences unrelated to physical sensation. They may occur in any sensory modality, and are often associated with mental illness.

DISEASES ASSOCIATED WITH NEURONAL DAMAGE/LOSS

Multiple sclerosis (MS) is one of a group of demyelinating diseases, meaning that the principal pathological process involves the progressive loss of myelin. In MS this can occur throughout the nervous system and may affect all myelinated neurons. There are broadly two patterns of progression in MS: the more common relapsing-remitting form (four out of five cases) involves periods of hiatus (relapse), coinciding with inflammation of regions of CNS white matter, followed by recovery, although an underlying trend of disease progression is still apparent, particularly in later stages. The progressively disabling form (about one in five cases) involves a slow but steady deterioration of function. In either case, progression is often slow, although eventually white matter in the brain, especially that surrounding the ventricles, will be lost. More recent evidence indicates that in addition to demyelination, the axons themselves may be damaged by the disease process (Waxman, 2005). Early signs include loss of (or disturbed) sensation in hands or lower limbs, and loss of, or impaired, muscle control. Blurred vision is also a common early feature. As the disease progresses, more widespread paralysis (and loss of sensation) will be seen, and there may be cognitive changes as well.

Although MS is described as an auto-immune disease, the trigger for the self-harming immune response is, as yet, unknown. The drug beta-interferon is thought to work by modifying the responsiveness of the immune system (Arnason, 1999). Recently a second medicine, glatiramer acetate, has been developed to reduce relapse rate and intensity in the more common form of the disease. The mode of action is unclear but, like beta-interferon, it affects the immune response, promoting the release of anti-inflammatory substances such as interleukin 4.

As the name implies, **motor neuron disease** (MND) is more restricted in terms of its pathology, but also usually more aggressive, with death generally occurring within a few years of onset as the motor neurons that normally control respiration and swallowing become affected (death usually occurs as a result of respiratory failure). MND actually comprises a group of related disorders with variable course. One of the most common forms, amyotrophic lateral sclerosis (ALS), is also known as Lou Gehrig disease after the New York Yankees baseball player who developed this disorder. As motor neurons in the spinal cord and cranial nerves die, there is progressive and unremitting loss of muscle function. Intellectual abilities may remain intact until later stages of disease (Bruijn, Miller, & Cleveland, 2004), although cognitive impairments correlate with pyramidal cell loss in the premotor and prefrontal cortex in a proportion of cases (Maekawa et al., 2004), suggesting that MND is not in fact restricted to loss of motor neurons (see also Al Chalabi, 2006).

The cause(s) of MND remain a mystery, although a small proportion (< 5% of cases) are thought to be genetic (Boillee & Cleveland, 2004). Other possible causal factors include as yet unknown viruses, possible exposure to toxins, and even head injury. Nevertheless, the pathology of MND *is* known and appears to involve the over-expression of genes coding for a particular glutamate receptor (glutamate is a widespread neurotransmitter in the CNS). This leads to **excito-toxicity** in the glutamate system and resultant loss of tissue (Kawahara et al., 2004).

It might be noted that **poliomyelitis**, an infectious disease caused by a virus

KEY TERMS

Multiple sclerosis: A disease in which progressive loss of myelin leads to loss of function.

Motor neuron disease: One of a group of disorders characterised by progressive destruction of the motor neurons that control voluntary action.

Excito-toxicity: The process by which nerve cells are killed by excitatory substances.

Poliomyelitis (polio): A viral disease where motor neurons are damaged resulting in muscle weakness and/or paralysis.

and otherwise unrelated to MND, also targets motor neurons. Although rarely fatal, polio may leave lasting muscle wastage as a result of peripheral nerve damage and the resultant loss of innervation to muscles.

SPINAL DAMAGE

There are a number of rare diseases of the spinal cord but the most common damage to it results from accidental injury. Although the nerve tissue is normally well protected by the backbone that encases it, spinal injury often involves a displacement of vertebrae resulting in a "shearing effect" in which axons are literally torn apart. Transection of the spinal cord brings about a permanent paraplegia (lower body paralysis) in which there is loss of sensation and motor control of the body regions below the point of damage. Ironically, spinal reflexes below that point may still be intact, and even more pronounced as a result of loss of inhibitory influence from the brain. Transection in the neck region resulting from injury (usually breaking of the neck) is likely to bring about quadriplegia: paralysis of all four limbs and trunk.

CORTICAL MOVEMENT DISORDERS

HEMIPLEGIA

This condition has already been described as a loss of contralateral voluntary control. This means that an affected individual is no longer able to intentionally move parts of their body on the side opposite to that of the brain damage. The most common cause of hemiplegia is interruption of blood supply via the mid-cerebral artery, due to **aneurysm**, **haemorrhage**, or **clot** to the primary motor strip. Other causes include accidental head injury, epilepsy, and tumour. Hemiplegia can also occur after damage to subcortical structures, including the basal ganglia, which are also served by the mid-cerebral artery.

Usually with hemiplegia there will be a modest but discernible degree of recovery of function over time. This is because initial symptoms result not just from cell death due to loss of blood supply, but additionally from temporary loss of function in surrounding neurons. Diaschisis, as it is known, is in effect a short-term reduction in activity levels because of reduced inputs from the now-dead cells. These adjacent neurons may also be affected by a temporary change in blood supply. (However, exposure to excess blood in the event of haemorrhage can cause cell death.) Many neurons later appear to return to a normal or near normal level of functioning, leading to (partial) behavioural recovery of function. Functional improvement may also occur as recovering patients develop entirely new ways of achieving movement, making use of quite different brain regions. A primary aim of physiotherapy is to promote recovery of function in this way, by teaching the use of alternative muscle systems to achieve the same goal.

CEREBRAL PALSY

Cerebral palsy is not a unitary disorder, and may take a variety of forms encompassing many **signs** and **symptoms** depending on extent of damage. It

> **KEY TERMS**
> **Aneurysm:** A form of stroke caused by a blood vessel in the brain suddenly expanding then bursting.
>
> **Haemorrhage:** A general term for bleeding. In the brain, this may occur following an aneurysm, or other damage to a blood vessel.
>
> **Clot:** A solid deposit in the blood that may block a narrow blood vessel leading to a form of stroke.
>
> **Signs:** The indications of some abnormality or disturbance that are apparent to the trained clinician/observer (as opposed to symptoms, which are things an individual describes/ complains of).
>
> **Symptoms:** (See signs above.) Symptoms are the features of a disorder or disease that the individual reports/complains of.

usually results from trauma during late foetal development or birth. Because of its heterogeneous nature, it is difficult to talk in general terms about the condition. However, a hallmark is motor disturbance, which may include difficulties in making voluntary movements (ataxia), unwanted involuntary movements (athetoidy), and excessively tensed muscles (spasticity). These problems are probably also responsible for the speech difficulties that are often seen in cerebral palsy, although language difficulties may also be linked to more general intellectual impairment which is a frequent but by no means ubiquitous feature of the condition.

APRAXIA

The term refers to a collection of movement disorders in which the ability to perform certain purposeful actions on command is compromised. A diagnosis is made mainly on exclusionary grounds: for example, that the disturbance cannot be attributed to a deficit in the control of muscles. Thus, an apraxic individual may be unable to make a particular gesture when asked, but may make the same gesture spontaneously. To add to the confusion there are several ways of categorising apraxia, and some forms are also known by more than one name. A final concern is that apraxia often co-occurs with aphasia, and in such patients it is important to establish that an apparent apraxic deficit is not secondary to a primary language deficit, for example a failure to understand basic instructions.

Given these complications, some neuropsychologists (e.g., Heilman & Rothi, 1993) have found it instructive to revisit the original ideas of Liepmann, who first characterised different forms of apraxia over 100 years ago (Liepmann, 1905). In what he called ideo-motor apraxia, the patient makes errors when asked to "pantomime" particular actions such as hammering a nail or brushing teeth (Leiguarda & Marsden, 2000). The patient seems to have some basic knowledge of the required action, but not of the use of the relevant tool, a hammer or toothbrush in this example, and may thus use their fist (as a hammer) or their finger (as a toothbrush). Conversely, in ideational apraxia (sometimes called conceptual apraxia) patients may be able to make well-formed movements, which are nevertheless inappropriate and/or disorganised. Such individuals may also misuse tools, but additionally behave as if they have effectively lost the "idea" (memory representation?) of the requisite action sequence: they can neither correctly implement a movement to order nor recognise the same movements made by others (Heilman, Rothi, & Valenstein, 1982). Thus, in this conceptualisation, ideational apraxia would be regarded as the more serious (and rarer) condition (see Figure 5.10).

Problems with this taxonomy arise, however, when specific testing arrangements are taken into account. Although inability to imitate so-called "transitive" actions (actions in relation to specific objects) is regarded as a hallmark feature of apraxia (Buxbaum, Johnson-Frey, & Bartlett-Williams, 2005), some apraxic individuals who cannot initiate "pretend" actions (i.e., cannot "pantomime") can in fact imitate someone else carrying out the same action. Others may appear apraxic until they are given the actual objects with which to carry out the required action (Ietswaart, Carey, & Della Sala, 2006). Still others may struggle with transitive actions (such as stirring a drink with a spoon) but perform intransitive ones (such as waving or signalling *STOP!*) normally (Haaland & Flaherty, 1984). According to DeRenzi, Pieczuro, and Vignolo (1968), over half of all

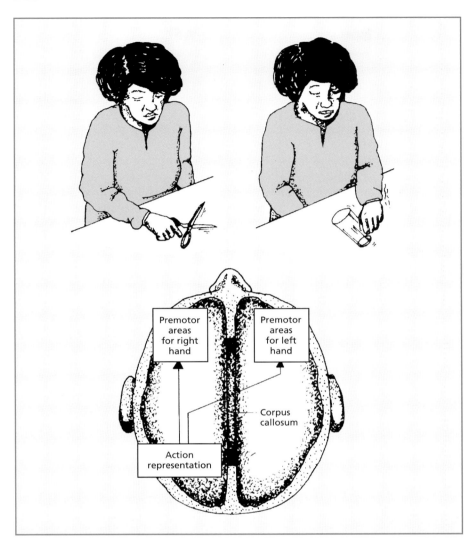

FIG. 5.10 Ideational apraxia. Movement of the left and right hands is coordinated by the right and left motor cortex. Patients with apraxia may be unable to engage in purposeful movement with one (or both) hand(s), being clumsy or otherwise responding inappropriately. However, damage restricted to the left parietal lobe is sufficient to induce bilateral ideational (limb) apraxia. In this condition, the patient seems to have lost their internal representations for movements, so can neither recognise actions by others, nor implement movements on instruction. Source: Gazzaniga et al. (1998). *Cognitive neuroscience: The biology of the mind* (Figure 10.32). Copyright © 1998 by W. W. Norton & Company, Inc. Used by permission of W. W. Norton & Company, Inc.

apraxic individuals show features of both ideo-motor and ideational apraxia (as traditionally conceptualised) and this has prompted some neuropsychologists to emphasise the similarities rather than the differences between Liepmann's two forms. To further complicate matters, re-examination of Liepmann's original work by Goldenberg (2003) indicates ambiguous use of the terms for the two forms of apraxia by both Liepmann and his colleague Pick (Pick, 1905). Today, the term "limb apraxia" is frequently used to encompass both conditions, although there is clearly a graduated scale of impairment. Damasio and Geschwind (1985) characterised this hierarchy as follows:

1   A failure to produce a correct movement in response to a verbal command.
2   A failure to correctly imitate a movement.
3   A failure to correctly perform a movement (or sequence of movements) in response to an observed object.
4   A failure to even correctly handle an object.

An advantage of grouping together Liepmann's two forms of apraxia under the single heading of "limb apraxia" is that it creates a clearer distinction with a third form also described by Liepmann—motor apraxia, now (confusingly) called limb-kinetic apraxia. Although this can co-occur with limb apraxia, in its isolated form there can be a bilateral loss of hand/finger dexterity which affects all types of movement (symbolic and non-symbolic; transitive and intransitive, etc.) without any marked "conceptual" impairment (Goldenberg, 2003).

Whatever the eventual resolution regarding a definitive taxonomy of apraxic disorders, the most severe presentations of bilateral limb apraxia are consistently associated with left parietal damage (Rizzolatti & Matelli, 2003). According to Heilman and Rothi, representations of movement plans are stored here (specifically in BA 40 on the left side, also known as the supra-marginal gyrus/inferior parietal lobule), and damage may either degrade or completely obliterate the representation, making both generation and recognition of gestures/actions either problematic or impossible. However, a small number of cases of limb apraxia have also been associated with damage to more anterior regions (still in the left hemisphere), such as the SMA or the PMC, or to the pathways connecting parietal and frontal regions. This suggests that normal praxis is mediated by a distributed network encompassing parietal, frontal, and possibly subcortical structures on the left side.

Other forms of apraxia have also been described: Unilateral callosal apraxia is associated with damage to the anterior part of the corpus callosum. This prevents motor commands from the left hemisphere travelling to the right side which, of course, controls the left hand. So callosal apraxia almost always affects the left hand in right-handed individuals. Constructional apraxia may follow right parietal damage. Limb movements are normal but individuals cannot generate representations of objects by building models or copying 3D geometric patterns. This is seen as a disorder of the organisation of complex spatial actions. Buccofacial (oral) apraxia is actually the most common apraxic condition and is characterised by an inability to produce particular oro-facial movements, such as sticking out one's tongue or blowing a kiss, on demand. It is invariably associated with specific localised damage to BA 44 of the left frontal lobe (part of Broca's area).

Finally, as we mentioned above, there are some intriguing points of overlap between some forms of apraxia and the mirror neuron system. Anatomically, for example, areas of damage seen in limb and buccofacial apraxia partially overlap with the mirror circuit in the left (but not right) hemisphere (Rizzolatti & Matelli, 2003). Both are, essentially, disorders of transitive gesture/actions, and hand and mouth transitive gestures are also likely to activate the mirror system (Buxbaum et al., 2005). Finally, many apraxic patients are unable to imitate gestures despite having normal (or near normal) capacity to plan and execute goal-directed movements with visual feedback (Ietswaart et al., 2006). These points of convergence are currently being explored by researchers.

SUBCORTICAL MOVEMENT DISORDERS

Within a period of a few months in the early 1980s, a group of young patients came to the attention of a hospital in California. All presented with profound Parkinson's disease-like symptoms including marked and unremitting akinesia (immobility). Research indicated that each individual was a drug addict and had recently used synthetic heroin contaminated with an impurity known as MPTP. This substance is converted in the brain to the closely related and highly toxic substance MPP, which has an affinity for cells that contain the dark pigment neuromelanin. The substantia nigra (as its name, from the Latin for "black substance", suggests) is rich in such cells, and these had been obliterated by the MPP. The individuals came to be known as "the frozen addicts". They had an unusually "pure" and enduring drug-induced form of **Parkinsonism** (Martin & Hayden, 1987).

Most neurological disorders that affect the basal ganglia are less clear-cut than the damage seen in the frozen addicts: in these disorders, damage tends to be localised, and/or progress slowly. Because of this selectivity, there is rarely complete loss of function. Rather, we find a raft of intriguing disorders in which movement is compromised rather than abolished. Actions may still be possible but they now occur in unregulated or poorly coordinated ways.

PARKINSON'S DISEASE (PD)

Of all the subcortical movement disorders this is perhaps the best understood. It affects relatively few people under 50, but the incidence steadily increases to about 1% in 60-year-olds and at least 2% in 85-year-olds. It is a progressive and relentless disorder and, although the symptoms may develop quite slowly, it is in principle a terminal illness. (Its progress is so slow that most people die of unrelated illnesses before PD has run its full course, thought to be at least 15 years.) The features of the disorder were recorded by the ancient Greeks, and the constellation of symptoms was known by its common name of "shaking palsy" for many years, before its full characterisation by the English physician James Parkinson. Incidentally he did not name it after himself. This honour was suggested by the famous French neurologist Charcot.

Through careful observation of affected individuals, Parkinson realised that the disorder that came to bear his name comprised a cluster of movement-related symptoms. These need not all be present for the diagnosis to be appropriate, and the severity of symptoms will become more pronounced over time. The symptoms in question comprised resting tremor, rigidity, bradykinesia–akinesia, and postural disturbance. This list has now been expanded, and the full range of Parkinson's features are clustered into what are often referred to as positive and negative symptoms (see Box 5.5).

Resting tremor is so called because it disappears or at least becomes less marked when the person engages in some deliberate act. It can usually be seen in the hands or lower limbs. The rigidity (sometimes called cog-wheel rigidity because an external force can induce "give", only for rigidity to reappear after a brief movement) is thought to be related to dysregulation of usually antagonistic

Box 5.5 The positive and negative symptoms of PD

Positive symptoms

Tremor at rest: alternating movements that usually disappear during deliberate actions. The "pill-rolling" action of fingers and thumb is common.

Muscular rigidity: caused by antagonistic muscles being tensed at the same time. This is apparent when limbs are manipulated passively (by someone else). A resistance, followed by loosening, then further resistance is often found, giving rise to the term "cog-wheel rigidity".

Involuntary movements: changes in posture, known as akathesia, may be almost continual, especially during inactivity. Involuntary turns to the side (of the head and eyes) are sometimes apparent.

Negative symptoms

Disordered posture: for example, the inability to maintain a body part (such as the head) in the appropriate position, or failure to correct minor imbalances that may cause the patient to fall.

Loss of spontaneous movement: akinesia is the inability to generate spontaneous intentional movement. A blank facial expression is another manifestation.

Slowness in movement: bradykinesia is a marked slowing of repetitive movements such as tapping or clapping.

Disordered locomotion: walking may be slow and poorly coordinated—more a shuffle than a stride.

Disturbed speech: bradykinesia also affects the production of speech, which may slow markedly, sound atonal, and be difficult to understand.

---

actions of flexor and extensor muscles. Under normal circumstances, as one muscle is tensed, the opposor muscle passively extends. Rigidity occurs because both muscles are tensed at the same time.

Akinesia and bradykinesia are two prominent negative symptoms that also merit close consideration. These terms describe absence or severe slowing of movement. They both become most apparent when the patient is required to act by his or her own volition. A classic illustration of akinesia is to play a game of "catch" with a Parkinson's patient. Gently toss a ball to him/her and they might catch it without difficulty; this would, of course, be a stimulus-driven action. Now ask the patient to throw the ball back. Although they will certainly understand the instruction, they may find this (internally driven action) impossible.

Bradykinesia might be observed by asking a PD patient to clap their hands together. Although, once again, the instruction will have been understood, they may find this simple task extremely effortful (starting somewhat hesitantly, and rapidly tailing off altogether). Curiously, some background music with a strong beat may do the trick—another case of an external cue driving the action. The mask-like visage of the Parkinson patient is a further tell-tale sign of either bradykinesia or akinesia affecting facial expression.

That this set of diverse symptoms all depend (in some way) on dysfunction in the basal ganglia circuitry has been known for over 30 years. Indeed, post-mortem studies had shown clear evidence of loss of tissue in the caudate/putamen region (particularly the putamen) even before this. The discovery by Hornykiewicz in 1966 that these changes may be secondary to loss of dopamine innervation from neurons originating in the substantia nigra-pc (and making up the nigro-striatal pathway) eventually led to the development of drug treatments aimed at replacing missing dopamine or restoring the balance between dopamine and the principal intrinsic striatal neurotransmitter ACh.

You might think that dopamine itself would be a suitable drug to treat PD. However, when taken orally most is quickly broken down in the gut. But a related substance, L-dopa, can be taken orally, does not get metabolised in the gut to the same extent, and is converted to dopamine by cells in the brain. This drug has therefore assumed a central role in the treatment of PD. It does not "cure" the disease, but it does provide some symptomatic relief, although its effects lessen as the disease progresses.

Two other developments in treatment for PD merit attention. Deep brain stimulation involves the surgical implantation of very fine electrodes into the basal ganglia (usually either the globus pallidus or the subthalamic nucleus; see Freund, 2005, for a concise review). Battery-powered tonic high-frequency electrical stimulation of these nuclei aims to reduce their outputs, thus lifting the inhibitory effect of the globus pallidus on the thalamus. Although still in its experimental stages, results so far suggest that this treatment may be especially effective in reducing bradykinesia (Anderson et al., 2005). A radically different treatment for PD involves the implantation of tissue from foetal brains. The idea (no matter how distasteful to some) is to implant cells that are dopaminergic (i.e., that manufacture and release dopamine). However, it is too early to judge the true effectiveness of this procedure: An initial review of more than 20 cases by Olanow, Kordower, and Freeman (1996) gave early cause for optimism, but more recent studies by Freed et al. (2001) and Olanow et al. (2003) suggest that the beneficial effects of grafts may be limited to young patients. More worryingly, Freed's group found that about 15% of treated patients may develop side effects that are as debilitating as the disease itself. A synopsis of foetal transplant research for PD is provided in Box 5.6.

Box 5.6 The viability of foetal transplants for Parkinson's disease

From 1987 to 2003, five reports were published detailing procedures to transplant tissue from (aborted) foetuses into the brains of individuals with advanced Parkinson's disease. The pooled sample included just 23 patients. The tissue itself comprised cells capable of producing and releasing dopamine, usually drawn from neuroblasts (cells able to divide into either neurons or glia) taken from several embryos, which were transplanted into multiple sites in, and adjacent to, the striatum. After a period of recovery it was possible to assess these patients both in terms of Parkinson's symptomatology, and functionally in terms of renewed dopamine activity and concomitant reduction in requisite L-dopa medication.

The results of these trials were very encouraging. Overall, grafted patients showed a significant improvement in motor function, a reduced need for medication, and an increase in the uptake of precursors for dopamine, strongly suggestive of increased dopamine turnover (use). These changes were maintained for more than 10 years in some patients.

However, each of these studies was "open-label", meaning that both patients and clinicians were aware of the treatment and its anticipated consequences. Moreover there were no control patients despite the fact that placebo effects can be prominent in PD. To overcome this problem, two placebo controlled trials were initiated and have now reported their findings (Freed et al., 2001; Olanow et al., 2003). To try to control for placebo effects, some patients in each trial even underwent "sham" surgery in which they were anaesthetised and operated on, but no tissue was implanted. Although the clinical procedures used in each of these studies differed in terms of amount and type of tissue implanted, and whether or not immunosuppressant drugs were given, the findings failed to replicate those of the earlier open-label trials. The Freed study reported some evidence for symptom reduction in younger patients although the average change across all patients did not reach statistical significance. This study used tissue from only two donors (somewhat less than the open-label trials) and no immunosuppressant medication. Moreover, two patients died after grafting. The Olanow study did employ immunosuppression, but the group used solid tissue rather than tissue in liquid suspension. There was no significant improvement in symptomatology at 24 months, although patients grafted with tissue from multiple ($n = 4$) donors fared better in the first 6 months post-surgery.

Winkler, Kirik, and Bjorklund (2005) have provided a concise summary of and commentary on tissue transplantation for PD, which to date (early 2007) has been conducted in about 400 patients worldwide. They conclude that while transplantation remains both a viable and promising approach, there are many parameters that require further research before a safe and effective standardised procedure can be developed. These include patient variables such as age, duration of illness, medication levels, and symptomatology; and methodological variables such as tissue source and type, and the duration of use of immunosuppression (see also Piccini et al., 2005).

Very recently, the prospect of using stem cells as an alternative tissue source has arisen, although as yet data concerning the effectiveness of this type of grafting have been restricted to work with animals.

HUNTINGTON'S DISEASE

Huntington's disease is a rare genetically determined disorder (which used to be known as Huntington's chorea). It leads to death within about 12–15 years of onset of symptoms. These usually take a characteristic course, although the exact transition point between "choreic" and "end-stage" is difficult to identify or predict. The "choreic" stage of Huntington's is marked by the presence of unusual and intrusive movements (so-called "choreform" movements) which may initially appear benign, taking the form of fidgeting or restlessness. But soon they become apparent in limbs, trunk, head, and neck, to the extent that they interfere with "normal" actions including walking, talking, and even swallowing. Psychological

KEY TERM
Huntington's disease: A rare, genetically determined, neurological disorder causing dementia and death due to progressive loss of neurons in the striatum.

and cognitive changes, which can sometimes lead to a misdiagnosis of mental illness, may also be apparent.

In the later stages of the disease involuntary movements may disappear, but so too do voluntary movements. The upshot is that "end-stage" Huntington's disease resembles, in certain respects, the negative symptoms of Parkinson's disease. The individual may be immobile, mute, bed-ridden, and even have difficulty breathing and swallowing. Memory and attentional impairments, **perseveration** and aphasia are also seen. Death is often due to **aspiration pneumonia**.

Although the disease remains rare, its pathology is now becoming better understood. In later stages there are widespread changes involving loss of tissue to several regions of cortex. These probably account for the psychological and cognitive changes that become progressively more prominent. However, these are thought to be secondary to more subtle and earlier changes in the striatum, or at least relatively independent of the main symptoms of movement disorder. Indeed, in early-stage Huntington's the only changes are found in the caudate, where a progressive loss of so-called "spiny" **interneurons**, initially in the medial region and later in more lateral regions, is observed. Because these neurons normally help to regulate the inhibitory output to the external part of the globus pallidus and substantia nigra, their demise brings about a dysregulation of the indirect (inhibitory) route through the basal ganglia, and the appearance of unwanted (disinhibited) involuntary movements (see Figure 5.4). However, as the disease progresses to affect neurons throughout the striatum, with up to 90% of spiny interneurons lost, the entire regulatory function of the basal ganglia is compromised, including the "enabling" facility of the direct route. At this point negative symptoms prevail, as intentional actions (including basic vegetative processes such as breathing and swallowing) no longer gain the "assent" of the basal ganglia.

Huntington's disease is caused by the presence of a single dominant gene on chromosome four which has mutated to become extra long by dint of the unwanted presence of multiple **trinucleotide repeats**. If one of your parents has Huntington's you have a 50% chance of developing it. You may therefore wonder why this disorder has persisted, as far as medical records tell us, for at least 300 years. The answer is that the symptoms do not appear until middle age (typically about 40) and most people have had children by that time. However, it is now possible to test for the presence of this mutant gene (Gusella & MacDonald, 1994), and many people with a family history opt to have the test, to help them decide in advance whether or not to start a family.

TICS, TOURETTE'S SYNDROME, AND OBSESSIVE-COMPULSIVE DISORDER

Tics are brief, involuntary, unpredictable, and purposeless repetitive gestures or movements that often seem to focus on the face and head. They may involve unusual facial grimacing, twitching, or other stereotyped actions. Sometimes vocal tics occur, wherein the individual makes clicks or grunts, or even barks. These are most common in children, and often disappear in adolescence. Evidence suggests that the appearance of tics is definitely associated with stress. If tics persist into adulthood the condition merges with Tourette's syndrome (TS).

TS is therefore a severe form of tic disorder. As well as the sort of tic already described, someone with Tourette's may display multiple involuntary mannerisms, echolalia (parrot-like mimicry) and, in the most severe cases, coprolalia (expletive use of foul language often of a sexual nature). Although this constellation of symptoms sounds bizarre, people with TS are not considered mentally ill, and usually have insight into their condition. Rather, they cannot "control" action plans (including lewd thoughts) which therefore intrude on their other activities. Their manifestation is made worse by anxiety or stress, and ameliorated to some extent by relaxation and the use of dopamine-blocking drugs.

Earlier, we described the features of tics and TS as involuntary. Strictly speaking this is not the case. Most "Touretters" can muster sufficient will-power to inhibit a tic or mannerism for a short while, but the longer they hold off, the worse the compulsion to engage in the action becomes. Although this seems a world away from "normal experience", Bradshaw and Mattingley (1995) have likened this "compulsion" to the infectious nature of yawning and the developing struggle to suppress it.

Our inclusion of obsessive-compulsive disorder (OCD) alongside tics and TS may, on the face of it, seem a little fanciful. After all, OCD is a psychiatric disorder appearing in DSM IV (the current classification system) in the same section as other anxiety-related conditions, and the symptoms of OCD seem to support this. As the name suggests, people with this disorder display a range of symptoms including obsessive repetitive thoughts or feelings, and/or the compulsion to engage in ritualistic behaviours such as repeatedly checking locks or endless hand washing. The obsessions or compulsions are so intense that they interfere with other more routine behaviours, so that day-to-day living becomes completely disrupted by them. If the individual is, for any reason, unable to engage in the behaviour, they are likely to experience spiraling levels of anxiety.

Yet there are, increasingly, doubts about the purely psychological origin of OCD. For one thing, psychological treatments tend to be relatively ineffective against it, whereas selective serotonin re-uptake inhibitor medications (SSRIs) can have dramatic effects in reducing or even eliminating the obsessional and compulsive behaviours (Goodman, 1999; Leonard, 1997). This has led to speculation that OCD may be related either to low levels of serotonin, or underactivity at serotonin synapses in the striatum. Serotonin is known to interact with dopamine in this region and is generally thought to have an inhibitory action. So an SSRI drug, which has the effect of boosting serotonin neurotransmission, will in effect replenish the inhibitory influence whose absence leads to obsessive and compulsive behaviours in the first place (Rapoport, 1990). Intriguingly, McDougle et al. (1994) have reported that the addition of a dopamine antagonist drug such as haloperidol alongside an SSRI is more effective than an SSRI alone in the pharmacological treatment for OCD. Second, there is considerable overlap between OCD, tics, and TS: Tics are, in effect, compulsive actions, and at least 25% of people with TS also meet the diagnostic criteria for OCD. Grados et al. (2001) have reported a family association between tic disorders (including TS) and OCD consistent with a common underlying genetic predisposition.

If all other treatments for OCD fail, a surgical procedure known as cingulotomy can lead to a reduction of symptoms in a proportion of those operated on (Martuza et al., 1990). The surgery involves lesioning the pathway that funnels cortical output from the cingulate gyrus and/or the orbitofrontal regions into the basal ganglia. Finally, deep brain stimulation of the subthalamic nucleus may (as with Parkinson's disease) alleviate some OCD symptoms (Abelson et al., 2005).

OTHER DISORDERS LINKED TO BASAL GANGLIA DYSFUNCTION

Two other disorders merit brief attention. Ballism (or the more common unilateral hemi-ballism) is a rare movement disorder linked directly to damage to the sub-thalamic nucleus, usually from a stroke. The main features of this condition are wild flinging-like movements of the limbs and sometimes the neck and head, which are so pronounced that they can cause severe injuries. Treatment involves dopamine-blocking drugs, and symptoms sometimes resolve after a period of recovery.

Sydenham's chorea is a complication that may develop following rheumatic fever in about one in five affected children. Hallmark features of this disorder are tics, twitches and other motoric signs such as sudden aimless movements in the head, trunk, and limbs (Black & Mink, 1999). Although the condition usually resolves within a few weeks, there are reports of children who have had recurrent episodes over a period of several years. An MRI study by Geidd et al. (1995) reported enlargement of the caudate, putamen, and globus pallidus which resolved as symptoms abated.

INTERIM COMMENT

At the beginning of this section we suggested that damage to the basal ganglia (or the loops between the basal ganglia and the rest of the brain) would not bring about the abolition of movement, but rather its dysregulation. This is exactly what we see in both Parkinson's and Huntington's diseases. In the former, loss of dopamine input to the striatum from the substantia nigra leads to a change in the balance between the direct and indirect routes. Remember that ordinarily, dopamine promotes activity in the direct route and inhibits the indirect route. So reduced dopamine innervation will tend to bias basal ganglia output in favour of the indirect route which works as a "brake" on actions (Gerfen, 2006), and we see the negative symptoms of bradykinesia and akinesia. The positive symptoms are thought to be related either to changes in output from the basal ganglia and thalamus to the spinal cord secondary to the changes in the striatum itself, or to functional changes to reciprocal connections (between the subthalamic nucleus and globus pallidus) within the basal ganglia itself (Hamani et al., 2003). In either case, disturbance in the normal dynamic balance within the basal ganglia leads to impairments in the control of movement.

In Huntington's disease there is intrinsic progressive cell loss within the striatum, particularly in the caudate. Initially the indirect pathway is more affected so the "brake" effect is reduced, leading to the intrusion of unwanted (disinhibited) choreic movements. However, in the final stages of Huntington's the loss of cells in the striatum is so extensive that most output is compromised, and the symptoms now resemble the negative features of Parkinson's disease. A similar disruption to the normal functioning of the indirect route is seen in ballism and hemi-ballism, in which the subthalamic nucleus is damaged and we see, as a consequence, dramatic unwanted movements superimposed on an otherwise normal behavioural repertoire.

In the case of tics, TS, and OCD, the basal ganglia and its inputs from the cortex again appear pivotal. Three structural imaging studies have reported reduced size of the caudate and/or putamen in TS (see Saxena et al., 1998, for a review). There are relatively few functional imaging studies in tics and TS, and their results are difficult to interpret (Albin & Mink, 2006). However, the available evidence points to underactivity in prefrontal and cingulate regions coupled with underactivity in the caudate (Moriarty et al., 1995), and increased dopamine innervation throughout the striatum (Singer et al., 2002). Dopamine-blocking drugs acting in the striatum will thus modify TS symptoms (Wolf et al., 1996). In the case of OCD, there is compelling evidence of overactivity in the orbitofrontal and cingulate regions and the caudate, especially if the individual is challenged or provoked by the object/situation that induces their symptoms (Breiter et al., 1996). Symptomatic relief may be achieved by severing the pathway connecting these regions, or by SSRI drugs, which potentiate serotonergic inhibition in the striatum and/or the orbitofrontal lobes. In this context, Sydenham's chorea could be conceptualised as a sort of temporary form of TS. It has also been linked to structural changes (swelling) in the basal ganglia, and symptoms can be lessened with the use of dopamine-blocking medications.

CHAPTER SUMMARY

At the start of this chapter, we warned that the nervous system's control of movement is complex, yet we are probably all guilty of taking for granted the skills that this control mechanism permits. These skills are not solely the domain of Olympic gymnasts or concert pianists: with very little practice we can all master skills currently quite beyond the scope of the most talented robots.

There are at least four major motor pathways carrying different types of motor information to various regions of the body. These in turn are innervated by different brain regions. At one time it was thought that there were two basic motor systems in the brain: the pyramidal and extra-pyramidal systems, controlling deliberate and automatic actions respectively. This distinction is not now thought especially helpful, because components of the two systems interact in the brain itself, and in the spinal cord and periphery.

In the brain, attention has focused on the various roles in movement of the cerebellum, the basal ganglia, and the cortex. The cerebellum is important for posture, balance, and skill acquisition, and it interacts with the spinal cord and the frontal lobes. The basal ganglia also interact with the frontal lobes with which they form a series of feedback loops. A current theory about basal ganglia function is that they play a vital role both in the selection of preferred actions and in terminating ongoing actions in anticipation of switching to a different action. The actions in question are ones that are internally generated, rather than those that are driven by external stimuli.

Cortical control of movement is essentially hierarchical. The primary motor strip is innervated by the SMA and PMC. These regions are, in turn, influenced by more anterior regions including, but extending beyond, the prefrontal cortex. There is increasingly strong evidence that the parietal lobes also have at least two important roles in movement control. Areas 5 and 7 seem to be important in adapting movements in light of sensory feedback, and the more lateral regions, especially on the left, may be involved in the storage of representations of movement plans. Damage to this region leads to limb apraxia, which is viewed as a problem of recognising or conceptualising movement plans in time/space.

In the frontal lobes, damage in the primary motor strip may cause weakness or loss of movement in very discrete contralateral muscles. Damage in the SMA and PMC disrupts internally or externally driven motor plans bilaterally. Prefrontal damage will be associated with absence of motor plans and other features of the dysexecutive syndrome (which we review in Chapter 11). A mirror neuron circuit encompassing frontal, parietal, and possibly other cortical regions has recently been discovered. In humans, the circuit becomes active both during observation of actions and when similar actions are undertaken by the observer.

Damage to components of the basal ganglia is usually associated with dysregulation of internally generated movements. Several well-characterised neurological disorders including Parkinson's and Huntington's diseases, and probably tics, Tourette's syndrome, and even OCD, are associated with damage, disease, or disorder to components of the basal ganglia and/or its connections with the thalamus and cortex.

CHAPTER 6

CONTENTS

6

Language and the brain

INTRODUCTION

Think for a moment of the complex range of computational skills that are involved in understanding and generating language. Yet by the age of 4 or 5 most children can understand language (in their "mother" tongue at least) spoken at a rate of several words per second. This stream of sounds is continuous—not conveniently broken up like words on a page—and the listener has to know the boundaries between words in order to make sense from them. By late adolescence most humans will have a working understanding of many thousands of words (up to 50,000 for English speakers). Humans start to produce language as soon as they begin to acquire their vocabulary. In fact, some psychologists argue that using language precedes knowledge of words, and they cite the verbal-babble interactions of mother and child as examples of pre-vocabulary "speech".

By about 2 to 3 years old, children can effortlessly generate completely novel utterances according to implicit grammatical rules, and conduct meaningful conversations both with other children and with adults. Language development also seems to occur in the most adverse circumstances: consider, for example, the acquisition of complex language in deaf children. Indeed, of all psychological attributes, language is surely the one that sets humans apart. Other animals may use gestures and sounds to communicate, but the complexity and sophistication of human language suggests that extensive regions of the brain must be dedicated to dealing with it.

Scientific interest in language dates back to the earliest attempts by researchers to study the brain in a systematic way, with the work of Dax, Broca, and Wernicke in the 19th century. Since then, interest in all aspects of language has intensified to the point where its psychological study (psycholinguistics) is now recognised as a discipline in its own right. The development of research tools such as the Wada test and, more recently, structural and functional imaging procedures has enabled researchers to examine language function in the brains of normal individuals (see Chapter 2). Perhaps predictably, this research has necessitated extensive revision of earlier ideas about how the brain deals with language; as usual, the more closely one looks, the more complicated things appear. However, despite the complexities, it is reassuring to note that research findings from several different perspectives are now producing converging results, and we review some of this work towards the end of this chapter.

Meanwhile, we start with a review of the classic neurological studies of aphasia. This is a "catch-all" term meaning disruption to, or loss of, language function(s). Aphasia of some sort is commonly seen following brain damage or disease (for example, 40% of stroke victims develop some form of temporary or enduring aphasia). It is also seen in Alzheimer's and Pick's diseases (two forms of age-related dementia), and it can occur following head injury (for example, after a road traffic accident).

The classic approach to aphasia provided a framework for differentiating between different forms of language impairment, both anatomically and functionally. However, it was developed on the basis of a small number of case studies, and long before the advent of the modern structural and functional imaging techniques. Their arrival confirmed suspicions that were already felt in some quarters, namely that the classic approach grossly oversimplified both the brain processes in language, and its neuroanatomical substrates (e.g., Caplan, 1987). To set the record straight, subsequent research approaches have tried to address each of these areas of concern (albeit without much collaborative "cross-talk" until recently). There has, for example, been a move by some researchers away from the strictly neurological approach that has focused on the organisation of the brain (for language), to an examination of the organisation of language itself. We summarise the main areas of interest in psycholinguistics later in the chapter, and pick up this theme again when introducing the cognitive neuropsychological approach.

In-vivo imaging research into language is also reviewed. This work has tended to support the view that language is predominantly served by a series of interconnected cortical regions in the left hemisphere, as the 19th-century neurologists first proposed. However, it has also shown that additional brain areas in both the left and right hemispheres are involved. The use of structural imaging techniques to study aphasia, as typified by the work of Dronkers and her colleagues, is also introduced. Like the functional imaging research, it has prompted revision and significant elaboration of earlier ideas about brain language systems.

THE CLASSIC NEUROLOGICAL APPROACH AND APHASIA

Franz Joseph Gall, working almost 200 years ago, noticed that some of his more articulate friends (an early example being a school chum) had protruding eyeballs! This, he subsequently reasoned, must be due to the brain behind the eyes having grown to accommodate a superior language faculty—and thus was born the idea that language "resided" in the frontal lobes. Gall's ideas about localisation of language gained support when Broca was introduced to a patient with a serious leg infection, right **hemiparesis** and loss of speech. As we mentioned in Chapter 1, the patient was known as "Tan" because this was the only "sound" he could utter (which he tended to do repeatedly). Broca realised that this patient could serve as a test of Gall's theory, and when he died, a rudimentary post-mortem of Tan's brain revealed evidence of marked damage to the left posterior frontal gyrus (see Figure 6.1 later). Actually, Broca noted that there was damage to other cortical regions too, but the brain was never dissected, so the true extent of Tan's lesion was not known. The area of *marked* damage quickly became known as Broca's

Key Term
Hemiparesis: Partial or complete loss of movement in one side of the body.

area, corresponding to BA 44, extending into BA 45, and Tan's disorder was coined "Broca's aphasia" by fellow neurologists. Broca himself referred to Tan's language disorder as "aphemia" (disruption of voluntary speech production), signifying his belief that Tan's was essentially a speech programming disorder similar to what might today be called **speech apraxia**.

In 1874 Karl Wernicke described two patients who had a quite different type of language disorder. Their speech was fluent but incomprehensible and they also had profound difficulties understanding spoken language. Wernicke later examined the brain of one of these patients and found damage in the posterior part of the superior temporal gyrus on the left (see Figures 1.2 and 6.1). He argued that this patient's comprehension difficulties arose because the damaged region in question would ordinarily be involved in the auditory memory of words. His incomprehensible output was attributed to ineffective monitoring of self-generated speech.

At the same time as characterising this second form of language disorder, which came to be known as Wernicke's aphasia, Wernicke himself developed a theory of how the various brain regions with responsibility for receptive and expressive language function interact. His ideas were taken up and developed by Lichtheim, and later by Geschwind, and we will consider their work later in the chapter. For consistency, we will adhere to the nomenclature of these early pioneers. However, it is important to note that the following descriptions differ somewhat from those of the original authors, having broadened over the years to accommodate a wider range of aphasic features as more cases have come to light. It should also be realised that many modern-day researchers avoid altogether the use of these names to identify aphasic conditions. This is because "connectionist models" of language, which initially brought about renewed interest in the classic forms of aphasia, have themselves been found wanting, chiefly for failing to capture the true complexities of language systems in the brain. We review some of these concerns later, but we start the following section with descriptions and illustrations of the classic aphasic conditions.

BROCA'S APHASIA

In Broca's aphasia, as with most neurological conditions, impairment is a matter of degree, but the core feature is a marked difficulty in producing coherent speech (hence the alternative names of "expressive" or "non-fluent" aphasia). Although Tan's speech was limited to the one "sound", most Broca's aphasic patients can speak a little, but they seem to have problems in finding the words they want to use, and prepositions, conjunctions, and other relational words (words like "in", "and", "but", "about", "above", and so on) are often omitted. As a result, speech is slow, effortful, non-fluent, and deliberate, and may have only a very simple grammatical structure. The term "**telegraphic speech**" has often been used as a short-hand description for Broca's aphasia speech ("...*in car*...*off to the*...*the match*...*City play*...*good watch*...*like City*...*"*).

Despite these problems, some aspects of language function are well preserved. Patients with Broca's aphasia may be able to use well-practised expressions without obvious difficulty ("*It never rains but it pours!*") and they may also be able to sing a well-known song faultlessly. Reading aloud may be relatively unaffected. These abilities demonstrate that the problem is not related to the "mechanics" of moving the muscles that are concerned with speech, and to underline this point,

KEY TERMS
Speech apraxia: A characteristic sign of Broca's aphasia in which articulatory problems are apparent and speech is peppered with neologisms or paraphasias.
Telegraphic speech: A name to describe the non-fluent "stop–start" agrammatic speech associated with Broca's aphasia.

some Broca's aphasic patients have similar "agrammatical" problems when trying to write. (See Box 6.1 for an illustration of some Broca's aphasia features.) The alternative name of "expressive" aphasia is a reminder that the most obvious features of this condition relate to difficulties in language production, especially of novel (as opposed to well-learned) utterances. The lack of fluency is attributed to a speech programming deficit (aphemia in Broca's terms): a loss of the ability to execute speech movements despite an absence of facial or vocal muscle paralysis.

Notwithstanding the previous discussion, some patients with Broca's aphasia also have comprehension difficulties. For example, while the sentence "*the boy watched the girl talk with friends*" would probably not cause problems, a sentence such as: "*the girl, whom the boy was watching, was talking with friends*" might be difficult. (The test is to see if the respondent knows who was watching whom.) At present, however, it is unclear whether such comprehension deficits are related to problems with grammatical processing of the more complex sentence, or to problems with working memory or even attention. Moreover, it is generally accepted that comprehension problems in Broca's aphasia are both qualitatively and quantitatively distinct from those seen in Wernicke's aphasia (Dronkers, Redfern, & Knight, 2000). Finally, most Broca's patients are aware of their own language difficulties and have "insight" into their condition.

Box 6.1 Broca's aphasia (adapted from Stirling, 1999)

Therapist: "Tell me about your recent holiday."
Patient: ". . . Well . . . Well now . . . (long pause). We . . . err . . . I . . . holiday . . . you know . . ."
Therapist: "What happened?"
Patient: ". . . Oh, we . . . err . . . holiday . . . you know . . . seaside . . ."
Therapist: "Tell me some more."
Patient: "Beautiful weather . . ." (shows off suntan on arm)
Therapist: "Where did you get that?"
Patient: (bursts into song) "Oh, I do like to be beside the seaside . . . Oh I do like to be beside the sea . . ." (broad grin)
Therapist: "Did you go with your sister?"
Patient: "Sister . . . yes . . . sister. To . . . On holi . . . holiday . . . In a cara . . . cara . . . cara- thingy . . . caravan! That's it! A cara . . . caravan."
Therapist: "Did you take her, or did she take you?"
Patient: "Hey! You're . . . you're . . . trying to catch . . . catch me out . . .!" (grins broadly again)
Therapist: "I just wondered who made the arrangements?"
Patient: "We . . . we . . . you know, we go there . . . every . . . each . . . you know . . . year. Same place, same time, same girl." (laughs at own joke)

Comment: This vignette includes instances of telegraphic and agrammatical speech, effortful word finding, faultless expression of familiar material, and insight. Can you identify an example of each?

Earlier, we referred to the location of "Broca's area" as being in the left frontal lobe just forward from the primary motor cortex on the posterior surface of the third frontal gyrus (BA area 44 and part of area 45: see Figure 6.1a), roughly in front of and slightly above the left ear. However, recent research indicates that Broca's aphasia probably depends on more extensive damage than Broca originally thought. Indeed, lesions to Broca's area alone do not necessarily produce lasting aphasia (Dronkers et al., 1992). Adjacent cortical regions and/or areas of cortex normally hidden from view in the sulci (folds) under the surface have also been implicated. The insula is one candidate region. We will return to Dronkers' research later in this chapter.

WERNICKE'S APHASIA

Wernicke's first patient had difficulty in understanding speech, yet could speak fluently although what he said usually did not make much sense. This form of aphasia clearly differed in several respects from that described by Broca. The problems for Wernicke's patient were related to comprehension and meaningful output rather than the agrammatical and telegraphic output seen in Broca's patients. The fluent but nonsensical speech of someone with Wernicke's aphasia is all the harder to understand because of two further characteristic features. One is the patient's use of non-words or made-up words (known as "neologisms"). A second is the use of "paraphasias"—words that are semantically related to the desired word, but nevertheless inappropriate (binoculars instead of glasses for example). Most Wernicke's aphasic patients also have little or no "insight" into their condition. They talk nonsense without realising it, being unaware that other people cannot understand them (see Box 6.2).

Box 6.2 Wernicke's aphasia (adapted from Stirling, 1999)

Therapist: "What's this for?" (shows patient a hammer)

Patient: "Oh Boy! That's a . . . that's a thingy for . . . thing for . . . for knocking things."

Therapist: "Yes, but what is it?"

Patient: "It? I dunno . . . Umm . . . It's a nisby thing though!" (chuckles to himself)

Therapist: "How about this?" (shows patient a nail)

Patient: "That? Well, see you have those all over the place . . . In the doors, on the floors . . . everywhere's got 'em . . ."

Therapist: "What is it?"

Patient: "Mmm . . . See, I don't really get there much see, so . . . you know, it's kind of hard for me to spray . . ."

Therapist: (hands patient the nail) "Do you recognise it now?"

Patient: "Let's see now . . . it's sort of sharp, and long . . . could be a screw . . ."

Therapist: "Do you use this (points to the hammer again) with that?" (points to the nail)

> *Patient:*   "Mmm. That's a good one! (laughs again) Let's see now, a screw and a nail eh? Maybe in a toolboss . . . Yes! That's it; they all go in the toolboss in the back of the shed you see. In the garden . . . the shed, in the toolboss."
>
> *Comment:* This vignette includes illustrations of paraphasia, neologisms, incoherent speech, and lack of insight. Can you identify one example of each?

Wernicke thought that the underlying deficit in this condition was one of being unable to link sound images to stored representations (memories and conceptual meanings) of words. Although he only performed a post-mortem on one of his aphasic patients, damage was evident in the left posterior temporal region immediately behind Heschl's gyrus (the primary auditory cortex). Heschl's gyrus was known to receive massive inputs from the inner ear and is where speech sounds undergo initial analysis. Wernicke thought that the processed speech sounds would then be fed into the areas of cortex just behind Heschl's gyrus (the area commonly referred to as Wernicke's area) to be referenced to actual words (see Figure 6.1a and b). More recent evidence suggests, once again, that this analysis is somewhat simplistic, and that other areas of the cortex, in addition to Wernicke's area, may be important in understanding spoken language—a point that we return to later.

CONNECTIONIST MODELS OF LANGUAGE

THE WERNICKE-LICHTHEIM-GESCHWIND MODEL

Broca's and Wernicke's work generated considerable interest among fellow researchers. In 1885, Lichtheim proposed what has come to be known as a "connectionist" model (also called a "localisationist" model) of language to explain the various forms of aphasia (seven in all) that had by then been characterised. Incidentally, the term "connectionist" implies that different brain centres are interconnected, and that impaired language function may result from damage either to one of the centres or to the pathways between centres. The model is thus similar to the idea of a "distributed control network" that we introduced in Chapter 1, although, as originally conceptualised, it operated strictly serially (i.e., without parallel processing).

In Lichtheim's model, Broca's and Wernicke's areas formed two points of a triangle. The third point represented a "concept" centre (see below) where word meanings were stored and where auditory comprehension thus occurred. Each point was interconnected, so that damage, either to one of the centres (points), or to any of the pathways connecting them, would induce some form of aphasia. Lichtheim's model explained many of the peculiarities of different forms of aphasia, and became, for a time, the dominant model of how the brain manages language comprehension and production (see Figures 6.1 and 6.2). Although it fell out of favour in the early part of the 20th century, the model received renewed impetus in the 1960s following Geschwind's work (e.g., Geschwind, 1967).

Wernicke had actually been the first to suggest that the region of brain he had identified would be anatomically linked to Broca's area, and he reasoned that there

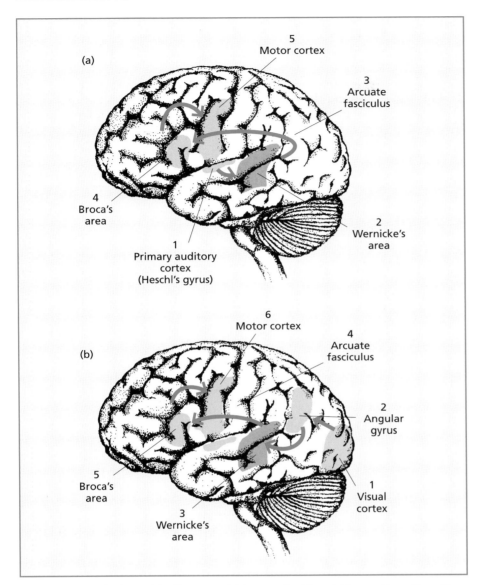

FIG. 6.1   Connectionist models of language. (a) A connectionist model for speaking a "heard" word. Sounds are initially coded in the primary auditory cortex (1) then fed to Wernicke's area (2) to be linked to meanings. The arcuate fasciculus (3) conveys information about the "heard" word forward to Broca's area (4) to evoke programmes for articulation. Output from Broca's area is supplied to the primary motor strip to produce the necessary muscle movements in the mouth and throat. (b) A connectionist model for speaking a "seen" word. As above except that following initial processing in the visual cortex (1), input is then relayed to the angular gyrus (2) where the visual image of the word is associated with the corresponding auditory pattern in the adjacent Wernicke's area.

could be a disconnection between the area for speech sounds (Wernicke's area) and the area for speech output (Broca's area), even if the two areas themselves were not damaged. The pathway in question is called the **arcuate fasciculus**, and Geschwind (1965) described a small number of aphasic individuals with *apparent*

KEY TERM
Arcuate fasciculus: Fibre bundle connecting Broca's and Wernicke's areas in the brain.

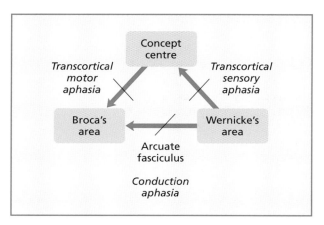

FIG. 6.2 Lichtheim's model in which Wernicke's area processed the sound image of words. This was fed forward via the arcuate fasciculus to Broca's area, which was responsible for the generation of speech output. Damage to this pathway led to conduction aphasia. A second route between Wernicke's and Broca's areas is via the concept centre, which Lichtheim envisaged as the part of the brain where meanings were stored. Damage to the pathway between Wernicke's area and the concept centre gave rise to transcortical sensory aphasia (marked by intact repetition skills but inability to understand auditory inputs). Damage to the pathway from the concept centre to Broca's area induced transcortical motor aphasia marked by a loss of spontaneous speech.

damage to it. Their disorder was known as "conduction aphasia" and, although comprehension and speech production were substantially preserved, the ability to repeat words, especially novel or unusual ones, was impaired (see Figure 6.1a and b, and Figure 6.2).

The exact location of the concept centre in Lichtheim's model was unclear, with Lichtheim himself arguing that concepts were actually distributed widely throughout the cortex. More recent interpretations (Geschwind, 1967) localised it to the left inferior parietal lobe encompassing the angular gyrus (see Figure 6.1a) and the region just anterior to this known as the supramarginal gyrus. This area is connected to (but separate from) Wernicke's area, and patients with damage to this region certainly have "receptive" language problems. However, this usually manifests as some form of "alexia" (loss of reading ability). On the other hand, damage to BA 37 (posterior medial temporal gyrus) in the left hemisphere *is* associated with lost access to semantic information about words that aphasic patients can nevertheless hear and repeat, making it a good candidate as the concept centre (Damasio & Damasio, 1989), or at least for word-level comprehension (Dronkers et al., 2004, and see below). (See Figure 6.1a and b, and Figure 2.1.)

Geschwind (1972) proposed that damage to the concept centre, or the connections between it and the other centres, readily explained the features of two further rare aphasic conditions: motor and sensory transcortical aphasia. The motor form, he argued, is similar to Broca's aphasia but, in addition, spontaneous speech is absent. Another feature is a marked tendency (which sometimes appears almost compulsive) to repeat things aloud (called "echolalia"). Damage to the pathway between the supplementary motor area (SMA) and Broca's area can bring about this disorder (Bradshaw & Mattingley, 1995). In the sensory form, difficulty with comprehension resembles that seen in Wernicke's aphasia but repetition is intact. Indeed, as with the motor form, echolalia may even be prominent. The loss of connections between Wernicke's area and BA 37 (which we mentioned earlier) may be responsible for transcortical sensory aphasia. To complete the picture, extensive damage to multiple parts of Lichtheim's system could account for global aphasia—a profound aphasic disorder affecting both comprehension and production of language. In sum, the Wernicke-Lichtheim-Geschwind connectionist model (circa 1972) provided an elaborated framework that could account for a range of both classic and more recently characterised forms of aphasia.

PROBLEMS WITH CONNECTIONIST MODELS

Despite its appeal, a number of observations soon emerged that could not easily be accommodated by the model. These coalesced under the headings of (a) lack of symptom specificity in aphasia, (b) failure to appreciate the true complexities of requisite language processes in the brain, and (c) poor correspondence with recent neuroanatomical observations. A special issue of the journal *Cognition* (vol 92, 2004) addressed, in detail, most of these concerns and the interested reader should refer to this source. For present purposes, one illustration from each area of concern will suffice. Consider symptom specificity: Wernicke's aphasia was characterised as a receptive language disorder, yet some patients with Wernicke's aphasia produce agrammatical speech (an expressive deficit). Broca's aphasia, on the other hand, was characterised as an expressive aphasia yet, as we noted earlier, some patients with Broca's aphasia also make comprehension errors (a receptive deficit). In short, the classic aphasic syndromes actually comprise variable (perhaps overlapping) clusters of symptoms, suggesting a much more complex "neural architecture" than the connectionist model permitted.

Stemming from this point, now consider brain language processes. At one time, language processing was fractionated only into receptive and expressive functions. Later, linguists began to distinguish between syntax, semantics, phonology, and so on (see below) yet these linguistic domains are, themselves, divisible into multiple subsystems, as illustrated by the work of Levelt et al. that we review later. Third, consider recent concerns about the neuroanatomy of language. It is now apparent that damage to Broca's area does not necessarily lead to Broca's aphasia, and that Wernicke's aphasia does not usually result from specific damage to Wernicke's area (Dronkers et al., 2004). Finally, while speech production *does* appear to be the responsibility of the left hemisphere (in right-handers), effective speech perception appears to require the collaboration of both hemispheres. Thus, despite its heuristic appeal the connectionist model has, in the view of Poeppel and Hickok (2004) among others, outlived its usefulness and is no longer tenable.

INTERIM COMMENT

The study of language impairment in people with brain damage has provided a wealth of information about the role(s) of mainly left-sided cortical regions in language operations. Yet long-standing ideas about the nature of different aphasic conditions (and how they may map onto these cortical regions) cannot be reconciled either with recent observations about the true complexities of language processing, or with data from imaging studies of language, some of which we review below.

The types of aphasia identified over 100 years ago are still seen today, although careful case study has revealed additional forms of language disorder that may be related to subtle lesions/damage to other components of the brain's language system. As we shall see, recent research has led neuropsychologists to conclude that the forms of aphasia identified by Broca and Wernicke depend on more extensive damage to either frontal or posterior regions than was initially thought. It also seems that other "centres" (and interconnecting pathways) in addition to Broca's and Wernicke's areas and the arcuate fasciculus contribute to a distributed control network responsible for the full range of language functions, which is considerably more complex than the triangular connectionist model of Lichtheim. Finally, it is worth mentioning again that there is potential danger in relying on the study of damaged brains to form an understanding of normal brain function.

THE PSYCHOLINGUISTIC APPROACH

Psycholinguistics is, primarily, the study of the structure of language in normal individuals rather than the study of language dysfunction in neurological patients. (We could describe it as a "top-down" approach, whereas the neurological approach is "bottom-up".) Linguists such as de Saussure (1917) and Chomsky (1957, 1965) developed theories about the form and structure of language that were relatively independent of the neurological work described in the previous section; in fact, the two approaches initially represented quite distinct levels of inquiry into the study of language. Although it is beyond the scope of this book to provide a detailed account of contemporary psycholinguistic thinking, an understanding of some concepts and terminology is important, and will inform our discussion of the neuropsychology of language.

Psycholinguists generally divide language into four major domains:

1   *Phonology* is the investigation of basic speech sounds (*ba, pa*, and *ta* are all phonemes).
2   The study of meaning in language is known as *semantics*.
3   Words are strung together to form sentences according to particular implicit rules of grammar, known as *syntax* (*syntactic* is the adjective).
4   The study of using language in a natural social setting is known as *pragmatics*.

Phonemes are combined to form words, and our word store, which includes information about pronunciation, meaning, and relations with other words, is known as our lexicon. The structure of our mental lexicon has been a major research topic in psycholinguistics and evidence suggests that it is partly organised in terms of meaning.

From this summary you can see that psycholinguistics has a distinct approach and different level of inquiry. However, it is still of interest to ask whether there is any common ground between it and the classic neurological approach. Earlier, for example, we noted how Wernicke's and other "posterior" aphasias involve speech that, despite being correctly structured, is difficult to understand. There is also poor comprehension. A psycholinguistic interpretation would be that these aphasias are related to deficits in *semantic* processing rather than to problems with the brain's *syntactic* mechanisms. This may in turn imply that semantic processing was a function of these posterior regions.

Similarly, we earlier described individuals with damage to frontal regions (including Broca's area) as having non-fluent agrammatical aphasia. In psycholinguistic terms, this type of aphasia could be attributed to impaired *syntactic* processing. We know that some non-fluent aphasic patients have difficulties in understanding language, which would imply a problem with semantics too; however, these problems really become apparent when understanding depends on precise grammatical analysis in the absence of other semantic clues. Patients with Broca's aphasia would, for example, probably be able to distinguish between the meaningful sentence "*the boy ate the cake*" and the meaningless sentence "*the cake ate the boy*". Actually, Linebarger, Schwartz, and Saffran (1983) have shown that patients with Broca's aphasia can also distinguish accurately between grammatical and agrammatical sentences. So, it seems that the problem for individuals with this form of aphasia is not that grammatical processing mechanisms have been lost, but rather that they cannot be easily or quickly accessed.

INTERIM COMMENT

Psycholinguistics is a complex discipline and one that has been somewhat isolated. Progress has certainly been made in identifying the structure and form of language(s), its universal features, its acquisition, and so on, but until recently this work has tended to ignore pathologies of language. More recently, neuropsychologists have begun to draw parallels between aphasic disorders and disruption to specific linguistic processes. These data provide evidence of a double dissociation between semantic and syntactic processes, and illustrate clearly that no single brain "language centre" exists. This approach has been the springboard for cognitive neuropsychologists to study individual cases of language disorder in detail and, in the process, further tease apart specific components of the language system that may be selectively impaired. Functional imaging has also provided a tool for bringing psycholinguistics closer to the neuropsychology of language, as researchers attempt to map psycholinguistic concepts. See Grodzinsky and Friederici (2006) for an example where psycholinguistic concepts, classic neuropsychology, and functional imaging are brought together to propose a "map for syntax".

THE MODERN ERA OF LANGUAGE RESEARCH

The cognitive neuropsychological approach mentioned earlier is a relatively recent development (dating back no more than 25 to 35 years) and is considered in the following section. However, this is just one of three important contemporary lines of investigation that we need to review. In addition, we must consider recent explorations of language functions in the brain using neuroimaging and neuro-physiological imaging techniques, and revisit some more carefully conducted neuroanatomical research.

THE COGNITIVE NEUROPSYCHOLOGY APPROACH

In this approach, which is exemplified in the work of Caplan (1992) and Ellis and Young (1996), researchers try to understand the true nature of language disturbances in relation to underlying cognitive dysfunctions. Although this approach has evolved from the psycholinguistic approach reviewed above, it differs in two important respects. First, it tries to relate language and cognitive processes, and second it focuses on pathologies of language rather than normal language. Cognitive neuropsychologists tend to focus on specific language impairments rather than **syndromal** (multi-faceted) conditions like Broca's and Wernicke's aphasia. One reason given for this approach (as we mentioned in Chapter 1) is that studying groups of people with Broca's or Wernicke's aphasia is pointless because the conditions are both broad and poorly defined (Ellis & Young, 1996). A second is that since brain damage is inherently variable, potentially informative individual differences are lost in "group"-based research (Caramazza, 1984). Thus on both counts, so the argument goes, it makes more sense to conduct detailed case study investigations on individuals with very specific language impairments.

KEY TERM

Syndromal: A feature of a syndrome, the latter being a term for a disorder or condition (such as split-brain syndrome) characterised by a cluster of interrelated signs and symptoms rather than one defining feature.

Although cognitive neuropsychologists have made progress in understanding many aspects of language impairment, we will illustrate their approach with reference to just one condition—**anomia**—defined here as a specific problem in naming objects. (Note that, confusingly, the term "anomia" is also sometimes used to identify a general word-finding problem.) If you followed the descriptions of the classic aphasias that we gave earlier you will be aware that some form of anomia is common to both Wernicke's and Broca's aphasias, which, on the face of it, is not a promising start. Yet detailed case study reveals several subtly different forms of anomia, and thorough neuropsychological testing indicates that they may have quite distinct origins in terms of cognitive dysfunction.

Consider first patient JBR, reported by Warrington and Shallice (1984). He had developed widespread temporal lobe damage following **herpes simplex** infection. He was impaired at naming living things (such as a daffodil or lion) but not inanimate objects (like torch or umbrella). However, his problem was not limited to naming because he also struggled to understand the spoken names of items that he himself couldn't name. Compare JBR with Hart et al.'s patient MD, who also had a deficit in naming animate objects, yet could sort pictures of animate and inanimate items well, and could also discriminate heard and read words from each category (Hart, Berndt, & Caramazza, 1985). This subtle distinction suggests that whereas JBR might have incurred loss (or degradation) of semantic knowledge of specific categories, MD had retained the semantic representations but his access to it from pictures or actual objects was impaired.

A third anomic patient, JCU, reported by Howard and Orchard-Lisle (1984), seemed at first glance to have a widespread generalised anomia for objects from various categories, yet could often be prompted to name items correctly if given the initial phoneme (sound) of the word. However, he was also prone to naming semantically related items if given the wrong phoneme! For example, when asked to name a tiger, and given the phoneme "L", he incorrectly said *lion*.

In contrast, patient EST, studied by Kay and Ellis (1987), had pronounced anomia with no apparent damage to semantic representations, a profile similar to classic Broca's aphasia. Although he clearly struggled to name objects from many categories, he nevertheless retained semantic information about items, voluntarily providing associated semantic information about an object even if the name eluded him. This suggests that EST's anomia was related to a problem in generating the actual words (perhaps through inaccessibility to his speech output lexicon) rather than any loss of semantic representation. To reinforce this view, patients like EST know when they have generated an approximation to the required word rather than the word itself, and will comment to this effect, saying, "*that's not quite it . . . it's like that but I forget what it actually is*".

Another word production disturbance, often encountered in Wernicke's aphasia, is known as "neologistic jargonaphasia". Patient RD studied by Ellis, Miller, and Sin (1983) was anomic, especially for rare or unusual items, yet evidence from other tests indicated that he retained semantic knowledge of the unnameable items. He could name items he had used before or was very familiar with, but for other items he generated phonological approximations—neologisms that sounded similar to the target word ("peharst" for "perhaps" for example). The major difference between EST and RD is that the former could understand speech well, but RD could not—in fact, his comprehension had to be assessed using written words. His neologisms are likely to be the result of a failure

KEY TERMS
Anomia: Inability to name objects or items.
Herpes simplex: Infection with this virus can affect brain function, leading to permanent damage.

TABLE 6.1 THE UNDERLYING DIFFICULTIES OF FIVE ANOMIC PATIENTS

Patient	Can understand speech	Can generate speech	Can name living things	Can name inanimate things	Has semantic knowledge about things	Likely understanding problem
JBR	Yes	Yes	Only poorly	Yes	Not about living things	Loss of semantic knowledge for specific categories
MD	Yes	Yes	Not fruit or vegetables	Yes	Yes	Loss of access (via pictures or objects) to preserved semantic knowledge
JCU	Yes	Yes	No (unless prompted with auditory cues)	No (unless prompted with auditory cues)	Partial at best	Object recognition and comprehension relatively intact but a general non-specific impairment to semantic representations
EST	Yes	Yes (but only high-frequency words)	No	No	Yes	Loss of access to speech output lexicon for low-frequency words
RD	No	No (produces neologisms)	No	No	Yes	Failure to understand speech or monitor own speech

to properly monitor his own speech, which would explain his lack of awareness of his own errors.

These types of observation have enabled researchers to develop detailed models of the cognitive processing stages involved (in this instance) in object naming. We can see, for example, that JBR's anomia appeared to be related to a problem with specific components of his semantic system, and represents a deficit in object recognition (see Chapter 8). Other operations were intact. EST, on the other hand, had problems accessing his speech output lexicon, especially for rare words, while the lexicon itself and his semantic system were probably intact. These examples also show us that, with appropriate testing, subtle differences can be identified in the form of anomia that a patient presents with. We have summarised the cases described above in Table 6.1.

In recent years, the insights provided by the cognitive neuropsychological approach have led to the development of possible treatments for anomia. Various approaches can be used. For example, patients can be taught compensatory strategies, whereby intact processes are used to support impaired ones. For individuals whose impairment is more extensive, targeted teaching tasks can lead to improvements in performance, at least for certain words. Just as cognitive neuropsychology theory can inform therapy, the success (or otherwise) of therapeutic approaches can inform cognitive neuropsychology theory. Nickels (2002) provides a good theoretical overview of the issues, while Laganaro, DiPietro, and Schnider (2006) present a more recent example focusing on three different patients with different patterns of deficit who responded to treatment in different ways.

INTERIM COMMENT

Earlier we said that the cognitive neuropsychological approach focused on language dysfunction in brain-damaged individuals. However, Ellis and Young (1996) have pointed out that the anomic disturbances seen in brain-damaged individuals are, in certain respects, simply more pronounced forms of disturbance that we all experience from time to time. Slips of the tongue, malapropisms, spoonerisms, and the "tip of the tongue" phenomenon are all features of "normal" language usage (see Freud, 1901), and may be related to brief disruptions of the same processes (or components) that are more severely affected in cases of clinical anomia. The cognitive neuropsychological approach has developed rapidly as researchers exploit in-vivo imaging techniques for exploring brain–language relations, as discussed in the following section.

NEUROPHYSIOLOGICAL APPROACHES

Structural and functional in-vivo imaging techniques such as CT, MRI, and PET (see Chapter 2) are gradually leading to important discoveries about many aspects of brain function, and language is no exception. CT and structural MRI scan data tend to reinforce the classic post-mortem findings of extensive damage and loss of tissue in frontal areas in people with Broca's aphasia, and posterior damage in individuals with Wernicke's aphasia (Damasio & Damasio, 1989; Naeser & Hayward, 1978). See the section on neuroanatomy later in this chapter for some more detailed studies. When PET is used to examine "resting" brain function, patients with non-fluent (Broca's type) aphasia show underactivation in left frontal regions, while patients with fluent aphasia show underactivation in more posterior regions. However, when anatomical and activation data are compared in the same individuals, underactivity is sometimes observed in areas that are not damaged. Moreover, the functional measures correlate more closely with language disturbance than do the anatomical measures. This is a reminder that visible anatomical lesions may only reveal part of the story.

PET and fMRI have also been used to examine functional activity in normal individuals while they undertake different types of linguistic task. Compared to other areas of neuropsychology, PET continued to be relatively widely used even as fMRI became more popular. There are two reasons for this. First some of the critical areas in language research are areas that are particularly prone to artefacts in MRI imaging. Second, fMRI is an extremely noisy procedure and in studies employing spoken language as stimulus material this presents a significant technical challenge—it is obviously essential that participants can hear the stimulus input clearly! However, over the last few years technological advances in MRI physics and stimulus presentation have overcome both of these problems at many imaging centres and therefore fMRI is now more widely used for language studies.

Since the initial pioneering PET studies of normal language (Petersen et al.'s 1988 study of word generation, for example, is widely regarded as a "classic"), hundreds of neuroimaging studies of language have been published. Taken together, these have significantly refined our understanding of the brain basis of normal language. For example, Vigneau et al. (2006) published a meta-analysis based on 260 articles published between 1992 and 2004. This led them to conclude that language is represented in large-scale distributed control networks in the left hemisphere. For example, Figure 6.3 shows brain activations associated with semantic processing.

A detailed review by Demonet, Thierry, and Cardebet (2005) subdivided neuroimaging language research into certain core processes. They reviewed research on single word processing as well as research on sentence and discourse processing. We will return to the latter issue later in this chapter when we consider laterality. For single word processing, Demonet et al. identified five distinct research areas: spoken word perception, visual word perception (reading words), semantic processing (extracting meaning), spoken output, and written output. Figures 6.4a and b show the brain activations associated with processing spoken and visual words respectively. While an exploration of all these areas is beyond our scope, certain illustrative examples highlight the advances that neuroimaging methods have brought about. Neuroimaging of spoken word perception has shed new light on classical aphasia-based models of comprehension, suggesting that the left posterior superior temporal gyrus (Wernicke's area) is functionally heterogeneous. Wise et al. (1999, 2001) report two distinct subregions. One is activated during both perception and production of speech and appears to serve as a temporary buffer for the storage of speech sounds. Another is activated during articulatory speech movements and appears to act as an interface between speech sounds and the motor codes needed to generate them.

Studies of reading single words have also produced informative results. For example, Jobard, Crivello, and Tzourio-Mazoyer (2003) showed that distinct regions of the left posterior inferior frontal gyrus (Broca's area) are activated depending on whether participants are reading regular or irregular words. The reading of irregular words is thought to be dependent on a direct association between the visual form of the word and its meaning, since "sounding out" the word phoneme by phoneme does not produce a recognisable word (if you read the word "yacht" by making the component sounds, you generate something that makes no sense; to understand the word you have to recognise the visual form and translate that directly to meaning). Interestingly, this distinction is relevant to studies of reading different languages. For languages like English, where there are many irregularities, word reading activates subtly different regions than languages like Italian, where letter-to-sound conversion is much more reliable (Paulesu et al., 2000).

A number of the earlier neuroimaging studies selected tasks that were adjudged to be "simple". For example, Petersen et al.'s classic PET study of 1988 chose word generation. However, psycholinguists such as Levelt (1989) have long argued that word generation is, in fact, a task of considerable complexity involving

Left   Right

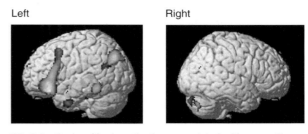

FIG. 6.3 Regional brain activations associated with semantic processing. This figure demonstrates a network of interacting cortical structures, predominantly on the left side. We are very grateful to Professor Cathy Price of the Wellcome Trust Centre for Neuroimaging, London, for providing these images.

(a)   (b)

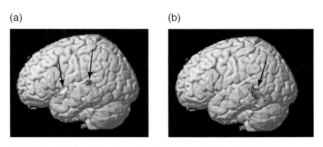

FIG. 6.4 Regional brain activations associated with lexical processing of (a) auditory words and (b) visual words. (a) Activations associated with listening to words compared to listening to reversed words; (b) activations associated with viewing words compared with viewing false fonts (strings of pseudo-letter symbols). We are very grateful to Professor Cathy Price of the Wellcome Trust Centre for Neuroimaging, London, for providing these images.

multi-tiered processing components. Although the precise details of Levelt's theory need not concern us (but see Levelt, Roelofs, & Meyer, 1999, for further information), a version of his model of word generation does merit consideration and is summarised in Box 6.3.

Box 6.3 A summary of Levelt's model of word generation

- First, the speaker needs to be aware of the social context in which word generation is occurring, to remember the rules of the experimental task, and to know what is expected of him/her.
- Next, there must be some conceptual preparation, which may depend on semantic processing of the stimulus material that is to be responded to: e.g., *"generate a verb which relates to the following noun"*.
- Since there may be many alternatives (i.e., lots of potential verbs), the mental lexicon must be accessed, and some form of selection undertaken.
- Once selected, the mental representation of the word must be articulated. But word articulation is itself a compound task, involving the sequential processing of phonemes.
- These in turn permit the generation of syllables. (Although most spoken English is based on reassembling no more than 500 syllables, the language itself contains about 50,000 words.)
- Quite how these are translated into sounds is not known, but it is clear that the actual articulation process is flexible—people can make themselves understood with their mouth full, or when smoking a cigarette for example!
- Humans can produce about 12 speech sounds per second, and this involves the precise coordinated control of at least 100 different muscles.
- Generated speech is also monitored by the speaker and, if necessary, corrected for errors, sometimes before the errors are even articulated.
- Speech is also effortlessly adjusted for volume and speed of delivery to suit the particular environment.

This summary makes it abundantly clear that the task of selecting a single word (in response to a picture, word, or other stimulus) involves multiple processing stages, and is in fact an enormously complex undertaking. According to Indefrey and Levelt (2000), it is still possible to make sense of functional imaging data by taking advantage of the fact that most studies have used slightly different experimental procedures. For example, some, like Petersen et al.'s, have used verb/word generation. Others have employed word repetition, or picture naming. Sometimes, word generation has been overt, while in other studies silent, or delayed. The different procedures involve different core processing stages; so, for example, word repetition does not make demands on conceptual preparation. Similarly, the first core process implicated in reading pseudo-words (non-words that sound like words) is phonological encoding, and so on. Thus, it is possible to tease apart the individual components involved in different word generation studies, and Indefrey and Levelt (2000) have presented such a provisional meta-analysis. More recent functional imaging studies have used more subtle experimental designs and more carefully chosen control tasks that acknowledge the complexity of even apparently "simple" language tasks.

fMRI and PET have also provided valuable tools for assessing language processing in individuals whose language abilities are in some way abnormal. Most obviously this involves the use of neuroimaging in aphasic patients, although this approach has been relatively little used. This may reflect the heterogeneity of patients preventing the usual neuroimaging group studies, however Price et al. (1999) made a convincing case for applying neuroimaging to single case studies. Another interesting angle has been to study individuals who are not aphasic but who have atypical language abilities. For example, there have been studies of multilingual people. Kim et al. (1997) showed that in bilingual people who learned their second language as adolescents or later, distinct regions of the left inferior frontal gyrus represent the two languages. However, in people who were exposed to both languages from early childhood, there is far less distinction. This finding has important implications for understanding language development. Another interesting study group are the congenitally deaf. These people have never been exposed to spoken language and use sign language to communicate. Sign language is effectively their native language. The striking finding of neuroimaging is that sign language recruits remarkably similar brain areas to oral language (Neville et al., 1998), suggesting that these brain regions are biased to represent language even in a non-auditory form.

NEUROANATOMICAL RESEARCH

The "neurological/neuroanatomical" approach was an obvious choice for the early researchers who relied on case studies of individuals with brain damage. Cases of Broca's and Wernicke's aphasia have been reported and described for over 100 years and are relatively commonplace today. Each is widely accepted as a legitimate clinical entity. But the real question is not how many cases of these syndromes conform to the description and anatomical model of Lichtheim, but how many do not. This matter has been carefully explored by Dronkers and her colleagues at the University of California (Dronkers et al., 2000; Dronkers, Redfern, & Ludy, 1995). Her starting point was the realisation that certain problems with the connectionist model have been routinely "forgotten" in the quest to find supportive evidence for it. For example, as we mentioned earlier, the grammar-based comprehension difficulty of many Broca's cases does not fit well with the idea of this aphasia as a disturbance of expressive language function. Moreover, the connectionist model has somewhat conveniently ignored the fact that many patients with Wernicke's aphasia make significant recoveries, ending up with few lasting comprehension problems despite obvious posterior damage. As we also mentioned earlier, the true neuroanatomical locations of Broca's and Wernicke's areas have even been questioned.

By 1992, Dronkers' group had detailed evidence on 12 right-handed Broca's aphasic patients, two of whom had lesions that spared Broca's area. Ten more cases were identified in whom damage to Broca's area was apparent, but who had no true Broca's aphasic features. In a similar vein, Dronkers et al. (1995) reported seven cases of Wernicke's aphasia, of whom two had no damage to Wernicke's area at all, and seven additional cases with damage to Wernicke's area but without the persistent features of Wernicke's aphasia.

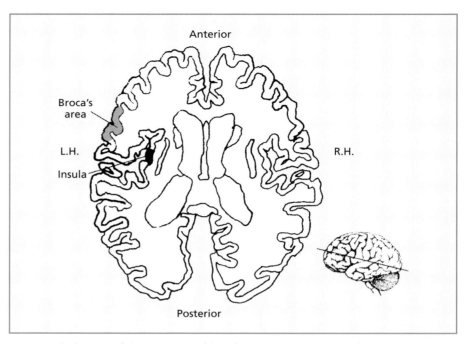

FIG. 6.5   The location of the superior tip of the left insula. This region, identified by Dronkers et al., is consistently damaged in aphasic patients with speech apraxia. Broca's area is indicated for reference.

Dronkers' patient pool has grown to over 100 very clearly defined and extensively imaged people with aphasia, and it has been possible to look for anatomical commonalities within aphasic groups. For example, every person who met the full diagnostic criteria for Broca's aphasia had damage to a specific part of a deep cortical region in the left frontal lobe known as the insula (the superior tip, see Figure 6.5), though posterior inferior frontal gyrus (IFG) damage was not ubiquitous (actually found in 85% of cases: Dronkers, 2000). The immediate conclusion from this observation might be that the insula (rather than the IFG) is the true location of Broca's area—but this would be incorrect because the research group also had a small number of patients with damage to the superior tip of the insula who did not have Broca's aphasia. However, they all had speech apraxia (an articulatory speech programming disorder encountered earlier, in which the individual may produce neologisms—i.e., approximations to the correct word, or distortions of it, rather than the word itself). This is, of course, a prominent though not defining feature of Broca's aphasia. The most parsimonious explanation for this finding is that if, as is often the case, frontal damage includes this region of the insula, the individual is likely to experience speech apraxia as one of the features of their aphasia.

Dronkers' work has stimulated renewed interest in the anatomical substrate(s) of Broca's aphasia, although her conclusions have not gone unchallenged. For example, Hillis et al. (2004) failed to find an association between left insular damage (assessed by MRI) and speech apraxia, but they did find a strong association between the disorder and underactivity in the left posterior inferior frontal gyrus (i.e., Broca's area). A strength of this study was the large sample ($n = 80$) of both acute and chronically speech-apraxic patients—an important consideration because stroke-induced speech apraxia is often transient, showing substantial recovery over a period of months. Dronkers' cases were chronic, suggesting much larger areas of stroke damage, but also making it more likely that her findings were partly artifactual, because the insula is particularly susceptible to large mid-cerebral artery strokes.

Borovsky et al.'s (2007) study of anatomical correlates of conversational speech deficits perhaps moves us closer to a satisfactory conclusion to this debate: This group reported that both poor fluency and low complexity were associated with lesions in a cluster of left anterior locations including the insula, inferior frontal gyrus, primary motor cortex, and underlying white matter. They suggest that these form a network mediating the production of complex and fluent speech, and that further specificity (localisation) is not currently possible; Broca's area, for example, being anatomically large and functionally diverse, should be subdivided (which neither Hillis's or Borovsky's imaging procedures permitted) in order to truly map structure to function.

Dronkers' group has also explored the anatomical basis of the comprehension difficulties often reported in Broca's aphasia (see Bates et al., 2003). Almost all such cases have damage to anterior regions of the superior temporal gyrus (on the left). This area is frequently damaged in Broca's aphasia but is, of course, in the temporal rather than frontal lobe. At present it is difficult to ascertain whether this region is truly a grammar "node" in the language network, or part of a working memory network that is needed to process longer sentences. However, functional imaging studies by Mazoyer et al. (1993) and Bavelier et al. (1997) have also confirmed the importance of this region in sentence comprehension in normal individuals. As for Broca's area itself, it seems to serve a number of functions including, for example, a role in verbal working memory, in addition to its involvement in the programming of motor control of speech production, the function that Broca originally ascribed to it. However, concerns remain about the anatomical boundaries of this region: In a fascinating recent MRI re-analysis of the actual brains of Broca's first two patients (Leborgne and Lelong) by Dronkers et al. (2007), damage *was* apparent in the left inferior frontal gyrus (BA 44 and 45) but also in left medial structures and associated white matter tracts. Clearly, progress in establishing the exact role(s) of Broca's area will be contingent on a consensus about both its boundaries and if/how it should be subdivided.

In the case of Wernicke's aphasia, enduring symptoms are only found in individuals with extensive damage to the posterior regions of the mid-temporal gyrus and underlying white matter. Smaller lesions, either in Wernicke's area itself or to other posterior temporal sites, usually produce only transient aphasic features that resolve in a matter of months. According to Dronkers et al. (1998), damage to Wernicke's area alone is more likely to be associated with repetition deficits than comprehension problems. The authors have suggested that this deficit could primarily be an auditory short-term memory problem in which the individual cannot hold on to the **echoic trace** of an item long enough to repeat it.

In a more recent study (Dronkers et al., 2004), 64 patients with left hemisphere brain damage were studied using a combination of neuropsychological and structural imaging techniques. This revealed five brain regions involved in language comprehension and, notably, neither Broca's nor Wernicke's areas were among them. However the regions identified were adjacent to either Broca's or Wernicke's area and Dronkers therefore suggests that the classical findings were actually due to damage to these closely adjacent regions. A critical region identified in this

KEY TERM

Echoic trace: A form of very short-term auditory memory (a sort of acoustic after-image) thought to last no more than 1 or 2 seconds.

study was the middle temporal gyrus. Patients with damage to this region had the most pronounced comprehension deficits and the authors suggest that this region is involved in word-level comprehension. Damage to the other regions, including other regions of temporal cortex and inferior and mid-frontal cortex, is proposed to cause sentence-level comprehension problems. The patients in Dronkers' study showed different patterns of deficit depending on which region, or combination of regions, was damaged and this raises the obvious possibility that differences in presentation of "classic" Broca's and Wernicke's aphasias may reflect differences in the extent of damage within these closely connected regions. Dronkers believes that none of the five regions identified is dedicated to sentence comprehension per se, but that they work together as a network supporting language comprehension.

Dronkers' approach has shown that it is possible to draw conclusions about brain–language relations if one has access to aphasic individuals with carefully characterised symptoms/features and anatomically accurate information about brain lesions. The work of her group indicates that, in addition to Broca's and Wernicke's areas and the arcuate fasciculus, many other regions, mainly on the left in the temporal lobe, contribute to both receptive and expressive language functions. It also generates hypotheses about normal language function that can be tested by functional brain imaging. Like Levelt, Dronkers et al. (2000) acknowledge that the neuropsychology of language has, for too long, been guided by an oversimplified model of how the brain deals with language. The emerging model must integrate the new language areas with the traditional ones, but also factor in attentional, executive, and working memory processes in order to provide a more realistic framework of brain–language networks.

INTERIM COMMENT

Three recent lines of research have taken our understanding of the neuropsychology of language well beyond the revised connectionist model of the early 1970s. The cognitive neuropsychology approach has shown how, by careful observation and neuropsychological testing, it is possible (and informative) to distinguish between subtly different forms of language dysfunction. The neuroimaging approach has not only tended to reinforce, but also to extend classic models of how the brain processes language. In particular, this approach has led to the identification of brain regions not previously thought to be involved in language. The neuroanatomical approach of Dronkers et al., Hillis et al., and Borovsky et al. has shown how it is possible to relate loss of function to cortical damage, provided that patients are thoroughly tested and the damage is precisely mapped. A picture emerging from all three approaches is that language itself is far more complicated than the early researchers thought. Thus, the neural networks serving language comprise many more discrete regions, albeit mainly on the left side, than earlier models suggested. Additionally, functional imaging suggests that these regions function as extensively interconnected networks.

LANGUAGE AND LATERALITY

From our review of brain–language research, it would be reasonable to conclude that language is mediated by a series of interconnected regions in the left hemisphere. This pattern of "distributed control" is found in almost all right-handers, and the majority of left-handers (Rasmussen & Milner, 1977). Over 100 years ago Broca declared *"nous parlons avec l'hemisphere gauche"*, and both the functional and structural imaging findings bear this out to a certain extent, as does much of the research on language function in the split-brain syndrome and data derived from the Wada test (see Chapters 2 and 3).

So is the left hemisphere *the* language hemisphere? Not exclusively. Although hundreds of neuroimaging studies have revealed strong left-sided activity in language tasks, many have also shown activity (usually to a lesser extent) in corresponding regions on the right. For example, Figure 6.6 shows a bilateral network of brain regions involved in speech production. Indeed, there is evidence to show that certain aspects of language are managed, perhaps predominantly, by the right hemisphere. One aspect that appears to be the preserve of the right hemisphere is the processing of emotional aspects of language. For example, individuals with right hemisphere damage, and with otherwise intact language skills, may speak in a monotone, despite *understanding* the emotional connotations of what they are saying (Behrens, 1988). The region of right cortex in question is in the equivalent location to Broca's on the left. In other words, damage to Broca's area impairs fluent speech. Damage to the equivalent area on the right impairs emotionally intoned (**prosodic**) speech, which instead is said to be "aprosodic". More posterior right-sided damage (in regions roughly equivalent to Wernicke's area on the left side) can lead to difficulties in the interpretation of emotional tone. PET studies with normal individuals have also highlighted this double dissociation: speech production requiring emotional tone activates frontal regions on the right (Wallesch et al., 1985), whereas comprehension of emotionally intoned speech activates posterior regions on the right (Lechevalier et al., 1989). Obviously, the actual message may convey enough meaning to be understood without having to decode the emotional tone too, but sometimes appreciation of tone is critical in understanding the true message. "Thanks very much!" can mean "thank you" or "thanks for nothing" depending on the speaker's tone of voice. The right hemisphere's interpretation of "prosodic cues" appears to be closely related to more fundamental skills in detecting tonal differences, or changes to pitch, which are also mediated primarily by the right hemisphere: Stirling, Cavill, and Wilkinson (2000) reported a left ear (right hemisphere) advantage in normal individuals for the detection of emotional tone in a dichotic listening task (this sort of experiment is described in Chapter 9 and illustrated in Figure 9.1), a finding that reinforces the view that the processing of emotional voice cues may be preferentially a right hemisphere task.

There is growing evidence linking inferential skills (filling in the blanks, or "putting two and two

> **KEY TERM**
> **Prosodic:** An adjective to describe emotionally intoned language. (Aprosodic speech is devoid of emotional intonation, or monotone.)

Left

Right

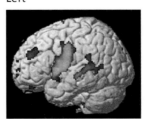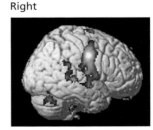

FIG. 6.6 Bilateral brain activations associated with speech production. This figure clearly demonstrates that some normal language functions rely on neuronal activity in both left and right hemisphere regions. We are very grateful to Professor Cathy Price of the Wellcome Trust Centre for Neuroimaging, London, for providing these images.

together") and even "sense of humour" to the right hemisphere too. Individuals with right hemisphere damage are less adept at following the thread of a story (Kaplan et al., 1990) or understanding the non-literal aspects of language, such as metaphors (Brownell, 1988). They also struggle to rearrange sentences into coherent paragraphs (Schneiderman, Murasugi, & Saddy, 1992). Functional imaging has revealed greater right- than left-sided activation associated with "higher-level" language tasks, such as understanding metaphors (Sotillo et al., 2005), detecting inconsistencies in stories (Ferstl, Rinck, & von Cramon, 2005) and drawing inferences from text (Mason & Just, 2004). The idea that the right hemisphere may be critically involved in more abstract aspects of language is one that is gaining ground and is, in certain respects, reminiscent of the idea (discussed in Chapter 3) that the two hemispheres have different processing styles. Jung-Beeman (2005) has proposed that the two hemispheres allow a two-pronged approach to the comprehension of natural language. The left hemisphere is involved in rapid interpretation and tight links, while the right hemisphere underpins broader meaning and recognition of distant semantic and conceptual relations.

A final interesting point concerning language lateralisation is that the right hemisphere can sometimes support the recovery of language function following brain damage. This is particularly true in children, as we discussed in Chapter 3. In fact, children who have had their entire left hemisphere removed to treat epilepsy can regain most language abilities (Vargha-Khadem et al., 1997) and this must be mediated by the right hemisphere. In some cases adults can also regain some degree of language function after left hemisphere damage, due to the corresponding region on the right taking over the function (e.g., Blank et al., 2003). One interpretation of these observations is that language areas exist on the right and, if necessary, these can become more finely tuned to perform tasks that are normally the province of left-lateralised regions.

CHAPTER SUMMARY

The classic neurological approach to understanding the role of the brain in language relied on case studies of people with localised damage, usually to the left hemisphere. Broca and Wernicke described differing forms of aphasia, the prominent features of the former being non-fluent agrammatical speech, and those of the latter being fluent but usually unintelligible speech. Their work led to the development of Lichtheim's "connectionist" model of language, which emphasised both localisation of function and the connections between functional areas. Connectionist models gained renewed impetus with the work of Geschwind in the 1960s.

Three new lines of inquiry—the cognitive neuropsychology approach, functional neuroimaging research, and the neuroanatomical work of Dronkers and colleagues—have prompted new ideas about the networks of brain regions that mediate language. The cognitive neuropsychological approach has underlined the subtle differences in cognitive processes that may give rise to specific language disorders. The functional imaging research has identified a wider set of left brain (and some right brain) regions that are clearly active as participants undertake language tasks. The newer structural imaging work has also prompted this conclusion, as well as necessitating a re-evaluation of the functional roles of Broca's and Wernicke's areas. The emerging view from these diverse research approaches is that language is a far more complex and sophisticated skill than was once thought. Many left-sided cortical regions collaborate in a truly distributed network to facilitate receptive and expressive language functions. Their work is supplemented by right hemisphere regions with particular responsibilities for higher-level aspects of language processing.

CHAPTER 7

CONTENTS

7

Memory and amnesia

(contributed by Andrew Parker)

INTRODUCTION

Memory has been investigated extensively by those involved in neuropsychological research. This research has taken many forms encompassing practically all types of memory, ranging from information that is processed for the briefest of periods of time to memory across the lifespan. This chapter assesses the contribution that neuropsychologists have made both through the study of those individuals with brain damage and by use of neuroimaging procedures with healthy volunteers. Memory itself, at a most general level, refers to our ability to acquire, retain, and retrieve information (see Figure 7.1a). This information is stored in the brain, and thus analysis of those who have sustained damage to the brain, or techniques that allow us to image brain activity, provide us with means by which we can understand memory.

The fact that memories are stored somewhere in the brain, *and* that they consist of activities involved in acquiring, storing, and retrieving information, points to two general theoretical approaches that have provided guiding frameworks in the study of memory. The first approach has often been labelled the *systems* approach and takes the view that different types of memory are located within different regions of the brain (e.g., Cohen & Squire, 1980; Schacter & Tulving, 1994). The second approach has been called the *process* approach and takes the view that memory is composed of different processes that may recruit similar or different neural regions depending on the task facing the individual (e.g., Cermak, 1994; Roediger, Weldon, & Challis, 1989; Verfaellie & Keane, 2002). Of course this dichotomy simplifies many aspects of past and ongoing research; memory is likely to consist of multiple neural regions and multiple processes (Parkin, 1999). In light of this, the current chapter emphasises the idea that memory consists of both systems and processes and that both views are important for a comprehensive understanding of this topic.

The chapter starts with a consideration of short-term and **working memory** before moving onto long-term memory. This outline appears to emphasise the memory systems approach, and indeed in some ways it does. However, this is purely for the sake of exposition, as the reader will soon become aware of how

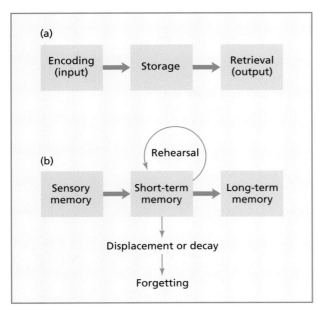

FIG. 7.1 (a) A generic model of the main information processing activities associated with memory. (b) A schematic diagram of Atkinson and Shiffrin's model of human memory. According to this model, sensory input was conceptualised as passing from a sensory register into short-term storage. If the material was rehearsed it would be consolidated into long-term memory. Otherwise it would quickly be forgotten.

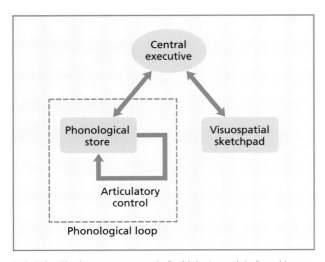

FIG. 7.2 The key components in Baddeley's model of working memory. The central executive coordinates activity in the two slave systems to keep in mind visuospatial or auditory-verbal information.

these "so-called" systems operate, and thus of the processing activities performed by these systems.

SHORT-TERM MEMORY AND WORKING MEMORY

The idea of short-term memory (STM) has a long history but its most influential form was developed by Atkinson and Shiffrin (1968). Their "modal model" of memory (see Figure 7.1) distinguishes between a sensory memory store (which stores sensory impressions for very brief periods of time), a short-term memory store (which can hold information over longer periods through mental rehearsal), and a long-term memory store (into which information is passed following processing by the short-term store). The model proposes that the memory stores (systems) are essentially unitary: that is, indivisible into separate subcomponents. However this notion has been subject to revision following empirical investigations into both short-term and long-term memory.

With respect to short-term storage, the concept of a unitary STM system presented a number of problems and has undergone subsequent revisions. These revisions eventually led to an alternative conception in which STM is composed of a number of subsystems. This multi-component model, referred to as working memory, is most closely associated with the work of Alan Baddeley and colleagues (e.g., Baddeley, 1986; Baddeley & Hitch, 1974). The structure of working memory is illustrated in Figure 7.2. It consists of a central executive whose function is to direct and regulate the flow of information, and allocate attention and processing operations within the two "slave" systems, so-called because they are essentially controlled by the central executive. These slave systems are the visuospatial sketchpad (which serves the function of integrating and processing spatial and visual information over short periods) and the phonological loop (which serves the function of storing and processing verbal auditory information over short periods). Although the model was initially proposed on the basis of research with individuals without brain damage, the study of both neuropsychological patients and the use of neuroimaging with healthy controls has been useful in its subsequent testing and development.

NEUROPSYCHOLOGICAL EVIDENCE FOR COMPONENTS OF WORKING MEMORY

The visuospatial sketchpad is the subsystem responsible for the temporary storage and manipulation of visual and spatial information. One particular neuropsychological test used to assess visuospatial memory is the Corsi block test (see Chapter 2). In this task nine identical blocks are arranged in front of the participant in such a manner that there is no apparent order or pattern to their placement. Following this, the experimenter taps the blocks in a particular sequence (e.g., touches block 3 followed by 5, 2, 8, etc.). The participant is then required to immediately reproduce this sequence. This measures visuospatial working memory, as the participant has to retain the spatial sequence in order to achieve accurate reproduction. DeRenzi, Faglioni, and Previdi (1977) found that patients with damage to the right posterior parietal region were significantly impaired on this task. However, the parietal regions do not act by themselves in terms of processing spatial information—the right frontal cortex is also important. For example, Pigott and Milner (1994) tested performance on a task that required short-term memory for chequerboard-like patterns. In this, participants were presented with a random array of black and white squares. After a short delay the participant was shown the same pattern with one of the squares missing. It was found that those with right frontal damage were impaired at remembering the spatial position of the missing square. Neuroimaging work also suggests a role for frontal regions in visuospatial working memory. For example, Smith, Jonides, and Koeppe (1996) presented to participants arrays of dots on a computer screen for 200 ms. Following a 3-second delay, a circle appeared either in the same or in a different location to one of the dots. Participants were asked to decide if the circle would have covered one of the dots if it had been present at the same time. It was found that this task led to activation in the right frontal lobe.

The label "visuospatial" suggests a combination of both visual and spatial processing. In everyday life most visual perceptions contain both visual and spatial information, which may in turn suggest that such features are processed together in the brain. However, it is now becoming clear that the visual and spatial components of working memory can be dissociated. For example, Owen et al. (1995) reported that damage to the anterior temporal lobes impairs visual working memory, while leaving spatial working memory intact. Conversely, Levine, Warach, and Farah, (1985) reported that damage to the parietal lobes selectively impairs spatial memory tasks. This double dissociation provides strong evidence that the visuospatial sketchpad needs to be subdivided into separate visual and spatial components. The visual component is important for processing the identity of the object, while the spatial component is important for processing the relative location of objects or features of object. Overall, these studies testify to the importance of neuropsychological research in advancing our understanding of this component of working memory.

Neuroimaging with healthy controls has also revealed that separate regions are implicated in the processing of visual and spatial information, with visual working memory associated with activations in inferior occipitotemporal regions and spatial working memory associated with activations in parietal regions (Courtney et al., 1996; Postle, Druzgal, & D'Esposito, 2003).

In Baddeley's model the phonological loop actually comprises a passive storage system called the phonological store and an active rehearsal mechanism called the articulatory control process. The former is responsible for the temporary storage of speech-based sounds which decay rapidly unless refreshed by the articulatory control process. An everyday example of the phonological loop would be holding a phone number in one's memory just long enough for a call to be made; the number is held in the passive store in speech-based form and refreshed by subvocal rehearsal. Studies of brain-damaged individuals support the idea that the phonological loop consists of two components. For example, it is possible to observe patients with damage to the phonological store without damage to the articulatory control process (e.g., Caterina & Cappa, 2003; Vallar & Baddeley, 1984). Neuroimaging work also provides broad support for the model, as different activations are associated with the phonological store, in BA 40 on the left, and the rehearsal process, in BA 44/45 also on the left (Awh et al., 1996; and see previous chapter). However, the location of these subsystems is far from being resolved. For example, Chein, Ravizza and Fiez (2003) argued that the putative location of the phonological store around BA 40 may not be an accurate reflection of the functions of this region as it is often activated by non-verbal stimuli, which is inconsistent with its role in phonological processing.

Recent work in neuroimaging has revealed some interesting findings about auditory non-verbal working memory that are not encompassed by Baddeley's model. Arnot et al. (2005) found support for the idea that the neural processes that support working memory for the identity of a sound differ from those that support working memory for localising a sound. In their experiment, participants were presented with two sounds in succession and performed one of two tasks. In one task, participants were asked if the second sound was the same as the first. In the other task, participants were asked if the second sound was in the same spatial location as the first. Arnot et al. found that working memory for the identity of the sound activated a region in the left superior temporal gyrus. In contrast, working memory for spatial location activated parietal cortex, posterior temporal lobe, and the superior frontal sulcus. Thus the processing associated with auditory non-verbal working memory appears to be functionally segregated, with different processing requirements being performed by different neural regions or pathways. In some sense this finding is similar to the results obtained for visuospatial working memory in which the neural regions associated with the processing of object identity are different from those associated with object location (see Chapter 8 for a review of dorsal and ventral streams, and Box 7.1 for a description of a recent modification to Baddeley's working memory model: the episodic buffer).

Box 7.1 Additions to the working memory model: the episodic buffer

Although the working memory (WM) model has stood the test of time and received considerable support, a number of changes and adaptations have been made that further refine the original ideas about short-term storage and processing. One important change has been the addition of a new component called the episodic buffer (Baddeley & Wilson, 2002). This component was added for two main reasons: first, because of the need for WM to have some means of integrating visual and verbal codes (which, remember, are processed by separate subsystems); second, because of the need for the temporary storage of information that exceeds the capacity of the two slave subsystems. The latter came to light from the finding that immediate memory span for prose passages is much greater than that for unrelated lists of words. Originally, this fact was attributed to long-term memory. However, Baddeley and Wilson (2002) reported a group of amnesic individuals who, despite having impaired long-term memory, displayed normal levels of prose recall if asked to remember the passages immediately without any form of interference or delay. If the superiority of prose recall is dependent on long-term memory, then the amnesic individuals should clearly be deficient when tested on this task. Baddeley and Wilson claimed that the reason for unimpaired recall of prose was due to the operation of the episodic buffer, which is able to hold and integrate relatively large amounts of information over short periods and act as an intermediary between the two slave systems and long-term memory. This conception of the episodic buffer is not without its critics. Gooding, Isaac, and Mayes (2005) point out that as a theoretical construct it is as yet somewhat underspecified and difficult to test. Also, there is currently no means of assessing the independent contributions of the episodic buffer and long-term memory to prose recall. As a consequence the validity of the episodic buffer awaits the test of time and future research.

The central executive is considered to be responsible for the attentional control of the other working memory subsystems as outlined above. It is thought to be primarily dependent on the dorsolateral prefrontal regions such that damage here impairs performance on experimental tasks that depend on executive control and processing (Stuss & Knight, 2002). Research has revealed that the executive may actually comprise a number of subprocesses, each associated with a different neural region (Baddeley, 2002; Shallice, 2002, 2004). More details on the frontal lobes and executive functioning can be found in Chapter 11.

INTERIM COMMENT

On the whole, neuropsychological research has provided good support for the idea that working memory comprises a number of subcomponents with each involved in the processing or storage of different forms of information. What is becoming increasingly clear is that these subcomponents are widely distributed across diverse neural regions. A challenge for future research is to answer the question of how these subcomponents interact in order to perform the everyday tasks in which working memory is so crucially important.

LONG-TERM MEMORY

GENERAL BACKGROUND

Amnesia refers to a particular cognitive deficit in which long-term memory is selectively impaired (Victor, Adams, & Collins, 1971). There are two broad

KEY TERM
Amnesia: General term for loss of memory. Anterograde amnesia is loss of memory following some trauma. Retrograde amnesia is loss of memory for a period of time prior to trauma.

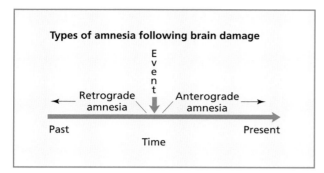

Types of amnesia following brain damage

FIG. 7.3   A schematic diagram that illustrates the distinction between anterograde and retrograde amnesia. Anterograde amnesia refers to memory loss following the event that brought about the brain damage. Retrograde amnesia refers to memory loss of information that precedes the event that brought about the brain damage.

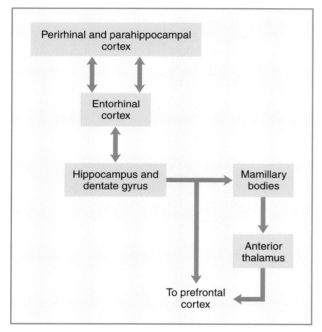

FIG. 7.4   The major structures and connections of the medial temporal lobes.

classes or subtypes of global memory impairments referred to as anterograde and retrograde amnesia (see Figure 7.3).

Anterograde amnesia is essentially a memory deficit for the acquisition of new information or new learning since the time of the brain damage. Thus those with anterograde amnesia will have problems remembering what they did the previous day or even a few moments ago. It can be considered a deficit in the ability to update memory, and in many respects those with this form of amnesia effectively live in the past as no (or very few) new memories are laid down. This type of amnesia is typically associated with damage to the medial temporal lobe (MTL) and associated structures, namely the hippocampus, the dentate gyrus, the entorhinal cortex, the perirhinal cortex, and the parahippocampal cortex (Zola-Morgan & Squire, 1993) (see Box 7.2 and Figure 7.4). Some of these structures are connected to other neural regions important for memory such as the thalamus, mamillary bodies, and prefrontal cortex.

Retrograde amnesia refers to an impairment in remembering information from the time prior to the onset of the damage. In terms of neuropsychological research, these two types of amnesia are often investigated separately, with theoretical emphasis and empirical studies designed to assess or characterise the nature of one or the other form. This chapter will deal with each in turn and attempt to consider how research with brain-damaged individuals and neuroimaging work has advanced what we know about the neural basis of long-term memory.

ANTEROGRADE AMNESIA AND NON-DECLARATIVE MEMORY

Perhaps the most famous case of anterograde amnesia is that of patient HM. He was unfortunate enough to suffer from severe epilepsy, and efforts to treat this conventionally (with medications) were unsuccessful. The decision was made to remove the focus of his seizures and this entailed the surgical removal of much of the medial temporal lobe regions in both hemispheres. The operation took place in the early 1950s and left HM with a very severe form of anterograde amnesia. As a consequence of being unable to update his memory, HM was mentally "stuck" in the 1950s (Corkin, 1984). Thus he failed to recognise people he had recently encountered even when these individuals had been in frequent contact with him. He also reread magazines and newspapers because he failed to recognise the fact that he had read them before. On several occasions he made his

Box 7.2 Causes of amnesia

A brief overview of some of the causes of amnesia is provided below. However the list is not exhaustive and memory loss is also known to be associated with electro-convulsive therapy (ECT), dementia, and epileptic seizures to name just a few. In spite of this, the causes outlined below are important as these have been the most informative in the neuropsychological investigation of memory.

The Korsakoff syndrome

Amnesia can actually result from nutritional deficiency that is often associated with chronic alcoholism. Alcohol interferes with the gastrointestinal transport of

the vitamin thiamine. Thiamine itself plays an important role in cerebral metabolism and thus a reduction in the amount of thiamine reaching the brain has serious consequences for healthy neural functioning. The memory disorder resulting from thiamine depletion is called the Korsakoff syndrome or sometimes the Wernicke-Korsakoff syndrome (after the two researchers, Carl Wernicke and Sergei Korsakoff, who were initially involved in studying this disorder). The precise neuropathology associated with this syndrome is still the subject of investigation but research has implicated the neural structures within the diencephalon (including the mamillary bodies and the thalamus) and even the frontal lobes (Colchester et al., 2001; and see Box 7.3 later in this chapter).

Hypoxia

Hypoxia refers to an inadequate supply of oxygen to the tissues (including neural tissue). Hypoxia can result from heart disorders, carbon monoxide poisoning, arterial disorders, and impaired respiratory function. The neuropathology associated with hypoxia is variable and often widespread (Caine & Watson, 2000) but in terms of memory disorders the hippocampus, thalamus, and fornix are often implicated (Aggleton & Saunders, 1997; Kesler et al., 2001; Reed et al., 1999).

Vascular disorders

The brain needs a constant supply of blood and this is carried to the brain by a dedicated vascular system. This vascular system consists of a number of major arteries that branch outwards throughout the brain into smaller and smaller arteries, which eventually merge with veins that carry the blood back to the heart. Interruptions to the supply of blood can occur for a number of reasons, such as a blockage from a blood clot or *embolism*, or damage to the walls of the artery. In both these cases, the cessation of the supply of blood leads to the brain being deprived of oxygen and nutrients, and brings about cell death. Depending on which arteries are damaged or blocked, different neural regions or structures can be affected. With respect to memory disorders, the important arteries are those that supply the hippocampus, thalamus, mamillary bodies, and basal forebrain (O'Conner & Verfaellie, 2002; von Cramon, Hebel, & Schuri, 1985).

Viral infections

Infection with the herpes simplex virus can bring about memory disorders as a consequence of herpes simplex encephalitis. Neuropathological features of this disease include widespread bilateral temporal lobe damage (Colchester et al.,

2001). As structures important for memory reside in the temporal lobe regions (more specifically the medial temporal lobes) then it is not surprising that herpes simplex encephalitis can bring about severe memory impairments.

Head injuries

As the name suggests this form of injury results from a blow to the head in one form or another. The injury can be either penetrating (e.g., gunshot wound) or closed. In the case of closed head injury, diffuse damage across widespread neural regions can occur as a result of compression of the brain, the shearing of axons, and haemorrhaging. Closed head injuries can often bring about post-traumatic amnesia which can last from minutes, following very mild injury, to months, following more severe injury.

way back to a previous address following a move to a new house (Milner, 1966; Scovile & Milner, 1957) because he was unable to update his memory for his new address.

In spite of this impairment, HM's IQ was above normal, as were his language and perceptual abilities (Scovile & Milner, 1957). Furthermore, if asked to keep a string of digits in mind (such as a phone number) he was able to do so very successfully if allowed to make use of mental rehearsal. However if rehearsal was prevented, his performance dropped to almost zero (Milner, 1966). HM had some degree of retrograde impairment but this was small in comparison to the severity of his anterograde deficit. For example, he was able to recognise the faces of people who became famous *before* but not after his surgery (Marslen-Wilson & Teuber, 1975). However, it has recently been demonstrated that HM has acquired small amounts of new knowledge. For example, O'Kane, Kesinger, and Corkin, (2004) found that he knew a small number of facts about celebrities who had only become famous since his operation. In addition he was able to reconstruct an accurate floor plan of the house he moved into since the onset of the amnesia, presumably due to what amounts to thousands of learning trials (Corkin, 2002). In general, HM showed impaired abilities on recall and recognition memory tasks under conditions that do not allow for extended practice or learning. However he demonstrated intact abilities for perceptual and motor skills learning (Corkin, 2002).

The study of HM raises a number of questions relating to amnesia. Two of these are addressed below: (1) What are the patterns of intact and impaired performance in amnesia? (2) What precisely is the contribution of the medial temporal lobe (MTL) to memory? Although amnesic individuals such as HM are deficient in acquiring new memories they are not deficient in all aspects of new learning. By examining the patterns of performance across a wide range of experimental tasks, research into amnesia has been a valuable source of information with regard to unravelling the complexity of long-term memory systems and processes.

One way to think about this is the distinction made between declarative and non-declarative memory (Squire & Knowlton, 2000). Declarative memory (sometimes called explicit memory) refers to memory for events, episodes, and facts (see Figure 7.5). This type of memory is accompanied by conscious awareness that memory is being used in order to perform some task. For example, if someone is asked to recall a list of words, or what they did yesterday, then that person will be

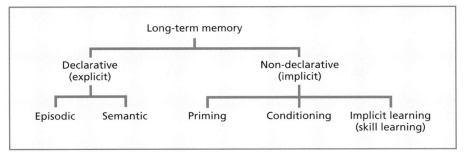

FIG. 7.5 A schematic diagram that illustrates the distinction between declarative and non-declarative memory (adapted from Squire, 2004).

aware that they are using memory in order to recall the information. Non-declarative memory (sometimes called implicit memory), on the other hand, is a form of memory that is observed and expressed though performance without any necessary dependence on awareness. In this case, the individual uses memory without any conscious awareness that memory is guiding or directing their performance. A typical example could be something like riding a bicycle. The ability to ride a bicycle is learned and then expressed through performance (actually riding it without falling off). This behaviour does not demand that the individual recall consciously the actual act of learning. Instead learning is expressed in an automatic fashion. Non-declarative memory comes in many forms and appears to be remarkably preserved in amnesic individuals (Squire 2004). Priming, classical conditioning and implicit learning are three examples of non-declarative memory, which are outlined below.

PRIMING

Priming refers to the influence of a previous study episode on current performance in terms of accuracy or speed of performance. When psychologists refer to implicit memory, more often than not they mean priming. Priming does not demand awareness of the study episode or the ability of the individual to remember any of the details of the study phase of the experiment. This fact makes it a form of non-declarative memory. For example, imagine a participant in an experiment being presented with a set of words (including, e.g., CHORD). Later they are given a set of word fragments (e.g., C H_ R _) and asked to say what word comes to mind when they read the fragments. Research has shown that participants are more likely to complete a word fragment with one presented earlier than an equally likely alternative such as CHARM, even though they do not consciously attempt to recall the studied words (Hayman & Tulving, 1989; Roediger et al., 1992). It is as if the words simply "pop into mind" in an automatic fashion. This popping into mind of previously studied stimuli is an example of priming. The same phenomenon can be observed in amnesic individuals. For example, Tulving, Hayman, and MacDonald (1991) studied priming in patient KC, who had very dense amnesia resulting from damage to the MTL. KC was presented with a list of words during the study phase of an experiment and then given a test of word fragment completion. Tulving et al. found that in spite of not being able to consciously remember any of the words, KC's performance was unimpaired on the word fragment completion task. Essentially, it was as if KC had

KEY TERM
Priming: The (possibly subconscious) influence of some preliminary event or stimulus on subsequent responding.

no deficit at all when memory was tested using an implicit test of memory—KC was just as likely as healthy respondents to complete word fragments with previously studied words. This suggests that whatever memory systems or processes are responsible for these priming effects, they are not dependent on the integrity of the MTL.

Cognitive research has indicated that the priming effects observed on tests such as word fragment completion are based on the perceptual characteristics of the word. Thus if the words are initially *heard* and then tested *visually*, priming is reduced (Rajaram & Roediger, 1993). This perhaps indicates that such priming effects are dependent on neural regions involved in vision and perception. Research with brain-damaged individuals and neuroimaging of healthy controls has provided broad support for this idea. For example, Gabrieli et al. (1995a) found priming effects to be reduced in a patient with damage to the right occipital lobes. Subsequent work has indicated that the left occipital lobe can also support priming (Yonelinas et al., 2001). With respect to neuroimaging research, priming effects on tasks like word fragment completion are associated with *decreased* activations in regions involved in perceptual processing, such as the occipital lobes and the ventral surface of the occipital/temporal region (Bäckman et al., 1997; Koutstaal et al., 2001). The fact that decreased activations were found may sound unusual but it is thought to be due to decreased metabolic demands or synaptic strengthening following the initial processing of the word during the study phase (Wagner, Bunge, & Badre, 2004).

Intact priming effects in amnesia are not limited to relatively low-level perceptual tasks as described above. In addition, performance on memory tasks that require conceptual or meaningful semantic processing is also spared. An example of such a task is word association. In this, participants are presented with words such as "belt" or "noisy". Later, during testing, they are presented with related words such as "strap" or "quiet" and asked to free-associate by saying whatever words come to mind. Participants without brain damage are more likely to respond with the meaningfully related words that were presented earlier in the experiment (e.g., strap – belt, quiet – noisy). Levy, Stark, and Squire (2004) assessed this form of priming, called conceptual priming, in amnesic patients and found it to be entirely intact in these respondents too, even when conscious recognition of the presented words was no greater than chance.

Again, this would appear to indicate that priming effects are not dependent on the medial temporal lobes but instead the contribution of some other neural region which has now been identified by neuroimaging. Wagner et al. (1997) found that when individuals were required to make conceptual or semantic judgements about words, the left prefrontal cortex became activated. Furthermore, when asked to make the same judgement to the words on a second occasion, a relative decrease in the activation was observed in this same area. This decrease in activation is considered to be the neural signature of priming effects, and parallels that found with perceptual tasks.

CLASSICAL CONDITIONING

Some recent work has focused on whether another form of non-declarative memory is also intact in amnesic individuals. **Classical conditioning** is a relatively simple form of associative learning that has been studied in humans using the eyeblink conditioning paradigm (see Figure 7.6). In its simplest form this involves present-

KEY TERM
Classical conditioning: A simple form of learning where a previously neutral stimulus (e.g., a light) becomes associated with a motivationally salient stimulus (e.g., food) through repeat presentation.

ing a conditioned stimulus such as a light or tone just before a puff of air, the unconditioned stimulus, is directed to the eye. The unconditioned stimulus automatically causes an eyeblink response. Following this pairing procedure, the light or tone alone also brings about an eyeblink response (the "conditioned" response). Gabrieli et al. (1995b) found that amnesic individuals with damage to the MTL had no difficulty in learning the conditioned eyeblink response in spite of profound declarative memory impairments.

The **cerebellum** seems to be the critical neural region for this type of non-declarative memory. For example, Woodruff-Pak, Papka, and Ivry (1996) found that patients with cerebellar damage were impaired at acquiring the classically conditioned eyeblink response. In addition, Coffin et al. (2005) noted that the cerebellum is particularly susceptible to the toxic effects of prenatal alcohol exposure. In line with this, they found that children with established prenatal alcohol exposure were also impaired at learning a classically conditioned eyeblink response. Neuroimaging research is supportive of the findings with brain-damaged patients. Using PET, Schreurs et al. (1997) found changes in cerebellar activity during the learning and extinction of classically conditioned responses.

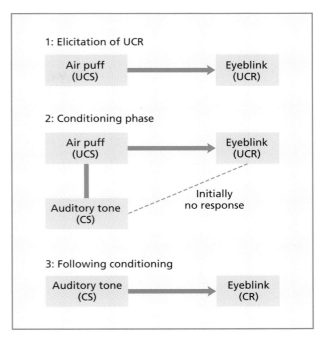

FIG. 7.6   The eyeblink conditioning paradigm, in which the unconditioned stimulus (UCS) is a small puff of air directed towards the eye. This elicits an eyeblink response. This response does not need to be learned and thus is called the unconditioned response (1). During conditioning (2), a conditioned stimulus such as an auditory tone is paired with the puff of air. Following this procedure the auditory tone comes to elicit the eyeblink response (3).

IMPLICIT LEARNING

Implicit learning is essentially learning without awareness. This form of learning has been assessed by a number of experimental procedures, one of which is the serial reaction time task. This may, for example, involve the presentation of a light in one of four horizontal locations. Each location is associated with a response button which respondents are required to press when the light flashes. The lights flash according to a particular sequence or pattern of which the participant is unaware. In spite of being unaware of this sequence, participants' reaction times become faster with practice. This is taken to indicate implicit learning of the sequence. Studies with amnesic individuals indicate that their performance on this task is spared despite profound recognition memory deficits (Reber & Squire, 1994). Another interesting task, developed only recently, is a variation of the radial arm maze initially used in rodent studies of learning. This task involves the presentation of a central circular area on a computer screen. Stemming outwards from this are a number of rectangular arms. A dot is presented at the end of one of the arms and the respondent is required to move the screen cursor down the arm using a computer mouse. Once this is done, a dot appears in another arm and the participant is required to trace the cursor back along the first arm and then down the arm that now has a dot within it. Again, unbeknown to the respondent, the appearance of the dot is not in fact random, but follows a predetermined sequence. Implicit learning is indicated by decreased reaction times to move

KEY TERM
Cerebellum: Region at the base of the brain that is important in sensory and motor functions.

around the maze. It has been demonstrated that those with selective damage to the hippocampus were able to acquire this skill in the absence of knowledge of how the skill was acquired (Hopkins, Waldram, & Kesner, 2004).

The above studies demonstrate that whatever neural systems underlie such learning abilities, they are not dependent on MTL structures. Instead, learning of this sort appears to be dependent on the striatum and substantia nigra: both components of the basal ganglia (see Chapter 5 for more details on this structure). Studies of individuals with damage to these structures, such as patients with Huntington's or Parkinson's disease, find impaired performance on such implicit learning tasks (Helmuth, Mayr, & Daum, 2000; Knopman & Nissen, 1991). The importance of the basal ganglia in implicit learning is backed up by neuroimaging research that demonstrates changes in basal ganglia activity over the course of learning structured, compared to random, sequences (Thomas et al., 2004).

INTERIM COMMENT

The research outlined above is broadly consistent with the idea that preserved memory functions in amnesia are of the non-declarative type. One of the main characteristics of non-declarative memory is that it is a form of non-conscious memory (Squire & Knowlton, 2000). For example most amnesic patients demonstrate priming effects, classical conditioning, and implicit learning without any form of conscious memory for the initial study or learning episode. This may appear to indicate that the primary deficit in amnesia is to conscious memory with all forms of non-conscious memory intact. However this may not be the whole story, as amnesic patients can sometimes show impairments in certain tasks of non-conscious memory. For example, they show impairments on a number of tasks including priming effects for fragmented pictures (Verfaellie et al., 1996), more complex forms of classical conditioning (McGlinchey-Berroth et al., 1997), and the later stages of skill learning (Knowlton, Squire, & Gluck, 1994). As a consequence the characterisation of intact learning abilities in amnesia as being one of non-conscious memory is likely to be too simplistic, and no generally agreed conclusions have yet been formed.

ANTEROGRADE AMNESIA AND DECLARATIVE MEMORY

The medial temporal lobes have been shown to be important for declarative memory. Damage to these structures brings about an anterograde deficit. Considered below are a range of neuropsychological investigations that add to our understanding of declarative memory and show how the study of the hippocampus can help to redefine the nature of conscious remembering.

EPISODIC AND SEMANTIC MEMORY

Declarative memory, as noted earlier, refers to memory for events and facts. Memory for events is often called episodic memory and memory for facts is often called semantic memory (Tulving, 1983). Some researchers claim that the amnesic deficit is one that specifically pertains to episodic memory (Parkin, 1982). This is argued because amnesic patients have no problems with using language or answering general knowledge questions. As both of these depend on the use of semantic memory, it would seem reasonable to conclude that semantic memory is intact. However, when amnesic individuals are presented with a list of words to recall, or asked about what they did yesterday, then their performance is likely to be severely impaired. In both of these instances, the amnesic person is being asked to remember a specific event or episode. This, of course, depends on episodic memory. As amnesic individuals are clearly impaired on tasks of this kind, it would seem reasonable to conclude that episodic memory is impaired. In theoretical terms it could be said that amnesia provides support for the distinction between episodic and semantic memory.

Unfortunately this conclusion is somewhat premature and thought needs to be given to an alternative explanation. In the above example, the typical amnesic patient could be considered successful at retrieving information that was learned *prior* to the onset of the amnesia (this would be general world knowledge or semantic information learned earlier in their life) but unsuccessful at learning and recalling new information *after* the onset of amnesia. If this is true then the amnesia may simply be a new learning deficit rather than one that can be seen as supporting the episodic–semantic distinction. Support for the episodic–semantic distinction would be more conclusive if amnesic individuals were able to learn new semantic information in the absence of new episodic information. Current findings are somewhat ambiguous on this issue. An early study by Gabrieli, Cohen, and Corkin (1988) found HM to be severely impaired at learning new semantic facts and this does not support the episodic–semantic distinction (but see more recent research on HM by O'Kane, et al., 2004). However other research has demonstrated some degree of support. Tulving et al. (1991) and Westmacott and Moscovitch (2001) both found that new semantic learning could take place in amnesic individuals albeit at a rather slow pace. This conflict may have been resolved by Bayley and Squire (2005) who suggest that new learning of semantic information may take place but only if some of the structures in the MTL remain undamaged. When destruction is more widespread then new semantic learning is absent.

THE ROLE OF THE HIPPOCAMPUS

The role of the hippocampus has been extensively studied in both animals and humans and is known to be centrally important for declarative memory. However, declarative memory can take different forms and can be assessed by different means. One form is related to the recognition of a stimulus such as a word, picture, or face based on its overall familiarity. Another is often called recollection and is based on the retrieval of more detailed information, typically in the form of an association between two or more stimuli. Both types of declarative memory are accompanied by conscious awareness but differ in our experience of remembering. This distinction, between *familiarity* and *recollection*, can be easily illustrated. A typical example is to imagine seeing someone you recognise. Unfortunately you cannot remember their name or any other details about them—this represents *familiarity*-based recognition. Later, you recall their name and perhaps where you have seen them before. This is *recollection*-based memory. These two components of declarative memory can be measured in a number of ways. One technique involves comparing item recognition memory (e.g., memory for a list of words) with free recall. The idea behind this is that item recognition can be based on familiarity (if a word on the test list seems familiar then respond "yes", i.e., I saw this word earlier). However free recall requires the retrieval of associations between the stimuli and cannot be based on familiarity alone. Another technique involves comparing item recognition and associative recognition. For the latter, rather than measuring memory for single stimuli, the experimenter presents pairs of words during the study phase (e.g., stay–pool; hall–thin; rage–firm). Later, during the recognition test, some of these pairs are presented again, in the same pairs as before (e.g., stay–pool), whereas others are re-paired (e.g., rage–thin; hall–form). The participant has to try to distinguish those pairs presented unchanged from those that have been rearranged. As a consequence, associative recognition, by its very nature, requires the retrieval (recollection) of associations.

The distinction between familiarity-based memory and recollection has become very important recently as neuropsychologists have attempted to uncover the neural regions responsible for each of these. Some argue that the hippocampus is important for all forms of declarative memory, both familiarity and recollection (Squire & Knowlton, 2000). However, others argue that the hippocampus is important only for recollection (Aggleton & Brown, 1999, 2006). These ideas can be examined in individuals with selective damage to the hippocampus. If the hippocampus is required for both familiarity and recollection then selective damage to this structure should impair both forms of memory. But if the hippocampus is required for only recollection, then it should be possible to observe dissociations between recollection and familiarity. Evidence in favour of the idea that the hippocampus is important for all forms of declarative memory was presented by Reed and Squire (1997). They tested a group of patients with selective bilateral damage to the hippocampal region and found impairments on tests of even single item recognition. More recently, Stark and Squire (2003) compared memory for single items and memory for associations between items in a group of patients with bilateral damage to the hippocampal region and found impairments on both types of test. Thus, on the basis of these findings it would appear that the hippocampus *is* needed for *both* familiarity and recollection, thus supporting the ideas of Squire and colleagues.

However, these findings have not gone unchallenged. For example, Mayes et al. (2002) and Holdstock et al. (2002) studied patient YR who, like the patients mentioned above, has bilateral damage to the hippocampus. YR was assessed across a range of tests designed to tap familiarity and recollection. The researchers found that her memory abilities were impaired when tested with recall-type tasks (recollection) but preserved on tests of recognition (familiarity). In addition Holdstock et al. (2005) tested patient BE, who also has selective bilateral hippocampal damage, and found his associative recognition and recall performance to be more impaired than single item recognition. Accordingly, both YR and BE provide evidence for the theory of Aggleton and Brown (1999, 2006).

INTERIM COMMENT

Theories about hippocampal function have been the focus of investigation in the animal modelling literature. Of course it is not possible to ask animals if they are conscious of a specific event or are able to recollect details of some particular experience. As a consequence, understanding hippocampal functioning in animals has, of necessity, taken a different route. However, elements of both the human and animal research can be seen to map onto one another. For example, largely on the basis of work with rodents, Eichenbaum (2002) has advanced the idea that the hippocampus is important for the acquisition and expression of *relational* memories. An important property of relational memory is that associations are formed between multiple elements of an episode but, in spite of being associated, these elements maintain their own independent identity. Thus an association between A and B is not "fused" in some rigid and inseparable representation but rather stored in a manner that allows each element to be accessed, compared, and processed in relation to other elements. These relational representations can be altered, added to, and changed over time. Thus relational representations formed by the hippocampus are said to be flexible. For example, if A is related to B, and B is related to C, then a flexible representation of these pairings allows one to make an inference about the relationship between A and C even though they have never been paired together.

The research with brain-damaged individuals reviewed earlier provides some support for the relational account of hippocampal function, as do some recent neuroimaging studies that find greater hippocampal activation during the formation and remembering of stimulus pairings. In addition, it has been shown that solving problems of the type A–B, B–C, A–C also leads to greater activity in the hippocampus (Heckers et al., 2004).

So where do all these findings leave the debate regarding the functions of the hippocampus? Unfortunately, the picture is still unclear and only further research is likely to clarify it. In terms of research on amnesia this will be an interesting debate to keep an eye on, as it will help to sharpen our understanding of the precise functions of the hippocampus and the contribution it makes to declarative memory. (See also Box 7.3.)

Box 7.3 The diencephalon and amnesia

Damage to the diencephalon, which comprises the thalamus and hypothalamus (including the mamillary bodies), typically results in memory impairments. In part this is known on the basis of research with Korsakoff amnesia. However, as this syndrome produces pathology that is more widespread and not limited to the diencephalon, then the precise contribution of this structure remains uncertain. Of course what we need to do is to assess the memory performance of individuals with more circumscribed lesions. Kishiyama et al. (2005) presented a patient (RG) with bilateral damage to the thalamus following a stroke. Testing revealed impaired recognition memory across a range of materials including words, pictures, and faces. Theoretically, these results are of importance because they demonstrate that damage to the thalamus can bring about reductions in memory performance. More specifically, as the thalamus receives afferents from the hippocampus these two structures can be thought of as comprising a neural circuit in which damage to either component can bring about amnesia (Aggleton & Brown, 1999, 2006). As the thalamus itself comprises a number of distinct nuclei, it has been proposed that different mnemonic processes are subserved by different nuclei. For example, Aggleton and Brown (1999, 2006) claim that the anterior nuclei are important for recollection, while the medial dorsal nuclei are important for familiarity-based recognition. Unfortunately this has yet to receive support from human studies and some evidence actually runs contrary to its proposal. In particular, Edelstyn, Hunter, and Ellis (2006) found that damage to the medial dorsal thalamic nuclei did not impair familiarity-based recognition.

MEMORY PROCESSES

So far, this chapter has dealt with research that provides broad support for the idea of memory systems. The notion that memory systems differ with regard to how they process information has been implicit in much of the foregoing, and research with brain-damaged individuals has highlighted the importance of component processes involved in different types of memory task. This section deals with the concept of memory processes in a more explicit manner and considers how such ideas from mainstream cognitive psychology have been integrated and advanced by neuroscience research. One of the most significant achievements of the cognitive approach to learning and memory relates to the development of theories and ideas about encoding and retrieval processes, and how these interact to influence memory performance. Functional imaging procedures have, in a sense, enhanced cognitive psychology by revealing the neural processes underlying memory formation and remembering. In other words, it is now possible to "see" the hypothetical processes postulated by cognition researchers.

ENCODING

Encoding refers to those cognitive activities or processes that are responsible for creating a representation of the event or episode to be remembered. Early work in cognitive psychology demonstrated that the manner in which a stimulus is encoded has direct implications for whether that stimulus will be remembered. For example, Craik and Lockhart (1972) found that performing "deep" meaningful processing on a set of words (e.g., Is a "cat" a mammal?) enhanced memory for those words compared to a condition where shallow processing was performed (e.g., Is the word "cat" printed in upper- or lower-case letters?). Craik and Lockhart claimed that memory was nothing more than the remnants of prior processing activity and that deeper processing led to more durable and robust memory traces. The idea of levels of processing has been advanced by neuroimaging studies in which participants perform either a deep or shallow processing task on a set of stimuli (e.g., words) while in the scanner. Collectively the results indicate that a number of areas are active in the deep processing condition compared to the shallow processing condition. These include the hippocampus and adjacent MTL regions and the left prefrontal cortex (see Cabeza & Nyberg, 2000, for a review). Some studies have found hemispheric differences such that greater left (vs right) activations are typical when the stimuli are words (vs patterns) (Wagner et al., 1998). Thus different encoding processes that are known to influence memory appear to be associated with different neural regions.

As deep processing is associated with both enhanced memory and enhanced activations in particular neural regions, it should be possible to predict the memorability of a stimulus by the magnitude of these activations. For example, Fletcher et al. (2003) required participants to perform a deep or shallow processing task on a set of words while being scanned. Later, the participants were asked to recall as many of the words as possible. The researchers found a number of things: First, deep encoding led to greater activations in left medial temporal lobes and the left lateral prefrontal cortex. Second, the amount of activation in these areas actually predicted which words would be recalled; the greater the amount of activation, the more likely the word would be recalled.

Some more recent work indicates that successful memory encoding is related to the *interaction* between the hippocampus and other cortical regions to which it connects; greater interactions lead to greater probability of recall success (Ranganath et al., 2005). Other research has shown that not only can we predict which words will be recalled by monitoring neural activity during the encoding of the word, but the neural activations that occur milliseconds *before* a word is encoded can also predict memory success (Otten et al., 2006).

The focus so far has been on encoding. However, memory is as much about retrieval as it is about encoding (Tulving, 1983). What has neuroimaging research told us about the act of retrieving information from memory?

RETRIEVAL

Retrieval refers to accessing information stored in memory. In cognitive research, retrieval can be broken down into a number of subcomponents called retrieval mode, ecphory, and recollection (Tulving, 1983). For further details see Box 7.4.

Box 7.4 Components of memory retrieval

Retrieval mode refers to a form of "mental set" in which the individual directs attention to the act of remembering, and makes use of cues in order to recall information. For example, suppose someone asks me if Zack was at the fancy dress party I went to last week. The name "Zack", the event "party", and the time "last week" all act as potential retrieval cues. In attempting to answer the question I will put them all together and prepare to probe my memory of the event. Ecphory is the term used to refer to the interaction between the retrieval cue and the stored memory trace. For example, the stored memory trace of who was at the party will interact with the retrieval cues "Zack", "party", etc. and allow me to recover the stored information of who was at the party. Recollection is when the individual becomes aware of the information retrieved. In this case I become aware that Zack was indeed at the party, as I recall him swinging from the chandelier in an astronaut suit. As with encoding, these processes are unobservable but neuroimaging procedures may again allow us to "see" some of these activities and help to establish a neural basis for retrieval.

Retrieval mode was examined by Lepage et al. (2000). They found a number of regions to be activated, including the right prefrontal cortex (and to a much lesser extent the left prefrontal region), during retrieval. This was found whether or not retrieval was successful, and was taken to indicate the neurocognitive processes underlying the establishment and maintenance of the "mental set" in which attention is directed to the act of remembering. The involvement of the right prefrontal region has taken on added significance given the fact that numerous studies appear to show similar activations during episodic memory retrieval (see below).

Distinguishing between ecphory and recollection is difficult, and research has tended to compare whether different areas of the brain are activated when retrieval is successful (in which case *both* ecphory and recollection have presumably taken place) to conditions in which the retrieval is unsuccessful (in which case ecphory and recollection have not taken place). For example, Stark and Squire (2000) compared which regions of the brain were active when participants recognised words (or pictures) presented earlier during the experiment, compared to words (or pictures) that were not presented earlier. The assumption was that stimuli presented earlier would lead to ecphory and recollection whereas new stimuli would not lead to such processes. Stark and Squire found significant activation in the left hippocampus during word recognition, and bilateral activation of the hippocampus during picture recognition. However, a potential problem with this study is that participants may not have recognised some of the words and pictures presented earlier. What is needed in order to "image" ecphory and recollection is to compare activations that occur when participants actually recognise the stimuli to activations in which participants fail to recognise the stimuli. This requires the use of event-related fMRI (see Chapter 2). Using this method Dobbins et al. (2003) found that correct recognition responses were associated with enhanced activations in the left hippocampus and the parietal cortex. The finding of enhanced neural responses in the hippocampus is to be expected on the basis of work with brain-damaged individuals. However the significance of the parietal activations is somewhat unclear even though it has been observed in a number of experiments (McDermott & Buckner, 2002; Rugg, 2004).

ENCODING AND RETRIEVAL INTERACTIONS

On the basis of the previous discussion it may be thought that encoding and retrieval are two entirely separate processes. However, cognitive research has come to place emphasis on how these two processes interact with each other in order to enhance memory. The manner in which encoding and retrieval processes interact has been the focus of much research and forms the foundation of a particular framework called *transfer appropriate processing* or TAP for short. TAP has its roots in memory research dating back to the 1970s but has been more formally specified by Roediger and colleagues (e.g., Roediger et al., 1989). Basically, TAP states that the most important factor determining successful memory is the extent to which encoding and retrieval processes overlap. If retrieval processes overlap or recapitulate the same mental processes that occurred during encoding, then memory will be successful. For example, Morris, Bransford, and Franks (1977) presented participants with words such as EAGLE and asked them to perform one of two tasks on these words: a semantic-meaningful task (e.g., Is an eagle a large bird?) or a rhyming task (e.g., Does eagle rhyme with legal?). Later, participants were given one of two tests of memory: one presumed to rely on meaning (a recognition test) and one thought to rely on the sounds of the words (deciding if the test words sounded similar to the studied words). It was found that performance on the test that depended on meaning was enhanced by the earlier meaning-based encoding task, while performance on the sound test was enhanced by the earlier rhyme-based encoding task.

Presumably, the reason why encoding–retrieval overlap is important is that retrieval reflects the recovery or reactivation of the memory trace laid down during encoding. This idea has been assessed by neuroimaging research. Vaidya et al. (2002) made use of fMRI in order to examine whether the cognitive/neural processes used to encode pictures of objects into memory were also active when retrieving this information. Participants were scanned while encoding words and pictures into memory and also later while retrieving this information. It was found that during the encoding of pictures a number of neural regions became activated, including the fusiform gyrus and inferior temporal gyrus bilaterally, and the left mid-occipital gyrus. During retrieval a subset of these regions became active once again, most notably in the left hemisphere. These regions are known to play a role in aspects of object recognition and Vaidya et al. speculated that during retrieval these regions became reactivated as information about an object's shape and its meaning was being processed.

INTERIM COMMENT

Research with neuroimaging has revealed that encoding and retrieval processes may be implemented in different hemispheres of the brain. The so called HERA (hemispheric encoding and retrieval asymmetry) model was originally proposed by Tulving et al. (1994) and Nyberg, Cabeza, and Tulving (1996) and was meant to summarise a number of findings indicating that the left prefrontal region showed greater activation during encoding while the right prefrontal region showed greater activation during retrieval. Although subject to some criticisms (Lee et al., 2000) these findings have been shown to be remarkably robust (Habib, Nyberg, & Tulving, 2003). It would seem that although encoding and retrieval processes do activate similar neural regions, as predicted by TAP, the extent of overlap is partial. Some of the differences are related to the manner in which processing activity is lateralised.

RETROGRADE AMNESIA AND AUTOBIOGRAPHICAL MEMORY

As mentioned earlier, retrograde amnesia refers to an impairment in remembering information from the time prior to the onset of the disorder or injury to the brain. Although it often co-occurs with anterograde amnesia (Kapur, 1999) it can also occur in relative isolation and is then called focal retrograde amnesia (e.g., Kapur et al., 1989). Most often, impairments are greatest for more *recent* events leading up to the injury or disease (Squire, 1992). This produces a situation in which memory for more distant events, such as those in childhood, is actually better than memory for more recent events. This is the reverse of what is found in those without retrograde amnesia, who display superior memory for more recent events. The temporal extent of the retrograde impairment can vary quite widely. For some individuals the impairment may be for the previous few months or years. For very severe cases, the extent of impairment can be across the whole lifespan (Cermak & O'Connor, 1983).

In addition, individuals with retrograde amnesia can often display a range of deficits in recalling pre-morbid memories. These can include: (1) memory for personal episodes and events from their lives such as a birthday party or holiday, (2) personal semantic information such as who they are, their characteristic traits and preferences, (3) public and news events, such as who won the general election on some particular date, and also famous people and personalities, such as politicians and TV stars. Interestingly, on some occasions deficits can be more severe for certain types of memory. For example, Manning (2002) examined patient CH who had retrograde amnesia resulting from hypoxia following a cardiac arrest. Testing revealed that CH had relatively preserved new learning abilities (i.e., limited anterograde amnesia), however memory for autobiographical information was particularly impaired, and more so for personal events and episodes.

When asked to recall an autobiographical memory many people report recalling visual images of the event or seeing what happened (Brewer, 1995). It is now thought that visual imagery may play an important role in the retrieval of memory for personal events and experiences (autobiographical memory) and that it enables us to mentally relive and re-experience our past (Rubin, Schrauf, & Greenberg, 2003). If this is true, then individuals who are deficient with respect to processing visual information may also have impaired access to their auto-biographical memories and feel unable to relive those memories. Recent studies are consistent with this idea. Greenberg et al. (2005) studied patient MS, a man with a visual processing deficit (agnosia) who had sustained damage to a number of regions including the temporal and occipital lobes. Not only did MS display a severe retrograde deficit, but the autobiographical memories he did manage to recall were unlike those of control participants in a number of ways. For example, when rating his memories in terms of how real or vivid they felt, MS was sig-nificantly impaired. His memories were simply lacking in the types of detail and recollective experience that make our memories of incidents and events so compelling.

Why should visual imagery play such an important role in the retrieval of our past? A neuroscientific explanation relates to the way in which memories are stored and retrieved. Memories, especially autobiographical memories, are com-plex and often involve the interplay of a number of different senses such as vision, audition, olfaction, etc. (Hodges, 2002). Damasio (1989) advanced a theoretical account that argued that the processing and storage of such a variety of infor-mation takes place not in one neural region but across multiple regions, with each involved in processing a different aspect of the original event. For humans at least, the visual sense is particularly important. When it comes to retrieving auto-biographical memory then multiple neural regions become activated and provide the basis of our re-experiencing the event. These interacting regions can be seen as being dependent on one another and, as a consequence, damage to one region can effectively disrupt the activation process from spreading to other neural regions. This may either prevent memory retrieval, or at least disrupt the retrieval of some of the details of the experienced event. Damasio's theory has been used on a number of occasions to account for aspects of the retrograde deficit (e.g., Hunkin, 1997) and, in relation to patient MS, the explanation could be that damage to the regions of brain responsible for visual processing (e.g., occipital lobes) disrupts retrieval processes and prevents access to either autobiographical memory or to the types of details that lead to vivid recollection (Greenberg et al., 2005). Interestingly, the MTL would still appear to be important for more vivid and detailed recollection. For example, Steinvorth, Levine, and Corkin (2005) found that patient HM, although able to retrieve distant memories, often substituted gist for specific details. Thus the ability to recall personal experiences and almost "relive the moment" depends on the intact functioning of multiple neural regions.

NEUROIMAGING OF AUTOBIOGRAPHICAL MEMORY

The idea that autobiographical memory is dependent on a diverse set of interacting neural regions has received some support from neuroimaging research. In a review, Maguire (2002) reported that autobiographical retrieval leads to the activation of a network of areas including temporal and parietal regions, the medial frontal cortex, the cerebellum, and the hippocampus. However, different experimental studies often reveal different activations. Maguire claims that this is likely to be due to a number of factors such as the variety of means by which autobiographical memories are elicited, the relative recency of the memories, differences in the amount of effort required to recall a memory, and the amount of time allowed for each recall and response. All these differences make comparisons and generalisations quite difficult and clearly much research needs to be carried out in this important and interesting area.

As mentioned earlier, patients with retrograde amnesia often display a temporal gradient of memory loss affecting more recent (vs more distant) memories. According to some researchers, the reason for this is that following the encoding of an event, memories undergo a slow consolidation process and this is dependent on the hippocampus (Squire, 1992; Teng & Squire, 1999). Thus, initially, a newly formed memory is actually quite unstable. Consolidation processes work to make the memory stable and increase its strength and resistance to forgetting. More specifically, it has been proposed that the hippocampus is responsible for retrieving only relatively recent memories. Following the passage of time, and the consolidation process, it becomes possible to retrieve memories independently of the hippocampus. This idea has received support from research with animals and humans. For example, Zola-Morgan and Squire (1990) trained monkeys to discriminate between a set of different objects over a period of weeks. Following lesions to the hippocampus the monkeys were tested on their memory for the previously learned objects. If the hippocampus is required for the retrieval of more recent memories, then lesions to this structure should produce a greater impairment for the most recently acquired objects. This was indeed the case: memory was most impaired for the objects learned a few days before and was best for those acquired weeks before. In humans, Bayley, Hopkins, and Squire (2003) presented amnesic individuals, whose pathology was limited to the hippocampal region, with the cue-word autobiographical memory test. They were asked to recall memories from the first third of their lives prior to the onset of their amnesia. Compared to control participants, the quality and details of the memories retrieved were virtually identical. Thus it would appear that the recall of more distant memories is not dependent on an intact and fully functioning hippocampus.

The idea that the hippocampus is not required for more distant memories is not without its dissenters. For example, Nadel and Moscovitch (1997) and Moscovitch and Nadel (1998) propose that the hippocampus is required for the retrieval of both recent *and* remote memories. They note that the temporal gradient of memory loss in some retrograde amnesia cases extends back decades, sometimes up to 30 years. They suggest it is implausible that any form of physiological consolidation process would take this amount of time, extending sometimes over the entire life of the individual. Their alternative hypothesis is that the hippocampus is always involved in the encoding and retrieval of memories. Over time, memories are subject to reactivation with older memories, acquiring a greater number of reactivations. The reactivation process leads to multiple memory traces being formed within the hippocampus and surrounding cortex. When damaged, older (vs more recent) memories are more likely to be recalled because they are more resistant to loss as they possess multiple retrieval routes. Some recent neuroimaging work is consistent with the predictions of this theory: Bosshardt et al. (2005) found that recall of more distant memories resulted in the *increased* activity of the hippocampus. The consolidation theory of Squire and colleagues would predict a *smaller* amount of activation over extended periods of time because older memories are hypothesised to be less dependent on the hippocampus. As a consequence, it is not clear how the findings of Bosshardt et al. could be accounted for by the consolidation theory. (See Box 7.5 for a summary of the neurobiological events thought to underpin consolidation of memories at the cellular level.)

Box 7.5 Long-term potentiation and consolidation

Although the consolidation theory of Squire and colleagues has met some challenges, very few researchers would seriously question the idea that for memories to become stable they must undergo some form of consolidation process. Presumably this process takes the form of cellular and molecular changes at the synaptic level. In spite of being beyond the scope of this chapter, the molecular and cellular basis of memory consolidation has been the object of intensive research and is worth mentioning here. One candidate mechanism thought to be responsible for the consolidation of memories is called long-term potentiation (LTP). The process underlying LTP is complex but, at the risk of oversimplifying matters, it refers to the increased magnitude of the response of the postsynaptic neuron following stimulation by the presynaptic neuron (in experimental animals the action of the presynaptic neuron is mimicked by an electrical impulse). This increased response can be shown to last for hours or months (Barnes, 1979) and thus represents the record of *previous* neuronal activity. The reason for this is an increase in protein synthesis in the postsynaptic neuron (Bourne et al., 2006; Fonseca, Nagerl, & Bonhoeffer, 2006). Effectively, this leads to a modification or strengthening of the synapse (Martin & Morris, 2002). LTP has been shown to occur in the hippocampus and in the cortex (Bear & Kirkwood, 1993; Ivanco & Racine, 2000) and thus provides a molecular basis for plastic changes in these regions. Linking LTP to overt behavioural changes (learning and memory) has been demonstrated by findings that indicate impaired learning following drug-induced blockade of LTP (Davis, Butcher, & Morris, 1992) and that learning can bring about LTP-like changes (Mitsuno et al., 1994; Tsvetkov et al., 2002). As a consequence, LTP represents a potential mechanism for the enduring cellular and molecular changes underlying consolidation processes in learning and memory. Exactly how these cellular and molecular changes are reflected in the types of memory considered in this chapter is as yet unknown and represents a pressing challenge for neuroscientific research.

CHAPTER SUMMARY

This chapter has considered what neuropsychological research has told us about the *systems* and *processes* underlying short-term/working memory and long-term memory. Through the careful analysis of individuals with brain damage, and with the use of neuroimaging procedures, it will be appreciated that the concept of memory does indeed encompass and support the idea of multiple memory systems and sub-systems with multiple component processes. It is now clear that the human brain possesses the capacity to represent many different forms of information and that different neural regions performing different cognitive processes are responsible for this capacity. With respect to short-term memory, broad support has been gathered for the idea that multiple systems and processes are responsible for the maintenance and manipulation of information currently being processed. Neuroscientific research has assisted in the development and refinement of models of short-term and working memory. By the careful analysis of those individuals with brain damage, the idea of a unitary short-term memory does not stand up to scrutiny: Different regions of the brain are, for example, responsible for maintaining and manipulating verbal information and visuospatial information. Neuropsychological work has also provided the impetus for revisions of the working memory model and the incorporation of the so-called episodic buffer.

With respect to long-term memory, the idea of declarative and non-declarative memory has received considerable support. Furthermore, the precise nature of the subsystems and processes underlying these forms of memory is being worked out in ever finer detail. For example, non-declarative memory comprises a number of subsystems that dissociate from one another and are located in different neural regions. Declarative memory comprises a number of processes that enable conscious remembering of past events, and research suggests that these processes may be differentially dependent on different neural systems and pathways. Conscious recollection appears to be crucially dependent on the hippocampus, and vivid memories may require the additional involvement of neural regions involved in perception. However, this does not mean that our understanding of memory is complete—rather, that it is continuing to develop. Further growth will depend in part on the theoretical frameworks and ideas that we bring to bear on the empirical data, and on the discovery of new findings that may challenge these frameworks and preconceptions.

CHAPTER 8

CONTENTS

Visual object recognition and spatial processing

INTRODUCTION

The primacy of the visual system in humans is reinforced by the observation that up to half of the cerebral cortex is directly or indirectly involved in visual processing. It is important at the outset to try to distinguish between sensory mechanisms of vision and perceptual processes that permit recognition of the visual input. Essentially, visual sensation is about input "getting registered" in the brain. Perception is concerned with interpretation of that input (Mesulam, 1998). The latter is what principally concerns us here, and we will consider research findings from case studies of people who have lost certain perceptual functions, usually after damage or disease to key cortical regions, as well as findings from functional brain imaging.

Although the distinction between "sensation" and "perception" sounds clear-cut, it is, to some extent, artificial, because a good deal of "processing" of visual input takes place almost as soon as light enters the eye. In the retina, a network of cells interacts to provide the brain with evidence of contrast, colour, and boundaries (edges). Retinal output, in the form of millions of nerve impulses, travels via the optic nerve and tract to the lateral geniculate nuclei (one on each side) of the thalamus. Here, information from the two eyes begins to coalesce, with input from the central fovic retinal regions being separated from peripheral retinal regions. Most lateral geniculate output is relayed on to the primary visual cortex where two vast "sheets" of cells (in the left and right occipital lobes) map out the entire visual field (see Figure 3.4). Cells in this region are arranged in columns and respond preferentially, and in some cases exclusively, to particular types of visual input, such as the orientation of lines, colour information, and so on. Thanks in no small part to the pioneering work of Hubel and Weisel in the 1960s and 1970s, the route from eye to brain is reasonably well understood. We do not intend to provide detailed coverage of it in this chapter—readers wishing to learn more should refer to one of the many excellent reviews of this research area, such as Chapter 5 of Gazzaniga, Ivry, and Mangun (2002).

Neuropsychologists tend to be more interested in the processes after sensory registration that lead to perception. In order to begin to understand these stages of processing, we need to look beyond V1 and V2 of the occipital lobe to other cortical regions that are implicated in the interpretation of visual sensation. Separate cortical regions deal with colour and movement, and coordinate higher-order perceptual processes such as reading, object recognition, and facial recognition. In fact, "visual" areas exist throughout the occipital, parietal, and even temporal lobes.

There is substantial evidence that these areas divide (to some extent) into two separate processing streams, commonly referred to as the "what" and "where" streams (Ungerleider & Mishkin, 1982). Later in the chapter we introduce some brain disorders that seem to be anatomically and functionally linked to one or other stream. These are of interest in their own right, but they also provide clues about the sort of visual perceptual processing that must occur in "intact" brains. Normal visual perception can be studied more directly using functional imaging and we will also review some of this literature. However, we start with a brief review of Ungerleider and Mishkin's model of parallel, but functionally distinct, visual processing streams.

THE "WHAT" AND "WHERE" STREAMS AND VISUAL PERCEPTION

In the mammalian brain there is extensive output from the occipital lobes to other cortical regions that is carried primarily by two major pathways. The inferior route follows a ventral course (round the side and particularly underneath) into the temporal lobes, whereas the superior route takes a dorsal course (over the top) into posterior regions of the parietal lobes. In 1982, Ungerleider and Mishkin suggested that these anatomically distinct routes could also be distinguished in terms of the types of "processing" they mediated. On the basis of data gleaned largely from lesion studies and electrical recording in monkeys, they proposed that the ventral stream is specialised for object recognition and perception, whereas the dorsal stream is specialised for spatial perception—i.e., for determining the locations of objects and their positions relative to one another and to the viewer. The two streams operate in parallel to allow us to address the fundamental questions of "what" we are looking at, and "where" it is located in our field of vision (see Figure 8.1).

Pohl's (1973) discrimination learning study is typical of the research from which Ungerleider and Mishkin developed their model. It had two conditions: in the landmark task, monkeys learned to associate the presence of food in one of two food wells with a landmark such as a cone, which was always positioned near the baited well. After a period of learning the rule was reversed so that food now only appeared in the well farthest away from the cone. In the object discrimination condition, there were two landmarks such as a cone and a cube. In the training phase, food was only hidden in the food well near to one particular landmark, then when this had been learned, the relationship between cue and food was reversed. Pohl found evidence of a double dissociation: performance on the "spatial" landmark task was disrupted by parietal but not temporal lesions, whereas performance in the object discrimination was impaired by temporal but not parietal lesions (see Figure 8.2).

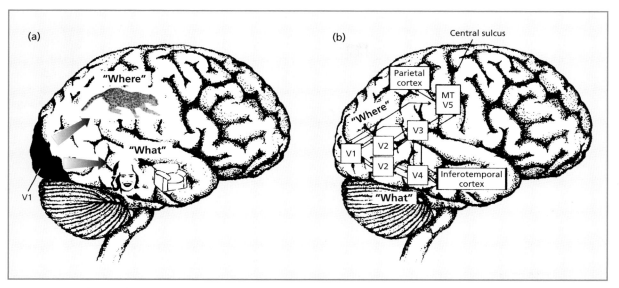

FIG. 8.1 The "what" and "where" streams of visual perception. (a) Ungerleider and Mishkin's "what" and "where" streams, and (b) a slightly more detailed flow diagram of some of the cortical regions implicated in these two processing streams.

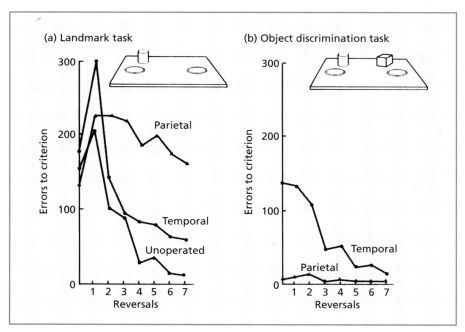

FIG. 8.2 Pohl's double dissociation study. In the landmark experiment, monkeys learned to associate the presence of food in a well identified by a particular marker (in this case, a cylinder). Once learned, the rule was reversed so that now the food was in the well farthest away from the marker. Although control animals and those with temporal lesions quickly learned the reversal, animals with bilateral parietal lobe lesions failed to improve. In the object discrimination experiment, monkeys learned to associate the presence of food with one of two markers (say, the cube). Once learned, the rule was reversed and the food was now associated with another object (the cylinder). Monkeys with parietal lesions were untroubled by this reversal, whereas those with bilateral temporal lobe lesions took several trials to learn the new association. The former experiment relies on processing in the "where" stream; the latter relies on processing in the "what" stream. Adapted from Pohl (1973).

Ungerleider and Mishkin's model has been largely supported by anatomical and lesion data in humans (e.g., Farah, 1990) as well as functional imaging (e.g., Haxby et al., 1991, 1994). For example, patient DF (reported by Milner & Goodale, 1995), who had incurred damage to the ventrolateral region of her occipital lobe as a result of carbon monoxide poisoning, had a profound difficulty in recognising and discriminating between simple objects such as different-sized cubes. However, her visually guided action towards an object (to grasp it for example) was normal. Conversely, patients with **optic ataxia** have preserved object recognition but cannot use visual information to guide their actions, leading to grossly defective grasping/reaching skills. This condition is almost always associated with damage to the superior parietal lobule (Battaglia-Mayer & Caminiti, 2002).

However the details of the model have been amended as our knowledge of cortical functions has increased. Anatomically, it is clear that more cortical modules are involved in the two streams than was initially thought. Moreover, modules within the two streams appear to interact with one another (i.e., send and receive projections) more extensively than Ungerleider and Mishkin anticipated (see below). Goodale and Milner (1992) mooted the possibility of a third pathway, projecting into the superior temporal sulcus area (STS) which contains many **polysensory** neurons (meaning that they respond to inputs from multiple sensory channels). It is therefore possible that this route would be important in the integration of perceptual information about stimuli arising from different sensory inputs, such as hearing and touch (Boussaoud, Ungerleider, & Desimone, 1990). Recent functional imaging studies support this notion (e.g., Taylor et al., 2006), but cross-modal integration remains incompletely understood.

Conceptually, the main challenge to the model has concerned the nature of information processing in the dorsal stream. Originally, Ungerleider and Mishkin proposed that this stream was dedicated to the identification of object location in space. But Goodale and Milner (1992) suggested that the real purpose of the dorsal stream was to guide an individual's on-line control of action. In other words, while knowing about the location of objects is an important component, some neurons in this pathway become particularly active only when a visual stimulus prompts a motor response, such as reaching for an object. This observation has led to the idea that the dorsal route really serves "how" rather than "where" functions (Milner & Goodale, 1995), and it is of interest to note that a major projection from the parietal lobe is to frontal areas, which, as we mentioned in Chapter 5, are critical in planning and controlling purposeful actions.

Yet another modification to Ungerleider and Mishkin's model was proposed by Turnbull, Beschin, and Della Sala (1997) and elaborated by Creem and Proffitt (2001). These authors argue that although there is good support for Milner and Goodale's re-labelling of the dorsal "where" stream as the "how" stream, it is important to recall that this route terminates in the *superior* parietal lobe and is primarily related to "egocentric" (viewer-centred) visually guided action. The *inferior* parietal lobule, on the other hand, is known to be associated with a range of visuospatial skills (some of which we describe later in this chapter) *not* directly concerned with action, such as mental rotation and 3D construction. Creem and Proffitt have characterised these as involving the manipulation of non-egocentric spatial representations. In other words, in humans (and it is important to

KEY TERMS

Optic ataxia: A deficit in reaching under visual guidance that cannot be explained by motor, somatosensory, or primary visual deficits.

Polysensory: Responsive to input from several modalities.

emphasise species-specific distinctions here given that Ungerleider and Mishkin's model was derived from primate studies), the parietal lobe may actually subserve both "how" and "where" functions in the superior and inferior regions respectively. Moreover, the latter may represent a point of interaction between Ungerleider and Mishkin's dorsal and ventral streams in situations where recognition of an object would be facilitated by knowledge of its visuospatial properties (see Figure 8.1b).

While debates about, and refinements of, the model are likely to continue for some time, the basic principle of separable dorsal and ventral processing streams for visual perception, specialised for what and where (or how), has become accepted as a tenet of brain organisation. In fact, recent evidence suggests that the same what/where segregation may be an organisational principle that extends to other perceptual domains such as audition (Alain et al., 2001) and touch (Reed, Klatzky, & Halgren, 2005).

INTERIM COMMENT

Ungerleider and Mishkin's model is accepted as offering a heuristic framework for understanding the lines of demarcation between object recognition and spatial processing. However, many neuropsychologists anticipate further revisions to the model as more is learned about the nuances of visual perception. The question of laterality, for example, is one unresolved issue: primate studies show that although both pathways receive bilateral inputs—because primates (including humans) tend to scan the visual field with both eyes—callosal lesions induce a greater impairment for ventral stream (what) processing than dorsal stream (where/how) processing. This suggests that processing in the latter pathway is somehow "more segregated" within each hemisphere. Confirmation of this distinction in humans is currently lacking although anecdotal evidence from cases of "hemineglect" (see Chapter 9) is broadly consistent with it, despite additional evidence for the "primacy" of the right hemisphere in these cases. We return to consider spatial processing in the dorsal stream later in this chapter. For the time being, we need to consider some of the characteristics of the ventral stream, and the effects that damage to different components of it can have on object recognition.

THE VENTRAL STREAM AND OBJECT RECOGNITION

Although we humans are inclined to take visual perception for granted, it is in fact an astonishingly complex process, or, more accurately, collection of processes, involving multiple computations, reconstructions, and integrations. For example, 3D objects in our field of vision are projected onto our retinas, which only work in 2D. So the brain must "reconstruct" a third dimension in order for us to see in 3D. Second, objects must be recognised as such irrespective of where their image falls on the retina, their distance from the viewer, and their orientation. For example, a tree is still usually *perceived* as a tree whether it is close to you or on the distant horizon. Third, you must also be able to recognise objects when they are moving in different directions. A horse moving across your line of vision projects a quite different image from one galloping directly towards you. Finally, your brain must be able to link the percept (of the horse for example) with stored representations of horses in order for you to make the semantic leap towards recognition of the object as a horse.

The ventral stream runs bilaterally from area V1 of the occipital lobes via areas V2 and V4 into the inferior regions of the temporal lobes (see Figure 8.1). If we examine the response characteristics of neurons in this stream, three clear trends emerge. First, neurons in posterior regions (at the beginning of the stream) fire in response to relatively simple stimulus characteristics such as width, shading, and texture, whereas neurons later on in the stream only respond to much more complex visual stimuli. Remarkably, some cells in anterior temporal regions only respond to very specific shapes of stimuli such as a hand, or even particular faces (Gross, Rocha-Miranda, & Bender, 1972). A second feature is that neurons further forward along the stream are less concerned with the physical position of objects in the visual field. We could describe cells in these forward regions as having large **receptive fields**, and in the case of some anterior temporal neurons almost the entire retina appears to be covered. So, no matter where the object falls on the retina, cortical cells will respond to an object to which they are tuned. A final point is that cells in this stream make considerable use of colour. This attribute is tremendously important for object recognition, not least because it often allows us to distinguish **figure** from **ground**, providing additional clues about the edges (and thus the shape) of objects (Zeki, 1980).

CLASSIC DESCRIPTIONS OF VISUAL AGNOSIA

In order to better understand the sort of processing that occurs in the ventral stream, it is helpful to consider classic neurological disorders that appear to stem from dysfunction or damage to it. In the 1890s, on the basis of a small number of detailed case studies, Lissauer described two forms of object recognition failure which he called apperceptive and associative agnosia. Today, we think that the two disorders are linked to damage at different stages in the ventral stream, and reflect different types of perceptual disturbance. Lissauer's binary classification of agnosias oversimplifies the true diversity of these conditions. However, the distinction at least provides a useful starting point for our consideration of visual agnosia.

Apperceptive agnosia

When shown a photograph of a cup, someone with this type of agnosia will probably be able to describe some of the physical features of it such as its size, colour, the presence of a handle, and so on. However, they will be unable to identify the object. In the most severe cases, when damage to occipital and surrounding posterior regions (especially in the right hemisphere) is widespread, patients with apperceptive agnosia cannot even copy simple shapes, match them, or discriminate between them. A case in point is Mr S (studied by Benson & Greenberg, 1969) who had become agnosic following accidental carbon monoxide poisoning. Although he clearly had some rudimentary impression of form, describing a safety-pin as "*silver and shiny like a watch or nail clippers*", he could not recognise objects, letters, numbers, or faces. He could, however, recognise objects from touch. Moreover, there was no evident deficit in his speech, memory, or comprehension.

People with apperceptive agnosia are described as being unable to put individual parts of a visual stimulus together to form what psychologists call a **percept**. The problem is regarded as "perceptual" rather than "sensory" because patients with apperceptive agnosia can usually describe individual elements of an object. They can see an object's form and features but they seem unable to "bind" individual components together into a meaningful whole.

Associative agnosia

Individuals with this form of agnosia can copy objects relatively well, and detect similar items from a visual display. In some cases they may even be able to sort items into groupings (animals, items of cutlery, tools, etc.). The problem in associative agnosia is an inability to identify (and name) specific objects. Consider the following situation: a patient is shown an assortment of cutlery. He picks up a fork and, when asked, draws a recognisable sketch of it. This shows that perception of the item is relatively complete, and therefore that the individual does not have apperceptive agnosia. He may, if asked, be able to find another similar item from the cutlery drawer. However, he would still be unable to identify the item as a fork. Moreover, if later asked to draw the object from memory, he might be unable to do so, although if actually asked to draw a fork, he probably could. Even at this point, he might not realise that the object he was holding and the drawing he has just made were of the same item. This problem is not necessarily related to general deficits in semantic memory because individuals with this form of agnosia can sometimes describe in great detail functional (or other semantic) information about objects from memory. One associative agnosic patient (MS) was unable to draw an anchor from memory, but was nevertheless able to define the item as "a brake for ships" (Ratcliff & Newcombe, 1982).

On the other hand, some people with associative agnosia *do* have problems with their semantic memory. Patient AB (studied by Warrington, 1975) could match objects and distinguish shapes, and he could also match different views of faces reasonably well. However, he was unable to name any of a series of 12 common objects shown to him. He could determine whether photographs depicted animals or objects, but he was unable to name or distinguish between different types of animal, suggesting some form of semantic memory deficit.

Insight into the nature of the cognitive deficit found in associative agnosia is provided by McCarthy and Warrington (1986). Their patient FRA suffered a stroke that affected left occipital and temporal regions. Amongst other "spared" perceptual skills such as being able to point to "named" objects, he could, additionally, colour in overlapping line drawings of objects (something that patients with apperceptive agnosia cannot do). However, he was unable to name any of them, and could provide only partial semantic information (at best) about just a few of them. This suggests that the core problem in associative agnosia is one of linking percepts to meaning. Object recognition is certainly more complete than for someone with apperceptive agnosia. However, the remaining problem is one of forming links between the "percept" and stored semantic information about such items.

> **KEY TERM**
> **Percept:** The "whole" that is perceived by putting together the constituent parts.

INTERIM COMMENT

Historically, a key distinction between apperceptive and associative agnosia has been whether or not individuals can copy drawings; generally people with associative agnosia can, but those with apperceptive agnosia cannot (but see below). Lissauer's distinction between the two forms can be related to processing in the ventral stream. Apperceptive agnosia occurs because of damage at an early stage in the ventral stream, and although many people with this form of agnosia have bilateral damage, cases of people with unilateral damage suggest that it is the right hemisphere that is most critical. People with this form of agnosia have only the most rudimentary visual perceptual functions, and damage to the occipital lobes and adjacent cortical regions such as the occipitotemporal border is often apparent. Associative agnosia is related to a somewhat later stage in perceptual processing in the ventral stream. The percept is relatively complete, but there is a problem linking it with relevant stored semantic information. This form of agnosia is much less common than apperceptive agnosia. However, rare instances indicate underlying damage either to semantic systems in posterior regions of the left hemisphere, or to the pathways connecting the occipito-temporal border regions of the right and left hemispheres (Janowiak & Albert, 1994; and see Figure 8.3).

RECENT CONCERNS ABOUT UNDERSTANDING VISUAL AGNOSIA

One unresolved problem concerning the classification of visual agnosia is a consequence of the inherently non-specific nature of brain damage. In Lissauer's original characterisations, both apperceptive and associative agnosia were considered to be "post-sensory" disorders. Yet the reality is that many people with visual agnosia have sensory impairments such as colour blindness or small blind spots (scotomas) *in addition* to their perceptual problems. This is particularly so in apperceptive agnosia, which is frequently associated with accidental carbon monoxide poisoning (see the case of Mr S discussed earlier). The poisoning also leads to widespread but minor lesions (sometimes called "salt and pepper" lesions) in posterior regions that are linked to sensory impairments such as those mentioned above. Clearly, it is important to ensure that the apparently perceptual deficits seen in agnosia are not, after all, caused by more fundamental sensory impairments as some writers have suggested (e.g., Bay, 1953).

However, the main problem with Lissauer's classification of visual agnosia is that it is too simple, and therefore fails to distinguish satisfactorily between subtly different forms of deficit. Consider first apperceptive agnosia: although the classic description emphasises the failure to bind together individual elements into a perceptual whole, cases have recently come to light where correct perception of the whole appears to depend on the orientation of the objects, the shading or shadowing that is apparent, or even the extent to which images are degraded. Some agnosic patients may, for example, be able to identify an object when viewed in a normal (standard) orientation, yet be unable to identify the same object if it is shown end-on, upside-down, or in some other unusual orientation. Patient JL, studied by Humphreys and Riddoch (1984), struggled to match normal views of

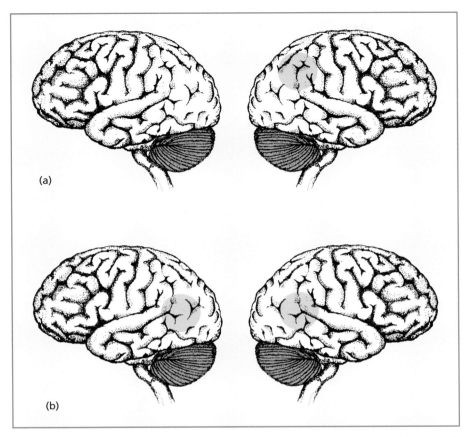

FIG. 8.3 Cortical regions typically damaged in apperceptive and associative agnosia. (a) Unilateral damage in posterior regions of the right hemisphere is more likely to be associated with apperceptive agnosia than equivalent damage on the left, although damage is, in fact, often bilateral. (b) In associative agnosia damage can be to either hemisphere, although the location is typically more ventral than that seen in apperceptive agnosia (in the vicinity of the occipital-temporal boundary).

objects with foreshortened views (end-on) (see Figure 8.4a). Moreover, when shown items from the Gollin picture test (1960), which comprises intact and partially degraded line drawings of familiar objects, some agnosic patients can identify the intact drawings but not the degraded ones (Warrington & Taylor, 1973, and see Figure 8.4b).

Associative agnosia also seems too simple a concept to account for the subtle differences in deficit that are observed in this condition. As we have seen, patient AB, studied by Warrington (1975), could draw and match objects, and was good at recognising unusual views of objects. However, he was profoundly impaired at object or picture naming, and was equally poor at describing functions of objects when given their names aurally. HJA, studied by Humphreys and Riddoch (1984), on the other hand, could define a carrot when asked to do so verbally, yet failed to identify a picture of one, guessing that it was a sort of brush. Moreover, he could often name objects by touch (when blindfolded) that he could not identify visually. These two examples illustrate that similar perceptual frailties may, on closer observation, take subtly different forms, and be related to different cognitive

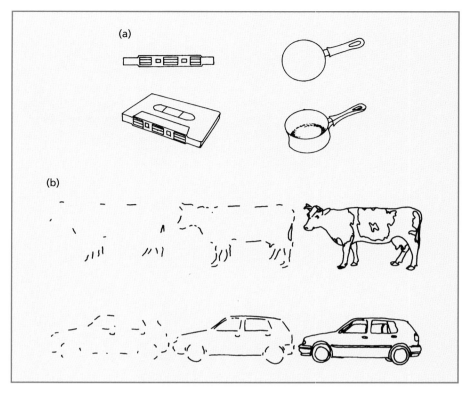

FIG. 8.4 Unusual views of objects. (a) All people find it easier to recognise objects when viewed from a "normal" angle. However, some people with agnosia cannot recognise objects at all when shown an "unusual" view. (b) The Gollin figures also present particular difficulties for some agnosic patients, although recognition of complete figures may be unaffected.

processing impairments. AB's problems involved semantic memory deficits, whereas HJA had an intact memory but seemed unable to access it from visually presented material.

Another problem is related to the question of how complete the percept actually is for individuals who would otherwise receive a diagnosis of associative agnosia. Recall that the acid test of this form has, historically, been whether or not the person can copy whole drawings. HJA, mentioned earlier, was able to produce an accurate copy of an etching of London, but the process took 6 hours and he completed the exercise in a laborious, slavish, line-by-line manner, which seemed to be independent of any "knowledge" of the actual form of objects in the sketch. Humphreys and Riddoch acknowledged that HJA was an unusual case. They argued that he had a particular problem in the integration of overall form with local detail, and other test findings showed that HJA was often "thrown" by the presence of detail in drawings or pictures that he was trying to copy or recognise: for example, he found silhouettes easier to recognise than line drawings. Of course, it is likely that normal individuals make extensive use of their semantic memory (which HJA could not do) when copying a drawing. This may make the copy less accurate, but a lot faster. The point is that, whichever way we look at it, HJA does not fit conveniently into either of Lissauer's agnosic types.

MODERN IDEAS ABOUT VISUAL AGNOSIA

Most researchers now acknowledge that Lissauer's classification is in need of revision and/or expansion. Farah (1990), for example, has proposed that visual object agnosia needs to be considered in relation to deficits in both word and face recognition (see below). Warrington has emphasised the importance of perceptual categorisation as a stage in object recognition that may be impaired in patients with apperceptive agnosia (Warrington & Taylor, 1978). Humphreys and Riddoch (1987, 2001) have argued that there are at least five subtypes of agnosia, and Ellis and Young (1996) also found it necessary to disaggregate Lissauer's two forms into several subtypes.

Riddoch and Humphreys' (2001) cognitive neuropsychological model of object recognition is an attempt to integrate case study reports (from their own patients, and those of Warrington, Farah, etc.) with an influential theory of visual perception proposed by Marr (1982). Although the details of his model need not concern us, it broadly comprises three sequential stages. The first is the generation of a unified "primal sketch" from the two 2D retinal images. It includes information about boundaries, contours, and brightness fluctuations, but not overall form. The second stage involves the generation of what Marr called a 2.5D image. This is viewer-centred (from the viewer's perspective), and contains information about form and contour, but neither object constancy (recognising an object as such whether it is near or far away, or even upside-down) nor perceptual classification. The final stage is the 3D representation. This is a true object- (rather than viewer-) centred mental representation. It is independent of the viewer's position, and specifies the real 3D shape of an object from any view, enabling true object recognition. Riddoch and Humphreys' model of object recognition is shown in Figure 8.5. For simplicity we have identified the stages sequentially:

- The initial parallel visual processing of objects is along the basic dimensions of colour, depth, and form. Motion features may also be processed if appropriate (if the object is moving). This stage of processing (motion excepted) essentially corresponds to Marr's primal sketch.
- The next stage involves grouping by colinearity (meaning identification of the edge of the object by dint of it having a common boundary).
- Then comes feature binding/multiple shape segmentation. This involves combining object features to form shapes, or breaking up compound images into component objects. Problems at this stage are more likely with overlapping or "busy" images where recognition depends on the correct binding of elements into a coherent image: see Figure 8.6a and b for examples of stimuli that may cause recognition difficulties at this stage.
- The next stage is equivalent to converting Marr's 2.5D sketch into a true viewpoint-independent 3D image. This stage is about the formation of constancy (see above), and remains somewhat controversial because some people with agnosia seem able to recognise objects despite being unable to match together conventional and unusual views of the same object.
- The next stage is a full structural description, tested by asking respondents whether or not presented pictures/drawings are of real objects. Some patients perform poorly on this task even though they may be good at matching different views of objects (see previous stage).

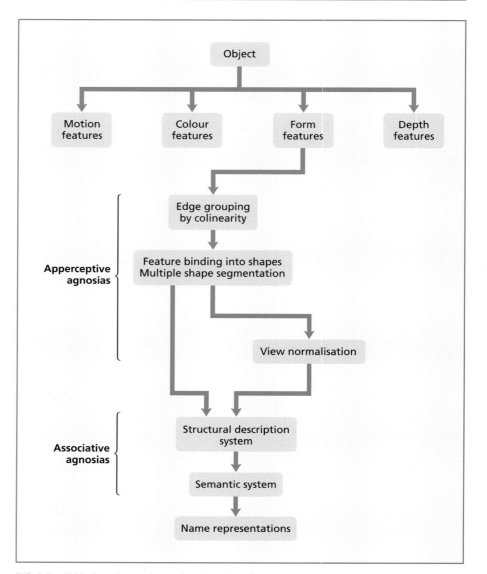

FIG. 8.5   Riddoch and Humphreys' (2001) model of visual object recognition. The model describes the component processes (and their connections) assumed to underpin normal and faulty object recognition. Adapted from Riddoch & Humphreys (2001) in B. Rapp (Ed.), *Handbook of cognitive neuropsychology*. Hove, UK: Psychology Press.

● In reality, the full structural description quickly meshes into the semantic system stage: individuals may be able to distinguish real from imaginary objects yet be unable to say which two items in an array of three (for example, hammer, nail, spanner) "go together". Some individuals with this problem can nevertheless provide detailed semantic information about the same objects if told their names, indicating that the problem is one of accessing the semantic system from the visual image.

● For other patients with agnosia, especially with category-specific semantic problems (see below), the basic deficit may either be loss of specific access (from the essentially intact visual image) or a semantic deficit, in which case the patient would not be able to elaborate on an item even when *told* what it was.

- The last stage in the model (name representations) is necessary to accommodate a small number of agnosic patients who clearly have semantic knowledge of objects but still cannot name them when they see them; a condition called **optical aphasia**.

Riddoch and Humphreys' modification and extension of Marr's model serves as a useful template for understanding the various forms of agnosia that have now been described in the literature and, inter alia, provides a heuristic model for visual object recognition in the intact brain. For example, Lissauer's apperceptive agnosia actually encompasses a series of disorders linked to failures (early) in the processing stream up to and including an inability to form either a primal sketch or a 2.5D viewer-centred image (e.g., Mr S). An inability to recognise degraded objects or unusual views of objects with preserved ability to recognise form (e.g., JL) may be specifically related to a failure, at the view normalisation stage, in forming a 3D object-centred image. Associative agnosia may occur either because of problems in accessing semantic memory despite the formation of an intact object-centred image (e.g., FRA), or because of impairments to semantic memory itself (e.g., AB).

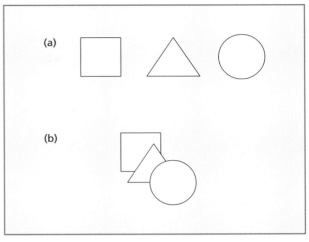

FIG. 8.6   Binding elements into a coherent image. Some apperceptive agnosic patients can recognise simple shapes when they are separate (a) but not when they overlap (b).

INTERIM COMMENT

Riddoch and Humphreys have offered a dynamic multi-stage scheme of visual object recognition that accounts for many of the apparent contradictions or inexactitudes of earlier models. However, the authors acknowledge that much more research is required to resolve remaining uncertainties about agnosic disorders and, in the process, about normal object recognition. One example relates to the formation of a true object-centred image. Recall that the copying style of agnosic patients like HJA, though accurate, was painstaking and laborious. Humphreys and Riddoch have taken this as an indication that HJA did not, in fact, have normal form recognition, because of his problems in integrating fine detail into the global form (a problem at the feature-binding stage in their model). This in turn implies that normal object recognition involves both the encoding of a global form and the integration of fine detail into that form. Humphreys and Riddoch coined the term **integrative agnosia** to describe HJA's deficit and suggested that such a "processing" failure was, in fact, a hallmark of many agnosic patients.

FUNCTIONAL IMAGING OF OBJECT RECOGNITION

PET and fMRI have provided us with the tools to examine the neural substrates of object recognition in normal people. Farah and Aguirre (1999) reviewed the results of 17 early imaging studies and their conclusions were somewhat disappointing. The meta-analysis revealed a lack of internal consistency and showed only that the posterior part of the brain was involved in object recognition. Farah and Aguirre argued that in spite of their uninspiring findings, imaging was a potentially exciting tool for exploring category specificity. This prediction has been borne out since, with a wealth of informative imaging results that are revolutionising our understanding of category-specific organisation at the neural level. We will review this literature later in the chapter.

fMRI has also provided evidence about other aspects of object recognition. For example, Bar and colleagues (Bar, 2004; Bar et al., 2006) have explored the role of the prefrontal cortex in exerting top-down control over object recognition. They suggest that very early in object recognition, prefrontal regions use coarse shape information to narrow the range of candidate objects, facilitating object recognition (see Figure 8.7). Carlson, Grol, and Verstraten (2006) have explored the temporal dynamics of object recognition, revealing multiple unique stages in the process, including support for Bar's top-down modulation. Thus, fMRI is providing evidence about the details of object recognition that classic neuropsychology simply cannot access. Imaging studies have also suggested that the neural basis of object recognition can be altered. Behrmann et al. (2005) performed lengthy training on a subject with long-standing agnosia and succeeded in improving some aspects of his object recognition skills. fMRI revealed that behavioural improvement was accompanied by functional reorganisation in the fusiform gyrus, part of the visual recognition system. This raises the possibility that some of the anomalies in the classic neuropsychological studies of agnosia may represent individual differences in the extent to which dynamic functional reorganisation occurs.

CATEGORY SPECIFICITY

Prior to the advent of functional imaging, an outstanding issue for the understanding of object recognition was that of category specificity. For some agnosic patients (for example, AB, whose case was reviewed earlier), impairment is linked to general deficits in semantic memory and inability to make intra-class distinctions. However, cases have come to light suggesting that category-specific semantic impairments may also occur in agnosia. A seminal series of papers by Warrington, Shallice, and McCarthy (Warrington & McCarthy, 1983, 1987; Warrington & Shallice, 1984) described a small number of agnosic patients with category-specific semantic deficits. For example, some had a naming deficit for living things, and others had a deficit for inanimate objects (see also Table 6.1). Other studies have since confirmed the existence of category specificity in patients. There have been various attempts to explain this phenomenon (see Caramazza & Mahon, 2003). One suggestion is that naming living things depends more on visual/perceptual information, while naming inanimate objects depends more on functional/associative information. There is some empirical support for this theory, but also evidence that is problematic (Caramazza & Shelton, 1998). We will return to this theory later when we review neuroimaging data. Although

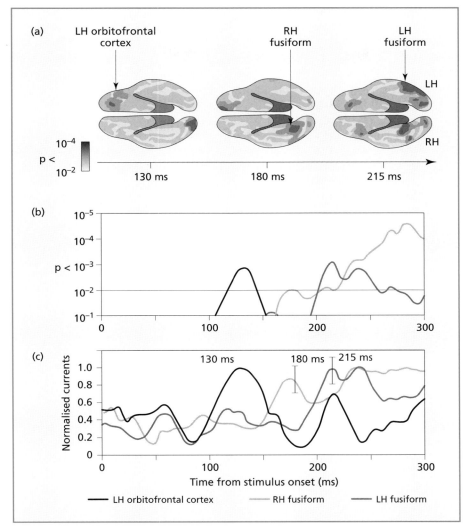

FIG. 8.7 Top-down control of object recognition. Orbitofrontal activity precedes temporal cortex activity. Source: Bar, M., et al. (2006). Top-down facilitation of visual recognition. *Proceedings of the National Academy of Sciences, 103,* 449–454. Reproduced with permission.

convincing evidence for category-specific deficits has only really emerged since the 1990s, one class of objects has always been considered special and distinct in the field of object recognition: faces.

RECOGNITION OF FACES AND PROSOPAGNOSIA

The ability to recognise faces is a skill that has long intrigued psychologists, partly because humans are so good at it. Consider the following lines of evidence. First, humans have a phenomenal memory for faces. Most readers will be aware of that "striking" moment of recognition when spotting the face of someone not encountered for many years. Second, research indicates that humans can memorise face information very quickly and with very little effort. People tested on Warrington's facial memory test, in which they look briefly at 50 anonymous black and white photographs of people, can correctly recognise most (or even all) of them in a later test. Third, although the distinctions between faces are subtle (all humans usually have two eyes, a nose, and a mouth), humans are able to scan large numbers of photographs very quickly to find one famous face. This last observation is a reminder that the key to effective face processing is "individuation"—that is, being able to distinguish between the subtle variations in form, size, shape, and alignment of the components of a human face.

A small number of people suffer from a specific form of agnosia that involves the inability to perceive faces. In **prosopagnosia** (as it is known) the degree of impairment is, as with object recognition, variable. In some cases, people may be unable to match pairs of faces, or say whether two photographs are of the same individual. In other cases, recognition of particular individuals such as film stars or members of the person's own family may be affected. In the most extreme and perplexing form of the disorder, the person may even lose the ability to recognise themselves from photographs or in the mirror.

Consider the following cases: Soldier S was studied by Bodamer (1947). Despite making an otherwise reasonable recovery following head injury, he was unable to recognise once-familiar faces. He could differentiate between faces and other objects, although he was prone to errors in recognising animals from photographs of their head, once misidentifying a dog as an unusually hairy person! When it came to humans, he complained that all faces looked very much alike, describing them as routinely flat white ovals with dark eyes. He was unable to interpret facial expressions although he could see movements (of a face) that led to changed expressions. He was unable to recognise his own face in a mirror.

Now consider Mr W, who was studied by Bruyer et al. (1983). He developed prosopagnosia in middle-age following a period of illness. He retained the ability to copy line drawings of faces, and he could match photographs of faces taken from different perspectives. He could also select faces correctly when given a verbal description, and his performance on this task deteriorated (as it would for normal subjects) if the faces were partly obscured. His particular problem only became apparent when he was asked to identify faces of either famous people or people he knew personally. For example, he identified only one of ten photographs of famous people. He also failed to recognise any familiar acquaintances from video vignettes, although he could recognise them from their names or even from hearing their voices. This showed that Mr W had "semantic knowledge" of these acquaintances, so his prosopagnosia was not simply an amnesic condition. Ellis and Young (1996) suggested that his problem was one of accessing memories about the person (including his/her name) from the image of the face. A fault in the operation of "facial recognition units" (the facial equivalent to object recognition units in their model of object recognition) would account for Mr W's prosopagnosia.

Prosopagnosia is a rare condition with a variable presentation. However, the deficits of Soldier S and Mr W suggest the existence of (at least two) different forms: Soldier S's problems are, in certain respects, analogous to the object recognition deficits seen in apperceptive agnosia; his basic perception of faces is impaired. Mr W's prosopagnosia, on the other hand, parallels the object recognition deficit of associative agnosia. His face perception seems relatively intact but

KEY TERM
Prosopagnosia: The form of agnosia in which the ability to perceive faces is affected.

he is unable to recognise (or in other ways semantically process) faces (a comparable vignette is presented in Box 8.1).

Box 8.1 A case study of prosopagnosia (adapted from Stirling, 1999)

Therapist: (shows patient a picture of a cow and horse) "Which is the horse?"
Patient: "That's easy . . . the one on the right without horns."
Therapist: (shows photograph of Elvis Presley) "Do you know who this is?"
Patient: "Is it a famous person?"
Therapist: "Yes."
Patient: "Is it the Pope?"
Therapist: "No, this person is no longer alive . . . Describe the face to me."
Patient: "Well, he's tall, and has got black hair swept back with lots of grease . . ."
Therapist: "Does he have a moustache?"
Patient: "No, but he has long sideburns . . . and a guitar."
Therapist: "It's Elvis Presley!" (Patient nods, but doesn't appear to connect the face to the name.)
Therapist: "Now, who's this?" (Shows photograph of patient's wife.)
Patient: "I dunno . . . some woman . . . about my age with grey hair and nice eyes . . ."
Therapist: "It's your wife." (Patient once again seems unable to connect the picture to the identification.)
Therapist: "OK. Who's this?" (Shows photograph of patient.)
Patient: "No idea . . ."
Therapist: "Describe him . . ."
Patient: "Well, he looks quite old, and has lost a lot of hair. He looks like he needs a holiday, with those bags under his eyes . . . A good long rest . . ."
Therapist: "It's you!"
Patient: "No . . . you are kidding me! It's a very poor photograph. I don't look a bit like that!"

CO-OCCURRENCE OF DIFFERENT FORMS OF AGNOSIA

Many people with prosopagnosia also show other abnormalities of object recognition, and when these conditions coincide the prosopagnosia is, typically, more severe. This has led to the suggestion that prosopagnosia is just a particular type of object recognition failure involving a breakdown of within-category recognition. However, the test of this hypothesis is not the number of individuals who show both forms of agnosia, but whether individuals can be found with one but not the other form. Cases of specific prosopagnosia have been well documented, although cases with impaired object recognition but intact face recognition are much rarer. However, they do exist; for example, patient CK studied by Moscovitch, Winocur, and Behrmann (1997) had profound object recognition but intact face recognition. This suggests a dissociation between object recognition and facial recognition, indicating that facial recognition is a separate skill that *need not* overlap with object recognition. Another case was reported by Assal, Favre, and Anders (1984). Their patient MX developed a marked agnosia for livestock (he was a farmer), places, and faces. Within 6 months his prosopagnosia had disappeared although he remained agnosic for animals. Prosopagnosic patient WJ (McNeil & Warrington, 1993) showed almost the exact opposite pattern of deficit. His performance on a version of the famous faces recognition test was at chance level, although his ability to recognise objects such as cars, breeds of dog, or flowers was normal. After developing the disorder, he acquired a flock of 36 sheep which could be identified by number. On a series of recognition tests WJ clearly retained his knowledge of individual sheep despite his profound prosopagnosia for human faces!

Farah (1990) has conducted a meta-analysis of the coincidence of object agnosia, prosopagnosia, and **acquired alexia** (inability to recognise written words after brain injury/damage) by reviewing every published study detailing cases of any of these disorders between 1966 and 1989. She hypothesised that alexia and prosopagnosia could be linked to fundamentally different deficits in analytical and holistic processing respectively, whereas object agnosia could result from deficits in either system. One prediction from this intriguing hypothesis is that object agnosia should not occur independent of either alexia or prosopagnosia (one or other must be present). The results of her analysis are shown in Table 8.1. Clearly, many people have deficits in all three areas. Numerous instances of alexia alone and prosopagnosia alone were also identified. But the most interesting findings were that only a single case of object agnosia alone could be identified, and there was one possible case of alexia and prosopagnosia without object agnosia. Since publication of this research a small number of additional "exceptions" have been reported, casting doubt on Farah's hypothesis. Nevertheless, the co-occurrence (and mutual exclusivity) of different forms of agnosia merits further investigation.

TABLE 8.1 THE RESULTS OF FARAH'S META-ANALYSIS	
Deficits in	**Number of patients**
Face, object, and word recognition	21
Faces and objects	14
Words and objects	15
Faces and words	1?
Faces only	Many
Objects only	1?

PROSOPAGNOSIA AND THE BRAIN

If we consider the question of location of brain damage and prosopagnosia, the following picture emerges: many cases have bilateral damage, and this is predominantly to occipital or temporal lobes. Of those people with prosopagnosia who have unilateral lesions, the vast majority have right hemisphere damage, again mainly to ventral occipital and/or temporal regions (DeRenzi et al., 1994). In fact Farah (1990) could find only four cases (6% of her sample) of prosopagnosia following unilateral left-sided damage. Overall, this is quite strong evidence of a specialised role for the right hemisphere in face recognition. This view is further supported by data from a small number of imaging case studies of prosopagnosia reported by Sergent and Signoret (1992). For two prosopagnosic patients with problems similar to Soldier S (see above) but no object agnosia, damage was localised to occipital and medial temporal regions of the right hemisphere. For two additional prosopagnosic patients with intact face perception but impaired access to memory (like Mr W), damage was found in more anterior regions of the right temporal lobe.

INTERIM COMMENT

In summary, the available neuropsychological evidence suggests that face recognition is more than just a sophisticated form of object recognition. Prosopagnosia also seems to be linked to damage to brain regions that may be specialised to deal preferentially with faces. These areas include ventral regions of the occipital and temporal lobes on the right side. One interpretation of these data is that posterior regions (early in the ventral stream) deal with the integrative process of putting together the face from its component parts, whereas areas further forward, but still on the right side, are concerned with identification, and linking this with other semantic and biographic information about the person. fMRI has provided a wealth of evidence about category specificity generally and face specificity in particular, which we will review in more detail below.

IMAGING CATEGORY SPECIFICITY

As we have indicated earlier, category specificity is the area of visual recognition where functional imaging has been most useful (so far). fMRI has shown quite clearly that distinct regions of the brain show a selectively enhanced response to objects within a visually similar class. As with the classic neuropsychology evidence, the fMRI literature has been particularly strong in identifying faces as a "special" class of objects. A small region of the fusiform gyrus (dubbed the "fusiform face area") is activated when respondents view faces but not non-face objects (Kanwisher, 2000). fMRI has also identified regional specificity in response to other object categories including such diverse examples as body parts (Downing et al., 2001), cars (Xu, 2005), and birds (Gauthier et al., 2000).

Debate continues about the extent to which these neural substrates for different objects overlap. The data suggest that some of the selective responses co-locate, although it has been argued that this represents a failure of spatial resolution of the technique. fMRI data in group studies have always undergone a degree of spatial "smoothing" and therefore studies may not have the sensitivity to distinguish regions that are small and closely adjacent. Perhaps more interestingly, the abundance of neuroimaging data has sparked theoretical debate about why category specificity might occur. In a series of experiments by Gauthier and colleagues, fMRI responses have been studied in subjects with a particular expertise in identifying a certain type of object (for example, birdwatchers or car buffs). These subjects were found to have a shift in levels of processing and category-selective regions, compared to non-expert subjects (see Figure 8.8). Further, Gauthier showed that similar shifts could be observed in non-expert subjects after a period of intensive training on a particular category. For these

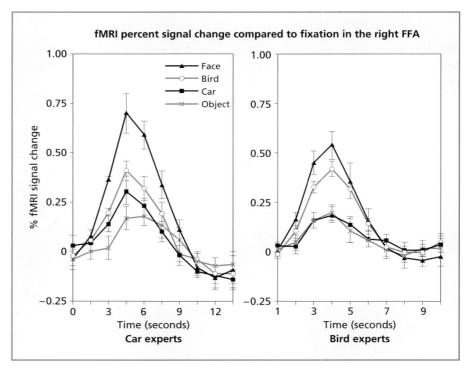

FIG. 8.8 Imaging modification of object recognition signal strength in expert subjects. Source: Xu, Y. (2005). Revisiting the role of the fusiform face area in visual expertise. *Cerebral Cortex, 15*, 1234–1242. Reproduced with permission.

expert and highly trained individuals, other classes of objects have acquired the "special" status that faces have for all of us—we are all experts at recognising faces (Tanaka, 2001). Gauthier and colleagues suggest that normal face recognition involves a different level of recognition from that of other objects, and thus the fusiform face area is not specific to faces but to the type of processing we normally apply to faces.

Other theories have focused on the computational requirements of recognising different classes of objects. For example, Malach, Levy, and Hasson (2002) argued that recognising stimuli like faces requires analysis of fine details and this is best served by regions that represent information from the central visual field. By contrast, identifying houses or places requires large-scale integration and this is best served by regions that represent peripheral visual field information. He suggested that certain types of category selectivity can be explained by these basic perceptual requirements.

Although theories are starting to emerge from the neuroimaging literature, it is an area that can still be characterised as involving "too much data but too few models" (Peissig & Tarr, 2006). In some ways, this is the complete reverse of the situation before functional imaging, when it could be argued there were not enough data but too many models. Now that we are not relying on extremely rare neuropsychological cases with unusual object recognition deficits, it seems reasonable to assume that our understanding of object recognition will continue to develop over the next few years.

SPATIAL FUNCTIONS AND THE "WHERE" STREAM

Earlier in this chapter we reviewed some of the evidence that led to Ungerleider and Mishkin's proposal of separate "what" and "where" visual processing streams. The agnosic conditions described earlier illustrate the effects of disturbances to functioning at different stages of the "what" (perhaps it should be what and who) stream, but we now need to consider the other stream, which is concerned with a range of spatial functions.

The "where" stream runs from the occipital cortex into the parietal lobe (see Figure 8.1). Output travels via V2 and V3 into area V5 (also known as the mid-temporal sulcus or MT). From there, it is channelled into various modular regions within the posterior parietal cortex. In V5, for example, we find cells that are exquisitely sensitive to stimuli moving in a particular direction irrespective of their exact location in the visual field. Cells in a parietal region known as V7 have even more extensive receptive fields and are selectively responsive to objects moving in particular directions at particular speeds. Other cells in the parietal region are responsive to a combination of input signalling spatial location of objects in the viewer's field of vision and the position of the viewer's own head and eyes. This is important because it allows the viewer to reference object location in space regardless of head or eye position or orientation. So, for example, you do not "see" the world as tilted when you bend your head to the left or right (Motter & Mountcastle, 1981).

As we mentioned in Chapter 3, the right hemisphere is often referred to as the spatial hemisphere although the left hemisphere also engages in spatial processing. The available evidence leads to the intriguing possibility that the left and right hemispheres may actually have complementary responsibilities when it comes to dealing with spatial information, and we revisit the question of "laterality" effects in spatial processing towards the end of the chapter. First, however, we need to consider briefly some basic spatial processes related to perception. Then we review some of the more integrative skills that nevertheless make substantial demands on spatial processing, such as constructional skills and negotiating routes. Finally, we consider briefly the general role of the left and right hemispheres in spatial memory.

BASIC SPATIAL PROCESSES

LOCALISING POINTS IN SPACE

Individuals with damage to superior regions of parietal cortex have difficulty reaching towards a visual stimulus (see our reference to optic ataxia earlier). Left-sided damage affects ability to reach towards the right side, and vice versa. If we remove the movement component, and simply measure perception of left- or right-side space (i.e., detection of stimuli in the left or right visual fields), we find that unilateral damage to the right parietal regions is most likely to adversely affect this ability.

DEPTH PERCEPTION

Local depth perception, meaning the ability to detect depth of close objects because of the different images falling on each eye (binocular disparity), can be disrupted by both right and left hemisphere lesions (Danta, Hilton, & O'Boyle, 1978). Global depth perception, which refers to detection of depth (as in a landscape) where binocular disparity for individual items is not helpful, appears to be disrupted by right hemisphere damage (Benton & Hecaen, 1970).

LINE ORIENTATION AND GEOMETRIC RELATIONS

The ability to judge angles or orientations of lines is affected following right (but not left) parietal damage (Benton, Hannay, & Varney, 1975). Similarly, the ability to remember novel complex shapes of geometric patterns (especially those that cannot be named) is also affected after right parietal damage.

MOTION

It is very rare for humans to lose their ability to detect motion yet retain other perceptual abilities. In the handful of well-documented cases, there is usually damage to both left and right parietal lobes. Patient MP, reported by Zihl, von Cramon, and Mai (1983), had extensive damage that included areas of the mid-temporal gyrus and adjacent regions of the parietal lobes on both sides. She described her motion blindness as like seeing movements as a series of jerky still photographs (similar to what we might see in strobe lighting conditions). Interestingly, other spatial skills such as localisation of objects in space were relatively spared, which supports the idea of distinct movement-processing modules in each hemisphere. Motion perception has also been studied using neuroimaging techniques and area V5 has been identified as particularly important. This region is also activated by illusory motion (Zeki, Watson, & Frackowiak, 1993) and the motion after-effect (Tootell et al., 1995) suggesting a role in the processing of perceived as well as actual motion. Conversely, in a recent study Moutoussis and Zeki (2006) showed V5, as well as parietal cortex, activation when motion occurred, regardless of whether or not respondents were consciously aware of it. So V5 processing may proceed even when participants are not aware of motion.

ROTATION

PET imaging research, both with normal participants engaged in tasks that involve mental rotation and analysis of the performance of brain-damaged participants on similar tasks, once again points to the involvement of the right parietal lobe. In a classic study by Deutsch et al. (1988) participants had to decide which hand a "cartoon man" was holding a ball in. The cartoon was shown in various orientations, and in front and rear view. Patients with right hemisphere lesions made more errors and had slower reaction times on this task. More recent fMRI studies have confirmed the importance of right parietal regions in mental rotation tasks, although some studies have suggested that the activation is more bilateral. One reason for this discrepancy may involve individual differences. An intriguing recent fMRI study has found sex differences in the neural basis of mental rotation. Hugdahl, Thomsen, and Ersland (2006) reported more parietal activation in male participants and more inferior frontal activation in female participants, potentially suggesting a systematic difference in how the task was performed.

CONSTRUCTIONAL SKILLS

The skills involved in completing constructional tasks are more complex than those needed to undertake the spatial-perceptual tests mentioned above. They involve spatial perception, but in addition require the production or generation of some tangible output. There are several standard neuropsychological assessments of these skills and evidence suggests that right parietal damage is most likely to impair performance on them. However, some caution is required in interpreting test results because, in moving away from the purely perceptual, we introduce other psychological factors. The following two tests certainly involve hand–eye coordination and attention, and arguably even memory (which depends on other cortical functions), in addition to spatial skills.

The Rey-Osterrieth complex figure is a detailed line drawing that looks a little like the Union Jack flag, with other elements such as extra triangles and lines attached (see Figure 8.9a). Participants simply have to copy the figure. Normal individuals often complete this task almost faultlessly within a few minutes. However, it presents major difficulties for some patients with damage in the right temporo-parietal region (Benton, 1967). Damage here also adversely affects individuals on the block design test (a test taken from the WAIS; see Chapter 2) in which participants have to copy a simple pattern by assembling coloured blocks (see Figure 8.9b). Right hemisphere patients sometimes even fail to appreciate that the configuration of the nine blocks must be 3×3. Left hemisphere damage can also affect block design performance but in this case the basic configuration is usually correct, and it is more likely that individual blocks will be incorrectly oriented.

Constructional skills are one of the areas where functional imaging has been of relatively little use. fMRI in particular does not lend itself to the study of these processes for simple mechanical reasons. When people are enclosed in an fMRI scanner, they cannot see their hands and the range of possible movements is extremely limited. Therefore, it is difficult to assess tasks depending on hand–eye coordination or complex manual construction.

ROUTE FINDING

Researchers have developed a number of tests to assess route finding. They range from simple **finger mazes** (where a blindfolded participant has to learn a route by trial and error, usually by guiding his/her finger through a small maze) to following directions using standardised maps. As with the construction tests mentioned earlier, in interpreting results we must be aware that the different tasks assess other skills in addition to basic spatial ones. Moreover, depending on the particular task, it may be possible to use non-spatial strategies as well as, or even instead of, spatial ones, which further complicates interpretation. An additional complication is that some people struggle with certain types of route-finding tasks and not with others. This has necessitated a distinction between those measures that tap perception of spatial relationships in extra-personal space (like finger mazes) and measures that require respondents to guide *themselves* in three-dimensional space.

Performance on variants of the finger maze is compromised following damage to the right parietal lobe (Milner, 1965), but in addition, where there is a signifi-cant memory demand (a complex maze for example), performance can be affected

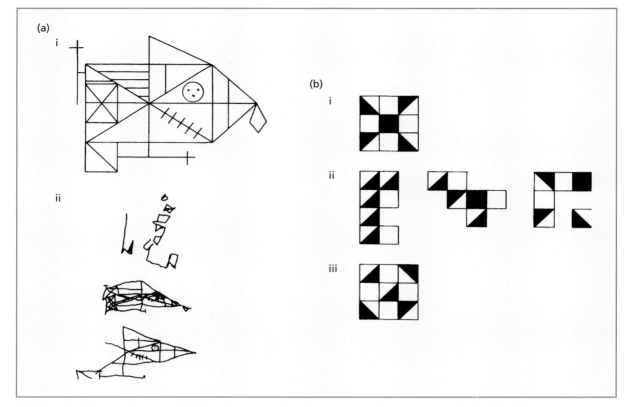

FIG. 8.9 Rey-Osterrieth figures and WAIS block design test. (a) This apparently simple copying task (i) is difficult for some patients with right temporal-parietal damage (ii). (b) In the WAIS block design test, respondents must "construct" the nine-square pattern (i) using individual blocks. Patients with right hemisphere damage (ii) are prone to errors in which they ignore the overall form of the pattern. Left hemisphere patients (iii) may get the overall form correct but get the detail wrong.

by damage to right temporal or frontal areas. A variant of the finger maze is where the participant has to find their way through a proper maze. In Semmes et al.'s (1955) maze test, nine dots are placed on the floor of a large room and participants are given a plan of the route (via the dots) to follow. For reference, one wall of the room is designated "north" and the person is not allowed to rotate the map as they follow the route. Typically, right parietal damage affects performance on this test (Semmes et al., 1963), although Ratcliff and Newcombe (1973) only found marked impairments in individuals with bilateral damage. A possible explanation for this is that in this type of task respondents can adopt different strategies. A "spatial" strategy is one way, but a verbal strategy (*turn right . . . go straight on . . . turn right again . . .*) can also be employed.

In Money's (1976) standardised road map test, participants are given a fictitious map that shows a route marked on it. At every junction they must "say" which direction (left, right, straight on) to go in. This test requires planning and memory as well as spatial skill, and performance is affected by damage to the frontal areas of the right hemisphere in addition to the more posterior parietal regions. Finally, there is even some evidence that basic geographic knowledge about entire countries can be adversely affected following right-sided damage.

Functional imaging has been widely used to study spatial navigation. Although parietal cortical regions have been shown to be involved in topographic processing, the main focus of imaging research has been on the hippocampus. This is a region that seems to be critically involved in complex route-finding tasks, whether using mazes or map-based navigation (see Figure 8.10). Indeed, structural imaging has suggested that individuals who have developed unusually acute navigational skills (London taxi drivers) actually have altered structure of the hippocampus (Maguire et al., 2000). A recent study has distinguished between route following (following well-learned paths between locations) and way finding (finding novel paths between locations) and has shown that they are associated with distinct neural substrates (Hartley et al., 2003). Way finding specifically activated right hippocampus in participants who navigated successfully. Posterior perceptual regions, including posterior parietal cortex, were also activated during way finding, regardless of performance.

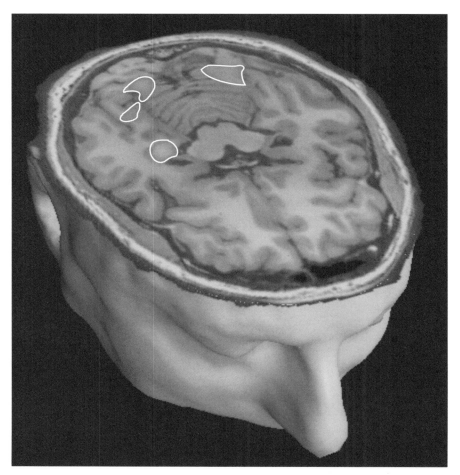

FIG. 8.10   Brain activations associated with spatial navigation. This image shows the brain responses in London taxi drivers when planning a route in virtual reality to deliver a (virtual) customer to their desired location. We are grateful to Dr Eleanor Maguire of the Wellcome Trust Centre for Neuroimaging, London, for providing this image [see Spiers, H. J. & Maguire E. A. (2006). *Neuroimage, 31*, 1826–1840].

INTERIM COMMENT

Taken together, these observations illustrate the range of spatial perceptual abilities that humans possess, and which we tend to take for granted until a problem arises. Spatial perception depends on the ability to form an internal representation of the outside world, and sometimes to locate oneself in it. The formation of that internal representation, and the ability to manipulate it or "mentally" move around it, depends on effective processing in the "where" stream.

SPATIAL MEMORY

Spatial memory span can be assessed using Corsi's block-tapping test, which we introduced in Chapter 2. The wooden blocks are conveniently numbered on the tester's side, but the side facing the participant is blank. The experimenter taps a sequence of blocks, which the respondent must immediately duplicate. The experimenter increases the length of the sequence (in the classic manner) in order to establish spatial memory span. DeRenzi and Nichelli (1975) have found that patients with posterior damage on either side have a reduced span. Tests that assess spatial working memory appear to tap right hemisphere function, and usually present particular difficulties for respondents with right frontal damage. Recall from the previous chapter a study by Smith et al. (1996) in which normal participants were shown a brief array of dots (for 200 ms) then 3 seconds later a circle appeared on the screen. Respondents had to decide whether (or not) the circle would have surrounded one of the dots. PET activation during this test (when compared with a non-working memory condition) was most marked in the right frontal lobe. When we move beyond short-term retention, we find evidence of marked impairment in people with more posterior right hemisphere damage. For example, if recall on the Corsi tapping test is delayed by as little as 16 seconds, patients with right temporal and parietal hemisphere damage show the largest deficits. A recent study by van Asselen et al. (2006) considered stroke patients with different lesion foci. It suggested that patients with right posterior parietal or right dorsolateral prefrontal lesions were impaired at keeping spatial information in memory over short time periods, while those with lesions to either right or left hippocampus were impaired at longer time intervals.

Spatial working memory could be considered a form of higher-level processing that is critically dependent on visual perception and visual experience. However, Vecchi et al. (2004) have shown that although they do not have normal visuospatial abilities, patients who are congenitally blind are capable of performing spatial working memory tasks. An fMRI study by Ricciardi et al. (2006) showed that the parietal and prefrontal regions activated during a visual and a tactile spatial working memory task were extremely similar. This suggests that aspects of spatial working memory depend on higher-order representations that are independent of basic sensory processes. Figure 8.11 shows right-lateralised brain responses associated with a visual spatial working memory task.

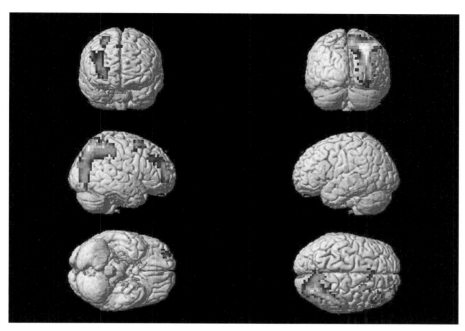

FIG. 8.11   Brain activations associated with spatial working memory. This image shows fMRI responses associated with the performance of an abstract spatial working memory task based on the CANTAB spatial working memory paradigm. Participants must search for coloured tokens in a spatial array, remembering where tokens have previously been found. We are grateful to our colleague Emma Pegg of the University of Manchester for providing this image.

THE LEFT HEMISPHERE AND SPATIAL PROCESSING

The fMRI literature on spatial processing has suggested that while right hemisphere structures may be predominantly involved, left hemisphere activity is also apparent. An insight into the operation of the left hemisphere in spatial tasks can be gleaned from observing the compensatory procedures adopted by individuals who have incurred right-sided damage. A classic case study of one such individual was reported by Clarke et al. (1993). Despite an extensive right-sided lesion resulting from a brain tumour, the Swiss woman in question hoped to become an architect, and the researchers were able to observe her as she tried to overcome (or circumvent) her spatial deficits by making greater use of left-sided functions. When copying arrays like the Rey-Osterrieth figure, she used a piecemeal strategy (akin to HJA's copying strategy described earlier). As a result, although basic elements of the figure were included, fine detail was often misplaced or omitted. She also used a feature-by-feature (as opposed to holistic) strategy in trying to recognise a series of Swiss towns from photographs. This worked well if a town had a distinctive or unique feature, but broke down when she tried to identify towns with similar but spatially distinct features. Related to these problems, her geographic knowledge and route-finding skills were also impaired, and in order to get around she developed a verbal point-by-point (landmarks) strategy. An fMRI study by Slotnick and Moo (2006) adds weight to these observations. They compared participants performing a categorical and a coordinate spatial memory task. The categorical task involved judgements like "one item is above another" while the coordinate task involved judgements like "one item is near another". Categorical spatial memory recruited left prefrontal cortex while coordinate spatial memory recruited right prefrontal cortex. This is evidence for hemispheric specialisation for different aspects of spatial memory, both of which may be recruited in the spatial processes we employ in everyday life.

INTERIM COMMENT

The weight of evidence considered in the previous sections underlines the importance of right hemisphere structures in processing all kinds of spatial information. However, we also saw that once we moved away from purely perceptual types of task it became possible to solve or complete tasks using various strategies—essentially spatial, verbal, or perhaps a combination of both. Studies such as that reported by Clarke et al. remind us that both hemispheres can participate in spatial processing. Spatial skills are not the exclusive preserve of the right hemisphere. We might describe the processing responsibilities of the left and right hemispheres as verbal and spatial respectively, but this confuses the issue in view of the fact that we have been talking about how each hemisphere contributes to dealing with spatial tasks. We might, alternatively, invoke the idea of processing styles (see Chapter 3), by comparing the holistic approach of the right hemisphere with the analytical style of the left. Once again, this does not entirely work because some of the spatial skills that are affected by right hemisphere damage (such as spatial location) make no particular demands on holistic skills. Kosslyn (1987) has suggested a cerebral division of labour such that the right hemisphere is specialised for dealing with "coordinate" spatial relations whereas the left is specialised for "categorical" spatial relations. fMRI has provided some support for this view.

CHAPTER SUMMARY

Visual perception of objects depends on activity in two parallel but separate processing streams. The "what" stream deals with object recognition and links with stored memories of related objects. The "where" stream deals with various aspects of spatial processing, both of perceived objects and of the individual in space. This distinction is apparent if you consider the situation of reaching to select a particular object from a group of items: the "where" stream guides your hand to the object, and the "what" stream allows you to select the correct object. The visual agnosias appear to result from disturbances to different stages of processing in the "what" stream. Lissauer's original distinction between apperceptive and associative agnosia is now considered an oversimplification of the true diversity of (object) agnosic conditions. Riddoch and Humphreys' model of object recognition is better able to explain many of these subtly distinct conditions.

Prosopagnosia often co-occurs with object agnosia, but the weight of available evidence suggests that it is a distinct condition that is linked anatomically to ventral regions in the right hemisphere. In fact, many neuropsychologists think that it actually comprises at least two disorders: one related to a failure to construct the facial image from its component parts, and a second concerned with an inability to relate facial images with semantic information about the person in question. fMRI studies of category specificity have identified distinct regions for the recognition of many different classes of objects. However, a coherent theoretical framework for understanding *why* these specialisations occur has yet to emerge.

Spatial processing is subserved by a dorsal stream that terminates in the parietal lobes. Damage to this stream affects the perception of objects in space, detection of motion, and mental rotation. This stream interacts with other cortical regions to mediate spatial constructional skills, route finding, and spatial memory. The hippocampus is also a crucial structure in route finding. Although available evidence tends to emphasise the importance of the right hemisphere for spatial processing, the left hemisphere can make important contributions to the overall processing effort through the employment of complementary processing styles.

CHAPTER 9

9

Attention and consciousness

INTRODUCTION

We intuitively know what it means to "attend" to a particular event, process, or stimulus sequence. We cannot pay attention to every item of input so we have to be choosy. In this sense, attention refers to selecting, focusing, and homing in on certain things, and ignoring, filtering out, or inhibiting others.

The concept of an "attentional spotlight" has often been mooted as a metaphor for this process (in the visual modality at least) but, as we shall see, it is only approximate. For example, although we usually look directly at whatever we are trying to attend to, it is possible to attend to an area of space that we are not directly gazing at (essentially looking out of the corner of one's eye; a phenomenon demonstrated by von Helmholtz over 100 years ago). A second problem is that it has now been demonstrated quite convincingly that, under certain circumstances, we can actually track several moving targets (up to four) at the same time (Cavanagh & Alvarez, 2005), raising the possibility of multiple spotlights, albeit ranging over a limited angle of visual field (i.e., close to one another). A third problem illustrated by LaBerge (1983) is that the attentional spotlight can be shown to have a narrower or wider "beam" depending on task requirements (respondents could be "pre-cued" to focus on a five-letter word or on the central letter of the same word)—an observation that led him to suggest as an alternative metaphor the "attentional zoom-lens".

LaBerge's work illustrates a further complication that must be taken into consideration in our efforts to understand the parameters of attention—that it can clearly be guided/directed by both task requirements and the goal(s) of the perceiver. A real-world example of this can be seen in the card game of "snap", in which the players attend to each card as it is dealt to see if it matches one of theirs, or the top card in the "pool". Some neuropsychologists have called this "endogenous" attention because "the spotlight" is being driven internally. Yet, conversely, our own experience tells us that no matter how hard we may try to focus our attention on one thing, we can easily be distracted by an unexpected but salient event or stimulus occurring elsewhere. When attention is disrupted or even re-directed by external influences, a sudden loud noise for example, neuropsychologists refer to this as exogenous attention (or orienting; see below). In other words, attention can be directed by both deliberate and accidental processes. Finally, under certain circumstances, attention can be directed to internally generated ideas, thoughts, or plans. This may involve nothing more sinister than day-dreaming, but it can quite easily merge into more pathological processes if it involves rumination or obsessive/recurrent thoughts. Conditions such as post-traumatic stress disorder, morbid jealously, and even depression have been linked to dysfunctional processing of this sort.

In the first edition of this book we bemoaned the absence of a unified theory of attention. In the intervening 5 years, psychologists have continued to work on the development of models to explain how different aspects of attention may work in "intact" individuals (e.g., Duncan, 2006). And neuropsychologists have focused on trying to unravel the brain regions that may be involved in attention, often through detailed investigations of individuals with neurological disorders in which attentional mechanisms seem to be damaged or impaired. Both these lines of inquiry are reviewed here. Functional imaging and ERP studies have also been informative, and these too are reviewed. Yet despite this valuable and often intriguing work, a unified theory arguably remains elusive. Nevertheless, Corbetta and Shulman's (2002) neuropsychological model (essentially, a development and elaboration of an earlier proposal from Posner, 1980) has attracted considerable attention (see also Corbetta et al., 2005) and we review it later in the chapter.

Then we briefly consider the vexed question of consciousness—an area of investigation "off-limits" for most psychologists and neuropsychologists for the last 100 years or so, yet in truth a nettle that just had to be grasped sooner or later. We consider some recent research and thinking about consciousness, and how it relates to attention, and even working memory. However, it is important to stress that in so doing, we are interpreting consciousness in a narrow sense, relating to conscious awareness, rather than in the broader sense which encompasses awareness of subjective experience and self-awareness.

TYPES OF ATTENTION

We start on a point of consensus: there seems to be broad agreement that the general domain of attention needs to be subdivided into at least four more specific areas—vigilance, arousal, divided attention, and selective attention (LaBerge, 1990).

Vigilance is about sustaining attention over time. Whenever you go to a lecture your vigilance is put to the test as you try to stay "on track" with the lecturer right to the end of the class. Exceptional vigilance skills are regarded as a prerequisite for air-traffic controllers, whose job involves the monitoring of plane movements depicted on a computer screen (Molloy & Parasuraman, 1996). Impairments in vigilance skill have been linked to neurological disease and possibly psychiatric disorder too. Vigilance involves selection, but the emphasis is on maintaining this focus for minutes or even hours, something that may require prolonged conscious effort. Neuropsychologists have referred to this as a "top-down" influence (endogenous, if you like) to distinguish it from the attention-grabbing effect of an unexpected loud noise which, in this taxonomy, would be a "bottom-up" (or exogenous) influence.

Arousal and *alertness* are terms that have usually been linked to physiological states that may vary in relation to attention. Consider your own circadian pattern of alertness for example. Every 24 hours you experience 6–8 hours of sleep during which time you are relatively unresponsive to external stimuli, although a clap of thunder or a loud firework may nevertheless disturb you. During your waking hours, you are more alert at some times than others. Research has shown that alertness generally improves through the day, reaching a peak in early evening, and then diminishing towards bedtime. Sudden unexpected events can interfere with your level of alertness when you are awake, just as they can when you are asleep. Researchers refer to the response that ensues as "orienting", and as we shall see, the evoking of an **orienting response** has been used as a research paradigm by psychologists trying to understand this aspect of attention

Divided attention would be addressed in tasks where there are at least two channels of input and the respondent has to try to "attend" to each one. Studies of divided attention have been useful in establishing an individual's processing capacity and limitations. That is to say, to what extent can an individual do two things at once? Practice and automaticity, task similarity and difficulty not surprisingly all affect dual-task performance.

Selective (focused) attention refers to the phenomenon alluded to at the start of the introduction. Our sensory apparatus is constantly bombarded with input, yet we more or less automatically seem able to invoke a process (the attentional spotlight?) that allows us to focus on one channel at the expense of others. As you read this page, we hope you are attending sufficiently carefully not to be distracted by the noises coming from outside, the smells wafting up from the kitchen, or the dull pain from that tooth that needs filling—not, at least, until we point them out to you. As we will see, understanding the mechanisms of selective attention has been a major goal of neuropsychologists, and we will inevitably focus on this work in the present chapter. Researchers have made extensive use of experiments in auditory selective attention and the related field of visual search to learn more about the way these attentional processes operate.

ISSUES IN PSYCHOLOGICAL INVESTIGATIONS OF ATTENTION

EARLY OR LATE SELECTIVE ATTENTION?

Most people will be aware of the effort required to converse with someone in a noisy and crowded room, and of suddenly becoming aware of a salient word or term used by another speaker on the far side of a room (Cherry, 1953; Moray, 1959). This apparently innocent experience (sometimes referred to as "the cocktail party phenomenon") shows that "unattended" material can, under certain circumstances, attract our attention. In the 1950s the pre-eminent model of attention held that "attended" material is selected at a very early stage of information processing (Broadbent, 1958), but the cocktail party phenomenon confounds this "early selection" model because the so-called unattended input must have undergone a certain amount of processing (up to semantic analysis) in order to cause a shift of our attention. If it had been subject to early selection, we might simply not have "heard" it.

An effective way of investigating selective attention experimentally is to use the dichotic listening paradigm. In a typical variant of this procedure a participant may be presented with two simultaneous streams of auditory (often verbal) input

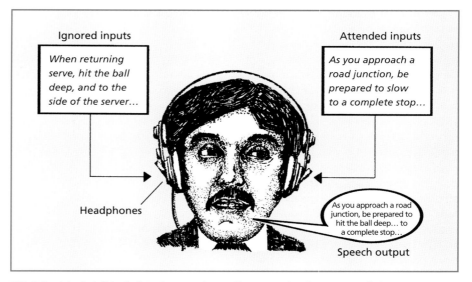

FIG. 9.1   A typical dichotic listening experiment. The respondent hears two verbal messages simultaneously but must repeat aloud only one of the "channels". Respondents usually notice little or nothing about the unattended input, but occasionally salient or personally significant material is recognised and sometimes even intrudes into the speech output. (Adapted from Gazzaniga et al., 2002.)

(one to each ear). By requiring the listener to "shadow" one channel (i.e., repeat aloud the stream of words in the "attended" channel, and thus have to attend to it) the experimenter can assess the extent to which information in the unattended channel "gets through", by later asking whether anything could be recalled from it. Not surprisingly, there is nearly always much better recall from the attended than the unattended channel, but in situations where the unattended channel material is "salient" or semantically related to the material in the attended channel, it is often recalled, and sometimes described (erroneously) as having been presented in the attended channel (Gray & Wedderburn, 1960). Like the cocktail party phenomenon, this suggests that material in the unattended channel may actually undergo quite extensive processing. Note that material would be presented too quickly for the result to be explained simply on the basis of rapid switching of attention (see Figure 9.1).

Although the evidence from dichotic listening experiments clearly supports some sort of selecting of attended over unattended material (because relatively little of the unattended message is recalled) it does not fit well with a strict "early selection" model of attention like Broadbent's, because some processing of the unattended material *does* take place. An alternative model was proposed by Treisman (1964) who argued that although a particular channel might be selected early on in the processing stream, the unattended channel, rather than being shut down, was "attenuated", meaning it received less attentional effort than the attended channel. Thus, salient or personally relevant material in this channel would not necessarily be lost and may undergo semantic processing, at which point a shift in attention to the unattended channel may occur. Treisman's model has received widespread support, even from Broadbent (1970), and is the dominant theory for selective attention in the auditory modality. Figure 9.2 illustrates the differences between the models of selective attention.

In studies of visual attention, the evidence also suggests that selection may occur relatively early in the processing stream, especially when attention is directed towards stimulus location. The logic of visual search studies is that the more "distractor" items present in a visual field, the longer it should take to identify the particular target. Consider, for example, a study by Treisman and Gelade (1980). Participants viewed a series of visual arrays comprising red Os and green Xs, and they had to identify the presence (or absence) of a red X. For such "conjunctive targets" (targets combining stimulus attributes shared by non-targets), the time taken to identify presence/absence is proportionate to the number of non-targets shown, because attention must be directed around the array item-by-item until the target is found. This shows that attention to a spatial location precedes identification, supporting the idea of early selection of location. A conjunctive search array similar to Triesman and Gelade's is shown in Figure 9.3a. This finding should be contrasted with the situation when the target is distinguishable on the basis of one solitary attribute: "*Find the Y among an array of Ks*". Now, the number of distractors is largely irrelevant, and

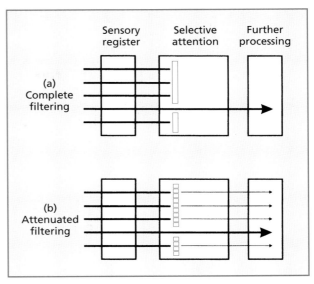

FIG. 9.2   Two filtering models of attention. (a) Following sensory registration, only one channel of input is selected for further processing. This is akin to Broadbent's model of early selective attention. (b) One channel is selected for "priority" processing. However, the other channels of input are not filtered out; rather they are attenuated. This is similar to Treisman's attenuation model of selective attention.

participants describe the target as "popping-out" from the array (see Figure 9.3b). This process has been called "pre-attentive", which is taken to mean that attention is not needed to find the target (although it is obviously invoked once the target has been found).

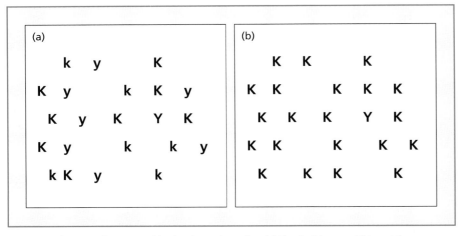

FIG. 9.3   The type of array used in visual search studies. (a) The "odd one out" target is a conjunctive one combining attributes of other targets. Visual search proceeds in a place-by-place manner until the target (upper case Y) is found. (b) The target (upper case Y) almost jumps out of this array. Little conscious effort is required to locate it, giving rise to the expression "pre-attentive" to characterise the processing requirements of the task.

Data from studies comparing these two experimental paradigms (with different numbers of distractor items, and more or fewer shared features between target and distractors) prompted Treisman and Gelade to propose that the "pop-out" phenomenon depended on parallel search, whereas conjunctive arrays relied on a serial search. Essentially, the argument went that the former task, being pre-attentive, is effortless and automatic, whereas the requirement to combine features (colour, shape, orientation, etc.), sometimes called feature binding, requires attentional effort, and probably early selection. Treisman developed her "feature integration theory" (FIT) to account for these findings. This theory has undergone various reformulations (Treisman, 1992, 1993, 1999) none of which entirely satisfies all critics (such as Duncan & Humphreys, 1992, and Wolfe, 1998). Among other concerns, researchers have questioned the assumption that pre-attentive stimulus coding (in the pop-out condition) can actually occur without any attentional effort. And they have pointed out that the degree of similarity among distractor items does, in fact, affect visual search times, contrary to FIT.

Arguably, a similar attentional process to that seen in "pop-out" can also be observed in studies of involuntary visual orienting (Posner & Cohen, 1984). In a typical experiment "irrelevant" visual stimuli (such as brief light flashes) would be presented to different locations in the visual field, interspersed with target stimuli to which the participant should respond. When a target stimulus falls in a similar location to a previous irrelevant light flash, reaction time to it is faster, indicating that the irrelevant stimulus somehow directed (researchers say "primed") attentional mechanisms to that particular spatial location, albeit involuntarily. However, this effect is only observed if the interval between irrelevant and target stimuli is brief (less than 300 ms). With longer intervals the effect is reversed leading to slower reaction times. This paradoxical effect is known as **inhibition of return** and serves a vital role in automatic visual orienting. If such a mechanism did not exist, we would probably find it difficult to attend voluntarily to anything for any period of time, being constantly distracted by new but irrelevant stimuli. The distinction between deliberate and incidental attentional processes appears critical, and we return to consider it later in this chapter.

A final twist in the "early versus late selection" debate comes from studies of "negative priming" (Tipper, 1985; Tipper, Weaver, & Houghton, 1994). In this paradigm, respondents view compound images (say, a red line drawing of a hammer on top of a second blue drawing of a cat) and have to name the blue object (and ignore the red one). If the ignored object then becomes the attended object on the next trial (i.e., a blue hammer appears superimposed with some other red object), participants are slower in naming it (the negative priming effect). This strongly suggests that the non-attended item was in fact meaningfully processed, not ignored as the FIT would predict. This, of course, implies that late selection is operating.

We revisit the question of early versus late selection when we review the concept of attention as a resource, and the question of "perceptual load" below. First, however, we consider whether attention is space- or object-based.

SPACE- OR OBJECT-BASED SELECTION?

Visual search studies such as Treisman and Gelade's show that voluntary attention can operate effectively when it is directed to particular points in space. Posner (1980) reported a classic study illustrating the advantage of space-based attention.

KEY TERM
Inhibition of return: When attention is directed to a location, there is a brief period when processing at that location is facilitated. Following facilitation, there is a period during which attention is inhibited from returning to that location. This is inhibition of return (IOR).

In this experiment, participants fixated on a central point on a computer screen with an empty box to the left and right of the fixation point. After a short delay, one of the two boxes briefly became illuminated. Then, after a further variable delay, a stimulus was presented either in the box that had been illuminated or in the other box. Reaction times to the stimulus were consistently faster when it appeared in the "cued" box than the "non-cued" one, a finding interpreted as showing how shifting attention (from the expected cued box to the non-expected uncued one) takes time. It is important to note that in this paradigm, participants fixated gaze on the central point at all times, so covert mechanisms rather than overt eye movements were responsible for this voluntary orienting effect (see Figure 9.4).

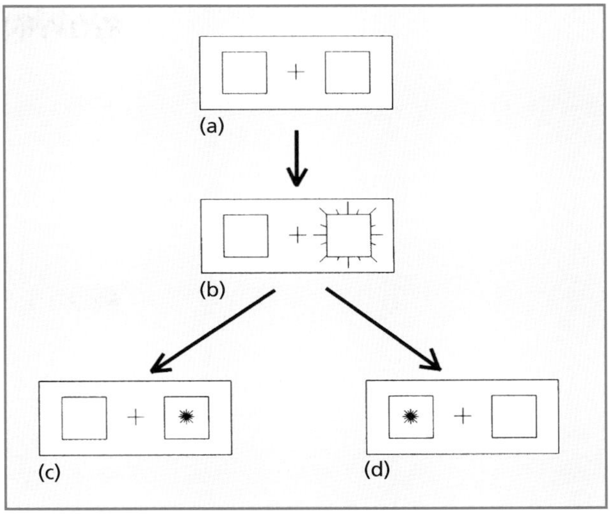

FIG. 9.4   An illustration of Posner's (1980) study. A participant fixates his or her gaze on the cross in between the two squares. One of the boxes is then "cued" (more brightly illuminated) for a brief period. The respondent knows that the cue usually correctly predicts the subsequent presentation of a target stimulus (an asterisk). Response speeds (reaction times) are significantly faster when the cue correctly predicts the location of the stimulus (c) than when it predicts the incorrect location (d).

On the other hand, as we saw above, object-based attention is apparent in studies of negative priming (Tipper, 1985; Tipper et al., 1994). A further illustration of object-based attention comes from a study by O'Craven, Downing, and Kanwisher (1999). Their participants viewed compound images of overlaid drawings similar to those in Tipper's study, except that one of the images was stationary and the other was moving slightly. They were told to attend either to the direction of the motion of the moving image, or to the stationary one. If attention is location based, participants would have to attend to both images because they are in the same location. If object-based attention operates, the attended item would receive more processing than the unattended one. Functional MRI of brain regions that became more active during this task supported the latter account: there was more activity in the fusiform face area (referred to in Chapter 8 as part of the temporal lobe associated with processing faces) when a face stimulus was attended to than ignored, and more activity in the para-hippocampal "place" area when a picture of a house had to be attended to than when it was ignored.

We might add that several observations from individuals with the neurological disorder "unilateral neglect", which we consider later in this chapter, support the ideas of both spatial- and object-based attention. Thus, overall, it seems that humans may deploy either attentional strategy in the visual modality, depending on the task requirements, including how easy or difficult it is. Indeed, looking beyond visual attention again, there appear to be several ways of directing (biasing) attention in the face of competing targets (location, feature, category, set, etc.) (Duncan, 2006). However, attention takes up "effort", which is not unlimited. We now consider the idea of attention as a resource.

ATTENTION AS A RESOURCE

Resource theory approaches to attention (Kahneman, 1973; Wickens, 1980) sidestep many of the arguments introduced thus far by proposing that there is a finite central pool of information-processing capacity available to the individual, which is allocated according to demand. At one extreme, stimuli may be so simple or infrequent that only a fraction of the resource is "used", and attention (as we have conceptualised it) is not really an issue, though vigilance may be. At the other extreme, tasks may be so complex or demanding that the entire resource is "used up" by just part of the input invoking attention to this material at the expense of the remainder. Thus, the greater the effort needed to attend to target material, the less likely non-target material is to be processed. It follows that the greater the similarity between competing tasks (as in the dichotic listening studies) the greater the likelihood that such inputs will, by competing for the same resource, induce interference and errors.

A key question in this approach is whether the resource base is a single reservoir available to the individual irrespective of stimulus characteristics on a "first-come, first-served" basis, or whether there are separate reservoirs set aside for different types of input. Wickens' model envisages several separate resource domains with distinct pools: early versus late processing, verbal versus spatial processing, auditory versus visual processing, and even in terms of the nature of the required response (for example, manual versus vocal). It would be true to say that while the question of a single or multiple resource pool(s) has yet to be resolved, the experimental evidence tends to support separate pools. For example, in dual-task studies (see our earlier reference to divided attention) in which respondents try to complete two tasks simultaneously, there is less interference and hence fewer errors when the tasks or responses involve different stimulus modalities. McLeod (1977) required participants to engage in a tracking task (performed manually) and simultaneously to undertake a tone identification task that, in one condition, required a vocal response and, in another, a manual one with their other hand. Performance on the tracking task was worse in the latter condition. Moreover, the ERP research (which we review below) shows that different brain regions seem to be involved in early and later stimulus processing.

Yet it is also true that there is nearly always *some* interference effect in dual-task studies, prompting Baddeley (1986) to suggest that there may be separate resource pools at subordinate processing levels, but at the highest processing level "the central executive" represents a non-specific attentional resource. Indeed, proponents of resource-based theories of attention have argued that information-processing capacity limitations (in attention) *are determined* by working memory capacity limits. The overlap between attentional and working memory systems is the subject of ongoing investigations (Kastner & Ungerleider, 2000), and we briefly revisit this issue later in this chapter (in the section *Attention and the brain*). For the time being we might simply note that overlapping cortical regions are active in both processes.

A slightly different take on this issue is represented in the work of Lavie and colleagues (Lavie, 1995, 2005; Lavie & Fox, 2000). She has argued that the critical consideration in allocating what is a finite attention resource is related to the perceptual "difficulty" or "complexity" of the task in hand—or the amount of perceptual "*load*", to use her term. In other words, with a very simple task plenty of attentional resource will be left over, permitting processing of other irrelevant or peripheral stimuli (in fact, this re-allocation happens automatically in her scheme). However, with more demanding tasks (big arrays, crowded images, and so on; an intrinsically heavy perceptual load, etc.) allocation of resource will dictate focused attention, early selection, and little or no processing of non-attended channels.

The effects of "perceptual load" intrinsic to a core task on distractor processing were illustrated in a functional imaging study by Rees, Frith, and Lavie (1997). Respondents had to monitor a string of words and decide either whether they were presented in upper or lower case (lower load), or how many syllables they contained (higher load). Irrelevant background motion evoked activity in motion-sensitive brain regions (area MT in particular) in lower- but not higher-load conditions. In other words, increasing the load of the core task led to less processing of the distractor stimuli. This effect has subsequently been found to hold in cross-modal situations where the load task is auditory but the irrelevant task is in the visual modality. However, and consistent with Baddeley's ideas outlined above, if *executive* control functions such as working memory are "loaded" by requiring the respondent to memorise six digits immediately before the target-detection task (as opposed to "loading" the core task itself), irrelevant low-priority distractors increase the interference with the target-detection task, leading to a consequent drop in performance (Lavie, 2005). So, it would appear that cognitive control is needed to maintain the distinction between targets and distractors, and if this is otherwise "engaged", performance on the core task will be adversely affected.

The "perceptual load approach" to understanding the allocation of attentional resources circumvents many of the earlier concerns about early/late filtering of unattended material or the operation of visual search strategies. However, the concept itself remains somewhat vague, and its relation to "the slave" and "central executive" components of working memory needs to be clarified.

INTERIM COMMENT

We know what we mean when we talk about attention, and there seem to be several ways of measuring it or invoking it. The process itself involves a biasing in favour of some particular aspect or feature of a stimulus at the expense of others: "biased competition" in Duncan's words. What we feel less sure about are its parameters—the extent to which it overlaps with alertness or working memory for instance. The material introduced in the previous section amply illustrates *the continued absence* of a cohesive framework on which to build psychological models of attention. Studies of selective attention lead to the conclusion that unattended material is not so much "filtered out" as "attenuated". In studies of visual search, attention may be "location" or "object" based, and we must also distinguish between voluntary and involuntary attentional mechanisms. Resource-based models raise the possibility that attentional mechanisms overlap closely with working memory systems, or at least that full effective deployment of an attentional resource depends on an unencumbered working memory system.

ATTENTION AND THE BRAIN

The psychological approach has provided a lot of data, but no truly unifying ideas about attention. In fact, it seems to have raised as many questions as it answers. In this section we consider contributions to our thinking about attention gleaned from more neurobiological approaches. Can an examination of brain structure and functioning inform our understanding of how attention operates?

BRAIN ACTIVATION AND ATTENTION

We can examine attentional processing in the nervous system by recording ERPs to attended and non-attended material. In a typical ERP study, the respondent may be instructed to attend to inputs to one ear and ignore those to the other. (At a later stage, the instructions can be reversed to avoid the possibility of differential ear sensitivity affecting results.) Typical findings from this type of study are illustrated in Figure 9.5. They suggest that the ERP to the attended channel begins to differentiate itself from the ERP to the unattended channel about 80 ms after stimulus onset (Andreassi, 1989), as indicated by a markedly enhanced N_1 wave. More recently, Woldorff and Hillyard (1991; Woldorff et al., 1993) found evidence of earlier cortical waveform changes in the 20 to 50 ms latency range. This means that attended material is being "treated" differently by regions of sensory cortex very soon after stimulus presentation.

With ERP studies in the visual modality it becomes possible to investigate "spatial" attention. In order to do this, researchers have adapted the paradigm developed by Posner, Snyder, and Davidson (1980) in which participants fixate on a central point but are cued to expect stimuli to the left or right of that point (see Figure 9.4). The ERP wave shows characteristic changes in amplitude which start about 70–90 ms after stimulus presentation (known as the P100 wave) when the stimulus appears in the "cued" location. The response is greater than when the same stimulus is presented but attention is focused elsewhere, suggesting an attentional amplification for the attended stimulus.

By combining ERP and ERF (event-related field) procedures (see Chapter 2), Mangun, Hillyard, and Luck (1993) have confirmed that the enhanced ERP is *cortical* in origin. In other words, by voluntarily directing attention towards particular stimuli, changes in ERP waveform (reflecting enhanced cortical activity)

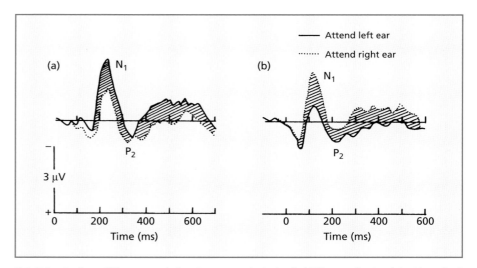

FIG. 9.5 Auditory ERPs to attended and non-attended stimuli. (a) The amplitude of the N_1 peak of the ERP is greater to a tone presented to the left ear when the respondent is attending to inputs to the left ear, than when the same tone is presented but the respondent is attending to inputs to the right ear. (b) This is not related to auditory acuity because the reverse effect can be observed if tones are now presented to the right ear. Adapted from Andreassi, J. L. (1989). *Psychophysiology: Human behaviour and physiological response* (2nd edn.). Hillsdale, NJ: Lawrence Erlbaum Associates Inc. Reproduced with permission.

can be seen well within one-tenth of a second. Interestingly, this technique can also be used to see if "involuntary" shifts in attention activate the same mechanisms. Hopfinger and Mangun (1998) have shown that when an unexpected and irrelevant sensory cue (which draws attention to part of the visual field) precedes the target stimulus by up to 300 ms, the ERP to the target stimulus is enhanced, but with longer intervals between the cue and target the effect is reversed (see our earlier reference to "inhibition of return"). This study strongly suggests that certain attentional processes evoked by voluntary cues are also evoked by involuntary ones. It is also a reminder that any effective model of attention must accommodate both deliberate and incidental influences on the direction of attention. We return to this matter later.

Several additional components of the ERP waveform, related to quite specific higher-level attentional processing, have also interested researchers. In chronological order, the N170 (a negative peak with a latency of between 170 and 200 ms) is strongest over right posterior temporal sites (Bentin et al., 1996) to facial images in general (including animal and cartoon faces). This is quickly superseded by a slightly later negative peak, the N250 (with a latency of about 250 ms), if the face is "meaningful", famous, or familiar (Herzmann et al., 2004). However, the most extensively researched such peak is the P300, a positive wave occurring roughly one-third of a second or later after stimulus presentation. This "late" wave seems to be related to the contextual meaning of the stimulus, and shows that attention can modify the brain's response for some time after a stimulus has been presented. A typical P300 study might require a respondent to listen out for infrequent high tones (so-called "odd-balls") presented in a series with more frequent low tones. The ERP to the "odd-ball" tones will show the typical positive shift (about one-third of a second after the stimulus is presented), while the non-salient low tones will not evoke this response. One crude way of distinguishing between ERP components is to envisage the early changes in terms of physical relevance, and the later ones as linked to semantic relevance (see Figure 9.6).

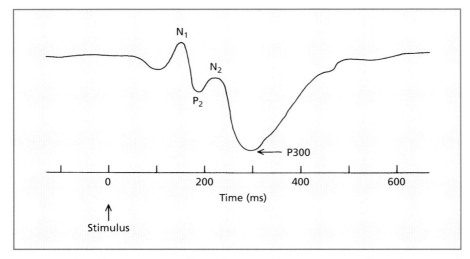

FIG. 9.6 Early and late components of an auditory ERP. The early components (up to about 200 ms) are thought to reflect cortical processing of relatively simple stimulus attributes such as intensity or pitch. Later components such as the P300 wave vary in relation to "significance" of stimuli and are thus thought to reflect higher-level (semantic) processing of stimuli.

Functional imaging has been less extensively used than ERPs to map brain attentional processes, mainly because of its comparatively poorer temporal resolution (see Chapter 2). Progress has nevertheless been made, and an fMRI study of object-based attention by O'Craven et al. (1999) was described earlier. You may recall that participants in this study viewed compound images of overlaid photographs in which one was stationary and the other was moving slightly, and they were told to attend either to the direction of the motion of the moving image, or only to the stationary one. Functional MRI of brain regions that became more active during this task indicated increased activity in the fusiform face area (referred to in Chapter 8 as part of the temporal lobe associated with processing faces) when a face stimulus was attended to than ignored, and more activity in the para-hippocampal "place" area when a picture of a house had to be attended to than when it was ignored. This study suggests that attention operates by facilitating the processing of the attended image rather than by inhibiting the unattended one.

An ingenious study by Egner and Hirsch (2005) has confirmed this facilitatory effect. The researchers used a version of the Stroop test in which images of famous actors or politicians were superimposed with the name of another either well-known actor or politician. In some trials the image and name were congruent (for example, both actors); on other trials they were incongruent (an image of an actor plus the name of a politician). Egner and Hirsch focused on trials that immediately followed an incongruent trial, when top-down attentional influences would be most pronounced. They recorded activity in the prefrontal cortex and fusiform face area on these trials, both when the face was the target (attended) stimulus, and when it was the distractor. Results indicated that fusiform activity was significantly enhanced on these attentionally "loaded" trials if participants were attending to faces, though not if the target was the name. Fusiform activation was clearly correlated with activation in the prefrontal cortex, suggesting that the former structure was receiving top-down control from the latter. (See also Nieuwehhuis & Yeung, 2005.)

Although, for reasons already explained, fMRI does not readily lend itself to the exploration and measurement of rapid brain activations associated with attentional processes, it has contributed, along with other methods described in Chapter 2, to the identification of key elements in an attentional circuit in the brain, which we now consider.

BRAIN STRUCTURES AND ATTENTION

There is no single attention "centre" in the brain. Instead, several regions are thought to form a distributed neural network that is collectively responsible for the attributes of attention considered so far. The network comprises brainstem, midbrain, and forebrain structures, and impaired attention may result from damage to any of these. However, as with most neural networks, it is also possible to predict the particular attentional dysfunction most directly linked to each component part of the system.

The ascending reticular activating system (ARAS)

This is a brainstem structure (actually a diffuse network itself) comprising neurons whose axons ascend through the midbrain to influence forebrain structures including the cortex. The system was once thought to be unitary, but is now known to involve several distinct neurotransmitter systems (groups of neurons that release different chemical messengers to influence other neurons). It includes a cholinergic (acetylcholine-releasing) pathway, a noradrenergic (noradrenaline-releasing) pathway, a dopaminergic (dopamine-releasing) pathway, and a serotonergic (serotonin-releasing) pathway. The axons of most of these neurons divide many times en route to the cortex, and the upshot of this cortical innervation is that a relatively small number of brainstem and midbrain neurons can affect the excitability of virtually every cortical neuron. Not surprisingly, this system has long been implicated in arousal and the sleep–wake cycle. Damage to the ARAS will profoundly disrupt circadian rhythms and can result in coma, or chronic vegetative state. Stimulation of the ARAS will, conversely, quickly wake a sleeping animal. Moreover, drugs such as amphetamine, which are known to be CNS stimulants, are thought to have particular influences on the neurons in the ARAS and the pathway from it to the cortex. These findings suggest at least two roles for the ARAS in the control of attention. Tonic (background) influences will affect vigilance performance, while phasic (brief) changes will be important in orienting.

The superior colliculi

These are two modest bumps on the dorsal side of the brainstem in the midbrain region. They appear to play a key role in controlling a particular but vital type of eye movement in which objects initially in the peripheral field of vision "capture" attention. Their role in visual attention is thus self-evident. The eye movements controlled by the superior colliculi are called express saccades—the eyes jump from their old focus of attention to a new one in one jerk rather than a smooth arc. Damage to these structures interferes with express saccades but not other slower eye movements. In **supranuclear palsy**, a neurodegenerative disorder that affects several subcortical regions including the superior colliculi, patients are unable to direct their gaze in the normal way, not looking at someone who is speaking, or turning to greet an approaching friend. This deficit has been referred to as a loss of "visual grasp", and a similar temporary effect can be induced by local administration of drugs that block the action of neurotransmitters in the superior colliculi (Desimone et al., 1990). Incidentally, the inferior colliculi (two additional bumps just beneath the superior colliculi) are thought to play a similar role in orienting the individual towards "salient" auditory stimuli.

The pulvinar region of the thalamus

This appears to play a vital role in filtering material to be attended to from the vast amounts of sensory input that the brain actually receives. The thalamus as a whole acts as a relay station for almost all sensory inputs en route to the cortex, and is therefore ideally situated to serve as a filter. This idea was supported in a study by LaBerge and Buchsbaum (1990). In one condition, participants had to attend to the presence/absence of a single letter. In a second condition, participants had to "look out" for the same letter embedded among other letters. The second task required more "attention" than the first because there was now a requirement to filter or sift through the array to find the target letter. Sure enough, the second condition brought about greater PET activation of the pulvinar than the first, even when stimulus complexity was accounted for. The application of drugs that interfere with pulvinar functioning also disrupts shifts of attention (Petersen, Robinson, & Morris, 1985). Moreover, people with damage to this thalamic region are likely to have attentional difficulties involving the ability to filter stimuli, attending to one input and ignoring others, and in the ability to "latch on" to new stimuli. The pulvinar receives an important input from the superior colliculi, and it is thought that the ability of incidental but salient visual stimuli to adjust the attentional spotlight alluded to earlier depends critically on this axis.

The cingulate gyrus

The cingulate gyrus (or just cingulate) is another cortical "node" in the brain's attentional network. It appears to be involved in several separate attentional processes: For instance, the cingulate as a whole provides an interface in which sensory inputs are linked to "emotional tone" (was the movement in the periphery of your visual field a tree bending in the wind or a mugger?). Additionally, the anterior regions of this structure are critically involved in response selection (ignore the wind-blown tree, but run away from the mugger!). The anterior cingulate (AC) becomes active in circumstances in which appropriate "correct" responses have to be selected in a deliberate (even effortful) manner. PET studies of participants undertaking the Stroop test reinforce this role for the AC. In one variant of this test, respondents are presented with a list of words spelling different colours. Some of the words are printed in the same colour that they spell, but others are printed in a different colour. On some trials participants have to name the word irrespective of the colour it is printed in, and on other trials they must name the ink colour irrespective of the word. The AC is much more active during colour naming than word naming (Pardo et al., 1990) because the former leads to a greater "interference" effect. This is caused by the tendency to read the word even though this is not required (referred to as a pre-potent response).

Hopfinger, Buonocore, and Mangun (2000) undertook an fMRI study of covert attention, employing a variant of Posner's classic paradigm (see Figure 9.4 above). They were able to look separately at "cue" (a directional arrow) and "target" processing effects (does a chequerboard display have grey/white squares?) because of an 8-second time-lag between cue and target. Cue presentation activated medial and dorsolateral frontal regions, inferior parietal and superior temporal regions, and the posterior cingulate gyrus (all bilaterally). Target processing, as expected, activated various sensory and motor regions, the ventrolateral frontal cortex and, critically, the anterior cingulate (see Figure 9.7). This study shows that the posterior and anterior cingulate can be dissociated into preparatory and response selection components respectively.

The parietal lobes

These are specialised for processing spatial relations and their role in attention is inferred from two independent research findings. First, parietal damage (on either side but especially the right) is associated with hemineglect, an attentional disorder in which half of the visual field is, effectively, ignored. (See later in this chapter.) Second, the P300 wave that we mentioned earlier is most marked in parietal regions. There is still debate about what exactly the P300 signifies, but one idea is that it reflects "attentional resource" allocated to a particular task. In other words,

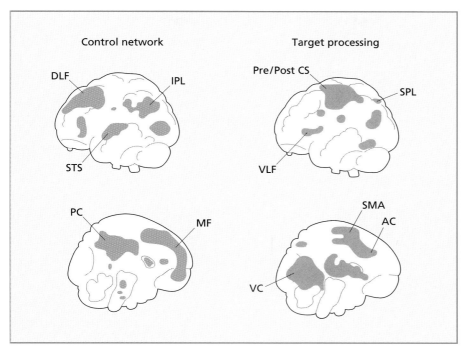

FIG. 9.7   Hopfinger's study of controlled spatial attention (Hopfinger et al., 2000). The left-hand upper and lower images indicate brain regions in a control network activated by cue presentation: medial and dorsolateral frontal regions, inferior parietal and superior temporal regions, and the posterior cingulate gyrus. Target processing, as expected, activated various sensory and motor regions, the ventrolateral frontal cortex and, critically, the anterior cingulate, indicated in the upper and lower images on the right. Posterior and anterior cingulate activations dissociated into preparatory and response selection components respectively. Note: all activations were bilateral, although only left hemisphere is shown. Source: Adapted by permission from Macmillan Publishers Ltd: *Nature Neuroscience* (Hopfinger, Buonocore, & Mangun, 2000), © 2000.

the more attention a person pays to particular stimuli, the larger the resultant P300. It is also noteworthy that individuals with damage to parietotemporal regions no longer generate P300s.

The frontal lobes

We have just seen that at least two regions of prefrontal cortex are implicated in attention control (Hopfinger et al., 2000). Top-down executive influences of this sort are inextricably linked to central executive working memory function, which we introduced in Chapter 7. Executive functions (in general) are also reviewed in Chapter 11, and the linkage between all three (executive functions, working memory, and attention) is explored separately below. However, other frontal regions not linked to executive functioning also appear to be important in influencing motoric aspects of attention. A form of neglect is seen in some individuals with premotor frontal damage, although this is somewhat different from the classic hemineglect syndrome to be discussed later. In the frontal form, individuals seem uninterested in making movements towards the neglected side—a motor as opposed to a sensory neglect (Buxbaum, 2006).

The frontal eye fields (FEFs)

Located laterally in the frontal lobes (BA 8), these are also important attentional nodes. These regions control voluntary gaze. This is important because we have already seen that the superior colliculi direct gaze in an involuntary manner towards unexpected stimuli. Clearly some mechanism is required to override this system, otherwise we would constantly be distracted by new stimuli. This job is performed by the frontal eye fields. As you might expect, damage to this region brings about a form of distractibility in which an individual's visual attention is constantly drawn to irrelevant visual stimuli. LaBerge has offered a neuroanatomical model of attentional control which includes many of the structures identified above. We summarise this model in Box 9.1.

Box 9.1 LaBerge's triangular model of attention

According to LaBerge (1995, 2000), attention comprises three elements: simple selection, preparation, and maintenance. Simple selection is typically brief, the goal usually being the identification of the selected item itself. Preparatory and maintenance functions are required to sustain attention in a more deliberate way over a short (preparatory) or longer (maintenance) period of time. Posner's spatial cues would be a means of evoking preparatory attention. Completing the Stroop test would be an example of maintained attention. LaBerge envisages attention as enhanced (excitatory) activity in discrete cortical association areas, which can be brought about by either top-down or bottom-up influences. Bottom-up control operates in two main ways: triggering shifts in attention, and directing attention to new locations. In each case, the processes are rapid and, effectively, involuntary. Attentional capture (the term used for this bottom-up process) encompasses those occasions when our attention is "grabbed" by some salient but peripheral event or stimulus. For LaBerge, it also accounts for the so-called pre-attentive visual search findings of Treisman and Gelade (1980) in which respondents report that non-conjunctive targets "pop-out" from the array (see Figure 9.3b). Once detected, the target then directs attention to itself, whereupon top-down influences (from the frontal lobes) "decide" whether or not to maintain attention to that item.

In LaBerge's "triangular" model of attention (see Figure 9.8), the three core components are the parietal lobe, the frontal lobe, and the pulvinar of the thalamus, although the model also implicates the visual cortex and the superior colliculi. An abrupt visual stimulus induces brief parietal activity, either directly or via the superior colliculi and thalamus. This is likened to a pre-attentive or orienting activation. The parietal lobe, which is assumed to be the anatomical location of spatial representations, has reciprocal (informational) connections with the frontal lobe. If the latter "chooses" to sustain (or even initiate) activity in the parietal lobe, it does so via the pulvinar, which can potentiate activity in particular cortical regions and inhibit it in others (LaBerge & Buchsbaum, 1990). The pathway from frontal to parietal lobe via the pulvinar is unidirectional, and is the means by which top-down "deliberate" control of attention can be effected.

LaBerge has subsequently modified his triangular model, making it more neuroanatomically (and less neuropsychologically) rooted (LaBerge 2002, 2006) by linking it with short- and long-term functional changes within cortical columns. However, some features of LaBerge's (2000) model resonate with Corbetta and Shulman's (2002) model of attention, which we review later in this chapter.

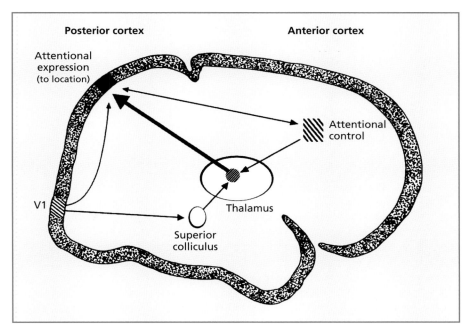

FIG. 9.8   LaBerge's triangular circuit of attention. Following preliminary processing in area V1 of the occipital cortex, a new visual stimulus may induce some "pre-attentive" registration in the parietal lobe, either by means of a direct input or via the superior colliculus and pulvinar of the thalamus. Sustained attention engages regions of the frontal lobe. Continued attentional control can be achieved by frontal output to the parietal lobe via the thalamus. (Adapted from LaBerge, 2000.)

ATTENTION, WORKING MEMORY, AND EXECUTIVE CONTROL

At present, there is no absolute agreement about which brain regions are critically implicated in either attention or working memory, but there *is* broad agreement that top-down attentional control involves the frontal lobes, and some frontal structures—the dorsolateral prefrontal cortex (DLPFC) and the anterior cingulate in particular—are involved in working memory and executive control (Chelazzi & Corbetta, 2000). A moment's thought suggests that working memory *must* be involved in (at least) top-down attention when a participant seeks to keep "in mind" information over a period of time that will guide his/her subsequent actions, as in the classic Posner et al. paradigm.

To underline the "common ground" between attentional mechanisms and working memory, PET and fMRI studies by Jonides et al. (1993), Smith et al. (1996), and Courtney et al. (1997) have all demonstrated a significant degree of overlap in both right parietal and frontal regions of activation during tasks of spatial attention and spatial working memory. Additionally, it has been known for some time that sustained effortful attention over longer periods (as required in the Stroop test) engages medial frontal structures including the anterior cingulate and the frontal eye fields (Posner & DiGirolamo, 1998) in addition to DLPFC regions associated with the central executive control of working memory.

More recently, three independent lines of evidence have reinforced the view that working memory, attention, and executive control share a good deal of common ground. For example, Kane et al. (2001) reported a study of visually presented letter identification that included an "**anti-saccade**" condition: shortly before each target letter was presented, an attention-attracting cue appeared on the side opposite to where the letter would subsequently appear. For optimal performance, respondents had to resist the temptation to shift attention (and move their eyes) towards the cue. The researchers found that respondents with the smallest working memory capacities were most likely to make persistent attentional errors; suggesting that a common attention-executive (top-down) system underpins the relationship between distractibility and poor working memory.

The imaging studies cited earlier produced impressive results but have been criticised on methodological grounds including, in at least one instance, the conflation of spatial memory and spatial attention tasks, leading to difficulties in interpreting the "apparent" convergence of their anatomical representations (in other words, the tasks were so similar that functional overlap was almost inevitable). In an effort to overcome this problem, LaBar et al. (1999) conducted an fMRI investigation in which the same respondents undertook a working memory task (with no spatial attentional component) and a spatial attention task in which any working memory component was controlled for. Although some brain regions were only activated in one or other of the tasks, several, including the frontal eye fields and supplementary motor regions of the frontal lobes, the intraparietal sulcus, and the thalamus, were equally activated by both: a finding that LaBar and colleagues interpreted as supporting the view that working memory and spatial attention are represented by partially overlapping neural networks. (See Figure 9.9 for an illustration of the method and findings of this study.)

Third, in an ERP study by Awh, Anllo-Vento, and Hillyard (2000), participants were required to undertake both a spatial working memory and a spatial attention task using (virtually) identical stimulus displays. In the former, they had to "remember" the position of three dots presented briefly to the left or right of a fixation point. Irrelevant chequerboard-patterned probes were briefly presented on the same or opposite side during the retention period, and ERPs were recorded to these. After about 8 seconds, another dot appeared on screen and participants had to say whether or not it occupied a location of one of the original three dots. This completed the trial although performance on this was of no interest to the researchers. In the spatial attention condition, the stimulus sequence was almost identical, but the instruction was to pay attention to the "side" in which the dots appeared (rather than their precise locations) and to press a button whenever a faint/dim dot (not shown in the memory condition) appeared on the same side. Once again irrelevant chequerboard probes appeared during the 8-second delay period and ERPs to these were recorded. The key questions were: (a) whether the task manipulations would induce enhanced ERPs to chequerboard stimuli on the "cued" side, and (b) whether these would be similar or different in the spatial working memory and spatial attention conditions. As expected, ERP enhancement was observed on the cued side, but of greater interest was the considerable

KEY TERM
Anti-saccade: Inhibition of a reflexive eye movement towards a light target.

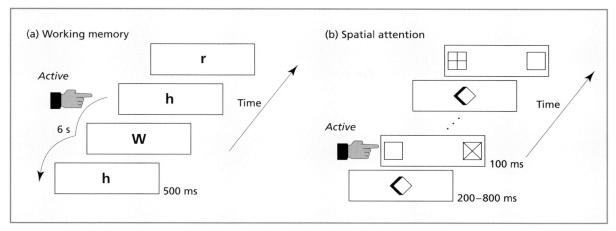

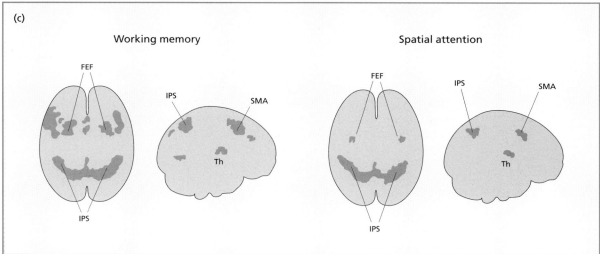

FIG. 9.9 LaBar et al.'s fMRI investigation of working memory and attention. (a) In the working memory task, respondents viewed a series of letters and had to press a button if the current letter was the same as the one shown two letters previously (called the 2-back paradigm; control condition not shown). (b) In the attention task the diamond figure with one side emboldened was the cue to signal a subsequent target: an X in a box. The cue signalled the correct direction on about 80% of trials (control condition not shown). (c) Although some brain regions (not shown) were only activated in one or other of the tasks, several, including the frontal eye fields and supplementary motor regions of the frontal lobes, the intraparietal sulcus, and the thalamus, were equally activated by both, suggesting that working memory and spatial attention are represented by partially overlapping neural networks. Source of (a) & (b): LaBar, K. S., Gitelman, D. R., Parrish, T. B., and Mesulam, M. M. (1999). Neuroanatomical overlap of working memory and spatial attention networks: a functional MRI comparison with subjects. *NeuroImage, 10*, 695–704. Reproduced with permission, © Elsevier, 1999.

overlap, both in terms of ERP amplitudes and location of maximum activation, in the two task conditions: a finding that the authors interpreted as providing strong support for a marked functional overlap in the mechanisms of spatial working memory and spatial attention.

Thus, evidence from studies employing three different methodologies (cognitive psychology, fMRI, and ERP) converges to illustrate the likely commonality between spatial attention, working memory, and executive control. To this we might add a reminder that placing "load" on working memory reduces available resource for focused attention, and increases the likelihood of being distracted by irrelevant stimuli or events (Lavie, 2005).

INTERIM COMMENT

Both ERP and functional imaging studies indicate that augmented processing of attended stimuli can be observed relatively soon after stimulus presentation (within 50–70 ms). Attended channels continue to receive preferential attentional treatment at later stages of processing up to and including the P300 wave, usually associated with responses to stimuli with "semantic significance". None of these studies supports the idea of active inhibition of unattended channels.

Attempts to identify cortical and subcortical structures involved in mediating attention have been quite informative, and LaBerge's triangular model attempts to integrate some of these structures into a network that accounts for both "bottom-up" and "top-down" control of attention. The available evidence suggests that "top-down" attentional control overlaps significantly with executive components of working memory, and although some of the earlier functional imaging studies have been criticised for failing to distinguish adequately between attentional and working memory tasks, converging evidence from more recent studies, employing a range of procedures, has reinforced the view that both working memory and attention involve partially overlapping neural networks distributed in frontal and parietal regions. However, progress in this area is hampered by continuing uncertainties about the structure of working memory and the parameters and categories of attention.

NEUROLOGICAL ATTENTIONAL DISORDERS

HEMINEGLECT

Hemineglect (also known as unilateral or spatial neglect) is a collection of related (but not identical) disorders usually associated with inferior parietal or medial temporal lobe damage (but see later). An individual with this condition effectively ignores (or fails to pay attention to) one side of space with respect to the midline of the head or body. This is sometimes called **egocentric neglect**, and appears to be associated with hypofunction (or damage) in the angular gyrus (Hillis et al., 2005). The angular gyrus is sometimes identified as a key part of the temporal-parietal junction [TPJ] area, which we consider below. Much less commonly, a patient may appear to consistently neglect the left or right side of objects regardless of where they appear in the visual field. This is sometimes called **allocentric neglect**, and it is associated with underactivity (or damage) in the superior temporal gyrus (Hillis et al., 2005). Moreover, it should be noted that, in rare instances, neglect may involve different spatial referents such as left/right foreground and distance, or even left/right upper and lower space (Behrmann, 2000). In fact, a very small number of neglect patients may even evince a dissociation in the form of left-sided neglect for near space and right-sided neglect for far space, or vice versa. To complete the picture, neglect in the auditory or even somatosensory modality may be apparent. However, visual hemineglect is far and away the most common form of disorder, and this is what we will focus on.

Hemineglect occurs in between 25–30% of stroke-affected individuals according to Appelros (2002). Nine out of ten have a right-sided injury and left-sided neglect. The regions most frequently implicated are the angular (and supramarginal) gyrus, superior temporal and inferior frontal lobes, and associated subcortical structures (Vallar, 1998). About 10% of neglect cases have left-sided damage and right hemineglect although, for reasons that are not entirely clear, this is usually less severe. Taken together, these observations lead to the conclusion that although left- and right-sided damage may lead to contralateral neglect, right-sided structures are somehow more critically involved. One long-standing explanation for this finding was that whereas the left parietal lobe is only responsible for attention on the right side of space, the right parietal lobe has an "executive" control for spatial attention on both sides. Thus, following right-sided damage, the left parietal lobe can still mediate attention to the right visual field, but attentional control of the left side is lost. Therefore, left-sided damage is typically less disabling because the intact right side can continue to exert some control over both sides (Weintraub & Mesulam, 1987). An alternative explanation has invoked the different processing styles of the left and right hemispheres (see Chapter 3). According to Robertson and Rafal (2000), the left parietal lobe is chiefly responsible for local shifts in attention whereas the right parietal lobe is involved in more global shifts. Thus, following right hemisphere damage, the patient is limited to the local attentional shifts of the left hemisphere, leading to the fixation with local detail and the loss of effective disengagement. Neither of these accounts is, in fact, entirely satisfactory, but the model proposed by Corbetta and Shulman (2002) (to be reviewed later) overcomes some of these intrinsic problems and provides the most complete explanation for these apparent asymmetries.

The extent of hemineglect is variable, and may range from a general apparent indifference towards objects on the left side, to denial of the very existence of that side of the body (Buxbaum, 2006). One of Sacks' patients had **anosognosia** (Sacks, 1985) and famously called a nurse in the middle of the night to ask her to help him throw his own left leg out of bed, thinking that "the alien leg" had been put there as a cruel joke by fellow patients! Less severely affected patients may simply ignore items in their left visual field. Moreover, there is usually some recovery in the months following injury/damage and so, typically, the neglect is most marked early on, becoming less pronounced, though not usually disappearing completely, as recovery ensues. The late German artist Anton Raederscheidt suffered a right-sided stroke but continued to paint even though he had an initially severe form of hemineglect (Butter, 2004; Wurtz, Goldberg, & Robinson, 1982). In a famous series of self-portraits it is possible to see the effects of his hemineglect and how this diminished over a period of months as he partially recovered after his stroke. In an interview his wife described how, in the early recovery period, she had to keep guiding him to the left side of the canvas, and it is clear from the paintings themselves that Raederscheidt's gradual reconstruction of the left side of his visual space was a deliberate "non-fluent" process.[1] The case of Anton Raederscheidt highlights an important subjective feature of hemineglect. The individual is not so much desperate to re-find the missing half of their visual field, as utterly uninterested in it. It just doesn't exist as far as they are concerned,

KEY TERM
Anosognosia: A condition in which a person who suffers impairment following brain damage seems unaware of or denies the existence of their handicap, even if the handicap is severe (blindness or paralysis).

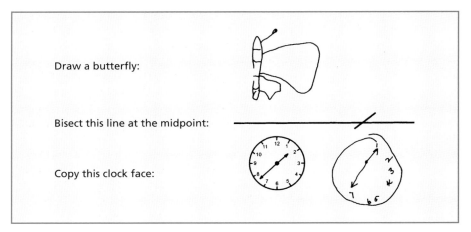

FIG. 9.10 Typical responses of hemineglect patients in drawing tasks.

and in Raederscheidt's case it had to be deliberately (and somewhat artificially) reconstructed.

What are the tell-tale signs of neglect in the visual modality, and why should it be classified as an attentional rather than perceptual disorder? Detecting neglect is quite straightforward: Ask the patient to copy some simple line drawings and the results will be similar to those shown in Figure 9.10. When probed about whether the drawing might be lacking certain details, the patient will usually deny this, saying that it is complete. On a simple line-bisection task (in which the respondent is required to indicate the midpoint of a series of uncalibrated horizontal lines of different lengths), the neglect patient typically places the bisecting line to the right of true centre (Marshall & Halligan, 1990). (This is the exact opposite of healthy controls who typically show a small left-oriented bias; sometimes called pseudo-neglect.) Finally, when asked to cross out every vowel shown on a sheet of random letters comprising both vowels and consonants, the neglect patient will "chalk up" many more hits on the right side of the array than on the left.

None of the previous observations entirely rules out the possibility that hemineglect may relate to sensory/perceptual rather than attentional deficits. However, three further lines of evidence strongly support the idea that it is an attentional disorder. For example, when identical objects are presented to both visual fields simultaneously, the "neglect" patient usually fails to report the object in the left visual field (a phenomenon known as "extinction"). However, if different objects are presented one at a time to each side, there will be normal or near-normal recognition even on the "neglected" side. Second, Mesulam (1985) reported that attention to objects on the neglected side can be improved by offering rewards for target detection there. And finally it has become clear that some processing of materials presented to the "neglect" side occurs even if the patient denies knowledge of that material. In one famous illustration by Marshall and Halligan (1988) a neglect patient was simultaneously shown two images of a house, identical except that the house presented on the left had flames coming out of some of its windows. The patient could not describe any differences between the images but, when asked to choose, expressed a clear preference to live in the house on the right!

The idea that hemineglect results from a lack of awareness of the existence of one side of visual space seems alien to those of us with intact attentional mechanisms, but it was further demonstrated in the reports by Bisiach and Luzzatti (1978) of two hemineglect cases. The researchers asked their patients to imagine that they were standing in a famous Milanese square opposite the entrance to the cathedral, and to report the various buildings and other landmarks that came to mind. (Both knew this location well, having lived in the city for many years before their illnesses.) Later, the same respondents were asked to imagine themselves standing on the cathedral steps looking back to their initial vantage point, and now to report buildings and landmarks (again in their mind's eye) that they could see from this new vantage point. The results of this study are represented in Figure 9.11. When the two patients imagined themselves standing opposite the cathedral, most of the identified landmarks were to the right. When they imagined themselves standing on the steps of the cathedral looking back, most of the identified landmarks were, once again, to the right. This study reveals some important features of "imaginal"

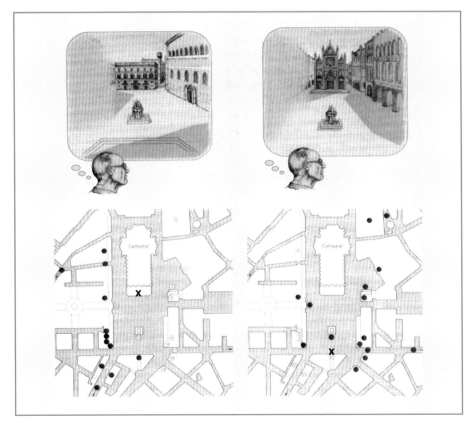

FIG. 9.11   Hemineglect and imaginal spatial attention. When asked to imagine the view from the steps of the cathedral (marked "x" on the left-hand map), both patients identified more landmarks and buildings to the right. When asked to imagine the view from the opposite end of the square (marked "x" on the right-hand map), both patients once again identified many more landmarks and buildings to the right. Source: Bisiach, E., & Luzzatti, C. (1978). Unilateral neglect of representational space. *Cortex, 14*, 129–133. As redrawn in *Cognitive neuroscience: The biology of the mind* (Figure 6.38) by M. S. Gazzaniga, R. Ivry, and G. R. Mangun: Copyright © 1998 by W. W. Norton & Company, Inc. Used by permission of W. W. Norton & Company, Inc.

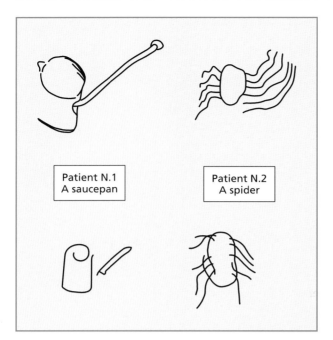

FIG. 9.12   Chokron et al.'s (2004) study of imaginal hemineglect. Respondents were invited to draw images of a saucepan and a spider from memory, either with their eyes open (upper figures) or closed (lower figures). In these illustrations, there is more evidence of symmetry/completion in the lower than upper figures. Source: Chokron, S., Colliot, P., and Bartolomeo, P. (2004). The role of vision in spatial representation. *Cortex, 40,* 281–290. Reproduced with permission.

hemineglect. First, it cannot be related to memory impairment because the total number of recalled landmarks was similar to the number generated by normal controls. Second, the attentional disturbance could not be caused by external cues because the entire test relied on imagery. The most parsimonious explanation of these findings is that the patients behaved as if they were missing the concept of one side of space—the left—even when they effectively rotated themselves through 180 degrees.

However, since this landmark case study, questions have been raised about the generalisability of its findings. For example, according to Gainotti, D'Erme, and Bartolomeo (1991), about two-thirds of neglect patients do not in fact have "neglect" for imaginal tasks like that of Bisiach and Luzzatti. Moreover, there have been no recorded cases of individuals with imaginal neglect but no conventional visual neglect as well. In a clever test to establish the importance of vision on imaginal spatial representation, Chokron, Colliot, and Bartolomeo (2004) asked six right-hemisphere-damaged neglect patients to draw a series of objects from memory with their eyes either open or closed. Some of the drawings are shown in Figure 9.12. In most, there is more evidence of neglect in the former than the latter condition. The authors suggested that this finding "highlighted" the importance of vision in capturing attentional control and holding it (inappropriately for these neglect patients) to the right side of space. At the very least this implies that the two forms of neglect (imaginal and conventional) may be dissociable (partly distinct) and that conventional visual neglect is the more problematic.

Corbetta et al. (2005) have shown that recovery from hemineglect maps onto measureable functional changes in the cortex. This group followed-up 11 stroke-induced neglect cases for 39 weeks. Reduced neglect was strongly associated with the reappearance of normalised activity levels on the right side. Interestingly, changes in activation were not restricted to the specific location of stroke, reminding us that damage in one location can influence (in this case, suppress) activity in anatomically distant but functionally linked locations. In other words, neglect (or its absence) is mediated by a network of structures rather than one specific/critical location. Recovery of function can, incidentally, be significantly enhanced through engagement with effective physiotherapies, which may soon be supplemented by computer-based virtual reality technologies (Kim et al., 2004). However, and perhaps somewhat counterintuitively, Chokron et al. (see above) raised the possibility of *suppressing* visual control (for example, by means of light deprivation) as a means of aiding recovery from unilateral neglect. This has yet to be tested but it would be the exact opposite of conventional therapies, in which a strong emphasis is placed on re-training visual awareness.

BALINT'S SYNDROME

This is a rare but very disabling condition in which the individual manifests one or more of a trio of symptoms that could easily be mistaken for blindness for all but a very restricted area of the visual field. Balint's cases may be unable to point or reach towards a visual target (called optic ataxia; see an earlier reference to this condition above), they seem unable to shift gaze voluntarily to a new target (called **ocular apraxia**), and they may be unable to easily identify different objects in the same region of visual field presented together (known as **simultanagnosia**). When, for example, a crossed spoon and fork were held out in front of a Balint's patient, he reported only the presence of the spoon, and then later after a repeat presentation, the fork, yet the objects overlapped. However, such individuals are not blind, and can actually "see" objects anywhere in the visual field *if* they can direct attention to that location—and therein lies the problem. The ocular apraxia means that Balint's patients cannot redirect their gaze to areas adjacent to their present focus of attention (although a redirection may occur involuntarily). It is this lack of voluntary control that defines Balint's syndrome as a profound spatial attentional disorder (Damasio, 1985).

Farah (1990) further illustrated the attentional deficit seen in Balint's individuals. When shown a complex meaningful picture similar to that in Figure 9.13 the patient could identify different elements of the picture as his attention switched *involuntarily* around the scene, but he could never grasp the full meaning of the picture because it was visually scanned in such a piecemeal way. So the attentional disorder in Balint's compromises the appreciation of spatial relationships, which will influence the understanding and interpretation of visual displays (Robertson & Rafal, 2000).

However, many Balint's patients also display impaired object recognition, especially when more than one object is presented, even if they overlap (see above). In fact, the problem may be in deciding what actually constitutes "an object" (essentially a "binding" problem). Consider the findings of Humphreys and Riddoch (1992) working with their Balint's patient GK. He viewed arrays comprising randomly positioned all-green or all-red dots, or a mixture of the two. In each case, GK usually only reported seeing one colour of dot. However, if the array was changed to show pairs of dots (one red and one green), the same distance apart as in the initial arrays but joined by a line to look a bit like a series of dumbbells, GK now usually reported seeing both colours of dot. In other words, the connecting line created a new "object" (dumbbell) which GK was able to attend to in its entirety.

Balint's is almost always associated with damage to dorsal occipital-parietal regions, although more recently collected anatomic data suggest, as was the case with hemineglect, that different features of the syndrome may be dissociable, and

FIG. 9.13   A picture/story stimulus similar to those used by Farah. When Balint's patients view figures similar to the one shown here, their inability to voluntarily scan the entire figure and appreciate the "story" that it depicts is apparent.

linked to distinct cortical regions (and white matter pathways that connect them; Rizzo & Vecera, 2002). Bilateral damage to the superior parietal lobule (a key area in the "where–how" stream described in Chapter 8) is frequently seen, which explains why Balint's syndrome is also known as dorsal simultanagnosia.

INTERIM COMMENT

Balint's syndrome and hemineglect demonstrate that our ability to construct a complete model of our visual world depends on being able to attend to different elements of it, to switch attention to new objects or new regions of space very quickly, and to use this specific information to build a relational map of the "big picture". In hemineglect, parietal damage means that this skill is lost (usually) for the contralateral visual field. As a result, attention appears to be focused on the remaining intact half. The person is not blind to the other half of the visual field, and can, under certain circumstances, see objects in it. But their attention is somehow "drawn" to one half of the visual field, and they do not even seem to "miss" the other half.

Balint's syndrome is a rarer and more disabling condition in which attentional control, even to half the visual field, is lost. Instead, we see a sort of single object-based attentional system operating without voluntary control. Although Balint's syndrome is not in any way related to tunnel vision, the experience of the disorder must be a little like only seeing visual stimuli from the end of a long tube, which roams around the visual field unpredictably. Balint's has been likened to having hemineglect on both sides, although this is an oversimplification of the links between the two disorders. Compared to hemineglect, there is usually much more widespread damage in Balint's, which is most likely to involve more dorsal regions, bilaterally.

A final point to note is that damage to the "where–how" stream affects not only spatial attention but also object recognition, reminding us that the dorsal route undoubtedly interacts with, and contributes to the functions of, the ventral stream in this process.

TOWARDS AN INTEGRATED MODEL OF ATTENTION

Posner and colleagues (Posner et al., 1987) proposed a model of visual attention that emphasised change and selection. They argued that the redirection of attention must involve at least three processes: disengagement (from the present focus), redirection (to the new stimulus), and engagement (with the new stimulus). The three elements, they suggested, depend on the sequential interaction of different brain structures: "*the disengage*" process depends on intact parietal functioning, "*the redirect*" on the superior colliculi, and "*the engage*" on the thalamus.

The evidence in support of this hypothesis merits consideration: as we have seen, patients with parietal damage find it difficult to disengage from an attended stimulus, and this problem is not related to "engage" deficits, which, under appropriate circumstances, can be shown to be normal. (See our discussion of hemineglect and Balint's syndrome.) We also noted earlier that patients with collicular damage, as seen in supranuclear palsy, have difficulties redirecting gaze, and that individuals with pulvinar thalamic damage struggle to "latch on" to new targets. A network comprising some of these structures was designated the posterior attentional system by Posner. Subsequently, Posner (1992) proposed a second attention network that becomes active during intentional (endogenous) processing, such as listening out for "salient" target words, or covertly awaiting the presentation of a visual target having been "cued" to attend to a particular location. Posner thought that this so-called anterior network comprised parts of the cingulate, medial, and dorsolateral frontal regions, and that it clearly overlapped considerably with the component structures that contribute to the executive functions of the frontal lobes (to be discussed in Chapter 11). Endogenous control of attention was achieved by its modulation of parietal regions.

Corbetta and Shulman (2002) have developed what has quickly become an influential model of attention. Like Posner, these researchers acknowledged the importance of both anterior and posterior influences on attention, but they have argued that both combine to mediate attention in real-world settings. Their approach is commendable for three reasons: First, they have relied on meta-analysis of (mainly) functional imaging studies. Thus, their conclusions are based on findings from several independent studies, each of which has employed somewhat different experimental methods, making consensus findings all the more noteworthy. Second, by pooling data, the resultant sample size is much more "respectable" than would be the case with single studies. Third, their model offers a plausible explanation for the laterality effects seen in hemineglect (Corbetta et al., 2005).

Corbetta and Shulman envisage two interacting "arms" in their attention network. One primarily operates as a top-down control system involved in preparing, applying, and controlling attention to stimuli and, if necessary, organising appropriate responses. This system also responds to the detection of stimuli, particularly if they are pre-cued. The second is viewed as a bottom-up network, specialised for the detection of behaviourally relevant, salient, but unexpected stimuli. Conceptually, the top-down arm is analogous to Posner's anterior system and the bottom-up arm analogous to his posterior system, although anatomically, quite different regions have been identified in the two models.

If we take a closer look at the top-down "arm", a meta-analysis of fMRI studies indicates a network of cortical regions that become activated when a respondent anticipates a stimulus (i.e., following a cue) and that remain activated during the preparatory period for up to about 10 seconds: this network includes the dorsal regions of the parietal lobe and posterior frontal lobe. If we extend the analysis to include studies where attention to actual stimulus attributes (colour, movement, shape, etc.) is required, similar areas of activation are seen in parietal regions, plus marked activation in BA 8 (the frontal eye fields; see above). Although these activations are generally bilateral, there is some evidence that where a change in motor response is dictated by a particular stimulus, increased activation is more marked in left posterior parietal regions, an observation that jibes well with our review of apraxia in Chapter 5. The main components of the top-down attention arm, referred to by Corbetta et al. as a dorsal system, are illustrated in Figure 9.14a.

Turning now to the bottom-up (or stimulus-driven) arm, Corbetta and Shulman conceptualise this system as a "circuit-breaker", capable of interrupting and even re-orienting attention in response to a salient or unexpected stimulus

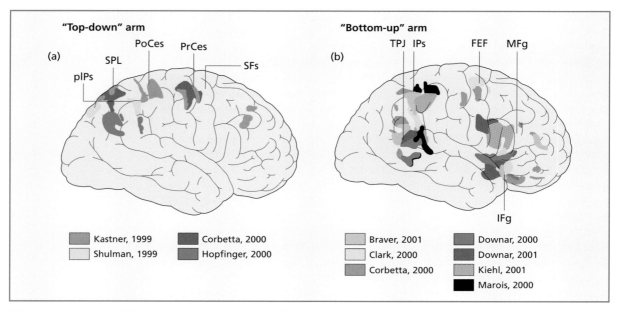

FIG. 9.14 Corbetta and Shulman's model of attention. (a) The bilateral top-down arm: results of a four-study meta-analysis indicate regions activated by cues preceding target stimuli. Areas of maximal activation included pIPs (posterior intraparietal sulcus), SPL (superior parietal lobule), PoCes and PrCes (post- and precentral sulcus), and SFs (superior central sulcus). Comparable left hemisphere activations were also found (not shown). (b) The right hemisphere bottom-up arm: results of a seven-study meta-analysis indicate regions in a ventral fronto-parietal network that are activated to unexpected stimuli. Areas of maximum activation included the TPJ (temporo-parietal junction), IPs (intraparietal sulcus), FEF (frontal eye field), and the MFg and IFg (medial and inferior frontal gyrus). Activation in the left hemisphere is much less pronounced (not shown). Source: Adapted by permission from Macmillan Publishers Ltd: *Nature Reviews Neuroscience* (Corbetta & Shulman, 2002), © 2002.

(such as a fire alarm or a flash of lightning). This arm involves a quite different set of cortical locations and is strongly (though not completely) lateralised to the right hemisphere. Parietal and frontal regions are implicated but these are more ventral (hence Corbetta et al.'s reference to this as the ventral system) than the regions in the mainly dorsal top-down arm (see Figure 9.14b). However, this "stimulus-driven" arm can exert powerful effects on the top-down arm: For example, low-frequency task-relevant stimuli such as rare distractors that are the same colour as attended stimuli will activate it, but will also activate the top-down circuit, presumably so that they can be evaluated and if necessary "deliberately" responded to. Task-irrelevant distractors on the other hand will only have this effect if they are very salient (e.g., the fire alarm). Key nodes in this arm are the right temporo-parietal junction (TPJ) and the right medial and inferior frontal gyri. Finally, there is some evidence that activity in this ventral system is partly mediated by a noradrenergic (NA) input from the locus coeruleus (part of the ascending reticular activating system; see above). There is, for example, a more dense NA innervation of the right than left thalamus. This observation is significant because NA release is thought to increase **signal to noise ratio** in threatening situations where effective attentional control may mean the difference between life and death.

In their 2002 paper, Corbetta and Shulman speculated that damage to the strongly right-lateralised stimulus-driven system was likely to be implicated in hemineglect (see our earlier discussion of this disorder). If this ventral system was

KEY TERM
Signal to noise ratio:
Degree to which relevant information can be perceived against a background of irrelevant information.

compromised, an individual might be indifferent to the left side because stimuli there would not exert their "circuit-breaker" effects. However, there is something wrong with this argument because it seems that the right temporo-parietal junction (TPJ) area actually responds equally well to unexpected stimuli on both sides, so damage here might be expected to cause bilateral deficits. Moreover, TPJ activation does not correlate with motor preparation, whereas most neglect cases show contralateral impairments in movement preparation and initiation. The authors were aware of these problems, and they suggested that hemineglect probably resulted from a more dynamic dysfunction (i.e., at least not localised only to the TPJ), although the anatomy of this network was not defined.

However, Corbetta et al. (2005) *were* able to describe in more detail the *network of dysfunction* implicated in the neglect syndrome. This study, which we introduced earlier, followed up a group of hemineglect patients during their recovery (for a period of 39 weeks), recording fMRI signals early on post-stroke, and again several months later. We summarised their research as suggesting that recovery was associated with "normalisation" of balanced cortical activity bilaterally. However, re-examination of their findings, especially relating to changes in activation over time, merits closer scrutiny. For example, dorsal parietal activation (part of the top-down attention system, you might recall) was markedly reduced on the right side and paradoxically *increased* on the left side shortly after stroke although neither site was itself damaged. This strongly suggests that the ventral arm ordinarily interacts with the dorsal arm to redirect attention, but following right-sided stroke, ipsilateral (same-sided) ventral–dorsal interaction is reduced, giving rise to a functional imbalance in which the left dorsal parietal lobe is relatively hyperactive. The right TPJ is crucial in this because damage to it (or to the ventral system of which it is part) will prevent it from sending the "circuit-breaker" signal to the dorsal arm (on the same side). So left-sided neglect results from two additive dysfunctional processes: First, stimuli on the left will be less likely to invoke "capture" because the right TPJ is compromised, and second, reduced activity here will bring about reduced activation in the dorsal system on the right, giving free rein to left posterior dorsal areas to influence top-down attention to the right side, and hence induce a marked rightward bias. A schematic (simplified) version of this model is shown in Figures 9.15a and b.

INTERIM COMMENT

Corbetta and colleagues have offered a neuropsychological model of attention that, in certain respects, builds on ideas first suggested by Posner and Mesulam. However, although their model has two "arms" (a top-down and a bottom-up component), these interact continuously in real-world settings to mediate directing attention (the dorsal arm), circuit breaking (the ventral arm), and re-orienting attention (ventral influence on the dorsal arm). In fact, it is, essentially, a unitary model with specialised component systems in it rather than two attentional control networks. In comparison with LaBerge's model it is less neuroanatomically rooted, and more concerned with cortical functions/ dysfunctions. However, like LaBerge's model it envisages attention as being "controlled" by a continuous interaction between top-down and bottom-up influences (particularly the effects of the latter on the former). It additionally offers a compelling explanation of many of the features of hemineglect.

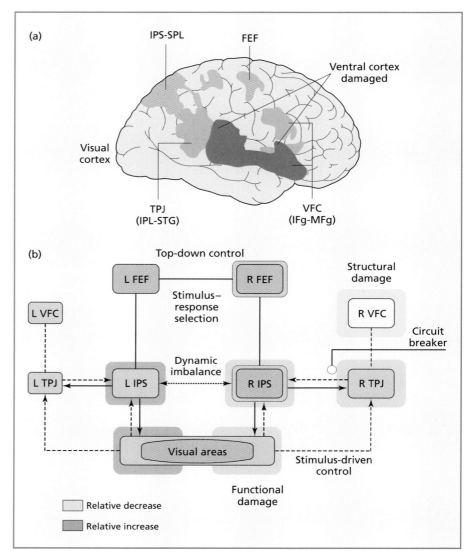

FIG. 9.15 Corbetta et al.'s (2005) explanation of hemineglect. (a) Major components of the dorsal (top-down) and ventral (bottom-up) attention arms (as depicted in 9.14a and b). The dark area represents location of lesions in the right hemisphere associated with hemineglect, encompassing an area extending from the TPJ (temporo-parietal junction) into VFC (ventrofrontal cortex). (b) Ventral damage in the right hemisphere exerts dual effects, depicted in this schematic diagram. Stimuli in the left visual field are unable to invoke "capture" because the right TPJ is compromised. Additionally, reduced right ventral activity leads to reduced activation in the dorsal system on the right, giving free rein to left posterior dorsal areas to influence top-down attention to the right side, and hence induce a marked rightward bias. Source: Adapted by permission from Macmillan Publishers Ltd: *Nature Neuroscience* (Corbetta, Kincade, Lewis, Snyder, & Sapir, 2005), © 2005.

On the other hand, it is a new model and needs to be tested empirically. Moreover, some puzzling features need to be clarified. For example, dorsolateral and cingulate regions do not feature at all in the 2002 model (and only the former features in the 2005 model), yet both regions have been implicated in executive control. The frontal eye fields, on the other hand, feature extensively in the general model, yet their primary function is thought to be related to the control of head and eye movements (Joseph, 2000) rather than executive control. One question for future research will be about the involvement of the frontal eye fields in non-visual attentional tasks. Additionally, a complete account of the attentional dysfunctions in hemineglect will need to consider (a) the different disturbances giving rise to egocentric and allocentric forms, and (b) how information in the neglected side still seems to undergo considerable "covert" processing.

CONSCIOUSNESS

Despite an upsurge in recent interest, a consensus definition of consciousness still eludes us. Nevertheless, we humans do at least know what it is like to *be* conscious—it seems to be restricted to when we are awake, and it involves "experience" of external stimuli (so-called "phenomenal awareness"); awareness of internal states and mental operations such as thoughts, feelings, and emotions and by extension a sense of self as "cognate"; and, arguably, awareness of other people's mental states too. Research in the area has recently been intense, indicating that consciousness is now a legitimate, and indeed urgent, domain of psychological enquiry. There are clearly important links between consciousness and neuropsychology, and we have included our discussion of it here because of the apparent intimate relationship between consciousness and attention (Maia & Cleeremans, 2005). However, as we mentioned in the introduction to this chapter, consciousness, at least as recently conceptualised (Blackmore, 2003), encompasses rather more than "focused attention": Pinker (1997) suggested three aspects meriting independent consideration:

- *Sentience or basic phenomenal awareness*: the private subjective experience of something.
- *Access to information*: being able to report on the contents of one's mental experiences.
- *Self-knowledge*: awareness of one's own mental state moment by moment, sometimes referred to as metacognition (thinking about one's thinking).

As you can see, even a consideration of the parameters of consciousness is complicated. Fortunately, many excellent articles and texts about various aspects of it have recently been published, and the reader keen to delve deeper is urged to refer to Dennett (1991), Chalmers (1995), Pinker (1997), Edelman and Tononi (2000), and Blackmore (2003) for highly accessible sources on consciousness in all its manifestations.

Perhaps we should also say at this point that we are taking it as axiomatic that consciousness, like all other aspects of cognition, is ultimately dependent on physical processes in our brain. In this sense, we are declaring our allegiance to what philosophers would call (some form of) "materialism", and simultaneously eschewing "dualism", the doctrine associated with René Descartes, who argued that the mind was a separate non-physical entity that interacted with the physical nervous system in the brain's pineal gland. These days, dualism has few supporters in the scientific fraternity (the neurophysiologist Sir John Eccles, who died in 1997, was a notable exception), although we also feel obliged to acknowledge that dualist ideas seem to be widely entrenched in the minds (or should that be brains?) of members of the lay public, given continued popular interest in religion, astrology, spiritualism, and so on.

Three disparate lines of enquiry have obliged us to broach the subject of consciousness: First it should be apparent from dipping into the various chapters in this book that changes in neuropsychological functioning are often accompanied by subjective (or even objective) changes to consciousness. Second, several additional lines of psychological and neuropsychological research (not already mentioned) have nevertheless begun to shed light on the nature of human consciousness: we review some of these below. And third, researchers have started to think about the structure of consciousness from a neuroscientific perspective—this quickly divides into two separate issues: From a practical point of view, what parts of the brain seem to be involved in consciousness? And from a conceptual point of view, what sort of neuronal architecture—network(s) of neurons—would be necessary for a "consciousness system" to operate?

Wilhelm Wundt's Leipzig facility, set up in 1879 to examine the contents of consciousness through introspection, is often regarded as the first "experimental psychology laboratory". Other 19th-century academics, notably Hughlings-Jackson, Helmhotz, Huxley, James, and even Freud, wrote extensively about consciousness, and in Freud's case about the "subconscious" mind too. However, the advent of behaviourism at the beginning of the 20th century, which we touched on in Chapter 1, heralded an era of psychological enquiry in which consciousnesss was not only frowned upon, but effectively put quite beyond the pale as an area of experimental investigation. Even the "father" of modern-day cognitive neuroscience, George Miller, warned in his classic text *Psychology: The science of mental life* (1962) that consciousness was a poorly defined and slippery concept that psychologists would do well to avoid if possible. Despite these warnings, many cognitive psychologists and neuropsychologists working in the latter parts of the 20th century felt that their work touched on aspects of consciousness: Baddeley, for example, thought of his working memory central executive as a "conscious" control system (Baddeley, 2001), and Sperry and colleagues were aware that data from their investigations of people who had undergone the split-brain surgical procedure (see Chapter 3) might also inform ideas about the nature of consciousness.

In fact, it is unclear quite when or how consciousness became, once again, an acceptable area of study for researchers, although the change certainly occurred within the working life of the first author. Some have argued that the widespread availability of in-vivo imaging techniques, permitting correlation between subjective experiences and objective brain activations, was a tipping point (e.g., Frith et al., 1991). In our view, another contributing factor has been the realisation (probably felt by most researchers at some stage in their careers) that the methods of conventional experimental neuropsychology mean that it can, for the most part, only address certain (arguably rather superficial) types of question. Whatever the reason or reasons, having languished on the sidelines of scientific psychology for more than a century, consciousness has quite suddenly become a respectable and even pressing domain of neuropsychological and neuroscientific inquiry.

However, we should also sound a note of caution because despite its newfound legitimacy, many researchers have argued that some aspects of consciousness will *always* remain beyond the parameters of psychological investigation. Indeed, returning for a moment to Pinker's tripartite conceptualisation of it, other authors, notably Chalmers (1995), have argued that the question of how physical processes in the brain give rise to conscious subjective experiences— sometimes called "qualia" (this would be "sentience" in Pinker's terms)—and whether such qualia are ever truly accessible to anyone other than the person having the experience, remains a moot point. One might ask, for example: Is my impression of the colour blue the same as yours? In Chalmers' terms, this is the "hard—others such as Searle (1992) might say intractable—problem" of consciousness, in comparison with access awareness and self-awareness, domains that lend themselves slightly more readily to experimental enquiry.

CONSCIOUSNESS AND NEUROPSYCHOLOGY

In this section we briefly review some of the material described elsewhere in this book that we consider to inform (or be relevant to) ideas about consciousness. To avoid unnecessary duplication, we simply list these to enable readers to refer back to such "points of interest" as they wish:

- In Chapter 1 we described some recent research on a region of medial parietal lobe known as the precuneus. One (of several) feature of this region is that it is more active when the respondent is awake but not actively engaged with an overt cognitive task: during meditation for example. It also becomes more active when there is a task requirement to manipulate imagery from a personal viewpoint or perspective. We suggested that a prudent interpretation of the functional significance of the precuneus may be that it is involved both in supporting self-referential mental representations and more generally in the modulation of consciousness, or even as an element in a wider consciousness network.

- In Chapter 3 we discussed some of the consequences of undergoing the split-brain procedure. One of the more intriguing findings to emerge from this work was that after surgery, the right and left hemispheres sometimes appeared to function as separate conscious entities. An early illustration of this was provided by Sperry (1968) who reported the anecdotal experience of a split-brain patient perplexed to be reaching into her cupboard with her right hand for a pink dress, only to find her left hand then reaching in for a blue one. In another example, a patient could not explain why he was drawing a picture of a car with his left hand; the actual reason was that an image of a vehicle had just been briefly presented to his (non-speaking) right hemisphere. Such observations initially prompted both Sperry and Gazzaniga to suggest that split-brain patients had dual consciousness; although Gazzaniga et al. (2002) later revised his views by suggesting that in fact only the left hemisphere is able to engage in "high-level" consciousness, roughly equivalent to Pinker's "self-knowledge"—an idea that we briefly return to towards the end of this chapter.

- In Chapter 4 we described the phantom limb phenomenon, and we suggested a number of mechanisms that might explain how it arises. Clearly people with "phantom" experiences would normally claim to have unimpaired consciousness, but their experiences are relevant to this discussion because such individuals develop a conscious (sentient) awareness for something that is, in fact, absent: a limb, breast, or genitals for example. Moreover, "dissociative-like" experiences can quickly be induced in intact individuals (as described in Box 4.2). These two examples illustrate that conscious awareness is not inextricably linked to sensory or even perceptual processing, but is in fact some way removed from both.

● In Chapter 7 the issue of consciousness cropped up several times in our review of memory and amnesia. First (as we noted earlier), the central executive component of working memory in Baddeley's model is widely regarded as an attentional control mechanism, and there has been an implicit assumption that the system as a whole plays a role in consciousness (Baddeley, 2001). Second, review of cases like HM suggests that amnesia may, in some instances, be restricted to remembering that depends on conscious retrieval of material, with "procedural memory" being preserved. And third, this debate has been broadened into consideration of other distinctions between declarative and non-declarative memory. Three experimental procedures—priming, classical conditioning, and implicit learning—have been used to explore effective memory (which does not appear to require conscious awareness) in healthy individuals.

● In this chapter we have reported several instances of abnormal or dysfunctional consciousness in the context of attention; hemineglect and Balint's syndrome are just two examples. In crude terms these disorders represent impaired conscious awareness (here we see the intimate link between consciousness and attention) for half, or all, of the visual field. Note also that in hemineglect at least, closer observation of the nature of the deficit again raises questions about the extent to which information on the neglected side is, in fact, being processed semantically despite not registering consciously.

● In Chapters 10 and 11 we will encounter further examples of neuropsychological cases or phenomena that inform particular aspects of consciousness, especially in Pinker's third domain of "self-knowledge". Damage to specific regions of the frontal lobes (medial orbital regions in particular) can impair appropriate social functioning (as in the case of Phineas Gage). Dorsolateral damage can affect access to information and thus "self-knowledge". And more widespread frontal damage (probably including damage to the anterior cingulate) can impair executive control more generally. The point of these examples is that deficits are apparent without the individuals being consciously aware of them. In the case of impaired social functioning this can, of course, have serious if unintended consequences, leading to confrontations with the police or worse.

INTERIM COMMENT

We have identified the above areas of interest to underline our earlier point that many of the things that neuropsychologists are interested in *say something* about the nature of (impaired) human consciousness. In the following section we consider some additional examples of psychological research (not reviewed elsewhere in this book) which also inform current thinking about consciousness. We hope we can convince you that no matter how difficult it may be to do research on consciousness, to continue to ignore it on the grounds that it is beyond investigation altogether would be misleading, if not negligent. On the contrary, the examples in both the previous section and the one that follows show that researchers are now beginning to chip away at the "consciousness edifice", and make real progress in the process.

However, two general points should be made before the next section. First, despite our intuitive sense of the importance of consciousness, we need to be aware that a vast amount of psychological processing occurs without conscious awareness. Having learned to drive a car, for example, you do not re-run the conscious agonies of coordinating your interaction with the clutch, brakes, and steering every time you get into a vehicle in the way you did when you were learning to drive. In fact the process of acquiring skills is marked by the gradual replacement of conscious (deliberate) control with more automatic control (Shiffrin & Schneider, 1977) which can be plotted and observed using functional imaging techniques (Petersen et al., 1998). If we go back to the driving analogy, you may well have experienced arriving safely in your car at your destination without very much (or even any?) recollection of the journey there (see Norman and Shallice's ideas on supervisory attention in Chapter 11). Second, we are also generally oblivious to (i.e., not consciously aware of) the intermediate component stages in most psychological processes in which we routinely engage. For example, we are not aware of the process of feature binding that takes place in the course of object recognition (Humphreys & Riddoch, 2001). Our sentience (to use Pinker's term again) is of the complete object (an antique spoon that someone is showing us for example), which, perversely, we may then begin to analyse consciously in a deconstructive way in terms of its individual features: how shiny it is, its feel, size, value, and aesthetic appeal, and so on. Similarly, the act of "reading" tends only to engage consciousness at the final stage of semantic processing of whole words or even sentences, not, for example, during feature detection of individual letters, although reading clearly involves letter identification.

An excellent example of how conscious awareness is about the complete "percept" rather than any intermediate processes leading to it is provided by the famous Rubin vase/silhouettes illusion (see Figure 9.16). No matter how many times you have seen it (and therefore know the trick), your brain does not allow you to see intermediate or mixed-up percepts; you either see the vase or the two faces. (See Windmann et al., 2006, for a review of attentional control over this and other bi-stable visual stimuli.)

PSYCHOLOGICAL OBSERVATIONS RELEVANT TO CONSCIOUSNESS

We now turn to consider briefly three paradigms from experimental psychology of relevance in our consideration of the nature of consciousness. These are *the readiness potential*, *attentional blink*, and *inattentional/change blindness*, which we describe below, and we comment on their importance for consciousness in the interim comment section that follows.

FIG. 9.16 The Rubin faces/vase illusion, one of several bi-stable illusions. At any one time, viewers report seeing either the faces or the vase, never an intermediate or ambiguous image.

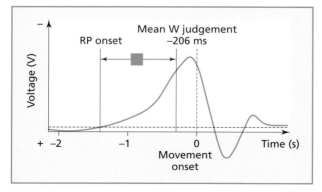

FIG. 9.17 Pooled results of Libet et al.'s study of the readiness potential (RP). The RP can be detected up to 1.5 seconds before movement onset, and up to 1 second before reported conscious awareness of intention to move (W judgement).

The readiness potential (bereitschaftspotential)

It is possible to record a negative ERP (usually from the SMA area of the frontal lobes) that builds up over a period of 1 or 2 seconds prior to an intended movement. Libet et al. (1983) adapted this paradigm by inviting respondents to make periodic key presses "whenever they felt the urge to", and additionally to indicate, by noting the position of a hand on a slow-moving clock face (which eliminated movement reaction time), the point at which they became "aware" of their "intention" to make a movement. Typical results for this experiment are shown in Figure 9.17. They indicated that conscious awareness of the intended movement typically occurred about 200 ms before the movement itself. A rather more surprising finding was that the readiness potential was detectable (as a negative-going voltage change) some 350 ms or more before this. In other words, conscious awareness of the intention to make a movement occurred at least a third of a second *after* electrical changes anticipating the movement were clearly measureable in the SMA. Sirigu and colleagues (2004) have recently confirmed Libet et al.'s original findings. Haggard and Eimer (1999) repeated this experiment with a further modification in which respondents could also choose which hand to make the movement with. Separate potentials were, additionally, recorded for each hand/hemisphere. Haggard and Eimer confirmed the occurrence of a readiness potential several hundred milliseconds before awareness of the intention to move, although "awareness" corresponded more closely to the lateralised potentials relating specifically to the particular hand about to make the movement. Conscious awareness thus seems to be more closely time-linked to selection of a specific movement than the general imperative to move, although it still came after it.

Attentional blink

In the simplest version of this paradigm, a respondent views pairs of visual stimuli such as short words or four-digit numbers. Each presentation appears only briefly (for about one-tenth of a second or less) and is immediately followed by an irrelevant mask (to eliminate visual after-traces called iconic images) before the second image is shown. If the gap between successive stimuli is less than 500 ms and the respondent has to "attend" to the first of the two images, there is a good chance that the second image will not be reported at all. For obvious reasons, this phenomenon has been dubbed "attentional blink". A recent study by Sergent et al. (2005) employed this paradigm and additionally recorded separate ERPs to both the first and second images. The researchers found that when the interstimulus interval (ISI: the gap between the first and second image) was about 250 ms, detection of the second image was severely compromised compared to another condition in which the ISI was about two-thirds of a second. Poor detection was related to ongoing processing of the first image, as reflected by the continuing ERP to it, and the absence of a separate fully developed ERP to the second image. In other words, respondents failed to detect the second image because they were still "consciously" processing the first. This effectively occupied their attention, causing them to neglect the second image. A schematic diagram illustrating Sergent et al.'s stimulus sequence is shown in Figure 9.18.

Inattentional/change blindness

Inattentional blindness may occur when a participant is paying attention to one particular task (say, a visual search task) but other non-task-relevant stimuli are periodically presented. When later quizzed as to whether anything else (other than the visual search stimuli) had appeared on screen, a significant proportion of participants will say no. Simons and Chabris (1999) described a dramatic and

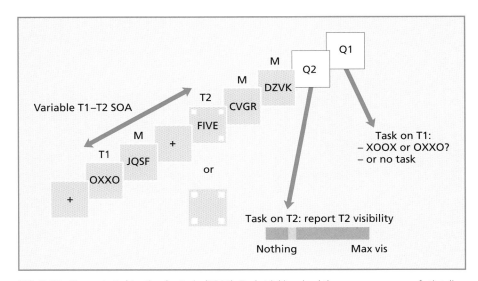

FIG. 9.18 Sergent et al.'s stimulus train (2005). Each trial involved the same sequence of stimuli. The critical ones are those presented at T1 (either OXXO or XOOX) and T2 (a number [FIVE in this example] or BLANK). Both are followed by a mask (M). The sequence is completed by two question cards: Q2 asks whether anything was seen at T2, and Q1 asks what was seen at T1. In this study the time gap between T1 and T2 was either 258 ms or 688 ms. Source: Reproduced by permission from Macmillan Publishers Ltd: *Nature Neuroscience* (Sergent, Baillet, & Dehaene, 2005), © 2005.

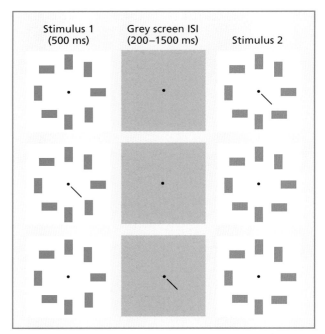

FIG. 9.19   The stimuli used in Simons' (2000) study of change blindness. Top row: when the cue is indicated by the pointer with the second image, change blindness is often apparent. Bottom row: when the cue is indicated as soon as the first image has been replaced with the grey screen, there is a marked reduction in change blindness. (For completeness the middle row shows Simons' control condition when attention was directed with the initial stimulus and little or no change blindness resulted.) Source: Simons, D. J. (2000). Current approaches to change blindness. *Visual Cognition, 7*, 1–15. Reproduced with permission.

humorous example of this phenomenon. Their respondents had to watch a short film of two teams of people playing "catch" with a ball: they were told to pay particular attention to just one of the teams. At one point, a person in a gorilla suit walked "into shot", beat their chest in authentic gorilla style, and walked off again. Despite this intrusion, about half the observers failed to spot anything untoward!

Change blindness is a closely related phenomenon that has recently been examined by Simons (2000) and reviewed by Rensink (2002). A respondent may be required to view a stimulus array similar to that shown in Figure 9.19 (top left-hand image) for 500 ms. This is followed by a grey screen mask which lasts for up to 1.5 seconds, to be followed by a second array that is either identical to, or subtly different from, the initial array (see Figure 9.19 right-hand image). Even when directed to the part of the array that might have been changed, about 50% of respondents failed to notice any difference. This "change blindness" should be compared with the situation in which the respondent is cued (with an arrow) to focus on part of the array when the grey mask appears (the first array has, of course, disappeared at this point). Now respondents nearly always correctly identify a change (see bottom row of Figure 9.19). "Spot-the-difference" games of the sort that sometimes appear in popular magazines essentially tap the same phenomenon.

INTERIM COMMENT

At first glance, these three examples may seem to be of little interest for students of consciousness. However, each actually says something rather important: Libet et al.'s observations indicate that changes in the brain related to an intended action precede conscious awareness of the intention to act. This has important consequences for people who believe in **free will** because it strongly suggests that the "intention" is already being processed before awareness kicks in. It also undermines a long-standing theory of how the brain works, attributable to Spinoza (1632–1677), and known as dual-aspect theory. This argues that the mental state of consciousness and physical brain activity form two sides of the same coin, so the temporal delay seen in Libet's paradigm would not be predicted by it (there should be no delay). However, we see that conscious awareness still has a potential benefit in this situation because it occurs in time to allow the respondent to stop (or modify) an action before it actually occurs.

Attentional blink shows us that conscious awareness of a stimulus (access awareness in Pinker's scheme) involves effort and uses up resources, which may curtail or even preclude attention to succeeding stimuli. Remember that

KEY TERM
Free will: A philosophical term for the capacity of rational agents to choose a course of action from among various alternatives.

attentional blink *only* operates if the person has to process (attend to) the first image. The phenomena of inattentional and change blindness have been interpreted as showing that, contrary to our intrinsic sense of having a complete image of *the world before us*, we actually have a somewhat partial view which, according to Lamme (2003), is nevertheless given privileged status by attention. If that status is achieved, other stimuli may go unnoticed. Thus once again we see the intimate relationship between conscious awareness and attention, and we return to this issue below.

CONSCIOUSNESS AND THE BRAIN

Two methods lend themselves to establishing the areas of the brain that subserve consciousness. First, we can simply compare activations in the brains of individuals with impaired, disordered, or altered consciousness to those recorded from normally conscious people. Second, we can compare, within individuals, levels of activation when they are performing a task (usually something fairly demanding) presumed to involve consciousness with levels of activation when they are resting. Although neither method is foolproof, reassuringly similar findings emerge from each line of research. Baars and colleagues (Baars, Ramsoy, & Laureys, 2003) employed the first, admittedly somewhat crude, method in measuring functional

changes (reduced PET activation compared to conscious control participants) in four types of unconsciousness: coma, persistent vegetative state, general anaesthesia, and sleep. Their findings are illustrated in Figure 9.20. In the three clinical states, fairly widespread bilateral hypo-metabolism was seen in a distributed network comprising dorsal and medial frontal and parietal regions. Similar, though less pronounced, reduced metabolic activity was observed in healthy individuals during slow-wave sleep.

Petersen et al.'s (1998) study, mentioned earlier, employed the second method. They compared PET activations in verbal (word generation) and spatial (maze-learning) tasks when respondents were naïve to each task, thus necessitating plenty of conscious effort, with activations once the tasks were learned. Their findings are illustrated in Figure 9.21. Although different regions were activated in the two tasks, frontal and parietal activation, common to both tasks during skill acquisition, clearly diminished with practice, implicating their involvement in conscious effort but not well-rehearsed tasks.

Obviously, Petersen et al.'s study is not specifically about consciousness; we are inferring that different levels of conscious effort would be required at different stages of skill acquisition, and participants were, of course, conscious throughout.

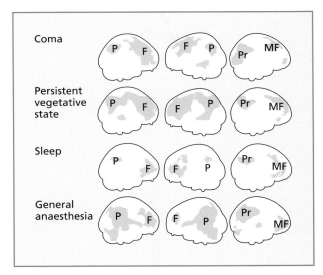

FIG. 9.20 Regions of hypofunction in different types of non-consciousness (Baars et al., 2003). Reduced PET activations (compared to conscious control participants) in four types of unconsciousness: coma, persistent vegetative state, general anaesthesia, and sleep. There is widespread bilateral hypo-metabolism in each clinical state in a distributed network comprising dorsal and medial frontal and parietal regions. Similar, though less pronounced, hypofunction was seen in healthy individuals during slow-wave sleep. Source: Baars, B. J., Ramsoy, T. Z., and Laureys, S. (2003). Brain, conscious experience and the observing self. *Trends in Neurosciences, 26,* 671–675. Adapted with permission, © Elsevier, 2003.

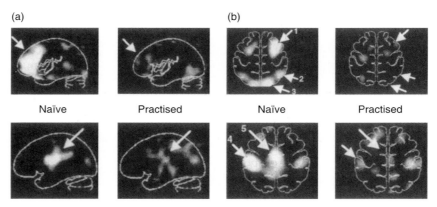

Naïve   Practised   Naïve   Practised

FIG. 9.21   Petersen et al.'s (1998) study of brain activation at the beginning of a task and once it has been learned. PET activations in (a) a verbal task and (b) a spatial task when respondents were naïve to each task (first and third columns) and when they had learned them (second and fourth columns). Frontal and parietal activation, common to both tasks during skill acquisition, clearly diminished in relation to reduced need for "conscious effort" once the skill was acquired. Source: Petersen, S. E., Van Meir, H., Fiez, J. A., and Raichle, M. E. (1998). The effects of practice on the functional anatomy of task performance. *Proceedings of the National Academy of Sciences*, 95, 853–860. Reproduced with permission.

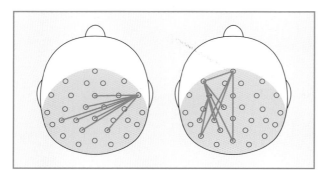

FIG. 9.22   Rodruguez et al.'s (1999) study of EEG phase synchrony to face and non-face stimuli. A schematic diagram depicting EEG desynchrony (in the 180–360-ms latency period) in the left figure in response to the random doodle, and greater EEG synchrony in the right-hand figure during the same latency period to the image of a face. Source: Reprinted by permission from Macmillan Publishers Ltd: *Nature* (Rodriguez et al., 1999), © 1999.

Indeed, differentiating the effects of consciousness from other psychological processes such as familiarity, learning, attention, and so on is a particular problem for this sort of research. To try to circumvent this problem, McIntosh, Rajah, and Lobaugh (1999) devised a PET study involving a simple visual discrimination task in which participants learned to respond to one stimulus and ignore a second. There were, however, two tones, although respondents were not explicitly briefed about these: one signalled the imminent presentation of a visual stimulus and the other the absence of a stimulus. There were three blocks of trials to enable the researchers to plot any associative learning between auditory and visual stimuli; participants were subsequently divided into those who noticed the association and those who did not. The most pronounced differential level of activity to tones between the "aware" and "unaware" groups was recorded in the left prefrontal cortex (BA 9), suggesting that this region was related to conscious awareness of the significance of the tones. However, this formed part of a more extensive circuit which included the right prefrontal cortex, and superior temporal lobes, cerebellum, and occipital cortex (all bilaterally).

For a more detailed analysis of the temporal effects of conscious processing researchers employ EEG (or ERP) methods. For example, Rodriguez et al. (1999) used a 30-electrode EEG procedure to measure the degree of neuronal synchrony (coincidental firing of neurons at different cortical locations) to images that resembled faces when seen "the right way up" but appeared to be meaningless "doodles" when inverted. Their findings are illustrated schematically in Figure 9.22. Marked EEG synchrony was only seen for the faces. This was detectable for about 350 ms after the image had been shown and ranged over extensive regions of occipital, parietal, and frontotemporal cortex, especially on the left side. We should, however, sound a note of caution at this point because, whereas at one time long-range synchronous firing was thought to be *the* neuronal signature of consciousness (Crick & Koch, 1990), it is now regarded as a necessary *but not sufficient* feature of it, possibly related to "feature binding" (Enger & Singer, 2001), as happens when a viewer puts together facial features to perceive an entire face.

Other researchers have emphasised one additional feature of neuronal activation that distinguishes between conscious and unconscious experience—that it must be "recurrent" (i.e., bidirectional, also sometimes called "re-entrant"). Imagine a visual input exciting neurons further and further forward in the ventral processing stream (see Chapter 8): researchers think that conscious recognition of the stimulus will nevertheless only occur when recurrent excitation (back in the direction from which it came) occurs. This can be illustrated very easily with reference to backward masking. A mask presented about 40 ms after a target stimulus will prevent the target from being consciously perceived if its (the mask's) forward progress along the ventral pathway is sufficiently forceful to inhibit any recurrent processing of the target (Dehaene et al., 2001). Astonishingly, this can happen even if the mask itself is presented so briefly as to be invisible (Lamme, Zipser, & Spekreijse, 2002).

In summary, brain studies of consciousness prompt the following tentative conclusions: Consciousness seems to be associated with widespread increases in activation, sometimes likened to "amplification", in various cortical regions (and subcortical structures, particularly the thalamus, have also been implicated: e.g., Tononi & Edelman, 1998). The extent of this activation/amplification will vary depending on the nature of the task, although conscious effort invariably recruits frontal (and anterior cingulate) regions in addition to other temporal and parietal regions. At the neuronal level, long-range synchronous processing seems to be a necessary, but not sufficient, condition for consciousness. Extensive recurrent processing, on the other hand, may be both necessary and sufficient for it. A stimulus that fails to achieve such processing is unlikely to be consciously perceived.

GLOBAL WORKSPACE THEORY (GWT)

GWT emerged almost 20 years ago (Baars, 1988) as a conceptual model of high-level cognitive processing. Over the intervening period, as research into consciousness has gathered pace, both scientists and philosophers have realised that GWT may provide a heuristic account of the neural architecture of consciousness itself. Despite this, it is important to realise that GWT presently remains a conceptual rather than physiological model. Moreover, although we will describe the general features of GWT, many questions, some of which we also identify in Box 9.2, have yet to be satisfactorily answered. In other words, although there is considerable interest in GWT as a model of consciousness, there are several versions of it. We should also note that GWT is a "work in progress": accounts of it by the same authors have, in some instances, changed significantly over time (e.g., Dehaene, Kerszberg, & Changeux, 1998 vs Dehaene et al., 2006).

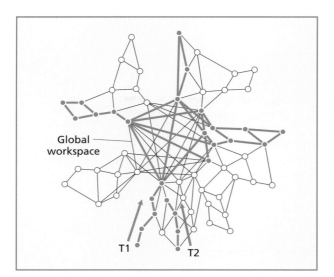

Global
workspace

T1   T2

FIG. 9.23 Dehaene's (2003) schematic of a global workspace network. Two stimuli (T1 and T2) compete for entry into the global workspace (depicted by the interconnected network). T1 gains access and is broadcast throughout the network. T2 is consequently prevented from accessing the workspace. Adapted from Dehaene, S., Sergent, C., and Changeux, J.-P. (2003). A neuronal network model linking subjective reports and objective physiological data during conscious perception. *Proceedings of the National Academy of Sciences, 100,* 8520–8525. Reproduced with permission.

A schematic diagram of a global workspace is shown in Figure 9.23. It is envisaged to be an extensive neuronal network probably involving prefrontal, anterior cingulate, and other thalamo–cortical interactions (as illustrated in Figure 9.24). The basic idea of GWT, as it applies to consciousness, is that at any given time we only have conscious access to a small proportion of all ongoing cognitive processing and there is a constant competition between (unconscious) cognitive processes for access to consciousness. These competing influences can, additionally, be biased by top-down (attentional) or bottom-up influences such as stimulus salience (a loud noise or a bright image). Cooney and Gazzaniga (2003, p. 162) have referred to the conscious awareness that results as:

> . . . *a fluctuating stream of transiently self-sustained, self-modifying workspace states, the characteristics of which are postulated to determine the contents of the subject experience of the individual* . . .

Access to the global workspace is not *just* competitive: it operates on a "winner-takes-all" basis. However, although conscious experiences may have fleetingly "won out" to reside here, their occupancy of the workspace is likely to be short-lived as other competing interests gain assent. Nevertheless, occupying the workspace does bestow two privileges: first because "winner-takes-all" operates, brief competing influences will, in effect, be prevented from gaining access unless they can "trump" the current "privileged" contents. This can be seen very clearly in the fate of the second stimulus in the "attentional blink" phenomenon, and is illustrated in Figure 9.23 by the failure of T2 (the second stimulus) to gain access to the workspace currently occupied by T1 (the first stimulus). Second, material currently in conscious awareness is "privileged" in the sense that it can be "broadcast" across the global workspace to be available to (and perhaps to influence) other modular processors such as those concerned with language output or attention.

Thus far our account of GWT would (we hope) be widely accepted by most consciousness researchers. The arguments begin (and quickly go way beyond the remit of this book) when we look more closely at the overlap between workspace occupancy and conscious awareness. To give just a flavour of the ongoing debates, consider the perspective of Baars and colleagues (Baars, 1998). They use the metaphor of "the theatre of the mind" to represent the sum of neuronal processing in the brain: Actors on the stage represent the potential contents of consciousness, and the "spotlight" of attention, falling on a few or even just one actor, represents full conscious awareness. In this scheme, attention is the means of bringing material into consciousness (the attentional spotlight). Baars later added the "active working memory elements" to his model (Baars, 2003), subsequently clarified by Baars and Franklin (2003) as encompassing "reportable" mental rehearsal and visual imagery, and the conscious elements of the central executive. This view has been even more forcefully stated by Maia and Cleermans (2005) who have suggested that attention, working memory, cognitive control (the central executive again?), and consciousness depend on a single mechanism, conceptualised as a global workspace with strong top-down control from the prefrontal cortex.

Now consider an alternative perspective such as that shared by psychologist Lamme (2003) and philosopher Block (2005). They have argued that there is a need to distinguish between the core and fringes of consciousness—called, by Lamme, access awareness and phenomenal awareness respectively. Access awareness would be equivalent to Baars' spotlight, but phenomenal awareness is proposed to account for instances when it seems that information is briefly available to the individual but "forgotten" or "erased" before it can be reported. (In fact, this also resonates with Pinker's distinction between *access to information* and *sentience* or basic phenomenal awareness.) For example, in Simons' change blindness study reviewed earlier, a cue presented *after* the first array had been replaced with the grey screen effectively eliminated the effect (i.e., no change blindness). So remnants of the no-longer-displayed array must have been briefly "accessible" when the cue appeared. Lamme, in fact, likened phenomenal awareness to "iconic" memory, whereas access awareness was likened to working memory. A consequence of Lamme's ideas is that many inputs may reach the conscious state of phenomenal awareness, and attention selects from these the inputs that will be consciously reported.

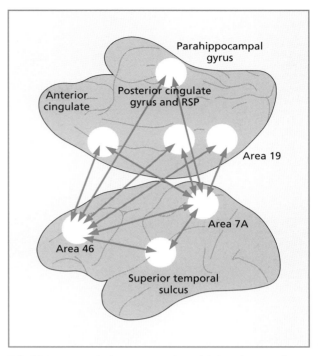

FIG. 9.24   Anatomical components in a global workspace. The global workspace is envisaged to extend bilaterally across much of the cerebral cortex. With permission, adapted from Goldman-Rakic (1988), the *Annual Review of Neuroscience, 11*, © 1988 by Annual Reviews.

To bring the debate up to date, consider the conflicting views of Dehaene et al. (2006) and Koch and Tsuchiya (2007). Dehaene et al. have argued that only true consciousness permits "reportability". If a respondent cannot provide a report of an event or stimulus, it cannot be considered to have entered consciousness. On this basis, Lamme's "phenomenal" consciousness is not true consciousness, and Dehaene et al. prefer to use the term "preconscious" for this type of processing. Information in preconsciousness nevertheless may cause "recurrent" excitation in the ventral stream which may last for a short period (perhaps 1 or 2 seconds) after removal of the stimulus, and may thus be accessible to true consciousness if top-down influences (such as a relevant cue) provide the necessary attentional amplification. In other words, a "trace"—in effect, a fleeting iconic (visual) or echoic (auditory) memory—may remain, and be available and accessible to true consciousness if attention is directed towards it, which is exactly what happens in the Simons "change blindness" paradigm. Incidentally, in this model, even recurrent excitation would be necessary *but not sufficient* for conscious awareness, which also requires top-down directed attention. As in Baars' model, attention is a mechanism for permitting entry into the global workspace, and thus into full

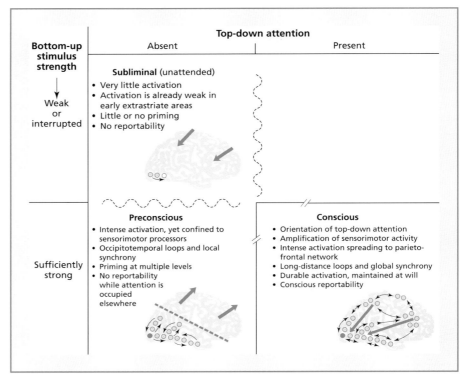

FIG. 9.25 Dehaene et al.'s (2006) tripartite model of consciousness and attention. Reportable conscious awareness is only possible if stimulus strength is sufficiently strong and top-down attention is directed to amplify it. If attention is directed elsewhere, strong stimulus strength alone will not be sufficient to bring about conscious awareness. However, this state of preconsciousness may lead to full conscious awareness if attention is redirected sufficiently quickly. Some stimuli never acquire sufficient strength to enter conscious awareness and are likely to remain subliminal and unattended. Source: Dehaene, S., Changeux, J. P., Naccache, L., Sackur, J., and Sergent, C. (2006). Conscious, preconscious and subliminal processing: A testable taxonomy. *Trends in Cognitive Sciences, 10*, 204–211. Reproduced with permission, © Elsevier, 2006.

consciousness, and the boundary between preconsciousness and full consciousness is sharp. Dehaene et al.'s (2006) model, which, for completion, also includes an illustration of subliminal (non-conscious) processing, is represented in Figure 9.25.

Koch and Tsuchiya, on the other hand, take issue with the idea that consciousness should be defined by reportability, citing a number of instances when attentional processing is apparent without consciousness: Male and female nude images attract the viewer's attention even when the images are rendered invisible (and thus unreportable) by means of a masking procedure called (appropriately perhaps) flash suppression (Jiang et al., 2006). Similarly, a degree of conscious processing seems possible with minimal top-down attention: as, for example, in dual-task studies where a core task that is occupying attention does not necessarily preclude correct identification of a briefly presented image in the periphery (Braun & Julesz, 1998).

At this stage of the debate, it is difficult to know whether the preceding arguments are a case of "splitting hairs" or the delineation of a crucial distinction with profound consequences for cognitive psychology and neuropsychology. After all, almost everyone agrees that the contents of our conscious experience are ordinarily constrained by what we pay attention to. However, one additional piece of evidence garnered by the oldest psychological research method of all, introspection, suggests to us that consciousness is not quite the black–white issue that Dehaene et al. have implied: When you scan a visual scene (panning round a room for instance) you remain aware of parts of the visual field beyond your focus of attention, although your ability to provide a verbal description of peripheral items might be impoverished compared with a description of your current focus of attention.

So the debate continues, and both "attention" and "consciousness" still resist clear and unequivocal definition. However, it is reassuring to note that psychologists, neuropsychologists, neuroscientists, and philosophers are collaborating in efforts to clarify these interconnected issues once and for all. We have identified some of the questions currently attracting attention in Box 9.2.

Box 9.2 Unresolved issues relating to GWT and consciousness

- What is the exact relationship between GWT and attention?
- What is the exact relationship between GWT and working memory?
- Are there different types/levels of consciousness within GWT?
- What, exactly, is the relationship between synchrony, recurrent excitation, and GWT?
- Must the global workspace itself always involve frontal activations to cause conscious awareness?

SELF-KNOWLEDGE/AWARENESS

Pinker's third component of consciousness is self-knowledge or awareness. This *should* be of interest to neuropsychology because as we have seen, for example in our review of hemineglect, brain damage may lead to a revision of the parameters of self-awareness by rendering patients "indifferent" to half their visual field or, in the case of anosognosia, one side of their own body. However, in the clinical setting, leaving aside the impoverished self-awareness seen in gross neurological disease (such as late-stage Alzheimer's), psychiatry has in fact arguably shown more interest in self-awareness. Impairments of this sort are apparent in cases of body-dysmorphic disorder (Albertini & Phillips, 1999), other delusional disorders (Blakemore & Frith, 2003), and, most intriguingly, in certain cases of schizophrenia (Spence et al., 1997; Stirling, Hellewell, & Ndlovu, 2001).

Earlier in this section, we mentioned that their observations of post-recovery split-brain patients initially led both Sperry and Gazzaniga to speculate about the possibility that such individuals experienced a form of dual consciousness. Because of concerns about the authenticity of the early findings, Gazzaniga has subsequently revised his views, developing an idea earlier mooted by Bever (1983) that the left hemisphere has an enhanced role in high-level self-awareness, as both an "interpreter" of why events (both external and internal) occur, and a selector of appropriate responses (Gazzaniga et al., 2002). As Gazzaniga has argued, such a system would offer enormous adaptive benefit, enabling information about different events to be woven together into a causal chain to guide future behaviour.

Gazzaniga's evidence is somewhat anecdotal (mostly from split-brain patients), but worthy of review nonetheless. For example, in the small number of patients with both left and right hemisphere language skills, the left hemisphere is better at making associative links between pairs of stimuli. When asked to choose one of six possible words linking two tachistoscopically presented words ("bleed" would, for example, link "pin" and "finger"; "oven" would link "bread" and "roast"), left hemisphere performance was significantly better than right. In another tachistoscopic study, patients were briefly presented with images to the right and left of a fixation point: a snowy scene to the left (going to the right hemisphere) and a chicken's foot to the right (going to the left hemisphere) for example. Then they were asked to choose one cartoon from an array of pictures on the table in front of them to go with each of the tachistoscopically presented images. In this example, one patient chose a picture of a chicken with their right hand and that of a shovel with their left, both ostensibly correct. But when asked why they had made those choices, the patient confabulated (made up part of their answer) by saying the chicken went with the chicken foot (correct) and the shovel was needed to clear out the chicken shed (incorrect). In a final example, if certain commands were flashed to the right hemisphere (i.e., left of the fixation point), some patients could read the words and follow the command, to laugh or walk for example. But when asked why they were laughing to themselves or walking out of the room, they generated confabulated answers such as "I just wanted some fresh air". Confabulation was absent when commands were presented to the left hemisphere. In each of these examples it appears that the left hemisphere is interpreting actions initiated by the right, which itself is contributing little to the interpretive process.

Cooney and Gazzaniga (2003) have extended this logic to explain "anosognosia for hemiplegia" (unawareness of left-sided paralysis, usually associated with right hemisphere damage): If the area of the brain that normally signals a problem (i.e., right parietal lobe) has itself been damaged, there is, in the authors' words, "no system to file a complaint" (Cooney & Gazzaniga, 2003, p. 164). As the patient no longer registers the existence of "left limbs", the intact (left hemisphere) interpreter system concludes that everything must be OK!

INTERIM COMMENT

Intriguing though these ideas are, it is difficult to evaluate Gazzaniga's hypothesis for two related reasons: First, the proposal is primarily derived from observations of a very small number of split-brain patients (we encountered this problem in Chapter 3). Second, the findings themselves rely heavily (though not exclusively) on verbal report, which, for most split-brain patients, means output from the left hemisphere. So the hypothesis could be confounded given the functional isolation of the left from the right hemisphere in this syndrome. Extending the hypothesis to include neurological conditions like anosognosia does not provide a true test of it (although the findings are certainly consistent with it) because once again most forms of hemineglect are related to right-sided damage. Finally, although some brain-damaged individuals are unaware of their own cognitive impairments and also prone to confabulation (Joseph, 2000), many with pronounced left hemisphere damage are both well aware of their impairments and "enjoy" full consciousness. An "interpreter" function for the left hemisphere therefore remains, for the time being, an interesting possibility rather than an established fact.

NOTE

1   Some of Raederscheidt's self-portraits can be viewed at www.physpharm.fmd.uwo.ca/undergrad/sensesweb/

CHAPTER SUMMARY

Attentional mechanisms allow us to make the most of the cognitive limitations of the brain, which has evolved to permit detailed processing of a relatively small proportion of all the potential incoming sensory (and self-generated) material to which it has access. As researchers have examined attentional processes it has become clear that "attention" is not a unitary phenomenon, and it probably needs to be partitioned into a series of related but distinct domains.

Researchers have made progress in examining the processes involved in selective attention, and an evolving view is that the diverse findings (relating to early/late and object/space based attention for example) can be best understood if attention is viewed as a resource with a finite capacity. There is continued interest in distinguishing between pre-attentive processes and voluntary orienting in different types of visual search.

Both ERP and functional imaging research confirm that "top-down" (attentional) influences can effect cortical processing within a very short period of time following stimulus onset, and this appears to be a facilitatory one for the selected material. However, both the cocktail party phenomenon and negative priming remind us that certain non-attended material can also influence high-level (semantic) processing.

Several cortical and subcortical structures appear to be involved in mediating attentional processes. Posner's and Mesulam's theories have been further refined by LaBerge (1995, 2000) into a model that distinguishes between bottom-up (automatic/incidental/pre-attentive) and top-down (deliberate/executive) control. There is a growing consensus that top-down attentional processes overlap significantly with the central executive function of working memory.

Recent research into the neurological disorders of hemineglect and Balint's syndrome is reviewed. Particular attention is paid to the underlying pathologies of these conditions in the context of established visual processing streams in the cortex. Corbetta and Shulman's model of attentional control in the brain is described and reviewed in some detail.

Recent developments in our understanding of how the brain might "mediate" consciousness are considered within Pinker's tripartite taxonomy. Material is drawn both from other parts of this book and from experimental work described elsewhere to illustrate that psychology and neuropsychology are making important contributions to debates about the nature of consciousness. Global workspace theory is introduced as a conceptual model of consciousness, and we offer a flavour of ongoing debates about the parameters of such a system, and implicitly of consciousness itself, and its links to/overlap with attention and working memory.

Finally, we introduce Gazzaniga's ideas about the highest level of human conscious control (an interpreter/integrator function of diverse inputs/outputs) which, he has argued, depends on a left hemisphere located (or biased) region of the workspace.

CHAPTER 10

CONTENTS

10

Emotion and motivation

INTRODUCTION

Emotion is fundamental to human experience. Every action we take, every decision we make, has an emotional context and therefore all our cognitive functions are coloured by our emotional state. Similarly, motivation is crucial to real-life function. We do not perform cognitive operations aimlessly for no reason. We do things that will achieve outcomes that we need or want, or to avoid outcomes that would be harmful or unpleasant. The vast majority of our behaviour is aimed at either obtaining rewards (which can be tangible or more abstract—as we will see, social approval, inclusion in a group, altruism, and perceived status can all be extremely rewarding) or avoiding punishments (which can, again, be tangible or more abstract). Emotional responses are crucial to motivated behaviour; if something elicits positive emotions we will seek it out, while if something elicits negative emotions we will avoid it.

In the 17th century, the philosopher Descartes used the famous phrase "I think, therefore I am" to suggest that thought is what makes us who we are. Three and a half centuries later, in his influential book *Descartes' error*, Antonio Damasio (1994) argued that it is not only thought that defines us, but, more fundamentally, *feeling*. Logical thought does not make us human, rather it is the interaction between what we think and how we feel that is at the core of who we are and what motivates us to behave in the ways we do. Thus to understand human neuropsychology, we must explore the topics of emotion and motivation.

Given that many cognitive neuroscientists now accept the importance of emotion and motivation in the study of behaviour, it is surprising that, until recently, this topic did not have a place in most cognitive neuroscience or neuropsychology textbooks. Indeed, the first edition of this book did not cover the topic. The study of emotion and motivation has been a huge growth area in the last 5–10 years and this is reflected in the inclusion of chapters in the most up-to-date texts. So why have emotion and motivation been sidelined for so long? In his recent book, Ward (2006) argued that traditional cognitive psychology theories were derived from computer-based models of information processing. And computers, of course, do not compute emotions and are not motivated to behave.

This is a reasonable explanation; however other factors may also be important. Most significantly, the advent of brain-imaging techniques has allowed us to access emotional and motivational function in a way that was not previously possible.

Emotions are not easy to measure empirically. People can describe how they feel (or don't feel) and psychologists can observe behaviour and characterise it as normal or abnormal by reference to expected behaviour. However, there is no objective "right or wrong" when it comes to emotion. Patients can be given a memory test, or an attention test, and an objective score can be derived from the number of correct and incorrect responses. In the realm of emotions, quantification is far more difficult. Similarly, although psychologists can qualitatively assess the extent to which a patient is motivated, objectively measuring that motivation is considerably harder. Some attempts to quantify emotional and motivational function will be discussed below.

Functional neuroimaging has revolutionised the study of human emotion and motivation. We can put people in a scanner and measure directly their brain responses to emotional information or to motivational cues. This has allowed us to develop brain-based models of emotional and motivational processing. These models are proving particularly valuable in psychiatry, as most psychiatric disorders are characterised by emotional disturbances. It has also led to new areas of research opening up, in particular the field of "social neuroscience" which considers the basis of interactive and social behaviour, which is so fundamental to human experience. Although social neuroscience is largely beyond the scope of this book, we will briefly consider some of the basic ideas and approaches at the end of this chapter.

DEFINITIONS AND MEASUREMENT OF EMOTION AND MOTIVATION

DEFINING EMOTION

There is a wealth of language available for describing emotions. If you try listing words that describe subtly different emotional states, you will quickly discover just how rich our emotional vocabulary is. When did you last feel happy, sad, pleased, sorry, excited, disappointed, anxious, upset, elated, nervous, frightened, optimistic, disgusted, outraged, angry, embarrassed, smug, or apathetic? You can recognise and relate to all these (and many more) distinct emotional states. How do we distil this vast emotional experience into concepts that are experimentally useful?

One approach that has been used in psychology is to consider two dimensions of emotional experience. The first is pleasantness or unpleasantness; most emotions can be characterised as more or less pleasant. The second is intensity; an emotional experience can vary in the extent of its impact. For example, losing a favourite scarf or the death of a family member are both events that may make us sad. However the sadness is of a different order of magnitude in the two cases. Osgood, Suci, and Tannanbaum (1957) suggested that emotions can be classified according to these two dimensions of valence (pleasant vs unpleasant) and arousal (intensity). Factor-analytical studies in the last 50 years have failed to improve on this basic dimensional model.

An alternative approach has been to try to reduce the vast number of subtly distinct emotional states to a small group of universal basic emotions. This approach has its origins in the work of Charles Darwin who studied the emotional experience of people from widely different cultures around the world. He concluded that a core set of emotions with evolutionary significance cut across cultural divides and are universally experienced. These same basic emotions can also be identified in animals. In an attempt to operationally define these basic emotions, Ekman and Friesen (1971) focused on recognition of facial expressions. They concluded that regardless of culture, six basic emotional expressions could be recognised: happy, sad, fearful, angry, disgusted, and surprised. Although many psychologists are uncomfortable with reducing emotional experience to these six basic emotions, and it is clearly a simplistic categorisation, Ekman's faces have been widely used in the recent study of emotion, as we shall see.

DEFINING MOTIVATION

The concepts of emotion and motivation are closely related. Indeed, some emotion theorists (e.g., Davidson et al. 1990) have used motivation to define emotion, suggesting that emotions can be characterised as those that make us approach and those that make us withdraw. Emotions can thus be seen as reactions that dictate our motivated behaviour. The study of motivation is associated with very precise definitions and concepts based on an extensive animal literature. It is an interesting irony that motivation has been very little studied in humans until the last few years—but, by contrast, the animal literature has long been dominated by studies involving motivation. The complexities of animal learning theory, although applicable to humans, are beyond the scope of this book. However, certain definitions are important to establish.

Motivated behaviour is any behaviour or action performed to obtain rewards or avoid punishments. A **reward** is defined as anything an animal will work for, while a **punishment** is defined as anything an animal will work to avoid or escape. **Reinforcement** is the process whereby behaviour is modified by rewards and punishments and a **reinforcer** is any stimulus that elicits behavioural modification. A reinforcer can be primary (or unconditioned) or secondary (or conditioned). A primary reinforcer elicits motivated behaviour without any learning, while a secondary reinforcer only elicits the response after learning or conditioning has occurred. The classic example comes from "Pavlov's dogs". Pavlov observed that dogs automatically salivate on tasting appetising food. Food is a primary or unconditioned reinforcer. Presented with a novel food, dogs will not automatically salivate until they have tasted the food and learned that it is pleasant. Once this conditioning has occurred, dogs will salivate on seeing the food before any tasting has taken place. Taking this further, Pavlov realised that he could train dogs to salivate on presentation of a light or a tone, if this initially abstract stimulus reliably predicted food. The light or tone is referred to as a secondary or conditioned reinforcer. Pavlov's experiments are examples of classical conditioning, where learning occurs without any intervening action from the animals. Another type of learning is **instrumental learning** where animals learn to perform an action to obtain a reward or avoid a punishment. Thus a rat presented with a lever and a food dispenser can be taught to press the lever to obtain food.

As an example to illustrate these concepts, consider a situation where an animal hears a tone signalling that they will be given an electric shock a few seconds later. However, if they press a lever they can escape the shock. Here, the shock is a punishment, the unpleasant unconditioned stimulus that the animal will work to avoid. The tone is a conditioned, secondary reinforcer, something that the animal has learned to associate with shock, via classical conditioning, and responds to accordingly. Pressing the lever is an instrumental response, a motivated behaviour that the animal has learned will avert an unpleasant outcome. To illustrate the link between emotion and motivation, bear in mind that this process is driven by the basic emotion of fear. Electric shock causes instinctive fear and the tone comes to elicit fear after conditioning has occurred.

Salivating dogs and lever-pressing rats may seem a long way from complex human behaviours. However, the same basic principles govern almost everything we do. Over our lives we learn which cues signal positive and negative outcomes, and we learn how our actions and behaviours can increase the probability of positive outcomes and decrease the probability of negative ones. The complexity of modern human life raises some interesting theoretical questions. For example, is money a primary or secondary reinforcer? Humans will work for money and, to a certain extent, this is because money is a means to an end. We use money to buy things that are essential to life. However, perhaps money itself has become a primary reinforcer, given that we will continue to work for more money long after our basic needs have been met. Such questions are the province of social neuroscience, which we will consider briefly at the end of this chapter.

MEASURING EMOTION

As discussed in the introduction, empirical measurement of emotion is less straightforward than measuring memory function or object recognition. However, various techniques for accessing emotional function have been used. Self-report has always been an important tool for assessing mood state, with **Likert scales** relatively widely used. A Likert scale is a questionnaire response format where people are asked to choose a number corresponding to how they feel about a particular statement (e.g., 1 = strongly agree, 4 = neutral, 7 = strongly disagree). A similar approach is a visual analogue scale, a line 10 cm long marked with an extreme position at either end. Participants place a cross at the position on the line that best represents how they feel (see Figure 10.1 for an example). However, any type of self-report is, by definition, subjective and therefore experimenters have sought alternative approaches to measuring emotion.

One popular approach is to introduce an emotional element to a standard cognitive task and study how the emotional context affects cognition. An example of this is the van Restorff effect. If people are given a list of words to memorise, they will typically remember the first few and the last few words better than words in the middle of the list. However, if an emotionally salient word is included in the middle of the list (for example, a swear word), most people will recall this word

KEY TERM

Likert scales: A simple measure of subjective experience. Participants must make a mark on a line that corresponds to how they feel.

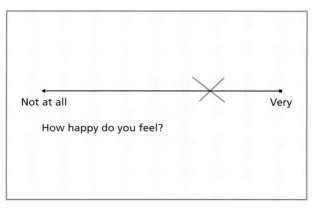

FIG. 10.1   An analogue scale for rating feelings.

much more easily than an emotionally neutral word in a similar position. The emotional content of the word is thus facilitating cognition. We will return to the effect of emotional context on cognitive processing later in this chapter.

Face emotion processing

A measure of emotional processing that is emerging as a literature standard is recognition of face emotion. The stimuli used are often Ekman's emotional faces or variants on them (see Figure 10.2). These are black and white photographs of actors making the expressions that correspond to the six basic emotions discussed above. One assessment tool based on Ekman's faces uses images that have been morphed using computer technology to express emotions to a gradual increasing extent. For example, mixing 10% of a fearful face with 90% of the same face with a neutral expression generates a face that is just very slightly fearful; 20% fear with 80% neutral gives a slightly more fearful expression, and so on up to 100% fearful. Participants can then be tested to determine at what point they recognise the fearful emotion. Most will not recognise a 10% fearful face as showing fear, but as the intensity of the fear in the face increases, the emotion will be recognised. This paradigm (Young et al., 1997), and variants of it, can be used to assess abnormalities in emotional recognition. For example, Dolan and Fullam (2006) have found that patients with antisocial personality disorder have impaired recognition of sad faces.

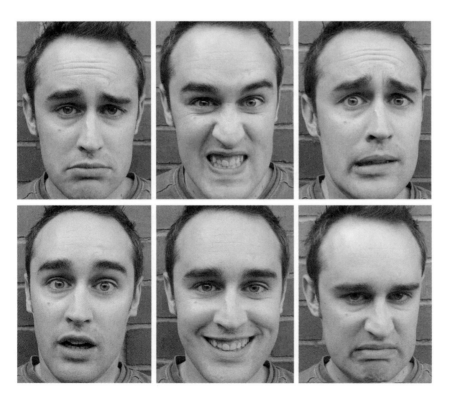

FIG. 10.2   The six universal expressions similar to those depicted in the Ekman face series (thanks to MTS).

FIG. 10.3 Examples of (a) positive and (b) negative emotional images. These photographs are typical of the emotionally arousing images found in the IAPS.

International Affective Picture System (IAPS)

It is possible to recognise emotional states in faces without experiencing an explicit emotional response. Thus it is possible to identify a face as sad or angry without feeling sadness or anger ourselves. Interestingly, fear may be something of an exception. From an evolutionary standpoint, fear in another human face is a cue telling us that a potentially threatening situation is present, which suggests that we too may have reason to be afraid. Think of those wildlife films where one animal in a herd spots a predator and makes a fearful response. The other animals in the herd instantly respond by showing fear, even if they haven't yet seen the predator themselves. However, in a laboratory context, the Ekman faces provide a test of how well participants recognise other people's emotions, rather than studying their own emotional responses. The IAPS pictures (Lang, Bradley, & Cuthbert, 1998) are a set of images designed to elicit an emotional response. Positive pictures include cute babies, kittens, etc. (things that make us instinctively think "aaah"). Negative pictures include scenes of decaying food, mutilated bodies, etc. (things that instinctively elicit a "yuck" response). These pictures have been extensively standardised using the dimensional measures of valence and arousal (see Figure 10.3).

Skin conductance

The IAPS pictures are designed to elicit emotional arousal. One way to measure this objectively, rather than relying on subjective report, is to use skin conductance response (SCR; also referred to as galvanic skin response or GSR). When we experience emotional arousal there is a slight change in the activity of the sweat glands which affects the electrical conductivity of the skin. This can be measured by placing sensitive electrodes on the tips of the fingers. Even subtle and transient arousal that is not apparent to an observer can be detected using this technique. For example, the IAPS pictures only elicit a fleeting emotional arousal effect, but this can be detected using SCR. A person whose emotional response is abnormal may not generate these SCR responses; for example, criminal psychopaths show some abnormalities in their responses to IAPS pictures (Levenston et al., 2000). You may recognise SCR as the technique underlying lie detector tests. The principle is exactly the same: Telling a lie causes a transient increase in emotional arousal and even if this is not apparent to the most skilled observer, the change in SCR can often be detected.

Mood induction techniques

Emotional pictures produce a fleeting emotional arousal effect. To achieve a longer-lasting change in emotional state, mood induction techniques have been developed. The aim of these is to elicit a short-term change in mood state; most typically, they attempt to elicit transient sad mood (often in studies relating to clinical depression). There are various ways this can be achieved and often a combination of methods is used to maximise the effect. Participants can be asked to think about sad events in their lives, or they may be played clips from sad films or sad pieces of music. Such approaches can successfully generate temporary sadness which influences cognitive performance and has a significant effect on brain function as measured by imaging techniques.

MEASURING MOTIVATION

As discussed above, motivated behaviour is behaviour that is aimed to obtain rewards or avoid punishments, and the study of motivated behaviour typically looks at how rewards and punishments affect learning. There is a huge literature in animal research but this has not readily translated to human neuropsychology. There are a number of reasons for this. First, punishments in humans present ethical problems. Electric shock can be used in animal studies but is not ethically acceptable in human studies. Primary rewards also present problems. An animal can be deprived of food for a period of time before an experiment, ensuring that a food reward is extremely motivating. Again this poses ethical problems in humans. Second, humans learn associations far more quickly than animals; it is much harder to study the process of acquisition when it occurs almost instantly. There are also many layers of prior conditioning and socialisation to deal with. For example, even a hungry human subject may not want to receive chocolate as a reward if they are trying to lose weight: unlike a hungry animal, which will always want food. Human subjects are also motivated in subtle ways by the social context of the study; for example, they may be trying to avoid looking stupid or, in some legal situations, they may want to appear less able to complete a task than they actually are. In spite of these problems, various experimental measures of motivated behaviour have been developed. Two of these are described below, the second of which has become probably the most widely used paradigm for studying reinforcement-related behaviour in human neuropsychology.

Conditioned preference paradigms

This is a paradigm that has been adapted directly from the animal literature. Subjects develop a conditioned preference for initially neutral stimuli if they are reliably associated with rewards (Baeyens, Hermans, & Eelen, 1993; Johnsrude et al., 1999; Niedenthal, 1990; Todrank et al., 1995). In the Johnsrude paradigm, participants are presented with abstract patterns in the context of a working memory task and these patterns are paired with food reward on a percentage of trials. In a second phase, participants are given a forced-choice preference test. Normal participants show a marked preference for the pattern paired most frequently with reward. Interestingly, because they believe they are performing a complex working memory test, their conscious attention is focused on this task and they are largely unaware of the reward-related contingencies. Thus although they reliably prefer the pattern most often paired with reward, if they are asked to explain their preference, they will say "I just like the shape of that one" or something similar. (You may notice similarities between this paradigm and "implicit learning" procedures described in Chapter 7.)

The Iowa gambling task

This is a more complex task developed by Damasio, Bechara, and colleagues that assesses how rewards and punishments influence decision making. Participants select cards from decks and receive rewards and punishments (in the form of play money) depending on their selections. The task is described in more detail in Box 10.1.

Box 10.1 The Iowa gambling task

Participants are shown four decks of cards. Unknown to them, two are high-risk decks and two are low-risk decks. The high-risk decks offer a prospect of immediate large rewards, but carry a cost of even larger long-term penalties. The low-risk decks offer smaller immediate rewards, but even smaller long-term penalties. Figure 10.4 shows a computerised version of this task. Over a series of trials, participants will gain most money by choosing cards from the low-risk rather than the high-risk decks. Participants repeatedly select cards from the four decks with the object of gaining as much money as possible. Initially the participant samples all four decks. They develop a short-lived preference for the high-risk decks based on the large rewards, but then as they experience the large punishments they start to prefer the safer low-risk decks.

This task was designed as a model for real-life decision-making situations where we must assess the risks associated with certain courses of action and weigh these against the potential benefits of those actions. Normal participants gradually learn the consequences of choosing from the different decks and then choose the low-risk decks on the majority of trials. Interestingly, they still occasionally opt for the high-risk decks, "gambling" on a favourable outcome. If SCR is measured while performing the task, these risky "gambles" are associated with elevated SCR indicating transient emotional arousal (Bechara et al., 1999). There is some debate about how soon people understand the contingencies of the task, with Maia and McClelland (2004) suggesting that understanding occurs earlier than Bechara et al. claim. Bechara et al. (2005) have suggested that this interpretation does not detract significantly from the theories they derive from using the task.

INTERIM COMMENT

Emotion and motivation are difficult to define and difficult to measure objectively. We can describe our emotional experiences in great and elaborate detail; however, obtaining an empirical measurement is extremely challenging. We have described various techniques for accessing emotional experience, but the reader will probably have realised that many of these approaches are rather oblique. We can produce a set of scores that provide a quantified description of a person's memory function, for example, but we cannot pin down their emotional function so easily. Although motivated behaviour has been widely studied in animals, it is less accessible to human research. There has been a dearth of paradigms for assessing motivated behaviour. The Iowa gambling task is emerging as a standard tool to study how rewards and punishments influence decision making; however this task only captures certain high-level aspects of motivated behaviour. As we shall see later, brain-imaging techniques provide an alternative approach for studying emotion and motivation, using paradigms that do not require an explicit behavioural measure. First, however, we will consider the classical neuropsychological literature on emotion and motivation.

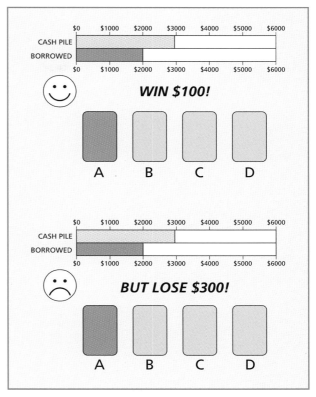

FIG. 10.4   The Iowa gambling task. Computerised version of the task showing a trial on which a participant receives a small reward but a large penalty after choosing one of the two high-risk decks. We are grateful to Professor Antoine Bechara of CALTECH for providing this figure.

EVIDENCE FROM NEUROLOGY AND NEUROPSYCHOLOGY

EFFECTS OF VENTRAL FRONTAL LESIONS ON BEHAVIOUR

One of the most famous cases in neurology is that of Phineas Gage. Details of Gage's case are given in Box 10.2. In brief, Gage was severely injured in an accident in 1848 which damaged his frontal lobes (see Figure 10.5). In spite of the dramatic nature of the accident, most of his mental faculties were well preserved afterwards. However, there were marked changes in his personality. This was the first case to suggest to neurologists that motivational and emotional functions could be impaired in isolation from marked cognitive impairments.

Gage's case has been revisited recently by Damasio (1994) who studied Gage's skull (stored at the Havard Medical School museum), and used imaging and computer techniques to reconstruct the brain lesion. The most extensive damage was to the ventromedial part of the anterior prefrontal cortex. Damasio (1994) also reported on the case of a "modern day Gage", a patient named Elliot who had

> ## Box 10.2 Phineas Gage
>
> Phineas Gage was a 25-year-old railroad worker in Vermont. In the summer of 1848 he was working on a railroad using explosives to blast a path through rock. The correct technique was to drill a hole, pack it with explosive, cover it in sand, "tamp" it down with an iron rod, light a fuse, and retreat to safety. Due to a momentary lapse in concentration the covering sand was not added to a particular hole and Gage tamped straight onto the explosive with the iron rod. There was an instant explosion which blew the iron rod up through Gage's cheek, his brain, and his skull before flying through the air and landing 100 yards away. Astonishingly, Gage was still conscious (though understandably rather stunned). He was able to talk while being transported to hospital and climbed out of the cart at the hospital by himself. He was patched up and treated for several subsequent infections, but within 2 months was pronounced cured. The vision in his left eye was affected, but otherwise his sensory processing, motor skills, language, and memory all seemed unimpaired. However, the accident had a dramatic effect on his personality. Although we are dependent on the rather moralistic accounts of the mid 19th century, it seems clear that Gage went from a pillar of the community to a rather feckless character who made very poor judgements and failed to function in society. The classic quote is "Gage was no longer Gage". The sad story of Phineas Gage ends in 1861 when he died of a series of intense seizures, doubtless a legacy of his accident.

surgery to remove a tumour from the orbital surface of the brain. After surgery his intellectual abilities were normal; however, he lost the social skills needed to function in the world. Furthermore, while he could describe the changes in his abilities, he appeared completely detached about them, describing them as if they were affecting someone else. Other patients with orbitofrontal lesions have also been described (Stuss et al., 1986) and social impairments are commonly reported. Patients have reduced social awareness and are less concerned about the societal rules governing behaviour. These are complex functions which we will return to later in the chapter. However, these neurological cases make it clear that normal emotional and motivational behaviour depends on the orbitofrontal cortex.

EFFECTS OF AMYGDALA LESIONS ON BEHAVIOUR

In animals, the effects of amygdala lesions have been extensively described. The term **Kluver-Bucy syndrome** (named after the scientists who first described it) is used to describe the multiple emotional and motivational deficits resulting from focal amygdala damage. In humans, however, focal damage to the amygdala is extremely rare. Although there are illnesses that do cause amygdala damage, the lesions are by no means confined to the amygdala but affect other structures as well. Neurosurgical procedures that selectively lesion the amygdala are occasionally used as a treatment for intractable epilepsy. Historically, psychosurgery has also used amygdalectomy to treat extreme aggression. Although it is important to remember that these cases are people whose brains were already

KEY TERM
Kluver-Bucy syndrome:
A collection of emotional impairments resulting from amygdala damage in animals.

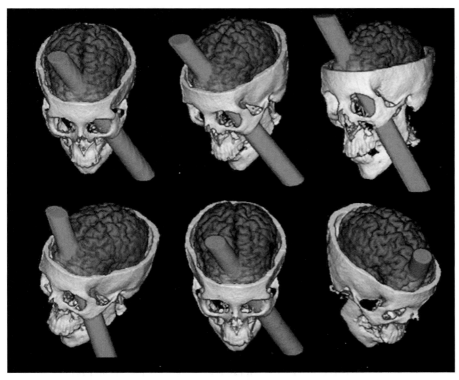

FIG. 10.5 Phineas Gage's accident. A computer-generated graphic depicting the path of the tamping rod (entering via the left cheek and exiting medially through the top of the skull). Source: Damasio, Grabowski, Frank, Galaburda, & Damasio (1994). Reprinted with permission from AAAS.

abnormal before the surgery, they do provide interesting information about the effects of amygdala damage. Sensory and cognitive functions are not typically affected to any significant extent. There is some evidence that amygdala lesions affect primary motivated behaviours, such as eating and sexual behaviour, at least temporarily. There is much stronger evidence that emotional behaviour is affected. Narabayashi et al. (1963) described 60 patients who had about one-third of their amygdala destroyed to treat aggression or hyperactivity. The majority of these patients showed decreased emotional excitability and "normalised" social function. They did not become emotionless but generally calmer and more cooperative. The effects of complete lesions of the amygdala have been somewhat mixed, but since these surgeries have only been performed on patients with extreme disturbances of emotional function prior to surgery, it is hard to interpret these findings. An interesting aside concerns the famous amnesic case HM (see Chapter 7) whose temporal lobes (including most of both hippocampi and amygdalae) were surgically removed. Although the neuropsychological focus has been on his memory deficits, a striking observation about his post-operative behaviour is that he was extremely placid and content at all times, even in circumstances where negative emotions might be expected (Corkin, 1984).

NEUROPSYCHOLOGICAL STUDIES OF EMOTION AND MOTIVATION

Amygdala damage and emotional faces

Patients with amygdala damage can recognise faces and can generate and communicate a normal range of facial expressions (Anderson & Phelps, 2000). However, they have selective impairments in their ability to recognise facial emotions. In studies of patients with bilateral amygdala damage, Adolphs et al. (1994, 1999) showed pictures of fearful faces and asked patients to rate how afraid the person was. Patients rated the degree of fear significantly lower than controls. This finding generalised to sadness (Adolphs & Tranel, 2004) and other negative emotions, but not to happiness. When patients with amygdala damage were asked to make more complex social judgements based on facial expression (how approachable or how trustworthy the person was) they also showed impairments (Adolphs, Tranel, & Damasio, 1998). Other expressions of social emotions (such as guilt and flirtatiousness) are also sensitive to amygdala damage (Adolphs, Baron-Cohen, & Tranel, 2002). More recently, Adolphs and colleagues have investigated these deficits in more detail and have suggested that patients with amygdala damage fail to process information conveyed in the eyes of faces. Eye information is particularly important in many emotions, including fear. In a single-case study they asked a patient with apparent fear recognition deficits to focus particularly on the eyes in the faces, and her deficit disappeared. However, the most recent study from this group adds another complicating factor (Gosselin et al., 2007). The same patient was found to be impaired at recognising scary music (and sad music to a lesser extent). Obviously eye information is irrelevant here and therefore the role of the amygdala in emotion recognition extends beyond evaluating information from eyes.

Amygdala damage and conditioned learning

Johnsrude et al. (2000) used the preference conditioning paradigm described earlier to assess performance in a group of patients with unilateral anterior temporal lobe resections. These patients all had some degree of amygdala damage, as well as damage to surrounding regions. A comparison group of patients with unilateral frontal lobe lesions were also assessed. Patients with frontal damage showed an impairment on the working memory task used to "mask" the conditioning procedure but established normal conditioned preferences for rewarded patterns. By contrast, the patients with amygdala lesions performed normally on the working memory task but showed severe impairments of preference conditioning. This clearly implicates the amygdala in human conditioned learning. The Johnsrude paradigm looks at conditioning with positive reinforcers. The amygdala has also been shown to be involved in negative conditioning in humans. Phelps et al. (1998) used a fear-conditioning paradigm in a patient with bilateral amygdala damage. A mild shock was paired with a visual stimulus on repeated trials. After the conditioning phase, the patient showed normal SCR response to the shock itself, but unlike control participants, she failed to show SCR response to the conditioned visual stimulus. The patient knew at a cognitive level that the stimulus predicted a shock, so this wasn't an inability to learn about relationships. However this knowledge failed to translate into an emotional response.

Orbitofrontal cortex and motivated decision making

The Iowa gambling task (described earlier) is probably the most widely used neuropsychological test of motivational function. Bechara et al. (1994) demonstrated significant impairments in patients with orbitofrontal lesions, with patients continuing to opt for high-risk decks. Strikingly, patients understood and could explain the contingencies. They had understanding of the task but did not use this to guide behaviour. Bechara et al. interpreted this as suggesting that orbitofrontal patients are insensitive to future consequences of behaviour, an explanation consistent with their observed everyday behaviour. This account has not been universally accepted; for example, Maia and McLelland (2004) have suggested that reversal learning impairments could explain Bechara's findings and this would be consistent with other reports of reversal learning deficits following orbitofrontal damage. However, in defence of their explanation, Bechara et al. (2005) cite the abnormal skin conductance responses (SCRs) observed in patients. Control participants showed elevated SCRs when they were about to make a high-risk choice. Patients with orbitofrontal lesions did not. Interestingly, they *did* show normal raised SCRs to receiving rewards and punishments.

Gambling impairments in orbitofrontal patients have also been reported by Rogers et al. (1999). Their participants were less able to make accurate judgements and more willing to take risks. Patients with bilateral amygdala lesions were also impaired on the Iowa task (Bechara et al., 1999) and failed to show anticipatory SCRs to risky choices. However, these patients also failed to show the normal elevation of SCRs in response to receiving rewards and punishments.

INTERIM COMMENT

The case study of Phineas Gage first showed that emotional and motivational behaviour could be affected broadly independently of cognitive function. Since then, further cases have confirmed that emotion and motivation constitute a dissociable domain of neuropsychological function. Two brain regions have emerged as particularly important: the amygdala and orbitofrontal cortex. The amygdala appears particularly important in controlling emotional recognition and conditioned learning, while the OFC controls decision making based on emotionally or motivationally salient information. As we shall see later, neuroimaging data have enabled us to observe the normal functioning of these two regions more closely. However, we will first consider how emotion interacts with other systems: first the somatic system and second the cognitive system.

THE INTERACTION BETWEEN SOMATIC AND EMOTIONAL SYSTEMS

The presence of elevated SCR responses to emotional stimuli makes it clear that emotional response can elicit changes in the physiological state of the body. SCR measures increased sweating, but increased heart rate and respiration rate are also observed in response to arousing stimuli. The relationship between the brain's and the body's response to emotional information has underpinned several important theories.

JAMES-LANGE THEORY OF EMOTION

William James and Carl Lange, two 19th-century psychologists, independently proposed that the feeling of emotion arises directly from the experience of bodily changes. The theory proposes that experiences elicit bodily changes and when we notice these we feel an emotion. Increased heart rate, sweating, etc. are thus not the *consequences* of emotional responses but the *causes* of them; we are afraid because our heart rate goes up rather than our heart rate going up because we are afraid. Lange was particularly forthright in his expression of the theory, claiming that vasomotor responses *are* emotions. However, there were various problems with this theory. First, it was felt at the time that the temporal pattern of events does not fit. Visceral changes were thought (wrongly as we now know) to be quite slow, while the feeling of emotion is very quick. Second, cutting nerves carrying visceral information to the brain in animals did not abolish their emotional responses. Third, visceral changes are similar for different types of emotional stimuli and this theory therefore struggled to explain the range of emotions we are capable of feeling.

CANNON-BARD THEORY OF EMOTION

Criticisms of the James-Lange theory led Cannon and Bard in the 1920s to propose that the feeling of emotion and the bodily sensations are independent. However, evidence subsequently suggested that the somatic and cerebral experiences of emotions interact with one another. In a famous (or infamous) experiment, Schachter and Singer (1962) demonstrated this interdependence. They told participants they were studying a vitamin supplement called Suproxin, when in fact they were injected with either adrenaline or placebo. Adrenaline is released by our hormonal system whenever we face a stressful situation, and increases blood pressure, heart rate, and respiration—all are indices of physiological arousal and therefore markers of the somatic experience of emotion. Schachter and Singer manipulated participants' interpretations of their physical sensations. Some were told that side effects of Suproxin were common and told what they might experience; others were given no information. The expectation was that the people who had been told about the "side effects" would attribute their experiences to the drug, while the naïve participants would be more likely to interpret their arousal as an emotion. Schachter and Singer went a step further and attempted to manipulate the emotion that these people would feel. The participants were required to wait in a room with another person, actually an experimental stooge. The stooge either displayed angry behaviour or was extremely happy and cheerful, in both cases engaging the participant in an interaction. Schachter and Singer observed and coded the actions taken by each participant, and also asked them to describe their emotion state. The participants who had taken the adrenaline but hadn't been told about its effects responded with emotions that matched those of the stooge (happy when the stooge was happy, but angry when he was angry). Those who had been warned of side effects and those who had taken a placebo did not display any pronounced emotion. This experiment shows that there is an interaction between physiological effects and situational cues in eliciting emotion, which is problematic for both the James-Lange and Cannon-Bard theories.

SCHACHTER-SINGER TWO-FACTOR THEORY

Based on their famous experiment, Schachter and Singer proposed a two-factor theory of emotion. This proposes that we don't automatically know when we are happy, angry, or afraid. What we feel is some generalised arousal, and to understand it we consider situational cues and use them to label what we are feeling. The two factors are therefore:

1 Some component of the situation must trigger non-specific arousal marked by increased heart rate, rapid breathing, etc.
2 The situation/environment is then analysed for cues telling us what has caused the emotion.

This theory provides a good explanation of the experimental finding; the adrenaline provides the arousal and the stooge situation provides the means of labelling that arousal as a defined emotion. Other experimental data also fit this theory. For example, in a bizarre experiment, Dutton and Aron (1974) had an attractive female experimenter interview male participants either on a normal floor or on a swaying rope bridge at a height. She gave her telephone number to the men. Of those interviewed on the bridge, over 60% called the woman, compared to fewer than 30% interviewed on solid ground. One of the stranger cognitive psychology experiments, this was interpreted as participants on the bridge experiencing fear but mis-attributing the arousal to attraction towards the woman.

Schachter and Singer's experiment and the resulting theory have been criticised for various reasons and it certainly seems clear that the theory is an over-simplification of emotional experience. A more modern attempt to link somatic states to emotional experience is Damasio's somatic marker hypothesis.

THE SOMATIC MARKER HYPOTHESIS

Damasio's theory (1994, 1996) revisits aspects of the James-Lange view in that it ascribes a critical role to bodily responses in generating emotional feelings. In brief, the argument is that an emotive stimulus in the environment elicits an associated physiological affective state. Experiences of these types of associations are stored as somatic markers. In future situations, somatic markers are automatically activated at a physiological level and bias cognitive processing and decision making. In some ways, Damasio's theory is a scientific formulation of the concept of a "gut instinct" based on prior experience. The biasing process may occur unconsciously or consciously, engaging higher cortical cognitive processing. Somatic markers are proposed to orientate us towards the most advantageous options, simplifying the decision process. At a neurobiological level, Damasio proposes that the amygdala and ventromedial prefrontal cortex are the core components of this hypothesised mechanism. The behaviour of patients with damage to the amygdala and, particularly, the OFC is consistent with the hypothesis. The poor decision making shown by OFC patients is hypothesised to reflect a failure of their somatic marker system to guide behaviour appropriately.

THE INTERACTION BETWEEN EMOTIONAL AND COGNITIVE SYSTEMS

Thus far, we have highlighted the dissociability of emotional and cognitive processing, for example, describing patients with intact cognitive function but impaired emotional decision making. However, it is clear that emotional and motivational factors influence cognition in a whole host of ways. Think about the days in your life that are most memorable and they are probably days when emotionally salient events occurred. Think how difficult it is to concentrate on a task when you are angry or sad. Or think how much more focused you may be on some cognitive activity if there is a tangible reward for good performance. These everyday examples highlight the fact that while cognition and emotion may be independent in many respects, they interact extensively in our day-to-day experience.

There is a considerable literature on emotional effects on cognition, which is beyond the scope of this chapter. However, we will consider a few illustrative examples of the interaction between emotion and memory. We know anecdotally that emotionally arousing events are more readily remembered. The effect of emotional arousal on memory has been studied experimentally by Cahill and McGaugh (among others). In one study (1995) they showed two groups of participants 12 images, each accompanied by a single sentence of narration. Many aspects of the stories were similar but there was a key difference in emotional content. One version of the story was uneventful, involving a boy and his mother visiting his father in the hospital where he worked. They see an emergency accident drill on the way and the boy ends up staying with his father at the hospital while his mother goes to run some errands. In the other version of the story, the boy is actually involved in a car accident and sustains serious injuries. He is admitted to the hospital and stays there when his mother goes home. In a memory test 2 weeks after being shown the stories, both groups were tested for their recall of specific details. The people who viewed the emotionally arousing story were able to recall more details and this was due to them having significantly stronger memories for the emotional parts of the story. In a follow-up study, Cahill and McGaugh gave a **beta blocker** to participants before presenting them with the emotional story. This drug blocks the effect of stress hormones on the brain and it effectively abolished the emotional enhancement of memory. Further, Cahill et al. (1995) showed that patients with amygdala damage do not show the normal facilitation of memory for the emotional version of the story, suggesting that the effect is normally mediated by the amygdala.

We have so far considered how emotion may enhance memory, however emotion can also have the oppposite effect. One example of this is "memory narrowing" whereby people remember less detail of an emotional scene or situation. Reisberg and Heuer (2004) have argued that emotional arousal leads to a narrowing of attention, such that peripheral information is less likely to be attended to and therefore more likely to be forgotten. A real-life example is what is termed "weapon focus" in crime investigation. Witnesses to a crime can often remember a weapon in great detail, because it is the most emotionally salient detail. However their recall of other aspects of the scene is far poorer than might be expected. Another way in which emotion can impair memory is emotion-induced forgetting, whereby emotionally arousing stimuli can lead to amnesia for

KEY TERM
Beta blocker: A drug that blocks the effects of adrenaline and noradrenaline.

either preceding events or subsequent events. If people are shown lists of words or pictures, they are significantly less likely to remember the stimuli appearing before or after arousing stimuli than other items in the list (e.g., Hurlemann et al., 2005).

Emotional effects on memory (and other aspects of cognition) have aroused interest in the study of depression (see Murphy, Sahakian, & O'Carroll, 1998, for review). In general, memory recall tends to be congruent with one's current mood, so depressed people are more likely to remember sad information. This has been shown empirically in a number of studies, with depressed patients routinely showing enhanced processing of negative information. It may also be of great clinical significance, effectively creating a vicious circle of negative cognition. Once someone is depressed, their memory and attentional systems are biased towards sad information and this focus on "the negative" serves to enhance and exacerbate the initial depression.

INTERIM COMMENT

We have discussed briefly some of the ways in which emotion and motivation interact with bodily states and with cognitive processing. While emotion can be viewed as an independent aspect of function, dependent on distinct neural systems (including the amygdala and ventromedial frontal cortex as key components), it is clear that the full complexity of human emotional experience depends on the interaction of this system with others. Damasio's somatic marker hypothesis is a currently influential account on the role our bodily representations play in our emotional life, and many modern researchers believe that physiological arousal, emotion, and cognition conspire to drive our more complex social behaviours. In Damasio's words, "The action of biological drives, body states and emotions may be an indispensable foundation for rationality" (1994, p. 200). Indirect evidence suggests that the amygdala and ventromedial frontal cortex are critical mediators of this interaction and neuroimaging techniques have allowed us to look directly at how these structures regulate motivation and emotion.

NEUROIMAGING OF EMOTION AND MOTIVATION

As we discussed in the introduction, emotion and motivation have been somewhat neglected realms of neuropsychology, perhaps reflecting the problem of studying these functions using classic neuropsychological approaches. Functional imaging has provided us with the means to study these processes without even needing objective measures. In a simple experiment, one could image a person observing emotional faces compared with neutral faces. We have no measure of what the person is doing, but the neuroimaging results will tell us whether areas of their brain are significantly more activated when the faces are emotional. This in turn tells us something about the neuropsychology of emotion. Thus functional imaging has led to an even greater explosion of data in this area than in the other domains of neuropsychology discussed in this book.

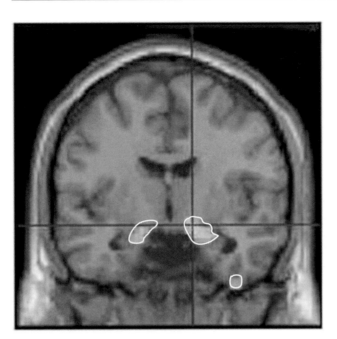

FIG. 10.6   Amygdala activation to emotional faces. Enhanced neural response in the amygdala associated with viewing aversive Ekman faces (sad, angry, fearful; see Figure 10.2) compared with neutral face expressions. Data obtained at the Neuroscience and Psychiatry Unit, Manchester.

NEUROIMAGING OF EMOTION
Imaging studies of face emotion

Imaging studies of emotion have predominantly looked at responses to emotional faces, often using the Ekman stimuli of the six basic emotions (see Figure 10.6). For fearful faces, amygdala response has been widely reported (Whalen et al., 2001), with increasing intensity of fearful expression resulting in increasing activity (Morris et al., 1996). In addition to the amygdala, fearful expressions have also been reported to activate the thalamus, anterior cingulate, and anterior insula (Morris et al., 1998). Facial expressions of anger activate regions of the temporal and prefrontal cortices, including anterior cingulate (Blair et al., 1999; Sprengelmeyer et al., 1998). Sadness, in contrast, activates right-sided temporal lobe regions and the amygdala (Blair et al., 1999). The processing of disgust has consistently been associated with insula response, increasing activity correlating with increasing intensity of disgust (Phillips et al., 1997). Disgust has also been shown to activate areas of the basal ganglia (Posamentier & Abdi, 2003). Happiness is the only positive emotion of the six and, interestingly, increasing happiness in stimuli has been associated with decreasing amygdala response (Morris et al., 1996).

Of the six basic emotions, surprise is the least investigated and has some distinct qualities. Specifically, surprise can be described as a "transitory emotion", in that it is briefly experienced and can change into other expressions depending on the nature of the surprise (Posamentier & Abdi, 2003). You may be surprised to see a long-lost friend and the surprise gives way to happiness. By contrast, you may be surprised to find your car windscreen smashed and the surprise gives way to anger. Kim and colleagues (2003) investigated brain responses to surprised facial expressions in relation to how they were rated (positive–negative) by participants. Negative ratings of surprised facial expressions elicited enhanced activation in the right amygdala, while positive ratings were associated with larger signal changes in ventral prefrontal regions.

Neuroimaging thus reveals a common network of regions involved in processing face emotion information, with some variation depending on the emotion involved. More recent studies have looked at face emotion processing in various patient groups as well as how social factors may influence normal face processing. One example of this is a study by Lieberman et al. (2005) who observed how race affects emotion processing. This study reported differential amygdala activity depending on the race of people depicted in the stimulus materials (photographs) and that of participants. Meanwhile Kaplan, Freedman, and Iacoboni (2007) have reported differences in responses to politicians' faces depending on the political affiliation of participants. These studies hint at the wide range of cultural and social factors that may influence how we process face emotion.

Imaging studies of other emotional stimuli

Face stimuli have been more widely used in imaging studies than other emotional stimuli. However there have been studies with emotional pictures and film clips. Lane et al. (1997) studied responses to emotional pictures using PET. Pleasant and unpleasant emotions were both associated with enhanced blood flow in regions including medial prefrontal cortex and thalamus. Unpleasant emotion additionally activated regions including parahippocampal gyrus, hippocampus, and amygdala. Pleasant emotion additionally activated part of the caudate. Similarly Paradiso et al. (1997) reported common activations for film clips eliciting different emotions, with some additional emotion-specific activations within the limbic system.

Emotional words have also been investigated. Whalen et al. (1998) found that the ventral anterior cingulate responded preferentially to emotionally toned words in a version of the Stroop paradigm. A similar finding has been observed in a study using an emotional go–no-go task with verbal stimuli (Elliott et al., 2000). In these studies, the valence of the words was incidental to the cognitive task. Direct evaluation of emotional valence of words (unpleasant and pleasant) has been shown to activate areas including ventral cingulate cortex, and left DLPFC. The evaluation of unpleasant words additionally activated subcortical regions, including the thalamus, caudate, and amygdala (Maddock, Garrett, & Buonocore, 2003). More recently, technical advances in stimulus delivery have allowed participants to listen to auditory input during noisy fMRI scanning. This has led to an interest in music as an emotional stimulus. For example, Koelsch et al. (2006) reported that unpleasant (permanently dissonant) music evoked response in amygdala, hippocampus, parahippocampal gyrus, and temporal poles. By contrast, pleasant music evoked responses in regions including inferior frontal gyrus and ventral striatum.

Imaging emotion generation

The studies described above have considered how the brain responds to external emotional stimuli, whether faces, pictures, words, or music. In general these studies have shown that both positive and negative emotional stimuli are mediated by neural responses in temporal and prefrontal cortices and limbic structures. Negative emotions tend to be more associated with amygdala responses while positive emotions may elicit differential prefrontal and striatal responses. Some of the stimuli used in these experiments may also have affected the emotional state of participants. Emotional film clips and music, in particular, can be used as part of mood-induction procedures as they can evoke a transient state of emotional experience. Happy music can lift our mood for example, while a frightening film clip may cause us to feel genuine fear. Neuroimaging studies have also looked more explicitly at the experience of emotion. Reiman et al. (1997) used either film clips or recall of personal experiences to generate emotional states in participants and found that the internal and external generation of emotion depended on subtly different brain regions. In a more direct attempt to separate perception of emotional content from subjective experience of emotion it was found that amygdala response was specific to perceiving emotion, while hippocampal and prefrontal responses were associated with subjective feelings of emotion (Garrett & Maddock, 2006). These studies are beginning to explore the subtleties of emotional experience in a way that is inaccessible to classic neuropsychology. As we shall see in the last section of this chapter, understanding how emotion is perceived and generated has enormous implications for psychiatry.

NEUROIMAGING OF MOTIVATION

Imaging primary reinforcers: Taste and smell

In much of the animal electrophysiological literature studying reward processing, the rewards used are either appetising food or drink. Imaging studies of people eating or drinking are problematic because they involve large amounts of head movements, and an important prerequisite of good imaging data is that participants keep their heads still! So, rather than studying people actually eating, an alternative approach has been to use tastes and smells strongly associated with food. An fMRI study of taste and smell stimuli (Francis et al., 1999) demonstrated neuronal responses in the medial OFC in response to the taste of glucose and to the smell of vanilla. The OFC is known to contain taste and smell receptors and it is possible that this is simply an effect of sensory stimulation. However, evidence that OFC also mediates motivational aspects of taste and smell comes from a follow-up fMRI study by O'Doherty et al. (2000). Even if you do not recognise the term, you will be familiar with an effect known as "sensory-specific satiety". If you have just eaten a large amount of a particular food, the reward value of that food rapidly diminishes; after one chocolate biscuit you may be very keen to have another but after five or six, your desire to eat more is substantially reduced. O'Doherty et al. scanned participants before and after eating a large meal and then presented smells of foods that were part of the meal and foods that were not. The OFC response was significantly reduced for foods that were part of the meal. This is evidence that the OFC codes motivational as well as sensory properties. Small et al. (2001) studied a similar phenomenon in people eating chocolate during PET scanning. Participants were fed large amounts of chocolate and asked to rate how pleasant it was at regular intervals. As expected, it became steadily less pleasant and, as the ratings decreased, activation in medial OFC diminished. Recently a study of five food flavours (O'Doherty et al., 2006) demonstrated differential responses in human ventral striatum that directly reflected subjective preferences for the flavours.

Imaging studies of financial reward and loss

In the neuroimaging context, most studies of reinforcement have used financial rewards. As we discussed earlier, money is not a primary reinforcer in the classic sense; it has no intrinsic physiological value, but it does have enormous social value, and is a strong behavioural motivator in most modern societies. From an empirical viewpoint, money is a very useful reinforcer, as various parameters (size of reward, probability of reward, etc.) can be systematically and objectively varied. One of the first studies of financial reward was a PET study (Thut et al., 1997) in which participants performed a simple cognitive task under the two conditions. In one they were simply told "OK" while in the other they received money for accurate performance. Financial reward was associated with activation in regions of an extended reward system, including midbrain, thalamus, dorsolateral PFC, and OFC.

In a more sophisticated study, Delgado et al. (2000) examined neuronal responses to receiving financial rewards and punishments. Participants were presented with a series of computerised cards on which they knew a number from 1 to 9 would appear, and had to guess whether the number would be greater or less than 5. They won money for correct guesses and lost money for incorrect guesses. Increased responses were seen in the dorsal and ventral striatum after a reward, while decreased responses were seen after a punishment. A similar study (Elliott, Friston, & Dolan, 2000) also assessed responses to winning and losing money and reported striatal responses to winning.

Imaging has also been used to look at important variables that affect motivation. One such variable is anticipation of financial reward. For example, Breiter et al. (2001) compared anticipation and outcome on a rewarded task and found that neural responses in regions including the extended amygdala, ventral striatum, and OFC were seen for anticipation as well as outcome. Another variable in reward studies is reward value, and O'Doherty et al. (2001) showed that medial OFC response correlated with amount of abstract ("play") money won on a task. We have also demonstrated a relationship between medial OFC response and reward value (Elliott et al., 2003). (See Figure 10.7.)

The most recent imaging studies of financial reward have used increasingly complex mathematical modelling to look at reward prediction (Knutson & Cooper, 2005; O'Doherty et al., 2006). These studies are predicated on the fact that reinforcement is critically dependent on the extent to which outcomes match expectations. If you fully expect to receive a reward, your response to it may be more muted than if it was at least partly unexpected. In fact if you do not receive an expected reward, the experience feels more like a punishment. Similarly, if you don't receive an expected punishment, you may feel almost as though you had received a reward (the positive experience of "getting away with it"). Thus reward and punishment responses in the brain are extensively modulated by expectations, and new modelling and analysis techniques in functional imaging are allowing these relationships to be explored.

Imaging gambling tasks

Neuropsychologically, the Iowa gambling task has been an important tool for studying how people translate knowledge of reinforcement contingencies into appropriate behavioural choices. Remember that patients with OFC damage understood the contingencies of the task, but failed to translate this knowledge into advantageous decision making. The Iowa task is extremely complicated and hard to use in an imaging context because there are so many variables to control. However, other gambling tasks have been used. Ernst et al. (2004) devised a "wheel of fortune" task where participants were presented with a circular spinner with blue and red segments of varying sizes. The size of the segments reflected the probability of winning on that colour and boxes below the spinner showed how large a win would be associated with each colour. Three types of condition were used:

1   High risk/high reward (e.g., a 10% chance of winning $7 vs a 90% chance of winning $1).

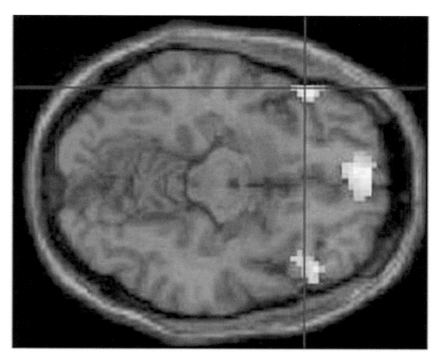

FIG. 10.7   Orbitofrontal activations to financial reward. Neural responses in the orbitofrontal cortex associated with varying the value of financial reward in a cognitive task. Data obtained at the Neuroscience and Psychiatry Unit, Manchester.

2   Moderate risk/moderate reward (e.g., a 30% chance of winning $2 vs a 70% chance of winning $1).
3   Equal risk/equal reward (a 50% chance of winning $1 on blue vs a 50% chance of winning $1 on red).

Participants chose the colour representing their preferred option. Ernst et al., found that the OFC was significantly responsive when participants were making their decision and that this response was particularly enhanced for high-risk choices. Rogers et al. (2004) also showed that the OFC was involved in making decisions on a gambling task.

These results essentially confirm the findings of studies in lesion patients. However fMRI allows us to explore the role of the OFC in more depth. Given the temporal resolution of fMRI it is possible to separate out some of the component processes of gambling tasks to determine exactly what the OFC is doing. In the Ernst et al. (2004) study, the OFC activity specifically related to the decision-making stage of the task. By contrast, once the decision had been made, anticipation of reinforcement was associated with activity in the ventral striatum. Studies have also allowed differences in individual behaviour on gambling tasks to be studied. Among normal people there is considerable variation in how willing someone is to take a risk. Some people are characterised as "loss averse" which means that they are less likely to make risky choices that could lead to a substantial loss. Tom et al. (2007) found that individual differences in loss aversion on a gambling task were predicted by neural responses in ventral striatum and prefrontal cortex. Studies like this hint at how fMRI can potentially be used to characterise normal variation in emotional and motivational behaviour, which is an extremely interesting area not accessible to classical neuropsychology.

INTERIM COMMENT

Functional neuroimaging has revolutionised the study of emotion and motivation in humans. In studies of emotion, imaging has confirmed the importance of the amygdala and ventromedial prefrontal cortex, highlighting a particular role for the amygdala in the recognition and experience of negative emotions. However, imaging has also identified a wider network of mostly temporal and frontal regions involved in emotion and has been able to characterise dissociable roles for these regions depending on the exact emotional context. For example, distinct regions have been associated with the perception compared to the experience of different emotions. In studies of motivation, the OFC has again emerged as a critical region, but imaging has also clearly demonstrated the importance of striatal structures. With increasingly sophisticated modelling and analysis techniques, it is becoming possible to identify the neural correlates of different components of human reward systems and thus gain a deeper understanding of motivated behaviour.

SOCIAL NEUROSCIENCE

Historically, neuropsychology has focused principally on how humans function in isolation; how we attend our environment, how we recognise things, how we remember things, and so on. Perhaps the one exception has been the study of language where almost any attempt to analyse communication necessarily involves considering the participant interacting with someone else. However, much of our real-life behaviour involves a highly sophisticated level of social interaction. This may be explicit, as when we are interacting with a group of other people in an overtly social situation. But it may also be implicit. Imagine sitting on your own thinking about your current concerns: maybe you're trying to make a decision about whether to apply for a particular job; maybe you're trying to remember a conversation you had last week; maybe you're trying to decide what to do at the weekend. All these things require you to think about social interactions. All involve you thinking within parameters imposed by your social and cultural experiences and values. We are intensely social animals and the social context affects most of what we do. In considering the social context of our behaviour, emotion and motivation are critical concepts. Social interactions involve emotional responses and social factors are important motivators of behaviour. For most of us, social acceptance and approval are very important and, consciously or not, play an important role in guiding our decisions and behaviour. The recent boom in emotional and motivational neuroscience has therefore led to the emergence of a new cognitive discipline. Over the last 2 or 3 years, the term "social neuroscience" has started to be widely used. Specifically, social neuroscience is the study of the brain basis of social behaviour. There are many fascinating issues and topics within this new discipline and we only consider a few illustrative examples here.

THEORY OF MIND AND EMPATHY

Theory of mind is the ability to represent the mental states of other people, to appreciate their beliefs about the world, which may be distinct from our own. Imagine you are out with a friend and while they are at the bar you move their bag out of someone else's way. When your friend comes back and reaches for their bag, you will realise that they don't know it is somewhere different and will point them to it. This seems trivial but is a vital skill. The bag was at position A. It is now at position B. You know that because you moved it there. But you also know that your friend wasn't there when the bag was moved to B, so you realise that they still think it is at A. You are seeing the world from your friend's perspective. Very young children don't have this ability. Imagine the same situation with two 3-year-olds (transposing the action to a playgroup rather than a bar of course!). When the owner of the bag returns, the child who has moved it will not think to tell them. That child knows that the bag is now at position B and in their mind that is just a fact about the world that *everyone* should know.

Normal children develop theory of mind and it represents an important developmental milestone. Children with autism may not develop normal theory of mind. Influential theories of autism (see work by Frith and Baron-Cohen or example) suggest that a core deficit is impaired theory of mind. One paradigm that has been used with children is the "Sally-Anne task" (Baron-Cohen, Leslie, & Frith, 1985). Children are introduced to two characters (Sally and Anne). Sally puts a marble in a basket while Anne is watching. Anne then leaves the room and Sally moves the marble from the basket to a box. Anne then comes back. The child being tested is then asked "Where will Anne look for the marble?" Over the age of 4, normal children will reply "In the basket". Autistic children typically reply "In the box". When questioned they show that they can remember that the marble was in the basket initially, but they fail to grasp that Anne's belief about the marble is different from the reality of where it now is. This finding has been reproduced in a number of studies. The autistic child or adult finds it very difficult to represent the mental states of others and appreciate that they may be different from their own. It should be noted that there may be other deficits associated with autism, and also that the theory of mind difficulties can be overcome in individuals, but it does appear to be significant in most autistic people.

Theory of mind has been studied using neuroimaging. A meta-analysis of imaging studies by Frith and Frith (2003) identified three crucial brain regions—the temporal poles, medial prefrontal cortex, and temporo-parietal junction—which play distinct but interconnected roles in normal theory of mind. These areas can be activated by various different paradigms involving theory of mind. For example, one study by Gallagher et al. (2000) looked at responses to cartoons. Certain cartoons involve theory of mind in order to get the joke, while others do not. Cartoons involving theory of mind resulted in greater activation of medial prefrontal cortex. Similar results were seen for story comprehension, where some stories involved a theory of mind component and others did not.

The concept of empathy is somewhat related to theory of mind. It also involves seeing the world from another person's point of view but is more concerned with feeling what they feel. If you see another person in distress, you will probably experience some fellow feeling. If the distressed person is someone you are close to, this may be particularly strong. In extreme cases, some people report feeling actual physical pain corresponding to the physical pain being experienced by a loved one. See Figure 10.8 for an example of a simple task probing empathy and theory of mind. Empathy has also been investigated using functional imaging and has been shown to depend on brain regions implicated in emotion: medial and ventral prefrontal cortex, temporal poles, and amygdala (Farrow et al., 2001; Lamm, Batson, & Decety, 2007; Vollm et al., 2006). See Figure 10.9 for

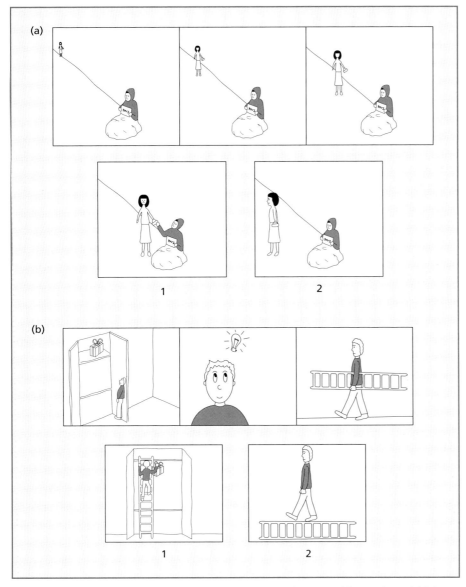

FIG. 10.8   Empathy and theory of mind cartoons. Stimuli used to assess (a) empathy and (b) theory of mind. Participants are asked to choose the frame (1 or 2) that best completes the cartoon. For the empathy cartoon, this involves choosing the picture that makes the person feel better, while for the theory of mind cartoon, it involves appreciating the intentions of the person. We are grateful to Dr Birgit Vollm, University of Manchester, for providing this figure.

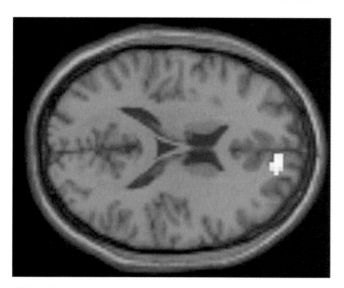

FIG. 10.9 Neural responses to empathy and theory of mind cartoons. Neural responses in medial prefrontal cortex to cartoons requiring an empathetic response. We are grateful to Dr Birgit Vollm, University of Manchester, for providing this figure.

medial prefrontal activation associated with empathy.

MIRROR NEURONS

In Chapter 5 we introduced the idea of mirror neurons, a type of brain cell that responds similarly when we perform an action or when we witness someone else perform the same action (see Box 5.5). Mirror neurons were first discovered in monkeys in the early 1990s. An Italian research team found individual neurons in the brains of macaques that fired both when the monkeys grabbed an object and when they watched another monkey grab the same object. Rizzolatti and colleagues, who made this initial discovery, believe that mirror neurons can explain how and why theory of mind and empathy may occur. If watching an action and performing that action can evoke the same response at a single neuron level, it is entirely plausible that watching an action and performing an action could also elicit the same *feelings* in people. From there it is a short conceptual step to understanding how observing an emotion can cause us to *feel* the emotion. Wicker et al. (2003) performed an imaging study of participants while they inhaled an unpleasant odour (butyric acid, which smells like rotten butter) and while they viewed a film of an actor pulling a disgusted face. The anterior insula was activated in both situations. Similarly, Keyser and colleagues have found that the same area of the somatosensory cortex was active both when participants were lightly touched on the leg with a soft stimulus, and when they viewed pictures of someone else being touched in the same spot. Also of interest is whether mirror neurons respond not only to other people's actions or emotions, but also to the *intent* behind those actions. Iacoboni et al. (2005) used fMRI to examine participants as they watched videos of a hand picking up a teacup. In one video, the teacup appeared on a table amid a pot of tea and plate of biscuits, suggesting that the hand was grasping the cup to take a sip as part of afternoon tea. In the other video, the table was messy and scattered with crumbs suggesting that tea-break was over and the hand was clearing the table. In a third video the cup was alone, with no context. Mirror neurons in the premotor cortex and other brain areas reacted more strongly to the same action when it occurred in a meaningful context, suggesting that the neurons are important for understanding intentions as well as actions. While this research is still preliminary, it is looking increasingly likely that mirror neurons will provide a crucial line of evidence for understanding social neuroscience.

SOCIAL COOPERATION

Another issue that has been studied in social neuroscience is how brain networks mediate social cooperation. Much of what we do is in collaboration with other people and therefore cooperation is an important social function. One tool that has been used to study cooperation in the neuroscience context is the Prisoner's Dilemma game. This is a paradigm borrowed from economics and has many variants. In the classic game there are two players, each of whom must imagine they have been imprisoned for a crime committed in conjunction with someone else. Both participants must choose whether to come clean or deny everything. The choices made by both influence their prison terms. For neuroscience purposes, a version of the game is generally used where the prison aspect is replaced by winning and losing money. Players can cooperate or defect. If both defect, both win a small amount of money. If both cooperate, both win an intermediate amount. If one cooperates and one defects, the cooperator wins nothing and the defector wins the largest amount. On a single trial it pays to defect. However if players complete a series of trials, the best strategy to maximise gain is mutual cooperation. If players establish mutual trust and cooperate each time, they always win the intermediate amount. When two normal participants play the game, mutual cooperation is generally the strategy that develops over a series of trials. However, the paradigm can be experimentally manipulated by making one of the participants an experimental stooge who may adopt a more or less aggressive strategy. The response of the true participant to different strategies can then be observed. In a functional imaging version of the paradigm, mutual cooperation has been associated with reward areas (medial OFC and striatum), suggesting that social cooperation is intrinsically rewarding (Rilling et al., 2002). Playing against a more aggressive player results in different activation patterns (Rilling et al., 2007), which also depend on personality variables. Interestingly, playing against a computer, rather than a human player, results in less extensive neural responses. The game is logically the same with a computer, but the social context is different. These results therefore highlight the importance of social context in determining patterns of neural response.

UNDERSTANDING SOCIAL NORMS

Our final example concerns various studies of social norms. These are studies that look at how our brain responses have been socialised by the implicit rules of socially acceptable behaviour. In a study by Berthoz et al. (2002), participants were presented with stories that involved the violation of a conventional social norm (for example, someone spitting food across the table at a dinner party because they didn't like the taste). These norm violations were associated with activation of lateral orbitofrontal regions. An interesting recent direction in social norm studies is "altruistic punishment". The premise of these studies is that in situations where someone else has broken a social or moral rule, we feel that punishment is appropriate and perhaps even desirable. DeQuervain et al. (2004) found that reward regions of the striatum were activated when participants administered an altruistic punishment, suggesting that punishing transgression is positively reinforcing. Singer et al. (2006) performed a two-stage study. In the first stage, participants played interactive games with other people, some of whom played fairly while others did not. Participants were then imaged while watching those other people apparently experiencing electric shock. When people perceived as fair were "shocked", empathy-related activations were observed; these were considerably reduced when people perceived as unfair were "shocked". Studies like this are beginning to tell us a great deal about how our social behaviour is mediated at a neuronal level.

IMPAIRMENTS OF EMOTION, MOTIVATION, AND SOCIAL FUNCTION

PSYCHIATRIC DISORDERS

Elsewhere in this book we have referred to the neuropsychological problems experienced by patients with psychiatric disorders. Cognitive dysfunction is a symptom of many psychiatric problems. However, almost by definition, psychiatric disorders are primarily emotional and a whole book (or several books) could be devoted to the emotional and motivational problems experienced by patients. People who are depressed have emotionally biased memory systems, as we have discussed. They also have profound problems with motivation; depressed patients may say that they simply cannot be bothered to engage in daily activities. Figure 10.10 shows attenuated brain responses in medial prefrontal regions associated with a motivational task in depressed patients. Bipolar depression (or "manic depression") is a distinct subtype of depressive disorder, characterised by both depressive episodes and episodes of mania. In the manic phase of the disorder, patients may be inappropriately euphoric and highly aroused, suggesting a complex imbalance in emotional systems. Mania has not been widely studied using imaging techniques, as this patient population is very difficult to obtain reliable images from.

Meanwhile, patients with anxiety disorders show disproportionate fear in certain situations. This is most obvious in patients with specific phobias who can be incapacitated by irrational fears about particular stimuli. Patients with

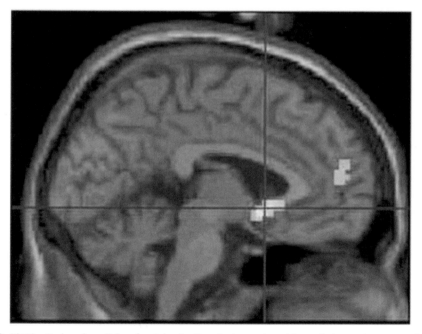

FIG. 10.10   Reduced medial prefrontal activations in depression. Attenuated neural responses in medial prefrontal regions in a depressed patient performing a financially rewarded task compared to a task with no rewards. Data obtained at the Neuroscience and Psychiatry Unit, Manchester.

addictions, whether to drugs, gambling, or sex, have a biased motivational system, such that they look to a particular stimulus for rewards to an extent that is detrimental to their social function. Eating disorders can also be characterised in terms of dysfunctional motivational states, such that the desire to achieve a perceived social ideal of slimness disrupts the basic physiological drive to eat.

If we consider the wider field of social neuroscience, more examples emerge. As we have seen, people with autism or Asperger's syndrome typically have problems with theory of mind. They find it extremely difficult to view the world from someone else's perspective. Meanwhile, people with antisocial personality disorder are thought to have deficits in empathy. They may be able to interpret the world from another rational point of view, but they do not have any sense of fellow-feeling. Finally, schizophrenic individuals who are paranoid or delusional can be thought of as interpreting social situations and interactions according to a completely skewed version of reality.

CHAPTER SUMMARY

Emotion and motivation are rapidly growing areas of study in cognitive neuroscience. Traditionally emotion and motivation have been difficult to study in a laboratory setting because they are such subjective concepts that are extremely difficult to quantify. In spite of these difficulties, some techniques have emerged allowing neuropsychologists to characterise emotional and motivational function in patients with circumscribed brain damage. From the classic case of Phineas Gage through to the modern series of studies by Damasio, Bechara, and colleagues, it is clear that two critical brain regions are the amygdala and ventromedial prefrontal cortex. Patients with damage to these regions typically have relatively spared cognitive function but pronounced impairments in emotion, motivation, and social function. Although these neuropsychological cases suggest a degree of independence between cognition and emotion, it is clear that the full range of emotional experience depends on interactions between cognition and emotion, as well as somatic responses. Emotion is associated with bodily responses as well as feelings, and both of these can colour how we perceive, interpret, and remember the world around us. Thus theories of emotion have attempted to explain the interactions with somatic states and with cognitive function.

Neuroimaging has led to huge advances in our understanding of emotion and motivation. These techniques essentially provide a human analogue of the electrophysiological techniques that have been a pillar of emotion and motivation research in animals. We can now look directly at what happens in people's brains as they experience different emotions or motivational contexts, without needing empirical measures of performance. Imaging studies of emotion have confirmed the importance of the amygdala and ventral frontal regions, as well as other limbic and frontal areas, but have also allowed more detailed exploration of how responses within this network depend on which emotion is involved, whether it is just perceived or actually experienced, and how it is generated. Ventral frontal regions and the amygdala also form part of the motivation circuitry, as well as striatal structures and other prefrontal areas. Researchers are now exploring how this human reward network responds under different conditions and how the different regions interact in different aspects of reward processing.

The explosion of interest in emotion and motivation has led to the emergence of a new discipline of social neuroscience. Our social interactions are dependent on emotional and motivational factors and neuroscientists are now starting to explore this wider context. For many, this is an extremely exciting new direction as it takes neuropsychology out of a sterile laboratory or clinical context and explores how our real-life behaviours are mediated by brain function. Social functions, as well as the basic component processes of emotion and motivation, are abnormal in many psychiatric disorders and therefore understanding these processes also has important implications for psychiatric research.

CHAPTER 11

CONTENTS

Executive functions

INTRODUCTION

The development of sophisticated neuropsychological testing techniques and the advent of in-vivo imaging have led to increased interest in the role of cortical regions, particularly the frontal lobes, in what neuropsychologists call "executive function(s)". However, it is important at the outset to be clear about the term itself, and the relationship between executive functions and the frontal lobes. Executive functions refer to a set of psychological attributes that are supervisory, controlling, and organisational. Although these skills are all critical for normal everyday behaviour, their somewhat abstract nature means that routine psychological assessments such as IQ tests or measures of sensory perception may fail to detect any executive dysfunctions. Executive functions include the ability to plan, initiate, and terminate actions, to think in abstract or conceptual terms, to adapt to changing circumstances, and to respond in socially appropriate ways. Individuals with impaired executive function show deficits in higher-level cognitive operations that require planning, flexible thought, and coordination of different subprocesses. Baddeley (1986) has used the term "dysexecutive syndrome" to identify these impairments.

At one time, psychologists used the terms "executive" and "frontal" in an almost interchangeable way because they believed that frontal lobe damage alone led to executive dysfunction. While this is often the case, we now need to qualify this relationship in two important though related ways. First, we should remember that the frontal lobes receive information from, and send information to, most other cortical regions and many subcortical systems (such as the basal ganglia, the limbic system, and the cerebellum) as well. Second, and consistent with the idea of distributed control, we find that damage to regions other than the frontal lobes can sometimes lead to executive dysfunction, although it remains the case that frontal damage is most frequently associated with it. For example, disorders characterised by basal ganglia pathology (Parkinson's disease being the most studied example) are often associated with deficits in executive function. The basal ganglia and frontal cortex are extensively interconnected and it seems that executive function depends on the functional integrity of this circuitry, rather than of the frontal lobes per se.

A further point should be made before consideration of the nature and causes of executive dysfunction. That is, executive function is less completely defined and understood than, for example, memory or attention. As yet, there is no clear agreement on the underlying causes of some of the executive deficits we will review, and therefore explanatory models of executive dysfunction (some of which we consider later in this chapter) may seem circular, overlapping, or of limited general application. Nevertheless, any comprehensive model of executive function must give due consideration to the range of psychological skills the frontal lobes and their connections subserve.

DOMAINS OF EXECUTIVE DYSFUNCTION

There remains considerable disagreement among researchers as to how to partition executive function (see, for example, Roberts, Robbins, & Weiskrantz, 1998). Historically, a sort of "mass-action" approach to frontal lobe function has been favoured, with the region assumed to act as a unit in the coordination of executive functions. More recently though, neuropsychologists have used dissociations to tease apart apparently independent components of executive function. Even so, it remains a matter of debate as to how many such components we need to consider. One way of looking at different aspects of executive dysfunction is to partition them into three domains, and we will consider:

1   impairments in the initiation, maintenance, and cessation of actions (action control);
2   impairments in abstract and conceptual thinking;
3   impairments in the ability to organise behaviour towards a goal.

However, readers should note that these "functional" domains do not map particularly well onto distinct "structural" frontal regions, so further revision of the fractionation of executive functions is likely in the future (see further discussion later in the chapter).

IMPAIRMENTS IN ACTION CONTROL

People with frontal damage often display what neuropsychologists call "psychological inertia" (Lezak, 1983). Although this can take a variety of forms, there are two basic components. First, appropriate actions may simply not be initiated: an individual may, for example, neglect personal hygiene, or there may be a marked reduction in self-initiated speech, even with repeated prompting. The individual seems indifferent to, and uninterested in, the world around them, and often (though not always) oblivious to their own indifference.

The second component of psychological inertia is characterised by difficulty in terminating or amending behaviour once started. It can be observed in the laboratory as well as social settings. The drawings in Figure 11.1a illustrate the attempts of one "frontal" patient to complete the "memory for designs test" (Graham & Kendall, 1960) in which a set of simple geometric shapes are shown one at a time for a few seconds, and the respondent then has to draw each one as soon as the design is covered up. Although the actual designs vary considerably in their complexity and format, the drawings by the frontal patient all look very similar (in comparison with the drawings in Figure 11.1b by a control participant), which is indicative of **perseverative** responding: repeating the same behaviour, or type of behaviour, again and again.

Both inertia and perseveration can also be seen in the pattern of responding of some individuals in tests of verbal fluency. When asked to name as many items as quickly as possible beginning with the letter "F", a patient with executive impairments may first generate words comparatively slowly, and then get "stuck in a rut" by generating only words that are interrelated; such as "*finger . . ., fingernail . . ., fingers . . .*" and so on. Sometimes erroneous (but semantically related) intrusions such as "*ring-finger*" may slip in.

Another behavioural manifestation of executive dysfunction (which overlaps in some ways with the next category of disorder) has been described by L'hermitte (1983) and L'hermitte, Pillon, and Serdaru (1986). The "environmental dependency syndrome" (as it has come to be known) describes a pattern of behaviour in which environmental cues trigger responses irrespective of their appropriateness at the time. For example, when shown into a room in which there was a table with a hammer, nails, and some pictures, one of L'hermitte's patients started hanging the pictures; another patient left to her own devices in a kitchen began washing the dirty dishes. This pattern of behaviour is sometimes referred to as "stimulus-driven" or "utilisation" behaviour, because the apparent impulsivity of such patients is influenced by immediate circumstances rather than the broader social context. Parents will recognise this as a common feature of child behaviour (perhaps not the washing up), and it is interesting to note that, in neurodevelopmental terms, the frontal lobes are one of the last cortical regions to mature (in late adolescence). However, "utilisation" can lead to embarrassingly inappropriate social behaviour in adults with frontal lobe damage, as happened when L'hermitte showed one of his patients a disposable cardboard bedpan, only for the patient to commence using it!

IMPAIRMENTS IN ABSTRACT AND CONCEPTUAL THINKING

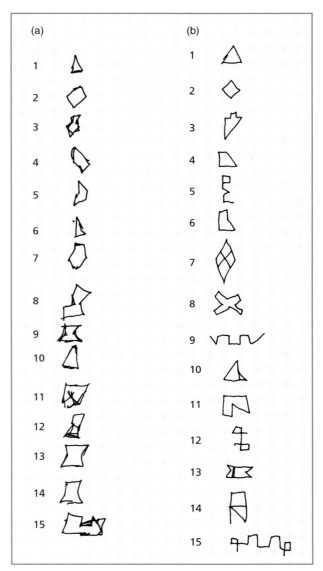

FIG. 11.1 The memory for designs test. The respondent views a series of abstract figures one at a time for a few seconds each. Immediately after each presentation, they try to draw the design. A control participant's drawings are shown in the right column (b). Although they are not perfect, this person scored zero errors. The drawings of the same figures by a patient with frontal lobe damage are shown in the left column (a). The patient's drawings provide an indication of perseverative responding: each drawing looks similar to the previous one. The patient's error score was > 20, which is indicative of marked damage.

A similar pattern of fixated or inflexible thinking is also seen in other manifestations of executive dysfunction. The Wisconsin card sort test (WCST) (see Chapter 2) was developed to examine concept formation and the ability of participants to overcome the tendency to perseverate. In this test the respondent must sort a pack of cards one card

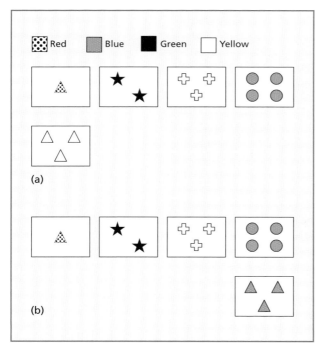

FIG. 11.2 Typical responses in the WCST. In (a) the unstated rule was "sort by colour". The participant's response is incorrect because they actually sorted by shape. In (b) the unstated rule was also "sort by colour", which the respondent did correctly even though the card differed from the matching cards in respect of both shape and number.

at a time so that each matches one of four "key" cards in some way. Each card differs in three dimensions (see Figure 11.2): the number of objects shown on the card (one, two, three, or four), the shape of the objects (circles, triangles, squares, or stars), and their colour (red, green, blue, or yellow). So, for each card, a participant can match it according to shape, number, or colour. As the participant places a card in a pile underneath one of the four key cards, they are told only whether or not the card matches according to the criterion the experimenter "has in mind". The idea is that by using this feedback, the individual will quite quickly learn (i.e., infer) the matching criterion, and sort subsequent cards according to it. After a number of correct sortings, the experimenter changes the matching criterion. (In some procedures, this is done without warning, but in the modified procedure, Nelson, 1976, participants are explicitly told that the former matching rule no longer applies.) People with frontal lobe damage generally learn to sort much more slowly than normal people but, in particular, they make many more perseverative errors, meaning that they continue to sort according to the previous matching criterion even though it no longer applies. This is most obviously apparent in Nelson's modified procedure (in which participants are specifically told that the rule has changed though not what it has changed to). Despite this instruction, some frontal patients will continue to sort according to the obsolete rule, showing an inability to think flexibly and change behaviour to adapt to the "new situation".

A variant of the WCST developed by Delis et al. (1992) required participants to sort sets of six cards each showing an object/drawing/word into two equal piles. The cards could be sorted according to several criteria including shape, shading, category of word written on each, and so on. Frontal patients struggled with this test in two characteristic ways. First, they were not very good at sorting the cards into meaningful groups at all, and second, even if they could sort as per the instructions, they struggled to describe the actual rule they were using.

Other tests that assess conceptual thinking are the Brixton and Hayling tests (Burgess & Shallice, 1997). In the Brixton test, participants must predict which of an array of numbered circles will be filled in on the next trial. This is determined by one of several simple rules and periodically the relevant rule is changed. Thus participants must learn a rule, apply it, and update it as necessary. Frontal patients make more errors on this task than controls or patients with posterior lesions (Shallice & Burgess, 1996).

The Hayling task consists of two sets of 15 sentences, each with the last word missing. The sentences are designed to strongly cue a particular final word. In the first task (Hayling A) participants must complete the sentence as quickly as possible with an appropriate word. For example: He mailed the letter without a . . . (stamp).

In the second task (Hayling B) participants must complete the sentence with any inappropriate word. For example: He mailed the letter without a . . . (gorilla).

This second condition is much more difficult, requiring participants to inhibit a cued prepotent response and to generate an entirely novel response. Patients with frontal damage are impaired on both Haylings A and B, but it is suggested that different fundamental processes underpin the impairments (Shallice & Burgess, 1996) with Hayling B capturing important aspects of executive function.

IMPAIRMENTS IN GOAL-ORIENTED BEHAVIOUR

Goal-oriented behaviour comprises various core aspects. One component is sequencing: we must generate a sequential plan of action incorporating various subcomponents in an appropriate order. Second, successful behaviour requires self-monitoring, essentially the process of checking that we are on track to achieve the desired result. Both of these components are sensitive to frontal lobe damage.

Sequential planning

Research suggests that individuals with frontal lobe damage struggle with tasks that, for successful completion, must be broken down into a series of subroutines to be completed in the right order. Problems may arise because of composite difficulties in sequential planning, memory, self-monitoring, and of course not losing sight of the overall goal (see Box 11.1).

Box 11.1 "Tea for two"

Consider the executive components involved in making a cup of tea:

- First there is, self-evidently, an overall goal that must be borne in mind as the tea-maker goes about their task.
- The task can be broken down into a number of subcomponents. What materials and items will be needed, and where are they in the kitchen?
- What is the appropriate sequence of actions? The kettle must be filled, the tea should go in the pot, milk in the cups, and so on.
- What about contingency plans? Perhaps the milk in the jug is sour? Is there more in the fridge? Is there any powdered milk? Did anyone want sugar? Are there any sweeteners instead?

The point of this example is to illustrate the range of psychological skills implicated in even this simple task: Our tea-maker has to have a strategy: they must sequence different elements of the task in the correct order; they must remember what has already been done, and what yet needs to be done; and finally they must be able to adapt the task to changing circumstances (if needs be) to fulfil the overall goal.

The example of making a cup of tea illustrates the vital importance of "temporal" sequencing in planning many actions. A study by Milner (1982) neatly illustrates the particular difficulty some frontal patients have in distinguishing between more and less recent events. Participants viewed a sequence of simple line drawings of objects one at a time. Every so often a test card would be shown that had two objects on it. On recognition trials, the respondent had to decide which of the two objects had appeared in the preceding sequence (one had appeared but the other was new). In recency trials, the respondent had to decide which of the two objects had appeared most recently. The recognition rate of frontal patients was comparable with that of control participants, but recency judgements were significantly impaired. In other words, frontal patients could not remember the order in which the material was viewed. Incidentally, there was also a laterality effect evident in this study giving rise to a double dissociation. Patients with left frontal damage fared worse with verbal material than with drawings, and patients with right frontal damage did worse with drawings than words.

The previous study shows that frontal patients struggle to memorise sequences—but do they also struggle in planning sequential actions? Petrides and Milner (1982) developed a disarmingly simple procedure to test this. Respondents were required simply to point to any item in a 3×2 array that they had not pointed to before. The array always contained the same six items, but their location was changed on successive trials. Frontal patients made significantly more errors than controls, suggesting a marked impairment in planning of sequential actions. Of course, this task relies heavily on working memory (remembering what you have already pointed to, in order to avoid doing it again), and we saw in Chapter 7 that central executive component of working memory is mediated by the dorsolateral prefrontal cortex (DLPFC).

Impaired planning of sequential action is also seen in tasks such as the "Tower of London" puzzle (Shallice, 1982). In this test there are three coloured balls, and three prongs. One can hold three balls, the second two balls, and the third just one ball. On each trial the balls are placed in the standard starting position and the participant must move them to a different specified finishing position in the least possible number of moves. Some trials require only two moves, while others require ten or more to reach the final configuration. Frontal patients are worse than controls on both simple and complex trials, although the gap widens on complex trials. The behaviour of frontal patients seems aimless and devoid of strategy. Even when they do solve the puzzle, it is as if they have stumbled across the answer rather than thinking it through step-by-step (see Figure 11.3). A computerised variant of the Tower of London task, dubbed the "Stockings of Cambridge" (part of the CANTAB battery; see Chapter 2) has been used to show explicitly that not only do patients with frontal damage solve fewer problems than controls, but they also solve problems less efficiently, tending to take more moves than the optimum number.

Self-monitoring

When neuropsychologists refer to self-monitoring, they are really talking about the reflexive skill of self-inquiry: "How am I getting along with this task?", "What was it I just did?", "How close am I to successful completion?" Time and again, both anecdotal and experimental evidence points to frailties in this intrinsic ability

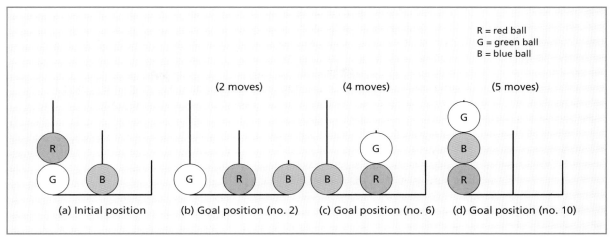

FIG. 11.3   The "Tower of London" test. Respondents may only move one ball from the top of a prong at a time. From a standard starting position (a) the participant might be asked to rearrange the balls in various ways that require two (b), four (c), or more (d) moves. Patients with dorsolateral prefrontal damage probably struggle on this test because their ability to plan a sequence of actions is compromised.

in patients with frontal damage. Anecdotally, case reports frequently allude to the frontal patient's inability to "keep on track" during prolonged tasks. When asked to copy one of several drawings on a page, they may start accurately, but then integrate material from one or more of the other drawings into their own. In a classic "real-life" study of the derailment that is seen in the goal-oriented behaviour of frontal patients, Shallice and Burgess (1991) set three patients a set of relatively simple tasks to complete. These included shopping for certain items, finding out some information about four queries (the price of a pack of tomatoes, etc.), and keeping an appointment. This was specifically not a memory test and respondents had a list of the tasks and instructions to follow. Nevertheless, each patient had difficulty completing the assignment. In one case an item could not be purchased because the shop did not stock the individual's favourite brand; in another, items were selected but not paid for; or, worse still, an entire component of the assignment was ignored. This is a particularly good illustration of the problems frontal patients have in achieving goals. They start with the best intentions, but are easily distracted, and are unable to get back on track because of an apparent lack of awareness about being blown off-course.

TASK SWITCHING AND MULTI-TASKING

The preceding section on goal-directed behaviour focuses on situations where a person has a single goal in mind and must sequence their actions to achieve that goal. However, executive functions are also thought to be called on in situations where people are required to perform more than one task, thus maintaining multiple goals. Typical examples of this are task switching (where people move between distinct tasks) and multi-tasking (where they attempt to carry out more than one task at the same time.

TASK SWITCHING

Everyday life requires frequent switching between different tasks. If I sit at my desk writing an email and the phone rings, I stop writing and pick up the phone. I must switch task from writing to one person to talking to another and it may take a moment to adjust to the change. This phenomenon can be studied in an experimental setting by using two (or more) simple tasks and switching between trials of each task. Rogers and Monsell (1995) devised a task where participants looked at a grid of four squares on a computer screen. A letter/number pairing (e.g., L4 or G9) appeared in each square of the grid in turn, moving in a clockwise direction (thus L4 top left, G9 top right, A6 bottom right, P3 bottom left, etc.). When the pair was at the top participants had to decide if the letter was a vowel or consonant, and when the pair was at the bottom they had to decide if the number was odd or even. On two of the four trials participants were doing the same task as the last trial; on the other two they were switching to a different task. On trials where participants switched, they made more errors and their reaction times were significantly longer. This reaction time difference is referred to as a "switch cost" (see Figure 11.4).

There are several interesting characteristics of the switch cost which tell us more about the nature of task switching (Monsell 2003). First, the switch cost is reduced but not eliminated if people are given a chance to prepare for the switch. Second, although the switch trials are particularly slowed, performance overall is slower in a task-switching block of trials than in a single-task block, suggesting longer-term as well as transient effects of switching. Third, switch costs are most pronounced when participants switch from a hard to an easy task, as compared with an easy to hard switch. These observations have led theorists to suggest a number of mechanisms that are important in task switching. Monsell and others have suggested that participants must undergo a process of reconfiguring their task set, a "mental gear change". However this reconfiguration must depend, in part, on presentation of the trigger stimulus, in order to explain the residual switch cost even when preparation is allowed. The finding of greater switch costs when moving from hard to easy suggests that inhibition of the old task may be more important than activating the new one when performing a switch. A harder task that requires more processing resources may be harder to inhibit.

It should be clear that task switching, requiring as it does mental flexibility and active maintenance of behavioural goals, falls within the definition of executive function, and should depend on intact frontal lobes. Rogers et al. (1998) have shown that patients with prefrontal damage (especially left-sided) have difficulties performing task-switching paradigms. Aron, Robbins, and Poldrack (2004) have suggested an interesting dissociation between left and right prefrontal regions in task switching. Patients with focal right-sided lesions appeared to have particular problems inhibiting the old task, while those with left-sided lesions were poor at maintaining control of the appropriate task set.

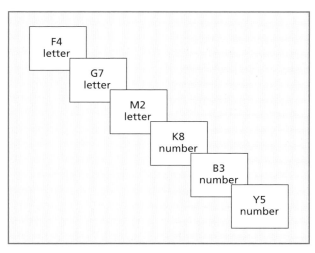

FIG. 11.4 A typical task-switching paradigm. Participants see a letter and a number on the screen and are prompted to name either the letter or the number. Where they have to switch from one to the other (on the fourth trial in this example), their reaction time is elevated, representing a so-called "switch cost".

MULTI-TASKING

Like task switching, multi-tasking is also an integral component of everyday life. If, instead of typing an email, I am making a cup of tea when the phone rings, I am likely to continue with that while holding a conversation. Most of us can perform two tasks at once with reasonable competence as long as at least one of the tasks is relatively routine. However, as the tasks become more demanding, attempting to do two (or more) things at once typically leads to impaired performance on one or both tasks. The debate on mobile phone use while driving highlights this point. Using a hand-held mobile phone is now banned in many countries because it has been shown to impair driving performance and thus increase the likelihood of accidents. However, many experts argue that even using a hands-free system has a significant negative effect on driving performance. Although the concept of switch costs does not apply when we are performing two tasks in parallel, capacity limitations make it likely that neither task is being performed with optimum efficiency.

Burgess and colleagues (see Burgess, 2000, for review) have suggested that multi-tasking is prototypical of situations where we have to organise and structure behaviour in the face of multiple goals. They characterise certain patients as displaying "strategy application disorder", which specifically compromises their ability to multi-task. These patients are unimpaired on many laboratory tests of function, including IQ tests and the classic executive function tests, such as Wisconsin Card sorting and verbal fluency. Burgess et al. (2000) reported that patients with this specific disorder typically have lesions to the most anterior part of the prefrontal cortex, suggesting that this region is critical for coordinating multiple behavioural goals.

ISSUES WITH "EXECUTIVE TESTS"

Current research on the neuropsychology of executive function is raising a number of issues about the classic executive tests. In the previous sections, we have illustrated/described a number of features of impaired executive function in terms of characteristic performance deficits on tests undertaken both in the laboratory or clinic and in real-world settings. In Shallice and Burgess's study for example, the researchers designed tasks based on patients' real-life experiences. This raises the issue of **ecological validity**. Burgess et al. (2006) have recently argued that traditional tests of executive function are largely derived from conceptual frameworks that have become outdated. They suggest that these tests were aimed more at theoretical research than clinically useful research and, especially given that the theories in question have been substantially revised, there is a case for developing and using new measures that are more ecologically valid. Such measures have a direct relevance to the problems encountered by patients in their everyday lives. Examples from Burgess's research group include the "Multiple Errands" and "Six Elements" tasks, which simulate real-life situations where cognitive flexibility, working memory, etc. are required. In considering this issue, it is also important to distinguish between tests to characterise deficits in frontal patients and tests that engage frontal mechanisms in normal people. The best tests for one application may not be the best for the other.

KEY TERM
Ecological validity:
Characteristic of experiments where the methods, materials and setting approximate the real-life situation that is under study.

An additional concern about traditional tests of executive function is that multiple versions of tests have often been developed. For example, Unterrainer et al. (2003) explicitly demonstrated that performance on the Tower of London task depended on the exact instructions given. The length of training sessions and the use of cueing or prompting also have significant effects on performance. These findings led Unterrainer and Owen (2006) to call for standardised versions of the classic frontal tasks to allow inter-study comparisons.

INTERIM COMMENT

In the previous sections we described three principal domains of executive dysfunction. Individuals have difficulty initiating and terminating actions, and often seem indifferent to their own "inertia". Sometimes, their behaviour is guided more by immediate circumstances than any grand plan, and we see evidence of utilisation or stimulus-driven behaviour. Dysexecutive cases also have difficulties with tasks that demand flexibility and adaptation of behaviour, and, as a result, may show marked perseveration. Finally, they seem to have particular problems with complex tasks that need to be broken down into smaller sequential tasks in order to be completed successfully.

Our list of executive dysfunctions is meant to be illustrative rather than comprehensive and, even with our examples, it is possible to argue that the domains overlap. For instance, poor planning may be linked to a tendency to engage in stimulus-driven behaviour, and perseveration may be related to "loss of goal" because both rely on impaired memory. Nevertheless, the overall impression of someone with executive dysfunction is of an individual whose thinking has undergone fundamental changes that may impact on almost every other aspect of behaviour. In the following sections we try to address these issues from a different "bottom-up" perspective, by considering in a little more detail what we know about the brain systems and regions that may be involved in executive function, and how damage or dysfunction to these areas is related to impaired executive function.

UNDERLYING MECHANISMS OF EXECUTIVE FUNCTION

When asked to define executive function, a neuropsychologist will typically resort to listing various higher-level cognitive processes that are believed to depend on "executive function". However, defining a single process that under-pins all these examples has proved much more challenging. Certain influential theorists have attempted to reduce executive function to a lowest common denominator. For example, Goldman-Rakic (1987) argued that representational working memory held the key to understanding prefrontal control of behaviour. However, perhaps the prevalent view today is that executive functions are multifactorial. In fact, in studies using batteries of tests designed to assess executive function, a highly consistent finding is that the degree of correlation between different executive tests is small and often statistically insignificant. This suggests that the concept of "executive function" is not unitary and requires further fractionation. Having reviewed the available literature, Baddeley (1996) proposed that what he termed the "central executive" served four different functions: allocating resources to perform two tasks simultaneously, the capacity to switch strategies, the capacity to selectively attend to one source of input while inhibiting the effect of others, and the capacity to manipulate information stored in long-term memory.

More recently, Miyake et al. (2000) used a statistical technique called latent variable analysis to determine the extent to which aspects of executive function may be distinct. The three processes considered (shifting, updating, and inhibition) were found to be moderately correlated but still clearly separable. The authors concluded that component processes falling under the umbrella of executive function are distinguishable but not completely independent. Subsequent work from the same group has made the situation still more complicated, as Friedman and Miyake (2004) have demonstrated that one of the previously defined components—inhibition—can itself be further fractionated into distinct but somewhat correlated subcomponents. Specifically, resistance to proactive interference (that is, the impact of previous learning on performance) was dissociated from prepotent response inhibition (the need to restrain oneself from making an established motor response). Both of these were further dissociated from distractor interference (the impact of task-irrelevant distraction on performance). Clearly the exact nature of executive function, or functions, and the inter-relationships between components are still incompletely understood. The complexity of this area of neuropsychology is exacerbated by the fact that tests of executive function are, by definition, complex cognitive tasks that almost invariably depend on non-executive as well as executive processes.

THE BRAIN AND EXECUTIVE FUNCTION/DYSFUNCTION

In spite of the debate surrounding the definition and fractionation of executive function, the combination of traditional neuropsychology and functional neuroimaging has allowed researchers to gain more understanding about the brain basis of executive functions. To illustrate this, we will focus on three tasks tapping into the three domains of executive function discussed earlier in this chapter. Given that executive functions are thought to be subserved by the prefrontal cortex, key questions are whether executive tasks are *sensitive* to frontal function and whether they are *specific* to frontal function.

THE BRAIN AND ACTION CONTROL: VERBAL FLUENCY

Verbal fluency is a commonly used measure of executive function, in part because it is an extremely quick and simple task to administer. In the phonemic version of the task (mentioned earlier), participants are given a letter of the alphabet and asked to generate as many words as possible beginning with that letter in a set time period. Several meta-analyses (e.g., Henry & Crawford, 2004) have shown that patients with frontal lobe lesions consistently demonstrate impaired performance on phonemic verbal fluency tasks. The impairment is typically more severe when the lesion is either bilateral or left lateralised. However, verbal fluency impairments do not seem to be specific to frontal lobe patients, as patients with non-frontal lesions also perform poorly on the task (e.g., Perret, 1974). Again left-sided lesions produce more pronounced impairments.

Neuroimaging can explore which regions within the frontal lobes are important for a task. Studies of verbal fluency have produced somewhat inconsistent results, perhaps reflecting differences in the exact nature of the cognitive activation tasks used. However, in general terms, studies suggest that key regions are the left dorsolateral prefrontal cortex (DLPFC), anterior cingulate, and left inferior frontal gyrus (e.g., Frith, 1995; Paulesu et al., 1997). Non-frontal regions have also been identified, in particular the thalamus.

THE BRAIN AND ABSTRACT/CONCEPTUAL THINKING: WCST

We described the WCST earlier in this chapter. It assesses cognitive flexibility, thought to depend on the core subprocesses of shifting and updating. A recent review (Alvarez & Emory 2006) assessed 25 studies of the effects of different brain lesions on WCST performance. Although the majority of studies found that frontal patients performed worse on the WCST than either controls or patients with non-frontal lesions, this was by no means a universal finding. In particular, there are a number of studies reporting negligible differences between the performance of patients with frontal and non-frontal damage, suggesting that the WCST may be sensitive to prefrontal damage, but not a specific index of it.

This conclusion is largely supported by the neuroimaging literature (see Barcelo & Knight, 2001, for review). Typically WCST performance is associated with widespread and bilateral activation of the prefrontal cortex, in particular the DLPFC. However, this frontal activation is part of a distributed network of activity that also includes posterior and subcortical brain regions.

THE BRAIN AND GOAL-DIRECTED BEHAVIOUR: TOWER OF LONDON

The Tower of London and related tasks were described earlier in this chapter. They are tests of planning thought to particularly assess components of executive function related to goal-directed behaviour. Unterrainer and Owen (2006) have recently reviewed the neuropsychological and neuroimaging literature on this task. Numerous studies have reported impaired planning abilities in patients with frontal lobe lesions. Indeed, a more sophisticated componential analysis of performance by Owen et al. (1995) suggests that inhibition impairments may play a crucial role. It appears that patients begin to move the coloured balls around before they have fully thought through an appropriate solution. However, once again, although the sensitivity of the task seems well established, the specificity is more debatable. For example, studies of patients with basal ganglia disorders such as Parkinson's disease show significant impairments on the task. This is consistent with the idea mentioned earlier, that executive dysfunctions may depend on disruptions to fronto–subcortical circuitry, rather than specific frontal damage.

The neuroimaging literature supports a role for prefrontal regions in Tower of London performance (see Figure 11.5). The DLPFC seems particularly important, with similar levels of activation in the right and left hemispheres. However, once again, non-frontal regions are also involved, including basal ganglia structures, premotor cortex, and posterior parietal cortex (e.g., Van den Heuvel et al., 2003).

THE BRAIN AND TASK SWITCHING/MULTI-TASKING

Neuroimaging has also been used to study task switching and multi-tasking, again confirming the involvement of prefrontal regions but additionally implicating non-frontal regions. Lateral prefrontal cortex and anterior cingulate are critically involved in task switching, but studies also report increased posterior parietal and (sometimes) basal ganglia activation (e.g., Braver, Reynolds, & Donaldson, 2003; Liston et al., 2006; Yeung et al., 2006). Imaging studies of multi-tasking have confirmed the importance of anterior prefrontal regions, as suggested by the neuropsychological literature (e.g., Burgess, Scott, & Frith, 2003), however few imaging studies have explicitly addressed multi-tasking, not least because the physical constraints of a scanner limit the available paradigms.

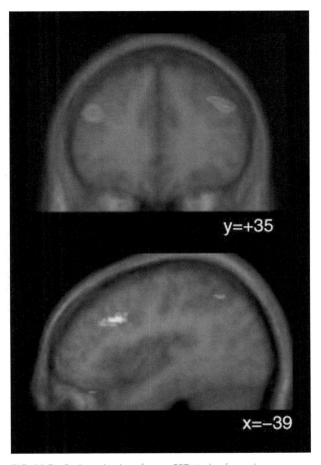

FIG. 11.5 Brain activations from a PET study of people performing a computerised Tower of London task. We are very grateful to Dr Adrian Owen of the MRC Cognition and Brain Sciences Unit, Cambridge for providing this image.

INTERIM COMMENT

In the examples discussed above it is clear that the evidence from neuropsychology and neuroimaging confirms the sensitivity of classic executive function tests to frontal lobe function. However, it is also clear that these tests are not specific to frontal function. Other regions are activated during normal performance, and non-frontal lesions can result in impairments of task performance. Two important issues arise from this brief review. First, although we have alluded to different prefrontal regions thus far, we have focused on frontal vs non-frontal. Treating the frontal lobe as a single area is obviously grossly simplistic. Neuroimaging studies have helped us address the issue of whether different aspects of executive function depend on different frontal regions. The second issue is how we refine our understanding of frontal involvement in executive function to account for the lack of specificity discussed above. In the next part of this chapter we will look at these two issues in more detail.

SPECIALISATION WITHIN THE PREFRONTAL CORTEX

Given the complexity of both executive function and frontal lobe neuroanatomy, it is perhaps surprising how little research effort has been dedicated to exploring the mappings between them. However, with the emergence of neuroimaging techniques more studies have attempted to localise components of executive processing. Given that there is no coherent and accepted theory that clearly fractionates executive function into separable processes, this literature is inevitably hamstrung to some extent. Nevertheless, certain important themes can be identified, some of which are reviewed briefly below.

THE SUPERVISORY ATTENTIONAL SYSTEM AND ANTERIOR CINGULATE

Norman and Shallice (1986) proposed a model of executive function that they termed the "supervisory attentional system" (see Figure 11.6). This model was proposed to explain goal-directed behaviour where achieving an overall goal depends on successful and orderly completion of several subgoals. For example, if you are decorating a room there are a number of smaller subroutines that must be completed to achieve this goal. The ordering of these subroutines is quite important: there is no point painting a wall before filling in cracks in it; and laying a new carpet before painting the walls is asking for trouble. Representations of how to complete the subroutines are stored in memory, along with thousands of other learned actions. In order to decorate the room, a decorator must inhibit irrelevant representations, and select and correctly sequence the appropriate ones. For a professional decorator, correctly ordering these representations (or "schemas" as Norman and Shallice termed them) is a relatively automatic and passive process termed "contention scheduling". For an amateur, contention scheduling alone is unlikely to be sufficient; the process will also require a higher level of planning. Norman and Shallice suggest that this depends on a supervisory attentional system (SAS). The SAS can bring order to the task in hand when a higher level of control is called for. It can also override contention scheduling, where necessary, to bring flexibility to complex task performance. For example, if our professional decorator discovers an unexpected problem, his or her SAS will come into play in order to solve the problem and complete the task.

Early neuroimaging experiments attempted to localise the SAS within the prefrontal cortex. PET studies in the 1990s suggested that the anterior

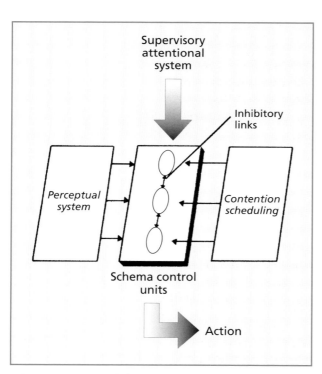

FIG. 11.6 Norman and Shallice's supervisory attentional system in which certain components within an overall plan of action are mutually inhibitory (you cannot stir the tea without already having picked up the spoon, for example). This relatively passive organisational process is known as contention scheduling. However, it can be "overridden" by a supervisory attentional process if required (if, for example, your guest advises you that he or she no longer takes milk or sugar).

cingulate may be a critical region. Corbetta et al. (1991) showed that when participants had to watch for changes in one stimulus parameter (shape, colour, or movement), posterior cortical regions were activated. However, when they had to simultaneously monitor all three parameters, the region most strongly activated was the anterior cingulate. In another study (Frith et al., 1991) greater anterior cingulate activation was seen when participants had to generate a random sequence of finger movements compared to producing a cued sequence. These, and other studies, suggest a role for the anterior cingulate in action control. However, this region is also involved in many other aspects of function (see examples elsewhere in this chapter, and indeed elsewhere in this book). Moreover, the original SAS model has been re-evaluated in more recent years to explain executive function (Shallice & Burgess, 1996). This model suggests processes for examining schema as well as eight separable executive processes for implementing, monitoring, and updating schema as appropriate. Their "supervisory system" thus involves multiple components which are likely to relate to the function of multiple brain regions.

RESPONSE SELECTION AND LEFT DORSOLATERAL PREFRONTAL CORTEX

In the PET experiment of Frith et al. (1991) described above, greater anterior cingulate activation was seen when participants generated their own sequence of finger movements. The left dorsolateral prefrontal cortex was also involved. In a verbal version of the task, left DLPFC was activated when participants freely generated words rather than simply repeating them. Jahanshahi et al. (1995) showed that left DLPFC was also more activated if participants had to choose when to make a specific response. Thus choosing when to respond, as well as which response to make, seems to depend on the left DLPFC. In a later study, Jahanshahi and Rothwell (2000) asked participants to generate random response sequences (a demanding thing to do!) at faster and faster rates. Performance broke down at faster rates and there was an accompanying drop in left (but not right) DLPFC activity. These observations led Frith, Jahanshahi, and others to propose that the left DLPFC has a specific role in response selection and specification.

WORKING MEMORY AND LATERAL PREFRONTAL CORTEX

An influential hypothesis suggests that the ventrolateral prefrontal cortex (VLPFC) and DLPFC play distinct roles in working memory (Owen, 1997). Specifically the VLPFC is proposed to control the retrieval of representations from posterior cortical regions, while the DLPFC is proposed to control the monitoring and manipulation of these representations. Various imaging studies have supported this idea. For example, Wagner et al. (2001) demonstrated VLPFC activation but very little DLPFC activation associated with rote rehearsal in working memory. Elaborative rehearsal, which involves the manipulation of material in working memory, preferentially activated the DLPFC. However, other studies have argued against such a simple separation, suggesting a greater degree of functional overlap.

Neither the DLPFC nor VLPFC is uniquely activated by working memory tasks. Duncan and Owen (2000) performed a meta-analysis of neuroimaging studies of executive function (see Figure 11.7). Their analysis covered a wide range

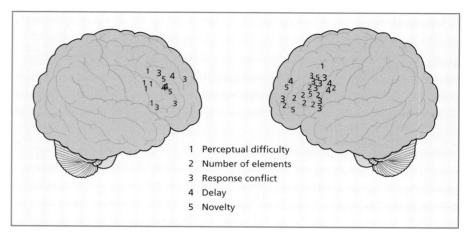

FIG. 11.7   Similar regional brain activations from various studies using different executive tasks, from a meta-analysis by Duncan and Owen (2000). We are grateful to Dr Adrian Owen of the MRC Cognition and Brain Sciences Unit, Cambridge for providing this image.

of tasks and considered the extent to which the tasks activated similar regions. In spite of the diversity of the tasks, three main clusters of activation could be identified across the studies: the dorsal anterior cingulate, mid DLPFC, and mid VLPFC. One possible interpretation of these findings is that the three regions form a common network that is recruited by diverse cognitive demands. Another explanation is that the three regions subserve distinct functions, but functions that are sufficiently abstract to be involved in different cognitive tasks. For example, working memory processes are often involved in complex tasks: the WCST is not seen as an implicit test of working memory, although participants clearly need to hold in mind the current rule and remember recent selections when working out a new rule. Similarly the Tower of London is typically seen as a test of planning, but generating a solution involves remembering previous moves in the sequence and thus working memory processes are implicitly recruited. As already discussed, DLPFC and VLPFC are both implicated in working memory and are therefore likely to be involved in any task with working memory components, explicit or implicit. Similarly, the anterior cingulate has been widely implicated in sustained attention, response selection, and inhibition of competing inappropriate responses. Some or all of these processes may be components of many complex tasks. As astute readers may have realised, there is a tendency for arguments and theories in this area to become somewhat circular, and further research is required to refine the concepts.

DISTRIBUTED CONTROL NETWORKS

As discussed above, executive function research has run into a number of difficulties. First, executive function and frontal lobe function have been used interchangeably, but it is clear that many paradigmatic tests of executive function are not specific to the frontal lobes. Second, attempts to fractionate executive functions into component subprocesses dependent on different brain regions have produced disappointing results.

Neuroimaging is beginning to suggest that the reason for these difficulties may be that thinking about a one-to-one mapping between structure and function is inappropriate for executive functions. This is intuitively plausible as these functions are by definition extremely complex and multi-faceted. Various recent meta-analyses have suggested that executive functions are mediated by networks incorporating multiple cortical regions, both frontal and posterior, whose functions are collaborative and overlapping (Goldman-Rakic, 1998; Mesulam, 1998). Carpenter and Just (1999) showed that the component regions involved in executive task performance depended on the level of difficulty (or "cognitive load"; see our discussion of this in Chapter 8). This suggests that understanding the brain basis of executive function is by no means a simple mapping exercise. Instead it involves understanding how multiple brain regions can be flexibly combined depending on task requirements and, potentially, also on individual skills and experiences. Different people may take different strategic approaches to an executive task, and therefore recruit different brain regions.

Understanding the interaction between brain regions involves a new approach to functional imaging data. Structural equation modelling or, more recently, dynamic causal modelling can be used to look at "effective connectivity": that is, the dynamically changing functional interactions between regions in a connected network. Studies using this approach have demonstrated that the strength of connections between regions involved in executive function is modulated by task demands (Funahashi, 2001). In a further recent development, event-related fMRI has shown that the frontal activation associated with particular tasks has distinct temporal properties. Some activations are sustained while others are more transient. Understanding the brain basis of executive function must take these temporal differences into account (Collette et al., 2006).

INTERIM COMMENT

Functional neuroimaging has changed the way we think about executive function over the last 10 years. In many areas of neuropsychology, PET and fMRI have been used as tools in a mapping exercise: determining which brain regions are responsible for which functions. In the area of executive function, it has become clear that seeking one-to-one mapping between structure and function is unlikely to be a fruitful way forward. Instead researchers are using more sophisticated analysis techniques to explore the connectivity between regions in distributed networks and determine how these connections are modulated by task demands. This approach has been applied to other aspects of function too, but the need for it is perhaps clearest for the high-level functions we term "executive".

EXECUTIVE DYSFUNCTION AND PSYCHIATRIC DISORDERS

THE RISE AND FALL OF FRONTAL LOBOTOMIES

In view of what has been said so far about damage to the frontal lobes and associated impaired function, it is both ironic and (for psychiatry) somewhat embarrassing to record that some of the earliest attempts to modify presumed brain disorder among psychiatric patients involved wholesale removal (or isolation) of frontal tissue. The development of the procedure that came to be known as the frontal lobotomy or leucotomy represents one of the darkest times in the history of psychiatry, yet merits retelling if only to serve as a reminder to avoid making the same sort of mistake ever again.

The procedure itself was introduced in the early 1930s by the respected Portuguese neurologist Egas Moniz. Of course at that time there were no effective treatments for any of the major psychiatric disorders, and in Moniz's defence it must be said that clinicians were desperate for access to any therapeutic procedures that offered hope of favourable outcome, or even a measure of effective control. Moniz heard of the work by two American researchers who reported a change to the "personality" of a chimpanzee whose frontal lobes they had removed. From being uncooperative and aggressive, the chimp became docile and pliant after surgery. Moniz reasoned that the same effect might offer relief for severely agitated mental patients. However, he was uneasy about operating on the whole of the frontal lobes so modified the procedure to encompass only the prefrontal areas.

Moniz eventually settled on a surgical procedure in which a hole was drilled in the side of the patient's forehead, and a probe with a retractable blade (a leucotome) inserted and moved through an arc, lesioning all the tissue it encountered. After World War II the technique was adopted (and simplified) by Freeman in the United States. The "lobotomy" (as it now came to be known) could be administered (under anaesthesia) in a doctor's surgery in a matter of minutes. Over the next few years thousands of lobotomies were carried out using Freeman's procedure, and, to compound insult with injury, Moniz received the Nobel prize for physiology and medicine in 1949.

It is, of course, easy to be wise after the event. Records show that a small number of aggressive agitated patients did become more cooperative and manageable after surgery. Some depressed and extremely anxious patients also showed a reduction in their symptoms, but often exchanged these for the behavioural inertia that we described earlier. Proper clinical trials were never instigated even though the procedure itself was used on an ever-wider cross-section of psychiatric patients. It was, for example, used extensively for a period as a treatment for schizophrenia, yet no formal evaluative study of its effectiveness for such patients was ever conducted, and so far as we can tell, anecdotally, it seemed to do little good and clearly made symptoms worse for some schizophrenic patients.

The procedure eventually fell out of favour, largely because of the development in the early 1950s of effective drugs for schizophrenia, and then later for depression and the anxiety disorders. Today psycho-surgical procedures are still occasionally carried out as a last-ditch treatment for intractable depression or drug-resistant obsessive-compulsive disorder. The most common procedure is anterior cingulotomy involving a small disconnecting lesion between the anterior cingulate and subcortical structures. A more recent technique that also targets the anterior cingulate is deep brain stimulation. Mayberg et al. (2005) have used implanted electrodes to disrupt cingulate activity, leading to marked improvement in severely depressed patients.

PSYCHIATRIC DISORDERS, THE FRONTAL LOBES, AND NEUROIMAGING

The link between psychiatry and the frontal lobes is evident when psychiatric symptoms are compared to those caused by frontal lobe lesions. The term pseudo-psychopathy has been coined to identify some of the disinhibited features, especially in the social domain, that frontal patients may exhibit. A second syndrome, called pseudo-depression, was also characterised by Blumer and Benson (1975) to encompass the apathy, indifference, withdrawal, and loss of initiative seen in some frontal patients. These descriptors are, of course, also applicable to many people with chronic schizophrenia. Patients with schizophrenia have been reliably shown to have impairments on classic tests of frontal function; for example, Figure 11.8 shows performance on a Tower of London task. Neuroimaging research has confirmed that people with this diagnosis often have functional abnormalities indicative of frontal impairment (Stirling, Hellewell, & Quraishi, 1998). Underactivation of the frontal lobes (during the completion of tasks that lead to activation in control respondents) is now a relatively robust finding in schizophrenia and seems most closely linked to the presence of negative symptoms. However, many classic imaging studies of schizophrenia are plagued by confounds (Weinberger, Berman, & Frith, 1996) and the general consensus today is that there is no clear focal pathology. Instead, connectivity models of schizophrenia have gained more and more credence (Andreasen, Paradiso, & O'Leary, 1998; Frith, 1997). Effective connectivity analyses have clearly demonstrated abnormalities in schizophrenic patients performing executive tasks (Fletcher et al., 1999; Meyer-Lindenberg et al., 2001). Newer techniques of white matter and diffusion tensor imaging have confirmed the presence of connectivity disruption even in very young patients (White et al., 2007) and those with new-onset illness (Federspiel et al., 2006). These observations underpin a new generation of neurodevelopmental and neuropathological theories of schizophrenia (e.g., Carlsson & Carlsson, 2006; Rubia, 2002; Stephan, Baldeweg, & Friston, 2006).

In the case of clinical depression, as with schizophrenia, functional changes are apparent in the frontal lobes but the picture is more complicated than was first thought (Drevets et al., 1997). Regions of the prefrontal cortex may be hypo- or hyperactive in response to cognitive challenges. Again, it seems that a model of depression based on an interconnected network with frontal, limbic, and sub-cortical components provides a more complete picture (Mayberg, 2003)

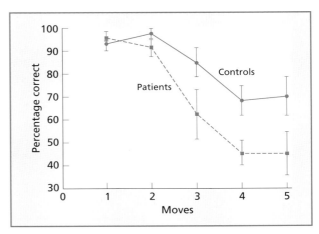

FIG. 11.8   Tower of London performance in schizophrenia. The performance of a group of 12 patients and 12 age- and IQ-matched controls on a computerised Tower of London task. In spite of relatively preserved general intellectual function, this group of patients performed poorly on more difficult problems (those requiring more moves) suggesting executive dysfunction. Data acquired in collaboration with Professor Barbara Sahakian and Dr Peter McKenna, University of Cambridge.

CHAPTER SUMMARY

The raft of well-documented impairments of executive function can be categorised in a variety of ways. Nevertheless, the list will include problems in the initiation and cessation of actions, impaired strategy formation, and loss of goal-oriented behaviour.

No single theory of frontal lobe impairment can currently account for the range of dysfunctions associated with them. Impairments in action control, abstract thinking, and goal-oriented behaviour are all observed in patients with prefrontal damage. Patients may also have difficulties with task switching and multi-tasking. However, although there are plenty of examples, there is no clear theoretical framework for understanding whether the concept of executive function can be broken down into separable components.

Neuroimaging research has demonstrated, unsurprisingly, that classic executive functions are mediated by prefrontal regions. However, attempts to localise specific components of executive function to specific frontal regions have met with limited success. Further, many studies find that executive functions involve posterior and subcortical regions, as well as prefrontal cortices. Influential recent research is therefore moving away from a functional segregation approach to prefrontal mapping and concentrating instead on functional integration. In other words, researchers are not looking for one-to-one mappings between structure and function, but identifying interconnected networks of regions that mediate these complex functions. This approach is in its infancy but promises significant advances in our understanding of the brain's most complicated activities.

Surgical lesioning of frontal regions of the brain was introduced as a treatment for severe mental illness in the 1930s. Although no properly controlled evaluation studies of the procedure were ever conducted, the lobotomy continued to be employed until the mid-1950s. More recently it has become apparent that a significant proportion of people meeting diagnostic criteria for either schizophrenia or depression show abnormalities of prefrontal function. A new generation of neuroanatomical models of psychiatric disorders propose that they are characterised by disrupted connectivity with networks involving frontal, limbic, and subcortical structures.

APPENDIX

CONTENTS

A primer of nervous system structure and function

INTRODUCTION

Almost all recent textbooks of physiological or biopsychology (many of which are listed in the "Further reading" section after this appendix) provide up-to-date detailed and well-illustrated accounts of the "workings" of the mammalian nervous system. Rather than reiterate this material in full here, we aim to provide the minimum grounding to help contextualise the material covered in the preceding chapters. We have pitched this appendix at a level to suit readers not already familiar with nervous system structure and function so, if what follows whets your appetite to learn more about the brain, spinal cord, and other components of the nervous system, so much the better. If, on the other hand, you are approaching this appendix with some trepidation, remember that many important ideas in neuropsychology pre-date our current level of understanding of brain physiology. Thus, an encyclopaedic knowledge of the nervous system is not a prerequisite for the neuropsychologist, although a basic understanding probably is.

We know that, like other parts of the nervous system, the brain and spinal cord are made up of different types of component nerve cell, so a starting point is to learn how these work and communicate with each other. Inevitably, our prime interest is the brain—a structure that has been described as the most complicated known to man. It therefore makes sense to divide it up into separate regions, each of which will be briefly considered in turn. Since neuropsychology is usually concerned with functions and operations that have cortical origins, the cortex clearly deserves special consideration. This structure is the outer surface of the brain, and, in evolutionary terms, the most recently developed region. It too is usually divided up, first in terms of left or right side (or cortical hemisphere), and then, in relation to the particular bones of the skull that cover and protect it, into lobes. As you will see, cortical lobes can also be distinguished in terms of some of the psychological functions they mediate (see Figure A1).

Knowing some of the basic terminology about the layout of the nervous system will also be advantageous. For example, brain regions are often described

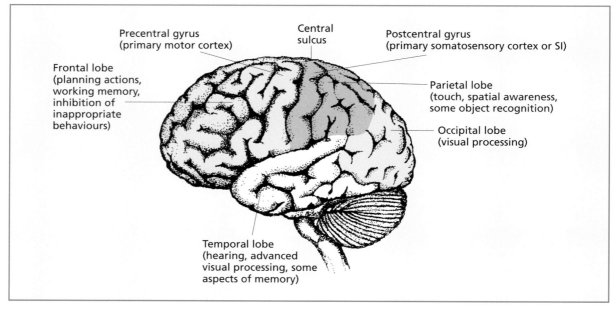

FIG. A1   The lobes of the cortex, showing the anatomical locations (and some functional specialisms) of the four cortical lobes.

in terms of their location, particularly in relation to other regions. So, allowing for the fact that humans walk upright rather than on all fours, dorsal means towards the back, and ventral the underside. Rostral means towards the front (head end), and caudal towards the bottom or tail end. Lateral is to the side, whereas medial is to the middle. If a particular structure has a front and rear section, we might refer to these as the anterior and posterior (pituitary gland for example). Finally, inferior means below, and superior above.

NEURONS AND GLIA

Our entire nervous system is made up of two fundamentally different classes of cell: neurons and neuroglia or just glia (which is the plural of glial cell) (see Figure A2). Neurons are responsible for conveying tiny electrical (or nerve) impulses around the nervous system and communicating, via synaptic transmission, with other neurons or, in the periphery, with muscles. Neurons themselves do not move, but they can convey nerve impulses along their length very efficiently and quickly (see Figure A3).

Although no one has ever actually counted them, it is estimated that the adult human brain contains between 100 and 150 billion neurons (1 billion = 1000 million), and glia are thought to outnumber neurons by 10 to 1! Glia play a range of vital supporting roles but are probably not directly involved in either conveying nerve impulses or in synaptic transmission. For example, in the central nervous system one type of glial cell (known as an oligodendrocyte) literally wraps itself around the "cable" part of a neuron (the axon), rather like a carpet is wrapped round a central cardboard tube, to provide a form of insulation known as a **myelin sheath**. (Schwann cells do a similar job in the peripheral nervous system.)

KEY TERM
Myelin sheath: A wrapping of insulation found on axons of many neurons giving a characteristic white appearance and leading to faster nerve impulse propagation.

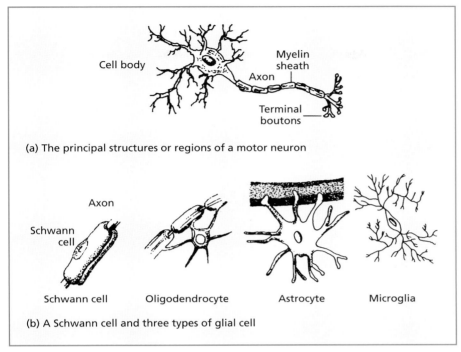

(a) The principal structures or regions of a motor neuron

(b) A Schwann cell and three types of glial cell

FIG. A2   A neuron (a) and glia (b). Not all neurons look like the one shown (a), but all have a cell body, an axon (that usually branches), and terminal boutons. This neuron is myelinated, and several dendrites are apparent as processes (outgrowths) of the cell body. A Schwann cell and three types of glial cell are illustrated (b). See the text for an explanation of their principal functions.

Another type of glial cell (known as microglia) *can* move around the nervous system, and they act rather like vacuum cleaners, removing (and digesting) dead or damaged tissue, and filling what would otherwise be empty space with scar tissue (see Raivich, 2005). Astrocytes surround blood vessels in the brain, and are involved in regulating the transfer of substances (glucose, oxygen, hormones, and potentially harmful toxins) between blood and brain.

As with glial cells, there are a variety of different types of neuron, some of which are found throughout the nervous system, and others that are only found in very discrete locations. For example, amacrine cells are found only in the retina, whereas interneurons are widespread throughout the brain and spinal cord. However, because most neurons carry nerve impulses and engage in synaptic transmission, it is helpful (though not entirely accurate) to think of them as all working in the same way.

NERVE IMPULSES AND SYNAPTIC TRANSMISSION

Most physiological or biopsychology textbooks include elegant descriptions of these processes, and the interested reader should consult these sources for detailed information. However, the points summarised in Boxes A1 and A2 may help to provide a clearer idea of the basics of both "within" and "between" neuron communication. When considering these points, remember that nerve impulses can travel the length of your body (2 metres or so) within about 20 ms, and that synaptic transmission can occur in an even shorter period of time. So, although our account of the processes may seem long winded, they actually happen incredibly quickly. Remember, too, that scientists estimate that the average central nervous system neuron (not that any such thing really exists) probably receives several thousand converging inputs, and can in turn influence about the same number of neurons (i.e., several thousand) via its dividing axon (**divergence**). For some neurons whose role is specifically to control the activity levels of others (such as neurons in our brainstem that modulate overall brain arousal level), the degree of divergence is such that a single neuron may synaptically influence at least a quarter of a million other neurons. See Figure A3 for an illustration of an active neuron and a schematic synapse, and Figure A4 for an illustration of "summation" of excitatory and inhibitory influences on a receiving (post-synaptic) neuron.

> **KEY TERM**
> **Divergence:** In the nervous system, the principle that because axons may branch many times, a single neuron can influence a large number of targets (usually other neurons).

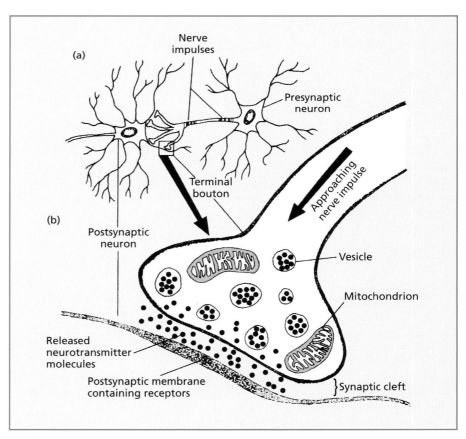

FIG. A3   A neuron conveying a volley of nerve impulses (a) and a schematic synapse (b). When nerve impulses arrive in the terminal bouton region, a sequence of events is triggered culminating in the release of neurotransmitter into the synaptic cleft.

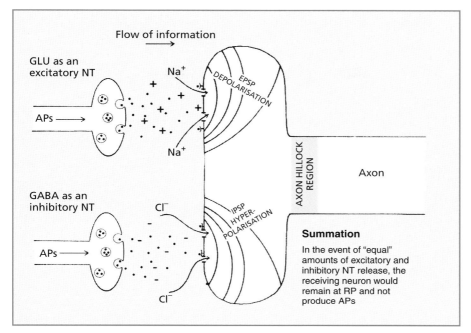

FIG. A4   The convergence of an excitatory and inhibitory input onto a receiving neuron, grossly simplified. Two neurons converge on a single "receiving" neuron. One releases the excitatory neurotransmitter (GLU) and the other releases the inhibitory neurotransmitter (GABA). Whether or not the receiving neuron fires will depend on the relative influences of the two competing inputs.

Box A1 Nerve impulses

- Think of nerve impulses as tiny electrical "blips" that travel along the surface of the cable part (the axon) of neurons. Most are formed at the axon hillock—a region where the cell body "becomes" the axon. This type of conduction is regarded as "active" in comparison with the "passive" conduction of information that occurs along dendrites and over a neuron's cell body.

- A neuron is able to generate its own nerve impulses (when stimulated), which, once formed, travel at a fixed speed and amplitude (size) in a given neuron, although speed and size of nerve impulse may vary between neurons. In fact, many neurons actually display spontaneous excitability or firing, so the critical issue is how this rate changes as the neuron itself is influenced by other neurons, events, or stimuli.

- In the human nervous system large myelinated neurons (such as motor neurons) can convey nerve impulses at over 100 metres per second; small diameter non-myelinated neurons (such as interneurons in the spinal cord) may propagate nerve impulses at less than 1 metre per second.

- Nerve impulses tend to occur in volleys (bursts) rather than alone. Thus a few nerve impulses may indicate a weak stimulus; more will signal a strong stimulus. Frequency coding, as this is known, appears to be a general feature of nervous system functioning. However, note that inverse frequency coding operates at some locations in the nervous system—for example, the firing of some neurons in the retina is inhibited by strong light.

- Nerve impulses conform to the "all or none" law, meaning they either occur fully or not at all. You cannot have a partial action potential.
- When a nerve impulse is at a particular point along an axon, its presence "excites" the region of axon just in front of it, effectively causing the impulse to move on to the next region of axon. This is analogous to a "domino" effect where a falling domino in one position causes the domino next to it to fall, and so on. The main difference is that, in neurons, "fallen" dominoes quickly pick themselves up ready to be knocked down again by the next passing nerve impulse.
- A variety of factors can influence a neuron and determine whether or not it produces nerve impulses, but in the brain and spinal cord the most likely influence is from other neurons via synaptic transmission.

Box A2 Synaptic transmission

- Action potentials arriving at the terminal bouton region of a neuron induce the neuron to discharge chemical messengers (called neurotransmitters) into the space between it and the "receiving" neuron. This extremely narrow gap (typically, about 30 nanometres) is called the synaptic cleft, and it contains extra-cellular fluid (water with ions and enzymes).
- Neurotransmitters are stored ready for release in tiny sacks called vesicles, present in the terminal bouton region of neurons. Neurons manufacture their own neurotransmitters from the breakdown products of food.
- There are many different neurotransmitters (some researchers have estimated over 1000 exist in our own nervous systems) but the vast majority of synapses are mediated by one of a core group of about 10, which includes acetylcholine (ACh), noradrenaline (NA), serotonin (5HT), dopamine (DA), gamma-aminobutyric acid (GABA), and glutamate (GLU). Some neurons release more than one neurotransmitter: a phenomenon called "co-release". This is most likely to involve one of the core neurotransmitters mentioned above plus a specialised (and probably localised) second substance from the "peptide" class of neurotransmitters. Substance P and VIP are two examples.
- Some released molecules of neurotransmitter diffuse across the cleft and find their way to particular receptor sites on the surface of the receiving neuron into which they fit (like a key in a lock). This diffusion is passive: the neurotransmitter molecules are not propelled in any way to the other side of the cleft.
- Their presence in the receptor can cause the receiving neuron to become excited, making it more likely to generate its own nerve impulses (an excitatory synapse). This is often mediated by the opening of channels in the receiving neuron's membrane that permit the influx of positively charged Na (sodium) ions.
- At other synapses, a neurotransmitter may have the opposite effect, causing the receiving neuron to become less excited, reducing the likelihood of it producing action potentials (an inhibitory synapse). This effect is mediated

either by the influx of negatively charged Cl (chloride) ions or the efflux (movement out) of positively charged K (potassium) ions.

- Some neurotransmitters (such as GLU) seem to be exclusively excitatory, and others such as GABA exclusively inhibitory (see Figure A4). Other neuro-transmitters can be excitatory at certain synapses and inhibitory at others. Such opposite effects are possible because there are different receptor types for certain neurotransmitters. For example, ACh has an excitatory influence at so-called nicotinic ACh receptors and an inhibitory influence at muscarinic ACh receptors. There are thought to be at least five DA receptors and as many as nine 5HT receptors in our own nervous systems.
- The action of a neurotransmitter is quickly terminated either by it being broken down by enzymes present in the cleft, or by being pumped back into the terminal bouton of the sending neuron (a process called re-uptake).

DEVELOPMENTAL AND AGEING ASPECTS

Where do neurons and glia come from and how do they end up where they are? The answer to the first question is straightforward. Like all cells in our body, neurons and glia are the products of cell division, ultimately traceable back to the single fertilised egg which begins to divide shortly after conception. However, the second part of the question is, with a few exceptions, currently unanswerable, except to say that during development, cells migrate (move), divide, and in certain cases selectively die (Toga, Thompson, & Sowell, 2006). The neurons and glia remaining are our nervous system!

One thing we can be sure of is that the maximum number of neurons an individual ever has reaches a peak relatively early in life—there is little evidence of further widespread neuron proliferation after the age of 2. The fact that many neurons are already present explains (in part) why a newborn baby's head is large in comparison with the rest of its body. The number of neurons appears to remain relatively static throughout childhood and then begins to decline in adolescence, and it has been estimated that by the age of 15 or so, humans are losing thousands of neurons every day (up to 85,000 according to Pakkenberg & Gundersen, 1997). This apparently alarming figure must be set alongside the vast number we start off with. If you consider a lifespan of 80 years, you will find that the loss of neurons at age 80 is less than 10% of the total, assuming a normal healthy life. Accelerated cell loss is, of course, a feature of several neurological disorders including Alzheimer's and Parkinson's diseases.

Unlike neurons, glial cells do increase in number throughout childhood and adolescence, and even in adulthood. In the corpus callosum (a structure in the middle of the brain that was discussed in Chapter 3), the amount of myelination increases (i.e., more oligodendrocytes form myelin sheaths) annually, with the structure only reaching full maturity at about 18 years. Incidentally, on a more sinister note, most brain tumours arise as a result of uncontrolled division of glial cells, not neurons.

In the last few years it has become clear that certain neurons in the adult mammalian nervous system may also undergo cell division to produce new cells. In rodents this has now been established at two locations: the olfactory bulb and the dentate gyrus in the hippocampus (see Ziv et al., 2006; and Hack et al., 2005). Although it is unlikely that cell proliferation here does much to counter the overall loss of neurons, the finding is important because it raises the possibility of being able to control (particularly, to switch on) cell division in other brain regions where marked loss of tissue has occurred (see below). At time of writing, neurogenesis in the adult human brain is assumed, rather than unequivocally proved, to occur at the same sites (Eriksson et al., 1998).

Before we leave the issue of lifespan changes, it is important to realise that for a nervous system to work effectively it is not just the number of neurons that is important, but how they interconnect with each other. We know that in the mammalian nervous system (including our own), neurons communicate predominantly via chemical synapses. Although the absolute number of neurons declines with age from adolescence onwards, the number of connections or synapses between neurons *can* increase, and certainly does not follow the declining neuron count. Some researchers estimate that most of the physical growth of the human brain after the age of about 2, not attributable to myelination, reflects the formation of new connections, and synaptic contacts (Toga et al., 2006).

Certainly, when there is brain damage later in life, loss of cells may be compensated for by the formation of new synapses (called synaptogenesis). In Parkinson's disease (discussed in Chapter 5), there is progressive loss of a particular type of neuron, but it is not until about three-quarters of these cells have died that the characteristic symptoms of tremor and rigidity appear. Researchers think that in the period of disease prior to symptom onset the remaining healthy cells continually form new synapses onto target cells, in effect replacing the inputs from the neurons that have died. This is known to involve axonal sprouting, meaning that existing neurons produce new shoots or branches that, in turn, make new synaptic contacts. Thus when we said earlier that neurons do not move, this is not strictly true for a neuron's axon, which may grow new branches several millimetres long to extend its sphere of influence.

DIVIDING UP THE NERVOUS SYSTEM

Because the nervous system stretches from the top of your head to the tip of your toes, it makes sense to divide it up into more manageable chunks. One important distinction is between the central (CNS) and peripheral nervous system (PNS). For mammals, the CNS is the brain and spinal cord, and the PNS is everything else. Sometimes it is useful to further subdivide the peripheral nervous system into the branch in which neurons carry nerve impulses to voluntary muscles (i.e., ones you can consciously control), and the branch carrying nerve impulses to muscles such as the heart and gut, which are not under voluntary control. The former is referred to as the skeletal nervous system and the latter as the autonomic nervous system (ANS).

Another way of subdividing the nervous system is to take into account the direction of nerve impulses conveyed along particular neurons. Afferent (or sensory) neurons carry nerve impulses towards the brain. Efferent neurons carry impulses away from the brain, and in the case of motor neurons, towards muscles.

A further useful distinction differentiates neurons with and without myelin sheaths. The sheath (which actually only covers the axon part of the neuron) dramatically improves speed of conduction, and the myelin gives these neurons a characteristic pinky-white appearance, hence the term "white matter". Incidentally, this structure is not continuous, being broken every 1–2 mm of axon at regions known as nodes of Ranvier, where the exchange of ions (mainly Na and K) necessary to propagate the nerve impulse can occur. Unmyelinated neurons convey action potentials much more slowly, and have a pinky-grey appearance. So too do cell bodies, giving rise to the term "grey matter".

Quite often, cell bodies of neurons will be clumped together in one location. (They don't actually touch one another but lie in very close proximity to each other.) These clumps are known as ganglia or nuclei. Similarly, the cable parts of neurons (the axons) often run side-by-side from one part of the nervous system to another. Once again, they don't actually merge into a single structure, but they do lie next to each other. Bundles of axons are known as tracts or nerves. It is important to remember just how small and densely packed axons can be. The human optic nerve is made up almost exclusively of myelinated axons, and is about the same diameter as a piece of cooked spaghetti. Yet it comprises axons of over 2 million individual retinal ganglion cells conveying information in the form of nerve impulses from the retina into the brain.

THE CENTRAL NERVOUS SYSTEM

In mammals, the central nervous system (CNS) includes all nerve tissue that is encased in bone. Although neuropsychology is understandably preoccupied with the cortex and its functions, it is important to realise that the cortex itself is only one part of the brain (many other brain structures in addition to cortex are highlighted in Figure A5). We will consider the brain shortly, but for completeness, we need briefly to consider the other major element of the CNS: The spinal cord nestles within the vertebrae, and is made up of both grey and white matter. It is a continuous structure but is also highly segmented, meaning that there is very precise delineation of input and output at each level (or vertebra). Sensory

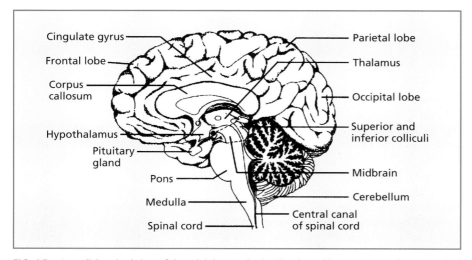

FIG. A5   A medial sagittal view of the adult human brain. The dotted lines represent the anatomical positions of the notional divisions between the hindbrain, midbrain, and forebrain. Clearly, the latter has expanded at the expense of the former two regions in the course of evolution for many higher mammals.

information from a clearly mapped-out region of body (known as a dermatome) enters towards the rear (or dorsal regions) of the spinal cord, at the particular level (vertebra). Motor output from the cord leaves via the ventral (frontal) roots, again to innervate muscles predominantly within the specified dermatome.

The grey matter comprises, for the most part, unmyelinated interneurons. These tend to influence other neurons only locally, either at the level in question, or perhaps in an adjacent segment. The white matter, on the other hand, surrounds the central grey matter, and comprises vast tracts of myelinated axons conveying both afferent and efferent information. Some of these run the entire length of the spinal cord although any given neuron only carries information in one direction. As we saw in Chapter 4, the dorsal columns carry relatively precise "sensory" information from the periphery towards the brain, and the ventral columns carry "motor" output in the opposite direction to muscles.

THE HINDBRAIN

This comprises the medulla, pons, and cerebellum. The medulla is, in effect, the continuation of the spinal cord in the cranium. However, in addition to the pathways to and from the cord it contains a series of regions that control basic vegetative processes such as respiration, heart rate, and certain reflexes. Brain death is assessed by the absence of electrical activity in this lowest region of the brain. More ventrally are found the pyramidal decussations: bundles of axons in pyramidal shapes that convey output signals from the brain to motor neurons whose cell bodies are located in the spinal cord itself. The term "decussation", meaning "crossing", reminds us that descending fibres cross from the left side to the right (and vice versa) at this level in the brainstem to bring about the familiar pattern of contralateral control.

The pons lies just rostral to (above) the medulla, and is ventral to the cerebellum. It is the main link between the cerebellum and the rest of the brain, particularly the cortex. It also has a role in certain aspects of both visual and auditory processing and, among other things, helps to coordinate eye movements in relation to balance. Several of the cranial nerves "exit" from this structure, including the trigeminal nerve, a mixed nerve that carries sensory information from the face and innervates muscles in the lower face and jaw. This region of brainstem also contains a significant portion of the reticular formation, which plays a key role in mediating the level of excitability (arousal) of large swathes of cortex.

The cerebellum is the large bilaterally symmetrical "walnut"-like structure on the dorsal (back) part of the brainstem roughly at the level of the ears. It is connected to the pons by three contiguous stalks called the cerebellar peduncles, two of which convey information into the cerebellum, and a third which conveys output via the thalamus to the cortex, and additionally to the brainstem. Structurally, the cerebellum comprises a midline region called the vermis and lateral regions comprising a wrinkled outer cortex and underlying white matter. This has a characteristic matrix-like appearance consequent on the way two major classes of intrinsic cerebellar neuron—Purkinje cells and the parallel fibres of granule cells—interact here. A series of four pairs of deep cerebellar nuclei are embedded in the cerebellum, serving as relay points for both inputs to and outputs from it.

Among other functions, this structure is concerned with balance, and the learning and execution of skilled movements, particularly those "enacted" through time: in other words, skills such as playing a piano, or performing some complex gymnastic routine, in which the sequence of controlling muscles has to be precisely coordinated. People with bilateral damage to their cerebellum often appear drunk, even to the point of slurring their speech, which after all depends on the coordination (in time) of muscles in the throat and mouth. They may also display a "staggering" gate. People with unilateral damage display these problems too, but usually just on the ispilateral (same) side as the damage.

THE MIDBRAIN

Here, we find the thalamus and hypothalamus, the tegmentum, and the tectum, the latter comprising four little bumps on the dorsal surface of the brainstem above the cerebellum. The bottom two (the inferior colliculi) are concerned with auditory processing, and especially in turning the head towards an auditory stimulus. The top two (the superior colliculi) do a similar job, but for visual processing (see Chapter 8). The tegmentum (the brainstem region immediately beneath the tectum) contains a diverse set of structures and nuclei including the frontal (rostral) section of the reticular formation, the periaqueductal grey area (PAG), the ventral tegmental area (VTA), the red nucleus, and the substantia nigra (SN).

The hypothalamus is involved in controlling behaviours that help the body to maintain an equilibrium or satisfy its needs. It will be no surprise to learn that it is the nerve centre (no pun intended) for the control of eating, drinking, temperature regulation, and sex. It also includes control regions for the autonomic nervous system and, in collaboration with the pituitary gland, helps to coordinate much of the endocrine (hormone) system. Not only does it secrete so-called releasing-factor hormones to control the anterior pituitary, but it also produces and supplies the hormones released by the posterior pituitary, and additionally controls their release from it.

The thalamus—a bilateral structure resembling (in adult humans) two avocado stones joined side by side, at a point called the massa intermedia—is a relay station for sensory information coming into the brain. By relay station we mean that input from a particular modality such as vision enters the thalamus, or more specifically a particular nucleus of it, where it may undergo some preliminary/intermediate processing, before being sent on to the cortex for further detailed analysis. The lateral geniculate nuclei receive input from the eyes, and relay it to the occipital lobes; the medial geniculate nuclei receive auditory input and relay it on to the temporal lobes.

THE FOREBRAIN

The basal ganglia and limbic system

Two other systems of neurons need mention at this point. The basal ganglia (see Chapter 5) comprise not one but several interconnected structures (the caudate, putamen, globus pallidus, the subthalamic nucleus, and substantia nigra). While it is not necessary to remember their names, it is helpful to have an idea of how this network of structures collectively helps to control movement, and we describe this in Chapter 5. The basal ganglia do not, for example, directly initiate movement;

rather, in combination with the motor cortex, they determine which possible actions actually get put into effect, by permitting some and inhibiting others. Researchers now think that the basal ganglia serve as a sort of gatekeeper for motor plans that originate in the cortex, and damage to any of the component structures (or the pathways that connect them) will impair the control of movement.

The limbic system, named by MacLean (1949), comprises—in addition to the cingulate gyrus which is a region of cortex just above the corpus callosum— several different interconnected subcortical structures, including the hippocampus, amygdala, septum, and hypothalamus. It is, in certain respects, the *emotional* equivalent of the *motor* basal ganglia: Activity in the limbic system selectively imbues behaviour with emotional tone (fear, anger, pleasure, and so on). Like the basal ganglia, the limbic system seems not to work in isolation, but rather in collaboration with both lower (brainstem) and higher (cortical) brain centres. Damage or abnormal functioning in the limbic system may be associated with both inappropriate emotional responding and impaired detection and/or identification of emotion-laden stimuli. In higher mammals, including man, certain limbic structures seem to have evolved to additionally mediate learning and memory (the hippocampus) and attention (the anterior cingulate gyrus). Damage to the limbic system may be related to certain psychiatric disorders including schizophrenia, depression, and anxiety. Like the basal ganglia, the limbic system is conventionally regarded as a "forebrain" structure.

The cortex

Viewing the external surface of an intact human brain, you might expect to see the brainstem, the cerebellum, and cortex. The cortex seems to cover much of the rest of the brain, although it is actually a forebrain (front) structure. It has a bumpy, folded appearance. The bumps are called gyri (singular: gyrus), the shallower folds or indents are called sulci (singular: sulcus), and the deeper ones are called fissures. Gyri, sulci, and fissures dramatically increase the surface area of the cortex. In fact, about two-thirds of cortical tissue is hidden in these folds. If you could flatten out the human cortex, it would cover an area of about 2500 square centimetres.

"Cortex" means bark, and it is a very apt term in this case, for the adult human cortex is between 1.5 and 4.5 mm thick. Its pinky-grey appearance tells us that it is made up primarily of cell bodies (remember cell bodies do not have myelin sheaths), which are usually arranged in a series of between four and six layers parallel to the surface. Immediately underneath the cortex the appearance changes to white, indicating vast tracts of myelinated neuron axons conveying information to and from the cortex and between one cortical region and another.

Like many other brain structures the cortex is often described as being "bilaterally symmetrical", which means that the left and right sides are like mirror images of each other. However, as we mention in Chapter 3, this is only approximately true, and several important anatomical distinctions between the left and right side are apparent on closer inspection. The two sides of the cortex are sometimes referred to as hemispheres, and again the term is apt: taken as a whole, the cortex looks a little like a partly inflated ball. However, it is important to note that each hemisphere contains many subcortical structures as well. The hemispheres are connected to each other by a number of pathways, of which the largest by far is the corpus callosum (see Figure A6). This structure is actually a massive band of axons running from one side of the cortex to the other. Although it is only about 10 cm long and no more than 1 cm in thickness, it comprises well over 500,000,000 myelinated axons. The relative isolation of the two hemispheres is best demonstrated by the observation that it is possible to insert a thin probe at any point along the longitudinal fissure (which separates them) and the first thing you would touch is the corpus callosum about 3 to 4 cm down.

We mentioned earlier that the cortex itself is made up primarily of cell bodies, and one of the largest and most prominent types of cortical cell is the so-called pyramidal cell (see Figure A7). This type of neuron has a very extensive branch-like structure. The branches are known as dendrites, and are the part of the neuron most likely to receive inputs from other neurons. Under a microscope these pyramidal cells look a little like Christmas trees, with the top branches corresponding to dendrites, and the lower, broader, part comprising a cell body and further sideways-pointing dendrites. The stem and roots of the tree would be the axon, which leaves the cortex to form a strand of white matter. Pyramidal cells are oriented at 90 degrees to the surface of the cortex, and clusters of these cells are sometimes called columns. Indeed, a regular feature of cortical organisation is its so-called column structure.

Sensory, motor, and association cortex

Another way of distinguishing between different parts of the cortex has, historically, been according to function. Some (discrete) cortical regions clearly have primary sensory or motor responsibilities—for example, Brodmann's areas 1, 2, 3a, and 3b constitute the primary somatosensory cortex (see Chapter 4), and BA 4 is the primary motor strip (see Chapter 5). Other (more extensive) regions don't have primary sensory or motor responsibilities, and the term "association cortex" has been used for many years as a "catch-all" for these cortical areas. Yet research shows that relatively little associating (or combining) of sensory input actually takes place here. Rather, much association cortex is involved in what amounts to a more elaborate processing of information. For example,

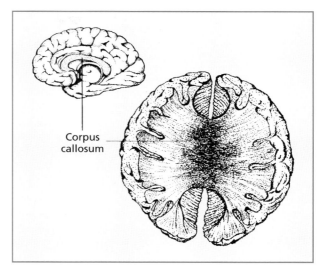

FIG. A6 The corpus callosum.

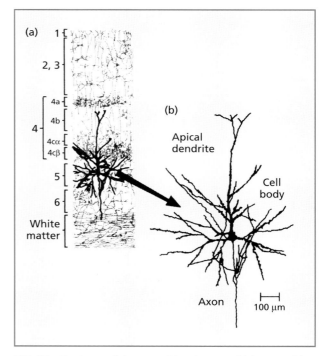

FIG. A7 The layers of the cortex (a) and a pyramidal neuron (b). Most regions of cortex appear laminated; neuroanatomists typically identify six layers. In this figure, one pyramidal neuron has been highlighted. It has an extensive dendritic structure that permeates several cortical layers, a centrally located cell body, and an axon, which descends and ultimately leaves the cortex via layer six. Adapted from Rosenzweig et al. (1999). *Biological psychology*. Sunderland, MA: Sinauer Associates Inc. Reproduced with permission.

the primary visual cortex deals with sensory registration, while regions of visual association cortex ("modules" in Fodor's terms) are concerned with (among other things) colour perception, object recognition, and movement (see Chapter 8). However, some associating *does* occur in association cortex, in the following sense at least: regions of the temporal lobe association cortex enable us to "imagine" the appearance of a person whose voice we hear, and parts of our parietal association cortex enable us to "draw" images of objects we cannot see, but can feel.

THE LOBES OF THE CORTEX

Another way of identifying cortical regions is in relation to the cranial bones that they lie beneath. In the higher mammals, including man, we differentiate between four lobes, or eight if you include both hemispheres (see Figure A1). Not only can the lobes be distinguished by their anatomical location, but they also separate *to some extent* in terms of the psychological processes with which they are concerned.

Frontal lobes

If you think of the human brain as looking a little like a boxing glove from the side, then the frontal lobes comprise the part of the glove that the fingers would occupy. They account for more than 30% of the entire complement of cortical brain cells, and are the part of the cortex that is more highly developed in humans than in any other primate. The frontal lobes are also the last to mature and there is evidence of continuing synaptogenesis and myelination into late adolescence.

At one time, the main function of these lobes was thought to be that of controlling movement, which they achieve in a highly organised hierarchical manner. The primary motor strip (BA 4) sends outputs that ultimately "drive" motor neurons controlling individual muscles: fine movements in the fingers and joints of your hand, for example. The region of frontal lobe anterior to (in front of) BA 4, called the supplementary area and merging into the premotor cortex has control over BA 4, so can organise concerted (bilateral) movements, such as holding a bottle and twisting off the cap. The region anterior to it is known as prefrontal cortex. This area is also involved in movement but only in terms of planning, intending, and "willing" it.

As we have learned more about frontal lobe function, it has become clear that, in addition to their key role(s) in movement control, they are also involved in many other aspects of behaviour including planning (in an abstract sense: for example, strategy), generating ideas, problem solving, working memory, and personality (see Chapter 11). Specialised compartments of the frontal lobe also contribute to the control of voluntary eye movements (the frontal eye fields) and expressive language (Broca's area). We describe the role of the frontal lobes in movement in Chapter 5 and some of their "executive" functions in Chapter 11.

Parietal lobes

The parietal lobes are located immediately posterior to (behind) the frontal lobes, and are separated from them by the central sulcus, the groove running across the top of the brain (roughly from ear to ear but by no means in a straight line). These lobes have important sensory functions, especially in relation to somatosensation, and also vision, and on the left, language, which we describe in some detail in Chapters 4 and 6; they are also critical for attention (see Chapter 8).

The first strip of parietal lobe (the gyrus furthest forward) is the primary somatosensory cortex (also known as S1, encompassing BA 1, 2, and 3). Neurons here respond to touch sensation from very discrete body regions, and the entire body is "mapped" contralaterally onto this cortical strip. For example, touch receptors in your right hand will send nerve impulses that end up in your left primary somatosensory strip. Different adjacent columns of neurons here will respond to input from each finger (and each part of each finger!). Further back (i.e., further away from the central sulcus), more posterior regions of parietal lobe are involved in more "integrative" sensory functions: linking, for example, touch with visual information or with memory. Damage here can lead to a disorder known as astereognosis, which is marked by the inability to recognise objects by touch. The parietal lobes are also involved in visuospatial processing, some aspects of language processing, and attention. The left parietal lobe also has a motor function.

Parietal damage, particularly on the right side, can give rise to the condition known as neglect of the left visual field (see Chapter 8). More discrete damage is associated with difficulties in object recognition, spatial orientation, and even basic geographic knowledge/memory. Left parietal damage is associated with apraxia. As discussed in Chapter 1, the precuneus (posterior medial parietal lobe) may have a particular role in referencing "the self" in 3D space, and perhaps even in self-consciousness.

Occipital lobes

The left and right occipital lobes are tucked behind and underneath the parietal lobes at the back of the cortex. Visual input from the lateral geniculate nucleus of the thalamus terminates in V1 (so-called striate occipital cortex). Damage here almost always results in a marked visual impairment, and can lead to cortical blindness. For example, extensive damage to V1 on the right will result in blindness in the left visual field (everything to the left of centre as you look straight ahead). Surrounding V1, the "extrastriate" areas of the occipital lobe (V2, 3, and 4) comprise modules (Fodor's term again) concerned with the perception of form, movement, movement direction, location, and colour; at least 30 such modules can be found here according to Zeki et al. (1991). V2 is also the starting point for two major processing routes projecting into the dorsal parietal, the ventral parietal, and temporal lobes, and dubbed (respectively) the "where" and "what" streams by Ungerleider and Mishkin (1982). Some of these functions are described in more detail in Chapter 8.

Temporal lobes

In our boxing glove analogy, the temporal lobe would be the thumb (except you have one lobe on each side). The anterior part of this lobe is separated from the frontal lobe (which it lies to the side of), but the rear (posterior) sections are bounded by the parietal and occipital lobes, and the actual boundaries are not clearly defined by sulci. Three gyri can be identified in the temporal lobe, known as the superior (upper), medial (mid), and inferior (lower) gyri respectively. The posterior region of the superior temporal gyrus is the primary auditory cortex, also known as Heschl's gyrus, with input coming mainly from the ear on the opposite side of the body. On the left side, adjacent regions, especially behind the primary auditory cortex, are involved in the recognition of language sounds. On the right side, the equivalent regions are involved in interpreting non-verbal speech sounds such as tone, rhythm, and emotion.

However, the temporal lobes are not just concerned with auditory processing. Lower (inferior) regions, for example, are involved in visual object recognition. In general, cells in different parts of the inferior temporal gyrus respond to rather specific visual stimuli such as faces, objects, or types of animal, suggesting that stored representations (memories) of items may be located in a highly organised and compartmentalised way here. We consider some of the evidence in support of this idea in Chapter 8. An illustration of the range of functions with which the temporal lobes are involved is that a tumour here can give rise to auditory, visual, or even olfactory (smell) hallucinations (Liddle, 1997).

CHAPTER SUMMARY

The brain, like other parts of the nervous system, is made up of neurons and glia, although neurons alone carry nerve impulses around the nervous system. To begin to understand how the brain works it makes sense to divide it up, and the principal component parts of the hindbrain, midbrain, and forebrain have been introduced. It is also helpful to divide up the cortex in terms of both the anatomical location of the lobes and their diverse functions. However, it is very important to remember that a "hallmark" feature of brain function is, in fact, the interactivity and collaboration between different regions. The brain *does not* work as a series of independent functioning elements, as the localisationists once believed. Rather, even the most simple of behaviours (wiggling one of your fingers for example) will involve the collaborative activation and interaction of multiple cortical and subcortical regions. Obviously, such collaboration can be doubled and redoubled (several times) when we consider neuronal control of more sophisticated behaviours such as "willed action selection" (see Chapter 5), expressive language (see Chapter 6), or risk taking (see Chapter 10).

No matter how many times we describe the brain to our students, we both still marvel at the sheer complexity of it, and we hope you share our sense of wonder. We are also amazed that such a complicated structure goes wrong so infrequently. However, when brain damage, disorder, or disease does occur it can sometimes shed considerable light on the functioning of the normal intact brain. You only have the one, so take care of it!

FURTHER READING

CHAPTER 1

Caramazza, A. (1984). The logic of neuropsychological research and the problem of patient classification in aphasia. *Brain and Language, 21*, 9–20.

Catani, M., & ffytche, D. H. (2005). The rises and falls of disconnection syndromes. *Brain, 128*(10), 2224–2239.

Cavanna, A. E., & Trimble, M. R. (2006). The precuneus: A review of its functional anatomy and behavioural correlates. *Brain, 129*, 564–583.

Coltheart, M. (2001). Assumptions and methods in cognitive neuropsychology. In B. Rapp (Ed.), *Handbook of cognitive neuropsychology*. Philadelphia: Psychology Press.

Ellis, A. W., & Young, A. W. (1996). *Human cognitive neuropsychology: A textbook with readings*. Hove, UK: Psychology Press.

Selnes, O. A. (2001). A historical overview of contributions from the study of deficits. In B. Rapp (Ed.), *Handbook of cognitive neuropsychology*, Hove, UK: Psychology Press.

CHAPTER 2

Carter, R., & Frith, C. D. (1999). *Mapping the mind*. Berkeley, CA: University of California Press.

Frackowiak, R. S. J. (Ed. in chief) (2004). *Human brain function* (2nd ed.). Amsterdam: Elsevier Academic Press. *(Detailed chapters on imaging methodology and also useful review chapters on aspects of function which serve as further reading for the other chapters of our book.)*

Hugdahl, K. (Ed.) (2003). *Experimental methods in neuropsychology*. Boston: Kluwer Academic Publishers.

Parkin, A. (1999). *Explorations in cognitive neuropsychology*. Hove, UK: Psychology Press.

CHAPTER 3

Brown, W. S., Paul, L. K., Symington, M., & Dietrich, R. (2005). Comprehension of humour in primary agenesis of the corpus callosum. *Neuropsychologia, 43*, 906–916.

Corballis, M. C. (2003). From mouth to hand: Gesture, speech, and the evolution of right-handedness. *Behavioral and Brain Sciences, 26*, 199–260.

Gazzaniga, M. S. (2002). The split brain revisited. In *The hidden mind* [*Scientific American* special issue, *April*, 27–31].

Kimura, D. (2002). Sex differences in the brain. *Scientific American*, May 13.

Mevorach, C., Humphreys, G. Q., & Shalev, L. (2005). Attending to local form while ignoring global aspects depends on handedness: Evidence from TMS. *Nature Neuroscience, 8*(3), 276–277.

Springer, S. P., & Deutsch, G. (1998). *Left brain, right brain: Perspectives from cognitive neuroscience* (5th ed.). New York: W. H. Freeman.

Tranel, D., Damasio, H., Denburg, N. L., & Bechara, A. (2005). Does gender play a role in functional asymmetry of ventromedial prefrontal cortex? *Brain, 128*, 2872–2881.

CHAPTER 4

Buonomano D. V., & Merzenich, M. M. (1998). Cortical plasticity: From synapses to maps. *Annual Review of Neuroscience*, *21*, 149–186.

Flor, H., Nikolajsen, L., & Jensen, T. S. (2006). Phantom limb pain: A case of maladaptive CNS plasticity? *Nature Reviews: Neuroscience*, *7*, 873–881.

Mogilner, A., Grossman, J. A., Ribary, U., Joliot, M., Volkman, J., Rapaport, D., et al. (1993). Somatosensory cortical plasticity in adult humans revealed by magnetoencephalography. *Proceedings of the National Academy of Sciences*, *90*, 3593–3597.

Nudo, R. J., Milliken, G. W., Jenkins, W. M., & Merzenich, M. M. (1996). Use dependent alterations of movement representations in primary motor cortex of adult squirrel monkeys. *Journal of Neuroscience*, *16*, 785–807.

Ptito, M., Moesgaard, S. M., Gjedde, A., & Kupers, R. (2005). Cross-modal plasticity revealed by electrotactile stimulation of the tongue in the congenitally blind. *Brain*, *128*, 606–614.

Wittenberg, G. F., Chen, R., Ishii, K., Bushara, K. O., Taub, E., Gerber, L. H., et al. (2003). Constraint induced therapy in stroke: Magnetic-stimulation motor maps and cerebral activation. *Neurorehabilitation and Neural Repair*, *17*, 48–57.

CHAPTER 5

Bradshaw, J. L., & Mattingley, J. B. (1995). *Clinical neuropsychology: Behavioural and brain science*. London: Academic Press.

Heilman, K. M., Rothi, L. J., & Valenstein, E. (1982). Two forms of ideomotor apraxia. *Neurology*, *32*, 342–346.

Hochberg, L. R., Serruya, M. D., Friehs, G. M., Mukland, J. A., Saleh, M., Caplian, A. H., et al. (2006). Neural ensemble control of prosthetic devices by a human with tetraplegia. *Nature*, *442*, 164–171.

Ohyama, T., Nores, W. L., Murphy, M., & Mauk, M. D. (2003). What the cerebellum computes. *Trends in Neurosciences*, *26*, 222–227.

Rizzolatti, G., & Buccino, G. (2004). The mirror-neuron system and its role in imitation and language. In S. Dehaene, G. R. Duhamel, M. Hauser, & G. Rizzolatti (Eds.), *From monkey brain to human brain*. Cambridge, MA: MIT Press.

Tekin, S., & Cummings, J. L. (2002). Frontal–subcortical neuronal circuits and clinical neuropsychiatry: An update. *Journal of Psychosomatic Research*, *53*, 647–654.

Wichmann, T., & Delong, M. R. (1996). Functional and pathophysiological models of the basal ganglia. *Current Opinion in Neurobiology*, *6*, 751–758.

Winkler, C., Kirik, D., & Bjorklund, A. (2005). Cell transplantation in Parkinson's disease: How can we make it work. *Trends in Neurosciences*, *28*, 86–92.

CHAPTER 6

Demonet, J. F., Thierry, G., & Cardebet, D. (2005). Renewal of the neurophysiology of language: Functional neuroimaging. *Physiological Reviews*, *85*, 49–95.

Dronkers, N. F., Wilkins, D. P., Van Valin, R. D., Redfern, B. B., & Jaeger, J. J. (2004). Lesion analysis of the brain areas involved in language comprehension. *Cognition*, *92*, 145–177.

Ellis, A. W., & Young, A. W. (1996). *Human cognitive neuropsychology: A textbook with readings*. Hove, UK: Psychology Press.

Indefrey, P., & Levelt, W. J. (2000). The neural correlates of language production. In M. S. Gazzaniga (Ed.), *The new cognitive neurosciences* (2nd ed.), London: MIT Press.

Poeppel, D., & Hickok, G. (2004). Towards a new functional anatomy of language. *Cognition*, *92*, 1–12.

Vigneau, M., Beaucousin, V., Herve, P. Y., Duffau, H., Crivello, F., Houde, O., et al. (2006). Meta-analyzing left hemisphere language areas: Phonology, semantics and sentence processing. *Neuroimage*, *30*, 1414–1432.

CHAPTER 7

Aggleton, J. P., & Brown, M. W. (2006). Interleaving brain systems for episodic and recognition memory. *Trends in Cognitive Sciences*, *10*, 455–463.

Arnot, S. R., Grady, C. L., Hevenor, S. J., Graham, S., & Alain, C. (2005). The functional organisation of auditory working memory as revealed by fMRI. *Journal of Cognitive Neuroscience*, *15*, 819–831.

Corkin, S. (2002). What's new with the amnesic patient HM? *Nature Reviews Neuroscience, 3,* 153–160.

Eichenbaum, H., Yonelinas, A. P., & Ranganath, C. (2007). The medial temporal lobe and recognition memory. *Annual Review of Neuroscience, 30,* 123–152.

Greenberg, D. L., Eacott, M. J., Brechin, D., & Rubin, D. C. (2005). Visual memory loss and autobiographical amnesia: A case study. *Neuropsychologia, 43,* 1493–1502.

Squire, L. R. (2004). Memory systems of the brain: A brief history and current perspective, *Neurobiology of Learning and Memory, 82,* 171–177.

CHAPTER 8

Buxbaum, L. J. (2006). On the right (and left) track: 20 years of progress in studying hemispatial neglect. *Cognitive Neuropsychology, 23*(1), 184–201.

Farah, M. J. (1990). *Visual agnosia: Disorders of object recognition and what they tell us about normal vision.* Cambridge, MA: MIT Press.

Farah, M. J., & Aguirre, G. K. (1999). Imaging visual recognition: PET and fMRI studies of the functional anatomy of human visual recognition. *Trends in Cognitive Sciences, 3*(5), 179–186.

Humphreys, G. W., & Riddoch, M. J. (1992). Interactions between objects and space-vision revealed through neuropsychology. In D. E. Meyers & S. Kornblum (Eds.), *Attention and performance XIV* (pp. 143–162). Hillsdale, NJ: Lawrence Erlbaum Associates Inc.

Peissig, J. J., & Tarr, M. J. (2007). Visual object recognition: Do we know more now than we did 20 years ago? *Annual Review of Psychology, 58,* 75–96.

CHAPTER 9

Baars, B. J. (2003). *The conscious access hypothesis: Global workspace theory and brain dynamics.* Cambridge, MA: MIT Press.

Conney, J. W., & Gazzaniga, M. S. (2003). Neurological disorders and the structure of human consciousness. *Trends in Cognitive Sciences, 7,* 161–165.

Corbetta, M., Kincade, M. J., Lewis, C., Snyder, A. Z., & Sapir, A. (2005). Neural basis and recovery of spatial attention deficits in spatial neglect. *Nature Neuroscience, 8,* 1603–1610.

Duncan, J. (2006) Brain mechanisms of attention. *Quarterly Journal of Experimental Psychology, 59*(1), 2–27.

LaBerge, D. (2000). Attentional networks. In M. S. Gazzaniga (Ed.), *The new cognitive neurosciences* (pp. 711–724). Cambridge, MA: MIT Press.

Lavie, N. (2005). Distracted and confused? Selective attention under load. *Trends in Cognitive Sciences, 9,* 75–82.

CHAPTER 10

Damasio A. (1994) *Descartes' error: Emotion, reason and the human brain.* New York: Putnam Publishing.

Frith, C. D., & Wolpert, D. M. (2004). *The neuroscience of social interaction: Decoding, influencing, and imitating the actions of others.* Oxford, UK: Oxford University Press.

O'Doherty, J. (2004) Reward representations and reward-related learning in the human brain: Insights from human neuroimaging. *Current Opinion in Neurobiology, 14,* 769–776.

CHAPTER 11

Duncan, J., & Owen, A. M. (2000). Common regions of the human frontal lobe recruited by diverse cognitive demands. *Trends in Neurosciences, 23,* 475–483.

Gazzaniga, M. S. (Ed.) (2004). *The cognitive neurosciences III* (pp. 943–956). Cambridge, MA: MIT Press.

LeDoux, J. (1996). *The emotional brain.* New York: Simon & Shuster.

Roberts, A. C., Robbins, T. W., & Weiskrantz, L. (1998). *The prefrontal cortex.* Oxford, UK: Oxford University Press.

Shallice, T. (2004). The fractionation of supervisory control. In J. M. Unterrainer and A. M. Owen (2006). Planning and problem solving: From neuropsychology to functional neuroimaging. *Journal of Physiology (Paris), 99,* 308–317.

GENERAL READING

Banich, N. (2004). *Cognitive neuroscience and neuropsychology*. New York: Houghton Mifflin.

Carlson, N. R. (2007). *Physiology of behavior* (9th ed.). Boston: Allyn & Bacon.

Ellis, A. W., & Young, A. W. (1996). *Human cognitive neuropsychology: A textbook with readings*. Hove, UK: Psychology Press.

Gazzaniga, M. S. (2000). *Cognitive neuroscience, a reader*. Oxford, UK: Blackwell

Gazzaniga, M. S. (Ed.) (2004). *The cognitive neurosciences III*. Cambridge, MA: MIT Press.

Gazzaniga, M. S., Ivry, R. B., & Mangun, G. R. (2003). *Cognitive neuroscience: The biology of the mind* (2nd ed.). New York: W. W. Norton & Co.

Kolb, B., & Whishaw, I. Q. (2003). *Fundamentals of human neuropsychology* (5th ed.). New York: Freeman & Co.

Springer, S. P., & Deutsch, G. (2000) *Left brain; right brain: Perspectives from cognitive neuroscience* (5th ed.). New York: Freeman & Co.

Ward, J. (2006). *The student's guide to cognitive neuroscience*. Hove, UK: Psychology Press.

NEUROPSYCHOLOGY ON THE WORLD WIDE WEB

There is a wealth of information about neuropsychology to be accessed via the internet. A simple GOOGLE search using a key term such as *Parkinson's disease* or *aphasia* will produce hundreds of "hits" to explore. The GOOGLE images option permits access to thousands of figures, photographs, and diagrams: These can be downloaded although some will be subject to copyright. GOOGLE Scholar will be useful if you want to start a literature search: It gives access to many full-text journal articles of interest to neuropsychologists. WIKIPEDIA is also worth browsing as a first step, although in our experience, entries are of more variable quality. However, for more detailed information we have provided below a selection of specific sites for you to explore. At time of writing all of these were fully functional, and offered open-access to most contents.

http://www.neuroguide.com
A links page with a comprehensive search facility, table of contents, and opportunities to sign up for newsletters—many useful links.

http://neuropsychologycentral.com
Mainly links, but the site also offers an in-house and web search facility.

http://home.epix.net/~tcannon1/ Neuropsychology.htm
Professor Cannon's homepage with lots of links to journals, other neuropsychology information pages, and links and information on specific brain disorders.

http://www.lib.uiowa.edu/hardin/md/neuro.html
A links page to many other neuropsychology sites regularly updated by staff at the Hardin Library, University of Iowa. Lots of information about neurological disorders.

http://lbc.nimh.nih.gov
The website of the laboratory of brain cognition, National Institute for Mental Health (NIMH), with lots on functional neuroimaging, and other neuroscience material.

http://www.brainsource.com
A web site prepared by neuropsychologist Denis Swiercinsky, offering numerous links. Particularly good for information on neuropsychological testing.

http://faculty.washington.edu/chudler/ehc.html
Prof Eric Chudler's webpage which contains links to search engines, information about neuropsychological disorders, and much more. A link to the kids-page is also worth a visit!

http://www.cogneuro.ox.ac.uk/links/
Links to many other academic sites from the McDonnell Centre for Cognitive Science, University of Oxford.

http://www.psychology.org/links/ Underlying_Reductionistic_Machinery/ Neuropsychology/
This takes you to an Encyclopedia of Psychology, with many useful links to research methods and clinical disorders.

http://neurophys.wisc.edu/neurosci.html
More links from the University of Wisconsin.

http://mindbrain.ucdavis.edu/labs/Whitney-new/
Many useful links to brain imaging, and other current neuroscience research at U. C. Davis.

**http://www.med.harvard.edu/publications/
On_The_Brain/**
Access to the Harvard-Mahoney Neuroscience Institute newsletters (with an extensive back catalogue).

**http://www.ion.ucl.ac.uk/national_hospital/
national_hospital.htm**
The homepage of the Institute of Neurology, Queens Square, London. Many useful and interesting links.

http://www.neuropsychologyarena.com
The Neuropsychology Arena provides researchers, instructors, and students in neuropsychology with information on the range of books and journals produced by Psychology Press, LEA, Taylor & Francis, and Routledge. It also offers other helpful resources, such as information about conferences, societies, and blogs.

GLOSSARY

Ablation: the surgical removal of brain tissue.

Acquired alexia: loss of reading ability in a previously literate person.

Agnosia: loss of ability to recognise objects, persons, sounds, shapes, or smells in spite of intact sensory function.

Alexia: inability to read.

Allocentric neglect: consistent processing errors on one side of individual stimuli (either right or left) regardless of location with respect to the viewer.

Alzheimer's disease: a form of dementia involving progressive loss of psychological functions as a result of widespread loss of cortical and sub-cortical neurons.

Amnesia: general term for loss of memory. Antero-grade amnesia is loss of memory following some trauma. Retrograde amnesia is loss of memory for a period of time prior to trauma.

Aneurysm: a form of stroke caused by a blood vessel in the brain suddenly expanding and then bursting.

Angular gyrus: a region of cortex on the temporal/parietal border roughly equivalent to Brodmann's area 39. The left side is probably involved in reading (sentences).

Anomia: inability to name objects or items.

Anosognosia: a condition in which a person who suffers impairment following brain damage seems unaware of or denies the existence of their handicap, even if the handicap is severe (blindness or paralysis).

Anterior cingulate: a midline frontal lobe structure implicated in attention, response inhibition, and emotional response (especially to pain).

Anterograde amnesia: a form of memory loss where new events are not stored in long-term memory.

Anti-saccade: inhibition of a reflexive eye movement towards a light target.

Aphasia: deficit in the production and/or comprehension of language.

Apraxia: the inability to carry out certain motor acts on instruction without evident loss of muscle tone (acts may be performed spontaneously, for example).

Arborial structure: the branching pattern of neuronal dendrites.

Arcuate fasciculus: fibre bundle connecting Broca's and Wernicke's areas in the brain.

Aspiration pneumonia: bronchial infection and congestion that affects ability to breathe and can lead to death.

Astereognosis: an agnosic condition in which objects cannot be recognised by touch alone.

Autism: a developmental disorder characterised by aloofness, automaticity, and aphasia.

Axon: long, thin projection from a neuron that carries electrical impulses from the cell body.

Behaviourism: the school of psychology founded by Thorndike and popularised by Skinner, which places emphasis on the acquisition of behaviour through learning and reinforcement.

Beta blocker: a drug that blocks the effects of adrenaline and noradrenaline.

Biopsy: the removal of tissue (in a living individual) for analysis.

Brainstem: the lower part of the brain, adjoining and structurally continuous with the spinal cord.

Brodmann area: a region of the cortex defined on the basis of cytoarchitecture.

Cerebellum: region at the base of the brain that is important in sensory and motor functions.

Cerebral cortex: the outer surface of the brain which has, in higher mammals, a creased and bumpy appearance

Classical conditioning: a simple form of learning where a previously neutral stimulus (e.g., a light) becomes associated with a motivationally salient stimulus (e.g., food) through repeat presentation.

Clinical neuropsychology: a branch of clinical psychology that specialises in the assessment of patients with focal brain injury or neuro-cognitive deficits.

Clot: a solid deposit in the blood that may block a narrow blood vessel leading to a form of stroke.

Cognitive neuropsychology: a branch of neuro-psychology that studies how brain structure and function relate to specific psychological processes.

Conduction aphasia: aphasia in which the principal deficit is an inability to repeat spoken language.

Convergence: in the nervous system, the process of many (converging) inputs influencing one component (for example, a neuron).

Converging operations: the use of several research methods to solve a single problem so that the strengths of one method balance out the weaknesses of the others.

Coronal (as in section): the orientation of a brain slice if you were looking "face on" and the brain was sliced vertically.

Critical periods: the early stages of an organism's life during which it displays a heightened sensitivity to certain environmental stimuli, and develops in particular ways.

D_1 receptors: a class of dopamine receptor found particularly in the frontal lobes and striatum.

D_2 receptors: another class of dopamine receptor found particularly in the striatum and pituitary.

Descartes: French philosopher famous for his ideas about the separate identities of mind and body.

Diaschisis: sudden loss of function in a region of the brain connected to, but at a distance from, a damaged area.

Disconnection: the general term for a group of dis-orders thought to be caused by damage to a pathway between two undamaged regions (e.g., split-brain syndrome).

Distal: far away; as opposed to proximal, meaning near to.

Divergence: in the nervous system, the principle that because axons may branch many times, a single neuron can influence a large number of targets (usually other neurons).

Dopamine: a catecholamine neurotransmitter found in the brain.

Dyslexia: a specific reading difficulty found in a person with otherwise normal intelligence.

Echoic trace: a form of very short-term auditory memory (a sort of acoustic after-image) thought to last no more than 1 or 2 seconds.

Ecological validity: characteristic of experiments where the methods, materials and setting approximate the real-life situation that is under study.

Egocentric neglect: consistent errors to one side of the viewer (right or left).

Epilepsy: the term for a group of neurological disorders characterised by synchronised but excessive neuronal activity.

Equipotentiality: the term associated with Lashley, broadly meaning that any region of cortex can assume responsibility for a given function (memory being the function of interest for Lashley).

Excito-toxicity: the process by which nerve cells are killed by excitatory substances.

Figure (as in figure and ground): the figure is the prominent or core feature of an array.

Finger maze: a piece of apparatus in which the (usually blindfolded) respondent must negotiate a route from A to B. Typically the maze comprises a grooved piece of wood with one correct route and a series of blind alleys. The respondent pushes their finger along the "correct" path.

Fluent aphasia: another name for Wernicke's aphasia. Language is fluent but nonsensical.

Free will: a philosophical term for the capacity of rational agents to choose a course of action from among various alternatives.

Gestalt: a collection of physical, biological, psycho-logical, or symbolic entities that creates a uni-fied concept, configuration, or pattern.

Ground (as in figure and ground): the ground is the background or peripheral element of an array.

Gyri: elongated bumps (convexities) in the cortex (singular: gyrus).

Haemorrhage: a general term for bleeding. In the brain, this may occur following an aneurysm, or other damage to a blood vessel.

Hallucinations: perceptual experiences unrelated to physical sensation. They may occur in any sensory modality, and are often associated with mental illness.

Hemiparesis: partial or complete loss of movement in one side of the body.

Hemiplegia: loss of sensory awareness from, and muscle control of, one side of the body.

Herpes simplex: infection with this virus can affect brain function, leading to permanent damage.

Homotopical: occurring at the same relative location.

Huntington's disease: a rare, genetically determined, neurological disorder causing dementia and death due to progressive loss of neurons in the striatum.

Hyperactivity: in neurological terms, excess functional activity. In behavioural terms, a developmental disorder marked by excess excitability, inattentiveness, restlessness, and reckless/antisocial behaviour.

Ictal focus: the point of origin of epileptic activity, often a discrete region of damaged cortical tissue.

Inhibition of return: when attention is directed to a location, there is a brief period of when processing at that location is facilitated. Following facilitation, there is a period during which attention is inhibited from returning to that location. This is inhibition of return (IOR).

Instrumental learning: a type of learning where an animal learns to perform an action to obtain reinforcement.

Integrative agnosia: a condition characterised by impaired object recognition due to problems in integrating or combining elements of objects.

Interneurons: the name for neurons that receive input from neurons and send their output to other neurons, found throughout the CNS.

In-vivo imaging techniques: a range of imaging techniques that explore structure and/or function in living subjects.

Ipsilateral: same-sided. An unusual anatomical "wiring" arrangement in which brain function is linked to behaviour function on the same side (the norm being contralateral or opposite side control).

Kinaesthetic: anything related to the sensation of body movement/location. Sensory information about the status of joints and muscles.

Kluver-Bucy syndrome: a collection of emotional impairments resulting from amygdala damage in animals.

Lateral inhibition: a relatively common feature of nervous system "wiring" in which active neurons tend to suppress activity of adjacent neurons.

Lesion: a cut in (or severing of) brain tissue. This may occur as the result of an accident or may be part of a surgical procedure.

Lexicon: loosely equates to stored vocabulary, that is, one's long-term memory of native-tongue words (estimated to be about 50,000 for English speakers).

Likert scales: a simple measure of subjective experience. Participants must make a mark on a line that corresponds to how they feel.

Lobectomy: surgical removal of all or part of a cortical lobe (as in temporal lobectomy for removal of the temporal lobe).

Localisation of function: the concept that different parts of the brain carry out different functions and, conversely, that not all parts of the brain do the same thing.

Long-term potentiation: the enduring increase in functional activity (at synapses) that may be related to memory storage in the brain.

Mass-action: the principle (alongside equipotentiality) that cortical regions of the brain are inherently non-specialised, and have the capacity to engage in any psychological function.

Meninges: the system of membranes that enclose the central nervous system.

Meta-analysis: a research technique in which data from similar but separate projects are pooled into a single data set to increase statistical power.

Midline: anatomically, in mammals, the imaginary line separating the left from the right side.

Mind–body problem: explaining what relationship, if any, exists between mental processes and bodily states.

Modularity: the idea (attributed to Fodor) that psychological functions such as language and perception can be broken down into multiple components that may, in turn, depend on the effective processing of discrete brain regions.

Module: a core unit in an integral modular system (see above).

Motor neuron disease: one of a group of disorders characterised by progressive destruction of the motor neurons that control voluntary action.

Multiple sclerosis: a disease in which progressive loss of myelin leads to loss of function.

Myelin sheath: a wrapping of insulation found on axons of many neurons giving a characteristic white appearance and leading to faster nerve impulse propagation.

Neurogenesis: the process by which neurons are generated.

Neuron cell bodies: the central parts of neurons (nerve cells) that contain the nucleus.

Neurotransmitters: a heterogeneous group of chemical messengers usually manufactured by, stored in, and released by neurons that can influence the excitability of other neurons (or muscles).

Ocular apraxia: the inability to move the eyes voluntarily to objects of interest despite unrestricted eye movements and normal visual fields

Open head injuries: head injuries involving damage to the cranium so that the brain is exposed or visible. Often compared with "closed head injury" in which brain damage has occurred although the cranium has not been penetrated: for example, dementia pugilistica (brain damage associated with boxing).

Optic ataxia: a deficit in reaching under visual guidance that cannot be explained by motor, somatosensory, or primary visual deficits

Optical aphasia: a deficit in naming objects viewed visually in spite of intact semantic knowledge of them.

Orienting response: a spontaneous reaction to a stimulus in which the head and/or body are moved so that the source of the stimulus may be examined.

Parallel information processing: the idea that the brain processes two sources of information simultaneously.

Paralysis: loss of movement in a body region (such as a limb).

Parietal lobe: region of cortex behind the frontal lobes and above the occipital lobes. It plays key roles in spatial function and attention.

Parkinson's disease: a neurological disorder in which movements become slowed or are lost altogether. Rigidity and tremor are also found. Associated with loss of cells in and around the basal ganglia.

Parkinsonism: signs and symptoms that resemble Parkinson's disease. Certain drugs (such as neuroleptics) can induce these as a side effect.

Percept: the "whole" that is perceived by putting together the constituent parts.

Perseveration: the tendency to repeat the same (or similar) response despite it no longer being appropriate.

Perseverative (see above): a response may be perseverative in the sense of being an unnecessary or inappropriate regurgitation of an earlier response.

Poliomyelitis (polio): a viral disease where motor neurons are damaged resulting in muscle weakness and/or paralysis.

Polysensory: responsive to input from several modalities.

Priming: the (possibly subconscious) influence of some preliminary event or stimulus on subsequent responding.

Prosodic: an adjective to describe emotionally intoned language. (Aprosodic speech is devoid of emotional intonation, or monotone.)

Prosopagnosia: the form of agnosia in which the ability to perceive faces is affected.

Psychoanalysis: the school of psychology initiated by Freud that emphasises the role(s) of unresolved subconscious conflicts in psychological disorder.

Punishment: in animal learning, anything an animal will work to avoid.

Radio-ligand: a radioactive biochemical marker that binds to a specific receptor type in the brain.

Receptive fields: the area of external influence on any given internal sensory element. Typically, for example, cells in your fovea (central field of vision) have much smaller receptive fields than those in the periphery.

Receptor sites: molecular structures on (or in) the membranes of neurons that neurotransmitter substances (and hormones) can "influence" when they occupy them, usually by making the neuron more or less excited.

Reinforcement: typically some form of reward (positive reinforcement) or punishment (negative reinforcement) that affects the likelihood of a response being repeated.

Reinforcer: a stimulus that elicits a change in behaviour.

Retrograde amnesia: a form of memory loss where people are unable to remember events that happened before the onset of amnesia.

Reward: in animal learning, anything that an animal will work to obtain.

Sagittal: sideways, as in sagittal brain scans taken from the side of the head.

Sensory nerves: nerves carrying action potentials from sensory receptors towards the CNS (e.g., the optic nerve).

Signal to noise ratio: degree to which relevant information can be perceived against a background of irrelevant information.

Signs: the indications of some abnormality or disturbance that are apparent to the trained clinician/observer (as opposed to symptoms, which are things an individual describes/complains of).

Silent synapses: synapses that are not currently transmitting neuronal signals.

Simultanagnosia: inability to recognise multiple elements in a simultaneously displayed visual presentation.

Somatosensory: sensation relating to the body's superficial and deep parts, as contrasted to specialised senses such as sight.

Spatial neglect: a condition in which damage to one side of the brain causes a deficit in attention to the opposite side of space.

Speech apraxia: a characteristic sign of Broca's aphasia in which articulatory problems are apparent and speech is peppered with neologisms or paraphasias.

Stroke: a catch-all term for disturbances of the blood supply to the brain. Most commonly, strokes are caused by obstruction to, or rupture of, blood vessels in the brain.

Striatum: a collective name for the caudate and putamen, key input regions in the basal ganglia.

Subcortical: the portion of the brain immediately below the cerebral cortex.

Substantia nigra: another component of the basal ganglia. Neurons originating in the substantia nigra terminate in the striatum, where they release the neurotransmitter dopamine.

Sulci: the smaller folds or indents on the surface of the cortex (singular: sulcus). Larger ones are called fissures.

Supranuclear palsy: one of the so-called subcortical dementias in which there is progressive tissue loss in the basal ganglia and midbrain structures such as the superior and inferior colliculi.

Symptoms (see Signs above): symptoms are the features of a disorder or disease that the individual reports/complains of.

Synapses: the tiny fluid-filled gaps between neurons where synaptic transmission (see below) may occur. Typically 20–30 nanometres (millionths of a millimetre) wide.

Syndromal: a feature of a syndrome, the latter being a term for a disorder or condition (such as split-brain syndrome) characterised by a cluster of interrelated signs and symptoms rather than one defining feature.

Syntax: the rules governing the structure of sentences.

Tachistoscope: an item of psychological equipment with which visual material can be presented to respondents for very brief exposure times (these days often replaced by digital computers).

Telegraphic speech: a name to describe the non-fluent "stop–start" agrammatic speech associated with Broca's aphasia.

Temporal lobe: the region of the cortex (on both sides of the brain) running forward horizontally above and in front of the ear, known to be involved in language, memory, and visual processing.

Thalamus: a multi-functional subcortical brain region.

Theory of mind: the ability to attribute mental states to others and to understand that others have beliefs that are different from one's own.

Transduction: process by which a cell converts one kind of signal or stimulus into another.

Trinucleotide repeats: stretches of DNA in a gene that contain many repeats of the same three-nucleotide sequence. A genetic cause of neurological disorders.

Ultrasound: an antenatal procedure for generating images of unborn children.

Voluntary gaze: intentional adjustments of eyes in the deliberate process of attending to a feature in the visual field.

Wada test: a test that involves the administration of a fast-acting barbiturate (via the carotid artery) to one hemisphere at a time, to determine, among other things, the hemisphere that is dominant for language.

White matter: parts of the brain comprising axons of nerve cells, mainly responsible for neuronal transmission rather than information processing.

Working memory: a form of short-term memory, first characterised by Alan Baddeley, which allows a person to hold "on-line" (and manipulate) a certain amount of information for a few seconds after it has been presented: for example, keeping a phone number in mind until you have dialled it.

REFERENCES

Abelson, J. L., Curtis, G. C., Sager, O., Albucher, M., Harrigan, S., Taylor, B., & Martis, B. G. (2005). Deep brain stimulation for refractory obsessive-compulsive disorder. *Biological Psychiatry, 57,* 510–516.

Adolphs R., Baron-Cohen, S., & Tranel, D. (2002). Impaired recognition of social emotions following amygdala damage. *Journal of Cognitive Neuroscience, 14,* 1264–1274.

Adolphs R., & Tranel, D. (2004). Impaired judgments of sadness but not happiness following bilateral amygdala damage. *Journal of Cognitive Neuroscience, 16,* 453–462.

Adolphs, R., Tranel, D., & Damasio, A. R. (1998). The human amygdala in social judgment. *Nature, 393,* 470–474.

Adolphs, R., Tranel, D., Damasio, H., & Damasio, A. (1994). Impaired recognition of emotion in facial expressions following bilateral damage to the human amygdala. *Nature, 372,* 613–614.

Adolphs, R., Tranel, D., Hamann, S., Young, A. W., Calder, A. J., Phelps, E. A., et al. (1999). Recognition of facial emotion in nine individuals with bilateral amygdala damage. *Neuropsychologia, 37,* 1111–1117.

Aggleton, J. P., Bland J. M., Kentridge, R. W., & Neave, N. J. (1994). Handedness and longevity: Archival study of cricketers. *British Medical Journal, 309,* 1681–1684.

Aggleton, J. P., & Brown, M. W. (1999). Episodic memory, amnesia, the hippocampal–anterior thalamic axis. *Behavioral and Brain Sciences, 22,* 425–489.

Aggleton, J. P., & Brown, M. W. (2006). Interleaving brain systems for episodic recognition memory. *Trends in Cognitive Sciences, 10,* 455–463.

Aggleton, J. P., Kentridge, R. W., & Neave, N. J. (1993). Evidence for longevity differences between left handed and right handed men: An archival study of cricketers. *Journal of Epidemiology and Community Health, 47,* 206–209.

Aggleton, J. P., & Saunders, R. C. (1997). The relationships between temporal lobe diencephalic structures implicated in anterograde amnesia. *Memory, 5,* 49–71.

Al Chalabi, A. (2006). Motor neuron disease. *Advances in Clinical Neuroscience and Rehabilitation, 6,* 7–8.

Alain, C., Arnott, S. R., Hevenor, S., Graham, S., & Grady, C. L. (2001). What and where in the human auditory cortex. *Proceedings of the National Academy of Science USA, 98,* 12301–12306.

Albertini, R. S., & Phillips, K. A. (1999). 33 cases of body-dysmorphic disorder in children and adolescents. *Journal of the American Academy of Child and Adolescent Psychiatry, 38,* 453–459.

Albin, R. L., & Mink, J. W. (2006). Recent advances in Tourette syndrome research. *Trends in Neurosciences, 29,* 175–182.

Albin, R. L., Young, A. B., & Penny, J. B. (1989). The functional anatomy of basal ganglia disorders. *Trends in Neurosciences, 12,* 366–375.

Albin, R. L., Young, A. B., & Penny, J. B. (1995). The functional anatomy of disorders of the basal ganglia. *Trends in Neurosciences, 18,* 63–64.

Albuquerque, E. X., Hudson, C. S., Mayer, R. F., & Satterfield, J. R. (1976). Studies of human myasthenia gravis: Electrophysiological and ultrastructural evidence compatible with antibody attachment to acetylcholine receptor complex. *Proceedings of the National Academy of Sciences, 73,* 4584–4588.

Alexander, G. E., DeLong, M. R., & Strick, P. L. (1986). Parallel organisation of functionally segregated circuits linking basal ganglia and cortex. *Annual Review of Neuroscience, 9,* 357–381.

Allard, T., Clark, S. A., Jenkins, W. M., & Merzenich, M. M. (1991). Reorganisation of somatosensory area 3b representation in adult owl monkeys after digit syndactyly. *Journal of Neurophysiology, 66,* 1048–1058.

Alvarez, J. A., & Emory, E. (2006). Executive function and the frontal lobes: A meta analytic review. *Neuropsychology Review, 16*(1), 17–42.

Anderson, A. K., & Phelps, E. A. (2000). Expression without recognition: Contributions of the human amygdala to emotional communication. *Psychological Science, 11,* 106–111.

Anderson, R. A., Burdick, J. W., Musallam, S., Pesaran, B., & Cham, J. G. (2004). Cognitive neural prosthetics. *Trends in Cognitive Sciences, 8,* 486–493.

Anderson, V. C., Burchiel, K. J., Hogarth, P., Favre, J. P., & Hammerstad, J. P. (2005). Pallidal vs subthalamic nucleus deep brain stimulation in Parkinson's disease. *Archives of Neurology, 62,* 554–560.

Andreasen, N. C., Paradiso, S., & O'Leary, D. S. (1998). Cognitive dysmetria as an integrative theory of schizophrenia: A dysfunction in cortical-subcortical-cerebellar circuitry? *Schizophrenia Bulletin, 24*(2), 203–218.

Andreassi, J. L. (1989). *Psychophysiology: Human behaviour and physiological response* (2nd ed.). Hillsdale, NJ: Lawrence Erlbaum Associates Inc.

Annett, M. (1985). *Left, right, hand and brain.* London: Lawrence Erlbaum Associates Ltd.

Annett, M. (1987). Handedness as chance or as species-characteristic. *Behavioral and Brain Sciences, 10,* 263–264.

Annett, M. (2002). *Handedness and brain asymmetry: The right shift theory.* New York: Psychology Press.

Appelros, P. (2002). Neglect and anosognosia after first-ever stroke: Incidence and relationship to disability. *Journal of Rehabilitation Medicine, 34,* 215–230.

Arnason, B. G. (1999). Treatment of multiple sclerosis with interferon beta. *Biomedical Pharmacotherapy, 53,* 344–350.

Arnot, S. R., Grady, C. L., Hevenor, S. J., Graham, S., & Alain, C. (2005). The functional organisation of auditory working memory as revealed by fMRI. *Journal of Cognitive Neuroscience, 15,* 819–831.

Aron, A. R., Robbins, T. W., & Poldrack, R. A. (2004). Inhibition and the right inferior frontal cortex. *Trends in Cognitive Sciences, 8,* 170–177.

Assal, G., Favre, C., & Anders, J. P. (1984). Non-reconnaissance d'animaux familiers chez un paysan: Zooagnosie ou prosopagnosie pour les animaux. *Revue Neurologique, 140,* 580–584.

Atkinson, R. C., & Shiffrin, R. M. (1968). Human memory: A proposed system and its control processes. In K. W. Spence & J. T. Spence (Eds.), *The psychology of learning and motivation, Vol 2.* London: Academic Press.

Awh, E., Anllo-Vento, L., & Hillyard, S. A. (2000). The role of spatial selective attention in working memory for locations: Evidence from event related potentials. *Journal of Cognitive Neuroscience, 12,* 840–847.

Awh, A., Jonides, J., Smith, E. E., Schumacher, E. H., Koeppe, R. A., & Katz, S. (1996). Dissociation of storage rehearsal in verbal working memory: Evidence from positron emission tomography. *Psychological Science, 7,* 25–31.

Aziz-Zadeh, L., Koski, L., Zaidel, E., Mazziotta, J., & Iacoboni, M. (2006). Lateralisation of the human mirror neuron system. *Journal of Neuroscience, 26,* 2964–2970.

Baars, B. J. (1988). *A cognitive theory of consciousness.* Cambridge, UK: Cambridge University Press.

Baars, B. J. (1998). A non-Cartesian theatre in the brain: Recent findings are broadly supportive of a global workspace theory. *Ciencia e Cultura, 50*(2), 32–33.

Baars, B. J. (2003). *The conscious access hypothesis: Global workspace theory and brain dynamics.* Cambridge, MA: MIT Press.

Baars, B. J., & Franklin, S. (2003). How consciousness, experience and working memory interact. *Trends in Cognitive Sciences, 7,* 166–172.

Baars, B. J., Ramsoy, T. Z., & Laureys, S. (2003). Brain, conscious experience and the observing self. *Trends in Neurosciences, 26,* 671–675

Backlund, H., Morin, C., Ptito, A., Bushnell, M. C., & Olausson, H. (2005). Tactile functions after cerebral hemispherectomy. *Neuropsychologia, 43,* 332–339.

Bäckman, L., Almkvist, O., Erson, J., Nordberg,

A., Winblad, B., Reineck, R., et al. (1997). Brain activation in young older adults during implicit explicit retrieval. *Journal of Cognitive Neuroscience, 9,* 378–391.

Baddeley, A. (1996). Exploring the central executive. *Quarterly Journal of Experimental Psychology, 49A,* 5–28.

Baddeley, A. D. (1986). *Working memory.* Oxford, UK: Clarendon Press.

Baddeley, A. D. (2001). The concept of episodic memory. *Philosophical Transactions of the Royal Society (B): Biological Sciences, 356,* 1345–1350.

Baddeley, A. D. (2002). Fractionating the central executive. In D. T. Stusss & R. T. Knight (Eds.), *Principles of frontal lobe function* (pp. 246–260). New York: Oxford University Press.

Baddeley, A. D., & Hitch, G. J. (1974). Working memory. In G. H. Bower (Ed.), *The psychology of learning and motivation, Vol 8.* London: Academic Press.

Baddeley, A. D., & Wilson, B. (2002). Prose recall amnesia: Implications for the structure of working memory. *Neuropsychologia, 40,* 1737–1743.

Baeyens, F., Hermans, D., & Eelen, P. (1993). The role of CS–US contingency in human evaluative conditioning. *Behavioural Research and Therapy, 31,* 731–737.

Bar, M. (2004). Visual objects in context. *Nature Reviews: Neuroscience, 5*(8), 617–629.

Bar, M., Kassam, K. S., Ghuman, A. S., Boshyan, J., Schmidt, A. M., Dale, A. M., et al. (2006). Top-down facilitation of visual recognition. *Proceedings of the National Academy of Sciences, 103,* 449–454.

Barcelo, F., & Knight, R. T. (2001). Both random and perseverative errors underlie WCST deficits in prefrontal patients. *Neuropsychologia, 40,* 349–356.

Barnes, C. A. (1979). Memory deficits associated with senescence: A neurophysiological behavioral study in the rat. *Journal of Comparative and Physiological Psychology, 93,* 74–104.

Baron-Cohen, S. (2003). *The essential difference: The truth about the male and female brain.* New York: Basic Books.

Baron-Cohen, S., Leslie, A., & Frith, U. (1985). Does the autistic child have a "theory of mind"? *Cognition, 21,* 37–46.

Bates, E., Wilson, S. M., Saygin, A. P., Dick, F., Sereno, M. I., Knight, R. T., et al. (2003). Voxel based lesion symptom mapping. *Nature: Neuroscience, 6*(5).

Bartholomeus, B. (1974). Effects of task requirements on ear superiority for sung speech. *Cortex, 10,* 215–223.

Battaglia-Mayer, A., & Caminiti, R. (2002). Optical ataxia as a result of the breakdown of the global tuning fields of parietal neurons. *Brain, 125,* 225–237.

Bavelier, D., Corina, D., Jezzard, P., Padmanabhan, S., Clark, V. P., Karni, A., et al. (1997). Sentence reading: A functional MRI study at 4 tesla. *Journal of Cognitive Neuroscience, 9*(5), 664–686.

Bavelier, D., & Neville, H. J. (2002). Cross-modal plasticity: Where and how? *Nature Reviews: Neuroscience, 3,* 443–452.

Bavelier, D., Tomann, A., Hutton, C., & Mitchell, D. (2000). Visual attention to periphery is enhanced in congenitally deaf individuals. *Journal of Neuroscience, 20,* 1–6.

Bay, E. (1953). Disturbances of visual perception and their examination. *Brain, 76,* 515–551.

Bayley, P. J., Hopkins, R. O., & Squire, L. R. (2003). Successful recollection of remote autobiographical memories by amnesic patients with medial temporal lobe lesions. *Neuron, 38,* 135–144.

Bayley, P. J., & Squire, L. R. (2005). Failure to acquire new semantic knowledge in patients with large medial temporal lobe lesions. *Hippocampus, 15,* 273–280.

Bear, M. F., & Kirkwood, A. (1993). Neocortical long-term potentiation. *Current Opinion in Neurobiology, 3,* 197–202.

Bechara, A., Damasio, A. R., Damasio, H., & Anderson, S. W. (1994). Insensitivity to future consequences following damage to human prefrontal cortex. *Cognition, 50,* 7–15.

Bechara, A., Damasio, H., Damasio, A. R., & Lee, G. P. (1999). Different contributions of the human amygdala and ventromedial prefrontal cortex to decision making. *Journal of Neuroscience, 19,* 5473–5481.

Bechara, A., Damasio, H., Tranel, D., & Damasio, A. R. (2005). The Iowa Gambling Task and the somatic marker hypothesis: Some questions and answers. *Trends in Cognitive Science, 9,* 159–162

Behrens, S. (1988). The role of the right hemisphere in the production of linguistic stress. *Brain and Language, 33,* 104–107.

Behrmann, M. (2000). Spatial reference frames and hemispatial neglect. In M. S. Gazzaniga (Ed.), *The new cognitive neurosciences* (pp. 651–666). Cambridge, MA: MIT Press.

Behrmann, M., Marotta, J., Gauthier, M. J., & Tarr, T. J. (2005). Behavioural change and its neural correlates in visual agnosia after expertise training. *Journal of Cognitive Neuroscience, 17*, 554–568.

Bennett, E. L., Diamond, M. L., Krech, D., & Rosenzweig, M. R. (1964). Chemical and anatomical plasticity of brain. *Science, 146*, 610–619.

Benson, D. F., & Greenberg, J. P. (1969). Visual form agnosia. *Archives of Neurology, 20*, 82–89.

Bentin, S., Allison, T., Puce, A., Perez, E., & McCarthy, G. (1996). Electrophysiological studies of face perception in humans. *Journal of Cognitive Neuroscience, 8*, 551–565.

Benton, A. L. (1967). Constructional apraxia and the minor hemisphere. *Confina Neurologica, 29*, 1–16.

Benton, A. L., Hannay, H. J., & Varney, N. R. (1975). Visual perception of line direction in patients with unilateral brain disease. *Neurology, 25*, 907–910.

Benton, A. L., & Hecaen, H. (1970). Stereoscopic vision in patients with unilateral cerebral disease. *Neurology, 20*, 1084–1088.

Berthoz, S., Armony, J. L., Blair, R. J., & Dolan, R. J. (2002). An fMRI study of intentional and unintentional (embarrassing). Violations of social norms. *Brain, 125*, 1696–1708.

Bever, T. G. (1983). Cerebral lateralisation, cognitive asymmetry and human consciousness. In E. Perecman & J. Brown (Eds.), *Cognitive processing in the right hemisphere*. New York: Academic Press.

Bisiach, E., & Luzzatti, C. (1978). Unilateral neglect of representational space. *Cortex, 14*, 129–133.

Black, K. J., & Mink, J. W. (1999). Neuropsychiatry of movement disorders. *Current Opinion in Psychiatry, 12*, 313–319.

Blackmore, S. (2003). *Consciousness: An introduction*. London: Hodder & Stoughton.

Blair R. J., Morris J. S., Frith C. D., Perrett D. I., & Dolan, R. J. (1999). Dissociable neural responses to facial expressions of sadness and anger. *Brain, 122*, 883–893.

Blakemore, S. J., Bristow, D., Bird, G., Frith, C., & Ward, J. (2005). Somatosensory activations during the observation of touch and a case of touch–vision synaesthesia. *Brain, 128*, 1571–1583.

Blakemore, S. J., & Frith, C. (2003). Self-awareness and action. *Current Opinion in Neurology, 13*, 219–224.

Blank, S. C., Bird, H., Turkheimer, F., & Wise, R. J. (2003). Speech production after stroke: The role of the right opercularis. *Annals of Neurology, 15*, 310–320.

Bleie, T. (2004). Evolution, brains, and the predicament of sex in human cognition. *Sexualities, Evolution and Gender, 5*, 149–189.

Bliss, T. V., & Lomo, T. (1973). Long-lasting potentiation of synaptic transmission in the dentate area of the anaesthetised rabbit following stimulation of the perforant pathway. *Journal of Physiology, 232*, 331–356.

Block, N. (2005). Two neural correlates of consciousness. *Trends in Cognitive Sciences, 9*, 46–52.

Blumer, D., & Benson, D. F. (1975). Personality changes with frontal and temporal lobe lesions. In D. F. Benson & D. Blumer (Eds.), *Psychiatric aspects of neurological disease* (pp. 151–170). New York: Grune & Stratton.

Bodamer, J. (1947). Die prosopagnosie. *Archiv für Psychiatrie und Nervenkrankheiten, 179*, 6–53.

Boillee, S., & Cleveland, D. W. (2004). Gene therapy for ALS delivers. *Trends in Neurosciences, 27*, 235–237.

Bolam, J. P., & Magill, P. J. (2004). Current thinking in basal ganglia research. *Trends in Neurosciences, 27*, 1.

Borovsky, A., Saygin, A. P., Bates, E., & Dronkers, N. (2007). Lesion correlates of conversational speech production deficits. *Neuropsychologia, 45*, 2525–2533.

Bosshardt, S., Degonda, N., Schmidt, C. F., Boesiger, P., Nitsch, R. M., Hock, C., et al. (2005). One month of human memory consolidation enhances retrieval-related hippocampal activity. *Hippocampus, 15*, 1026–1040.

Botvinick, M. M., Cohen, J. D., & Carter, C. S. (2004). Conflict monitoring and anterior cingulate cortex: An update. *Trends in Cognitive Sciences, 8*, 539–546.

Bourne, J. N., Sorra, K. E., Hurlburt, J., & Harris, K. M. (2006). Polyribosomes are increased in spines of CA1 dendrites 2 h after the induction of LTP in mature rat hippocampal slices. *Hippocampus, 17*, 1–4.

Bourne, V. J. (2005). Lateralised processing of positive facial emotion: Sex differences in strength of hemispheric dominance. *Neuropsychologia, 43*, 953–956.

Boussaoud, D., Ungerleider, L. G., & Desimone, R. (1990). Pathways for motion analysis: Cortical connections of the medial superior temporal and fundus of the superior temporal visual areas in the macaque. *Journal of Comparative Neurology, 296*, 462–495.

Bradshaw, J. L., & Mattingley, J. B. (1995). *Clinical neuropsychology: Behavioural and brain science.* London: Academic Press.

Brancucci, A., Babiloni, C., Rossini, P. M., & Romani, G. L. (2005). Right hemisphere specialization for intensity discrimination of musical and speech sounds. *Neuropsychologia, 43*, 1916–1923.

Brass, M., & Heyes, C. (2005). Imitation: Is cognitive neuroscience solving the correspondence problem? *Trends in Cognitive Sciences, 9*(10), 489–495.

Braun, J., & Julesz, B. (1998). Withdrawing attention at little or no cost: Detection and discrimination tasks. *Perception and Psychophysics, 60*, 1–23.

Braver, T., Reynolds, J., & Donaldson, D. (2003). Neural mechanisms of transient and sustained cognitive control during task switching. *Neuron, 39*, 713–726.

Breiter, H. C., Aharon, I., Kahneman, D., Dale, A., & Shizgal, P. (2001). Functional imaging of neural responses to expectancy and experience of monetary gains and losses. *Neuron, 30*, 619–639.

Breiter, H. C., Rauch, S. L., Kwong, K. K., Baker, J. R., Weiskoff, R. M., Kennedy, D. N., et al. (1996). Functional magnetic resonance imaging of symptom provocation in obsessive compulsive disorder. *Archives of General Psychiatry, 53*, 595–606.

Brewer, W. F. (1995). What is recollective memory? In D. D. Rubin (Ed.), *Remembering our past: Studies in autobiographical memory* (pp.19–66). Cambridge, UK: Cambridge University Press.

Broadbent, D. (1958). *Perception and communication.* London: Pergamon Press.

Broadbent, D. A. (1970). Stimulus set and response set: Two kinds of selective attention. In D. I. Motofsky (Ed.), *Attention: Contemporary theory and analysis* (pp. 51–60). New York: Appleton Century Crofts.

Broca, P. (1861). Remarques sur la siège de la faculté du langage articule. *Bulletin de la Société Anatomique de Paris, 16*, 343–357.

Brodmann, K. (1909). Vergleichende Lokalisationslehreder Grosshirnrinde in ihren prinzipien Dargestellt auf Grund des Zellenbaues. Leipzig: J. A. Barth. [In G. von Bonin (Ed.), *Some papers on the cerebral cortex* (pp. 201–230). Springfield, IL: Charles C. Thomas (1960).]

Brown, J., Cooper-Kuhn, C. M., Kemperman, G., Van Praag, H., Winkler, J., Gage, F., et al. (2003). Enriched environment and physical activity stimulate hippocampal but not olfactory bulb neurogenesis. *European Journal of Neuroscience, 17*, 2042–2046.

Brown, W. S., Paul, L. K., Symington, M., & Dietrich, R. (2005). Comprehension of humour in primary agenesis of the corpus callosum. *Neuropsychologia, 43*, 906–916.

Brownell, H. (1988). Appreciation of metaphoric and connotative word meaning by brain-damaged patients. In C. Chiarello (Ed.), *Right hemisphere contributions to lexical semantics* (pp. 19–31). New York: Springer-Verlag.

Bruijn, L. T., Miller, T. M., & Cleveland, D. W. (2004). Unraveling the mechanisms involved in motor neuron degeneration in ALS. *Annual Review of Neuroscience, 27*, 723–749.

Bruyer, R., Laterre, C., Seron, X., Feyereisen, P., Strypstein, E., Pierrard, E., et al. (1983). A case of prosopagnosia with some preserved covert remembrance of familiar faces. *Brain and Cognition, 2*, 257–284.

Buccino, G., Binkofski, F., Fink, G. R., Fadiga, L., & Fogassi, L. (2001). Action observation activates premotor and parietal areas in a somatotopic manner: An fMRI study. *European Journal of Neuroscience, 13*, 400–404.

Buchel, C., Morris, J., Dolan, R. J., & Friston, K. J. (1998). Brain systems mediating aversive conditioning: An event related fMRI study. *Neuron, 20*, 947–957.

Buonomano, D. V., & Merzenich, M. M. (1998). Cortical plasticity: From synapses to maps. *Annual Review of Neuroscience, 21*, 149–186.

Burgess, P. W. (2000). Strategy application disorder: The role of the frontal lobes in human multitasking. *Psychological Research, 63*, 279–288.

Burgess, P. W., Alderman, N., Forbes, C., Costello, A., Coates, L. M., Dawson, D. R., et al. (2006). The case for the development and use of ecologically valid measures of executive function in experimental and clinical neuropsychology. *Journal of the International Neuropsychological Society, 12*, 194–209.

Burgess, P. W., Scott, S. K., & Frith, C. D. (2003). The role of the rostral frontal cortex (area 10). in prospective memory: A lateral versus medial dissociation. *Neuropsychologia, 41*, 906–918.

Burgess, P. W., & Shallice, T. (1997). *The Hayling and Brixton Tests*. Bury St Edmonds, UK: Thames Valley Test Company Ltd.

Burgess, P. W., Veitch, E., Costello, A., & Shallice, T. (2000). The cognitive and neuroanatomical correlates of multitasking. *Neuropsychologia, 38*, 848–863.

Butter, C. M. (2004). Anton Raederscheidt's distorted self-portraits and their significance for understanding balance in art. *Journal of the History of the Neurosciences, 13*, 66–78.

Buxbaum, L. J. (2006). On the right (and left). track: 20 years of progress in studying hemispatial neglect. *Cognitive Neuropsychology, 23*, 184–201.

Buxbaum, L. J., Johnson-Frey S. H., & Bartlett-Williams, M. (2005). Deficient internal models for planning hand–object interactions in apraxia. *Neuropsychologia, 43*, 917–929.

Cabeza, R., & Nyberg, L. (2000). Imaging cognition II: An empirical review of 275 PET fMRI studies. *Journal of Cognitive Neuroscience, 12*, 1–47.

Cabranes, J. A., DeJuan, R., Encinas, M., Marcos, A., Gil, P., Fernandez, C., et al. (2004). Relevance of functional imaging in the progression of mild cognitive impairment. *Neurological Research, 26*, 496–501.

Cahill, L., Babinsky, R., Markowitsch, H., & McGaugh, J. L. (1995). The amygdala and emotional memory. *Nature, 377*, 295–296.

Cahill, L., & McGaugh, J. L. (1995). A novel demonstration of enhanced memory associated with emotional arousal. *Consciousness and Cognition, 4*, 410–421.

Caine, D., & Watson, J. D. (2000). Neuropsychological neuropathological sequelae of cerebral anoxia: A critical review. *Journal of the International Neuropsychological Society, 6*, 86–99.

Cajal, R. Y. (1913). *Degeneration and regeneration of the nervous system* [R. M. Day trans., 1928]. London: Open University Press.

Cajal, R. Y. (1937). *Recuerdos de mi Vida*. Cambridge, MA: MIT Press.

Cameron, H. A., & McKay, R. D. (2001). Adult neurogenesis produces a large pool of new granule cells in the dentate gyrus. *Journal of Comparative Neurology, 435*, 406–417.

Caplan, D. (1987). *Neurolinguistics and linguistic aphasiology: An introduction*. Cambridge, UK: Cambridge University Press.

Caplan, D. (1992). *Language: Structure, processing and disorders*. Cambridge, MA: MIT Press.

Caramazza, A. (1984). The logic of neuropsychological research and the problem of patient classification in aphasia. *Brain and Language, 21*, 9–20.

Caramazza, A. (1986). On drawing inferences about the structure of normal cognitive systems from the analysis of patterns of impaired performance: The case for single patient studies. *Brain and Cognition, 5*, 41–66.

Caramazza, A., & Mahon, B. Z. (2003). The organization of conceptual knowledge: The evidence from category-specific semantic deficits. *Trends in Cognitive Sciences, 7*, 354–361.

Caramazza, A., & Shelton, R. S. (1998). Domain-specific knowledge systems in the brain: The animate–inanimate distinction. *Journal of Cognitive Neuroscience, 10*, 1–34.

Carlen, M., Cassidy, R. M., Brismar, H., Smith, G. A., Enquist, L. W., & Frisen, J. (2002). Functional integrity of adult-born neurons. *Current Biology, 12*(7), 606–608.

Carlson, N. R. (2007). *Physiology of Behavior* (9th ed). New York: Pearson Education.

Carlson, T., Grol, M. J., & Verstraten, F. A. (2006). Dynamics of visual recognition revealed by fMRI. *Neuroimage, 15*, 892–905.

Carlsson, A., & Carlsson, M. L. (2006). A dopaminergic deficit hypothesis of schizophrenia: The path to discovery. *Dialogues in Clinical Neuroscience, 8*(1), 137–142.

Carpenter, P. A., & Just, M. A. (1999). Modeling the mind: High field fMRI-activation during cognition. *Topics in Magnetic Resonance Imaging, 10*, 16–36.

Catani, M., & ffytche, D. H. (2005). The rises and falls of disconnection syndromes. *Brain, 128*(10), 2224–2239.

Caterina, M. C., & Cappa, A. (2003). Segregation of the neural correlates of language and phonological short-term memory. *Cortex, 39*, 913–925.

Cavanagh, P., & Alvarez, G. A. (2005). Tracking multiple targets with multifocal attention. *Trends in Cognitive Sciences, 9*, 349–354.

Cavanna, A. E., & Trimble, M. R. (2006). The precuneus: A review of its functional anatomy and behavioural correlates. *Brain, 129*, 564–583.

Cermak, L. S. (1993). Automatic versus controlled processing and the implicit task performance of amnesic patients. In P. Graf & M. E. J. Masson (Eds.), *Implicit memory: New directions in cognition, development, neuropsychology* (pp. 287–301). Hillsdale, NJ: Lawrence Erlbaum Associates Inc.

Cermak, L. S., & O'Connor, M. (1983). The anterograde retrograde retrieval ability of a patient with amnesia due to encephalitis. *Neuropsychologia, 21,* 213–234.

Chalmers, D. J. (1995). The puzzle of conscious experience. *Scientific American, 258,* 62–68.

Chang, F. L., & Greenhough, W. T. (1982). Lateralised effects of monocular training on dendritic branching in adult split-brain rats. *Brain Research, 232,* 283–292.

Chaytor, N., Schmitter-Edgecombe, M., & Burr, R. (2006). Improving the ecological validity of executive functioning asesment. *Archives of Clinical Neuropsychology, 21,* 217–227.

Chein, J. M., Ravizza, S. M., & Fiez, J. A. (2003). Using neuroimaging to evaluate models of working memory and their implications for language processing. *Journal of Neurolingustics, 16,* 315–339.

Chelazzi, L., & Corbetta, M. (2000). Cortical mechanisms of visuospatial attention in the primate brain. In M. S. Gazzaniga (Ed.), *The new cognitive neurosciences* (pp. 667–686). Cambridge, MA: MIT Press.

Cherry, E. C. (1953). Some experiments on the recognition of speech with one or two ears. *Journal of the Acoustic Society of America, 25,* 975–979.

Chokron, S., Colliot, P., & Bartolomeo, P. (2004). The role of vision in spatial representation. *Cortex, 40,* 281–290.

Chomsky, N. (1957). *Syntactic structures.* The Hague: Mouton.

Chomsky, N. (1965). *Aspects of the theory of syntax.* Cambridge, MA: MIT Press.

Christensen, A-L. (1979). *Luria's neuropsychological investigation* (2nd ed). Copenhagen: Ejnar Munksgaards Vorlag.

Chung, M. K., Dalton, K. M., & Davidson, R. (2004). Less white matter concentration in autism: 2D voxel based morphometry. *Neuroimage, 23,* 242–251.

Clarke, S., Assal, G., & DeTribolet, N. (1993). Left-hemisphere strategies in visual recognition, topographical orientation and time planning. *Neuropsychologia, 31,* 99–113.

Coffin, J. M., Baroody, S., Schneider, K., & O'Neill, J. (2005). Impaired cerebellar learning in children with prenatal alcohol exposure: A comparative study of eyeblink conditioning in children with ADHD dyslexia. *Cortex, 41,* 389–398.

Cohen, L. G., Celnik, P., Pascual-Leone, A., Corwell, B., Falz, L., Dambrosia, J., et al. (1997). Functional relevance of cross-modal plasticity in blind humans. *Nature, 389,* 180–183.

Cohen, N. J., & Squire, L. R. (1980). Preserved learning retention of pattern analyzing skill in amnesia: Dissociation of knowing how–knowing that. *Science, 210,* 207–209.

Colchester, A., Kingsley, D., Lasserson, D., Kendall, B., Bello, F., & Rush, C. (2001). Structural MRI volumetric analysis in patients with organic amnesia I. Methods and comparative findings across diagnostic groups. *Journal of Neurology, Neurosurgery and Psychiatry, 71,* 13–22.

Collette, F., Hogge, M., Salmon, E., & Van der Linden, M. (2006). Exploration of the neural substrates of executive functioning by functional imaging. *Neuroscience, 139,* 209–221.

Coltheart, M. (2001). Assumptions and methods in cognitive neuropsychology. In B. Rapp (Ed.), *Handbook of cognitive neuropsychology.* Philadelphia: Psychology Press.

Coltheart, M., Inglis, L., Cupples, L., Michie, P., Bates, A., & Budd, B. (1998). A semantic subsystem specific to the storage of information about visual attributes of animate and inanimate objects. *Neurocase, 4,* 353–370.

Cooney, J. W., & Gazzaniga, M. S. (2003). Neurological disorders and the structure of human consciousness. *Trends in Cognitive Sciences, 7,* 161–165.

Corballis, M. C. (1991). *The lop-sided ape: Evolution of the generative mind.* Oxford, UK: Oxford University Press.

Corballis, M. C. (2003). From mouth to hand: Gesture, speech, and the evolution of right-handedness. *Behavioral and Brain Sciences, 26,* 199–260.

Corballis, P. M., Funnell, M. G., & Gazzaniga, M. S. (1999). A dissociation between spatial and identity matching in callosotomy patients. *Neuroreport, 10,* 2183–2187.

Corbetta, M., Kincade, M. J., Lewis, C., Snyder, A. Z., & Sapir, A. (2005). Neural basis and recovery of spatial attention deficits in spatial neglect. *Nature: Neuroscience, 8,* 1603–1610.

Corbetta, M., Miezen, F. M., Dobmeyer, S., Shulman, G. L., & Petersen, S. E. (1991). Selective and divided attention during visual discriminations of shape, colour and speed:

Functional anatomy by PET. *Journal of Neuroscience, 11*, 2383–2402.

Corbetta, M., & Shulman, G. L. (2002). Control of goal-directed and stimulus-driven attention in the brain. *Nature Reviews: Neuroscience, 3*, 201–215.

Coren, S. (1992). *The left-hander syndrome*. New York: Free Press.

Coren, S. (1995). Family patterns of handedness: Evidence for indirect inheritance mediated by birth stress. *Behaviour Genetics, 25*, 517–524.

Corkin, S. (1984). Lasting consequences of bilateral medial temporal lobectomy: Clinical course experimental findings in H.M. *Seminars in Neurology, 4*, 249–259.

Corkin, S. (2002). What's new with the amnesic patient H.M.? *Nature Reviews: Neuroscience, 3*, 153–160.

Corsi, P. M. (1972). Human memory and the medial temporal region of the brain. *Dissertation Abstracts International, 34*, 891B.

Courtney, S. M., Ungerleider, L. G., Keil, K., & Haxby, J. V. (1996). Object spatial visual working memory activates separate neural systems in the human cortex. *Cerebral Cortex, 6*, 39–49.

Courtney, S. M., Ungerleider, L. G., Keil, K., & Haxby, J. V. (1997). Transient and sustained activity in a distributed neural system for human working memory. *Nature, 386*, 608–611.

Craik, F. I. M., & Lockhart, R. S. (1972). Levels of processing: A framework for memory research, *Journal of Verbal Learning and Verbal Behavior, 11*, 671–684.

Creem, S. H., & Proffitt, D. R. (2001). Defining the cortical visual systems: "what", "where" and "how". *Acta Psychologica, 107*, 43–68.

Crick, F., & Koch, C. (1990). Towards a neurobiological theory of consciousness. *Seminars in Neuroscience, 2*, 263–275.

Damasio, A. (1994). *Descartes' error: Emotion, reason and the human brain*. New York: Putnam Publishing.

Damasio, A., & Geschwind, N. (1985). Anatomical localization in clinical neuropsychology. In J. A. M. Frederiks (Ed.), *Handbook of clinical neurology* (pp. 7–22). Amsterdam: Elsevier.

Damasio, A. R. (1985). Disorders of complex visual processing: Agnosia, achromatopsia, Balint's syndrome, and related difficulties of orientation and construction. In M. M. Mesulam (Ed.), *Principles of behavioural neurology* (pp. 259–288). Philadelphia: F. A. Davis.

Damasio, A. R. (1989). Time-locked multiregional retroactivation: A systems level proposal for the neural structures of recall recognition. *Cognition, 33*, 25–62.

Damasio, A. R. (1996). The somatic marker hypothesis and the possible functions of the prefrontal cortex. *Philosophical Transactions of the Royal Society of London B, 351*, 1413–1420.

Damasio, H., & Damasio, A. R. (1989). *Lesion analysis in neuropsychology*. New York: Oxford University Press.

Damasio, H., Grabowski, T., Frank, R., Galaburda, A. M., & Damasio, A. R. (1994). The return of Phineas Gage: Clues about the brain from the skull of a famous patient. *Science, 264*, 1102–1105.

Danta, G., Hilton, R. C., & O'Boyle, D. J. (1978). Hemisphere function and binocular depth perception, *Brain, 101*, 569–590.

Dapretto, M. (2006). Understanding emotions in others: Mirror neuron dysfunction in children with autism spectrum disorders. *Nature: Neuroscience, 9*, 28–30.

Davidson, R. J., Ekman, P., Saron, C., Senulis, J., & Friesen, W. V. (1990). Emotional expression and brain physiology I: Approach/withdrawal and cerebral asymmetry. *Journal of Personality and Social Psychology, 58*, 330–341.

Davis, S., Butcher, S. P., & Morris, R. G. (1992). The NMDA receptor antagonist D-2-amino-5-phosphopentanoate (D-AP5) impairs spatial learning LTP in vivo at intercerebral concentrations comparable to those that block LTP in vitro. *Journal of Neuroscience, 12*, 21–34.

de Saussure, F. (1916). *Cours de linguistique generale* [Eds. C. Bally & A. Sechehaye]. Lausanne & Paris: Payot. [Trans. W. Baskin, *Course in general linguistics*, Glasgow: Fontana/Collins, 1977.]

Dehaene, S., Changeux, J. P., Naccache, L., Sackur, J., & Sergent, C. (2006). Conscious, preconscious and subliminal processing: A testable taxonomy. *Trends in Cognitive Sciences, 10*, 204–211.

Dehaene, S., Kerszberg, M., & Changeux, J. P. (1998). A neuronal model of a global workspace in effortful cognitive tasks. *Proceedings of the National Academy of Sciences, 95*, 14529–14534.

Dehaene, S., Naccache, L., Cohen, L., LeBihan, D., Mangin, J. F., Poline, J. B., et al. (2001). Cerebral mechanisms of word masking and unconscious repetition priming. *Nature Neuroscience, 4*, 752–758.

Dehaene, S., Sergent, C., & Changeux, J.-P. (2003). A neuronal network model linking subjective reports and objective physiological data during conscious perception. *Proceedings of the National Academy of Sciences, 100,* 8520–8525.

Dejerine, J. (1892). Contribution a l'étude anatomo-pathologique et clinique des différentes variétés de cécité verbale. *Comptes Rendus des Séances de la Société de Biologie et de ses Filiales, 4,* 61–90.

Delgado, M. R., Nystrom, L. E., Fissell, C., Noll, D. C., & Fiez, J. A. (2000). Tracking the haemodynamic response to reward and punishment in the striatum. *Journal of Neurophysiology, 84,* 3072–3077.

Delis, D. C., Robertson, L. C., & Efron, R. (1986). Hemispheric specialisation of memory for visual hierarchical stimuli. *Neuropsychologia, 24*(2), 205–216.

Delis, D. C., Squire, L. R., Bihrle, A., & Massman, P. (1992). Componential analysis of problem solving ability: Performance of patients with frontal lobe damage and amnesiac patients on a new sorting test. *Neuropsychologia, 30,* 683–697.

Demonet, J. F., Thierry, G., & Cardebet, D. (2005). Renewal of the neurophysiology of language: Functional neuroimaging. *Physiological Reviews, 85,* 49–95.

Dennett, D. C. (1991). *Consciousness explained.* Boston: Little, Brown.

DeQuervain D. J., Fischbacher, U., Treyer, V., Schellhammer, M., Schnyder, U., Buck, A., et al. (2004). The neural basis of altruistic punishment. *Science, 305,* 1254–1258.

DeRenzi, E., Faglioni, P., & Previdi, P. (1977). Spatial memory hemispheric locus of lesion. *Cortex, 13,* 424–433.

DeRenzi, E., & Nichelli, P. (1975). Verbal and non-verbal short-term memory impairment following hemispheric damage. *Cortex, 11,* 341–354.

DeRenzi, E., Perani, D., Carlesimo, G. A., Silveri, M. C., & Fazio, F. (1994). Prosopagnosia can be associated with damage confined to the right hemisphere: An MRI and PET study and a review of the literature. *Neuropsychologia, 32,* 893–902.

DeRenzi, E., Pieczuro, A., & Vignolo, L. A. (1968). Ideational apraxia: A quantitative study. *Neuropsychologia, 6,* 41–52.

DeRenzi, E., & Vignolo, L. A. (1962). The token test: A sensitive test to detect disturbances in aphasics. *Brain, 85,* 665–678.

Descartes, R. (1664). *Traite de l'homme.* Paris: Angot.

Desimone, R., Wessinger, M., Thomas, L., & Schneider, W. (1990). Attentional control of visual perception: Cortical and sub-cortical mechanisms. *Cold Spring Harbour Symposia on Quantitative Biology, 55,* 963–971.

Deutsch, G., Bourbon, W., Papanicolaou, A., & Eisenberg, H. (1988). Visuo-spatial tasks compared during activation of regional cerebral blood flow. *Neuropsychologia, 26,* 445–452.

DiPellegrino, G., Fadiga, L., Fogassi, L., Gallese, V., & Rizzolatti, G. (1992). Understanding motor events: A neurophysiological study. *Experimental Brain Research, 91,* 176–180.

Dobbins, I. G., Rice, H. J., Wagner, A. D., & Schacter, D. L. (2003). Memory orientation success: Separable neurocognitive components underlying episodic recognition. *Neuropsychologia, 41,* 318–333.

Dobkin, B. H. (1993). Neuroplasticity: Key to recovery after central nervous system injury. *Western Journal of Medicine, 159,* 56–60.

Dolan M., & Fullam R. (2006). Face affect recognition deficits in personality-disordered offenders: Association with psychopathy. *Psychological Medicine, 36,* 1563–1566.

Downing, P. E., Jiang, Y. H., Shuman, M., & Kanwisher, N. (2001). A cortical area selective for visual processing of the human body. *Science, 293,* 2470–2473.

Drevets, W. C., Price, J. L., Simpson, J. R., Todd, R. D., Reich, T., Vannier, M., et al. (1997). Subgenual prefrontal cortex abnormalities in mood disorders. *Nature, 386,* 824–827.

Dronkers, N. F. (2000). The pursuit of brain–language relationships. *Brain and Language, 71,* 59–61.

Dronkers, N. F., Plaisant, O., Iba-Zizen, M. T., & Cabanis, E. A. (2007). Paul Broca's historic cases: High resolution MR imaging of the brains of Leborgne and Lelong, *Brain, 130,* 1432–1441.

Dronkers, N. F., Redfern, B. B., & Knight, R. T. (2000). The neural architecture of language disorders. In M. S. Gazzaniga (Ed.), *The new cognitive neurosciences* (pp. 949–958). Cambridge, MA: MIT Press.

Dronkers, N. F., Redfern, B. B., & Ludy, C. A. (1995). Lesion localisation in chronic Wernicke's aphasia. *Brain and Language, 51*(1), 62–65.

Dronkers, N. F., Redfern, B. B., Ludy, C., & Baldo, J. (1998). Brain regions associated with conduction aphasia and echoic rehearsal. *Journal of the International Neuropsychology Society, 4*(1), 23–24.

Dronkers, N. F., Shapiro, J. K., Redfern, B., & Knight, R. T. (1992). The role of Broca's area in Broca's aphasia. *Journal of Clinical and Experimental Neuropsychology, 14*, 52–53.

Dronkers, N. F., Wilkins, D. P., Van Valin, R. D., Redfern, B. B., & Jaeger, J. J. (2004). Lesion analysis of the brain areas involved in language comprehension. *Cognition, 92*(1–2), 145–177.

Duncan, J. (2006). Brain mechanisms of attention. *Quarterly Journal of Experimental Psychology, 59*(1), 2–27.

Duncan, J., & Humphreys, G. (1992). Beyond the search surface: Visual search and attentional engagement. *Journal of Experimental Psychology: Human Perception and Performance, 18*(2), 578–588.

Duncan, J., & Owen, A. M. (2000). Common regions of the human frontal lobe recruited by diverse cognitive demands. *Trends in Neurosciences, 23*, 475–483.

Dutton, D. G., & Aron, A. P. (1974). Some evidence for heightened sexual attraction under conditions of high anxiety. *Journal of Personality and Social Psychology, 30*, 510–517.

Edelman, G. M., & Tononi, G. (2000). *A universe of consciousness.* New York: Basic Books.

Edelstyn, N. M. J., Hunter, B., & Ellis, S. J. (2006). Bilateral dorsolateral thalamic lesions disrupt conscious recollection. *Neuropsychologia, 44*, 931–938.

Egner, T., & Hirsch, J. (2005). Cognitive control mechanisms resolve conflict through cortical amplification of task-relevant information. *Nature: Neuroscience, 8*, 1784–1790.

Ehde, D. M., Czerneicki, J. M., & Smith, D. G. (2000). Chronic phantom sensation, phantom pain, residual limb pain, and other regional pain after lower limb amputation. *Archives of Physical Medicine and Rehabilitation, 81*, 1039–1044.

Eichenbaum, H. (2002). *The cognitive neuroscience of memory: An introduction.* Oxford, UK: Oxford University Press.

Ekman, P., & Friesen, W. E. (1971). Constants across cultures in the face and emotion. *Journal of Personality and Social Psychology, 17*, 124–129.

Elgh, E., Larsson, A., Eriksson, S., & Nyberg, L. (2003). Structure–function correlates of cognitive decline in aging. *International Psychogeriatrics, 15*, 121–133.

Elliott, R., Friston, K. J., & Dolan, R. J. (2000). Dissociable neural responses associated with reward, punishment and risk-taking behaviour *Journal of Neuroscience, 20*, 6159–6165.

Elliott, R., Newman, J. L., Longe, O. A., & Deakin, J. F. W. (2003). Differential response patterns in the striatum and orbitofrontal cortex to financial reward in humans: A parametric fMRI study. *Journal of Neuroscience, 23*, 303–307.

Elliott, R., Rubinsztein, J. S., Sahakian, B. J., & Dolan, R. J. (2000). Selective attention to emotional stimuli in a verbal go/no-go task: An fMRI study. *Neuroreport, 11*, 1739–1744.

Ellis, A. W., Miller, D., & Sin, G. (1983). Wernicke's aphasia and normal language processing: A case study in cognitive neuropsychology. *Cognition, 15*, 111–144.

Ellis, A. W., & Young, A. W. (1996). *Human cognitive neuropsychology: A textbook with readings.* Hove, UK: Psychology Press.

Ellis, L., & Engh, T. (2000). Handedness and age of death: New evidence on a puzzling relationship. *Journal of Heath Psychology, 5*(4), 561–565.

Engel, A. G. (1984). Myasthenia gravis and myasthenic syndromes. *Annals of Neurology, 16*, 519–535.

Enger, A. K., & Singer, W. (2001). Temporal binding and the neural correlates of sensory awareness. *Trends in Cognitive Sciences, 5*, 16–25.

Eriksson, P. S., Perfilieva, E., Bjork-Eriksson, T., Alborn, A. M., Nordborg, C., Peterson, D. A., et al. (1998). Neurogenesis in the adult human hippocampus. *Nature: Medicine, 4*, 1313–1317.

Ernst, M., Nelson, E. E., McClure, E. B., Monk, C. S., Munson, S., Eshel, N., et al. (2004). Choice selection and reward anticipation: An fMRI study. *Neuropsychologia, 42*, 1585–1597.

Evarts, E. V. (1974). Sensory motor cortex activity associated with movement is triggered by visual as compared to somesthetic inputs. In F. O. Schmitt & F. G. Worden (Eds.), *The neurosciences: Third study program.* Cambridge, MA: MIT Press.

Farah, M. J. (1990). *Visual agnosia: Disorders of object recognition and what they tell us about normal vision.* Cambridge, MA: MIT Press.

Farah, M. J., & Aguirre, G. K. (1999). Imaging visual recognition: PET and fMRI studies of the functional anatomy of human visual recognition. *Trends in Cognitive Sciences, 3*(5), 179–186.

Farrow, T. F., Zheng, Y., Wilkinson, I. D., Spence, S. A., Deakin, J. F., Tarrier, N., et al. (2001). Investigating the functional anatomy of empathy and forgiveness. *Neuroreport, 12*, 2433–1438.

Federspiel, A., Begre, S., Kiefer, C., Schroth, G., Strik, W. K., & Dierks, T. (2006). Alterations of white matter connectivity in first-episode schizophrenia. *Neurobiology of Disease, 22*(3), 702–709.

Ferstl, E. C., Rinck, M., & von Cramon, D. Y. (2005). Emotional and temporal aspects of situation model processing during text comprehension: An event-related fMRI study. *Journal of Cognitive Neuroscience, 17,* 724–739.

Fine, I., Finney, E. M., Boynton, G. M., & Dobkins, K. R. (2005). Comparing the effects of auditory deprivation and sign language within the auditory and visual cortex. *Journal of Cognitive Neuroscience, 17,* 1621–1637.

Finney, E. M., & Dobkins, K. R. (2001). Visual contrast sensitivity in deaf versus hearing populations: Exploring the perceptual consequences of auditory deprivation and experience with a visual language. *Cognitive Brain Research, 11,* 171–183.

Finney, E. M., Fine, I., & Dobkins, K. R. (2001). Visual stimuli activate auditory cortex in the deaf. *Nature: Neuroscience, 4,* 1171–1173.

Fletcher, P. C., Happe, F., Frith, U., Baker, S. C., Dolan, R. J., Frackowiak, R. S., et al. (1995). Other minds in the brain: A functional imaging study of "theory of mind" in story comprehension. *Cognition, 57,* 109–128.

Fletcher, P. C., McKenna, P. J., Friston, K. J., Frith, C. D., & Dolan, R. J. (1999). Abnormal cingulated modulation of frontal-temporal connectivity in schizophrenia. *Neuroimage, 9*(3), 337–342.

Fletcher, P. C., Stephenson, C. M. E., Carpenter, A., Donovan, T., & Bullmore, E. Y. (2003). Regional brain activations predicting subsequent memory success: An event-related fMRI study of the influence of encoding tasks. *Cortex, 39,* 1009–1026.

Flor, H., Birbaumer, N., Schulz, R., Grusser, S. M., & Mucha, R. F. (2002). Pavlovian conditioning of opioid and non-opioid pain inhibitory mechanisms in humans. *European Journal of Pain, 6,* 395–402.

Flor, H., Nikolajsen, L., & Jensen, T. S. (2006). Phantom limb pain: A case of maladaptive CNS plasticity? *Nature Reviews: Neuroscience, 7,* 873–881.

Flourens, M. J. P. (1824). *Recherches expérimentales sur les propriétés et les functions du système nerveux dans les animaux vertebres.* Paris: Balliere.

Fodor, J. A. (1983). *The modularity of mind: An essay on faculty psychology.* Cambridge, MA: MIT Press.

Fonseca, R., Nagerl, U. V., & Bonhoeffer, T. (2006). Neuronal activity determines the protein synthesis dependence of long-term potentiation. *Nature: Neuroscience, 9,* 478–480.

Francis, S., Rolls, E. T., Bowtell, R., McGlone, F., O'Doherty, J., Browning, A., et al. (1999). The representation of pleasant touch in the brain and its relationship with taste and olfactory areas. *Neuroreport, 10,* 453–459.

Francks, C., Fisher, S. E., Marlow, A. J., Macphie, I. L., Taylor, K. E., Richardson, A. J., et al. (2003). Familial and genetic effects on motor coordination, laterality, and reading-related cognition. *Americal Journal of Psychiatry, 160,* 1970–1977.

Franco, L., & Sperry, R. W. (1977). Hemisphere lateralisation for cognitive processing of geometry. *Neuropsychologia, 15,* 107–114.

Franz, E., Ivry, R., & Gazzaniga, M. S. (1996). Dissociation of spatial and temporal coupling in the bimanual movements of callosotomy patients. *Psychological Science, 7,* 306–310.

Freed, C. R., Greene, P. E., Breeze, R. E., Tsai, W. Y., DuMouchel, W., Kao, R., et al. (2001). Transplantation of embryonic dopamine neurons for severe Parkinson's disease. *New England Journal of Medicine, 344,* 710–719.

Freud, S. (1901). *The psychopathology of everyday life.* London: T. Fisher Unwin.

Freund, H. (1984). Pre-motor areas in man. *Trends in Neurosciences, 7,* 481–483.

Freund, H. J. (2005). Long-term effects of deep brain stimulation in Parkinson's disease. *Brain, 128,* 2222–2223.

Friedman, L. (1989). Mathematics and the gender gap: A meta-analysis of recent studies on sex differences in mathematical tasks. *Review of Educational Research, 59*(2), 185–213.

Friedman, N. P., & Miyake, A. (2004). The relations among inhibition and interference control functions: A latent variable analysis. *Journal of Experimental Psychology (General), 133*(1), 101–135.

Frith, C. D. (1997). Brain mechanisms associated with top-down processes in perception. *Philosophical Transactions of the Royal Society B, 352,* 1221–1230.

Frith, C. D. (1995). Regional brain activity in chronic schizophrenic patients during the performance of a verbal fluency task. *British Journal of Psychiatry, 167,* 343–349.

Frith, C. D., Friston, K., Liddle, P. F., & Frackowiak, R. S. (1991). Willed action and the prefrontal cortex in man: A study with PET. *Proceedings of the Royal Society of London; Biological Sciences, 244*, 241–246.

Frith U., & Frith C. D. (2003). Development and neurophysiology of mentalising. *Philosophical Transactions of the Royal Society of London B, 358*, 459–472.

Fritsch, G., & Hitzig, E. (1870). On the electrical excitability of the cerebrum. In G. VonBonin (Ed.), *The cerebral cortex*. Springfield IL: C.C. Thomas. [1960.]

Funahashi, S. (2001). Neural mechanisms of executive control by the prefrontal cortex. *Neuroscience Research, 39*(2), 147–165.

Gabbard, C., Hart, S., & Gentry, V. (1995). General motor proficiency and handedness in children. *Journal of Genetic Psychology, 156*, 411–416.

Gabrieli, J. D. E., Cohen, N. J., & Corkin, S. (1988). The impaired learning of semantic knowledge following bilateral medial temporal-lobe resection. *Brain and Cognition, 7*, 157–177.

Gabrieli, J. D. E., Fleischman, D. A., Keane, M. M., Reminger, S., & Morrell, F. (1995a). Double dissociation between memory systems underlying explicit implicit memory in the human brain. *Psychological Science, 6*, 76–82.

Gabrieli, J. D. E., McGlinchley-Berroth, R., Carillo, M. C., Gluck, M. A., Cermak, L. S., & Disterhoft, J. F. (1995b). Intact delay-eyeblink conditioning in amnesia. *Behavioral Neuroscience, 109*, 819–827.

Gainotti, G., D'Erme, P., & Bartolomeo, P. (1991). Early orientation of attention towards the half space ipsilateral to the lesion in patients with unilateral brain damage. *Journal of Neurology, Neurosurgery, and Psychiatry, 54*, 1082–1089.

Gall, F. J., & Spurzheim, J. (1810–1819). *Anatomie et physiologie du système nerveux en général, et du cerveau particulier*. Paris: Schoell.

Gallagher, H. L., Happe, F., Brunswick, N., Fletcher, P. C., Frith, U., & Frith, C. D. (2000). Reading the mind in cartoons and stories: An fMRI study of "theory of mind" in verbal and non-verbal tasks. *Neuropsychologia, 38*, 11–21.

Gallese, V., Fadiga, L., Fogassi, L., & Rizzolatti, G. (1996). Action recognition in the premotor cortex. *Brain, 119*, 593–609.

Garrett, A. S., & Maddock, R. J. (2006). Separating subjective emotion from the perception of emotion-inducing stimuli: An fMRI study. *Neuroimage, 33*, 263–274.

Gauthier, I., Skudlarski, P., Gore, J. C., & Anderson, A. W. (2000). Expertise for cars and birds recruits brain areas involved in face recognition. *Nature: Neuroscience, 3*, 191–197.

Gazzaniga, M. S. (1989). Organisation of the human brain [review]. *Science, 245*, 947–952.

Gazzaniga, M. S. (2000). Cerebral specialization and inter-hemispheric communication. Does the corpus callosum enable the human condition? *Brain, 123*, 1293–1326.

Gazzaniga, M. S. (2002). The split brain revisited. *Scientific American [special issue, The hidden mind], April*, 27–31.

Gazzaniga, M. S., & Hillyard, S. A. (1971). Language and spatial capacity of the right hemisphere. *Neuropsychologia, 9*, 273–280.

Gazzaniga, M. S., Ivry, R. B., & Mangun, G. R. (1998). *Cognitive neuroscience: The biology of the mind*. New York: W. W. Norton & Co.

Gazzaniga, M. S., Ivry, R. B., & Mangun, G. R. (2002). *Cognitive neuroscience: The biology of the mind* (2nd ed.). New York: W. W. Norton & Co.

Gazzaniga, M. S., & Smylie, C. S. (1983). Facial recognition and brain asymmetries: Clues to underlying mechanisms. *Annual Review of Neurology, 13*, 536–540.

Gazzaniga, M. S., & Sperry, R. W. (1967). Language after section of the cerebral commissures. *Brain, 90*, 131–148.

Geffen, G., & Butterworth, P. (1992). Born with a split brain: The 15-year development of a case of congenital absence of the corpus callosum. In S. Schwartz (Ed.), *Case studies in abnormal psychology* (pp. 113–117). New York: John Wiley.

Geidd, J. N., Rapoport, J. L., Kruesi, M. J., Parker, C., Schapiro, M. B., Allen, A. J., et al. (1995). Sydenham's chorea: Magnetic resonance imaging of the basal ganglia. *Neurology, 45*, 2199–2202.

Georgopoulos, A. P., Taira, M., & Lukashin, A. (1993). Cognitive neurophysiology of the motor cortex. *Science, 260*, 47–52.

Gerfen, C. R. (2006). Indirect pathway neurons lose their spines in Parkinson's disease. *Nature: Neuroscience, 9*, 157–158.

Gerloff, C., Corwell, B., Chen, R., Hallett, M., & Cohen, L. G. (1997). Stimulation over the human supplementary motor area interferes with the organisation of future elements in complex motor sequences. *Brain, 120*, 1587–1602.

Geschwind, N. (1965). Disconnexion syndromes in animals and man. *Brain*, *88*, 237–294.

Geschwind, N. (1967). The varieties of naming errors. *Cortex*, *3*, 97–112.

Geschwind, N. (1972). Language and the brain. *Scientific American*, *226*(4), 76–83.

Geschwind, N., & Behan, P. (1982). Left-handedness: Association with immune disease, migraine, and developmental learning disorder. *Proceedings of the National Academy of Sciences, USA*, *79*, 5097–5100.

Goldenberg, G. (2003). Apraxia and beyond: Life and work of Hugo Liepman. *Cortex*, *39*, 509–524.

Goldman-Rakic, P. (1998). The physiological approach: Functional architecture of working memory and disordered cognition in schizophrenia. *Biological Psychiatry*, *46*, 650–661.

Goldman-Rakic, P. S. (1987). Circuitry of primate prefrontal cortex and regulation of behaviour by representational memory. In F. Plum (Ed.), *Handbook of physiology: The nervous system, 5.* Bethesda, MD: American Physiology Society.

Gollin, E. S. (1960). Developmental studies of visual recognition of incomplete objects. *Perceptual and Motor Skills*, *11*, 289–298.

Goodale, M. A., & Milner, A. D. (1992). Separate visual pathways for perception and action. *Trends in Neurosciences*, *15*, 22–25.

Gooding, P. A., Isaac, C. L., & Mayes, A. R. (2005). Prose recall amnesia: More implications for the episodic buffer. *Neuropsychologia*, *43*, 583–587.

Goodman, W. K. (1999). Obsessive-compulsive disorder: Diagnosis and treatment. *Journal of Clinical Psychiatry*, *60*(suppl. 18), 27–32.

Gosselin, N., Peretz, I., Johnsen, E., & Adolphs, R. (2007). Amygdala damage impairs emotion recognition from music. *Neuropsychologia*, *45*, 236–244.

Grados, M. A., Riddle, M. A., Samuels, J. F., Liang, K. Y., Hoehn-Saric, R., Bienvenu, O. J., et al. (2001). The familial phenotype of obsessive-compulsive disorder in relation to tic disorders: The Hopkins OCD family study. *Biological Psychiatry*, *50*, 559–565.

Graham, F. K., & Kendall, B. S. (1960). Memory for designs test. *Perceptual and Motor Skills*, *11*, 147–188.

Gray, J. A., & Wedderburn, A. A. (1960). Grouping strategies with simultaneous stimuli. *Quarterly Journal of Experimental Psychology*, *12*, 180–184.

Greenberg, D. L., Eacott, M. J., Brechin, D., & Rubin, D. C. (2005). Visual memory loss autobiographical amnesia: A case study. *Neuropsychologia*, *43*, 1493–1502.

Grillner, S., Hellgren, J., Menard, A., Saitoh, K., & Wikstrom, M. A. (2005). Mechanisms for selection of basic motor programs: Roles of the striatum and pallidum. *Trends in Neurosciences*, *28*, 364–370.

Grodzinsky, Y., & Friederici, A. D. (2006). Neuroimaging of syntax and syntactic processing. *Current Opinion in Neurobiology*, *16*, 240–246.

Gross, C. G., Rocha-Miranda, C. E., & Bender, D. B. (1972). Visual properties of neurons in inferotemporal cortex of the macaque. *Journal of Neurophysiology*, *35*, 96–111.

Gusella, J. F., & MacDonald, M. E. (1994). Hunting for Huntington's disease. *Molecular Genetic Medicine*, *3*, 139–158.

Haaland, K. Y., & Flaherty, D. (1984). The different types of limb apraxia errors made by patients with left vs right hemisphere damage. *Brain and Cognition*, *3*, 370–384.

Habib, R., Nyberg, L., & Tulving, E. (2003). Hemispheric asymmetries of memory: The HERA model revisited. *Trends in Cognitive Sciences*, *7*, 241–245.

Hack, M. A., Saghatelyan, A., de Chevigny, A., Pfeifer, A., Ashery-Padan, R., Lledo, P. M., et al. (2005). Neuronal fate determinants of adult olfactory bulb neurogenesis. *Nature: Neuroscience*, *8*, 856–872.

Haggard, P., & Eimer, M. (1999). On the relation between brain potentials and the awareness of voluntary movements. *Experimental Brain Research*, *126*, 128–133.

Halpern, D. F. (2005). Sex, brains and hands— Gender differences in cognitive abilities. eskeptic.com05-03-15.html

Halpern, D. F., & Coren, S. (1988). Do right-handers live longer? *Nature*, *333*, 213.

Halpern, D. F., Haviland, M. G., & Charles, D. (1998). Handedness and sex differences in intelligence: Evidence from the Medical College Admission Test. *Brain and Cognition*, *38*(1), 87–101.

Hamani, C., Saint-Cyr, J. A., Fraser, J., Kaplitt, M., & Lozano, A. M. (2003). The subthalamic nucleus in the context of movement disorders. *Brain*, *127*, 4–20.

Hardyck, C., & Petrinovich, L. F. (1977). Left-handedness. *Psychological Bulletin*, *84*, 383–404.

Hart, J., Berndt, R. S., & Caramazza, A. (1985). Category specific naming deficit following cerebral infarction. *Nature, 316*, 439–440.

Hartley, T., Maguire, E. A., Spiers, H. J., & Burgess, N. (2003). The well-worn route and the path less traveled: Distinct neural bases of route following and way-finding in humans. *Neuron, 37*(5), 877–888.

Hatta, T., & Koike, M. (1991), Left hand preference in frightened mother monkeys in taking up their babies. *Neuropsychologia, 29*, 207–209.

Hausmann, M., Becker, C., Gather, U., & Gunturkun, O. (2002). Functional cerebral asymmetries during the menstrual cycle: A cross-sectional and longitudinal analysis. *Neuropsychologia, 40*, 808–816.

Haxby, J. V., Grady, C. L., Horwitz, B., Ungerleider, L. G., Mishkin, M., Carson, R. E., et al. (1991). Dissociation of object and spatial visual processing pathways in human extrastriate cortex. *Proceedings of the National Academy of Sciences: USA, 88*, 1621–1625.

Haxby, J. V., Horwitz, B., Ungerleider, L. G., Maisog, J. M., Pietrini, P., & Grady, C. L. (1994). The functional organization of the human extrastriate cortex: A PET rCBF study of selective attention to faces and locations. *Journal of Neuroscience, 14*, 6336–6353.

Hayman, C. A. G., & Tulving, E. (1989). Contingent dissociation between recognition fragment completion: the method of triangulation. *Journal of Experimental Psychology: Learning, Memory and Cognition, 15*, 228–240.

Hebb, D. O. (1949). *The organisation of behaviour: A neuropsychological theory*. New York: Wiley.

Heckers, S., Zalesak, M., Weiss, A. P., Ditman, T., & Titone, D. (2004). Hippocampal activations during transitive inference in humans. *Hippocampus, 14*, 153–162.

Heilman, K. M., & Rothi, L. J. (1993). Apraxia. In K. M. Heilman and E. Valenstein (Eds.), *Clinical Neuropsychology* (3rd ed., pp. 141–164). Oxford, UK: Oxford University Press.

Heilman, K. M., Rothi, L. J., & Valenstein, E. (1982). Two forms of ideomotor apraxia. *Neurology, 32*, 342–346.

Heiser, M., Iacoboni, M., Maeda, F., Marcus, J., & Mazziotta, J. C. (2003). The essential role of Broca's area in imitation. *European Journal of Neuroscience, 17*, 1123–1128.

Helmuth, L. L., Mayr, U., & Daum, I. (2000). Sequence learning is Parkinson's disease: A comparison of spatial attention number response sequences. *Neuropsychologia, 38*, 1443–1451.

Henry, J. D., & Crawford, J. R. (2004). A meta-analytic review of verbal fluency performance following focal cortical lesions. *Neuropsychology, 18*, 284–295.

Henson, R. (2006). Forward inference using functional neuroimaging: dissociations versus associations. *Trends in Cognitive Neurosciences, 10*, 64–69.

Hepper, P. G., McCartney, G. R., & Alyson, S. E. (1998). Lateralised behaviour in first trimester human foetuses. *Neuropsychologia, 36*(2), 531–534.

Hepper, P. G., Shalidullah, S., & White, R. (1991). Handedness in the human foetus. *Neuropsychologia, 29*(11), 1107–1111.

Hepper, P. G., Wells, D. L., & Lynch, C. (2005). Prenatal thumb sucking is related to postnatal handedness. *Neuropsychologia, 43*, 313–315.

Herzmann, G., Schweinberger, S. R., Sommer, W., & Jentzsch, I. (2004). What's special about personally familiar faces? A multimodal approach. *Psychophysiology, 41*, 688–701.

Hickmott, P. W., & Steen, P. A. (2005). Large scale changes in dendritic structure during reorganisation of adult somatosensory cortex. *Nature: Neuroscience, 8*, 140–142.

Hicks, R. A., Johnson, C., Cuavas, T., Deharo, D., & Bautista, J. (1994). Do right-handers live longer? An updated assessment of baseball player data. *Perceptual and Motor Skills, 78*, 1243–1247.

Hilgetag, C. C., Theoret, H., & Pascual-Leone, A. (2001). Enhanced visual spatial attention ipsilateral to rTMS-induced "virtual lesions" of human parietal cortex. *Nature: Neuroscience, 4*, 953–957.

Hillis, A. E., Newhart, M., Heider, J., Barker, P. B., Herskovits, E. H., & Degaonkar, M. (2005). Anatomy of spatial attention: Insights from perfusion imaging and hemispatial neglect in acute stroke. *Journal of Neuroscience, 25*, 3161–3167.

Hillis, A. E., Work, M., Barker, P. B., Jacobs, M. A., Breese, E. L., & Maurer, K. (2004). Re-examining the brain regions crucial for orchestrating speech articulation. *Brain, 127*, 1479–1487.

Hiscock, M., Israelian, M., Inch, R., Jacek, C., & Hiscock-Kalil, C. (1994). Is there a sex difference in human laterality? I. An exhaustive survey of visual laterality studies from six neuropsychology journals. *Journal of Clinical and Experimental Neuropsychology, 16,* 423–435.

Hiscock, M., Israelian, M., Inch, R., Jacek, C., & Hiscock-Kalil, C. (1995). Is there a sex difference in human laterality? II. An exhaustive survey of visual laterality studies from six neuropsychology journals. *Journal of Clinical and Experimental Neuropsychology, 17,* 590–610.

Hochberg, L. R., Serruya, M. D., Friehs, G. M., Mukland, J. A., Saleh, M., Caplian, A. H., et al. (2006). Neural ensemble control of prosthetic devices by a human with tetraplegia. *Nature, 442,* 164–171.

Hodges, J. R. (2002). Pure retrograde amnesia exists but what is the explanation? *Cortex, 38,* 674–677.

Hoffman, R. E., & Cavus, I. (2002). Slow transcranial magnetic stimulation, long term depotentiation and brain hyperexcitability disorders. *American Journal of Psychiatry, 159,* 1093–1102.

Holdstock, J. S., Mayes, A. R., Gong, Q. Y., Roberts, N., & Kapur, N. (2005). Item recognition is less impaired than recall associative recognition in a patient with selective hippocampal damage. *Hippocampus, 15,* 203–215.

Holdstock, J. S., Mayes, A. R., Roberts, N., Cezayirli, E., Isaac, C. L., O'Reilly, R., et al. (2002). Under what conditions is recognition spared relative to recall after selective hippocampal damage in humans? *Hippocampus, 12,* 341–351.

Holloway, R. L., & Lacoste, M-C. (1986). Sexual dimorphism in the human corpus callosum: An extension and replication study. *Human Neurobiology, 5,* 87–91.

Hopfinger, J. B., Buonocore, M. H., & Mangun, G. R. (2000). The neural mechanisms of top-down attentional control. *Nature: Neuroscience, 3,* 284–291.

Hopfinger, J. B., & Mangun, G. R. (1998). Reflexive attention modulates processing of visual stimuli in human extra-striate cortex. *Psychological Science, 9,* 441–447.

Hopkins, R. O., Waldram, K., & Kesner, R. P. (2004). Sequences assessed by declarative procedural tests of memory in amnesic patients with hippocampal damage. *Neuropsychologia, 42,* 1877–1886.

Hornykiewicz, O. (1966). Dopamine (3-hydroxytyramine). and brain functions. *Pharmacological Review, 18,* 925–964.

Howard, D., & Orchard-Lisle, V. (1984). On the origin of semantic errors in naming: Evidence from the case of a global aphasic. *Cognitive Neuropsychology, 1,* 163–190.

Hubel, D. H., & Weisel, T. N. (1977). Functional architecture of macaque monkey visual cortex. *Proceedings of the Royal Academy, London, Series B, 198,* 1–59.

Hugdahl, K., Thomsen, T., & Ersland, L. (2006). Sex differences in visuospatial processing: An fMRI study of mental rotation. *Neuropsychologia, 44*(9), 1575–1583.

Humphreys, G. W., & Riddoch, M. J. (1984). Routes to object constancy: Implications for neurological impairments of object constancy. *Quarterly Journal of Experimental Psychology, 36A,* 385–415.

Humphreys, G. W., & Riddoch, M. J. (1987). *To see but not to see: A case study of visual agnosia.* Hove, UK: Lawrence Erlbaum Associates Ltd.

Humphreys, G. W., & Riddoch, M. J. (1992). Interactions between objects and space-vision revealed through neuropsychology. In D. E. Meyers & S. Kornblum (Eds.), *Attention and performance XIV* (pp. 143–162). Hillsdale, NJ: Lawrence Erlbaum Associates Inc.

Humphreys, G. W., & Riddoch, M. J. (2001). Detection by action: Neuropsychological evidence for action-defined templates in search. *Nature: Neuroscience, 4,* 84–88.

Hunkin, N. M. (1997). Focal retrograde amnesia: Implications for the organisation of memory. In A. J. Parkin (Ed.), *Case studies in the neuropsychology of memory* (pp. 63–82). Hove, UK: Psychology Press

Hurlemann, R., Hawellek, B., Matusch, A., Kolsch, H., Wollersen, H., Madea, B., et al. (2005). Noradrenergic modulation of emotion-induced forgetting and remembering. *Journal of Neuroscience, 25,* 6343–6349.

Hutsler, J., Galuske, R. A., & Ralf, A. W. (2003). Hemispheric asymmetries in cerebral cortical networks. *Trends in Neurosciences, 26*(8), 429–435.

Hyde, J. S., Fennema, E., & Lamon, S. J. (1990). Gender differences in mathematics performance: A meta-analysis. *Psychological Bulletin, 107*(2), 139–155.

Iacoboni, M., Molnar-Szakacs, I., Gallese, V., Buccino, G., Mazziotta, J. C., & Rizzolatti, G. (2005). Grasping the intentions of others with one's own mirror neuron system. *PLOS Biology, 3,* 529–535.

Iacoboni, M., Woods, R. P., Brass, M., Bekkering, H., Mazziotta, J. C., & Rizzolatti, G. (1999). Cortical mechanisms of human imitation. *Science, 286*, 2526–2528.

Ietswaart, M., Carey, D. P., & Della Salla, S. (2006). Tapping, grasping and aiming in ideomotor apraxia. *Neuropsychologia, 44*, 1175–1184.

Indefrey, P., & Levelt, W. J. (2000). The neural correlates of language production. In M. S. Gazzaniga (Ed.), *The new cognitive neurosciences* (2nd ed.). London: MIT Press.

Isaacs, E., Christie, D., Vargha-Khadem, F., & Mishkin, M. (1996). Effects of hemispheric side of injury, age at injury, and presence of seizure disorder on functional ear and hand asymmetries in hemiplegic children. *Neuropsychologia, 34*(2), 127–137.

Ivanco, T. L., & Racine, R. J. (2000). Long-term potentiation in the reciprocal corticohippocampal corticocortical pathways in the chronically implanted freely moving rat. *Hippocampus, 10*, 143–152.

Jahanshahi, M., Jenkins, I. H., Browne, R. G., Marsden, C. D., Passingham, R. E., & Brooks, D. J. (1995). Self-initiated versus externally triggered movements: An investigation using measurements of regional cerebral blood flow with PET and movement related potentials in normals and Parkinson's disease subjects. *Brain, 118*, 913–933.

Jahanshahi, M., & Rothwell, J. (2000). Transcranial magnetic stimulation studies of cognition: An emerging field. *Experimental Brain Research, 13*, 1–9.

Janowiak, J., & Albert, M. L. (1994). Lesion localization in visual agnosia. In A. Kertesz (Ed.), *Localisation and neuroimaging in neuropsychology*. London: Academic Press.

Jeannerod, M. (1994). The representing brain: Neural correlates of motor intention and imagery. *Behavioral and Brain Sciences, 17*, 187–245.

Jeeves, M. A., & Temple, C. M. (1987). A further study of language function in callosal agenesis. *Brain and Language, 32*, 325–335.

Jenkins, I. H., Brooks, D. J., Nixon, P. D., Frackowiak, R. S., & Passingham, R. E. (1994). Motor sequence learning: A study with positron emission tomography. *Journal of Neuroscience, 14*, 3775–3790.

Jiang, Y., Costello, P., Fang, F., Huang, M., & He, S. (2006). A gender and sexual orientation-dependent spatial attention effect of invisible images. *Proceedings of the National Academy of Sciences, 103*, 17048–17052.

Jobard, G., Crivello, F., & Tzourio-Mazoyer, N. (2003). Evaluation of the dual-route theory of reading: A meta analysis of 35 neuroimaging studies. *Neuroimage, 20*, 693–712.

Johnsrude, I. S., Owen, A. M., White, N. M., Zhao, W. V., & Bohbot, V. (2000). Impaired preference conditioning after anterior temporal lobe resection in humans. *Journal of Neuroscience, 20*, 2649–2656.

Johnsrude, I. S., Owen, A. M., Zhao, W. V., & White, N. M. (1999). Conditioned preference in humans: A novel experimental approach. *Learning and Motivation, 30*, 250–264.

Jonides, J., Smith, E. E., Koeppe, R. A., Awh, E., Minoshima, S., & Mintun, M. A. (1993). Spatial working memory in humans as revealed by PET. *Nature, 363*, 623–625.

Joseph, R. (2000). *Neuropsychiatry, neuropsychology, clinical neuroscience*. New York: Academic Press.

Jung-Beeman, M. (2005). Bilateral brain processes for comprehending natural language. *Trends in Cognitive Sciences, 9*, 512–518

Kaas, J. H. (1983). What if anything is S1? Organisation of first somatosensory area of cortex. *Physiological Reviews, 63*, 206–231.

Kaas, J. H., Krubitzer, L. A., Chino, Y. M., Langston, A. L., Polley, E. H., & Blair, N. (1990). Reorganisation of retinotopic cortical maps in adult mammals after lesions of the retina. *Science, 248*, 229–231.

Kahn, D. M., & Krubitzer, L. (2002). Massive cross-modal cortical plasticity and the emergence of a new cortical area in developmentally blind mammals. *Proceedings of the National Academy of Sciences, 99*, 11429–11434.

Kahneman, D. (1973). *Attention and effort*. Englewood Cliffs, NJ: Prentice Hall.

Kaminski da Rosa, V. (1984). Managing the right-half brain of salary review. *Supervisory Management, 29*, 8–11.

Kandel, E., Schwartz, J. H. & Jessell, T. M. (Eds.) (1991). *Principles of neural science* (3rd ed.). New York: Elsevier.

Kane, M. J., Bleckley, M. K., Conway, A. R., & Engle, R. W. (2001). A controlled-attention view of working memory capacity. *Journal of Experimental Psychology (General), 130*, 169–183.

Kanwisher, N. (2000). Domain specificity in face perception. *Nature: Neuroscience, 3*, 759–763.

Kaplan, J. A., Fein, D., Morris, R., & Delis, D. C. (1990). The effects of right hemisphere damage on pragmatic interpretation of conversational remarks. *Brain and Language, 38,* 315–333.

Kaplan J. T., Freedman, J., & Iacoboni, M. (2007). Us versus them: Political attitudes and party affiliation influence neural response to faces of presidential candidates. *Neuropsychologia, 45,* 55–64.

Kapur, N. (1999). Syndromes of retrograde amnesia: A conceptual empirical synthesis. *Psychological Bulletin, 125,* 800–825.

Kapur, N., Young, A., Bateman, D., & Kennedy, P. (1989). Focal retrograde amnesia: A long term clinical neuropsychological follow-up. *Cortex, 25,* 387–402.

Karni, A., Meyer, G., Rey-Hipolito, C., Jezzard, P., Adams, M., Turner, R., et al. (1998). The acquisition of skilled motor performance: Fast and slow experience-driven changes in primary motor cortex. *Proceedings of the National Academy of Sciences, 95,* 861–868.

Kastner, S., & Ungerleider, L. G. (2000). Mechanisms of visual attention in the human cortex. *Annual Review of Neuroscience, 9,* 315–341.

Kawahara, Y., Ito, K., Sun, H., Aizawa, H., Kanazawa, I., & Kwak, S. (2004). Glutamate receptors: RNA editing and death of motor neurons. *Nature, 427,* 801.

Kay, J., & Ellis, A. W. (1987). A cognitive neuropsychological case study of anomia: Implications for psychological models of word retrieval. *Brain, 110,* 613–629.

Kennerley, S. W., Sakai, K., & Rushworth, M. F. (2004). Organisation of action sequences and the role of the pre-SMA. *Journal of Neurophysiology, 91,* 978–993.

Kesler, S. R., Hopkins, R. O., Blatter, D. D., Edge-Booth, H., & Bigler, E. D. (2001). Verbal memory deficits associated with fornix atrophy in carbon monoxide poisoning. *Journal of the International Neuropsychological Society, 7,* 640–646.

Kilshaw, D., & Annett, M. (1983). Right and left hand skill: Effects of age, sex, and hand preference. *British Journal of Psychology, 74,* 253–281.

Kim, H., Somerville, L. H., Johnstone, T., Alexander, A. L., & Whalen, P. J. (2003). Inverse amygdala and medial prefrontal cortex responses to surprised faces. *Neuroreport, 14,* 2317–2322.

Kim, K., Kim, J., Ku, J., Kim, D.J., Chang, W. H., Shin, D. I., et al. (2004). A virtual reality assessment and training system for unilateral neglect. *Cyberpsychology and Behaviour, 7,* 742–749.

Kim, K. H., Relkin, N. R., Lee, K. M., & Hirsch, J. (1997). Distinct cortical areas associated with native and second languages. *Nature, 388,* 171–174.

Kimura, D. (1973). The asymmetry of the human brain. *Scientific American, 228,* 70–78.

Kimura, D. (1992). Sex differences in the brain. *Scientific American, 267*(3), 118–125.

Kimura, D. (2002). Sex differences in the brain. *Scientific American,* May 13.

Kimura, D. (2004). Human sex differences in cognition: Fact, not predicament. *Sexualities, Evolution and Gender, 6,* 45–53.

Kimura, D., & Hampson, E. (1994). Cognitive pattern in men and women is influenced by fluctuations in sex hormones. *Current Directions in Psychological Science, 3,* 57–61.

Kingstone, A., & Gazzaniga, M. S. (1995). Subcortical transfer of higher order information: More illusory than real? *Neuropsychology, 9,* 321–328.

Kishiyama, M. M., Yonelinas, A. P., Kroll, N. E. A., Lazzara, M. M., Nolan, E. C., Jones, E. G., et al. (2005). Bilateral thalamic lesions affect recollection familiarity based recognition memory judgments. *Cortex, 41,* 778–788.

Knecht, S., Deppe, M., Dräger, B., Bobe, L., Lohmann, H., Ringelstein, E-B., et al. (2000a). Language lateralization in healthy right-handers. *Brain, 123,* 74–81.

Knecht, S., Dräger, B., Deppe, M., Bobe, L., Lohmann, H., Flöel, A., et al. (2000b). Handedness and hemispheric language dominance in healthy humans. *Brain, 123,* 2512–2518.

Knopman, D., & Nissen, M. J. (1991). Procedural learning is impaired in Huntington's disease: Evidence from the serial reaction time task. *Neuropsychologia, 29,* 245–254.

Knowlton, B. J., Squire, L. R., & Gluck, M. A. (1994). Probabilistic classification learning in amnesia. *Learning and Memory, 1,* 106–120.

Knutson, B., & Cooper, J. C. (2005). Functional magnetic resonance imaging of reward prediction. *Current Opinion in Neurology, 18,* 411–417.

Koch, C., & Tsuchiya, N. (2007). Attention and consciousness: Two distinct brain processes. *Trends in Cognitive Sciences, 11,* 16–22.

Koelsch, S., Fritz, T., Van Cramon, D. Y., Muller,

K., & Friederici, A. D. (2006). Investigating emotion with music: An fMRI study. *Human Brain Mapping, 27*, 239–250.

Koepp, M. J., Gunn, R. N., Lawrence, A. D., Cunningham, V. J., Dagher, A., Jones, T, et al. (1998). Evidence for striatal dopamine release during a video game. *Nature, 393*, 266–268.

Kolb, B., & Whishaw, I. Q. (1980). *Fundamentals of human neuropsychology* (1st ed.). New York: Freeman & Co.

Kolb, B., & Whishaw, I. Q. (1996). *Fundamentals of human neuropsychology* (4th ed.). New York: Freeman & Co.

Kolb, B., & Whishaw, I. Q. (2003). *Fundamentals of human neuropsychology* (5th ed.). New York: Freeman & Co.

Kopiez, R., Galley, N., & Lee, J. I. (2006). The advantage of a decreasing right-hand superiority: The influence of laterality on a selected musical skill (sight reading achievement). *Neuropsychologia, 44*, 1079–1087.

Kosslyn, S., & Anderson, R. (1992). *Frontiers in cognitive neuroscience*. Cambridge, MA: MIT Press.

Kosslyn, S. M. (1987). Seeing and imagining in the cerebral hemispheres: A computational approach. *Psychological Review, 94*, 148–175.

Koutstaal, W., Wagner, A. D., Rotte, M., Maril, A., Buckner, R. L., & Schacter, D. L. (2001). Perceptual specificity in visual object priming: Functional magnetic resonance imaging evidence for laterality differences in the fusiform cortex. *Neuropsychologia, 39*, 184–199.

Kuypers, H. G. (1981). Anatomy of descending pathways. In V. B. Brooks (Ed.), *Handbook of physiology, Vol. 7: The nervous system* (pp. 579–666). Bethesda, MD: American Physiology Society.

L'hermitte, F. (1983). Utilisation behaviour and its relation to lesions of the frontal lobes. *Brain, 106*, 237–255.

L'hermitte, F., Pillon, B., & Serdaru, M. (1986). Human autonomy and the frontal lobes. Part 1: Imitation and utilisation behaviour: A neuropsychological study of 75 patients. *Annals of Neurology, 19*, 326–334.

LaBar, K. S., Gitelman, D. R., Parrish, T. B., & Mesulam, M. M. (1999). Neuroanatomical overlap of working memory and spatial attention networks: A functional MRI comparison with subjects. *Neuroimage, 10*, 695–704.

LaBerge, D. (1983). The spatial extent of attention to letters and words. *Journal of Experimental Psychology: Human Perception and Performance, 9*, 371–379.

LaBerge, D. (1990). Thalamic and cortical mechanisms of attention suggested by recent positron emission tomographic experiments. *Journal of Cognitive Neuroscience, 2*, 358–372.

LaBerge, D. (1995). *Attentional processing: The brain's art of mindfulness*. Cambridge, MA: Harvard University Press.

LaBerge, D. (2000). Attentional networks. In M. S. Gazzaniga (Ed.), *The new cognitive neurosciences* (pp. 711–724). Cambridge, MA: MIT Press.

LaBerge, D. (2002). Attentional control: Brief and prolonged. *Psychological Research, 66*, 220–233.

LaBerge, D. (2006). Apical dendrite activity in cognition and consciousness. *Consciousness and cognition, 15*, 235–257.

LaBerge, D., & Buchsbaum, M. S. (1990). Positron emission tomographic measurements of pulvinar activity during an attention task. *Journal of Neuroscience, 10*, 613–619.

Laganaro, M., DiPietro, M., & Schnider, A. (2006). What does recovery from anomia tell us about the underlying impairment: The case of similar anomic patterns and different recovery. *Neuropsychologia, 44*(4), 534–545.

Lambertz, N., Gizewski, E. R., de Greiff, A., & Forsting, M. (2005). Cross-modal plasticity in deaf subjects dependent on the extent of hearing loss. *Brain Research: Cognitive Brain Research, 25*, 884–890.

Lamm, C., Batson, C. D., & Decety, J. (2007). The neural substrate of human empathy: Effects of perspective-taking and cognitive appraisal. *Journal of Cognitive Neuroscience, 19*, 42–58.

Lamme, V. A. F. (2003). Why visual attention and awareness are different. *Trends in Cognitive Sciences, 7*, 12–18

Lamme, V. A. F., Zipser, K., & Spekreijse, H. (2002). Masking interrupts figure–ground signals in V1. *Journal of Cognitive Neuroscience, 14*, 1–10.

Landers, M. (2004). Treatment-induced neuroplasticity following focal injury to the motor cortex. *International Journal of Rehabilitation Research, 27*, 1–5.

Lane, R. D., Reiman, E. M., Bradley, M. M., Lang, P. J., Ahern, G. L., Davidson, R. J., et al. (1997). Neuroanatomical correlates of pleasant and unpleasant emotion. *Neuropsychologia, 35,* 1437–1444.

Lang, P. J., Bradley, M. M., & Cuthbert, B. N. (1998). *International affective picture system (IAPS): Affective ratings of pictures and instruction manual. Technical Report A-6.* Gainesville, FL: University of Florida.

Lashley, K. S. (1930). Basic neural mechanisms in behaviour. *Psychological Review, 37,* 1–24.

Lavie, N. (1995). Perceptual load as a necessary condition for selective attention. *Journal of Experimental Psychology: Human Perception and performance, 21,* 451–468.

Lavie, N. (2005). Distracted and confused? Selective attention under load. *Trends in Cognitive Sciences, 9,* 75–82.

Lavie, N., & Fox, E. (2000). The role of perceptual load in negative priming. *Journal of Experimental Psychology. Human Perception and Performance, 26,* 1038–1052.

Leask, S. J., & Crow, T. J. (2001). Word acquisition reflects lateralisation of hand skill. *Trends in Cognitive Sciences, 5,* 513–516.

Lechevalier, B., Petit, M. C., Eustache, F., Lambert, J., Chapon, F., & Vaider, F. (1989). Regional cerebral blood flow during comprehension and speech (in cerebrally healthy subjects). *Brain and Language, 37,* 1–11.

Lee, C. H., Robbins, T. W., Pickard, J. D., & Owen, A. M. (2000). Asymmetric frontal activation during episodic memory: The effects of stimulus type on encoding retrieval. *Neuropsychologia, 38,* 677–692.

Lee, L. J., Lo, F. S., & Erzurumlu, R. S. (2005). NMDA receptor-dependent regulation of axonal and dendritic branching. *Journal of Neuroscience, 25,* 2304–2311

Leiguarda, R. C., & Marsden, C. D. (2000). Limb apraxia: Higher order disorders of sensory-motor integration. *Brain, 123,* 860–879.

Leonard, H. L. (1997). New developments in the treatments of obsessive-compulsive disorder. *Journal of Clinical Psychiatry, 58*(suppl. 14), 39–45.

Lepage, M., Ghaffar, O., Nyberg, L., & Tulving, E. (2000). Prefrontal cortex episodic memory retrieval mode. *Proceedings of the National Academy of Sciences, USA, 97,* 506–511.

Levelt, W. J. (1989). *Speaking: From intention to articulation.* Cambridge, MA: MIT press.

Levelt, W. J., Roelofs, A., & Meyer, A. S. (1999). A theory of lexical access in speech production. *Behavioral and Brain Sciences, 22,* 1–38.

Levenston, G. K., Patrick, C. J., Bradley, M., &

Lang, P. J. (2000). The psychopath as observer: Emotion and attention in picture processing. *Journal of Abnormal Psychology, 109,* 373–385.

Levine, D. N., Warach, J., & Farah, J. (1985). Two visual systems in mental imagery: Dissociation of "what" "where" in imagery disorders due to bilateral posterior cerebral lesions. *Neurology, 35,* 1010–1018.

Levine, S. C., Banich, M. T., & Koch-Weser, M. (1988). Face recognition: A general or specific right hemisphere capacity? *Brain and Cognition, 8,* 303–325.

Levy, D. A., Stark, C. E. L., & Squire, L. R. (2004). Intact conceptual priming in the absence of declarative memory. *Psychological Science, 15,* 680–686.

Levy, J. (1969). Possible basis for the evolution of lateral specialisation of the human brain. *Nature, 224,* 614–615.

Levy, J., & Trevarthen, C. W. (1976). Metacontrol of hemisphere function in human split brain patients. *Journal of Experimental Psychology: Human Perception and Performance, 2,* 299–312.

Levy, J., Trevarthen, C. W., & Sperry, R. W. (1972). Perception of bilateral chimeric figures following "hemispheric deconnection". *Brain, 95,* 61–78.

Lewin, C., & Herlitz, A. (2002). Sex differences in face recognition: Women's faces make the difference. *Brain and Cognition, 50,* 121–128.

Lewis, J. W. (2006). Cortical networks related to human use of tools. *The Neuroscientist, 12,* 211–231.

Lezak, M. D. (1983). *Neuropsychological assessment.* New York: Oxford University Press.

Libet, B., Gleason, C. A., Wright, E. W., & Pearl, D. K. (1983). Time of conscious intention to act in relation to onset of cerebral activity (readiness potential).: The unconscious initiation of a freely voluntary act. *Brain, 106,* 623–642.

Lichtheim, L. (1885). On aphasia. *Brain, 7,* 433–484.

Liddle, P. F. (1997). Dynamic neuroimaging with PET, SPET or fMRI. *International Review of Psychiatry, 9,* 331–337.

Lieberman, M. D., Hariri, A., Jarcho, J. M., Eisenberger, N. I. & Bookheimer, S. Y. (2005). An fMRI investigation of race-related amygdala activity in African-American and Caucasian-American individuals. *Nature: Neuroscience, 8,* 720–722.

Liégeois, F., Connelly, A., Helen Cross, J., Boyd, S.

G., Gadian, D. G., Vargha-Khadem, F., et al. (2004). Language reorganization in children with early-onset lesions of the left hemisphere: An fMRI study. *Brain, 127,* 1229–1236

Liepmann, H. (1905). Der weiter Krankheitsverlauf bei dem Einseitig, Apraktischen und der Gehirnbefund auf Grund von Serienschnitten. *Monatschrift für Psychiatrie und Neurologie, 17,* 283–311.

Linebarger, M., Schwartz, M., & Saffran, E. (1983). Sensitivity to grammatical structure in so-called agrammatic aphasics. *Cognition, 13,* 361–392.

Lissauer, H. (1890). Ein Fall von Seelenblindheit nebst einem Beitrage zur Theorie derselben. *Archiv für Psychiatrie und Nervenkrankheiten, 21,* 222–270.

Liston, C., Matalon, S., Hare, T. A., Davidson, M. C., & Casey, B. J. (2006). Anterior cingulated and posterior parietal cortices are sensitive to dissociable forms of conflict in a task-switching paradigm. *Neuron, 50*(4), 643–653.

Lotze, M., Flor, H., Grodd, W., Larbig, W., & Birbaumer, N. (2001). Phantom movements and pain: An fMRI study of upper-limb amputees. *Brain, 124,* 2268–2277.

Lotze, M., Grodd, W., Birbaumer, N., Erb, M., Huse, E., & Flor, H. (1999). Does use of a myoelectric prosthesis prevent cortical reorganisation and phantom limb pain? *Nature: Neuroscience, 2,* 501–502.

Luria, A. R. (1966). *Higher cortical functions in man.* New York: Basic Books.

Luria, A. R. (1973). *The working brain: An introduction to neuropsychology.* Harmondsworth, UK: Penguin Books.

Maccoby, E., & Jacklin, C. (1974). *The psychology of sex differences.* Stanford, CA: Stanford University Press.

MacLean, P. D. (1949). Psychosomatic disease and the "visceral brain": Recent developments bearing on the Papez theory of emotion. *Psychosomatic Medicine, 11,* 338–353.

Maddock, R. J., Garrett, A. S. & Buonocore, M. H. (2003). Posterior cingulate cortex activation by emotional words: fMRI evidence from a valence decision task. *Human Brain Mapping, 18,* 30–41.

Maeda, F., Kleiner-Fisman, G., & Pascual-Leone, A. (2002). Motor facilitation while observing hand actions: Specificity of the effect and role of observer's orientation. *Journal of Neurophysiology, 87,* 1329–1335.

Maekawa, S., Al-Sarraj, S., Kibble, M., Landau, S., Parnavelas, D., Everall, I., et al. (2004). Cortical selective vulnerability in motor neuron disease: A morphometric study. *Brain, 127,* 1237–1251.

Maguire, E. A. (2002). Neuroimaging studies of autobiographical event memory. In A. Baddeley, M. A. Conway, & J. Aggleton (Eds.), *Episodic memory: New directions in research* (pp. 164–180). New York: Oxford University Press.

Maguire, E. A., Gadian, D. G., Johnsrude, I. S., Good, C. D., Ashburner, J., Frackowiak, R. S., et al. (2000). Navigation-related structural change in the hippocampi of taxi drivers. *Proceedings of the National Academy of Sciences, USA, 97,* 4398–4403.

Maia, T. V., & Cleeremans, A. (2005). Consciousness: Converging insights from connectionist modeling and neuroscience. *Trends in Cognitive Sciences, 9,* 397–404.

Maia, T. V., & McClelland, J. L. (2004). A reexamination of the evidence for the somatic marker hypothesis: What participants really know in the Iowa gambling task. *Proceedings of the National Academy of Sciences, USA, 101,* 16075–16080

Malach, R., Levy, I., & Hasson, U. (2002). The topography of high-order human object areas. *Trends in Cognitive Sciences, 6,* 176–184.

Malouin, F., Richards, C. L., Jackson, P. L., Dumas, F., & Doyon, J. (2003). Brain activations during motor imagery of locomotor-related tasks: A PET study. *Human Brain Mapping, 19,* 47–62.

Mangun, G. R., Hillyard, S., & Luck, S. (1993). Electrocortical substrates of visual selective attention. In D. E. Meyer & S. Kornblum (Eds.), *Attention and performance (XIV): Synergies in experimental psychology, artificial intelligence and cognitive neuroscience* (pp. 219–242). Cambridge, MA: MIT Press.

Manning, L. (2002). Focal retrograde amnesia documented with matching anterograde retrograde procedures. *Neuropsychologia, 40,* 28–38.

Marr, D. (1982). *Vision: A computational investigation into the human representation and processing of visual information.* San Francisco: Freeman.

Marshall, J. C., & Halligan, P. W. (1988). Blindsight and insight into visuospatial neglect. *Nature, 336,* 766–767.

Marshall, J. C., & Halligan, P. W. (1990). Line bisection in a case of visual neglect: psychophysical studies with implications for theory. *Cognitive Neuropsychology, 7,* 107–130.

Marslen-Wilson, W. D., & Teuber, H. L. (1975). Memory for remote events in anterograde amnesia: Recollection of public figures from news photographs. *Neuropsychologia, 13*, 347–352.

Martin, S. J., & Morris, R. G. M. (2002). New life in an old idea: The synaptic plasticity memory hypothesis revisited. *Hippocampus, 12*, 609–636.

Martin, W. R., & Hayden, M. R. (1987). Cerebral glucose and dopa metabolism in movement disorders. *Canadian Journal of Neurological Sciences, 14*, 448–451.

Martuza, R. L., Chiocca, E. A., Jenike, M. A., Giriunuas, I. E., & Ballantine, H. T. (1990). Stereotactic radiofrequency thermal cingulectomy for obsessive compulsive disorder. *Journal of Neuropsychiatry and Clinical Neurosciences, 2*, 331–336.

Mason, R. A., & Just, M. A. (2004). How the brain processes causal inferences in text. *Psychological Science, 15*, 1–7.

Mathews, G. A., Fane, B. A., Pasterski, V. L., Conway, G. S., Brook, C., & Hines, M. (2004). Androgenic influences on neural asymmetry: Handedness and language lateralisation in individuals with congenital adrenal hyperplasia. *Psychoneuroendocrinology, 29*, 810–822.

Matsuzaka, Y., & Tanji, J. (1996). Changing directions of forthcoming arm movements: Neuronal activity in the pre-supplementary area of monkey cerebral cortex. *Journal of Neurophysiology, 76*, 2327–2342.

Mayberg, H. S. (2003). Modulating dysfunctional limbic-cortical circuits in depression: Towards development of brain-based algorithms for diagnosis and optimised treatment. *British Medical Bulletin, 65*, 193–207.

Mayberg, H. S., Lozano, A. M., Voon, V., McNeely, H. E., Seminowitz, D., Hamani, C., et al. (2005). Deep brain stimulation for treatment resistant depression. *Neuron, 45*, 651–660.

Mayes, A. R., Holdstock, J. S., Isaac, C. L., Hunkin, N. M., & Roberts, N. (2002). Relative sparing of item recognition in a patient with damage limited to the hippocampus. *Hippocampus, 12*, 525–540.

Mazoyer, B. M., Tzourio, N., Frak, V., Syrota, A., Murayama, N., Levrier, O., et al. (1993). The cortical representation of speech. *Journal of Cognitive Neuroscience, 5*, 467–479.

McCarthy, R., & Warrington, E. K. (1986). Visual associative agnosia: A clinico-anatomical study of a single case. *Journal of Neurology, Neurosurgery, and Psychiatry, 49*, 1233–1240.

McDermott, K. B., & Buckner, R. L. (2002). Functional neuroimaging studies of memory retrieval. In L. R. Squire & D. L. Schacter, (Eds.), *Neuropsychology of memory* (pp. 166–173). New York: Guilford Press.

McDougle, C. J., Goodman, J. F., Leckman, J. F., Lee, N. C., Heninger, G. R., & Prince, L. H. (1994). Haloperidol addition in fluvoxamine-refractory obsessive compulsive disorder: A double blind placebo-controlled study in patients with and without tics. *Archives of General Psychiatry, 51*, 302–308.

McGlinchey-Berroth, R., Carrillo, M. C., Gabrieli, J. D. E., Brawn, C. M., & Disterhoft, J. F. (1997). Impaired trace eyeblink conditioning in bilateral medial-temporal lobe amnesia. *Behavioral Neuroscience, 111*, 873–882.

McGlone, J. (1980). Sex differences in human brain asymmetry: A critical survey. *Behavioral and Brain Sciences, 3*(2), 215–263.

McHaffie, J. G., Stanford, T. R., Stein, B. E., Coizet, P., & Redgrave, P. (2005). Subcortical loops through the basal ganglia. *Trends in Neurosciences, 28*, 401–407.

McIntosh, A. R., Rajah, M. N., & Lobaugh, N. J. (1999). Interactions of prefrontal cortex in relation to awareness in sensory learning. *Science, 284*, 1531–1533.

McLeod, P. (1977). A dual task response modality effect: Support for multiprocessor models of attention. *Quarterly Journal of Experimental Psychology, 29*, 651–667.

McManus, I. C. (1992). *Right hand, left hand.* London: Weidenfeld & Nicholson.

McNeil, J. E., & Warrington, E. K. (1993). Prosopagnosia: A face specific disorder. *Quarterly Journal of Experimental Psychology, 46A*, 1–10.

Melzak, R. (1992). Phantom limbs. *Scientific American, 266*(4), 120–126.

Merzenich, M., & Jenkins, W. M. (1995). Cortical plasticity, learning and learning dysfunction. In B. Julesz & I. Kovacs (Eds.), *Maturational windows and adult cortical plasticity* (pp. 2–24). Reading, MA: Addison-Wesley.

Merzenich, M. M., & Kaas, J. H. (1980). Principles of organisation of sensory-perceptual systems in mammals. In J. M. Sprague & A. N. Epstein (Eds.), *Progress in psychobiology and physiological psychology, 9*. New York: Academic Press.

Mesulam, M. M. (Ed.) (1985). *Principles of*

behavioural neurology. Philadelphia: F. A. Davis.

Mesulam, M. M. (1998). From sensation to cognition. *Brain, 121*, 1013–1052.

Mevorach, C., Humphreys, G. Q., & Shalev, L. (2005). Attending to local form while ignoring global aspects depends on handedness: Evidence from TMS. *Nature: Neuroscience, 8*(3), 276–277.

Meyer-Lindenberg, A., Poline, J. B., Kohn, P. D., Holt, J. L., Egan, M. F., Weinberger, D. R., et al. (2001). Evidence for abnormal cortical functional connectivity during working memory in schizophrenia. *American Journal of Psychiatry, 158*, 1809–1817.

Miller, G. A. (1962). *Psychology, The science of mental life*. New York: Harper & Row.

Miller, G. A. (2003). The cognitive revolution: A historical perspective. *Trends in Cognitive Sciences, 7*(3), 141–144.

Milner, A. D., & Goodale, M. A. (1995). *The visual brain in action*. Oxford, UK: Oxford University Press.

Milner, B. (1965). Visually guided maze learning in man: Effects of bilateral hippocampal, bilateral frontal and unilateral cerebral brain lesions. *Neuropsychologia, 3*, 317–338.

Milner, B. (1966). Amnesia following operation on the temporal lobes. In C. W. M. Whitty & O. L. Zangwill (Eds.), *Amnesia* (pp. 109–133). London: Butterworth.

Milner, B. (1982). Some cognitive effects of frontal lobe lesions in man. *Philosophical Transactions of the Royal Society of London, 298*, 211–226.

Minati, L., & Aquino, D. (2006). Probing neural connectivity through diffusion tensor imaging. *Cybernetics and Systems, 37*, 263–268.

Mirescu, C., Peters, J. D., & Gould, E. (2004). Early life experience alters response of adult neurogenesis to stress. *Nature: Neuroscience, 7*(8), 841–846.

Mitchell, R. L. C., & Crow, T. J. (2005). Right hemisphere language functions and schizophrenia: the forgotten hemisphere? *Brain, 128*, 963–978.

Mitsuno, K., Sasa, M., Ishihara, K., Ishikawa, M., & Kikuchi, H. (1994). LTP of mossy fibre-stimulated potentials in CA3 during learning in rats. *Physiology and Behavior, 55*, 633–638.

Miyake, A., Friedman, N. P., Emerson, M. J., Witzki, A. H., Howerter, A., & Wager, T. (2000). The unity and diversity of executive functions and their contributions to complex frontal lobe tasks: A latent variable analysis. *Cognitive Psychology, 41*, 49–100.

Mogilner, A., Grossman, J. A., Ribary, U., Joliot, M., Volkman, J., Rapaport, D., et al. (1993). Somatosensory cortical plasticity in adult humans revealed by magnetoencephalography. *Proceedings of the National Academy of Sciences, 90*, 3593–3597.

Molloy, R., & Parasuraman, R. (1996). Monitoring an automated system for a single failure: Vigilance and task complexity effects. *Human Factors, 38*, 311–322.

Money, J. A. (1976). *A standardised road map test of directional sense: Manual*. San Rafael, CA: Academic Therapy Publications.

Moniz, E. (1937). Prefrontal leucotomy in the treatment of mental disorders. *American Journal of Psychiatry, 93*, 1379–1385.

Monsell, S. (2003). Task switching. *Trends in Cognitive Sciences, 7*, 134–140.

Moray, N. (1959). Attention in dichotic listening: Effective cues and the influence of instructions. *Quarterly Journal of Experimental Psychology, 9*, 56–60.

Moriarty, J., Campos-Costa, D., Schmitz, B., Trimble, M. R., Ell, P. J., & Robertson, M. (1995). Brain perfusion abnormalities in Gilles de la Tourette's syndrome. *British Journal of Psychiatry, 167*, 249–254.

Morris, C. D., Bransford, J. D., & Franks, J. J. (1977). Levels of processing versus transfer appropriate processing. *Journal of Verbal Learning and Verbal Behavior, 16*, 519–533.

Morris, J. S., Friston, K. J., Buchel, C., Frith, C. D., Young, A. W., Calder, A. J., et al. (1998). A neuromodulatory role for the human amygdala in processing emotional facial expressions. *Brain, 121*, 47–57.

Morris, J. S., Frith, C. D., Perrett, D. I., Rowland, D., Young, A. W., Calder, A. J., et al. (1996). A differential neural response in the human amygdala to fearful and happy facial expressions. *Nature, 383*, 812–815.

Morris, R. D., Hopkins, W. D., & Bolser-Gilmore, L. (1993). Assessment of hand preference in two language-trained chimpanzees: A multi-method analysis. *Journal of Clinical and Experimental Psychology, 15*, 487–502.

Moscovitch, M., & Nadel, L. (1998). Consolidation the hippocampal complex revisited: In defence of the multiple-trace model. *Current Opinion in Neurobiology, 8*, 297–300.

Moscovitch, M., Winocur, G., & Behrmann, M. (1997). What is special about face recognition? Nineteen experiments on a person with visual object agnosia and dyslexia but normal face recognition. *Journal of Cognitive Neuroscience, 9*, 555–604.

Motter, B. C., & Mountcastle, V. B. (1981). The functional properties of light sensitive neurons of the posterior parietal cortex studied in waking animals. *Journal of Neuroscience, 1*, 3–36.

Moutoussis, K., & Zeki, S. (2006). Seeing invisible motion: A human fMRI study. *Current Biology, 16*, 574–579.

Murphy, F. C., Sahakian, B. J., & O'Carroll, R. E. (1998). Cognitive impairment in depression: Psychological models and clinical issues. In D. Ebert & K. P. Ebmeier (Eds.), *New models for depression* (pp. 1–33). Basel: Karger.

Nadel, L., & Moscovitch, M. (1997). Memory consolidation, retrograde amnesia and the hippocampal complex. *Current Opinion in Neurobiology, 7*, 217–227.

Naeser, M. A., & Hayward, R. W. (1978). Lesion localisation in aphasia with cranial computed tomography and the Boston Diagnostic Aphasia Exam. *Neurology, 28*, 545–551.

Narabayashi, H., Nagao, T., Saito, Y., Yoshida, N., & Naghata, M. (1963). Stereotactic amygdalotomy for behavioural disorders. *Archives of Neurology, 9*, 1–16.

Navon, D. (1977). Forest before trees: The precedence of global features in visual processing. *Cognitive Psychology, 9*, 353–383.

Nelson, H. E. (1976). A modified card sorting test sensitive to frontal lobe defects. *Cortex, 12*, 313–324.

Nelson, H. E. (1982). *National Adult Reading Test: Test manual.* Windsor, UK: NFER-Nelson.

Neville, H. J., Bavelier, D., Corina, D., Rauschecker, J., Karni, A., Lalwani, A., et al. (1998). Cerebral organization for language in deaf and hearing subjects: Biological constraints and effects of experience. *Proceedings of the National Academy of Sciences, 95*, 922–929.

Nickels, L. (2002). Therapy for naming disorders: Revisiting, revising and reviewing. *Aphasiology, 16*, 935–979.

Niedenthal, P. M. (1990). Implicit perception of affective information. *Journal of Experimental Social Psychology, 26*, 505–527.

Nieuwehhuis, S., & Yeung, N. (2005). Neural mechanisms of attention and control: Losing our inhibitions? *Nature: Neuroscience, 8*, 1631–1632.

Norman, D. A., & Shallice, T. (1986). Attention to action: Willed and automatic control of behaviour. In R. J. Davidson, G. E. Schwartz, & D. Shapiro (Eds.), *Consciousness and self-regulation, 4* (pp. 1–18). New York: Plenum Press.

Nottebohm, F. (1980). Brain pathways for vocal learning in birds: A review of the first 10 years. *Progress in Psychobiology, Physiology and Psychology, 9*, 85–114.

Nudo, R. J., Milliken, G. W., Jenkins, W. M., & Merzenich, M. M. (1996). Use dependent alterations of movement representations in primary motor cortex of adult squirrel monkeys. *Journal of Neuroscience, 16*, 785–807.

Nyberg, L., Cabeza, R., & Tulving, E. (1996). PET studies of encoding retrieval: The HERA model. *Psychonomic Bulletin and Review, 3*, 135–148.

O'Conner, M., & Verfaellie, M. (2002). The amnesic syndrome: Overview and subtypes. In A. D. Baddeley, M. D. Kopelman, & B. A Wilson (Eds.), *Handbook of memory disorders.* Chichester, UK: John Wiley.

O'Craven, K., Downing, P., & Kanwisher, N. (1999). fMRI evidence for objects as the units of attentional selection. *Nature, 401*, 584–587.

O'Doherty, J. (2004). Reward representations and reward-related learning in the human brain: Insights from human neuroimaging. *Current Opinion in Neurobiology, 14*, 769–776.

O'Doherty, J., Kringelbach, M. L., Rolls, E. T., Hornak, J., & Andrews, C. (2001). Abstract reward and punishment in the human orbitofrontal cortex. *Nature: Neuroscience, 4*, 95–102.

O'Doherty, J., Rolls, E.T., Francis, S., Bowtell, R., McGlone, F., Kobal, G., et al. (2000). Sensory-specific satiety-related olfactory activation of the human orbitofrontal cortex *Neuroreport, 11*, 893–897.

O'Doherty, J. P., Buchanan, T. W., Seymour, B., & Dolan, R. J. (2006). Predictive neural coding of reward preference involves dissociable responses in human ventral midbrain and ventral striatum. *Neuron, 49*, 157–166.

O'Kane, G., Kesinger, E. A., & Corkin, S. (2004). Evidence for semantic learning in profound amnesia: An investigation with patient HM. *Hippocampus, 14*, 417–425.

O'Leary, D. D., Ruff, N. L., & Dyck, R. H. (1994). Developmental, critical period plasticity, and adult reorganisation of mammalian somatosensory systems. *Current Opinion in Neurobiology, 4*, 535–544.

Ohyama, T., Nores, W. L., Murphy, M., & Mauk,

M. D. (2003). What the cerebellum computes. *Trends in Neurosciences*, *26*, 222–227.

Olanow, C. W., Goetz, C. G., Kordower, J. H., Stoessel, A. J., Sossi, V., & Brin, F. M. (2003). A double-blind controlled trial of bilateral fetal nigral transplantation in Parkinson's disease. *Annals of Neurology*, *54*, 403–414.

Olanow, C. W., Kordower, J. H., & Freeman, T. B. (1996). Fetal nigral transplantation as a therapy for Parkinson's disease. *Trends in Neurosciences*, *19*(3), 102–109.

Osgood, C. E., Suci, G. J. & Tannenbaum, P. H. (1957). *The measurement of meaning*. Urbana, IL: University of Illinois Press.

Otten, L. J., Quale, A. H., Akram, S., Ditewig, T. A., & Rugg, M. D. (2006). Brain activity before an event predicts later recollection. *Nature: Neuroscience*, *9*, 489–491.

Owen, A. M. (1997). The functional organisation of working memory processes within human lateral cortex: The contribution of functional neuroimaging. *European Journal of Neuroscience*, *9*, 1329–1339.

Owen, A. M., Sahakian, B. J., Semple, J., Polkey, C. E., & Robbins, T. W. (1995). Visuo-spatial short term recognition memory and learning after temporal lobe excisions, frontal lobe excisions, or amygdalo-hippocampectomy in man. *Neuropsychologia*, *33*, 1–24.

Pakkenberg, B., & Gundersen, H. J. (1997). Neocortical neuron number in humans: Effects of sex and age. *Journal of Comparative Neurology*, *384*, 312–320.

Paradiso, S., Robinson, R. G., Andreasen, N. C., Downhill, J. E., Davidson, R. J., Kirchner, P. T., et al. (1997). Emotional activation of limbic circuitry in elderly normal subjects in a PET study. *American Journal of Psychiatry*, *154*, 384–389.

Pardo, J. V., Pardo P. J., Janer, K. W., & Raichle, M. E. (1990). The anterior cingulate cortex mediates processing selection in the Stroop attentional conflict paradigm. *Proceedings of the National Academy of Sciences*, *87*, 256–259.

Parkin, A. J. (1982). Residual learning capability in organic amnesia. *Cortex*, *18*, 417–440.

Parkin, A. J. (1999). Component processes versus systems: Is there really an important difference? In J. K. Foster & M. Jelicic (Eds.), *Memory: Systems, process or function?* (pp. 273–287). Oxford, UK: Oxford University Press.

Pascual-Leone, A., & Torres, F. (1993). Plasticity of the sensory motor cortex representation of

the reading finger in Braille readers. *Brain*, *116*, 39–52.

Passingham, R. E. (1981). Broca's area and the origin of human vocal skills. *Philosophical Transactions of the Royal Society, B*, *29*(2), 167–175.

Paulesu, E., Goldacre, B., Scifo, P., Cappa, S. F., Gilardi, M. C., Castiglioni, I., et al. (1997). Functional heterogeneity of left inferior frontal cortex as revealed by fMRI. *Neuroreport*, *8*(8), 2011–2016.

Paulesu, E., McCrory, E., Fazio, F., Menoncello, N., Brunswick, N., Cappa, S. F., et al. (2000). A cultural effect on brain function. *Nature: Neuroscience*, *3*, 91–96.

Peissig, J. J., & Tarr, M. J. (2007). Visual object recognition: Do we know more now than we did 20 years ago? *Annual Review of Psychology*, *58*, 75–96.

Penfield, W., & Rasmussen, T. L. (1950). *The cerebral cortex of man: A clinical study of localisation of function*. New York: Macmillan.

Perret, E. (1974). The left frontal lobe of man and the suppression of habitual responses in verbal categorical behaviour. *Neuropsychologia*, *12*, 323–330.

Persson, P. G., & Allerbeck, P. (1994). Do left-handers have increased mortality? *Epidemiology*, *5*, 337–340.

Petersen, S. E., Fox, P. T., Posner, M. I., Mintun, M., & Raichle, M. E. (1988). Positron emission tomographic studies of the cortical anatomy of single word processing. *Nature*, *331*, 585–589.

Petersen, S. E., Robinson, D. L., & Morris, J. D. (1985). Pulvinar nuclei of the behaving rhesus monkey: Visual responses and their modulation. *Journal of Neurophysiology*, *54*, 867–886.

Petersen, S. E., Van Meir, H., Fiez, J. A., & Raichle, M. E. (1998). The effects of practice on the functional anatomy of task performance. *Proceedings of the National Academy of Sciences*, *95*, 853–860.

Petrides, M., & Milner, B. (1982). Deficits on subject-ordered tasks after frontal and temporal lobe lesions in man. *Neuropsychologia*, *20*, 249–262.

Phelps, E. A., Labar, D. S., Anderson, A. K., O'Connor, K. J., Fulbright, R. K., & Spencer, D. S. (1998). Specifying the contributions of the human amygdala to emotional memory: A case study. *Neurocase*, *4*, 527–540.

Phillips, M. L., Young, A. W., Senior, C., Brammer, M., Andrew, C., Calder, A. J., et al. (1997). A specific neural substrate for perceiving facial expressions of disgust. *Nature, 389,* 495–498.

Piccini, P., Pavese, N., Hagell, P., Reimer, J., Bjorklund, A., Oertel, W. H., et al. (2005). Factors affecting the clinical outcome after neural transplantation in Parkinson's disease. *Brain, 128,* 2977–2986.

Pick, A. (1905). *Studien zur motorischen Apraxie und ihr nahestendee Erscheinungen; ihre Bedeutung in der Symptomatologie psychopathischer Symptomkomplexe.* Leipzig und Wein: Franz Deuticke.

Pigott, S., & Milner, B. (1994). Capacity of visual short-term memory after unilateral frontal or anterior temporal-lobe resection. *Neuropsychologia, 32,* 969–981.

Pinker, S. (1997). *How the mind works.* New York: Norton.

Poeppel, D., & Hickok, G. (2004). Towards a new functional anatomy of language. *Cognition, 92,* 1–12.

Pohl, W. (1973). Dissociation of spatial discrimination deficits following frontal and parietal lesions in monkeys. *Journal of Comparative and Physiological Psychology, 82,* 227–239.

Poldrack, R. A. (2006). Can cognitive processes be inferred from neuro-imaging data? *Trends in Cognitive Sciences, 10,* 59–63.

Popper, K. (1934). *The logic of scientific discovery.* London: Taylor & Francis.

Posamentier, M. T., & Abdi, H. (2003). Processing faces and facial expressions. *Neuropsychology Review, 13,* 113–143.

Posner, M. I. (1980). Orienting of attention. *Quarterly Journal of Experimental Psychology, 32,* 3–25.

Posner, M. I. (1992). Attention as a cognitive and neural system. *Current Directions in Psychological Science, 1,* 11–14.

Posner, M. I., & Cohen, Y. (1984). Components of visual orienting. In H. Bouma & D. Bouwhuis (Eds.), *Attention and performance X* (pp. 531–556). London: Lawrence Erlbaum Associates Ltd.

Posner, M. I., & DiGirolamo, G. J. (1998). Attention and cognitive neuroscience: An overview. In M. S. Gazzaniga (Ed.), *The new cognitive neurosciences* (pp. 623–631). Cambridge, MA: MIT Press.

Posner, M. I., Inhoff, A. W., Freidrich, F. J., & Cohen, A. (1987). Isolating attentional systems: A cognitive anatomical analysis. *Psychobiology, 15,* 107–121.

Posner, M. I., Snyder, C. R., & Davidson, J. (1980).

Attention and the detection of signals. *Journal of Experimental Psychology, 109,* 160–174.

Postle, B. R., Druzgal, T. J., & D'Esposito, M. (2003). Seeking the neural substrates of visual working memory storage. *Cortex, 39,* 927–946.

Previc, F. H. (1991). A general theory concerning the prenatal origins of cerebral lateralisation in humans. *Psychological Review, 98,* 299–334.

Price, C. J., Mummery, C. J., Moore, C. J., Frackowiak, R. S., & Friston, K. J. (1999). Delineating necessary and sufficient neural systems with functional imaging studies of neuropsychological patients. *Journal of Cognitive Neuroscience, 11,* 371–382.

Ptito, M., Moesgaard, S. M., Gjedde, A., & Kupers, R. (2005). Cross-modal plasticity revealed by electrotactile stimulation of the tongue in the congenitally blind. *Brain, 128,* 606–614.

Pulvermuller, F., Neininger, B., Elbert, T., Mohr, B., Rockstroh, B., Koebbel, P., et al. (2001). Constraint-induced therapy of chronic aphasia after stroke. *Stroke, 32,* 1621–1630.

Raivich, G. (2005). Like cops on the beat: The active role of resting microglia. *Trends in Neurosciences, 28*(11), 571–573.

Rajaram, S., & Roediger, H. L. (1993). Direct comparison of four implicit memory tests. *Journal of Experimental Psychology: Learning, Memory and Cognition, 19,* 765–776.

Ramachandran, V. S. (1994). Phantom limbs, neglect syndromes and Freudian psychology. *Review of Neurobiology, 37,* 291–333.

Ramachandran, V. S. (2006). *Mirror neurons and imitation learning as the driving force behind "the great leap forward" in human evolution.* Retrieved from: http://www.edge.org/3rd_culture/rama/rama_p1.html

Ramnani, N., & Miall, R. C. (2004). A system in the brain for predicting the actions of others. *Nature: Neuroscience, 7,* 85–90.

Ranganath, C., Heller, A., Cohen, M. X., Brozinsky, C. J., & Riseman, J. (2005). Functional connectivity with the hippocampus during successful memory formation. *Hippocampus, 15,* 997–1005.

Rapoport, J. L. (1990). Obsessive compulsive disorder and basal ganglia dysfunction. *Psychological Medicine, 20,* 465–469.

Rasmussen, T., & Milner, B. (1977). The role of early left brain injury in determining lateralisation of cerebral speech function. *Annals of the New York Academy of Sciences, 299,* 355–369.

Ratcliff, G., & Newcombe, F. (1973). Spatial

orientation in man: Effects of left, right and bi-lateral posterior cerebral lesions. *Journal of Neurology, Neurosurgery, and Psychiatry, 36,* 448–454.

Ratcliff, G., & Newcombe, F. (1982). Object recognition: Some deductions from the clinical evidence. In A. W. Ellis (Ed.), *Normality and pathology in cognitive functions* (pp. 147–171). London: Academic Press.

Reber, P. J., & Squire, L. R. (1994). Parallel brain systems for learning with without awareness. *Learning and Memory, 1,* 217–229.

Recanzone, G. H., Schreiner, C. E., & Merzenich, M. M. (1993). Plasticity in the frequency representation of primary auditory cortex following discrimination training in adult owl monkeys. *Journal of Neuroscience, 13,* 87–104.

Redgrave, P., Prescott, T. J., & Gurney, K. (1999). The basal ganglia: A vertebrate solution to the selection problem? *Neuroscience, 89,* 1009–1023.

Reed, C. L., Klatzky, R. L., & Halgren, E. (2005). What vs where in touch: An fMRI study. *Neuroimage, 25,* 718–726.

Reed, J. M., & Squire, L. R. (1997). Impaired recognition memory in patients with lesions limited to the hippocampal formation. *Behavioral Neuroscience, 111,* 667–675.

Reed, L. J., Marsden, P., Lasserson, D., Sheldon, N., Lewis, P., & Stanhope, N. (1999). FDG-PET analysis findings in amnesia resulting from hypoxia. *Memory, 7,* 599–612.

Rees, G., Frith, C. D., & Lavie, N. (1997). Modulating irrelevant motion perception by varying attentional load in an unrelated task. *Science, 278,* 1616–1619.

Reiman, E. M., Lane, R. D., Ahern, G. L., Schwartz, G. E., Davidson, R. J., Friston, K. J., et al. (1997). Neuroanatomical correlates of externally and internally generated human emotion. *American Journal of Psychiatry, 154,* 918–925.

Reisberg, D., & Heuer, F. (2004). Memory for emotional events. In D. Reisberg & P. Hertel, (Eds.), *Memory and emotion* (pp. 3–41). New York: Oxford University Press.

Reitan, R. M., & Wolfson, D. (1993). *The Halstead-Reitan Neuropsychological test battery: Theory and clinical interpretation.* Tucson, AZ: Neuropsychology Press.

Renner, M. J., & Rosensweig, M. R. (1987). *Enriched and impoverished environments: Effects on brain and behaviour.* New York: Springer-Verlag.

Rensink, R. A. (2002). Change detection. *Annual Review of Psychology, 53,* 245–277.

Ricciardi, E., Bonino, D., Gentili, C., Sani, L., Pietrini, P., & Vecchi, T (2006). Neural correlates of spatial working memory in humans: A functional magnetic resonance imaging study comparing visual and tactile processes. *Neuroscience, 139*(1), 339–349.

Riddoch, M. J., & Humphreys, G. W. (2001). Object recognition. In B. Rapp (Ed.), *Handbook of cognitive neuropsychology.* Hove, UK: Psychology Press.

Rilling, J. K., Glenn, A. L., Jairam, M. R., Pagnoni, G., Goldsmith, D. R., Elfenbein, H. A., et al. (2007). Neural correlates of social cooperation and non-cooperation as a function of psychopathy. *Biological Psychiatry, 61,* 1260–1271.

Rilling, J. K., Gutman, D. A., Zeh, T. R., Pagnoni, G., Berns, G. S., and Kitts, C. D. (2002). A neural basis for social cooperation. *Neuron, 35,* 395–405.

Ringo, J. L., Doty, R. W., Demeter, S., & Simard, P. Y. (1994). Time is of the essence: A conjecture that hemispheric specialisation arises from interhemispheric conduction delay. *Cerebral Cortex, 4,* 331–343.

Rizzo, M., & Vecera, S. P. (2002). Psychoanatomical substrates of Balint's syndrome. *Journal of Neurology, Neurosurgery, and Psychiatry, 72,* 162–186.

Rizzolatti, G., & Buccino, G. (2004). The mirror-neuron system and its role in imitation and language. In S. Dehaene, G. R. Duhamel, M. Hauser, & G. Rizzolatti (Eds.), *From monkey brain to human brain.* Cambridge, MA: MIT Press.

Rizzolatti, G., Fadiga, L., Gallese, V., & Fogassi, L. (1996). Premotor cortex and the recognition of motor actions. *Cognitive Brain Research, 3,* 131–141.

Rizzolatti, G., Fogassi, L., & Gallese, V. (2001). Neurophysiological mechanisms underlying the understanding and imitation of action. *Nature Reviews: Neuroscience, 2,* 661–667.

Rizzolatti, G., & Matelli, M. (2003). Two different streams form the dorsal visual system. *Experimental Brain Research, 153,* 146–157.

Robbins, T. W., James, M., Owen, A. M., Sahakian, B. J., McInnes, L., & Rabbitt, P. M. (1994). Cambridge Neuropsychological Test Automated Battery (CANTAB): A factor analytic study of a large sample of normal elderly volunteers. *Dementia, 5*(5), 266–281.

Roberts, A. C., Robbins, T. W., & Weiskrantz, L. (1998). *The prefrontal cortex*. Oxford, UK: Oxford University Press.

Robertson, D., & Irvine, D. (1989). Plasticity of frequency organisation in auditory cortex of guinea pigs with partial unilateral deafness. *Journal of Comparative Neurology, 282*, 456–471.

Robertson, L. C., & Rafal, R. (2000). Disorders of visual attention. In M. S. Gazzaniga (Ed.), *The new cognitive neurosciences* (pp. 633–650). Cambridge, MA: MIT Press.

Roder, B., Teder-Salejarvi, W., Sterr, A., & Rosler, F. (1999). Improved auditory spatial tuning in blind humans. *Nature, 400*, 162–166.

Rodriguez, E., George, N., Lachaux, J., Martinerie, J., Renault, B., & Varela, F. J. (1999). Perception's shadow: Long distance synchronization of human brain activity. *Nature, 397*, 430–433.

Roediger, H. L., Weldon, M. S., & Challis, B. H. (1989). Explaining dissociations between implicit explicit measures of retention: A processing account. In H. L. Roediger & F. I. M. Craik (Eds.), *Varieties of memory consciousness: Essays in honour of Endel Tulving* (pp. 3–41). Hillsdale, NJ: Lawrence Erlbaum Associates Inc.

Roediger, H. L., Weldon, M. S., Stadler, M. A., & Riegler, G. I. (1992). Direct comparison of two implicit memory tests: Word fragment word stem completion. *Journal of Experimental Psychology: Learning, Memory and Cognition, 18*, 1251–1269.

Rogers, R. D., & Monsell, S. (1995). Costs of a predictable switch between simple cognitive tasks. *Journal of Experimental Psychology: General, 124*, 207–231.

Rogers, R. D., Owen, A. M., Middleton, H. C., Williams, E. J., Pickard, J. D., Sahakian, B. J., et al. (1999). Choosing between small likely rewards and large, unlikely rewards activates inferior and orbital prefrontal cortex. *Journal of Neuroscience, 19*, 9029–9038.

Rogers, R. D., Ramnani, N., Mackay, C., Wilson, J. L., Jezzard, P., Carter, C. S., et al. (2004). Distinct portions of anterior cingulate cortex and medial prefrontal cortex are activated by reward processing in separable phases of decision-making cognition. *Biological Psychiatry, 55*(6), 594–602.

Rogers, R. D., Sahakian, R. A., Hodges, J. R., Polkey, C. E., Kennard, C., & Robbins, T. W. (1998). Dissociating executive mechanisms of task control following frontal lobe damage and Parkinson's disease. *Brain, 121*, 815–842.

Roland, P. E. (1993). *Brain activation*. New York: Wiley-Liss.

Roland, P. E., Larson, B., Lassen, N. A., & Skinhoje, E. (1980). Supplementary motor area and other cortical areas in organisation of voluntary movements in man. *Journal of Neurophysiology, 43*, 118–136.

Rose, S. P. (1992). *The making of memory*. New York: Bantam.

Rosenbaum, D. A., Slotta, J. D., Vaughan, J., & Plamondon, R. (1991). Optimal movement selection. *Psychological Science, 2*, 86–91.

Rubia, K. (2002). The dynamic approach to neurodevelopmental psychiatric disorders: Use of fMRI combined with neuropsychology to elucidate the dynamics of psychiatric disorders, exemplified in ADHD and schizophrenia. *Behavioural Brain Research, 130*, 47–56.

Rubin, D. C., Schrauf, R. W., & Greenberg, D. L. (2003). Belief recollection in autobiographical memories. *Memory and Cognition, 31*, 887–901.

Rugg, M. D. (2004). Retrieval processes in human memory. In M. S. Gazzaniga (Ed.), *The cognitive neurosciences III* (pp. 727–737). Cambridge, MA: MIT Press.

Rushworth, M. F., Walton, M. E., Kennerley, S. W., & Bannerman, D. M. (2004). Action sets and decisions in the medial frontal cortex. *Trends in Cognitive Sciences, 8*, 410–417.

Sacks, O. (1985). *The man who mistook his wife for a hat*. New York: Summit Books.

Sadato, N., Pascual-Leone, A., Grafman, J., Ibanez, V., Deiber, M. P., Gold, G., et al. (1996). Activation of the primary visual cortex by Braille reading blind subjects. *Nature, 380*, 526–528.

Saxena, S., Brody, A. L., Schwartz, J. M., & Baxter, L. R. (1998). Neuro-imaging and frontal-subcortical circuitry in obsessive-compulsive disorder. *British Journal of Psychiatry, 173*(suppl. 35), 26–37.

Schacter, D. L., & Tulving, E. (1994). What are the memory systems of 1994? In D. L. Schacter & E. Tulving (Eds.), *Memory systems 1994* (pp. 1–38). Cambridge, MA: MIT Press.

Schachter, S., & Singer, J. E. (1962). Cognitive, social and physiological determinants of emotional state. *Psychological Review, 69*, 79–99.

Schachter, S. C., & Ransil, B. J. (1996). Handedness distributions in nine professional groups. *Perceptual and Motor Skills, 82*, 51–63.

Schneiderman, E. I., Murasugi, K. G., & Saddy, J. D. (1992). Story arrangement ability in right brain damaged patients. *Brain and Language*, *43*, 107–120.

Schreurs, B. G., McIntosh, A. R., Bahro, M., Herscovith, P., Sunderl, T., & Molchan, S. E. (1997). Lateralization behavioral correlation of changes in regional cerebral blood flow with classical conditioning of the human eyeblink response. *Journal of Neurophysiology*, *77*, 2153–2163.

Schwartz, A. B. (2004). Cortical neural prosthetics. *Annual Review of Neuroscience*, *27*, 487–507.

Scovile, W. B., & Milner, B. (1957). Loss of recent memory after bilateral hippocampal lesions. *Journal of Neurology, Neurosurgery, and Psychiatry*, *20*, 11–21.

Searle, J. (1992). *The rediscovery of the mind*. Cambridge, MA: MIT Press.

Selnes, O. A. (2001). A historical overview of contributions from the study of deficits. In B. Rapp (Ed.), *Handbook of cognitive neuropsychology*, Hove, UK: Psychology Press.

Semmes, J., Weinstein, S., Ghent, L., & Teuber, H. L. (1955). Spatial orientation: Analysis of locus of lesion. *Journal of Psychology*, *39*, 227–244.

Semmes, J., Weinstein, S., Ghent, L., & Teuber, H. L. (1963). Impaired orientation in personal and extra-personal space. *Brain*, *86*, 747–772.

Sengelaub, D. R., Muja, N., Mills, A. C., Myers, W. A., Churchill, J. D., & Garraghty, P. E. (1997). Denervation-induced sprouting of intact peripheral afferents into cuneate nucleus of adult rats. *Brain Research*, *769*, 256–262.

Sergent, C., Baillet, S., & Dehaene, S. (2005). Timing of the brain events underlying access to consciousness during the attentional blink. *Nature: Neuroscience*, *8*, 1391–1399

Sergent, J. (1982). The cerebral balance of power: Confrontation or cooperation? *Journal of Experimental Psychology: Human Perception and Performance*, *8*, 252–272.

Sergent, J. (1990). Further incursions into bicameral minds. *Brain*, *113*, 537–568.

Sergent, J., & Signoret, J. L. (1992). Functional and anatomical decomposition of face processing: Evidence from prosopagnosia and PET study of normal individuals. *Philosophical Transactions of the Royal Society of London, B*, *335*, 55–62.

Shah, A., & Lisak, R. P. (1993). Immunopharmacologic therapy in myasthenia gravis. *Clinical Neuropharmacology*, *16*, 97–103.

Shallice, T. (1982). Specific impairments in planning. *Philosophical Transactions of the Royal Society of London*, *298*, 199–209.

Shallice, T. (2002). Fractionation of the supervisory system. In D. T. Stuss & R. T. Knight (Eds.), *Principles of frontal lobe function* (pp. 261–277). New York: Oxford University Press.

Shallice, T. (2004). The fractionation of supervisory control. In M. S. Gazzaniga (Ed.), *The cognitive neurosciences III* (pp. 943–956). Cambridge, MA: MIT Press.

Shallice, T., and Burgess, P. (1996). The domain of supervisory process and temporal organisation of behaviour. *Philosophical Transactions of the Royal Society of London, B*, *351*, 1405–1412.

Shallice, T., & Burgess, W. (1991). Deficits in strategy and application following frontal lobe damage in man. *Brain*, *114*, 727–741.

Sheng, M., & Kim, M. J. (2002). Post synaptic signalling and plasticity mechanisms. *Science*, *298*, 776–780.

Shiffrin, R. M., & Schneider, W. (1977). Controlled and automatic human information processing: II. Perceptual learning, automatic attending, and a general theory. *Psychological Review*, *84*, 127–190.

Simons, D. J. (2000). Current approaches to change blindness. *Visual Cognition*, *7*, 1–15.

Simons, D. J., & Chabris, C. F. (1999). Gorillas in our midst: Sustained inattentional blindness for dynamic events. *Perception*, *28*, 1059–1074.

Singer, H. S., Szymanski, S., Giuliano, J., Yokoi, F., Dogan, A. S., Brasic, J. R., et al. (2002). Elevated intra-synaptic dopamine release in Tourette's syndrome measured by PET. *American Journal of Psychiatry*, *159*, 1329–1336.

Singer, T., Seymour, B., O'Doherty, J. P., Stephan, K. E., Dolan, R. J., & Frith, C. D. (2006). Empathic neural responses are modulated by the perceived fairness of others. *Nature*, *439*, 466–469.

Sirigu, A., Daprati, E., Cianca, S., Giraux, P., Nighoghossian, N., Posada, A., et al. (2004). Altered awareness of voluntary action after damage to the parietal cortex. *Nature: Neuroscience*, *7*, 80–84.

Slotnick, S. D., & Moo, L. R. (2006). Prefrontal cortex hemispheric specialization for categorical and coordinate visual spatial memory. *Neuropsychologia*, *44*, 1560–1568.

Small, D. M., Zatorre, R. J., Daghar, A., Evans, A. C., & Jones-Gotman, M. (2001). Changes in brain activity related to eating chocolate: From pleasure to aversion. *Brain*, *124*, 1720–1733.

Smith, E. E., & Jonides, J. (1994). Working memory in humans: Neuropsychological evidence. In M. S. Gazzaniga (Ed.), *The cognitive neurosciences* (pp. 1009–1020). Cambridge, MA: MIT Press.

Smith, E. E., Jonides, J., & Koeppe, R.A. (1996). Dissociating verbal and spatial working memory using PET. *Cerebral Cortex, 6*, 11–20.

Sommer, I. E. C., Aleman, A., Bouma, A., & Kahn, R. S. (2004). Do women really have more bilateral language representation than men? A meta-analysis of functional imaging studies. *Brain, 127*, 1845–1852.

Sotillo, M., Carretie, L., Hinojosa, J. A., Tapia, M., Mercado, F., Lopez-Martin, S., et al. (2005). Neural activity associated with metaphor comprehension: Spatial analysis. *Neuroscience Letters, 373*, 5–9.

Spence, S. A., Brooks, D. J., Hirsch, S. R., Liddle, P. F., Meehan, J., & Grasby, P. M. (1997). A PET study of voluntary movement in schizophrenic patients experiencing passivity phenomena (delusions of alien control). *Brain, 120*, 1997–2011.

Sperry, R. W. (1968). Hemisphere deconnection and unity of conscious awareness. *American Psychologist, 23*, 723–733.

Sperry, R. W., Gazzaniga, M. S., & Bogen, J. E. (1969). Inter-hemispheric relationships: The neocortical commissures; syndromes of hemisphere disconnection. In P. J. Vinken & G. W. Bruyn (Eds.), *Handbook of clinical neurology, 4* (pp. 273–290). New York: John Wiley & Sons.

Sprengelmeyer, R., Rausch, M., Eysel, U. T., & Przuntek, H. (1998). Neural structures associated with recognition of facial expressions of basic emotions. *Proceedings of the Royal Society of London Series B—Biological Sciences, 265*, 1927–1931.

Springer, S. P., & Deutsch, G. (1998). *Left brain, right brain: Perspectives from cognitive neuroscience* (5th ed.). New York: W. H. Freeman.

Squire, L. R. (1992). Memory and the hippocampus: A synthesis of findings with rats, monkeys humans. *Psychological Review, 99*, 195–231.

Squire, L. R. (2004). Memory systems of the brain: A brief history current perspective. *Neurobiology of Learning and Memory, 82*, 171–177.

Squire, L. R., & Knowlton, B. J. (2000). The medial temporal lobe, the hippocampus, the memory systems of the brain. In M. S. Gazzaniga (Ed.), *The new cognitive neurosciences* (pp. 765–779). Cambridge, MA: MIT Press.

Stark, C. E. L., & Squire, L. R. (2000). Functional resonance imaging (fMRI) activity in the hippocampal region during recognition memory. *Journal of Neuroscience, 20*, 7776–7781.

Stark, C. E. L., & Squire, L. R. (2003). Hippocampal damage equally impairs memory for single items memory for conjunctions. *Hippocampus, 13*, 281–292.

Steg, G., & Johnels, B. (1993). Physiological mechanisms and assessment of motor disorders in Parkinson's disease. In H. Narabayashi, T. Nagatsu, N. Yanagisawa, & Y. Mizuno (Eds.), *Advances in neurology*. New York: Raven Press.

Steinvorth, S., Levine, B., & Corkin, S. (2005). Medial temporal lobe structures are needed to re-experience remote autobiographical memories: Evidence from H.M. and W.R. *Neuropsychologia, 43*, 479–496.

Stephan, K. E., Baldeweg, T., & Friston, K. J. (2006). Synaptic plasticity and disconnection in schizophrenia. *Biological Psychiatry, 59*, 929–939.

Stirling, J. (1999). *Cortical functions*, London: Routledge.

Stirling, J. D., Cavill, J., & Wilkinson, A. (2000). Dichotically presented emotionally intoned words produce laterality differences as a function of localisation task. *Laterality, 5*(4), 363–371.

Stirling, J. D., Hellewell, J. S., & Ndlovu, D. (2001). Self-monitoring dysfunction and the positive symptoms of schizophrenia. *Psychopathology, 34*, 198–202.

Stirling, J. D., Hellewell, J. S., & Quraishi, N. (1998). Self-monitoring and the schizophrenic symptoms of alien control. *Psychological Medicine, 28*, 675–683.

Stuss, D. T., Benson, D. F., Clermont, R., Della Malva, C. L., Kaplan, E. S., & Weir, W. S. (1986). Language functioning after bilateral prefrontal leukotomy. *Brain and Language, 28*, 66–70.

Stuss, D. T., & Knight, R. T. (2002). *Principles of frontal lobe function*. New York: Oxford University Press.

Svendsen, F., Tjolsen, A., & Hole, K. (1998). AMPA and NMDA receptor dependent spinal LTP after nociceptive tetanic stimulation. *Neuroreport, 9*, 1185–1190.

Tanaka, J. W. (2001). The entry point of face recognition: Evidence for face expertise. *Journal of Experimental Psychology (General)*, *130*(3), 534–543.

Taub, E., Uswatte, G., & Elbert, T. (2002). New treatments in neurorehabilitation founded on basic research. *Nature Reviews: Neuroscience, 3*, 228–236

Taylor, K. I., Moss, H. E., Stamatakis, E. A., & Tyler, L. K. (2006). Binding crossmodal object features in peripheral cortex. *Proceedings of the National Academy of Sciences, 103*, 8239–8244.

Taylor, L. B. (1969). Localisation of cerebral lesions by psychological testing. *Clinical Neurosurgery, 16*, 269–287.

Tekin, S., & Cummings, J. L. (2002). Frontal-subcortical neuronal circuits and clinical neuropsychiatry: An update. *Journal of Psychosomatic Research, 53*, 647–654.

Temple, C. (1993). *The brain*. Harmondsworth, UK: Penguin Books.

Temple, C. N., & Ilsley, J. (1993). Phonemic discrimination in callosal agenesis. *Cortex, 29*(2), 341–348.

Teng, E., & Squire, L. R. (1999). Memory for places learned long ago is intact after hippocampal damage. *Nature, 400*, 675–677.

Thomas, K. M., Hunt, R. H., Vizueta, N., Sommer, T., Durston, S., Yang, Y., et al. (2004). Evidence of developmental differences in implicit sequence learning: An fMRI study of children adults. *Journal of Cognitive Neuroscience, 16*, 1339–1351.

Thomasius, R., Zapletalova, P., Petersen, K., Buchert, R., Andersen, B., Wartberg, L., et al. (2006). Mood, cognition and serotonin transporter availability in current and former ecstasy (NMDA) users: The longitudinal perspective. *Journal of Psychopharmacology, 20*, 211–225.

Thut, G., Schultz, W., Roelcke, U., Nienhusdmeier, M., Missimer, J., Maguire, R. P., et al. (1997). Activation of human brain by monetary reward. *Neuroreport, 8*, 1225–1228.

Tipper, S. P. (1985). The negative priming effect: Inhibitory priming by ignored objects. *Quarterly Journal of Experimental Psychology, 37*A, 571–590.

Tipper, S. P., Weaver, B., & Houghton, G. (1994). Behavioural goals determine inhibitory mechanisms of selective attention. *Quarterly Journal of Experimental Psychology, 47*A, 809–840.

Todrank, J., Byrnes, D., Wrzesniewski, A., & Rozin, P. (1995). Odors can change preferences for people in photographs: A cross-modal evaluative conditioning study with olfactory USs and visual CSs. *Learning and Motivation, 26*, 116–140.

Toga, A. W., Thompson, P. M., & Sowell, E. R. (2006). Mapping brain maturation. *Trends in Neurosciences, 29*, 148–159.

Tom, S. M., Fox, C. R., Trepel, C., & Poldrack, R. A. (2007). The neural basis of loss aversion in decision-making under risk. *Science, 315*, 515–518.

Tonnessen, F. E., Lokken, A., Hoien, T., & Lundberg, I. (1993). Dyslexia, left-handedness, and immune disorders. *Archives of Neurology, 50*(4), 411.

Tononi, G., & Edelman, G. M. (1998). Consciousness and complexity. *Science, 282*, 1846–1851.

Tootell, R. B., Reppas, J. B., Dale, A. M., Look, R. R., Sereno, M. I., Malach, R., et al. (1995). Visual motion after-effect in human cortical area MT revealed by functional magnetic resonance imaging. *Nature, 375*, 139–141.

Tranel, D., Damasio, H., Denburg, N. L., & Bechara, A. (2005). Does gender play a role in functional asymmetry of ventromedial prefrontal cortex? *Brain, 128*, 2872–2881

Treisman, A., & Gelade, G. (1980). A feature-integration theory of attention. *Cognitive Psychology, 12*, 97–136.

Treisman, A. M. (1964). Verbal cues, language and meaning in selective attention. *American Journal of Psychology, 77*, 206–219.

Treisman, A. M. (1992). Spreading suppression or feature integration? A reply to Duncan and Humphreys (1992). *Journal of Experimental Psychology: Human Perception and Performance, 18*, 589–593.

Treisman, A. M. (1993). The perception of features and objects. In A. Baddeley & L. Weiskrantz (Eds.), *Attention: Selection, awareness and control*. Oxford, UK: Clarendon Press.

Treisman, A. M. (1999). Feature binding, attention and object perception. In G. W. Humphreys, J. Duncan, & A. Treisman (Eds.), *Attention, space and action*. Oxford, Oxford University Press.

Tsvetkov, E., Carlezon, W. A., Benes, F. M., Kel, E. R., & Bolshakov, V. Y. (2002). Fear conditioning occludes LTP-induced presynaptic enhancement of synaptic transmission in the cortical pathway to the lateral amygdala. *Neuron, 34*, 289–300.

Tulving, E. (1983). *Elements of episodic memory*. Oxford, UK: Clarendon.

Tulving, E., Hayman, C. A. G., & MacDonald, C. A. (1991). Long-lasting perceptual priming semantic learning in amnesia: A case experiment. *Journal of Experimental Psychology: Learning, Memory and Cognition*, *17*, 595–617.

Tulving, E., Kapur, S., Craik, F. I. M., Moscovitch, M., & Houle, S. (1994). Hemispheric encoding/retrieval asymmetry in episodic memory. *Proceedings of the National Academy of Sciences, USA*, *91*, 2016–2020.

Turnbull, O. H., Beschin, N., & Della Sala, S. (1997). Agnosia for object orientation: Implications for theories of object recognition. *Neuropsychologia*, *35*, 153–163.

Turner, A. M., & Greenhough, W. T. (1985). Differential rearing effects on rat visual cortex synapses: I. Synaptic and neuronal density and synapses per neuron. *Brain Research*, *329*, 195–203.

Tyszka, J. M., Grafton, S. T., Chew, W., Woods, R. P., & Colletti, P. M. (1994). Parcelling of medial frontal motor areas during ideation and movement using functional resonance imaging at 1.5 tesla. *Annals of Neurology*, *35*, 746–749.

Ugurbil, K., Toth, L., & Kim, D.S. (2003). How accurate is magnetic resonance imaging of brain function? *Trends in Neurosciences*, *26*, 108–114.

Umilta, M. A., Kohler, E., Gallese, V., Fogassi, L., Fadiga, L., Keysers, C., et al. (2001). "I know what you are doing": A neurophysiological study. *Neuron*, *31*, 155–165.

Ungerleider, L. G., & Mishkin, M. (1982). Two cortical visual systems. In D. J. Ingle, M. A. Goodale, & R. J. W. Mansfield (Eds.), *Analysis of visual behaviour* (pp. 549–586). Cambridge, MA: MIT Press.

Unterrainer, J. M., & Owen, A. M. (2006). Planning and problem solving: From neuropsychology to functional neuroimaging. *Journal of Physiology (Paris)*, *99*, 308–317.

Unterrainer, J. M., Rahm, B., Leonhart, R., Ruff, C. C., & Halsband, U. (2003). The Tower of London: The impact of instructions, cueing, and learning on planning abilities. *Brain Research: Cognitive Brain Research*, *17*, 675–683.

Vaidya, C. J., Zhao, M., Desmond, J. E., & Gabrieli, J. D. E. (2002). Evidence for cortical encoding specificity in episodic memory: Memory-induced re-activation of picture processing areas. *Neuropsychologia*, *40*, 2136–2143.

Vallar, G. (1998). Spatial hemineglect in humans. *Trends in Cognitive Sciences*, *2*, 87–97.

Vallar, G., & Baddeley, A. D. (1984). Phonological short-term store, phonological processing sentence comprehension. A neuropsychological case study. *Cognitive Neuropsychology*, *1*, 121–141.

Van Asselen, M., Kessels, R. P., Japp, K. L., Neggers, S. F., Frijns, C. J., & Postma, A. (2006). Neural correlates of human wayfinding in stroke patients. *Brain Research*, *1067*, 229–238.

Van den Heuvel, O. A., Groenewegen, H. J., Barkhof, F., Lazeron, R. H., van Dyck, R., & Veltman, D. J. (2003). Frontostriatal system in planning complexity: A parametric functional magnetic resonance version of Tower of London task. *Neuroimage*, *18*, 367–374.

Van Empelen, R., Hennekens-Schinkel, A., Buskens, E., Helders, J. M., & van Nieuwenhuizen, O. (2004). Functional consequences of hemispherectomy. *Brain*, *127*, 2071–2079.

Vargha-Khadem, F., Carr, L. J., Isaacs, E., Brett, E., Adams, C., & Mishkin, M. (1997). Onset of speech after left-hemispherectomy in a nine year old boy. *Brain*, *120*, 159–182.

Vecchi, T. A., Cattaneo, Z. A., Monegato, M. A., Pece, A. B., Cornoldi, C. C., & Pietrini, P. D. (2004). Why Cyclops could not compete with Ulysses: Monocular vision mental images. *Neuroreport*, *17*(7), 723–726.

Verfaellie, M., Gabrieli, J. D. E., Vaidya, C. J., & Croce, P. (1996). Implicit memory for pictures in amnesia: Role of etiology priming task. *Neuropsychology*, *10*, 517–537.

Verfaellie, M., & Keane, M. M. (2002). Impaired preserved memory processes in amnesia. In L. R. Squire & D. L. Schacter (Eds.), *Neuropsychology of memory* (3rd ed., pp. 35–46). New York: Guilford Press.

Victor, M., Adams, R. D., & Collins, G. H. (1971). *The Wernicke-Korsakoff syndrome*. Philadelphia: F. A. Davis.

Vigneau, M., Beaucousin, V., Herve, P. Y., Duffau, H, Crivello, F., Houde, O., et al. (2006). Meta-analyzing left hemisphere language areas: Phonology, semantics and sentence processing. *Neuroimage*, *30*, 1414–1432.

Vogel, J. J., Bowers, C. A., & Vogel, D. S. (2003). Cerebral lateralization of spatial abilities: A meta-analysis. *Brain and Cognition*, *52*, 197–204.

Vogt, O., & Vogt, C. (1903). Zur anatomischen Gliederung des Cortex Cerebri. *Journal of Psychology and Neurology*, *2*, 160–180.

Vollm, B., Richardson, P., Stirling, J., Elliott, R., Dolan, M., Chaudhry, I., et al. (2004). Neurobiological substrates of antisocial and borderline personality disorder: Preliminary results of an fMRI study. *Criminal Behaviour and Mental Health*, *14*, 39–54.

Vollm, B., Taylor, A. N. W., Richardson, P., Corcoran, R., Stirling, J., McKie, S., et al. (2006). Neuronal correlates of theory of mind and empathy: A functional magnetic resonance imaging study in a nonverbal task. *Neuroimage*, *19*, 90–98.

Von Cramon, D. Y., Hebel, N., & Schuri, U. (1985). A contribution to the anatomical basis of thalamic amnesia. *Brain*, *108*, 993–1008.

Wada, J., & Rasmusssen, T. (1960). Intracarotid injection of sodium amytal for the lateralisation of cerebral speech dominance. *Journal of Neurosurgery*, *17*, 266–282.

Wagner, A. D., Bunge, S. A., & Badre, D. (2004). Cognitive control, semantic memory, priming: Contributions from the prefrontal cortex. In M. S. Gazzaniga (Ed.), *The cognitive neurosciences III* (pp. 709–725). Cambridge, MA: MIT Press.

Wagner, A. D., Desmond, J. E., Demb, J. B., Glover, G. H., & Gabrieli, J. D. E. (1997). Semantic repetition priming for verbal pictorial knowledge: A functional MRI study of left inferior prefrontal cortex. *Journal of Cognitive Neuroscience*, *9*, 714–726.

Wagner, A. D., Pare-Blagoev, E. J., Lark, J., & Poldrack, R. A. (2001). Recovering meaning: Left prefrontal cortex guides controlled semantic retrieval. *Neuron*, *31*, 329–338.

Wagner, A. D., Poldrack, R. A., Eldridge, L. L., Desmond, J. E., Glover, G. H., & Gabrieli, J. D. E. (1998). Material-specific lateralization of prefrontal activation during episodic encoding retrieval. *Neuroreport*, *9*, 3711–3717.

Wallesch, C. W., Henriksen, L., Kornhuber, H. H., & Paulson, O. B. (1985). Observations on regional cerebral blood flow in cortical and sub-cortical structures during language production in normal man. *Brain and Language*, *25*, 224–233.

Ward, J. (2006). *The student's guide to cognitive neuroscience*. Hove, UK: Psychology Press.

Warren, J. M., Abplanalp, J. M., & Warren, H. B.

(1967). The development of handedness in cats and rhesus monkeys. In H. W. Stevenson, E. H. Hess, & H. L. Rheingold (Eds.), *Early behaviour: Comparative developmental epproaches*. New York: John Wiley & Sons.

Warrington, E. K. (1975). The selective impairment of semantic memory. *Quarterly Journal of Experimental Psychology*, *27*, 187–199.

Warrington, E. K., & McCarthy, R. (1983). Category specific access dysphasia. *Brain*, *106*, 859–878.

Warrington, E. K., & McCarthy, R. (1987). Categories of knowledge: Further fractionation and an attempted integration. *Brain*, *110*, 1273–1296.

Warrington, E. K., & Shallice, T. (1984). Category specific semantic impairments. *Brain*, *107*, 829–854.

Warrington, E. K., & Taylor, A. M. (1973). The contribution of the right parietal lobe to object recognition. *Cortex*, *9*, 152–164.

Warrington, E. K., & Taylor, A. M. (1978). Two categorical stages of object recognition. *Perception*, *7*, 695–705.

Waxman, S. (Ed.) (2005). *Multiple sclerosis as a neuronal disease*. London: Academic Press.

Wechsler, D. (1981). *Manual for the Wechsler Adult Intelligence Scale–revised*. San Antonio, TX: Psychological Corporation.

Wechsler, D. (1999). *Wechsler Abbreviated Scale of Intelligence, Harcourt Assessment*. San Antonio, TX: Psychological Corporation.

Weiller, C., & Rijntjes, M. (1999). Learning, plasticity and recovery in the central nervous system. *Experimental Brain Research*, *128*, 134–138.

Weinberger, D. R., Berman, K. F., & Frith, C. D. (1996). Pre-frontal function in schizophrenia: Confounds and controversies *Philosophical Transactions: Biological Sciences*, *351*, 1495–1503.

Weintraub, S., & Mesulam, M. M. (1987). Right cerebral dominance in spatial attention. *Archives of Neurology*, *44*, 621–625.

Wernicke, C. (1874). *Der Aphasische Symptomenkomplexe*. Breslau, Poland: Cohn & Weigert.

Westmacott, R., & Moscovitch, M. (2001). Names words without meaning: Incidental postmorbid semantic learning in a person with extensive bilateral medial temporal damage. *Neuropsychology*, *15*, 586–596.

Whalen, P. J., Bush, G., McNally, R. J., Wilhelm, S., McInerney, S. C., Jenike, M. A., et al. (1998).

The emotional counting Stroop paradigm: A functional magnetic resonance imaging probe of the anterior cingulate affective division. *Biological Psychiatry*, *44*, 1219–1228.

Whalen, P. J., Shin, L. M., McInerney, S. C., Fischer, H., Wright, C. I., & Rauch, S. L. (2001). A functional MRI study of human amygdala responses to facial expressions of fear versus anger. *Emotion*, *1*, 70–83.

White, T., Kendi, A. T., Lehericy, S., Kendi, M., Karatekin, C., Guimaraes, A., et al. (2007). Disruption of hippocampal connectivity in children and adolescents with schizophrenia: A voxel based diffusion tensor imaging study. *Schizophrenia Research*, *90*(1–3), 302–307.

Wichmann, T., & DeLong, M. R. (1996). Functional and pathophysiological models of the basal ganglia. *Current Opinion in Neurobiology*, *6*, 751–758.

Wickens, C. D. (1980). The structure of attentional resources. In R. Nickerson & R. Pew (Eds.), *Attention and performance VIII* (pp. 87–113). Hillsdale, NJ: Lawrence Erlbaum Associates Inc.

Wicker, B., Keysers, C., Plailly, J., Royet, J. P., Gallese, V., & Rizzolatti, G. (2003). Both of us disgusted in my insula: The common neural basis of seeing and feeling disgust. *Neuron*, *40*, 655–664.

Wilson, B. A. (1993). Ecological validity of neuropsychological assessment: Do neuropsychological indexes predict performance in everyday activities? *Applied and Preventive Psychology*, *2*, 209–215.

Windmann, S., Wehrmann, M., Calabrese, P., & Gunturkun, O. (2006). Role of the prefrontal cortex in attentional control over bistable vision. *Journal of Cognitive Neuroscience*, *18*, 456–471.

Winkler, C., Kirik, D., & Bjorklund, A. (2005). Cell transplantation in Parkinson's disease: How can we make it work. *Trends in Neurosciences*, *28*, 86–92.

Wise, R. J., Green, J., Buchel, C., & Scott, S. K. (1999). Brain regions involved in articulation. *Lancet*, *353*, 1057–1061.

Wise, R. J., Scott, S. K., Blank, S. C., Mummery, C. J., & Warburton, E. (2001). Identifying separate neural sub-systems within Wernicke's area. *Brain*, *124*, 83–95.

Witelson, S. F. (1985). The brain connection: The corpus callosum is larger in left-handers. *Science*, *229*, 665–668.

Wittenberg, G. F., Chen, R., Ishii, K., Bushara, K. O., Taub, E., Gerber, L. H., et al. (2003). Constraint induced therapy in stroke: Magnetic-stimulation motor maps and cerebral activation. *Neurorehabilitation and Neural Repair*, *17*, 48–57.

Woldorff, M. G., Gallen, C. C., Hampson, S. A., Hillyard, S. A., Pantev, C., Sobel, D., et al. (1993). Modulation of early sensory processing in human auditory cortex during auditory selective attention. *Proceedings of the National Academy of Sciences*, *90*, 8722–8726.

Woldorff, M. G., & Hillyard, S. A. (1991). Modulation of early auditory processing during selective listening to rapidly presented tones. *Electroencephalography and Clinical Neurophysiology*, *79*(3), 170–191.

Wolf, S. S., Jones, D. W., Knable, M. B., Gorey, J. G., Lee, K. S., Hyde, T. M., et al. (1996). Tourette syndrome: Prediction of phenotypic variation in monozygotic twins by caudate nucleus D2 receptor binding. *Science*, *273*, 1225–1227.

Wolfe, J. M. (1998). Visual search. In H. Pasher (Ed.), *Attention*. Hove, UK: Psychology Press.

Wood, R., Gurney, K., & Redgrave, P. (2001). Direct pathway connections to globus pallidus in a computational model of the basal ganglia. *British Neuroscience Association Abstracts*, *16*, 90.

Woodruff-Pak, D., Papka, M., & Ivry, R. B. (1996). Cerebellar involvement in eyeblink conditioning in humans. *Neuropsychology*, *10*, 443–458.

Woolsey, T. A., & Wann, J. R. (1976). Areal changes in mouse cortical barrels following vibrissal damage at different postnatal ages. *Journal of Comparative Neurology*, *170*, 53–66.

Wurtz, R. H., Goldberg, M. E., & Robinson, D. L. (1982). Brain mechanisms of visual attention, *Scientific American*, *246*, 124–135.

Xu, Y. (2005). Revisiting the role of the fusiform face area in visual expertise. *Cerebral Cortex*, *15*, 1234–1242.

Yeung, N., Nystrom, L. E., Aronson, J. A., & Cohen, J. D. (2006). Between-task competition and cognitive control in task switching. *Journal of Neuroscience*, *26*, 1429–1438.

Yonelinas, A. P., Kroll, N. E. A., Baynes, K., Dobbins, I. G., Frederick, C. M., Knight R. T., et al. (2001). Visual implicit memory in the left hemisphere: Evidence from patients with callosotomies' right occipital lobe lesions. *Psychological Science*, *12*, 293–298.

Young, A. W., Rowland, D., Calder, A. J., Etcoff, N. L., Seth, A., & Perrett, D. I. (1997). Facial expression megamix: Tests of dimensional and category accounts of emotion recognition. *Cognition, 63*, 271–313.

Zaidel, E. (1978). Auditory language comprehension in the right hemisphere following cerebral commissurotomy and hemispherectomy: A comparison with child language and aphasia. In A. Caramazza & E. B. Zurif (Eds.), *Language acquisition and language breakdown: Parallels and divergencies*. Baltimore: Johns Hopkins Press.

Zeki, S. (1980). The representation of colours in the cerebral cortex. *Nature, 284*, 412–418.

Zeki, S. M., Watson, D. G., & Frackowiak, R. S. (1993). Going beyond the information given: The relation of illusory visual motion to brain activity. *Proceedings of the Royal Society of London, B, 252*, 212–222.

Zeki, S. M., Watson, J. D., Lueck, C. J., Friston, K. C., Kennard, C., & Frackowiak, R. S. (1991). A direct demonstration of functional specialisation in human visual cortex. *Journal of Neuroscience, 11*, 641–649.

Zihl, J., von Cramon, D., & Mai, N. (1983). Selective disturbance of movement vision after bilateral brain damage. *Brain, 106*, 313–340.

Ziv, Y., Ron, N., Butovsky, O., Landa, G., Sudai, E., Greenberg, N., et al. (2006). Immune cells contribute to the maintenance of neurogenesis and spatial learning abilities in adulthood. *Nature: Neuroscience, 9*, 268–276.

Zola-Morgan, S., & Squire, L. R. (1990). The primate hippocampal formation: Evidence for a time-limited role in memory storage. *Science, 250*, 288–290.

Zola-Morgan, S., & Squire, L. R. (1993). Neuroanatomy of memory. *Annual Review of Neuroscience, 16*, 547–563.

AUTHOR INDEX

SUBJECT INDEX